Commonly Used Editor Commands

vi

To enter the vi screen editor, type **vi**. If you want to work on a specific file, type **vi filename**. You can use the following commands after you access the editor. The ^ represents the Control key; for example, ^C means press the Control key while you press C.

^C	Interrupt a search or global command.
^G	File status.
^L	Redraw screen.
^V	Input a literal character.
^W	Move to next screen.
^Z	Suspend editor.
^[\<Esc>	Leave input made, return to command mode.
^^	Switch to previous file.
$	Move to last column.
%	Move to match.
&	Repeat substitution.
'	Move to mark (to first nonblank).
(	Move back a sentence.
)	Move forward a sentence.
+	Move down by lines (to first nonblank).
,	Reverse last F, f, T, or t search.
-	Move up by lines (to first nonblank).
.	Repeat the last command.
/	Search forward.
0	Move to a space, move right by columns.
;	Repeat last F, f, T, or t search.
?	Search backward.
@	Execute buffer.
A	Append to the line.
F	Character in line backward search.
H	Move to count lines from screen top.
I	Insert at line beginning.
L	Move to screen bottom.
M	Move to screen middle.
N	Search.
Q	Switch to ex mode.
R	Replace characters.
U	Restore the current line.
Y	Copy line.
ZZ	Save file and exit.
a	Append after cursor.
b	Move back a word.
i	Insert before cursor.
j	Move down by lines.
k	Move up by lines.
m	Set mark.
n	Repeat last search.
o	Append after line.
p	Insert from buffer.
r	Replace character.
s	Substitute character.
u	Undo last change.
x	Delete character.
z	Redraw window.
{	Move back a paragraph.
}	Move forward a paragraph.
~	Reverse case.

Emacs

The EMACS editor is a screen editor. To enter the editor, type **emacs**. If you want to work on a specific file, type **emacs filename**. After you access the editor, you can use the following commands.

Basic Cursor and Screen Control Commands

Control+l	Clear screen and redisplay everything.
Control+f	Move forward a character.
Control+b	Move backward a character.
Control+n	Move to next line.
Control+p	Move to previous line.
Esc+a	Move back to beginning of sentence.
Esc+e	Move forward to end of sentence.
Esc+<	Go to beginning of file.
Esc+>	Go to end of file.
Esc+r	Move cursor to the line in the middle of window.
Esc+f	Move cursor forward one word.
Esc+b	Move backward one word.
Control+g	Stop an active operation or erase a numeric argument or the beginning of a command.
Control+x 1	Retain one window (kill all other windows).
Control+x Control+c	Exit Emacs editor.
Control+z	Temporarily exit to shell.
Control+x \<n>	Split screen into *n* windows.
Control+X o	Switch between the windows.
Control+h a	Access the apropos help system.
Control+x k	Remove help text.

Major Mode Commands

Esc+x fundamental	Activates fundamental mode.
Esc+x text-mode	Activates text mode.
Control+h m	Access help on current major mode.

Minor Mode Commands

Esc+x auto-fill-mode	Toggle autofill on or off.
Esc+x auto-save-mode	Toggle autosave on or off.
Esc+x	Toggle overwrite mode on or off.

Editing Commands

Control+d	Delete the character to the right of the point.
Delete key	Erase the character to the left of the point.
Control+x u	Undo the most recent change.
Control+y	Yank back killed text.
Control+x s	Save some buffers.
Control+x Control+s	Save file.

Search and Replace Commands

Control+s+Esc+Control+w	Search for text in the forward direction.
Control+r Esc Control+w	Search for text in the backward direction.
Esc+%	Search for text and prompt for replace.
\<Esc>	Exits without replacing any more text.
Control+x Control+f	Find a file.

sed

The sed editor is a stream editor; sed commands are entered at the shell prompt to process one or more lines in one or more files.

SYNOPSIS

```
sed [-an] command [file ...]
sed [-an] [-e command] [-f command_file] [file ...]
```

The following command options are available:

- **-a**   The files listed as parameters for the "w" functions are created or truncated before any processing begins, by default. The -a option causes sed to delay opening each file until a command containing the related "w" function is applied to a line of input.

- **-e** *command*   Append the editing commands specified by the command argument to the list of commands.

- **-f** *command file*   Append the editing commands found in the file *command file* to the list of commands. The editing commands should each be listed on a separate line.

- **-n**   By default, each line of input is echoed to the standard output after all of the commands have been applied to it. The -n option suppresses this behavior.

The form of a sed command is as follows:

```
[address[,address]]function[arguments]
```

NINE UNIX COMMANDS YOU'LL USE A LOT

cd
Change working directory.

```
cp [ -ip ] file1 file2
cp [ -ipr ] file ... directory
```
Copy files.
- **-i**   Inquire whether a file will be overwritten by the copy.
- **-p**   Preserve modes (ignore umask) and modification times.
- **-r**   Recursively copy directories.

```
grep [ -bchilnosvw ][ -f file ][ -e ] expr [ files ]
```
Search a file for a pattern.
- **-b**   Block number is printed before each line.
- **-c**   Count of matches is printed instead of actual lines.
- **-h**   Headers are not printed before each line.
- **-i**   Ignore case in comparisons.
- **-l**   List only the filenames that contain a match, once each.
- **-n**   Number each line with its line number.
- **-o**   Output headers on every line.
- **-s**   Silent mode. Only a status is returned.
- **-v**   All lines except those that match.
- **-w**   Word mode. Expression is searched for as a word.
- **-e** *expr*   Expression to use is *expr*.
- *files*   Files to search in.

lp
Print text files.

```
ls [ -acdfgilqrstu1CFLMR ] name ...
```
List contents of directory.
- **-a**   List all entries; in the absence of this option, entries whose names begin with a period (.) are not listed.
- **-c**   Use time when file status was last changed.
- **-d**   If argument is a directory, list only its name.
- **-f**   Force each argument to be interpreted as a directory and list the name found in each slot. This option turns off -l, -t, -s, and -r, and turns on -a.
- **-g**   Include the group ownership of the file.
- **-i**   Print the *i*-number in the first column of the report.
- **-l**   List in long format.
- **-r**   Reverse the order of sort.
- **-s**   Give size of each file in kilobytes .
- **-t**   Sort by time modified (latest first).
- **-u**   Use time of last access instead of last modification.
- **-C**   Force multicolumn output; this is the default when output is to a terminal.

- **-F**   Cause directories to be marked with a trailing /, sockets with a trailing =, symbolic links with a trailing @, and executable files with a trailing *.
- **-L**   If argument is a symbolic link, list the file or directory of the link references rather than the link itself.
- **-M**   List in Macintosh format.
- **-R**   Recursively list subdirectories encountered.
- **-1**   Force one-entry-per-line output format.

```
man -k [ -M path ] [ -m path ] keyword ...
man [ -acw ] [ -M path ] [ -m path ] [ section ] name ...
```
Find and display reference manual pages.
- **-a**   All of the manual pages are displayed instead of only the first one.
- **-c**   Copy the manual page to standard out instead of using more.
- **-w**   Which manual pages would display are listed.
- **-k**   Keyword lookup of description lines (same as apropos command).
- **-M** *path*   Search *path* instead of $MANPATH.
- **-m** *path*   Search *path* in addition to $MANPATH.

```
mkdir dirname ...
```
Make directories.
- *dirname*   Name of the directories to create.

```
more [ -cdflMsu ] [ -# ] [ +# ] [ +/pat ] [ name ... ]
```
Browse or page through a text file.
- **-c**   Clear the screen before displaying each page.
- **-d**   Display user-friendly messages.
- **-f**   Folding is not done on lines.
- **-l**   ^L (form-feed) is not treated as an end of screen.
- **-s**   Squeeze multiple blank lines into one blank line.
- **-u**   Underlining is suppressed.
- **-#**   Number of lines per page.
- **+#**   Start displaying # lines into the file.
- **+/pat**   Start displaying two lines before the pattern *pat* is found.
- *name*   Name of the file to display

```
mv [ -if ] file1 file2
mv [ -if ] file ... directory
```
Moves (renames) *file1* to *file2* and removes any pre-existing *file2*. The second form moves multiple files into a directory.
- **-i**   Inquire whether *file2* should be removed if one already exists.
- **-f**   Force the move without question.
- *file1*   Name of the file to rename.
- *file2*   Name of the new file.

UNIX
UNLEASHED

Sams Development Team

SAMS
PUBLISHING

201 West 103rd Street, Indianapolis, IN 46290

Contents

Part III Programming

Part IV Process Control

Foreword

Given life by Turing Award winning Bell Labs computer scientist Ken Thompson at Murray Hill, N.J., in August 1969, UNIX spent its early years as a research curiosity. When I met up with Unix in the summer of '82, however, it already possessed the one characteristic that destined it to dominate a major chunk of the world's market for operating systems—portability. UNIX kicked off the era of open systems, the first wholesale paradigm shift in the history of computing, by being the first portable operating system.

Portability is so crucial because it symbolizes everything that open systems is about, and is the critical computing ingredient for the Information Age. You may hear people use the word primarily to talk about their applications that can run on more than one type of computer platform, but, at its highest level of abstraction, portability is much more. When you think about using standard network interfaces to pass data between different computers, that's portability of information; running applications across a range of devices from desktop to mainframe—or even supercomputer—is portability across scale; and the ability to swap out old technology for the latest technical advances without dramatically affecting the rest of your installation is portability through time. All this is necessary to support the extremely sophisticated levels of information malieability that corporations need to make the Information Age really work.

UNIX was always technically cool, advanced, insanely great, etc. So cool that Bell Labs began giving it away to colleges and universities in 1975 because they thought it would be a good recruitment tool—they believed graduate computer engineers would want to work at the place that produced such an elegant piece of technology. But UNIX's all-important portability didn't come about until 1977. Before that, UNIX's technical qualities alone had lured many Bell operating company department heads to Murray Hill, where they learned about UNIX from its small team of creators and began deploying it on Digital Equipment Corporation computers throughout the Bell System. By 1977, AT&T found itself buying a much larger percentage of Digital's annual output than seemed comfortable. (AT&T didn't want to be responsible for a precipitous drop in Digital's fortunes if it had to stop buying for any reason.) So that year, UNIX's creators ported UNIX for the first time, to a non-Digital computer whose only significant characteristic was that it was a non-Digital computer.

After that, UNIX was portable, and entrepreneurs ported it to new microcomputers like crazy. That's when I came on the scene, as a computer industry news reporter covering all that entrepreneurial energy. Even in 1982, the manifest destiny felt by the people in the UNIX industry was clear. And the idea of a common operating system atop different hardware platforms so powerfully fired the imaginations of information systems managers in major corporations that, today, UNIX has become their de facto server operating system.

Given that you've purchased or are considering this book, you already know that UNIX is ubiquitous. What UNIX is not, however—even with the modern graphical user interfaces that paint a pretty face on it—is easy to program or administer compared to DOS or NetWare. Just as a 747 is a bit more complicated to run than, say, a glider, UNIX's increased flexibility and power come with the price of greater complexity.

This book, which delves deeply into the underpinnings of UNIX systems and offers detailed information on many different brands of UNIX, can be your first step on an enjoyable journey into the powerful, technically elegant world of open, portable computing.

Mike Azzara, associate publisher/editorial director, *Open Systems Today.*

About the Authors

Susan Peppard was born many years ago in New York City. She attended New York University where she studied French literature and picked up a couple of degrees. When this failed to produce splendid job offers, she turned to computers (big, blue, room-sized machines, sporting 30 KB of memory).

Today, 30 years later, she confines her computer-related activities to writing on and about them and playing games. She is a documentation consultant (technical writer) and lives in New Jersey with a horrible black dog, an innocuous grey cat, and—between semesters—varying configurations of her children. She and UNIX met in 1985 and have been living together happily ever since.

Pete Holsberg saw his first computer in 1960, as a graduate student at Rutgers, and they have plagued him ever since. While at Rutgers, he was exposed to both analog and digital computers. He went to work for Electronic Associates, Inc., Princeton, New Jersey on leaving Rutgers. EAI was the world's largest manufacturer of analog and hybrid computers.

He later joined Mercer College, Trenton, New Jersey in 1970 as associate professor of electrical engineering and was given responsibility for the PDP-8/I lab. He was instrumental in bringing microcomputers to the campus in 1981; these were used in electronics engineering technology education. Currently, he is systems administrator for the college's UNIX lab, consultant to the college's Academic Computing Committee, secretary of the college's LAN Computing Committee, advisor to the Educational Technology Users Group for faculty and staff, and coordinator for electronics curricula.

Pete has authored a textbook on C for electronics engineering technology for Macmillan and a book on UNIX tools for Macmillan Computer Publishing. He has written invited chapters in a number of MCP books, and has been the technical editor or technical reviewer for many of MCP's UNIX book offerings.

Pete lives in Ewing, New Jersey with his wife, Cathy Ann Vandegrift and their four computers. They sail and enjoy the New Jersey Symphony Orchestra. Pete has a private pilot's license and is an avid autocross racer and tennis hacker. Cathy is a Realtor.

James C. Armstrong, Jr., is a software engineer with ten years of industry experience with UNIX and C. He is currently working as a technical editor at Advanced Systems, and also works free-lance for several other companies in the San Francisco Bay area. He can be reached at james@sagamartha.com.

Salim M. Douba is a network consultant with Proterm Data Systems Ltd./USConnect, Ottawa, Ontario, Canada. He is also an independent certified NetWare Instructor (CNI) teaching NetWare operating systems and advanced courses. He holds a master's degree in electrical engineering from the American University of Beirut. His experience and main career interests have primarily been in Internetworking and multiplatform integration. He is reachable on CompuServe on 70573,2351.

S. Lee Henry writes a systems administration column for *SunExpert Magazine*, and manages systems and networking for the physics and astronomy department at Johns Hopkins University. She is on the board of directors of the Sun User Group and has been a UNIX programmer and administrator for over twelve years.

Ron Rose is an international management consultant with 20 years of data processing management experience. He has led large-scale data processing installations in Asia, Europe, and the United States, and he has managed several software product start-up efforts. He completed a master's in information systems from Georgia Institute of Technology, after completing undergraduate work at Tulane University and the University of Aberdeen, Scotland. His current position is as a director for Bedford Associates, Inc., in Norwalk, Connecticut, where he leads groups that provide Open Systems and Lotus Notes products, along with related high-performance UNIX systems-integration work. He also has appeared on national television (CNBC) as a management consultant on technology issues.

Richard E. Rummel, CDP, is the president of ASM Computing, Jacksonville, Florida, which specializes in UNIX software development and end user training. He has been actively employed in the computer industry for 20 years. Married for 21 years, he is the father of two children, a dog, and a cat.

Scott Parker has worked as a UNIX system administrator and an ORACLE Database administrator and developer for several companies.

Ann Marshall is a UNIX computer professional specializing in relational database management and system administration. A free-lance writer in her spare time, she has written articles about the RS/6000 in *RS/Magazine*. She received her undergraduate degree in economics and English from Vanderbilt University and obtained her master's degree in computer science from the University of Alabama in Huntsville. Outside of computers, Ann's hobbies include travel, reading, and writing fiction. You can reach Ann on CompuServe at 71513,335.

Ron Dippold graduated from Rose-Hulman Institute of Technology with a degree in electrical engineering and computer science. He is employed as a senior engineer at Qualcomm, Inc., of San Diego, CA. He is the author of several computer books and is a technical editor for many more. He served as a computer columnist and consulting editor for *ComputerEdge Magazine*.

When **Chris Negus** isn't playing soccer or listening to Indigo Girls, he's usually writing about UNIX. Despite contributions to dozens of books and articles on UNIX, he still maintains that he is not a geek. In the past decade, Chris has worked for AT&T Bell Laboratories, UNIX System Laboratories, and Novell as a UNIX consultant. He most recently coauthored Novell's Guide to UNIXWare for Novell Press. Presently, Chris is a partner in C & L Associates, a UNIX consulting company in Salt Lake City.

John Valley lives in Richmond, Virginia with his wife Terri and his Labrador retriever, Brandon. Mr. Valley currently operates a small practice as an independent consultant for UNIX and Windows tools and applications. With more than twenty years of experience in the computer industry, his background ranges from Cobol business applications and mainframe operating system development to UNIX tools and Windows programming. He teaches courses in C/C++ programming and UNIX fundamentals.

Mr. Valley is largely self-taught, having started as a night shift computer operator in 1972. After serving time as a Cobol applications programmer and mainframe systems programmer, he signed on with Nixdorf Computer Software Corporation (now defunct) to write operating system code. Soon promoted to project leader, he supervised the company's product design efforts for four years. Almost by coincidence, he encountered the UNIX environment in 1985 and quickly became a devotee of UNIX and C programming.

He has published three books on UNIX topics: *UNIX Programmer's Reference* (Que; 1991), *UNIX Desktop Guide to the Korn Shell* (Hayden; 1992), and *C Programming for UNIX* (Sams; 1992).

Jeff Smith is a psychology major who took a wrong turn and ended up working with computers. Jeff has worked with UNIX systems since 1982 as a programmer and systems administrator. He has administered mail, news, security, and the domain name system on several varieties of UNIX including 2.9BSD, 4.3BSD, Dynix, SunOS, and AIX. Currently, he manages a network of 180 Sun workstations at Purdue University.

Dave Taylor has been working with UNIX since 1980, when he first logged in to a Berkeley-based DEC VAX computer while an undergraduate at the University of California, San Diego. Since then, he's used dozens of different UNIX systems and has contributed commands incorporated into HP's HP-UX UNIZ operating system and UC Berkeley's BSD 4.4 UNIX release. His professional experience includes positions as research scientist at Hewlett-Packard Laboratories in Palo Alto, California; software and hardware reviews editor for *SunWorld Magazine*; interface design consultant for XALT Software; and president of Intuitive Systems. He has published more than 300 articles on UNIX, Macintosh, and technical computing topics, and also the book *Global Software*, addressing the challenges and opportunities for software internationalization from a marketing and programming viewpoint. He is well-known as the author of the Elm Mail System, the most popular screen-based electronic mail package in the UNIX community.

Currently he is working as a consultant for Intuitive Systems in West Lafayette, Indiana, while pursuing a graduate degree in educational computing at Purdue University and working on a new interface to the FTP program.

Sydney S. Weinstein, CDP, CCP, is a consultant, columnist, lecturer, author, professor and president of Myxa Corporation, an Open Systems technology company specializing in helping companies move to and work with Open Systems. He has more than 15 years of experience with UNIX dating all the way back to Version 6. He is a contributing editor for *C Users Journal* and was a contributing author for *UNIX Programmer's Reference* (Que, 1990). He can be contacted care of Myxa Corporation, 3837 Byron Road, Huntingdon Valley, PA 19006-2320 or via electronic mail using the Internet/USENET mailbox syd@Myxa.com (dsinc!syd for those who cannot do Internet addressing).

Dave Till holds a master's degree in computer science from the University of Waterloo (a well-respected institution), majoring in programming language design. He also has substantial experience developing compilers and compiler technology, and has several years of technical writing experience.

Introduction

by Scott Parker

Are you:

New to UNIX and looking for a book to help you get acquainted with UNIX?

Not so new to UNIX but looking to expand your knowledge?

A programmer looking for a guide to UNIX as a reference and a teaching guide for Perl, awk, and the shells?

A beginning system administrator looking to learn how to install UNIX or how to connect your UNIX to a network?

A system administrator looking for a reference guide or maybe just wanting to expand your knowledge?

A curious soul wanting to know everything about UNIX?

If any of these is true, you are holding the right book. *UNIX Unleashed* was written to cover all the bases. We started this book with the mission of giving you, the reader, a complete book on UNIX. In this book you will find

A tutorial for those who are new to UNIX. As you learn more about UNIX and get more and more comfortable, this book will be there to help you become a UNIX power user.

How to navigate the file system and how to use mail.

Instructive lessons on how to use vi, EMACS, sed.

How to program in the Bourne Shell, C Shell, and Korn Shell.

How to program in awk and Perl.

How to create your own man pages and formatted text.

How to install UNIX and power it down.

How to administer the file system, user accounts, the network, security system, mail, news, and devices.

Organization

Part I starts with a tutorial on "Finding Your Way Around UNIX." Robert and Rachel Sartin, Jeff Smith, Rick Rummel, Pete Holsberg, Ron Dippold and Dave Taylor give an introduction to operating systems. In Part I, you will find a step-by-step tutorial on how to log on the UNIX system and how to do some basic commands. There is also a complete introduction to all the file listing commands, file tools, and editing text files. You will also find a quick guide to navigating the network and methods to communicate with other systems on your network.

In Part II, "Hunt for Shells," Rick Rummel and John Valley teach you how to develop shell scripts for the Bourne Shell, Korn Shell, and C Shell.

In Part III, "Programming," Ann Marshall, David Till, and James Armstrong teach you how to program awk and Perl and how to use the UNIX C compiler.

In Part IV, "Process Control," Robert and Rachel Sartin give you an introduction to how to control your programs on UNIX. Here you find how to start a job (program) and how to kill it.

In Part V, "Text Formatting and Printing," James Armstrong and Susan Peppard give instruction on how to use these powerful macros, and how to create text with graphs, pictures, equations, etc. Learn how to create man pages and how to print postscript.

In Part VI, "Advanced File Utilities," Robert and Rachel Sartin and S. Lee Henry teach you how to put your programs or text into version control, how to back up and archive your work for protection against hard disk crashes, and more.

In Part VII, "System Administration," Sydney Weinstein, Chris Negus, Scott Parker, Ron Rose, Salim Douba, Jeff Smith, and James Armstrong teach the basics of UNIX System Administration. Here you will learn how to install UNIX, how to create user accounts, how to partition disk drives, and how to administer security, mail, uucp, and news.

Finally, in Part VIII, "UNIX Flavors and Graphical User Interfaces," S. Lee Henry and Kamran Husain give an overview of the history of UNIX and where it is going. You will learn how to navigate X Window and, for the more advanced, how to program in the GUI environment.

IN THIS PART

1

PART

Finding Your Way Around UNIX

Operating Systems

1

By Rachel and Robert Sartin

What Is an Operating System?

An operating system is an important part of a computer system. You can view a computer system as being built from three general components: the hardware, the operating system, and the applications. (See Figure 1.1.) The hardware includes pieces such as a central processing unit (CPU), a keyboard, a hard drive, and a printer. You can think of these as the parts you are able to touch physically. Applications are why you use computers; they use the rest of the system to perform the desired task (for example, play a game, edit a memo, send electronic mail). The operating system is the component that on one side manages and controls the hardware and on the other manages the applications.

FIGURE 1.1.

Computer system components.

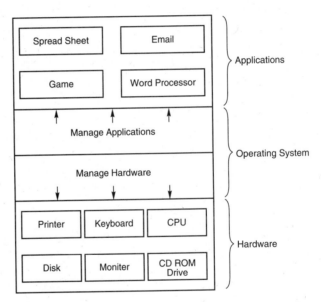

When you purchase a computer system, you must have at least hardware and an operating system. The hardware you purchase is able to use (or *run*) one or more different operating systems. You can purchase a bundled computer package, which includes the hardware, the operating system, and possibly one or more applications. The operating system is necessary in order to manage the hardware and the applications.

When you turn on your computer, the operating system performs a series of tasks, presented in chronological order in the next few sections.

Hardware Management, Part 1

One of the first things you do, after successfully plugging together a plethora of cables and components, is turn on your computer. The operating system takes care of all the starting functions that must occur to get your computer to a usable state. Various pieces of hardware need to be initialized. After the start-up procedure is complete, the operating system awaits further instructions. If you shut down the computer, the operating system also has a procedure that makes sure all the hardware is shut down correctly. Before turning your computer off again, you might want to do something useful, which means that one or more applications are executed. Most boot ROMs do some hardware initialization but not much. Initialization of I/O devices is part of the UNIX kernel.

Process Management

After the operating system completes hardware initialization, you can execute an application. This executing application is called a *process*. (See Chapter 18, "What Is a Process?") It is the operating system's job to manage execution of the application. When you execute a program, the operating system creates a new process. Many processes can exist simultaneously, but only one process can actually be executing on a CPU at one time. The operating system switches between your processes so quickly that it can appear that the processes are executing simultaneously. This concept is referred to as *time-sharing* or *multitasking*.

When you exit your program (or it finishes executing), the process *terminates*, and the operating system manages the termination by reclaiming any resources that were being used.

Most applications perform some tasks between the time that the process is created and the time that it terminates. To perform these tasks, the program makes requests to the operating system and the operating system responds to the requests and allocates necessary resources to the program. When an executing process needs to use some hardware, the operating system provides access for the process.

Hardware Management, Part 2

To perform its task, a process may need to access hardware resources. The process may need to read or write to a file, send data to a network card (to communicate with another computer), or send data to a printer. The operating system provides such services for the process. This is referred to as *resource allocation*. A piece of hardware is a resource, and the operating system allocates available resources to the different processes that are running.

See Table 1.1 for a summary of different actions and what the operating system (OS) does to manage them.

Table 1.1. Operating system functions.

Action	OS Does This
You turn on the computer	Hardware management
You execute an application	Process management
Application reads a tape	Hardware management
Application waits for data	Process management
Process waits while other process runs	Process management
Process displays data on screen	Hardware management
Process writes data to tape	Hardware management
You quit, the process terminates	Process management
You turn off the computer	Hardware management

From the time you turn on your computer until you turn it off, the operating system is coordinating the operations. As hardware is initialized, accessed, or shut down, the operating system manages these resources. As applications execute, request, and receive resources, or terminate, the operating system takes care of these actions. Without an operating system, no application can run and your computer is just an expensive paperweight.

The UNIX Operating System

The previous section looked at an operating system in general. This section looks at a specific operating system: UNIX. UNIX is an increasingly popular operating system. Traditionally used on minicomputers and workstations in the academic community, UNIX is now available on personal computers, and the business community has started to choose UNIX for its openness. Previous PC and mainframe users are now looking to UNIX as their operating system solution. This section looks at how UNIX fits into the operating system model.

UNIX, like other operating systems, is a layer between the hardware and the applications that run on the computer. It has functions that manage the hardware and functions that manage executing applications. So what's the difference between UNIX and any other operating system? Basically two things: internal implementation and the interface that is seen and used by users. For the most part this book ignores the internal implementation. If you wish to know these details, many texts exist that cover them. The interface is what this book describes in detail. The majority of UNIX users need to be familiar with the interface and need not understand the internal workings of UNIX.

The UNIX system is actually more than strictly an operating system. UNIX includes the traditional operating system components. In addition, a standard UNIX system includes a set of libraries and a set of applications. Figure 1.2 shows the components and layers of UNIX. Sitting above the hardware are two components: the file system and process control. Next is the set of libraries. On top are the applications. The user has access to the libraries and to the applications. These two components are what many users think of as UNIX, because together they constitute the UNIX interface.

FIGURE 1.2.

The layers of UNIX.

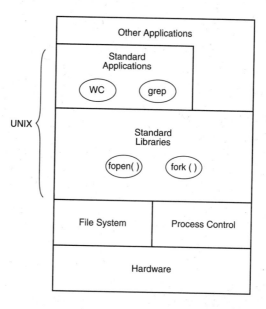

The part of UNIX that manages the hardware and the executing processes is called the kernel. In managing all hardware devices, the UNIX system views each device as a file (called a device file). This allows the same simple method of reading and writing files to be used to access each hardware device. The file system (explained in more detail in Chapter 3, "The UNIX File System: Go Climb a Tree") manages read and write access to user data and to devices, such as printers, attached to the system. It implements security controls to protect the safety and privacy of information. In executing processes (see Chapter 18), the UNIX system allocates resources (including use of the CPU) and mediates accesses to the hardware.

One important advantage that results from the UNIX standard interface is application portability. Application portability is the ability of a single application to be executed on various types of computer hardware without being modified. This can be achieved if the application uses the UNIX interface to manage its hardware needs. UNIX's layered design insulates the application from the different types of hardware. This allows the software developer to support the single application on multiple hardware types with minimal effort. The application writer has lower development costs and a larger potential customer base. Users not only have more applications available, but can rely on being able to use the same applications on different computer hardware.

UNIX goes beyond the traditional operating system by providing a standard set of libraries and applications that developers and users can use. This standard interface allows application portability and facilitates user familiarity with the interface.

The History of UNIX

How did a system such as UNIX ever come to exist? UNIX has a rather unusual history that has greatly affected its current form.

The Early Days

In the mid-1960s, AT&T Bell Laboratories (among others) was participating in an effort to develop a new operating system called Multics. Multics was intended to supply large-scale computing services as a utility, much like electrical power. Many people who worked on the Bell Labs contributions to Multics later worked on UNIX.

In 1969, Bell Labs pulled out of the Multics effort, and the members of the Computing Science Research center were left with no computing environment. Ken Thompson, Dennis Ritchie, and others developed and simulated an initial design for a file system that later evolved into the UNIX file system. An early version of the system was developed to take advantage of a PDP-7 computer that was available to the group.

An early project that helped lead to the success of UNIX was its deployment to do text processing for the patent department at AT&T. This project moved UNIX to the PDP-11 and resulted in a system known for its small size. Shortly afterward, the now famous C programming language was developed on and for UNIX, and the UNIX operating system itself was rewritten into C. This then radical implementation decision is one of the factors that enabled UNIX to become the open system it is today.

AT&T was not allowed to market computer systems, so it had no way to sell this creative work from Bell Labs. Nonetheless, the popularity of UNIX grew through internal use at AT&T and licensing to universities for educational use. By 1977 commercial licenses for UNIX were being granted, and the first UNIX vendor, Interactive Systems Corporation, began selling UNIX systems for office automation.

Later versions developed at AT&T (or its successor, Unix System Laboratories, now owned by Novell) included System III and several releases of System V. The two most recent releases of System V, Release 3 (SVR3.2) and Release 4 (SVR4; the most recent version of SVR4 is SVR4.2) remain popular for computers ranging from PCs to mainframes.

All versions of UNIX based on the AT&T work require a license from the current owner, UNIX System Laboratories.

Berkeley Software Distributions

In 1978 the research group turned over distribution of UNIX to the UNIX Support Group (USG), which had distributed an internal version called the Programmer's Workbench. In 1982 USG introduced System III, which incorporated ideas from several different internal versions of and modifications to UNIX, developed by various groups. In 1983 USG released the original UNIX System V, and thanks to the divestiture of AT&T, was able to market it aggressively. A series of follow-on releases continued to introduce new features from other versions of UNIX, including the internal versions from the research group and the Berkeley Software Distribution.

While AT&T (through the research group and USG) developed UNIX, the universities that had acquired educational licenses were far from inactive. Most notably, the Computer Science Research Group at the University of California at Berkeley (UCB) developed a series of releases known as the Berkeley Software Distribution, or BSD. The original PDP-11 modifications were called 1BSD and 2BSD. Support for the Digital Equipment Corporation VAX computers was introduced in 3BSD. VAX development continued with 4.0BSD, 4.1BSD, 4.2BSD, and 4.3BSD, all of which (especially 4.2 and 4.3) had many features (and much source code) adopted into commercial products. Various later releases from UCB have attempted to create a publicly redistributable version of UNIX (prior releases had source code available only to source licensees). Notably, the "Second Networking Release" (Net2) was intended to make available all the parts of the Berkeley Software Distribution that were not subject to license restrictions. UNIX System Laboratories (USL) brought a lawsuit against the University and a company called Berkeley Software Design, Incorporated (BSDI). USL claimed license infringements by the BSD releases and BSDI's BSD/386 product, which was based in part on the BSD code. Recently the lawsuit was settled; the result is that BSDI is shipping BSD/386, and a new 4.4-Lite release of BSD, which requires no license from USL, will be available from UCB.

UNIX and Standards

Because of the multiple versions of UNIX and frequent cross-pollination between variants, many features have diverged in the different versions of UNIX. With the increasing popularity of UNIX in the commercial and government sector came the desire to standardize the features of UNIX so that a user or developer using UNIX could depend on those features.

The Institute of Electrical and Electronic Engineers created a series of standards committees to create standards for "An Industry-Recognized Operating Systems Interface Standard based on the UNIX Operating System." The results of two of the committees are important for the general user and developer. The POSIX.1 committee standardizes the C library interface used to write programs for UNIX. (See Chapter 17, "C Language.") The POSIX.2 committee standardizes the commands that are available for the general user. (See especially Chapter 4, "Listing Files," Chapter 5, "Popular Tools," Chapter 6, "Popular File Tools," Chapter 7, " Editing Text Files," Chapter 10, "What Is a Shell?" Chapter 11, "Bourne Shell," Chapter 12, "Korn Shell," Chapter 13, "C Shell," Chapter 14, "Which Shell Is Right for You? Shell Comparison," and Chapter 15, "Awk, Awk.")

In Europe, the X/Open Consortium brings together various UNIX-related standards, including the current attempt at a Common Open System Environment (COSE) specification. X/Open publishes a series of specifications called the X/Open Portability Guide, currently at Version 4. XPG4 is a popular specification in Europe, and many companies in the United States supply versions of UNIX that meet XPG.

The United States government has specified a series of standards based on XPG and POSIX. Currently FIPS 151-2 specifies the open systems requirements for federal purchases.

UNIX for Mainframes and Workstations

Many mainframe and workstation vendors make a version of UNIX for their machines. The best way to get information on these is directly from the manufacturer.

UNIX for Intel Platforms

Thanks to the great popularity of personal computers, there are a great number of UNIX versions available for Intel platforms. Choosing from the versions and trying to find software for the version you have can be a tricky business because the UNIX industry has not settled on a complete binary standard for the Intel platform. There are two basic categories of UNIX systems on Intel hardware, the SVR4-based systems and the older, more established SVR3.2 systems.

SVR4 vendors include NCR, IBM, Sequent, SunSoft (which sells Solaris for Intel), and Novell (which sells UnixWare). The Santa Cruz Operation (SCO) is the main vendor in the SVR3.2 camp. Vendors in the first camp are working toward cleaning up the standards to gain full "shrink-wrap portability" between their versions of UNIX. The goal is that this will make UNIX-on-Intel applications available, shrink-wrapped for any version of UNIX, just as you can now buy applications for MS-DOS or Microsoft Windows. SCO UNIX currently has a much larger base of available applications and is working to achieve binary compatibility with UnixWare.

Source Versions of "UNIX"

Several versions of UNIX and UNIX-like systems have been made that are free or extremely cheap and include source code. These versions have become particularly attractive to the modern-day hobbyist, who can now run a UNIX system at home for little investment and with great opportunity to experiment with the operating system or make changes to suit his or her needs.

An early UNIX-like system was MINIX, by Andrew Tanenbaum. His books *Operating Systems: Design and Implementations* describes MINIX and includes a source listing of the original version of MINIX. The latest version of MINIX is available from the publisher. MINIX is available in binary form for several machines (PC, Amiga, Atari, Macintosh, and SPARCStation).

In addition to the BSD386 product from BSDI, there is a free version of UNIX also based on the BSD releases, and called, confusingly, 386BSD. This is an effort by Bill and Lynne Jolitz to create a system for operating system research and experimentation. The source is freely available, and 386BSD has been described in a series of articles in *Dr. Dobbs' Journal.*

Another popular source version of UNIX is Linux. Linux was designed from the ground up by Linus Torvalds to be a free replacement for UNIX, and it aims for POSIX compliance. There are current efforts to make Linux reliably run both SVR3.2 and SVR4 binaries. There is also a project called WINE to create Microsoft Windows emulation capability for Linux.

Making the Change to UNIX

Many people considering making the transition to UNIX have a significant base of PC-based MS-DOS and Microsoft Windows applications. There have been a number of efforts to create programs or packages on UNIX that would ease the migration by allowing users to run their existing DOS and Windows applications on the same machine on which they run UNIX. Products in this arena include SoftPC and SoftWindows from Insignia, WABI from SunSoft, and WINE for Linux and 386BSD.

Introduction to the UNIX Philosophy

As described in the section "The History of UNIX," UNIX has its roots in a system that was intended to be small and supply orthogonal common pieces. Although most UNIX systems have grown to be fairly large and monolithic applications are not uncommon, the original philosophy still lives in the core commands available on all UNIX systems. There are several common key items throughout UNIX:

- Simple, orthogonal commands
- Commands connected through pipes
- A (mostly) common option interface style
- No file types

For detailed information on commands and connecting them together, see the chapters on shells (Chapters 10–14) and common commands (Chapters 5–9 and Chapter 15).

Simple, Orthogonal Commands

The original UNIX systems were very small, and the designers tried to take every advantage of those small machines by writing small commands. Each command attempted to do one thing well. The tools could then be combined (either with a shell script or a C program) to do more complicated tasks. One command, called wc, was written solely to count the lines, words, and characters in a file. To count all the words in all the files, you would type wc * and get output like that in Listing 1.1.

Listing 1.1. Using a simple command.

```
$ wc *
    351    2514   17021 minix-faq
   1011    5982   42139 minix-info
   1362    8496   59160 total
$
```

Commands Connected Through Pipes

To turn the simple, orthogonal commands into a powerful toolset, UNIX enables the user to use the output of one command as the input to another. This connection is called a *pipe*, and a series of commands connected by pipes is called a *pipeline*. For example, to count the number of lines that reference MINIX in all the files, one would type grep MINIX * ¦ wc and get output like that in Listing 1.2.

Listing 1.2. Using a pipeline.

```
$ grep MINIX * ¦ wc
    105     982    6895
$
```

A (Mostly) Common Option Interface Style

Each command has actions that can be controlled with *options*, which are specified by a hyphen followed by a single letter option (for example, -l). Some options take *option arguments*, which are specified by a hyphen followed by a single letter, followed by the argument (for example, -h Header). For example, to print on pages with 16 lines each all the lines in the file `minix-info` that mention *Tanenbaum*, you would enter `wc minix-info ¦ pr -l 16` and get output like that in Listing 1.3.

Listing 1.3. Using options in a pipeline.

```
$ grep Tanenbaum minix-info ¦ pr -l 16


Feb 14 16:02 1994     Page 1


[From Andy Tanenbaum <ast@cs.vu.nl> 28 August 1993]
     The author of MINIX, Andrew S. Tanenbaum, has written a book describing
     Author:     Andrew S. Tanenbaum
                               subjects.ast (list of Andy Tanenbaum's
                                Andy Tanenbaum since 1987 (on tape)
Version 1.0 is the version in Tanenbaum's book, "Operating Systems: Design




$
```

The bad news is that some UNIX commands have some quirks in the way they handle options. As more systems adopt the standards mentioned in the section "The History of UNIX," you will find fewer examples of commands with quirks.

No File Types

UNIX pays no attention to the contents of a file (except when you try to run a file as a command). It does not know the difference between a spreadsheet file and a word processor file. The meaning of the characters in a file is entirely supplied by the command(s) that uses the file. This concept is familiar to most PC users, but was a significant difference between UNIX and other earlier operating systems. The power of this concept is that any program can be used to operate on any file. The downside is that only a program that understands the file format can fully decode the information in the file.

Summary

UNIX has a long history as an open development environment. More recently, it has become the system of choice for both commercial and some personal uses. UNIX performs the typical operating system tasks, but also includes a standard set of commands and library interfaces. The building-block approach of UNIX makes it an ideal system for creating new applications.

Getting Started: Basic Tutorial

2

By Rachel and Robert Sartin

IN THIS CHAPTER

Logging In

If you're used to working with personal computers, then you're probably used to having a box with a floppy drive, a hard disk, and a monitor on your desk. You just turn it on and type away. UNIX workstations are similar to personal computers. A UNIX workstation might have a floppy drive, a hard disk, and a very large monitor. On a larger UNIX system, you might just have a terminal. Large UNIX systems allow multiple logins at a time. In these situations, the computer system has different parts in different places. Regardless of your situation, you will have at least one input device (a keyboard) and at least one output device (a video monitor). These pieces are physically connected to that computer.

User Account Setup

After a UNIX system is booted, you cannot simply start using it as you do a PC. Before you can access the computer system, someone—usually the system administrator—must configure the computer for your use. If you are running UNIX on your PC at home, you will most likely need to do these things for yourself. If you are a UNIX novice trying to set up your home computer system, you can refer to Chapter 33, "UNIX Installation Basics." If you are using a computer system in your place of work, your employer may have a person or persons whose specific job it is to administer all the systems. If this is the case, you will have to coordinate with a staff member to set up your system account. The company may have an application form on which you can request such things as a certain user name, a temporary password, which shell you want to use (see Chapter 14, "Which Shell Is Right for You"), what your default group is, what groups you should belong to, and which mail aliases you should be added to. Many of these things will depend on what work you will be doing and whom you will be working with.

No matter who sets up your computer account, you must know two things before you can use the system: your user name and your password. If you don't know what these are, you must stop and find out what has been assigned to you. The user name is a unique name that identifies you to the system. It is often related to your real name, such as your first name, your last name, or a combination of first initial and last name (for example, "frank," "brimmer," or "fbrimmer," respectively). If you get to request a user name, try to choose something that makes others think of you alone, and is not vague or common enough to cause confusion with others. The system administrator will verify that no one else on your system has this name before allowing you to have it. The password that you request or that has been assigned to you is a temporary string that allows you to initially access the computer system. The initial password isn't of any real importance because you should change it to something of your choice the first time you log in to the system (see "Managing Your Password" later in this chapter).

The other items on the account application form are harder for a novice user to determine. Asking a peer who uses the same system for the values his or her account has might be a good place to start. The system administrator may be able to help you figure out what values you should have. But don't worry; these are all easily changed later if you wish.

Logging In to the System

Now that you know your user name (say it's "brimmer") and password (say it's "new_user"), you can access the system. When you sit down in front of a UNIX workstation, you are expected to log in to the system. The system prompts (asks) you for your user name by printing `login:`. You should then enter your user name. Next, UNIX will prompt you for your password by printing `Password:`. Enter your password. As you type your password, don't be alarmed if the characters you type are not displayed on your screen. This is normal and is for your protection. No one else should know your password, and this way no one can look at your screen when you login and see your password.

```
login: brimmer
Password:
Please wait...checking for disk quotas

Marine biology word of the day:
Cnidaria (n.) Nigh-DARE-ee-uh (L. a nettle)  - a phylum of basically
radially symmetrical marine invertebrates including corals, sea
anemones, jellyfish and hydroids. This phylum was formerly known
as Coelenterata.
$
```

> **TIP:** Some keyboards have a key labeled "Return." Some have a key labeled "Enter." If your keyboard has both, then "Return" is probably the correct key to use.

> **TIP:** On some systems, erase is # and kill is @. On others, erase is Backspace or Delete and kill is Control+U or Control+X.

If you typed everything correctly and the system administrator has everything set up correctly, you are now logged in and may use the system. If you get a message saying `Login Incorrect`, then you may have typed your user name or password incorrectly. If you make a mistake during your user name, the Backspace key and the Delete key may not undo this mistake for you. The easiest thing to do is to start over by pressing Enter twice to get to a new `login:` prompt.

Other error messages you might receive are No Shell, No Directory, or Cannot Open Password File. If you see any of these messages, or if multiple attempts at logging in always produce the Login Incorrect message, contact your system administrator for help.

> **TIP:** The No Shell message means that UNIX is not able to start the command interpreter, which was configured when your account was set up. Depending on the UNIX system, your login may complete successfully and the default shell will be used. If this happens, you can use the chsh command, which will change the shell specified in your account. See Part II, "Hunt For Shells," for more information about various shells. The No Directory message means that UNIX cannot access your home directory, which was specified when your account was set up. Again, depending on the system, your login may complete successfully, placing you in a default directory. You may need to then enlist the help of the system administrator to create your home directory or change the home directory value for your account. See Chapter 3, "The UNIX File System: Go Climb a Tree," regarding directories and specifically your home directory. The Cannot Open Password File message means that UNIX is having a problem accessing the system password file, which holds the account information (user name, password, user id, shell, group, and so on) for each user. If there is a problem with this file, no user can log in to the system. Contact your system administrator if you see this message.

If your system is configured to use a graphical user interface (GUI), you probably have a login screen. This screen performs the same function as the command-line prompts but is presented as a graphical display. The display probably has two boxes for you to fill in, each with a label. One box is for your user name and the other is for your password.

After Login Succeeds

After a successful login, several messages appear on your screen. Some of these may be the date and time of your last login, the system's informative message (called the "Message of the Day"), and a message informing you whether you have (electronic) mail. The Message of the Day can be an important message to watch because it is one way that administrators communicate with the system users. The next scheduled down time (when no one can use the system) is an example of information that you might see here.

After all the messages scroll by, the system is ready and waiting for you to do something. This ready-and-waiting condition is signified by a prompt followed by a cursor. Typical prompts are $ or %. The dollar-sign prompt is commonly used by Bourne and Korn shells and the percent sign by c-shells. The value of this prompt (your primary prompt) can be changed if you wish. The person who set up your account may have already configured a different prompt value. To change this prompt, you need to change the value of the environment variable PS1 (for Bourne and Korn) or prompt (for C shell). (See the section "Configuring Your Environment" in this chapter for details on environment variables.) The cursor (the spot on the screen where the next character you type is displayed) is commonly an underline (_) or a box, either of which can be blinking. The cursor you see may vary from system to system.

Different Privileges for Different Users

If you are administering your own personal system, it is still important for you to set up a personal account for yourself, even though your system will come configured with some type of administrative account. This account should be used to do system-wide administrative actions. It is important to be careful when using this account because it has special privileges. UNIX systems have built-in security features. Most users cannot set up a new user account or do other administrative procedures. The user "root" is a special user, sometimes called super-user, which can do anything at all on the system. This high degree of power is necessary to fully administer a UNIX system, but it also allows its user to make a mistake and cause system problems. For this reason, you should set up a personal account for yourself that does not have root privilege. Then, your normal, day-to-day activities will affect only your personal environment and you will be in no danger of causing system-wide problems. In a multiuser, nonpersonal environment, you will most likely have only user (and not super-user) privileges. This security is even more important when more than one person is involved because one mistake by the root can affect every user and the entire system.

UNIX also has security to help prevent different users from harming each other on a multiuser system. Each user "owns" his or her environment and can selectively let groups or all others have access to this work. If you are doing private work in one area that no one else should be allowed to see, then you should restrict access to the owner (you). If you and your team members are working on a group project, you can restrict access to the owner (you) and everyone in your group. If this work should be shared with many or all people on the system, then you should allow access to everyone.

Logging Out

When you are done using the system, you should log out. This will prevent other people from accidentally or intentionally getting access to your files. It will also make the system available for their use.

The normal way to log out from almost any shell is to type exit. This causes your shell to exit, or stop running. When you exit from your login shell, you log out. If you are using csh, you can also type logout; if you are in a login shell, then csh will log out. Some shells, depending on your configuration, will also log you out if you type the end-of-file character (typically Control+D; see "Working on the System" later in this chapter).

If you have a graphical user interface, your logout procedure may be different. Please consult your manuals or online help to learn about logging out of your GUI.

Using Commands

During the login process described in the section, "Logging In" UNIX performs several actions that prepare you and the system for each other. These include performing system accounting, initializing your user environment, and starting a command interpreter (commonly called a *shell*). Commands are how you tell the system to do something. The command interpreter recognizes these commands and passes the information off to where it is needed. UNIX systems originally came with a command interpreter called the Bourne Shell (usually referred to as *sh*, though some systems ship Korn or POSIX as *sh*—see the Note that follows). This shell is still available on most UNIX computer systems. A newer shell that is common to most UNIX systems is the C Shell (referred to as *csh*). Another commonly used, but not as pervasive, shell is the Korn Shell (referred to as *ksh*). Among different shells, there is some variation of the commands that are available. Refer to Part II, "Hunt for Shells," for details on these UNIX shells.

> **NOTE:** What's in a name?
>
> There are a number of different common shells on various UNIX operating systems. The most common are as follows:
>
> | | |
> |---|---|
> | sh | The Bourne shell is the most common of all the shells. (May be installed as bsh.) |
> | sh | The POSIX shell is much like the Korn shell. The POSIX standard requires it to be installed as sh. Some vendors install it as /bin/sh. Some put it in a special directory and call it sh, leaving the Bourne shell as /bin/sh. |
> | ksh | The Korn shell is a derivative of the Bourne shell, which adds history and command-line editing. (Sometimes installed as sh.) |
> | csh | The C shell is based on the popular C language. |
> | bash | The Born Again shell is less common. |
> | tcsh | This is a version of the C shell with interactive command-line editing. |

What Is a Command?

A UNIX command is a series of characters that you type. These characters consist of words that are separated by whitespace. Whitespace is the result of typing one or more Space or

Tab keys. The first word is the name of the command. The rest of the words are called the command's arguments. The arguments give the command information that it might need, or specify varying behavior of the command. To invoke a command, simply type the command name, followed by arguments (if any), to indicate to the shell that you are done typing and are ready for the command to be executed, press Enter.

Try it out. Enter the date command. The command's name is "date" and it takes no arguments. Therefore, type date and press Enter and see what happens. You should see that the computer has printed the current date and time. If the date or time does not match reality, ask the system administrator to fix it. How about trying a command that has arguments? Try the echo command. The name of the command is "echo" and it takes a series of arguments. The echo command will then write, or echo, these arguments out to your screen. Try creating a command that will write your first and last name on the screen. Here is what these commands and output look like on our system:

```
$ date
Sat Mar  5 11:11:00 CST 1994
$ echo Arnold Brimmer
Arnold Brimmer
$
```

> **NOTE:** Some commands such as echo are part of the particular shell you are using. These are called *built-ins*. In this case, the commands are not standard from one shell to another. Therefore, if you learn one shell and then later have to (or want to) switch to using a different shell, you may have to learn new commands (and unlearn others). Other commands are standard UNIX commands and do not depend on what shell you are using. These should be on every UNIX system. The remaining commands are nonstandard UNIX and may or may not be on a particular UNIX system.

UNIX commands use a special type of argument called an option. An option commonly takes the form of a dash (made by using the minus sign key) followed by one or more characters. The options provide information to the command. Most of the time, options are just a single character following a dash. Two of the other lesser used forms are a plus sign rather than a minus sign, and a word following a dash rather than a single character. The following paragraph shows a common command with two of its common options. The ls command lists the files in your current directory.

First, try the ls command with no arguments. Then, try it with the -a option and note that the directory listing contains a few files that start with a period. These hidden files get listed by the ls command only if you use the -a option. Next, try the ls command with the -1 option. This option changes the format of the directory listing so that each file is displayed along with some relevant details. Finally, try the `ls` command with both of these options, so that your command is as follows: `ls -a -l`.

```
$ ls
visible
$ ls -a
.            ..           .hidden   visible
$ ls -l
total 0
-rw-rw-rw-   1 sartin   uu              0 Mar  5 12:58 visible
$ ls -a -l
total 16
drwxrwxrwx   2 sartin   uu           1024 Mar  5 13:03 .
drwxr-xr-x  37 sartin   uu           3072 Mar  5 13:03 ..
-rw-rw-rw-   1 sartin   uu              0 Mar  5 12:58 .hidden
-rw-rw-rw-   1 sartin   uu              0 Mar  5 12:58 visible
$
```

A command developer often tries to choose option letters that are meaningful. Regarding the `ls` command, you might think of the `-a` as meaning that "all" files should be listed (including the special files starting with period). And you might think of the `-l` option as meaning a "long" directory listing because the format is changed so that each line contains one file along with its details. This makes for a longer listing.

Redirecting Input and Output

One very pervasive concept in UNIX is the redirection of commands' input and output. Before looking at redirection, though, it is a good idea to look at input and output without modification. UNIX uses the word standard in this subject to mean the default or normal mode. Thus, UNIX has the term *standard input*, which means input coming from the default setting, and the term *standard output*, which means output going to the normal place. When you first log in to the system, and your shell executes, your standard input is set to be what you type at the keyboard, and your standard output is set to be your display screen. With this in mind, follow along with the example.

The `cat` command takes any characters from standard input, and then echoes them to standard output. For example, type the `cat` command, with no arguments. Your cursor should be sitting on the next line without a prompt. At this point, the `cat` command is waiting for you to enter characters. You can enter as many as you like, and then you should specify that you are finished. Type a few words and then press Return. Now type the special character, Control+D (hold down the Control key while typing the D key). This is the "eof" control character. (See "Working on the System" later in this chapter for a description of control characters.) The words you typed should be on your screen twice— once caused by you entering them from the keyboard, and next as the `cat` command outputs them to your screen. This first step used standard input (from you typing on the keyboard), and standard output (the command results being printed on the screen).

```
$ cat
s
A few words
<CTRL><D>
A few words
$ cat > scotty
Meow, whine
meow
<CTRL><D>
$ cat < scotty
Meow, whine
meow
$ cat scotty
Meow, whine
meow
$
```

Although this simple case may not seem terribly useful yet, wait to see its use as you add redirection.

UNIX shells have special characters that signify redirection. Only the basics are covered here. Refer to Part II, "Hunt for Shells," for details on each shell's redirection syntax. Output redirection is signified by the > character and input redirection is signified by the < character. Output is commonly redirected to and input is redirected from a file. Now, continue with the rest of the example.

Next, try the cat command using output redirection, leaving standard input alone. Enter cat > *filename*. The filename is a name of your choice. Once again, the cat command should be waiting for input (coming from standard input, which is your keyboard) at the beginning of the next line. Enter a few words, as you did before, press Return, and then, at the start of the next line, press Control+D. The words you typed didn't show up on your screen because you redirected the output of the cat command. The output was directed to go to the file *filename*. But how do you know it is there? In order to verify this, use the cat command with input redirection—which is the next order of business.

> **CAUTION:** <Ctrl><D> must be specified as the first character of an input line for it to be seen as "eof."

To see the contents of the file *filename*, you would like the input of the cat command to come from that file, and the output to go to the screen so that you can see it. Therefore, you want to redirect standard input and leave the output alone. Enter cat < *filename*. This time, the cat command did not wait for you—because you were not supplying the input. The file supplied the input. The cat command printed the contents of the file to the screen.

TIP: Note the subtle distinction between these two commands: `cat > filename` and `cat < filename`. You can remember the difference by verbalizing which way the sign points; does it point into the command or out of the command? Into the command is input redirection and out of the command is output redirection.

The `cat` command allows you to specify a filename to use as input. Try showing the contents of the file this (more common) way: enter `cat filename`. Many commands are designed similarly—they have an argument that is used to specify a file as the input. Because of this common command design, redirecting input in this way is not nearly as common as redirecting the output.

UNIX was developed with the philosophy of having simple commands that do well-defined, simple things. Then, by combining these simple commands, the user could do very powerful things. Pipes are one of the ways UNIX allows users to combine several commands. The pipe is signified by the vertical bar (¦) symbol. A pipe is a means of taking the output of one command and redirecting it as the input of another command. Say that you want to know how many files you have in your current directory. Recall that the `ls` command will list all the files in your current directory. You could then count the number of files. But UNIX has a command that counts the number of characters, words, and lines of input and displays these statistics. Therefore, you can combine these two commands to give you the number of files in your directory. One way you could do this is as follows: `ls -l ¦ wc -l`. Analyzing this command, you can see that the first part is something familiar. The `ls -l` command gives a directory listing in long format. In fact, it prints one file per line. The `wc -l` command gives the number of lines that are in the input. Combining the two commands via a pipe takes the output of the first command (the long directory listing) and gives it to the input of the second command. The output of the second command (which is not redirected—it goes to standard output) is displayed on your screen.

These basic forms of redirection allow you to be very versatile as you learn a few commands at a time. Try to learn a command and use it with various options and arguments, then add redirection of input and output. And finally, combine commands with pipes. This approach should help you to feel comfortable with the commands and their varied uses.

Configuring Your Environment

In order to make using the shell easier and more flexible, UNIX uses the concept of an *environment*. Your environment is a set of values. You can change these values, add new values, or remove existing values. These values are called *environment variables*—environment because they describe or define your environment, and variables because they can change.

Viewing and Setting Environment Variables

Every user's environment looks a little different. Why don't you see what your environment looks like? Type the env command with no arguments. The output formatting and variable names depend on which shell you are using and how your system is configured. A typical environment might include some of the following:

```
$ env
HOME=/u/sartin
LOGNAME=sartin
MAIL=/usr/mail/sartin
MANPATH=/usr/man:/usr/contrib/man:/usr/local/man
PATH=/bin/posix:/bin:/usr/bin:/usr/contrib/bin:/usr/local/bin
SHELL=/bin/sh
TERM=vt100
TZ=CST6CDT
$ echo $HOME
/u/sartin
$
```

Sometimes the number of variables in your environment grows quite large, so much so that you don't want to see all of the values displayed when you are interested in just one. If this is the case, you can use the echo command to show an environment variable's current value. To specify that a word you type should be treated differently—as a value of an environment variable—you immediately precede the variable name with a dollar sign ($). Be careful not to type any whitespace between the $ and the word. One of the variables in the example is HOME. You probably have this variable in your environment, too. Try to display its value using echo.

> **NOTE:** If you use csh, some environment variables are automatically copied to and from csh variables. These include HOME, TERM, and PATH, which csh keeps in home, term, and path.

You can create a new environment variable by simply giving it a value. If you give an existing variable a value, the old value is overwritten. One difficulty in setting environment variables is that the way you set them depends on the shell you are using. To see how to set environment variables, look at the details about the shell you are using in Part II, "Hunt For Shells."

In order for your screen to display the output correctly, the environment variable TERM needs to have a reasonable value. This variable name comes from the times when terminals were used as displays (before PCs and graphics displays were common). Different terminals supported varying output control. Therefore, UNIX systems have various terminal types that they support. These are not standard, so you need to find out which terminal type to use from your support personnel. If you are using a PC to connect to a UNIX system, your PC is running a terminal emulation tool. Most of these tools have the capability to emulate several types of terminal. The important point here is to make sure that your emulator and your TERM variable are the same (or compatible). Start by seeing what your TERM variable is set to by entering echo $TERM. Refer to your PC terminal emulation manual and ask your system administrator for help to make sure that this is set up correctly.

> **TIP:** Many terminal emulators (including the Microsoft Windows "Terminal" program) support either "VT100" or ANSI standard terminal control sequences. Try setting TERM to vt100 or ansi for this type of terminal emulator.

Using Shell Startup Files

Where do all these environment variables come from? Well, the system sets up various ones for you. And each user commonly sets up others during the login process. Yes, you may be doing this without even knowing it. During the startup, which happens at login, a shell is started. This shell automatically looks in a special place or two for some startup information. One of these places is in your home directory. The startup information in your home directory is found in special files. The specific shell you are using will determine the name of the particular file. When the shell starts up, it examines this file and performs whatever actions are specified. One of the common actions is to give values to environment variables. This action is called *initializing* or *setting* the values.

One environment variable that is commonly set in a user's shell startup file is the PATH variable (or lowercase path for C-shell users). This variable's value is a list of places (directories) on the system where the shell should look to locate a command. Each command you type is physically located as a file somewhere on your file system. It is possible for the same command name to be located in different places (and to have either the same or different behavior when executed). Say that you have a program called my_program that is stored in your home directory, and your friend has a program called my_program, which is in her home directory. If you type my_program at the prompt, the shell needs to know where to look to find the storage location of my_program. The shell looks at the value of the PATH variable and uses the list of directories as an ordered directory search list. The first directory that has a my_program stops the search, and the shell executes that file. Because all files within a single directory must be unique, this gives a straightforward and sufficient method for finding executables (commands).

You probably want $HOME/bin to be toward the beginning of your PATH directory list, whereas you may want your friend's binary directory to be toward the end, or not listed at all. This way, when you type my_program, you will execute your my_program rather than hers. You can do all types of things in shell startup files in addition to setting environment variable values. If you want, you can add an echo command that prints out a greeting or reminds you to do something. One common item that is configured inside a shell startup file is the setup of your control characters. (See "Working on the System" later in this chapter.) These startup files are a powerful tool for you, the user of the shell, to configure the behavior of the shell automatically. Shell startup files are covered in more detail in Part II, "Hunt for Shells."

> **TIP:** It is a good idea to create a bin directory in your HOME and store executables there. Include $HOME/bin in your path.

Configuring with *rc* files

The idea of having a file that is read on startup is not only used by the shells. In fact, many commands have special files containing configuration information that the user can modify. The general class of files is called *rc* files. This comes from the naming convention of these files. Most of these files end with the letters *rc*. Some of the more common files are .exrc, .mailrc, and .cshrc. These are all dot files; that is, they begin with a period (dot). The significance of starting a filename with a dot is that this file is not displayed during normal directory listing. If you want to see these files, use the -a option to the ls command. The .exrc file is used by the vi and ex editors (see Chapter 7, "Text Editing with vi, EMACS, and sed"). The .mailrc file is used by various electronic mail tools (see Chapter 9, "Communicating with Others"). The .cshrc file is the C-shell startup file just discussed. The rc files are normally found in your home directory; that is, the default location for most of these files. Look at which rc files you have in your home directory (use the ls -a command). Then examine the contents of one of the files (use the cat *filename* command).

Your environment has a great effect on the use of your system. It is initialized during login with a shell startup file, and it grows and changes as you create new variables and change existing ones. Your environment affects every command you execute. It is important to get your environment set up to make your common actions easy. Spend the time to do this now and you will be glad you did later.

Managing Your Password

During login, UNIX asked you to enter your password. If this is your first time on this computer, your password was configured by the system administrator. One of the very first things you should do after logging in is change your password so that no one, not even the system administrator, knows what it is. You can do this via the `passwd` command. But before you do this, you should put some thought into what you want your password to be. Here are some points to consider:

1. It should be easy for you to remember. If you forget what your password is, no one, not even the system administrator, can look it up for you. The only thing the system administrator can do is to reset your password to a value. This wastes the administrator's time as well as yours.

2. It shouldn't be easy for anyone to figure out. Do not make it anyone's name or birth date, or your user name, or any of these spelled backwards. It is also wise to avoid something that appears in a dictionary. A good idea would be to include at least one nonalphabetic character (for example, a period or a dollar sign).

3. Make it a reasonable length. Some systems impose a minimum number of characters for a password. At least 5 characters is adequate. There isn't usually a limit as to the maximum number of characters, but only the first 8 are significant. The ninth character and after are ignored when checking to see whether you typed your password correctly.

4. Change your password once in a while. Some systems check the last time you changed your password. If a time limit has been reached, you will be notified that your password has expired as you log in. You will be prompted to change it immediately and won't be allowed to log in until you successfully get it changed. This time limit is system imposed. Changing your password every few months is reasonable.

5. Don't write it down or tell it to anyone. Don't write it on scraps of paper. Don't tell your mother. Don't write it in your calendar. Don't write it in your diary. Don't tell your priest. Don't put it in a dialup terminal configuration file. Nowhere. Nobody. Maybe in your safe deposit box.

After you have thought about what you want your password to be, you can change it with the `passwd` command. Try it now; you can change your password as often as you like. Enter `passwd`. First, a prompt asking you to enter your old password is displayed. Type your old password and press Return. Next, you are prompted for your new password. Type it in and press Enter. Finally, you are prompted to re-enter your new password. This confirmation helps avoid changing your password if you made a typing error. If you make a mistake entering your old password, or if the two new password entries are not identical, then no change is made. Your old password is still in effect. Unless you make the same mistake both times that you enter the new password, you are in no danger of erroneously changing your password.

Working on the System

Most keys on the keyboard are fairly obvious. If you type the S key, an s character appears on your screen. If you hold down the Shift key and type the S key, a capital s character (S) appears on your screen. In addition to the letters and digits, the symbols, some of which are above the digits, are familiar—such as the percent sign (%) and the comma (,). There are some UNIX and system-specific special characters in addition to these, which you should become familiar with. They will help you manage your work and typing more effectively. The general type of character is called a *control character.* The name comes from the way in which you type them. First, locate the Control key—there should be one or maybe two on your keyboard. It may be labeled *Ctrl* or some other abbreviation of the word *Control.* This key is used like the Shift key. You press it but don't release it. While the Control key is depressed, you type another key, often a letter of the alphabet. If you type the Q key while the Control key is held, this is called Control+Q, and is commonly written ^Q (the caret symbol, which is found above the digit 6, followed by the alphabetic character).

> **NOTE:** When you see the notation ^Q, this does NOT mean to hold the Control and Shift down while pressing Q. All you do is to hold down the Control key while pressing Q.

UNIX uses these control keys for various common keyboard actions. They can come in very handy. But the hard part is that different systems have different default Control key settings for these actions. Therefore, first you should find out what your current settings are, and then you can change them if you wish. In order to look at what your current settings are, use the `stty` command. Enter `stty -a` at your command prompt and look at the results. Refer to the next example for an output of this command.

> **TIP:** If you're typing and nothing is showing on your screen, a ^S (or *stop control character*) inadvertently may have been typed. Try typing ^Q (or *start control character*) and see whether your typed characters now appear.

```
$ stty -a
speed 9600 baud; line = 0; susp <undef>; dsusp <undef>
rows = 44; columns = 120
intr = ^C; quit = ^\; erase = ^H; kill = ^X; swtch <undef>
eof = ^D; eol = ^@; min = 4; time = 0; stop = ^S; start = ^Q
-parenb -parodd cs8 -cstopb hupcl cread -clocal -loblk -crts
-ignbrk -brkint -ignpar -parmrk -inpck -istrip -inlcr -igncr icrnl -iuclc
ixon -ixany -ixoff -rtsxoff -ctsxon -ienqak
isig icanon iexten -xcase echo echoe echok -echonl -noflsh
opost -olcuc onlcr -ocrnl -onocr -onlret -ofill -ofdel -tostop tab3
$
```

Referring to the preceding example of stty output, look for the section that has the words erase, kill, and eof. Associated with each word is a control character. Find the similar part of your stty output. Keep this handy as you read the next topics.

Erase

Look at the word erase in the stty output. Next to this word is ^H (verbalized as Control+H). Therefore, on my system, Erase, which means to back up over the last character typed, is done by typing ^H. The Erase key is how you can fix your typing errors. Remember to look at your stty -a output because your system may be configured differently than this example. Try it out on your system. First, type a character you wish to erase, say, an A. Now type your Control, Backspace, or Delete key associated with your Erase. If everything goes right, your cursor should have backed up to be on top of your A and the next key you type will be where the A was. Try typing a correct series of keys, say date<Return>, to make sure that the control character actually worked. If you get a message similar to "A^Hdate not found", then Erase is not working. To make it work correctly, pick the key you want associated with Erase and input the following (assuming that you have picked the backspace key):

```
$ stty erase '^H'
$
```

Now, try entering the date command again and deleting the *A* in dAte and replacing it with *a*.

> **NOTE:** Depending on your display, erasing characters may not actually make the character disappear. Instead, it may reposition the cursor so that the next keystroke overwrites the character.

The Erase key is one of the most used control keys, because typing without mistakes is difficult to do. Therefore, most keyboards have one or more special keys that are suited to this job. Look for keys labeled "Delete" or "Backspace." One of these usually works as an erase key. Try typing some characters and seeing what happens when you then press Backspace or Delete. Normally the Backspace key is set up to be ^H, so, if your erase is configured to be ^H, Backspace most likely will work.

Kill

The Kill control character is similar to the Erase control character, in that it allows you to back up over typing mistakes. Whereas Erase backs up one character at a time, Kill backs up all the way to the prompt. Therefore, if you are typing a really long command and you realize, toward the end, that you forgot to do some other command first, you can start over by typing the control character associated with Kill. If you can't see what your Kill is set to, redo the stty command. In the stty output example, the system has kill set to ^X. Again, remember that your system can be configured differently than this example. Now, try typing several characters followed by your Kill control character and see what happens. All the characters should be erased and your cursor should be after the prompt.

Stop and Start

Two other commonly used control characters are Stop and Start. Their normal values are ^S and ^Q, respectively. Stop allows you to temporarily pause what is happening on your screen, and Start allows you to resume activity following a stop. This is useful if text is scrolling on your screen too fast for you to read. The Stop control character will pause the scrolling indefinitely so that you can read at your leisure. You might try this during your next login while the Message of the Day is scrolling by (see the section earlier in this chapter called "Logging In"). But remember to be prepared and be swift, because that text can scroll by quite quickly. Try to stop the scrolling, and then don't forget to continue the scrolling by typing your Start control character.

NOTE: On modern GUIs and high-speed connections Stop and Start give very poor control of output. This is because the output is so fast an entire screen may go by before you type the Stop character.

eof

The eof control character is used to signal the end of input. The letters *eof* come from *end of file*. The normal value of the eof control character is ^D, but be sure to verify this using the stty command. You can see how the eof character is used in the section called "Redirecting Input and Output" earlier in this chapter.

There are several other control characters that we will not look at here. You should refer to the stty command in your system documentation for information. Or better yet, keep reading because we will show you how to find information about commands via the UNIX online help facility.

The stty command is also used to set the value of control characters. You can simply enter stty erase '^H' to change your Erase character to Backspace. Do not enter a Control+H here; rather, enter '^H'. Some shells, including the original Bourne shell, treat the caret specially, so you may need the quotes. (Double quotation marks would also work in this example.) Try changing the value of your Erase control character and then use the stty -a command to make sure it happened.

> **TIP:** Remember that typing the end of file character to your shell might log you out of the system!

Online Help

One of the most important things to know about UNIX or any computer system is how to get help when you don't know how to use a command. Many commands will give you a *usage message* if you incorrectly enter the command. This message shows you the correct syntax for the command. This can be a quick reminder of the arguments and their order. For many commands, you can get the usage message by using the option -?. The usage message often does not give you any semantic information.

The UNIX command man is a powerful tool that gives you complete online access to the UNIX manuals. In its simplest form, the man command takes one argument, the name of the command or manual entry on which you need information. Try using the man command now—perhaps you could use one of the previous commands you were interested in as the argument. Or, if you want to get a head start on this section, you might try entering man man to get information on the man help facility itself.

The manual entry is called a *man page*, even though it is often more than one page long. There are common sections to man pages. Depending on the command, some or all of the sections may be present. At the start of the man page is the Name. This is usually a one-liner that gives the command's name along with a phrase describing what it does. Next is the Synopsis, which gives the command's syntax including its arguments and options. In the Synopsis, if an argument is enclosed in square brackets ([ ]), then that argument is optional. If two elements of the syntax are separated with a vertical bar (¦), then either one or the other (but not both) of the items is allowed.

```
$ man page
```

Depending on the man page, there are several more sections that you may see. A few of the more common are Description, Files, and See Also. The Description section contains the details of the command's usage. It describes each option, argument, and the interrelations and accepted values of each. This will help you to learn exactly how the command should be used. The Files section contains a list of the UNIX files used by this command. You may want to look at the contents of these files to help you understand some of the command's behaviors. The See Also section can be very important when you either want to learn more on a similar topic or don't have quite the right man page. This section lists pointers to related or dependent commands.

The man command has a very useful option, especially for users who are unfamiliar with UNIX. This option is -k and is used to find all commands that have to do with a word you supply following the -k. For instance, if you would like to find out information on printing, you might enter the command man -k print. The man command then searches a special database, called the *whatis* database, for commands and descriptions that contain the word *print*. During the search, if *print* or any word that contains *print* (such as *printing*) is found, this command is displayed on your screen. Therefore, the final result is a list of all commands having to do with *print*. Then you can use the man command to find out the details about any or all of the commands on this list. On some systems, another way to do this search is via the command apropos, which is equivalent to man -k.

Although having the complete set of manual entries online is extremely useful, it also takes a fairly large amount of disk space. One option that some people use to help lower the amount of disk space needed is to have the manual entries stored on one machine that everyone can access via the network. Because of this, the manual entries may not be stored in the directories expected. In order to show the man command where the entries are stored, you can set the MANPATH variable (see the section "Viewing and Setting Environment Variables" that appeared earlier in this chapter).

Another potential problem you might see when trying to use man has to do with the -k option. Recall that the -k option searches the whatis database for a keyword you specify. This works only if the system administrator has created this database ahead of time. The system administrator does this via the catman command. If the database has not yet been created, you will see an error regarding the whatis database not being found whenever you use the -k option (or the apropos command). Ask your system administrator to fix this.

Summary

The start of this chapter helped you prepare for what needs to happen before and during login. The section "Configuring Your Environment" looked at your environment and how you can configure it. Look at the manual entry for the shell you're using to find out more about environments. Also read Part II, "Hunt for Shell," for shell details. The section on "Managing Your Password" discussed how managing your password via the passwd command is important for security reasons. Look at the manual entry for passwd if you need more information. The "Working on the System" section helped make your typing easier through the use of control characters. The stty man page is a good place to look for more information on control characters. The section on online help is probably the most important section of this chapter; by describing the man command, it showed you how to access the UNIX manual online. Using this, you can look up anything you want or need. The commands that you saw in the "Using Commands" section are in the online manual. Use the man command and learn more about them. With this as a start, you should be comfortable with the basics.

The UNIX File System: Go Climb a Tree

By Jeff Smith

When you work with UNIX, one way or another you spend most of your time working with files. In this chapter, you learn how to create and remove files, copy and rename them, create links to them, and use directories to organize your files so that you can find them later. You also learn how to view your files, list their names and sizes, and move around in the UNIX file tree. Finally, this chapter shows how you can choose to share or restrict the information in your files.

One of UNIX's greatest strengths is the consistent way in which it treats files. Although some operating systems use different types of files that each require unique handling, you can handle most UNIX files the same. For instance, the cat command, which displays a disk file on your terminal screen, can also send the file to the printer. As far as cat (and UNIX) are concerned, the printer and your terminal look the same, and they look like any other UNIX file. UNIX also doesn't distinguish between files that you create and the standard files that come with the operating system—as far as UNIX is concerned, a file is a file is a file. This consistency makes it easy to work with files because you don't have to learn special commands for every new task. Often, as in the cat example, you can use the same command for several purposes. This makes it easy to write UNIX programs because you usually don't have to worry whether you're talking to a terminal, a printer, or an ordinary file on a disk drive.

The Types of UNIX Files

There are three types of UNIX files: regular files, directories, and device files. *Regular files* hold executable programs and data. *Executable programs* are the commands (such as cat) that you enter. *Data* is information that you store for later use. Such information can be virtually anything: a USENET news article with a promising-looking recipe for linguini, a book that you are writing, a homework assignment, or a saved spreadsheet.

Directories are files that contain other files and subdirectories, just as a filing cabinet's drawers hold related folders. Directories help you organize your information by keeping closely related files in the same place so you can find them later. For instance, you might save all your spreadsheets in a single directory instead of mixing them with your linguini recipes and book chapters.

As in the cat example, files can also refer to computer hardware such as terminals and printers. These *device files* can also refer to tape and disk drives, CD-ROM players, modems, network interfaces, scanners, and any other piece of computer hardware. Under UNIX, even the computer's memory is a file.

Although UNIX treats all files similarly, some require slightly unique treatment. For example, UNIX treats directories specially in some ways. Also, because they refer directly to the computer's hardware, device files sometimes must be treated differently from ordinary files. For instance, most files have a definite size in bytes—the number of characters they contain. Your terminal's keyboard is a device file, but how many characters does it hold? The question of file size doesn't make sense in this case. Despite these differences, UNIX commands usually don't distinguish among the various types of files.

Creating, Listing, and Viewing Files

You can create files in many ways, even if you don't yet know how to use a text editor. One of the easiest ways is to use the `touch` command, as follows:

```
$ touch myfile
```

This command creates an empty filenamed `myfile`.

An empty file isn't much good except as a place holder that you can fill in later. If you want to create a file that contains some text, you can use either the `echo` or `cat` command. The `echo` command is a simple but useful command that prints its command-line arguments to *stdout*, the *standard output* file, which by default is your terminal screen. For instance, enter the following:

```
$ echo Will Rogers
Will Rogers
```

The words `Will Rogers` are echoed to your terminal screen.

You can save the words by using your shell's *file redirection* capability to redirect echo's standard output to a different file:

```
$ echo Will Rogers > cowboys
```

Notice that the preceding command does not send output to your terminal; the greater-than sign tells your shell to *redirect* echo's output into cowboys.

You can view the contents of cowboys with cat, as follows:

```
$ cat cowboys
Will Rogers
```

If you want to add more text to a file, use *two* greater-than signs:

```
$ echo Roy Rogers >> cowboys
```

Now cat shows both lines:

```
$ cat cowboys
Will Rogers
Roy Rogers
```

> **CAUTION:** When you use the greater-than sign to create a file, your shell creates a zero-length file (just as touch does) and then fills it. If the file already exists, your shell first destroys its contents to make it zero-length. You must use two greater-than signs to append new text to a file or you will destroy your earlier work.

The cat command doesn't just display files. It also can create them by using shell redirection. If you plan to enter several lines of text, cat is more convenient than echo:

```
$ cat > prufrock
Let us go then, you and I,
When the evening is spread out against the sky
Like a patient etherised upon a table;
```

Then press Ctrl+D. This keystroke is the default *end-of-file* character; it tells cat that you are done typing.

Now you have a filenamed prufrock, and you can view it by using the cat command:

```
$ cat prufrock
Let us go then, you and I,
When the evening is spread out against the sky
Like a patient etherised upon a table;
```

Note that cat does not print the end-of-file character when you display the file.

> **NOTE:** When you create a file with cat, you can use your *character-erase, word-erase,* and *line-kill* characters (see Chapter 7, "Text Editing with vi, EMACS, and sed Files") to correct typing mistakes in the current line. After you press Enter, you cannot make corrections. To correct such a mistake, you must learn to use a text editor (see Chapter 7).

It may seem odd that cat both creates and displays files, but this is normal for UNIX; that is, it's normal for commands not to know one type of file from another. The name cat derives from the word *catenate*, which means to connect in a series or to link together. The cat command doesn't care which file it receives as input or where the output goes. Because UNIX handles your terminal keyboard and screen as ordinary files, when you enter cat cowboys, cat catenates cowboys to your terminal screen, and when you enter cat > prufrock, the command catenates what you enter into a disk file. You can even run cat without specifying an input or output file:

```
$ cat
Let us go then, you and I,
Let us go then, you and I,
When the evening is spread out against the sky
When the evening is spread out against the sky
```

Press Ctrl+D to insert an end-of-file.

The cat command echos to your screen every line that you enter before Ctrl+D because, by default, cat uses your terminal keyboard as its input file and your screen as its output file. Like other UNIX commands, cat treats files quite consistently and therefore is very flexible.

The cat command works well for short files that fit on a single terminal screen, but if you try to display a longer file, all but the last lines of it scroll off your screen. To view long files, you can temporarily freeze your terminal screen by typing Ctrl+S and restart it by typing Ctrl+Q. However, if your terminal is fast, you may not be able to stop it quickly enough. *Pagers* like pg and more pause after every screen. (See Chapter 4, "Listing Files.")

Now that you have some files, you may want to list them or view their names. The ls (*list files*) command can display each file's name, size, and time of creation, and also which users have permission to view, modify, and remove them.

If you want to know only the names of the files, enter the following:

```
$ ls
cowboys prufrock
```

If you have many files, you may want to view only some of them. If you want ls to list specific files, you can specify their names on the command line:

```
$ ls prufrock
prufrock
```

This output isn't very useful; you already know the name of the file, so there's not much point in listing it. However, you can use ls in this way to find out whether a certain file exists. If the file doesn't exist, ls prints an error message, as follows:

```
$ ls alfred_j
alfred_j: No such file or directory
```

The message No such file or directory means exactly what it says: You don't have a filenamed alfred_j.

A better application of this feature of ls is to use your shell's *metacharacters* or *wild cards* to list a file when you know only part of its name. (For more information on *metacharacters* and *wild cards*, see Chapter 11, "Bourne Shell," Chapter 12, "Korn Shell," and Chapter 13, "C Shell.") With shell wild cards, you can specify parts of filenames and let your shell fill in the rest. Suppose that you can't remember the name of the file that includes the linguini recipe, but you remember that it starts with the letter *l.* You could enter **ls** and then search through a list of all your files to find the one that you want. However, the following command makes the search easier:

```
$ ls l*
linguini    local_lore
```

The l* argument narrows your listing by telling ls that you're interested only in files that begin with an l, followed by zero or more of any other characters. The ls command ignores the files cowboys and prufrock, and lists only those files beginning with the letter l.

Wild cards are a powerful method for narrowing your file listings. Throughout this chapter, you'll see many uses for wild cards. Because they are a characteristic of your shell and not the commands you invoke from your shell, wild cards work equally well with other commands, such as cat. For instance, you could enter the following command to display both your linguini recipe and the file local_lore:

```
$ cat l*
```

However, different shells may use different wild cards, or use the same ones in different ways. This chapter provides examples only of the wild cards that are common to all shells. To learn how your shell uses wild cards, see Chapters 12 ("Korn Shell") and 13 ("C Shell") and your shell's manual page.

The UNIX File Tree

As mentioned in the introduction to this chapter, your personal files usually contain data—information that you want the computer to save when you're not logged in. If you use UNIX for a long time, you'll accumulate hundreds or even thousands of files, and thousands more system files that are a standard part of UNIX. How can you keep all these files organized and find the ones that you want when you need them?

The designers of UNIX solved this problem by using directories to organize the UNIX file system into a structure that is shaped like an upside-down tree. Directories enable you to keep related files in one place, where you see them only when you want—after all, you needn't clutter your file listings with recipes when you're working with a spreadsheet.

Figure 3.1 shows part of the file tree for a typical UNIX system. In this drawing, which looks somewhat like an upside-down tree, names like home and jane are followed by a slash (/), which indicates that they are directories, or files of files. Note that ordinary files, such as cowboys and prufrock, are not followed by a slash. Such files are called *leaves* because they aren't connected to anything else. The connecting lines are the *paths* through the UNIX file tree. You can move around the tree by following the paths.

FIGURE 3.1.

The file tree for a typical UNIX system.

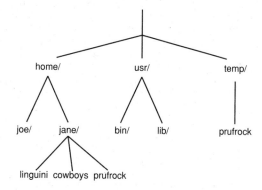

Notice also that two files are named prufrock. How can two files have the same name? And when you enter **cat prufrock**, how does UNIX know which one you want? Don't worry—your shell can distinguish one prufrock file from the other, for two reasons.

First, UNIX shells always remember their *current working directory* (CWD). The CWD is the directory in the file tree that you're in at any particular time. If you move somewhere else in the tree, the CWD changes. For example, if you're in the directory jane and you enter **cat prufrock**, you see the prufrock file that is attached to that directory; if you're in the tmp directory, you see the file attached to that directory.

Second, although so far you have named files by using relative pathnames, UNIX translates these pathnames into fully qualified pathnames. *Fully qualified pathnames* (or *full pathnames*) begin with a slash. Every file in the file tree has a unique, fully qualified pathname, which you construct by following the connecting lines from the root to the file. For instance, the following is the fully qualified pathname of the file prufrock in the directory jane:

/home/jane/prufrock

To construct this unique name, you follow the path from the *root* directory (/) through the directories home and jane, and end with the file prufrock. UNIX uses the slash to separate the different parts of the pathname. This character is also the special name for the root of the tree. Because it has this special meaning, the slash is one of the few characters that you cannot use in a UNIX filename.

For the file prufrock in the directory tmp, the fully qualified pathname is the following:

/tmp/prufrock

You construct this pathname the same way that you constructed that of the prufrock file in the jane directory. This time, you climbed down the file tree from the root directory to the directory tmp and then to the file prufrock, adding slash characters to separate the directories. Even though both files end in the name prufrock, UNIX can tell them apart because each has a unique pathname.

Relative pathnames begin with something other than the slash character. Using relative pathnames is usually convenient when specifying files that are in your CWD—for example, `cat prufrock`. But what if you want to refer to a file that is not in your CWD? Suppose that your CWD is `/home/jane` and you want to look at the file `/tmp/prufrock`. You can do this in two ways. First, you can enter the following command:

```
$ cat /tmp/prufrock
```

This command tells your shell unambiguously which file you want to see.

Secondly, you can tell your shell to move through the file tree to `/tmp` and then use a relative pathname. For example, if your shell's command to change your CWD is `cd`, you would enter the following:

```
$ cd /tmp
```

(Note that, unlike `cat` and `ls`, `cd` is "silent" when it succeeds. Most UNIX commands print nothing when all goes well.) Now your CWD is the directory `/tmp`. If you enter **cat prufrock**, you see the contents of the file `/tmp/prufrock` rather than `/home/jane/prufrock`.

As noted earlier, the name `/` has special significance to UNIX because it separates the components of pathnames and is the name of the file tree's root directory. For convenience, every UNIX directory also has two special names: . (*dot*) and .. (*dot-dot*). By convention, `ls` doesn't show these filenames because they begin with dot, but you can use the `-a` option to list these files, as follows:

```
$ ls -a
.    ..    cowboys    prufrock
```

Dot is a synonym for the CWD, and dot-dot for the CWD's parent directory. If your CWD is `/home/jane` and you want to move to `/home`, you can enter either

```
$ cd /home
```

or

```
$ cd ..
```

The result of both commands is the same. When you enter **cd /home**, your shell begins with the root directory and moves down one level to `/home`. When you enter **cd ..**, your shell starts in `/home/jane` and moves up one level; if you enter the command again, you move up to the parent directory of `/home`, which is `/`. If you enter the command once again, where do you go—hyperspace? Don't worry. Because `/` doesn't have a parent directory, its dot-dot entry points back on itself, so your CWD is still `/`. In the UNIX file system, the root directory is the only directory whose dot-dot entry points to itself.

Along with your CWD, your shell also remembers your *home* directory. This is the directory in which you automatically begin when you first log in. You spend most of your time in the home directory, because it is the directory in which you keep your files. If you get lost climbing around the file tree with cd, you can always return to your home directory by typing the cd command without any arguments:

```
$ cd
```

Your home directory looks like any other directory to UNIX—only your shell considers the home directory to be special.

Now that you are familiar with the cd command, you can move around the file tree. If you forget where you are, you can use the pwd (*print working directory*) command to find out. This command doesn't take any command-line arguments. The following example demonstrates how to use cd and pwd to move around the file tree and keep track of where you are:

```
$ pwd
/home/jane
$ cd /tmp
$ pwd
/tmp
$ cd
$ pwd
/home/jane
```

Of course, while you're moving around, you might also want to use ls and cat to list and view files. Moving around the file tree to view the standard system files distributed with UNIX is a good way to learn more about the UNIX file tree.

File and Directory Names

Unlike some operating systems, UNIX gives you great flexibility in how you name files and directories. As previously mentioned, you cannot use the slash character because it is the pathname separator and the name of the file tree's root directory . However, almost everything else is legal. Filenames can contain alphabetic (both upper- and lowercase), numeric, and punctuation characters, control characters, shell wild-card characters (such as *), and even spaces, tabs, and newlines. However, just because you *can* do something doesn't mean you *should*. Your life will be much simpler if you stick with upper- and lowercase alphabetics, digits, and punctuation characters such as ., -, and _.

> **CAUTION:** Using shell wild-card characters such as * in filenames can cause problems. Your shell expands such wild-card characters to match other files. Suppose that you create a filenamed * that you want to display with cat, and you still have your files cowboys and prufrock. You might think that the command cat * will do the trick, but remember that * is a shell wild card that matches anything.

Your shell expands * to match the files *, cowboys, and prufrock, so cat displays all three. You can avoid this problem by *quoting* the asterisk with a backslash:

```
$ cat \*
```

Quoting, which is explained in detail in Chapters 12 ("Korn Shell") and 13 ("C Shell"), temporarily removes a wild card's special meaning and prevents your shell from expanding it. However, having to quote wild cards is inconvenient, so you should avoid using such special characters in filenames.

You also should avoid using a hyphen or plus sign as the first character of a filename, because command options begin with those characters. Suppose that you name a file -X and name another unix_lore. If you enter **cat** *, your shell expands the * wild card and runs cat as follows:

```
$ cat -X unix_lore
```

The cat command interprets -X as an option string rather than a filename. Because cat doesn't have a -X option, the preceding command results in an error message. But if cat did have a -X option, the result might be even worse, as the command might do something completely unexpected. For these reasons, you should avoid using hyphens at the beginning of filenames.

Filenames can be as long as 255 characters in System V Release 4 UNIX. Unlike DOS, which uses the dot character to separate the filename from a three character suffix, UNIX does not attach any intrinsic significance to dot—a filenamed lots.of.italian.recipes is as legal as lots-of-italian-recipes. However, most UNIX users follow the dot-suffix conventions listed in Table 3.1. Some language compilers like cc require that their input files follow these conventions, so the table labels these conventions as "Required" in the last column.

Table 3.1. File suffix conventions.

Suffix	Program	Example	Required
.c	C program files	ls.c	Yes
.f	FORTRAN program files	math.f	Yes
.pl	Perl program files	hose.pl	No
.h	*include* files	term.h	No
.d, .dir	The file is a directory	recipes.d,	No
		recipes.dir	No

Suffix	Program	Example	Required
.gz	A file compressed with the GNV project's gzip	foo.gz	Yes
.Z	A compressed file	term.h.Z	Yes
.zip	A file compressed with PKZIP	book.zip	Yes

Choosing good filenames is harder than it looks. Although long names may seem appealing at first, you may change your mind after you enter `cat lots-of-italian-recipes` a few times. Of course, shell wild cards can help (as in `cat lots-of*`), but as you gain experience, you'll find that you prefer shorter names.

Organizing your files into directories with well-chosen names can help. For instance, Figure 3.2 shows how Joe organizes his recipes.

FIGURE 3.2.

Organizing your files within a directory.

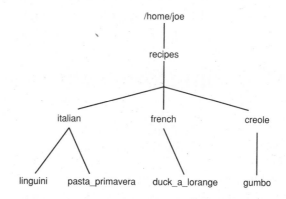

Joe could have put all his recipes in a single directory, but chose to use the directories `italian`, `french`, and `creole` to separate and categorize the recipes. Instead of using filenames like `recipe-italian-linguini`, he can use `cd` to move to the directory `recipes` and then move to the subdirectory `italian`; then Joe can use `ls` and `cat` to examine only the files that he wants to see. You may think that Joe is carrying this organizing a bit too far (after all, he has only four recipes to organize), but he's planning for that happy day when he's collected several thousand.

Similarly, if you keep a journal, you might be tempted to put the files in a directory named `journal` and use filenames like `Dec_93` and `Jan_94`. This approach isn't bad, but if you intend to keep your journal for ten years, you might want to plan ahead by removing the year from the filename and making it a directory in the pathname, as shown in Figure 3.3.

FIGURE 3.3.

Organizing your file for a
`journal` *directory.*

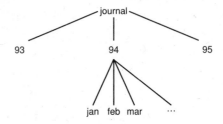

By using this approach, you can work with just the files for a particular year. To get to that year, however, you have to use one more `cd` command. Thus you must consider the trade-off between having to enter long filenames and having to climb around the file tree with `cd` to find your files. You should experiment until you find your own compromise between too-long filenames and too many levels of directories.

Creating Directories with *mkdir*

Now that you know the advantages of organizing your files into directories, you'll want to create some. The `mkdir` (*make directory*) command is one of the simplest UNIX commands. To create a single directory named `journal`, enter the following:

```
$ mkdir journal
```

(Like `cd`, `mkdir` prints no output when it works.) To make a subdirectory of `journal` named `94`, enter the following:

```
$ mkdir journal/94
```

Or if you prefer, you can enter the following:

```
$ mkdir journal
$ cd journal
$ mkdir 94
```

Working with Files

Now that you know how to create, list, and view files, create directories, and move around the UNIX file tree, it's time to learn how to copy, rename, and remove files.

Copying Files with cp

To copy one or more files, you use the cp command. You might want to use cp to make a backup copy of a file before you edit it, or to copy a file from a friend's directory into your own.

Suppose that you want to edit a letter but also keep the first draft in case you later decide that you like it best. You could enter the following:

```
$ cd letters
$ ls
andrea zach
$ cp andrea andrea.back
$ ls
andrea andrea.back zach
```

(When it works, cp prints no output, following the UNIX tradition that "no news is good news.")

Now you have two identical files: the original andrea file and a new filenamed andrea.back. The first file that you give to cp is sometimes called the *target*, and the second the *destination*. The destination can be a file (as in the preceding example) or a directory. For instance, you might decide to create a subdirectory of letters in which to keep backups of all your correspondence:

```
$ cd letters
$ mkdir backups
$ ls
andrea backups zach
$ cp andrea backups
$ ls backups
andrea
```

Note that the destination of the cp command is simply backups, not backups/andrea. When you copy a file into a directory, cp creates the new file with the same name as the original unless you specify something else. To give the file a different name, enter it as follows:

```
$ cp andrea backups/andrea.0
$ ls backups
andrea.0
```

As you can see, ls works differently when you give it a directory rather than a file as its command-line argument. When you enter ls *some_file*, ls prints that file's name if the file exists; otherwise, the command prints the following error message:

```
some_file: No such file or directory
```

If you enter ls *some_dir*, ls prints the names of any files in *some_dir*; otherwise, the command prints nothing. If the directory doesn't exist, ls prints the following error message:

```
some_dir: No such file or directory
```

You can also use cp to copy several files at once. If plan to edit both of your letters and want to save drafts of both, you could enter the following:

```
$ cd letters
$ ls
andrea backups zach
$ cp andrea zach backups
$ ls backups
andrea zach
```

When copying more than one file at a time, you must specify an existing directory as the destination. Suppose that you enter the following:

```
$ cd letters
$ ls
andrea     backups     zach
$ cp andrea zach both
cp: both not found
```

The cp command expects its last argument to be an existing directory, and prints an error message when it can't find the directory.

If what you want is to catenate two files into a third, use cat and shell redirection:

```
$ cat andrea zach > both
```

You can also use the directory names dot and dot-dot as the destination in cp commands. Suppose that a colleague has left some files named data1 and data2 in the system temporary directory /tmp so that you can copy them to your home directory. You could enter the following:

```
$ cd
$ cp /tmp/data1 .
$ cp /tmp/data2 .
$ ls
data1 data2
```

Alternatively, because the destination is dot, a directory, you can copy both files at once:

```
$ cp /tmp/data1 /tmp/data2 .
$ ls
data1 data2
```

To copy the files to the parent directory of your CWD, use dot-dot rather than dot.

By default, cp *silently* overwrites (destroys) existing files. In the preceding example, if you already have a filenamed data1 and you type **cp /tmp/data1 .**, you lose your copy of data1 forever, replacing it with /tmp/data1. You can use cp's -i (*interactive*) option to avoid accidental overwrites:

```
$ cp -i /tmp/data1 .
cp: overwrite ./data1(y/n)?
```

When you use the -i option, cp asks whether you want to overwrite existing files. If you do, type **y**; if you don't, type **n**. If you're accident-prone or nervous, and your shell enables you to do so, you may want to create an *alias* that always uses cp -i (see Chapters 12 and 13, "Korn Shell" and "C Shell").

Moving Files with *mv*

The mv command moves files from one place to another. Because each UNIX file has a unique pathname derived from its location in the file tree, moving a file is equivalent to renaming it: you change the pathname. The simplest use of mv is to rename a file in the current directory. Suppose that you've finally grown tired of typing **cat recipe-for-linguini** and want to give your fingers a rest. Instead, you can enter the following:

```
$ mv recipe-for-linguini linguini
```

There is an important difference between cp and mv: cp leaves the original file in its place, but mv removes it. Suppose that you enter the following command:

```
$ mv linguini /tmp
```

This command removes the copy of linguini in your CWD. So, if you want to retain your original file, use cp instead of mv.

Like cp, mv can handle multiple files if the destination is a directory. If your journal is to be a long-term project, you may want to put the monthly files in subdirectories that are organized by the year. Enter the following commands:

```
$ cd journal
$ ls
Apr_93 Dec_93 Jan_93 Jun_93 May_93 Oct_93
Aug_93 Feb_93 Jul_93 Mar_93 Nov_93 Sep_93
$ mkdir 93
$ mv *_93 93
$ ls
93
$ ls 93
Apr_93 Dec_93 Jan_93 Jun_93 May_93 Oct_93
Aug_93 Feb_93 Jul_93 Mar_93 Nov_93 Sep_93
```

Note that, by default, ls sorts filenames in dictionary order down columns. Often, such sorting is not what you want. The following tip suggests ways that you can work around this problem. Also note that mv, like other UNIX commands, enables you to use shell wild cards such as *.

> **TIP:** You can work around `ls`'s default sorting order by prefixing filenames with punctuation (but not hyphens or plus signs), digits, or capitalization. For instance, if you want to sort the files of month names in their natural order, prefix them with 00, 01, and so on:
>
> ```
> $ cd journal/93
> $ ls
> 01_jan 03_mar 05_may 07_jul 09_sep 11_nov
> 02_feb 04_apr 06_jun 08_aug 10_oct 12_dec
> ```

Like `cp`, `mv` *silently* overwrites existing files by default:

```
$ ls
borscht        strudel
$ mv borscht strudel
$ ls
strudel
```

This command replaces the original file `strudel` with the contents of `bortsch`, and `strudel`'s original contents are lost forever. If you use `mv`'s `-i` option, the `mv` command, like `cp`, asks you before overwriting files.

Also like `cp`, `mv` requires that you specify dot or dot-dot as the destination directory. In fact, this requirement is true of *all* UNIX commands that expect a directory argument.

Removing Files with *rm*

You can remove unwanted files with `rm`. This command takes as its arguments the names of one or more files, and removes those files—forever. Unlike operating systems like DOS, which can sometimes recover deleted files, UNIX removes files once and forever. Your systems administrator may be able to recover a deleted file from a backup tape, but don't count on it. (Besides, systems administrators become noticeably cranky after a few such requests.) Be especially careful when using shell wild cards to remove files—you may end up removing more than you intended.

> **TIP:** Shell wild-card expansions may be dangerous to your mental health, especially if you use them with commands like `rm`. If you're not sure which files will match the wild cards that you're using, first use `echo` to check. For instance, before entering **rm a***, first enter **echo a***. If the files that match a* are the ones that you expect, you can enter the `rm` command, confident that it will do only what you intend.

To remove the file andrea.back, enter the following command:

```
$ rm andrea.back
```

Like cp and mv, rm prints no output when it works.

If you are satisfied with your edited letters and want to remove the backups to save disk space, you could enter the following:

```
$ cd letters/backups
$ ls
andrea zach
$ rm *
$ ls
```

Because you have removed all the files in the subdirectory backups, the second ls command prints nothing.

Like cp and mv, rm has an interactive option, -i. If you enter **rm -i** *, rm asks you whether you really want to remove each individual file. As before, you type **y** for yes and **n** for no. This option can be handy if you accidentally create a filename with a nonprinting character, such as a control character. Nonprinting characters don't appear in file listings, and they make the file hard to work with. If you want to remove the file, enter **rm -i** *; then type **y** for the file you that you want to remove, while typing **n** for the others. The -i option also comes in handy if you want to remove several files that have such dissimilar names that you cannot specify them with wild cards. Again, simply enter **rm -i** *, and then type **n** for each file that you *don't* want to remove.

Working with Directories

A directory is simply a special kind of file. Some of the operations that work with files also work with directories. However, some operations are not possible, and others must be done differently for directories.

Creating Multiple Directories with *mkdir*

As mentioned in the section "Creating Directories with mkdir," you make directories with the mkdir command. In that section, you created a single directory, journal. However, mkdir can also create multiple directories at once. For example, to create two directories named journal and recipes, enter the following command:

```
$ mkdir journal recipes
```

The mkdir command can even create a directory *and* its subdirectories if you use its -p option:

```
$ mkdir -p journal/94
```

Removing a Directory with *rmdir*

To remove an empty directory, use `rmdir`. Suppose that you made a typing mistake while creating a directory and want to remove it so that you can create the right one. Enter these commands:

```
$ mkdir jornal
$ rmdir jornal
$ mkdir journal
```

The `rmdir` command removes only empty directories. If a directory still has files, you must remove them before using `rmdir`:

```
$ rmdir journal
rmdir: journal: Directory not empty
$ rm journal/*
$ rmdir journal
```

Actually, `rm` *can* remove directories if you use its `-r` (*recursive*) option. This option tells `rm` to descend the file tree below the directory, remove all the files and subdirectories below it, and finally remove the directory itself. So, before you use this option, be sure that you mean to remove all the files and the directory. If you decide that you'll never eat Creole-style cuisine again, you can remove those recipes by entering the following:

```
$ cd recipes
$ rm -r creole
```

TIP: The `rm` command is like a chainsaw: It's a good tool, but one with which you can saw off your leg if you're not careful. The `-r` option is particularly dangerous—especially if you use it with shell wild cards—because it lops off entire branches of the file tree. If you have a directory of precious files that you don't want to accidentally remove, create a filenamed `-no-rm-star` in the same directory by entering the following:

```
$ echo just say no > -no-rm-star
```

Now suppose that this directory also has two precious files named p1 and p2. If you enter **rm** *, your shell expands the wild card and runs the rm command with the following arguments:

```
rm -no-rm-star p1 p2
```

Because rm doesn't have an option `-no-rm-star`, it prints an error message and quits without removing your precious files. Note, however, that this also makes it difficult for you to use wild cards with *any* UNIX commands in this subdirectory because the shell always expands filenames before passing them to commands.

Renaming Directories with *mv*

You can also use mv to rename directories. For instance, to correct a mistyped mkdir command, you would have to rename the directory:

```
$ mkdir jornal
$ mv jornal journal
```

This command works even if the directory isn't empty.

> **NOTE:** Some file commands do not work with directories, or require that you use different options, such as the -r option to rm. For instance, to copy a directory, you must use cp -r to copy recursively the directory and all its files and subdirectories. Suppose that you want to copy your Hungarian recipes to /tmp so that your friend Joe can add them to his collection:
>
> ```
> $ cd recipes
> $ ls hungarian
> chicken_paprika goulash
> $ cp -r hungarian /tmp
> $ ls /tmp
> hungarian
> $ ls /tmp/hungarian
> chicken_paprika goulash
> ```
>
> Again, because the destination of the copy is a directory (/tmp), you need not specify the full pathname /tmp/hungarian.
>
> Another difference between directories and files is that the ln command (discussed later in this chapter in the section "Hard and Symbolic Links") refuses to make a hard link to a directory.

Keeping Secrets—File and Directory Permissions

UNIX is a multiuser operating system, which means that you share the system with other users. As you accumulate files, you'll find that the information that some contain is valuable; some files you want to share, and others you prefer to keep private. UNIX file and directory permissions give you a flexible way to control who has access to your files.

All UNIX files have three types of permissions—*read*, *write*, and *execute*—associated with three classes of users—*owner*, *group* and *other* (sometimes called *world*).

Read permission enables you to examine the contents of files with commands such as cat, write permission enables you to alter the contents of a file or truncate it, and execute permission is necessary to run a file as a command. Each of the three permissions can be granted or withheld individually for each class of user. For instance, a file might be readable and writable by you, readable by other members of your group, but inaccessible to everyone else, or it might be readable and writable only by you.

The ls command shows your file and directory permissions, and the chmod (*change mode*) command changes them.

The -l option tells ls to make a long listing, such as the following:

```
$ cd recipes/german
$ ls -l
-rw-r--r-r  1 joe   user1   2451 Feb  7 07:30 strudel
-rw-r--r-r  1 joe   user1   4025 Feb 10 19:12 borscht
drwxr-xr-r  2 joe   user1    512 Feb 10 19:12 backups
```

Figure 3.4 shows the parts of the long listing. The file permissions, owner, and group are the parts that are most important for information security.

FIGURE 3.4.

The ls command's long listing.

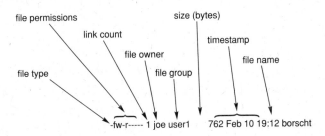

To know who can access a file and in what ways, you must know the owner and the group and then examine the *file permission string*. The permission string is ten characters long. The first character indicates the file type, which is a hyphen (-) for regular files, d for a directory, and l for a symbolic link. (Symbolic links are discussed later in this chapter, in the section "Hard and Symbolic Links." The following note describes the other file types.)

NOTE: The following is a complete list of the UNIX file types:

-	Regular file
d	Directory
l	Symbolic link
c	Character special file
b	Block special file
p	Named pipe

You're already familiar with regular files and directories, and symbolic links are discussed in the section "Hard and Symbolic Links." Character and block special files are device files, which were described in the introductory section of this chapter. You create device files with the `mknod` command, which is covered in Chapter 35, "File System Administration."

Named pipes enable you to communicate with a running program by reference to a file. Suppose that you have a continuously running program named `quoted` (also known as a *daemon*) that accepts requests to mail you a joke- or a quote-of-the-day. The commands that the program accepts might be `send joke` and `send quote`. Such a daemon could open a named pipe file in a standard place in the UNIX file tree, and you could send its requests with `echo`:

```
$ echo send joke > quoted_named_pipe
```

The `quoted` program would continuously read the file *quoted_named_pipe*; when you echo into that file your request for a joke, the program would mail one to you.

The next nine characters are three groups of three permissions for owner, group, and other. Each group of three shows read (`r`), write (`w`), and execute (`x`) permission, in that order. A hyphen indicates that the permission is denied. In Figure 3.4, the permission string for the file `borscht` looks like this:

```
-rw-r----
```

The first character is a hyphen, so `borscht` is a regular file, not a directory. The next three characters, `rw-`, show permissions for the owner, `joe`. Joe can read and write the file, but execute permission is turned off because `borscht` is not a program. The next three characters, `r--`, show the permissions for other people in the group `user1`. Members of this group can read the file, but cannot write or execute it. The final three hyphen characters, `---`, show that read, write, and execute permissions are off for all other users.

You may wonder how files are assigned to a certain group. When you create files, UNIX assigns them an owner and a group. The owner will be your login name and the group will be your default (or login) group. Each UNIX user belongs to one or more groups, and when you log in you are put automatically into your default group. Files that you create are owned by you and assigned to your default group. If you are a member of other groups, you can use the `chgrp` command to change the group of an existing file to one of your other groups.

Suppose that your login name is karen, your default group is user1, and you're also a member of the group planners, which is supposed to brainstorm new products for your company. You want your planners coworkers to see your memos and project plans, but you want to keep those documents secret from other users. You also have another directory, jokes, that you want to share with everyone, and a directory called musings, in which you keep private notes. The following commands create the directories and set appropriate directory permissions:

```
$ cd
$ mkdir jokes memos musings
$ ls -l
total 6
drwx------ 2 karen user1      512 Jan 3 19:12 jokes
drwx------ 2 karen user1      512 Jan 3 19:12 memos
drwx------ 2 karen user1      512 Jan 3 19:12 musings
$ chgrp planners memos
$ chmod g+rx memos
$ chmod go+rx jokes
$ ls -l
total 6
drwxr-xr-x 2 karen user1      512 Jan  3 19:12 jokes
drwxr-x--- 2 karen planners   512 Jan  3 19:12 memos
drwx------ 2 karen user1      512 Jan  3 19:12 musings
```

The mkdir command creates the directories with default permissions that depend on Karen's umask. (The section "Default File and Directory Permissions—Your umask," later in this chapter, explains the umask.) Only the owner, Karen, can read, write, and execute the directories. She wants the memos directory to be accessible to other members of the group planners (but no one else), so she uses chgrp to change its group to planners and then uses chmod to add group-read and group-execute permissions. For the directory jokes, she uses chmod again to add read and execute permission for everyone. She leaves the directory musings alone because it already has the permissions she wants.

The chmod command expects two or more arguments, a permission specification, and one or more files:

```
$ chmod permissions file(s)
```

You can specify *permissions* either *symbolically* or *absolutely*. The preceding example provides examples of symbolic permissions, which are intuitively easy to work with. They consist of one or more of the characters ugo, followed by one of +-=, and finally one or more of rwx. The ugo characters stand for *user* (the file's owner), *group*, and *other*. As before, rwx stands for *read, write,* and *execute* permissions. You use the plus (+) and minus (-) signs to add or subtract permissions, and the equals sign (=) to set permissions absolutely, regardless of the previous ones. You can combine these strings any way you want. Table 3.2 shows some examples.

Table 3.2 *Symbolic* options to `chmod`.

Option	Result
u+rwx	Turn on owner read, write, and execute permissions
u-w	Remove owner write permission
go+x	Add execute permission for group or other
o-rwx	Remove all other permissions
o-w, og+r	Remove owner write permission and set other and group permissions to read (no write or execute permission)
u+rwx, og+x	Set owner read, write, and execute permission, and execute permission for all other users
ugo+rwx	Turn on all permissions for all users

The examples in Table 3.2 show only a few of the ways in which you can combine symbolic permissions. Note that you can specify different permissions for owner, group, and other in the same command, by using comma-separated permission specifications, as in the fifth and sixth examples.

Also note that the equals sign works differently than the plus and minus signs. If you type **chmod g+w memo1**, `chmod` adds group write permission to that file but leaves the read and execute permissions as they were, whether they were on or off. However, if you type **chmod g=w memo1**, you turn on write permission and turn off read and execute permissions, even though you don't mention those permissions explicitly:

```
$ ls -l memo1
-rw-r--r-- 1 karen    planners   1721 May 28 10:14 memo1
$ chmod g+w memo1
$ ls -l memo1
-rw-rw-r-- 1 karen    planners   1721 May 28 10:14 memo1
$ chmod g=w memo1
$ ls -l memo1
-rw--w-r-- 1 karen    planners   1721 May 28 10:14 memo1
```

The first `chmod` turns on write permission for members of the group `planners`, which is probably what Karen wants. The second `chmod` sets write permission but turns off read and execute permissions. It makes no sense to give a file write permission without also giving it read permission, so the first command is better.

Setting permissions properly may seem intimidating at first, but after you work with them a little, you'll feel more comfortable. Create some files with `touch`, and then experiment with various `chmod` commands until you have a good feel for what it does. You'll find that it looks more complicated on paper than in practice.

After you become comfortable with symbolic modes, you may want to move on to absolute modes, which are given as numbers. Numeric modes save you some typing because you can specify all three classes of permission with three digits. And, because these specifications are absolute, you don't have to worry about the file's current permissions; new ones are set without regard to the old ones. In this way, using absolute modes is similar to using the equals sign with symbolic modes.

When you use absolute modes, you set owner, group, and other permissions in one fell swoop. You specify numeric permissions with three digits that correspond to owner, group, and other. Execute permission has the value 1, write permission 2, and read permission 4. To create a numeric permission specification, you add, for each class of user, the permission values that you want to grant. Suppose that you have a filenamed `plan-doc2` that you want to make readable and writable by you and other members of your group, but only readable by everyone else. As Table 3.3 shows, you calculate the correct numeric mode for the `chmod` command by adding the columns.

Table 3.3. Calculating numeric `chmod` options.

Permission	Owner	Group	Other
Read	4	4	4
Write	2	2	-
Execute	-	-	-
Total	6	6	4

In Table 3.3, the resulting numeric mode is 664, the total of the columns for owner, group, and other. The following command sets those permissions regardless of the current ones:

```
$ ls -l plan-doc2
-r--------   1 karen    planners   1721 Aug 14 11:28 plan_doc2
$ chmod 664 plan_doc2
$ ls -l plan-doc2
-rw-rw-r-- 1 karen    planners   1721 Aug 14 11:28 plan_doc2
```

Now suppose that Karen has a game program named `trek`. She wants everyone on the system to be able run the program, but she doesn't want anyone to alter or read it. As the owner, she wants to have read, write, and execute permission. Table 3.4 shows how to calculate the correct numeric mode.

Table 3.4. Calculating another set of numeric chmod options.

Permission	Owner	Group	Other
Read	4	-	-
Write	2	-	-
Execute	1	1	1
Total	7	1	1

Because the three columns add up to 711, the correct chmod command is as follows:

```
$ chmod 711 trek
$ ls -l trek
-rwx--x--1 1 karen    user1    56743 Apr 9 17:10 trek
```

Numeric arguments work equally well for files and directories.

Default File and Directory Permissions— Your *umask*

How are default file and directory modes chosen? Consider the following commands, for example:

```
$ touch myfile
$ mkdir mydir
```

What permissions will be assigned to myfile and mydir by default, and how can you control those defaults? After all, you don't want to type a chmod command every time that you create a file or directory—it would be much more convenient if they were created with the modes that you most often want.

Your umask (*user-mask*) controls default file and directory permissions. The command umask sets a new umask for you if you're dissatisfied with the one that the system gives you when you log in. Many users include a umask command in their login start-up files (.profile or .login). To find out your current umask, just type **umask**:

```
$ umask
022
```

To change your umask, enter **umask** and a three digit number that specifies your new umask. For instance, to change your umask to 027, enter the following command:

```
$ umask 027
```

UNIX determines the default directory modes by subtracting your umask from the octal number 777. Therefore, if your umask is 027, your default directory mode is 750.

The result of this arithmetic is a mode specification like that which you give chmod, so the effect of using the umask command is similar to using a chmod command. However, umask never sets file execute bits, so you must turn them on with chmod, regardless of your umask. To find the corresponding file permissions, you subtract your umask from 666. For example, if your umask is 022, your default file modes will be 644.

Table 3.5 shows some typical umasks and the default file and directory modes that result from them. Choose one that is appropriate for you and insert it into your login start-up file. Table 3.5 shows file and directory modes both numerically and symbolically, and umask values range from the most to the least secure.

Table 3.5. Typical umask values.

umask Value	Default File Mode	Default Directory Mode
077	600 (rw-------)	700 (rwx------)
067	600 (rw-------)	710 (rwx--x---)
066	600 (rw-------)	711 (rwx--x--x)
027	640 (rw-r-----)	750 (rwxr-xr-x)
022	644 (rw-r--r--)	755 (rwxr-xr-x)
000	666 (rw-rw-rw-)	777 (rwxrwxrwx)

Perhaps the best way to understand umask values is to experiment with the commands umask, touch, mkdir, and ls to see how they interact, as in the following examples:

```
$ umask 066
$ touch myfile
$ mkdir mydir
$ ls -l
-rw-------1 karen      user1     0 Feb 12 14:22 myfile
drwx--x--1 2 karen     user1   512 Feb 12 14:22 mydir
$ rm myfile
$ rmdir mydir
$ umask 027
$ touch myfile
$ mkdir mydir
$ ls -l
-rw-r----- 1 karen     user1     0 Feb 12 14:23 myfile
drwxr-x---  2 karen     user1   512 Feb 12 14:23 mydir
```

The umask command may seem confusing, but it's important. You must choose a umask that provides the default file and directory permissions that are right for you. Otherwise, you'll spend all your time changing file and directory permissions, or leave your files and directories with insecure permissions.

Hard and Symbolic Links

The ln (*link*) command creates both *hard* and *symbolic* links. When you refer to the file "prufrock" in the command cat prufrock, UNIX translates the filename into an internal name. Because UNIX uses a different representation for its internal bookkeeping, you can refer to files by more than one name. A hard link is an alternative name for a file. Suppose you have a file data and you use ln to make a hard link to it called data2:

```
$ ln data data2
$ ls
data   data2
```

The name data2 now refers to exactly the same *internal* file as data. If you edit data, the changes will be reflected in data2 and vice versa. Data2 is *not* a copy of data1 but a different name for the same file. Suppose that Karen enters:

```
$ ln memo1 memo2
```

Karen now has two filenames—memo1 and memo2—that refer to the same file. Since they refer to the same internal file, they are identical except for their names. If she removes memo1, memo2 remains because the underlying file that memo2 refers to is still there. UNIX removes the internal file only after you remove all of the filenames that refer to it, in this case both memo1 and memo2. You can now see that rather than saying that rm removes a file, it's more accurate to say that it removes the file's name from the file system. When the last name for a file is gone, UNIX removes the internal file.

What good are hard links? Sometimes people working together on projects share files. Suppose that you and Joe work on a report together and must edit the same file. You want changes that you make to be reflected in Joe's copy automatically, without having Joe copy the file anew each time you change it. You also want Joe's changes to be reflected in the copy. Instead of trying to synchronize two separate files, you can make a hard link to Joe's file. Changes he makes will be reflected in your version and vice versa because you both are working with the *same file* even though you use different names for it.

A symbolic link (also known as a *symlink*) allows you to create an alias for a file, a sort of signpost in the file system that points to the real file someplace else. Suppose that you frequently look through your friend Joe's Italian recipes, but you are tired of typing:

```
$ cat /home/joe/recipes/italian/pizza/quattro_stagione
```

You could copy his recipes to your home directory, but that would waste disk space and you would have to remember to check for new recipes and copy those as well. A better solution is to create a symbolic link in your home directory that points to Joe's directory. You use ln's -s option to create symbolic links:

```
$ cd
$ ln -s /home/joe/recipes/italian italian
$ ls italian
linguini  pasta_primavera
```

Your symbolic link `italian` now points to Joe's recipes, and you can conveniently look at them.

There are some important differences between hard and symbolic links. First, you can't make a hard link to a directory, as in the example above. Hard links cannot cross disk partitions, and you can't make a hard link to a file in a *network* file system. Symbolic links can do all of these jobs.

Hard links must refer to a real file, but symbolic links may point to a file or directory that doesn't exist. Suppose that you have a symbolic link to your colleague's file `/home/ann/work/project4/memos/paper.ms` and she removes it. Your symlink still points to it, but the file is gone. As a result, commands like `ls` and `cat` may print potentially confusing error messages:

```
$ ls
paper.ms
$ cat paper.ms
cat: paper.ms not found
```

Why can't `cat` find `paper.ms` when `ls` shows that it's there? The confusion arises because `ls` is telling you that the symbolic link `paper.ms` is there, which it is. `Cat` looks for the real file—the one the symbolic link *points to*—and reports an error because Ann removed it.

A final difference is that permission modes on symbolic links are meaningless. UNIX uses the permissions of the file (to which the link *points*) to decide whether you can read, write, or execute the file. For example, if you don't have permission to `cat` a file, making a symlink to it won't help; you'll still get a `permission denied` message from `cat`.

Summary

In this chapter you've learned a lot: the basics of creating and manipulating files and directories, some shell tricks, and a fair amount about the UNIX file system. While it may seem overwhelming now, it will quickly become second nature as you work with UNIX files. However, you've only scratched the surface—you'll want to consult the manual pages for `echo`, `cat`, `ls`, `cp`, `rm`, `mv`, `mkdir`, `chmod`, and `ln` to get the details. UNIX provides a cornucopia of powerful file manipulation programs, text editors, production-quality text formatters, spelling checkers, and much more. Read on and practice.

Listing Files

4

IN THIS CHAPTER

This chapter covers some useful commands and constructs that help you better manage your data files. As a system matures, the file system becomes an eclectic collection of data files—some old, some new, some borrowed, some blue. The file system maintains information about data files such as file ownership, the size of the file, and the access dates. All of this information is useful in helping to manage your data. You'll learn more about ls, the directory list command. In addition, you'll learn about the find command, which you can use to locate files even when you don't know the complete path name.

Sometimes you want to limit the scope of a command so that the output from the command is more focused. You accomplish this by using partial filenames and some special wildcard characters. This chapter discusses three ways of causing the system to make filename substitutions.

You'll also look at two of the most powerful features of UNIX—redirection and piping—which are methods for rerouting the input and output of most commands.

Listing Files and Directories: *ls* Revisited

As you learned in Chapter 3, "The UNIX File System: Go Climb a Tree," the ls command lists the names of files and directories. This section reviews the basics of ls and provides examples of its options.

ls: The Short and Long of It

In its simplest form, the ls command without arguments displays the names of the files and directories in the current working directory in alphabetical order by name. For example,

```
$ ls
```

```
21x         LINES.dat    LINES.idx   PAGES.dat   PAGES.idx
acct.pds    marsha.pds   p11         t11         users
```

On some systems, the default output from ls is a single column of output. Most of the examples in this chapter use the columnar format to conserve space.

The ls command can also accept a filename as a command line parameter. For example,

```
$ ls marsha.pds
```

```
marsha.pds
```

If the command line parameter is a directory name, all the files in that directory are listed. For example,

```
$ ls users
```

```
dave        marsha      mike
```

Notice that the files are listed in order by collating sequence. That is, files beginning with numbers come first; files beginning with uppercase characters come next; and files beginning with lowercase characters come last. Also notice that although this format displays your filenames in a compact fashion, it doesn't give you much information about the files. You can get more detail about the files by requesting a long listing with the -l option. For example,

```
$ ls -l

-rwxr-xr--   1 asm      adept        512 Dec 14 16:16 21x
-rw-rw-r--   1 marsha   adept       1024 Jan 20 14:14 LINES.dat
-rw-rw-r--   1 marsha   adept       3072 Jan 20 14:14 LINES.idx
-rw-rw-r--   1 marsha   adept        256 Jan 20 14:14 PAGES.dat
-rw-rw-r--   1 marsha   adept       3072 Jan 20 14:14 PAGES.idx
-rw-rw-r--   1 marsha   acct         240 May  5  1992 acct.pds
-rw-rw-r--   1 marsha   adept       1024 Nov 22 15:42 marsha.pds
-rwxrwxr--   4 root     sys       243072 Aug 22  1991 p11
-rwxrwxr--   4 root     sys       256041 Aug 22  1991 t11
drw-rw-r--   1 marsha   adept       3072 Oct 12 11:42 users
```

A long listing displays seven columns of information about each file. In the first line of the listing,

-rwxr-xr--	indicates the file's type and permissions
1	indicates the number of links to the file
asm	is the user ID of the file's owner
adept	is the group ID of the group that the owner belongs to
512	is the size of the file in bytes
Dec 14 16:16	is the time stamp—the date and time when the file was last modified
21x	is the name of the file (refer to Figure 3.4 in Chapter 3)

The first and second columns require a bit more explanation. The first column is a ten-character field that indicates the file's mode—its type and its permissions. In the first line of the list, the file's mode is -rwxr-xr--. The first character tells the file type, which is a hyphen (-) for regular files, and d for directories. In this example, the first nine items in the list are all ordinary files, and the last item is a directory.

The next nine characters of the entry are the file's permissions—three sets of three characters that control which users may access a file and what they can do with it. The first set of three characters controls what the file's owner can do; the second set of three characters controls what others in the group can do; and the third set of three characters controls what all other users can do. Each set of three characters shows read (r), write (w), and execute (x) permission, in that order. A hyphen (-) means that the permission is denied.

The second column of the long listing is the number of links to this file. All the files except two—p11 and t11—are pointed to only from this directory. p11 and t11 have entries in three other directories, for a total of four links.

You should refer to the "Keeping Secrets—File and Directory Permissions" section in Chapter 3 for a complete description of file types and for further details on file permissions. File links are covered in the "Hard and Symbolic Links" section of Chapter 3.

Other *ls* Options

The `ls` command has several options. This section covers many of the ones more frequently used.

Showing Hidden Files with *-a*

The `ls` option doesn't normally list files that begin with a period. Suppose that the directory displayed in the previous section also contained a file named `.profile`. In that case, you would see

```
$ ls -a

.                       .profile    21x         LINES.dat
LINES.idx   PAGES.dat   PAGES.idx   acct.pds    marsha.pds
p11         t11         users
```

Note that the files . and .. represent the current and parent directories, respectively.

You can combine options, as in this example:

```
$ ls -al
-rw-r--r--   1 marsha   adept      2156 Jul 19 1991  .
-rw-r--r--   1 marsha   adept      2246 Jul 19 1991  ..
-rw-r--r--   1 marsha   adept       117 Jul 19 1991  .profile
-rwxr-xr--   1 asm      adept       512 Dec 14 16:16 21x
-rw-rw-r--   1 marsha   adept      1024 Jan 20 14:14 LINES.dat
-rw-rw-r--   1 marsha   adept      3072 Jan 20 14:14 LINES.idx
-rw-rw-r--   1 marsha   adept       256 Jan 20 14:14 PAGES.dat
-rw-rw-r--   1 marsha   adept      3072 Jan 20 14:14 PAGES.idx
-rw-rw-r--   1 marsha   acct        240 May  5 1992  acct.pds
-rw-rw-r--   1 marsha   adept      1024 Nov 22 15:42 marsha.pds
-rwxrwxr--   4 root     sys      243072 Aug 22 1991  p11
-rwxrwxr--   4 root     sys      256041 Aug 22 1991  t11
drw-rw-r--   1 marsha   adept      3072 Oct 12 11:42 users
```

Showing File Types with *-F*

Another useful option is `-F`, which distinguishes directory and executable files from ordinary files. The `-F` option causes a slash (/) to be appended to the filename for directories and an asterisk (*) to be appended to files which are executable. For example,

```
$ ls -F
21x*         LINES.dat   LINES.idx   PAGES.dat   PAGES.idx
acct.pds     marsha.pds  p11*        t11*        users/
```

Listing Files Whose Names Contain Nonprintable Characters with -q

When a file is created, the filename can inadvertently acquire nonprintable characters. Suppose that a filename contained a backspace character (represented here as ^H). The file named abcd^Hefg would display in a normal ls command as abcefg. Because you cannot see the backspace character, you might be confused about the actual filename. With the ls -q option, this filename would display as abcd?efg.

Even if you don't know what the mystery character is, you can still work with the file by using filename substitution (discussed in the next section). If you need to know the exact nature of the mystery character, you can use the -b option, which causes the nonprintable character to print in octal mode. With the -b option, the filename would display as abcd\010efg, in which \010 is the octal representation of a backspace.

Other Useful *ls* Options

Additional ls options include the following:

- -u Used with -l, causes the last access time stamp to be displayed instead of the last modification time.
- -s Used with -l, gives the file size in blocks instead of bytes.
- -t Sorts the output by time stamp instead of name. Used with -u sorts the output by access time.
- -r Reverses the order of the output. By itself, displays the output in reverse alphabetic order, used with -t, displays the output by the most recent time stamp.
- -x Forces the output into multicolumn

Using Metacharacters When Referring to Filenames

So far you've learned how to work with files by referring to their complete names. Sometimes, however, it is useful to refer to several files without having to name each one of them. Likewise, if you can remember only part of a filename, it is useful to list all the files whose names contain that part. UNIX provides *metacharacters*, also known as wildcards, which enable you to refer to files in these ways.

There are two metacharacters: the question mark (?) and the asterisk (*). In addition to metacharacters, filename substitution can be done on character sets. For more information about metacharacters, see Chapter 11, "Bourne Shell," Chapter 12, "Korn Shell," and Chapter 13, "C Shell."

Pattern Matching on a Single Character

In filename substitution, the question mark (?) stands for any single character. Consider the following directory:

```
$ls

21x         LINES.dat    LINES.idx    PAGES.dat    PAGES.idx
acct.pds    marsha.pds   p10          p101         p11
t11         z11
```

You can use the question mark (?) in any position. For example,

```
$ ls ?11
p11    t11    z11
```

You can also use more than one question mark in a single substitution. For example,

```
$ ls p??
p10    p11
```

The following command gives you all three-character filenames:

```
$ ls ???
21x    p10    p11    t11    z11
```

Suppose that you wanted to list all of the files that begin with LINES. We could do this successfully with

```
$ ls LINES.???

LINES.dat    LINES.idx
```

Now suppose that you wanted to find the files that end in .pds. The following two commands illustrate how to do this:

```
$ ls ????.pds
acct.pds
$
$ ls ?????.pds
marsha.pds
```

Pattern Matching on a Group of Characters

In the previous example, to list all of the files ending in .pds using single character substitution, you would have to know exactly how many characters precede the period. To overcome this problem, you use the asterisk (*), which matches a character string of any length, including a length of zero. Consider the following two examples:

```
$ ls *.pds
acct.pds    marsha.pds
```

```
$ ls p10*
p10    p101
```

As with single character substitution, more than one asterisk (*) can be used in a single substitution. For example,

```
$ ls *.*
LINES.dat    LINES.idx    PAGES.dat    PAGES.idx    acct.pds
marsha.pds
```

Pattern Matching on Character Sets

You have seen how you can access a group of files whose names are similar. What do you do, though, if you need to be more specific? Another way to do filename substitution is by matching on character sets. A character set is any number of single alphanumeric characters enclosed in square brackets—[and].

Suppose that you wanted a list of all the filenames that start with p or t followed by 11. You could use the following command:

```
$ ls [pt]11
p11    t11
```

You can combine character sets with the metacharacters. To list the names of all the files that begin with p or t, you could use

```
$ ls [pt]*
p10        p101        p11        t11
```

Now suppose that you wanted a list of all the filenames that begin with an uppercase alphabetic character. You could use

```
$ ls [ABCDEFGHIJKLMNOPQRSTUVWXYZ]*
LINES.dat    LINES.idx    PAGES.dat    PAGES.idx
```

If you're guessing that there might be a better way to do this, you're right. When the characters in a character set substitution are in sequence, you can use a hyphen (-) to denote all of the characters in the sequence. Therefore, you can abbreviate the previous command in this way:

```
$ ls [A-Z]*
```

If a character sequence is broken, you can still use the hyphen for the portion of the character set that is in sequence. For example, the following command lists all the three-character filenames that begin with p, q, r, s, t, and z:

```
$ ls [p-tz]??
p10    p11    t11    z11
```

How File Substitution Works

It is important to understand how file substitution actually works. In the previous examples, the `ls` command doesn't do the work of file substitution—the shell does. (Refer to Chapter 10, "What Is a Shell," for more information.) Even though all the previous examples employ the `ls` command, any command that accepts filenames on the command line can use file substitution. In fact, using the simple `echo` command is a good way to experiment with file substitution without having to worry about unexpected results. For example,

```
$ echo p*
p10 p101 p11
```

When a metacharacter is encountered in a UNIX command, the shell looks for patterns in filenames that match the metacharacter. When a match is found, the shell substitutes the actual filename in place of the string containing the metacharacter so that the command sees only a list of valid filenames. If the shell finds no filenames that match the pattern, it passes an empty string to the command.

The shell can expand more than one pattern on a single line. Therefore, the shell interprets the command

```
$ ls LINES.* PAGES.*
```

as

```
$ ls LINES.dat LINES.idx PAGES.dat PAGES.idx
```

There are file substitution situations that you should be wary of. You should be careful about the use of whitespace (extra blanks) in a command line. If you enter the following command, for example, the results might surprise you:

```
$ ls LINES. *
LINES.: not found
21x          LINES.dat    LINES.idx    PAGES.dat    PAGES.idx
acct.pds     marsha.pds   p10          p101         p11
t11          z11
```

What has happened is that the shell interpreted the first parameter as the filename `LINES.` with no metacharacters and passed it directly on to `ls`. Next, the shell saw the single asterisk (*), and matched it to any character string, which matches every file in the directory. This is not a big problem if you are simply listing the files, but it could mean disaster if you were using the command to delete data files!

Unusual results can also occur if you use the period (.) in a shell command. Suppose that you are using the

```
$ ls .*
```

command to view the hidden files. What the shell would see after it finishes interpreting the metacharacter is

```
$ ls . ... .profile
```

which gives you a complete directory listing of both the current and parent directories.

When you think about how filename substitution works, you might assume that the default form of the `ls` command is actually

```
$ ls *
```

However, in this case the shell passes to `ls` the names of directories, which causes `ls` to list all the files in the subdirectories. The actual form of the default `ls` command is

```
$ ls .
```

The *find* Command

One of the wonderful things about UNIX is its unlimited path names. A directory can have a subdirectory that itself has a subdirectory, and so on. This provides great flexibility in organizing your data.

Unlimited path names have a drawback, though. To perform any operation on a file that is not in your current working directory, you must have its complete path name. Disk files are a lot like flashlights: You store them in what seem to be perfectly logical places, but when you need them again, you can't remember where you put them. Fortunately, UNIX has the `find` command.

The `find` command begins at a specified point on a directory tree and searches all lower branches for files that meet some criteria. Since `find` searches by path name, the search crosses file systems, including those residing on a network, unless you specifically instruct it otherwise. Once it finds a file, `find` can perform operations on it.

Suppose you have a file named `urgent.todo`, but you cannot remember the directory where you stored it. You can use the `find` command to locate the file.

```
$ find / -name urgent.todo -print
/usr/home/stuff/urgent.todo
```

The syntax of the `find` command is a little different, but the remainder of this section should clear up any questions.

The `find` command is different from most UNIX commands in that each of the argument expressions following the beginning path name is considered a Boolean expression. At any given stop along a branch, the entire expression is true—file found—if all of the expressions are true; or false—file not found—if any one of the expressions is false. In other words, a file is found only if all the search criteria are met. For example,

```
$ find /usr/home -user marsha -size +50
```

is true for every file beginning at /usr/home that is owned by Marsha and is larger than 50 blocks. It is not true for Marsha's files that are 50 or fewer blocks long, nor is it true for large files owned by someone else.

An important point to remember is that expressions are evaluated from left to right. Since the entire expression is false if any one expression is false, the program stops evaluating a file as soon as it fails to pass a test. In the previous example, a file that is not owned by Marsha is not evaluated for its size. If the order of the expressions is reversed, each file is evaluated first for size, and then for ownership.

Another unusual thing about the find command is that it has no natural output. In the previous example, find dutifully searches all the paths and finds all of Marsha's large files, but it takes no action. For the find command to be useful, you must specify an expression that causes an action to be taken. For example,

```
$ find /usr/home -user me -size +50 -print
/usr/home/stuff/bigfile
/usr/home/trash/bigfile.old
```

first finds all the files beginning at /usr/home that are owned by me and are larger than 50 blocks. Then it prints the full path name. (Actually, the full path name of the found files is sent to the standard output file, which is discussed later in this chapter.)

The argument expressions for the find command fall into three categories:

- Search criteria
- Action expressions
- Search qualifiers

Although the three types of expressions have different functions, each is still considered a Boolean expression and must be found to be true before any further evaluation of the entire expression can take place. (The significance of this is discussed later.) Typically, a find operation consists of one or more search criteria, a single action expression, and perhaps a search qualifier. In other words, it finds a file and takes some action, even if that action is simply to print the path name. The rest of this section describes each of the categories of the find options.

Search Criteria

The first task of the find command is to locate files according to some user-specified criteria. You can search for files by name, file size, file ownership, and several other characteristics.

Finding Files with a Specific Name: -name fname

Often, the one thing that you know about a file for which you're searching is its name. Suppose that you wanted to locate—and possibly take some action on—all the files named core. You might use the following command:

```
$ find / -name core -print
```

This locates all the files on the system that exactly match the name core, and it prints their complete path names.

The -name option makes filename substitutions. The command

```
$ find /usr/home -name "*.tmp" -print
```

prints the names of all the files that end in .tmp. Notice that when filename substitutions are used, the substitution string is enclosed in quotation marks. This is because the UNIX shell attempts to make filename substitutions before it invokes the command. If the quotation marks were omitted from "*.tmp" and if the working directory contained more than one *.tmp file, the actual argument passed to the find command might look like this:

```
$ find /usr/home -name a.tmp b.tmp c.tmp -print
```

This would cause a syntax error to occur.

Locating Files of a Specific Size: -size n

Another useful feature of find is that it can locate files of a specific size. The -size n expression is a good example of a search criterion that is evaluated numerically. The numeric portion of the expression may be integers in the form n, -n, or +n. An integer without a sign matches if the file is exactly n. An integer preceded by a minus sign matches if the requested file is smaller than n. An integer preceded by a plus sign matches if the file is larger than n. For example,

```
$ find / -size +100 -print
```

prints the names of all the files that are more than 100 blocks long.

In the -size expression, the integer may be suffixed with the character c. With the suffix, the match is made on the file size in characters. Without the suffix, the match is made on the file size in blocks. Therefore, the command

```
$ find / -size -512c -print
```

prints the names of all the files that are less than 512 bytes long.

Other search criteria include:

-user uname   Looks for files that are owned by the user with the login name of uname. If uname is numeric it is compared to the user number.

`-group gname`	Looks for files that are owned by a member of the group gname. If gname is numeric, it is compared to the group number.
`-atime n`	Looks for files that were last accessed n days ago. n must be an integer. It can take the form n, -n, or +n.
`-mtime n`	Looks for files that were last modified n days ago. n must be an integer.
`-perm onum`	Looks for files whose permission flags match the octal number onum. If onum is preceded by a minus sign, the match will be made if the permission flag has the bit(s) set that matches the bit(s) in onum. For example, the expression `-perm -100` will be true for any file that is executable by its owner.
`-links n`	A match if the file has n links. n must be an integer. It can take the form n, -n, or +n.
`-type x`	Looks for files that are of type *x*. Valid values for *x* are: b for a block special file, c for a character special file, d for a directory, p for a `fifo` (named pipe), and f for an ordinary file.
`-newer fname`	Looks for files that have been modified more recently than the file `fname`.
`-local`	Looks for files that reside on the local system as opposed to a remote site.

Action Expressions

Once the `find` command has located a file, it must be told what to do with it. These are called action expressions.

Displaying the Path Names of Found Files: *-print*

As you know, it does little good to locate a file, and then take no action. One commonly used action is the `-print` expression, which causes the complete path name to be printed when a file is found. This is useful if you want to check for the existence of a file before deciding to take some other action.

Executing a UNIX Command on the Found Files: *-exec cmd \;*

Sometimes you know what action you want to take once you find a file. In those cases, you can use the expression

`-exec` *cmd* `\;`

where *cmd* is any UNIX command. \; tells the find command to take the action specified between -exec and \;. find then continues to evaluate argument expressions.

The most powerful aspect of the find command is the unique file substitution method found within the -exec cmd expression. In any cmd statement, the argument {} is replaced with the name of the currently matched file. For example, suppose that the command

```
$ find /usr/home -name core -print
```

gives the following results:

```
/usr/home/dave/core
/usr/home/marsha/core
/usr/home/mike/core
```

The command

```
$ find /usr/home -name core -exec rm {} \;
```

has the same effect as issuing these commands:

```
$ rm /usr/home/dave/core
$ rm /usr/home/mike/core
$ rm /usr/home/marsha/core
```

Executing a UNIX Command on Found Files, But Querying First: -ok cmd \;

The -ok expression works exactly like the -exec expression, except that the execution of the command is optional. When it encounters an -ok expression, the find program displays the generated command, with all substitutions made, and prints a question mark. If the user types y, the command is executed.

Writing Found Files to a Device: -cpio device

The -cpio device action expression causes a file to be written to a given device in cpio form. For example, the command

```
$ find /usr/home -cpio -o >/dev/rmt0
```

writes all the files in /usr/home and all its subdirectories to the magnetic tape device /dev/rmt0. This is a good way to back up data files. It is a shorthand equivalent of

```
$ find /usr/home -print | cpio >/dev/rmt0
```

Search Qualifiers

There are times when you may want the find command to alter its normal search path. This is accomplished by adding search qualifiers to the find command.

Searching for Files on Only the Current File System: *-mount*

The `-mount` search qualifier restricts the search to the file system named in the starting point. For example, the command

```
$ find / -mount -type d -print
```

prints the names of all the directories in only the root file system.

Altering the Search Path with *-depth*

The `-depth` search qualifier alters the seek order to a `depth-first` search. The `find` command processes the files in a directory before it processes the directory itself. This helps in finding files to which the user has access, even if his access to the directory is restricted. To see the difference, try the following two commands. Remember that `-print` is always true.

```
$ find /usr -print
$ find /usr -depth -print
```

Combining Search Criteria

You can combine search criteria in a single command. Because the expressions in a `find` command are evaluated from left to right and the search fails when any one expression fails, the effect is a logical AND. For example, the command

```
$ find /usr/home -name "*.tmp" -atime +7 -exec rm {} \;
```

removes all the files that end in `.tmp` and that have not been accessed in the last 7 days.

Suppose, though, that you wanted to locate files ending in either `.tmp` or `.temp`. You could use the expression `-name "*mp"`, but you might find files that you didn't expect. The solution is to combine search criteria in a logical OR expression. The syntax is

```
\( expression -o expression \)
```

The `\` in front of the parentheses is an escape character; it prevents the shell from misinterpreting the parentheses. The following command line, for example, finds files ending in either `.tmp` or `.temp`:

```
$ find /usr/home \( -name "*.tmp" -o -name "*.temp" \)
```

Negating Expressions to Find Files That Don't Meet Criteria

Suppose that Marsha wanted to see whether anyone was putting files into her personal directory. She could use the negation operator (`!`), as in

```
$ find /usr/home/marsha ! -user marsha -print
$ /usr/home/marsha/daves.todo
```

Specifying More Than One Path to Search

By specifying a directory in which the `find` command should begin searching, you can control the scope of the search. The `find` command actually takes a list of directories to be searched, but you must specify all paths before you supply any expression arguments. For example, the command

```
$ find /usr/home/mike /usr/home/dave
```

produces a list of all the files in Mike's and Dave's directories and in your current working directory.

> **NOTE:** You must specify at least one directory for a search. To specify the current directory for a search, use `.pathname`.

Controlling Input and Output

One thing common to almost all computer programs is that they accept some kind of input and produce some kind of output. UNIX commands are no different. In this section, you'll discover how you can control the source of input and the destination of output.

One reason why UNIX is so flexible is that each program is automatically assigned three standard files: the standard input file, the standard output file, and the standard error file. Programmers are not restricted to using only these files. However, programs and commands that use only the standard files permit maximum flexibility. The three standard files also can be redirected. When it is not redirected, the standard input file is the user's keyboard, and both standard output and standard error go to the user's screen.

Output Redirection

Two operators enable you to redirect output to a file: > and >>. The > operator either creates a new file that contains the redirected output, or overwrites an existing file with the redirected output. The >> operator appends the new output to the end of the specified file. That is, if the file already contains data, the new output is added to the end of it.

To divert the standard output from your screen, use the > operator. Consider the directory used in an example at the beginning of this chapter. To redirect the output to a file named `dirfile`, you would use the command

```
$ ls >dirfile
```

Now you could use `dirfile` in another command. For example,

```
$ cat dirfile

21x
LINES.dat
LINES.idx
PAGES.dat
PAGES.idx
acct.pds
dirfile
marsha.pds
p11
t11
users
```

> **NOTE:** Notice that the specified output file, `dirfile`, already appears in the listing. This is because the first thing that `ls` does is to open its output file.

> **NOTE:** When the output of `ls` is redirected, the default output is in a single column. This is useful if the result is to be processed by another command that looks for one filename per line.

The > operator causes a new file to be created. If you had already created a file named `dirfile`, it would be deleted and replaced with the new data. If you wanted to add the new data to the old `dirfile`, you could use the >> operator. For example:

```
$ ls -x >dirfile
$ ls -x >>dirfile
$ cat dirfile

21x         LINES.dat   LINES.idx   PAGES.dat   PAGES.idx
acct.pds    dirfile     marsha.pds  p11         t11
users
21x         LINES.dat   LINES.idx   PAGES.dat   PAGES.idx
acct.pds    dirfile     marsha.pds  p11         t11
users
```

Input File Redirection

There are two possible sources of input for UNIX commands. Programs such as `ls` and `find` get their input from the command line in the form of options and filenames. Other programs, such as `cat`, can get their data from the standard input as well as from the command line. Try the `cat` command with no options on the command line:

```
$ cat
```

There is no response. Because no files are specified with the command, `cat` waits to get its input from your keyboard, the standard input file. The program will accept input lines from the keyboard until it sees a line which begins with Ctrl+D, which is the end-of-file signal for standard input.

To redirect the standard input, you use the < operator. For example, if you wanted `cat` to get its input from `dirfile`, you could use the command

```
$ cat <dirfile
```

The difference between this command and

```
$ cat dirfile
```

is a subtle one. In filenames provided as options to a command, you can use filename substitution. When redirecting input, you must use the name of an existing file or device. Therefore, the following command is a valid UNIX command:

```
$ cat dir*
```

You cannot, however, use the following command, for it is an invalid UNIX command:

```
$ cat <dir*
```

Redirecting Error Messages

Most commands have two possible types of output: normal or standard output, and error messages. Normally, error messages display to the screen, but error messages can also be redirected.

Earlier in this chapter, you saw the following example with a space between the partial filename and the metacharacter:

```
$ ls LINES. *
```

```
LINES.: not found
21x          LINES.dat    LINES.idx    PAGES.dat    PAGES.idx
acct.pds     marsha.pds   p10          p101         p11
t11          z11
```

It appears that all of the output in this example is on the standard output. However, if you change the command slightly, you get different results:

```
$ ls LINES. * >dirfile
LINES.: not found
```

What has happened is that the legitimate output from the `ls` command has been redirected to `dirfile`, and the error message has been sent to the standard error file.

To redirect error messages, use the > operator prefixed with a 2. For example,

```
$ ls LINES. * 2>errmsg
```

```
21x         LINES.dat    LINES.idx    PAGES.dat    PAGES.idx
acct.pds    marsha.pds   p10          p101         p11
t11         z11
```

Now the error message has been directed to the file errmsg, and the legitimate output has gone to the standard output file.

You can redirect both standard output and standard error for the same command. For example,

```
$ ls LINES. * >dirfile 2>errmsg
```

You cannot redirect the same standard file twice. For example, the following command is invalid:

```
$ ls >dirfile >anotherdir
```

If you wanted to discard all error messages, you could use the following form:

```
$ ls LINES. * >dirfile  2>/dev/null
```

NOTE: The standard error redirection operator (2>) is actually the same operator as standard output redirection (>). When a UNIX program opens files, they are given integer numbers. The three standard files are numbered 0, 1, and 2.

0 is assumed for input redirection. 1 is assumed for output redirection; therefore, redirection of standard output can also be written as 1>. Redirection is not restricted to only the first three files. However, to redirect higher-numbered files, the user would need to know how they are used within the program.

NOTE: Note for C shell users. In the C shell, error messages cannot be redirected separately from standard output. In the C-shell you can include error output with standard output by adding an ampersand (&) to the redirection symbol.

```
$ ls LINES. * >& dirfile
```

This command would redirect both standard output and error messages to dirfile.

Using Pipes to Pass Files Between Programs

Suppose that you wanted a directory listing that was sorted by the mode—file type plus permissions. To accomplish this, you might redirect the output from ls to a data file and then sort that data file. For example,

```
$ ls -l >tempfile
$ sort <tempfile

-rw-rw-r--  1 marsha    adept       1024 Jan 20 14:14 LINES.dat
-rw-rw-r--  1 marsha    adept       3072 Jan 20 14:14 LINES.idx
-rw-rw-r--  1 marsha    adept        256 Jan 20 14:14 PAGES.dat
-rw-rw-r--  1 marsha    adept       3072 Jan 20 14:14 PAGES.idx
-rw-rw-r--  1 marsha    acct         240 May  5  1992 acct.pds
-rw-rw-r--  1 marsha    adept       1024 Nov 22 15:42 marsha.pds
-rw-rw-r--  1 marsha    adept          0 Jan 21 10:22 tempfile
-rwxr-xr--  1 asm       adept        512 Dec 14 16:16 21x
-rwxrwxr--  4 root      sys       243072 Aug 22  1991 p11
-rwxrwxr--  4 root      sys       256041 Aug 22  1991 t11
drw-rw-r--  1 marsha    adept       3072 Oct 12 11:42 users
```

Although you get the result that you wanted, there are three drawbacks to this method:

- You might end up with a lot of temporary files in your directory. You would have to go back and remove them.

- The sort program doesn't begin its work until the first command is complete. This isn't too significant with the small amount of data used in this example, but it can make a considerable difference with larger files.

- The final output contains the name of your tempfile, which might not be what you had in mind.

Fortunately, there is a better way.

The pipe symbol (|) causes the standard output of the program on the left side of the pipe to be passed directly to the standard input of the program on the right side of the pipe symbol. Therefore, to get the same results as before, you can use the pipe symbol. For example,

```
$ ls -l | sort

-rw-rw-r--  1 marsha    adept       1024 Jan 20 14:14 LINES.dat
-rw-rw-r--  1 marsha    adept       3072 Jan 20 14:14 LINES.idx
-rw-rw-r--  1 marsha    adept        256 Jan 20 14:14 PAGES.dat
-rw-rw-r--  1 marsha    adept       3072 Jan 20 14:14 PAGES.idx
-rw-rw-r--  1 marsha    acct         240 May  5  1992 acct.pds
-rw-rw-r--  1 marsha    adept       1024 Nov 22 15:42 marsha.pds
-rwxr-xr--  1 asm       adept        512 Dec 14 16:16 21x
-rwxrwxr--  4 root      sys       243072 Aug 22  1991 p11
-rwxrwxr--  4 root      sys       256041 Aug 22  1991 t11
drw-rw-r--  1 marsha    adept       3072 Oct 12 11:42 users
```

You have accomplished your purpose elegantly, without cluttering your disk. It is not readily apparent, but you have also worked more efficiently. Consider the following example:

```
$ ls -l | sort >dirsort & ; ps

  PID TTY  STAT  TIME COMMAND
13678 003  R     2:13 sh
15476 003  R     0:01 ls
15477 003  R     0:00 sort
15479 003  R     0:00 ps
```

Both ls and sort are executing simultaneously, which means that sort can begin processing its input, even before ls has finished its output. A program, such as sort, that takes standard input and creates standard output is sometimes called a *filter*.

The capability to string commands together in a pipeline, combined with the capability to redirect input and output, is part of what gives UNIX its great power. Instead of having large, comprehensive programs perform a task, several simpler programs can be strung together, giving the end user more control over the results. It is not uncommon in the UNIX environment to see something like this:

```
$ cmd1 <infile | cmd2 -options | cmd3 | cmd4 -options >outfile
```

Summary

In this chapter, you learned how to use UNIX commands to list filenames with ls and to locate files based on search criteria with find. You also learned how to supply partial filenames to a command by using filename substitution. Finally, you learned how to reroute input and output by using standard file redirection and piping.

Popular Tools

5

By Pete Holsberg

IN THIS CHAPTER

UNIX is known not only for its longevity and versatility as an operating system, but also for the variety and number of utility programs that UNIX publishers provide. UNIX users have long called these programs *tools* because of the neat little things each one does and for their capability to be combined into more specialized utilities. (See Chapters 11, 12, and 13 for information on shell programming.)

Tools usually provide information or manipulate files and their contents. This chapter deals with the most general of information-provider tools—a pocketful of handy things that you use all the time and those special few that you keep at hand for certain special jobs. These tools enable you to do mathematical calculations without your pocket or desk calculator, check the time and date, get information about yourself and other users, find out details about commands on your system, and check your disk space. After dealing with these tools for a while, you'll find yourself using them without thinking, just as you might use one of the attachments on your Swiss Army knife.

Making Calculations with dc and bc

UNIX has two calculator programs that you can use from the command line: dc and bc. The dc (*desk calculator*) program uses *Reverse Polish Notation* (RPN), familiar to everyone who has used Hewlett-Packard pocket calculators, and the bc (*basic calculator*) program uses the more familiar algebraic notation. Both programs perform essentially the same calculations.

Calculating with bc

The basic calculator, bc, can do calculations to any precision that you specify. Therefore, if you know how to calculate pi and want to know its value to 20, 50, or 200 places, for example, use bc. This tool can add, subtract, multiply, divide, and raise a number to a power. It can take square roots, compute sines and cosines of angles, calculate exponentials and logarithms, and handle arctangents and Bessel functions. In addition, it contains a programming language whose syntax looks much like that of the C programming language (see Chapter 17, "C Language"). This means that you can use the following:

- Simple and array variables
- Expressions
- Tests and loops
- Functions that you define

Also, bc can take input from the keyboard, from a file, or from both.

Here are some examples of bc receiving input from the keyboard:

```
$ bc
2*3
6
```

To do multiplication, all you have to do is enter the two values with an asterisk between them. To exit from bc, just type **Ctrl+d**. However, you can also continue giving bc more calculations to do.

Here's a simple square root calculation (as a continuation of the original bc command):

```
sqrt(11)
3
```

Oops! The default behavior of bc is to treat all numbers as integers. To get *floating-point* numbers (that is, numbers with decimal points in them), use the scale command. For example, the following input tells bc that you want it to set four decimal places and then try the square root example again:

```
scale=4
sqrt(11)
3.3166
```

In addition to setting the number of decimal places with scale, you can set the number of significant digits with length.

You need not always use base-10 for all your calculations, either. For example, suppose that you want to calculate the square root of the base-8 (*octal*) number, 11. First change the input base to 8 and then enter the same square root command as before to do the calculation:

```
ibase=8
sqrt(11)
3.0000
Ctrl+D
$
```

This result is correct because octal 11 is decimal 9 and the square root of 9 is 3 in both octal and decimal.

> **TIP:** If you want to change back to base 10, you must supply the octal value of 10 to the ibase command. It's simpler to exit from bc—by pressing **Ctrl+D**—and then restart the program.

You can use a variable even without a program:

```
$ bc
x=5
10*x
50
```

Here's a simple loop in bc's C-like syntax:

```
y=1
while(y<5){
y^2
y=y+1
}
1
4
9
16
```

The first line sets y to the value 1. The next four lines establish a loop: the middle two lines repeat as long as the value of y is less than 5 (`while(y<5)`). Those two repeated lines cause bc to print the value of y-squared and then add one to the value of y. Note that bc doesn't display the value of a variable when it's on a line with an equals sign (or a `while` statement). Also, note the positions of the braces.

> **CAUTION:** Because bc is fussy about spaces and the placement of parentheses and braces, you may not get what you want the first time that you enter it. Unfortunately, the bc tool that you have and the one used for the examples in this book may differ.

Here's another, more compact kind of loop. It sets the initial value for y, tests the value of y, and adds one to the value of y, all on one line:

```
for (y = 1; y <= 5; y = y + 1){
3*y
}
3
6
9
12
15
```

Initially, y is set to 1. Then the loop tests whether the variable is less than or equal to 5. Because it is, bc performs the calculation 3*y and prints 3. Next, 1 is added to the present value of y, making it 2. That's also less than 5, so bc performs the 3*y calculation, which results in 6 being printed. y is incremented to 3, which is then tested; because 3 is less than 5, 3*y is calculated again. At some point, bc increments y to 6, which is neither less than 5 nor equal to it, so that the loop terminates with no further calculation or display.

You can define and use new functions for the bc program. A bc function is a device that can take in one or more numbers and calculate a result. For example, the following function, s, adds three numbers:

```
define s(x,y,z){
return(x+y+z)
}
```

To use the s function, you enter a command such as the following:

```
s(5,9,22)
36
```

Each variable name and each function name must be a single lowercase letter. If you are using the math library, bc -l, (discussed below), the letters a, c, e, j, l, and s are already used.

If you have many functions that you use fairly regularly, you can type them into a text file and start bc by entering bc myfile.bc (where *myfile* is the name of text file). The bc program then knows those functions and you can invoke them without having to type their definitions again. If you use a file to provide input to bc, you can put comments in that file. When bc reads the file, it ignores anything that you type between /* and */.

If scale is 0, the bc program does *modulus division* (using the % symbol), which provides the remainder that results from the division of two integers, as in the following example:

```
scale=4
5/2
2.5000
5%2
0
scale=0
5/2
2
5%2
1
```

If scale is not 0, the numbers are treated as floating point even if they are typed as integers.

In addition to including C's increment operators (++ and −), bc also provides some special assignment operators: +=, -=, *=, /=, and ^=. See Chapter 17, "C Language," for further explanation.

The built-in math functions include the following:

Function	Returns
a(x)	The arc tangent of x
c(x)	The cosine of x
e(x)	e raised to the x power
j(n,x)	The Bessel function of n and x, where n is an integer and x is any real number
l(x)	The natural logarithm of x
s(x)	The sine of x

To use these math functions, you must invoke bc with the -l option, as follows:

```
$ bc -l
```

Calculating with dc

As mentioned earlier, the desk calculator, dc, uses RPN, so unless you're comfortable with that notation, you should stick with bc. Also, dc does not provide a built-in programming language, built-in math functions, or the capability to define functions. It can, however, take its input from a file.

If you are familiar with stack-oriented calculators, you'll find that dc is an excellent tool. It can do all the calculations that bc can and it also lets you manipulate the stack directly.

To display values, you must enter the p command. For example, to add and print the sum of 5 and 9, enter

```
5
9
+p
14
```

See your UNIX reference manual (different versions use different titles), or if you have them, view the on-line man pages for details on dc.

Finding the Date and Time

When used by an ordinary user, the date command does only one thing: it displays the date and the time. The system administrator can use date to set the date and the time.

Here's how you use date to find out the current date and time:

```
$ date
Sat Sep 28 1:45:58 EDT 1991
```

This is the simplest form of executing the date command, but not the most useful. This command has many options that let you extract any part of the usual output and display that part alone or with other parts.

First, look at the individual options. Unlike most UNIX commands, which usually have single letters as options, date's options are strings of characters. The option string begins with a plus sign (+) and each option is preceded with a percent sign (%). You can include ordinary text in the option string, as you will see in the next example.

TIP: You should enclose the option string in either single or double quotation marks so that the shell won't interpret any characters in the ordinary text portion that it believes are special.

The a option outputs the abbreviated name of the day, and the A option provides the unabbreviated name:

```
$ date +%a

Sat

$ date +%A

Saturday
```

The b option outputs the abbreviated name of the month, and the B option provides the unabbreviated name:

```
$ date +%b

Sep

$ date +%B

September
```

The d option provides the day of the month in two-digit numeric form, and the e option outputs the day of the month with a space preceding the day for days 1 to 9. In the following example, the date is the 28th day of the month:

```
$ date +%d

28

$ date +%e

28
```

If you execute these two commands again early the next month—on the fourth, for example—you would see the following:

```
$ date +%d

4

$ date +%e

 4
```

The D option outputs the common numerical date format (month/day/year) used in the United States:

```
$ date +%D

09/28/91
```

Other options—c, x, and X—output the date in the format for whichever country was specified when SVR4 was installed. If you designated a country other than the United States during installation, try these options on your own; their output differs for different countries.

The options H and I output the hour in numeric form: H in 24 hour or military form, and I in 12 hour form.

```
$ date +%H

13

$ date +%I

1
```

The j option is rather interesting. It outputs the so-called "Julian" date—the day as one of the 365 days of the year (or 366 in a leap year). The following example shows the j option returning the date for September 28:

```
$ date +%j

271
```

This option is useful when calculating the elapsed time between two dates.

The U and W options both output the week as one of the 52 weeks of the year (or 53 in a leap year). They differ in that U begins the week with Sunday and W begins the week with Monday. When executed on September 29, 1991, date produces the following:

```
$ date +%U

39

$ date +%W

39
```

The m option outputs the month as one of the 12 months of the year:

```
$ date +%m

09
```

The M option gives the minutes value in the range of 00 to 59, and the S option shows the seconds value in the range of 00 to 61 (to allow for a "leap second" or two):

```
$ date +%M

48

$ date +%S

41
```

The R option combines the H and M options, and the T option combines H, M, and S:

```
$ date +%R

13:48

$ date +%T

13:48:51
```

The p option outputs either AM or PM, and r combines I, M, S, and p:

```
$ date +%p

AM

$ date +%r

1:48:25 AM
```

The w option shows the day of the week as a number between 0 and 6, with 0 representing Sunday:

```
$ date +%w

6
```

The y option shows the year as a number between 00 and 99, and the Y option shows the year as a four-digit value:

```
$ date +%y

91

$ date +%Y

1991
```

The Z option outputs the abbreviated time zone name for your computer. In the following example, the computer is located in the Eastern time zone, but during Daylight Savings Time:

```
$ date +%Z

EDT
```

You can combine two or more options along with text strings to produce more descriptive outputs, such as the following:

```
$ date "+Today is %A, the %e of %B, %Y"

Today is Saturday, the 28 of September, 1991
```

Displaying a Monthly or Yearly Calendar with *cal*

The cal command is very simple but quite handy when you need to see the calendar of any month (or all 12) in any given year. Used with no arguments, cal simply prints a calendar of the current month:

```
$ cal
    February 1994
 S  M Tu  W Th  F  S
          1  2  3  4  5
 6  7  8  9 10 11 12
13 14 15 16 17 18 19
20 21 22 23 24 25 26
27 28

$
```

If you specify a year, as in cal 1993, you get a calendar for all 12 months, but if you specify a month and a year, as in cal 4 1992, you get just that month.

> **CAUTION:** If you specify a year as a two-digit number, cal gives you the calendar for that year. In other words, cal 93 produces a calendar for the year 93, not the year 1993.

> **Historical Note:** In 1752 the calendar was adjusted to account for the "discovery" of leap year by eliminating 11 days (September 3 through September 13). Type cal 9 1752 to see the strangest month of all!

Getting Information About Users

To get information about users (including yourself), you can use several commands. The who command reports on users who are presently logged in, and finger reports on anyone who has an account on the computer. The id command reports information about the user who invokes it.

The *who* Command

The who command normally reports certain information about logged-in users. By using its options, you can specify that it report information about the processes initiated by init, and that it report reboots, changes to the system clock, and logoffs. (See chapters 18 and 35 for more information on processes and `init`.) If you invoke `who` with no options or arguments, you get the following output:

```
$ who

juucp      tty00      Sep 28 11:13
pjh        slan05     Sep 28 12:08
```

The output shows that two users are currently logged in: the user `juucp`, who logged in at 11:13, and the user `pjh`, who logged in at 12:08. Notice that `juucp` is logged in on a *tty* line (actually, `juucp` is a neighboring site that is called in over a modem) and that `pjh` logged in over a network (STARLAN, which is shortened to `slan` in `who`'s output).

NOTE: The term tty is short for *teletypewriter*, the first kind of terminal to be connected to a UNIX computer system. Even though terminals have advanced significantly, the terminology has not changed. A "neighboring site" is a computer that is located nearby.

The `-u` option adds the "time since the last activity" (also called the *idle time*) and the process ID number for each logged-in user. A "process ID number" or PID is an interger number assigned by UNIX to uniquely identify a given process (usually, a process is a program that is running). PIDs are needed in UNIX because they allow—yea, encourage—simultaneous running of multiple processes. (See Part IV, "Process Control," for more information.)

```
$ who -u

juucp      tty00      Sep 28 11:13    .     5890
pjh        slan05     Sep 28 12:08    .     7354
```

NOTE: If the user has been active within the last minute, `who` displays a dot (.) for the idle time.

The `-T` option reports a plus sign (+) if you are able to send messages to the user's terminal, or a minus sign (-) if it is not:

```
$ who -T

juucp      + tty00      Sep 28 11:13
pjh        + slan05     Sep 28 12:08
```

The `-q` (*quick*) option simply shows login IDs and a count of the logged-in users:

```
$ who -q

juucp    pjh
# users=2
```

There's a special case for who: who am i. This case is useful if you are logged in from several terminals under different accounts, and you forget which one you are currently using:

```
$ who am i

pjh        slan05      Sep 28 12:08
```

The *finger* Command

You can use the finger command with or without arguments. Without arguments, finger's output looks a little like who's:

```
$ finger
Login      Name             TTY        Idle    When      Where
pjh        Pete Holsberg    pts000     6d  Mon 13:03
ajh        Alan Holsberg    sxt/002        Sat 15:00
```

This output lists all currently logged users—with a heading line—plus the user's full name and the name of the remote computer (in the "Where" column) if the person is logging in over a network.

This command is more useful if you give it a person's login ID as an argument, as in the following example:

```
$ finger lam
Login name: lam                    In real life: Pak Lam dp168
Directory: /home/stu/lam           Shell: /usr/bin/ksh
On since Feb 23 19:07:31 on pts016   from pc2
2 days 21 hours Idle Time
No unread mail
No Plan.
```

Here, finger displays personal information for the user lam: his real name, home directory, which shell he uses, and when he last logged in and from which computer (pc2). The last line indicates that he does not have a text file called .plan in his home directory. The finger command displays the contents of .plan and .project if they exist. As you can see, users can reveal as much or as little of themselves as they choose.

If your computer is on a network and you know another person's e-mail address, you can display information about that person by issuing a command such as the following:

```
$ finger holsberg@pilot.njin.net
```

The finger command provides many options that can suppress one or more fields of the normal, long output. However, because finger responds so quickly, simply disregarding that extra information when it appears onscreen is easier than learning the appropriate option.

The *id* Command

The id command reports four things: the user ID number, login name, group ID number, and group name of the person who invokes it. If the *real* and *effective IDs* (see Chapter 44, "System Security") are not the same, id prints both sets of values.

> **NOTE:** id is often used in shell scripts to restrict the use of a shell by a certain user or group of users.
>
> When a system administrator creates an account for a user, that user is given a login ID and also placed in a group. This is important because UNIX provides access to files according to whether the user is the owner of the file and whether the user belongs to the group that has been granted access to the file.

In the following example, the user ID is 102, the login name is pjh, and the user belongs to the root group, which is group number 0:

```
$ id
uid=102(pjh) gid=0(root)
```

Switching Accounts with *su*

If you have more than one account on a system, you need not log out of one and then log into the second to use the second account. Instead, you can simply use the su (*switch user*) command. The system administrator uses su frequently to check a user's complaint, because su enables the administrator to become that user and run the programs that were causing problems.

The usual su command syntax is

```
su - userID
```

The minus sign tells su to cause the current user to take on the identity, *userID*. To do this, su executes the user's shell—as specified in the *shell field* of /etc/passwd—and invokes /etc/profile and that user's .profile file. The su command then displays the user's normal environment. If the user omits the minus sign, su invokes the user's shell, but the environment is the same as before. Of course, before you can switch to another user, you must know that user's password—unless you are the system administrator, in which case your privileges enable you to assume identities without using passwords.

> **NOTE:** /etc/profile and .profile are files that control the working environment of each user.

Suppose, the system administrator wishes to become user lam:

```
#su - lam
$
```

To reassume identity as sysadm, he merely logs out of lam's account.

Learning More About Commands with *man*

UNIX supplies information about its commands in two forms: reference manuals (printed documentation called *man pages*) and online files. To use the man pages, you simply find the appropriate reference manual and look up the command. However, reference manuals seem to have lives of their own and are never to be found where you last put them. That's when online man pages—and the man command—become useful.

The simplest form of the man command takes a single argument: the name of the command in which you are interested. For example, here's the man page for man:

```
NAME
      cat - concatenate and print files

SYNOPSIS
      cat [-u] [-s] [-v [[-t] [-e]] file . . .

DESCRIPTION
      cat reads each file in sequence and writes it on  the  standard output.
Thus

          cat file

      prints the contents of file on your terminal, and

          cat file1 file2 >file3

      concatenates file1 and file2,  and  writes  the  results  in file3.   If
no input file is given, or if the argument - is encountered, cat  reads  from
the  standard  input.    cat processes supplementary code set characters
according to the locale specified in the LC_CTYPE environment  variable  [see
      LANG on environ(5)].

      The following options apply to cat:

      -u          The output is not buffered.  (The default  is  buffered output.)
```

-s   **cat** is silent about non-existent files.

-v   Causes non-printing characters (with the exception of tabs, new-lines, and form-feeds) to be   printed visibly. **ASCII** control characters (octal 000 - 037) are printed as ^n, where n is the   corresponding **ASCII** character in the range octal 100 - 137 (@, A, B, C, . . ., X, Y, Z, [,   \,], ^, and _); the DEL character (octal 0177) is printed ^**?**. Other non-printable characters are   printed as **M-x**, where x is the **ASCII** character specified by the low-order seven bits. All   supplementary code set characters are considered to be printable.

The following options may be used with the -v option:

-t   Causes tabs to be printed as ^**I**'s and formfeeds to be printed as ^**L**'s.

-e   Causes a **$** character to be printed at the end of each line (prior to the new-line).

The -t and -e options are ignored if the -v option is not specified.

FILES
   /usr/lib/locale/locale**/LC_MESSAGES/uxcore.abi**
   language-specific   message   file   [See **LANG** on **environ**(5).]

SEE ALSO
   cp(1), **pg**(1), **pr**(1)

The **NAME** section gives the name of the command and a brief description of what it does.

The **SYNOPSIS** section shows the command's syntax by listing all possible options and arguments. Arguments to **cat** are the names of one or more files. The fact that *file* is written in italic type means that *file* is merely a placeholder for the name of an actual file. The **cat** command has three options and one of them has two "sub-options". The brackets around options indicate that they are optional. For example, the command could be any one of the following:

   cat file
   cat -u file
   cat -s file
   cat -u -s file (or **cat -s -u file**)
   cat -us file (or **cat -su file**)
   cat -v file
   cat -v -t file (or **cat -vt file**)
   cat -v -e file (or **cat -ve file**)
   cat -v -t -e file (or **cat -vte file**)
   cat -u -v -t file (or **cat -uvt file**)

and so on. With three options and two suboptions, there are many possible combinations. Note that the order of writing the options doesn't matter and options can be combined so that only one dash (-) need be written. While these are generally true, there are some Unix commands that require a particular order, some that do not permit combinations and even a few that require a specific order and deny any combinations.

The **DESCRIPTION** section is the heart of the manual page. It describes each option and argument, and frequently contains one or more examples. However, its explanations are frequently sprinked with referenced to other commands, so that in general it is difficult to learn about a command from its man page.

```
      The FILES section lists other files that are used or related to the
command.
      The SEE ALSO section lists related commands. The numbers in parentheses
refer to the section of the manual in which the command will be found. Among
the most important are:
      Section 1 - User Commands
      Section 1C - Basic Networking Commands
      Section 1M - Administration Commands
      Section 2 - System Calls
      Section 3 - BSD Routines
      Section 3C - C Library Functions
      Section 3M - Math Library Functions
      Section 3S - Standard I/O Functions
      Section 4 - File Formats
      Section 5 - Miscellaneous
      Section 6 - (not included)
      Section 7 - Special Files
      Section 8 - System Maintenance Procedures
```

As a user or adminstrator, you will be most interested in section 1 (which contains 1, 1C and 1M). Programmers will be interested in 2, 3 and possibly 4.

Some man pages have the following additional sections:

The NOTES section is self-explanatory.

The DIAGNOSTICS sections contains explanations of error messages that the command may cause to be displayed. Not enough commands have a DIAGNOSTICS section!

The WARNINGS section describes anything that may limit the use of a command.

The BUGS section tells of known problems that have not been fixed in the current version of the command.

Finding Information About Disk Utilization with *du* and *df*

Occasionally, a user needs to know how much disk space his or her files occupy—perhaps the system administrator has sent e-mail requesting that the user is approaching some sort of limit. Frequently, the system administrator needs the same information for all users or on all parts of one or more disks, and frequently needs information on the overall utilization in all file systems. UNIX provides two commands that report that information: du and df.

Summarizing Disk Usage with *du*

The du command reports the number of disk blocks used for each directory and subdirectory, and the files found there. It has an option to display the number of blocks of just the "top level" directory.

> **NOTE:** A *block* is the smallest piece of a disk that can be allocated to a file. Frequently, the size of a block is 512 bytes (but the size depends on things that the system administrator did when setting up the disks). A file that is 1 byte long and a file that is 511 bytes long each occupies one block. A 513 byte file and a 1,023 byte file each occupies two blocks. That is, every 512 bytes of a file occupy a disk block, plus one block for the last piece that less than 512 bytes.

Here are some sample executions. First, issue the command to display what you have in the directory hierarchy, from the current directory on down:

```
$ ls -lR

total 259
drwxr-xr-x   2 pjh      other          48 Oct 17  1990 unixbin
-rw-r--r--   1 pjh      root       130137 May 10  1993 vpix.img

./unixbin:
total 16
-rw-rw-rw-   1 pjh      other        7576 Apr  8  1993 rununix.exe
```

The current directory has one regular file (vpix.img) and one directory file (unixbin), and the subdirectory has one regular file (rununix.exe).

Now find out the total disk usage:

```
$ du -s

274     .
```

That's 274 blocks, or somewhere between 13,312 and 13,823 bytes.

Use the following command to find out how many blocks are in the subdirectory:

```
$ du

17      ./unixbin
274     .
```

Then find out how many blocks each file has:

```
$ du -a

16      ./unixbin/rununix.exe
17      ./unixbin
256     ./vpix.img
274     .
```

> **NOTE:** The total for a directory or directory hierarchy includes the blocks that the directory files themselves occupy.

Reporting Blocks and Files with *df*

The df command helps the system administrator maintain the file systems on the disks. The command displays information about *mounted* and *unmounted resources*, types of *file systems*, and numbers of *inodes*. It also deals with *special devices* rather than easily identifiable directory paths. Most of these terms have little meaning to the ordinary user, but they are discussed in Chapter 35. However, if a user wants to see what's going on with the disk's file systems, the system permits it.

Multiple options are available with df. In this section, you'll see some of these options demonstrated and explained. But first, here is a typical result that you get when you invoke df with no options:

```
$ df

/                    (/dev/root      ):  381964 blocks   58845 files
/proc                (/proc          ):       0 blocks     128 files
/dev/fd              (/dev/fd        ):       0 blocks       0 files
/stand               (/dev/dsk/c0t0d0sa):   12643 blocks     194 files
/var                 (/dev/dsk/c0t0d0sb):  961502 blocks   64499 files
/tmp                 (/dev/dsk/c0t0d0sd):  191308 blocks   24560 files
/usr                 (/dev/dsk/c0t1d0s3):  772900 blocks   53842 files
/home                (/dev/dsk/c0t1d0s4):  923256 blocks   63303 files
/.NetWare            (/.NetWare      ):       0 blocks     499 files
```

The first column is the path name of the file system. This system's special device name appears in the second column. The third column reports the number of disk blocks available on each disk partition. Finally, the last column displays the number of files that can be added to each partition. When setting up a new disk, the system administrator partitions it into file systems and allocates several blocks and *inodes* (or files) to each file system according to how that partition will be used. For details, see Chapter 35, "File System Administration."

The -b option shows the free space in kilobytes rather than blocks:

```
$ df -b

Filesystem           avail
/dev/root            190982
/proc                0
/dev/fd              0
/dev/dsk/c0t0d0sa    6321
/dev/dsk/c0t0d0sb    480751
/dev/dsk/c0t0d0sd    95654
/dev/dsk/c0t1d0s3    386450
/dev/dsk/c0t1d0s4    461628
/.NetWare            0
```

The -k option shows some details about allocated space—how much has been used and how much is available—in kilobytes:

```
$ df -k
```

```
filesystem            kbytes   used     avail   capacity   mounted on
/dev/root             316416   125434   190982  40%        /
/proc                 0        0        0       0%         /proc
/dev/fd               0        0        0       0%         /dev/fd
/dev/dsk/c0t0d0sa     10240    3918     6321    38%        /stand
/dev/dsk/c0t0d0sb     509952   29201    480751  6%         /var
/dev/dsk/c0t0d0sd     102368   6714     95654   7%         /tmp
/dev/dsk/c0t1d0s3     512000   125550   386450  25%        /usr
/dev/dsk/c0t1d0s4     512976   51348    461628  10%        /home
/.NetWare             0        0        0       0%         /.NetWare
```

If you are curious about file systems, the -n option tells you the name of the file system type used for each partition. (Again, see Chapter 35 for details.)

```
$ df -n
```

```
/                 : vxfs
/proc             : proc
/dev/fd           : fdfs
/stand            : bfs
/var              : vxfs
/tmp              : vxfs
/usr              : vxfs
/home             : vxfs
/.NetWare         : nucam
```

Finally, the -t option shows used blocks and files, and the total allocation for each file system:

```
$ df -t
```

```
/                 (/dev/root        ):    381964 blocks    58845 files
                            total:        632832 blocks    65520 files
/proc             (/proc            ):         0 blocks      128 files
                            total:             0 blocks      202 files
/dev/fd           (/dev/fd          ):         0 blocks        0 files
                            total:             0 blocks       50 files
/stand            (/dev/dsk/c0t0d0sa):     12643 blocks      194 files
                            total:         20480 blocks      200 files
/var              (/dev/dsk/c0t0d0sb):    961502 blocks    64499 files
                            total:       1019904 blocks    65536 files
/tmp              (/dev/dsk/c0t0d0sd):    191308 blocks    24560 files
                            total:        204736 blocks    24576 files
/usr              (/dev/dsk/c0t1d0s3):    772900 blocks    53842 files
                            total:       1024000 blocks    65536 files
/home             (/dev/dsk/c0t1d0s4):    923256 blocks    63303 files
                            total:       1025952 blocks    65536 files
/.NetWare         (/.NetWare        ):         0 blocks      499 files
                            total:             0 blocks      500 files
```

Summary

UNIX provides several small programs that you can use to quickly obtain information that you frequently need. These programs include the following:

- bc, dc—calculator programs
- date and cal—to display time and date
- finger, who and id—provide user information
- man and apropos—explains commands
- su—"switch user"
- du and df—display information about disk contents

These commands are rather specialized commands that, in general, retrieve information about different parts of the system: users, files, directories, clock, and so on. The basis of information storage in UNIX is the *file*, so Chapter 6, "Popular File Tools," explores the somewhat more specialized commands for working with files—particularly text files.

Popular File Tools

6

By Pete Holsberg

IN THIS CHAPTER

Files are the heart of UNIX. Unlike most other operating systems, UNIX was designed with a simple, yet highly sophisticated, view of files: Everything is a file. Information stored in an area of a disk or memory is a file; a directory is a file; the keyboard is a file; the screen is a file.

This single-minded view makes it easy to write tools that manipulate files, because files have no structure—UNIX sees every file merely as a simple stream of bytes. This makes life much simpler for both the UNIX programmer and the UNIX user. The user benefits from being able to send the contents of a file to a command without having to go through a complex process of opening the file. In a similar way, the user can capture the output of a command in a file without having previously created that file. And perhaps most importantly, the user can send the output of one command directly to the input of another, using memory as a temporary storage device or file. Finally, users benefit from UNIX's unstructured files because they are simply easier to use than files that must conform to one of several highly structured formats.

Determining the Nature of a File's Contents with *file*

A user—especially a power user—must take a closer look at a file before manipulating it. If you've ever sent a binary file to a printer, you're aware of the mess that can result. Murphy's Law assures that every binary file includes a string of bytes that does one or more of the following:

- Spew a ream of paper through the printer before you can shut it off, printing just enough on each page to render the paper fit only for the recycling bin
- Put the printer into a print mode that prints all characters at 1/10 their intended size
- Lock your keyboard
- Dump core—that is, create a file consisting of whatever was in memory at that instant of time!

In a similar way, sending a binary file to the screen can lock the keyboard, put the screen in a mode that changes the displayed character set to one that is clearly not English, dump core, and so on.

While it's true that many files already stored on the system—and certainly every file you create with a text editor (see Chapter 7)—are text files, many are not. UNIX provides a command, file, that attempts to determine the nature of the contents of files when you supply their file names as arguments. You can invoke the file command in one of two ways:

```
file [-h] [-m mfile] [-f ffile] arg(s)
file [-h] [-m mfile] -f ffile
```

The `file` command performs a series of tests on each file in the list of `arg(s)` or on the list of files whose names are contained in the file `ffile`. If the file being tested is a text file, `file` examines the first 512 bytes and tries to determine the language in which it is written. The identification is worded by means of the contents of a file called `/etc/magic`. If you don't like what's in the file, you can use the `-m mfile` option, replacing `mfile` with the name of the "magic file" you'd like to use. (Consult your local magician for suitable spells and potions!) Here are the kinds of text files that Unixware Version 1.0's `file` command can identify:

- Empty files
- SCCS files
- `troff` (typesetter runoff) output files
- Data files
- C program text files (with or without garbage)
- FORTRAN program text files (with or without garbage)
- Assembler program text files (with or without garbage)
- `[nt]roff`, `tbl`, or `eqn` input text (with or without garbage)
- Command text files (with or without garbage)
- English text files (with or without garbage)
- ASCII text files (with or without garbage)
- PostScript program text files (with or without garbage)

Don't be concerned if you're not familiar with some of these kinds of text. Many of them are peculiar to UNIX and are explained in later chapters.

If the file is not text, `file` looks near the beginning of the file for a *magic number*—a number or string that is associated with a file type; an arbitrary value that is couple with a descriptive phrase. Then `file` uses `/etc/magic`, which provides a database of magic numbers and kinds of files, or the file specified as *mfile* to determine the file's contents. If the file being tested is a *symbolic link*, `file` follows the link and tries to determine the nature of the contents of the file to which it is linked. The `-h` option causes `file` to ignore symbolic links.

The `/etc/magic` file contains the table of magic numbers and their meanings. For example, here is an excerpt from Unixware Version 1.0's `/etc/magic` file. The number following `uxcore:` is the magic number, and the phrase that follows is the file type. The other columns tell `file` how and where to look for the magic number:

```
>16   short    2         uxcore:231   executable
0     string             uxcore:648   expanded ASCII cpio archive
0     string             uxcore:650   ASCII cpio archive
>1    byte     0235      uxcore:571   compressed data
0     string             uxcore:248   current ar archive
0     short    0432      uxcore:256   Compiled Terminfo Entry
0     short    0434      uxcore:257   Curses screen image
0     short    0570      uxcore:259   vax executable
0     short    0510      uxcore:263   x86 executable
0     short    0560      uxcore:267   WE32000 executable
0     string   070701    uxcore:565   DOS executable (EXE)
0     string   070707    uxcore:566   DOS built-in
0     byte     0xe9      uxcore:567   DOS executable (COM)
0     short    0520      uxcore:277   mc68k executable
0     string             uxcore:569   core file (Xenix)
0     byte     0x80      uxcore:280   8086 relocatable (Microsoft)
```

CAUTION: Human beings cannot read any of the files listed in this excerpt, so you should not send any of these files to the screen or the printer. The same is true for any of the previously listed text files that have garbage.

Browsing Through Text Files with *more* (page), and *pg*

After you identify a file as being a text file that humans can read, you may want to read it. The cat command streams the contents of a file to the screen, but you must be quick with the Scroll Lock (or equivalent) key so that the file content does not flash by so quickly that you cannot read it (your speed-reading lessons notwithstanding). UNIX provides a pair of programs that present the contents of a file one screen at a time.

The more(page) programs are almost identical, and will be discussed as if they were a simple program. The only differences are the following:

- page clears the screen automatically between pages, but more does not.

- more provides a two-line overlap from one screen to the next, while page provides only a one-line overlap.

Both more and page have several commands, many of which take a numerical argument that controls the number of times the command is actually executed. You can issue these commands while using the more or page program (see the syntax below), and none of these commands are echoed to the screen. Table 6.1 lists the major commands.

```
more [-cdflrsuw] [-lines] [+linenumber] [+/pattern] [file(s)]
page [-cdflrsuw] [-lines] [+linenumber] [+/pattern] [file(s)]
```

Table 6.1. Commands for more(page)

Command	Meaning
nSpacebar	If no positive number is entered, display the next screenfull. If an n value is entered, display n more lines.
nReturn	If no positive number is entered, display another line. If an n value is entered, display n more lines. (Depending on your keyboard, you can press either the Return or Enter key.)
n^D, nd	If no positive number is entered, scroll down 11 more lines. If an n value is given, scroll the screen down n times.
nz	Same as nSpacebar, except that if an n value is entered, it becomes the new number of lines per screenfull.
n^B, nb	Skip back n screensfull and then print a screenfull.
q, Q	Exit from more or page.
=	Display the number of the current line.
v	Drop into the editor (see Chapter 7) indicated by the EDITOR environment variable (see Chapters 11, 12, 13), at the current line of the current file.
h	Display a Help screen that describes all the more or page commands.
:f	Display the name and current line number of the file that you are viewing.
:q, :Q	Exit from more or page (same as q or Q).
_ (dot)	Repeat the previous command.

After you type the more and page programs' commands, you need not press the Enter or Return key (except, of course, in the case of the nReturn command). The programs execute the commands immediately after you type them.

You can invoke more(page) with certain options that specify the program's behavior. For example, these programs can display explicit error messages instead of just beeping. Table 6.2 lists the most commonly used options for more and page.

Table 6.2. Options for `more` and `page`

Option	Meaning
`-c`	Clear before displaying. To display screens more quickly, this option redraws the screen instead of scrolling. You need not use this option with page.
`-d`	Display an error message instead of beeping if an unrecognized command is typed.
`-r`	Display each control character as a two-character pattern consisting of a caret followed by the specified character, as in ^C.
`-s`	Replace any number of consecutive blank lines with a single blank line.
`-lines`	Make *lines* the number of lines in a screenfull.
`+n`	Start at line number *n*.
`+/pattern`	Start two lines above the line that contains the regular expression *pattern*. (Regular expressions are explained in the next section.)

The `more(page)` program is a legacy from the Berkeley version of UNIX. System V variants give us `pg`, another screen-at-a-time file viewer. The `pg` program offers a little more versatility by giving you more control over your movement within a file (you can move both forward and backward) and your search for patterns. The program has its own commands and a set of command-line options. Table 6.3 lists the more frequently used commands. Unlike `more` and `page`, the `pg` program requires that you always press the Return or Enter key to execute its commands.

`$pg [options] file`

Table 6.3. Commands for `pg`

Command	Meaning
*n*Return	If no *n* value is entered or if a value of +1 is entered, display the next page. If the value of n is –1, display the previous page. If the value of *n* has no sign, display page number n. For example, a value of 3 causes pg to display page 3. (Depending on your keyboard, you can press either the Return or Enter key.)
*n*d, ^D	Scroll half a screen. The value *n* can be positive or negative. So, for example, 2d will scroll full screen forward, and -3d will scroll one and a half screens back.

Command	Meaning
nz	Same as *n*Return except that if an *n* value is entered, it becomes the number of lines per screenfull.
., ^L	Redisplay (clear the screen and then display again) the current page of text.
$	Displays the last screenfull in the file.
n/pattern/	Search forward for the *n*th occurrence of *pattern*. (The default value for *n* is 1.) Searching begins immediately after the current page and continues to the end of the current file, without wrap-around.
n?pattern?	Search backward for the nth occurrence of *pattern*. (The default value for *n* is 1.) Searching begins immediately before the current page and continues to the beginning of the current file, without wrap-around.
h	Display an abbreviated summary of available commands.
q, Q	Quit pg.
!command	Execute the shell command *command* as if it were typed on a command line.

Addressing is the ability to specify a number with a sign or a number without a sign. A number with no sign provides *absolute* addressing; for example, pressing 3 followed by the Return key displays page 3. A number with a sign provides *relative* addressing; that is, the command moves you to a line relative to the current line.

The pg program has several startup options that modify its behavior. Table 6.4 describes the most frequently used options.

Table 6.4. Some of pg's Startup Options

Options	Meanings
-n	Change the number of lines per page to the value of *n*. Otherwise, the number of lines is determined automatically by the terminal. For example, a 24-line terminal automatically uses 23 lines per page.
-c	Clear the screen before displaying a page.

continues

Table 6.4. continued

Options	Meanings
-n	Remove the requirement that you press Return or Enter after you type the command. Note: Some commands will still require that you press Enter or Return.
-p *string*	Change the prompt from a colon (:) to *string*. If *string* contains the two characters %d, they are replaced by the current page number when the prompt appears.
-r	Prevent the use of !command and display an error message if the user attempts to use it.
-s	Print all messages and prompts in standout mode (which is usually inverse video).
+*n*	Start the display at line number *n*.
+/*pattern*/	Start the display at the first line that contains the regular expression *pattern*. Regular expressions are explained in the next section.

Each of the commands discussed in this section can accept a list of file names on the command line, and display the next file when it reaches the end of the current file.

Searching for Strings with the *grep* Family

Suppose that you want to know whether a certain person has an account on your system. You can use more, page, or pg to browse through /etc/passwd looking for that person's name, but if your system has many users, that can take a long time. Besides, an easier way is available: grep. It searches one or more files for the pattern of the characters that you specify and displays every line in the file or files that has that pattern in it.

grep stands for *global/regular expression/print*; that is, search through an entire file (do a global search) for a specified regular expression (the pattern that you specified) and display the line or lines that contain the pattern.

Before you can use grep and the other members of the grep family, you must explore regular expressions, which are what gives the grep commands (and many other UNIX commands) their power. After that, you will learn all of the details of the grep family of commands.

Regular Expressions

A regular expression is a sequence of ordinary characters and special operators. Ordinary characters include the set of all uppercase and lowercase letters, digits, and other commonly used characters: the tilde (~), the back quotation mark ('), the exclamation mark (!), the "at" sign (@), the pound sign (#), the underscore (_), the hyphen (-), the equals sign (=), the colon (:), the semicolon (;), the comma (,), and the slash (/). The special operators are backslash (\), dot (.), asterisk (*), left square bracket ([), caret (^), dollar sign ($), right square bracket (]).

By using regular expressions, you can search for general strings in a file. For example, you can tell grep to show you all lines in a file that contain any of the following: the word Unix, the word UNIX, a pattern consisting of four digits, a ZIP code, a name, nothing, or all the vowels in alphabetic order.

You can also combine two strings into a *pattern*. For example, to combine a search for Unix and UNIX, you can specify a word that begins with U, followed by n or N, followed by i or I, and ending with x or X.

Several UNIX commands use regular expressions to find text in files. Usually you supply a regular expression to a command to tell that command what to search for. Most regular expressions match more than one text string.

There are two kinds of regular expressions: *limited* and *full* (sometimes called *extended*). Limited regular expressions are a subset of full regular expressions, but UNIX commands are inconsistent in the extended operations that they permit. At the end of this discussion, you'll find a table that lists the most common commands in UNIX System V Release 4 that use regular expressions, along with the operations that they can perform.

The simplest form of a regular expression includes only ordinary characters, and is called a *string*. The grep family (grep, egrep, and fgrep) matches a string wherever it finds the regular expression, even if it's surrounded by other characters. For example, the is a regular expression that matches only the three-letter sequence t, h, and e. This string is found in the words the, therefore, bother, and many others.

Two of the members of the grep family use regular expressions—the third, fgrep, operates only on strings:

grep   The name means to search globally (throughout the entire file) for a regular expression and print the line that contains it. In its simplest form, grep is called as follows:

grep regular_expression filename

When grep finds a match of regular_expression, it displays the line of the file that contains it and then continues searching for a subsequent match. Thus, grep displays every line of a file that contains a text string that matches the regular expression.

egrep

You call this member exactly the same way as you call grep. However, this member uses an extended set of regular expression operators, that will be explained later, after you master the usual set.

> **CAUTION:** None of these commands alter the original file. Output goes to stdout (by default, stdout is the screen). To save the results, you must redirect the output to a file.

The contents of the following file are used in subsequent sections to demonstrate how you can use the grep family to search for regular expressions:

```
$ cat REfile

A regular expression is a sequence of characters taken
from the set of uppercase and lowercase letters, digits,
punctuation marks, etc., plus a set of special regular
expression operators. Some of these operators may remind
you of file name matching, but be forewarned: in general,
regular expression operators are different from the
shell metacharacters we discussed in Chapter 1.

The simplest form of a regular expression is one that
includes only letters. For example, they would match only
the three-letter sequence t, h, e. This pattern is found
in the following words: the, therefore, bother. In other
words, wherever the regular expression pattern is found
-- even if it is surrounded by other characters -- it will
be matched.
```

Regular Expression Characters

Regular expressions match patterns that consist of a combination of ordinary characters, such as letters, digits, and various other characters used as operators. You will meet examples of these below. A character's use often determines its meaning in a regular expression. All programs that use regular expressions have a *search pattern*. The editor family of programs (vi, ex, ed, and sed; see Chapter 7, "Editing Text Files") also has a *replacement pattern*. In some cases, the meaning of a special character differs depending on whether it's used as part of the search pattern or in the replacement pattern.

A Regular Expression with No Special Characters

Here's an example of a simple search for an regular expression. This regular expression is a character string with no special characters in it.

```
$ grep only REfile
```

```
includes only letters. For example, the would match only
```

The sole occurrence of `only` satisfied `grep`'s search, so `grep` printed the matching line.

Special Characters

Certain characters have special meanings when used in regular expressions, and some of them have special meanings depending on their position in the regular expression. Some of these characters are used as placeholders and some as operators. Some are used for both, depending on their position in the regular expression.

- ■ The dot (.), asterisk (*), left square bracket ([) and backslash (\) are special except when they appear between a left and right pair of square brackets ([ ]).
- ■ A circumflex or caret (^) is special when it's the first character of a regular expression, and also when it's the first character after the opening left square bracket in a left and right pair of square brackets.
- ■ A dollar sign ($) is special when it's the last character of a regular expression.
- ■ A pair of delimiters, usually a pair of slash characters (//), is special because it delimits the regular expression.

NOTE: Any character not used in the current regular expression can be used as the delimiter, but the slash is traditional.

- ■ A special character preceded by a backslash is matched by the character itself. This is called escaping. When a special character is escaped, the command recognizes it as a literal—the actual character with no special meaning. In other words, as in file-name matching, the backslash cancels the special meaning of the character that follows it.

Now let's look at each character in detail.

Matching Any One Character

The dot matches any one character except a *newline*. For example, consider the following:

```
$ grep 'w.r' REfile
from the set of uppercase and lowercase letters, digits,
you of file name matching, but be forewarned: in general,
in the following words: the, therefore, bother. In other
words, wherever the regular expression pattern is found
```

> **NOTE:** The regular expression w.r appears within a set of apostrophes (referred to by UNIXees as "single quotes"). Their use is mandatory if grep is to function properly. If they are omitted, the shell (see Chapters 11, 12, and 13) may interpret certain special characters in the regular expressio as if they were "shell special characters" rather than "grep special characters" and the result will be unexpected.

The pattern w.r matches wer in lowercase on the first displayed line, by war in forewarned on the second, by wor in words on the third, and by wor in words on the fourth. Expressed in English, the sample command says "Find and display all lines that match the following pattern: w followed by any character except a newline followed by r."

You can form a somewhat different one-character regular expression by enclosing a list of characters in a left and right pair of square brackets. The matching is limited to those characters listed between the brackets. For example, the pattern

```
[aei135XYZ]
```

matches any one of the characters a, e, i, 1, 3, 5, X, Y, or Z.

Consider the following example:

```
$ grep 'w[fhmkz]' REfile
```

```
words, wherever the regular expression pattern is found
```

This time, the match was satisfied only by the wh in wherever, matching the pattern "w followed by either f, h, m, k, or z."

If the first character in the list is a right square bracket (]), it does not terminate the list—that would make the list empty, which is not permitted. Instead,] itself becomes one of the possible characters in the search pattern. For example, the pattern

```
[]a]
```

matches either] or a.

If the first character in the list is a circumflex (also called a caret), the match occurs on any character that is *not* in the list:

```
$ grep 'w[^fhmkz]' REfile
```

```
from the set of uppercase and lowercase letters, digits,
you of file name matching, but be forewarned: in general,
shell metacharacters we discussed in Chapter 1.
includes only letters. For example, the would match only
in the following words: the, therefore, bother. In other
words, wherever the regular expression pattern is found
-- even if it is surrounded by other characters -- it will
```

The pattern "w followed by anything *except* f, h, m, k, or z" has many matches. On line 1, we in lowercase is a "w followed by anything except an f, an h, an m, a k, or a z." On line 2, wa in forewarned is a match, as is the word we on line 3. Line 4 contains wo in would, and line 5 contains wo in words. Line 6 has wo in words as its match. The other possible matches on line 6 are ignored because the match is satisfied at the beginning of the line. Finally, at the end of line 7, wi in will matches.

You can use a minus sign (-) inside the left and right pair of square brackets to indicate a range of letters or digits. For example, the pattern

```
[a-z]
```

matches any lowercase letter.

> **NOTE:** You cannot write the range "backward"; that is, _ [z-a] is illegal.

Consider the following example:

```
$ grep 'w[a-f]' REfile

from the set of uppercase and lowercase letters, digits,
you of file name matching, but be forewarned: in general,
shell metacharacters we discussed in Chapter 1.
```

The matches are we on line 1, wa on line 2, and we on line 3. Look at REfile again and note how many potential matches are omitted because the character following the w is not one of the group *a through f.*

Furthermore, you can include several ranges in one set of brackets. For example, the pattern

```
[a-zA-Z]
```

matches any letter, lower- or uppercase.

Matching Multiples of a Single Character

If you want to specify precisely how many of a given character you want the regular expression to match, you can use the escaped left and right curly brace pair (\{___\}). For example, the pattern

```
X\{2,5\}
```

matches at least two but not more than five Xs. That is, it matches XX, XXX, XXXX, or XXXXX. The minimum number of matches is written immediately after the escaped left curly brace, followed by a comma (,) and then the maximum value.

If you omit the maximum value (but not the comma), as in

```
X\{2,\}
```

you specify that the match should occur for *at least* two Xs.

If you write just a single value, omitting the comma, you specify the exact number of matches, no more and no less. For example, the pattern

```
X\{4\}
```

matches only XXXX. Here are some examples of this kind of regular expression:

```
$ grep 'p\{2\}' REfile
```

```
from the set of uppercase and lowercase letters, digits,
```

This is the only line that contains "pp."

```
$ grep 'p\{1\}' REfile
```

```
A regular expression is a sequence of characters taken
from the set of uppercase and lowercase letters, digits,
punctuation marks, etc., plus a set of special regular
expression operators. Some of these operators may remind
regular expression operators are different from the
shell metacharacters we discussed in Chapter 1.
The simplest form of a regular expression is one that
includes only letters. For example, the would match only
the three-letter sequence t, h, e. This pattern is found
words, wherever the regular expression pattern is found
```

Notice that on the second line, the first "p" in "uppercase" satisfies the search. The grep program doesn't even see the second "p" in the word because it stops searching as soon as it finds one "p."

Matching Multiples of a Regular Expression

The asterisk (*) matches zero or more of the preceding regular expression. Therefore, the pattern

```
X*
```

matches zero or more Xs: nothing, X, XX, XXX, and so on. To ensure that you get at least one character in the match, use

```
XX*
```

For example, the command

```
$ grep 'p*' REfile
```

displays the entire file, because every line can match "zero or more instances of the letter p." However, note the output of the following commands:

```
$ grep 'pp*' REfile
```

```
A regular expression is a sequence of characters taken
from the set of uppercase and lowercase letters, digits,
punctuation marks, etc., plus a set of special regular
expression operators. Some of these operators may remind
regular expression operators are different from the
shell metacharacters we discussed in Chapter 1.
The simplest form of a regular expression is one that
includes only letters. For example, the would match only
the three-letter sequence t, h, e. This pattern is found
words, wherever the regular expression pattern is found
```

```
$ grep 'ppp*' REfile
```

```
from the set of uppercase and lowercase letters, digits,
```

The regular expression ppp* matches "pp followed by zero or more instances of the letter p," or, in other words, "two or more instances of the letter p."

The extended set of regular expressions includes two additional operators that are similar to the asterisk: the plus sign (+) and the question mark (?). The plus sign is used to match one or more occurrences of the preceding character, and the question mark is used to match zero or one occurrences. For example, the command

```
$ egrep 'p?' REfile
```

outputs the entire file because every line contains zero or one p. However, note the output of the following command:

```
$ egrep 'p+' REfile
```

```
A regular expression is a sequence of characters taken
from the set of uppercase and lowercase letters, digits,
punctuation marks, etc., plus a set of special regular
expression operators. Some of these operators may remind
regular expression operators are different from the
shell metacharacters we discussed in Chapter 1.
The simplest form of a regular expression is one that
includes only letters. For example, the would match only
the three-letter sequence t, h, e. This pattern is found
words, wherever the regular expression pattern is found
```

Another possibility is [a-z]+. This pattern matches one or more occurrences of any lowercase letter.

Anchoring the Match

A circumflex (^) used as the first character of the pattern anchors the regular expression to the beginning of the line. Therefore, the pattern

```
^[Tt]he
```

matches a line that begins with either The or the, but does not match a line that has a The or the at any other position on the line. Note, for example, the output of the following two commands:

```
$ grep '[Tt]he' REfile
```

```
from the set of uppercase and lowercase letters, digits,
expression operators. Some of these operators may remind
regular expression operators are different from the
The simplest form of a regular expression is one that
includes only letters. For example, the would match only
the three-letter sequence t, h, e. This pattern is found
in the following words: the, therefore, bother. In other
words, wherever the regular expression pattern is found
-- even if it is surrounded by other characters -- it is
```

```
$ grep '^[Tt]he' REfile
```

```
The simplest form of a regular expression is one that
the three-letter sequence t, h, e. This pattern is found
```

A dollar sign as the last character of the pattern anchors the regular expression to the end of the line, as in the following example:

```
$ grep '1\.$' REfile
```

```
shell metacharacters we discussed in Chapter 1.
```

This anchoring occurs because the line ends in a match of the regular expression. The period in the regular expression is preceded by a backslash, so the program knows that it's looking for a period and not just any character.

Here's another example that uses REfile:

```
$ grep '[Tt]he$' REfile
```

```
regular expression operators are different from the
```

The regular expression .* is an idiom that is used to match zero or more occurrences of any sequence of any characters. Any multicharacter regular expression always matches the longest string of characters that fits the regular expression description. Consequently, .* used as the entire regular expression always matches an entire line of text. Therefore, the command

```
$ grep '^.*$' REfile
```

prints the entire file. Note that in this case the anchoring characters are redundant.

When used as part of an "unanchored" regular expression, that idiomatic regular expression matches the longest string that fits the description, as in the following example:

```
$ grep 'C.*1' REfile
```

```
shell metacharacters we discussed in Chapter 1.
```

The regular expression C.*1 matches the longest string that begins with a C and ends with a 1.

Another expression, d.*d, matches the longest string that begins and ends with a d. On each line of output in the following example, the matched string is highlighted with italics:

```
$ grep 'd.*d' REfile
```

```
from the set of uppercase and lowercase letters, digits,
shell metacharacters we discussed in Chapter 1.
includes only letters. For example, the would match only
words, wherever the regular expression pattern is found
-- even if it is surrounded by other characters -- it is
```

You've seen that a regular expression command such as grep finds a match even if the regular expression is surrounded by other characters. For example, the pattern

```
[Tt]he
```

matches the, The, there, There, other, oTher, and so on (even though the last word is unlikely to be used). Suppose that you're looking for the word The or the and do not want to match other, There, or there. In a few of the commands that use full regular expressions, you can surround the regular expression with escaped angle brackets (\<___\>). For example, the pattern

```
\<the\>
```

represents the string the, where t follows a character that is not a letter, digit, or underscore, and where e is followed by a character that is not a letter, digit, or underscore. If you need not completely isolate letters, digits, and underscores, you can use the angle brackets singly. That is, the pattern \<the matches anything that begins with the, and ter\> matches anything that ends with ter.

You can tell egrep (but not grep) to search for either of two regular expressions as follows:

```
$ egrep 'regular expression-1 | regular expression-2' filename
```

Regular Expression Examples

When you first look at the list of special characters used with regular expressions, constructing search-and-replacement patterns seems to be a complex process. A few examples and exercises, however, can make the process easier to understand.

Example 1: Matching Lines That Contain a Date

A standard USA date consists of a pattern that includes the capitalized name of a month, a space, a one- or two-digit number representing the day, a comma, a space, and a four-digit number representing the year. For example, Feb 9, 1994 is a standard USA date. You can write that pattern as a regular expression:

```
[A-Z][a-z]* [0-9]\{1,2\}, [0-9]\{4\}
```

You can improve this pattern so that it recognizes that May—the month with the shortest name—has three letters, and that September has nine:

```
[A-Z][a-z]\{3,9\} [0-9]\{1,2\}, [0-9]\{4\}
```

Example 2: Matching Social Security Numbers

Social security numbers also are highly structured: three digits, a dash, two digits, a dash, and four digits. Here's how you can write a regular expression for social security numbers:

```
[0-9]\{3\}-[0-9]\{\2\}-[0-9]\{4\}
```

Example 3: Matching Telephone Numbers

Another familiar structured pattern is found in telephone numbers, such as 1-800-555-1212. Here's a regular expression that matches that pattern:

```
1-[0-9]\{3\}-[0-9]\{3\}-[0-9]\{4\}
```

Details Of *grep* Family

The grep family consists of three members:

grep	This command uses a limited set of regular expressions. See table.
egrep	Extended grep. This command uses full regular expressions (expressions that have string values and use the full set of alphanumeric and special characters) to match patterns. Full regular expressions include all the limited regular expressions of grep (except for \(and \)), as well as the following ones (where *RE* is any regular expression):

RE+	Matches one or more occurrences of *RE*. (Contrast that with *RE**, which matches zero or more occurrences of *RE*.)
RE?	Matches zero or one occurrence of *RE*.
RE1 ¦ *RE2*	Matches either *RE1* or *RE2*. The ¦ acts as a logical OR operator.
(*RE*)	Groups multiple regular expressions.

The section "The egrep Command" provides examples of these expressions.

fgrep	Fast grep. This command searches for a string, not a pattern. Because fgrep does not use regular expressions, it interprets $, *, [,], (,), and \ as ordinary characters. Modern implementations of grep appear to be just as fast as fgrep, so using fgrep is becoming obsolete—except when your search involves the previously mentioned characters.

NOTE: The $, *, [,], (,), and \ regular expression metacharacters also have special meaning to the shell, so you must enclose them within single quotation marks to prevent the shell from interpreting them. (See Chapters 11, 12, and 13.)

The *grep* Command

The most frequently used command in the family is grep. Its complete syntax is

```
$grep [options] RE [file(s)]
```

where *RE* is a limited regular expression. Table 6.5 lists the regular expressions that grep recognizes.

The grep command reads from the specified file on the command line or, if no files are specified, from standard input. Table 6.5 lists the command-line options that grep takes.

Table 6.5. Command-Line Options for grep

Option	Result
-b	Display, at the beginning of the output line, the number of the block in which the regular expression was found. This can be helpful in locating block numbers by context. (The first block is block zero.)
-c	Print the number of lines that contain the pattern, that is, the number of matching lines.
-h	Prevent the name of the file that contains the matching line from being displayed at the beginning of that line. NOTE: When searching multiple files, grep normally reports not only the matching line but also the name of the file that contains it.
-i	Ignore distinctions between uppercase and lowercase during comparisons.
-l	Print one time the name of each file that contains lines that match the pattern—regardless of the actual number of matching lines in each file—on separate lines of the screen.
-n	Precede each matching line by its line number in the file.
-s	Suppress error messages about nonexistent or unreadable files.
-v	Print all lines except those that contain the pattern. This reverses the logic of the search.

Here are two sample files on which to exercise grep:

```
$ cat cron
```

```
In SCO Xenix 2.3, or SCO UNIX, you can edit a
crontab file to your heart's content, but it will
not be re-read, and your changes will not take
effect, until you come out of multi-user run
level (thus killing cron), and then re-enter
multi-user run level, when a new cron is started;
or until you do a reboot.

The proper way to install a new version of a
crontab (for root, or for any other user) is to
issue the command "crontab new.jobs", or "cat
new.jobs | crontab", or if in 'vi' with a new
version of the commands, "w ! crontab". I find it
easy to type "vi /tmp/tbl", then ":0 r !crontab
-l" to read the existing crontab into the vi
buffer, then edit, then type ":w !crontab", or
"!crontab %" to replace the existing crontab with
what I see on vi's screen.
```

```
$ cat pax
```

```
This is an announcement for the MS-DOS version of
PAX version 2. See the README file and the man
pages for more information on how to run PAX,
TAR, and CPIO.

For those of you who don't know, pax is a 3 in 1
program that gives the functionality of pax, tar,
and cpio. It supports both the DOS filesystem
and the raw "tape on a disk" system used by most
micro UNIX systems. This will allow for easy
transfer of files to and from UNIX systems. It
also supports multiple volumes. Floppy density
for raw UNIX type read/writes can be specified on
the command line.

The source will eventually be posted to one of
the source groups.

Be sure to use a blocking factor of 20 with
pax-as-tar and B with pax-as-cpio for best
performance.
```

The following examples show how to find a string in a file:

```
$ grep 'you' pax
```

```
For those of you who don't know, pax is a 3 in 1
```

```
$ grep 'you' cron
```

```
In SCO Xenix 2.3, or SCO UNIX, you can edit a
crontab file to your heart's content, but it will
not be re-read, and your changes will not take
effect, until you come out of multi-user run
or until you do a reboot.
```

Note that you appears in your in the second and third lines.

You can find the same string in two or more files by using a variety of options. In this first example, case is ignored:

```
$ grep -i 'you' pax cron

pax:For those of you who don't know, pax is a 3 in 1
cron:In SCO Xenix 2.3, or SCO UNIX, you can edit a
cron:crontab file to your heart's content, but it will
cron:not be re-read, and your changes will not take
cron:effect, until you come out of multi-user run
cron:or until you do a reboot.
```

Notice that each line of output begins with the name of the file that contains a match. In the following example, the output includes the name of the file and the number of the line of that file on which the match is found:

```
$ grep -n 'you' pax cron

pax:6:For those of you who don't know, pax is a 3 in 1
cron:1:In SCO Xenix 2.3, or SCO UNIX, you can edit a
cron:2:crontab file to your heart's content, but it will
cron:3:not be re-read, and your changes will not take
cron:4:effect, until you come out of multi-user run
cron:7:or until you do a reboot.
```

The following example shows how to inhibit printing the lines themselves:

```
$ grep -c 'you' pax cron

pax:1
cron:5
```

The following output shows the matching lines without specifying the files from which they came:

```
$ grep -h 'you' pax cron

For those of you who don't know, pax is a 3 in 1
In SCO Xenix 2.3, or SCO UNIX, you can edit a
crontab file to your heart's content, but it will
not be re-read, and your changes will not take
effect, until you come out of multi-user run
or until you do a reboot.
```

The following specifies output of "every line in pax and cron that does not have [Yy][Oo][Uu] in it":

```
$ grep -iv 'you' pax cron

pax:This is an announcement for the MS-DOS version of
pax:PAX version 2. See the README file and the man
pax:pages for more information on how to run PAX,
pax:TAR, and CPIO.
pax:
pax:program that gives the functionality of pax, tar,
pax:and cpio. It supports both the DOS filesystem
```

```
pax:and the raw "tape on a disk" system used by most
pax:micro UNIX systems. This will allow for easy
pax:transfer of files to and from UNIX systems. It
pax:also support multiple volumes. Floppy density
pax:for raw UNIX type read/writes can be specified on
pax:the command line.
pax:
pax:The source will eventually be posted to one of
pax:the source groups.
pax:
pax:Be sure to use a blocking factor of 20 with
pax:pax-as-tar and B with pax-as-cpio for best
pax:performance.
cron:level (thus killing cron), and then re-enter
cron:multi-user run level, when a new cron is started;
cron:
cron:The proper way to install a new version of a
cron:crontab (for root, or for any other user) is to
cron:issue the command "crontab new.jobs", or "cat
cron:new.jobs ¦ crontab", or if in 'vi' with a new
cron:version of the commands, "w ! crontab". I find it
cron:easy to type "vi /tmp/tbl", then ":0 r !crontab
cron:-l" to read the existing crontab into the vi
cron:buffer, then edit, then type ":w !crontab", or
cron:"!crontab %" to replace the existing crontab with
cron:what I see on vi's screen.
```

Note that blank lines are considered to be lines that do not match the given regular expression.

The following example is quite interesting. It lists every line that has r.*t in it and of course it matches the longest possible string in each line. First, let's see exactly how the strings are matched. The matching strings in the listing are highlighted in italics so that you can see what grep actually matches:

```
$ grep 'r.*t' pax cron
```

```
pax:This is an announcement for the MS-DOS version of
pax:PAX version 2. See the README file and the man
pax:pages for more information on how to run PAX,
pax:For those of you who don't know, pax is a 3 in 1
pax:program that gives the functionality of pax, tar,
pax:and cpio. It supports both the DOS filesystem
pax:and the raw "tape on a disk" system used by most
pax:micro UNIX systems. This will allow for easy
pax:transfer of files to and from UNIX systems. It
pax:also support multiple volumes. Floppy density
pax:for raw UNIX type read/writes can be specified on
pax:The source will eventually be posted to one of
pax:Be sure to use a blocking factor of 20 with
pax:pax-as-tar and B with pax-as-cpio for best
cron:In SCO Xenix 2.3, or SCO UNIX, you can edit a
cron:crontab file to your heart's content, but it will
cron:not be re-read, and your changes will not take
cron:level (thus killing cron), and then re-enter
cron:multi-user run level, when a new cron is started;
cron:or until you do a reboot.
cron:The proper way to install a new version of a
```

```
cron:crontab (for root, or for any other user) is to
cron:issue the command "crontab new.jobs", or "cat
cron:new.jobs ¦ crontab", or if in 'vi' with a new
cron:version of the commands, "w ! crontab". I find it
cron:easy to type "vi /tmp/tbl", then ":0 r !crontab
cron:-l" to read the existing crontab into the vi
cron:buffer, then edit, then type ":w !crontab", or
cron:"!crontab %" to replace the existing crontab with
```

You can obtain for free a version of grep that highlights the matched string, but the standard version of grep simply shows the line that contains the match.

If you are thinking that grep doesn't seem to do anything with the patterns that it matches, you are correct. But in Chapter 7, "Editing Text Files," you will see how the sed command does replacements.

Now let's look for two or more 1s (two 1s followed by zero or more 1s):

```
$ grep '111*' pax cron
```

```
pax:micro UNIX systems. This will allow for easy
pax:The source will eventually be posted to one of
cron:crontab file to your heart's content, but it will
cron:not be re-read, and your changes will not take
cron:level (thus killing cron), and then re-enter
cron:The proper way to install a new version of a
```

The following command finds lines that begin with The:

```
$ grep '^The' pax cron
```

```
pax:The source will eventually be posted to one of
cron:The proper way to install a new version of a
```

The next command finds lines that end with n:

```
$ grep 'n$' pax cron
```

```
pax:PAX version 2. See the README file and the man
pax:for raw UNIX type read/writes can be specified on
cron:effect, until you come out of multi-user run
```

You can easily use the grep command to search for two or more consecutive uppercase letters:

```
$ grep '[A-Z]\{2,\}' pax cron
```

```
pax:This is an announcement for the MS-DOS version of
pax:PAX version 2. See the README file and the man
pax:pages for more information on how to run PAX,
pax:TAR, and CPIO.
pax:and cpio. It supports both the DOS filesystem
pax:micro UNIX systems. This will allow for easy
pax:transfer of files to and from UNIX systems. It
pax:for raw UNIX type read/writes can be specified on
cron:In SCO Xenix 2.3, or SCO UNIX, you can edit a
```

The *egrep* Command

As mentioned earlier, egrep uses full regular expressions in the pattern string. The syntax of egrep is the same as that for grep:

```
$egrep [options] RE [files]
```

where *RE* is a regular expression.

The egrep command uses the same regular expressions as the grep command, except for \(and \), and includes the following additional patterns:

RE+	Matches one or more occurrence(s) of *RE*. (Contrast this with grep's *RE** pattern, which matches zero or more occurrences of *RE*.)
RE?	Matches zero or one occurrence of *RE*.
RE1 ¦ RE2	Matches either *RE1* or *RE2*. The ¦ acts as a logical OR operator.
(RE)	Groups multiple regular expressions.

The egrep command accepts the same command-line options as grep (see Table 6.6) as well as the following additional command-line options:

-e *special_expression*	Search for a special expression (that is, a regular expression that begins with a -)
-f *file*	Put the regular expressions into *file*

Here are a few examples of egrep's extended regular expressions. The first finds two or more consecutive uppercase letters:

```
$ egrep '[A-Z][A-Z]+' pax cron

pax:This is an announcement for the MS-DOS version of
pax:PAX version 2. See the README file and the man
pax:pages for more information on how to run PAX,
pax:TAR, and CPIO.
pax:For those of you who don't know, PAX is a 3-in-1
pax:and cpio. It supports both the DOS filesystem
pax:micro UNIX systems. This allows for easy
pax:transfer of files to and from UNIX systems. It
pax:for raw UNIX type read/writes can be specified on
```

The following command finds each line that contains either DOS or SCO:

```
$ egrep 'DOS¦SCO' pax cron

pax:This is an announcement for the MS-DOS version of
pax:and cpio. It supports both the DOS filesystem
cron:In SCO Xenix 2.3, or SCO UNIX, you can edit a
```

The next example finds all lines that contain either new or now:

```
$ egrep 'n(e¦o)w' cron

multi-user run level, when a new cron is started;
The proper way to install a new version of a
```

```
issue the command "crontab new.jobs", or "cat
new.jobs ¦ crontab", or if in 'vi' with a new
```

The *fgrep* Command

The fgrep command searches a file for a character string and prints all lines that contain the string. Unlike grep and egrep, fgrep interprets each character in the search string as a literal character, because fgrep has no metacharacters.

The syntax of fgrep is

```
fgrep [options] string [files]
```

The options you use with the fgrep command are exactly the same as those that you use for egrep, with the addition of -x, which prints only the lines that are matched in their entirety.

As an example of fgrep's -x option, consider the following file named sample:

```
$ cat sample
this is
a
file for testing
egrep's x
option.
```

Now, invoke fgrep with the -x option and a as the pattern.

```
$ fgrep -x a sample
a
```

That matches the second line of the file, but

```
$ fgrep -x option sample
```

outputs nothing, as option doesn't match a line in the file. However,

```
$ fgrep -x option. sample
option.
```

matches the entire last line.

Sorting Text Files

UNIX provides two commands that are useful when you are sorting text files: sort and uniq. The sort command merges text files together, and the uniq command compares adjacent lines of a file and eliminates all but one occurrence of adjacent duplicate lines.

The *sort* Command

The sort command is useful with database files—files that are line- and field-oriented—because it can sort or merge one or more text files into a sequence that you select.

The command normally treats a blank or a tab as a delimiter. If the file has multiple blanks, multiple tabs, or both between two fields, only the first is considered a delimiter; all the others belong to the next field. The -b option tells sort to ignore the blanks and tabs that are not delimiters, discarding them instead of adding them to the beginning of the next field.

The normal ordering for sort follows the ASCII code sequence.

The syntax for sort is

```
$sort [-cmu] [-ooutfile] [-ymemsize] [-zrecsize] [-dfiMnr] [-btchar]
    [+pos1 [-pos2]] [file(s)]
```

Table 6.6 describes the options of sort.

Table 6.6. The sort Command's Options

Option	Meaning
-c	Tells sort to check only whether the file is in the order specified.
-u	Tells sort to ignore any repeated lines (but see the next section, "The uniq Command").
-m	Tells sort to merge (and sort) the files that are already sorted. (This section features an example.)
-zrecsize	Specifies the length of the longest line to be merged and prevents sort from terminating abnormally when it sees a line that is longer than usual. You use this option only when merging files.
-ooutfile	Specifies the name of the output file. This option is an alternative to and an improvement on redirection, in that outfile can have the same name as the file being sorted.
-ymemsize	Specifies the amount of memory that sort uses. This option keeps sort from consuming all the available memory. -y0 causes sort to begin with the minimum possible memory that your system permits, and -y initially gives sort the most it can get. memsize is specified in kilobytes.
-d	Causes a dictionary order sort, in which sort ignores everything except letters, digits, blanks, and tabs.
-f	Causes sort to ignore upper- and lowercase distinctions when sorting.
-i	Causes sort to ignore nonprinting characters (decimal ASCII codes 0 to 31 and 127).

Option	Meaning
-M	Compares the contents of specified fields as if they contained the name of month, by examining the first three letters or digits in each field, converting the letters to uppercase, and sorting them in calendar order.
-n	Causes sort to ignore blanks and sort in numerical order. Digits and associated characters—the plus sign, the minus sign, the decimal point, and so on—have their usual mathematical meanings.
-r	When added to any option, causes sort to sort in reverse.
-t*char*	Selects the delimiter used in the file. (This option is unnecessary if the file uses a blank or a tab as its delimiter.)
+*pos1* [-*pos2*]	Restricts the key on which the sort is based to one that begins at field *pos1* and ends at field *pos2*. For example, to sort on field number 2, you must use +1 -2 (begin just after field 1 and continue through field 2).

In addition, you can use - as an argument to force sort to take its input from stdin.

Here are some examples that demonstrate some common options. The file auto is a tab-delimited list of the results of an automobile race. From left to right, the fields list the class, driver's name, car year, car make, car model, and time:

```
$ cat auto

ES    Arther    85    Honda      Prelude    49.412
BS    Barker    90    Nissan     300ZX      48.209
AS    Saint     88    BMW        M-3        46.629
ES    Straw     86    Honda      Civic      49.543
DS    Swazy     87    Honda      CRX-Si     49.693
ES    Downs     83    VW         GTI        47.133
ES    Smith     86    VW         GTI        47.154
AS    Neuman    84    Porsche    911        47.201
CS    Miller    84    Mazda      RX-7       47.291
CS    Carlson   88    Pontiac    Fiero      47.398
DS    Kegler    84    Honda      Civic      47.429
ES    Sherman   83    VW         GTI        48.489
DS    Arbiter   86    Honda      CRX-Si     48.628
DS    Karle     74    Porsche    914        48.826
ES    Shorn     87    VW         GTI        49.357
CS    Chunk     85    Toyota     MR2        49.558
CS    Cohen     91    Mazda      Miata      50.046
DS    Lisanti   73    Porsche    914        50.609
CS    McGill    83    Porsche    944        50.642
AS    Lisle     72    Porsche    911        51.030
ES    Peerson   86    VW         Golf       54.493
```

If you invoke sort with no options, it sorts on the entire line:

```
$ sort auto

AS   Lisle     72   Porsche   911       51.030
AS   Neuman    84   Porsche   911       47.201
AS   Saint     88   BMW       M-3       46.629
BS   Barker    90   Nissan    300ZX     48.209
CS   Carlson   88   Pontiac   Fiero     47.398
CS   Chunk     85   Toyota    MR2       49.558
CS   Cohen     91   Mazda     Miata     50.046
CS   McGill    83   Porsche   944       50.642
CS   Miller    84   Mazda     RX-7      47.291
DS   Arbiter   86   Honda     CRX-Si    48.628
DS   Karle     74   Porsche   914       48.826
DS   Kegler    84   Honda     Civic     47.429
DS   Lisanti   73   Porsche   914       50.609
DS   Swazy     87   Honda     CRX-Si    49.693
ES   Arther    85   Honda     Prelude   49.412
ES   Downs     83   VW        GTI       47.133
ES   Peerson   86   VW        Golf      54.493
ES   Sherman   83   VW        GTI       48.489
ES   Shorn     87   VW        GTI       49.357
ES   Smith     86   VW        GTI       47.154
ES   Straw     86   Honda     Civic     49.543
```

To alphabetize a list by the driver's name, you need sort to begin with the second field (+1 means skip the first field). Sort normall treats the first blank (space or tab) in a sequence of blanks as the field separator, and consider that reht rest of the blanks are part of the next field. This has no effect on sorting on the second field because there is an equal number of blanks between the class letters and driver's name. However, whenever a field is "rapped"—for example, driver's name, car make, and car model—the next field will include leading blanks:

```
$ sort +1 auto

DS   Arbiter   86   Honda     CRX-Si    48.628
ES   Arther    85   Honda     Prelude   49.412
BS   Barker    90   Nissan    300ZX     48.209
CS   Carlson   88   Pontiac   Fiero     47.398
CS   Chunk     85   Toyota    MR2       49.558
CS   Cohen     91   Mazda     Miata     50.046
ES   Downs     83   VW        GTI       47.133
DS   Karle     74   Porsche   914       48.826
DS   Kegler    84   Honda     Civic     47.429
DS   Lisanti   73   Porsche   914       50.609
AS   Lisle     72   Porsche   911       51.030
CS   McGill    83   Porsche   944       50.642
CS   Miller    84   Mazda     RX-7      47.291
AS   Neuman    84   Porsche   911       47.201
ES   Peerson   86   VW        Golf      54.493
AS   Saint     88   BMW       M-3       46.629
ES   Sherman   83   VW        GTI       48.489
ES   Shorn     87   VW        GTI       49.357
ES   Smith     86   VW        GTI       47.154
ES   Straw     86   Honda     Civic     49.543
DS   Swazy     87   Honda     CRX-Si    49.693
```

Note that the key to this sort is only the driver's name. However, if two drivers had the same name, they would have been further sorted by the car year. In other words, +1 actually means skip the first field and sort on the rest of the line.

Here's a list sorted by race times:

```
$ sort -b +5 auto
```

```
AS    Saint     88    BMW        M-3       46.629
ES    Downs     83    VW         GTI       47.133
ES    Smith     86    VW         GTI       47.154
AS    Neuman    84    Porsche    911       47.201
CS    Miller    84    Mazda      RX-7      47.291
CS    Carlson   88    Pontiac    Fiero     47.398
DS    Kegler    84    Honda      Civic     47.429
BS    Barker    90    Nissan     300ZX     48.209
ES    Sherman   83    VW         GTI       48.489
DS    Arbiter   86    Honda      CRX-Si    48.628
DS    Karle     74    Porsche    914       48.826
ES    Shorn     87    VW         GTI       49.357
ES    Arther    85    Honda      Prelude   49.412
ES    Straw     86    Honda      Civic     49.543
CS    Chunk     85    Toyota     MR2       49.558
DS    Swazy     87    Honda      CRX-Si    49.693
CS    Cohen     91    Mazda      Miata     50.046
DS    Lisanti   73    Porsche    914       50.609
CS    McGill    83    Porsche    944       50.642
AS    Lisle     72    Porsche    911       51.030
ES    Peerson   86    VW         Golf      54.493
```

The -b means do not treat the blanks between the car model (e.g. M-3) and the race time as part of the race time.

Suppose that you want a list of times by class. You try the following command and discover that it fails:

```
$ sort +0 -b +5 auto
```

```
AS    Lisle     72    Porsche    911       51.030
AS    Neuman    84    Porsche    911       47.201
AS    Saint     88    BMW        M-3       46.629
BS    Barker    90    Nissan     300ZX     48.209
CS    Carlson   88    Pontiac    Fiero     47.398
CS    Chunk     85    Toyota     MR2       49.558
CS    Cohen     91    Mazda      Miata     50.046
CS    McGill    83    Porsche    944       50.642
CS    Miller    84    Mazda      RX-7      47.291
DS    Arbiter   86    Honda      CRX-Si    48.628
DS    Karle     74    Porsche    914       48.826
DS    Kegler    84    Honda      Civic     47.429
DS    Lisanti   73    Porsche    914       50.609
DS    Swazy     87    Honda      CRX-Si    49.693
ES    Arther    85    Honda      Prelude   49.412
ES    Downs     83    VW         GTI       47.133
ES    Peerson   86    VW         Golf      54.493
ES    Sherman   83    VW         GTI       48.489
ES    Shorn     87    VW         GTI       49.357
ES    Smith     86    VW         GTI       47.154
ES    Straw     86    Honda      Civic     49.543
```

This command line fails because it tells sort to skip nothing and sort on the rest of the line, then sort on the sixth field. To restrict the first sort to just the class, and then sort on time as the secondary sort, use the following expression:

```
$ sort +0 -1 -b +5 auto

AS    Saint      88   BMW        M-3        46.629
AS    Neuman     84   Porsche    911        47.201
AS    Lisle      72   Porsche    911        51.030
BS    Barker     90   Nissan     300ZX      48.209
CS    Miller     84   Mazda      RX-7       47.291
CS    Carlson    88   Pontiac    Fiero      47.398
CS    Chunk      85   Toyota     MR2        49.558
CS    Cohen      91   Mazda      Miata      50.046
CS    McGill     83   Porsche    944        50.642
DS    Kegler     84   Honda      Civic      47.429
DS    Arbiter    86   Honda      CRX-Si     48.628
DS    Karle      74   Porsche    914        48.826
DS    Swazy      87   Honda      CRX-Si     49.693
DS    Lisanti    73   Porsche    914        50.609
ES    Downs      83   VW         GTI        47.133
ES    Smith      86   VW         GTI        47.154
ES    Sherman    83   VW         GTI        48.489
ES    Shorn      87   VW         GTI        49.357
ES    Arther     85   Honda      Prelude    49.412
ES    Straw      86   Honda      Civic      49.543
ES    Peerson    86   VW         Golf       54.493
```

This command says skip nothing and stop after sorting on the first field, then skip to the end of the fifth field and sort on the rest of the line. In this case, the rest of the line is just the sixth field.

Here's a simple merge example. Notice that both files are already sorted by class and name.

```
$ cat auto.1

AS    Neuman     84   Porsche    911        47.201
AS    Saint      88   BMW        M-3        46.629
BS    Barker     90   Nissan     300ZX      48.209
CS    Carlson    88   Pontiac    Fiero      47.398
CS    Miller     84   Mazda      RX-7       47.291
DS    Swazy      87   Honda      CRX-Si     49.693
ES    Arther     85   Honda      Prelude    49.412
ES    Downs      83   VW         GTI        47.133
ES    Smith      86   VW         GTI        47.154
ES    Straw      86   Honda      Civic      49.543
```

```
$ cat auto.2

AS    Lisle      72   Porsche    911        51.030
CS    Chunk      85   Toyota     MR2        49.558
CS    Cohen      91   Mazda      Miata      50.046
CS    McGill     83   Porsche    944        50.642
DS    Arbiter    86   Honda      CRX-Si     48.628
DS    Karle      74   Porsche    914        48.826
DS    Kegler     84   Honda      Civic      47.429
DS    Lisanti    73   Porsche    914        50.609
```

```
ES   Peerson   86   VW        Golf      54.493
ES   Sherman   83   VW        GTI       48.489
ES   Shorn     87   VW        GTI       49.357
```

```
$ sort -m auto.1 auto.2
```

```
AS   Lisle     72   Porsche   911       51.030
AS   Neuman    84   Porsche   911       47.201
AS   Saint     88   BMW       M-3       46.629
BS   Barker    90   Nissan    300ZX     48.209
CS   Carlson   88   Pontiac   Fiero     47.398
CS   Chunk     85   Toyota    MR2       49.558
CS   Cohen     91   Mazda     Miata     50.046
CS   McGill    83   Porsche   944       50.642
CS   Miller    84   Mazda     RX-7      47.291
DS   Arbiter   86   Honda     CRX-Si    48.628
DS   Karle     74   Porsche   914       48.826
DS   Kegler    84   Honda     Civic     47.429
DS   Lisanti   73   Porsche   914       50.609
DS   Swazy     87   Honda     CRX-Si    49.693
ES   Arther    85   Honda     Prelude   49.412
ES   Downs     83   VW        GTI       47.133
ES   Peerson   86   VW        Golf      54.493
ES   Sherman   83   VW        GTI       48.489
ES   Shorn     87   VW        GTI       49.357
ES   Smith     86   VW        GTI       47.154
ES   Straw     86   Honda     Civic     49.543
```

For a final example, pass1 is an excerpt from /etc/passwd and Sort it on the user ID field—field number 3. Specify the -t option so that the field separator used by sort is the colon, as used by /etc/passwd.

```
$ cat pass1
```

```
root:x:0:0:System Administrator:/usr/root:/bin/ksh
slan:x:57:57:StarGROUP Software NPP Administration:/usr/slan:
labuucp:x:21:100:shevett's UPC:/usr/spool/uucppublic:/usr/lib/uucp/uucico
pcuucp:x:35:100:PCLAB:/usr/spool/uucppublic:/usr/lib/uucp/uucico
techuucp:x:36:100:The 6386:/usr/spool/uucppublic:/usr/lib/uucp/uucico
pjh:x:102:0:Peter J. Holsberg:/usr/pjh:/bin/ksh
lkh:x:250:1:lkh:/usr/lkh:/bin/ksh
shevett:x:251:1:dave shevett:/usr/shevett:/bin/ksh
mccollo:x:329:1:Carol McCollough:/usr/home/mccollo:/bin/ksh
gordon:x:304:20:gordon gary g:/u1/fall91/dp168/gordon:/bin/csh
grice:x:273:20:grice steven a:/u1/fall91/dp270/grice:/bin/ksh
gross:x:305:20:gross james l:/u1/fall91/dp168/gross:/bin/ksh
hagerho:x:326:20:hagerhorst paul j:/u1/fall91/dp168/hagerho:/bin/ksh
hendric:x:274:20:hendrickson robbin:/u1/fall91/dp270/hendric:/bin/ksh
hinnega:x:320:20:hinnegan dianna:/u1/fall91/dp163/hinnega:/bin/ksh
innis:x:262:20:innis rafael f:/u1/fall91/dp270/innis:/bin/ksh
intorel:x:286:20:intorelli anthony:/u1/fall91/dp168/intorel:/bin/ksh
```

Now run sort with the delimiter set to a colon:

```
$ sort -t: +2 -3 pass1
```

```
root:x:0:0:System Administrator:/usr/root:/bin/ksh
pjh:x:102:0:Peter J. Holsberg:/usr/pjh:/bin/ksh
labuucp:x:21:100:shevett's UPC:/usr/spool/uucppublic:/usr/lib/uucp/uucico
```

```
lkh:x:250:1:lkh:/usr/lkh:/bin/ksh
shevett:x:251:1:dave shevett:/usr/shevett:/bin/ksh
innis:x:262:20:innis rafael f:/u1/fall91/dp270/innis:/bin/ksh
grice:x:273:20:grice steven a:/u1/fall91/dp270/grice:/bin/ksh
hendric:x:274:20:hendrickson robbin:/u1/fall91/dp270/hendric:/bin/ksh
intorel:x:286:20:intorelli anthony:/u1/fall91/dp168/intorel:/bin/ksh
gordon:x:304:20:gordon gary g:/u1/fall91/dp168/gordon:/bin/csh
gross:x:305:20:gross james l:/u1/fall91/dp168/gross:/bin/ksh
hinnega:x:320:20:hinnegan dianna:/u1/fall91/dp163/hinnega:/bin/ksh
hagerho:x:326:20:hagerhorst paul j:/u1/fall91/dp168/hagerho:/bin/ksh
mccollo:x:329:1:Carol McCollough:/usr/home/mccollo:/bin/ksh
pcuucp:x:35:100:PCLAB:/usr/spool/uucppublic:/usr/lib/uucp/uucico
techuucp:x:36:100:The 6386:/usr/spool/uucppublic:/usr/lib/uucp/uucico
slan:x:57:57:StarGROUP Software NPP Administration:/usr/slan:
```

Note that 35 comes after 329, because sort does not recognize numeric characters as being numbers. You want the user ID field to be sorted by numerical value, so correct the command by adding the -n option:

```
$ sort -t: -n +2 -3 pass1
```

```
root:x:0:0:System Administrator:/usr/root:/bin/ksh
labuucp:x:21:100:shevett's UPC:/usr/spool/uucppublic:/usr/lib/uucp/uucico
pcuucp:x:35:100:PCLAB:/usr/spool/uucppublic:/usr/lib/uucp/uucico
techuucp:x:36:100:The 6386:/usr/spool/uucppublic:/usr/lib/uucp/uucico
slan:x:57:57:StarGROUP Software NPP Administration:/usr/slan:
pjh:x:102:0:Peter J. Holsberg:/usr/pjh:/bin/ksh
lkh:x:250:1:lkh:/usr/lkh:/bin/ksh
shevett:x:251:1:dave shevett:/usr/shevett:/bin/ksh
innis:x:262:20:innis rafael f:/u1/fall91/dp270/innis:/bin/ksh
grice:x:273:20:grice steven a:/u1/fall91/dp270/grice:/bin/ksh
hendric:x:274:20:hendrickson robbin:/u1/fall91/dp270/hendric:/bin/ksh
intorel:x:286:20:intorelli anthony:/u1/fall91/dp168/intorel:/bin/ksh
gordon:x:304:20:gordon gary g:/u1/fall91/dp168/gordon:/bin/csh
gross:x:305:20:gross james l:/u1/fall91/dp168/gross:/bin/ksh
hinnega:x:320:20:hinnegan dianna:/u1/fall91/dp163/hinnega:/bin/ksh
hagerho:x:326:20:hagerhorst paul j:/u1/fall91/dp168/hagerho:/bin/ksh
mccollo:x:329:1:Carol McCollough:/usr/home/mccollo:/bin/ksh
```

The *uniq* Command

The uniq command compares adjacent lines of a file. If it finds duplicates, it passes only one copy to stdout.

> **CAUTION:** Duplicate adjacent lines imply that the file was sorted before it was given to uniq for processing. Make sure that you sort a file before you feed it to uniq.

Here is uniq's syntax:

```
uniq [-udc [+n] [-m]] [input.file [output.file]]
```

The following examples demonstrate the options. The sample file contains the results of a survey taken by a USENET news administrator on a local computer. He asked users what newsgroups they read (*newsgroups* are a part of the structure of USENET News, an international electronic bulletin board), used cat to merge the users' responses into a single file, and used sort to sort the file. ngs is a piece of that file.

```
$ cat ngs

alt.dcom.telecom
alt.sources
comp.archives
comp.bugs.sys5
comp.databases
comp.databases.informix
comp.dcom.telecom
comp.lang.c
comp.lang.c
comp.lang.c
comp.lang.c
comp.lang.c++
comp.lang.c++
comp.lang.postscript
comp.laserprinters
comp.mail.maps
comp.sources
comp.sources.3b
comp.sources.3b
comp.sources.3b
comp.sources.bugs
comp.sources.d
comp.sources.misc
comp.sources.reviewed
comp.sources.unix
comp.sources.unix
comp.sources.wanted
comp.std.c
comp.std.c
comp.std.c++
comp.std.c++
comp.std.unix
comp.std.unix
comp.sys.3b
comp.sys.att
comp.sys.att
comp.unix.questions
comp.unix.shell
comp.unix.sysv386
comp.unix.wizards
u3b.sources
```

To produce a list that contains no duplicates, simply invoke uniq:

```
$ uniq ngs

alt.dcom.telecom
alt.sources
comp.archives
comp.bugs.sys5
```

```
comp.databases
comp.databases.informix
comp.dcom.telecom
comp.lang.c
comp.lang.c++
comp.lang.postscript
comp.laserprinters
comp.mail.maps
comp.sources
comp.sources.3b
comp.sources.bugs
comp.sources.d
comp.sources.misc
comp.sources.reviewed
comp.sources.unix
comp.sources.wanted
comp.std.c
comp.std.c++
comp.std.unix
comp.sys.3b
comp.sys.att
comp.unix.questions
comp.unix.shell
comp.unix.sysv386
comp.unix.wizards
u3b.sources
```

This is the desired list. Of course, you can get the same result by using the sort command's -u option while sorting the original file.

The -c option displays the so-called *repetition count*—the number of times each line appears in the original file:

```
$ uniq -c ngs
      1 alt.dcom.telecom
      1 alt.sources
      1 comp.archives
      1 comp.bugs.sys5
      1 comp.dcom.telecom
      1 comp.databases
      1 comp.databases.informix
      4 comp.lang.c
      2 comp.lang.c++
      1 comp.lang.postscript
      1 comp.laserprinters
      1 comp.mail.maps
      1 comp.sources
      3 comp.sources.3b
      1 comp.sources.bugs
      1 comp.sources.d
      1 comp.sources.misc
      1 comp.sources.reviewed
      2 comp.sources.unix
      1 comp.sources.wanted
      2 comp.std.c
      2 comp.std.c++
      2 comp.std.unix
      1 comp.sys.3b
```

```
2 comp.sys.att
1 comp.unix.questions
1 comp.unix.shell
1 comp.unix.sysv386
1 comp.unix.wizards
1 u3b.sources
```

The -u command tells uniq to output only the truly unique lines; that is, the lines that have a repetition count of 1:

$ uniq -u ngs

```
alt.dcom.telecom
alt.sources
comp.archives
comp.bugs.sys5
comp.databases
comp.databases.informix
comp.dcom.telecom
comp.lang.postscript
comp.laserprinters
comp.mail.maps
comp.sources
comp.sources.bugs
comp.sources.d
comp.sources.misc
comp.sources.reviewed
comp.sources.wanted
comp.sys.3b
comp.unix.questions
comp.unix.shell
comp.unix.sysv386
comp.unix.wizards
u3b.sources
```

The -d option tells uniq to output only those lines that have a repetition count of 2 or more:

$ uniq -d ngs

```
comp.lang.c
comp.lang.c++
comp.sources.3b
comp.sources.unix
comp.std.c
comp.std.c++
comp.std.unix
comp.sys.att
```

The uniq command also can handle lines that are divided into fields by a separator that consists of one or more spaces or tabs. The -*m* option tells uniq to skip the first *m* fields. The file mccc.ngs contains an abbreviated and modified newsgroup list in which every dot (.) is changed to a tab:

$ cat mccc.ngs

```
alt     dcom    telecom
alt     sources
comp    dcom    telecom
```

```
comp     sources
u3b      sources
```

Notice that some of the lines are identical except for the first field, so sort the file on the second field:

```
$ sort +1 mccc.ngs > mccc.ngs-1
```

```
$ cat mccc.ngs-1
```

```
alt     dcom     telecom
comp    dcom     telecom
alt     sources
comp    sources
u3b     sources
```

Now display lines that are unique except for the first field:

```
$ uniq -1 mccc.ngs-1
```

```
alt     dcom     telecom
alt     sources
```

The uniq command also can ignore the first *m* columns of a sorted file. The +*n* option tells uniq to skip the first *n* columns. The new file mccc.ngs-2 has four characters in each of its first fields on each line:

```
$ cat mccc.ngs-2
```

```
alt .dcom.telecom
comp.dcom.telecom
alt .sources
comp.sources
u3b .sources
```

```
$ uniq +4 mccc.ngs-2
```

```
alt .dcom.telecom
alt .sources
```

Compressing Files—compress, uncompress, and zcat

While investigating storage techniques, some computer science researchers discovered that certain types of files are stored quite inefficiently in their natural form. Most common among these "offenders" is the text file, which is stored one ASCII character per byte of memory. An ASCII character requires only seven bits, but almost all memory devices handle a minimum of eight bits at a time—that is, a byte. (A bit is a binary digit—the 1 or 0 found on electronic on/off switches.) Consequently, the researchers found that 12.5 percent of the memory device is wasted. These researchers further studied the field of language patterns, and found that they could code characters into even smaller bit patterns according to how frequently they are used.

The result of this research is a programming technique that compresses text files to about 50 percent of their original lengths. Although not as efficient with files that include characters that use all eight bits, this technique can indeed reduce file sizes substantially. Because the files are smaller, storage and file transfer can be much more efficient.

There are three UNIX commands associated with compression: `compress`, `uncompress`, and `zcat`. Here is the syntax for each command:

```
compress [ -cfv ] [ -b bits ] file(s)
uncompress [ -cv ] [ file(s) ]
zcat [ file(s)]
```

The options for these commands are listed in Table 6.7.

Table 6.7. Options for the Compression commands

Options	Meaning
-c	Writes to `stdout` instead of changing the file.
-f	Forces compression even if the compressed file is no smaller than the original.
-v	Displays the percentage of reduction for each compressed file.
-b bits	Tells `compress` how efficient to be. By default, `bits` is 16, but you can reduce it to as little as 9 for compatibility with computers that are not sufficiently powerful to handle full, 16-bit compression.

Normally, `compress` shrinks the file and replaces it with one that appends the extension `.Z` to the file name. However, things can go wrong; for example, the original file name might have 13 or 14 characters, or the compressed file could be the same size as the original when you have not specified the `-f` option. You can use `uncompress` to expand the file and replace the `.Z` file with the expanded file that has an appropriate name (usually the name is that of the compressed file, except without the `.Z` extension). The `zcat` command temporarily uncompresses a compressed file and prints it.

Incidentally, note that all three of these utilities can take their input from `stdin` through a pipe. For example, suppose that you retrieve a compressed `tar` archive (see Chapter 32, "Backing Up") from some site that archives free programs. If the compressed file were called `archive.tar.Z`, you could then uncompress it and separate it into its individual files with the following command:

```
$ zcat archive.tar * ¦ tar -xf -
```

Printing with *pr*

The pr command is the "granddaddy" of all of the programs that format files. It can separate a file into pages of a specified number of lines, number the pages, put a header on each page, and so on. This section looks at some of the command's more useful options (see Table 6.8).

> Incidentally, pr has nothing to do with actual printing on a printer. The name was used originally because the terminals of that time were printers—there were no screens as we know them today. You'll learn about true printing in the next section, "Printing Hard Copy Output."

The syntax for the pr command is as follows:

```
pr -m [-N [-wM] [-a]] [-ecK] [-icK] [-drtfp] [+p] [ -ncK] [-oO] [-lL]
[-sS] [-h header] [-F] [file(s)]
```

Table 6.8. Options for the pr Command

Option	Meaning
+p	Begin the display with page number p. If this is omitted, display begins with page 1.
-N	Display in N columns.
-d	Double-space the display.
-ecK	Expand tabs to character positions K+1, 2K+1, 3K+1, etc. Normally, tabs expand to positions 8, 16, 24, etc. If a character is entered for "c", use it as the tab character.
-ncK	Number each line with a K-digot number (default value is 5; e.g., 1, 2, 3, etc.). If a character is entered for "c", use it instead of a tab immediately following the K-digit number.
-wM	Set the width of each column to M characters when displaying two or more columns (default is 72).
-oO	Offset each line by O character positions to the right.
-lL	Set the length of a page to L lines (default is 66).
-h header	Use header as the text of the header of each page of the display in place of the name of the file. Note: there nust be a space between the h and the first character of the actual header string.

Option	Meaning
-p	Pause at the end of each page and ring the terminal bell. Proceed on receipt of a carriage return
-f	Use a form-feed character instead of a sequence of line feeds to begin a new page. Pause before displaying the first page on a terminal.
-r	Do not print error messages about files that cannot be opened.
-t	Omit the 5-line header and the 5-line trailer that each page normally has. Do not space to the beginning of a new page after displaying the last page. Takes precedence over -h *header*.
-sS	Separate columns by the character entered for S instead of a tab.
-F	Fold lines to fit the width of the column in multi-column display mode, or to fit an 80-character line.
-m	Merge and display up to eight files, one per column. May not be used with -*N* or -a

Here is the sample file that you'll use to examine pr:

```
$ cat names

allen christopher
babinchak david
best betty
bloom dennis
boelhower joseph
bose anita
cacossa ray
chang liang
crawford patricia
crowley charles
cuddy michael
czyzewski sharon
delucia joseph
```

The pr command normally prints a file with a five-line header and a five-line footer. The header, by default, consists of these five lines: two blank lines; a line that shows the date, time, filename, and page number; and two more blank lines. The footer consists of five blank lines. The blank lines provide proper top and bottom margins so that you can pipe the output of the pr command to a command that sends a file to the printer. The pr command normally uses 66-line pages, but to save space the demonstrations use a page length of 17: five lines of header, five lines of footer, and seven lines of text.

Use the `-l` option with a 17 argument to do this:

```
$ pr -l17 names

Sep 19 15:05 1991   names Page 1


allen christopher
babinchak david
best betty
bloom dennis
boelhower joseph
bose anita
cacossa ray


(Seven blank lines follow.)

Sep 19 15:05 1991   names Page 2


chang liang
crawford patricia
crowley charles
cuddy michael
czyzewski sharon
delucia joseph
```

Notice that pr puts the name for the file in the header, just before the page number. You can specify your own header with `-h`:

```
$ pr -l17 -h "This is the NAMES file" names

Sep 19 15:05 1991   This is the NAMES file Page 1


allen christopher
babinchak david
best betty
bloom dennis
boelhower joseph
bose anita
cacossa ray


(Seven blank lines follow.)

Sep 19 15:05 1991   This is the NAMES file Page 2


chang liang
crawford patricia
crowley charles
cuddy michael
czyzewski sharon
delucia joseph
```

The header that you specify replaces the file name.

NOTE: There must be a space between `-h` and the start of the header string. Also, if the header string contains spaces, you must quote the entire string.

Multicolumn output is a `pr` option. Note how you specify two-column output (`-2`):

```
$ pr -l17 -2 names

Sep 19 15:05 1991  names Page 1


allen christopher        chang liang
babinchak david          crawford patricia
best betty               crowley charles
bloom dennis             cuddy michael
boelhower joseph         czyzewski sharon
bose anita               delucia joseph
cacossa ray
```

You can number the lines of text; the numbering always begins with 1:

```
$ pr -l17 -n names

Sep 19 15:05 1991  names Page 1


     1    allen christopher
     2    babinchak david
     3    best betty
     4    bloom dennis
     5    boelhower joseph
     6    bose anita
     7    cacossa ray

(Seven blank lines follow.)

Sep 19 15:05 1991  names Page 2


     8    chang liang
     9    crawford patricia
    10    crowley charles
    11    cuddy michael
    12    czyzewski sharon
    13    delucia joseph
```

Combining numbering and multicolumns results in the following:

```
$ pr -l17 -n -2 names

Sep 19 15:05 1991  names Page 1


     1    allen christopher      8    chang liang
     2    babinchak david        9    crawford patricia
     3    best betty            10    crowley charles
     4    bloom dennis          11    cuddy michael
```

```
5     boelhower joseph          12    czyzewski sharon
6     bose anita                13    delucia joseph
7     cacossa ray
```

pr is, good for combining two or more files. Here are three files created from fields in
/etc/passwd:

$ cat p-login

```
allen
babinch
best
bloom
boelhow
bose
cacossa
chang
crawfor
crowley
cuddy
czyzews
delucia
diesso
dimemmo
dintron
```

$ cat p-home

```
/u1/fall91/dp168/allen
/u1/fall91/dp270/babinch
/u1/fall91/dp163/best
/u1/fall91/dp168/bloom
/u1/fall91/dp163/boelhow
/u1/fall91/dp168/bose
/u1/fall91/dp270/cacossa
/u1/fall91/dp168/chang
/u1/fall91/dp163/crawfor
/u1/fall91/dp163/crowley
/u1/fall91/dp270/cuddy
/u1/fall91/dp168/czyzews
/u1/fall91/dp168/delucia
/u1/fall91/dp270/diesso
/u1/fall91/dp168/dimemmo
/u1/fall91/dp168/dintron
```

$ cat p-uid

```
278
271
312
279
314
298
259
280
317
318
260
299
300
```

```
261
301
281
```

The -m option tells pr to merge the files:

```
$ pr -m -120 p-home p-uid p-login

Oct 12 14:15 1991    Page 1


/u1/fall91/dp168/allen   278        allen
/u1/fall91/dp270/babinc  271        babinch
/u1/fall91/dp163/best    312        best
/u1/fall91/dp168/bloom   279        bloom
/u1/fall91/dp163/boelho  314        boelhow
/u1/fall91/dp168/bose    298        bose
/u1/fall91/dp270/cacoss  259        cacossa
/u1/fall91/dp168/chang   280        chang
/u1/fall91/dp163/crawfo  317        crawfor
/u1/fall91/dp163/crowle  318        crowley

(Seven blank lines follow.)

Oct 12 14:15 1991    Page 2


/u1/fall91/dp270/cuddy   260        cuddy
/u1/fall91/dp168/czyzew  299        czyzews
/u1/fall91/dp168/deluci  300        delucia
/u1/fall91/dp270/diesso  261        diesso
/u1/fall91/dp168/dimemm  301        dimemmo
/u1/fall91/dp168/dintro  281        dintron
```

You can tell pr what to put between fields by using -s and a character. If you omit the character, pr uses a tab character.

```
$ pr -m -120 -s p-home p-uid p-login

Oct 12 14:16 1991    Page 1


/u1/fall91/dp168/allen   278 allen
/u1/fall91/dp270/babinch     271 babinch
/u1/fall91/dp163/best    312 best
/u1/fall91/dp168/bloom   279 bloom
/u1/fall91/dp163/boelhow     314 boelhow
/u1/fall91/dp168/bose    298 bose
/u1/fall91/dp270/cacossa     259 cacossa
/u1/fall91/dp168/chang   280 chang
/u1/fall91/dp163/crawfor     317 crawfor
/u1/fall91/dp163/crowley     318 crowley

(Seven blank lines follow.)

Oct 12 14:16 1991    Page 2


/u1/fall91/dp270/cuddy   260 cuddy
/u1/fall91/dp168/czyzews     299 czyzews
```

```
/u1/fall91/dp168/delucia      300  delucia
/u1/fall91/dp270/diesso  261  diesso
/u1/fall91/dp168/dimemmo      301  dimemmo
/u1/fall91/dp168/dintron      281  dintron
```

The -t option makes pr act somewhat like cat. By including the -t option, you can specify the order of merging, and even tell pr not to print (or leave room for) the header and footer:

```
$ pr -m -t -s p-uid p-login p-home

278   allen     /u1/fall91/dp168/allen
271   babinch   /u1/fall91/dp270/babinch
312   best      /u1/fall91/dp163/best
279   bloom     /u1/fall91/dp168/bloom
314   boelhow   /u1/fall91/dp163/boelhow
298   bose      /u1/fall91/dp168/bose
259   cacossa   /u1/fall91/dp270/cacossa
280   chang     /u1/fall91/dp168/chang
317   crawfor   /u1/fall91/dp163/crawfor
318   crowley   /u1/fall91/dp163/crowley
260   cuddy     /u1/fall91/dp270/cuddy
299   czyzews   /u1/fall91/dp168/czyzews
300   delucia   /u1/fall91/dp168/delucia
261   diesso    /u1/fall91/dp270/diesso
301   dimemmo   /u1/fall91/dp168/dimemmo
281   dintron   /u1/fall91/dp168/dintron
```

Printing Hard Copy Output

Displaying the results of your work on your terminal is fine, but when you need to present a report for management to read, nothing beats printed output.

Three general types of printers are available:

- Dot-matrix printers are usually very fast, but do not offer the print quality required for formal reports.
- Inkjet printers are not quite as fast, but do offer better letter quality.
- Laser printers provide the best print quality, and some are also quite fast. The two main types of laser printers, HP and PostScript, use different languages to convert your text file to something that the printer's engine can convert to hard copy.

Your system administrator can tell you which printers are available on your computer, or you can use the lpstat command to find out yourself. (This command is described later in this section.)

Requesting To Print

UNIX computers are multiuser computers, and there may be more users on a system than there are printers. For that reason, every print command that you issue is placed in a queue, to be acted on after all the ones previously issued are completed. To cancel requests, you use the `cancel` command.

The *lp* Command

Normally, the System V `lp` command has the following syntax:

```
lp [options] [files]
```

This command causes the named files and the designated options (if any) to become a print request. If no files are named in the command line, `lp` takes its input from the standard input so that it can be the last command in a pipeline. Table 6.9 contains the most frequently used options for `lp`.

Table 6.9. Options for `lp` Command

Option	Meaning
`-m`	Send mail after the files have been printed (see Chapter 9, "Communicating with Others").
`-d dest`	Choose `dest` as the printer or class of printers that is to do the printing. If `dest` is a printer, then `lp` prints the request only on that specific printer. If `dest` is a class of printers, then `lp` prints the request on the first available printer that is a member of the class. If `dest` is any, then `lp` prints the request on any printer that can handle it. For more information see the discussion below on `lpstat`.
`-n N`	Print `N` copies of the output. The default is one copy.
`-o option`	Specify a printer-dependent option. You can use the `-o` option as many times consecutively as you want, as in `-o option1 -o option2 . . . -o optionN`, or by specifying a list of options with one `-o` followed by the list enclosed in double quotation marks, as in `-o "option1 option2 . . . optionN"`. The options are as follows:
	nobanner Do not print a banner page with this request. Normally, a banner page containing the user-ID, file name, date, and time is printed for each print request, to make it easy for several users to identify their own printed copy.

continues

Table 6.9. Options for `lp` **Command**

Option	Meaning
`lpi=N`	Print this request with the line pitch set to *N*.
`cpi=pica¦elite¦compressed`	Print this request with the character pitch set to pica (representing 10 characters per inch), elite (representing 12 characters per inch), or compressed (representing as many characters per inch as a printer can handle).
`stty=stty-option-list`	A list of options valid for the `stty` command. Enclose the list with single quotation marks if it contains blanks.
`-t title`	Print *title* on the banner page of the output. The default is no title. Enclose *title* in quotation marks if it contains blanks.
`-w`	Write a message on the user's terminal after the files are printed. If the user is not logged in, or if the printer resides on a remote system, send a mail message instead.

To print the file sample on the default printer, type:

```
$ lp sample
request id is lj-19 (1 file)
```

Note the response from the printing system. If you don't happen to remember the request id later, don't worry; lpstat will tell it to you, as long as it has not finished printing the file. Once the system has finished printing, your request has been fulfilled and no longer exists.

Suppose your organization has a fancy, all-the-latest-bells-and-whistles-and-costing-more-than-an-arm-and-a-leg printer, code-named the_best in the Chairman's secretary's office in the next building. People are permitted to use it for the final copies of important documents so it is kept fairly busy. And you don't want to have to walk over to that building and climb 6 flights of stairs to retrieve your print job until you know it's been printed. So you type

```
$ lp -m -d the_best final.report.94
request id is the_best-19882 (1 file)
```

You have asked that the printer called the_best be used and that mail be sent to you when the printing has completed. (This assumes that this printer and your computer are connected on some kind of network that will transfer the actual file from your computer to the printer.)

The *cancel* Command

You may want to cancel a print request for any number of reasons, but only one command enables you to do it—the cancel command. Usually, you invoke it as follows:

```
cancel [request-ID(s)]
```

where request-ID(s) is the print job number that lp displays when you make a print request. Again, if you forget the request-ID, lpstat (see the section on lpstat) will show it to you.

Getting Printer and Print Request Status

The lpstat command gives the user information about the print services, including the status of all current print requests, the name of the default printer, and the status of each printer.

The syntax of lpstat is very simple:

```
$lpstat [options] [request-ID(s)]
```

When you use the lp command, it puts your request in a queue and issues a *request ID* for that particular command. If you supply that ID to lpstat, it reports on the status of that request. If you omit all IDs and use the lpstat command with no arguments, it displays the status of all your print requests.

Some options take a parameter list as arguments, indicated by [list] below. You can supply that list as either a list separated by commas, or a list enclosed in double quotation marks and separated by spaces, as in the following examples:

```
-p printer1,printer2
```

```
-u "user1 user2 user3"
```

If you specify all as the argument to an option that takes a list or if you omit the argument entirely, lpstat provides information about all requests, devices, statuses, and so on, appropriate to that option letter. For example, the following commands both display the status of all output requests:

```
$ lpstat -o all
```

```
$ lpstat -o
```

Here are some of the more common arguments and options for `lpstat`:

-d	Report what the system default destination is (if any).
-o [*list*]	Report the status of print requests. *list* is a list of printer names, class names, and request IDs. You can omit the -o.
-s	Display a status summary, including the status of the print scheduler, the system default destination, a list of class names and their members, a list of printers and their associated devices, and other, less pertinent information.
-p [*list*] [-D] [-l]	If the -D option is given, print a brief description of each printer in *list*. If the -l option is given, print a full description of each printer's configuration.
-t	Display all status information: all the information obtained with the -s option, plus the acceptance and idle/busy status of all printers and the status of all requests.
-a [*list*]	Report whether print destinations are accepting requests. *list* is a list of intermixed printer names and class names.

Comparing Directories with *dircmp*

The `dircmp` command examines the contents of two directories—including all subdirectories—and displays information about the contents of each. It lists all the files that are unique to each directory and all the files that are common. The command specifies whether each common file is different or the same by comparing the contents of each of those files.

The syntax for `dircmp` is

```
dircmp [-d] [-s] [-wn] dir1 dir2
```

The options are as follows:

-d	Perform a `diff` operation on pairs of files with the same names (see the section "The `diff` Command" later in this chapter).

-s	Suppress messages about identical files.
-w*N*	Change the width of the output line to *N* columns. The default width is 72.

As an example, suppose that the two directories have the following contents:

```
./phlumph:
total 24
-rw-r--r--   1 pjh      sys          8432 Mar  6 13:02 TTYMON
-rw-r--r--   1 pjh      sys            51 Mar  6 12:57 x
-rw-r--r--   1 pjh      sys           340 Mar  6 12:55 y
-rw-r--r--   1 pjh      sys           222 Mar  6 12:57 z

./xyzzy:
total 8
-rw-r--r--   1 pjh      sys           385 Mar  6 13:00 CLEANUP
-rw-r--r--   1 pjh      sys            52 Mar  6 12:55 x
-rw-r--r--   1 pjh      sys           340 Mar  6 12:55 y
-rw-r--r--   1 pjh      sys           241 Mar  6 12:55 z
```

Each directory includes a unique file and three pairs of files that have the same name. Of the three files, two of them differ in size and presumably in content. Now use dircmp to determine whether the files in the two directories are the same or different, as follows:

```
$ dircmp xyzzy phlumph

Mar  6 13:02 1994  xyzzy only and phlumph only Page 1

./CLEANUP                       ./TTYMON

(Many blank lines removed to save space.)
Mar  6 13:02 1994  Comparison of xyzzy phlumph Page 1

directory       .
different        ./x
same             ./y
different        ./z

(Many blank lines removed to save space.)

$
```

Note that dircmp first reports on the files unique to each directory and then comments about the common files.

```
$ dircmp -d xyzzy phlumph

Mar  6 13:02 1994  xyzzy only and phlumph only Page 1


./CLEANUP                       ./TTYMON

(Many blank lines removed to save space.)

Mar  6 13:02 1994  Comparison of xyzzy phlumph Page 1

directory       .
```

```
different      ./x
same           ./y
different      ./z

(Many blank lines removed to save space.)

Mar  6 13:02 1994  diff of ./x in xyzzy and phlumph Page 1

3c3
< echo "root has logged out..."
--
> echo "pjh has logged out..."

(Many blank lines removed to save space.)

Mar  6 13:02 1994  diff of ./z in xyzzy and phlumph Page 1

6d5
<        j) site=jonlab ;;

(Many blank lines removed to save space.)
$
```

At this point, you may want to refer back to the section "The `diff` Command" later in this chapter.

Encrypting a File with the *crypt* Command

If you have sensitive information stored in text files that you wish to give to other users you may want to encrypt them to make them unreadable by casual users. UNIX system owners of the Encryption Utilities, which are available only to purchasers in the United States, can encrypt a text file—in any way they see fit—before they transmit it to another user or site. The person who receives the encrypted file needs a copy of the `crypt` command and the password used by the person who encrypted the message in the first place.

The usual syntax for the `crypt` command is

$crypt [key] < clearfile > encryptedfile

where *key* is any phrase. For example

`crpyt "secret agent 007" <mydat> xyzzy`

will encrypt the contents of `my dat` and write the result to `xyzzy`.

> **TIP:** This approach requires that you type key, the *encryption key*, at your keyboard, in which case someone nearby might notice it. You can define your encryption key in an environment variable (see Chapters 11, 12, and 13) called CRYPTKEY.

Then use the following syntax:

```
$crypt -k < clearfile > encryptedfile
```

The encryption key need not be complex. In fact, the longer it is, the more time it takes to do the decryption. A key of three lowercase letters causes decryption to take as much as five minutes of machine time—and possibly much more on a multiuser machine.

> **CAUTION:** Do not concatenate encrypted files, even if they were encrypted with the same key. If you try to do so, you will successfully decrypt only the first file.
>
> Also, do not pipe the output of crypt through any program that changes the settings of your terminal. Otherwise, when crypt finishes, the output will be in a strange state.

Printing the Beginning or End of a File with *head* and *tail*

By default, the head command prints the first 10 lines of a file to stdout (by default, the screen):

```
$ head names
```

```
allen christopher
babinchak david
best betty
bloom dennis
boelhower joseph
bose anita
cacossa ray
chang liang
crawford patricia
crowley charles
```

You can specify the number of lines that head displays, as follows:

```
$ head -4 names
```

```
allen christopher
babinchak david
best betty
bloom dennis
```

To view the last few lines of a file, use the tail command. This command is helpful when you have a large file and want to look at at the end only. For example, suppose that you want to see the last few entries in the log file that records the transactions that occur when files are transferred between your machine and a neighboring machine. That log file may be large, and you surely don't want to have to read all the beginning and middle of it just to get to the end.

By default, `tail` prints the last 10 lines of a file to `stdout` (by default, the screen). Suppose that your names file consist of the following:

```
$ cat names

allen christopher
babinchak david
best betty
bloom dennis
boelhower joseph
bose anita
cacossa ray
chang liang
crawford patricia
crowley charles
cuddy michael
czyzewski sharon
delucia joseph
```

The `tail` command limits your view to the last 10 lines:

```
$ tail names

bloom dennis
boelhower joseph
bose anita
cacossa ray
chang liang
crawford patricia
crowley charles
cuddy michael
czyzewski sharon
delucia joseph
```

You can change this display by specifying the number of lines to print. For example, the following command prints the last five lines of names:

```
$ tail -5 names

crawford patricia
crowley charles
cuddy michael
czyzewski sharon
delucia joseph
```

The `tail` also can *follow* a file; that is, it can continue looking at a file as a program continues to add text to the end of that file. The syntax is

```
tail -f logfile
```

where *logfile* is the name of the file being written to. If you're logged into a busy system, try one of the following forms:

```
$ tail -f /var/uucp/.Log/uucico/neighbor
```

```
$ tail -f /var/uucp/.Log/uuxqt/neighbor
```

where `neighbor` is the name of a file that contains log information about a computer that can exchange information with yours. The first is the log file that logs file-transfer activity between your computer and *neighbor*, and the second is the log of commands that your computer has executed as requested by *neighbor*.

The `tail` command has several other useful options:

+n	Begin printing at line n of the file.
b	Count by blocks rather than lines (*blocks* are either 512 or 1,024 characters long).
c	Count by characters rather than lines.
r	Print from the designated starting point in the reverse direction. For example, `tail -5r` *file* prints the next-to-last five lines of the file. You cannot use option r cannot be used with option f.

Pipe Fitting with *tee*

In UNIX pipelines, you use the `tee` command just as a plumber uses a tee-fitting in a water line: to send output in two directions simultaneously. Fortunately, electrons behave different than water molecules, because `tee` can send all its input to both destinations. Probably the most common use of `tee` is to siphon off the output of a command and save it in a file while simultaneously passing it down the pipeline to another command.

The syntax for the `tee` command is

```
$tee [-i] [-a] [file(s)]
```

The `tee` command can send its output to multiple files simultaneously. With the `-a` option specified, `tee` appends the output to those files instead of overwriting them. The `-i` option prevents the pipline from being broken. To show the use of `tee`, type the comman that follows:

```
$ lp /etc/passwd ¦ tee status
```

This command causes the file `/etc/passwd` to be sent to the default printer, prints a message about the print request on the screen and simultaneously captures that message in a file called `status`. The `tee` sends the output of the `lp` command to two places: the screen and the named file.

Updating a File's Time and Date with *touch*

The touch command updates the access and modification time and date stamps of the files mentioned as its arguments. (See Chapters 4 and 35 for more information on the time and date of a file.) If the file mentioned does not exist, it is immediately created as a 0-byte file with no contents. You can use touch to protect files that might otherwise be removed by cleanup programs that delete files that have not been accessed or modified within a specified number of days.

Using touch, you can change the time and date stamp in any way you choose, if you include that information in the command line. Here's the syntax:

```
$touch [ -amc ] [ mmddhhmm[yy] ] file(s)
```

This command returns to the terminal an integer number that represents the number of files whose time and/or date could not be changed.

With no options, touch updates both the time and date stamps. The options are as follows:

-a	Update the access time and date only.
-m	Update the modification time and date only.
-c	Do not create a file that does not exist.

The pattern for the time-date stamp—*mmddhhmm*[*yy*]—consists of the month (01–12), day (01–31 as appropriate), hour (00–23), minute (00–59) and, optionally, year (00–99). Therefore, the command

```
$ touch 0704202090 fireworks
```

changes both access and modification time and dates of the file fireworks to July 4, 1990, 8:20 P.M.

Splitting Files with *split* and *csplit*

There are occasions when you have a text file that's too big for some application. For example, suppose you habe a 2MB file that you want to copy to a 1.4MB floppy disk. You will have to use split (or csplit) to divide it into two (or more) smaller files.

The syntax for split is

```
$ split [ -n ] [ in-file [ out-file ] ]
```

This command reads the text file *in-file* and splits it into several files, each consisting of *n* lines (except possibly the last file). If you omit *-n*, split creates 1,000-line files. The names of the small files depend on whether or not you specify *out-file*. If you do, these files are named *out-file*aa, *out-file*ab, *out-file*ac, and so on. If you have more than 26 output files, the 27th is named as *out-file*ba, the 28th as *out-file*bb, and so forth. If you omit *out-file*, split uses x in its place, so that the files are named xaa, xab, xac, and so on.

To recreate the original file from a group of files named xaa and xab, etc., type

```
$ cat xa* > new-name
```

It may be more sensible to divide a file according to the context of its contents, rather than on a chosen number of lines. UNIX offers a *context splitter*, called csplit. This command's syntax is

```
$ csplit [ -s ] [ -k ] [ -f out-file ] in-file arg(s)
```

where in-file is the name of the file to be split, and out-file is the base name of teh ouput files.

The *arg(s)* determine where each file is split. If you have N args, you get N+1 output files, named *out-file*00, *out-file*01, and so on, through *out-file*N (with a 0 in front of N if N is less than 10). N cannot be greater than 99. If you do not specify an *out-file* argument, csplit names the files xx00, xx01, and so forth. See below for an example where a file is divided by context into five files.

The -s option suppresses csplit's reporting of the number of characters in each output file. The -k option prevents csplit from deleting all output files if an error occurs.

Suppose that you have a password file such as the following. It is divided into sections: an unlabeled one at the beginning, followed by UUCP Logins, Special Users, DP Fall 1991, and NCR.

```
$ cat passwd
```

```
root:x:0:0:System Administrator:/usr/root:/bin/ksh
reboot:x:7:1:---:/:/etc/shutdown -y -g0 -i6
listen:x:37:4:x:/usr/net/nls:
slan:x:57:57:StarGROUP Software NPP Administration:/usr/slan:
lp:x:71:2:x:/usr/spool/lp:
_:-              :6:6:    ============================    :6:
_:-              :6:6:    ==   UUCP Logins                :6:
_:-              :6:6:    ============================    :6:
uucp:x:5:5:0000-uucp(0000):x:
nuucp:x:10:10:0000-uucp(0000):/usr/spool/uucppublic:/usr/lib/uucp/uucico
zzuucp:x:37:100:Bob Sorenson:/usr/spool/uucppublic:/usr/lib/uucp/uucico
asyuucp:x:38:100:Robert L. Wald:/usr/spool/uucppublic:/usr/lib/uucp/uucico
knuucp:x:39:100:Kris Knigge:/usr/spool/uucppublic:/usr/lib/uucp/uucico
_:-              :6:6:    ============================    :6:
_:-              :6:6:    ==   Special Users              :6:
_:-              :6:6:    ============================    :6:
msnet:x:100:99:Server Program:/usr/net/servers/msnet:/bin/false
install:x:101:1:x:/usr/install:
```

```
pjh:x:102:0:Peter J. Holsberg:/usr/pjh:/bin/ksh
hohen:x:346:1:Michael Hohenshilt:/usr/home/hohen:/bin/ksh
reilly:x:347:1:Joan Reilly:/usr/home/reilly:/bin/ksh
_:-              :6:6:     ============================    :6:
_:-              :6:6:     ==   DP Fall 1991               :6:
_:-              :6:6:     ============================    :6:
gordon:x:304:20:gordon gary g:/u1/fall91/dp168/gordon:/bin/csh
lewis:x:288:20:lewis prince e:/u1/fall91/dp168/lewis:/bin/ksh
metelit:x:265:20:metelitsa natalya:/u1/fall91/dp270/metelit:/bin/ksh
nadaraj:x:307:20:nadarajah kalyani:/u1/fall91/dp168/nadaraj:/bin/ksh
nado:x:266:20:nado conan j:/u1/fall91/dp270/nado:/bin/ksh
_:-              :6:6:     ============================    :6:
_:-              :6:6:     ===  NCR  =================      :6:
_:-              :6:6:     ============================    :6:
antello:x:334:20:antello ronald f:/u1/fall91/ff437/antello:/bin/ksh
cilino:x:335:20:cilino michael a:/u1/fall91/ff437/cilino:/bin/ksh
emmons:x:336:20:emmons william r:/u1/fall91/ff437/emmons:/bin/ksh
foreste:x:337:20:forester james r:/u1/fall91/ff437/foreste:/bin/ksh
hayden:x:338:20:hayden richard:/u1/fall91/ff437/hayden:/bin/ksh
```

You might want to split this file so that each section has its own file. To split this file into multiple files, you must specify the appropriate arguments to `csplit`. Each takes the form of a text string surrounded by slash (/) marks. The `csplit` command then copies from the current line up to, but not including, the argument. The following is the first attempt at splitting the file with `csplit`:

```
$ csplit -f PA passwd /UUCP/ /Special/ /Fall/ /NCR/

270
505
426
490
446
```

Note that there are four args: uucp, special, fall, and ncr. There will be five files created: PA01 will contan everything from the beginning of passwd, to (but not including) the first line that contains uucp. PA02 will contain everything from the first line containing uucp up to (but not including) the line that contains special, and so on. Five files are created: the first has 270 characters, the second has 505 characters, and so on. Now let's see what they look like:

```
$ cat PA00

root:x:0:0:System Administrator:/usr/root:/bin/ksh
reboot:x:7:1:--:/:/etc/shutdown -y -g0 -i6
listen:x:37:4:x:/usr/net/nls:
slan:x:57:57:StarGROUP Software NPP Administration:/usr/slan:
lp:x:71:2:x:/usr/spool/lp:
_:-              :6:6:     ============================    :6:
```

```
$ cat PA01

_:-              :6:6:     ==   UUCP Logins                :6:
_:-              :6:6:     ============================    :6:
uucp:x:5:5:0000-uucp(0000):x:
nuucp:x:10:10:0000-uucp(0000):/usr/spool/uucppublic:/usr/lib/uucp/uucico
```

```
zzuucp:x:37:100:Bob Sorenson:/usr/spool/uucppublic:/usr/lib/uucp/uucico
asyuucp:x:38:100:Robert L. Wald:/usr/spool/uucppublic:/usr/lib/uucp/uucico
knuucp:x:39:100:Kris Knigge:/usr/spool/uucppublic:/usr/lib/uucp/uucico
_:-             :6:6:    ==============================    :6:
```

`$ cat PA02`

```
_:-             :6:6:    ==    Special Users            :6:
_:-             :6:6:    ==============================    :6:
msnet:x:100:99:Server Program:/usr/net/servers/msnet:/bin/false
install:x:101:1:x:/usr/install:
pjh:x:102:0:Peter J. Holsberg:/usr/pjh:/bin/ksh
hohen:x:346:1:Michael Hohenshilt:/usr/home/hohen:/bin/ksh
reilly:x:347:1:Joan Reilly:/usr/home/reilly:/bin/ksh
_:-             :6:6:    ==============================    :6:
```

`$ cat PA03`

```
_:-             :6:6:    ==    DP Fall 1991              :6:
_:-             :6:6:    ==============================    :6:
gordon:x:304:20:gordon gary g:/u1/fall91/dp168/gordon:/bin/csh
lewis:x:288:20:lewis prince e:/u1/fall91/dp168/lewis:/bin/ksh
metelit:x:265:20:metelitsa natalya:/u1/fall91/dp270/metelit:/bin/ksh
nadaraj:x:307:20:nadarajah kalyani:/u1/fall91/dp168/nadaraj:/bin/ksh
nado:x:266:20:nado conan j:/u1/fall91/dp270/nado:/bin/ksh
_:-             :6:6:    ==============================    :6:
```

`$ cat PA04`

```
_:-             :6:6:    ===    NCR    ==================    :6:
_:-             :6:6:    ==============================    :6:
antello:x:334:20:antello ronald f:/u1/fall91/ff437/antello:/bin/ksh
cilino:x:335:20:cilino michael a:/u1/fall91/ff437/cilino:/bin/ksh
emmons:x:336:20:emmons william r:/u1/fall91/ff437/emmons:/bin/ksh
foreste:x:337:20:forester james r:/u1/fall91/ff437/foreste:/bin/ksh
hayden:x:338:20:hayden richard:/u1/fall91/ff437/hayden:/bin/ksh
```

This is not bad, but each file ends or begins with one or more lines that you don't want. The csplit command enables you to adjust the split point by appending an offset to the argument. For example, /UUCP/-1 means that the split point is the line before the one on which UUCP appears for the first time. Add -1 to each argument, and you should get rid of the unwanted line that ends each of the first four files:

`$ csplit -f PB passwd /UUCP/-1 /Special/-1 /Fall/-1 /NCR/-1`

```
213
505
426
490
503
```

You can see that the first file is smaller than the previous first file. Perhaps this is working. Let's see:

`$ cat PB00`

```
root:x:0:0:System Administrator:/usr/root:/bin/ksh
```

```
reboot:x:7:1:--::/:/etc/shutdown -y -g0 -i6
listen:x:37:4:x:/usr/net/nls:
slan:x:57:57:StarGROUP Software NPP Administration:/usr/slan:
lp:x:71:2:x:/usr/spool/lp:
```

$ cat PB01

```
_:-                   :6:6:   ==============================   :6:
_:-                   :6:6:   ==  UUCP Logins                  :6:
_:-                   :6:6:   ==============================   :6:
uucp:x:5:5:0000-uucp(0000):x:
nuucp:x:10:10:0000-uucp(0000):/usr/spool/uucppublic:/usr/lib/uucp/uucico
zzuucp:x:37:100:Bob Sorenson:/usr/spool/uucppublic:/usr/lib/uucp/uucico
asyuucp:x:38:100:Robert L. Wald:/usr/spool/uucppublic:/usr/lib/uucp/uucico
knuucp:x:39:100:Kris Knigge:/usr/spool/uucppublic:/usr/lib/uucp/uucico
```

$ cat PB02

```
_:-                   :6:6:   ==============================   :6:
_:-                   :6:6:   ==  Special Users                :6:
_:-                   :6:6:   ==============================   :6:
msnet:x:100:99:Server Program:/usr/net/servers/msnet:/bin/false
install:x:101:1:x:/usr/install:
pjh:x:102:0:Peter J. Holsberg:/usr/pjh:/bin/ksh
hohen:x:346:1:Michael Hohenshilt:/usr/home/hohen:/bin/ksh
reilly:x:347:1:Joan Reilly:/usr/home/reilly:/bin/ksh
```

$ cat PB03

```
_:-                   :6:6:   ==============================   :6:
_:-                   :6:6:   ==  DP Fall 1991                 :6:
_:-                   :6:6:   ==============================   :6:
gordon:x:304:20:gordon gary g:/u1/fall91/dp168/gordon:/bin/csh
lewis:x:288:20:lewis prince e:/u1/fall91/dp168/lewis:/bin/ksh
metelit:x:265:20:metelitsa natalya:/u1/fall91/dp270/metelit:/bin/ksh
nadaraj:x:307:20:nadarajah kalyani:/u1/fall91/dp168/nadaraj:/bin/ksh
nado:x:266:20:nado conan j:/u1/fall91/dp270/nado:/bin/ksh
```

$ cat PB04

```
_:-                   :6:6:   ==============================   :6:
_:-                   :6:6:   ===  NCR  ===================     :6:
_:-                   :6:6:   ==============================   :6:
antello:x:334:20:antello ronald f:/u1/fall91/ff437/antello:/bin/ksh
cilino:x:335:20:cilino michael a:/u1/fall91/ff437/cilino:/bin/ksh
emmons:x:336:20:emmons william r:/u1/fall91/ff437/emmons:/bin/ksh
foreste:x:337:20:forester james r:/u1/fall91/ff437/foreste:/bin/ksh
hayden:x:338:20:hayden richard:/u1/fall91/ff437/hayden:/bin/ksh
```

This is very good indeed. Now, to get rid of the unwanted lines at the beginning, you have csplit advance its current line without copying anything. A pair of arguments, /UUCP/-1 and %uucp%, tells csplit to skip all the lines beginning with the one that precedes the line containing UUCP, to the one that precedes the line containing uucp. This causes csplit to skip the lines that begin with _:-. The following displays the full command:

```
$ csplit -f PC passwd /UUCP/-1 %uucp% /Special/-1 %msnet% \
/Fall/-1 %dp[12][67][80]% /NCR/1%ff437%
```

```
213
334
255
321
332
```

Note the backslash (/) at the end of the first line fo the command. This is simply a continuation character—it tells the shell that the carriage return (or Enter) that you're about
to press is not the end of the command, but that you'd like to continue typing on the next
line on the scree. Also note that any argument can be a regular expression. Here are the
resulting files:

$ cat PC00

```
root:x:0:0:System Administrator:/usr/root:/bin/ksh
reboot:x:7:1:--:/:/etc/shutdown -y -g0 -i6
listen:x:37:4:x:/usr/net/nls:
slan:x:57:57:StarGROUP Software NPP Administration:/usr/slan:
lp:x:71:2:x:/usr/spool/lp:
```

$ cat PC01

```
uucp:x:5:5:0000-uucp(0000):x:
nuucp:x:10:10:0000-uucp(0000):/usr/spool/uucppublic:/usr/lib/uucp/uucico
zzuucp:x:37:100:Bob Sorenson:/usr/spool/uucppublic:/usr/lib/uucp/uucico
asyuucp:x:38:100:Robert L. Wald:/usr/spool/uucppublic:/usr/lib/uucp/uucico
knuucp:x:39:100:Kris Knigge:/usr/spool/uucppublic:/usr/lib/uucp/uucico
```

$ cat PC02

```
msnet:x:100:99:Server Program:/usr/net/servers/msnet:/bin/false
install:x:101:1:x:/usr/install:
pjh:x:102:0:Peter J. Holsberg:/usr/pjh:/bin/ksh
hohen:x:346:1:Michael Hohenshilt:/usr/home/hohen:/bin/ksh
reilly:x:347:1:Joan Reilly:/usr/home/reilly:/bin/ksh
```

$ cat PC03

```
gordon:x:304:20:gordon gary g:/u1/fall91/dp168/gordon:/bin/csh
lewis:x:288:20:lewis prince e:/u1/fall91/dp168/lewis:/bin/ksh
metelit:x:265:20:metelitsa natalya:/u1/fall91/dp270/metelit:/bin/ksh
nadaraj:x:307:20:nadarajah kalyani:/u1/fall91/dp168/nadaraj:/bin/ksh
nado:x:266:20:nado conan j:/u1/fall91/dp270/nado:/bin/ksh
```

$ cat PC04

```
antello:x:334:20:antello ronald f:/u1/fall91/ff437/antello:/bin/ksh
cilino:x:335:20:cilino michael a:/u1/fall91/ff437/cilino:/bin/ksh
emmons:x:336:20:emmons william r:/u1/fall91/ff437/emmons:/bin/ksh
foreste:x:337:20:forester james r:/u1/fall91/ff437/foreste:/bin/ksh
hayden:x:338:20:hayden richard:/u1/fall91/ff437/hayden:/bin/ksh
```

The program, therefore, has been a success.

In addition, an argument can be a line number (typed as an argument but without slashes)
to indicate that the desired split should take place at the line before the specified number.

You also can specify a repeat factor by appending *{number}* to a pattern. For example, /login/{8} means use the first eight lines that contain login as split points.

Comparing Files with *cmp* and *diff*

So far, you have seen UNIX commands that work with a single file at a time. However, often a user must compare two files and determine whether they are different, and if so, just what the differences are. UNIX provides commands that can help:

■ The cmp command compares two files, and then simple reports the character number and line number where they differ.

■ The diff command compares two files and tells you exactly where the files differ and what you must do to make them agree.

The cmp command is especially useful in shell scripts (see Chapters 11, 12 and 13). The diff command is more specialized in what it does and where you can use it.

The *cmp* Command

The simplest command for comparing two files, cmp, simply tells you whether the files are different or not. If they are different, it tells you where in the file it spotted the first difference, if you use cmp with no options. The command's syntax is

```
$ cmp [ -l ] [ -s ] file1 file2
```

The -l option gives you more information. It displays the number of each character that is different (the first character in the file is number 1), and then prints the octal value of the ASCII code of that character. (You will probably not have any use for the octal value of a character until you become a shell programming expert!) The -s option prints nothing, but returns an appropriate result code (0 if there are no differences, 1 if there are one or more differences). This option is useful when you write shell scripts (see Chapters 11, 12, and 13).

Here are two files that you can compare with cmp:

```
$ cat na.1

allen christopher
babinchak david
best betty
bloom dennis
boelhower joseph
bose anita
cacossa ray
delucia joseph

$ cat na.2
```

```
allen christopher
babinchak David
best betty
boelhower joseph
bose
cacossa ray
delucia joseph
```

Note that the first difference between the two files is on the second line. The D in David in the second file is the 29th character, counting all newline characters at the ends of lines.

```
$ cmp na.1 na.2

na.1 na.2 differ: char 29, line 2

$ cmp -l na.1 na.2

cmp:
      29 144 104
      68 141  12
      69 156 143
      70 151 141
      71 164 143
      72 141 157
      73  12 163
      74 143 163
      76 143  40
      77 157 162
      78 163 141
      79 163 171
      80 141  12
      81  40 144
      82 162 145
      83 141 154
      84 171 165
      85  12 143
      86 144 151
      87 145 141
      88 154  40
      89 165 152
      90 143 157
      91 151 163
      92 141 145
      93  40 160
      94 152 150
      95 157  12
```

This is quite a list! The 29th character is octal 144 in the first file and octal 104 in the second. If you look them up in an ASCII table, you'll see that the former is a *d*, and the latter is a *D*. Character 68 is the first a in anita in na.1 and the newline after the space after bose in na.2.

Now let's try the -s option on the two files:

```
$ cmp -s na.1 na.2

$ echo $?
```

1

The variable ? is the shell variable that contains the result code of the last command, and $? is its value. The value 1 on the last line indicates that cmp found at least one difference between the two files. (See Chapters 11, 12, and 13.)

Next, for contrast, compare a file with itself to see how cmp reports no differences:

```
$ cmp -s na.1 na.2

$ echo $?

0
```

The value 0 means that cmp found no differences.

The *diff* Command

The diff command is much more powerful than the cmp command. It shows you the differences between two files by outputting the editing changes (see Chapter 7, "Editing Text Files") that you would need to make to convert one file to the other. The syntax of diff is one of the following lines:

```
$ diff [-bitw] [-c ¦ -e ¦ -f ¦ -h ¦ -n] file1 file2

$ diff [-bitw] [-C number] file1 file2

$ diff [-bitw] [-D string] file1 file2

$ diff [-bitw] [-c ¦ -e ¦ -f ¦ -h ¦ -n] [-l] [-r] [-s] [-S name] dir1 dir2
```

The three sets of options—cefhn, -C *number*, and -D *string*—are mutually exclusive. The common options are

-b	Ignores trailing blanks, and treats all other strings of blanks as equivalent to one another.
-i	Ignores uppercase and lowercase distinctions.
-t	Preserves indentation level of the original file by expanding tabs in the output.
-w	Ignores all blanks (spaces and tabs).

Later in this section you'll see examples that demonstrate each of these options.

First, let's look at the two files that show what diff does:

Let's apply diff to the files na.1 and na.2 (the files with which cmp was demonstrated):

```
$ diff na.1 na.2

2c2
< babinchak david
---
> babinchak David
4d3
```

```
< bloom dennis
6c5
< bose anita
- - -
> bose
```

These editor commands are quite different from those that `diff` printed before. The first four lines show

```
 2c2
< babinchak david
- - -
> babinchak David
```

which means that you can change the second line of `file1` (na.1) to match the second line of `file2` (na.2) by executing the command, which means change line 2 of `file1` to line 2 of `file2`. Note that both the line from `file1`—prefaced with <—and the line from `file2`—prefaced with >—are displayed, separated by a line consisting of three dashes.

The next command says to delete line 4 from `file1` to bring it into agreement with `file2` up to—but not including—line 3 of `file2`. Finally, notice that there is another change command, 6c5, which says change line 6 of `file1` by replacing it with line 5 of `file2`.

Note that in line 2, the difference that `diff` found was the d versus D letter in the second word.

You can use the -i option to tell `diff` to ignore the case of the characters, as follows:

```
$ diff -i na.1 na.2

4d3
< bloom dennis
6c5
< bose anita
- - -
> bose
```

The -c option causes the differences to be printed in context; that is, the output displays several of the lines above and below a line in which `diff` finds a difference. Each difference is marked with one of the following:

- An exclamation point (!) indicates that corresponding lines in the two files are similar but not the same.
- A minus sign (-) means that the line is not in `file2`.
- A plus sign (+) means that the line is in `file2` but not in `file1`.

Note in the following example that the output includes a header that displays the names of the two files, and the times and dates of their last changes. The header also shows either stars (***) to designate lines from the first file, or dashes (- - -) to designate lines from the second file.

```
$ diff -c na.1 na.2

*** na.1      Sat Nov  9 12:57:55 1991
--- na.2      Sat Nov  9 12:58:27 1991
***************
*** 1,8 ****
  allen christopher
! babinchak david
  best betty
- bloom dennis
  boelhower joseph
! bose anita
  cacossa ray
  delucia joseph
--- 1,7 ----
  allen christopher
! babinchak David
  best betty
  boelhower joseph
! bose
  cacossa ray
  delucia joseph
```

After the header comes another asterisk-filled header that shows which lines of *file1* (na.1) will be printed next (1,8), followed by the lines themselves. You see that the babinchak line differs in the two files, as does the bose line. Also, bloom dennis does not appear in *file2* (na.2). Next, you see a header of dashes that indicates which lines of *file2* will follow (1,7). Note that for the *file2* list, the babinchak line and the bose line are marked with exclamation points. The number of lines displayed depends on how close together the differences are (the default is three lines of context). Later in this section, when you once again use diff with p1 and p2, you'll see an example that show how to change the number of context lines.

diff can create an ed script (see Chapter 7) that you can use to change *file1* into *file2*. First you a execute a command such as the following:

```
$ diff -e na.1 na.2

6c
bose
.
4d
2c
babinchak David
.
```

Then you redirect this output to another file using a command such as the following:

```
$ diff -e na.1 na.2 > ed.scr
```

Edit the file by adding two lines, w and q (see Chapter 7), which results in the following file:

```
$ cat ed.scr

6c
```

```
bose
.
4d
2c
babinchak David
.
w
q
```

Then you execute the command:

$ ed na.1 < ed.scr

This command changes the contents na.1 to agree with na.2.

Perhaps this small example isn't very striking, but here's another, more impressive one. Suppose that you have a large program written in C that does something special for you; perhaps it manages your investments or keeps track of sales leads. Further, suppose that the people who provided the program discover that it has bugs (and what program doesn't?). They could either ship new disks that contain the rewritten program, or they could run diff on both the original and the corrected copy and then send you an ed script so that you can make the changes yourself. If the script were small enough (less than 50,000 characters or so), they could even distribute it through electronic mail.

The -f option creates what appears to be an ed script that changes *file2* to *file1*. However, it is not an ed script at all, but a rather puzzling feature that is almost never used:

$ diff -f na.1 na.2

```
c2
babinchak David
.
d4
c6
bose
.
```

Also of limited value is the -h option, which causes diff to work in a "half-hearted" manner (according to the official *AT&T UNIX System V Release 4 Users Reference Manual*). With the -h option, diff is supposed to work best—and fast—on very large files having sections of change that encompass only a few lines at a time and that are widely separated in the files. Without -h, diff slows dramatically as the sizes increase for the files on which you are apply diff.

$ diff -h na.1 na.2

```
2c2
< babinchak david
- - -
> babinchak David
4d3
< bloom dennis
6c5
```

```
< bose anita
---
> bose
```

As you can see, `diff` with the `-h` option also works pretty well with original files that are too small to show a measurable difference in `diff`'s speed.

The `-n` option, like `-f`, also produces something that lokks like an `ed` script, but isn't and is also rarely used. The `-D` option permits C programmers (see Chapter 17) to produce a source code file based on the differences between two source code files. This is useful when uniting a program that is to be compiled on two different computers.

Summary

This chapter introduced some tools that enable you to determine the nature of the contents of a file and to examine those contents. Other tools extract selected lines from a file and sort the structured information in a file. Some tools disguise the contents of a file, and others compress the contents so that the resultant file is half its original size. Other tools compare two files and then report the differences. These commands are the foundation that UNIX provides to enable users to create even more powerful tools from relatively simple ones.

However, none of these tools enables you to create a file that is exactly—to the tiniest detail—what you want. The next chapter discusses just such tools—UNIX's text editors.

Text Editing with *vi*, EMACS, and *sed*

7

By Dave Taylor

IN THIS CHAPTER

The *vi* Editor

If you like primitive tools, you've already figured out that you can use a combination of << and cat to add lines to a file, and you can use sed and file redirection to modify the contents of a file. These tools are rough and awkward, and when it's time to either create new files or modify existing ones, you need a screen-oriented editor. In UNIX, the screen editor of choice is called vi.

There are a number of editors that may be included with your UNIX system, including ed, ex, vi, and EMACS. The latter two use the entire screen, a big advantage, and both are powerful editors. This section focuses on vi, however, because it's easier and, perhaps more importantly, it's guaranteed to always be part of UNIX. Most vendors omit EMACS, forcing you to find it yourself.

In this section, you will learn how to start and quit vi, simple character motion in vi, how to move by words and pages, how to insert text into the file, how to search within a file, how to have vi start out right, the key colon commands in vi.

In some ways, an editor is like another operating system living within UNIX. If you're used to Windows or Macintosh editors, you'll be unhappy to find that vi doesn't know anything about your mouse. Once you spend some time working with vi, however, it will grow on you. By the end of this section, you will be able to create and modify files on your UNIX system to your heart's content.

How to Start and Quit *vi*

Most UNIX commands do their work, display their results, and quit. Among the few exceptions are more and pg, where you work within the specific program environment until you have viewed the entire contents of the file being shown, or until you quit. The vi editor is another program in this small category of *environments*, programs that you move in and use until you explicitly tell the program to quit.

Before you start vi for the first time, you must learn about two aspects of its behavior. The first is that vi is a *modal* editor. A mode is like an environment. Different modes in vi interpret the same key differently. For example, if you're in *insert mode*, pressing the A key adds an *a* to the text, whereas in *command mode*, pressing the A key enters a, a single key abbreviation for the *append* command. If you ever get confused about what mode you're in, press the Esc key on your keyboard. Pressing Esc always returns you to the command mode (and if you're already in command mode, it beeps to remind you of that fact).

TIP: In vi, the Enter key is a specific command (meaning move to the beginning of the next line). As a result, you never need to press Enter to have vi process your command.

NOTE: EMACS is a *modeless* editor. In EMACS, the A key always adds the letter a to the file. Commands in EMACS are all indicated by holding down the Ctrl key while pressing the command key; for example, Ctrl+C deletes a character.

The second important characteristic of vi is that it's a screen-oriented program. It *must* know what kind of terminal, computer, or system you're using to work with UNIX. This probably won't be a problem for you, because most systems are set up so that the default terminal type matches the terminal or communications program you're using. Here you will learn how to recognize when vi cannot figure out what terminal you're using, and what to do about it.

You can start vi in a number of different ways, and you will learn about lots of helpful alternatives later. Right now you will learn the basics. The vi command by itself starts the editor, ready for you to create a new file. The vi command with a filename starts vi with the specified file, so you can modify that file immediately.

To begin, enter vi at the prompt. If all is working well, the screen will clear, the first character on each line will become a tilde (~), and the cursor will be sitting at the top-left corner of the screen:

```
% vi
_
~
~
~
~
~
~
~
~
~
```

Type a colon character. Doing so moves the cursor to the bottom of the screen and replaces the last tilde with a colon:

```
~
~
~
~
```

```
~
~
~
:_
```

Press the q key and the Enter key, and you should be back at the shell prompt:

```
~
~
~
~
~
~
~
~
:q
%
```

If that operation worked without a problem, go ahead and append your command to your
.login or .profile file. If the operation did not work, you received the unknown-termi-
nal-type error message. You might see this on your screen:

```
% vi
"unknown": Unknown terminal type
I don't know what type of terminal you are on. All I have is "unknown"
[using open mode]
_
```

Alternatively, you might see this:

```
% vi
Visual needs addressible cursor or upline capability
:
```

Don't panic. You can fix this problem. The first step is to get back to the shell prompt. To
do this, do exactly what you did in the first step: type :q and press Enter. You should then
see this:

```
% vi
"unknown": Unknown terminal type
I don't know what type of terminal you are on. All I have is "unknown"
[using open mode]
:q
%
```

The problem here is that vi needs to know the type of terminal you're using, but it can't
figure that out on its own. Therefore, you need to tell this to the operating system by setting the TERM environment variable. If you know what kind of terminal you have, use that
value; otherwise, try the default of vt100:

```
% setenv TERM vt100
```

If you have the $ prompt, which means you're using the Bourne shell (sh) or Korn shell
(ksh) rather than the C shell (csh), try this:

```
$ TERM=vt100 ; export TERM
```

Either way, you can now try entering vi again, and it should work. If it does work, append the command (whichever of these two commands was successful for you) to your .login file if you use csh, or to .profile if you use sh or ksh:

```
% echo "setenv TERM vt100" >> .login
```

or

```
$ echo "TERM=vt100 ; export TERM" >> .profile
```

This way, the next time you log in, the system will remember what kind of terminal you're using.

If this didn't work, it's time to talk with your system administrator about the problem or to call your UNIX vendor to find out what the specific value should be. If you are connected through a modem or other line, and you are actually using a terminal emulator or communications package, then you might also try using ansi as a TERM setting. If that fails, call the company that makes your software and ask them what terminal type the communications program is emulating.

Great! You have successfully launched vi, seen what it looks like, and even entered the most important command: the quit command. Now create a simple file and start vi so it shows you the contents of the file:

```
% ls -l > demo
% vi demo
total 29
drwx------  2 taylor          512 Nov 21 10:39 Archives/
drwx------  3 taylor          512 Dec  3 02:03 InfoWorld/
drwx------  2 taylor         1024 Dec  3 01:43 Mail/
drwx------  2 taylor          512 Oct  6 09:36 News/
drwx------  4 taylor          512 Dec  2 22:08 OWL/
-rw-rw----  1 taylor          126 Dec  3 16:34 awkscript
-rw-rw----  1 taylor          165 Dec  3 16:42 bigfiles
drwx------  2 taylor          512 Oct 13 10:45 bin/
-rw-rw----  1 taylor            0 Dec  3 22:26 demo
-rw-rw----  1 taylor        12556 Nov 16 09:49 keylime.pie
-rw-rw----  1 taylor         8729 Dec  2 21:19 owl.c
-rw-rw----  1 taylor          199 Dec  3 16:11 sample
-rw-rw----  1 taylor          207 Dec  3 16:11 sample2
drwx------  2 taylor          512 Oct 13 10:45 src/
drwxrwx--   2 taylor          512 Nov  8 22:20 temp/
-rw-rw----  1 taylor          582 Nov 27 18:29 tetme
~
~
~
~
~
~
~
"demo" 17 lines, 846 characters
```

You can see that vi reads the file specified on the command line. In this example, my file is 17 lines long, but my screen can hold 25 lines. To show that some lines lack any text, vi uses the tilde on a line by itself. Finally, note that, at the bottom, the program shows the name of the file, the number of lines it found in the file, and the total number of characters.

Type :q again to quit vi and return to the command line for now. When you type the colon, the cursor will flash down to the bottom line and wait for the q, as it did before.

You have learned the most basic command in vi—the :q command—and survived the experience. It's all downhill from here.

Simple Character Motion in vi

Getting to a file isn't much good if you can't actually move around in it. Now you will learn how to use the cursor control keys in vi. To move left one character, press the h key. To move up, press the k key. To move down, press the j key. To move right a single character, use the l key. You can move left one character by pressing the Backspace key, and you can move to the beginning of the next line with the Enter key.

Launch vi again, specifying the demo file:

```
% vi demo
total 29
drwx------   2 taylor        512 Nov 21 10:39 Archives/
drwx------   3 taylor        512 Dec  3 02:03 InfoWorld/
drwx------   2 taylor       1024 Dec  3 01:43 Mail/
drwx------   2 taylor        512 Oct  6 09:36 News/
drwx------   4 taylor        512 Dec  2 22:08 OWL/
-rw-rw----   1 taylor        126 Dec  3 16:34 awkscript
-rw-rw----   1 taylor        165 Dec  3 16:42 bigfiles
drwx------   2 taylor        512 Oct 13 10:45 bin/
-rw-rw----   1 taylor          0 Dec  3 22:26 demo
-rw-rw----   1 taylor      12556 Nov 16 09:49 keylime.pie
-rw-rw----   1 taylor       8729 Dec  2 21:19 owl.c
-rw-rw----   1 taylor        199 Dec  3 16:11 sample
-rw-rw----   1 taylor        207 Dec  3 16:11 sample2
drwx------   2 taylor        512 Oct 13 10:45 src/
drwxrwx--   2 taylor        512 Nov  8 22:20 temp/
-rw-rw----   1 taylor        582 Nov 27 18:29 tetme
~
~
~
~
~
~
~
"demo" 17 lines, 846 characters
```

You should see the cursor sitting on top the t in total on the first line, or perhaps flashing underneath the t character. Perhaps you have a flashing box cursor or one that shows up in a different color. In any case, that's your starting spot in the file.

Press the h key once to try to move left. The cursor stays in the same spot and vi beeps to remind you that you can't move left any farther on the line. Try the k key to try to move up; the same thing will happen.

Now try pressing the j key to move down a character:

```
                total 29
drwx------  2 taylor       512 Nov 21 10:39 Archives/
drwx------  3 taylor       512 Dec  3 02:03 InfoWorld/
drwx------  2 taylor      1024 Dec  3 01:43 Mail/
```

Now the cursor is on the d directory indicator on the second line of the file.

Press the k key to move back up to the original starting spot.

Using the four cursor control keys (h, j, k, and 1), move around in the file for a little bit until you are comfortable with what's happening on the screen. Now try using the Backspace and Enter keys to see how they help you move around.

Move to the middle of a line:

```
total 29
drwx------  2 taylor       512 Nov 21 10:39 Archives/
drwx------  3 taylor       512 Dec  3 02:03 InfoWorld/
drwx------  2 taylor      1024 Dec  3 01:43 Mail/
```

Here you're middle digit in the file size of the second file in the listing. Here are two new cursor motion keys: the 0 (zero) key moves the cursor to the beginning of the line, and $ moves it to the end of the line. First, press 0:

```
total 29
drwx------  2 taylor       512 Nov 21 10:39 Archives/
drwx------  3 taylor       512 Dec  3 02:03 InfoWorld/
drwx------  2 taylor      1024 Dec  3 01:43 Mail/
```

Now press $ to move to the end of the line:

```
total 29
drwx------  2 taylor       512 Nov 21 10:39 Archives/
drwx------  3 taylor       512 Dec  3 02:03 InfoWorld/
drwx------  2 taylor      1024 Dec  3 01:43 Mail/
```

If you have arrow keys on your keyboard, try using them to see if they work the same way the h, j, k, and 1 keys work. If the arrow keys don't move you around, they might have shifted you into insert mode. If you type characters and they're added to the file, you need to press the Esc key to return to command mode. Wrap this up by leaving this edit session. Because vi now knows that you have modified the file, it will try to ensure that you don't quit without saving the changes:

```
~
~
:q
No write since last change (:quit! overrides)
```

Use :q! (shorthand for :quit) to quit without saving the changes.

> **NOTE:** In general, if you try to use a colon command in vi and the program complains that it might do something bad, try the command again, followed by an exclamation point. This is like saying, "Do it anyway!"

Stay in this file for the next section if you'd like, or use :q to quit.

Moving about a file using these six simple key commands is, on a small scale, much like the entire process of using the vi editor when working with files. Stick with these simple commands until you're comfortable moving around, and you will be well on your way to becoming proficient with vi.

Moving by Words and Pages

The description of the EMACS editor mentioned that because it's always in insert mode, all commands must include the Ctrl key. Well, it turns out that vi has its share of *Ctrl+key commands*, commands that require you to hold down the Ctrl key and press another key. In this section, you will learn about Ctrl+F, Ctrl+B, Ctrl+U, and Ctrl+D. These move you forward or backward a screen, and up or down half a screen of text, respectively.

Here are a few more commands: Ctrl+w moves you forward word by word, Ctrl+b moves you backward word by word, and the uppercase versions of these two commands have very similar, but not identical, functions.

To see how this works, you need to create a file that is larger than your screen. An easy way to do this is to save the output of a common command to a file over and over until the file is long enough. The system I use has lots of users, so I needed to use the who command just once. You might have to append the output of who to the big.output file a couple of times before the file is longer than 24 lines. (You can check by using wc, of course.)

```
% who > big.output; wc -l big.output
    40
% vi big.output
                 leungtc  ttyrV   Dec  1 18:27    (magenta)
tuyinhwa ttyrX   Dec  3 22:38   (expert)
hollenst ttyrZ   Dec  3 22:14   (dov)
brandt   ttyrb   Nov 28 23:03   (age)
holmes   ttyrj   Dec  3 21:59   (age)
yuxi     ttyrn   Dec  1 14:19   (pc115)
frodo    ttyro   Dec  3 22:01   (mentor)
labeck   ttyrt   Dec  3 22:02   (dov)
chenlx2  ttyru   Dec  3 21:53   (mentor)
leungtc  ttys0   Nov 28 15:11   (gold)
chinese  ttys2   Dec  3 22:53   (excalibur)
cdemmert ttys5   Dec  3 23:00   (mentor)
yuenca   ttys6   Dec  3 23:00   (mentor)
janitor  ttys7   Dec  3 18:18   (age)
mathisbp ttys8   Dec  3 23:17   (dov)
```

```
janitor  ttys9   Dec  3 18:18   (age)
cs541    ttysC   Dec  2 15:16   (solaria)
yansong  ttysL   Dec  1 14:44   (math)
mdps     ttysO   Nov 30 19:39   (localhost)
md       ttysU   Dec  2 08:45   (muller)
jac      ttysa   Dec  3 18:18   (localhost)
eichsted ttysb   Dec  3 23:21   (pc1)
sweett   ttysc   Dec  3 22:40   (dov)
"big.output" 40 lines, 1659 characters
```

Because I have only a 25-line display and the output is 40 lines long (you can see that on the status line at the bottom), there is more information in this file than the screen can display at once.

To see the next screenful, hold down the Ctrl key, press the F key, and then let both go. In future, when I indicate Ctrl+F that's what I mean you should do.

```
eichsted ttysb   Dec  3 23:21   (pc1)
sweett   ttysc   Dec  3 22:40   (dov)
wellman  ttysd   Dec  3 23:01   (dov)
tuttleno ttyse   Dec  3 23:03   (indyvax)
wu       ttysf   Dec  3 23:10   (term01)
daurismj ttysg   Dec  3 23:10   (dov)
cs414    ttysh   Dec  3 23:12   (xds)
cq       ttysi   Dec  3 23:13   (expert)
cdemmert ttysk   Dec  3 22:37   (xsun22)
jrlee    ttysn   Dec  3 22:53   (mac1)
fitzgejs ttyso   Dec  3 23:18   (dov)
doerrhb  ttysp   Dec  3 23:20   (dov)
cdemmert ttysq   Dec  3 23:00   (xsun22)
frazierw ttysr   Dec  3 23:01   (dov)
buckeye  ttyss   Dec  3 23:20   (mac2)
mtaylor  ttyst   Dec  3 23:22   (dov)
look     ttysu   Dec  3 23:12   (age)
janitor  ttysw   Dec  3 18:29   (age)
ajones   ttysx   Dec  3 23:23   (rass)
~
~
~
~
```

Notice that the entire screen was rewritten, and that the familiar tilde characters have popped up again to indicate the end of the file.

By default, vi has a two-line overlap when you move from screen to screen. If you look carefully, you can see that both eichsted and sweett show up on both screens of data. This doesn't mean that they appear twice in the file; rather, vi is trying to help you not get lost while you wander through the file.

Now, what do you think will happen if you press Ctrl+U?

```
leungtc  ttys0   Nov 28 15:11   (gold)
chinese  ttys2   Dec  3 22:53   (excalibur)
cdemmert ttys5   Dec  3 23:00   (mentor)
yuenca   ttys6   Dec  3 23:00   (mentor)
janitor  ttys7   Dec  3 18:18   (age)
```

```
mathisbp ttys8    Dec  3 23:17   (dov)
janitor  ttys9    Dec  3 18:18   (age)
cs541    ttysC    Dec  2 15:16   (solaria)
yansong  ttysL    Dec  1 14:44   (math)
mdps     ttysO    Nov 30 19:39   (localhost)
md       ttysU    Dec  2 08:45   (muller)
jac      ttysa    Dec  3 18:18   (localhost)
eichsted ttysb    Dec  3 23:21   (pc1)
sweett   ttysc    Dec  3 22:40   (dov)
wellman  ttysd    Dec  3 23:01   (dov)
tuttleno ttyse    Dec  3 23:03   (indyvax)
wu       ttysf    Dec  3 23:10   (term01)
daurismj ttysg    Dec  3 23:10   (dov)
cs414    ttysh    Dec  3 23:12   (xds)
cq       ttysi    Dec  3 23:13   (expert)
cdemmert ttysk    Dec  3 22:37   (xsun22)
jrlee    ttysn    Dec  3 22:53   (mac1)
fitzgejs ttyso    Dec  3 23:18   (dov)
```

The command has moved you up half a screen. Notice where eichsted and sweett are now. Instead of the text being replaced at once, as when you used Ctrl+F, the text was scrolled downward a line at a time, each new line being added as the program went along. The Ctrl+U command might work either way—one line or an entire screen at a time— for you.

Now it's time to try moving around in this file word by word. Find the w key on your keyboard and press it once to see what happens.

```
leungtc  ttys0    Nov 28 15:11   (gold)
chinese  ttys2    Dec  3 22:53   (excalibur)
cdemmert ttys5    Dec  3 23:00   (mentor)
```

Now press w six times more, noting that the cursor stops three times in the field to indicate what time the user logged into the system (15:11 in this listing). Now your cursor should be sitting on the parenthesized field:

```
leungtc  ttys0    Nov 28 15:11   (gold)
chinese  ttys2    Dec  3 22:53   (excalibur)
cdemmert ttys5    Dec  3 23:00   (mentor)
```

It's time to move backward. Press b a few times; your cursor moves backward to the beginning of each word.

What happens if you try to move backward but you're already on the first word of the line, or try to move forward but you're already on the last word?

Using the various keys you've learned, move back to the beginning of the line beginning with leungtc, which you used in the last exercise:

```
leungtc  ttys0    Nov 28 15:11   (gold)
chinese  ttys2    Dec  3 22:53   (excalibur)
cdemmert ttys5    Dec  3 23:00   (mentor)
```

This time press the uppercase letter W, rather than the lowercase w, to move through this line. Can you see the difference? Notice what happens when you hit the time field and the parenthesized words. Instead of pressing w seven times to move to the left parenthesis before gold, you can press W just five times.

Try moving backward using the B command. Notice that the B command differs from the b command the same way the W command differs from the w command.

Moving about forward and backward word by word, being able to move half screens or full screens at a time, and being able to zero in on specific spots with the h, j, k, and l cursor-motion keys give you quite a range of motion. Practice using these commands in various combinations to move your cursor to specific characters in your sample file.

Inserting Text into the File with *i, a, o,* and *O*

Being able to move around in a file is useful. The real function of an editor, however, is to enable you to easily add and remove—in editor parlance, insert and delete—information. The vi editor has a special *insert mode*, which you must use in order to add to the contents of the file. There are four different ways to shift into insert mode, and you will learn about all of them in this section.

The first way to switch to insert mode is to enter the letter i, which, mnemonically enough, inserts text into the file. The other commands that accomplish more or less the same thing are a, which appends text to the file; o, which opens up a line below the current line; and O, which opens up a line above the current line.

This time you want to start with a clean file, so quit from the big.output editing session and start vi again, this time specifying a nonexistent file called buckaroo:

```
% vi buckaroo
~
~
~
~
~
~
~
~
~
~
~
~
~
~
~
~
~
~
~
~
~
~
"buckaroo" [New file]
```

Notice that vi reminds you that this file doesn't exist; the bottom of the screen says New file instead of indicating the number of lines and characters.

Now it's time to try using insert mode. Press k once:

```
~
~
~
~
```

The system beeps at you because you haven't moved into insert mode yet, and k still has its command meaning of moving down a line (and of course, there isn't another line yet).

Press the i key to move into insert mode, and then press the k key again:

```
k_
~
~
~
```

There you go! You've added a character to the file.

Press the Backspace key, which will move the cursor over the letter k:

```
k
~
~
~
```

Now see what happens when you press Esc to leave insert mode and return to the vi command mode:

```
~
~
~
```

Notice that the k vanished when you pressed Esc. That's because vi only saves text you've entered to the left of or above the cursor, not the letter the cursor is resting on.

Now move back into insert mode by pressing i and enter a few sentences from a favorite book of mine:

```
"He's not even here," went the conservation.
"Banzai."
"Where is he?"
"At a hotpsial in El paso."
"What? Why werent' we informed? What's wrong with him?"_
~
~
```

> **NOTE:** Movie buffs will perhaps recognize that this text comes from the book *Buckaroo Banzai*. The film *The Adventures of Buckaroo Banzai Across the Eighth Dimension* is based on this very fun book.

I've deliberately left some typing errors in the text here. Fixing them will demonstrate some important features of the vi editor. If you fixed them as you went along, that's okay, and if you added errors of your own, that's okay, too!

Press Esc to leave insert mode. Press Esc a second time to ensure that it worked; remember that vi beeps to remind you that you're already in command mode.

Now use the cursor motion keys (h, j, k, and l) to move the cursor to any point on the first line:

```
"He's not even here," went the conservation.
"Banzai."
"Where is he?"
"At the hotpsial in El paso."
"What? Why werent' we informed? What's wrong with him?"
~
~
```

It turns out that there's a line of dialogue missing between the line you're on and `"Banzai."` One way to enter the line would be to move to the beginning of the line `"Banzai."`, insert the new text, and press Enter before pressing Esc to quit insert mode. But vi has a special command—o—to open a line immediately below the current line for inserting text. Press o on your keyboard and follow along:

```
"He's not even here," went the conservation.
_
"Banzai."
"Where is he?"
"At the hotpsial in El paso."
"What? Why werent' we informed? What's wrong with him?"
~
~
```

Now type the missing text:

```
"He's not even here," went the conservation.
"Who?"_
"Banzai."
"Where is he?"
"At the hotpsial in El paso."
"What? Why werent' we informed? What's wrong with him?"
~
~
```

That's it. Press Esc to return to command mode.

The problem with the snippet of dialogue you're using is that there's no way to figure out who is talking. Adding a line above this dialogue helps identify the speakers. Again, use cursor motion keys to place the cursor on the top line:

```
"He's not _even here," went the conservation.
"Banzai."
"Where is he?"
"At the hotpsial in El paso."
```

```
"What? Why werent' we informed? What's wrong with him?"
~
~
```

Now you face a dilemma. You want to open up a line for new text, but you want the line to be *above* the current line, not below it. It happens that vi can do that, too. Instead of using the o command, use its big brother O instead. When you press O, here's what you see:

```
_
"He's not even here," went the conservation.
"Banzai."
"Where is he?"
"At the hotpsial in El paso."
"What? Why werent' we informed? What's wrong with him?"
~
~
```

Type the new sentence and press Esc.

```
I found myself stealing a peek at my own watch and overhead
General Catbird's
aide give him the latest._
"He's not even here," went the conservation.
"Banzai."
"Where is he?"
"At the hotpsial in El paso."
"What? Why werent' we informed? What's wrong with him?"
~
~
```

Now the dialogue makes a bit more sense. The conversation, overheard by the narrator, takes place between the general and his aide.

There are a few words missing in one of the lines, so the next task is to insert them. Use the cursor keys to move the cursor to the fifth line, just after the word "Where":

```
I found myself stealing a peek at my own watch and overhead
General Catbird's
aide give him the latest.
"He's not even here," went the conservation.
"Banzai."
"Where_is he?"
"At the hotpsial in El paso."
"What? Why werent' we informed? What's wrong with him?"
~
~
```

At this juncture, you need to add the words "the hell" to make the sentence a bit stronger (and correct). You can use i to insert the text, but then you end up with a trailing space. Instead, you can add text immediately after the current cursor location by using the a key to append the information. When you press a, the cursor moves one character to the right:

```
I found myself stealing a peek at my own watch and overhead
General Catbird's
aide give him the latest.
```

```
"He's not even here," went the conservation.
"Banzai."
"Where is he?"
"At the hotpsial in El paso."
"What? Why werent' we informed? What's wrong with him?"
~
~
```

Here's where vi can be difficult to use. You're in insert mode, but there's no way for you to know that. When you type the letters you want to add, the screen shows that they are appended. But what if you think you're in insert mode when you're actually in command mode? One trick you could use to ensure you're in insert mode is to press the command key a second time. If the letter "a" shows up in the text, simply backspace over it; now you know that you're in append mode. When you're done entering the new characters, and you're still in append mode, here's what your screen looks like:

```
I found myself stealing a peek at my own watch and overhead
General Catbird's
aide give him the latest.
"He's not even here," went the conservation.
"Banzai."
"Where the hell is he?"
"At the hotpsial in El paso."
"What? Why werent' we informed? What's wrong with him?"
~
~
```

Notice that the cursor stayed on the "i" in "is" throughout this operation. Press Esc to return to command mode. Notice that the cursor finally hops off the "i" and moves left one character.

To differentiate between the i and a commands, remember that the *insert* command always adds the new information immediately before the cursor, whereas *append* adds the information immediately after the cursor.

With this in mind, try to fix the apostrophe problem in the word "werent'" on the last line. Move the cursor to the "n" in that word:

```
"Where the hell is he?"
"At the hotpsial in El paso."
"What? Why werent' we informed? What's wrong with him?"
~
```

Now, to put the apostrophe immediately after the current character, do you want to use the insert command (i) or the append (a) command? If you said "Append," give yourself a pat on the back! Press a to append the apostrophe:

```
"Where the hell is he?"
"At the hotpsial in El paso."
"What? Why werent' we informed? What's wrong with him?"
~
```

Press the ' key once and press Esc.

Quit `vi`. Use `:q`, and the program reminds you that you haven't saved your changes to this new file:

```
~
~
No write since last change (:quit! overrides)
```

To write the changes, you need a new command, so I'll give you a preview of a set of colon commands you will learn later in this chapter. Type `:` (the colon character), which moves the cursor to the bottom of the screen.

```
~
~
:_
```

Now press `w` to write out the file, and then press the Enter key:

```
~
~
"buckaroo" 8 lines, 271 characters
```

It's okay to leave `vi` now. Use `:q` to quit and you're safely back at the command prompt. A quick `cat` confirms that the tildes were not included in the file itself:

```
%
% cat buckaroo
I found myself stealing a peek at my own watch and overhead
General Catbird's
aide give him the latest.
"He's not even here," went the conservation.
"Banzai."
"Where the hell is he?"
"At the hotpsial in El paso."
"What? Why weren't' we informed? What's wrong with him?"
%
```

As you can tell, the `vi` editor is quite powerful, and it has a plethora of commands. Just moving about and inserting text, you have learned 24 commands, as summarized in Table 7.1.

Table 7.1. Summary of `vi` motion and insertion commands.

Command	Meaning
0	Move to beginning of line.
$	Move to end of line.
a	Append text—move into insert mode after the current character.
^b	Back up one screen of text.
B	Back up one space-delimited word.
b	Back up one word.

Command	*Meaning*
Backspace	Move left one character.
^d	Move down half a page.
Esc	Leave insert mode, return to command mode.
^f	Move forward one screen of text.
h	Move left one character.
i	Insert text—move into insert mode before the current character.
j	Move down one line.
k	Move up one line.
l	Move right one character.
O	Open new line for insert above the current line.
o	Open new line for insert below the current line.
Enter	Move to beginning of next line.
^u	Move up half a page.
W	Move forward one space-delimited word.
w	Move forward one word.
:w	Write the edit buffer to the system.
:q	Quit vi and return to the UNIX prompt.
:q!	Quit vi and return to the system, throwing away any changes made to the file.

WARNING: In this table, I've introduced a simple shorthand notation that's worth explaining. UNIX users often use a caret followed by a character instead of the awkward Ctrl+c notation. Therefore, ^f has the same meaning as Ctrl+F. Expressing this operation as ^f does not change the way it's performed: you'd still press and hold down the Ctrl key and then press the lowercase F key. It's just a shorter notation.

You've already learned quite a few commands, but you've barely scratched the surface of the powerful vi command!

Deleting Text

You now have many of the pieces you need to work efficiently with the vi editor, to zip to any point in the file, or to add text wherever you like. Now you need to learn how to delete characters, words, and lines.

The simplest form of the delete command is the x command, which functions as though you are writing an X over a letter you don't want on a printed page: it deletes the character under the cursor. Press x five times and you delete five characters. Deleting a line of text this way can be quite tedious, so vi has some alternate commands. (Are you surprised?) One command that many vi users don't know about is the D, or *delete through end of line*, command. Wherever you are on a line, pressing D immediately deletes everything after the cursor to the end of that line of text.

If there's an uppercase D command, you can just bet there's a lowercase d command too. The d command is the first of a set of more sophisticated vi commands, which are followed by a second command that indicates what you'd like to do with the command. You already know that w and W move you forward a word in the file; they're known as *addressing commands* in vi. You can follow d with one of these addressing commands to specify what you would like to delete. For example, to delete a line, simply press dd.

Sometimes you might get a bit overzealous and delete more than you anticipated. That's not a problem—well, not too much of a problem—because vi remembers the state of the file prior to the most recent action taken. To undo a deletion (or insertion, for that matter), use the u command. To undo a line of changes, use the U command. Be aware that once you've moved off the line in question, the U command is unable to restore it!

Start vi again with the big.output file you used earlier:

```
leungtc   ttyrV    Dec  1 18:27   (magenta)
tuyinhwa  ttyrX    Dec  3 22:38   (expert)
hollenst  ttyrZ    Dec  3 22:14   (dov)
brandt    ttyrb    Nov 28 23:03   (age)
holmes    ttyrj    Dec  3 21:59   (age)
yuxi      ttyrn    Dec  1 14:19   (pc)
frodo     ttyro    Dec  3 22:01   (mentor)
labeck    ttyrt    Dec  3 22:02   (dov)
chenlx2   ttyru    Dec  3 21:53   (mentor)
leungtc   ttys0    Nov 28 15:11   (gold)
chinese   ttys2    Dec  3 22:53   (excalibur)
cdemmert  ttys5    Dec  3 23:00   (mentor)
yuenca    ttys6    Dec  3 23:00   (mentor)
janitor   ttys7    Dec  3 18:18   (age)
mathisbp  ttys8    Dec  3 23:17   (dov)
janitor   ttys9    Dec  3 18:18   (age)
cs541     ttysC    Dec  2 15:16   (solaria)
yansong   ttysL    Dec  1 14:44   (math)
mdps      ttysO    Nov 30 19:39   (localhost)
md        ttysU    Dec  2 08:45   (muller)
jac       ttysa    Dec  3 18:18   (localhost)
eichsted  ttysb    Dec  3 23:21   (pc1)
```

```
sweett   ttysc   Dec  3 22:40   (dov)
"big.output" 40 lines, 1659 characters
```

Press the x key a few times to delete a few characters from the beginning of the file:

```
gtc ttyrV   Dec  1 18:27   (magenta)
tuyinhwa ttyrX   Dec  3 22:38   (expert)
hollenst ttyrZ   Dec  3 22:14   (dov)
brandt   ttyrb   Nov 28 23:03   (age)
holmes   ttyrj   Dec  3 21:59   (age)
```

Now press u to undo the last deletion:

```
ngtc ttyrV   Dec  1 18:27   (magenta)
tuyinhwa ttyrX   Dec  3 22:38   (expert)
hollenst ttyrZ   Dec  3 22:14   (dov)
brandt   ttyrb   Nov 28 23:03   (age)
holmes   ttyrj   Dec  3 21:59   (age)
```

If you press u again, what do you think will happen?

```
gtc ttyrV   Dec  1 18:27   (magenta)
tuyinhwa ttyrX   Dec  3 22:38   (expert)
hollenst ttyrZ   Dec  3 22:14   (dov)
brandt   ttyrb   Nov 28 23:03   (age)
holmes   ttyrj   Dec  3 21:59   (age)
```

The undo command alternates between the last command having happened or not having happened. To explain it a bit better, the undo command is an action unto itself, so the second time you press u, you're undoing the undo command that you just requested. Press the u key a few more times if you need to convince yourself that this is the case.

It's time to make some bigger changes to the file. Press dw twice to delete the current word and the next word in the file. It should look something like this after the first dw:

```
ttyrV   Dec  1 18:27   (magenta)
tuyinhwa ttyrX   Dec  3 22:38   (expert)
hollenst ttyrZ   Dec  3 22:14   (dov)
brandt   ttyrb   Nov 28 23:03   (age)
holmes   ttyrj   Dec  3 21:59   (age)
```

Then it should look like this after the second dw:

```
Dec  1 18:27   (magenta)
tuyinhwa ttyrX   Dec  3 22:38   (expert)
hollenst ttyrZ   Dec  3 22:14   (dov)
brandt   ttyrb   Nov 28 23:03   (age)
holmes   ttyrj   Dec  3 21:59   (age)
```

Press u. You see that you can only undo the most recent command. At this point, though, because you haven't moved from the line you're editing, the U, or undo a line of changes, command will restore the line to its original splendor:

```
leungtc  ttyrV   Dec  1 18:27   (magenta)
tuyinhwa ttyrX   Dec  3 22:38   (expert)
hollenst ttyrZ   Dec  3 22:14   (dov)
brandt   ttyrb   Nov 28 23:03   (age)
holmes   ttyrj   Dec  3 21:59   (age)
```

Well, in the end, you really don't want to see some of these folk. Fortunately, you can delete lines with the dd command. What if I want to delete the entries for chinese and janitor, both of which are visible on this screen?

The first step is to use the cursor keys to move down to any place on the line for the chinese account, about halfway down the screen:

```
chenlx2  ttyru   Dec  3 21:53   (mentor)
leungtc  ttys0   Nov 28 15:11   (gold)
chinese  ttys2   Dec  3 22:53   (excalibur)
cdemmert ttys5   Dec  3 23:00   (mentor)
yuenca   ttys6   Dec  3 23:00   (mentor)
janitor  ttys7   Dec  3 18:18   (age)
mathisbp ttys8   Dec  3 23:17   (dov)
```

If your cursor isn't somewhere in the middle of this line, move it so that you too are not at an edge.

Instead of removing this line completely, perhaps you'd rather just remove the date, time, and name of the system (in parentheses) instead. To accomplish this, you don't need to press dw a bunch of times, or even x a lot of times, but rather just D to delete through the end of the line:

```
chenlx2  ttyru   Dec  3 21:53   (mentor)
leungtc  ttys0   Nov 28 15:11   (gold)
chinese  ttys2   _
cdemmert ttys5   Dec  3 23:00   (mentor)
yuenca   ttys6   Dec  3 23:00   (mentor)
janitor  ttys7   Dec  3 18:18   (age)
mathisbp ttys8   Dec  3 23:17   (dov)
```

Oh, that's not quite what you wanted to do. No problem, the undo command can fix it. Simply pressing the u key restores the text you deleted:

```
chenlx2  ttyru   Dec  3 21:53   (mentor)
leungtc  ttys0   Nov 28 15:11   (gold)
chinese  ttys2   Dec  3 22:53   (excalibur)
cdemmert ttys5   Dec  3 23:00   (mentor)
yuenca   ttys6   Dec  3 23:00   (mentor)
janitor  ttys7   Dec  3 18:18   (age)
mathisbp ttys8   Dec  3 23:17   (dov)
```

The problem is that you used the wrong command to delete the two entries chinese and janitor from the file. Instead of using the D command, you should use dd. Pressing dd once has these results:

```
Dec  1 18:27     (magenta)
tuyinhwa ttyrX   Dec  3 22:38   (expert)
hollenst ttyrZ   Dec  3 22:14   (dov)
brandt   ttyrb   Nov 28 23:03   (age)
holmes   ttyrj   Dec  3 21:59   (age)
yuxi     ttyrn   Dec  1 14:19   (pc)
frodo    ttyro   Dec  3 22:01   (mentor)
labeck   ttyrt   Dec  3 22:02   (dov)
```

```
chenlx2  ttyru    Dec  3 21:53    (mentor)
leungtc  ttys0    Nov 28 15:11    (gold)
cdemmert ttys5    Dec  3 23:00    (mentor)
yuenca   ttys6    Dec  3 23:00    (mentor)
janitor  ttys7    Dec  3 18:18    (age)
mathisbp ttys8    Dec  3 23:17    (dov)
janitor  ttys9    Dec  3 18:18    (age)
cs541    ttysC    Dec  2 15:16    (solaria)
yansong  ttysL    Dec  1 14:44    (math)
mdps     ttys0    Nov 30 19:39    (localhost)
md       ttysU    Dec  2 08:45    (muller)
jac      ttysa    Dec  3 18:18    (localhost)
eichsted ttysb    Dec  3 23:21    (pc1)
sweett   ttysc    Dec  3 22:40    (dov)
wellman  ttysd    Dec  3 23:01    (dov)
```

Notice that a new line of information has been pulled onto the screen at the bottom to replace the blank line that you removed. If you try using the u command now, what happens? You're almost done. A few presses of the Enter key and you're down to the entry for the janitor account. Using dd removes that line too:

```
Dec  1 18:27     (magenta)
tuyinhwa ttyrX    Dec  3 22:38    (expert)
hollenst ttyrZ    Dec  3 22:14    (dov)
brandt   ttyrb    Nov 28 23:03    (age)
holmes   ttyrj    Dec  3 21:59    (age)
yuxi     ttyrn    Dec  1 14:19    (pc)
frodo    ttyro    Dec  3 22:01    (mentor)
labeck   ttyrt    Dec  3 22:02    (dov)
chenlx2  ttyru    Dec  3 21:53    (mentor)
leungtc  ttys0    Nov 28 15:11    (gold)
cdemmert ttys5    Dec  3 23:00    (mentor)
yuenca   ttys6    Dec  3 23:00    (mentor)
mathisbp ttys8    Dec  3 23:17    (dov)
janitor  ttys9    Dec  3 18:18    (age)
cs541    ttysC    Dec  2 15:16    (solaria)
yansong  ttysL    Dec  1 14:44    (math)
mdps     ttys0    Nov 30 19:39    (localhost)
md       ttysU    Dec  2 08:45    (muller)
jac      ttysa    Dec  3 18:18    (localhost)
eichsted ttysb    Dec  3 23:21    (pc1)
sweett   ttysc    Dec  3 22:40    (dov)
wellman  ttysd    Dec  3 23:01    (dov)
tuttleno ttyse    Dec  3 23:03    (indyvax)
```

Each line below the one deleted moves up a line to fill in the blank space, and a new line, for tuttleno, moves up from the following screen.

Now you want to return to the buckaroo file to remedy some of the horrendous typographic errors! It doesn't matter whether you save the changes you've just made to the file, so use :q! to quit, discarding these edit changes to the big.output file. Entering vi buckaroo starts vi again:

```
I found myself stealing a peek at my own watch and overhead
General Catbird's
aide give him the latest.
```

```
"He's not even here," went the conservation.
"Banzai."
"Where the hell is he?"
"At the hotpsial in El paso."
"What? Why weren't' we informed? What's wrong with him?"
~
~
~
~
~
~
~
~
~
~
~
~
~
"buckaroo" 8 lines, 271 characters
```

There are a few fixes you can make in short order. The first is to change "conservation" to "conversation" on the third line. To move there, press the Return key twice and then use W to zip forward until the cursor is at the first letter of the word you're editing:

```
I found myself stealing a peek at my own watch and overhead
General Catbird's
aide give him the latest.
"He's not even here," went the conservation.
"Banzai."
"Where the hell is he?"
```

Then use the dw command:

```
I found myself stealing a peek at my own watch and overhead
General Catbird's
aide give him the latest.
"He's not even here," went the .
"Banzai."
"Where the hell is he?"
```

Now enter insert mode by pressing i and type in the correct spelling of the word "conversation." Then press Esc:

```
I found myself stealing a peek at my own watch and overhead
General Catbird's
aide give him the latest.
"He's not even here," went the conversation.
"Banzai."
"Where the hell is he?"
```

That's one fix. Now move down a few lines to fix the atrocious misspelling of "hospital":

```
"Banzai."
"Where the hell is he?"
"At the hotpsial in El paso."
"What? Why weren't' we informed? What's wrong with him?"
~
```

Again, use dw to delete the word, then i to enter insert mode. Type "hospital" and press Esc, and all is well on the line:

```
"Banzai."
"Where the hell is he?"
"At the hospital in El paso."
"What? Why weren't' we informed? What's wrong with him?"
~
```

Well, almost all is well. The first letter of "Paso" needs to be capitalized. Move to it by pressing w:

```
"Banzai."
"Where the hell is he?"
"At the hospital in El paso."
"What? Why weren't' we informed? What's wrong with him?"
~
```

It's time for a secret vi expert command! Instead of pressing x to delete the letter, i to enter insert mode, P as the correct letter, and Esc to return to command mode, there's a much faster way to transpose case: the ~ command. Press the ~ character once, and here's what happens:

```
"Banzai."
"Where the hell is he?"
"At the hospital in El Paso."
"What? Why weren't' we informed? What's wrong with him?"
~
```

Cool, isn't it? Back up to the beginning of the word again, using the h command, and press ~ a few times to see what happens. Notice that each time you press ~, the character's case switches (transposes) and the cursor moves to the next character. Press ~ four times and you should end up with this:

```
"Banzai."
"Where the hell is he?"
"At the hospital in El pASO."
"What? Why weren't' we informed? What's wrong with him?"
~
```

Back up to the beginning of the word and press ~ four more times until the word is correct.

One more slight change and the file is fixed! Move to the last line of the file, to the extra apostrophe in the word "weren't'," and use the x key to delete the offending character. The screen should now look like this:

```
I found myself stealing a peek at my own watch and overhead
General Catbird's
aide give him the latest.
"He's not even here," went the conversation.
"Banzai."
"Where the hell is he?"
"At the hospital in El Paso."
```

```
"What? Why weren't we informed? What's wrong with him?"
~
~
~
~
~
~
~
~
~
~
~
~
~
~
```

That looks great! It's time to save it for posterity. Use `:wq`, a shortcut that has `vi` write out the changes, and then immediately quit the program:

```
~
~
~
"buckaroo" 8 lines, 270 characters
%
```

Not only have you learned about the variety of deletion options in `vi`, but you have also learned a few simple shortcut commands: `~`, which transposes case, and `:wq`, which writes out the changes and quits the program all in one step.

You should feel pleased; you're now a productive and knowledgeable `vi` user, and you can modify files, making easy or tough changes. Go back to your system and experiment further, modifying some of the other files. Be careful, though, not to make changes in any of your dot files (for example, `.cshrc`), lest you cause trouble that would be difficult to fix!

Searching within a File

With the addition of two more capabilities, you'll be ready to face down any `vi` expert, demonstrating your skill and knowledge of the editor. Much more importantly, you'll be able to really fly through files, moving immediately to the information you desire.

The two new capabilities are for finding specific words or phrases in a file and for moving to specific lines in a file. Similar to searching for patterns in more and page, `/pattern` searches forward in the file for a specified pattern, and `?pattern` searches backward for the specified pattern. To repeat the previous search, use the `n` command to tell `vi` to search again, in the same direction, for the same pattern.

You can easily move to any specific line in a file using the `G`, or *go to line*, command. If you press a number before you press `G`, the cursor will move to that line in the file. If you press `G` without a line number, the cursor will zip you to the very last line of the file by default.

Start vi again with the big.output file:

```
leungtc  ttyrV   Dec  1 18:27   (magenta)
tuyinhwa ttyrX   Dec  3 22:38   (expert)
hollenst ttyrZ   Dec  3 22:14   (dov)
brandt   ttyrb   Nov 28 23:03   (age)
holmes   ttyrj   Dec  3 21:59   (age)
yuxi     ttyrn   Dec  1 14:19   (pc)
frodo    ttyro   Dec  3 22:01   (mentor)
labeck   ttyrt   Dec  3 22:02   (dov)
chenlx2  ttyru   Dec  3 21:53   (mentor)
leungtc  ttys0   Nov 28 15:11   (gold)
chinese  ttys2   Dec  3 22:53   (excalibur)
cdemmert ttys5   Dec  3 23:00   (mentor)
yuenca   ttys6   Dec  3 23:00   (mentor)
janitor  ttys7   Dec  3 18:18   (age)
mathisbp ttys8   Dec  3 23:17   (dov)
janitor  ttys9   Dec  3 18:18   (age)
cs541    ttysC   Dec  2 15:16   (solaria)
yansong  ttysL   Dec  1 14:44   (math)
mdps     ttysO   Nov 30 19:39   (localhost)
md       ttysU   Dec  2 08:45   (muller)
jac      ttysa   Dec  3 18:18   (localhost)
eichsted ttysb   Dec  3 23:21   (pc1)
sweett   ttysc   Dec  3 22:40   (dov)
"big.output" 40 lines, 1659 characters
```

Remember that you used :q! to quit earlier, so your changes were not retained.

To move to the very last line of the file, press G once:

```
cdemmert ttysk   Dec  3 22:37   (xsun)
jrlee    ttysn   Dec  3 22:53   (mac1)
fitzgejs ttyso   Dec  3 23:18   (dov)
doerrhb  ttysp   Dec  3 23:20   (dov)
cdemmert ttysq   Dec  3 23:00   (xsun)
frazierw ttysr   Dec  3 23:01   (dov)
buckeye  ttyss   Dec  3 23:20   (mac2)
mtaylor  ttyst   Dec  3 23:22   (dov)
look     ttysu   Dec  3 23:12   (age)
janitor  ttysw   Dec  3 18:29   (age)
ajones   ttysx   Dec  3 23:23   (rassilon)
~
~
~
~
~
~
~
~
~
~
~
~
~
```

To move to the third line of the file, press 3 followed by G:

```
leungtc  ttyrV   Dec  1 18:27   (magenta)
tuyinhwa ttyrX   Dec  3 22:38   (expert)
hollenst ttyrZ   Dec  3 22:14   (dov)
```

```
brandt    ttyrb    Nov 28 23:03   (age)
holmes    ttyrj    Dec  3 21:59   (age)
yuxi      ttyrn    Dec  1 14:19   (pc)
frodo     ttyro    Dec  3 22:01   (mentor)
labeck    ttyrt    Dec  3 22:02   (dov)
chenlx2   ttyru    Dec  3 21:53   (mentor)
leungtc   ttys0    Nov 28 15:11   (gold)
chinese   ttys2    Dec  3 22:53   (excalibur)
cdemmert  ttys5    Dec  3 23:00   (mentor)
yuenca    ttys6    Dec  3 23:00   (mentor)
janitor   ttys7    Dec  3 18:18   (age)
mathisbp  ttys8    Dec  3 23:17   (dov)
janitor   ttys9    Dec  3 18:18   (age)
cs541     ttysC    Dec  2 15:16   (solaria)
yansong   ttysL    Dec  1 14:44   (math)
mdps      ttysO    Nov 30 19:39   (localhost)
md        ttysU    Dec  2 08:45   (muller)
jac       ttysa    Dec  3 18:18   (localhost)
eichsted  ttysb    Dec  3 23:21   (pc1)
sweett    ttysc    Dec  3 22:40   (dov)
```

Notice that the cursor is on the third line of the file.

Now it's time to search. From your previous travels in this file, you know that the very last line is for the account ajones, but instead of using G to move there directly, you can search for the specified pattern by using the / search command.

Pressing / immediately moves the cursor to the bottom of the screen:

```
md        ttysU    Dec  2 08:45   (mueller)
jac       ttysa    Dec  3 18:18   (localhost)
eichsted  ttysb    Dec  3 23:21   (pc1)
sweett    ttysc    Dec  3 22:40   (dov)
/_
```

Now you can type in the pattern *ajones*:

```
md        ttysU    Dec  2 08:45   (mueller)
jac       ttysa    Dec  3 18:18   (localhost)
eichsted  ttysb    Dec  3 23:21   (pc1)
sweett    ttysc    Dec  3 22:40   (dov)
/ajones_
```

When you press Return, vi spins through the file and moves you to the first line it finds that contains the specified pattern:

```
cdemmert  ttysk    Dec  3 22:37   (xsun)
jrlee     ttysn    Dec  3 22:53   (mac1)
fitzgejs  ttyso    Dec  3 23:18   (dov)
doerrhb   ttysp    Dec  3 23:20   (dov)
cdemmert  ttysq    Dec  3 23:00   (xsun)
frazierw  ttysr    Dec  3 23:01   (dov)
buckeye   ttyss    Dec  3 23:20   (mac2)
mtaylor   ttyst    Dec  3 23:22   (dov)
look      ttysu    Dec  3 23:12   (age)
janitor   ttysw    Dec  3 18:29   (age)
ajones    ttysx    Dec  3 23:23   (rassilon)
~
```

```
~
~
~
~
~
~
~
~
~
~
~
```

If you press n to search for this pattern again, a slash appears at the very bottom line to show that vi understood your request. But the cursor stays exactly where it is, which indicates that this is the only occurrence of the pattern in this file.

You notice that the account janitor has all sorts of sessions running. To search backward for occurrences of their account, use the ? command:

```
~
~
?janitor_
```

The first search moves the cursor up one line, which leaves the screen looking almost the same:

```
cdemmert ttysk   Dec  3 22:37   (xsun)
jrlee    ttysn   Dec  3 22:53   (mac1)
fitzgejs ttyso   Dec  3 23:18   (dov)
doerrhb  ttysp   Dec  3 23:20   (dov)
cdemmert ttysq   Dec  3 23:00   (xsun)
frazierw ttysr   Dec  3 23:01   (dov)
buckeye  ttyss   Dec  3 23:20   (mac2)
mtaylor  ttyst   Dec  3 23:22   (dov)
look     ttysu   Dec  3 23:12   (age)
janitor  ttysw   Dec  3 18:29   (age)
ajones   ttysx   Dec  3 23:23   (rassilon)
~
~
~
~
~
~
~
~
~
~
~
?janitor
```

Here's where n, or *next search*, can come in handy. If you press n this time and there is another occurrence of the pattern in the file, vi moves you directly to the match:

```
yuxi     ttyrn   Dec  1 14:19   (pc)
frodo    ttyro   Dec  3 22:01   (mentor)
labeck   ttyrt   Dec  3 22:02   (dov)
chenlx2  ttyru   Dec  3 21:53   (mentor)
```

```
leungtc   ttys0    Nov 28 15:11   (gold)
chinese   ttys2    Dec  3 22:53   (excalibur)
cdemmert  ttys5    Dec  3 23:00   (mentor)
yuenca    ttys6    Dec  3 23:00   (mentor)
janitor   ttys7    Dec  3 18:18   (age)
mathisbp  ttys8    Dec  3 23:17   (dov)
janitor   ttys9    Dec  3 18:18   (age)
cs541     ttysC    Dec  2 15:16   (solaria)
yansong   ttysL    Dec  1 14:44   (math)
mdps      ttysO    Nov 30 19:39   (localhost)
md        ttysU    Dec  2 08:45   (muller)
jac       ttysa    Dec  3 18:18   (localhost)
eichsted  ttysb    Dec  3 23:21   (pc1)
sweett    ttysc    Dec  3 22:40   (dov)
wellman   ttysd    Dec  3 23:01   (dov)
tuttleno  ttyse    Dec  3 23:03   (indyvax)
wu        ttysf    Dec  3 23:10   (term01)
daurismj  ttysg    Dec  3 23:10   (dov)
cs414     ttysh    Dec  3 23:12   (xds)
```

When you're done, quit vi by using :q.

There are not dozens, but *hundreds* of commands in vi. Rather than overwhelm you with all of them, even in a table, I have opted instead to work with the most basic and important commands.

How to Start vi Correctly

The vi command wouldn't be part of UNIX if it didn't have some startup options available, but there really are only two worth mentioning. The -R flag sets up vi as a read-only file to ensure that you don't accidentally modify a file. The second option doesn't start with a hyphen, but with a plus sign: any command following the plus sign is used as an initial command to the program. This is more useful than it may sound. The command vi +$ sample, for example, starts the editor at the bottom of the file sample, and vi +17 sample starts the editor on the 17th line of sample.

First, this is the read-only format:

```
% vi -R buckaroo
I found myself stealing a peek at my own watch and overhead
General Catbird's
aide give him the latest.
"He's not even here," went the conversation.
"Banzai."
"Where the hell is he?"
"At the hospital in El Paso."
"What? Why weren't we informed? What's wrong with him?"
~
 ~
 ~
 ~
 ~
 ~
```

```
~
~
~
~
~
~
~
~
"buckaroo" [Read only] 8 lines, 270 characters
```

Notice the addition of the [Read only] message on the status line. You can edit the file, but if you try to save the edits with :w, you will see this:

```
~
~
"buckaroo" File is read only
```

Quit vi with :q!.

Next, recall that janitor occurs in many places in the big.output file. Start vi on the file line that contains the pattern janitor in the file:

```
% vi +/janitor big.output
brandt     ttyrb    Nov 28 23:03    (age)
holmes     ttyrj    Dec  3 21:59    (age)
yuxi       ttyrn    Dec  1 14:19    (pc)
frodo      ttyro    Dec  3 22:01    (mentor)
labeck     ttyrt    Dec  3 22:02    (dov)
chenlx2    ttyru    Dec  3 21:53    (mentor)
leungtc    ttys0    Nov 28 15:11    (gold)
chinese    ttys2    Dec  3 22:53    (excalibur)
cdemmert   ttys5    Dec  3 23:00    (mentor)
yuenca     ttys6    Dec  3 23:00    (mentor)
janitor    ttys7    Dec  3 18:18    (age)
mathisbp   ttys8    Dec  3 23:17    (dov)
janitor    ttys9    Dec  3 18:18    (age)
cs541      ttysC    Dec  2 15:16    (solaria)
yansong    ttysL    Dec  1 14:44    (math)
mdps       ttysO    Nov 30 19:39    (localhost)
md         ttysU    Dec  2 08:45    (muller)
jac        ttysa    Dec  3 18:18    (localhost)
eichsted   ttysb    Dec  3 23:21    (pc1)
sweett     ttysc    Dec  3 22:40    (dov)
wellman    ttysd    Dec  3 23:01    (dov)
tuttleno   ttyse    Dec  3 23:03    (indyvax)
wu         ttysf    Dec  3 23:10    (term01)
"big.output" 40 lines, 1659 characters
```

This time notice where the cursor is sitting.

Finally, launch vi with the cursor on the third line of the file buckaroo:

```
% vi +3 buckaroo
I found myself stealing a peek at my own watch and overhead
General Catbird's
aide give him the latest.
"He's not even here," went the conversation.
"Banzai."
```

```
"Where the hell is he?"
"At the hospital in El Paso."
"What? Why weren't we informed? What's wrong with him?"
~
~
~
~
~
~
~
~
~
~
~
~
~
~
"buckaroo" 8 lines, 270 characters
```

Again, notice where the cursor rests.

At times it can be helpful to know these two starting options. In particular, I often use +/ *pattern* to start the editor at a specific pattern, but you can use vi for years without ever knowing more than just the name of the command itself.

The Key Colon Commands in vi

Without too much explanation, you have learned a few colon commands, commands that begin with a colon. The colon immediately zooms the cursor to the bottom of the screen for further input. These commands are actually a subset of quite a large range of commands, all part of the ex editor that lives inside the vi visual interface. (That's why vi is known as an *interface* to an editor, rather than an editor itself.)

The colon commands that are most helpful are :w, which writes the buffer back to the system; :w *filename*, which writes the buffer to the specified file; :q, which quits the editor; :q!, which quits regardless of whether any changes have occurred; :r *filename*, which reads another file into the editor; :e *filename*, which switches to the specified file; and :n, which moves to the next file in a list of files.

Start vi again, this time specifying more than one file on the command line; vi quickly indicates that you want to edit more than one file:

```
% vi buckaroo big.output
2 files to edit.
```

Then it clears the screen and shows you the first file:

```
I found myself stealing a peek at my own watch and overhead
General Catbird's
aide give him the latest.
"He's not even here," went the conversation.
"Banzai."
```

```
"Where the hell is he?"
"At the hospital in El Paso."
"What? Why weren't we informed? What's wrong with him?"
~
~
~
~
~
~
~
~
~
~
~
~
~
~
~
"buckaroo" 8 lines, 270 characters
```

Using :w results in this:

```
~
~
~
"buckaroo" 8 lines, 270 characters
```

Instead, try writing to a different file, using :w newfile:

```
~
~
:w newfile_
```

When you press Return, you see this:

```
~
~
"newfile" [New file] 8 lines, 270 characters
```

Now pay attention to where the cursor is in the file. The :r, or *read file*, command always includes the contents of the file *below* the current line. Just before you press Return, then, here's what your screen looks like:

```
I found myself stealing a peek at my own watch and overhead
General Catbird's
aide give him the latest.
"He's not even here," went the conversation.
"Banzai."
"Where the hell is he?"
"At the hospital in El Paso."
"What? Why weren't we informed? What's wrong with him?"
~
~
~
~
~
~
~
~
```

```
~
~
~
~
~
~
:r newfile_
```

Pressing Return yields this:

```
I found myself stealing a peek at my own watch and overhead
General Catbird's
I found myself stealing a peek at my own watch and overhead
General Catbird's
aide give him the latest.
"He's not even here," went the conversation.
"Banzai."
"Where the hell is he?"
"At the hospital in El Paso."
"What? Why weren't we informed? What's wrong with him?"

aide give him the latest.
"He's not even here," went the conversation.
"Banzai."
"Where the hell is he?"
"At the hospital in El Paso."
"What? Why weren't we informed? What's wrong with him?"
~
~
~
~
~
~
~
```

This can be a helpful way to include one file within another, or to build a file that contains lots of other files.

Now that you've garbled the file, save it to a new file, buckaroo.confused:

```
~
~
:w buckaroo.confused_
```

Press Return:

```
~
~
"buckaroo.confused" [New file] 16 lines, 540 characters
```

Now it's time to move to the second file in the list of files given to vi at startup. To do this, I use the :n, or *next file*, command:

```
~
~
:n_
```

Pressing Return results in the next file being brought into the editor to replace the text removed earlier:

```
leungtc  ttyrV   Dec  1 18:27  (magenta)
tuyinhwa ttyrX   Dec  3 22:38  (expert)
hollenst ttyrZ   Dec  3 22:14  (dov)
brandt   ttyrb   Nov 28 23:03  (age)
holmes   ttyrj   Dec  3 21:59  (age)
yuxi     ttyrn   Dec  1 14:19  (pc)
frodo    ttyro   Dec  3 22:01  (mentor)
labeck   ttyrt   Dec  3 22:02  (dov)
chenlx2  ttyru   Dec  3 21:53  (mentor)
leungtc  ttys0   Nov 28 15:11  (gold)
chinese  ttys2   Dec  3 22:53  (excalibur)
cdemmert ttys5   Dec  3 23:00  (mentor)
yuenca   ttys6   Dec  3 23:00  (mentor)
janitor  ttys7   Dec  3 18:18  (age)
mathisbp ttys8   Dec  3 23:17  (dov)
janitor  ttys9   Dec  3 18:18  (age)
cs541    ttysC   Dec  2 15:16  (solaria)
yansong  ttysL   Dec  1 14:44  (math)
mdps     ttysO   Nov 30 19:39  (localhost)
md       ttysU   Dec  2 08:45  (muller)
jac      ttysa   Dec  3 18:18  (localhost)
eichsted ttysb   Dec  3 23:21  (pc1)
sweett   ttysc   Dec  3 22:40  (dov)
"big.output" 40 lines, 1659 characters
```

In the middle of working on this, you suddenly realize that you need to make a slight change to the recently saved buckaroo.confused file. That's where the :e command comes in handy. Using it, you can switch to any other file:

```
~
~
:e buckaroo.confused_
```

Press Return:

```
I found myself stealing a peek at my own watch and overhead
General Catbird's
I found myself stealing a peek at my own watch and overhead
General Catbird's
aide give him the latest.
"He's not even here," went the conversation.
"Banzai."
"Where the hell is he?"
"At the hospital in El Paso."
"What? Why weren't we informed? What's wrong with him?"

aide give him the latest.
"He's not even here," went the conversation.
"Banzai."
"Where the hell is he?"
"At the hospital in El Paso."
"What? Why weren't we informed? What's wrong with him?"
~
~
~
```

```
~
~
~
~
"buckaroo.confused" 16 lines, 540 characters
```

Table 7.2 summarizes the basic vi commands you learned in this section.

Table 7.2. Basic vi commands.

Command	Meaning
0	Move to beginning of line.
$	Move to end of line.
/pattern	Search forward for the next line using a specified pattern.
?pattern	Search backward for the next line using a specified pattern.
a	Append text—move into insert mode after the current character.
^b	Back up one screen of text.
B	Back up one space-delimited word.
b	Back up one word.
Backspace	Move left one character.
^d	Move down half a page.
D	Delete through end of line.
d	Delete—dw = delete word, dd = delete line.
Esc	Leave insert mode, return to command mode.
^f	Move forward one screen of text.
G	Go to the last line of the file.
nG	Go to the nth line of the file.
h	Move left one character.
i	Insert text—move into insert mode before the current character.
j	Move down one line.
k	Move up one line.
l	Move right one character.
n	Repeat last search.
O	Open new line for insert above the current line.
o	Open new line for insert below the current line.

Command	Meaning
Return	Move to beginning of next line.
^u	Move up half a page.
U	Undo—replace current line if changed.
u	Undo the last change made to the file.
W	Move forward one space-delimited word.
w	Move forward one word.
x	Delete a single character.
:e *file*	Edit a specified file without leaving vi.
:n	Move to the next file in the file list.
:q	Quit vi and return to the UNIX prompt.
:q!	Quit vi and return to the system, throwing away any changes made to the file.
:r *file*	Read the contents of a specified file, including it in the current edit buffer.
:w *file*	Write the contents of the buffer to a specified file.
:w	Write the edit buffer to the system.

Advanced *vi* Tricks, Tools, and Techniques

In the last section you learned some fifty vi commands, which enable you to easily move about in files, insert text, delete other text, search for specific patterns, and move from file to file without leaving the program. This section expands your expertise by showing you some more powerful vi commands.

To be honest, you can do fine in vi without ever reading this section. You already know how to insert and delete text, save or quit without saving, and search for particular patterns, even from the command line as you start vi for the first time! On the other hand, vi is like any other complex topic. The more you're willing to study and learn, the more the program will bow to your needs. This means you can accomplish a wider variety of different tasks on a daily basis.

The Change and Replace Commands

In the last section, you fixed a variety of problems by deleting words and replacing them with new words. A much smarter way to do this is to use either the change or the replace commands.

Each command has a lowercase and uppercase version, and each is quite different from the other. The r command replaces the character that the cursor is sitting upon with the next character you type, whereas the R command puts you into *replace mode*, so that anything you type overwrites whatever is already on the line. By contrast, C replaces *everything* on the line with whatever you type. The c change command is the most powerful of them all. It works just like the d command. You can use the c command with any address command, and it allows you to change text through that address, whether it's a word, line, or even the rest of the document.

Start vi with the buckaroo.confused file.

```
I found myself stealing a peek at my own watch and overhead
General Catbird's
I found myself stealing a peek at my own watch and overhead
General Catbird's
aide give him the latest.
"He's not even here," went the conversation.
"Banzai."
"Where the hell is he?"
"At the hospital in El Paso."
"What? Why weren't we informed? What's wrong with him?"

aide give him the latest.
"He's not even here," went the conversation.
"Banzai."
"Where the hell is he?"
"At the hospital in El Paso."
"What? Why weren't we informed? What's wrong with him?"


~
~
~
~
~
~
"buckaroo.confused" 16 lines, 540 characters
```

Without moving the cursor at all, press R. Nothing happens, or so it seems. Now type the words Excerpt from "Buckaroo Banzai" and watch what happens:

```
Excerpt from "Buckaroo Banzai"at my own watch and overhead
General Catbird's
I found myself stealing a peek at my own watch and overhead
General Catbird's
aide give him the latest.
"He's not even here," went the conversation.
```

Now press Esc and notice that what you see on the screen is *exactly* what's in the file.

This isn't, however, quite what you want. You could use either D or d$ to delete through the end of the line, but that's a bit awkward. Instead, use 0 to move back to the beginning of the line:

```
Excerpt from "Buckaroo Banzai" at my own watch and overhead
General Catbird's
I found myself stealing a peek at my own watch and overhead
```

```
General Catbird's
aide give him the latest.
"He's not even here," went the conversation.
```

This time, press C to change the contents of the line. Before you even type a single character of the new text, notice what the line now looks like:

```
Excerpt from "Buckaroo Banzai" at my own watch and overhead
General Catbird'$
I found myself stealing a peek at my own watch and overhead
General Catbird's
aide give him the latest.
"He's not even here," went the conversation.
```

Here's where a subtle difference comes into play! Look at the very last character on the current line. When you pressed C, the program replaced the "s" with a "$" to show the range of the text to be changed by the command. Press the Tab key once, and then type `Excerpt from "Buckaroo Bansai" by Earl MacRauch.`

```
        Excerpt from "Buckaroo Bansai" by Earl MacRauchhead General Catbird'$
I found myself stealing a peek at my own watch and overhead
General Catbird's
aide give him the latest.
"He's not even here," went the conversation.
```

This time, watch what happens when you press Esc:

```
Excerpt from "Buckaroo Bansai" by Earl MacRauch
I found myself stealing a peek at my own watch and overhead
General Catbird's
aide give him the latest.
"He's not even here," went the conversation.
```

There's another mistake. It should be *Buckaroo Banzai*, not *Bansai*. This is a chance to try the new r command.

Use cursor control keys to move the cursor to the offending letter. Use b to back up words and then h a few times to move into the middle of the word. Your screen now looks like this:

```
            Excerpt from "Buckaroo Bansai" by Earl MacRauch
I found myself stealing a peek at my own watch and overhead
General Catbird's
aide give him the latest.
"He's not even here," went the conversation.
```

Now press r. Again, nothing happens; the cursor doesn't move. Press r again to make sure it worked:

```
        Excerpt from "Buckaroo Banrai" by Earl MacRauch
I found myself stealing a peek at my own watch and overhead
General Catbird's
aide give him the latest.
"He's not even here," went the conversation.
```

That's no good. It replaced the "s" with an "r," which definitely isn't correct. Press rz, and you should have the following:

```
           Excerpt from "Buckaroo Banzai" by Earl MacRauch
I found myself stealing a peek at my own watch and overhead
General Catbird's
aide give him the latest.
"He's not even here," went the conversation.
```

Okay, those are the easy ones. Now it's time to see what the c command can do for you. In fact, it's incredibly powerful. You can change just about any range of information from the current point in the file in either direction!

To start, move to the middle of the file, where the second copy of the passage is found:

```
           Excerpt from "Buckaroo Banzai" by Earl MacRauch
I found myself stealing a peek at my own watch and overhead
General Catbird's
aide give him the latest.
"He's not even here," went the conversation.
"Banzai."
"Where the hell is he?"
"At the hospital in El Paso."
"What? Why weren't we informed? What's wrong with him?"

aide give him the latest.
"He's not even here," went the conversation.
"Banzai."
"Where the hell is he?"
"At the hospital in El Paso."
"What? Why weren't we informed? What's wrong with him?"



      ~
      ~
      ~
      ~
      ~
      ~
      ~
"buckaroo.confused" 16 lines, 540 characters
```

Change the word "aide" that the cursor is sitting on to "The tall beige wall clock opted to." First press c and note that, like many other commands in vi, nothing happens. Now press w to change just the first word. The screen should look like this:

```
"At the hospital in El Paso."
"What? Why weren't we informed? What's wrong with him?"

aid$ give him the latest.
"He's not even here," went the conversation.
"Banzai."
```

Again, the program has replaced the last character of the change to a $. Now type The tall beige wall clock opted to. Once you reach the $, the editor stops overwriting characters and starts inserting them instead, so the screen now looks like this:

```
"At the hospital in El Paso."
"What? Why weren't we informed? What's wrong with him?"

The tall beige wall clock opted to_give him the latest.
"He's not even here," went the conversation.
"Banzai."
```

Press Esc and you're done (though you can undo the change with the u or U commands, of course).

Tall and beige or not, this section makes no sense now, so change this entire line using the $ motion command. First use 0 to move to the beginning of the line and then press c$:

```
"At the hospital in El Paso."
"What? Why weren't we informed? What's wrong with him?"

The tall beige wall clock opted to give him the latest$
"He's not even here," went the conversation.
"Banzai."
```

This is working. The last character changed to the dollar sign. Press Esc, and the entire line is deleted:

```
"At the hospital in El Paso."
"What? Why weren't we informed? What's wrong with him?"


_
"He's not even here," went the conversation.
"Banzai."
```

There are still five lines below the current line. You could delete them and then type in the information you want, but that's primitive. Instead, the c command comes to the rescue. Move down one line, press c5, and press Return. Watch what happens:

```
"At the hospital in El Paso."
"What? Why weren't we informed? What's wrong with him?"



~
~
~
~
~
~
~
~
~
~
~
~
6 lines changed
```

In general, you can always change the current and next line by using c followed by Return (because the Return key is a motion key too, remember). By prefacing the command with a number, you changed the range from two lines to five.

You might be asking, "Why *two* lines?" The answer is subtle. In essence, anytime you use the c command you change the current line plus any additional lines that might be touched by the command. Pressing Return moves the cursor to the following line; therefore, the current line (starting at the cursor location) through the following line are changed. The command should probably just change to the beginning of the following line, but that's beyond our control!

Now press Tab four times, type in (page 8), and press the Esc key. The screen should look like this:

```
"Where the hell is he?"
"At the hospital in El Paso."
"What? Why weren't we informed? What's wrong with him?"


                         (page 8)
~
~
~
```

What if you change your mind? That's where the u command comes in handy. A single press of the key and the original copy is restored:

```
            Excerpt from "Buckaroo Banzai" by Earl MacRauch
I found myself stealing a peek at my own watch and overhead
General Catbird's
aide give him the latest.
"He's not even here," went the conversation.
"Banzai."
"Where the hell is he?"
"At the hospital in El Paso."
"What? Why weren't we informed? What's wrong with him?"


"He's not even here," went the conversation.
"Banzai."
"Where the hell is he?"
"At the hospital in El Paso."
"What? Why weren't we informed? What's wrong with him?"


~
~
~
~
~
~
~
5 more lines
```

The combination of replace and change commands adds a level of sophistication to an editor you might have thought could only insert and delete. There's much more to cover, so don't stop now!

Numeric Repeat Prefixes

You have now seen two commands that were prefixed by a number to cause a specific action. The G command moves you to the very last line of the file, unless you type in a number first. If you type in a number, the G command moves to the specified line number. Similarly, pressing a number and then the Return key causes vi to repeat the key the specified number of times.

Numeric repeat prefixes are actually widely available in vi, and this is the missing piece of your navigational tool set.

Move back to the top of the buckaroo.confused file. This time, use 1G to move there, rather than a bunch of k keys or other steps. The top of the screen now looks like this:

```
        Excerpt from "Buckaroo Banzai" by Earl MacRauch
I found myself stealing a peek at my own watch and overhead
General Catbird's
aide give him the latest.
"He's not even here," went the conversation.
```

Now move forward 15 words. Instead of pressing w 15 times, enter 15w.

```
       Excerpt from "Buckaroo Banzai" by Earl MacRauch
I found myself stealing a peek at my own watch and overhead
General Catbird's
aide give him the latest.
"He's not even here," went the conversation.
```

Now move down seven lines by pressing the 7 key followed by the Return key. Use o to give yourself a blank line and press Esc again:

```
"Where the hell is he?"
"At the hospital in El Paso."
"What? Why weren't we informed? What's wrong with him?"


_

"He's not even here," went the conversation.
"Banzai."
```

You want to put "Go Team Banzai!" on the bottom, repeated three times. Can you guess how to do it? Simply press 3i to move into insert mode, and then type Go Team Banzai!. The screen looks like this:

```
"Where the hell is he?"
"At the hospital in El Paso."
"What? Why weren't we informed? What's wrong with him?"

Go Team Banzai! _

"He's not even here," went the conversation.
"Banzai."
```

Pressing Esc has a dramatic result:

```
"Where the hell is he?"
"At the hospital in El Paso."
"What? Why weren't we informed? What's wrong with him?"

Go Team Banzai! Go Team Banzai! Go Team Banzai!

"He's not even here," went the conversation.
"Banzai."
```

Now get rid of all the lines below the current line. There are many different ways to do this, but you're going to try to guess how many words are present and give dw a repeat count prefix to delete that many words. (Actually, you don't need to know the number of words, because vi will repeat the command only while it makes sense to do so).

I press 75dw and the screen instantly looks like this:

```
                    Excerpt from "Buckaroo Banzai" by Earl MacRauch
I found myself stealing a peek at my own watch and overhead
General Catbird's
aide give him the latest.
"He's not even here," went the conversation.
"Banzai."
"Where the hell is he?"
"At the hospital in El Paso."
"What? Why weren't we informed? What's wrong with him?"

Go Team Banzai! Go Team Banzai! Go Team Banzai!


~
~
~
~
~
~
~
~
~
~

7 lines deleted
```

Try the undo command here to see what happens!

Almost all commands in vi can work with a numeric repeat prefix, even commands that you might not expect to work, such as the i insert command. Remember that a request can be accomplished in many ways. To delete five words, for example, you could use 5dw or d5w. Experiment on your own, and you'll get the idea.

Numbering Lines in the File

It's very helpful to have an editor that works with the entire screen, but sometimes you only need to know what line you're currently on. Further, sometimes it can be very help-ful to have all the lines numbered on the screen. With vi, you can do both of these—the former by pressing ^g (remember, that's Ctrl+G) while in command mode, and the latter by using a complex colon command, `:set number`, followed by Return. To turn off the display of line numbers, simply type `:set nonumber` and press Return.

You're still looking at `buckaroo.confused` in vi. The screen looks like this:

```
          Excerpt from "Buckaroo Banzai" by Earl MacRauch
I found myself stealing a peek at my own watch and overhead
General Catbird's
aide give him the latest.
"He's not even here," went the conversation.
"Banzai."
"Where the hell is he?"
"At the hospital in El Paso."
"What? Why weren't we informed? What's wrong with him?"

Go Team Banzai! Go Team Banzai! Go Team Banzai!

~
~
~
~
~
~
~
~
~
~

7 lines deleted
```

Can you see where the cursor is? To find out what line number the cursor is on, press ^g. The information is listed on the status line at the bottom:

```
~
~
~
"buckaroo.confused" [Modified] line 10 of 11, column 1   --90%--
```

There's lots of information here. Included here is the name of the file (`buckaroo.confused`), an indication that vi thinks you've changed it since you started the program (`[Modified]`), the current line (`10`), total lines in the file (`11`), what column you're in, and, finally, an estimate of how far into the file you are.

Eleven lines? Count the display again. There are 12 lines. What's going on? The answer will become clear if you turn on line numbering for the entire file. To do this, type `:`, which zips the cursor to the bottom of the screen, where you then enter the `set number` command:

```
~
~
~
:set number_
```

Pressing Return causes the screen to change, thus:

```
 1           Excerpt from "Buckaroo Banzai" by Earl MacRauch
 2   I found myself stealing a peek at my own watch and overhead General Catbird's
 3   aide give him the latest.
 4   "He's not even here," went the conversation.
 5   "Banzai."
 6   "Where the hell is he?"
 7   "At the hospital in El Paso."
 8   "What? Why weren't we informed? What's wrong with him?"
 9
10   Go Team Banzai! Go Team Banzai! Go Team Banzai!
11
~
~
~
~
~
~
~
~
~
~
~
```

Now you can see why vi only figures that there are 11 lines, even though it seems by the screens shown here that there are 12 lines.

To turn off the line numbering, use the opposite command, :set nonumber, followed by Return.

There are definitely times when being able to include the number of each line is helpful. One example is if you are using awk and it's complaining about a specific line being in an inappropriate format (usually by saying syntax error, bailing out! or something similar).

Search and Replace

Though most of vi is easy to learn and use, one command that always causes great trouble for users is the search and replace command. The key to understanding this command is to remember that there's a line editor (ex) hidden underneath vi. Instead of trying to figure out some arcane vi command, it's easiest to just drop to the line editor and use a simple colon command—one identical to the command used in sed—to replace an old pattern with a new one. To replace an existing word on the current line with a new word (the simplest case), use :s/*old*/*new*/. If you want to have all occurrences on the current line matched, you need to add the g suffix (just as with sed): :s/*old*/*new*/g.

To change all occurrences of one word or phrase to another across the entire file, the command is identical to the preceding command, except that you must add a prefix indicating the range of lines affected. Recall that $ is the last line in the file, and that ranges are specified (in this case, as in sed) by two numbers separated by a comma. It should be no surprise that the command is :1,$ s/*old*/*new*/g.

You're still working with the buckaroo.confused file, so your screen should look very similar to this:

```
            Excerpt from "Buckaroo Banzai" by Earl MacRauch
I found myself stealing a peek at my own watch and overhead
General Catbird's
aide give him the latest.
"He's not even here," went the conversation.
"Banzai."
"Where the hell is he?"
"At the hospital in El Paso."
"What? Why weren't we informed? What's wrong with him?"

Go Team Banzai! Go Team Banzai! Go Team Banzai!

~
~
~
~
~
~
~
~
~
~
~
~
~
```

The cursor is on the very first line. Rename Earl. Type :. The cursor immediately moves to the bottom. Then type s/Earl/Duke/. Pressing Return produces this:

```
            Excerpt from "Buckaroo Banzai" by Duke MacRauch
I found myself stealing a peek at my own watch and overhead General Catbird's
aide give him the latest.
"He's not even here," went the conversation.
```

As you can see, this maneuver was simple and effective.

Maybe developmental psychology is your bag. Instead of having this Banzai character, you want your fictional character to be called Bandura. You could use the previous command to change the occurrence on the current line, but you really want to change all occurrences within the file.

This is no problem. Type :1,$ s/Banzai/Bandura/ and press Return. Here's the result:

```
            Excerpt from "Buckaroo Bandura" by Duke MacRauch
I found myself stealing a peek at my own watch and overhead
General Catbird's
aide give him the latest.
"He's not even here," went the conversation.
"Bandura."
"Where the hell is he?"
"At the hospital in El Paso."
"What? Why weren't we informed? What's wrong with him?"
```

```
Go Team Bandura! Go Team Banzai! Go Team Banzai!

~
~
~
~
~
~
~
~
~
~
~
~
```

The result is not quite right. You forgot the trailing g, so vi changed only the very first occurrence on each line, making the "go team" exhortation rather confusing.

To try again, type :1,$ s/Banzai/Bandura/g and press Return. The screen changes as desired:

```
        Excerpt from "Buckaroo Bandura" by Duke MacRauch
I found myself stealing a peek at my own watch and overhead
General Catbird's
aide give him the latest.
"He's not even here," went the conversation.
"Bandura."
"Where the hell is he?"
"At the hospital in El Paso."
"What? Why weren't we informed? What's wrong with him?"

Go Team Bandura! Go Team Bandura! Go Team Bandura!

~
~
~
~
~
~
~
~
~
~
7 substitutions
```

Notice that vi also indicates the total number of substitutions in this case.

Press u to undo the last change.

Search and replace is one area where a windowing system, like that on a Macintosh or a PC running Windows, comes in handy. A windowing system offers different boxes for the old and new patterns, and shows each change and a dialog box asking, "Should I change this one?" Alas, this is UNIX and it's still designed to run on ASCII terminals.

Key Mapping with the *:map* Command

As you have worked through the various examples, you might have tried pressing the arrow keys on your keyboard or perhaps the Ins or Del keys. Odds are likely that the keys not only didn't work, but instead caused all sorts of weird things to happen!

The good news is that vi has a facility that enables you to map any key to a specific action. If these *key mappings* are saved in a file called .exrc in your home directory, the mappings will be understood by vi automatically each time you use the program. The format for using the map command is :map *key command-sequence*. (In a nutshell, mapping is a way of associating an action with another action or result. For example, by plugging your computer into the right wall socket, you could map the action of flipping the light switch on the wall with the result of having your computer turn on.)

You can also save other things in your .exrc file, including the :set number option if you're a nut about seeing line numbers. More interestingly, vi can be taught abbreviations, so that each time you press the abbreviation, vi expands it. The format for defining abbreviations is :abbreviate *abbreviation expanded-value*. Finally, any line that begins with a double quote is considered a comment and is ignored.

It's finally time to leave the buckaroo.confused file, and restart vi, this time with the .exrc file in your home directory:

```
% cd
% vi .exrc
_
~
~
~
~
~
~
~
~
~
~
~
~
~
~
~
~
~
~
~
~
~
~
".exrc" [New file]
```

Before you actually add any information to this new file, define a few abbreviations to make life a bit easier. To do this, press :, which moves the cursor to the bottom of the screen. Then define tyu as a simple abbreviation for the lengthy phrase `Teach Yourself UNIX in a Few Minutes`:

```
~

~

~
:abbreviate tyu Teach Yourself UNIX in a Few Minutes_
```

Pressing Return moves the cursor back to the top.

Now try the abbreviation. Recall that in the `.exrc`, lines beginning with a double quote are comments and are ignored when `vi` starts up. Press `i` to enter insert mode, and then type `" Sample .exrc file as shown in tyu`. The screen looks like this:

```
" Sample .exrc file as shown in tyu_
~
~
```

As soon as you press Return or enter a space or punctuation character, the abbreviation is expanded. In this case, move to the next line by pressing Return:

```
" Sample .exrc file as shown in Teach Yourself UNIX in a Few Minutes
~
~
~
```

Press Esc to leave the insert mode.

This feature can also be used to correct common typos you make. Many people have a bad habit of typing "teh" instead of "the." Because `vi` is smart about abbreviation expansion, you can abbreviate "the" as "teh" and not get into trouble:

```
~

~
:ab teh the_
```

> **TIP:** You don't have to type "abbreviation" each time. The first two letters are sufficient for `vi` to figure out what's going on.

Press Return. Now whenever you make that typo, the editor will fix it. To demonstrate this, add a second comment to this file. Adding a comment is easy because you're still at the beginning of the second line. When you press `i` and type `" (subtly different from the example in teh`, you get the following result:

```
" Sample .exrc file as shown in Teach Yourself UNIX in a Few Minutes
" (subtly different from the example in the_
~
~
```

If you enter another character instead of pressing the spacebar, `vi` is smart enough *not* to expand the abbreviation. Try it yourself. After pressing the `h` key again, you'll see this:

```
" Sample .exrc file as shown in Teach Yourself UNIX in a Few Minutes
" (subtly different from the example in tehh_
~
~
```

Because you're still in insert mode, however, you can backspace and replace the spare h with a space, which instantly fixes the spelling. Finally, type book) and press Esc to return to command mode.

There's one more nifty abbreviation trick. Type :ab by itself and press Return. vi shows you a list of the abbreviations currently in effect:

```
~
~
:ab
tyu     tyu     Teach Yourself UNIX in a Few Minutes
teh     teh     the
[Hit any key to continue] _
```

Okay, now you can move on to key mapping.

Key mapping is as easy as defining abbreviations, except you must remember one thing: any control character entered *must* be prefaced with a ^v so that vi doesn't interpret it immediately. The Esc key is included in this list, too.

To map the Clear key to the D function, which, as you recall, deletes text through the end of the current line, type :map, followed by a single space:

```
~
~
:map
```

> **WARNING:** If you use many different terminals, you may have to remap the Clear (Clr) key.

Now you need to type the ^v; otherwise, when you press the Clear key, it will send an *Escape sequence* that will confuse vi to no end. Press ^v:

```
~
~
:map ^
```

The cursor is floating over the caret, which indicates the next character typed should be a control character. Instead of pressing any specific character, however, simply press the Clear key. The result is that it sends the Escape sequence, and vi captures it without a problem:

```
~
~
:map ^[OP_
```

Now type another space, because the *key* part of the key mapping has been defined. Then type the command to which vi should map the Clear key:

```
~
~
:map ^[OP D_
```

Press Return, and it's done! To test the key mapping, move back to the phrase `Few Min-utes` in the first line:

```
" Sample .exrc file as shown in Teach Yourself UNIX in a Few Minutes
"  (subtly different from the example in the book)
~
~
```

To clear this line, you need only press Clear.

To save this as a permanent key mapping in this `.exrc` file, duplicate each keystroke, but this time do it in insert mode instead of at the bottom of the screen. The result is a file that looks like this:

```
" Sample .exrc file as shown in Teach Yourself UNIX in a
"  (subtly different from the example in the book)
:map ^[OP D_
~
~
```

Mapping the arrow keys is done the same way, and typing `:ab` and then pressing Return shows all abbreviations. Typing `:map` and then Return demonstrates that you already have your arrow keys mapped to the `vi` motion keys:

```
~
~
:map
up       ^[[A    k
down     ^[[B    j
left     ^[[D    h
right    ^[[C    l
^[OP     ^[OP    D
[Hit any key to continue] _
```

You can see that sometimes the system can be smart about defining specific keys by name rather than by value, but the end result is the same. You can now use the arrow keys and Clear key, and `vi` knows what they mean.

Here's a final demonstration of what you can do with keyboard mapping. You'll often encounter a simple, tedious activity you must do over and over. An example might be surrounding a specific word with quotes to meet a style guideline. This sounds more painful than it need be, because a simple key mapping can automate the entire process of quoting the current word.

You know that `^a` isn't used by `vi`, so you can map that to the new quote-a-single-word command, making sure that you use `^v` before each control character or Esc. Type the characters `:map ^v^a i":`

```
~
~
:map ^A i"_
```

Press ^v and then the Esc key. To insert a double quote, you need to have vi go into insert mode (the i), type the quote, and receive an Esc to leave insert mode. The e command moves to the end of the current word, so type that, followed by the commands needed to append the second double quote. The final map now looks like this:

```
~
~
:map ^A i"^[ea"^[_
```

Press Return and it's done. Now move to the beginning of a word and try the new key mapping for ^a.

There are a variety of customizations you can use with the vi editor, including teaching it about special keys on your keyboard and defining task-specific keys to save time. You can use it to abbreviate commonly used words or phrases to save time or avoid typographical errors. Be cautious when working with the .exrc file, however, because if you enter information that isn't valid, it can be a bit confusing to fix it. Always try the command directly before using it in a special key mapping, and you'll stay out of trouble.

Moving Sentences and Paragraphs

You've learned quite a variety of different commands for moving about in files, but there are two more vi movement commands for you to try. So far, movement has been based on screen motion, but vi hasn't particularly known much about the information in the file itself: press k and you move up a line, regardless of what kind of file you're viewing.

The vi editor is smarter than that, however. It has some movement commands that are defined by the text you're currently editing. Each of these is simply a punctuation character on your keyboard, but each is quite helpful. The first is), which moves the cursor forward to the beginning of the next sentence in the file. Use the opposite, (, and you can move to the beginning of the current sentence in the file. Also worth experimenting with is }, which moves forward a paragraph in the file, and {, which moves backwards a paragraph.

To try this out, create a new file. Start vi and type the following text:

```
% cat dickens.note
                    A Tale of Two Cities
                        Preface

When I was acting, with my children and friends, in Mr Wilkie Collins's
drama of The Frozen Deep, I first conceived the main idea of this
story.  A strong desire was upon me then, to
embody it in my own person;
and I traced out in my fancy, the state of mind of which it would
necessitate the presentation
to an observant spectator, with particular
care and interest.
```

```
As the idea became familiar to me, it gradually shaped itself into its
present form.  Throughout its execution, it has had complete possession
of me; I have so far verified what
is done and suffered in these pages,
as that I have certainly done and suffered it all myself.

Whenever any reference (however slight) is made here to the condition
of the French people before or during the Revolution, it is truly made,
on the faith of the most trustworthy
witnesses.  It has been one of my hopes to add
something to the popular and picturesque means of
understanding that terrible time, though no one can hope
to add anything to the philosophy of Mr Carlyle's wonderful book.

Tavistock House
November 1859
```

When you start vi on this file, here's what your initial screen looks like:

```
                     A Tale of Two Cities
                           Preface

When I was acting, with my children and friends, in Mr Wilkie Collins's
drama of The Frozen Deep, I first conceived the main idea of this
story.  A strong desire was upon me then, to
embody it in my own person;
and I traced out in my fancy, the state of mind of which it would
necessitate the presentation
to an observant spectator, with particular
care and interest.

As the idea became familiar to me, it gradually shaped itself into its
present form.  Throughout its execution, it has had complete possession
of me; I have so far verified what
is done and suffered in these pages,
as that I have certainly done and suffered it all myself.

Whenever any reference (however slight) is made here to the condition
of the French people before or during the Revolution, it is truly made,
on the faith of the most trustworthy
witnesses.  It has been one of my hopes to add
something to the popular and picturesque means of
"dickens.note" 28 lines, 1122 characters
```

Move to the beginning of the first paragraph of text by typing /When and pressing Return. Now the screen looks like this:

```
                     A Tale of Two Cities
                           Preface

When I was acting, with my children and friends, in Mr Wilkie Collins's
drama of The Frozen Deep, I first conceived the main idea of this
story.  A strong desire was upon me then, to
embody it in my own person;
```

Press) once. The cursor moves to the beginning of the next sentence:

```
When I was acting, with my children and friends, in Mr Wilkie Collins's
drama of The Frozen Deep, I first conceived the main idea of this
```

```
story.  A strong desire was upon me then, to
embody it in my own person;
and I traced out in my fancy, the state of mind of which it would
necessitate the presentation
```

Try the (to move back a sentence. You end up back on the "W" in "When" at the beginning of the sentence. Repeatedly pressing (and) should let you fly back and forth through the file, sentence by sentence. Notice what occurs when you're at the top few lines of the title.

> **WARNING:** A little experimentation will demonstrate that vi defines a sentence as anything that occurs at the beginning of a block of text (for example, When I was...), or as any word that follows a punctuation character followed by *two* spaces. This is a bit unfortunate, because modern typographic conventions have moved away from using two spaces after the end of a sentence. If you only use one space between sentences—as I have for this book—moving by sentence is less helpful.

You can move back to the opening word of the first paragraph by pressing n to repeat the last search pattern. The screen now looks like this:

```
                    A Tale of Two Cities
                         Preface

When I was acting, with my children and friends, in Mr Wilkie Collins's
drama of The Frozen Deep, I first conceived the main idea of this
story.  A strong desire was upon me then, to
embody it in my own person;
and I traced out in my fancy, the state of mind of which it would
necessitate the presentation
to an observant spectator, with particular
care and interest.

As the idea became familiar to me, it gradually shaped itself into its
present form.  Throughout its execution, it has had complete possession
of me; I have so far verified what
is done and suffered in these pages,
as that I have certainly done and suffered it all myself.

Whenever any reference (however slight) is made here to the condition
of the French people before or during the Revolution, it is truly made,
on the faith of the most trustworthy
witnesses.  It has been one of my hopes to add
something to the popular and picturesque means of
"dickens.note" 28 lines, 1122 characters
```

To move to the next paragraph, press } once:

```
                    A Tale of Two Cities
                         Preface

When I was acting, with my children and friends, in Mr Wilkie Collins's
drama of The Frozen Deep, I first conceived the main idea of this
```

```
story.  A strong desire was upon me then, to
embody it in my own person;
and I traced out in my fancy, the state of mind of which it would
necessitate the presentation
to an observant spectator, with particular
care and interest.

As the idea became familiar to me, it gradually shaped itself into its
present form.  Throughout its execution, it has had complete possession
of me; I have so far verified what
is done and suffered in these pages,
as that I have certainly done and suffered it all myself.

Whenever any reference (however slight) is made here to the condition
of the French people before or during the Revolution, it is truly made,
on the faith of the most trustworthy
witnesses.  It has been one of my hopes to add
something to the popular and picturesque means of
"dickens.note" 28 lines, 1122 characters
```

Press the { key and you move right back to the beginning of the previous paragraph. In fact, you can easily fly back and forth in the file by using sequences of } (or a numeric repeat prefix like 2} to get there faster).

These two motion commands are helpful when you're working with stories, articles, or letters. Anytime you're working with words rather than commands (as in the .exrc file), these commands are worth remembering.

By the way, try d) to delete a sentence, or c} to change an entire paragraph. Remember that you can always undo the changes with u if you haven't done anything else between the two events.

Access UNIX with *!*

This final section on vi introduces you to one of the most powerful, and least known, commands in the editor: the ! Escape-to-UNIX command. When prefaced with a colon (:!, for example), it enables you to run UNIX commands without leaving the editor. More importantly, the ! command itself, just like d and c, accepts address specifications and feeds that portion of text to the command, and then replaces that portion with the results of having run that command on the text.

You should still be in the dickens.intro file. Start by double-checking what files you have in your home directory. To do this, type :!, which moves the cursor to the bottom line:

```
of the French people before or during the Revolution, it is truly made,
on the faith of the most trustworthy
witnesses.  It has been one of my hopes to add
something to the popular and picturesque means of
:!_
```

Type ls -CF and press Return, as if you were at the % prompt in the command line:

```
of the French people before or during the Revolution, it is truly made,
on the faith of the most trustworthy
witnesses.  It has been one of my hopes to add
something to the popular and picturesque means of
:!ls -CF
Archives/           big.output        dickens.note      src/
InfoWorld/          bigfiles          keylime.pie       temp/
Mail/               bin/              newfile           tetme
News/               buckaroo          owl.c
OWL/                buckaroo.confused sample
awkscript           demo              sample2
[Hit any key to continue] _
```

Press Return and you're back in the editor. You have quickly checked what files you have in your home directory. (Your fileage may vary.)

Now for some real fun. Move back to the beginning of the first paragraph and add the text "Chuck, here are my current files:" to it. Press Return *twice* before using the Esc key to return to command mode:

```
                    A Tale of Two Cities
                         Preface

Chuck, here are my current files:

_

When I was acting, with my children and friends, in Mr Wilkie Collins's
drama of The Frozen Deep, I first conceived the main idea of this
story.  A strong desire was upon me then, to
```

Notice that the cursor was moved up a line. You're now on a blank line, and the line following is also blank.

To feed the current line to the UNIX system and replace it with the output of the command, vi offers an easy shortcut: !!. As soon as you type the second ! (or, more precisely, once vi figures out the desired range specified for this command), the cursor moves to the bottom of the screen and prompts with a single ! character:

```
of the French people before or during the Revolution, it is truly made,
on the faith of the most trustworthy
witnesses. It has been one of my hopes to add
something to the popular and picturesque means of
!_
```

To list all the files in your directory, again type ls -CF and press Return. After a second, vi adds the output of that command to the file:

```
                    A Tale of Two Cities
                         Preface

Chuck, here are my current files:
Archives/           bigfiles          newfile
InfoWorld/          bin/              owl.c
Mail/               buckaroo          sample
News/               buckaroo.confused sample2
```

```
OWL/                  demo                  src/
awkscript             dickens.note          temp/
big.output            keylime.pie           tetme
```

```
When I was acting, with my children and friends, in Mr Wilkie Collins's
drama of The Frozen Deep, I first conceived the main idea of this
story.  A strong desire was upon me then, to
embody it in my own person;
and I traced out in my fancy, the state of mind of which it would
necessitate the presentation
to an observant spectator, with particular
care and interest.

As the idea became familiar to me, it gradually shaped itself into its
present form.  Throughout its execution, it has had complete possession
6 more lines
```

Notice that this time that the status on the bottom indicates how many lines were added to the file.

Press u to undo this change. Notice that the vi status indicator on the bottom line says there are now six fewer lines.

Move back to the "W" in "When." You are now ready to learn one of the most useful commands in vi. This command gives you the ability to hand a paragraph of text to an arbitrary UNIX command.

This time, use a sed command, sed 's/^/> /', which prefaces each line with >. Ready? This is where the } command comes in handy, too. To accomplish this trick, type !}, moving the cursor to the bottom of the screen. Then type the sed command as you saw earlier: sed 's/^/> /'. Pressing Return feeds the lines to sed. The sed command makes the change indicated and replaces those lines with the output of the sed command. Voilà! The screen now looks like this:

```
                    A Tale of Two Cities
                         Preface

Chuck, here are my current files:


> When I was acting, with my children and friends, in Mr Wilkie Collins's
> drama of The Frozen Deep, I first conceived the main idea of this
> story.  A strong desire was upon me then, to
> embody it in my own person;
> and I traced out in my fancy, the state of mind of which it would
> necessitate the presentation
> to an observant spectator, with particular
> care and interest.

As the idea became familiar to me, it gradually shaped itself into its
present form.  Throughout its execution, it has had complete possession
of me; I have so far verified what
is done and suffered in these pages,
as that I have certainly done and suffered it all myself.
```

```
Whenever any reference (however slight) is made here to the condition
of the French people before or during the Revolution, it is truly made,
!sed 's/^/> /'
```

Here are a few more examples of ways to interact with UNIX while within vi. First, you don't really want the prefix to each line, so choose u to undo the change.

You want the system to actually tighten up the lines, ensuring that a reasonable number of words occur on each line without any lines being too long. On the majority of systems, there is a command called either fmt or adjust to accomplish this. To figure out which works on your system, simply use the :! command and feed a word or two to the fmt command to see what happens:

```
Whenever any reference (however slight) is made here to the condition
of the French people before or during the Revolution, it is truly made,
:!echo hi ¦ fmt
[No write since last change]
hi
[Hit any key to continue] _
```

In this case, fmt worked as expected, so you can be sure that the command exists on your system. If the response was command unknown, adjust is a likely synonym. If neither exist, complain to your vendor!

Armed with this new command, you can try another variant of !}, this time by feeding the entire paragraph to the fmt command. You're still at the beginning of the word "When" in the text. When you type the command !}fmt, the paragraph is cleaned up, and the screen changes to this:

```
                    A Tale of Two Cities
                         Preface

Chuck, here are my current files:


When I was acting, with my children and friends, in Mr Wilkie Collins's
drama of The Frozen Deep, I first conceived the main idea of this
story.  A strong desire was upon me then, to embody it in my own
person; and I traced out in my fancy, the state of mind of which it
would necessitate the presentation to an observant spectator, with
particular care and interest.

As the idea became familiar to me, it gradually shaped itself into its
present form.  Throughout its execution, it has had complete possession
of me; I have so far verified what
is done and suffered in these pages,
as that I have certainly done and suffered it all myself.

Whenever any reference (however slight) is made here to the condition
of the French people before or during the Revolution, it is truly made,
on the faith of the most trustworthy
witnesses.  It has been one of my hopes to add
2 fewer lines
```

Again, vi tells you that the number of lines in the file have changed as a result of the command. In this situation, tightening up the paragraph actually reduced it by two display lines, too.

This command is so helpful that you may want to have it bound to a specific key with the keymap command. A typical way to do this in an .exrc might be this:

```
:map ^P !}fmt^M
```

The ^M is what vi uses to record an Return keypress. (Remember that you need to use ^v beforehand.) With this defined in your .exrc, you can press ^p to format the current paragraph.

The awk command, discussed in Chapter 15, "Awk, Awk," can easily be used to extract specific fields of information. This can be tremendously helpful in vi. Rather than continuing with the dickens.intro file, however, quit vi and create a new file containing some output from the ls command:

```
% ls -CF
Archives/          big.output         dickens.note       src/
InfoWorld/         bigfiles           keylime.pie        temp/
Mail/              bin/               newfile            tetme
News/              buckaroo           owl.c
OWL/               buckaroo.confused  sample
awkscript          demo               sample2
% ls -l a* b* > listing
```

Now you can use vi listing to start the file with the output of the ls command:

```
-rw-rw----  1 taylor         126 Dec  3 16:34 awkscript
-rw-rw----  1 taylor        1659 Dec  3 23:26 big.output
-rw-rw----  1 taylor         165 Dec  3 16:42 bigfiles
-rw-rw----  1 taylor         270 Dec  4 15:09 buckaroo
-rw-rw----  1 taylor         458 Dec  4 23:22 buckaroo.confused
~
~
~
~
~
~
~
~
~
~
~
~
~
~
~
~
~
"listing" 5 lines, 282 characters
```

It would be nice to use this as the basis for creating a *shell script*, which is just a series of commands that you might type to the shell directly, all kept neatly in a single file. A shell script can show you both the first and last few lines of each file, with the middle chopped out.

The commands you want to have occur for each file entry are these:

```
echo ==== filename ====
head -5 filename; echo ...size bytes...; tail -5 filename
```

Do this with a combination of the ! command in vi and the awk program with the awk command:

```
awk '{ print "echo ==== "$8" ===="; print "head "$8"; echo
..."$4" bytes...; tail "$8}'
```

With the cursor on the very top line of this file, you can now press !G to pipe the entire file through the command. The cursor drops to the bottom of the screen. Type in the awk script shown previously and press Return. The result is this:

```
echo ==== awkscript ====
head -5 awkscript; echo ...126 bytes...; tail -5 awkscript
echo ==== big.output ====
head -5 big.output; echo ...1659 bytes...; tail -5 big.output
echo ==== bigfiles ====
head -5 bigfiles; echo ...165 bytes...; tail -5 bigfiles
echo ==== buckaroo ====
head -5 buckaroo; echo ...270 bytes...; tail -5 buckaroo
echo ==== buckaroo.confused ====
head -5 buckaroo.confused; echo ...458 bytes...; tail -5 buckaroo.confused~
~
~
~
~
~
~
~
~
~
~
~
!awk '{ print "echo ==== "$8" ===="; print "head "$8"; echo
..."$4" bytes...; tail "$8}'
```

If you now quit vi and ask sh to interpret the contents, here's what happens:

```
% chmod +x listing
% sh listing
==== awkscript ====
{
        count[length($1)]++
}
END {
        for (i=1; i < 9; i++)
...126 bytes...
}
```

```
END {
        for (i=1; i < 9; i++)
            print "There are " counti " accounts with " i " letter names."
}
==== big.output ====
leungtc  ttyrV   Dec  1 18:27   (magenta)
tuyinhwa ttyrX   Dec  3 22:38   (expert)
hollenst ttyrZ   Dec  3 22:14   (dov)
brandt   ttyrb   Nov 28 23:03   (age)
holmes   ttyrj   Dec  3 21:59   (age)
...1659 bytes...
buckeye  ttyss   Dec  3 23:20   (mac2)
mtaylor  ttyst   Dec  3 23:22   (dov)
look     ttysu   Dec  3 23:12   (age)
janitor  ttysw   Dec  3 18:29   (age)
ajones   ttysx   Dec  3 23:23   (rassilon)
==== bigfiles ====
12556   keylime.pie
8729    owl.c
1024    Mail/
582     tetme
512     temp/
...165 bytes...
512     Archives/
207     sample2
199     sample
126     awkscript


==== buckaroo ====
I found myself stealing a peek at my own watch and overhead
General Catbird's
aide give him the latest.
"He's not even here," went the conversation.
"Banzai."
"Where the hell is he?"
...270 bytes...
"Banzai."
"Where the hell is he?"
"At the hospital in El Paso."
"What? Why weren't we informed? What's wrong with him?"


==== buckaroo.confused ====
        Excerpt from "Buckaroo Bandura" by Duke MacRauch
I found myself stealing a peek at my own watch and overhead
General Catbird's
aide give him the latest.
"He's not even here," went the conversation.
"Bandura."
...458 bytes...
"At the hospital in El Paso."
"What? Why weren't we informed? What's wrong with him?"


Go Team Bandura! Go Team Bandura! Go Team Bandura!

%
```

Clearly the ! command opens up vi to work with the rest of the UNIX system. There's almost nothing that you can't do within the editor, whether it's add or remove prefixes, clean up text, or even show what happens when you try to run a command or reformat a passage within the current file. Remember, you can run spell without leaving vi, too. Be careful, though, because spell will replace the entire contents of your file with the list of words it doesn't know. Fortunately, u can solve that problem.

A summary of the commands you have learned in this section is shown in Table 7.3.

Table 7.3. Advanced vi commands.

Command	Meaning
!!	Replace current line with output of UNIX command.
!}	Replace current paragraph with the results of piping it through the specified UNIX program or programs.
(	Move backward one sentence.
)	Move forward one sentence.
C	Change text through the end of line.
c	Change text in the specified range—cw changes the following word, whereas c} changes the next paragraph.
e	Move to the end of the current word.
^g	Show current line number and other information about the file.
R	Replace text until Esc.
r	Replace the current character with the next pressed.
^v	Prevent vi from interpreting the next character.
{	Move backward one paragraph.
}	Move forward one paragraph.
:!	Invoke specified UNIX command.
:ab a bcd	Define abbreviation a for phrase bcd.
:ab	Show current abbreviations, if any.
:map a bcd	Map key a to the vi commands bcd.
:map	Show current key mappings, if any.
:s/old/new/	Substitute new for old on the current line.
:s/old/new/g	Substitute new for all occurrences of old on the current line.
:1,$s/old/new/g	Substitute new for all occurrences of old.
:set nonumber	Turn off line numbering.
:set number	Turn on line numbering.

Clearly, vi is a very complex and sophisticated tool, allowing you to not only modify your text files but also customize the editor for your keyboard. Just as important, you can access all the power of UNIX while within vi.

With this section and the last, you now know more about vi than the vast majority of people using UNIX today. There's a second popular editor, however; one that is *modeless* and that offers its own interesting possibilities for working with files and the UNIX system. It's called EMACS, and if you have it on your system, it's definitely worth a look.

The EMACS Editor

The only screen-oriented editor that's guaranteed to be included with the UNIX system is vi, but that doesn't mean that it's the only good editor available. An alternative editor that has become quite popular in the last decade (remember that UNIX is almost twenty-five years old) is called EMACS. This section teaches you the fundamentals of this powerful editing environment.

Remember that EMACS is modeless, so be prepared for an editor that is quite unlike vi. Because it's modeless, there's no insert or command mode. The result is that you have ample opportunity to use the Ctrl key.

> **NOTE:** Over the years, I have tried to become an EMACS enthusiast, once even forcing myself to use it for an entire month. I had crib sheets of commands taped up all over my office. At the end of the month, I was able to edit almost half as fast as I could in vi, which I've used thousands of times in the past fourteen years that I've worked in UNIX. I think EMACS has a lot going for it, and generally I think that modeless software is better than modal software. The main obstacle I see for EMACS is that it's begging for pull-down menus like those in a Mac or Windows program. Using Ctrl, Meta, Shift+Meta, and other weird key combinations just isn't as easy for me. On the other hand, your approach to editing may be different, and you may not have years of vi experience affecting your choice of editing environments. I encourage you to give EMACS a fair shake by working through all the examples I have included. You may find it matches your working style better than vi.

Launching EMACS and Inserting Text

Starting EMACS is as simple as starting any other UNIX program. Simply type the name of the program, followed by any file or files you'd like to work with. The puzzle with EMACS is figuring out what it's actually called on your system, if you even have it.

Once in EMACS, it's important to take a look at your computer keyboard. EMACS requires you to use not just the Ctrl key, but another key known as the *Meta key*, a sort of alternative Ctrl key. If you have a key labelled Meta or Alt on your keyboard, that's the one. If, like me, you don't, press Esc every time a Meta key is indicated.

Because there are both Ctrl and Meta keys in EMACS, the notation for indicating commands is slightly different. Throughout this chapter, a control key sequence has been shown either as Ctrl+F or ^f. EMACS people write this differently to allow for the difference between the Ctrl and Meta keys. In EMACS notation, ^f is shown as C-f, where C- always means Ctrl. Similarly, M-x is the Meta key plus x. If you don't have a Meta key, the sequence is Esc, followed by x. Finally, some arcane commands involve both the Ctrl and Meta keys being pressed simultaneously with the other key involved. The notation is C-M-x. This indicates that you need to either press and hold down both the Ctrl and Meta keys while pressing x, or, if you don't have a Meta (or Alt) key, press Esc followed by C-x.

With this notation in mind, leave EMACS by pressing C-x C-c (Ctrl+X, followed by Ctrl+C).

First, see if your system has EMACS available. The easiest way to find out is to type emacs at the command line and see what happens.

```
% emacs
emacs: Command not found.
%
```

This is a good indication that EMACS isn't available. If your command worked and you now are in the EMACS editor, move down to step 2.

A popular version of EMACS, called GNU EMACS, comes from the Free Software Foundation. To see if you have this version, type gnuemacs or gnumacs at the command line.

If this fails to work, you can try one more command before you accept that EMACS isn't part of your installation of UNIX. Online documentation for UNIX is accessible through the man command. The actual database of documents also includes a primitive but helpful keyword search capability, accessible by specifying the -k option (for *keyword searches*) at the command line. To find out if you have EMACS, enter the following:

```
% man -k emacs
gnuemacs (11)   - GNU project Emacs
%
```

This indicates that GNU EMACS is on the system and can be started by entering gnuemacs at the command line.

Rather than start with a blank screen, quit the program (C-x C-c) and restart EMACS with one of the earlier test files, dickens.note:

```
% gnuemacs dickens.note
_                    A Tale of Two Cities
                          Preface
```

```
When I was acting, with my children and friends, in Mr Wilkie Collins's
drama of The Frozen Deep, I first conceived the main idea of this
story. A strong desire was upon me then, to
embody it in my own person;
and I traced out in my fancy, the state of mind of which it would
necessitate the presentation
to an observant spectator, with particular
care and interest.

As the idea became familiar to me, it gradually shaped itself into its
present form. Throughout its execution, it has had complete possession
of me; I have so far verified what
is done and suffered in these pages,
as that I have certainly done and suffered it all myself.

Whenever any reference (however slight) is made here to the condition
of the French people before or during the Revolution, it is truly made,
on the faith of the most trustworthy
witnesses. It has been one of my hopes to add
----Emacs: dickens.note          (Fundamental)----Top-------------------
```

As you can see, it's quite different from the display shown when vi starts up. The status line at the bottom of the display offers useful information as you edit the file at different points. It also displays the name of the file at all times, a feature that can be surprisingly helpful. EMACS can work with different kinds of files. Here you see by the word "Fundamental" in the status line that EMACS is prepared for a regular text file. If you're programming, EMACS can offer special features customized for your particular language.

Quit EMACS by using the C-x C-c sequence, but let a few seconds pass after you press C-x to see what happens. When you press C-x, the bottom of the screen suddenly changes to this:

```
on the faith of the most trustworthy
witnesses. It has been one of my hopes to add
----Emacs: dickens.note          (Fundamental)----Top-------------------
C-x-
```

Confusingly, the cursor remains at the top of the file, but EMACS reminds you that you've pressed C-x and that you need to enter a second command once you've decided what to do. Press C-c and immediately exit EMACS.

Already you can see there are some dramatic differences between EMACS and vi. If you're comfortable with multiple key sequences like C-x C-c to quit, you're going to enjoy learning EMACS. If not, stick with it anyway. Even if you never use EMACS, it's good to know a little bit about it.

How to Move Around in a File

Files are composed of characters, words, lines, sentences, and paragraphs, and EMACS has commands to help you move around in them. Most systems have the arrow keys enabled, which means you won't need some of the key sequences, but it's best to know them all anyway.

The most basic motions are `C-f` and `C-b`, which are used to move the cursor forward and backward one character, respectively. Switch those to the Meta command equivalents and the cursor will move word by word: `M-f` moves the cursor forward a word and `M-b` moves it back a word. Pressing `C-n` moves the cursor to the next line, `C-p` moves it to the previous line, `C-a` moves it to the beginning of the line, and `C-e` moves it to the end of the line. (The vi equivalents for these are `l`, `h`, `w`, and `b` for moving forward and backward a character or word; `j` and `k` for moving up or down a line; and `0` or `$` to move to the beginning or end of the current line. Which makes more sense to you?)

To move forward a sentence you can use `M-e`, which actually moves the cursor to the end of the sentence. Pressing `M-a` moves it to the beginning of the sentence. Notice the parallels between Ctrl and Meta commands: `C-a` moves the cursor to the beginning of the line, and `M-a` moves it to the beginning of the sentence.

Scrolling within the document is accomplished by using `C-v` to move forward a screen and `M-v` to move back a screen. To move forward a page (usually 60 lines of text; this is based on a printed page of information), you can use either `C-x ]` or `C-x [` for forward or backward motion, respectively.

Finally, to move to the very top of the file, use `M-<`, and to move to the bottom, use `M->`.

Go back into EMACS and locate the cursor. It should be at the very top of the screen:

```
         _                   A Tale of Two Cities
                       Preface

When I was acting, with my children and friends, in Mr Wilkie Collins's
drama of The Frozen Deep, I first conceived the main idea of this
story. A strong desire was upon me then, to
embody it in my own person;
and I traced out in my fancy, the state of mind of which it would
necessitate the presentation
to an observant spectator, with particular
care and interest.

As the idea became familiar to me, it gradually shaped itself into its
present form. Throughout its execution, it has had complete posession
of me; I have so far verified what
is done and suffered in these pages,
as that I have certainly done and suffered it all myself.

Whenever any reference (however slight) is made here to the condition
of the French people before or during the Revolution, it is truly made,
on the faith of the most trustworthy
witnesses. It has been one of my hopes to add
----Emacs: dickens.note          (Fundamental)----Top----------------------
```

Move down four lines by using `C-n` four times. You should now be sitting on the "d" in "drama":

```
                     Preface

When I was acting, with my children and friends, in Mr Wilkie Collins's
[d]rama of The Frozen Deep, I first conceived the main idea of this
```

```
story. A strong desire was upon me then, to
embody it in my own person;
and I traced out in my fancy, the state of mind of which it would
```

Next, move to the end of this sentence by using the M-e command (just like vi, EMACS expects two spaces to separate sentences):

```
When I was acting, with my children and friends, in Mr Wilkie Collins's
drama of The Frozen Deep, I first conceived the main idea of this
story._ A strong desire was upon me then, to
embody it in my own person;
and I traced out in my fancy, the state of mind of which it would
```

Now type in the following text: I fought the impulse to write this novel vociferously, but, dear reader, I felt the injustice of the situation too strongly in my breast to deny. Don't press Return or Esc when you're done. The screen should now look similar to this:

```
drama of The Frozen Deep, I first conceived the main idea of this
story. I fought the impulse to write this novel vociferously, but, dear reader,\
 I felt
the injustice of the situation too strongly in my breast to deny_  A strong des\
ire was upon me then, to
embody it in my own person;
and I traced out in my fancy, the state of mind of which it would
necessitate the presentation
```

You can see that EMACS wrapped the line when it became too long (between the words "felt" and "the"), and because the lines are still too long to display, a few of them end with a backslash. The backslash isn't actually a part of the file; with it, EMACS is telling you that those lines are longer than you might expect.

Now try to move back a few letters by pressing Backspace.

Uh-oh! If your system is like mine, the Backspace key doesn't move the cursor back a letter at all. Instead it starts the EMACS help system, where you're suddenly confronted with a screen that looks like this:

```
You have typed C-h, the help character. Type a Help option:

A  command-apropos.  Give a substring, and see a list of commands
              (functions interactively callable) that contain
              that substring. See also the  apropos  command.
B  dEscribe-bindings. Display table of all key bindings.
C  dEscribe-key-briefly. Type a command key sequence;
              it prints the function name that sequence runs.
F  dEscribe-function. Type a function name and get documentation of it.
I  info. The  info  documentation reader.
K  dEscribe-key. Type a command key sequence;
              it displays the full documentation.
L  view-lossage. Shows last 100 characters you typed.
M  dEscribe-mode. Print documentation of current major mode,
              which dEscribes the commands peculiar to it.
N  view-emacs-news. Shows emacs news file.
S  dEscribe-syntax. Display contents of syntax table, plus explanations
T  help-with-tutorial. Select the Emacs learn-by-doing tutorial.
```

```
V  dEscribe-variable. Type name of a variable;
               it displays the variable's documentation and value.
W  where-is. Type command name; it prints which keystrokes
               invoke that command.
--**-Emacs: *Help*                  (Fundamental)----Top----------------------
A B C F I K L M N S T V W C-c C-d C-n C-w or Space to scroll: _
```

To escape the help screen, press Esc. Your screen should be restored. Notice that the filename has been changed and is now shown as `*Help*` instead of the actual file. The status line also shows what file you're viewing, but you aren't always viewing the file you want to work with.

The correct keys to move the cursor back a few characters are `C-b`. Use them to back up. Then use `C-f` to move forward again to the original cursor location.

Check that the last few lines of the file haven't changed by using the EMACS move-to-end-of-file command `M->`. (Think of file redirection to remember the file motion commands). Now the screen looks like this:

```
Whenever any reference (however slight) is made here to the condition
of the French people before or during the Revolution, it is truly made,
on the faith of the most trustworthy
witnesses. It has been one of my hopes to add
something to the popular and picturesque means of
understanding that terrible time, though no one can hope
to add anything to the philosophy of Mr Carlyle's wonderful book.

Tavistock House
November 1859
_
```

```
--**-Emacs: dickens.note            (Fundamental)----Bot----------------------
```

Changing the words of Charles Dickens was fun, so save these changes and quit. If you try to quit the program with `C-x C-c`, EMACS reminds you that there are unsaved changes:

```
--**-Emacs: dickens.note            (Fundamental)----Bot----------------------
Save file /users/taylor/dickens.note? (y or n)  _
```

Pressing y saves the changes, and n quits without saving the changes. If you instead decide to return to the edit session, Esc cancels the action entirely. Pressing n reminds you a second time that the changes are going to be lost if you don't save them.

```
--**-Emacs: dickens.note            (Fundamental)----Bot----------------------
Modified buffers exist; exit anyway? (yes or no)  _
```

This time type yes and, finally, you're back on the command line.

Entering text in EMACS is incredibly easy. It's as if the editor is always in insert mode. The price that you pay for this, however, is that just about anything else you do requires Ctrl or Meta sequences: even the Backspace key did something other than what you wanted. (You could fix the problem with key mapping so that pressing that key results in a C-b command, but then you couldn't get to the help information.)

The motion commands are summarized in Table 7.4.

Table 7.4. EMACS motion commands.

Command	Meaning
M->	Move to end of file.
M-<	Move to beginning of file.
C-v	Move forward a screen.
M-v	Move backward a screen.
C-x]	Move forward a page.
C-x [	Move backward a page.
C-n	Move to the next line.
C-p	Move to the previous line.
C-a	Move to the beginning of the line.
C-e	Move to the end of the line.
M-e	Move to the end of the sentence.
M-a	Move to the beginning of the sentence.
C-f	Move forward a character.
C-b	Move backward a character.
M-f	Move forward a word.
M-b	Move backward a word.

How to Delete Characters and Words

Inserting text into an EMACS buffer is quite simple, and once you get the hang of it, moving about in the file isn't too bad either. How about deleting text? The series of Ctrl and Meta commands that allow you to insert text are a precursor to all commands in EMACS, and it should come as no surprise that C-d deletes the current character, M-d deletes the next word, M-k deletes the rest of the current sentence, and C-k deletes the rest of the current line. If you have a key on your keyboard labeled DEL, RUBOUT, or Delete, you're in luck, because DEL deletes the previous character, `M-DEL` deletes the previous word, and `C-x DEL` deletes the previous sentence.

I have a Delete key, but it's tied to the Backspace function on my system. Every time I press it, it actually sends a `C-h` sequence to the system, not the DEL sequence. The result is that I cannot use any of these backwards deletion commands.

Restart EMACS with the `dickens.note` file and move the cursor to the middle of the fifth line (remember, `C-n` moves to the next line, and `C-f` moves forward a character). It should look like this:

```
                     Preface

When I was acting, with my children and friends, in Mr Wilkie Collins's
drama of The Frozen Deep, I first conceived the main idea of this
story. A strong desire [w]as upon me then, to
embody it in my own person;
and I traced out in my fancy, the state of mind of which it would
necessitate the presentation
to an observant spectator, with particular
```

Notice that my cursor is on the "w" in "was" on the fifth line here.

Press `C-d C-d C-d` to remove the word "was." Now simply type came to revise the sentence slightly. The screen should now look like this:

```
                     Preface

When I was acting, with my children and friends, in Mr Wilkie Collins's
drama of The Frozen Deep, I first conceived the main idea of this
story. A strong desire came_upon me then, to
embody it in my own person;
and I traced out in my fancy, the state of mind of which it would
necessitate the presentation
to an observant spectator, with particular
```

Now press DEL once to remove the last letter of the new word and press e to reinsert it. Instead of backing up a character at a time, instead use `M-DEL` to delete the word just added. The word is deleted, but the spaces on either side of the word are retained.

```
                     Preface

When I was acting, with my children and friends, in Mr Wilkie Collins's
drama of The Frozen Deep, I first conceived the main idea of this
story. A strong desire _upon me then, to
embody it in my own person;
and I traced out in my fancy, the state of mind of which it would
necessitate the presentation
to an observant spectator, with particular
```

Try another word to see if you can get this sentence to sound better. Type crept to see how it reads.

On the other hand, it's probably not good to revise classic stories like *A Tale of Two Cities*, so the best move is to delete this entire sentence. If you press `C-x DEL`, will it do the right thing? Remember, `C-x DEL` deletes the previous sentence. Press `C-x DEL` and the results are helpful, if not completely what you want to accomplish:

```
                         Preface

When I was acting, with my children and friends, in Mr Wilkie Collins's
drama of The Frozen Deep, I first conceived the main idea of this
story. _upon me then, to
embody it in my own person;
and I traced out in my fancy, the state of mind of which it would
necessitate the presentation
to an observant spectator, with particular
```

That's okay. Now you can delete the second part of the sentence by using the `M-k` command. Now the screen looks like what you want:

```
When I was acting, with my children and friends, in Mr Wilkie Collins's
drama of The Frozen Deep, I first conceived the main idea of this
story. _

As the idea became familiar to me, it gradually shaped itself into its
present form. Throughout its execution, it has had complete posession
of me; I have so far verified what
```

Here's a great feature of EMACS! You just realized that deleting sentences is just as wildly inappropriate as changing words, so you want to undo the last two changes. If you were using `vi` you'd be stuck, because `vi` remembers only the last change; but EMACS has that beat. With EMACS, you can back up as many changes as you'd like, usually until you restore the original file. To step backwards, use `C-x u`.

The first time you press `C-x u`, the screen changes to this:

```
When I was acting, with my children and friends, in Mr Wilkie Collins's
drama of The Frozen Deep, I first conceived the main idea of this
story. _upon me then, to
embody it in my own person;
and I traced out in my fancy, the state of mind of which it would
necessitate the presentation
to an observant spectator, with particular
care and interest.

As the idea became familiar to me, it gradually shaped itself into its
present form. Throughout its execution, it has had complete posession
```

The second time you press it, the screen goes even further back in your revision history:

```
When I was acting, with my children and friends, in Mr Wilkie Collins's
drama of The Frozen Deep, I first conceived the main idea of this
story. A strong desire crept_upon me then, to
embody it in my own person;
and I traced out in my fancy, the state of mind of which it would
necessitate the presentation
to an observant spectator, with particular
care and interest.

As the idea became familiar to me, it gradually shaped itself into its
present form. Throughout its execution, it has had complete posession
```

Finally, pressing C-x u three more times causes the original text to be restored:

```
                     A Tale of Two Cities
                          Preface

When I was acting, with my children and friends, in Mr Wilkie Collins's
drama of The Frozen Deep, I first conceived the main idea of this
story. A strong desire [c]ame upon me then, to
embody it in my own person;
and I traced out in my fancy, the state of mind of which it would
necessitate the presentation
to an observant spectator, with particular
care and interest.

As the idea became familiar to me, it gradually shaped itself into its
present form. Throughout its execution, it has had complete posession
of me; I have so far verified what
is done and suffered in these pages,
as that I have certainly done and suffered it all myself.

Whenever any reference (however slight) is made here to the condition
of the French people before or during the Revolution, it is truly made,
on the faith of the most trustworthy
witnesses. It has been one of my hopes to add
--**-Emacs: dickens.note         (Fundamental)----Top----------------------
Undo!
```

Regrettably, if you don't have a DELETE key, some of the deletion commands will be unavailable to you. Generally, though, EMACS has as many ways to delete text as vi has, if not more. The best feature is that, unlike vi, EMACS remembers changes from the beginning of your editing session. You can always back up as far as you want by using the C-x u undo request.

The delete keys are summarized in Table 7.5.

Table 7.5. Deletion commands in EMACS.

Command	Meaning
DEL	Delete the previous character.
C-d	Delete the current character.
M-DEL	Delete the previous word.
M-d	Delete the next word.
C-x DEL	Delete the previous sentence.
M-k	Delete the rest of the current sentence.
C-k	Delete the rest of the current line.
C-x u	Undo the last edit change.

Search and Replace in EMACS

Because EMACS reserves the last line of the screen for its own system prompts, searching and replacing is easier than in vi. Moreover, the system prompts for the fields and asks, for each occurrence, whether to change it or not. On the other hand, this command isn't a simple key press or two, but rather it is an example of a *named EMACS command*.

Searching forward for a pattern is done by pressing C-s and searching backwards with C-r (the mnemonics are *search forward* and *reverse search*). To leave the search once you've found what you want, press Esc. To cancel the search, returning to your starting point, use C-g.

> **WARNING:** Unfortunately, you might find that pressing C-s does very strange things to your system. In fact, ^s and ^q are often used as *flow control* on a terminal, and by pressing the C-s key, you're actually telling the terminal emulator to stop sending information until it sees a C-q. If this happens to you, you need to try to turn off *XON/XOFF* flow control. Ask your system administrator for help.

Query and replace is really a whole new feature within EMACS. To start a query and replace, use M-x query-replace. EMACS will prompt for what to do next. Once a match is shown, you can type a variety of different commands to affect what happens: y makes the change; n means to leave it as is, but move to the next match; Esc or q quits replace mode; and ! automatically replaces all further occurrences of the pattern without further prompting.

You're still looking at the dickens.note file, and you have moved the cursor to the top-left corner by using M-<. Somewhere in the file is the word "Revolution," but you're not sure where. Worse, every time you press C-s, the terminal freezes up until you press C-q because of flow control problems. Instead of searching forward, search backward by moving the cursor to the bottom of the file with M-> and then pressing C-r.

```
----Emacs: dickens.note          (Fundamental)----Bot------------------------
I-search backward:
```

As you type each character of the pattern Revolution, the cursor dances backward, matching the pattern as it grows longer and longer, until EMACS finds the word you seek:

```
Whenever any reference (however slight) is made here to the condition
of the French people before or during the [R]evolution, it is truly made,
on the faith of the most trustworthy
witnesses. It has been one of my hopes to add
something to the popular and picturesque means of
understanding that terrible time, though no one can hope
to add anything to the philosophy of Mr Carlyle's wonderful book.
```

```
Tavistock House
November 1859
```

```
----Emacs: dickens.note          (Fundamental)----Bot---------------------
I-search backward: Revol
```

Now try the query-replace feature. Move to the top of the file with M-<, and then type in M-x, which causes the notation to show up on the bottom status line:

```
of the French people before or during the Revolution, it is truly made,
on the faith of the most trustworthy
witnesses. It has been one of my hopes to add
--**-Emacs: dickens.note          (Fundamental)----Top---------------------
M-x _
```

Then type the words query-replace and press Return. EMACS understands that you want to find all occurrences of a pattern and replace them with another. EMACS changes the prompt to this:

```
of the French people before or during the Revolution, it is truly made,
on the faith of the most trustworthy
witnesses. It has been one of my hopes to add
--**-Emacs: dickens.note          (Fundamental)----Top---------------------
Query replace: _
```

Now type in the word that you want to replace. To cause confusion in the file, change French to Danish. Maybe *A Tale of Two Cities* really takes place in London and Copenhagen! To do this, type French and press Return. The prompt again changes to this:

```
of the French people before or during the Revolution, it is truly made,
on the faith of the most trustworthy
witnesses. It has been one of my hopes to add
--**-Emacs: dickens.note          (Fundamental)----Top---------------------
Query replace French with: _
```

Enter Danish and again press Return.

```
as that I have certainly done and suffered it all myself.

Whenever any reference (however slight) is made here to the condition
of the French_people before or during the Revolution, it is truly made,
on the faith of the most trustworthy
witnesses. It has been one of my hopes to add
--**-Emacs: dickens.note          (Fundamental)----Top---------------------
Query replacing French with Danish:
```

It may not be completely obvious, but EMACS has found a match (immediately before the cursor) and is prompting you for what to do next. The choices here are summarized in Table 7.6.

Table 7.6. Options during query and replace.

Command	Meaning
y	Change this occurrence of the pattern.
n	Don't change this occurrence, but look for another.
q	Don't change. Leave query-replace completely (you can also use Esc for this function).
!	Change this occurrence and all others in the file.

Opt to make this change, and all other possible changes in the file, by pressing !. The screen changes to tell you that there were no more occurrences:

```
Whenever any reference (however slight) is made here to the condition
of the Danish_people before or during the Revolution, it is truly made,
on the faith of the most trustworthy
witnesses. It has been one of my hopes to add
--**-Emacs: dickens.note          (Fundamental)----Top----------------------
Done
```

Searching in EMACS is awkward, due in particular to the flow control problems that you may incur because of your terminal. However, searching and replacing with the query-replace command is much better and more powerful than the vi alternative. Your assessment of EMACS all depends on what features you prefer.

Using the EMACS Tutorial and Help System

Unlike vi and, indeed, most of UNIX, EMACS includes its own extensive built-in documentation and a tutorial to help you learn about using the package. As noted earlier, the entire help system is accessed by pressing C-h. Pressing C-h three times brings up the general help menu screen. There is also an information browser called *info* (accessed by pressing C-h i) and a tutorial system you can start by pressing C-h t.

EMACS enthusiasts insist that the editor is modeless, but in fact it does have modes of its own. You used one just now, the query-replace mode. To obtain help on the current mode that you're working in, you can use C-h m.

Press C-h C-h C-h, and the entire screen is replaced with this:

```
You have typed C-h, the help character. Type a Help option:

A  command-apropos.  Give a substring, and see a list of commands
            (functions interactively callable) that contain
```

```
                   that substring. See also the  apropos  command.
B  dEscribe-bindings. Display table of all key bindings.
C  dEscribe-key-briefly. Type a command key sequence;
                it prints the function name that sequence runs.
F  dEscribe-function. Type a function name and get documentation of it.
I  info. The  info  documentation reader.
K  dEscribe-key. Type a command key sequence;
                it displays the full documentation.
L  view-lossage. Shows last 100 characters you typed.
M  dEscribe-mode. Print documentation of current major mode,
                which dEscribes the commands peculiar to it.
N  view-emacs-news. Shows emacs news file.
S  dEscribe-syntax. Display contents of syntax table, plus explanations
T  help-with-tutorial. Select the Emacs learn-by-doing tutorial.
V  dEscribe-variable. Type name of a variable;
                it displays the variable's documentation and value.
W  where-is. Type command name; it prints which keystrokes
                invoke that command.
--**-Emacs: *Help*              (Fundamental)----Top----------------------
A B C F I K L M N S T V W C-c C-d C-n C-w or Space to scroll: _
```

What now? There are actually 17 different options from this point, as shown in Table 7.7.

Table 7.7. EMACS help system command options.

Command	Meaning
A	List all commands matching the specified word.
B	List all key mappings (EMACS calls them *key bindings*).
C	DEscribe any key sequence pressed, instead of doing it.
F	DEscribe the specified function.
I	Start up the info browser.
K	Fully dEscribe the result of a particular key sequence.
L	Show the last 100 characters you typed.
M	DEscribe the current mode you're in.
S	List a command syntax table.
T	Start the EMACS tutorial.
V	Define and dEscribe the specified variable.
W	Indicate what keystroke invokes a particular function.
C-c	EMACS copyright and distribution information.
C-d	EMACS ordering information.
C-n	Recent EMACS changes.
C-w	EMACS warranty.

Choose K and then press M-< to see what that command really does. The first thing that happens after you enter K is that the table of help information vanishes, to be replaced by the original text. Then the prompt appears along the bottom:

```
of the Danish_people before or during the Revolution, it is truly made,
on the faith of the most trustworthy
witnesses. It has been one of my hopes to add
--**-Emacs: dickens.note           (Fundamental)----Top-----------------------
DEscribe key:-
```

Pressing M-< brings up the desired information:

```
                    A Tale of Two Cities
                         Preface

When I was acting, with my children and friends, in Mr Wilkie Collins's
drama of The Frozen Deep, I first conceived the main idea of this
story. A strong desire came upon me then, to
embody it in my own person;
and I traced out in my fancy, the state of mind of which it would
necessitate the presentation
to an observant spectator, with particular
----Emacs: dickens.note~          (Fundamental)----Top-----------------------
beginning-of-buffer:
Move point to the beginning of the buffer; leave mark at previous position.
With arg N, put point N/10 of the way from the true beginning.
Don't use this in Lisp programs!
(goto-char (point-min)) is faster and does not set the mark.




----Emacs: *Help*            (Fundamental)----All-----------------------
Type C-x 1 to remove help window.
```

A quick C-x 1 removes the help information when you're done with it.

There is a considerable amount of help available in the EMACS editor. If you're interested in learning more about this editor, the online tutorial is a great place to start. Try C-h t to start it and go from there.

Working with Other Files

By this point it should be no surprise that there are about a million commands available within the EMACS editor, even though it can be a bit tricky to get to them. There are many file-related commands too, but this section focuses on just a few essential commands so you can get around in the program. The EMACS help system can offer lots more. (Try using C-h a file to find out what functions are offered in your version of the program.)

To add the contents of a file to the current edit buffer, use the command C-x i. It will prompt for a filename. Pressing C-x C-w prompts for a file to write the buffer into, rather than the default file. To save to the default file, use C-x C-s (that is, if you can: the C-s might again hang you up, just as it did when you tried to use it for searching). If that doesn't work, you can always use the alternative C-x s. To move to another file, use C-x C-f. (EMACS users never specify more than one filename on the command line. They use C-x C-f to move between files instead). What's nice is that when you use the C-x C-f command, you load the contents of that file into another buffer, so you can zip quickly between files by using the C-x b command to switch buffers.

Without leaving EMACS, press C-x C-f to read another file into the buffer. The system then prompts you as follows:

```
of the Danish people before or during the Revolution, it is truly made,
on the faith of the most trustworthy
witnesses. It has been one of my hopes to add
----Emacs: dickens.note          (Fundamental)----Top--------------------
Find file: ~/ _
```

Type buckaroo and the editor opens up a new buffer, moving you to that file:

```
[I] found myself stealing a peek at my own watch and overhead
General Catbird's
aide give him the latest.
"He's not even here," went the conversation.
"Banzai."
"Where the hell is he?"
"At the hospital in El Paso."
"What? Why weren't we informed? What's wrong with him?"
```

```
----Emacs: buckaroo            (Fundamental)----All--------------------
```

Now flip back to the other buffer with C-x b. When you enter that command, however, it doesn't automatically move you there. Instead it offers this prompt:

```
--**-Emacs: buckaroo           (Fundamental)----All--------------------
Switch to buffer: (default dickens.note) _
```

When you press ?, you receive a split screen indicating what the possible answers are:

```
I found myself stealing a peek at my own watch and overhead
General Catbird's
aide give him the latest.
"He's not even here," went the conversation.
"Banzai."
```

```
"Where the hell is he?"
"At the hospital in El Paso."
"What? Why weren't we informed? What's wrong with him?"



--**-Emacs: buckaroo             (Fundamental)----All-----------------------
Possible completions are:
*Buffer List*                    *Help*
*scratch*                        buckaroo
dickens.note




----Emacs:  *Completions*         (Fundamental)----All-----------------------
Switch to buffer: (default dickens.note) _
```

The default is okay, so press Return and go back to the Dickens file. One more C-x b; this time the default is buckaroo, so again press Return to move back.

You're in the buckaroo file, and you want to see what happens if you read dickens.note into this file. This is done easily. Move the cursor to the end of the file with M-> and then press C-x i, answering dickens.note to the prompt Insert file: ~/. Pressing Return yields the following screen display:

```
I found myself stealing a peek at my own watch and overhead
General Catbird's
aide give him the latest.
"He's not even here," went the conversation.
"Banzai."
"Where the hell is he?"
"At the hospital in El Paso."
"What? Why weren't we informed? What's wrong with him?"

                      A Tale of Two Cities
                          Preface

When I was acting, with my children and friends, in Mr Wilkie Collins's
drama of The Frozen Deep, I first conceived the main idea of this
story. A strong desire came upon me then, to
embody it in my own person;
and I traced out in my fancy, the state of mind of which it would
necessitate the presentation
to an observant spectator, with particular
care and interest.

As the idea became familiar to me, it gradually shaped itself into its
present form. Throughout its execution, it has had complete posession
--**-Emacs: buckaroo              (Fundamental)----Top-----------------------
```

It's time to quit and split. To do this, press C-x s and wait for an EMACS prompt or two. The first one displayed is this:

```
As the idea became familiar to me, it gradually shaped itself into its
present form. Throughout its execution, it has had complete posession
--**-Emacs: buckaroo            (Fundamental)----Top--------------------
Save file /users/taylor/buckaroo? (y or n) _
```

Answer y to save this muddled file. It returns you to the top of the file, and a quick C-x C-c drops you back to the system prompt.

This has only scratched the surface of EMACS, a fantastically powerful editor. The best way to learn more is to work through the online tutorial in the editor or to peruse the information available in the help system.

You have now learned quite a bit about the EMACS editor. Some capabilities exceed those of the vi editor, and some are considerably more confusing. Which of these editors you choose is up to you, and your choice should be based on your own preferences for working on files. You should spend some time working with the editor you prefer to make sure you can create simple files and modify them without any problems.

The *sed* Command

In this section, you get to put on your programming hat and learn about a powerful command that can be customized infinitely and used for a wide variety of tasks. sed is a program for modifying information traveling through a UNIX pipeline.

Changing Things En Route with *sed*

I'm willing to bet that when you read about learning some UNIX programming tools in this section, you got anxious, your palms started to get sweaty, your fingers shook, and the little voice in your head said, "It's too late! We can use a pad and paper! We don't need computers at all!"

Don't panic.

If you think about it, you've been programming all along in UNIX. When you enter a command to the shell, you're programming the shell to immediately perform the task specified. When you specify file redirection or build a pipe, you're really writing a small UNIX program that the shell interprets and acts upon. Frankly, when you consider how many different commands you now know and how many different flags there are for each of those commands, you've got quite a set of programming tools under your belt already. So onward!

With a ¦ symbol called a *pipe*, and commands tied together called *pipelines*, is it any wonder that the information flowing down a pipeline is called a *stream*? For example, the command cat test ¦ wc means that the cat command opens the file test and streams it to the wc program, which counts the number of lines, words, and characters therein.

To modify the information in a pipeline, then, it seems reasonable to use a *stream editor*, and that's exactly what the sed command is! In fact, its name comes from its function: stream editor.

Here's the bad news. The sed command is built on an old editor called ed, the same editor that's responsible for the grep command. Remember? The global/regular expression/print eventually became grep. A microcosm of UNIX itself, commands to sed are separated by a semicolon.

There are many different sed commands, but this section focuses on using sed to substitute one pattern for another and to extract ranges of lines from a file. The general format of the substitution command is: s/old/new/flags, where old and new are the patterns you're working with, s is the abbreviation for the substitute command, and the two most helpful flags are g (to replace all occurrences *globally* on each line) and n (to tell sed to replace only the first *n* occurrences of the pattern). By default, lines are listed to the screen, so a *sed expression* like 10q will cause the program to list the first 10 lines and then quit (making it an alternative to the command head -10). Deletion is similar: the command is prefaced by one or two *addresses* in the file, reflecting a request to delete either all lines that match the specified address or all in the range of first to last.

The format of the sed command is sed followed by the expression in quotes and, optionally, the name of the file to read for input.

Here's an easy example. Use grep to extract some lines from the /etc/passwd file and replace all colons with a single space. The format of this command is to substitute each occurrence of : with a space, or s/:/ /:

```
% grep taylor /etc/passwd ¦ sed -e 's/:/ /'
taylorj ?:1048:1375:James Taylor:/users/taylorj:/bin/csh
mtaylor ?:769:1375:Mary Taylor:/users/mtaylor:/usr/local/bin/tcsh
dataylor ?:375:518:Dave Taylor,,,,:/users/dataylor:/usr/local/lib/msh
taylorjr ?:203:1022:James Taylor:/users/taylorjr:/bin/csh
taylorrj ?:662:1042:Robert Taylor:/users/taylorrj:/bin/csh
taylorm ?:869:1508:Melanie Taylor:/users/taylorm:/bin/csh
taylor ?:1989:1412:Dave Taylor:/users/taylor:/bin/csh
```

This doesn't quite do what you want. You neglected to append the global instruction to the sed command to ensure that it would replace all occurrences of the pattern on each line. Try it again, this time adding a g to the instruction.

```
% grep taylor /etc/passwd ¦ sed -e 's/:/ /g'
taylorj ? 1048 1375 James Taylor /users/taylorj /bin/csh
mtaylor ? 769 1375 Mary Taylor /users/mtaylor /usr/local/bin/tcsh
dataylor ? 375 518 Dave Taylor,,,, /users/dataylor /usr/local/lib/msh
taylorjr ? 203 1022 James Taylor /users/taylorjr /bin/csh
taylorrj ? 662 1042 Robert Taylor /users/taylorrj /bin/csh
taylorm ? 869 1508 Melanie Taylor /users/taylorm /bin/csh
taylor ? 1989 1412 Dave Taylor /users/taylor /bin/csh
```

A more sophisticated example of substitution with sed is to modify names, replacing all occurrences of Taylor with Tailor:

```
% grep taylor /etc/passwd ¦ sed -e 's/Taylor/Tailor/g'
taylorj:?:1048:1375:James Tailor:/users/taylorj:/bin/csh
mtaylor:?:769:1375:Mary Tailor:/users/mtaylor:/usr/local/bin/tcsh
dataylor:?:375:518:Dave Tailor:/users/dataylor:/usr/local/lib/msh
taylorjr:?:203:1022:James Tailor:/users/taylorjr:/bin/csh
taylorrj:?:662:1042:Robert Tailor:/users/taylorrj:/bin/csh
taylorm:?:869:1508:Melanie Tailor:/users/taylorm:/bin/csh
taylor:?:1989:1412:Dave Tailor:/users/taylor:/bin/csh
```

The colons have returned, which is annoying. Use the fact that a semicolon can separate multiple sed commands on the same line and try it one more time:

```
% grep taylor /etc/passwd ¦ sed -e 's/Taylor/Tailor/g;s/:/ /g'
taylorj ? 1048 1375 James Tailor /users/taylorj /bin/csh
mtaylor ? 769 1375 Mary Tailor /users/mtaylor /usr/local/bin/tcsh
dataylor ? 375 518 Dave Tailor /users/dataylor /usr/local/lib/msh
taylorjr ? 203 1022 James Tailor /users/taylorjr /bin/csh
taylorrj ? 662 1042 Robert Tailor /users/taylorrj /bin/csh
taylorm ? 8692 1508 Melanie Tailor /users/taylorm /bin/csh
taylor ? 1989 1412 Dave Tailor /users/taylor /bin/csh
```

This last sed command can be read as "each time you encounter the pattern Taylor replace it with Tailor, even if it occurs multiple times on each line. Then, each time you encounter a colon, replace it with a space."

Another example of using sed is to rewrite the output of the who command to be a bit more readable. Consider the results of entering who on your system:

```
% who
strawmye ttyAc   Nov 21 19:01
eiyo     ttyAd   Nov 21 17:40
tzhen    ttyAg   Nov 21 19:13
kmkernek ttyAh   Nov 17 23:22
macedot  ttyAj   Nov 21 20:41
rpm      ttyAk   Nov 21 20:40
ypchen   ttyAl   Nov 21 18:20
kodak    ttyAm   Nov 21 20:43
```

The output is a bit confusing; sed can help:

```
% who ¦ sed 's/tty/On Device /;s/Nov/Logged in November/'
strawmye On Device Ac   Logged in November 21 19:01
eiyo     On Device Ad   Logged in November 21 17:40
tzhen    On Device Ag   Logged in November 21 19:13
kmkernek On Device Ah   Logged in November 17 23:22
macedot  On Device Aj   Logged in November 21 20:41
rpm      On Device Ak   Logged in November 21 20:40
ypchen   On Device Al   Logged in November 21 18:20
kodak    On Device Am   Logged in November 21 20:43
```

This time, each occurrence of the letters tty is replaced with the phrase On Device. Similarly, Nov is replaced with Logged in November.

The sed command can also be used to delete lines in the stream as it passes. The simplest version is to specify only the command:

```
% who ¦ sed 'd'
%
```

There's no output because the command matches all lines and deletes them. Instead, to delete just the first line, simply preface the d command with that line number:

```
% who ¦ sed '1d'
eiyo      ttyAd   Nov 21 17:40
tzhen     ttyAg   Nov 21 19:13
kmkernek ttyAh   Nov 17 23:22
macedot   ttyAj   Nov 21 20:41
rpm       ttyAk   Nov 21 20:40
ypchen    ttyAl   Nov 21 18:20
kodak     ttyAm   Nov 21 20:43
```

To delete more than just the one line, specify the first and last lines to delete, separating them with a comma. The following deletes the first three lines:

```
% who ¦ sed '1,3d'
macedot   ttyAj   Nov 21 20:41
rpm       ttyAk   Nov 21 20:40
ypchen    ttyAl   Nov 21 18:20
kodak     ttyAm   Nov 21 20:43
```

There's more to deletion than that. You can also specify patterns by surrounding them with slashes, just the substitution pattern. To delete the entries in the who output between eiyo and rpm, the following would work:

```
% who ¦ head -15 ¦ sed '/eiyo/,/rpm/d'
root       console Nov  9 07:31
rick       ttyAa   Nov 21 20:58
brunnert  ttyAb   Nov 21 20:56
ypchen     ttyAl   Nov 21 18:20
kodak      ttyAm   Nov 21 20:43
wh         ttyAn   Nov 21 20:33
klingham  ttyAp   Nov 21 19:55
linet2     ttyAq   Nov 21 20:17
mdps       ttyAr   Nov 21 20:11
```

You can use patterns in combination with numbers too, so if you wanted to delete the text from the first line to the line containing kmkernek, here's how you could do it:

```
% who ¦ sed '1,/kmkernek/d'
macedot   ttyAj   Nov 21 20:41
rpm       ttyAk   Nov 21 20:40
ypchen    ttyAl   Nov 21 18:20
kodak     ttyAm   Nov 21 20:43
```

Another aspect of sed is that the patterns are actually *regular expressions*. Don't be intimidated, though. If you understood the * and ? in filename wildcards, you've learned the key lesson of regular expressions: special characters can match zero or more letters in the pattern. Regular expressions are slightly different from *shell patterns*, because regular expressions more powerful (though more confusing). Instead of using the ? to match a character, use the . character.

Within this context, it's rare that you need to look for patterns sufficiently complex to require a full regular expression, which is definitely good news. The only two characters you want to remember for regular expressions are ^, which is the imaginary character before the first character of each line, and $, which is the character after the end of each line.

What does this mean? It means that you can use sed to list everyone reported by who that doesn't have *s* as the first letter of his or her account. You can also eliminate all blank lines from a file with sed. Return to the testme file:

```
% cat testme
Archives/             OWL/                    keylime.pie
InfoWorld/            bin/                    src/
Mail/                 bitnet.mailing-lists.Z  temp/
News/                 drop.text.hqx           testme


Archives/             OWL/                    keylime.pie
InfoWorld/            bin/                    src/
Mail/                 bitnet.mailing-lists.Z  temp/
News/                 drop.text.hqx           testme


Archives/             OWL/                    keylime.pie
InfoWorld/            bin/                    src/
Mail/                 bitnet.mailing-lists.Z  temp/
News/                 drop.text.hqx           testme
```

Now use sed to clean up this output.

```
% sed '/^$/d' < testme
Archives/             OWL/                    keylime.pie
InfoWorld/            bin/                    src/
Mail/                 bitnet.mailing-lists.Z  temp/
News/                 drop.text.hqx           testme
Archives/             OWL/                    keylime.pie
InfoWorld/            bin/                    src/
Mail/                 bitnet.mailing-lists.Z  temp/
News/                 drop.text.hqx           testme
Archives/             OWL/                    keylime.pie
InfoWorld/            bin/                    src/
Mail/                 bitnet.mailing-lists.Z  temp/
News/                 drop.text.hqx           testme
%
```

These commands can be used in combination, of course; one sed command can be used to remove all blank lines, all lines that contain the word keylime, and substitute BinHex for each occurrence of hqx:

```
% cat testme | sed '/^$/d;/keylime/d;s/hqx/BinHex/g'
InfoWorld/            bin/                    src/
Mail/                 bitnet.mailing-lists.Z  temp/
News/                 drop.text.BinHex                testme
InfoWorld/            bin/                    src/
Mail/                 bitnet.mailing-lists.Z  temp/
News/                 drop.text.BinHex                testme
InfoWorld/            bin/                    src/
Mail/                 bitnet.mailing-lists.Z  temp/
News/                 drop.text.BinHex                testme
%
```

If you've ever spent any time on an electronic network, you've probably seen either electronic mail or articles wherein the author responds to a previous article. Most commonly, all the lines of the original message are included, each prefixed by >. It turns out that sed is the appropriate tool either to add a prefix to a group of lines or to remove a prefix from lines in a file:

```
% cat << EOF > sample
Hey Tai! I've been looking for a music CD and none of
the shops around here have a clue about it. I was
wondering if you're going to have a chance to get into
Tower Records in the next week or so?
EOF
%
% sed 's/^/> /' < sample > sample2
% cat sample2
> Hey Tai! I've been looking for a music CD and none of
> the shops around here have a clue about it. I was
> wondering if you're going to have a chance to get into
> Tower Records in the next week or so?
%
% cat sample2 ¦ sed 's/^> //'
Hey Tai! I've been looking for a music CD and none of
the shops around here have a clue about it. I was
wondering if you're going to have a chance to get into
Tower Records in the next week or so?
%
```

Recall that the caret (^) signifies the beginning of the line, so the first invocation of sed searches for the beginning of each line and replaces it with >, saving the output to the file sample2. The second use of sed—wherein you remove the prefix—does the opposite search, finding all occurrences of "> " that are at the beginning of a line and replacing them with a null pattern (which is what you have when you have two slash delimiters without anything between them).

I've only scratched the surface of the sed command here. It's one of those commands where the more you learn about it, the more powerful you realize it is. But, paradoxically, the more you learn about it, the more you'll really want a graphical interface to simplify your life.

> **NOTE:** The only sed command I use is substitution. I figure that matching patterns is best done with grep, and it's very rare that I need to delete specific lines from a file anyway. One helpful tip is that sed can be used to delete from the first line of a file to a specified pattern, meaning that it can easily be used to strip headers from an electronic mail message. Specify the pattern 1,/^$/d.

Getting Around
the Network

8

*By Rachel and
Robert Sartin*

IN THIS CHAPTER

The "information superhighway" has received a lot of attention recently. Much of this "network of the future" is with us today. This chapter introduces you to the basic UNIX software that is used today to connect hundreds of thousands of machines together in the Internet and USENET.

Connecting machines in a network gives you even more computing and information resources than you can get from simply having a computer at your desk or in your computing center. With a network of machines connected together, you will be able to share data files with co-workers, send electronic mail, play multiuser games with people from all over the world, read USENET news articles, contribute to worldwide discussions, perform searches for software or information you need, and much more. In this chapter you will learn about the two most common ways to connect UNIX machines together in a network: UUCP and TCP/IP. On this simple base exists a worldwide network of machines and services that has the potential to greatly increase your productivity. By learning to use these services effectively, you will open the door to new possibilities using your computer. This chapter only begins to probe the extent of available software and resources. Please refer to the Sams Publishing book *Internet Unleashed* for even more information on this topic.

What Is a Network?

A *network* is a system of two or more computers connected to one another. In this chapter you will learn about some of the common ways to network UNIX machines together. At the simplest end of the scale, a network can be two UNIX machines connected to each other using a serial line (typically through a modem) and running *UUCP*, the UNIX-to-UNIX Copy Program. More complicated network configurations run *TCP/IP*, the Transfer Control Protocol/Internet Protocol, the common name for the protocol family used on the Internet, a collection of networks that allows you to connect your computer to hundreds of thousands of other computers.

UUCP—The Basic Networking Utilities

Early in the history of UNIX, it became apparent that it would be advantageous to connect UNIX machines so that they could share some resources. One of the attempts to connect machines together resulted in the UUCP protocol, which allows you to connect two UNIX machines to each other using a serial line (often with a modem attached). The primary focus of UUCP is to allow files to be copied between two UNIX machines, but there are services built on top of UUCP that allow execution of certain commands, such as news and mail commands, thus enabling more sophisticated processing. You can use UUCP to send electronic mail between two UNIX machines and to transmit and receive USENET news articles. The most common release of UUCP available now is often called either *BNU*, the Basic Networking Utilities—the System V version of UUCP, or HoneyDanBer (HDB). There are other freely available and commercial implementations of UUCP. Although UUCP originated on UNIX and was designed specifically for copying between UNIX machines, there are now versions of UUCP that run on MS-DOS and other platforms.

> **NOTE:** Just in case your UNIX machine does not include UUCP, there is a freely available version of UUCP (Taylor UUCP) on the CD-ROM. You can build this version on your UNIX machine and it will interoperate with HDB UUCP.

TCP/IP—LAN, WAN, and the Internet

In the 1970s, the United States Department of Defense began a research program called DARPA, the Defense Advanced Research Projects Administration. One of the efforts of DARPA was to create an *Internet*, an interconnected set of networks, that would allow research labs across the country to interact. This network was called the ARPAnet and the protocol that ran the interconnections was and is called *IP*, or Internet Protocol. Since the original ARPAnet, internetworking has grown incredibly and there is now a huge and difficult-to-define thing called the Internet that allows interconnections between computers all over the world. The Internet includes hundreds of thousands of machines (because of the amorphous nature of the Internet, it is difficult even to get an accurate count) connected through a series of public and private networks.

The Internet Protocol allows the sending of packets between any two computers that are connected to the Internet. IP supplies only a primitive service and further levels of protocol exist that use IP to perform useful functions. Two very common protocols are *TCP/IP* and *UDP/IP*. TCP/IP connects two programs in much the same way a serial line connects two computers. UDP/IP, the User Datagram Protocol/IP, supplies a simple way of sending short messages between two programs. Most interesting user programs that use IP networking use TCP to create a connection, so "TCP/IP" is often used to refer to the interconnection protocol on the Internet.

Names and Addresses

To use machines and resource on the network, you need to locate them. Hostnames use a hierarchical naming space that allows each hostname to be unique, without forcing it to be obscure or unpronounceable. For example, `ftp.uu.net` is the name of one host on the Internet. IP itself uses *Internet addresses*, unique identifiers of Internet hosts, which are usually written in *dot notation*, four numbers (each between 0 and 255), separated by periods. For example, `192.48.96.9` is the address (as of this writing) of the host `ftp.uu.net`, which is covered in the section "Transferring Files—`rcp`, `ftp`, `uucp`."

What's in a Name?

Hostnames on the Internet are a series of "words" separated by periods, or *dots*. The dots separate different parts of the name. The naming system used is called the *domain naming system* (DNS) because it separates responsibility for unique names into administrative domains. The administrator of each domain is responsible for managing and assigning unique names within that domain. The management of the *top-level* or *root* domain, the extreme right word in a hostname, is responsible for the naming conventions. The best way to understand hostnames is to start out by reading them right to left, one word at a time. See Figure 8.1 for a sketch of the hierarchical name space used in these examples.

FIGURE 8.1.

A tree of hostnames.

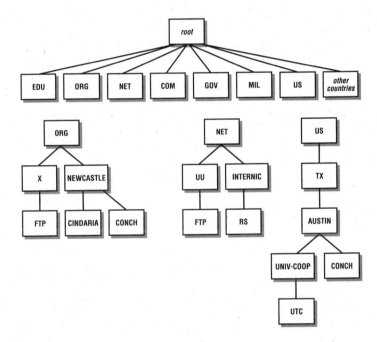

Look at the hostname `ftp.uu.net`. Reading right to left, the first word is `net`, which means that the hostname is a network service provider; see Table 8.1 for explanations of this and other top-level names. The next word is `uu`. Within `.net`, `uu` belongs to UUNET Communications, a company that supplies networking services. Elsewhere in the domain naming space, the name `uu` may mean something else.

Table 8.1. Top-level domains.

Domain	Meaning
EDU	Educational. Colleges and Universities.

continues

Domain	Meaning
ORG	Organizations. Nonprofit and not-for profit.
NET	Networks. Networking services providers (some under COM).
COM	Commercial. Businesses.
GOV	Government. United States government offices.
MIL	Military. The U.S. Armed Forces.
cc	Countries. *cc* is an ISO country code.
US	An example of a country code. The United States.

NOTE: Due in part to the history of the ARPAnet, most hosts in the United States (and some international organizations and businesses) are under EDU, ORG, NET, COM, GOV, or MIL. Many hosts in other countries are under a top-level domain that is the two-character ISO country code for the country. To further confuse things, the United States has a U.S. zone that includes local organizations, primary and secondary schools, and local governments.

Look at the hostnames conch.newcastle.org and conch.austin.tx.us. The org means that the name belongs to an organization. The newcastle means that Newcastle Associates is the owner. Finally, conch is a particular host in Newcastle's network. In the second name, us means the United States, tx means Texas, austin means the city Austin, and conch is a particular hostname. Note that the two machines are completely different machines with different owners. They happen to share one component of their name, but that is not a problem because of the hierarchical namespace presented by DNS.

In fact, there are many repetitions of names. There are many machines on the Internet that have ftp as the first part of their domain names, and many that have www as the first part of their names. The advantage of using the DNS is that these repetitions are not in conflict. It has been said about names that "all the good ones are taken," but the DNS allows you to reuse some of the good ones in a different context. Try using Figure 8.1 to figure out these hostnames:

```
ftp.x.org
ftp.uu.net
ftp.newcastle.org
rs.internic.net
utc.univ-coop.austin.tx.us
```

Notice that `utc.univ-coop.austin.tx.us` has a different number of components than some of the other names you looked at. The DNS can grow by creating a deeper tree. The owner of a domain may add new domains to make it easier to add more hosts.

> **NOTE:** In addition to having an official name, some hosts have *aliases* as well. The alias is simply another name for the host. For example, `ftp.x.org` is actually an alias for the current machine being used for ftp by `x.org`.

Using Shorter Names

Usually, the DNS is configured to use a *search path* for hostnames that don't end in a dot. This lets you use shorter names for hosts in your search path. Typically, your DNS will be configured to search your domain and then search progressively up to the root domain. Check your system documentation to see if you can change the DNS search path. If you were on `cnidaria.newcastle.org` and used the name `newcstle.net`, it would try the following names, matching the first one that exists:

- `newcstle.net.newcastle.org`
- `newcstle.net.org`
- `newcstle.net`

> **TIP:** Because of the search algorithm, you may see faster network access if you use full names ending in a dot for machines outside your local domain.

Decoding Addresses and Ports

Although DNS names are a reasonably convenient way for humans to refer to hosts, the Internet Protocol needs to use a 32-bit Internet address to find a host on the network. For example, as of this writing the host `ftp.uu.net` has the Internet Address `192.48.96.9`. Internet address are usually written using *dot names*, with four numbers between 0 and 255, separated by dots. Note that each of the four numbers is 8 bits, so you end up with a 32-bit Internet address.

It is not enough just to connect to the correct machine. You also need to connect to the correct program. TCP/IP and UDP/IP use *ports* to specify where a connection will go. In order to make a connection to a remote computer, there has to be some program listening on the correct port. If you think of IP addresses as being like phone numbers, a *port number* is like an extension. Once your IP message reaches the correct machine, the port number enables it to be delivered to the correct program.

When a new protocol is adopted as a standard, it is assigned a port number that will always be used for that protocol. For example, the login protocol used to implement `rlogin` is assigned port 513, and `telnet` is assigned port 23. You can examine the assignments of ports to protocols by looking at the file `/etc/services` on your machine. If you are running NIS (the Network Information System, formerly called the Yellow Pages), you can run the command `ypcat services` to look at the map.

Look at what happens when you run the command `rlogin remotehost`. If `remotehost` is willing to accept `rlogin` requests, there is a program waiting for connections on port 513 on `remotehost`; this program (called `inetd`) will handle all of the work on `remotehost` that needs to be performed to allow you to use `rlogin` (`inetd` does this by handing the incoming connection to a program called `rlogind`, which implements the protocol). The `rlogin` program on your host attempts to open a connection to port 513 on the `remotehost`. The program monitoring port 513 on `remotehost` will accept the connection and let your `rlogin` program perform the setup necessary to perform a login.

Converting Names to Addresses

You have seen what hostnames look like and what the low-level Internet address and port numbers are, but you still need to learn how names get converted to addresses.

Hostname conversion is usually handled by the domain naming system, which, in addition to specifying what hostnames look like, specifies a protocol for translating hostnames to addresses. First look at a hostname conversion of the name `ftp.x.org`. When your local host tries to convert the name `ftp.x.org` to an IP address, it contacts a *nameserver*, a machine that has DNS mappings loaded and is prepared to answer questions about them. Your nameserver is also configured with information about how to contact other nameservers so it can look up names that it doesn't already know.

A Brief Introduction to NIS

When implementing a network, one of the common problems that arises is management of `passwd` and group files. Some organizations wish to have a common user and group list for all or most hosts in a network. The Network Information Service, introduced by Sun, is one way to solve this problem. NIS allows sharing of `passwd`, group, and other information between hosts that share administrative control. Other (commercial and freely available) solutions to this problem exist, but none have yet become as widespread as NIS.

If you are running NIS, you should use the command `ypcat passwd` to examine the `passwd` information on your system. The actual `/etc/passwd` file will not list all of the users who can log in to a machine running NIS. If you are using NIS to manage `passwd` files, your password will be the same on any machine in your network that runs NIS. NIS may also be used to create an environment where you can share files transparently between systems. This is done using the network file system, NFS, which enables you to mount a file system from a mount computer and access it as if it were local. Some computing environments configure NIS so that your HOME is always the same directory, no matter what machine you use. This means that your files will be accessible no matter what machine in the network you are using. Check with your system administrators to find out if NIS is running and if it is being used to handle automounting of home (and other) directories.

I'm on the Wire—*rlogin, telnet, cu*

With the three services rlogin, telnet, and cu, you can connect to a remote computer over the network. rlogin uses the login service to connect using the TCP/IP protocol over the network, telnet uses the telnet service to connect using the TCP/IP protocol over the network, and cu connects over a phone line.

Before Using *rlogin, rsh,* and *rcp*

Before you use rlogin, some user configuration may be needed. The same configuration is used for rsh and rcp. You should refer to these details when reading the next section as well. For reference, *loc-host* is used as the local machine name and *rem-host* is the name of the remote machine.

Two files on the remote machine affect your remote access ability: /etc/hosts.equiv and .rhosts in the remote user's home directory. The hosts.equiv file contains a list of hostnames. Each machine in this list is considered to be a trusted host. Any user who has an account on both *loc-host* and *rem-host* is allowed to access the remote machine from the local machine without question. The "without question" is important and means that the user does not have to supply a password for access.

> **TIP:** System administrators should seriously consider disabling the rlogin and rexec protocols on machines that are directly connected to the Internet since the authentication used on these protocols is very weak. At the very least, be extremely careful about entries in /etc/hosts.equiv and any .rhosts files.

The .rhosts file in the remote user's home directory contains a list of trusted host and user pairs. This is similar to the trusted hosts of the hosts.equiv file, but gives a finer grain of control. Each entry grants trusted access to one particular user on a particular host rather than to all common users on a particular host. Lines in .rhosts that name only a machine will grant access to a user with the same login name. The user on *loc-host* can access *rem-host* without question (that is, without specifying a password). The user authentication is done by the protocol.

Usually only the system administrator can change the values in the /etc/hosts.equiv file. Since this file allows many users access, this is a system configuration file. But each user can set up his or her own .rhosts file. This file must live in the user's home directory and be owned by the user (or by root). The ownership restrictions are security measures preventing a user from gaining access to another user's account.

Listing 8.1 and Listing 8.2 show examples of the hosts.equiv and .rhosts files. These two files are located on the machine called flounder, and the .rhosts file is owned by user rob and is located in his home directory. The two hosts listed in the /etc/hosts.equiv file, manatee and dolphin, are trusted hosts to flounder. Any user with an account on manatee and flounder may remotely access flounder from manatee without specifying a password. Likewise, any user with an account on dolphin and flounder may remotely access flounder from dolphin without specifying a password.

Listing 8.1. /etc/hosts.equiv **and** $HOME/.rhosts **files.**

```
manatee
dolphin
```

Listing 8.2. /users/rob/.rhosts **on machine** flounder.

```
french-angel
rob yellowtail
rob dolphin
rob dolphin
root dolphin
diane stingray
rob stingray
root flying-gurnard
root
```

The .rhosts file of the user rob contains a list of users on a remote machine who may access flounder as user rob without specifying a password. That sentence packed several important points together that need expanding:

■ **The .rhosts file of user rob.** This implies that the machine flounder has a user account, with rob as the user name. The home directory of user rob (the example implies it is /users/rob) has a file named .rhosts that is owned by rob.

■ **Users on a remote machine who may access flounder.** Each entry in the list is a pair of names—the machine name and the associated user name. This pair of names describes one particular user who may access flounder. That user must be accessing flounder from the specified machine. It is not enough for the user to simply have an account on the machine; the remote access must be initiated from that machine (by that user).

■ **As user rob.** This is probably the most subtle of all the points, so be careful here. Any of the users who are in the list may access rob's account on flounder, as rob. They "become" rob on flounder even if they were a different user on the initiating machine. This is effectively the same as giving rob's password on machine flounder to this user. Because of this, be extremely selective about entries in your .rhosts files!

■ **Without specifying a password.** Some services (rlogin) allow for the possibility of a password prompt. If the user authentication was not successful via the equivalence files, the service is able to fall back on the prompt method of authentication. So the ability to access a remote host without specifying a password may not be needed. Other services (rsh and rcp) do not have a way to prompt for a password. In order to use these services, the access must be configured so that specifying a password is unnecessary.

Using Listing 8.2, for each of the following scenarios, decide if the user would be able to access flounder—as rob—without a password. Assume that each user has an account on the local machine in the question, as well as on flounder.

1. User root on machine stingray?

2. User root on machine manatee?

3. User root on machine french-angel?

4. User frank on machine dolphin?

5. User frank on machine stingray?

6. User frank on machine tarpon?

7. User diane on machine manatee?

8. User diane on machine dolphin?

9. User diane on machine flying-gurnard?

10. User rob on machine yellowtail?

11. User rob on machine dolphin?

12. User rob on machine manatee?

13. User rob on machine flying-gurnard?

Here are the answers:

1. Yes; rob's .rhosts file has an entry stingray root.

2. No; rob's .rhosts file does not have an entry manatee root. However, root from manatee could access flounder—as root—without a password, because manatee is listed in /etc/hosts.equiv.

3. No; rob's .rhosts file does not have an entry french-angel root.

4. No; rob's `.rhosts` file does not have an entry `dolphin frank`. However, `frank` from `dolphin` could access `flounder`—as `frank`—without a password, because `dolphin` is listed in `/etc/hosts.equiv`.

5. No; rob's `.rhosts` file does not have an entry `stingray frank`.

6. No; rob's `.rhosts` file does not have an entry `tarpon frank`.

7. No; rob's `.rhosts` file does not have an entry `manatee diane`. However, `diane` from `manatee` could access `flounder`—as `diane`—without a password, because `manatee` is listed in `/etc/hosts.equiv`.

8. Yes; rob's `.rhosts` file has an entry `stingray diane`.

9. No; rob's `.rhosts` file does not have an entry `flying-gurnard diane`.

10. Yes; rob's `.rhosts` file has an entry `yellowtail rob`.

11. Yes; the `/etc/hosts.equiv` file has an entry `dolphin`. Note that if the system administrator removed this entry, this answer would still be yes because of the `dolphin rob` entry in his `.rhosts` file.

12. Yes; the `/etc/hosts.equiv` file has an entry `manatee rob`.

13. No; the `/etc/hosts.equiv` file does not have an entry `flying-gurnard` nor does rob's `.rhosts` file have an entry `flying-gurnard rob`.

Using *rlogin*

If you need or wish to be logged in to a computer that is away from your current location, `rlogin` can help you. The `rlogin` application establishes a remote login session from your machine to another machine that is connected via the network. This machine could be next door, next to you on your desk, or even on a different continent. When you successfully execute an `rlogin` from your screen, whether it is a terminal, or one window of your graphical display, the shell that prompts you and the commands you enter are executing on the remote machine just as if you sat down in front of the machine and entered `login`.

Establishing an *rlogin* Connection

The `rlogin` command takes a mandatory argument that specifies the remote host. Both the local and remote host must have `rlogin` available for a connection to be established. If this is the case, the local `rlogin` will connect to the specified remote machine and start a login session.

During a nonremote login, the login process prompts you for two things: your user name and your password. Your user name identifies you to the computer and your password authenticates that the requester is really you. During an `rlogin`, the `rlogin` protocol takes care of some (or even all) of this identification/authorization procedure for you. The `rlogin` protocol initiates the login session on the remote host for a particular user. By default, this user is the same as the local user (that is, you). In this case, you never have to type in your user name. However, if you wish to log in to the remote host as a different user, you may override the default user name by using the `-l` option to specify a user name.

The `rlogin` protocol may even take care of the authentication for you. If you (or your system administrator) have made the proper entry in the `/etc/hosts.equiv` or your `$HOME/.rhosts` file, no authentication is necessary (that is, you will not be prompted for your password). If these files do not have entries for your host and user name, a password prompt will be printed just like in a local login attempt.

Let's look at a few examples. Assume that your user name is `rachel` and the local machine to which you're logged in is called `moray-eel`. To log in as yourself on machine `flounder` you would enter this:

```
$rlogin flounder
```

The connection to `flounder` would take place, and a login session would be initiated for user `rachel` (and fail if user `rachel` doesn't exist on `flounder`). Next, the `rlogin` protocol checks the special files to see if authentication is necessary. If `moray-eel` is listed in the file `/etc/hosts.equiv` or in `~rachel/.rhosts`, no authentication is needed.

To log in to `flounder` as user `arnie` you would enter `rlogin -l arnie flounder`.

Here the login session is initiated with the user name `arnie`. If user `arnie` exists on `flounder`, the special files are checked for authentication. Since the user name for the remote login is different than the local user name, the `/etc/hosts.equiv` file does not provide authentication. If the file `~arnie/.rhosts` has an entry `moray-eel rachel`, no authentication is necessary (that is, login succeeds without password). If this entry does not exist, the password prompt will appear and you must enter the password associated with user `arnie`. This is not a prompt for your password.

Failed Connect

Several things may go wrong when you try to connect to a remote machine via `rlogin`. Some of these are problems that are out of your control. In these instances, you should contact a system administrator to help you solve the problem.

In cases where authentication is necessary, you might enter the password incorrectly. If this happens, the result is the same as in a local login attempt. The login process lets you try again by prompting first for your user name and then your password. Note that this is the only situation in which you must supply your user name if you're trying to `rlogin` as yourself.

For most other problems you will need your system administrator's help. See the section "Troubleshooting" for ways to identify the cause of the problem. Any details about the problem symptoms will help the person who is responsible for fixing the problem. Some of the problems you might see are the following:

- The user account does not exist on the remote.
- Your local host is not connected to the remote via the network.
- The remote host is down.
- The remote host does not support `rlogin`.
- The network between the local and remote hosts is having problems.

Using the Remote Login Session

After a successful remote login, the `rlogin` protocol initiates your session using some information from your local session. This saves you the trouble of having to initialize your environment totally from scratch. Your terminal type (the value of the TERM environment variable) is propagated. Other information, such as baud rate and your screen (window) size, may also be propagated, depending on what the local and remote hosts support.

Then the login process proceeds as if you were actually directly connected to this machine. All of the information and files are taken from the remote. The remote password file contains the user account information, including the login shell to be executed and the starting (HOME) directory. All shell start-up files (found on the remote) execute, which further initializes your environment. When the start-up completes, the shell prompt you see is the shell that is running on the remote host.

> **NOTE:** In some LAN environments, the network is configured such that your HOME directory is on a remote file server that is mounted on each machine you access. In this case, you actually have just one physical HOME directory, and thus just one set of dot files (for example, `.login`). This results in the same login environment for you on each machine. However, this makes writing your dot files a little more complicated because you need to take into account all the different machines to accommodate.

> **TIP:** Because the remote prompt and local prompt may look alike, you may wish to include *hostname* in your prompt variable (PS1). If you're ever in doubt about what host the shell prompt is coming from, use the *hostname* command.

When you see the remote prompt, you can enter any commands you would in a local environment. The `rlogin` protocol transfers input and output between the local and remote hosts. This transfer is transparent to you. Sometimes you may notice slow performance, depending on the network speed and load.

During your remote session, you may want to access your local machine. You could just exit your remote session, at which point you would be back at your local prompt. But if you aren't finished using the remote, using `exit` followed by another `rlogin`, possibly multiple times, is tedious. There is a better way—using the escape character.

Using the Escape Character

The `rlogin` protocol provides an escape character that, when typed as the first character on the command line, is treated specially. The default escape character is the tilde (~) character, but you may change this on the `rlogin` command line via the `-e` option. If the character immediately following the escape character is one that the local `rlogin` process recognizes, it performs the function associated with this character. Otherwise the escape character (and the remaining characters) are executed on the remote.

The `~.` character sequence is the command to disconnect from remote. This is not a graceful disconnect, as in an `exit`. It immediately disconnects from the remote. This should only be used when, for some reason, you are unable to execute the `exit` command.

If the local `rlogin` was executed by a job-control shell (C shell or Korn shell), then you can suspend the `rlogin` by the escape sequence ~*susp*, where *susp* is your suspend control character, usually Ctrl+Z. This is very convenient. It saves the multiple `exit` followed by another `rlogin` sequence you would otherwise need for accessing the local machine. In a graphical user interface environment, having two windows—one for the `rlogin` and one locally—solves this problem as well.

It is possible to `rlogin` to one machine, then `rlogin` from there to another machine. You can use multiple escape characters to denote any one of the machines in this chain. As an example, say you are locally logged in to Host A. You are using a job-control shell with suspend set to Ctrl+Z. From Host A, you `rlogin` to Host B. From there you log in to Host C. And from there you `rlogin` to host D. At this point, everything you enter is going all the way to D to execute. In order to reach any host in the chain, just associate one escape character with each host. You must start with your local host, and then go in the same order as the `rlogin`s. In this example, a single ~ refers to Host A, ~~ refers to Host B, ~~~ refers to Host C.

To suspend the `rlogin` from Host B to Host C you would type ~~^Z. This will leave you in your original shell on Host B. In order to return to `rlogin` you would use the `fg` command as with any suspended process.

To disconnect the `rlogin` from Host C to Host D you would type ~~~..

One very common escape sequence, which is not supported on all platforms, is the shell escape, ~!. Typing this sequence causes the rlogin to give you a subshell on the machine that is referred to by ~. You can use multiple escape characters to denote any host within a chain of rlogins. To return to the rlogin, simply exit the subshell.

> **NOTE:** There is a difference between ~*susp* and ~!. The suspend command will put rlogin in the background and let you interact with your original shell (the one from which you ran rlogin). The shell escape will start a new shell as a child of rlogin. (See Figure 8.2.)

FIGURE 8.2.

Processes for suspend and shell escape.

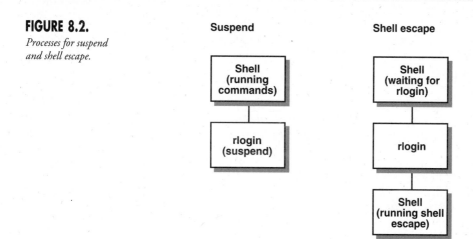

Using Telnet

The telnet service is used to communicate with a remote host via the telnet protocol. Invoking telnet with the remote host as an argument causes telnet to connect to that host. The remote telnet server usually initiates a login just as you would get on a terminal connected to the machine. After your login name and password are entered and verified, you will see the shell prompt on the remote machine. All commands and input you enter go to the remote; all output you receive comes from the remote.

If you wish to enter telnet command mode while you are connected to a remote, type the escape character. The default escape character is Ctrl+], but this can be changed via the set command. To return to the remote connection, simply execute a command. A set command will do this. If you have nothing you want to send or set, do a send nop. The nop argument stands for *no operation*.

If you enter telnet without any arguments, you will start up the telnet service in command mode. You will see a special telnet prompt (telnet>). You can enter any of the telnet commands. Following is a list of some of the most common commands you might use. Refer to your system's manual for `telnet`, for a complete list.

open	Connects to specified host.
close	Disconnects from host and returns to command mode.
quit	Closes the connection (if one exists) and exits telnet.
set	Changes the value for a given argument.
send	Sends a command to the remote and returns to remote connection.
display	Shows current setting of telnet configuration.
status	Shows current status of telnet connection.
?	Gives help.

The following sections look at some of these in a bit more detail.

open

The `open` command takes two parameters, host and port. The host, which is mandatory, can be a hostname or an IP address. This specifies the remote host to which a connection is to be established. This remote host must be reachable via the network and must support the telnet service. The port, which is optional, specifies the port number to use in connecting to the remote host. By default, the port to which telnet connects is the well-known telnet port (23). When a connection on the remote comes in on the telnet port, the remote's telnet service handles the connection. The remote telnet service assumes that the local connector wants to log in and invokes the login process on this connection. You can use this feature to do certain kinds of debugging and troubleshooting. For example, to connect to the mail server on a machine, you could enter `telnet` *hostname* `smtp` (or replace `smtp` with 25 if the first doesn't work). This will connect you directly to the Simple Mail Transfer Protocol on *hostname* and you can use this connection to troubleshoot mail problems. Sometimes network services are offered by telnet to a specific port number. For example, many `gopher` and WWW providers offer a special port for telnet access to the service.

In this default mode, a telnet `open` is somewhat like an `rlogin`. A remote login is initiated on the remote host. But the telnet protocol, unlike `rlogin`, does not perform any conveniences for you. It does not propagate any of your local environment. It does not perform any part of the login procedure (user identification and authentication).

If the first thing you will use telnet for is an `open` command, you do not need to enter telnet command mode at all. On the telnet command line, you can enter a host followed optionally by a port number. This causes telnet to immediately do an `open` with the command-line arguments.

close

The `close` command terminates the open connection (if one exists). On some versions of telnet, this does not exit telnet command mode. So if you are connected to Host B but decide you really want to be connected to Host C, enter `close` and then enter an `open B` command.

quit

The `quit` command should be used when you are finished using telnet. This will perform a close on the open connection (if one exists). Then it terminates the telnet service, returning you to your local shell prompt.

set

Telnet has several internal variables used for configuration. You can use the `set` command to change these values. To see the current variable values, use the `display` command. The telnet escape character can be changed via set.

> **TIP:** You can set certain special characters (such as `erase`) with telnet, but these settings may only work if you run telnet in line mode. Line mode is often used for connecting to remote machines that have line-oriented user interfaces and allows you to compose an entire line of text input before sending it to the remote (when you press return). You should probably not use line mode when connecting to a UNIX machine since interactive commands (such as `vi`), job control, and some shell history (`ksh` interactive command editing) rely on receiving characters as they are typed.

?

The question mark (?) is a telnet command that, without arguments, gives a list of all the telnet commands. This is useful if you've forgotten the name of a command. To get help about a specific command, use `?` with the command as an argument. The `?` can also be used as an argument to the `set`, `send`, and `toggle` commands to list the valid arguments of the command.

Before Using cu

Before you can use `cu`, your system administrator will need to configure the appropriate devices and machines for UUCP access. Check your system's UUCP documentation for information on how to do this.

Using *cu*

The cu service calls up another system. This service is used only to connect two computers via phone lines. Your local host must have an outgoing modem and the remote host must have a modem that supports incoming calls.

Your system administrator may have configured the parameters necessary to call up certain systems. This configuration is kept in the file /etc/uucp/Systems.

> **NOTE:** The actual file depends on which version of UUCP you have. This is correct for SVR4. Since the location may vary, consider this the "systems" file.

You can enter cu *system-name* to dial the remote host. If the remote host has not been configured in the /etc/uucp/Systems file, you can specify the necessary parameters on the command line. The cu *phone-number* command will call up the specified phone number. For example, cu 9=14085551212 will call using the ad device and give it the phone number 914085551212. The equals sign specifies that a pause is desired before the next digit is dialed.

You can also call up using a local device by specifying it with the -1 option. You can use the -1 option to specify the device to use for making the connection. This is generally used only for hardwired connections: cu -1 *dev* dir will connect directly to the line named dev.

Transferring Files—*rcp, ftp, uucp*

Files are the basis for everything you do in UNIX. When you execute a command (aside from Shell built-ins), the associated file contains the executing instructions. When you store or retrieve information, the data is kept in one or more files. The UNIX interface to hardware devices is through device files. Files are pervasive. Therefore, having the necessary files within your reach is extremely important.

Sometimes files you need are not stored on your local machine. Client-server environments are designed to provide a means of sharing files among many machines. When machines on a LAN are configured to share files (via the network), many more files become reachable to you. If you are using NFS, some directories on your system will be mounted from remote machines. These directories and files will be available as part of the normal UNIX file system, and you need no special techniques to access them.

Not all UNIX environments are configured this way. Even those that are may not share all file systems of all machines. Many files exist outside of a local LAN environment. In these cases, you may want to obtain a copy of a file from somewhere other than your local environment. You could use the tools in `I'm on the wire` to remotely log in and access them. But if you need to execute the file locally, or wish to have your own copy of the file, you need to copy the remote file to your local system.

The next section presents several tools to do remote copies. Your local configuration, the remote configuration, the way the remote and local configurations are connected, as well as your personal preference will determine which tool you choose.

Using *rcp*

Before you read this subsection, you should review the section "Before Using `rlogin`, `rsh`, and `rcp`." For `rcp` to work, you must configure the remote machine(s) so that user authentication is not necessary. For each remote you access via `rcp`, an entry in one or both of `/etc/hosts.equiv` and `$HOME/.rhosts` is mandatory. This is because `rcp` does not have a mechanism for in-process authentication (unlike `rlogin`).

Once the configuration is complete, you can use `rcp` in much the same way you use the `cp` command. Each command basically says to "copy File A to Location B." The `rcp` command adds some syntax that enables you to specify remote machines and users.

Specifying a Remote File

You can specify a remote file in several different ways. In general, unless a hostname is specified, the file is considered local. If the character string has a colon (`:`) before any slashes (`/`), the string before the colon specifies the remote host and the string after the colon specifies the file path. Here are three forms of the complete remote file specification:

```
hostname:filepath
user@hostname:filepath
user@hostname.domain:filepath
```

The file path in each can be an absolute path, a relative path, or blank. If it is relative, is it relative to the remote user's HOME directory. The remote user is considered the same as the local user unless explicitly included in the remote specification. In the second and third forms above, the remote user is explicitly included.

If the file path is absolute, this is an absolute path on the remote system. If the file path is blank, the user's HOME directory is assumed.

The hostname can be a simple name or an alias of the remote machine, or it can be a host domain name as in the third form above.

If you wish to use a different user account on the remote machine, you can specify the remote file, including the user name. The user name must refer to an account on the remote machine, and the user's `$HOME/.rhosts` file must contain the proper entry for your local machine.

Understanding the *rcp* Command Line Syntax

The rcp command line is flexible; to support this flexibility, there are a few variations of the command line:

- **rcp single-file dest.** In this variation, the first argument, single-file, is a single file. This file is copied to the destination dest. If dest is an existing directory, the file dest/single-file is created. If dest is an existing file, dest is overwritten with single-file. Otherwise the file dest is created by copying single-file.

- **rcp sources dest.** In this variation, the first argument, sources, is one or more files and/or directories. dest must be a directory. Only the members of sources that are files are copied to the destination dest. If dest is an existing directory, the files are copied under directory dest. It is unwise to specify a dest directory that does not exist with this form of the rcp command. The results vary from system to system. See the next form for copying a single directory.

- **rcp -r sources dest.** By adding the option -r, the files in source as well as the directories (and all their subdirectories) are copied to dest.

  If sources is a single directory, it is okay to specify a destination dest that doesn't exist. The directory will be created for you. This is probably what you want. Beware of this situation, because if dest *does* exist, the copied directory will be placed as a subdirectory of dest.

  If sources is multiple directories and/or files, dest must be an existing directory. If it doesn't exist, the results are not specified and differ from one UNIX system to another.

  Each version of the rcp command line supports an additional option, -p. This option causes rcp to preserve the modification times as well as the modes when the copy is made.

Using ftp

The ftp service is the interface to the file transfer protocol. This service provides a connection service to a remote computer along with file manipulation functions including sending and receiving files. It also provides user authentication, unlike rcp. It supports different file types.

To connect with a remote host, you can simply type ftp *hostname*. The *hostname* can either be a hostname or an Internet address. If you do not specify a remote host on the command line, you enter ftp command mode. Then you can use the open command to initiate a connection.

By default, when a connection is initiated via ftp, the remote ftp server starts up the login process. You must enter a valid user name and password in order to access the remote system. Once you have been authenticated, you are connected to the remote ftp server and it awaits your commands.

The ftp service has a large number of commands. Several common commands are covered in Table 8.2. For complete details, refer to your system's manual for ftp.

Table 8.2. Common ftp service commands.

Connection-Related Commands

open	Open a connection to specified host.
close	Close current open connection.
quit	Close current open connection and exit ftp.

File Transfer–Related Commands

binary	Change the file representation type to binary.
ascii	Change the file representation type to ascii.
put	Transfer a single file from the local to the remote host.
mput	Transfer multiple files from the local to the remote host.
get	Transfer a single file from the remote to the local host.
mget	Transfer multiple files from the remote to the local host.

File- and Directory-Management Commands

cd	Change remote's current working directory (UNIX cd).
lcd	Change the local's current working directory (UNIX cd).
cdup	Change remote's current working directory to be the parent directory (UNIX cd ..).
dir	List the remote's current working directory (UNIX ls).
pwd	Print the remote's current working directory (UNIX pwd).
mkdir	Make a new directory on the remote (UNIX mkdir).
rmdir	Delete a directory on the remote (UNIX rmdir).
rename	Change the name of a remote file or directory (UNIX mv).
delete	Delete a remote file (UNIX rm, with one file specified).
mdelete	Delete multiple remote files (UNIX rm, with multiple files).

Miscellaneous Commands

?	Obtain help about ftp.
!	Escape shell.

Connection-Related Commands

The ftp connection-related commands are fairly straightforward. The open command tries to connect to the ftp server on the specified remote host. The close command terminates the open connection (if one exists) and then returns to command mode. This is usually used when you want to connect to a different host, so you will commonly follow it with an open. The quit command closes the connection and then exits ftp.

File Transfer–Related Commands

The ftp service defines several file representation types for transfer. The two most common are ascii and binary. By default, the type is set to ascii. Any file that is plain ASCII text can be transferred using ascii type. Binary files, like a compiled and linked executable file, must be transferred using binary type. Be sure to set the correct type before transferring any files.

> **TIP:** Transferring ASCII text files between UNIX machines is slightly faster with binary type, but using binary type to transfer an ASCII text file between a UNIX and a non-UNIX machine may corrupt the file.

> **TIP:** If you are having trouble decoding or executing a binary file you get elsewhere, check to make sure you used binary type transfer.

The get and mget commands transfer files from the remote to the local host. The put and mput commands transfer files from the local to the remote host. Both get and put transfer one file per command. On both of these commands you may specify the destination for the file copy. If the destination is not specified, the file is placed in the current working directory. Both mget and mput transfer multiple files per command. The files are placed in the current working directory.

File- and Directory-Management Commands

The file- and directory-management commands are analogous to UNIX file and directory commands. In Table 8.2, the UNIX command that is analogous to the ftp command is given in parentheses. Remember that all of these commands, except lcd, operate on the remote file system. If you need to perform more in-depth local file management, use the shell escape command (!) to escape to a local shell prompt.

Miscellaneous Commands

The ? command provides help about ftp commands. If you want help about a specific command, you can specify this command as the first argument to the ?. The shell escape command (!) is used to start a subshell on the local machine. This is very useful if you need to perform some operations on your local host while you are connected to a remote ftp server. After you are finished working on the local host, simply exit the (sub)shell and you will return to ftp.

Configuring with .netrc

The ftp command can automatically perform the login to remote ftp servers and initialize your connection. It does this by reading in the .netrc file in your home directory. You can configure the login, password, and account (some ftp servers allow or require an extra account specification at authentication time) to use for a particular machine. In the following example from the .netrc file, automatic login is included as anonymous for several popular servers:

```
machine dg-rtp.rtp.dg.com login anonymous password sartin@pencom.com
machine town.hall.org login anonymous password sartin@pencom.com
machine ftp.uu.net login anonymous password sartin@pencom.com
machine rtfm.mit.edu login anonymous password sartin@pencom.com
machine ftp.x.org login anonymous password sartin@pencom.com
machine prep.ai.mit.edu login anonymous password sartin@pencom.com
machine ftp.ncsa.uiuc.edu login anonymous password sartin@pencom.com
machine emx.cc.utexas.edu login anonymous password sartin@pencom.com
machine boombox.micro.umn.edu login anonymous password sartin@pencom.com
machine rs.internic.net login anonymous password guest
```

TIP: Most versions of ftp will use your .netrc for password information only if the file is readable by you only. For password security this file should be unreadable by others or, better yet, should contain no sensitive passwords.

Anonymous ftp

There is a special login for ftp that allows you to anonymously access files on part of a remote machine. Anonymous access is not entirely anonymous, since some machines will log the connection, the password used, and all files retrieved. To use anonymous ftp, you use the login anonymous (on some machines, the login ftp will work) and supply any non-empty string for the password.

TIP: Some machines do password validation on anonymous logins. Most require that you supply a valid e-mail address.

Once you have successfully logged in as anonymous you will be granted limited access to the anonymous ftp subtree on the remote machine. All of the commands described in this section can be used. Some sites have a directory called /incoming (or a directory named incoming somewhere in the ftp tree) where you will be able to put files. Many sites put the publicly accessible files under /pub.

Using *uucp, uuto,* and *uupick*

The file copying tools, uucp, uuto, uupick, are part of the Basic Networking Utilities software release. These may not be on your UNIX system. Even if they are, more recent networking services (for example, ftp and rcp) are preferred. If you are interested in using the uu tools, check your system documentation to see if they are supported.

Following, for the sake of completeness, is a brief summary of these tools. For details, check your system's manual entry for each command.

uucp

The UUCP service copies one or more files from one UNIX machine to another UNIX machine. Use the uuname command to see what remote machines you can reach via uucp. uucp uses an older host naming scheme in the form *hostname!filepath*. To copy a local file, *myfile*, to remote machine *rem-host* to directory /tmp, enter the command uucp *myfile rem-host!*/tmp/.

uuto and *uupick*

The uuto tool sends a file to a specific user on a remote UNIX host. The file is deposited in a special place on the specified remote host. In order for the remote user to receive this file, she or he must use the uupick tool. The remote host and user are specified by the syntax *rem-host!username*. To send the local file *myfile* to user arnie on machine sturgeon enter the command uuto *myfile* sturgeon!arnie

Then user arnie must use the uupick tool to receive the file.

When you are ready to receive files that were sent via uuto, simply enter the uuto command without any arguments. Each file that has been sent to you is displayed, one at a time. As each is displayed, you have the choice of skipping it, moving it, deleting it, or printing it.

Other Networking Services

This section gives a very abbreviated introduction to some other services that are currently available on the Internet. These services give you access to the wealth of information available on the Internet, including source code, current weather information, financial data, computer conferences on a wide variety of topics, and some more frivolous programs, including a computerized tarot reader.

> **CAUTION:** These programs will only be useful to you if you are connected to the Internet and have a gateway that allows you to make outgoing connections. Check your local network configuration to be sure.

> **CAUTION:** These programs can be addictive. Make sure you get enough sleep and social activity between your net surfing excursions.

archie

The `archie` program offers access to a large list of files that are available via anonymous ftp. When you run an `archie` *string* search, the server will search for a name that is an exact match for *string* in its list of archives and will return the matches to you. You can modify the search behavior by specifying one of the following:

-c	Case-sensitive substring search.
-r	Regular expression search.
-s	Case-insensitive substring match. For example, if you were looking for the source to xmosaic, you could enter archie -s xmosaic. The output lists a large number of sites that have xmosaic available via anonymous ftp. Here is part of the response from archie -s xmosaic:

```
Host ftp.engr.ucf.edu

    Location: /pub/linux-mirrors/tsx11/binaries/usr.bin.X11.nomirror
        FILE -rw-r--r--    497473  Dec 26 18:06  xmosaic-1.2.term.tar.z
```

For each host that had a match of the string there is a list of locations that had matches. The best way to use `archie` output is to look for a host "near" you (for example, your service provider, someone in the same city/state as your service provider, someone in the same country) and use ftp to retrieve the desired files.

gopher

The University of Minnesota has developed a program called `gopher`, that you can use to retrieve information over the Internet. They report (in the `00README` file available by anonymous ftp from `boombox.umn.edu` in `/pub/gopher/00README`):

```
The internet Gopher uses a simple client/server protocol that can be used to publish and
search for information held on a distributed network of hosts. Gopher clients have a
```

seamless view of the information in the gopher world even though the information is
distributed over many different hosts. Clients can either navigate through a hierarchy
of directories and documents -or- ask an index server to return a list of all documents
that contain one or more words. Since the index server does full-text searches every
word in every document is a keyword.

If you want to test a gopher client without setting up your own gopher server you should
configure the client to talk to "gopher.micro.umn.edu" at port 70. This will allow you
to explore the distributed network of gopher servers at the University of Minnesota. You
can try the Unix client by telneting to consultant.micro.umn.edu and logging in as
"gopher".

WorldWide Web

In 1991 the European Laboratory for Particle Physics began a project that turned into the
WorldWide Web, also known as WWW or W3. WWW is fairly hard to pigeonhole, and
the best way to become familiar with it is to explore it. WWW is a set of software, conventions, servers, and a protocol (HTTP) for organizing information in a hypertext structure. It allows linking of pictures (both still and moving), sounds, and text of various kinds
into a web of knowledge. You can start at any place (a particularly good place to start is
the default home page at NCSA or a copy of it, using xmosaic) and choose the links that
interest you. Information is located using a *Uniform Resource Locator* (URL), which generally looks like this: *protocol://hostname/path*. The *protocol* tells how to access the
data (and is often http, which indicates the HyperText transfer protocol). The *hostname*
tells the name of the host to access. The *path* gives a host-specific location for the resource;
paths often look like normal UNIX filenames. A big difference between a URL path and
a filename is that a URL path often points to information that is generated on the fly (for
example, a current weather report), and the actual data returned may depend on what
features your WWW client supports. By exploring the Web, you will be able to find information ranging from your personal biorhythms to common questions about the
PowerPC to an archive of SCUBA diving destination reports.

The National Center for Supercomputing Applications at the University of Illinois has
developed World Wide Web interfaces called Mosaic. The UNIX version runs with Motif
widgets using X11 and is called xmosaic.

Troubleshooting TCP/IP

Sometimes you may find that your attempts at making network connection are not working. Some of the common errors for each command were covered in the sections "I'm on
the Wire—rlogin, telnet, cu" and "Transferring Files—rcp, ftp, uucp." This section covers
some system-level troubleshooting you might want to try if you are having trouble making network connections using TCP/IP (rlogin, telnet, rcp, ftp, and the commands
mentioned in the section "Other Services"). The suggestions here will help solve simple

problems and will help classify problems. See Chapter 37, "Networking," for more information on troubleshooting network problems.

nslookup to Check Address Mapping

One common failure in trying to make network connections is either having the wrong hostname or encountering an error or delay in the name service. One way to check the validity of the hostname is to try using the `nslookup` command. The simplest way to run the `nslookup` command is `nslookup` *hostname*:

```
$ nslookup ftp.uu.net.
Name Server: lazerus.pencom.com
Address:  198.3.201.57

Name:    ftp.uu.net
Address:  192.48.96.9

$ nslookup no.such.name.org
Name Server: lazerus.pencom.com
Address:  198.3.201.57

*** lazerus.pencom.com can't find no.such.name.org: Non-existent domain
$
```

This will query the DNS for the name of *hostname* (`ftp.uu.net` in the first example, `no.such.name.org` in the second).

> **TIP:** When a machine is newly added to the DNS, it may take a while before the nameservers learn about it. During that time, you may get "unknown host" errors. The person who adds a new host to the DNS should be able to give an estimate of how long to wait before a DNS failure should be considered an error.

Is There Anybody Out There? (ping)

If you can find the address of a host but your connections are failing, it may be because the host is unreachable or down. Sometimes you may get a "host unreachable" or "network unreachable" error. You will get these messages when the software that manages interconnections was able to determine that it could not send a packet to the remote host. The network routing software has internal tables that tell it how to reach other networks and hosts and these error messages indicate that there is no table entry that lets you reach the desired network or host.

When a host is simply down, you may get connection time-outs. You may want to try using the `ping` command to test if a host is running. The `ping` command sends a special kind of message called an *Internet control echo request message* or *ICMP echo request* (ICMP is the Internet control message protocol). This message asks the remote computer to send back an echo reply that duplicates the data of the echo request message. The low-level networking software of the remote computer will handle responding to an echo request, so a machine should be able to respond to a ping as long as the network software is running.

In the following example, we use ping to check the status of two hosts:

```
$ /etc/ping conch 100 10
PING conch.pencom.com: 100 byte packets
100 bytes from 198.3.200.86: icmp_seq=0. time=3. ms
100 bytes from 198.3.200.86: icmp_seq=1. time=4. ms
100 bytes from 198.3.200.86: icmp_seq=2. time=3. ms
100 bytes from 198.3.200.86: icmp_seq=3. time=5. ms
100 bytes from 198.3.200.86: icmp_seq=4. time=4. ms
100 bytes from 198.3.200.86: icmp_seq=5. time=8. ms
100 bytes from 198.3.200.86: icmp_seq=6. time=3. ms
100 bytes from 198.3.200.86: icmp_seq=7. time=3. ms
100 bytes from 198.3.200.86: icmp_seq=8. time=3. ms
100 bytes from 198.3.200.86: icmp_seq=9. time=3. ms

conch.pencom.com PING Statistics--
10 packets transmitted, 10 packets received, 0% packet loss
round-trip (ms)  min/avg/max = 3/3/8

$ /etc/ping brat 100 10
PING brat.pencom.com: 100 byte packets

--brat.pencom.com PING Statistics--
10 packets transmitted, 0 packets received, 100% packet loss
$
```

In the first example, the 100 says to use 100 bytes of data in each message and the 10 says to use 10 messages. All 10 message were returned. The second example shows what happens when you attempt to ping a host that is not up.

Once you determine that the remote host is not responding, you can either attempt to get the machine back up or wait until later to use it. If the machine is on your LAN, it should be fairly easy to go to it and start it running or talk to a local administrator. If the machine is somewhere remote, you may need to phone or e-mail someone to get assistance. If the machine is a resource on the Internet that is offered by some other school or company, you should probably just wait until it is running again unless your need is urgent (for both you and the remote administrator).

Summary

In this chapter, you have learned how UNIX machines are networked and how to take advantage of that networking. You have learned to log in to remote machines, copy files, begin to surf the Internet, and troubleshoot minor problems. By using these network services, you will be able to perform useful work on networked systems and explore the "information superhighway."

Communicating with Others

By Ron Dippold

The Internet would be useful as simply a data-sharing device—being able to FTP to another site and grab a program is quite useful, as is being able to log on to another machine using telnet. But there's a special type of data that comprises most of the appeal of the Internet—person-to-person communication. You can talk with people around the world, a message at a time or even in real-time.

This chapter covers the following topics regarding communications:

E-mail	Electronic mail enables you to exchange messages with anyone who is a member of any of the major information networks. It's faster and cheaper than snail-mail (the Post Office), and it's often cheaper and more convenient than a phone call.
USENET	Whereas e-mail is person-to-person messaging, USENET is person-to-millions-of-persons messaging on literally thousands of different topics. This is more information per day than any person can read completely, even if all they did was read it.
Talk	Simple person-to-person chat.
IRC	Internet Relay Chat is a multiple-person discussion forum, much like a CB radio channel. It is reportedly more addictive than drugs.

Electronic Mail (E-Mail)

E-mail is one of the most important applications of the Internet as far as companies, schools, and government agencies are concerned. Since these are the entities that heavily influence Internet development by deciding to hook up and offer Internet to their members, it's often considered one of the most important (if not the most important) service the Internet offers. For major online services such as CompuServe, GEnie, or SprintMail, which offer their users access to the Internet for mailing purposes, it's the only Internet service.

Basic Concepts

The basic principle behind e-mail is simple. You write a message using your computer, send it to another computer user, and it appears on that user's computer, where the user reads it. You probably know from experience that composing the letter is not a major technical chore, nor is reading it. The first problem is the same one you encounter with all computer data—organizing your data, in this case e-mail. The second problem is how to format the information—how do you send a program by mail? The third problem, which is far larger, is exactly how you get your message from your machine in Walla Walla, Washington, United States, to your friend's computer in Reykjavik, Iceland. And, since he's probably sharing his Internet computer with other people, how you get it to his account.

Internet Mail Is More Than Internet

The Internet proper is composed of computers tied together at all times by direct links. If your computer is "on the Internet" and my computer is "on the Internet," our machines should be able to exchange data without any dialing involved.

If you think about messages, however, you'll see that individual messages are transferable between machines that connect only occasionally. Each machine can save up messages that need to be sent, then exchange messages when they connect. Bulletin board systems (BBSes) do this routinely. This concept is exploited by many systems that offer "Internet Mail"—the systems can exchange e-mail with other Internet sites even though they are not part of the Internet itself. They do this by occasionally connecting to a system that is really on the Internet and exchanging mail. This is an important concept.

A computer system does not actually have to be part of the Internet to offer Internet Mail access. Since true Internet access is expensive, if you need only e-mail access you will be able to obtain it much more cheaply than true Internet access. There is probably at least one BBS in your area that offers Internet Mail access cheaply, sometimes even for free.

Mail will be slower on such systems. Since they only connect to a true Internet machine occasionally (maybe only once a day), all your outgoing mail and any incoming mail for you is held until this occurs. This introduces a delay of several hours. Since the delivery time for e-mail from one Internet machine to another is often measured in minutes, this is a substantial difference. If you want more, you pay more.

E-Mail Is Text

As far as Internet is concerned, e-mail is plain text, nothing more: This means all letters a through z, numbers 0 through 9, and various punctuation. You can't just send a program using e-mail. Various computers along the way will almost certainly eliminate over half of the message, if it gets transferred at all.

This imposes certain limitations—if you want to do anything special, such as carry other information about the message other than just the basic content, you have to do it within this constraint.

E-Mail Formats

A message from you to another person will probably travel through several machines. Typically, mail from your computer goes to the mail computer for your site, then to your service provider's computer, then to a large "backbone" site. From there it goes to another backbone site, to the recipient's service provider, to the recipient's site, then to the recipient's computer. Obviously, you need some way of addressing mail to a specific person—just sending mail to "John Smith" isn't going to work.

You need some delivery information to go along with the message, but you don't want to modify the vital contents of the message. If you're sending the latest Lorena Bobbitt joke to a friend, you don't want a piece of it chopped off (or otherwise modified).

On the Macintosh, a similar problem is solved by splitting a file into its Resource and Data forks. OS/2 uses extended attributes. You can't do this with the Internet, because e-mail is text only, by definition. You get around this problem by defining every piece of e-mail to consist of two basic pieces—a header and a body.

Internet mail consists of a header and a body. The header comes first, and contains all the information about the message, such as who it came from and who it's for. The end of the header is given by a completely blank line—not even any spaces. The body of the message, which consists of the actual message content, follows.

Actually, a message can consist of a header only. This isn't usual, but it's common enough, usually due to user error, that you shouldn't be surprised to see it.

E-Mail Addressing

How do you get mail to a person on another computer, considering that the mail probably has to pass through several computers?

One way is to list the computers the mail should pass through with the recipient. This is done on the Internet by an almost obsolete format known as UUCP bang-path:

```
comp01!comp02!comp03!username
```

It's called a bang-path because of the exclamation points: bang! bang! bang! Computer people, UNIX types especially, love short names. Exclamation is four syllables, and bang is only one. Plus, it's easier to spell. Thus, a mail path delimited by bangs is a bang-path.

This indicates that you want the mail to pass successively through the computers known as `comp01`, `comp02`, and `comp03`. Once on `comp03` it should go to user `username`. This type of addressing is simple if you know exactly where your mail is going, and it makes it easy for systems along the way to figure out where to send your mail next; but it is a crawling horror otherwise. Imagine if you had to address your snail-mail (post office) mail like this— from my mailbox to my local post office, then the central office, then the regional office, then another regional office, then the central office, then the local office, then the recipient's mailbox. What if one of the offices along the way changes? Oh yes, the names of the offices can each be only six letters long (a UUCP host name limitation).

The post office uses a different concept—each person is identified by country, state, city, and address. A parallel system for the post office (the ZIP code) makes sorting faster for humans, and it guards against sloppy writing causing too many problems. To get a message to someone from anywhere in the world, you just identify them with this information. You don't need to care about the path it takes to get there.

The more standard Internet version of this is domain name addressing, often just called Internet addressing. It looks like this:

```
localname@domain
```

Both pieces are extensible, although `localname` is usually just your user ID. The domain is read from right to left and specifies a series of progressively smaller logical domains (such as country, state, city, then street address). Here's an example:

```
jfaceless@wubba.sales.hugeco.com
```

The far right of the domain, `com`, indicates that this is a commercial site. The period separates it from the next item in the domain. `hugeco` is the name of the entity, in this case HugeCo, Ltd. `sales` specifies a specific department or site within the entity. Finally, `wubba` is the specific computer within the site.

This is known as a "fully-qualified domain name"—the address includes complete information on how to reach good old Joe Faceless, right down to the specific machine. Usually you don't have to be this specific. If there's only one `jfaceless` account within the company, for instance, HugeCo's mail computers should be smart enough to figure out how to route incoming mail to him. In this case, the Internet address he would proudly put on all his business cards would be this:

```
jfaceless@hugeco.com
```

Obviously, if `rawthah@harvard.edu` sends mail to `jfaceless@hugeco.com`, *someone* needs to figure out how to get it to him—this is the province of domain name servers. Let these computers do the work, and you usually don't have to worry about it.

By Internet convention, capitalization in the domain name is ignored. So you could use `HugeCo.Com`, `HUGECO.COM`, or `hugeco.com`. They're all the same. The same thing should happen with the user name as well, but this is not required, and if the site is using poor software it may consider `JFaceless` and `jfaceless` to be different users. It's safest always to preserve the case.

The far-right component of the domain is known as the top-level domain name. The most common in the United States are `edu` (educational sites), `com` (commercial sites), `gov` (government sites), and `mil` (military sites). For other countries, the top-level domain is the two-letter ISO country code. For example, `hans@bratwurst.edu.de` is a user in Germany. This isn't foolproof, as there are sites in Canada that don't bother with using the `.ca` code for Canada.

Sometimes you'll see something like this:

```
uuhost!foobar%yowza@ancient.edu
```

This indicates that once the mail gets to the site `ancient.edu` some other form of addressing takes over. You usually see this when dealing with an ancient system, or when transferring mail with another network.

E-Mail Headers

As explained earlier, the header of a message contains all the information about the message. This generally includes who the message is from, who the message is going to, the date the message was sent, a message subject, and information about computers the message has passed through. These are the usual items, and there can be more. It's not unusual for the header of the message to be larger than the actual contents of the message!

Header Format

A header item looks like this:

```
keyword: value
```

`keyword` identifies the specific type of information this header item contains. It must start at the beginning of the line. `value` contains the actual value of this item. It can stretch over multiple lines—this is indicated by starting following lines with white space (a tab or space).

Here's a common header item:

```
From: wakko@watertower.com
```

This identifies that the message is from `wakko@watertower.com`. Generally, the item is referred to by keyword, so this would be legitimately referred to as the *From header* of the message. This is opposed to just the *header*, which consists of all the header items in the message.

Here's an example of a header including a multiline header item:

```
From: luke@yoda.jedi.edu
Subject: Note how this subject is split and the
 subsequent lines are started with spaces, as
 opposed to the keywords, which are flush left
To: darth@deathstar.empire.gov
```

Minimal Header Items

Technically, the only header item you need to send mail to someone is the To header:

```
To: userid@domain
```

Normally, however, you will be asked for a Subject header when you compose the message. The recipient can view just the subject for a quick idea of what the message is about.

In addition, your mail program will probably add a Date header giving the time the message was sent, and a From header indicating your address. Here's a typical message just before it's sent:

```
From: cerebus@aardvarks.sim.com
To: astoria@regency.com
Date: Wed, 13 Sep 1312 13:43:12 -0300 (PST)
Subject: Talking

    Cerebus is sick of your ceaseless talking. The
    next time he sees you, Cerebus will use his sword,
    then talk.
```

As your message travels from machine to machine, each machine along the way will add some routing information.

Common Header Items

The best way to learn about common headers you will see on messages you receive is to examine an actual message. Most of this is an actual header from a message received by me, with names and addresses tampered with sufficiently to prevent the actual sender from getting strange e-mail.

```
From nihil@eniac.seas.void.edu Wed Feb  1 08:15:01 1993
Flags: 000000000015
Received: from phones.com (phones.com [229.46.62.22]) by
    happy.phones.com (8.6.5/QC-BSD-2.1) via ESMTP;
    id IAA13973 Wed, 1 Feb 1993 08:14:59 -0800 for
    <rdippold@happy.phones.com>
Received: from linc.cis.void.edu (root@LINC.CIS.VOID.EDU
    [230.91.6.8]) by phones.com (8.6.5/QC-main-2.3) via ESMTP;
    id IAA14773 Wed, 1 Feb 1993 08:14:56 -0800 for
    <rdippold@phones.com>
Received: from eniac.seas.void.edu (nihil@ENIAC.SEAS.VOID.EDU
    [230.91.4.1]) by linc.cis.void.edu (8.6.5/VOID 1.4) with
    ESMTP id LAA17163 for <rdippold@phones.com>
    Wed, 1 Feb 1993 11:14:45 -0500
Received: from localhost by eniac.seas.void.edu
    id LAA24236; Wed, 1 Feb 1993 11:14:44 -0500
From: nihil@eniac.seas.void.edu (Ex Nihilo Nihil Fit)
Sender: nihil@ocean.void.edu
Reply-To: nihil@void.edu,nihil@freenet.com
Cc: group-stuff@uunet.UU.NET
Cc: james@foobar.com
Message-Id: <199302011614.LAA24236@eniac.seas.void.edu>
Subject: Re: Apple IIe/IIgs Software and books for SALE...
To: rdippold@phones.com (Ron Dippold)
Date: Wed, 1 Feb 93 11:14:44 EST
In-Reply-To:    <CMM.342342.rdippold@happy.phones.com>;
    from "Ron Dippold" at Feb 1, 93 1:00 am
X-Mailer: ELM [version 2.3 PL11-void1.13]
Mime-Version: 1.0
Content-Type: text/plain; charset=US-ASCII
Content-Transfer-Encoding: 7bit
Content-Length: 10234
```

I told you headers could be large…normally they're not this big, but this is a good example of all the major header items you need to know.

Here's the first line:

```
From nihil@eniac.seas.void.edu Wed Feb  1 08:15:01 1993
```

This line is actually added by my local mail program. It is used both as a quick message summary (who and when) and as a way to separate messages. A typical mail file is just a big text file, so you need some way to tell the start of one message from the end of the next. For most places, this is the text `From` at the start of a line. This also means that if you try to place a `From` at the start of a line of text in your actual message, your mail program should place a > or some other character before it so that it doesn't falsely indicate the start of a new message.

```
Flags: 000000000015
```

Again, this is used by the local mail program. Each message can have several different statuses, such as deleted, unread, and flagged for further attention. This varies from program to program.

```
Received: from phones.com (phones.com [229.46.62.22]) by
    happy.phones.com (8.6.5/QC-BSD-2.1) via ESMTP;
    id IAA13973 Wed, 1 Feb 1993 08:14:59 -0800 for
    <rdippold@happy.phones.com>
```

Remember that each machine that receives mail adds its own Received header to the top of the message. This is the first such header in the message, so it must be the last mail transfer. The machine `happy.phones.com` (where my mail is located) received the message from `phones.com` (our company gateway) on February 1, 1993. The transfer was done using sendmail 8.6.5 (you can't know from this header that it was sendmail) and the protocol used was ESMTP. The intended recipient is listed last—this can change as the message goes through gateways, so it's helpful for tracking mail problems.

```
Received: from linc.cis.void.edu (root@LINC.CIS.VOID.EDU
    [230.91.6.8]) by phones.com (8.6.5/QC-main-2.3) via ESMTP;
    id IAA14773 Wed, 1 Feb 1993 08:14:56 -0800 for
    <rdippold@phones.com>
```

Here's the mail transfer that got the message from `void.edu` to my site. It's a direct connection with no intermediaries.

```
Received: from eniac.seas.void.edu (nihil@ENIAC.SEAS.VOID.EDU
    [230.91.4.1]) by linc.cis.void.edu (8.6.5/VOID 1.4) with
    ESMTP id LAA17163 for <rdippold@phones.com>
    Wed, 1 Feb 1993 11:14:45 -0500
```

Here the mail machine (`linc.cis`) at `void.edu` received the mail from another machine at `void.edu` (`eniac.seas`).

```
Received: from localhost by eniac.seas.void.edu
    id LAA24236; Wed, 1 Feb 1993 11:14:44 -0500
```

Finally, here's the original sending of the message. One interesting piece of information that can be gleaned from this whole exchange is how long it took the mail to get from the sender to me. The message was sent at `11:14:44 -0500` and was received at `08:14:59 - 0800` on the same day. The `-0500` and `-0800` show the time zone differences. To get equivalent times for both messages, you add 5 hours to the time of the sending and add 8 hours to the time of receipt, to get 16:14:44 and 16:14:59, respectively. The message arrived in 15 seconds!

```
From: nihil@eniac.seas.void.edu (Ex Nihilo Nihil Fit)
```

This is who sent me the message. The portion in parentheses is a comment. It usually contains the person's name, but in this case is a saying in Latin.

```
Sender: nihil@ocean.void.edu
```

`Sender` is the "authenticated identity" of the person who sent the message. This is where the sending computer tells you that, as nearly as it can determine, this is the account that actually sent the message, regardless of what the From header says. This is useful if one person is authorized to send mail for another, such as a secretary, or if one member of a group is sending a message for the whole group. If the Sender header is the same as the From header, it doesn't need to be added. In this case, `Nihil` sent mail from a machine within his organization different from the one given in his address. This isn't a big deal. If the From and Sender headers are radically different, however, the mail may be a forgery.

```
Reply-To: nihil@void.edu,nihil@freenet.com
```

The Reply-To header specifies who your reply should go to if you respond. Your mail software should be smart enough to do this automatically. There are usually two reasons for using a Reply-To header. The first is if the address given in the From header is broken and you can't fix it—usually because your mail administrator doesn't know what he or she is doing or doesn't care. The second is if your primary address is somewhat unreliable. `Nihil` has another mail account at `freenet.com`—if for some reason `void.edu` goes offline, he can still get much of his mail at his freenet account.

```
Cc: group-stuff@zznet.ZZ.NET
Cc: james@foobar.com
```

The message was also sent to `group-stuff@zznet.ZZ.NET` and `james@foobar.com`. You can choose whether to include them in your reply. This also could have been done in a single header statement:

```
Cc: group-stuff@zznet.ZZ.NET,james@foobar.com
```

Either form is acceptable. Headers such as From or Sender, however, should appear only once in the entire header.

```
Message-Id: <199302011614.LAA24236@eniac.seas.void.edu>
```

It is very helpful when trying to track a message for debugging, cancellation, or other purposes if every message has a unique identification. The method of generating this unique ID varies from site to site. There should never be another message with this specific ID generated by any machine anywhere on the network. Using `@eniac.seas.void.edu` makes it a local problem only.

```
Subject: Re: Apple IIe/IIgs Software and books for SALE...
```

This is the subject of the message. My mail program shows me a one-line summary of each message, including the From, Date, and Subject headers.

```
To: rdippold@phones.com (Ron Dippold)
```

This is who the message was sent to (me, in this case). Sometimes your local computer will strip off the `@phones.com` part.

```
Date: Wed, 1 Feb 93 11:14:44 EST
```

This is the date the mail was originally sent. EST is Eastern Standard Time—another way of giving the time zone.

```
In-Reply-To:  <CMM.342342.rdippold@happy.phones.com>;
    from "Ron Dippold" at Feb 1, 93 1:00 am
```

This message is a reply to a message that I sent with the message ID given above.

```
X-Mailer: ELM [version 2.3 PL11-void1.13]
```

The sender used the Elm Mail System to send this piece of mail. This can be useful in debugging, but usually it's a bit of self-promotion by the mail program.

```
Mime-Version: 1.0
Content-Type: text/plain; charset=US-ASCII
Content-Transfer-Encoding: 7bit
```

This deals with something that will be discussed later, MIME message format. Briefly, this says that the message contains only 7-bit text, which is nothing out of the ordinary.

```
Content-Length: 10234
```

The length of the body of the message (not shown here) is 10,234 characters.

Other Header Items

There are some other header items that might be occasionally useful for you to know:

```
Bcc: recipient
```

Bcc is *blind carbon copy.* This is like the Cc header, except that those who are sent the message because their address appears in the Cc or From headers don't see that the message was sent to those specified in the Bcc header. Use this to send a copy of a message to someone without letting the others know you're sending it.

```
Keywords: keyword, keyword
```

These are keywords relating to the message. This is mostly a comment field—some mail programs will let you search on *keyword*.

```
Comments: comments
```

This allows you to make comments on the message without actually including them in the body of the message.

```
Encrypted: software keyhelp
```

This indicates that the message body is encrypted with encryption software, and the optional keyhelp helps with selecting the key to decode with. Note that the header itself cannot be encrypted since it contains vital routing information.

Date Fields

Dates used in headers look like this:

```
Wed, 1 Feb 93 11:44 -500
```

The day of week (Wed) is optional. The time is given as 24 hour format (00:00–23:59) local time. The last field is the time zone in one of several formats.

```
UT or GMT      Universal/Greenwich Mean Time
EST or EDT     Eastern time zone
CST or CDT     Central time zone
MST or MDT     Mountain time zone
PST or PDT     Pacific time zone
-HHMM          HH hours and MM minutes earlier than UT
+HHMM          HH hours and MM minutes later than UT
```

If EST is Eastern Standards time and EDT is Eastern Daylight Time, you can figure out the abbreviations for the Central, Mountain, and Pacific time zones. The -HHMM format is probably the least confusing....-0500 makes it much easier to translate the time to local time than does EST.

You may also see the following military codes used:

```
Z       Universal Time
A       UT - 1 hour
M       UT - 12 hours
N       UT + 1 hour
Y       UT + 12 hours
```

Don't Sweat the Headers

If all this header information is giving you information overload, don't sweat it. The really important fields are From, To, Date, and Subject, and it's pretty obvious what those mean. The other information is there in case you need it.

Mail Programs

There are actually several components involved in sending mail. First there's the hardware: Mail has to be physically transferred somehow, either along a dedicated phone line, via satellite, or over a modem. Then there's the link layer: The systems on either end of the hardware connection have to agree on how to communicate with each other. Next is the transport agent: Mail transport agents (MTAs) worry about all the complexities involved in routing mail and sending mail from one site to another. Finally, there's the user agent: The mail user agent (MUA) is the software you use to read all your mail, manipulate it, and send your mail. This is what people usually mean when they talk about a "mail program."

The first three layers aren't usually your concern, unless the MTA places some special constraints on what you can send. You're concerned with the user agents.

There are many mail programs you can use. This chapter does not cover any one program, but it covers the elements that are common to them all.

Your Mail Files

Normally, you have a mail account on whatever computer handles your mail. Often, you can do other things with your account besides access your mail, but that's not important for now. All your new mail, known as incoming mail, is kept in what is usually called a mail spool file. It's quite common for your computer to occasionally look at the spool file and notify you if you have new mail. This is your clue to run your mail program.

Your mail program then grabs all the incoming mail and displays it for your edification. If you don't delete the mail, it is placed in your mailbox file. This is not the same as your incoming mail file—the mailbox file holds all your old mail. Many users eventually outgrow the single mailbox and have several for different subjects, but there is almost always a default mailbox used whenever you run your mail program, and this is what is referred to as "your mailbox."

If you send mail to someone else, it is sent directly to your site's mail computer, which can do what it pleases with the mail—it either sends it on immediately or saves the mail up to save in batches.

Using Mail Programs

As mentioned earlier, there are many mail programs, each with their own quirks. But they try to accomplish the same task and tend to present the messages in a similar format. Learning about one mail program will give you the concepts needed to use almost any program in existence.

Message Summaries

Almost every program in existence summarizes your messages like this:

```
FA    1) 14-Dec Tanya Harding      Where can I get a lead pipe? (2457 chars)
F     2) 11-Jan Ken Bibb        rdippold.ps.gz (1/1) (17464 chars)
F     4)  8-Feb Neil Gaiman       Greek Mythology (2576 chars)
F D   5) 10-Feb clinton@whiteho This is a stickup (13786 chars)
FA    6) 15-Feb Robbin Hughes     Re: REX test driver (1451 chars)
U     7) 16-Feb The King       Re: Chili Donuts (2653 chars)
```

There's one line per message. Again, the information for each message won't always be presented in exactly the same format, but the contents should be similar. From left to right for this mail program (named `mm90`). These lines give the following information:

- **Message flags.**   Each message has several state variables associated with it. In this case, the flags are whether the message is unread (U), whether I have answered the message (A), whether the message is deleted (D), and whether I have flagged the message for further attention (F). Some programs let you give each message one of several priority levels.

- **Message number.**   It helps to be able to refer to a message by a unique identifier for printing, reading, or deleting. Usually, the mail program just calls the first message in your mailbox 1 and counts up from there.

- **Date.**   This tells when the message was sent, from the Date header of the message.

- **Name.**   This is the name of the person who sent the mail, from the From header. If no name is given, the Internet address of the person is used.

- **Subject.**   When the sender entered the message, his or her mail program asked for a message subject. It's shown here. If there's not enough room, the subject is truncated.

- **Length.**   This shows how large the message is. Here it's given in characters— other programs give it in number of lines.

Reading New Messages

All mail programs have a "read new mail" command. Usually, you use just r or press Enter. This shows you your new messages one at a time. When you're reading each message you have several options available, such as replying or deleting the message.

Operating on Old Messages

The same functions that are available when you're reading a message are usually available when you're not reading any particular message, and can apply to a single old message or to a group of them. As an example, when you're reading a message you can tell the mail program to delete the message. When you're not reading any messages you should be able to tell the mail program "Delete message number 4" or even "Delete messages 4 through 6."

Messages are usually given by number, but if you're using a mail program that uses a mouse you may be able to select messages by clicking on them.

Common Mail Functions

Here's the standard list of mail functions you should learn how to do in your program:

- **Read message(s).**   Obviously, if you can't do this, not much else matters.
- **Delete message(s).**   Mailboxes can become very cluttered with old mail and you can even "lose" important mail because it's so buried in junk. You need to be able to get rid of mail you don't care about.
- **Flag message(s).**   You should be able to flag messages as being important. The mail program should then make them stand out in some way so you remember to deal with them later.
- **Send message.**   You should be able to send mail to other people.
- **Reply to message.**   You should be able to easily send a response to the person who sent you a piece of mail, and include a portion of the sender's message text for reference.
- **Save message(s) to file.**   You'll probably get mail that contains important information you want to use in another program. You should be able to save the body of a message to file, which you can then manipulate at will.
- **Switch to other mailbox.**   If you start getting enough mail, you may find it handy to create other mailboxes. Perhaps one for the Bulgarian cooking mailing list of which you're a member. Your mail program should be able to handle several mailboxes.
- **Move message(s) to other mailbox.**   If you have multiple mailboxes, it should be possible to move mail from one to another.

Mail Configuration File

Since how you handle your mail involves a lot of personal preference, almost all mail programs have many options that can be set. So that you don't have to set these every time you run your mail program, most mail programs have some sort of configuration file that is read every time the program starts.

You should definitely look into how to set this up for your mail program—while doing so you will often find many options you didn't even know about. For instance, many programs will let you set aliases; for example, you can use just `bill` instead of `wblowhard@longname.deep.stuff.edu`. The mail program turns the alias into the full name.

Common Mail Programs

There are dozens of mail programs out there, and they can't all be covered here. Instead, this chapter touches on a few common ones.

Mail (Berkeley Mail)

Most UNIX boxes come with a simple program known just as `mail`, or as `mailx`. This is some variation on the mail program from Berkeley UNIX, so it's sometimes called Berkeley Mail. This program is minimal in functionality and presentation, but it works, and many people still use it. If you like `mail` I would recommend that you upgrade to `mm90`, which is discussed in the section, "mm90 (Mail Manager 0.90)."

`mail` has the capability of being used in a noninteractive mode. You can send a file to someone in this way:

```
mail -s "subject" recipient < messagefile
```

Again, on some systems you need to use `mailx`. `mail`. `recipient` is who to send it to, `subject` is some message subject, and `messagefile` is the name of the file to send. You also can send the output of a program in a similar fashion:

```
program commands ¦ mail -s "subject" recipient
```

You could instead save the output of the program to a file first, but why introduce an additional step if you don't need to?

The Elm Mail System

If you're the type of person who likes full-screen, menu-driven (and other hyphenated adjectives) interfaces, Elm might be up your alley. It was created as an easy-to-use UNIX mail program, but actually has a fair amount of configurability and power. The support programs that come with it might be worth getting on their own. And if you like printed manuals, it comes with over a hundred pages of documentation in PostScript format.

The Elm system is probably not standard on your system, so you'll have to get it yourself or beg your sysadmin for it. You can anonymous ftp it from `ftp.uu.net` under `/networking/mail/elm`, or from `wuarchive.wustl.edu` under `/mirrors/elm`. The packed source code is about a megabyte. You'll need to compile it and answer a few system configuration questions.

Messages are displayed in a format close to the "standard" one-message-per-line format described earlier, but now you can use your arrow keys to scroll about the messages and just press a key to inflict your wishes on the current message. The online help isn't bad—just press ? at any time.

TIP: Elm tip 1: Press o from the main menu to get the options screen. Press > and Elm creates a file named `.elm/elmrc`—this is a special options file that you can edit with `vi` or `emacs` (or whatever you use). Most of these options aren't easily set from inside Elm. Be sure to read the `Ref.guide` file for more information on these options.

TIP: Elm tip 2: Elm can act as a command-line mailer just like Berkeley mail does—it even uses the same syntax:

```
elm -s "subject" recipient < messagefile
```

TIP: Elm tip 3: Don't ignore the support programs that come with Elm. A few of the most useful ones are the following:

`autoreply` answers all your incoming e-mail with an automatic reply. This is good if your mailbox is backlogged, or if you go on vacation or otherwise want to let people know that you're behind on reading your mail.

`filter` saves your incoming e-mail to different incoming mailboxes, deletes it, forwards it, and so on, based on the content of the e-mail message or its headers. This is useful if you subscribe to a mailing list or get lots of mail on a particular subject.

`frm` lists From and Subject headers for each message, one line per message. This is useful for quickly checking your incoming e-mail.

`messages` gives a quick count of the messages in your mailbox.

`newmail` and `wnewmail` are programs that immediately inform you when new e-mail has arrived. `wnewmail` runs in a window.

`readmsg` takes selected messages from a mailbox and sends them to standard output. This is good for quickly extracting and processing mail messages in bizarre ways.

There's even a USENET group for Elm: `comp.mail.elm`.

Pine

If Elm is still too complex for you, Pine is next on the list. Pine stands for *Pine is not Elm* (trust me, this is considered prime mail humor), and it's somewhat similar to Elm...but different.

It uses the same one-message-per-line, scroll-through-them-and-use-hotkeys-to-act-on-them principles as Elm, but Pine makes things a little easier. The number of features is less overwhelming, and there's a concerted effort to keep the same keys performing the same functions from screen to screen. Several items (such as address books) you'll have to "suffer" through with Elm rate their own full-screen editors in Pine. Pine even comes with its own text editor, Pico, which can be used as a general text editor. For the faint of heart, it's certainly an improvement over emacs or vi.

And there's good news on the installation, if you're lucky. You can anonymous ftp to `ftp.cac.washington.edu` and look in the `/mail` directory. Precompiled versions for AIX3.2, HP/UX 9.01, Linux, NeXTstep, Solaris 2.2 (SPARC), and SunOS 4.1.3 (SPARC) are available in the `UNIX-BINARIES` subdirectory, if you're lucky enough to be using one of these. If you need to compile your own version, get `pine.tar.Z` and warm up your C compiler.

Future versions of Pine will include built-in configuration, but if you want to set some Pine options, run it once, then use a text editor to edit the file `.pinerc` in your home directory. The configuration items are explained fairly well. There's not a whole lot to do here, but make sure you set `personal-name`, `smtp-server` (if you're using SMTP), and `inbox-path` (usually `/usr/spool/mail/yourid`).

Remote Mail Clients

The "Common Mail Programs" section has generally assumed that you will run your mail program on the computer that contains your Internet mail. In many cases, however, you will wish to do all your mail reading on your personal computer, both because you may be charged for all the time you are logged onto your mail account, and because the programs on Macs and PCs are much friendlier than those on many UNIX systems.

What you want is a program that will call the system that receives your mail (or that will connect to it by whatever means necessary), grab all your new mail, and disconnect. Then you can read your mail at your leisure and enter new messages. If there are any new messages, the program should call your mail system and give it the new messages for delivery. As you have probably guessed, these programs exist and are known as mail clients.

The big difference between this approach and the "read your mail on your Internet computer" approach is that your mailbox is kept on your personal computer instead of on the Internet computer.

Obviously, there has to be a way for your mail client to talk to your Internet computer and transfer messages. There are several standards for this.

SMTP—Simple Mail Transfer Protocol

Simple Mail Transfer Protocol (SMTP), or some variation of it (such as Extended SMTP) is used by computers on the Internet which handle mail to transfer messages from one machine to another. It's a one-way protocol—the SMTP client contacts the SMTP server and gives it a mail message.

Most mail client programs support SMTP for sending outgoing mail, simply because it's very easy to implement. Few mail clients support SMTP for incoming mail, because normally your mail computer can't contact your personal computer at will to give it mail. It's possible if your personal computer happens to be permanently networked to the mail computer via EtherNet, for instance, or if your mail computer knows how to use a modem to call your personal computer, but in most cases this isn't done.

POP3 (Post Office Protocol 3)

The standard protocol used by most mail clients to retrieve mail from a remote system is one of the post office protocols, either POP2 or usually its successor POP3. These protocols enable your mail client to grab new messages, delete messages, and do other things necessary for reading your incoming mail. POP only requires a rather "stupid" mail server in the sense that your mail client needs to have most of the intelligence needed for managing mail. It's a very simple protocol, and is offered by most mail clients.

POP3 is somewhat insecure in that your mail client needs to send your account name and password every time it calls. The more you do this, the greater the chance that someone with a network snooper might get both. (I'm not trying to scare you, but it's possible.) An extension known as APOP uses a secure algorithm known as MD5 to encrypt your password for each session.

Finally, note that standard POP3 has no way to *send* mail back to the mail server. There is an optional extension to POP3 known as XTND XMIT that allows this, but both the client and the server have to support it. Generally, a mail client uses SMTP to send messages and POP3 to retrieve them.

Desirable Features in Mail Clients

Here are some useful features to look for when shopping for a mail client:

■ **Delete on retrieve.** The client should have the option to automatically delete mail on the server after it has been downloaded. If you only read mail using your client, you don't want a huge mail file building up on the server. On the other hand, if you only occasionally use your mail client you might want to leave your mail messages on the host so you can access them with your UNIX mail program.

■ **Header only retrieve.**   You can tell quite a bit about a message just by looking at the message header. If reconnecting to your server is easy, you might want to have your mail program download only the header. Then, if you want to see the actual text of the message, the program will download that. This can be very useful if some idiot mails you a humongous file—you can be spared the time it takes to download the whole thing to your computer.

■ **Name server support.**   A machine name such as `mailserv.bozo.edu` is actually just a logical name for a computer that is truly identified by its IP number, something that looks like 130.029.13.12. Obviously, the machine name is easier to remember, and if anything happens to mailserv that requires the machine to move to a new IP address (such as a hardware upgrade), the administrators can map the name to the new IP address and you won't even notice. Those who are accessing the machine by number will have to find the new number and enter it. To turn the name into an IP number, though, your client needs to be smart enough to use a domain name server, which keeps track of what numbers go to what names.

■ **POP3.**   This is the standard way for a mail client to retrieve mail from the mail server. If your client doesn't support this, it darn well better have some way to retrieve mail that your mail server understands (for example, IMAP2 or PCMAIL).

■ **Retrieve on start-up.**   The client should enable you to immediately contact your mail server and retrieve all unread mail whenever you start it, because this will probably be your most common operation.

■ **Separate SMTP server.**   In some cases you will need to use a different machine to send mail (using SMTP) than you use to retrieve mail (using POP3). A good mail client should let you specify a different server for each.

■ **SMTP.**   This is the standard way for a mail client to give mail to the mail server. If your mail client doesn't understand SMTP, it should have some special protocol that your mail server understands to do the same thing (unless you don't want to send mail, of course). Some mail clients support SMTP connections as a way to receive messages, which can be useful if you expect your computer to be hooked up to the network all the time.

■ **TCP/IP, SLIP, or PPP.**   Your client should be able to access whatever network your mail host is on. Otherwise you'll just be talking to yourself. TCP/IP and TCP/SLIP are the most common network protocols mail programs are likely to need, and PPP is becoming more popular. If you have a SLIP or PPP driver that looks like TCP/IP to your mail program, all it needs is TCP/IP support.

■ **Timed retrieval.** The client should be able to automatically connect to your mail server and check for new mail every so often, and beep if it finds new mail. If you're calling in using a modem, you might want to make this every few hours, or even once a day, but if you're directly networked with the server (perhaps via EtherNet), you might want to check every five minutes.

■ **Other mail items.** A good mail client makes reading your mail as easy as possible. You shouldn't have to give up any of the features you enjoy under a UNIX mail program. These include a good text editor, header field filtering, an address book (aliases), and multiple mailboxes.

A Few Mail Clients

Again, there are dozens of mail clients out there. If your organization has standardized on one of the big ones, such as cc:Mail, Microsoft Mail, Lotus Notes, or BeyondMail, you're already familiar with one. These clients are a bit more "homegrown" on the Internet and have at least a demo version you can try first, before you buy the real (and expensive) program.

CommSet

Actually, this is a bit more than a mail client—it's an entire TCP/IP (plus SLIP and PPP) suite for DOS. All its components are in one package, which allows multiple-window, simultaneous sessions. You can have ftp in one window, telnet in another, and run `mail` or gopher in another. This isn't a big deal under UNIX, OS/2, or Windows, but it's pretty nice for a single-tasking system such as DOS. I'm including it here because its low price makes it worth looking at if you're searching for a mailer under DOS. This is what I use when I need TCP/IP under DOS.

You can anonymous ftp a demo version of CommSet from `ftp.cybercon.nb.ca`, or you can send mail to `info@cybercon.nb.ca` requesting information. The final price (before educational discount) should be around $99.

Eudora

Disclaimer: I work for QUALCOMM—in a different department, but I thought you should know...

Eudora is a full-featured mail client for Macs or PCs running Windows. It comes in two sub-flavors: Version 1 of Eudora is free, and Version 2 and above are commercial. Obviously, Version 2 has nifty features not available in 1, but 1 is pretty powerful by itself.

Eudora is fully windows-, menu-, and icon-driven, so you are bound to like this program. Eudora pretty much has it all—features galore. The only thing I could ask for is a native OS/2 version...

To test the free versions of Eudora, anonymous ftp to `ftp.qualcomm.com`. The PC version is under `/pceudora/windows` (get all the files). The Mac version is under `/mac/eudora`. For a Mac you need to decide which version you want to try—if you have System 6, get 1.3. Otherwise grab 1.4 (or higher).

Single-copy pricing is about $65, with an educational discount available. Send e-mail to `eudora-sales@qualcomm.com` for more info, or call 1-800-2-Eudora.

Pegasus Mail

Pegasus Mail runs on Novell and supports HMS and SMTP. It has DOS, Windows, and Macintosh versions, which gives you a wide range of platforms with a single program. There are a number of utilities available for use with it, such as Mercury, which is an SMTP gateway for Novell. It's fairly flexible in allowing you to set up user-defined mail gateways and has a large features list.

It's got its own text editor, which is integrated with the rest of the program, although if you're attached to your text editor (I couldn't give up QEdit), you can define your own external editor.

To find all the versions and add-on utilities, you can anonymous ftp to `risc.ua.edu`, under `/pub/network/pegasus`. The software is free! If you want manuals, it'll cost you $150 for a five-copy license. That's only $30 apiece. You can contact David Harris by fax in New Zealand at (+64) 3 453-6612, or send inquiries to `david@pmail.gen.nz`.

Pine

Didn't we just cover this? Yep…this is a DOS version of the UNIX Pine mail program. You can have the same mail interface on your UNIX and DOS platforms. Pine's big limitation is that it doesn't support POP3—it only supports IMAP2 and SMTP. For more information on Pine, see the section, "Common Mail Programs," where the UNIX version is discussed.

To get it, anonymous ftp to `ftp.cac.washington.edu` and look in the `/mail/PC-PINE` directory. Grab the file that's appropriate for your networking software: FTP's PC/TCP (`pcpine_f.zip`), the generic packet driver using built-in Waterloo TCP/IP (`pcpine_p.zip`), Novell's LANWorkPlace (`pcpine_n.zip`), or Sun's PC/NFS (`pcpine_s.zip`). If you don't have one of these, try the Waterloo TCP/IP version—it should only require the basic packet drivers.

ECSMail

ECSMail is impressive for its wide range of support. It includes not only a mail client, but mail transport and handling services, so you can build a complete mail system. All the components run under UNIX, OS/2, OpenVMS, or Windows NT, and mail clients are available for MS-DOS, Windows, and the Mac (System 7). We're talking enterprise-wide solution here, if you're into that level of standardization.

Contact ECS (in Canada) by calling 1-403-420-8081, or send mail to ECS Sales at `ecs-sales@edm.isac.ca`.

Other Mail Programs/Clients

This isn't all that's available for mail, by a long shot. Read the USENET group `comp.mail.misc` for more information.

Internet E-Mail Gateways

Internet Mail is more than just Internet. Because Internet is everywhere, it interests all the right people. In this case, the right people are all the other services that offer electronic mail and who want a piece of the action.

In theory, the Internet is a competitor with all the existing services such as AT&T Mail, CompuServe, and the rest. In practice, it's a neutral competitor—it's not some guided, malevolent entity that is trying to do away with any of the other services. Rather, it competes just by its existence; it offers more information and more connectivity than most of the services can ever hope to offer. Smart information services finally realized that this could be put to their advantage—anyone who cares to can join the Internet, and a service that joins the Internet has advantages over its competitors.

One huge advantage is connectivity. As soon as a mail service adds a computer (known as a gateway) that can transfer from its system to the Internet and vice versa, its users can exchange mail with anyone on the service or with anyone on the Internet. That's a lot of people. So a lot of services are now offering some sort of mail gateway. Even Prodigy, which was somewhat late to grasp the possibilities, has one now.

Instead of GEnie needing to install a special gateway to talk to Prodigy, and one to CompuServe, and one to SprintMail, and one to BubbaNet, it can set up and maintain just one gateway to the Internet through which everything flows. Given the glacial speed with which most of the online services implement upgrades like this, requiring only a single gateway is a good thing.

So now anyone can send e-mail anywhere! All is fluffy and bright and beautiful, right? Well, not quite...

Addressing Issues

It turns out that the services that connect to the Internet keep their same old account names and horrible mail systems. CompuServe's octal account addresses are as much of an anachronism as punch cards, but because of the company's current investment, they're not going to change it. (The Cubs will win the World Series first.) And you can't just send a mail message to a CompuServe account using an Internet-style address. A CompuServe ID looks something like this:

```
77777,777
```

In Internet addressing, a comma separates members of a list so you can't use the comma in the Compuserve address. There's a way around that (use a period instead of a comma) but you have to know that in advance. Someone trying to send mail to a system has to deal with those quirks. Hence this section, which details the translation that has to be done between the major networks.

Again, an Internet e-mail address looks something like this:

```
user@machine.site.domain
```

Any address to a mail gateway is going to be some variation (minor or major) on this theme.

Other Gateway Issues

There are a few "gotchas" you should know about before starting on your gateway quest. With luck, they'll never affect you, but the pessimistic might claim that Murphy's Law almost guarantees they will at some time.

Cash, Money, Moolah

Some of these services charge money for every mail message that gets sent or is received. And with their pricing plans in such flux (a year is the normal lifespan), it's impossible to keep track of more than a few at a time. However, since the Internet has no billing mechanisms and the commercial systems do, the users of the commercial systems end up paying for the mail. So be careful when sending mail to these poor slobs. If they ask you for it that's one thing, but unsolicited mail is another.

Furthermore, sending large files across any of the gateways is usually frowned upon.

Case Sensitivity

By custom, Internet addresses are case insensitive. That is, mail to `bozo@clown.edu` is the same as mail to `BOZO@CLOWN.EDU` or `BozO@CloWN.EdU`. Not all of the information services are so enlightened. Wherever possible, keep upper- and lowercase exactly as you are given them by the recipient, just in case. Chances are it doesn't matter, but why take those chances?

X.400 Addressing

The Internet uses what is formally known as RFC-822 addressing. Many large commercial services specializing in electronic mail use something known as an X.400 gateway to talk to the Internet. Those addresses look something like this:

```
/A=value/B=value/C=value
```

This style is usable from the Internet, because RFC-822 allows slashes and equals signs. In fact, there's the opposite problem: RFC-822 allows many characters to be used in addressing that cause an X.400 gateway to go into convulsions. This includes the @ character—because this appears in all Internet-style mail addresses, there's an obvious problem.

Whenever the Internet address has a "special" character, you need to use the following translation table:

Internet	X.400
@	(a)
%	(p)
!	(b)
"	(q)
_	(u)
(	(l)
)	(r)

For any other special character, such as #, substitute (*xxx*), where *xxx* is the three-digit decimal ASCII code for the character. For #, you would use (035).

For example, then, to convert the Internet address

```
oldvax!Mutt#Jeff@cartoon.com
```

into something that can be sent from an X.400 service such as MCI Mail, you need to turn it into this:

```
oldvax(b)Mutt(035)Jeff(a)cartoon.com
```

What a pain...but it works.

> **NOTE:** By the way, the ! is replaced with (b) because computer users like short names, and refer to an exclamation point as a "bang." Bang! Bang! Bang!

Gateway Translation Specifics

Using the following instructions should be fairly easy. To send mail to CompuServe from an Internet mail account, see the translation instructions in the section "CompuServe."

Parts of the address that you have to replace with appropriate information are given in *italics*. For instance, with

`userid@aol.com`

you need to replace `userid` with the recipient's account name or number. `domain` is the part of the Internet address after the @.

If you are sending mail from one service to another through the Internet, for example from WWIVNet to CompuServe, you will have to do two translations. First, check the section "CompuServe" and see how to translate the ID "From Internet." Then check the section "WWIVNet" and see how to translate that address "To Internet." If you do this from one strange network to another, the name may be a crawling horror, but at least it should be possible.

America Online

America Online (AOL) is a major commercial information system that recently joined the Internet (although it has had Internet e-mail for a while). Its Internet e-mail is seamless from an Internet point of view...

From Internet: America Online looks just like any other normal Internet site.

`userid@aol.com`

Example: `jjones@aol.com`

To Internet: There's no need to do anything special; just use the regular Internet format.

`userid@domain`

Example: `bsmith@wubba.edu`

To Others: America Online lets you use special abbreviated domains for mail to AppleLink, CompuServe, or GEnie. Send your mail to `userid@applelink`, `userid@cis`, or `userid@genie`, respectively.

Example: `11111.2222@cis`

AppleLink

AppleLink is Apple Computer's network.

From Internet: Use standard Internet addressing:

`userid@applelink.apple.com`

Example: `exnihil@applelink.apple.com`

To Internet: This is a bit nastier. You must address it like this:

`user@domain@internet#`

The whole thing must fit in 35 characters or less, so some addresses may be flat out impossible by normal methods. That's life...

Example: `bsmith@wubba.edu@internet#`

AT&T Mail

AT&T Mail is a commercial e-mail service provided by AT&T. You know who they are. AT&T mail doesn't use an X.400 gateway, thankfully.

From Internet: Use standard Internet addressing:

`userid@attmail.com`

To Internet: Use the following:

`internet!domain!userid`

Note the backward order here—this is the old bang-path type addressing. Oh well.

Example: `internet!wubba.edu!bsmith`

BITNET

BITNET is an old academic network that is becoming less important as more and more of it gets sucked into Internet, but you still might have to use it to contact someone at an educational site.

From Internet: Use the following addressing:

`userid%bitnetsitename.bitnet@gateway`

bitnetsitename is the name of the BITNET site where the person's account resides. *gateway* is the name of a site that is both on the Internet and on BITNET and can route mail between them. A commonly used one is `mitvma.mit.edu`, but you may have a closer one you can use. Ask your administrator.

Example: `jjones%uxavax.bitnet@mitvma.mit.edu`

To Internet: Oh boy...each BITNET site varies in the mail software it uses. If you're lucky, you can just use the Internet address and the gatewaying will happen automatically:

`userid@domain`

If that doesn't work, try this:

`userid%domain@gateway`

If neither of these methods works, ask your administrator.

Example: `bsmith%wubba.edu@mitvma.mit.edu`

BIX

BIX is the *Byte* magazine Information eXchange, a commercial service oriented toward techies and/or *Byte* magazine readers. It's been bought by Delphi, but still operates as a separate source.

From Internet: Use standard Internet addressing:

`userid@bix.com`

Example: `jjones@bix.com`

To Internet: You'll need to use the Internet Services menu option from the main menu, then use standard Internet addressing:

`userid@domain`

CompuServe

CompuServe is a very large commercial system. It's so large that it hasn't yet felt the pressure to join the Internet except by offering a mail gateway.

From Internet: Use standard Internet addressing with one difference: CompuServe IDs are in the form *77777,7777*. Since Internet dislikes commas in addresses, you need to change the comma to a period:

`77777.7777@compuserve.com`

Example: 12345.677@compuserve.com

To Internet: You need to add a prefix to the standard Internet addressing:

`>INTERNET:userid@domain`

Example: `>INTERNET:bsmith@wubba.edu`

Delphi

Delphi was the first of the large commercial services to really embrace Internet. It looks like any standard Internet site as far as Internet Mail is concerned:

From Internet: Use the following addressing:

`userid@delphi.com`

Example: `jjones@delphi.com`

To Internet: There's no need to do anything special; just use the regular Internet format:

`userid@domain`

Example: `bsmith@wubba.edu`

Easylink

This is another commercial system from AT&T.

From Internet: Use the following addressing:

`userid@eln.attmail.com`

To Internet: As far as I can tell (from the AT&T types I spoke to), this isn't currently available.

Envoy-100

This is Telecom Canada's commercial service with X.400 gatewaying.

From Internet: Use the following addressing:

`uunet.uu.net!att!attmail!mhs!envoy!userid`

Remember that I told you the bang-path format is almost obsolete? That's not true here yet.

Example: `uunet.uu.net!att!attmail!mhs!envoy!12345`

To Internet: Brace yourself…you need to use the following addressing:

`[RFC-822="userid(a)domain"]INTERNET/TELEMAIL/US`

(a) replaces @ because X.400 doesn't like the @ character. For other special X.400 characters, see the section "X.400 Addressing."

Example: `[RFC-822="bsmith(a)wubba"]INTERNET/TELEMAIL/US`

FidoNet

FidoNet is a large international BBS network—sort of the Internet for the BBSing crowd. It's not as fast as the Internet, but access is usually very cheap, and chances are there's a FidoNet BBS in your area.

Because it's run over phone lines, the BBS operators will rack up long-distance charges for any mail transferred, so please don't send large messages to FidoNet sites. Many sites will even chop your messages to 8000 or 16000 bytes, so much of your message won't get through.

From Internet: First, you need to know the network address of the BBS your recipient is on. It will be in a form such as `Z:N/F.P`. Then send the mail to the following address:

`userid@pP.fF.nN.zZ.fidonet.org`

If the network address of the BBS doesn't have a `P` component, leave the `pP.` part out of the address. For the `userid` replace any nonalphanumeric characters (such as spaces) with periods (.).

Example: `Jim_Jones@p4.f3.n2.z1.fidonet.org`

To Internet: Use standard Internet addressing with a suffix:

`userid@userid ON gateway`

The `gateway` is a special FidoNet site that acts as a gateway to Internet. You can use `1:1/31` unless you find a better one.

Example: `bsmith@wubba.edu ON 1:1/31`

GEnie

GEnie is General Electric's commercial information service.

From Internet: Use standard Internet addressing:

`userid@genie.geis.com`

Example: `jjones@genie.geis.com`

To Internet: Use standard Internet addressing with a suffix:

`userid@domain@INET#`

Example: `bsmith@wubba.edu@INET#`

Gold 400

Gold 400 is British Telecom's commercial X.400 system.

From Internet: Use the following addressing:

`userid@org_unit.org.prmd.gold-400.gb`

You'll need to have the recipient tell you his or her `userid`, `org_unit` (organization unit), `org` (organization), and `prmd` (private mail domain).

Example: `jjones@foo.bar.baz.gold-400.gb`

To Internet: Again, see the section "X.400 Addressing" to see how to handle nonstandard characters in addresses, but here's the format:

```
/DD.RFC-822=userid(a)domain%%/O=uknet/PRMD=uk.ac/ADMD=gold 400/C=GB
```

Example: `/DD.RFC-822=bsmith(a)wubba.edu/O=uknet/PRMD=uk.ac/ADMD=gold 400/C=GB`

KeyLink

KeyLink is Telecom Australia's commercial X.400 mail service.

From Internet: Use the following addressing:

```
userid@org_unit.org.telememo.au
```

You'll need to have the recipient tell you his or her *userid*, *org_unit* (organization unit), and *org* (organization). The *org_unit* might not be used—in that case, just eliminate it and the period that follows it.

Example: `jjones@froboz.grue.telememo.au`

To Internet: Again, see the section "X.400 Addressing" to see how to handle nonstandard characters in addresses, but this is the general format:

```
(C:au,A:telememo,P:oz.au,"RFC-822":"name - <userid(a)domain>")
```

name isn't actually used for delivery, just as a comment.

Example: `(C:au,A:telememo,P:oz.au,"RFC-822":"Bubba Smith - <bsmith(a)wubba.edu>")`

MCI Mail

MCI Mail is MCI's commercial e-mail service.

From Internet: There are several options. Each MCI user has a name (`Jim Jones`) and a phone number (`123-4567`) associated with his or her account. The number is unique to that account, so you can always send mail to an address such as the following:

```
number@mcimail.com
```

Example: `1234567@mcimail.com`

If you know there is only one J Jones with an account at MCI Mail, you can send mail to

```
FLast@mcimail.com
```

where *F* is the first initial and *Last* is the last name. Or, if you know there is only one Jim Jones you can send mail to

```
First_Last@mcimail.com
```

where *First* is the first name and *Last* is the last name. Note the underscore between them.

Example: `Jim_Jones@mcimail.com`

To Internet: When MCI prompts you with `To:` enter

`$$name (EMS)`

`name` isn't actually used for mail delivery, but you can put the person's real name here. MCI then prompts you with `EMS:`. Respond with

`INTERNET`

Then MCI asks for `Mbx:` and here you can enter the real Internet address:

`userid@domain`

PRODIGY

Prodigy is a large commercial service, Prodigy Information Services (jointly developed by Sears and IBM).

From Internet: Use standard Internet addressing:

`domain@prodigy.com`

Example: `jone45a@prodigy.com`

To Internet: This is a little tougher. Support for doing this isn't integrated into the standard Prodigy software, so you need to use their special offline Mail Manager program. It works only for IBM PC users and it'll cost you $4.95. When online, Jump to 'ABOUT MAIL MANAGER' and proceed from there.

SprintMail

Hmm…AT&T and MCI have commercial mail services. Sprint has to have one, if only for the principle of the matter. Actually, to be fair, Sprint has always been one of the more network-oriented phone companies. You may have used their Telenet network.

From Internet: Use this addressing:

`/G=first/S=last/O=organization/ADMD=TELEMAIL/C=US/@sprint.com`

`first` and `last` are the recipient's first and last names, of course, and `organization` is the recipient's SprintMail organization name.

Example: `/G=Chris/S=Smith/O=FooInc/ADMD=TELEMAIL/C=US/@sprint.com`

To Internet: Use this addressing:

`C:USA,A:TELEMAIL,P:INTERNET,"RFC-822":<userid(a)domain>) DEL`

Again, see the section "X.400 Addressing" to see how to handle nonstandard characters in addresses.

Example: `C:USA,A:TELEMAIL,P:INTERNET,"RFC-822":<bsmith(a)wubba.edu>) DEL`

WWIVNet

WWIVNet is the largest of several networks for BBSes running WWIV (World War IV) software. Traffic from node to node is long distance in several places, and the gateway site uses long distance as well, so please be courteous and don't send or receive anything large (over 8 KB or so).

From Internet: Use this addressing:

`userid-node@wwiv.tfsquad.mn.org`

You'll need to find out from your recipient his or her *userid* and *node*—they'll both be numbers.

Example: `99-8765@wwiv.tfsquad.mn.org`

To Internet: Use this addressing:

This is almost standard Internet format, but you replace the @ with a # and add a suffix:

`userid#domain@506`

Example: `bsmith#wubba.edu@506`

Other Gateways

There are other gateways around and more are sure to appear. Most services offering this type of gateway should have at least some clue of how the address translation needs to be done—ask the service if you need to know.

Finding Addresses

How do you find someone's e-mail address? Usually the best way is just to ask the person, but I've met several people who know they have an account but don't know exactly what their mail address is! They do most of their work locally and receive no outside mail.

Send Reverse Mail

If you're the solid type who knows your e-mail address, you can have the unfortunate type who doesn't know his or hers send you e-mail. If that person is on another network, you may have to do the translation as detailed in the section "Internet E-Mail Gateways." When you get the mail, 95% of the time the From header will include the address information you need, including all the network translation crud. The only way to be sure is to try it.

If that doesn't work, you can try examining the Received and Reply-To headers to see exactly what's going on.

Directories

There are many places that keep mail address compilations. If the person you are looking for belongs to a commercial system, you may have to log on to that system (or have someone else do it for you) and look up the account.

For many Internet addresses, you can send mail to the Internet address `whois@whois.internic.net` with just `help` as the body of the message.

For BITNET addresses, send mail to the Internet address `listserv@bitnic.bitnet` with `send bitnet servers` as the body of the message. This should give you a current list of BITNET nameservers you can query.

To find someone in the communications field, try RPI's address server. Send mail to Internet address `comserve@vm.its.rpi.edu` with `help` as the body of the message.

UNINNETT of Norway maintains an X.500 address registry service. Send mail to Internet address `directory@uninett.no` with `help` as the body of the message.

PSI runs an X.500 service at Internet address `whitepages@wp.psi.com` with `help` as the message body.

USENET Address Server

MIT keeps track of every person who has ever posted an article to USENET since the late 1980s (many USENET readers would be shocked to know this). This includes those from other networks who use a news gateway. If the person you are looking for has posted an article to USENET since then, he or she might be in this database.

Send mail to the Internet address `mail-server@rtfm.mit.edu`. In the body of the message, put this:

```
send usenet-addresses/key1 key2 key...
```

The keys should include all the words you think might appear in the address, usually parts of the person's name. In many cases you will use only *key1*. The keys are case insensitive.

You can try the following:

```
send usenet-addresses/dippold
```

to return several entries. The server will return only 40 matches, so if your keys are overly general ("Smith") you will need to give more keys, such as a first name, to narrow the search.

You can do several searches at once by placing several send usenet-addresses/*keys* lines in the message.

Your Address and Business Card

What's on your business card? Probably your name, company, position, phone and fax numbers, your address, and maybe some spiffy design.

Well, the business card of the 1990s also includes your Internet address. E-mail is almost always cheaper, faster, and more convenient than a fax or snail-mail. Putting your e-mail address on your business cards is one of the best ways to encourage people to use it. Not only is this useful, it's got more than a certain amount of trendiness, if you like that. With everybody and their cousin "discovering" the Internet, it's hip, it's happening, it's all the right adjectives. The trend may pass, but the e-mail address will still be useful.

Now, how do you give your address on your business card? I've heard people recommend "E-mail Address," "E-mail," "Internet," and other variations. My suggested solution is simple and elegant: just give your address without giving it any kind of label at all. The "@" should start frantic alarms ringing in the head of anyone who would know how to use your address, and if they don't know what it means, no explanation you can fit on your card is going to help.

For best results, give the address in Internet format, even if your account is on another service. If you're on CompuServe as ID 11111,2222, give your address as 11111.2222@compuserve.com rather than as CompuServe ID: 11111,2222. With the first format anyone who can send Internet mail can reach you, and CompuServe users will be smart enough to realize that the first part is your CompuServe ID. The second format requires that someone know how to do the 11111,2222 to 11111.2222@compuserve.com conversion, and they haven't all read this book. Of course, this assumes that you want non-CompuServe people sending you mail.

Mailing Lists

With e-mail you can carry on a conversation with another person. But why not with three others? Easy enough—just use the Cc header or specify multiple recipients on the To header. What about hundreds? Well, that might be tough. But what if there were enough interest in something (such as the band REM) that someone agreed to serve as a central dispatch point? All mail to that account would be sent to all other people in the discussion. This is known as a mailing list, and they are quite popular. The REM list mentioned has over 800 subscribers.

Clutter

The first thing you have to realize is that when you join (subscribe to) a mailing list, all of a sudden you're going to have a lot of messages in your mailbox. Can you handle the extra time it's going to take to read these new messages? Are you paying for mail? Many people don't comprehend exactly what they're getting into when they sign up for a mailing list. Remember to save the instructions on how to unsubscribe from the group, so you don't send your unsubscribe request to all the members of the group and feel like a fool.

Finding Lists

First you need to find some lists. Every month several informative postings are made to the USENET group news.answers, describing hundreds of mailing lists and how to subscribe to them. David Lawrence posts "Mailing Lists Available in USENET." Stephanie da Silva posts "Publicly Accessible Mailing Lists." If you have USENET access, news.answers is your best bet. Perhaps some of the people you correspond with know of some lists.

If neither approach works, you can use the uga.cc.uga.edu mailserver described in the following section.

LISTSERV Sites

LISTSERVers are nifty automatic programs that handle much of the drudgery involved in maintaining a mailing list. There are several such LISTSERVs, but you need only one to get started. I suggest you use listserv@uga.cc.uga.edu. Others include listserv@mizzou1.missouri.edu, listserv@jhuvm.bitnet, listserv@vm1.nodak.edu, listserv@ucsd.edu, listserv@unl.edu, LISTSERV@PSUVM.PSU.EDU, and LISTSERV@SJSUVM1.SJSU.EDU.

Commands to these sites are simple. You can give a new instruction on each line of the body if you like, although generally most of your requests will consist of a single line.

To start with, try sending mail to listserv@uga.cc.uga.edu with only the text help in the body of the message (the subject doesn't matter). You should get back a list of valid commands. Probably the most interesting for you will be listserv refcard, which returns a reference card and lists global, which returns a *big* list of all known mailing lists on many LISTSERVers—it's over 300,000 bytes. You're in mailing list heaven! If that's too big, try just lists.

Joining and Dropping

If your mailing list is managed by a LISTSERVer, joining a list is easy. Send mail to listserv@domain, with the following message line:

```
SUB LISTNAME Firstname Lastname
```

LISTNAME is the name of the list, such as HUMOR. *Firstname* and *Lastname* are your first and last names.

To sign off the list, use this:

```
SIGNOFF LISTNAME
```

Do *not* send your unsubscribe request to the mailing list itself. You'll just irritate people and they'll laugh at you.

If you would rather get one mailing a day—consisting of all the posts to the mailing list in one big chunk—rather than receiving dozens of little messages during the day, use this:

```
SET LISTNAME DIGEST
```

To get each piece as it is sent, use this:

```
SET LISTNAME MAIL
```

There are other commands—the `help` command should get them for you.

If the mailing list isn't being handled by a LISTSERVer, you're at the mercy of the mailing list maintainer as to how subscriptions are handled.

Generally, the address to send messages to for a mailing list is this:

```
listname@domain
```

The address to send messages to for subscribing and unsubscribing is this:

```
listname-request@domain
```

However, you can't always count on these. Sigh. In this case you have to rely on the instructions for the specific list, which you need to get from the maintainer or a friend.

Automatic Mail Sorting

I'm not going to go into too much detail about mail sorting because it's a rather complex subject, but sometimes you get to the point where you can't treat your incoming mail file as a single entity.

I get literally hundreds of messages a day, and I would go insane if I didn't use a program known as a mail filter. These look at your incoming mail, and based on criteria you set regarding the contents of header items or message text, they sort the mail into several mailboxes before you even see them.

For instance, I subscribe to several mailing lists. I route messages from each of these into a separate mailbox for reading at my leisure. I have USENET voting ballots arriving all the time—these go into a special voting file for processing by the voting software. Everything that's left goes into my general mailbox for normal reading.

Actually, mail filters can often do more than this. You can use them to selectively forward mail to other users, or to send automatic responses to certain messages. You can even have them send only a single informational message to anyone who mails you while you're on vacation, no matter how many messages they send you during that time.

The drawback to a filter program is that they can be tough to set up, unless you're using a mail client with the capability built in (for example, Eudora). You need to carefully check your configuration files to make sure you aren't accidentally dropping messages on the floor!

procmail

procmail is probably the most popular of the mail filters. You have quite a bit of control over your messages, and can even pass them through other programs, such as a formatter, before they are saved. It can execute other programs on demand, and can be used to run simple mailing lists or mail servers. It's been extensively tested, it is stable, and it is fast. Be careful, though, that you don't accidentally tell it to send some of your mail into a black hole.

You can get the latest version by anonymous ftp to `ftp.informatik.rwth-aachen.de` as `pub/unix/procmail.tar.Z`.

deliver

Although procmail is the king of the hill for mail filter programs, I personally like deliver. You write shell scripts to handle all incoming messages. This requires more work on your part, usually, than would procmail, but it's very clean, almost infinitely flexible, and limits what you can do with your e-mail only to how well you can program scripts. The speed shouldn't be too much of a concern on that fast machine of yours.

I found deliver by anonymous ftp at `sunsite.unc.edu` as `/pub/Linux/distributions/slackware/nl/deliver.tgz`.

mailagent

I can't recommend or condemn this program, as I'm not that familiar with it, but it's another well-known e-mail filter. This one is written in the perl language, which again means that you can do anything with your e-mail by extending mailagent yourself (if you know perl). It comes with quite a few built-in features. I'd suggest this if you know perl. Anonymous ftp to `ftp.eff.org` and get `/pub/net-tools/perl-mailagent.tar.Z`.

Elm

Elm comes with a support program named `filter`, which does mail filtering. See the section "The Elm Mail System" to see where to get this.

Sending Programs and Graphics

As mentioned before, standard Internet mail allows only normal text in the message body, nothing fancy like programs or graphics. This is just one of the ways the Internet is showing its age.

However, as soon as someone realizes there's a limitation, someone else comes up with a way to circumvent it. There are two major ways this particular problem is dealt with: the quick hack and the long-term solution.

uuencode

This is the quick hack. uuencode is a program that takes a program or an 8-bit file (such as a GIF) and encodes it as 6-bit printable characters. Because all Internet mail sites are supposed to pass normal ASCII printable characters unmodified, the data should make it through to the other side.

Here's a simple example. The file `test1` contains the text `This is a test`. Run it through uuencode and place the result in `test1.uue`:

```
uuencode test1 test1 > test1.uue
```

This is the standard uuencode command format: first the name of the file you want to encode, then the name the file will be given when it is unpacked on the other end, and then the command to send the output to a file. Normally, you want the file to have the same name when it is unpacked as it does now, so both names (`test1` and `test1`) will usually be the same in any uuencode you do. When you cat `test1.uue` you get this:

```
begin 660 test1
.5&AI<R!I<R!A('1E<W1!
end
```

The first line contains uuencode's begin signal, then the UNIX file permissions of the file, then the name to which the file should be unpacked. The second line contains the encoded data, which consists of all printable characters. Finally, a blank line and `end` (to end the file). You can freely send this through almost any mail system.

You can even send the uuencoded data directly to someone else without an intermediate file:

```
uuencode ttt.exe ttt.exe | mail -s "Tic Tac Toe" mybuddy
```

> **NOTE:** The uuencoded file will be about 35 percent larger than the original file. About 33 percent of that comes from converting 8-bit bytes to 6-bit bytes; the other 2 percent comes from control information in the encoding.

uudecode

Now that you have the encoded program, you have to decode it. For that you use uudecode.

First, save the e-mail message to a file. In mm90 I'd use move `test1.uue` (the .uue just reminds you that it's a uuencoded file). Then decode it:

```
uudecode test1.uue
```

It's as simple as that. Well, not quite. A lot of other crud, such as message headers, ended up in the `test1.uue` file. Sometimes the sender adds some commentary before the data. uudecode is supposed to find the beginning of the actual uuencoded data in the file, but sometimes it gets confused, and you might have to use your editor to trim off everything before the begin line and after the end line.

Now look at the resulting file with cat `test1`:

```
This is a test
```

It worked! You could have just sent this sentence through the mail, of course, but programs should work this same way, but it's tough to show their contents in print, except as a hex dump. This would probably send weaker readers screaming, hence the example shows just the simple sentence.

split

Wait! All is not paradise. test1 was a short file. What if you want to send a 200,000 byte file? Add the 35 percent, and we have 270,000 bytes after the file is encoded. That's a hefty message by any estimation. Although you usually won't run into the problem with normal messages, some sites have a limit on message size, usually around 64,000 bytes. If you send your file as one big chunk, only a fourth of it may get there. What you need to do is split it up into smaller chunks.

You can do this manually, but there's a UNIX program that will do the job for you: split. Just tell split the number of lines you want in each piece, and it'll go snicker-snack, sending that big file galumphing back. The number of lines doesn't tell you the size exactly, but you can experiment. I find that using 800 lines per piece will give you nice, safe 50,000 byte chunks. Here's how it works:

```
uuencode bigfile bigfile > bigfile.uue
    split -800 bigfile.uue splits
```

```
mail -s "Bigfile.uue 1/3" mybuddy < splitsaa
mail -s "Bigfile.uue 2/3" mybuddy < splitsab
mail -s "Bigfile.uue 3/3" mybuddy < splitsac
rm bigfile.uue splits??
```

The hidden piece of the puzzle is that `split` takes the number of lines and the file to split, then a base name for the output files. In this case it's `splits`. It then names the resulting files `splitsaa`, `splitsab`, `splitsac`, and if necessary, all the way up to `splitszz`. This gives you 676 pieces. If that's not enough, you're cleaning your house with a toothbrush—you should probably use another method to transfer the files. The subjects with 1/3, 2/3, and 3/3 are just to let the receiver know how many pieces total there are and which piece of the whole each message is.

Now the receiver has to save all the messages into a big file, edit out everything except the uuencoded stuff, then run uudecode on the resulting file. It's cumbersome, but it works. If you do this a lot you can use a program that automates the uuencode splitting, mailing, and recombining. There's a program for everything.

Getting *uuencode* for Your System

If you're on a UNIX system, uuencode, uudecode, and `split` should come standard. If you're using DOS or a Mac, you'll have to get one from a friend or via ftp.

If you're using DOS, anonymous ftp to `oak.oakland.edu`. Go to the directory `/pub/msdos/decode` and grab `uuexe525.zip`. This is a very nice uuencode and uudecode for the PC that is actually superior to the standard UNIX version. For instance, it will automatically reorder the pieces of the file if they're out of order.

If you're using a Mac, anonymous ftp to `sumex-aim.stanford.edu` and grab `/info-mac/cmp/uu-lite-15.hqx`. It's a very full-featured uuencoder for the Mac.

For *any* computer for which you have a C compiler available, you can anonymous ftp to `oak.oakland.edu`. Go to the directory `/pub/misc/unix` and grab `uuencode.c` and `uudecode.c`. This is the portable C source for the standard uuencode and uudecode and should work on almost any computer. The portable C versions of uuencode and uudecode are simple but are always there.

MIME

No, silent weirdos in whiteface haven't invaded Internet. MIME is a specification for the extension of Internet mail to include attachments of programs, data, and multimedia. This is one of the long-term solutions.

You should be able to use one MIME application to mail full-motion video with sound to someone who can use a MIME application to play it back. In reality it's not quite that easy except in some very specific cases (such as the exact same program being used on both ends). However, it has advanced to the stage where many mail programs are MIME compatible enough that they can encode and decode files, as well as pictures, enclosed with a mail message.

This can be a useful feature if you're going to be sending a large number of files via mail, although, of course, the sender has to support it as well.

Au Revoir, E-Mail

Whew! There's a lot to talk about regarding e-mail (and there's more yet to learn). If you've read this section and understand a good portion of it, you know more about mail than the great majority of Internet users. And if you're using it as a reference, I hope it serves well. Here we fondly bid farewell to e-mail and move on to something even bigger.

USENET

Ah, USENET! Consumer of more person-hours than the great pyramids of Egypt. An information (and noise) source of unimaginable proportions.

What Is USENET?

When you say USENET people tend to think of Internet. What is it, really?

Analogies

The best way to describe USENET is in terms of e-mail (since you've just read that subject to death). Think of your mailbox, with all its new and old messages. Imagine what it might be like if everyone on Internet could read that mailbox, enter new messages, and leave replies. Now imagine having 5,000 mailboxes. That's USENET.

Or think of USENET as a huge set of public bulletin boards that millions of people read. Occasionally these folks write their own notices to nail to the church door, as it were. That's USENET.

Okay, you want to get away from cheesy analogies. USENET is a huge public messaging system. It is divided into thousands of discussions of different subjects—each separate piece is known as a newsgroup, or group. When someone enters a message while "in" a group, that message goes to all other USENET sites in the world, and people reading that same group can read the message and reply to it if they care to. Generally, there are dozens of different conversations ("threads") going on in any particular group—each is distinguished by a subject name, much like the Subject in a mail message. There are thousands of new messages posted each day. That's USENET.

USENET Is Not Internet

USENET is commonly thought of as being the same thing as the Internet, but they're not the same thing. The Internet is an international network of computers tied together via dedicated lines. USENET is just one of the services that uses the Internet. If you're familiar with bulletin board systems (BBSes), you might think of the Internet as the BBS hardware, and USENET as the message bases.

Not all computers on the Internet have USENET (it can take a lot of space!). Not all computers carrying USENET groups are on the Internet—like e-mail, some systems call Internet systems to exchange USENET messages. Don't say one when you mean the other.

USENET Is Usenet Is NetNews

Frankly, capitalization standards on Internet are quite relaxed. You can call it USENET, you can call it Usenet, you can call it UseNet. People will know what you mean. If you call it UsEnEt, people will start edging nervously for the exits. You can even refer to it by the ancient moniker Netnews (or NetNews). People will understand what you mean.

You can call the subject groupings into which USENET is divided groups or newsgroups. Please don't call them BBoards, as for some reason this upsets some inhabitants.

USENET Is Too Big

USENET comprises tens of megabytes of new posts a day and over 5,000 groups. Nobody can read it all, even if they go with an IV and read 24 hours a day. Your goal is to find as much possible useful information on subjects that interest you in the time you allot for yourself each day.

USENET Is an Information Bonanza

If you're interested in something, it's probably talked about in some group on USENET, and the amount of information is staggering. It can quickly become your prime information source for several of your interest areas.

USENET Is a Noise Overload

That information is buried among lots of noise—things you aren't interested in or posts that are of no use to anybody and may even be designed to confuse. Your goal is to separate the wheat from the chaff with maximum efficiency—hopefully keeping the wheat.

USENET Is a Controlled Anarchy

USENET isn't an anarchy in the popular sense of being total chaos. But while anarchy excludes outside control, it doesn't preclude self-control, and USENET is a web of written and unwritten agreements on the proper rules of behavior. Your goal is to avoid violating these codes of behavior until you know enough about them to decide when they can be broken.

USENET Sounds Intimidating

Well, it can be intimidating, especially if you just jump in as though you're on a local BBS discussion group. However, there are tried and true ways to ease painlessly into USENET, and I'm here to help you with those. I can help you attain your goals.

Underlying Concepts

This isn't a technical overview of USENET, but there are a few concepts you should know before you begin.

USENET Messages

USENET messages are much like the Internet mail messages described earlier this chapter—they consist of a header, which has information about the message, and the body, which has the actual message. They even use the same format as mail messages, and most of the same headers are valid. There are a few new ones, which are covered in the following sections.

The USENET Distribution Model

Every computer that gets USENET keeps a database of USENET messages. When a new message is entered, it is sent to neighboring USENET sites using NNTP (Network News Transfer Protocol). These distribute the post to other sites, until it is on every machine on USENET. There are various mechanisms to prevent a message from showing up on the same machine more than once, which we don't need to get into here. Only occasionally does a broken machine (usually a FidoNet gateway) regurgitate old articles back onto the Net.

Because posts can take different paths to reach different machines, there's no guarantee that you'll see a specific post before you see the reply to the post. For example, someone posts a message from Machine A, which sends the post through slow Machine B to get to your machine. It also sends the post to another machine, C, which gets it immediately. Someone there replies to it quickly, and C sends out the post to its neighbors, including Machine D. Machine D sends the reply on to you, where you see it immediately. In the meantime, the original post still hasn't gotten past Machine B to your computer. This is fairly common, although the scenario is usually more complicated. Don't be alarmed.

I said that all machines get all posts. Well, sort of...because USENET is so huge, many sites only carry a subset of all the available groups. A site won't get posts for groups it doesn't care about, or if it does, it won't keep them. In addition, there's something called a Distribution header that you can put in your message to try to restrict its distribution to a geographical area, such as San Diego. This is useful for messages that affect only San Diego.

Newsgroup Names

Newsgroups are named like this:

```
comp.sys.ibm.pc.games.action
```

This is a hierarchy reading down from left to right. Reading the group name, you have a *comp*uter group for computer *sys*tems from *ibm*, the *pc*s to be exact. You're talking about *games* for those systems, more specifically *action* games.

Here's another one:

```
talk.politics.guns
```

You have a group for *talk* about *politics*, more specifically *gun control*. I'll talk more about these hierarchies later.

The newsgroup with which your post is associated is given in the header of the message, in the Newsgroups item. It looks like this:

```
Newsgroups: news.announce.newgroups
```

That's not much of a concept, but here's a mindblowing concept if you're used to traditional BBSes. Each post can go in multiple groups! If I do this:

```
Newsgroups: alt.usenet.future,news.groups
```

my post will appear in both groups. This is known as crossposting. While you should know it is possible, you shouldn't actually do this until you've looked around a while, because frivolous crossposting is frowned on.

In fact, there's another header that can be used to send any replies back to a specific group. For instance, you might make a wide informational post to several groups, but specify that the discussion (if any) should be only in a single group. This is the Followup-To header. Together, the headers look like this:

```
Newsgroups: rec.arts.comics.misc,rec.arts.comics.strips,
   rec.arts.comics.animation
 Followup-To: rec.arts.comics.animation
```

Remember from the e-mail header discussion that one header can spread over several lines, as long as succeeding lines are indented. That's what you did to split `Newsgroups` over two lines. All replies to the post will go to `rec.arts.comics.animation`, unless the person replying overrides that.

Crossposting can be abused, but more on that later.

Threads

An original post and all the replies to it are considered to be a single "thread" of conversation. This can actually look more like a Christmas tree than a straight line, as there are replies to replies, and replies to those replies, which branch off until each sub-branch dies of finality or boredom.

Each USENET message has a Subject associated with it that is supposed to summarize the contents of the message (although this is often not the case). One way to track a thread is to note the message subjects, which those who reply to the post are supposed to preserve until the discussion wanders too far from the original subject. The only way to fully keep track of threads is to use a threaded newsreader, which is discussed in the next section.

Newsreaders

The first item of business is which program you will use to read USENET. Your choice of these programs (known as newsreaders) can hugely impact how you read the Net, how much information you get out of it, and how much garbage you have to sludge through.

rn (readnews)

rn is free, so there's a good chance the system you use to read mail has it, and a good chance that it will be offered to you as your default newsreader. Avoid using it if you can!

Back when rn was first written, one person could read every single message posted to USENET and still have time for a life. It reflects those simpler times—its default is to dive in and show you all the messages in the group, one at a time.

This sounds reasonable, but it's a fact that the majority of the posts on most newsgroups you will read are of no interest to you. "What?!" you cry. "I could never get enough information on *Mystery Science Theater 3000*!" You wouldn't think so, but there will come a time when you no longer wish to slog through every post on the group and become choosy about which posts you read. rn does not let you do this easily. Since popular groups can get over 100 messages a day, rn's preference for showing you every single message really wastes your time.

Message Overview and Threading

Just how much of your time rn wastes is evident the first time you run another news program that first gives you an overview of the group. It provides you with a summary line for each post, just as a mail program does—it gives you the poster's name, the subject, and possibly the message size. Scroll through the pages of summaries and choose which posts look interesting. When you're done choosing, read the posts you've selected.

This is already a major shift in concept—instead of having to read everything to decide what you don't want to read, you are choosing which few posts look interesting.

Now I'll add another concept to that—the newsreader should keep track of which posts are related to each other and group them, so you can select or ignore whole groups of posts at once. It can do this by noticing the threads and subject names mentioned before.

These two changes account for an almost unbelievable difference in speed between a good threaded newsreader and something line rn. Now that I've gotten good at determining which threads look promising and which don't, I can read USENET literally 100 times faster than I could before. I'll recommend some right after this...

Kill Files

What if you knew a particular subject were of no interest to you, and that you would never read a post by that name again? It's a waste of time for the newsreader to even offer it to you. This goes doubly for certain people who do nothing but generate noise on USENET. It'd be nice never to see any of their posts.

This is what a kill file is for. In its most primitive form, you give it a subject or poster whom you never wish to hear from again. Usually you'll be allowed a little bit of fine-tuning—you may wish to kill that subject only in one particular newsgroup.

In a group where over half the discussion is about something you don't care about (for instance, a particular author on a fantasy group), having the newsreader kill all articles relating to that author can save you time and make you less likely to lose valuable articles in the crush.

There's also the opposite of a kill file. If you know you will want to read every posting on a particular subject or from a particular person, a selection file lets you have the newsreader automatically mark them for reading. This isn't quite as common as the kill file.

Which Newsreader?

This is one of those religious preference questions, similar to "What's the best editor?" I would say that any newsreader that has the following features is a contender:

- Offers a message overview that lets you select messages to read before actually reading any.
- Enables you to group posts together by common subject and/or thread.
- Lets you specify authors or subjects that will be automatically killed by the newsreader so you never see them. You should be able to do this for one group or for all groups.
- Lets you do the opposite—automatically select certain authors or subjects.

The rest is just gravy, although I'm tempted to add "Is very configurable" to the list.

Unfortunately, compiling and configuring a new newsreader can be a very hairy business, especially if you're new to USENET. For now, you might have to use whatever your system has available—if there's nothing but rn, pester your administrator.

NN (No News)

NN (No News [Is Good News]) has probably the largest number of users of any newsreader other than rn. It's fast, flexible, very configurable, has very nice kill and selection options, sorts messages in several ways, and offers several ways to manage the old messages. It's even got its own group, news.software.nn. This is definitely worth a look.

Other UNIX Readers

Other UNIX readers that are worth looking at (if your site offers them) are TRN, STRN, and TIN. They meet or exceed the criteria given. You can also read the USENET group news.software.readers for the latest information.

Other Readers

For other systems, you should be reading the USENET groups comp.os.msdos.mail-news and news.software.readers. There are, most likely, programs out there for your system. For instance, there's Trumpet for DOS and WinTrumpet for Windows. If you have a complete TCP/IP package, you might want to see if it includes a mail reader (other than rn).

Offline Readers

Just as you can use a mail client to do your mail processing offline, you can use an offline reader to do your USENET processing offline. This is useful if you're paying by the minute for your connect time. See the group alt.usenet.offline-reader for help with these.

Finding Your Groups

How do you find the groups that interest you? Say you want to find a beer group. Now what?

The Hierarchies

As mentioned earlier, group names are arranged in hierarchies from left to right. The left item is known as the top-level of the hierarchy. In the case of a group such as this:

`alt.tv.animaniacs`

it is said that the group is "in the `alt` hierarchy" (or "`alt.` hierarchy"). The Net is organized into seven major hierarchies, one anarchic hierarchy, and a bunch of smaller, less important hierarchies.

The Big Seven Hierarchies

The big seven hierarchies are the following:

`comp.`	**Computer topics.** This ranges from programming to hardware to peripherals to folklore. Most popular computer systems and operating systems have their own set of groups here.
`misc.`	**Miscellaneous.** When nobody can figure out where to put a new group, it often ends up under `misc.`. For example, the `misc.jobs` groups don't clearly belong in any of the other six hierarchies, so they go under `misc.`.
`news.`	**The business of USENET.** This is where people talk about USENET administration, propose new groups, and argue about when USENET is going to die of its own excesses.
`rec.`	**Recreational topics.** This is where most of the hobbyist stuff, such as `rec.crafts.jewelry`, goes. It also contains artistic and music discussions, crafts, and more in that vein.
`sci.`	**Science.** This is where the math and physics types hang out. Medical, too, such as `sci.med.radiology`.
`soc.`	**Social topics.** This is a grab bag of many cultural groups for different regions, such as `soc.culture.chile`, social research groups, religious discussion groups, and alternative lifestyle groups. It's something of a milder version of the talk hierarchy.

`talk.`   **Heated debate.**   Incredibly vicious personal attacks by people (most of whom seemingly haven't even heard of the concept of "critical thinking") that go on interminably about all the things you would expect—politics and religion. See `talk.politics.mideast`, for example. No debate here is ever really ended.

These hierarchies are sometimes known as USENET proper and are considered by many news administrators to be the only "real" hierarchies. For a new group to be created in any of these seven hierarchies, it has to go through a group interest polling procedure that discourages overly frivolous group creation. More on this later.

The Sewer of .alt

Actually, some of my favorite groups are in the `.alt` hierarchy, but it has a mixed reputation. Unlike the big seven hierarchies, anyone who cares to send a group creation message for a new group can make an `.alt` group. This is often followed by someone else sending out a group removal message if they consider the group outrageous, but still it's a lot looser than the big seven groups. For instance, one group in the `alt.` hierarchy is `alt.barney.dinosaur.die.die.die`. The `alt.` hierarchy is also controversial because groups such as `alt.sex.stories` reside here, and because of the `alt.binaries.pictures` groups, which involve huge amounts of message space chewed up by pictures. Because of all the hassles involved with `alt.`, many sites don't carry any of the groups.

I consider that a shame, because `alt.` is also a haven for groups that can't find a home in the big seven hierarchies. For instance, discussions of TV shows are generally considered transitory, since interest in the show will probably eventually die out. For this reason, people are unwilling to vote to place a group for a show such as "Twin Peaks" in the big seven hierarchies, so they end up in the fertile `alt.tv` section of the `alt.` hierarchy, where they are the source of years of enjoyment to many (I feel like a commercial).

`alt.` is also nice because groups can be quickly created, unlike in the big seven, where it takes two months. So a group such as `alt.current-events.la-quake` can be created overnight in response to special situations.

`alt.` has become somewhat more organized in the past year. Anyone can create a new group, but anyone can also send out a removal message, and there are several `alt.` volunteer police who will summarily do so if the group hasn't been proposed on `alt.config` or if it's clearly a joke group. This has cut down on the number of "triple-word" joke groups, such as `alt.french.captain.borg.borg.borg`, which were first made popular by the group `alt.swedish.chef.bork.bork.bork`. But it isn't the big seven by a long shot, and I'd hate to see the day when it is.

The Other Hierarchies

Anybody can create a hierarchy for a specialized reason (all you have to do is persuade other sites to carry the groups), and there are often good reasons for doing so. Especially useful are hierarchies for regional groups. For instance, there are many `ca.` groups for discussion of California topics (for example, `ca.politics`). This keeps local stuff where the rest of the Net doesn't have to read it. Cities that have active Net communities often have their own hierarchies, such as `sdnet.` for San Diego. The same goes for universities (`ucsd.`) and companies.

There are other hierarchies that are intended to be more widely spread, but are limited for other reasons. Many of the BITNET mailing lists are echoed on USENET in the `bit.` groups. Much child education discussion goes on in the `k12.` groups.

A few hierarchies have made a bid for the big seven but have failed. `trial.` and `us.` both failed from lack of interest, although at this time people are trying to resurrect the `us.` hierarchy.

Where Do I Go?

Back to your original question—how do you know where to go for a particular subject? There are several ways.

First, your newsreader may be smart enough to find part of a group name. If I tell NN to go to group `beer`, for instance, it asks me if I mean `alt.beer` or `rec.food.drink.beer`. In this way I just found two groups, and if I look for brewing I'll find more.

Dave Lawrence posts "List of Active Newsgroups" and "Alternative Newsgroup Hierarchies" to `news.groups` and `news.answers`. This is the mother lode—all "official" groups (although with `alt.` "official" doesn't mean much), each with a short description. Get it if you can.

Your newsreader probably has a way to show you a list of all groups. This might take some digging to find. (It's `:show groups all` in NN.)

Next, you can look through a file your newsreader leaves in your home directory, named `.newsrc` or something similar. This is just a list of group names, but they might give you some hints.

You can always ask for help on the group `news.groups.questions`, which is just for this sort of question.

Netiquette

This is perhaps the most important piece of this USENET section. You can muddle through the rest, but your use of netiquette (*Net etiquette*—more geek hilarity) determines how you are perceived by others on the Net—and a reputation can be a very hard thing to get rid of. You may be shocked to engage in a debate and find someone dredging up a post from six months ago that you're not too proud of.

The Net doesn't have rules, per se, but it has customs that are often stronger than the force of law would be. People routinely violate U.S. laws on USENET because they consider them to be a joke—and most of the other users seem to agree, so they ignore it. But violate the USENET customs and watch out.

Of course, there comes a time when any given rule should be broken, but until you get the nuances down, try to respect the customs.

I hope I'm not being too intimidating here. USENET is a wonderful place once you're acclimated to it. You just need a little help getting over the initial growing pains, and reading this will hopefully help. I'm going to tell you some horror stories, yes, but just so you can learn from them.

Newbie

If you're reading this, you're probably a newbie. That's USENET slang for "new person." It's not a bad thing to be a newbie, nor is it a hanging offense (or even something most people will look down at you for). People just treat newbies with a bit more caution, because they know that people who haven't grasped the local customs are more likely to commit a faux pas.

Even if you've been posting on your local BBS or FidoNet for 10 years, you're still a newbie. The customs are unique. Welcome to the Jungle, please obey our laws.

Newbie No More

This piece of advice is probably worth the whole price of the book if you're going to be on USENET for a while: The best way to learn the customs of USENET at absolutely no risk to yourself is just to read it without posting for six weeks.

You can watch newbies who weren't so cautious commit the same blunders that you might have done and get upbraided, just because they, unlike you, didn't know. You can see the conversational tactics that are used by the pros, when they'll press a point and when they'll back off. You also get the feel of each group—each one has its own special ambience.

The length of time you should read before posting varies according to what you feel comfortable with. Most people on USENET are actually full-time "lurkers"—they just read and don't post. Sometimes this is by choice, sometimes it's due to software or administrative limitations. But it's estimated that there are more than 100 readers of a group for every person who posts to it.

Signature Files

Most newsreaders enable you to attach a signature to every post you make. It takes the contents of the file `.signature` in your home directory and attaches it to the end of the post. This is intended to be used for identification purposes—perhaps your name and place of work if it's not obvious from the header. Or sometimes it's used for disclaimers.

By far, the most common use is as a small personality statement—this usually involves your name, Internet address, a favorite quote, and maybe a small picture drawn with text characters. I often identify people by their signatures, rather than by looking at the header, since they're immediately recognizable by general look.

Some people always go overboard, however, and this results in huge signatures with big ugly fonts, ASCII graphics, loads of stupid quotes, three different addresses, five phone numbers…you get the picture. Suddenly, the signature is a significant amount of information (done in wretched style) that has to be ignored every time, even as it pushes the real content of the post off the page. After seeing this a dozen times, people get irritated.

There's even a group dedicated to ragging on people with horrendous signatures, and even some standard "scoring" guidelines. You lose points for having the following in your signature:

- BUAG (Butt Ugly ASCII Font—big letters made up of multiple characters)
- A border all the way around it
- A border partially around it
- A bad quote
- Duplicate mail addresses
- Lots of wasted space
- Bad misspellings
- More than four signature lines
- Bad pictures "drawn" with text
- A big, ugly Amiga check mark
- Quotes from the group Rush (because of sheer overuse)
- A "map" of Australia
- High-bit characters
- Tab damage (You need to use spaces instead of tabs so it won't look horrible on systems that handle tabs differently, or if the signature is quoted.)

Readers of this group (`alt.fan.warlord`) take great pride in their skill at tearing bad signatures apart. But here's my hint for the day: If your signature is four or fewer lines, as called for by netiquette, nobody is going to care what you put in it.

Going over four lines makes it open season. Luckily, four lines is more than enough for almost any "vital" information you'd need to put there.

Excessive Quoting

Because of the nature of the Net, it's easy to lose track of where you were in a conversation or debate. If someone just replies, "That's the stupidest thing I ever heard!" you may have a hard time determining just who they were talking about or which side they're taking. Comments need a bit of context.

For that reason, most news software "quotes" the entire previous message into your editor for you. It does this by putting a quote character, usually a >, to the left of each line of text. You are supposed to trim this message down to the bare essentials necessary for context to be established for your following comments.

A lot of people seem to be incapable of grasping this concept. In the most heinous cases, they quote pages and pages of a previous message, including the person's signature, only to add a single line comment such as "This is stupid." Please trim your quotes. It means less space spent storing redundant data, it means people can read your message quicker, which makes them happier, and it makes your comments much more understandable.

It's up to your personal preference, but I've generally found that I never need more than about four lines of text from the previous message for any point I wish to make. In responding to a complex message it's quite acceptable to quote some text, reply to it, quote some more text, reply to it, and so on. You can even quote the entire message doing this in a few cases, but since you're doing it to establish context for each of your quotes, it's considered acceptable.

Also, watch how deep the quotes go. Someone quoting your message will also quote text you quoted—that text then has a >> in front of it. Too many levels of this gets confusing and makes it more likely that someone will be misattributed.

One final caution—while your quoting doesn't have to preserve the full context of the person's message, using "selective quoting" to make it appear that someone argued a point they never argued is viewed with much the same approval as hitting a pregnant woman. You're in trouble if you do this. And if you ever actually modify the text of a quote, lordy help you...

Pyramid Schemes

Occasionally, you'll see something about "Make Money Fast," usually with the name Dave Rhodes somewhere in it. *Don't Do It!*

This chain letter never goes away, and since the people who post it tend to be very obnoxious about where they post it (some even post it to every single group on USENET—

think about that), people are not tolerant of this at all. You'll get a few thousand upset e-mail messages that will probably shut down your machine and make your administrator less than amiable. Also, it may be illegal.

Excessive Crossposting

Earlier, I showed how to make a post go to several groups at once, which is known as crossposting. Crossposting is hardly ever necessary, and only once in a blue moon is it necessary to crosspost to more than four groups at once except for special informational USENET postings.

Newbies usually mess up on crossposting a plea for help—they're not sure where to ask for it, so they crosspost to any group that looks like it might have something to do with it. They always manage to hit a few inappropriate groups, and between the complaints about the crossposting and the alienation of those who might have helped due to the crossposting, the newbie doesn't get the question answered.

Take the time to look at a few messages in each group to see if it looks appropriate. If you find one that looks right, post to that *one* group asking your question. You can note that you're not 100 percent sure if you're in the right place and ask for better directions. People are usually very friendly to this type of posting. And, of course, you can ask on the group `news.groups.questions` where you should direct your questions.

Read the FAQ!

One day, the people of USENET noted that new users all tended to ask the same few questions. They decided to create a Frequently Asked Questions List (FAQ—the L just didn't sound good), which would present the answers to these questions, just preventing them from being asked over and over and over and over and over and over and, well…

That worked pretty well, and now many groups have FAQs. This means that if you pop up on a group and ask a question that is in the FAQ, you're going to get some very negative responses ("Read the FAQing FAQ!") If you enter a new group for the purpose of asking a question, make sure you look for a post with "FAQ" in the title. If you find any, read them first. Your answers (and answers to questions you hadn't even thought of yet) may be in there.

If you're looking for information in general, most FAQs are posted to `news.answers`. You can go there and browse all the beautiful FAQs.

Keep the Flaming to a Minimum

In Net parlance, a *flame* is a heated attack on someone or something. An extended series of exchanged flames (flames are catching, it seems) are a *flamewar*.

An occasional flame is usually warranted and cleans out your system, but be careful of letting it get away with you. Some people have a reputation of being much too quick to flame—even an honest mistake might earn you a litany of your mother's dating habits from this kind of person. Others have the reputation of enjoying flaming just for the sake of doing it. Actually, there's a whole group for these people (`alt.flame`).

If you ever want to acquire a reputation as being a cool-headed, capable debater, however, watch yourself. I find it useful to let the message sit for five minutes, then come back to it. You may find, as I do, that a nonantagonistic-appearing message is actually more damaging to the other person's case. And if you watch carefully, you can see what the Net pros have learned: how to flame with a precise acetylene torch, deftly vaporizing someone's ill-thought post with facts, style, and wit. This is much more devastating than the standard "Oh, yeah? Moron!" type of argument.

Don't Bluff

Trying to pretend you know something you don't is bound for failure on the Net much more often than you might think. There are a large number of well-informed people on the Net (some seem to be virtual information sinks on certain subjects), and chances are good that someone who knows more than you do is going to call your bluff.

This extends to less drastic claims as well—if you're going to make a claim, you had better be prepared to back it up. It's not known as the Net of a Million Lies for nothing, and most users who have been there awhile tend to be a bit skeptical. And then there are the people who actively oppose your position and have the facts to argue their side…

It's somewhat sad to see someone backing down from an ill-advised position, so be careful. And if you should ever be caught in an out-and-out falsehood, you might as well start humming a funeral march.

Whew!

Looking back on that list of "Don't do this," "Beware of that" is a bit exhausting. Again, I don't want you to be afraid of USENET—the worst that will probably happen if you do screw up royally is that someone writes you a nasty letter. Remember, you can absorb all this by osmosis just by reading newsgroups for a period of time before you post to them.

USENET Miscellany

Wait, I'm not done with you yet—I have so much more to give! This section contains some random bits of advice and frequently asked questions.

Creating a New Group

This one comes up often. "Hey, there's no group for discussing indigo feebles! How do I start one?"

In this case, I doubly recommend reading both `news.announce.newgroups` and `news.groups` for a three-month period before you try to create your own group. This seems extreme, but it's a whole new level of politics, written and unwritten rules, and various subtleties.

To help, you should grab the posts "How to Create a USENET Newsgroup" and the "USENET Newsgroup Creation Companion" from `news.groups`. The first is the official guidelines, the second is a helper I wrote.

Basically, creating a new group boils down to this: You issue a Request for Discussion (RFD), crossposted to `news.announce.newgroups`, `news.groups`, and any interested groups. It should give the proposed name of your group, its charter, and why it should be created. Follow-up discussion will take place in `news.groups`.

If the discussion yields any major changes to the name or charter, you'll need to issue a second RFD explaining the changes. This repeats until a consensus is reached.

The Call for Votes (CFV) can be held 30 days after the first RFD. You should contact the USENET Volunteer Votetakers (UVV) at rdippold@qualcomm.com to have your vote run by an experienced group of neutral votetakers. The UVV will take care of the voting, which runs 22 days. At the end of this time, the votes are tallied. If your proposed group has at least 100 more YES votes regarding its creation than it has NO votes, and if there are twice as many YES votes as NO votes, then the group passes and will be created by the `news.announce.newgroups` moderator after five days or so.

All this is a massive oversimplification, but it gives you some idea of the work involved, and the time period (two months). You might consider whether you want an `alt.` hierarchy group instead (read `alt.config`) or if you want to start a mailing list.

How Can I Get That Person Off the Net?

Uh oh…someone called you some nasty names or said something you consider offensive. Now what? Well, now you deal with it by yourself. Among the advantages of the Net is that someone with an unpopular viewpoint can't be kicked off just because their philosophy isn't in line with what the Acceptable Opinions Squad have decided are the required ways of thinking this year. This is somewhat of a disadvantage in that some people use it as just an excuse to be rude. You're an adult—you can presumably figure out some way to deal with it, such as just ignoring the person. If you go complaining to someone's administrator just because they called you a name, you're probably going to be disappointed, not to mention mocked.

There are a few situations in which it is considered okay to contact someone's administrator: if you receive an actual threat of violence and think it's serious, or if you are clearly defrauded by said person in a transaction that was arranged on the Net. You can probably see the trend here—if there was actual (or threatened) damage that occurred in the real world, you certainly might be justified.

Recommend Some Newsgroups!

I showed you earlier how to retrieve the posting of all the newsgroups and their short descriptions. I could really send my page count through the roof by just including that here, but I'll settle for recommending a few varied ones that might interest you:

alt.binaries.*	This is where all the pictures and other data are posted. You can get pictures, sounds, and music files among these groups.
alt.config	This is where group creation in the alt. hierarchy is discussed.
alt.culture.usenet	Yes, USENET has a culture, though this group is spotty.
alt.fan.pratchett	Getcher real live author here! Terry Pratchett, author of the sidesplitting *Discworld* books, chats with his fans.
alt.folklore.computers	This is anything you wanted to know (or didn't) about the history of computers. Some of it is even true.
alt.folklore.urban	Randy Beaman knew this kid who drank Pop Rocks and soda at the same time, and his head exploded! Okay, bye. Folk tales...
alt.internet.services	This shows what's where on the Internet.
alt.quotations	This is just what it looks like—lots of quotations.
comp.risks	This is the RISKS digest—examining the risks involved with technology.
comp.sys.*	Do you have a computer? It's probably got its own groups under comp.sys. Even the redoubtable HP 48 calculator has its own.
control	This is where newsgroup creation and removal actually takes place. It's interesting to watch if you read alt.config or news.groups.

`news.answers`	All the FAQs get posted here. It's information central.
`news.future`	Shows the future of the Net—a bit whiny, but sometimes interesting.
`news.groups`	This is for the discussion of USENET group creation and is the focus of a lot of USENET politics.
`news.newusers.questions`	This is just what it looks like. Ask away! Or at least read this for a while.
`news.software.readers`	Is your newsreader up to snuff?
`rec.arts.movies`	There's lots of information here about, like, movies.
`rec.humor.oracle`	This is the USENET oracle. It's definitely something different.
`talk.politics.misc`	Newbies seem to like to talk politics, but be careful! This is one of the most cutthroat groups on the Net.

Watch Out for Pranks

You may take USENET utterly seriously, or you may treat is as a playground for pranks. Most people fall somewhere in between, but there are a lot of people who lean towards the latter.

If you see something that seems too strange to be true, it probably is. Check the Newsgroups header line and look at the crossposts—if it's posted to a bizarre group, chances are someone's being funny. If you post a heated response, you'll just end up looking silly.

Look carefully at the Followup-To header—a favorite of those soft in the head is to send your reply to `misc.test`, `alt.dev.null`, or some totally inappropriate group. Whenever you reply to a message, you should always get in the habit of noticing which Newsgroups your message is being sent to so you don't get caught by something like this.

This baiting of the gullible is known as "trolling" and is quite a pastime on some groups, such as `alt.folklore.urban`. Basically, there are subjects that have come up so often that they're beyond Frequently Asked Questions and into "Good Grief!" status. After the subject has been dormant for awhile, someone who's been on the group awhile will make a post that ostensibly asks for information or makes a claim related to the subject. It'll be a post of the type that will make all newbies immediately want to write "Geesh, what are you? Stupid?" The group oldies will, of course, obtain great entertainment value from these posts. The more insulting, the better. You've been reeled in. How do you tell a troll from someone actually saying something stupid? Often, you can't unless you've been reading the group for awhile.

USENET Adieu

Obviously, I could go on for 200 pages about USENET. But you've got more than enough information now to fortify you. I think you'll find that USENET can be quite rewarding.

Talk

After those long e-mail and USENET sections, this piece seems almost naked.

Talk is a simple utility available on many networked systems. It allows you to "converse" in real-time with someone else. Anything you type automagically appears in one-half of the screen, anything the other person types appears in the other. It's easy to use:

```
talk userid@domain
```

If that person is logged on, he or she should get a message saying that someone wants to talk, and that the person should either enter *answer* or talk *youruserid@yourdomain* to talk to you.

When you're done, press Ctrl+C to exit. The first one to do this wins.

Talk is not as convenient as just calling the person. But sometimes you don't know the other person's number, sometimes you don't have a free phone line, or perhaps the person is long distance. Talk is cheap. (Ow! Lethally bad pun there...)

Internet Relay Chat (IRC)

I'd feel guilty if I didn't tell you about this, although I can hear hundreds of system administrators yelling "No, don't!" IRC is simply live multiple-person "chat" via the keyboard. That's it. Oh yes, it's apparently more addictive than cocaine, without the benefits.

Well, maybe that's a little harsh, but you would have to see the depths to which some people have become IRC-addicted to believe it. It's amazing how such a simple concept can be so captivating.

Basic IRC Structure

First, someone sets up an IRC server. Then those who wish to access it use their IRC client software.

The IRC "universe" consists of hundreds of channels with names such as #initgame. Users join (using their client software) in a channel that interests them and are then in conversation with everyone else who is on that same channel. You can talk with everyone or direct your comments to certain individuals. This is a flexible format that allows something as free-form as a general babble to many pairs of private conversations to a game of IRC Jeopardy, which plays much like the TV show. Some channels are private.

IRC users have their own nicknames and become quite attached to them (since your reputation goes with your nickname, this is quite understandable). A nickname database, NickServ, has been set up to eliminate accidental collisions.

Getting IRC Clients

Before you can do anything you'll need an IRC client. You'll need to grab the source code appropriate for your machine and compile it. If you absolutely can't get the source code running, and can't get someone else to do it for you, you can use the IRC telnet server:

```
telnet bradenville.andrew.cmu.edu
```

This site can't handle too much of a load, so you should use it only as a last resort.

You can get the UNIX IRC client by anonymous ftp to cs.bu.edu under /irc/clients. Look to see which file the symbolic link CURRENT points to—it will be linked to the latest UNIX source code for ircII.

A PC client running under MS-DOS or Windows can anonymous ftp to cs.bu.edu and look under /irc/clients/msdos. You'll have your choice of several for DOS, or winirc for Windows.

A Mac client can anonymous ftp to cs.bu.edu and look under /irc/clients/macintosh. Grab the latest version of Homer you find there.

Connecting to a Server

Once you have your client, you need to figure out which IRC server you will be talking to. Anonymous ftp to cs.bu.edu and look under /irc/support. There should be a file named servers.940201 (the last number is the date, so that part will change). Grab this and look for a server that's close to you.

Then tell your client to connect to this server. With luck, it'll talk back to you and you'll be in the world of IRC.

Choosing Channels

Once you get on an IRC server, all commands start with a /.

/help gives you a list of commands. To get the new user help, do /help intro then /help newuser.

/list shows all the current IRC channels. It looks something like this, except that there will be a heck of a lot more channels:

```
*** Channel    Users  Topic
*** #wubba     3      Wherefore the wubba?
*** #hoffa     5      i know where the body is
*** #litldog   2      where oh where has he gone
```

/names might be more interesting. It shows who's logged on each channel and whether it's a private or public channel:

```
Pub: #wubba       @wubba jblow jdoe
Prv: *    marla donald ivana bill hillary
Pub: #litldog    @yakko dot
```

Then use /join *channel* to participate on *channel*. Here you might do a /join #wubba.

/nick *nickname* enables you to change to a new nickname in case your old one is too stodgy.

/msg *nickname message* enables you to send a private *message* to *nickname*. Use the /query *nickname* to enter a private conversation with *nickname*. Use /query to exit it.

If you get ambitious and create a channel (using /join on a nonexistent channel creates it), be sure to look at the /mode command, which lets you determine the behavior of the channel.

Need Help?

/join #Twilight_zone is where IRC operators often hang out, and some are willing to help. Just ask your question—don't announce that you need to ask a question first.

Bad Moves

Don't use someone else's nickname if you can help it—people are very protective about them.

Never type anything that someone asks you to type if you aren't sure what it does. You might find that you've just given someone else control of your client!

Don't abuse the telnet server. If you're going to IRC a lot, get your own client.

Further Info

Anonymous ftp to cs.bu.edu and go to /irc/support. There's some interesting info here. IRC also has several alt. groups dedicated to it: alt.irc.corruption, alt.irc.ircii, alt.irc.lamers, alt.irc.opers, alt.irc.questions, alt.irc.recovery, and `alt.irc.undernet`. The corruption group probably won't be too interesting to you now, and you don't need the recovery group yet.

Good luck, and may you never op on request.

Is That It?

Is that all there is to UNIX communications? Well, that's 99% of it ...

To review, the Internet is the largest network in the world, comprising an international network of networks. Its lifeblood is data, and much of that data consists of user to user communications. The most basic and possibly the most fundamentally useful of these communications is Internet Mail, person-to-person messages. In fact, it is so useful that its reach far exceeds the reach of Internet itself, to other service providers such as Compuserve.

Internet Mail can be extended to multiple-person mailing lists, using list servers, but for public messaging, USENET is the preferred choice. It offers public posts on thousands of different subjects, with more being offered every day. You just need to explore the waters carefully at first and make sure you don't violate any of the customs.

Those two services constitute the vast majority of personal communications on the Internet, but there are other specialized applications, such as MUDs (Multi User Dungeons), mostly for real-time conversations. Two of the most popular are Talk, for single person to single person real-time "chatting" and Internet Relay Chat (IRC), for multiple person real-time conversations.

I'm sure that you will find that communication with others is a large part of your Internet experience.

2

PART

Hunt for Shells

What Is a Shell?

10

By Rick Rummel

Introduction

You can do many things without having an extensive knowledge of how they actually work. For example, you can drive a car without understanding the physics of the internal combustion engine. A lack of knowledge of electronics doesn't prevent you from enjoying music from a CD player. You can use a UNIX computer without knowing what the shell is and how it works. However, you will get a lot more out of UNIX if you do.

Three shells are typically available on a UNIX system: Bourne, Korn, and C shells. They are discussed in Chapters 11, 12, and 13. In this chapter, you'll learn

- What a shell is
- What a shell does for you
- How a shell relates to the overall system

The Kernel and the Shell

As the shell of a nut provides a protective covering for the kernel inside, a UNIX shell provides a protective outer covering. When you turn on, or "boot up," a UNIX-based computer, the program unix is loaded into the computer's main memory, where it remains until you shut down the computer. This program, called the kernel, performs many low-level and system-level functions. The kernel is responsible for interpreting and sending basic instructions to the computer's processor. The kernel is also responsible for running and scheduling processes and for carrying out all input and output. The kernel is the heart of a UNIX system. There is one and only one kernel.

As you might suspect from the critical nature of the kernel's responsibilities, the instructions to the kernel are complex and highly technical. To protect the user from the complexity of the kernel, and to protect the kernel from the shortcomings of the user, a protective shell is built around the kernel. The user makes requests to a shell, which interprets them, and passes them on to the kernel. The remainder of this section explains how this outer layer is built.

Once the kernel is loaded to memory, it is ready to carry out user requests. First, though, a user must log in and make a request. For a user to log in, however, the kernel must know who the user is and how to communicate with him. To do this, the kernel invokes two special programs, getty and login. For every user port—usually referred to as a tty—the kernel invokes the getty program. This process is called spawning. The getty program displays a login prompt and continuously monitors the communication port for any type of input that it assumes is a user name. Figure 10.1 shows a freshly booted UNIX system with six user ports.

FIGURE 10.1.

An active system with no users.

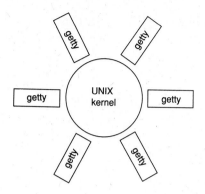

When getty receives any input, it calls the login program, as shown in Figure 10.2. The login program establishes the identity of the user and validates his right to log in. The login program checks the password file. If the user fails to enter a valid password, the port is returned to the control of a getty. If the user enters a valid password, login passes control by invoking the program name found in the user's entry in the password file. This program might be a word processor or a spreadsheet, but it usually is a more generic program called a shell.

FIGURE 10.2.

A user logs in.

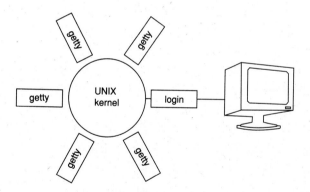

In the system shown in Figure 10.3, four users have logged in. Likewise, one user is in the process of logging in, and one port has no activity. Of the four active users, two are using the Bourne shell, one is using the Korn shell, and one has logged into a spreadsheet. Each user has received a copy of the shell to service his requests, but there is only one kernel. Using a shell does not prevent a user from using a spreadsheet or another program, but those programs run under the active shell. A shell is a program dedicated to a single user, and it provides an interface between the user and the UNIX kernel.

You don't have to use a shell to access UNIX. In Figure 10.3, one of the users has been given a spreadsheet instead of a shell. When this user logs in, the spreadsheet program starts. When he exits the spreadsheet, he is logged out. This technique is useful in situations where security is a major concern, or when it is desirable to shield the user from any interface with UNIX. The drawback is that the user cannot use `mail` or the other UNIX utilities.

FIGURE 10.3.

An active system.

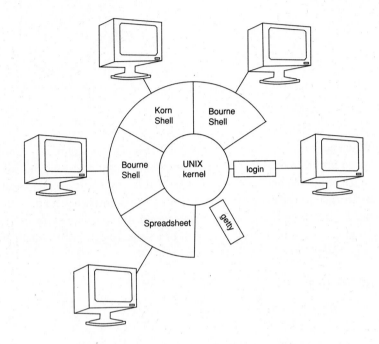

Because any program can be executed from the login—and a shell is simply a program—it is possible for you to write your own shell. In fact, three shells, developed independently, have become a standard part of UNIX. They are

- The Bourne shell, developed by Stephen Bourne
- The Korn shell, developed by David Korn
- The C shell, developed by Bill Joy

This variety of shells enables you to select the interface that best suits your needs or the one with which you are most familiar.

The Functions of a Shell

It doesn't matter which of the standard shells you choose, for all three have the same purpose: to provide a user interface to UNIX. To provide this interface, all three offer the same basic functions:

- Command line interpretation
- Program initiation

- Input-output redirection
- Pipeline connection
- Substitution of filenames
- Maintenance of variables
- Environment control
- Shell programming

Command Line Interpretation

When you log in, starting a special version of a shell called an interactive shell, you see a shell prompt, usually in the form of a dollar sign ($), a percent sign (%), or a pound sign (#). When you type a line of input at a shell prompt, the shell tries to interpret it. Input to a shell prompt is sometimes called a command line. The basic format of a command line is

```
command arguments
```

command is an executable UNIX command, program, utility, or shell program. The *arguments* are passed to the executable. Most UNIX utility programs expect *arguments* to take the following form:

```
options filenames
```

For example, in the command line

```
$ ls -l file1 file2
```

there are three arguments to `ls`, the first of which is an option, while the last two are file names.

One of the things the shell does for the kernel is to eliminate unnecessary information. For a computer, one type of unnecessary information is whitespace; therefore, it is important to know what the shell does when it sees whitespace. Whitespace consists of the space character, the horizontal tab, and the new line character. Consider this example:

```
$ echo part A     part B     part C
part A part B part C
```

Here, the shell has interpreted the command line as the `echo` command with six arguments and has removed the whitespace between the arguments. For example, if you were printing headings for a report and you wanted to keep the whitespace, you would have to enclose the data in quotation marks, as in

```
$ echo 'part A     part B     part C'
part A     part B     part C
```

The single quotation mark prevents the shell from looking inside the quotes. Now the shell interprets this line as the `echo` command with a single argument, which happens to be a string of characters including whitespace.

Program Initiation

When the shell finishes interpreting a command line, it initiates the execution of the requested program. The kernel actually executes it. To initiate program execution, the shell searches for the executable file in the directories specified in the PATH environment variable. When it finds the executable file, a subshell is started for the program to run. You should understand that the subshell can establish and manipulate its own environment without affecting the environment of its parent shell. For example, a subshell can change its working directory, but the working directory of the parent shell remains unchanged when the subshell is finished.

Input-output Redirection

Chapter 4, "Listing Files," introduced input-output redirection. It is the responsibility of the shell to make this happen. The shell does the redirection before it executes the program. Consider these two examples, which use the wc word count utility on a data file with 5 lines:

```
$ wc -l fivelines
5 fivelines
$ wc -l <fivelines
5
```

This is a subtle difference. In the first example, wc understands that it is to go out and find a file named fivelines and operate on it. Since wc knows the name of the file it displays it for the user. In the second example, wc sees only data, and does not know where it came from because the shell has done the work of locating and redirecting the data to wc, so wc cannot display the file name.

Pipeline Connection

Since pipeline connections are actually a special case of input-output redirection in which the standard output of one command is piped directly to the standard input of the next command, it follows that pipelining also happens before the program call is made. Consider this command line:

```
$ who ¦ wc -l
5
```

In the second example, rather than displaying its output on your screen, the shell has directed the output of who directly to the input of wc. Pipes are discussed in Chapter 4.

Substitution of Filenames

Chapter 4 explained how metacharacters can be used to reference more than one file in a command line. It is the responsibility of the shell to make this substitution. The shell makes this substitution before it executes the program. For example,

```
$ echo *
file1 file2 file3 file3x file4
```

Here, the asterisk is expanded to the five filenames, and it is passed to echo as five arguments. If you wanted to echo an asterisk, we would enclose it in quotation marks.

Maintenance of Variables

The shell is capable of maintaining variables. Variables are places where you can store data for later use. You assign a value to a variable with an equal (=) sign.

```
$ LOOKUP=/usr/mydir
```

Here, the shell establishes LOOKUP as a variable, and assigns it the value /usr/mydir. Later, you can use the value stored in LOOKUP in a command line by prefacing the variable name with a dollar sign ($). Consider these examples:

```
$ echo $LOOKUP
/usr/mydir

$ echo LOOKUP
LOOKUP
```

Note for C-shell users. Assigning values to variables in the C-shell differs from the Bourne and Korn shells. To assign a variable in the C-shell use the set command.

```
% set LOOKUP = /usr/mydir
```

Notice that spaces precede and follow the equal sign.

Like filename substitution, variable name substitution happens before the program call is made. The second example omits the dollar sign ($). Therefore, the shell simply passes the string to echo as an argument. In variable name substitution, the value of the variable replaces the variable name.

For example, in

```
$ ls $LOOKUP/filename
```

the ls program is called with the single argument /usr/mydir/filename.

Environment Control

When the `login` program invokes your shell, it sets up your environment, which includes your home directory, the type of terminal you are using, and the path that will be searched for executable files. The environment is stored in variables called environmental variables. To change the environment, you simply change a value stored in an environmental variable. For example, to change the terminal type, you change the value in the TERM variable, as in

```
$ echo $TERM
vt100
$ TERM=ansi
$ echo $TERM
ansi
```

> **Note for C-shell users.** C-shell assigns values to environment variables using the `setenv` command.
>
> ```
> % setenv TERM vt100
> ```

Chapter 11, "Bourne Shell," Chapter 12, "Korn Shell," and Chapter 13, "C Shell," contain more information on customizing your environment.

Shell Programming

You've seen that the shell is used to interpret command lines, maintain variables, and execute programs. The shell also is a programming language. By combining commands and variable assignments with flow control and decision making, you have a powerful programming tool. Using the shell as a programming language, you can automate recurring tasks, write reports and you can even build and manipulate your own data files. The next three chapters discuss shell programming in more detail.

Summary

The shell provides an interface between the user and the heart of UNIX—the kernel. The shell takes command lines as input, makes filename and variable substitution, redirects input and output, locates the executable file, and initiates programs. The shell maintains each user's environment variables. The shell also is a powerful programming language.

Bourne Shell

By Richard E.
Rummel

IN THIS CHAPTER

In this chapter, you learn how to get the most out of the Bourne shell, one of the most used of the UNIX shells. You also learn how to store data in your own variables, how to customize your environment with environment variables, and how to group commands together to form shell programs.

Shell Basics

The Bourne shell was written by Stephen Bourne at Bell Laboratories, where UNIX was originally developed. Because it is found on most UNIX systems, many software developers work under the assumption that the Bourne shell is available on a UNIX system. This use does not mean that it is the best shell, but simply that it is the most common. Other shells, most notably the Korn shell, were written to enhance the Bourne shell, so shell programs written for Bourne run under the Korn shell. In some literature, the Bourne shell is called the UNIX system Version 7 shell.

How the Shell Interprets Commands

The first exposure most people have to the Bourne shell is as an interactive shell. After logging on the system and seeing any messages from the system administrator, the user sees a shell prompt. For users other than the super-user, the default prompt for the interactive Bourne shell is a dollar sign ($). When you see the dollar sign ($), the interactive shell is ready to accept a line of input, which it interprets. When the super-user logs in, he or she sees the pound sign (#) as a prompt. It is a reminder that as super-user some of the built-in protections are not available and that extra care is necessary in this mode.

> **NOTE:** On UNIX systems the super-user, also referred to as root, is without restriction. The super-user can write to any directory and can remove any file. File permissions do not apply to the super-user. The password for the super-user is usually closely held by the system administrator.

The shell sees a line of input as a string of characters terminated with a newline character, which is usually the result of pressing Enter on your keyboard. The length of the input line has nothing to do with the width of your computer display. When the shell sees the newline character, it begins to interpret the line.

Entering Simple Commands

The most common form of input to the shell is the *simple command*, in which a command name is followed by any number of arguments. In the example

```
$ ls file1 file2 file3
```

ls is the command and *file1*, *file2*, and *file3* are the arguments. The command is any UNIX executable. It is the responsibility of the command, not the shell, to interpret the arguments. Many UNIX commands, but certainly not all, take the following form:

```
$ command -options filenames
```

Although the shell does not interpret the arguments of the command, the shell does make some interpretation of the input line before passing the arguments to the command. Special characters, when you enter them on a command line, cause the shell to redirect input and output, start a different command, search the directories for filename patterns, substitute variable data, and substitute the output of other commands.

Redirection of Input and Output

When the shell sees the input (<) or output (>) redirection characters, the argument following the redirection symbol is sent to the subshell that controls the execution of the command. When the command opens the input or output file that has been redirected, the input or output is redirected to the file.

```
$ ls -l >dirfile
```

In this example, the only argument passed on to ls is the option -l. The filename dirfile is sent to the subshell that controls the execution of ls. You can find more detail on input and output redirection in Chapter 4, "Listing Files."

Entering Multiple Commands on One Line

Ordinarily, the shell interprets the first word of command input as the command name and the rest of the input as arguments to that command. Three shell special characters—the semicolon (;), the ampersand (&), and the vertical bar (¦) or pipe—direct the shell to interpret the word following the symbol as a new command, with the rest of the input as arguments to the new command. For example, the command line

```
$ who -H; df -v; ps -e
```

is the equivalent of

```
$ who -H
$ df -v
$ ps -e
```

In the second case, however, the results of each command appear between the command input lines. When you use the semicolon to separate commands on a line, the commands are executed in sequence. The shell waits until one command is complete before executing the next.

If you separate commands on a line using the ampersand (&), the shell does not wait until one command is run before the second is started. If the ampersand is the last character on the input line, the last command is executed as a background job. To run the preceding series of commands concurrently, you enter the following:

```
$ who -H & df -v & ps -e
```

Whereas the semicolon serves merely as a command separator, the pipe symbol serves a different purpose. When the shell sees the pipe symbol, it takes the next word as a new command and redirects the standard output of the prior command to the standard input of the new command. For example, the command line

```
$ who ¦ sort
```

displays an alphabetized list of all logged-in users. The command line

```
$ who ¦ sort ¦ lp
```

prints a hard copy of the alphabetized list of all logged-in users. You can find more information on pipelines in Chapter 4, "Listing Files."

> **TIP:** When you're using pipelines, sometimes the order of the commands does not make a difference in the output, but it might make a difference in how efficiently the pipeline executes. The two commands
>
> ```
> sort /etc/inittab ¦ grep bin/sh
> grep bin/sh /etc/inittab ¦ sort
> ```
>
> accomplish the same thing, but the second pipeline operates more efficiently because it reduces the amount of data passed to sort.

Entering Commands Too Long for One Line

Sometimes command lines get quite lengthy. On some terminals, when you reach the edge of the display screen, the input autowraps to the next line, but depending on terminal settings, some do not. It would be nice if you could type part of a command on one line and enter the remainder of the command on a second line. You can accomplish by escaping the newline character.

Remember that the shell sees a line of input as a string of characters terminated with a newline character. But the newline character is also considered to be a white space character. If you end a line with a backslash (\), the next character, which is the newline character, is treated literally, meaning that the shell does not interpret the newline character as the end of the line of input. For example,

```
$ echo Now is the time for all good men      \_
to come to the aid of the party.
Now is the time for all good men to come to the aid of the party.
```

Filename Substitutions on the Command Line

Although the command separator, the pipe symbol, and the redirection symbols change the operational effects of a command line, they did not affect the arguments that were passed to the command. The substitution characters, on the other hand, cause a substitution to take place in the stream of arguments passed to a command. The most common substitution is *filename substitution*. When the shell's command-line interpreter sees one of the metacharacters—the asterisk (*), the question mark (?), or square brackets ([,])—the shell searches the directories for filenames that match a pattern indicated by the metacharacter.

The asterisk special character causes the shell to search the directory for filenames that match any pattern. The command

```
$ ls f*
file1
file1a
form
```

creates a listing of all filenames beginning with the letter *f.* The important point here is that the shell, not the ls command, did the directory search. In the following example, the ls command sees three arguments, and the preceding command line is the equivalent of

```
$ ls file1 file1a form
file1
file1a
form
```

The shell makes filename substitutions regardless of the command to be executed.

```
$ echo f*
file1 file1a form
```

The question mark metacharacter searches the directories for filenames that match the pattern with any single character substituted for the metacharacter. Square brackets cause a match to be made on any character appearing within the brackets. You can find more details on filename substitution in Chapter 4, "Listing Files."

Substitution of Variable Data

The second type of substitution that can take place is *variable substitution*. When the shell sees the dollar sign ($) character, the remainder of the word following the dollar sign is presumed to be a variable name. The shell then searches for any variables that have been defined for the current shell and substitutes the value of the variable in the command line. If the variable has not been defined, a null string, one containing no characters, is substituted on the command line. For example, the command

```
$ ls $HOME
```

lists the contents of the users' home directory, regardless of what the current working directory is. HOME is an environment variable. Variables are discussed in more detail in the next major section of this chapter. As in filename substitution, the ls command sees only the result of the substitution, not the variable name.

You can substitute variable names anywhere in the command line, including for the command name itself. For example,

```
$ dir=ls
$ $dir f*
file1
file1a
form
```

This example points out that the shell makes its substitutions before determining what commands to execute.

Substituting the Results of Commands in a Command Line

Sometimes it is useful to pass the output or results of one command as arguments to another command. You do so by using the shell special character, the back quotation mark ('). You use the back quotation marks in pairs. When the shell sees a pair of back quotation marks, it executes the command inside the quotation marks and substitutes the output of that command in the original command line. You most commonly use this method to store the results of command executions in variables. To store the five-digit Julian date in a variable, for example, you use the following command:

```
$ julian='date '+%y%j''
```

The back quotation marks cause the date command to be executed before the variable assignment is made. Back quotation marks can be extremely useful when you're performing arithmetic on shell variables; see "Shell Programming" later in this chapter.

Escaping from the Special Characters

By now, it should be clear that the shell looks for special characters in the input line before taking any other action. When it becomes necessary to use a special character in a command line, you can override, or "escape," the special action of the character by using an escape character. The escape characters are:

\   the backslash, which causes a single character to be escaped

'   the single quotation mark, which, used in pairs, causes a group of characters to be escaped

"   the double quotation mark, which, used in pairs, causes a group of characters to be escaped, but allows some special characters to perform their normal function

For example, UNIX does not forbid you to use special characters in filenames.

Suppose you have a directory with the following files:

```
file* file1 file2 file3
```

You want to display the contents of the first file, the one with the asterisk in its name. Enter the following command:

```
$ cat file*
```

You then get not only the file you want, but the rest of the files in the directory as well. Because you now understand how the shell interprets its input, performing filename substitution whenever it sees an asterisk, you know what the problem is but wonder how you can rectify the problem. If you try to remove the offending file with the command

```
$ rm file*
```

you remove far more than you want. Fortunately, the Bourne shell has provided a mechanism to get around this kind of problem.

Another special character that the shell looks for is the escape character, or backslash (\). When the shell sees the escape character, it takes the subsequent character literally; it does not attempt to interpret that character. In the preceding scenario, you can use the escape character to remove or even rename the offending file:

```
$ mv file\* filestar
```

Other characters that get special treatment by the shell are the white space characters. They are the tabs, spaces, and newlines, which make a separation between words. When more than one of these characters appears at a time, the shell strips the redundant white space characters from the input. For example,

```
$ echo This      word        is separated
This word is separated
```

Here, the result is probably not the desired effect.

Suppose you want to display a message with asterisks as attention getters, as in the following:

```
***** Program Error *****
```

To do so using escape characters would be cumbersome, as you can see in the following:

```
$ echo \*\*\*\*\* Program Error \*\*\*\*\*
***** Program Error *****
```

You may already have guessed that the shell has an easier way of displaying a message of this type. When you enclose a string of text within single quotation marks ('), the entire string is treated literally, as follows:

```
$ echo '***** Program Error *****'
***** Program Error *****
```

You can use this same method to retain white space:

```
$ echo 'This     word      is separated'
This     word      is separated
```

On some occasions, however, you may want part of a string to be treated literally and other parts to be interpreted by the shell.

```
$ USERS='who | wc -l'
$ echo '*** There are $USERS users logged into the system'
*** There are $USERS users logged into the system
```

You can overcome this problem by using the double quotation marks ("). The double quotation marks are not as restrictive as the single quotation marks. Within double quotation marks, the dollar sign ($), the backslash (\), and the back quotation marks (`) retain their shell meaning:

```
$ USERS='who | wc -l'
$ echo "*** There are $USERS users logged into the system"
There are 5 users logged into the system
```

Because the double quotation marks still allow the shell to interpret the back quotation marks, you can simplify the preceding example, as follows:

```
$ echo "*** There are `who | wc -l` users logged into the system"
There are 5 users logged into the system
```

Entering Data from the Shell

One of the useful features of a computer is its ability to process large volumes of data at one time. Often this data exists in the form of disk files. You have seen how you can provide a file name to a UNIX program in a command line, but what if the data does not exist in a file? For instance, you can use the UNIX `mail` utility to send a data file to another user, but often you just want to type in a short note to send to another user. Many UNIX programs allow data to be supplied to the program either from a disk file or from your keyboard.

When a UNIX program needs more data from the user than is practical to get from a command line, the program issues a *read request*. For most programs, a read terminates when a newline character is processed. In other words, a read request processes one line at a time. When the program is reading its data from a file, no response from the user is necessary for a read request, but when the program is reading its data from the keyboard, or *standard input*, the program pauses until the user enters a string of characters terminated with a newline character. Consider the following example:

```
$ head -2
Line 1
Line 1
```

```
Line 2
Line 2
$
```

Because no filename is supplied on the command line, and no input redirection has occurred, head is looking for its input from the standard input. After you enter the first line, head processes the line and sends it to the output file, which in this case is the standard output, creating the echo effect of the example. After you enter the second line, head displays that line and terminates because the command-line option requested only two lines. The natural operation of some programs is to process a file until it has processed the entire file. When a program looks for a complete file, and the file comes from the standard input, the user needs some way to indicate the end-of-data or end-of-file condition. In the Bourne shell, the end-of-file is indicated by Ctrl+d.

The file concatenation utility cat, processes an entire file at one time. In the following example, cat "sees" a file containing two lines.

```
$ cat
Line 1
Line 1
Line 2
Line 2
Ctrl+d
$
```

So if you wanted to send a short note to John, you might type:

```
$ mail John
John,
    Meet me at the mall at noon.
Rick
Ctrl+d
$
```

Shell Options

The Bourne shell is a computer program and like most programs it has several options. You are already familiar with the most common shell option, the interactive shell. Some options change the way the shell interprets command lines; others put limits on the user of the shell

The Restricted Shell

The restricted shell gives more control to the system administrator and restricts the options of the user. The restricted shell is useful in situations where security is vital or where the users lack sophistication. The restricted shell can be a user's default login shell. On many systems, the restricted shell is invoked by using /usr/bin/rsh, but this may vary;

consult your system's documentation. You may also invoke the restricted shell by using the -r flag when you're invoking the shell:

```
$ sh -r
```

In a restricted shell, the user cannot change directories (cd), change the PATH variable, specify a full pathname to a command, or redirect output.

The restricted user can execute shell programs that have access to these features. If the restricted shell calls a shell procedure, an unrestricted shell is invoked to carry out the commands. In this case, if the user has write permission in his or her working directory, he or she can write shell programs and bypass the restrictions. Normally, a restricted user is placed in a directory in which he or she has no write permission. Not having write permission in this directory does not mean that the user has no write permission anywhere, but because he or she cannot change directories or specify pathnames in commands, the user cannot write a shell script and later access it if he or she cannot write in the working directory.

Changing Shell Options with *set*

Although the restricted shell and the interactive shell are chosen when the shell is invoked, you can turn other options on and off using the set option. Following are some options you can set:

-e	Causes a noninteractive shell to exit if any subsequent command terminates with a nonzero exit status
-f	Disables filename substitution
-n	Causes the shell to read commands but not execute them
-u	Treats unset variables as errors when substituting
-x	Prints commands and their arguments as they are executed, showing the result of any substitutions

You turn on options with a hyphen (-) and turned them off with a plus (+).

For example, the shell normally looks at command line input and tries to substitute filenames when it encounters certain special characters, such as an asterisk (*). This default behavior can be changed with the set command using the -f option.

```
$ set -f
$ echo *
*
```

You can restore the default behavior by using set with the +f option.

```
$ set +f
$ echo *
file1 file2 ...
```

Variables

In algebra, variables are symbols which stand for some value. In computer terminology, variables are symbolic names which stand for some value. Earlier in this chapter, you saw how the variable HOME stood for the name of a user's home directory. If you enter the change directory command, cd, without an argument, cd takes you to your home directory. Does a generic program like cd know the location of every user's home directory? Of course not, it merely knows to look for a variable, in this case HOME, which stands for the home directory.

Variables are useful in any computer language because they allow you to define what to do with a piece of information without knowing specifically what the data is. A program to add two and two together is not very useful, but a program that adds two variables can be, especially if the value of the variables can be supplied at execution time by the user of the program. The Bourne shell has four types of variables: *user-defined variables, positional variables* or *parameters, predefined* or *special variables*, and *environment variables*.

Defining Your Own (User-Defined) Variables

As the name implies, user-defined variables are whatever you want them to be. Variable names are made up of alphanumeric characters and the underscore character, with the provision that variable names do not begin with one of the digits 0 through 9. (Like all UNIX names, variables are case sensitive. Variable names take on values when they appear in a command line to the left of an equal sign (=). For example, in the following command lines, COUNT takes on the value of 1, and NAME takes on the value of Stephanie:

```
$ COUNT=1
$ NAME=Stephanie
```

> **TIP:** Because most UNIX commands are lowercase words, shell programs have traditionally used all capital letters in variable names. It is certainly not mandatory to use all capital letters, but using them enables you to identify variables easily within a program.

To recall the value of a variable, precede the variable name by a dollar sign ($):

```
$ NAME=John
$ echo Hello $NAME
Hello John
```

You also can assign variables to other variables, as follows:

```
$ JOHN=John
$ NAME=$JOHN
$ echo Goodbye $NAME
Goodbye John
```

Sometimes it is useful to combine variable data with other characters to form new words, as in the following example:

```
$ SUN=Sun
$ MON=Mon
$ TUE=Tues
$ WED=Wednes
$ THU=Thurs
$ FRI=Fri
$ SAT=Satur
$ WEEK=$SAT
$ echo Today is $WEEKday
Today is
$
```

What happened here? Remember that when the shell's interpreter sees a dollar sign ($), it interprets all the characters until the next white space as the name of a variable, in this case WEEKday. You can escape the effect of this interpretation by enclosing the variable name in curly braces ({,}) like this:

```
$ echo Today is ${WEEK}day
Today is Saturday
$
```

You can assign more than one variable in a single line by separating the assignments with white space, as follows:

```
$ X=x Y=y
```

The variable assignment is performed from right to left:

```
$ X=$Y Y=y
$ echo $X
y
$ Z=z Y=$Z
$ echo $Y

$
```

You may notice that when a variable that has not been defined is referenced, the shell does not give you an error but instead gives you a null value.

You can remove the value of a variable using the unset command, as follows:

```
$ Z=hello
$ echo $Z
hello
$ unset Z
$ echo $Z

$
```

Conditional Variable Substitution

The most common way to retrieve the value of a variable is to precede the variable name with a dollar sign ($), causing the value of the variable to be substituted at that point.

With the Bourne shell, you can cause variable substitution to take place only if certain conditions are met. This is called conditional variable substitution. You always enclose conditional variable substitutions in curly braces ({ }).

Substituting Default Values for Variables

As you learned earlier, when variables that have not been previously set are referenced, a null value is substituted. The Bourne shell enables you to establish default values for variable substitution using the form

```
${variable:-value}
```

where *variable* is the name of the variable and *value* is the default substitution. For example,

```
$ echo Hello $UNAME
Hello
$ echo Hello ${UNAME:-there}
Hello there
$ echo $UNAME
$
$ UNAME=John
$ echo Hello ${UNAME:-there}
Hello John
$
```

As you can see in the preceding example, when you use this type of variable substitution, the default value is substituted in the command line, but the value of the variable is not changed. Another substitution construct not only substitutes the default value but also assigns the default value to the variable as well. This substitution has the form

```
${variable:=value}
```

which causes *variable* to be assigned *value* after the substitution has been made. For example,

```
$ echo Hello $UNAME
Hello
$ echo Hello ${UNAME:=there}
Hello there
$ echo $UNAME
there
$ UNAME=John
$ echo Hello ${UNAME:-there}
Hello John
$
```

The substitution value need not be literal; it can be a command in back quotation marks:

```
USERDIR={$MYDIR:-'pwd'}
```

A third type of variable substitution substitutes the specified value if the variable has been set, as follows:

```
${variable:+value}
```

If *variable* is set, then *value* is substituted; if *variable* is not set, then nothing is substituted. For example,

```
$ ERROPT=A
$ echo ${ERROPT:+"Error Tracking is Active"}
Error Tracking is Active
$ ERROPT=
$ echo ${ERROPT:+"Error Tracking is Active"}

$
```

Conditional Variable Substitution with Error Checking

Another variable substitution method allows for error checking during variable substitution:

```
${variable:?message}
```

If *variable* is set, its value is substituted; if it is not set, *message* is written to the standard error file. If the substitution is made in a shell program, the program immediately terminates. For example,

```
$ UNAME=
$ echo ${UNAME:?"UNAME has not been set"}
UNAME has not been set
$ UNAME=Stephanie
$ echo ${UNAME:?"UNAME has not been set"}
Stephanie
$
```

If no message is specified, the shell displays a default message, as in the following example:

```
$ UNAME=
$ echo ${UNAME:?}
sh: UNAME: parameter null or not set
$
```

Positional Variables or Parameters

You may recall that when the shell's command-line interpreter processes a line of input, the first word of the command line is considered to be an executable, and the remainder of the line is passed as arguments to the executable. If the executable is a shell program, the arguments are passed to the program as *positional variables*. The first argument passed to the program is assigned to the variable $1, the second argument is $2, and so on up to $9. Notice that the names of the variables are actually the digits 1 through 9; the dollar sign, as always, is the special character that causes variable substitution to occur.

The positional variable $0 always contains the name of the executable. Positional variables are discussed later in this chapter in the section "Shell Programming."

Special Variables in the Bourne Shell

The Bourne shell defines several variables that are always available. (You can find examples of how you can use these variables in the next major section of this chapter, "Shell Programming.") Following are some of the predefined variables:

$#   Contains the number of arguments passed to the program in the form of positional variables.

$$ Contains the process ID of the current process.

$?   Contains the exit status of the last command executed. Programs and commands customarily return an exit status of zero if the program is successful and return a nonzero value if an error occurs. But be careful, not all programs follow customs.

$*   Contains all the positional arguments passed to the program.

Environment Variables

Environment variables are variables that the shell or any other program can access to get information unique to a specific user. Any program can use environment variables. The vi editor, for example, checks the variable EXINIT for any standard options you want set every time you run vi. Consult the instructions of the specific programs for information on environment variables used by the program.

Several environment variables are created and used by the Bourne shell.

HOME   This variable is initialized when the interactive shell is executed by the login program. It contains the value of the user's home directory. If the cd command is executed without any arguments, the effect is cd $HOME.

IFS   This variable sets characters to be internal field separators, or the characters that separate words on a command line. By default, the internal field separators are the space, tab, and newline characters. Setting the IFS adds separators, but space, tab, and the newline character always separate fields.

MAIL   This variable specifies the complete pathname of the user's mailbox file.

MAILCHECK   This variable specifies in seconds how often the mailbox should be checked for incoming mail.

MAILPATH   This variable is a colon-separated list of mailbox files to be checked. Setting this variable can be useful for users who have more than one login name but want to have their mail checked, regardless of which name they have used to log in. The name of the mail file can be followed with a percent sign (%) and a message to be displayed when mail is received in that file.

PATH   This variable, usually set in your `.profile`, contains a list of directories that are searched for executables. If an executable, which is any utility, program, or shell program, is not in the PATH variable, it can only be executed by giving the full pathname of the executable file. The directories are searched in the order in which they appear in the PATH variable. If an executable file exists in more that one directory, the one found earliest in PATH is the one executed. See "Customizing the Shell" later in this chapter.

PS1   The value of the interactive shell prompt. The default value in the Bourne Shell is $.

PS2   The value of the secondary shell prompt. The default value is >.

TERM   This variable is not automatically created on all UNIX systems but is used by so many programs that it is considered a standard environment variable. TERM usually contains the type of terminal that you are using, such as `ansi` or `vt100`.

Preventing Variables from Being Changed

If a variable has had a value assigned, and you want to make sure that its value is not subsequently changed, you may designate a variable as a `readonly` variable with the following command:

```
readonly variable
```

From this point on, `variable` cannot be reassigned. This ensures that a variable won't be accidentally changed.

Making Variables Available to Subshells with export

When a shell executes a program, it sets up a new environment for the program to execute in. This is called a *subshell*. In the Bourne shell, variables are considered to be local variables; in other words, they are not recognized outside the shell in which they were assigned a value. You can make a variable available to any subshells you execute by exporting it using the export command. Your variables can never be made available to other users.

Suppose you wanted to change your shell prompt to something more meaningful than a dollar sign. You could do this by assigning a new value to the shell prompt variable PS1.

```
$ PS1="Enter Command: "
Enter Command:
```

Now, instead of a dollar sign, you get the descriptive phrase `Enter Command:` . Now suppose you start a new shell.

```
Enter Command: sh
$ exit
Enter Command:
```

When you started a new shell, the default shell prompt appeared. This is because the variable assignment to PS1 was made only in the current shell. To make the new shell prompt active in subshells, you must export it as in the following example.

```
$ PS1="Enter Command: "
Enter Command: export PS1
Enter Command: sh
Enter Command:
```

Now the variable PS1 is global, that is, it is available to all subshells. When a variable has been made global in this way, it remains available until you log out of the parent shell. You can make an assignment permanent by including it in your .profile, see "Customizing the Shell."

Shell Programming

In this major section, you learn how to put commands together in such a way that the sum is greater than the parts. You learn some UNIX commands that are useful mainly in the context of shell programs. You also learn how to make your program perform functions conditionally based on logical tests that you define, and you learn how to have parts of a program repeat until its function is completed. In short, you learn how to use the common tools supplied with UNIX to create more powerful tools specific to the tasks you need to perform.

What Is a Program?

A wide assortment of definitions exist for what is a computer program, but for this discussion, a computer program is an ordered set of instructions causing a computer to perform some useful function. In other words, when you cause a computer to perform some tasks in a specific order so that the result is greater than the individual tasks, you have programmed the computer. When you enter a formula into a spreadsheet, for example, you are programming. When you write a macro in a word processor, you are programming. When you enter a complex command like

```
$ ls -R / ¦ grep myname ¦ pg
```

in a UNIX shell, you are programming the shell; you are causing the computer to execute a series of utilities in a specific order, which gives a result that is more useful than the result of any of the utilities taken by itself.

A Simple Program

Suppose that daily you back up your data files with the following command:

```
$ cd /usr/home/myname; ls * ¦ cpio -o >/dev/rmt0
```

As you learned earlier, when you enter a complex command like this, you are programming the shell. One of the useful things about programs, though, is that they can be placed in a program library and used over and over, without having to do the programming each time. Shell programs are no exception. Rather than enter the lengthy backup command each time, you can store the program in a file named `backup`:

```
$ cat >backup
cd /usr/home/myname
ls * ¦ cpio -o >/dev/rmt0
Ctrl+d
```

You could, of course, use your favorite editor (see Chapter 7, "Editing Text Files"), and in fact with larger shell programs, you almost certainly will want to. You can enter the command in a single line, as you did when typing it into the command line, but because the commands in a shell program (sometimes called a *shell script*) are executed in sequence, putting each command on a line by itself makes the program easier to read. Creating easy-to-read programs becomes more important as the size of the programs increase.

Now to back up your data files, you need to call up another copy of the shell program (known as a subshell) and give it the commands found in the file `backup`. To do so, use the following command:

```
$ sh backup
```

The program `sh` is the same Bourne shell that was started when you logged in, but when a filename is passed as an argument, instead of becoming an interactive shell, it takes its commands from the file.

An alternative method for executing the commands in the file `backup` is to make the file itself an executable. To do so, use the following command:

```
$ chmod +x backup
```

Now you can back up your data files by entering the newly created command:

```
$ backup
```

If you want to execute the commands in this manner, the file `backup` must reside in one of the directories specified in the environment variable `$PATH`.

The Shell as a Language

If all you could do in a shell program was to string together a series of UNIX commands into a single command, you would have an important tool, but shell programming is much more. Like traditional programming languages, the shell offers features that enable you to make your shell programs more useful, such as: data variables, argument passing, decision making, flow control, data input and output, subroutines, and handling interrupts.

By using these features, you can automate many repetitive functions, which is, of course, the purpose of any computer language.

Using Data Variables in Shell Programs

You usually use variables within programs as place holders for data that will be available when the program is run and that may change from execution to execution. Consider the `backup` program:

```
cd /usr/home/myname
ls ¦ cpio -o >/dev/rmt0
```

In this case, the directory to be backed up is contained in the program as a literal, or constant, value. This program is useful only to back up that one directory. The use of a variable makes the program more generic:

```
cd $WORKDIR
ls * ¦ cpio -o >/dev/rmt0
```

With this simple change, any user can use the program to back up the directory that has been named in the variable `$WORKDIR`, provided that the variable has been exported to subshells. See "Making Variables Available to Subshells with `export`" earlier in this chapter.

Entering Comments in Shell Programs

Quite often when you're writing programs, program code that seemed logical six months ago may be fairly obscure today. Good programmers annotate their programs with comments. You enter comments into shell programs by inserting the pound sign (#) special character. When the shell interpreter sees the pound sign, it considers all text to the end of the line as a comment.

Doing Arithmetic on Shell Variables

In most higher level programming languages, variables are *typed*, meaning that they are restricted to certain kinds of data, such as numbers or characters. Shell variables are always stored as characters. To do arithmetic on shell variables, you must use the `expr` command.

The `expr` command evaluates its arguments as mathematical expressions. The general form of the command is as follows:

```
expr integer operator integer
```

Because the shell stores its variables as characters, it is your responsibility as a shell programmer to make sure that the integer arguments to `expr` are in fact integers. Following are the valid arithmetic operators:

+   Adds the two integers.

-   Subtracts the second integer from the first.

*   Multiplies the two integers.

/   Divides the first integer by the second.

%   Gives the modulus (remainder) of the division.

```
$ expr 2 + 1
3
$ expr 5 - 3
2
```

If the argument to expr is a variable, the value of the variable is substituted before the expression is evaluated, as in the following example:

```
$ $int=3
$ expr $int + 4
7
```

You should avoid using the asterisk operator (*) alone for multiplication. If you enter

```
$ expr 4 * 5
```

you get an error because the shell sees the asterisk and performs filename substitution before sending the arguments on to expr. The proper form of the multiplication expression is

```
$ expr 4 \* 5
20
```

You also can combine arithmetic expressions, as in the following:

```
$ expr 5 + 7 / 3
7
```

The results of the preceding expression may seem odd. The first thing to remember is that division and multiplication are of a higher precedence than addition and subtraction, so the first operation performed is 7 divided by 3. Because expr deals only in integers, the result of the division is 2, which is then added to 5, giving the final result 7. Parentheses are not recognized by expr, so to override the precedence, you must do that manually. You can use back quotation marks to change the precedence, as follows:

```
$ int=`expr 5 + 7`
$ expr $int / 3
4
```

Or you can use the more direct route:

```
$ expr `expr 5 + 7` / 3
4
```

Passing Arguments to Shell Programs

A program can get data in two ways: either it is passed to the program when it is executed as arguments, or the program gets data interactively. An editor such as vi is usually used in an interactive mode, whereas commands such as ls and expr get their data as arguments. Shell programs are no exception. In the section "Reading Data into a Program Interactively," you see how a shell program can get its data interactively.

Passing arguments to a shell program on a command line can greatly enhance the program's versatility. Consider the inverse of the backup program presented earlier:

```
$ cat >restoreall
cd $WORKDIR
cpio -i </dev/rmt0
Ctrl+d
```

As written, the program restoreall reloads the entire tape made by backup. But what if you want to restore only a single file from the tape? You can do so by passing the name of the file as an argument. The enhanced restore1 program is now:

```
# restore1 - program to restore a single file
cd $WORKDIR
cpio -i $1 </dev/rmt0
```

Now you can pass a parameter representing the name of the file to be restored to the restore1 program:

```
$ restore1 file1
```

Here, the filename file1 is passed to restore1 as the first positional parameter. The limitation to restore1 is that if you want to restore two files, you must run restore1 twice.

As a final enhancement, you can use the $* variable to pass any number of arguments to the program:

```
# restoreany - program to restore any number of files
cd $WORKDIR
cpio -i $* </dev/rmt0
```

```
$ restoreany file1 file2 file3
```

Because shell variables that have not been assigned a value always return null, or empty, if the restore1 or restoreany programs are run with no command-line parameters, a null value is placed in the cpio command, which causes the entire archive to be restored.

Consider the program in listing 11.1; it calculates the length of time to travel a certain distance.

Listing 11.1. Program example with two parameters.

```
# traveltime - a program to calculate how long it will
# take to travel a fixed distance
# syntax: traveltime miles mph
X60='expr $1 \* 60'
TOTMINUTES='expr $X60 / $2'
HOURS='expr $TOTMINUTES / 60'
MINUTES='expr $TOTMINUTES % 60'
echo "The trip will take $HOURS hours and $MINUTES minutes"
```

The program in listing 11.1 takes two positional parameters: the distance in miles and the rate of travel in miles per hour. The mileage is passed to the program as $1 and the rate of travel as $2. Note that the first command in the program multiplies the mileage by 60. Because the expr command works only with integers, it is useful to calculate the travel time in minutes. The user-defined variable X60 holds an interim calculation that, when divided by the mileage rate, gives the total travel time in minutes. Then, using both integer division and modulus division, the number of hours and number of minutes of travel time is found.

Now execute the traveltime for a 90-mile trip at 40 mph with the following command line:

```
$ traveltime 90 40
The trip will take 2 hours and 15 minutes
```

Decision Making in Shell Programs

One of the things that gives computer programming languages much of their strength is their capability to make decisions. Of course, computers don't think, so the decisions that computer programs make are only in response to conditions that you have anticipated in your program. The decision making done by computer programs is in the form of *conditional execution*: if a condition exists, then execute a certain set of commands. In most computer languages, this setup is called an if-then construct.

The *if-then* Statement

The Bourne shell also has an if-then construct. The syntax of the construct is as follows:

```
if command_1
then
  command_2
  command_3
fi
command_4
```

You may recall that every program or command concludes by returning an exit status.

The exit status is available in the shell variable $?. The if statement checks the exit status of its command. If that command is successful, then all the commands between the then statement and the fi statement are executed. In this program sequence, *command_1* is always executed, *command_2* and *command_3* are executed only if *command_1* is successful, and *command_4* is always executed.

Consider a variation of the backup program, except that after copying all the files to the backup media, you want to remove them from your disk. Call the program unload and allow the user to specify the directory to be unloaded on the command line, as in the following example:

```
# unload - program to backup and remove files
# syntax - unload directory
cd $1
ls -a | cpio -o >/dev/rmt0
rm *
```

At first glance, it appears that this program will do exactly what you want. But what if something goes wrong during the cpio command? In this case, the backup media is a tape device. What if the operator forgets to insert a blank tape in the tape drive? The rm command would go ahead and execute, wiping out the directory before it has been backed up! The if-then construct prevents this catastrophe from happening. A revised unload program is shown in listing 11.2.

Listing 11.2. Shell program with error checking.

```
# unload - program to backup and remove files
# syntax - unload directory
cd $1
if ls -a | cpio -o >/dev/rmt0
then
    rm *
fi
```

In the program in listing 11.2, the rm command is executed only if the cpio command is successful. Note that the if statement looks at the exit status of the last command in a pipeline.

Data Output from Shell Programs

The standard output and error output of any commands within a shell program are passed on the standard output of the user who invokes the program unless that output is redirected within the program. In the example in listing 11.2, any error messages from cpio would have been seen by the user of the program. Sometimes you may write programs that need to communicate with the user of the program. In Bourne shell programs, you usually do so by using the echo command. As the name indicates, echo simply sends its arguments to the standard output and appends a newline character at the end, as in the following example:

```
$ echo "Mary had a little lamb"
Mary had a little lamb
```

The echo command recognizes several special escape characters that assist in formatting output. They are as follows:

\b	Backspace
\c	Prints line without newline character
\f	Form Feed: advances page on a hard copy printer; advances to new screen on a display terminal
\n	Newline
\r	Carriage return
\t	Tab
\v	Vertical Tab
\\	Backslash
\0nnn	A one-, two-, or three-digit octal integer representing one of the ASCII characters

If you want to display a prompt to the user to enter the data, and you want the user response to appear on the same line as the prompt, you use the \c character, as follows:

```
$ echo "Enter response:\c"
Enter response$
```

The *if-then-else* Statement

A common desire in programming is to perform one set of commands if a condition is true and a different set of commands if the condition is false. In the Bourne shell, you can achieve this effect by using the if-then-else construct:

```
if command_1
then
    command_2
    command_3
else
    command_4
    command_5
fi
```

In this construct, *command_1* is always executed. If *command_1* succeeds, the *command_2* and *command_3* are executed; if it fails, *command_4* and *command_5* are executed.

You can now enhance the unload program to be more user friendly. For example,

```
# unload - program to backup and remove files
```

```
# syntax - unload directory
cd $1
if ls -a ¦ cpio -o >/dev/rmt0
then
    rm *
else
    echo "A problem has occurred in creating the backup."
    echo "The directory will not be erased."
    echo "Please check the backup device and try again."
fi
```

> **TIP:** Because the shell ignores extra whitespace in a command line, good program-
> mers use this fact to enhance the readability of their programs. When commands
> are executed within a `then` or `else` clause, indent all the commands in the clause
> the same distance.

Testing Conditions with *test*

You've seen how the `if` statement tests the exit status of its command to control the order in
which commands are executed, but what if you want to test other conditions? A command
that is used a great deal in shell programs is the `test` command. The `test` command examines
some condition and returns a zero exit status if the condition is true and a nonzero exit status
if the condition is false. This capability gives the `if` statement in the Bourne shell the same
power as other languages with some enhancements that are helpful in shell programming.

The general form of the command is as follows:

```
test condition
```

The conditions that can be tested fall into four categories: 1) String operators that test the
condition or relationship of character strings; 2) Integer relationships that test the numerical
relationship of two integers; 3) File operators that test for the existence or state of a file; 4)
Logical operators that allow for and/or combinations of the other conditions.

Testing Character Data

You learned earlier that the Bourne shell does not type cast data elements. Each word of
an input line and each variable can be taken as a string of characters. Some commands,
such as `expr` and `test`, have the capability to perform numeric operations on strings that
can be translated to integer values, but any data element can be operated on as a character
string.

You can compare two strings to see whether they are equivalent or not equivalent. You
also can test a single string to see whether it has a value or not. The string operators are as
follows:

> *str1* = *str2*   True if *str1* is the same length and contains the same characters as *str2*

str1 != str2   True if *str1* is not the same as *str2*

-n str1   True if the length of *str1* is greater than 0 (is not null)

-z str1   True if *str1* is null (has a length of 0)

str1   True if *str1* is not null

Even though you most often use test with a shell program as a decision maker, test is a program that can stand on its own as in the following:

```
$ str1=abcd
$ test $str1 = abcd
$ echo $?
0
$
```

Notice that unlike the variable assignment statement in the first line in the preceding example, the test command must have the equal sign surrounded by white space. In this example, the shell sends three arguments to test. Strings must be equivalent in both length and characters by character.

```
$ str1="abcd "
$ test "$str1" = abcd
$ echo $?
1
$
```

In the preceding example, str1 contains five characters, the last of which is a space. The second string in the test command contains only four characters. The nonequivalency operator returns a true value everywhere that the equivalency operator returns false.

```
$ str1=abcd
$ test $str1 != abcd
$ echo $?
1
$
```

Two of the string operations, testing of a string with no operator and testing with the -n operator, seem almost identical, as the following example shows.

```
$ str1=abcd
$ test $str1
$ echo $?
0
$ test -n $str1
$ echo $?
0
$
```

The difference between the two commands in the preceding example is a subtle one, but it points out a potential problem in using the test command, as shown in the following example of two different tests:

```
$ str1="      "
$ test $str1
```

```
$ echo $?
1
$ test "$str1"
$ echo $?
0
$ test -n $str1
test: argument expected
$ test -n "$str1
$ echo $?
0
```

In the preceding example, the first test is false. Why? Remember that the shell interpreter makes variable substitutions before it processes the command line, and when it processes the command line, it removes excess whitespace. Where $str1 does not have double quotation marks, the blanks are passed to the command line and stripped; when the double quotation marks are used, the blanks are passed on to test. What happens in the third test? When the interpreter removes the whitespace, test is passed only the -n option, which requires an argument.

Testing Numeric Data

The test command, like expr, has the capability to convert strings to integers and perform numeric operations. Whereas expr performs arithmetic on integers, test performs logical comparisons. The available numerical comparisons are as follows:

int1 -eq *int2*	True if *int1* is numerically equal to *int2*
int1 -ne *int2*	True if *int1* is not equal to *int2*
int1 -gt *int2*	True if *int1* is greater than *int2*
int1 -ge *int2*	True if *int1* is greater than or equal to *int2*
int1 -lt *int2*	True if *int1* is less than *int2*
int1 -le *int2*	True if *int1* is less than or equal to *int2*

This difference between numeric equivalency and string equivalency is shown in the following example, which defines two strings and then compares them using numeric equivalency first and then string equivalency.

```
$ str1=1234
$ str2=01234
$ test $str1 = $str2
$ echo $?
1
$ test $str1 -eq $str2
$ echo $?
0
$
```

In the second case here, the strings were converted to integers and found to be numerically equivalent, whereas the original strings were not.

Testing for Files

The third type of condition that `test` can examine is the state of files. Using the `test` command in your program, you can determine whether a file exists, whether it can be written to, and several other conditions. All the file test options return true, only if the file exists. The file test options are

`-r filenm`	True if the user has read permission
`-w filenm`	True if the user has write permission
`-x filenm`	True if the user has execute permission
`-f filenm`	True if `filenm` is a regular file
`-d filenm`	True if `filenm` is a directory
`-c filenm`	True if `filenm` is a character special file
`-b filenm`	True if `filenm` is a block special file
`-s filenm`	True if the size of `filenm` is not zero
`-t fnumb`	True if the device associated with the file descriptor `fnumb` (1 by default) is a terminal device

Combining and Negating *test* Conditions

The expressions that have been discussed thus far are called *primary* expressions because each tests only one condition. The characters following the hyphen are the operators, and the terms to the right and left of the operators are the arguments. Some of the operators, like the numeric comparison operators, are *binary* because they always have two arguments, one on the right and one on the left. Some of the operators, like the file test options, are *unary* because the operator takes only one argument, which is always placed on the right.

Sometimes you may not be interested in what is true, but in what is not true. To find out what is not true, you can use the unary negation operator, the exclamation (!), in front of any primary. Create an empty file and try some of the file operators shown in the following example:

```
$ cat >empty
Ctrl+d
$ test -r empty
$ echo $?
0
$ test -s empty
$ echo $?
1
$ test ! -s empty
$ echo $?
0
$
```

The primary expressions in a test command can be combined with a logical *and* operator, -a, or with a logical *or* operator, -o. When you use the -a operator, the combined expression is true if and only if both of the primary expressions are true. When you use the -o operator, the combined expression is true if either of the primary expressions is true. Using the empty file from above, test to see whether the file is readable and contains data:

```
$ test -r empty -a -s empty
$ echo $?
1
$
```

The combined expression is false. The first expression is true because the file is readable, but the second expression fails because the file has a size of 0.

A Shorthand Method of Doing Tests

Because the test command is such an important part of shell programming, and to make shell programs look more like programs in other languages, the Bourne shell has an alternative method for using test: you enclose the entire expression in square brackets ([ ]).

```
$ int1=4
$ [ $int1 -gt 2 ]
$ echo $?
0
$
```

Remember that even though it looks different, the preceding example is still the test command and the same rules apply.

Using test, you can make the unload program from listing 11.2 more user friendly, as well as more bullet proof, by making sure that a valid directory name is entered on the command line. The revised program is shown in listing 11.3.

Listing 11.3. Program using test for error checking.

```
# unload - program to backup and remove files
# syntax - unload directory
# check arguments
if [ $# -ne 1 ]
then
    echo "usage: unload directory"
    exit 1
fi
# check for valid directory name
if [! -d "$1" ]
then
    echo "$1 is not a directory"
    exit 2
fi
cd $1
```

continues

Listing 11.3. continued

```
ls -a | cpio -o >/dev/rmt0
if [ $? -eq 0 ]
then
    rm *
else
    echo "A problem has occurred in creating the backup."
    echo "The directory will not be erased."
    echo "Please check the backup device and try again."

    exit 3
fi
```

There are several items of interest in the revised program in listing 11.3. One is the introduction of the `exit` statement. The `exit` statement has two purposes: to stop any further commands in the program from being executed and to set the exit status of the program. By setting a nonzero exit status, subsequent programs can check the $? variable to see whether `unload` is successful. Notice that in the test to see whether the argument is a valid directory, the variable substitution is made within double quotation marks. Using double quotation marks prevents the `test` command from failing if the program were called with an argument containing only blanks; the test still fails, but the user does not see the error message from `test`. One other change to the program is to remove the actual backup command from the `if` statement and place it on a line by itself and then use `test` on the exit status to make the decision. Although using `if` to check the exit status of the backup is legitimate and probably more efficient, the meaning may be unclear to the casual observer.

Consider the `traveltime` program shown in listing 11.1. Suppose you execute the program with the following command line:

```
$ traveltime 61 60
The trip will take 1 hours and 1 minutes
```

Although this answer is correct, it may make your English teacher cringe. You can use numeric testing and `if-then-else` statements to make the output more palatable. The revised program is shown in listing 11.4.

Listing 11.4. Revised `traveltime` program.

```
# traveltime - a program to calculate how long it will
# take to travel a fixed distance
# syntax: traveltime miles mph
X60='expr $1 \* 60'
TOTMINUTES='expr $X60 / $2'
HOURS='expr $TOTMINUTES / 60'
MINUTES='expr $TOTMINUTES % 60'
if [ $HOURS -gt 1 ]
then
    DISPHRS=hours
else
```

```
    DISPHRS=hour
fi
if [ $MINUTES -gt 1 ]
then
    DISPMIN=minutes
else
    DISPMIN=minute
fi
echo "The trip will take $HOURS $DISPHRS \c"
if [ $MINUTES -gt 0 ]
then
    echo "and $MINUTES $DISPMIN"
else
    echo
fi
```

Now `traveltime` supplies the appropriate singular or plural noun depending on the amount of time:

```
$ traveltime 50 40
The trip will take 1 hour and 15 minutes
$ traveltime 121 60
The trip will take 2 hours and 1 minute
$ traveltime 120 60
The trip will take 2 hours
$
```

The Null Command

You have now enhanced the `unload` program to accept the name of a directory from the command line, to check for a valid directory name, and to give the user of the program more information on any errors that may occur. The only real difference between the `unload` function and the `backup` function is that `unload` removes the files from the directory after it has been archived. It would seem that a simple modification to `unload`—taking out the `rm` statement—would transform `unload` to an enhanced version of `backup`. The only problem is that the `rm` command is the only command following a `then` statement, and there must be at least one command following every `then` statement. The Bourne shell provides a solution with the *null* command. The null command, represented by a colon (:), is a place holder whose purpose is to fulfill a requirement where a command must appear. To change `unload` to `backup`, you replace the `rm` command with the null command and change some of the messages.

```
# backup - program to backup all files in a directory
# syntax - backup directory
# check arguments
if [ $# -ne 1 ]
then
    echo "usage: backup directory"
    exit 1
fi
# check for valid directory name
```

```
if [ ! -d "$1" ]
then
   echo "$1 is not a directory"
   exit 2
fi
cd $1
ls -a ¦ cpio -o >/dev/rmt0
if [ $? -eq 0 ]
then
   :
else
   echo "A problem has occurred in creating the backup."
   echo "Please check the backup device and try again."
```

Displaying the Program Name

In the previous two examples, a helpful message was displayed for the user who failed to enter any command-line arguments.

In this message, the name of the program is displayed as part of a literal string. However, if you renamed this program, this message would no longer be valid. In the Bourne shell, the variable $0 always contains the name of the program, as entered on the command line. You can now make the program more general, as in the following example:

```
if [ $# -ne 1 ]
then
   echo "usage: $0 directory"
   exit 1
fi
```

Nested *if* Statements and the *elif* Construct

Often you may want your program to do the following:

1. Check for a primary condition, and

    a. If the primary condition is true, perform an operation.

    b. If the primary condition is false, check a secondary condition.

        (1) If the secondary condition is true, perform another operation, but

        (2) If the secondary condition is false, check a third condition.

            (a) If the third condition is true, perform another operation.

You can do so by nesting if-else statements, as in the following syntax:

```
if command
then
   command
else
   if command
   then
      command
   else
      if command
```

```
        then
            command
        fi
    fi
fi
```

Nesting can be useful but can also be confusing, especially knowing where to place the `fi` statements. Because this kind of programming occurs frequently, the Bourne shell provides a special construct called `elif`, which stands for `else-if` and indicates a continuation of the main `if` statement. You could restate the sequence described above with `elif` statements, as follows:

```
if command
then
    command
elif command
then
    command
elif command
then
    command
fi
```

Either method produces the same results. You should use the one that makes the most sense to you.

Reading Data into a Program Interactively

Up to this point, all the input to your programs has been supplied by users in the form of command-line arguments. You can also obtain input for a program by using the `read` statement. The general syntax of the `read` statement is as follows:

```
read var1 var2 ... varn
```

When the Bourne shell encounters a `read` statement, the standard input file is read until the shell reads a newline character. When the shell interprets the line of input, it does not make filename and variable substitutions, but it does remove excess white space. After it removes white space, the shell puts the value of the first word into the first variable, and the second word into the second variable, and so on until either the list of variables or the input line is exhausted. If there are more words in the input line than in the variable list, the last variable in the list is assigned the remaining words in the input line. If there are more variables in the list than words in the line, the leftover variables are null. A *word* is a group of alphanumeric characters surrounded by whitespace.

In the following example, the `read` statement is looking for three variables. Since the line of input contains three words, each word is assigned to a variable.

```
$ read var1 var2 var3
Hello       my          friend
$ echo $var1 $var2 $var3
Hello my friend
```

```
$ echo $var1
Hello
$ echo $var2
my
$ echo $var3
friend
$
```

In the next example, the `read` statement is looking for three variables, but the input line consists of four words. In this case, the last two words are assigned to the third variable.

```
$ read var1 var2 var3
Hello my dear friend
$ echo $var1
Hello
$ echo $var2
my
$ echo $var3
dear friend
$
```

Finally, in this example, the input line contains fewer words than the number of variables in the `read` statement, so the last variable remains null.

```
$ read var1 var2 var3
Hello friend
$ echo $var1
Hello
$ echo $var2
friend
$ echo $var3

$
```

Suppose that you want to give the user of the `unload` program in Listing 11.3 the option to abort. You might insert these lines of code:

```
...
echo "The following files will be unloaded"
ls -x $1
echo "Do you want to continue: Y or N \c"
read ANSWER
if [ $ANSWER = N -o $ANSWER = n ]
then
    exit 0
fi
...
```

In the preceding example, you use the `\c` character in the user prompt so that the user's response appears on the same line as the prompt. The `read` statement will cause the program to pause until the operator responds with a line of input. The operator's response will be stored in the variable `ANSWER`. When you're testing the user's response, you use the `-o` operator so that the appropriate action is taken, regardless of whether the user's response is in upper- or lowercase.

The *case* Statement

Earlier in this section, you saw that the Bourne shell provided a special construct for a common occurrence by providing the `elif` statement to be used in place of nested `if-then-else` constructs. Another fairly common occurrence is a series of `elif` statements where the same variable is tested for many possible conditions, as in the following:

```
if [ variable1 = value1 ]
then
    command
    command
elif [ variable1 = value2 ]
then
    command
    command
elif [ variable1 = value3 ]
then
    command
    command
fi
```

The Bourne shell provides a cleaner and more powerful method of handling this situation with the `case` statement. The `case` statement is cleaner because it does away with the `elif`s and the `then`s. It is more powerful because it allows pattern matching, much as the command-line interpreter does. The `case` statement allows a value to be named, which is almost always a variable, and a series of patterns to be used to match against the value, and a series of commands to executed if the value matches the pattern. The general syntax of `case` is as follows:

```
case value in
    pattern1)
        command
        command;;
    pattern2)
        command
        command;;
    ...
    patternn)
        command;
esac
```

The case statement executes only one set of commands. If the value matches more than one of the patterns, only the first set of commands specified is executed. The double semi-colons (`;;`) after a command act as the delimiter of the commands to be executed for a particular pattern match.

In the program in listing 11.5, the `case` statement combines the three sample programs—`backup`, `restore`, and `unload`—into a single interactive program, enabling the user to select the function from a menu.

Listing 11.5. An interactive archive program.

```
# Interactive program to restore, backup, or unload
# a directory
echo "Welcome to the menu driven Archive program"
echo _
# Read and validate the name of the directory
echo "What directory do you want? \c"
read WORKDIR
if [ ! -d $WORKDIR ]
then
    echo "Sorry, $WORKDIR is not a directory"
    exit 1
fi
# Make the directory the current working directory
cd $WORKDIR
# Display a Menu
echo "Make a Choice from the Menu below"
echo _
echo "1  Restore Archive to $WORKDIR"
echo "2  Backup $WORKDIR "
echo "3  Unload $WORKDIR"
echo
# Read and execute the user's selection
echo "Enter Choice: \c"
read CHOICE
case "$CHOICE" in
    1) echo "Restoring..."
       cpio -i </dev/rmt0;;
    2) echo "Archiving..."
       ls ¦ cpio -o >/dev/rmt0;;
    3) echo "Unloading..."
       ls ¦ cpio -o >/dev/rmt0;;
    *) echo "Sorry, $CHOICE is not a valid choice"
       exit 1
esac
#Check for cpio errors
if [ $? -ne 0 ]
then
    echo "A problem has occurred during the process"
    if [ $CHOICE = 3 ]
    then
        echo "The directory will not be erased"
    fi
    echo "Please check the device and try again"
    exit 2
else
    if [ $CHOICE = 3 ]
    then
        rm *
    fi
fi
```

In the program in listing 11.5, notice the use of the asterisk (*) to define a default action if all the other patterns in the case statement fail to match. Also notice that the check for errors in the archive process occurs only once in the program. This check can be done in this program because the exit status of the case statement is always the exit status of the last command executed. Because all three cases end with the execution of cpio, and the default case ends with an exit statement, the exit status variable at this point in this program is always the exit status of cpio.

Another powerful capability of the case statement is to allow multiple patterns to be related to the same set of commands. You use a vertical bar (¦) as an *or* symbol in the following form:

```
pattern1 ¦ pattern2 ) command
                     command;;
```

You can further modify the interactive archive program to allow the user to make a choice by entering either the menu number or the first letter of the function, by changing the case statement:

```
read CHOICE
case "$CHOICE" in
   1 ¦ R ) echo "Restoring..."
           cpio -i </dev/rmt0;;
   2 ¦ B ) echo "Archiving..."
           ls ¦ cpio -o >/dev/rmt0;;
   3 ¦ U ) echo "Unloading..."
           ls ¦ cpio -o >/dev/rmt0;;
   *) echo "Sorry, $CHOICE is not a valid choice"
      exit 1
esac
```

Building Repetitions into a Program

Up to now, the programs you have looked at have had a top-to-bottom, linear progression. The program statements are executed from top to bottom. One of the most beneficial things about computer programs is their capability to process data in volume. For this to occur, the programming language must have some construct to cause portions of the program to be repetitive. In computer terminology, this construct is often called *looping*.

For example, suppose you had a computer file containing records with mailing addresses and ZIP codes and you wanted to print only records matching a specific ZIP code. You would want to write a program which reads a record, performs a matching test on the ZIP code, prints those that match, and then repeat the process until the data is exhausted. You could do this within a loop.

The Bourne shell has three different looping constructs built into the language. One of the key concepts in program looping is the termination of the loop. Many hours of computer time are wasted by programs that inadvertently go into infinite loops. The main difference between the shell's three looping constructs is the method by which the loop is terminated. The three types of loops are the while loop, the until loop, and the for loop; each is discussed separately in the following sections.

Repeating Within a *while* Loop

The while construct enables you to specify commands that will be executed *while* some condition is true.

The general format of the while construct is as follows:

```
while command
do
    command
    command
    ...
    command
done
```

Consider the following example in a program called squares in listing 11.6.

Listing 11.6. Example of a while loop.

```
# squares - prints the square of integers in succession
int=1
while [ $int -lt 5 ]
do
    sq='expr $int \* $int'
    echo $sq
    int='expr $int + 1'
done
echo "Job Complete"

$ squares
1
4
9
16
Job Complete
$
```

In the program in listing 11.6, as long as the value of int is less than five, the commands inside the loop are executed. On the fifth repetition, the test condition associated with the while statement returns a nonzero value, and the command following the done statement is executed.

In the interactive archive program in Listing 11.5, the user is allowed to make a single request and the program terminates. Using while, you can change the program to allow the user to enter multiple requests. The revised program is shown in listing 11.7.

Listing 11.7. Revised interactive archive program.

```
# Interactive program to restore, backup, or unload
# a directory
echo "Welcome to the menu driven Archive program"
```

```
ANSWER=Y
while [ $ANSWER = Y -o $ANSWER = y ]
do
    echo _
# Read and validate the name of the directory
    echo "What directory do you want? \c"
    read WORKDIR
    if [ ! -d $WORKDIR ]
    then
        echo "Sorry, $WORKDIR is not a directory"
        exit 1
    fi
# Make the directory the current working directory
    cd $WORKDIR
# Display a Menu
    echo "Make a Choice from the Menu below"
    echo _
    echo "1  Restore Archive to $WORKDIR"
    echo "2  Backup $WORKDIR "
    echo "3  Unload $WORKDIR"
    echo
# Read and execute the user's selection
    echo "Enter Choice: \c"
    read CHOICE
    case "$CHOICE" in
        1) echo "Restoring..."
           cpio -i </dev/rmt0;;
        2) echo "Archiving..."
           ls ¦ cpio -o >/dev/rmt0;;
        3) echo "Unloading..."
           ls ¦ cpio -o >/dev/rmt0;;
        *) echo "Sorry, $CHOICE is not a valid choice"
    esac
#Check for cpio errors
    if [ $? -ne 0 ]
    then
        echo "A problem has occurred during the process"
        if [ $CHOICE = 3 ]
        then
            echo "The directory will not be erased"
        fi
        echo "Please check the device and try again"
        exit 2
    else
        if [ $CHOICE = 3 ]
        then
            rm *
        fi
    fi
    echo "Do you want to make another choice? \c"
    read ANSWER
done
```

By initializing the ANSWER variable to Y, enclosing the main part of the program within a while loop, and getting a new ANSWER at then end of the loop in the program in listing 11.7, the user is able to stay in this program until he or she answers N to the question.

Repeating Within an *until* Loop

The `while` construct causes the program to loop as long as some condition is true. The `until` construct is the complement to `while`; it causes the program to loop until a condition is true. These two constructs are so similar, you can usually use either one. Use the one that makes the most sense in the context of the program you are writing.

The general format of the `until` construct is as follows:

```
until command
do
    command
    command
    ...
    command
done
```

You could have made the modification to the interactive archive program just as easily with an `until` loop by replacing the `while` with `until`:

```
until [ $ANSWER = N -o $ANSWER = n ]
```

Processing an Arbitrary Number of Parameters with *shift*

Before considering the `for` loop, it would be helpful to look at the `shift` command, since the `for` loop is really a shorthand use of `shift`.

In the examples presented so far, the number of positional parameters, or command-line arguments, is either presumed to be solitary or is passed on to a command as a whole using the $* variable. If a program needs to process each of the command-line arguments individually, and the number of arguments is not known, you can process the arguments one by one by using the `shift` command in your program. The `shift` command shifts the position of positional parameters by one; $2 becomes $1, $3 becomes $2, and so on. The parameter that was $1 before the `shift` command is not available after `shift`. The following simple program illustrates this concept:

```
# shifter
until [ $# -eq 0 ]
do
    echo "Argument is $1 and `expr $# - 1` argument(s) remain"
    shift
done
```

```
$ shifter 1 2 3 4
Argument is 1 and 3 argument(s) remain
Argument is 2 and 2 argument(s) remain
Argument is 3 and 1 argument(s) remain
Argument is 4 and 0 argument(s) remain
$
```

You may have noticed that the $# variable decremented each time the `shift` command was executed in the preceding example. Using this knowledge, you can use an `until` loop to process all the variables. Consider the example in listing 11.8, a program to sum an integer list supplied as command-line arguments.

Listing 11.8. An integer summing program.

```
# sumints - a program to sum a series of integers
#
if [ $# -eq 0 ]
then
    echo "Usage: sumints integer list"
    exit 1
fi
sum=0
until [ $# -eq 0 ]
do
    sum='expr $sum + $1'
    shift
done
echo $sum
```

Following is the execution of `sumints`:

```
$ sumints 12 18 6 21
57
$
```

You also can use the `shift` command for another purpose. The Bourne shell predefines nine positional parameters, $1 through $9. This does not mean that only nine positional parameters can be entered on the command line, but to access positional parameters beyond the first nine, you must use the `shift` command.

The `shift` command can take an integer argument that causes it to shift more than one position at a time. If you know that you have processed the first three positional parameters, for example, and you want to begin a loop to process the remaining arguments, you can make $4 shift to $1 with the following command:

```
shift 3.
```

Repeating Within a *for* Loop

The third type of looping construct in the Bourne shell is the `for` loop. The `for` loop differs from the other constructs in that it is not based on a condition being true or false. Instead the `for` loop executes one time for each word in the argument list it has been supplied. For each iteration of the loop, a variable name supplied on the `for` command line assumes the value of the next word in the argument list. The general syntax of the `for` loop is as follows:

```
for variable in arg1 arg2 ... argn
do
```

```
    command
    ...
    command
done
```

The following simple example illustrates the construct:

```
$ for LETTER in a b c d; do echo $LETTER; done
a
b
c
d
$
```

Because the argument list contained four words, the loop is executed exactly four times. The argument list in the `for` command does not have to be a literal constant; it can be from a variable substitution.

You can also write the `sumints` program in listing 11.8 using a `for` loop, by passing the command-line arguments to the `for` loop. The modified program appears in listing 11.9.

Listing 11.9. Modified integer summing program.

```
# sumints - a program to sum a series of integers
#
if [ $# -eq 0 ]
then
    echo "Usage: sumints integer list"
    exit 1
fi
sum=0
for INT in $*
do
    sum='expr $sum + $INT'
done
echo $sum
```

Getting Out of a Loop from the Middle

Normally, a looping construct executes all the commands between the do statement and the done statement. Two commands enable you to get around this limitation: the `break` command causes the program to exit the loop immediately, and the `continue` command causes the program to skip the remaining commands in the loop but remain in the loop.

A technique that is sometimes used in shell programming is to start an `infinite loop`, that is, a loop that will not end until either a `break` or `continue` command is executed. An infinite loop is usually started with either a `true` or `false` command. The `true` command always returns an exit status of zero, whereas the `false` command always returns a non-zero exit status. The loop

```
while true
do
   command
   ...
   command
done
```

executes until either your program does a break or the user initiates an interrupt. You can also write an infinite loop as follows:

```
until false
do
   command
   ...
   command
done
```

We could use this technique to make the interactive archive program of Listing 11.7 a little easier to use. The revised program is shown in listing 11.10.

Listing 11.10. Another version of the interactive archiver.

```
# Interactive program to restore, backup, or unload
# a directory
echo "Welcome to the menu driven Archive program"
while true
do
# Display a Menu
   echo
   echo "Make a Choice from the Menu below"
   echo _
   echo "1  Restore Archive"
   echo "2  Backup directory"
   echo "3  Unload directory"
   echo "4  Quit"
   echo
# Read the user's selection
   echo "Enter Choice: \c"
   read CHOICE
   case $CHOICE in
      [1-3] ) echo _
              # Read and validate the name of the directory
              echo "What directory do you want? \c"
              read WORKDIR
              if [ ! -d "$WORKDIR" ]
              then
                  echo "Sorry, $WORKDIR is not a directory"
              continue
              fi
              # Make the directory the current working directory
              cd $WORKDIR;;
          4) :;;
          *) echo "Sorry, $CHOICE is not a valid choice"
             continue _
   esac
   case "$CHOICE" in
```

continues

Listing 11.10. continued

```
    1) echo "Restoring..."
       cpio -i </dev/rmt0;;
    2) echo "Archiving..."
       ls ¦ cpio -o >/dev/rmt0;;
    3) echo "Unloading..."
       ls ¦ cpio -o >/dev/rmt0;;
    4) echo "Quitting"
       break;;
  esac
#Check for cpio errors
  if [ $? -ne 0 ]
  then
      echo "A problem has occurred during the process"
      if [ $CHOICE = 3 ]
      then
          echo "The directory will not be erased"
      fi
      echo "Please check the device and try again"
      continue
  else
      if [ $CHOICE = 3 ]
      then
          rm *
      fi
  fi
done
```

In the program in listing 11.1, the loop continues as long as `true` returns a zero exit status, which is always, or until the user makes selection four, which executes the `break` command and terminates the loop. Notice also, that if the user makes an error in choosing the selection or in entering the directory name, the `continue` statement is executed rather than the `exit` statement. This way, the user can stay in the program even if he or she makes a mistake in entering data, but the mistaken data cannot be acted on.

Notice also the use of two case statements. The first `case` statement requests that the operator enter a directory name only if option 1, 2, or 3 is selected. This example illustrates how pattern matching in a `case` statement is similar to that on a command line. In the first `case` statement, if the user selects option 4, the null command (:) is executed. Because the first `case` statement checks for invalid selections and executes a `continue` if an invalid selection is made, the second `case` statement need not check for any but valid selections.

Structured Shell Programming Using Functions

A common feature among higher level programming languages is the ability to group computer instructions together into functions that can be called from anywhere within the program. These functions are sometimes called *subroutines*. The Bourne shell also provides you this ability.

The general syntax of a function definition is as follows:

```
funcname ()
{
    command
    ...   _
    command;
}
```

Once it is defined, a function can be called from anywhere within the shell by using *funcname* as a command. There are two reasons you might want to group commands into a function. One good reason is to break a complex program into more manageable segments, creating a structured program. A structured program might take the following form:

```
# start program
setup ()
{  command list ; }_

do_data ()
{  command list ; }_

cleanup ()
{  command list ; }_

errors ()
{  command list ; }_

setup
do_data
cleanup
# end program
```

In the above example, `setup`, `do_data`, and `cleanup` are functions. When you look at a well-structured program, the names of the functions give you a fair idea of what the functions might do. If you were trying to analyze this, you might assume what the `setup` and `cleanup` functions do and concentrate on the `do_data` section.

> **TIP:** Always give variables and functions meaningful names. It may seem at the time you are writing a program that you will remember what the variables and functions are used for, but experience has proven that after the passage of time things are not always so clear. You should also remember that there will probably come a time when someone else will look at your programs, and that person will appreciate descriptive names.

Another legitimate reason for grouping commands into functions is that you may want to execute the same sequence of commands from several points within a program. At several points in the interactive archive program in listing 11.10, a non-fatal error occurs and the `continue` command is executed. You can give the user the option of continuing at each of these points with an interactive `continue` function named `icontinue`.

```
icontinue ()
{
while true
do
    echo "Continue? (y/n) \c"
    read ANSWER
    case $ANSWER in
        [Yy] ) return 0;;
        [Nn] ) return 1;;
        * ) echo "Answer y or n";;
    esac
done
}
```

Now you can replace the `continue` statements in the program with the `icontinue` function.

```
if icontinue then continue else break fi
```

All of the prompting, reading, and error checking are carried out by the `icontinue` function, instead of repeating these commands at every `continue` point. This example also illustrates the function's capability to return an exit status with `return`. If no `return` command is available within the function, the exit status of the function is the exit status of the last command in the function.

Shell functions are very much like shell programs—with one very important difference. Shell programs are executed by subshells, whereas shell functions are executed as part of the current shell. Therefore, functions can change variables that are seen in the current shell. Functions can be defined in any shell, including the interactive shell.

```
$ dir () { ls -l; }_
$ dir
-rw-rw-r—  1 marsha  adept   1024 Jan 20 14:14 LINES.dat
-rw-rw-r—  1 marsha  adept   3072 Jan 20 14:14 LINES.idx
-rw-rw-r—  1 marsha  adept    256 Jan 20 14:14 PAGES.dat
-rw-rw-r—  1 marsha  adept   3072 Jan 20 14:14 PAGES.idx
-rw-rw-r—  1 marsha  acct     240 May  5  1992 acct.pds
$
```

You have now defined `dir` as a function within your interactive shell. It remains defined until you log off or unset the function, as follows:

```
$ unset dir
```

Functions can also receive positional parameters, as in the following example:

```
$ dir () {_
> echo "Permission  Ln Owner    Group   File Sz Last Access"
> echo "----------  -- ----     ----    ------ ----------"
> ls -l $*;
>}
$ dir L*
Permission  Ln Owner    Group   File Sz Last Access
----------  -- ----     ----    ------ ----------_
```

```
-rw-rw-r--   1 marsha   adept      1024 Jan 20 14:14 LINES.dat
-rw-rw-r--   1 marsha   adept      3072 Jan 20 14:14 LINES.idx
```

In this example, the argument `L*` was passed to the `dir` function and replaced in the `ls` command for `$*`.

Normally, a shell script is executed in a subshell. Any changes made to variables in the subshell are not made in the parent shell. The dot (.) command causes the shell to read and execute a shell script within the current shell. You make any function definitions or variable assignments in the current shell. A common use of the dot command is to reinitialize login values by rereading the `.profile` file. For information about `.profile`, see "Customizing the Shell" later in this chapter.

```
$ . .profile
```

Handling the Unexpected with *trap*

When you're writing programs, one thing to keep in mind is that programs do not run in a vacuum. Many things can happen during a program that are not under the control of the program. The user of the program may press the interrupt key or send a `kill` command to the process, or the controlling terminal may become disconnected from the system. In UNIX, any of these events can cause a signal to be sent to the process. The default action when a process receives a signal is to terminate.

Sometimes, however, you may want to take some special action when a signal is received. If a program is creating temporary data files, and it is terminated by a signal, the temporary data files remain. In the Bourne shell, you can change the default action of your program when a signal is received by using the `trap` command.

The general format of the `trap` command is as follows:

```
trap command_string signals
```

On most systems, you can trap 15 signals. The default action for most is to terminate the program, but this action can vary, so check your system documentation to see what signals can occur on your system (Part IV, "Process Control" discusses signals in more detail). Any signal except 9 (known as the sure kill signal) can be trapped, but usually you are concerned only with the signals that can occur because of the user's actions. Following are the three most common signals you'll want to trap:

Signal	Description
1	Hangup
2	Operator Interrupt
15	Software Termination (kill signal)

If the command string contains more than one command, which it most certainly should, you must enclose the string in either single or double quotation marks. The type of quotation marks you use determines when variable substitution is made.

Suppose you have a program that creates some temporary files. When the program ends normally, the temporary files are removed, but receiving a signal causes the program to terminate immediately, which may leave the temporary files on the disk. By using the trap command in the following example, you can cause the temporary files to be removed even if the program does not terminate normally due to receiving a hangup, interrupt, or kill signal:

```
trap "rm $TEMPDIR/*$$; exit" 1 2 15
```

When the trap command is executed, the command string is stored as an entry in a table. From that point on, unless the trap is reset or changed, if the signal is detected, the command string is interpreted and executed. If the signal occurs in the program before the trap command is executed, the default action occurs. It is important to remember that the shell reads the command string twice—once when the trap is set and again when the signal is detected. This determines the distinction between the single and double quotation marks. In the preceding example, when the trap command line is read by the interpreter, variable substitution takes place for $TEMPDIR and $$. After the substitution, the resultant command string is stored in the trap table. If the trap command is changed to use single quotation marks

```
trap 'rm $TEMPDIR/*$$; exit' 1 2 15
```

when trap is executed, no variable substitution take place, and the command string

```
rm $TEMPDIR/*$$; exit
```

is placed in the trap table. When the signal is detected, the command string in the table is interpreted, and then the variable substitution takes place. In the first instance, $TEMPDIR and $$ have the value that they had at the time the trap was executed. In the second instance, $TEMPDIR and $$ assume the value that they have at the time the signal is detected. Make sure that you know which you want.

The command string for the trap command almost always contains an exit statement. If you don't include an exit statement, then the rm command is executed when the signal is detected, and the program picks right up where it left off when the signal occurred. Sometimes you might want the program to pick up where it left off instead of exiting. For example, if you don't want your program to stop when the terminal is disconnected, you can trap the hangup signal, specifying the null command, as shown in the following example:

```
trap : 1
```

You can set a trap back to the default by executing the trap command with no command string, like this:

```
trap 1
```

The following command has the effect of making the user press the interrupt key twice to terminate a program:

```
trap 'trap 2' 2
```

Conditional Command Execution with the And/Or Constructs

As you have already seen, often you can write a shell program more than one way without changing the results of the program. The until statement, for example, is simply a reverse way of using a while statement. You can cause commands to be conditionally executed using the if-then-else construct, but you also can accomplish conditional execution using the && and ¦¦ operators. In the C programming language, these symbols represent the *logical and* and the *logical or* operations respectively. In the Bourne shell, the && connects two commands in such a way that the second command is executed only if the first command is successful.

The general format of && is as follows:

```
command && command
```

For example, in the statement

```
rm $TEMPDIR/* && echo "Files successfully removed"
```

the echo command is executed only if the rm command is successful. You also can do this programming in an if-then statement like this one:

```
if rm $TEMPDIR/*
then
    echo "Files successfully removed"
fi
```

Conversely, the ¦¦ connects to commands in such a way that the second command is executed only if the first command is not successful, as in this command:

```
rm $TEMPDIR/* ¦¦ echo "Files were not removed"
```

The preceding is the programming equivalent of

```
if rm $TEMPDIR/*
then
    :
else
    echo "Files were not removed"
fi
```

You also can concatenate these operators. In the following command line, `command3` is executed only if both `command1` and `command2` are successful:

```
command1 && command2 && command3
```

You can also concatenate operators of different types. In the following command line, `command3` is executed only if `command1` is successful and `command2` is unsuccessful:

```
command1 && command2 ¦¦ command3
```

The `&&` and `¦¦` are simple forms of conditional command execution and are usually used only in cases where single commands are to be executed. Although the commands can be compound, if too many commands appear in this format, the program can be difficult to read. Generally, `if-then` constructs seem to be more clear if you use more than one or two commands.

Reading UNIX-Style Options

One of the nicer things about UNIX is that most of the standard commands have a similar command-line format:

```
command -options parameters
```

If you are writing shell programs for use by other people, it is nice if you use the same conventions. To help you do so, a special command is available in the Bourne shell for reading and processing options in this format: the `getopts` command, which has the following form:

```
getopts option_string variable
```

where `option_string` contains the valid single-character options. If `getopts` sees the hyphen (-) in the command input stream, it compares the character following the hyphen with the characters in `option_string`. If a match occurs, `getopts` sets `variable` to the option; if the character following the hyphen does not match one of the characters in `option_string`, `variable` is set to a question mark (?). If `getopts` sees no more characters following a hyphen, it returns a nonzero exit status. This capability enables you to use `getopts` in a loop.

The program in listing 11.11 illustrates how you use `getups` to handle options for the date command. The program creates a version of `date`, which conforms to standard UNIX style, and it adds some options.

Listing 11.11. A standardized date function `newdate`.

```
#newdate
if [ $# -lt 1 ]
then
   date
else
```

```
    while getopts mdyDHMSTjJwahr OPTION
    do
       case $OPTION
       in
          m) date '+%m ';;  # Month of Year
          d) date '+%d ';;  # Day of Month
          y) date '+%y ';;  # Year
          D) date '+%D ';;  # MM/DD/YY
          H) date '+%H ';;  # Hour
          M) date '+%M ';;  # Minute
          S) date '+%S ';;  # Second
          T) date '+%T ';;  # HH:MM:SS
          j) date '+%j ';;  # day of year
          J) date '+%y%j ';;# 5 digit Julian date
          w) date '+%w ';;  # Day of the Week
          a) date '+%a ';;  # Day abbreviation
          h) date '+%h ';;  # Month abbreviation
          r) date '+%r ';;  # AM-PM time
          \?) echo "Invalid option $OPTION";;
       esac
    done
fi
```

In the program in listing 11.11, each option is processed in turn. When getopts has processed all the options, it returns a nonzero exit status, and the while loop terminates. Notice that getopts allows options to be stacked behind a single hyphen, which is also a common UNIX form.

The following examples illustrate how newdate works:

```
$ newdate -J
94031
$ newdate -a -h -d
Mon
Jan
31
$ newdate -ahd
Mon
Jan
31
$
```

Sometimes an option requires an argument, which getopts also parses if you follow the option letter in *option_string* with a colon. When getopts sees the colon, it looks for a value following a space following the option flag. If the value is present, getopts stores the value in a special variable OPTARG. If it can find no value where one is expected, getopts stores a question mark in OPTARG and writes a message to standard error.

The program in listing 11.12 makes copies of a file and gives the copies a new name. The -c option takes an argument specifying the number of copies to make, and the -v option instructs the program to be verbose, that is to display the names of the new files as they are created.

Listing 11.12. duplicate **program.**

```
# Syntax: duplicate [-c integer] [-v] filename
#    where integer is the number of duplicate copies
#    and -v is the verbose option
COPIES=1
VERBOSE=N

while getopts vc: OPTION
do
   case $OPTION
   in
      c) COPIES=$OPTARG;;
      v) VERBOSE=Y;;
      \?) echo "Illegal Option"
          exit 1;;
   esac
done

if [ $OPTIND -gt $# ]
then
   echo "No file name specified"
   exit 2
fi

shift 'expr $OPTIND -1'

FILE=$1
COPY=0

while [ $COPIES -gt $COPY ]
do
   COPY='expr $COPY + 1'
   cp $FILE ${FILE}${COPY}
   if [ VERBOSE = Y ]
   then
       echo ${FILE}${COPY}
   fi
done
```

In the program in listing 11.12, allowing the user to enter options presents a unique problem; when you write the program, you don't know which of the positional parameters will contain the name of the file that is to be copied. The getopts command helps out by storing the number of the next positional parameter in the variable OPTIND. In the duplicate program, after getopts has located all the options, OPTIND is checked to make sure that a filename is specified and then the shift command makes the filename the first positional parameter.

```
$ duplicate -v fileA
fileA1
$ duplicate -c 3 -v fileB
fileB1
fileB2
fileB3
```

Customizing the Shell

The shell performs some very specific tasks and expects its input to follow some specific guidelines—command names first, for instance. But the Bourne shell does allow the user some control over his or her own environment. You can change the look of your shell and even add your own commands.

Customizing the Shell with Environment Variables

In the section "Variables" earlier in this chapter, you learned that one type of variable is called an environment variable. The shell refers to these variables when processing information. Changing the value of an environment variable changes how the shell operates. You can change your command-line prompt, get mail forwarded to you, and even change the way the shell looks at your input.

Changing Your Command-Line Prompt with PS

You can personalize your shell by changing the prompt your shell displays when it will accept commands. This is done by changing the value in the environment variable PS1. Suppose you wanted your command-line prompt to display your working directory. You could do this with:

```
$ PS1="'pwd'>"
/usr/home/teresa>cd /usr/home/john
/usr/home/teresa>
```

As you can see, you have changed the way your shell works. By writing your own shell programs and changing environment variables, you can create your own look. Notice though that the prompt does not change when you change directories. A function to do this is shown in the section "Adding Your Own Commands and Functions."

Adding Command-Line Separators with IFS

When a command line is entered in an interactive shell, each word on the command line is interpreted by the shell to see what action needs to be taken. By default, words are separated by spaces, tabs, and newline characters. You can add your own separators by changing the IFS environment variable, as in the following example:

```
$ IFS=':'
$ echo:Hello:My:Friend
Hello My Friend
$
```

Setting additional field separators does not void the default field separators; space, tab, and newline are always seen as field separators.

Checking Multiple Mailboxes with *MAILPATH*

Most users have only one mailbox for their electronic mail. Some users, however, may require multiple mailboxes (see Chapter 9, "Communicating with Others" for a discussion of electronic mail). For example, Dave wants to read mail addressed to him personally (which arrives to his personal user account), mail addressed to sysadm (which arrives to his system administrator account), and mail addressed to root (which arrives to his main account), but Dave can be logged in as only one of these accounts at any one time. Dave therefore can cause his current shell to check all three mailboxes by setting the environment variable MAILPATH, as follows:

```
$ MAILPATH="/usr/spool/mail/Dave:/usr/spool/mail/sysadm\
:/usr/spool/mail/root"
```

Now when mail is sent to any of these names, Dave receives the following message:

```
you have mail.
```

The only problem is that Dave does not know which mailbox to check when he receives this message. You can help solve Dave's problem by changing the mail message associated with each mailbox. You terminate the mailbox name in MAILPATH with a percent sign (%) and supply a message like this:

```
$ MAILPATH="/usr/spool/mail/Dave%Dave has mail\
:/usr/spool/mail/sysadm%sysadm has mail\
:/usr/spool/mail/root%root has mail
```

Automating Environment Changes

One problem with altering your environment by changing your environment variables is that when you log off, the changes are lost. You can give some permanence to your environment changes by placing the changes in your .profile.

Each time you log in to the Bourne shell, login looks in your home directory for the .profile file and executes the commands in that file. Any environment variables that you set and export in .profile are operative for subsequent operations, unless the user explicitly changes them.

But the .profile file can do more than just set environment variables, it is a shell program and can contain any of the commands that are valid in the Bourne shell.

Adding Your Own Commands and Functions

This chapter has shown how you can group UNIX commands together in files and create your own programs or shell scripts. Sometimes though, you don't achieve the desired results. The program in listing 11.13 changes the working directory, and at the same time changes the environment variable PS1, which contains the command-line prompt.

Listing 11.13. Change directory program `chdir`.

```
# Directory and Prompt Change Program
# Syntax: chdir directory

if [ ! -d "$1" ]
then
  echo "$1 is not a directory"
  exit 1
fi

cd $1
PS1="'pwd'> "
export PS1
```

When you execute the following `chdir` command from listing 11.13, nothing happens.

```
$ chdir /usr/home/teresa
$
```

There is no error message, yet the command-line prompt is not changed. The problem is that `chdir` is executed in a subshell, and the variable `PS1` that was exported is made available only to lower shells. To make `chdir` work like you want, it must be executed within the current shell. The best way to do that is to make it a function. You can write the function in your `.profile` file, but there is a better solution. Group your personal functions into a single file and load them into your current shell using the transfer command (.). Rewrite `chdir` as a function, changing the `exit` to `return`. The function definition file persfuncs is shown in listing 11.14.

Listing 11.14. Personal function file with `chdir` written as a function.

```
#Personal function file persfuncs
chdir ()
{
# Directory and Prompt Change Program
# Syntax: chdir directory

if [ ! -d "$1" ]
then
  echo "$1 is not a directory"
  return
fi

cd $1
PS1="'pwd'> "
export PS1;
}
$ . persfuncs
$ chdir /usr/home/teresa
/usr/home/teresa> chdir /usr/home/john
/usr/home/john> _
```

Keeping personal functions in a separate file makes them easier to maintain and debug than keeping them in your .profile.

You can make your personal functions a permanent part of your environment by putting the command

```
.persfuncs
```

in your .profile.

Specialized Topics

Debugging Shell Programs

When you begin to write shell programs, you will realize something that computer users have known for years: programmers make mistakes! Sometimes what seems to be a perfectly reasonable use of computer language produces results that are unexpected. At those times, it is helpful to have some method of tracking down your errors.

The Bourne shell contains a trace option, which causes each command to be printed as it is executed, along with the actual value of the parameters it receives. You initiate the trace option by using set to turn on the -x option or execute a shell with the -x option. The sumints program is reproduced in listing 11.15.

Listing 11.15. An integer summing program.

```
# sumints - a program to sum a series of integers
#
if [ $# -eq 0 ]
then
    echo "Usage: sumints integer list"
    exit 1
fi
sum=0
until [ $# -eq 0 ]
do
    sum='expr $sum + $1'
    shift
done
echo $sum
```

Running sumints with the trace option looks like this:

```
$ sh -x sumints 2 3 4
+ [ 3 -eq 0 ]
+ sum=0
+ [ 3 -eq 0 ]
```

```
+ expr 0 + 2
+ sum= 2
+ shift
+ [ 2 -eq 0 ]
+ expr 2 + 3
+ sum= 5
+ shift
+ [ 1 -eq 0 ]
+ expr 5 + 4
+ sum= 9
+ [ 0 -eq 0 ]
+ echo 9
9
$
```

The trace shows you each command that executes and the value of any substitutions that were made before the command was executed. Notice that the control words if, then, and until were not printed.

Grouping Commands

Commands to a shell can be grouped to be executed as a unit. If you enclose the commands in parentheses, the commands are run in a subshell; if you group them in curly braces ({}), they are run in the current shell. The difference in the two has to do with the effect on shell variables. Commands run in a subshell do not affect the variables in the current shell, but if commands are grouped and run in the current shell, any changes made to variables in the group are made to variables in the current shell.

```
$ NUMBER=2
$ (A=2; B=2; NUMBER='expr $A + $B'; echo $NUMBER)
4
$ echo $NUMBER
2
```

In the previous example, note that the variable NUMBER had a value of 2 before the command group was executed. When the command group was run inside of parentheses, NUMBER was assigned a value of 4, but after execution of the command group was complete, NUMBER had returned to its original value. In this next example, when the commands are grouped inside of curly braces, NUMBER will keep the value it was assigned during execution of the command group.

```
$ {A=2; B=2; NUMBER='expr $A + $B'; echo $NUMBER}
4
$ echo $NUMBER
4
$
```

Note that the second example looks somewhat like a function definition. A function is a named group of commands, which executes in the current shell.

Using the Shell Layer Manager *shl*

UNIX is a multi-programming operating system. Some UNIX systems take advantage of this feature, allowing the user to open several shells at one time, which they can accomplish using the shell layer manager `shl`. Only the active layer can get terminal input, but output from all layers is displayed on the terminal, no matter which layer is active, unless layer output is blocked.

A layer is created and named with `shl`. While the user is working in a layer, he or she can activate the shell manager by using a special character (Ctrl+Z on some systems). The shell layer manager has a special command-line prompt (>>>) to distinguish it from the layers. While in the shell layer manager, the user can create, activate, and remove layers. Following are the `shl` commands:

`create name`	Creates a layer called *name*
`delete name`	Removes the layer called *name*
`block name`	Blocks output from name
`unblock name`	Removes the output block for *name*
`resume name`	Makes *name* the active layer
`toggle`	Resumes the most recent layer
`name`	Makes *name* the active layer
`layers [-l] name ...`	For each *name* in the list, displays the process ID. The `-l` option produces more detail.
`help`	Displays help on the `shl` commands
`quit`	Exits `shl` and all active layers

Summary

In this chapter you have learned about many of the features of the Bourne shell. You have seen that the shell interprets and executes your commands, and how you can combine commands into shell programs to create your own tools.

Korn Shell

12

By John Valley

IN THIS CHAPTER

The previous chapter introduced the basics of UNIX shells and discussed the Bourne shell in particular. This chapter expands on the subject of shells by introducing the Korn shell—the second of the three main shell languages available to you. The third major shell language—the C shell—is discussed in Chapter 13.

The Korn shell is named after its author, David G. Korn of AT&T's Bell Laboratories, who wrote the first version of the program in 1986. The Korn shell is, therefore, a direct descendent of the Bourne shell. It is almost perfectly compatible with the Bourne shell. That is, with a few minor exceptions, any shell script written to be executed by the Bourne shell can be executed correctly by the Korn shell. The converse is, however, not true. As a general rule, Korn shell scripts cannot be processed correctly by the Bourne shell.

This upward compatibility provides a number of advantages, not the least of which is that it enables you to capitalize on your knowledge of the Bourne shell immediately. It also drastically reduces the amount of material that you need to learn in order to begin using the Korn shell.

Because the Korn shell is intended as a replacement for and an improvement on the Bourne shell, it is best discussed as a series of features added to the basic functionality of the Bourne shell. Many aspects of the shell's operation presented in Chapter 11, "The Bourne Shell," are not repeated here. Instead, this chapter summarizes the differences between the Bourne shell and the Korn shell.

The list of Korn shell enhancements is extensive, ranging from the profound to the picayune. The most dramatic enhancements are those that are intended to facilitate keyboard interaction with the shell, but there are also many important extensions to shell syntax and shell programming technique which should not escape your notice. Altogether, the enhancements can be collected into the following categories:

Command aliases: Aliases enable you to abbreviate frequently used commands without resorting to shell programming, thus improving your overall keyboard productivity.

Command history: Command history can be used alone or in conjunction with command editing to modify and reuse previously typed commands. It can also be used as a log of keyboard actions.

Command editing: The Korn shell provides two styles of command editing that enable you to revise and correct commands as you type them. Command editing can greatly reduce the amount of time you spend retyping commands.

Directory Management: The Korn shell provides extensions to the cd command, new pathname syntax, and new shell variables to facilitate switching between directories and to abbreviate long pathnames.

Arithmetic expressions: The Bourne shell offered minimal arithmetic capabilities. The Korn shell offers much greater power for handling numbers, even though a hand-held calculator is still a better tool for calculations.

Syntax improvements: The Korn shell offers improvements in the syntax of the if statement, the test built-in command, and the command substitution expression, which can improve the power and readability of your shell scripts.

Wildcard expressions: The Korn shell provides more wildcard formats to reduce your typing workload.

Coprocessing: The conventional pipe of the Bourne shell is expanded to permit more flexible programmed interaction between your shell script and the commands you invoke.

Job processing: The Korn shell includes batch job monitoring features to simplify running processes in the background and to enable you to do more things simultaneously.

Privileged mode switching: The Bourne shell provided no special features to capitalize on the set-uid capability of UNIX. The privileged mode of the Korn shell, on the other hand, enables you to switch the set-uid mode on and off and to develop procedures as shell scripts that previously required C language programming.

Although you haven't been introduced to the C shell yet, you'll find when you study it that many of the Korn shell features duplicate those of the C shell but with a different syntax. This is intentional. Although the C shell offers many desirable features, its general syntax is incompatible with the Bourne shell, making it somewhat of a square peg in a round hole in the UNIX world. The Korn shell solves this long-standing quandary in the UNIX world by offering the keyboard and shell programming features that people want but in a form compatible with the old, well established Bourne shell standard.

Shell Basics

As I mentioned earlier, the Korn shell is essentially a foundation equivalent to the Bourne shell with a new layer of goodies added on top. You can use the Korn shell as a one-for-one replacement of the Bourne shell, with no special knowledge of Korn shell features. Korn shell extensions do not come into play until you explicitly invoke them.

In particular, the Korn shell is identical to the Bourne shell in the following areas:

Redirection of input and output: The Bourne shell redirection operators <, <<, >, and >>, and the here document facility (<<*label*) all have identical syntax and work the same way.

Entering multiple commands on one line: The semicolon (;) marks the end of a shell statement. To enter multiple commands on one line, simply end each command but the last with a semicolon.

Filename substitutions: The Korn shell supports the familiar substitution characters *, ?, and [...], which when used in a word, cause the word to be replaced with all matching filenames. The Korn shell also supports additional filename matching patterns having the general form *(expression), and the tilde (~) abbreviation, but you need not use these extensions.

Substitution of variables: The Korn shell supports the variable substition form $name, as well as all the special variable references $*, $@, $$, $-, and $?, and the parameters $0 through $9. The special form ${name}, as well as the forms ${name[op]text} are also supported with their usual meaning. In addition, the Korn shell supports array variables ${name[index]}, special command substitutions $(...), and others. The extensions do not conflict with Bourne shell syntax, and you do not need to use them.

Command substitutions: The Bourne shell command substitution form `command` is fully supported in the Korn shell, with the same syntax and behavior as the Bourne shell format. The Korn shell also supports the variant syntax $(...) to simplify the use of command substitutions.

Escaping and quoting: The Korn shell recognizes quoted strings of the form "..." and '...', with the same meaning and effect. A single special character can be deprived of its meaning with the backslash (\); the backslash is removed from the generated command line, except when it appears within single quotes. There are no extensions to the standard escaping and quoting techniques.

Extending a command over multiple lines: To extend a command over multiple lines, end the line with a backslash (\). The backslash must be the last character of the line. The combination of the backslash, followed immediately by a newline character, is recognized and simply deleted from the command input. This is the same behavior as the Bourne shell.

The general philosophy of the Korn shell is to invoke extensions and special features with syntax that is not legal for the Bourne shell. As a result, any commands and shell scripts which are syntactically correct for the Bourne shell will be interpreted identically by the Korn shell. All Korn shell extensions use syntactic forms that do not appear in the Bourne shell language.

Features which are not invoked directly by commands, such as command history and command editing, are controlled instead by shell options. To use command editing, you must first issue the command set -o vi or set -o EMACS. If you don't, the Korn shell command line works the same as the Bourne shell. Also note that the set command follows the general philosophy: set -o is not valid in the Bourne shell and generates a syntax error.

The compatibility between the Bourne shell and Korn shell is nearly perfect, because it was one of the design objectives of the Korn shell that it should be able to execute system-provided shell scripts written for the Bourne shell, without the need to revise those scripts, or to invoke the Bourne shell to run them. This objective meant that even minor idiosyncracies of Bourne shell behavior could not be overlooked: the Korn shell design had to implement them all.

The upshot of all this is that the entire contents of Chapter 11, "Bourne Shell," applies equally well, without restriction or caveat and in its entirety, to the Korn shell.

Wildcard Expressions

The Bourne shell supports a number of syntactic forms for abbreviating a command-line reference to filenames. These forms are based on the idea of embedding one or more special pattern-matching characters in a word. The word then becomes a template for filenames and is replaced by all the filenames that match the template. The pattern-matching characters supported by the Bourne shell are *, ?, and the bracketed expression [. . .].

These pattern-matching characters are supported by the Korn shell, as well as a tilde expansion that uses the ~ character to shorten pathnames, and the extended pattern-matching expressions *(), ?(), +(), @(), and !(). The syntax of pattern-matching expressions is based on the recognition of unquoted parentheses—()—in a word. Parentheses are special to the shell in both the Bourne and Korn shells; they must be quoted to avoid their special meaning. The Bourne shell attaches no special significance to a word such as here+(by¦with), but it would complain about the parentheses. Thus, words containing embedded parentheses do not occur in the Bourne shell. The Korn shell, therefore, uses this syntax to extend wildcard pattern-matching without impairing Bourne shell compatibility.

Tilde Expansion

A word beginning with ~ (the tilde) is treated specially by the Korn shell. To avoid its special meaning, you must quote the tilde. Note that words containing a tilde in any position except for the first are treated normally. The tilde has special meaning only when it appears as the first character of a word.

The four different styles of tilde expansion are

~   Used by itself or when followed by a slash (/), the tilde is replaced by the pathname of your home directory. It is the same as writing $HOME or $HOME/.... For example,

```
$ echo ~
/usr/home/fran
```

```
$ echo ~/bin
/usr/home/fran/bin
```

```
$ bindir=~/bin
$ echo $bindir
~/bin
```

~string   A tilde followed by an alphanumeric string is replaced by the home directory of the named user. It is an error if no entry exists in the /etc/passwd file for string. For example,

```
$ echo ~bill
/usr/home/bill
```

~+   A tilde followed by a plus sign is replaced by the full pathname of the current directory. It is the same as writing $PWD or $PWD/.... For example,

```
$ pwd
/usr/lib
$ echo ~+/bin
/usr/lib/bin
```

~-   A tilde followed by a minus sign is replaced by the full pathname of the previous directory. It is the same as writing $OLDPWD or $OLDPWD/.... For example,

```
$ pwd
/usr/lib
$ cd ~/lib
/usr/home/fran/lib
$ echo ~-/bin
/usr/lib/bin
```

The tilde shorthand is a great time saver. The most common error people make when using it is that they forget that the tilde is recognized only at the beginning of a word, and that it can't be used in assignment expressions such as bindir=~/bin.

Pattern Expressions

A pattern expression is any word consisting of ordinary characters and one or more shell pattern-matching characters. The pattern-matching characters are the familiar *, ?, and [...] from the Bourne shell, as well as any of the following extended pattern-matching expressions:

(pattern[¦pattern]...)   Matches zero or more occurrences of the specified patterns. For example, time(sheet¦spent) matches the filenames time, timesheet, and timespent, but it doesn't match the filename timeused.

`+(pattern[¦pattern]...)`	Matches one or more occurrences of the specified patterns. For example, `time+(.x¦.y)` matches `time.x`, `time.x.x`, and `time.y`, but it doesn't match `time` or `time.x.y`.
`?(pattern[¦pattern]...)`	Matches no or one occurrence of any of the patterns. For example, `time?(.x¦.y)` matches `time`, `time.x`, and `time.y`, but it doesn't match `time.x.x`.
`@(pattern[¦pattern]...)`	Matches exactly one occurrence of the pattern. For example, `time@(.x¦.y)` matches `time.x` or `time.y`, but it doesn't match either `time` or `time.x.x`.
`!(pattern[¦pattern]...)`	Same as * except that strings that would match the specified patterns are not considered matches. For example, `time!(.x¦.y)` matches `time`, `time.x.y`, `time.0`, and everything beginning with `time` except for `time.x` and `time.y`.

Note that the definition of pattern expressions is recursive. Each form contains one or more pattern strings. This means that nested pattern expressions are legal. Consider, for example, `time*(.[cho]¦.sh)`. It contains the pattern `[cho]` inside the pattern expression. The pattern `time*(.*(sh¦obj))` matches either of the filenames `time.sh` or `time.obj`.

The main value of these extended pattern-matching expressions is in enabling you to select a subset of files without having to list each filename explicitly on the command line. Pattern expressions are also legal in other contexts where the shell does pattern matching, such as in the expression of the `case` statement.

Command Substitution

Another noteworthy enhancement provided by the Korn shell is a more convenient syntax for command substitutions. Remember from Chapter 11 on the Bourne shell that a string quoted with back-quotes (`'command'`) is replaced with the standard output of `command`. The backquote notation isn't easy to use, though. The Korn shell supports the following alternate form in addition to the standard Bourne shell backquote notation:

```
$(command-list)
```

Not only does the parenthesized form avoid the problem of recognizing backquotes on printed listings, but it also acts as a form of quoting or bracketing. You can use all the standard quoting forms inside the parentheses without having to use backslashes to escape quotes. Furthermore, the parenthesized form nests. You can use `$()` expressions inside `$()` expressions without difficulty.

An Improved *cd* Command

For directory movement, the Korn shell supports two new forms of the cd command:

```
cd -
cd oldname newname
```

The command cd - is especially helpful. It switches back to the directory you were in before your previous cd command. This command makes it easy for you to switch to another directory temporarily, and then to move back to your working directory by typing cd -. The PWD and OLDPWD variables are maintained to carry the full pathnames of your current and previous directory, respectively. You can use these variables for writing commands to reference files in a directory without typing the full pathname.

You can use the cd oldname newname command to change a component of the pathname of your current directory. Thus, it makes lateral moves in a directory structure somewhat easier. For example, if your current directory is /usr/prod/bin and you want to switch to the directory /usr/test/bin, just type the command cd prod test. Similarly, the command cd usr jjv switches from /usr/prod/bin to /jjv/prod/bin, assuming that the latter directory exists.

Aliases

The command aliasing feature of the Korn shell is certainly one of its most attractive and flexible enhancements over the Bourne shell. It's an enhancement you'll start using right away.

When you define a command alias, you specify a shorthand term to represent a command string. When you type the shorthand term, it is replaced during command execution with the string that it represents. The command string can be more than just a command name. It can define stock options and arguments for the command as well.

For example, you might have one or more preferred ways of listing your directory contents. Personally, I like to use the -FC options on my ls command when I just want to see what's in the directory. Typing the command ls -FC ... repeatedly all day long, though, would not be one of my favorite things to do. The command alias feature makes it easy to set up a short hand for the ls command. You do it like this:

```
$ alias lx='ls -FC'
```

Now whenever you enter lx on the command line, the command ls -FC is executed.

Defining Aliases

The `alias` command is a shell built-in, meaning that it is available to you only when running the Korn shell. It is not part of the UNIX operating system at large. You use the `alias` command to define new aliases and to list the command aliases currently in effect.

The general syntax of the `alias` command is

```
alias [ -tx ] [ name[=value] ... ]
```

The arguments of `alias` are one or more specifications, each beginning with an alias name. The alias name is the shorthand command that you enter at the terminal. Following an equal sign (=), you enter the text with which you want the shell to replace your shorthand. You should enclose the alias value string in single quotes to hide embedded blanks and special characters from immediate interpretation by the shell.

The Korn shell stores alias names and their definitions in an internal table kept in memory. Because it's not stored in a disk file, you lose your alias definitions whenever you log out or exit the Korn shell. To keep an alias from session to session, you need to define the alias in your login profile—a file in your home directory named `.profile`). There's nothing tricky about it. The same command that you enter at the keyboard to define an alias works just as well when issued from a login profile script. Thus, for aliases you want to use over and over, simply type the `alias` command in your login profile; you only have to do it once. (For more information about using the login profile, see the section called "Customizing" near the end of this chapter.)

The syntax of the `alias` command enables you to define more than one alias on a command. The general syntax is

```
alias name = value [name = value]...
```

You don't usually write multiple definitions on one `alias` command. This is because you usually think them up one at a time. In your login profile, it's a good idea to write only one alias definition per `alias` command. This makes it easier to add and delete alias definitions later.

After you've defined an alias, you might want to list the aliases in effect to see your new definition. Simply enter the `alias` command with no arguments. For example,

```
$ alias
true=let 1
false=let 0
lx=ls -FC
```

In all likelihood, there are a good many more alias definitions in effect than you defined. The Korn shell automatically defines a number of aliases when it starts up—such as when you log in—to provide convenient abbreviations for some Korn shell commands. The `true` and `false` definitions fall into this category. The UNIX operating system provides `true` and `false` commands, but as programs they must be searched for and loaded into memory to execute. As aliases the shell can execute them much more quickly, so these two particular aliases are provided as an easy performance enhancement for the many shell scripts you execute—usually unknowingly—throughout the day.

To use the `lx` command alias previously shown, use it as a new command name. For example,

```
$ lx
```

by itself lists all the files in the current directory in a neat columnar format, sorted for easy inspection. To list a directory other than the current directory, use the command

```
$ lx /usr/bin
```

After alias substitution, the shell sees the command `ls -FC /usr/bin`.

The ability to prespecify command options in an alias is a great help. Even better, you can usually augment or alter prespecified command options when you use the alias. Suppose, for example, that you want to add the command option `-a` when listing `/usr/bin` so that you can see all `dot` files in the directory. You might think that you have to type the full `ls` command, because the `lx` alias doesn't include an `-a` option letter. Not so. The following command works quite well:

```
$ lx -a /usr/bin
```

When the shell executes this command, it immediately replaces `lx` with the alias value string, obtaining the following internal form:

```
$ ls -FC -a /usr/bin
```

The `ls` command, like most other UNIX commands, is comfortable with command options specified in multiple words. In effect, the `-a` option has been added to the `-FC` options provided automatically by the alias.

Removing an Alias

To remove an alias that you or the Korn shell previously defined, use the `unalias` command:

```
$ unalias name [ name ... ]
```

Notice that just as you can define multiple aliases on one command line, you also can remove multiple aliases with one `unalias` command.

Writing an Alias Definition

One of my favorite aliases is the following one for the `pg` command:

```
$ alias pg='/usr/bin/pg -cns -p"Page %d:"'
```

The `pg` alias is instructive in a number of ways. Take a look at it in detail.

First, note that the alias name is `pg`. This is the same as the `pg` command itself, so in effect the alias hides the `pg` command. You can invoke the real UNIX `pg` command by using an explicit pathname—calling `/usr/bin/pg`—but not by the short command `pg`, which invokes the alias instead.

Choosing the same name for an alias as a real command name is unusual. It implies that you never want to execute the real command directly, and that you always want to dress it up with the options specified in the alias.

Because of the way I work, the options `-c`, `-n`, `-s`, and `-p` should have been built in to the command; I always want to use them. The `-c` option causes `pg` to clear the screen when it displays a new page. On a video terminal, this is more natural and faster than scrolling the lines. The `-n` option causes `pg` to execute a command key immediately without waiting for the Enter key. All `pg` commands are one letter long. The only reason not to use the `-n` option is to avoid the slack in performance that results from generating a terminal interrupt for each keypress, which the `-n` option requires. However, single-user workstations and modern high-performance computers don't notice the extra workload. Therefore, unless you're working on an old PDP-11, go ahead and specify the `-n` option for the convenience it adds. The `-s` option displays messages, such as the current page number, in highlighted mode, usually inverse video, which makes the non-text part of the display easier to notice or to ignore.

The `-p` option causes the `pg` command to display the page number at the bottom of each screen. I like page numbering because it gives me a rough idea of where I am in the displayed document. By default, the page number is displayed as a bare number, run on with the rest of the command line. The `pg` command, however, enables you supply a format for the page number. I specified `-p"Page %d:"`. It identifies the page number with the word `Page` and provides a colon (:) to separate the page number from the input command line.

Because the page number format string contains characters special to the shell—specifically, an embedded blank—it must be enclosed in quotes. The `alias` command also requires that the entire alias definition be enclosed in quotes. Therefore, I need a quote within a quote.

If you understood the discussion of quotes in the chapter on the Bourne shell, you should also realize that there are at least three ways to write this alias command:

```
$ alias pg='/usr/bin/ls -cns -p"Page %d:"'
```

```
$ alias pg="/usr/bin/ls -cns -p'Page %d'"
$ alias pg="/usr/bin/ls -cns -p\"Page %d\""
```

The first form is the form I chose for the example. The second embeds a single quoted string inside a double quoted string; it works just as well. The third form uses an escape character to embed a double quote inside a double quoted string. In this case, the shell strips off the backslashes before it stores the alias value. I avoid this form, because I don't like to use escape sequences unless I have to.

The point here is that alias definitions usually must be enclosed in quotes—unless the alias value is a single word. Thus, you must occasionally embed quoted strings inside a quoted string. You should recognize that this need can arise. Be prepared to handle it by making sure that you understand how the shell quoting mechanism works.

> **CAUTION:** If you do get a handle on how the shell quoting syntax works, it incites many otherwise nice people to brand you as a UNIX guru. So be careful.

Using Exported Aliases

The alias command supports a number of options, including -x (export) and -t (tracking).

An exported alias is much the same concept as an exported variable. Its value is passed into shell scripts that you invoke.

Exporting a command alias can be both helpful and harmful. For example, exporting the pg alias shown earlier would be helpful, because it would cause pg commands issued by a shell script—many UNIX commands are implemented as shell scripts—to work as I prefer. On the other hand, if you define an alias for the rm command that always prompts before deleting a file, you might be inundated with requests from system-supplied shell scripts to delete temporary files that you never heard of.

Use the command alias -x to display only those command aliases that are exported. Used in the form alias -x name, the alias name is redefined as an exported alias; it should have been defined previously. To define a new exported alias, use the full form alias -x name=value.

Using Tracked Aliases

By default, the Korn shell creates a tracked alias entry automatically for many of the commands that you invoke from the keyboard. This helps to improve performance. When an alias is tracked, the Korn shell remembers the directory where the command is found. Therefore, subsequent invocations don't have to search your PATH list for the command file. Essentially, the alias for the command is simply set to the full pathname of the command.

You can display the commands for which a tracked alias exists by using the command `alias -t`.

To request explicit tracking for a command that you use frequently, use the form `alias -t name`. If no alias already exists with the given name, the Korn shell does a path search and stores the full pathname of the command `name` as the alias value. Otherwise, the shell simply marks the alias as tracked for future reference.

Note that you generally don't set the tracked attribute for command aliases that you write—that is, where the alias name differs from the alias value. The values for tracked aliases should usually be set by the Korn shell itself. You can achieve the effect of a tracked alias by supplying the full pathname of the command in the alias value. This eliminates path searches. For example, the `lx` alias shown earlier would be better written as `alias lx='/usr/bin/ls -FC'`; it would achieve the same effect as tracking.

As a final example, suppose that the `vi` command is not in the list when you issue the command `alias -t`, but that you know you will be using the command fairly frequently. To request tracking for the `vi` command, simply issue the command `alias -t vi`.

One of the major reasons for the name *tracking* is that the Korn shell takes account of the possibility that your search path—the value of the `PATH` shell variable—may include the directory . (dot), a reference to your current directory. If you switch to another directory, commands that were available might become unavailable, or they might need to be accessed by a different pathname. Alias tracking interacts with the `cd` command to keep the full pathnames of tracked aliases current. In other words, alias tracking keeps track of the proper full pathname for commands as you switch from directory to directory and create, remove, or relocate executable files.

Shell Options

Being a rather sophisticated program, the Korn shell deals with many human interface issues that might be resolved in two or more ways. To help you use the shell in ways most convenient to you, the shell enables you to choose how it behaves by setting options.

There are two ways to set Korn shell options: on the `ksh` command when you invoke the shell and on the `set` command from within the shell once you've got it started. Options that you don't set explicitly take on a default value. Thus, you never need to bother with option settings unless you want to.

The `ksh` command is normally issued on your behalf by the UNIX login processor, using a template stored in the `/etc/passwd` file for your login name. Generally, the system administrator constructs the password entry for you, but unless he's very busy or very mean-spirited, he'll be happy to adjust your password entry to invoke the shell with your preferred settings. Of course, you can replace your login shell with the Korn shell at any time by using the following command:

```
$ exec ksh options ...
```

The exec statement that you encountered in your study of the Bourne shell does the same thing under the Korn shell. It replaces the current shell with the command named as its first argument—usually also a shell, but perhaps of a different type or with different options and arguments.

The syntax of the ksh command is

```
ksh [ [pm]aefhkmnpstuvx- ] [-cirs] [[pm]o option] ... [[pm]A name] [arg ...]
```

The `-c`, `-i`, `-r`, and `-s` options can be specified only on the ksh command line. All the other options can be specified on the set command as well.

The options specifiable only on the ksh command line are

-c	*Command:* The first (and only) arg is a command. The -c option prevents the shell from attempting to read commands from any other source. It merely executes the command given as arg and then exits. This option is not used often from the keyboard or from within shell scripts. It is most often used internally by programs written in the C language.
-i	*Interactive shell:* Forces the shell to behave as though its input and output are a terminal. Usually, you don't need to specify the -i option explicitly. Its main purpose is to prevent the abnormal termination of commands invoked by the shell from terminating the shell itself.
-r	*Restricted shell:* The Korn shell runs as a restricted shell and prevents the user from using the cd command or from invoking a command by its full pathname. This option is normally of interest only to the system administrator for setting up specialized user accounts.
-s	*Standard input:* The Korn shell doesn't activate the protections against abnormal termination given by option -i. The shell reads commands from standard input until end of file and then exits normally. This is a handy option, because it enables you to pipe a stream of commands to the shell for execution.

Additional options that you may specify on either the ksh command or the set command are listed below. Options can be specified with a letter in the usual way—for example, -a—or by name—for example, -o allexport. An option that has been set, either explicitly or by default, can be turned off with the + flag—as in +a or +o allexport.

-a   The equivalent option name is `allexport`. All variables are treated implicitly as exported variables. You don't need to invoke the `typeset -x` command or `export` alias to export the variable. A variable becomes eligible for export when it is first defined, whether by the `typeset` statement or by an assignment statement. The `typeset-x` command and `export` alias are permitted, but they have no additional effect.

-e   The equivalent option name is `errexit`. Any command returning a non-zero exit code causes immediate termination of the shell. When it is set within a shell script, only the shell script is terminated.

-f   The equivalent option name is `noglob`. Filename expansion is disabled. Wildcard expressions are treated literally and, with the -f option in force, have no special meaning or effect. You might use `set -f` and `set +f` to disable wildcard expansion for a short range of statements.

-h   The equivalent option name is `trackall`. Every command issued is automatically defined as a tracked alias, just as though you executed `alias -t xxx` in front of each command. The -h option is set on by default for non-interactive shells. Commands that specify a full pathname or that use names not valid as command alias names are not tracked.

-k   The equivalent option name is `keyword`. When -k is set, command arguments having the form `name=value` are stripped from the command line and are executed as assignment statements before the command is executed. The assignment is temporarily exported for the duration of the one command. The effect is equivalent to adding keyword arguments to the shell language and to UNIX commands and shell scripts that support this kind of argument. Most UNIX commands and shell scripts, however, do not support keyword arguments. Therefore, the -k option has little real application.

-m   The equivalent option name is `monitor`. -m runs commands that you launch in the background—using the & shell operator—in a separate process group, automatically reports the termination of such background jobs, and enables use of the `jobs` command for managing background jobs. If -m is not set, commands launched with the & operator execute in the same manner as with the Bourne shell, and job control is not in effect. The default is to enable this option automatically for interactive shells.

-n	The equivalent option name is noexec. -n causes the shell to read and process commands but not execute them. You can use this option in the form ksh -n shell-script-filename to check the syntax of a shell script. You'll probably not want to use this option with your login shell.
-p	The equivalent option name is privileged. The -p option is useful for script writers. A shell script file that has the set-uid bit, the set-gid bit, or both will, when invoked by the Korn shell, have the effective user-id and effective group-id set according to the file permissions, the owner-id, and the group-id; and the -p option will be on. In this mode, the shell script enjoys the permissions of the effective user-id and group-id, not those of the real user. Setting the -p option off—for example, with set +p—causes the Korn shell to set the effective user-id and group-id to those of the real user, effectively switching to the user's—not the file's—permissions. You can subsequently use the set -p command to revert to privileged mode. Not all versions of the Korn shell support this definition of the -p option; only the more recent UNIX operating system releases include this facility.
-s	When used on the set command, -s sorts the arg command arguments into alphabetical sequence before storing. Used on the ksh command, the -s option has the different meaning described earlier.
-t	The Korn shell, invoked with this option, reads and executes one command and then exits. You should set the -t option on the ksh command, not with the set command.
-u	The equivalent option name is nounset. -u causes the shell to generate an error message for a reference to an unset variable—for example, referring to $house when no value has previously been assigned to house. The default behavior is to replace the variable reference with the null string. This option is useful to script writers for debugging shell scripts.
-v	The equivalent option name is verbose. Each command is printed before scanning, substitution, and execution occur. This is useful for testing shell scripts when used in the form ksh -v shell-script-filename, or with set -v and set +v from within a shell script to force the display of a range of commands as they are being executed.
-x	The equivalent option name is xtrace. -x causes the Korn shell to display each command after scanning and

substitution but before execution. Each line is prefixed with the expanded value of the PS4 variable. Using this option enables you to see the effects of variable and command substitution on the command line. Used in the form `ksh -x shell-script-filename`, the -x option is a handy debugging tool for script writers.

— Used on either the ksh or set command, this option forces interpretation of the remaining words of the command line as arguments—not options—even for words beginning with - or +. The — option is often used on the set command for setting new values for the positional parameters, because it ensures that no substituted values are construed as set statement options.

In addition to the previous letter options, the -o keyletter supports the following additional named options:

bgnice	Requests the shell automatically to reduce the priority of background jobs initiated with the & shell operator, as though the nice command had been used.
EMACS	Invokes the EMACS editing mode. It is reset with set +o EMACS or set -o vi.
gmacs	Invokes the EMACS editing mode with the alternate definition of the Ctrl-t transpose function.
ignoreeof	Requests the shell to ignore an end of file character entered at the beginning of the command line. Ordinarily an EOF character entered in this position causes the shell to terminate. To avoid accidentally terminating the shell, you can set this option. You must use the exit command to terminate the shell and log out.
markdirs	Causes wildcard expansion to append a slash (/) to any generated pathnames that are the pathnames of directories.
noclobber	Modifies the behavior of the > redirection operator to inhibit the overwriting of existing files. If you name an existing file after >, the shell writes an error message and doesn't open the output file. Use >¦ to redirect output to an existing file when noclobber is set.
nolog	Inhibits the storing of functions in your command history file.
vi	Enables the vi editing mode with line input. Line input provides only a subset of the features of vi command editing, but it provides better performance than option viraw. You reset vi editing mode with set +o vi or set -o EMACS.

| viraw | Enables vi editing mode with character input. Character input provides all the features of the vi editing mode but with more overhead than option vi. |

The -A option can be used on either the ksh command line or the set command to define an array variable with initial values. When you specify -A, the next argument must be the name of the array variable to be initialized. Subsequent arguments are stored as consecutive elements of the array beginning with element 0. The -A option resets any previous value of the array variable before it assigns new values. Thus, the ending value of the array consists of only those arguments specified as arg.

The +A option assigns the arg values successively starting with element 0, but it doesn't reset any previous value of the array. Thus, if the array variable previously had twelve values and only six values were provided with +A, after execution the first six elements of the array would be the arg values and the last six elements would be left over from the previous value of the array.

The significance of the arg values depends on the options specified. If option -A is specified, the values are taken as initial array element values. If option -s or -i is specified, or if option -i defaults because the shell input is a terminal, the arg values are used to initialize the positional parameters $1, $2, and so on. If option -c is specified, the first arg is taken as a command string to be executed. If none of the options -A, -c, -i, or -s is specified, the first arg is taken as the name of a file of shell commands to be executed, and subsequent arg values are temporarily set as the positional parameters $1, $2, and so on, during the file's execution.

Command History

Command history and command editing are somewhat interrelated features. To employ fully all the benefits of command editing, however, you need an understanding of how command history works.

Command History is simply the automatic recording of commands that you enter in a numbered list. The list is kept in a special disk file in your home directory to preserve it from login session to session. Therefore, when you log in, the command history list from your previous session is available for reference and use. New commands you enter are added to the end of the list. To keep the list from growing overly large, the oldest commands at the beginning of the list are deleted when the list grows to a certain fixed size.

You don't need to do anything to activate the command history feature, nor do you need to specify its maximum size. Its operation is completely automatic. Your only mission, should you decide to accept it, is to use the list to make your life easier.

You can use the command history list in one of three ways. You can view the commands in the history list, using the `history` command. Use the `history` command when you can't remember whether you've already performed an action or if you want to refer to the syntax or operands of a previous command. You can resubmit a command from the list, using the r command. Except for very short commands, it's faster to resubmit a command you typed before with the r command than it is to type the command again. The r command provides several alternative ways for you to identify which command in the history list you want to reexecute. You can modify a command in the history list and then execute the modified command. You use the `fc` command to invoke this form of command editing. You can use any text editor you like to edit the chosen command. By default, the Korn shell invokes the crusty old `ed` command for you, but you can change the default to any text editor you want.

Please note that command editing with the `fc` command, although a convenient and useful feature of Command History, is not the same as the command editing feature discussed later in this chapter.

Now take a closer look at these commands for viewing and manipulating command history.

Displaying the Command History List

The `command` `history` command displays the commands in the command history list. Each command is listed with a line number preceding it. The line number uniquely identifies each command in the history list, and it is one way in which you can refer to a specific line in the history list.

```
$ history
[122] cd /usr/home/jim/src/payapp/pay001
[123] vi main.c
[124] cc -I../include -o main main.c
[125] fgrep include *.c ¦ grep '^#'
[126] vi checkwrite.c checkfile.c checkedit.c
[127] lint -I../include checkfile.c >errs; vi errs
[128] vi checkfile.c
[129] cc -I../include -o checks check*.c
[130] cp checks /usr/home/jim/bin
```

NOTE: The `history` command is actually an alias for the `fc` command—specifically, for `fc -l`.

The complete syntax for the history command is

```
history [first] [last]
```

For `first`, specify the first line to be displayed. You can designate a specific line directly by its line number—for example, `history 35`—or as a number of lines back from the current line—for example, `history -10`. You can also give the command name of the line from which the display should begin—for example, `history vi`. The Korn shell looks backward from the current line until it finds a command beginning with `vi` and then displays lines from that point forward.

For `last`, specify the last line to be displayed. If you omit `last`, history lines are displayed from `first` up to the current—most recently entered—line in the command history. You can use an actual line number, a relative line number, or a command name to designate the last line to be displayed.

If you omit both `first` and `last`, the Korn shell lists the last sixteen lines of history.

> **TIP:** You won't know what line numbers to use until you first list some history. Most people begin a search of command history without any operands. If you want to see more lines before line number 160, you might want to try `history 140`.

Reexecuting a Command from the History

The `r` command enables you to reexecute a command from the command history list. The `r` command itself isn't added to the history, but the command you reuse is added.

> **NOTE:** The `r` command is actually a preset alias for the `fc` command—specifically, for `fc -e -`.

The general syntax for `r` is

```
r [ old=new ] [ line ]
```

If you omit `line`, the most recently entered command is reexecuted.

Specify a line number (`25`), a relative line number (`-8`), or a command name (`vi`) for `line` to designate the command that you want to reuse. As with the `history` command, if you specify a command name, the most recently entered command with that name is reused.

You can modify a word or phrase of the reused command using the syntax `old=new`. For example, if the command history contained the following line

```
135 find /usr -type f -name payroll -print
```

you could reuse the find command, changing only the filename payroll to vendors, like this:

```
$ r payroll=vendors find
```

The r command echoes the line that will be executed, showing any changes that might have been made. For example, the r command above will yield the following output:

```
$ r payroll=vendors find
find /usr -type f -name vendors -print
```

Accessing the History List: *fc*

The fc (fix command) command is a built-in Korn shell command. It provides access to the command history list. Forms of the fc command enable you to display, edit, and re-use commands you previously entered. The Korn shell automatically defines the alias names history and r for you to reduce the amount of typing needed to perform simple history functions.

The syntax of the fc command is

```
fc [ -e editor ] [ -nlr ] [ first ] [ last ]
```

Invoked with no options, the fc command selects a line from the command history using the values of *first* and *last*, invokes the default command editor, and waits for you to edit the command or commands selected. When you exit the editor—either by filing the altered command text or by quitting the editor—the commands are executed.

The fc command actually copies the selected commands into a temporary file and passes the file to the text editor. The contents of the file after editing become the command or commands to be executed.

For example, if you enter the command

```
$ fc vi
```

where vi represents the value of first, the Korn shell copies the most recent vi command into a temporary file. The temporary file will have an unrecognizable name, such as /usr/tmp/fc13159, and is located in a directory designated for temporary files. The file that you actually edit is /usr/tmp/fc13159. Regardless of whether you change the text in file /msr/tmp/fc13159, the Korn shell executes its contents immediately after you exit the editor.

You can specify the command or commands to be processed in the following manner:

To process the command that you most recently entered—other than fc, of course—omit both first and last.

To select and process only one command, specify the command as the value of first and omit last.

To select a range of commands, specify the first command in the range with `first` and specify the last command in the range with `last`.

To designate a command by its line number position in the history list, use a plain number—for example, 219.

To designate a command preceding the most recent command in the history list, use a negative number. For example, in the command history list

```
135 mkdir paywork
136 mv paymast/newemps paywork
137 cd paywork
138 vi newemps
139 payedit newemps
```

the command `fc -2` selects the `vi` command.

To select a command by its name rather than by its position in the history list, use a command name or any prefix of a command name. The most recent command line that begins with the string that you specify will be selected. In the previous command history example, you could also select the `vi` command by entering `fc vi`.

The *first* and *last* command line selectors don't have to use the same formats. For example, you could select line 145 of the history list through the fifth-to-the-last line by entering fc 145 -5.

By default the fc command invokes a text editor on the selected lines and reexecutes them after editing. You can modify this default behavior with the following options:

-e	Use the `-e` option to override the Korn shell's default editor. For example, to use the vi editor to modify and reuse commands, type `fc -e vi ....` Use `fc -e vi ...` to override the default editor.
	The special format `-e -` means to suppress the use of an editor. The selected lines are executed immediately with no opportunity to change them. This form of the `fc` command—as in `fc -e - 135`—is equivalent to the r command. When you use this form, the second dash must be a word by itself. The command `fc -e - 135` immediately reexecutes line 135 of the command history, while the command `fc -e -135` attempts to edit the most recent command in the history list with an editor named `-135`, which probably doesn't exist. Alternatively, the command `fc -e- 135` generates another kind of error, for `-e-` isn't a valid option of the `fc` command.
-l	*List:* The selected lines are listed. No editor is invoked, and the lines are not reexecuted. The command `fc -l` is equivalent to the alias `history`.

-n   *Numbers:* Use the `-n` option to suppress the printing of line numbers in front of the command history. The `-n` option is meaningful only in combination with the `-l` option—for example, `fc -nl`.

-r   *Reverse:* The `-r` option causes the command history to be printed in reverse order. The most recently entered command is shown first, and successive lines show progressively older commands. Use the `-r` option in combination with the `-l` option—for example, `fc -lr`.

Command Editing

Command editing is arguably the most important extension of the Bourne shell included in the Korn shell. It is a great time-saver, and it makes the shell much easier to use for UNIX beginners.

The basic idea underlying command editing is to enable you to use common keys occurring on most terminal keyboards to correct keying errors as you enter a command.

To bring this basic idea to reality, the Korn shell must have some support from the terminal you're using. For example, if you're going to backspace and retype a character, it would be helpful if the terminal is capable of backspacing, erasing a character already displayed, and typing a new character in its place. For this reason, command editing is most useful with video display terminals. Hard-copy terminals such as teletypes are inappropriate for use with the command editing feature of the Korn shell.

The Korn shell supports two distinct styles of command editing: the `vi` edit mode—named after the `vi` text editor—and the EMACS editing mode—named after EMACS. If you're already familiar with either of these editors, you can begin to use command editing immediately.

Activating Command Editing Mode

Before you can use command editing, you first must activate it. Until you do so, the Korn shell command line works much the same as the Bourne shell. That is, everything you type goes into the command line indiscriminately as text, including control and function keys. This is a compatibility feature that you'll want to disable as soon as possible—typically, by activating command editing in your login profile.

To enable the `vi` editing mode, enter the following command line or place it in your `$.profile` (see "Customizing" later in this chapter):

```
set -o vi
```

To enable the EMACS editing mode, enter the following command line or place it in your `profile`:

```
set -o EMACS
```

If you're not familiar with either the `vi` or EMACS text editors but want to use command editing, read through the following sections and choose the editing interface that you find most natural.

vi Edit Mode

The `vi` edit mode uses the editing commands and methods of the `vi` text editor, although with some minor differences due to the fact that you're editing only one line of text and not an entire file.

The `vi` edit mode is activated when you enter the command

```
set -o vi
```

If you prefer to always use the `vi` edit mode, add the command to your `.profile`. Note, however, that you can't have the `vi` and EMACS edit modes both active at once. You can switch between them or shut them both off.

Just like the `vi` editor, `vi` command editing uses two modes: command and input. Normally, your keyboard is in input mode, and every character you type is entered into the command line. To enter command mode, press the Esc key. In command mode, the upper and lower case letters of the keyboard represent editing commands, and pressing a key causes an editing action. If no command corresponds to a given key, pressing it in command mode causes the terminal to beep. You cannot enter text in command mode. This error is the most common mistake beginners make with `vi`-style editing. It is a stumbling block that is responsible for the `vi` editor's miserable reputation as a text editor.

The Enter key always returns you to input mode. After you've made any editing changes to the line, you can press Enter no matter where your cursor is in the line to enter and execute the command.

One word of caution: Keystrokes that you type while in command mode are not displayed. You can see only the effect of an edit command, not the command itself. This can be unsettling when you're inexperienced with the `vi`-style of editing, or when you're entering a command of more than a couple keystrokes.

TIP: If you forget whether you're in command or edit mode, the invisible nature of command mode can make your keyboard appear to go wild, not responding to your inputs in any recognizable fashion. If this happens to you, the best thing to do is to try to cancel the current line completely with the `kill` function—normally the `@` or Ctrl-u keys. If all else fails, press the Enter key. The Enter key might give you an error message when it attempts to execute a garbled command, but at least it is guaranteed to return you to input mode.

The `vi` edit mode commands are summarized in Table 12.1. As you'll notice if you're already familiar with `vi`, nearly all of the `vi` commands are supported, even those which cause movement upward and downward in a file. Commands that move from one line to another actually cause movement in the history file. This enables you to browse through command history, select a command, modify it if necessary, and reenter it, all with a few simple keystrokes.

Some commands can be prefixed by a *count*—a non-zero number. A count causes the command to be automatically repeated that number of times. For example, `B` moves backward one word, but `12B` moves backward twelve words. If you don't specify a count, it defaults to one.

A few commands, notably `c` (*change*), `d` (*delete*), and `y` (*yank*), must be followed by a cursor motion command. Such commands are marked with the symbol →. The use of cursor motion commands is discussed following Table 12.2 below.

Table 12.1. `vi` command editing: command mode commands.

Command	Action
`a`	Inserts text after the cursor.
`A`	Inserts text at the end of the line.
`[n]b`	Moves backward one word.
`[n]B`	Moves backward one blank-delimited word.
`[n]cÆ`	Changes text.
`C`	Changes to end of line.
`[n]dÆ`	Deletes.
`dd`	Discards the entire current line.
`[n]D`	Deletes to end of line.
`[n]e`	Moves to end of current word.
`[n]E`	Moves to end of blank-delimited word.
`[n]fc`	Moves cursor to next c in current line.
`[n]Fc`	Moves cursor to previous c in current line.

continues

Table 12.1. continued

Command	Action
[n]G	Moves to the last—least recent—line in the command history. If nG is entered, it selects line n from the command history.
[n]h	Moves cursor one position to the left.
i	Inserts text before cursor.
I	Inserts text in front of the first nonblank character of the line.
[n]j	Moves down one line—that is, to a more recent history line. This command discards whatever you have typed on the current line.
[n]k	Moves up one line—that is, to a less recent history line. This command discards whatever you have typed on the current line.
[n]l	Moves cursor one position to the right.
n	Repeats the previous / or ? command.
N	Repeats the previous / or ? command but in the reverse direction. It causes a / command to be repeated as the equivalent ?, and ? to be repeated as the equivalent of /.
[n]p	Inserts text in the edit buffer after the current cursor position.
[n]P	Inserts text in the edit buffer before the current cursor position.
[n]rc	Replaces the current character with c. A repeat factor replaces n consecutive characters with c.
R	Replaces characters in the current line—replacement mode. This command differs from c in that it does not discard characters following the cursor; only as many characters as you type are replaced. You end replace mode by pressing Enter or Esc.
S	Deletes entire line and enters input mode.
tc	Moves cursor to the next c in the line.
Tc	Moves cursor to the previous c in the line.
u	Undoes the last text change. You can undo the previous u command. Successive u commands alternate between the original and the changed form of text.
U	Undoes all changes to the current line.
[n]v	Edits the current command—or line n of the history file—with the vi editor. When you exit vi, the edit file is executed as commands, one per line.

Command	Action
[n]w	Moves cursor to next word.
[n]W	Moves cursor to next blank-delimited word.
[n]x	Deletes characters after the cursor.
[n]X	Deletes characters before the cursor.
[n]yÆ	Yanks text into the edit buffer.
yy	Yanks the entire current line.
Y	Yanks text to end of line.
^	Moves cursor to the first character of the line that is not a space or tab.
0	Moves cursor to first position of the line.
$	Moves to last character of the line.
[n]-	Moves to the preceding line in the command history.
[n]+	Moves to the next line in the command history. Use + only when you have used - or k to move backward in the history file. Use G to skip back to the earliest line in the history file.
[n]¦	Moves to the nth character of the line—that is, to column n.
[n]_	(underscore) Inserts the last (nth) word of the previous command.
/string	Selects the most recent line in command history that contains string. string cannot be a regular expression. This command works in opposite direction to the vi editor.
/^string	Same as / except that it selects only a line that begins with string. That is, / will select a line that contains string anywhere in the line, but /^ will look only for lines that begin with string in column 1.
?string	Searches forward in the history file—that is, toward more recent lines—until it finds a line that contains string. The selected line replaces the current line. string cannot be a regular expression. This command works in opposite direction to the vi editor.
?^string	Same as /^ except that it works in the opposite direction.
;	Repeats the previous f, F, t, or T command.
,	Same as ; except that it works in the opposite direction.
~	Inverts the capitalization of the current character.
.	Repeats the previous text-modifying command.

continues

Table 12.1. continued

Command	Action
#	Inserts a pound sign (#) at the beginning of the line. If you then press Enter, the shell treats the line as a comment, and the line is added to command history.
=	Lists filenames in the current directory that begin with the same characters as the current word. The listed filenames are not inserted into the current line, nor is the current line changed. However, you can use the displayed information to select a file and finish typing a complete filename.
\	Appends characters to the word containing the cursor such that the word forms a valid pathname. The shell searches the current directory—or the directory specified by the incomplete word—for filenames that begin with the same characters as the word. Then it appends characters from the matching filenames until a full filename is formed, or, in the case of multiple matches, the filenames differ. This command is a handy way to abbreviate a filename or to enter a filename when you can remember only a few leading characters of the name.
*	Replaces the word with the list of filenames in the current directory—or in the directory specified by the word—that all begin with the same characters as the replaced word. This has the same effect as the wildcard expression string* if entered directly, except that the filenames are entered into the command line now instead of during shell processing.
Space	Moves cursor to the right. It doesn't change characters spaced over.
Backspace	Moves cursor to the left. It doesn't change characters backspaced over.
Enter	Executes the current command line.
Ctrl-l	Redraws the current line. This command is useful if the screen becomes garbled. It redraws only the display line used for command input, not the entire screen.

The vi command editing feature also suports a few control operations that you can use while in input mode. They are described in Table 12.2. Using one of these operations doesn't require you to switch to command mode first, and it doesn't switch you to command mode.

Table 12.2. vi **Command editing: input mode commands.**

Control	Action
Enter	Executes the command line. You can press Enter while in command mode or in input mode, regardless of the current cursor position. If the cursor is somewhere in the middle of the line, pressing Enter doesn't truncate the remainder of the line; the whole line is executed.
Erase	Normally, the # or Backspace key. This is the erase function defined with the stty command. The cursor is backspaced, and the character at that position is erased.
Kill	Normally, the @ or ^u (Ctrl-u) character. This is the kill function defined with the stty command. The current line is discarded; the input line is erased and the cursor returns to the start of the line. Notice that this differs from the normal shell action when command editing is not in effect. Normally, the kill function scrolls the discarded line up and starts a new line beneath it.
Ctrl-v	Escapes the next character. It enables you to enter the Erase, Kill, or \ character as data, avoiding the normal control function.
Ctrl-w	Deletes the previous word. It is similar to backspace, but it backspaces over the previous word instead of the previous character.
\	Escapes the next Erase or Kill character. It is similar to Ctrl-v, but it doesn't escape other commands.

Most vi commands can be preceded with a repeat factor, shown in the box as [n]. If you omit the repeat factor, the command executes its normal function one time. A repeat factor larger than one causes the command to repeat its action the specified number of times. Thus, 2W causes the cursor to skip forward not one but two words, and 7r. replaces seven characters starting at the cursor position with periods.

Commands shown with the symbol « require a cursor motion command following the main command letter. The c, d, and y commands must be followed by a cursor motion command to define the amount of text to be changed, deleted, or yanked. The cursor motion command can be any command that, if entered by itself, would move the cursor beyond the desired text. For example, dw deletes the current word. cte changes text up to, but not including, the next *e* in the line. y0 yanks the characters from the beginning of the line up to, but not including, the character at the cursor position.

Framing cursor motion commands to meet your text editing objectives is your responsibility. There are no prespecified limitations on the way to select a range of text; you are free to choose whatever comes naturally to you. Until you are comfortable with the use of cursor motion commands, however, stick to simple combinations, such as cw or cW to change a word.

The capitalized cursor movement commands B, E, and W differ from their lowercase counterparts in their choice of delimiters. The lower case b, e, and w commands consider a word to end at the next nonalphanumeric punctuation character—which can be a blank or tab, but also includes apostrophes, commas, and so on. The B, E, and W commands consider a word to be delimited strictly by blanks or tabs. They skip over—or select—punctuation characters as well as alphanumerics.

Most of the commands leave you in command mode. A few—a, A, c, C, i, I, R, and s— switch to input mode to enable you to enter text. If, after entering the text, you are ready to execute the command, simply press Enter. If you want to edit the line some more, however, you must switch back to command mode. In that case, press Esc after entering the desired text.

Not all commands supported by the vi editor are shown in Table 12.1. Commands not shown are not supported by the built-in vi edit mode of the Korn shell. Noteworthy omissions include the o and O (open) commands, the m (mark) command, and scrolling commands such as z, H, and M. These omissions are due to the difference between a command editor and a file editor. In a command editing context, they have no useful purpose.

If you want a fuller discussion of the vi text editing commands, refer to Chapter 7, "Editing Text Files."

EMACS Edit Mode

The EMACS edit mode is designed to parallel the editing interface offered by the EMACS editor. The EMACS editor is not so widely available as the vi editor, but many people feel its modeless full-screen editing style is more natural than vi. Be that as it may, a modal editing style is well suited to command editing. Even if you're already an EMACS devotee, you might want to try your hand at the vi edit mode before discarding it out of hand.

The EMACS edit mode is activated when you enter the command

```
set -o EMACS
```

If you prefer to always use the EMACS edit mode, you can add the command to your .profile. Note, however, that you can't have the EMACS and vi edit modes both active at once. You can switch between them or shut them both off.

Because the EMACS editing interface is modeless, you can always enter text into the current line. To perform an editing operation, you generally enter a command prefixed by the Esc key. Commands therefore generally require at least two keystrokes. Because the Escape key isn't conveniently located on most keyboards, entering a series of editing commands is quite a feat of gymnastics.

The EMACS keyboard commands are described in Table 12.3. The commands are listed in alphabetical order by the command letter, with special characters (*, =, and so on) listed first. All commands are one letter, preceded by Ctrl or Esc. As usual, you hold down the Ctrl key while pressing the command letter, but you press and release the Esc key before pressing the command letter key.

Many commands enable you to specify a repeat count in the form Esc n before the command. The repeat count either repeats the action of the command that number of times or specifies a column relative to which the command should operate. The value of *n* starts at 1. Esc 1 means execute the command once—it is the same as omitting Esc n—or column 1 of the current line.

> **CAUTION:** The EMACS editing mode edits lines, not commands. Command history might contain multiline commands, such as if or while, if you use such commands at the keyboard. The vi editing mode processes such commands as a single entity, but in the EMACS editing mode you might need to use the Ctrl-o (operate) command to step through multiline commands when you retrieve them from command history.

The EMACS command editing interface is an example of a user interface designed for an alien species, since it obviously requires the use of three hands to perform well. If you are a beginner or a casual user of command editing, you may nevertheless find EMACS editing mode preferable to the vi mode, because with EMACS there's no confusion between command mode versus input mode. As your proficiency and keyboard speed increase, however, the vi editing mode becomes a more attractive interface.

Table 12.3. *emacs* editing mode commands.

Esc n	*Key Sequence*	*Action*
	Enter	Executes the current line. On some terminals, it is labeled Return.
	Erase	The stty erase character. It deletes the character preceding the cursor.
Esc n	Erase	Backspaces *n* characters.
	Kill	Deletes the entire line. When entered twice in quick succession, it causes subsequent Kill characters to print blank lines.
	\	Escapes the next character, enabling the Erase,

continues

Table 12.3. *emacs continued.*

Esc n	Key Sequence	Action
		Kill, EOF, and Esc characters and Ctrl-x characters to be entered into the current line. The \ itself is discarded. Type \\ to enter a single backslash.
	Esc Esc	Appends characters to the current word to complete the pathname.
	Esc Space	Set a mark at the cursor position.
	Esc *	Performs pathname expansion on the current word as though an * were appended and replaces the word with the list of pathnames that match, if any.
	Esc =	Lists pathnames that match the current word, as though * were appended to the word. The current line is not changed.
	Esc <	Fetches the least recent line from command history.
	Esc >	Fetches the most recent line from command history.
	Esc .	Inserts the last word of your previous command at the current cursor position.
Esc n	Esc .	Inserts the nth word of your previous command at the cursor position.
	Esc _	Same as Esc . .
	Esc Ctrl-?	Same as Esc Ctrl-h. (Note 3)
Esc n	Esc Ctrl-?	Same as Esc Ctrl-h. (Note 3)
	Esc letter	Invokes the macro defined as an alias named _letter. (Note 6)
	Ctrl-] c	Moves cursor to next occurrence of character c in this line.
	Ctrl-a	Moves cursor to start of line.
	Ctrl-b	Moves cursor left one character.
Esc n	Ctrl-b	Moves cursor left n characters.
	Esc b	Moves cursor to beginning of word.
Esc n	Esc b	Moves back n-1 words.
	Ctrl-c	Make the current character uppercase.

Esc n	*Key Sequence*	*Action*
Esc n	Ctrl-c	Makes *n* characters uppercase.
	Esc c	Makes everything to end of current word uppercase. (Note 5)
Esc n	Esc c	Uppercase *n* words from cursor position. (Note 5)
	Ctrl-d	Deletes one character. (Note 1)
Esc n	Ctrl-d	Deletes *n* characters. (Note 1)
	Esc d	Deletes to the end of the current word.
Esc n	Esc d	Deletes to end of *n*th word right.
	Ctrl-e	Moves cursor to end of line.
	Ctrl-f	Move cursor right one character.
Esc n	Ctrl-f	Move cursor right *n* characters.
	Esc f	Move cursor right one word.
Esc n	Esc f	Move cursor right *n* words.
	Esc h	Same as Esc Ctrl-h.
Esc n	Esc h	Same as Esc n Esc Ctrl-h.
	Esc Ctrl-h	Deletes backward to beginning of current word. (Note 2)
Esc n	Esc Ctrl-h	Deletes backward to beginning of *n*th previous word. (Note 2)
	Ctrl-j	Same as Enter.
	Ctrl-k	Deletes to end of line.
Esc n	Ctrl-k	Deletes characters back to or up to column *n*.
	Ctrl-l	Redisplays the entire current line.
	Esc l	Makes all characters to end of current word lowercase. (Note 5)
Esc n	Esc l	Makes *n* words from cursor position lowercase. (Note 5)
	Ctrl-m	Same as Enter.
	Ctrl-n	Fetches the next line from the command history flie. Successive presses retrieve more recent lines in progression.
Esc n	Ctrl-n	Fetches the *n*th line forward from your present position in the command history file.

continues

Table 12.3. continued.

Esc n	Key Sequence	Action
	Ctrl-o	Executes the current line and then fetches the next line from command history. (Note 7)
	Ctrl-p	Replaces the current line with the last line of command history. Successive presses retrieve consecutively older lines from command history.
Esc n	Ctrl-p	Fetches the *n*th line back from command history.
	Esc p	Copies text from cursor to mark into an internal buffer.
	Ctrl-r string Enter	Searches command history for the most recent line containing string. To repeat the previous search, omit string.
Esc 0	Ctrl-r string Enter	Searches command history starting at the oldest line forward for the first occurrence of string. To repeat the previous search, omit string.
	Ctrl-r ^string Enter	Same as Ctrl-r, except that it matches string only at the beginning of a line.
Esc 0	Ctrl-r ^string Enter	Same as Esc 0 Ctrl-r, except that it matches string only at the beginning of a line.
	Ctrl-t	Transposes the current and next characters. (Note 4)
	Ctrl-u	Multiplies count of next command by 4. Thus, Ctrl-u Ctrl-f moves the cursor right four positions.
	Ctrl-v	Displays the current version of the Korn shell. To redisplay the current line, press any key.
	Ctrl-w	Deletes characters from cursor to mark.
	Ctrl-x Ctrl-x	Moves cursor to the mark position, setting a new mark at the old cursor position. This is called swap cursor and mark.
	Ctrl-y	Inserts most recently deleted text at the current cursor position.

1. If the Ctrl-d key is assigned to the EOF function with the stty command, it is interpreted as your EOF key when typed at the beginning of the line. Otherwise, it performs the delete function.

2. Most terminals generate Ctrl-h for the Backspace key. Some, however, generate ASCII DEL (0177). Therefore, the shorthand Esc Backspace might not work for your terminal.

3. The sequence Ctrl-? is not to be taken literally. It represents the ASCII DEL (0177) character. Most terminals generate the DEL character in response to the Delete key, in which case Esc Delete is a synonym for Esc Backspace.

4. If `set -o gmacs` is used instead of `set -o` EMACS, Ctrl-t transposes the current and previous character, not the current and next. This is the only difference between the EMACS and `gmacs` editing modes.

5. Changing character case also moves the cursor to the right, spacing over the changed character(s).

6. A macro is defined with the `alias` shell built-in command. Its name must begin with an underscore and must be followed by one letter. The value of the alias is processed as if you typed the characters of the value at the time of invoking the macro. Thus, sequences such as Ctrl-f in the alias value move the cursor at its current position. The letter used in the macro name should not be b, c, d, f, h, l, or p; these letters are already assigned to EMACS commands.

7. To use the `operate` (Ctrl-o) command, you must have previously established a position in the command history file using Ctrl-p, Ctrl-n, or other history command. Successive presses of Ctrl-o step through lines of command history in the forward—older to newer—direction, executing one line at a time. You have the opportunity to change each line before pressing Ctrl-o to execute it.

Variables

You were introduced to the concept of shell variables in Chapter 11, "Bourne Shell." Everything you learned there remains true for the Korn shell. However, the Korn shell provides some significant extensions to shell variable support. Among these are a greatly expanded set of variables having special meaning to the shell. These variables are often called *predefined* variables, because the shell provides an initial default value for them when you log in. The Korn shell also supports array variables and enhanced arithmetic on shell variables, both of which are a great boon to shell script writers. Naturally, the syntax of shell variable references is expanded to support these capabilities.

Predefined Variables

Variables having special meaning to the shell fall into two main groups: those which you can set to affect the behavior of the shell, and those which the shell sets for you to provide information.

Variables whose values are set by the shell include the familiar $@, $*, $#, $-, $?, and $$, as well as the new $!. The new variable $! provides the process ID of the last command you invoked. It differs from $$ in that the value of $$—your current process ID—is generally that of the shell itself and doesn't change, whereas the value of $! changes everytime you invoke a command. The values of the other shell variables have the same meaning as they do with the Bourne shell.

The following named variables are set by the Korn shell:

_	The full pathname of the last command you invoked. For example, after the command `ls *.c`, the value of `$_` is `/usr/bin/ls`.
ERRNO	The nonzero exit code of the last command that failed. This variable is similar to `$?`, but it differs in that its value changes only when a command fails. Successfully executed commands don't change the value of `$ERRNO`. This variable is primarily a diagnostic aid for use at the keyboard; it is of little use to shell scripts.
LINENO	The `LINENO` variable is meaningful only within a shell script. Its value is the line number of the line in the script currently being executed. You can assign a value to `LINENO`, but it will be changed by the next shell script you invoke—or, if inside a shell script, by the next line executed.
OLDPWD	The value of the `OLDPWD` variable is always the full pathname of the directory that was current immediately before the last `cd` command. In other words, repeated executions of cd `$OLDPWD` switch you back and forth between your current and previous directories. An important use of the `$OLDPWD` variable is to facilitate `cp` and `mv` commands. `cd someplace` followed by `cp filelist $OLDPWD` copies files to your original directory without your having to type the full directory pathname. Then use `cd $OLDPWD` to switch back to your original directory. (In the Korn shell, the shorthand `cd -` means the same thing as `cd $OLDPWD`.)
OPTARG	The value of `OPTARG` is set by the `getopts` command, a new built-in command provided by the Korn shell. (For more information, refer to the "Shell Programming" section later in this chapter.)
OPTIND	The value of `OPTIND` is set by the `getopts` command, a new built-in command provided by the Korn shell. (For more information, refer to the "Shell Programming" section later in this chapter.)
PPID	The value of `PPID` is the your current parent process-ID. That is, if `$$` is the current process-ID, `$PPID` is the process-ID of the parent process of `$$`. This variable is especially useful to shell script writers. It has little use at the keyboard. (Processes and process identifiers are discussed in Chapter 18, "What Is a Process?")

PWD

The full pathname of your current directory. Because of symbolic links, the value of $PWD isn't necessarily the same as the value printed by the pwd command. Suppose, for example, that a directory /usr/bin exists and that a symbolic link to / usr/bin exists named /bin. After cd /bin, the pwd command will print /usr/bin—the real pathname of the directory—but the statement print $PWD will print /bin—the pathname by which you reached the directory. (Links are explained in Chapter 3, "The UNIX File System: Go Climb a Tree.")

RANDOM

The value of $RANDOM is an integer in the range of 0 to 32,767. The value is different in a random way every time you examine it. This variable is not for general use, but a few game programs written in the Korn shell script language use this variable.

REPLY

The select statement, which is new with the Korn shell, sets the value of $REPLY to the user's input text. The read built-in command stores the user's typed input in $REPLY if you supply no variable names on the read command. (For more information, refer to the "Using the select Statement" section later in this chapter.)

SECONDS

The integer number of seconds since you invoked the Korn shell—usually since you logged in, unless you explicitly invoked the Korn shell with the ksh command. This variable simply records the wall-clock time the Korn shell has been running at your terminal.

The shell variables set by the Korn shell listed above don't require your attention. If you have a use for one of them, refer to it at your keyboard or in a shell script. You don't need to assign values to them, though. In some cases, you aren't even allowed to assign a value.

Some variables, however, require attention from you. In most cases, the Korn shell assigns a default value to these variables when it starts. You may override this default value in your login profile—a file named .profile in your home directory—or at any later time by using an assignment statement from the keyboard. The values of these variables affect the way the Korn shell works. Proper setup of these variables can enhance your effectiveness and productivity.

Variables used by the Korn shell are

CDPATH

The value of $CDPATH is a list of colon-separated directory pathnames. The value is referenced only by the cd command. Use the CDPATH variable to name a list of directories to be searched when you issue cd with a directory's simple filename.

The benefit of CDPATH is that it enables you to switch to a directory by giving only its filename instead of the full pathname. There is no default value for CDPATH.

> **NOTE:** I always put the following definition in my login profile:
>
> CDPATH=.:...:$HOME
>
> The command cd src looks first for a directory named src as a subdirectory in the current directory. Failing that, the cd command looks for src in the parent directory. If no directory named src is found in either place, it tries to change to src in my home directory. I find that proper use of the CDPATH variable saves a lot of typing.

COLUMNS
: The value of $COLUMNS defines the display width used by the Korn shell command edit mode—either vi or EMACS—as a view window for long lines, and as the screen width for printing the select list. The default value is 80.

EDITOR
: The value of $EDITOR is used primarily by programs other than the Korn shell. However, if you set the value of EDITOR (in your profile or at the keyboard), the Korn shell will inspect the value for a pathname ending in vi or emacs. If either value is found, the Korn shell automatically sets the corresponding vi or EMACS option, enabling command editing. This is only a convenience. You can still toggle the command edit mode by using the set -o command. There is no default value for EDITOR.

ENV
: The value of $ENV is the pathname of a shell script containing commands to be executed when the Korn shell is invoked. Note that the Korn shell is implicitly invoked every time you invoke a command written as a Korn shell script. You can also invoke the Korn shell from within other UNIX commands such as vi and pg. By placing alias, export, and set commands in a file and supplying the file's pathname as the value of $ENV, you can ensure that you have the same shell environment whenever you invoke the Korn shell. Keep the file pointed to by $ENV small, for its execution is added to the execution of every shell script you execute. (For more information, refer to the "Customizing" section later in this chapter.) There is no default value for ENV.

FCEDIT	The value of $FCEDIT is the pathname of the text editor to be invoked by the fc command. You can override the value of FCEDIT using the -e option on the fc command. The default value of FCEDIT is /bin/ed.
FPATH	The value of $FPATH is a colon-separated list of directories, the same format as for CDPATH and PATH. The directory list is searched for autoload function definitions. (Refer to the "Shell Programming" section later in this chapter for a discussion of autoload functions.) There is no default value for FPATH.
HISTFILE	HISTFILE is the filename of the Korn shell history file. If you want to specify an explicit filename for your history file, supply a value for HISTFILE in your login profile. The default value of HISTFILE is $HOME/.sh_history.
HISTSIZE	The value of HISTSIZE is an integer number specifying the maximum number of commands—not lines—to be retained in the history file. The shell may retain more than HISTSIZE commands in memory while you are working, but it will not accumulate more than HISTSIZE commands in the history file on disk. Note that a value you set for HISTSIZE is treated somewhat like a suggestion; depending on the specific version of the Korn shell you are using, it may act as a fixed upper limit to the number of commands remembered or as an at-least value. The default value of HISTSIZE is 128.
HOME	HOME with the Korn shell works the same as it does with the Bourne shell. The value of HOME is the pathname of your home directory. The value of HOME is used primarily by the cd command as the default directory when you specify no argument. It is also used by a great many commands and shell scripts. The variable is initialized by the UNIX login procedure before any shell is invoked. It is almost never proper for you to change the value of HOME. The default value of HOME is the sixth field of the /etc/passwd file entry for your login name.
IFS	IFS with the Korn shell works the same as it does with the Bourne shell. The value of IFS is zero or more characters to be treated by the shell as delimiters when parsing a command line into words. Rarely manipulated at the keyboard, the IFS variable can be altered in a shell script to parse a string into substrings using arbitrary delimiters. Improper alteration of the IFS variable can cause bizarre problems, so you should

always manipulate it with care and always restore it to its original value. The default value of IFS is the three characters Blank, Tab, and Newline in succession.

LINES
: The value of LINES is an integer number representing the number of lines displayed by your terminal. The Korn shell uses the value of LINES, if set, to limit the printing of select lists. (Refer to the "Using the select Statement" section later in this chapter.) If no value is set, select lists can be arbitrarily long, and some lines may scroll off the display. There is no default value for LINES.

MAIL
: MAIL with the Korn shell works the same as it does with the Bourne shell. The value is the pathname of a file to be monitored by the shell for a change in its date of last modification. If a change is noted, the shell issues the message You have mail at the next opportunity. There is no default value for MAIL. You should set MAIL to the name of your mail file in your login profile.

MAILCHECK
: The value of MAILCHECK is an integer number of seconds that specifies how often the shell should check for a change to the MAIL file. If MAILCHECK is not set or is zero, the shell checks at each command-line prompt for a change in the mail file. The default value of MAILCHECK is 600.

MAILPATH
: The value of MAILPATH is a colon-separated list of pathnames, each of which identifies a file to be monitored for a change in the date of last modification. A pathname can be suffixed with a question mark and message to customize the You have mail message—for example, MAILPATH=/var/spool/mail/jjv?New mail in /var/spool:/usr/mail/jjv?New mail in /usr/mail. Generally, you should set either the MAIL or the MAILPATH variable but not both. There is no default value for MAILPATH.

PATH
: PATH with the Korn shell works the same as it does with the Bourne shell. The default value is system dependent.

PS1
: PS1 is the primary prompt string. The Korn shell performs full substitution on the value of $PS1 before displaying it at the beginning of each command input line. You can, therefore, customize your prompt in the Korn shell environment to a much greater degree than when using the Bourne shell. For example, specify PS1='$PWD: ' to make your prompt be your current directory. (The quotes are important to prevent substitution of the value of PWD as part of the assignment; this

enables the substitution to occur later when the value of $PS1 is printed.) The default value is "$ ".

PS2
PS2 is the secondary prompt string. It is the same as with the Bourne shell. The default value is "> ".

PS3
PS3 selects a prompt string. The value of $PS3 is printed as the selection prompt by the select command. (Refer to the "Using the select Statement" section later in this chapter.)

PS4
PS4 debugs a prompt string. The value of $PS4 is scanned for variable substitution and is printed in front of each line displayed by the trace or -x option.

SHELL
SHELL is the pathname of the shell. The Korn shell sets a default value for $SHELL only if it is not set when ksh begins. The value isn't used directly by the Korn shell, but many other commands (such as vi and pg) use the value of $SHELL as the pathname of the shell to be called when invoking a subshell. If the $SHELL variable is defined when ksh begins and starts with an r, the Korn shell behaves as a *restricted* shell. That is, the user cannot invoke commands with a full pathname and cannot use the cd command.

TERM
The value of TERM is a symbolic alphanumeric string that identifies the type of your terminal. Not used by the Korn shell directly, the variable name TERM is reserved for general system use. The proper setting of $TERM is important to the proper and reasonable operation of your terminal, it and should be initialized appropriately when you log in. For the allowable values at your installation, consult your system administrator. There is no default value for TERM.

TMOUT
The value of TMOUT is an integer specifying the number of seconds after which no terminal activity should cause the Korn shell to automatically log out. A value of zero disables the automatic logout function.

VISUAL
The value of $VISUAL is used primarily by programs other than the Korn shell. However, if you set the value of VISUAL (in your profile or at the keyboard), the Korn shell will inspect the value for a pathname ending in vi or EMACS. If either value is found, the Korn shell automatically sets the corresponding vi or EMACS option, enabling command editing. This is only a convenience. You can still toggle the command edit mode using the set -o command. There is no default value for VISUAL.

As with the Bourne shell, variable names in the Korn shell begin with a letter or an underscore, and they contain an arbitrary number of letters, underscores, and digits. The variable name is a symbolic representation for the variable's value, which can be changed from time by an assignment statement, by the set, read, or select statements, as a by-product of the execution of shell built-in or other commands, or by the Korn shell itself. There is no arbitrary upper limit to the number of variables you can define and use, but the amount of memory available to the shell sets a practical (usually large) upper limit.

You can explicitly assign a value to a variable name using an assignment in the format name=value. Note that you don't write a dollar sign ($) in front of name when you write the assignment. The dollar sign is appropriate only when referring to the value of the variable.

The value of a variable is a string—that is, a sequence of alphanumeric and special characters—of arbitrary length. The Korn shell provides a number of extensions which enable the value of a variable to be manipulated in arithmetic ways. The variable's value is still stored as a string, however.

A variable retains its value from the time it is set—whether explicitly by you or implicitly by the Korn shell—until the value is changed or the shell exits. Note, however, that the value isn't passed to commands and shell scripts that you invoke unless the variable is marked for exportation. You mark a variable for exporting with the typeset shell built-in command or the export alias. Exported variables become part of the environment of all invoked commands.

Because the values of variables are retained internally in a memory table by the shell, all variables that the shell didn't inherit are automatically lost when the shell exits. For this reason, you cannot assign a value to a shell variable inside a shell script—one invocation of the shell—and expect the value to be retained after the shell script exits; the shell returns to a higher level shell. In other words, you can assign values to variables and export the variables to pass values downward to subshells of your current shell, but you cannot pass values upward to higher-level shells or shell scripts.

This limitation on the use of shell variables isn't normally visible to you at the keyboard. It normally arises in issues relating to shell programming. However, if you invoke the shell directly—by entering the sh, ksh, or csh command—or indirectly—by entering the shell environment from within another UNIX command, such as vi or pg—you should realize that any changes to the shell environment, including variable settings and aliases, will be lost when you return to your original shell level by exiting the subshell.

Referencing Variables

The Korn shell replaces strings that begin with $ and are followed by a reference expression appearing in command lines with the value of the reference expression. Any number of reference expressions may appear in the same command line. Adjacent references, when replaced, don't introduce new word boundaries into the command line. That is, a single word—command name, option, or argument—isn't split into two or more words by replacement even if the replaced value contains blanks, tabs, or other delimiter characters. You can use the eval shell built-in command when you want delimiters in the replacement text to cause further word splitting.

The valid reference expressions for the Korn shell are

`name`	`{name#pattern}`
`{name}`	`{name##pattern}`
`{name[n]}`	`{name%pattern}`
`{name[*]}`	`{name%%pattern}`
`{name[@]}`	`{#@}`
`{name:word}`	`{#*}`
`{name-word}`	`{#name}`
`{name=word}`	`{#name[*]}`
`{name?word}`	`{#name[@]}`
`{name+word}`	

name

The expression $name is replaced by the current value of the shell variable named name. If no value for the variable has been defined, the dollar sign and the variable name are replaced with the null string. For example,

```
$ today="January 13"
$ print Today is:$today.
Today is:January 13.
$ print Today is $tomorrow.
Today is:.
```

{name}

The expression ${name} is replaced by the current value of the shell variable named name. The braces help to separate the variable reference from surrounding text; they are discarded after substitution. You must use braces to reference a shell parameter greater than $9—for example, ${10} or ${12}—or to reference an array variable. For example,

```
$ Person1=John
$ Person2=Mike
$ print $Person1 and $Person2
John and Mike
$ print $Person1and$Person2
Person1and: not defined
$ print ${Person1}and$Person2
JohnandMike
```

{name[n]}

The value of the expression is the value of the *m*th element of the array variable name; it is null if the *m*th element isn't set. The first element of an array variable is `${name[0]}`.

{name[*]}

The value of the expression is the value of all the elements of the array variable name that are set, separated by blanks. Substitution occurs in the same way as for the special expression `$*` with regard to embedded blanks and word splitting. For example,

```
$ set -A planets Mercury Venus Earth Mars
$ planet[9]=Pluto
$ print ${planets[*]}
Mercury Venus Earth Mars Pluto
```

{name[@]}

The value of the expression is the value of all the elements of the array variable name that are set, separated by blanks. If elements of the array contain strings with embedded blanks and if the expression `${name[@]}` is contained inside quotes, the number of words in the substituted expression is equal to the number of non-null array elements. Otherwise, embedded blanks cause word splitting to occur, and the number of substituted words will be greater than the number of non-null array elements. For example,

```
$ set -A committee "B Jones" "M Hartly" "C Rogers"
$ for word in ${committee[@]}
> do
> print $word
> done
B
Jones
M
Hartly
C
Rogers
$ for word in "${committee[@]}"
> do
> print $word
> done
B Jones
M Hartly
C Rogers
```

{name:-word}

The expression is replaced by the value of variable name, if the variable has a value and the value is at least one character long. Otherwise, the expression is replaced by word. Note that word should not contain embedded blanks or tabs, although it may contain quoted strings.

Combine : with -, =, ?, or + to treat a variable with a null value—that is, a zero-length string—the same as an unset variable. Without :, the variable is tested only for whether it is set. For example,

```
$ month=January
$ print This month is ${month:-unknown}
This month is January
$ print This year is ${year:-unknown}
This year is unknown
```

{name-word}

The expression is replaced by the value of name, if the variable has a value. Otherwise, it is replaced by word. You can use ${name:-word} to ignore a value that is not set or is null. For example,

```
$unset month
$ month=January
$ print This month is ${month:unknown}
This month is January
$ print This year is ${year:unknown}
This year is unknown
```

{name=word}

The expression is replaced by the value of name, if the variable has a value. Otherwise, word is assigned as the value of word, and the expression is replaced by word. You can use ${name:=word} to assign word to name if the variable is either not set or is null. For example,

```
$ print This month is $month.
This month is .
$ print This month is ${month=January}.
This month is January.
$ print This month is $month.
This month is January.
```

{name?word}

The expression is replaced by the value of name, if the variable has a value. Otherwise, the string word is printed as an error message. An unset variable is recognized as an error and halts processing of the current command line. If the error is recognized inside a shell script, execution of the shell script is terminated. Use ${name:?word} to recognize either an unset or null value as an error. For example,

```
$ month=January
$ print This month is ${month?unknown}
This month is January
$ print This year is ${year?unknown}
ksh: year: unknown
```

{name+word}

The expression is replaced by the value of *word* if the variable *name* has a value. If the variable is not set, the expression is replaced by the null string. That is, if *name* has a value, it temporarily treats the value as though it were *word*. If *name* doesn't have a value, the expression has no value either. Use `${name:+word}` to treat a null value the same as an unset value. For example,

```
$ month=January
$ print This month is ${month+unknown}
This month is unknown.
$ print This year is ${year+unknown}
This year is .
```

{name#pattern}

The value of the expression is the value of *name* with the leftmost occurrence of *pattern* deleted. The shortest match for *pattern* is recognized. For *pattern*, specify a string that contains any character sequence, variable and command substitutions, and wildcard expressions. Only the first occurrence of *pattern* is deleted. For example,

```
$ print $PWD
/usr/home/valley
$ print ${PWD#*/}
usr/home/valley
```

{name##pattern}

The value of the expression is the value of *name* with the leftmost occurrence of *pattern* deleted. The longest possible match is recognized and deleted. For example,

```
$ print $PWD
/usr/home/valley
$ print ${PWD##*/}
valley
```

{name%pattern}

The value of the expression is the value of *name* with the shortest rightmost string matching *pattern* deleted. For example,

```
$ print $FNAME
s.myfile.c
$ print ${FNAME%.*}
s.myfile
```

{name%%pattern}

The value of the expression is the value of *name* with the longest rightmost string matching *pattern* deleted. For example,

```
$ print $FNAME
```

```
s.myfile.c
$ print ${FNAME%%.*}
s
```

{#@}

The value of the expression is the integer number of arguments that would be returned by $@.

{#*}

The value of the expression is the integer number of arguments that would be returned by $*. It is the same as $#.

{#name}

The value of the expression is the length of the string value of variable name. For example,

```
$ print $FNAME
s.myfile.c
$ print ${#FNAME}
10
```

{#name[*]}

The value of the expression is the number of elements of the array variable name that are set. For example,

```
$ set -A planets Mercury Venus Earth Mars
$ print ${#planets[*]}
4
```

{#name[@]}

{#name[@]} is the same as {#name[*]}.

Array Variables

An array variable is a variable with more than one value. Array variables are helpful for managing lists of strings, because you can reference an individual element in the list without resorting to string splitting techniques.

You can assign values to an array one at a time by using the assignment statement. For example,

```
$ planets[1]=Mercury
$ planets[2]=Venus
$ planets[3]=Earth
$ print ${planets[2]}
Venus
```

The general syntax name[subscript] is supported by the Korn shell for referring to elements of an array. For subscript, supply an integer number in the range of 0 through 511, or write a variable expression whose value is the desired element number. Element numbers begin at zero. Thus, the first element in an array is ${name[0]}.

You can use the -A option of the set command to set many array elements with one statement. For example, the previous code could be rewritten as

```
$ set -A planets Mercury Venus Earth
$ print ${planets[2]}
Venus
```

You can also substitute all the elements of an array by using the special notation ${name[*]} or ${name[@]}. For example,

```
$ set -A planets Mercury Venus Earth
$ planets[9]=Pluto
$ planets[7]=Uranus
$ print The known planets are: ${planets[*]}
The known planets are: Mercury Venus Earth Uranus Pluto
```

There are a few points to remember when using array variables:

If you reference the array variable without a subscript, the value of the reference is the first element of the array:

```
$ print $planets
Mercury
```

Array variables cannot be exported.

The special expression ${#name[*]} or ${#name[@]} can be used to get the number of non-null elements in an array. For example,

```
$ print There are ${#planets[*]} planets: ${planets[*]}
There are 5 planets: Mercury Venus Earth Uranus Pluto
```

You must use the brace-enclosed expression syntax to refer to elements of an array. Without the braces, the Korn shell interprets the expression in the same way the Bourne shell would. For example,

```
$ print The known planets are $planets[*]
The known planets are Mercury[*]
$ print The second planet from the Sun is $planets[2]
The second planet from the sun is Mercury[2]
```

Variable Arithmetic

An exciting new addition to the capabilities of the old Bourne shell offered by the Korn shell is the capability to do arithmetic. The Bourne shell provides no built-in calculating capability, so even the simplest arithmetic requires command substitutions that resort to calling other UNIX programs. The Korn shell adds some built-in capability to do basic arithmetic.

The two major tools you'll use when doing arithmetic inside the Korn shell are the type-set command and the let command. The typeset command provides number formatting capability and the capability to declare—or set aside—some variables for the special purpose of doing arithmetic. The let command is where all this magic really happens.

Using *typeset*

The Korn shell is still a very slow tool for doing repetitive calculations, even with the typeset statement. Floating-point—real numbers with decimal points and fractions and the like—isn't supported. Therefore, all your calculations must use integer values, and they will yield integer results. However, the shell arithmetic is sufficient to support programming concepts such as loop control with counters.

The typeset statement is an extension provided by the Korn shell to permit some amount of control over the format and usage of shell variables. When typeset is used for managing variables, its syntax is

```
typeset [ [pm]HLRZilrtux [n] ] [ name[=value] ] ...
```

The particular set of options that you use with the command determines the required format for the syntax of the command. Not all combinations of option letters are legal. Only the following options should be specified:

-i	Declares the variable to be of type integer. Use the optional *n* to specify the number base to which the value should be converted on substitution. The number is always carried in base 10, and only base 10 decimal values should be assigned to the variable. On substitution, however, the value is converted to the equivalent octal digit string. You may also specify one of the -L, -LZ, -R, or -RZ options for the named variable(s).
-l	The value of the named variable(s) should be converted to all lowercase letters when it is substituted. Don't specify this option together with -u. You must specify at least one name argument, and you may provide an optional initial value for some or all of the named variables.
-r	The named variable(s) will be treated as read-only, meaning that subsequent assignments of a value to the named variables will be inhibited. If the variable is to have a non-null value, you should supply a *value* for the listed variable names. You must name at least one variable to have the read-only attribute. You can use the -r option in combination with any of the other options.

-u	The value of the named variable(s) should be converted to all uppercase letters when it is substituted. Don't specify this option together with -1. You must specify at least one *name* argument, and you may provide an option initial value for some or all of the named variables.
-x	The named variables should be exported—made available—to shell scripts and subshells. Note that typeset -x is the only command provided by the Korn shell for establishing exported variables. A command alias is provided automatically at start-up by the shell named export, which is equivalent to the command typeset -x. Unlike the Bourne shell export statement, which permits only variable names, the Korn shell (using command alias) supports statements of the form export name=value ..., providing an initial value for each exported variable. If the variable already exists when the typeset -x command is given, the shell adds the export attribute to the variable. If a you define a new variable but specify no *value*, the variable is initialized to the null string and is marked exportable.
-L	The value of the named variable(s) should be left-justified and padded with blanks on the right to a length of *n* when it is substituted. Obviously, you must specify a field length *n*. For example, -L4 expands the variable value to four characters on substitution. You must specify at least one *name* argument, and you may provide an optional initial value for some or all of the named variables.
-LZ	Similar to -L, but it strips any leading zeroes from the variable value before substitution.
-R	The value of the named variable(s) should be right-justified and padded with blanks on the left to a length of *n* when it is substituted. You must specify a field length *n*. For example, -R4 expands the variable value to four characters on substitution. You must specify at least one *name* argument, and you may provide an optional initial value for some or all of the named variables. Don't specify the -L or -LZ options together with -R.
-RZ	Similar to -R, but it pads the value with zeroes on the left. If the value of the named variable contains only digits, the result is a numeric field of length *n*.
-Z	Same as -RZ.

-H   The -H option is supported only by versions of the Korn shell that execute on non-UNIX operating systems. When -H is specified, each of the *name* variables is presumed to be used to hold a filename or pathname. Assignment of a value to the variable causes mapping of the name to filename formats compatible with the host operating system. You can then use the variable as a filename argument on subsequent commands. You must specify one or more *name* arguments with this option. The -H option is ignored on UNIX operating systems.

Apart from exporting variables—usually by way of the export alias—the typeset command is mainly used for two purposes: setting up variables that you plan to use for calculation as integer variables, and defining special formatting options for variables.

Although the Korn shell doesn't require that a variable be declared as integer to do arithmetic with it, doing so provides some advantages. Calculations are more efficient when you use arithmetic variables in the let statement, because the shell can maintain the numeric value of the variable in an internal binary format, which is more suitable to the computer's math instructions. Likewise, there are contexts where the shell will recognize arithmetic operators in an expression if the expression contains integer variables, but it won't if the expression uses standard variables.

The general procedure for using typeset to define integer variables is straightforward. Before using variables for calculation, simply issue a typeset command to declare the variables as integers. For example,

```
typeset -i x y sum
read x y
let sum=x+y
print $sum
```

The Korn shell automatically defines an alias named integer which is equivalent to typeset -i:

```
alias integer="typeset -i"
```

You can use the alias to make your integer definitions more readable, as in the following revision of the previous example:

```
integer x y sum
read x y
let sum=x+y
print $sum
```

The second use of typeset—to set up output formatting options for variables—is of interest primarily to shell script writers who want to generate nicely formatted output. The formatting options -L, -R, -LZ, and -RZ are also of some use in generating filenames.

Suppose, for example, that you want to create a series of files that all end with a four-digit number. By writing the `typedef` statement

```
typeset -Z4 suffix
```

you can easily generate the required filenames by using code such as

```
typeset -Z4 suffix=0
while ...
do
   let suffix=suffix+1
   print sampfile.$suffix
done
```

The Korn shell automatically right-justifies the value of `$suffix` in a four-character field and fills the number out to four digits with leading zeros. Thus, it generates the series of filenames `sampefile.0001`, `sampfile.0002`, and so on.

Using *let*

Use `let` to perform an arithmetic calculation. The syntax for the `let` statement, the second major element in the shell's support for arithmetic, is simple. It is

```
let expr
```

For *expr*, write an expression that consists of terms and operators. A term is a variable or a literal integer number—for example, 3 or 512. A literal integer number is assumed to be written in base 10. You can specify another base using the format *radix#number*, where *radix* is the number base, and *number* is the value of the number. For a radix greater than 10, digits consist of the characters 0 through 9 and A through Z. For example, in radix 16 (hexadecimal), the digits are 0 through 9 and A through F.

Table 12.4 shows the arithmetic operators supported by the Korn shell for use in arithmetic expressions.

Table 12.4. Arithmetic operators in the Korn shell.

Operator	Expression	Value of Expression
-	-exp	Unary minus—the negative of exp
!	!exp	0 when exp is non-zero; Otherwise, 1
~	~exp	Complement of exp
*	exp1 * exp2	Product of exp1 and exp2
/	exp1 / exp2	Quotient of dividing exp1 by exp2
%	exp1 % exp2	Remainder of dividing exp1 by exp2
+	exp1 + exp2	Sum of exp1 and exp2

Operator	Expression	Value of Expression
-	exp1 - exp2	Difference of exp2 from exp1
<<	exp1 << exp2	exp1 is shifted left exp2 bits
>>	exp1 >> exp2	exp1 is shifted right exp2 bits
<=	exp1 <= exp2	1 if exp1 is less than or equal to exp2; otherwise, 0
>=	exp1 >= exp2	1 if exp1 is greater than or equal to exp2; otherwise, 0
<	exp1 < exp2	1 if exp1 is less than exp2; otherwise, 0
>	exp1 > exp2	1 if exp1 is greater than exp2; otherwise, 0
==	exp1 == exp2	1 if exp1 is equal to exp2; otherwise, 0
!=	exp1 != exp2	1 if exp1 is not equal to exp2; otherwise, 0
&	exp1 & exp2	Bitwise AND of exp1 and exp2
^	exp1 ^ exp2	Exclusive OR of exp1 and exp2
¦	exp1 ¦ exp2	Bitwise OR of exp1 and exp2
&&	exp1 && exp2	1 if exp1 is non-zero and exp2 is non-zero; otherwise, 0
¦¦	exp1 ¦¦ exp2	1 if exp1 is non-zero or exp2 is non-zero; otherwise, 0
=	var = exp	Assigns the value of exp to identifier id
+=	var += exp	Add exp to variable id
-=	var -= exp	Subtracts exp from variable id
*=	var *= exp	Multiplies var by exp
/=	var /= exp	Divides var by exp
%=	var %= exp	Assigns the remainder of var divided by exp to var
<<=	var <<= exp	Shifts var left exp bits
>>=	var >>= exp	Shifts var right exp bits
&=	var &= exp	Assigns the bitwise AND of var and exp to var
¦=	var ¦= exp	Assigns the bitwise OR of var and exp to var
^=	var ^= exp	Assigns the exclusive OR of var and exp to var

The Korn shell also supports expression grouping using parentheses. An expression in parentheses is evaluated as a unit before any terms outside the expression are evaluated. Parentheses are used to override the normal precedence of operators.

Operators in Table 12.4 are listed in decreasing order of precedence. The Korn shell uses the normal precedence for arithmetic operators, which you know from the C programming language or from the use of an ordinary calculator. Because of these precedence rules, the expression $a+b*y$ is computed by first multiplying $b*y$, and then adding the product to a, just as though the expression had been written $a+(b*y)$. With parentheses, you can change the order of calculation. For example, $(a+b)*y$ would be computed by first adding a and b, and then multiplying the sum by y.

The `let` command is a shell built-in command. Like any command, it sets an exit value. The exit value of the `let` command is 0 if the value of the last or only expression computed is non-zero. Conversely, if the last or only expression evaluates to 0, the exit value of the `let` command is 1. This strange inversion is an adaptation to the `if` statement, where a command setting a zero exit value is true—that is, causes execution of the `then` clause—and a command setting a non-zero exit value is false—that is, causes execution of the `else` clause.

For example, because of the `let` command's inverted exit value, the statement `if let "a == b"`, when a and b are equal, is considered true. The logical result of the equality comparison would be 1, which is equivalent to `if let 1`. The last expression has a value of 1. Therefore, the exit value from `let` is 0, and the `if` statement is considered true, thus invoking the `then` clause as expected.

Notice that you need to quote operators used in a `let` expression that are special to the shell. The command `let prod=x¦y` would give very strange results if it were written without quotes. The shell would see a pipe between the two commands `let prod=x` and `y`. Acceptable quoting is any of the following forms:

```
let "prod=x¦y"
let prod="x¦y"
let prod=x\¦y
```

Many Korn shell users use the convention of always quoting an expression in its entirety and, thereby, avoid the problem of shell metacharacters entirely.

Take another look at the syntax of the `let` command. Notice that each of its terms are arbitrary expressions. A command such as `let x+y` is valid, but it is ordinarily of little use. This is because the sum of variables x and y is computed but the result is thrown away. You should use an assignment expression—for example, `let sum=x+y`—to retain the result of the calculation in a variable named `sum` for later reference. The only time when it makes sense to evaluate an expression without assigning the result to a new variable is when the purpose of the `let` command is to set a command exit value—namely, for use in statements such as if and while. In these cases, however, you can use a more convenient form of the let statement: the (( )) expression.

A statement such as

```
if (( x+y < 25 ))
then ...
fi
```

is more clearly readable than the equivalent if let "x+y < 25". An additional advantage is that using quotes to hide operators is unnecessary inside an (( )) expression. The ((and)) operators are in effect a special kind of parentheses. They notify the Korn shell that the text they enclose is intended to be an arithmetic expression; this turns off the normal interpretation of metacharacters such as < and ¦, and it permits the unambiguous interpretation of these symbols as operators. Compatibility with the Bourne shell isn't compromised, for the ((and)) operators don't occur in shell scripts written for the Bourne shell.

You can use the (( )) expression form wherever the let command itself would be valid and in a number of other places as well. Unlike the let command, however, the (( )) syntax permits only one expression between the doubled parentheses.

You can use arithmetic expressions in any of the following contexts: as an array subscript, as arguments of the let command, inside doubled parentheses (( )), as the shift count in shift, as operands of the -eq, -ne, -gt, -lt, -ge, and -le operators in test, [, and [[commands, as resource limits in ulimit, or as the right-hand side of an assignment statement—but only when the variable name being assigned was previously defined as an integer variable with the typeset or integer statement.

Some Practical Examples of Arithmetic

Having reviewed all the basics of arithmetic in the Korn shell, you should take a look now at some specific examples. For instance,

```
$ x=4 y=5
$ print x+y
x+y
```

is an example of how not to use arithmetic expressions. The first command line assigns numeric values to the non-integer variables x and y. The print line attempts to print their sum, but the print command isn't one of the places where arithmetic expressions are supported. The result is fully compatible with the Bourne shell. The print statement simply echoes its arguments.

Now look at a first attempt to fix the problem:

```
$ let x=4 y=5
$ print $x+$y
4+5
```

The assignment statements have been changed to a `let` command, which has no significant affect on anything. The dollar signs on the `print` statement help the shell recognize that x and y are variables. The variable references are substituted with their respective values, but the Korn shell still persists in failing to recognize the presence of an expression on the `print` command argument. There is, in fact, no way to get the shell to recognize an expression and to evaluate it on a `print` command.

Here is a working solution:

```
$ integer x=4 y=5
$ let sum=x+y
$ print $sum
9
```

The key element of the solution is the use of the `let` statement to calculate the sum. It stores the calculated result in a new variable called `sum`, which can be referenced later.

You might think that using a hand calculator would be an easier way to do a simple arithmetic problem at the keyboard, and I would tend to agree with you. At the keyboard, a more effective approach is simply use the `expr` command. For example,

```
$ expr 4 + 5
9
```

expr achieves the same result at the keyboard, but it is of little use inside shell scripts, where the result of the `expr` calculation—written to standard output—isn't readily available for use.

Now consider this example of a counter-controlled loop:

```
integer i=0
while (( i<5 ))
do
    i=i+1
    print $i
done
```

This little program simply prints the numbers 1 through 5. Notice the use of an assignment statement instead of a `let` command to increment i. This works only because the variable i was previously declared an integer. The example works fine typed in at the keyboard. Try it.

For a more practical example, consider the following:

```
$ typeset -i16 hex
$ hex=125
$ print $hex
7D
```

Here, the variable hex has been declared to be integer and to be represented in base 16. The second line assigns a normal integer numeric value to the hex variable, and the third line prints it out. Magically, though, the effect of the 16 from the typeset command becomes clear: The value of hex is shown in hexadecimal (base 16) notation. Going the other way—that is, converting from hexadecimal to decimal—is just as easy:

```
$ integer n
$ n=16#7d
$ print $n
125
```

At the keyboard, once you've declared the hex and n variables, they remain in effect indefinitely. You can use them repeatedly to convert between hexadecimal. For example,

```
$ hex=4096; print $hex
1000
$ n=16#1000; print $n
4096
```

Shell Programming

Although the main thrust of the Korn shell's features is to enhance productivity at the keyboard, the Korn shell also provides a number of boons for writing shell scripts, making the Korn shell an attractive environment for program development. In this section, I review the Korn shell enhancements that apply to shell script writing. Of course, all the programming constructs of the Bourne shell are available, so the material in Chapter 11, "Bourne Shell," pertains equally to the Korn shell; it won't be repeated here.

The Korn shell extensions useful in writing shell scripts are conditional expressions, which enhance the flexibility of if, while, and until statements; array variables, integer variables, extended variable reference expressions, and arithmetic expressions; a new select statement for constructing a menu of prompts from which the user may select a choice; extended support for functions, including autoload functions; an enhanced form of the command expression—$(...)—that is simpler to use than the backquoted form '...', the command operator for coprocessing—¦&.

The section "Variables" earlier in this chapter discussed the Korn shell's extended variable support, including array variables, integer variables, variable reference expressions, and arithmetic expressions. The other new features are explained below.

Conditional Expressions

The if, while, and until statements support two new kinds of expressions. The (( )) doubled parentheses operator, which evaluates an arithmetic expression, enables you to perform complex arithmetic tests. A zero result is considered true, and a non-zero result is considered false. You may also write an extended conditional test expression as the argument of if, while, or until. A conditional test expression has the general form

```
[[ conditional-exp ]]
```

where `conditional-exp` is any of the forms shown in Table 12.2.

Notice that the conditional expression forms are similar to those of the `test` or `[ ]` expression. The Korn shell supports the `test` and `[ ]` expressions identically with how the Bourne shell does. The `[[ ]]` expression provides extended capabilities without compromising compatibility with the Bourne shell.

Table 12.5. Conditional expressions.

Expression	Condition When True
`-r file`	`file` exists.
`-w file`	`file` exists and has write permission enabled. The file might not be writable even if write permission is set, or if it is within a file system that has been mounted read-only.
`-x file`	`file` exists and has execute permission set. The file might not actually be executable. Directories usually have the execute permission flag set.
`-f file`	`file` exists and is a regular file.
`-d file`	`file` exists and is a directory.
`-c file`	`file` exists and is a character-special file.
`-b file`	`file` exists and is a block-special file.
`-p file`	`file` exists and is a named pipe.
`-u file`	The `set-uid` permission flag is set for `file`.
`-g file`	The `set-group-id` permission flag is set for `file`.
`-k file`	The `sticky` permission flag is set for `file`.
`-s file`	`file` has a size greater than zero.
`-L file`	`file` is a symbolic link.
`-O file`	`file` has an owner ID equal to the effective user ID of the current process.
`-G file`	`file` has a group ID equal to the effective group ID of the current process.
`-S file`	`file` is a socket.
`-t [ fildes ]`	The file descriptor `fildes`—whose default is 1—is a terminal.
`-o option`	The named option is set.
`-z string`	`string` is a zero-length string.

Expression	Condition When True
`-n string`	`string` is not a zero-length string.
`string`	`string` is not a zero-length, or null, string.
`string = pat`	`string` matches the pattern `pat`.
`string != pat`	`string` does not match the pattern `pat`.
`s1 < s2`	String `s1` is less than string `s2`. That is, `pat` collates before `s2`.
`s1 > s2`	String `s1` is greater than string `s2`. That is, `pat` collates after `s2`.
`file1 -nt file2`	File `file1` is newer than file `file2`.
`file1 -ot file2`	File `file1` is older than file `file2`.
`file1 -ef file2`	File `file1` is the same file as file `file2`.
`e1 -eq e2`	Expressions `e1` and `e2` are equal.
`e1 -ne e2`	Expressions `e1` and `e2` are not equal.
`e1 -gt e2`	Expression `e1` is greater than `e2`.
`e1 -ge e2`	Expression `e1` is greater than or equal to `e2`.
`e1 -lt e2`	Expression `e1` is less than `e2`.
`e1 -le e2`	Expression `e1` is less than or equal to `e2`.

Functions

The Korn shell fully supports Bourne shell functions. It also provides some extensions.

Defining Functions

In addition to the Bourne shell syntax, the Korn shell supports the following alternate syntax for defining a function:

```
function identifier
{
    command-list
}
```

Using Variables in Functions

The Korn shell allows a function to have local variables. A local variable exists only during the execution of the function and is destroyed when the function returns. A local variable can have the same name as a variable in the calling environment. During execution of the function, the local variable hides the outer variable. You define a local variable with the `typeset` command. For example,

```
function square
{
    typeset product
    let "product=$1*$1"
    print $product
    return
}
```

Using Traps in Functions

In the Bourne shell, traps set with the `trap` command remain in force after the function's return. In the Korn shell, traps set in the calling environment are saved and restored.

You can use the `typeset` command with option `-f` to manage functions. The `-f` option has four forms:

`typeset -f`	Lists the functions currently defined and their definitions. The predefined alias `functions` does the same thing.
`typeset -ft name ...`	Activates the `xtrace` option whenever function name is invoked. Tracing reverts to its former state when the function returns.
`typeset -fx name ...`	Defines functions as exported. Exported functions are inherited by shell scripts. However, a function cannot be exported to another instance of `ksh`. There is no method for passing function definitions through the command environment, as there is for variables.
`typeset -fu name ...`	Defines functions for autoload. A call to an autoload function before its definition is recognized as a function call when the function has been declared with `typeset`. The Korn shell searches the directories named in the `FPATH` variable for a file that has the same name as the function. If the Korn shell finds such a file, the function is loaded and executed, and the definition is retained as though an inline definition of the function had been read at that point.

Using Autoload Functions

Autoload functions provide superior performance versus conventional shell scripts, because they are retained in memory for fast execution on repeated calls, yet unreferenced functions incur no overhead other than processing of the `typeset -fu` command. You create autoload functions in much the same manner as shell scripts, except that the definition file should be in the form of a function. That is, it should begin with the statement `function name`. To use autoload functions, you must set the FPATH environment variable to the directory or directories to be searched—in the same manner as you set the PATH environment variable—and you must declare the functions in advance with the `typeset -fu` command.

Any function definition is eligible for use as an autoload function, although frequently used functions are preferred. Remember, once an autoload function has been read, its definition is retained in the shell's available memory. Large programs should be written as conventional shell scripts instead of as autoload functions, unless the program is heavily used.

Undefining Functions

To undefine a function, use the `unset` command:

```
unset -f name ....
```

The named functions are purged from memory, and any `typeset -fu` declaration for the named function is deleted. The `unset -f` command is not often used, but it is particularly useful when debugging a function. Using `unset -f` is the only way to force the shell to reread an autoload function definition file.

When To Use Functions

Functions are a handy way of creating new keyboard commands. Because a function executes as part of the current shell environment, a directory change made with the `cd` command remains in force after the function exits. This isn't true for ordinary commands and shell scripts. Because I almost always like to take a quick peek at a directory's contents after changing to it, I created the following short function definition and added it to my login profile:

```
function go
{
    cd $1
    /usr/bin/ls -FC
}
```

The go function, used in the form go *dirname*, not only changes to the directory but also prints a sorted listing so that I can see immediately what's in the directory.

Adding the go function to my login profile means that it's always present in the shell memory. Because go is a small function, this does no harm, considering how often I use it. For larger functions, it is better to store the function definition in a separate file and to replace the function definition in the profile with a `typeset -fu` declaration, thus making the function an autoload function.

Scanning Arguments with *getopts*

The Bourne shell provides negligible assistance with the processing of command-line options. As a result, many user-written shell scripts process options clumsily at best, and they often don't support the generalized UNIX command format for options. The `getopt` command, long a standard part of the UNIX command set, helps a little. The Korn shell, however, goes one step further by adding a built-in command called `getopts`, which provides the same power and flexibility to script writers that C programmers have long enjoyed.

The syntax of the `getopts` built-in command is straightforward:

```
getopts options var [ arg ... ]
```

For `options`, provide a string that defines the letters that can legally appear as command-line options. If an option letter can be followed by a value string, indicate this in the `options` string by following the letter with `:`. For example, `I:` represents the option syntax `-Istring`.

If `options` begins with `:`, the Korn shell provides user error handling. The invalid option letter is placed in `OPTARG`, and `var` is set to `?`. Without `:`, the `getopts` command issues an automatic error message on an invalid letter and sets `var` to `?` so that you can recognize that an error occurred and skip the invalid option, but it doesn't tell you what the invalid letter is.

For `var`, write the name of a variable to receive the option letter. The shell stores the letter in `var` when it identifies the letter as an option in the command line.

For `arg`, write the argument list from the command line that is to be scanned for options. The `arg` list is usually written in the form `$*` or `"$@"`.

For reasons of practicality, the `getopts` command cannot scan, identify, and process all option letters in a command on one invocation. Rather, each time you call `getopts`, you get the next option on the command line. Of course, `getopts` can't look at the real command line that invoked your shell script. It examines the `arg` list that you provide with `getopts`, stepping once through the list on each call.

When you call `getopts`, it starts by determining its current position in the `arg` list. If its current position is within a word and the word starts with `-`, the next character in the word is taken as an option letter. If this is your first call to getopts or the last invocation finished scanning a word, getopts examines the next *arg* for a leading hyphen.

In any case, when getopts identifies an option, it stores the letter in *var*. If the option takes a value string—indicated in the *option* string by being followed by :—the option value is scanned and stored in a predefined variable named OPTARG. If getopts has started a new *arg* variable, it increments the predefined variable OPTIND to indicate which argument it is working on—1, 2, and so on. It then updates its position in the argument list and exits.

After calling getopts, you inspect the *var* variable to find out which option has been identified. If the option takes a value, you'll find its value string in the predefined variable OPTARG. The return value from getopts is zero if it finds an option, or non-zero if it can find no more options in the command-line argument list.

The code for using getopts is almost a set piece that you need to memorize. Listing 12.1 is a shell program for scanning command-line options like those you might find in a script file. Here, the example merely prints the options it recognizes.

Listing 12.1. Scanning options with getopts.

```
# A routine to scan options
# ... allowable options are -a, -c, -R, -Aname, or -Iname.

while getopts :acRA:I: KEY $*
do
    case $KEY in
    a)    print Found option -a;;
    c)    print Found option -c ;;
    R)    print Found option -R ;;
    A)    print Found option -A, value is "'$OPTARG'" ;;
    I)    print Found option -I, value is "'$OPTARG'" ;;
    *)    print -u2 Illegal option: -$OPTARG
    esac
done
# Strip option arguments, leaving positional args
shift OPTIND-1
print ARGS: $*
```

The code in Listing 12.1 is executable. Enter the statements into a file and mark the file executable with chmod +x *filename* (refer to the "Keeping Secrets: File and Directory Permissions" section in Chapter 3). Then invoke the file's name with a sample set of option letters and arguments. You'll see the shell script's idea of the options and positional arguments that you entered.

There are two special points to note about Listing 12.1. First, the *option* string for the getopts command begins with a colon (:). When the *option* string begins with a colon, the `getopts` command provides user error handling; an unrecognized option letter is put into the `OPTARG` variable, and the *var* keyletter variable is set to ?. You can test explicitly for ? as the letter value, or you can simply provide your own error message for any unrecognized option letter.

If the *option* string doesn't begin with :, `getopts` provides its own error handling. Upon finding an unrecognized option letter, `getopts` prints an error message and sets *var* to ?, but it doesn't set the option letter in `OPTARG`. Therefore, although you can tell that an invalid option has been found, you don't know what the invalid letter is. Of course, an invalid option letter is simply any letter that doesn't appear in the *option* string.

Second, note the use of the `shift` statement to identify the remaining position arguments from the original command line. By itself, the `getopts` command doesn't strip words containing options from the *arg* list. However, after identifying options with `getopts`, you don't want to see them again when you examine the remaining positional arguments. You must throw the option words away yourself. The `shift` statement, inherited from the Bourne shell, does the job eminently well, assisted by the arithmetic expression handling syntax of the Korn shell. The expression `OPTIND-1` computes the number of positional arguments remaining on the command line. Notice that, because `OPTIND-1` occurs in the `shift` command line in the position of an expression, `OPTIND` is automatically recognized as a variable reference, and you don't need to write a dollar sign in front of it.

Using the *select* Statement

If you've ever written a shell script that enables the user to specify values either on the command line or to be prompted for them, you know what an elaborate piece of drudgery such a user-interface nicety can be. The Korn shell helps you out, though, with a new built-in command that automates the entire process—from printing a selection menu to prompting for the user's choice to reading it.

In fact, because the user might choose an illegal option—requiring you to repeat the menu selection process—or in case you want to display the menu repeatedly until the user decides to quit, the `select` statement is actually an iterative statement, much like `while` or `until`. You must use the `break` statement to terminate execution of `select`.

The syntax of the `select` statement is

```
select identifier [ in word ... ]
do command-list
done
```

The `select` statement first displays the word list (*word* ...) in one or more columns. If the `LINES` variable is set and specifies an integer number, it is taken as the maximum number of lines available for displaying the word list. If there are more items to display than this maximum, the list is broken into a multicolumn display. Each *word* is prefixed by a number starting at one. *word* may be a single word or a quoted string. It is scanned for variable and command substitutions prior to display.

In effect, the list of strings that you specify for *word* . . . becomes a series of menu items, which are automatically numbered and displayed for the user.

The select statement next displays the value of variable PS3 as a menu prompt. By default, the value of PS3 is #?, suggesting that the user should enter a number. If you want a different prompt, assign a value to PS3 before you execute the select statement.

The select statement next reads a reply from the user. The entire line entered by the user is saved in the special shell variable REPLY. If the user enters a null line—that is, presses Enter or Return without typing anything—select redisplays the list and issues the prompt again without invoking *command-list*. Otherwise, if the user entered a number, the variable named *identifier* is set to the *word* corresponding to that number. That is, entering 1 sets *identifier* to the first *word*; entering 2 sets *identifier* to the second *word*; and so on. If the number is greater than the number of words or if the user input isn't a number, *select* sets *identifier* to null. In any case, the *select* statement then executes *command-list*.

Consider the following example, in which the user is given a choice of colors from which to select. The select statement continues to execute until the user chooses one of the allowable color names.

```
PS3="Select color by number (e.g., 3):"
select color in Blue Green Yellow Red White Black Burnt-umber "Natural Wool"
do case $color in\
    Blue ¦ Green ¦ Yellow ¦ Red ¦ White ¦ Black ¦
    Burnt-umber ¦ "Natural Wool") break ;;
    *) print "Please enter a number from 1-8. Try again." ;;
    esac
done
print "Your color choice is: $color"
```

Notice the use of quotes to specify Natural Wool as one of the menu choices. If the words were not quoted, the select statement would view them as two separate menu items, and the user would be able to select either Natural (item 8) or Wool (item 9).

Also note that the example does nothing to execute the menu choice procedure repetitively until the user enters a valid selection. Iteration of select is automatic. It is the valid choices that must do something special to break out of the select loop—in this case, by executing the break statement.

Nothing prevents you from implementing a primitive menu-driven system with select. Listing 12.2 uses the select statement to offer the user a choice of application actions. The example continues to execute until the user chooses the Exit item. Then the select statement and any shell script in which it might be contained is terminated with the exit shell built-in command.

Listing 12.2. Implementing a menu system with `select`.

```
PS3=Choice?
select choice in "Enter Transactions" \
        "Print trial balance" \
        "Print invoices" \
        "Exit"
do case "$choice" in
    "Enter Transactions")   . daily-trans ;;
    "Print trial balance") . trial-balance ;;
    "Print invoices")       . invoices ;;
    "Exit")                 print "That's all, folks!"; exit ;;
    *)  print -u2 "Wrong choice. Enter a number (1-4)."
    esac
done
```

Using Coprocesses

The Bourne shell supports a minimal amount of communication between processes—typically, by way of the pipe operator. For example, you can invoke the ed line editor from a shell script to make a specific text change by using a command such as the one shown below.

```
(echo "/^Payroll
+1
i"
cat newlist
echo "."
echo "w"
echo "q"
) ¦ ed - paylist
```

This form of intertask communication is sufficient if you need only to pass some data to another command or to read its output. Suppose, however, that in the Listing 12.4 you wanted to provide for the case that the file `paylist` doesn't contain a line beginning with `Payroll` by skipping the `insert`, `write`, and `quit` editor commands. With the Bourne shell, you couldn't do this. With the Korn shell, you can maintain an interactive session with the `ed` command, with your program providing the instructions to `ed` and responding to its output.

To use coprocessing—a fancy term for the simultaneous execution of two procedures that read each other's output—you first must launch the program with which you want to communicate as a background process, by using the special operator `¦&`. The `¦&` operator is intended to suggest a combination of `&` (background execution) and `¦` (the pipe operator). When the background command is started, its standard and standard output are assigned to pipes connected to your own process—one for writing to the command and one for reading the command's output.

The simplest way of sending a line to the coprocess is to use the print -p command. The -p option tells print to write to the coprocess's input pipe. To read output from the coprocess, use read -p. Once again, the -p tells read to read from the coprocess pipe.

Using these facilities, you could rewrite the preceding procedure like this:

```
ed paylist ¦&
exec 3>&p
exec 4<&p
read -u4             # discard initial message line
print -u3 P          # Turn on prompting
print -u3 "/^Payroll" # search for the insert location
read -u3             # read prompt indicating success or failure
case "$REPLY" in
    '*'*) # search must have been successful
        print -u3 i
        cat text >&3 # file containing data to be inserted
        print -u3 .
        read -u4 # read the ending prompt
        print -u3 w; read -u4
        print -u3 q
        ;;
    *)   # not found
        print -u3 q
        echo "invalid paylist file"
        exit 1
        ;;
    esac
done
```

You should note the following in this example: The exec command (exec 3>&p) is used to move the coprocess input pipe from its default location to a numbered file descriptor. The exec command (exec 4<&p) is used again to move the coprocess output pipe to number file descriptor 4. Subsequent read and print commands specify the file descriptor as the source or sink of the operation, using the -u option. Ordinary UNIX commands can write to the coprocess by redirecting to file descriptor 3 (cat filename >&3).

> **NOTE:** Use read -p or print -p to read from or write to the coprocess *until* you have moved the coprocess input or output to a number file descriptor; *then* read or write to that file descriptor: read -u4 or print -u3.

Admittedly, the program using coprocessing is more complicated than the earlier version, but it is also safer. The Bourne shell version would have added new lines after the first line if the search for Payroll failed. The Korn shell version fails gracefully, without damaging the paylist file.

Notice that the Korn shell example of coprocessing in Listing 12.5 contains an incomplete `cat` command. This is because you need a special syntax to transcribe a file into the coprocess pipe. The standard Bourne shell syntax—`>filename` and `>&fildes`—is inadequate. This is because `>filename` and `>&fildes` provide you with no way to reference the coprocess input and output pipes.

Actually, by using a Korn shell feature designed especially to support coprocessing, you can use I/O redirection to send output to or read input from the background process with any UNIX command. The technique required is to switch the default input and output pipes created by the `¦&` operator to explicit file descriptors. You use the `exec` command to do this:

```
exec 3>&p
```

When used with the `exec` command, this special form of the output redirection operator causes the pipe for writing to the coprocess to be assigned to file descriptor 3. (The lack of a command on the `exec` statement, of course, tips off the Korn shell that you want to modify the current environment rather than execute another program.)

Similarly, the following code reassigns the pipe for reading from the coprocess:

```
exec 4<&p
```

If you place these lines at the front of the `ed` example, the `cat` command can be written in the familiar fashion—by using I/O redirection to an open file descriptor. For example,

```
cat newlist >&3
```

Of course, the new syntax for the `exec` statement is a terrible kludge, amounting to a form of syntactic code that is difficult to remember. However, the basic outlines of coprocessing, including the `¦&` operator and the `-p` options for `print` and `read`, are straightforward enough, as is the underlying concept. Coprocessing is a powerful capability, making it possible to do things in a shell script that previously required the C programming language. So sharpen up your coding pencils, and try your hand at coprocessing.

Customizing

It almost might be said that the term *shell* refers to what you have before you customize it—an empty shell. Of course, that's a gross exaggeration. The shell is more feature-laden than most programs you'll get an opportunity to shake a stick at. Still, the Korn shell permits so much customization that it's no exaggeration to say you might find another user's login environment so foreign as to be almost unusable by you. Indeed, some places try to place a limit on user customization.

There are many ways to adapt the Korn shell to your preferred way of working. Of course, bear in mind that if you're a beginning UNIX user, you might not have many preferences to cater to. As your familiarity with UNIX and with the Korn shell increases, you'll find many conveniences, shorthand methods, and customary usages that seem comfortable to you. The Korn shell helps you along by enabling you to encapsulate favorite behaviors into your login profile script and elsewhere.

Customizing the Korn shell begins with your login profile script, which is named `.profile` and which resides in your home directory. The file `$HOME/.profile` is of special importance because the Korn shell executes it every time you log in—or, more precisely, every time you launch an interactive shell.

Often the system administrator will place a starter `.profile` script in your home directory when he creates your login. Don't let yourself be cowed into thinking that there is anything sacrosanct in the hand-me-down `.profile` given to you. The contents of your `.profile` script affect only you. It is specific to your login name and home directory. Altering it could conceivably affect only those people who have your password and can log in with your login name. Almost always, that is only you. Therefore, you should feel free to add to, change, or delete anything in the `.profile` script, including deleting the whole file, if you want to. It doesn't matter to the shell. The `.profile` is supported only for your convenience; it isn't needed for Korn shell operation.

Your `.profile` script is, in fact, a shell script. Any shell programming techniques valid in a shell script are valid in the `.profile` script. If you're not a shell programmer, don't be daunted. Useful login profiles can be made up that contain nothing more than straightforward UNIX and shell commands, without an `if` or `while` statement in sight. If you know how to use shell conditional and iterative statements, so much the better. Don't, however, think that mastery of them is essential to writing good profile scripts. It isn't.

Your `.profile` script is an ideal place to put your favorite things. You might want to do the following things with your `.profile`. You should also observe the order in which the following are listed. Placing similar things together helps simplify the job of maintaining your `.profile`.

- Set control keys with the `stty` command.
- Set environment variables.
- Set local variables for shell control.
- Define aliases that you like to use.
- Define functions that you like to use, including autoload functions.
- Set your favorite shell options.
- Execute commands that you want to run each time you log in.

Setting Control Keys with *stty*

Use the `stty` command to establish the control keys that you prefer to use. The default Erase key is #, and the default Kill key is @. Both are bad choices because their use as terminal control characters conflicts with their use as ordinary text characters. You should redefine these keys with a statement similar to

```
stty erase '^H' kill '^U' intr '^C'
```

This example uses the caret (^) in front of an upper or lower case letter to designate a control key combination. Thus, `erase '^H'` specifies the Ctrl-h key combination as your backspace key. Of course, you would prefer to specify the actual characters generated by your backspace key as the value for the `erase` character—if you can figure out what it is. The presence of a caret forces the use of quote marks. The caret is special to the shell; without quotes, it will cause improper interpretation of the `stty` command. (For details about the `stty` command, refer to your UNIX user's reference manual.)

Setting Environment Variables

At the very least, you'll want to make sure that the variables `PATH` and `MAIL` have values. Usually, you'll want to set a great many more. If you use Bourne shell syntax, your variable settings will look like this:

```
PATH=/usr/bin:/usr/ucb:/usr/local/bin:$HOME/bin:
MAIL=/var/spool/mail/$LOGNAME
MAILCHECK=60
FCEDIT=/usr/bin/vi
VISUAL=/usr/bin/vi
export PATH MAIL MAILCHECK FCEDIT VISUAL
```

Alternatively, you can use the Korn shell `export` alias to avoid the need to remember to add each variable that you set to the `export` variable list—it does little good to set a variable if you don't export it. Using the `export` alias, the previous code would look like this:

```
export PATH=/usr/bin:/usr/ucb:/usr/local/bin:$HOME/bin:
export MAIL=/var/spool/mail/$LOGNAME
export MAILCHECK=60
export FCEDIT=/usr/bin/vi
export VISUAL=/usr/bin/vi
```

When you write your environment variable settings, keep in mind that some are automatically set by the UNIX login processor. Your system administrator can also provide a login script to set values before your `.profile` script runs. For example, the `PATH` and `MAIL` variables usually have initial values already set when your script starts. Overriding the default `PATH` variable is usually a good idea; you should have full control over your program search path, starting with its initial value. Overriding the default `MAIL` or `MAILPATH` variable is risky, unless you know what mail subsystems are in use.

Setting Local Variables for Shell Control

Local variables are variables that the shell uses but which don't be exported. They include FCEDIT—which designates the text editor to be used by the fc command—and the PS1 variable—which is your primary prompt string. You might also want to define a few local variables to hold the names of directories that you commonly access, which enables you to use cd $dir instead of the longer full pathname.

Defining Aliases

Define the aliases that you like to use. You must invent your own aliases; each user tends to have a different set. Most users, however, make up some aliases for the ls command. You can even redefine the default behavior of the ls command by defining an alias named ls. Here are some typical aliases that I like to use:

```
alias lx='/usr/bin/ls -FC'
alias l='/usr/bin/ls -l'
alias pg='/usr/bin/pg -cns -p"Page %d:"'
alias -t vi
```

Notice that in most cases I tend to use the full pathname for commands in the alias definition. I do this because it eliminates directory searches for the command, and it provides much the same effect as the Korn shell's alias tracking mechanism. Note also the explicit use of the alias -t command to request the shell to track the vi command. The shell looks up the full pathname of the vi command and defines an alias named vi for me so that the plain command vi has all the performance but none of the typing overhead of /usr/bin/vi.

Defining Functions

Define any functions that you like to use, including autoload functions. I use some function definitions as keyboard shorthand because a function can do things that an alias can't. For example, you might want to use the go function, described earlier in this chapter, for switching directories.

Setting Shell Options

If you find yourself frequently setting the same shell options at the command line, you could set them in your .profile instead. To set the preferred shell options, use the set command. For example, if you prefer to use the vi mode for command history and editing, and you want full job control support, you might add these two lines to your .profile:

```
set -o vi
set -o monitor
```

Executing Commands Every Time You Login

Execute commands that you like to run every time you login. For example, you might want to run the who command to find out who's currently logged in. Likewise, the df, which isn't present on all UNIX systems, displays the amount of free disk space available on mounted filesystems.

Executing Your *.profile* After Changing It

Whenever you change your .profile script, you should execute it before you log out. If you make an error in your script, you might have difficulty logging back in. To test your .profile script, you can run it with the . (dot) command:

```
$ . ./.profile
```

Be sure to leave a space after the first period: it's the command name, and ./.profile is the command argument. (Although .profile will usually be adequate by itself, you might need to use ./.profile if your current directory is not in the search path.) The dot command not only executes the script but also leaves any environment changes in effect after the script terminates.

Alternatively, you can run the script with ksh -v to have the shell execute the script and print each statement as it is executed:

```
$ ksh -v ./.profile
```

Using the -n option would cause the Korn shell to read your .profile and check it for syntax errors, but not execute the commands it contains.

Creating an *ENV* File

After you have your .profile set up the way you want, you're ready to tackle the environment file. The environment file is any file that contains shell scripts that you designate by assigning its pathname to the ENV variable. The shell automatically executes the ENV file whenever you start a new invocation of the shell, and when it executes a command. If you've ever shelled out from commands like pg and vi, you know that when you call the shell again, some environment settings, such as aliases, aren't carried over from your login shell. By placing aliases, function definitions, and even global variable settings in a separate file and setting ENV to its pathname in your .profile script, you can ensure that you have a consistent Korn shell environment at all times.

Don't get carried away, though. In some cases, the file designated by the pathname value of ENV is executed in front of shell commands that you call. Because many UNIX commands are implemented as shell scripts, this means that a large environment file can add surprising overhead to some unexpected places.

NOTE: As a rule, the environment file is executed as a preliminary step to invoking a shell script only when the shell script requires a new invocation of the Korn shell. This usually isn't the case when you invoke a shell script by its name.

To use an environment file create a file that contains the aliases, functions, and exported variable settings that you prefer. Then add the statement export `ENV=`*pathname*, where *pathname* is the full pathname of your environment file, to your `.profile`. The environment file will become effective the next time you log in. It will become effective immediately if you test your `.profile` with the following `.` command:

```
. .profile
```

Adding Settings for Other Programs to Your .profile

Customizing your environment doesn't stop with using the login profile and environment file to establish shell options and settings you want; it's also a handy place to put settings used by other programs. For example, one way to customize your `vi` editing environment is by defining a variable `EXINIT` that contains the commands `vi` will run every time you start it. You could place the `EXINIT` variable setting in your login profile to establish your preferred `vi` settings. Many UNIX commands respond to environment variables, which enables you to customize these commands in your login profile.

Job Control

The idea of a *job* may be somewhat foreign to UNIX users, for in UNIX most of the action is interactive. Nevertheless, even the Bourne shell provides basic tools for running background jobs, and UNIX the operating system has always provided such tools. The more recent releases of UNIX have even enhanced background job management.

The basic idea of a background job is simple. It's a program that can run without prompts or other manual interaction and can run in parallel with other active processes. With the Bourne shell, you launch a background job with the & operator. For example, the command `cc myprog.c &` compiles the source program `myprog.c` without tying up the terminal. You can do other work, even edit files with a full-screen editor, while the `cc` command works behind the scenes.

Enhancements to the `stty` command and the terminal driver in recent UNIX releases have added a new control key to your terminal: Suspend. Suspend is usually Ctrl-z. This new tool enables you to take an interactive program that you're currently running, such as a `vi` editing session, and to put it temporarily into the background. If the program wants to talk to your terminal, the system suspends the program. Otherwise, it continues running.

The Korn shell adds some tools that help you manage the family of processes you can accumulate. These tools consist of the `jobs`, `kill`, `wait`, `bg`, and `fg` commands.

To use the Korn shell's job control tools, you must have the `monitor` option enabled. Normally, the `monitor` option is enabled for you automatically; it's the default for interactive shells. If your operating system doesn't support job management, the default for the `monitor` option is off. Even without operating system support—the Suspend key and `stty` function is an operating system service, not a Korn shell service—you can still use some of the Korn shell's job control tools, but you must set the `monitor` option on yourself. You do that with the command `set -o monitor`.

The `jobs` command, which takes no arguments, simply lists the jobs that you currently have active. The output of `jobs` looks like this:

```
$ jobs
[1] + Running          xlogo&
[2] + Running          xclock -bg LightGreen&
[3] + Stopped          vi myprog.c
```

You use the `kill`, `bg`, and `fg` commands to manage jobs. When referring to a job, you use the job number shown in brackets in the output of `jobs`, preceded by a percent (%) sign. For example, `kill %1` would terminate the `xlogo` program that you currently have running. The `wait`, `kill`, `bg`, and `fg` commands can also refer to background jobs by their process ID, which you can generally obtain from the output of the `ps` command. However, the use of Korn shell job numbers is preferred, because they are simpler and safer to use than process IDs. Refer to Chapters 18 and 19 for more details on processes.

You create jobs in one of three ways by explicitly designating a command for background execution with the & operator; by switching a job into the background with the Korn shell `bg` command; or by pressing the Suspend key—usually Ctrl-z—while a foreground program is running.

By convention, a job started or switched into the background continues to run until it tries to read from your terminal. Then it is suspended by the operating system until you intervene. When it is in this state, the `jobs` command shows that the command is `Stopped`.

A job that has been stopped usually needs to talk to you before it can continue. In the previous `jobs` example, the `vi` command is shown to be stopped. The command won't continue until you reconnect it to your terminal. You do this with the `fg` command—for example, `fg %3` or `fg %vi`. The `vi` command then becomes the foreground process, and it resumes normal interactive execution with you.

NOTE: A full-screen program, such as `vi`, probably won't recognize that the screen no longer matches your last edit screen. You probably will need to press Ctrl-l to redraw the screen before you resume your edit session. Other programs that merely need your response to a prompt don't require any special action when you resume them with `fg`.

The full syntax of the `%` argument accepted by the `wait`, `kill`, `fg`, and `bg` commands is shown in Table 12.6.

Table 12.6. Job reference argument syntax.

Syntax	Meaning
`%number`	References job `number`
`%string`	References the job whose command begins with `string`
`%?string`	References the job whose command contains `string`
`%%`	The current job
`%+`	The current job (also %%)
`%-`	The previous job

The syntax of the Korn shell job control commands are summarized below.

Displaying Background Jobs and Their Status

Use the `jobs` command to display background jobs and their status. For example,

```
jobs [ -lp ] [ job ... ]
```

The `-l` option causes the `jobs` command to list the process ID for each job in addition to its job number. The `-p` option causes the `jobs` command to list only the process ID for each job instead of its job number.

If you omit the `job` arguments, `jobs` displays information about all background jobs, as in this example:

```
$ jobs
[1] + Running             xlogo&
[2] + Running             xclock -bg LightGreen&
[3] + Stopped             vi myprog.c
```

If you include `job` arguments, it displays information only for the specified jobs. For `job`, specify a process ID or a job reference beginning with `%`. For instance, to find out whether job 2 from the previous example is still running, you would enter this command:

```
$ jobs %2
[2] + Running             xclock -bg LightGreen&
```

Sending Signals to a Job

Use the `kill` command to send a signal to the specified jobs. Some signals cause a job to terminate. The TERM signal—also called signal 15, or interrupt—usually causes a job to terminate gracefully, whereas signal 9 always terminates a job but may leave files unclosed or wreak other havoc on the job that was in progress. You should use `kill -9` only when you cannot terminate the job any other way.

The `kill` command is normally a UNIX system command, but the Korn shell provides `kill` as a built-in command with enhanced capabilities. The Korn shell supports the basic functionality of the UNIX `kill` command transparently. Its syntax is

```
kill [ -signal ] job ...
```

For *signal* specify a signal number or a signal name. Signal numbers 1 through 15 are always valid. A signal name is one of a predefined list of mnemonic symbols that correspond to the valid signal numbers. Use `kill -1` to obtain a list of the valid signal names. The names TERM (terminate) and HUP (hang-up) are always valid. (Refer to your UNIX user's reference manual for more information about the `kill` and `signal` commands.)

> **NOTE:** The reason for the vagueness about signal names is that they vary from one version of UNIX to another. You'll have to use `kill -1` to find out the names that pertain specifically to your system.

For *job*, provide one or more process ID numbers or job references. Job references begin with `%`. You must provide at least one *job* argument with the `kill` command.

By way of example, suppose you have started an `xclock` process, displaying a clock on your X terminal screen:

```
$ xclock -bg LightGreen&
[4] + Running   xclock -bg LightGreen&
```

You can cancel the `xclock` window (a background job) with either of the following commands:

```
$ kill %4
```

or

```
$ kill %xclock
```

Suspending the Shell Until a Job Finishes

Use `wait` to suspend the shell until the specified job, if any, finishes. The visible effect of `wait` is simply to cause the shell not to issue another prompt to you. To get the prompt back if you decide not to wait, simply press Enter. This causes the shell to issue a prompt, and it terminates the wait command. The syntax of the wait command is

```
wait [ job ... ]
```

For job, specify one or more process ID numbers or job references that designate the job or jobs you want to wait for. If you specify no jobs, the shell waits until any job finishes. If you specify two or more jobs, the shell waits until all the specified jobs finish.

You won't use the wait command too often, but it is convenient when you have done all the interactive work you have and need the results of one or more background jobs before you continue. Without the wait command, you would have to execute the jobs command repetitively until the job or jobs that you wanted were marked Done.

One situation where the wait command comes in useful is when developing some formatted text files. You may want to run nroff or troff as background jobs, capturing the output to a disk file for review. While the nroff or troff job is running, you can edit other text files. However, when you have no other editing work to do, you'll need to wait for nroff or troff to finish because you have nothing else to do but review your previous work. A hypothetical console session might look like this:

```
$ vi chap1.nr
$ nroff -me chap1.nr >chap1.nrf &
[4] + Running     nroff -me chap1.nr
$ vi chap2.nr
$ nroff -me chap2.nr > chap2.nrf &
[5]   Running     nroff -me chap2.nr
$ jobs
[4]   Running     nroff -me chap1.nr
[5]   Running     nroff -me chap2.nr
$ wait
```

In this example, you overlapped editing of chap2.nr with formatted printing of chap1.nr. However, after finishing the edit of chap2.nr, you see by running the jobs command that both nroff jobs are still running. Since you have no more editing tasks to perform, you can use the wait command to wait until one of the two background jobs finishes. The shell will not issue another prompt until one of the two jobs is done, then you'll receive a Done message:

```
$ wait
[5]   Done        nroff -me chap2.nr
$
```

Moving Background Jobs into the Foreground

Use fg to move background jobs into the foreground. Foreground execution implies interactive processing in connection with the terminal. Therefore, using fg to bring more than one job into the foreground establishes a race condition. The first job to get your terminal wins, and the others revert to Stopped status in the background. The syntax for fg is

```
fg [ job ... ]
```

For *job*, specify one or more process ID numbers or job references. If you omit *job*, the current background process is brought into the foreground. The current job is the job that you most recently stopped or started.

The need to use the fg command often arises as a result of actions you take yourself. For example, suppose you are editing a text file with vi and, when trying to save the file and quit, you discover that you do not have write permission for the file. You can't save the file until you correct the condition, but you're currently stuck inside the editor. What do you do?

First, stop the vi editor session by pressing Ctrl-z. You'll immediately get the following console output:

```
[1]    Stopped      vi chap2.nr
$
```

Now, determine the cause of the problem and correct it. For the sake of brevity, we'll assume that the problem is nothing more than that you've tried to edit a file you've write-protected:

```
$ ls -l chap2.nr
-r—r—r—   1  barbara    user      21506 May 5 10:52
$ chmod u+w chap2.nr
$ ls -l chap2.nr
-rw-r—r—   1  barbara    user      21506 May 5 10:52
```

Finally, use the fg command to bring the vi edit session, currently stopped in background, back into execution:

```
$ fg %vi
```

You might need to type Ctrl-l (a vi editor command) to redraw the screen.

Moving Foreground Jobs into the Background

Use the bg command to place jobs currently in the Stopped status (as indicated by the jobs command) into the background and to resume execution. Note that a job will immediately switch back into the Stopped state if it requires terminal input. The syntax for bg is

```
bg [ job ... ]
```

For *job*, specify one or more process ID numbers or job references. A job reference begins with %. If you omit *job*, the command refers to the current job, which is the job that you most recently started or stopped.

In actual practice, you don't use the bg command to move a foreground job into the background, because there's no way to do so: the shell is not listening to your terminal while a foreground job is running. To get the shell's attention while a foreground command is running, you'll need to use Ctrl-z to stop (*suspend*) the foreground job.

Once you've stopped the job and have a shell prompt, you'll need to decide what to do with the job you stopped. You can perform other tasks, and when finished restart the stopped job with the fg command, as described earlier. But if the job you stopped is not interactive, that is, if it can run without constant input from you, then you can tell the shell to restart the job but leave it in the background.

As an example, suppose you've started a long-running format of a text file using the troff command:

```
$ troff -me chap1.nr > chap1.trf
```

If, after waiting a few minutes for the job to finish, you find that you want to do something else instead of just sitting there, you can use the following sequence to switch the troff command to background execution:

```
[ctrl-z]
$ bg
$
```

By default, the shell assumes you mean the job you last stopped. Now that the troff command is running in the background, you can do other work.

The net result of these actions is the same as if you had started the troff job in the background to begin with:

```
$ troff -me chap1.nr > chap1.trf &
```

Summary

This chapter presented the features of the Korn shell. Because the Korn shell has many features in common with Bourne Shell, only the features special to the Korn shell were discussed in this chapter.

The Korn shell is one of several shells available to you on most contemporary versions of the UNIX operating system. It is a newer, enhanced version of the original Bourne shell, with command history, command editing, command aliases, and job control to improve your keyboard productivity. It also offers a number of improvements for the shell script writer, including arithmetic variables and arithmetic expressions, array variables, a `select` statement for prompting the user with menus, and a coprocess mechanism for interactively executing other UNIX commands from within a shell script.

The initial impetus for construction of the Korn shell was to bring many of the enhancements in `csh` to users in a format consistent with the Bourne shell syntax and behavior. The C shell (`csh`) was implemented by the Berkeley group and was initially offered only in the BSD variant of UNIX. The Korn shell ported its extensions, together with many additional improvements, into the System V environment. Many people feel that the Korn shell is a successor to both the Bourne and C shells. It is now the shell of choice for use at the keyboard and for writing shell scripts.

The command history feature provides for capturing in a disk file each command as you execute it. The file is preserved across logins so that you have some of the context of your previous session when you next log in. You can use the command history file for reference or for reexecuting commands. When you reexecute a command, you can use it as it was originally written or you can modify it before execution. The `fc` command and the `history` and `r` aliases provide the user interface to the command history file.

The command editing feature provides two different text editor styles for editing commands as you write them. You must explicitly enable command editing to use it. By default the Korn shell manages the command line in the same way as the Bourne shell does. The `vi` edit mode implements most of the `vi` input and command modes, and it enables you to access and reuse commands stored in the command history file. The EMACS edit mode is compatible with the EMACS editor commands. Most users find either the `vi` or EMACS command editing mode to be more natural than the equivalent `bang` (!) notation of the C shell.

The command alias feature enables you to define new command names that stand for a leading portion of the command line of existing commands. The definition of an alias can replace not only the name of an existing command but also initial options and arguments of the command line. This greatly reduces the amount of typing needed for frequently executed commands. The feature also replaces the command tracking feature of the Bourne shell.

Extensions to wildcard file naming patterns provide more complex expressions that you can use to narrow in on the specific files you want to reference.

Features added for the benefit of the script writer are numerous and powerful. They eliminate some of the kludges that you used to have to deal with when writing new commands.

The typeset command provides a host of new features surrounding the use of shell variables. Array variables with the form ${*name*[n]} permit convenient processing of lists. Integer variables defined with typeset, the let command, and the (( )) expression notation enable you to do basic numeric calculations without having to leave the shell environment. You no longer have to resort to command substitution for the expr or bc commands.

An improved syntax for command substitution makes even this chore more palatable. The syntax $(...) for command replacement reduces the need for quoting substrings inside backquoted expressions. You can even nest them, which permits expressions such as $(...$(...)...) on the command line.

Coprocessing, a new feature of the shell, enables you to read and write from background commands, using them in interactive fashion. You can respond to error messages produced by the invoked command, and you can provide a programmed response. You launch a coprocess with the ¦& operator, using it in place of the & symbol. Once launched, a coprocess runs in parallel with your shell's process. To write to the command, use print -p. To read its output, use read -p. You can reassign the input and output pipes by using the exec *fd*>&p and exec *fd*<&p special commands. Now the script writer can do things previously possible only in the C programming language.

Another boon is the privileged shell mode. You can set the set-uid and set-gid flags on your shell scripts. You can use the set -o privileged or set -p option to toggle between the user's real user ID and the effective user ID. Use this feature to write special system services—for example, a tape library management system, a device allocation facility, or a file sharing system.

Last but not least, the Korn shell provides a way of getting around the problem of not being able to export aliases and functions. Using the ENV exported variable, you can define a miniprofile to be executed at each invocation of the shell. You no longer have to switch to the shell from vi, pg, or sdb only to find a bare-bones environment without your favorite aliases and functions.

All in all, the Korn shell seems to be just about the final word in command-line environments. Now your main concern will be whether compatibility constraints enable you to use the Korn shell for script writing. Although the Korn shell can execute Bourne shell scripts, the Bourne shell can't execute Korn shell scripts, and only the C shell can execute C shell scripts. At least you're free to use it for your keyboard environment, which is a step up for sure!

C Shell

13

By John Valley

IN THIS CHAPTER

As a UNIX user, you have a choice of shells available to you. These are the Bourne shell, the C shell, and the Korn shell. The C shell—the subject of this chapter—is one of the more popular shells available in UNIX. Chronologically, it was developed after the Bourne shell and before the Korn shell. The C shell incorporates many features of the Bourne shell and adds many new ones that make your UNIX sessions more efficient and convenient.

There are advantages and disadvantages to each shell. You may wish to review Chapter 14, "Which Shell Is Right for You?" to help you decide which one to use.

A Little History

The Bourne and Korn shells were created at AT&T's Bell Labs, which, not coincidentally, is also where UNIX originated. Bell Labs is not the only organization that contributed to the development of UNIX, however. The Department of Computer Science at the Berkeley campus, University of California, played a very important role.

As you might have already read, the early versions of UNIX were made available only to colleges and universities under a rather restrictive licensing arrangement: UNIX could be used outside of AT&T only for "research purposes." At Berkeley, interest in UNIX was very high. The computer science labs added many new features to UNIX and offered their version to other universities as well. The Berkeley version soon became the more popular version, not only because of its many new features and extensions, but also because Berkeley, unlike Bell Labs, offered maintenance and support to other user groups. Given this fact, it shouldn't be surprising that by the late 1970s, the BSD version (*Berkeley Software Distribution*) was the dominant variant of UNIX in use.

One of the additions to UNIX was a new shell, written by Bill Joy (also the author of the vi text editor). Joy did not pattern his shell after the Bourne shell; indeed, to judge by results, he apparently felt that the Bourne shell syntax was clumsy and nonintuitive. As a syntax model, he chose the C programming language. The C shell commands, especially if, while, and the other structured programming statements, are somewhat similar in syntax to the equivalent statements in C. A shell is quite a different animal from a compiler, however, so the C programming language served only as a model; many forms and structures in the C shell have nothing to do with the C programming language.

Because the C shell is not just an extension of the Bourne shell syntax, this chapter will cover all aspects of C shell operation; it can therefore be read independently from Chapter 11, "Bourne Shell," and Chapter 12, "Korn Shell."

Invoking C Shell

Each time you log in to UNIX, you're placed in an interactive shell referred to as your *login* shell. If your login shell is C shell, you can tell by its command-line prompt: the percent sign (%). The C shell prompt differs from the dollar sign prompt ($) of the Bourne shell to remind you that you're using the C shell. You can customize your keyboard prompt when using the C shell; for more information see the definition of prompt in the section titled "Variables" later in this chapter.

If your login shell is not C shell, and C shell is available on your system, you can invoke it as an interactive shell from the command line. Even when you're already running the C shell, there will be times when you want to launch the C shell again, for example to run a shell script or to temporarily change the shell's options. To invoke the C shell interactively, use the following command:

```
$ csh
%
```

NOTE: The csh command is usually located in either the /bin or the /usr/bin directory. Because both directories are usually in your search path, you shouldn't have any trouble finding the csh command if your system has it. If you don't find it right away, you might look in the directory /usr/ucb (standard home for BSD components in a UNIX System V system), or in /usr/local/bin, home for programs your shop has acquired that weren't provided with the original system. Remember, though, that the C shell was for many years available only to those shops using the BSD variant of UNIX; unlike the Bourne shell, there is no guarantee that you will have the csh command on your system.

The csh command also supports a number of options and arguments (described later in this chapter in the section titled "Shell Options"), but most of them are not relevant to running an interactive shell.

Whenever csh is invoked, whether as the login shell or as a subshell, it loads and executes a profile script named .cshrc. If it is a login shell, the C shell will also execute a profile script on startup named .login, and another on exit named .logout. Note that the .login script is executed after .cshrc, not before. For additional information about C shell profile scripts, see the section titled "Customizing Your Shell Environment" later in this chapter.

Most versions of the C shell import environment variables such as *PATH* into local array variables at startup. The C shell does not refer to the public environment variables (including *PATH*) for its own operation. This means that usually you'll want to maintain the *path* variable for directory searches, not *PATH*. Some versions of the C shell do not properly import environment variables, with confusing results. If it appears that you have no search path set, but the *PATH* variable is set and accurate (as shown by echo $PATH), check that the variable *path* has a matching value. If not, you'll need to import critical environment variables into local variables yourself.

> **NOTE:** If you are familiar with Bourne shell, you won't notice much difference working with the C shell unless you use advanced shell features such as variables, command replacement, and so on.
>
> Important differences do exist, however. Among these are the set of punctuation characters having special meaning to the shell (often called *metacharacters*). The C shell is sensitive to all the special characters of the Bourne shell, as well as the tilde (~), the commercial at sign (@), and the exclamation point (!). Don't forget to quote or escape these characters when writing commands unless you intend their special shell meaning. (See the section "Quoting and Escaping from Special Characters" for a discussion of the details.)

Shell Basics

When you enter commands at the shell prompt, you are providing input to the shell. The shell sees a line of input as a string of characters terminated with a newline character that is usually the result of pressing return on your keyboard. That input can be anything from a single, simple command to multiple commands joined with command operators. Each command line that you enter is actually a shell *statement*. In addition to providing input to the shell manually by entering shell statements on the command line, you can also provide input to the shell by putting shell statements into a file and executing the file.

The next section covers the basics of interacting with the shell by entering shell statements on the command line. (Of course, anything that you can enter on the command line can also be put into a file for later, "canned" execution. Such files are called *shell scripts*.) The section following is titled "Shell Statements—A Closer Look," which provides a more detailed, technical look at components of shell statements. If you plan to write shell scripts, you'll definitely want to read this section.

When you finish this section, you will feel like you know a lot about the shell, but this is just the beginning. In addition to its basic service of providing a means to instruct the computer, the shell also provides a number of tools you can use to expedite your work flow. These tools, or *features* of the shell, are described in subsequent sections of this chapter.

Executing Commands—The Basics

C shell accepts several types of commands as input: UNIX commands, built-in shell commands, user-written commands, and command aliases. This section describes the different types of commands you can execute and the various ways you can execute commands.

Command Names as Shell Input

As you know, you execute a command by entering the command's name. The C shell supports any of the following as command names:

- *Built-in C shell command.* The shell provides a number of commands implemented within the shell program itself: invoking a built-in command therefore executes very quickly because no program files need to be loaded. A built-in command is always invoked by a simple name, never by a pathname.

  Because the shell first checks a command name for built-in commands before searching for a file of the same name, you cannot redefine a built-in command with a shell script. The next section, "Built-In Shell Commands," briefly describes each one; detailed descriptions with examples of how to use these commands are presented in the task-oriented sections of this chapter.

- *Filename.* You can specify the filename or a relative or absolute pathname of a file as a command. The file must be marked executable and must be either a binary load file or a shell script in the C shell language. The C shell cannot process shell scripts written for the Bourne or Korn shells. (See the section titled "Shell Programming" later in this chapter for notes about using shell scripts with the C shell.)

  All UNIX commands are provided as executable files in the /bin or /usr/bin directories. You invoke a UNIX command by entering its filename or full pathname.

  Examples of invoking an executable program file include the following:

  ```
  % cat big.script
  % /usr/bin/cat big.script
  % /usr/ucb/cc myprog.c
  % ../paylist paymast
  ```

- *Command alias.* A command alias is a name you define using the alias shell built-in command.

  An alias can have the same name as a shell built-in command or an executable file. You can always invoke an executable file having the same name as an alias by using the file's full pathname. An alias having the same name as a built-in command, however, effectively hides the built-in command. Aliases are described in detail in the section titled "Aliases" later in this chapter.

Built-In Shell Commands

C shell provides a number of commands implemented within the shell program itself. Built-in commands execute very quickly because no external program file needs to be loaded. Table 13.1 lists the commands alphabetically along with a brief description of each one. The remainder of this chapter groups these commands into subsections dedicated to particular tasks you'll perform in the shell and describes how to use each command.

Table 13.1. Built-in commands for C shell.

Command	Description
alias	Define or list a command alias
bg	Background execution
break	Breaking out of a loop
breaksw	Exit from a switch statement
case	Begin a case in switch
cd	Change directory
chdir	Change directory
continue	Begin the next loop iteration immediately
default	Label for the default case in switch
dirs	List the directory stack
echo	Echo arguments to standard output
eval	Rescan a line for substitutions
exec	Invoke a new shell
exit	Exit from the current shell
fg	Switch a job to foreground execution
foreach	Looping control statement
glob	Echo arguments to standard output
goto	Alter the order of command execution
hashstat	Print hash table statistics
history	List command history
if	Conditional execution
jobs	List active jobs
kill	Signal a process
limit	Respecify maximum resource limits

Command	Description
login	Invoke the system login procedure
logout	Exit from a login shell
newgrp	Change your group ID
nice	Control background process dispatch priority
nohup	Prevent termination on logout
notify	Request notification of background job status changes
onintr	Process interrupt within a shell script
popd	Return to a previous directory
pushd	Change directory with pushdown stack
rehash	Rehash the directory search path
repeat	Repetitively execute a command
set	Display or change a variable
setenv	Set environment variable
shift	Shift parameters
source	Interpret a script in the current shell
stop	Stop a background job
suspend	Stop the current shell
switch	Conditional execution
time	Time a command
umask	Display or set the process file creation mask
unalias	Delete a command alias
unhash	Disable use of the hash table
unlimit	Cancel a previous limit command
unset	Delete shell variables
unsetenv	Delete environment variables
wait	Wait for background jobs to finish
while	Looping control
%job	Foreground execution
@	Expression evaluation

Executing Simple Commands

The most common form of input to the shell is the *simple command*, where a command name is followed by any number of arguments. For example, in the following command line

```
% chdir dirname
```

chdir is the command and *dirname* is the argument. It is the responsibility of the command, not the shell, to interpret the arguments. Many commands, but certainly not all, take the form

```
% command -options filenames
```

Although the shell does not interpret the arguments of the command, the shell does make some interpretation of the input line before passing the arguments to the command. Special characters entered on a command line cause the shell to redirect input and output, start a different command, search the directories for filename patterns, substitute variable data, and substitute the output of other commands.

Entering Multiple Commands on One Line

Ordinarily, the shell interprets the first word of command input as the command name and the rest of the input as arguments to that command. The semicolon (;) directs the shell to interpret the word following the symbol as a new command, with the rest of the input as arguments to the new command. For example, the command line

```
% who -H; df -v; ps -e
```

is the equivalent of

```
% who -H
% df -v
% ps -e
```

except that in the second case the results of each command would appear between the command input lines.

When the semicolon is used to separate commands on a line, the commands are executed in sequence. The shell waits until one command is complete before executing the next. You can also execute commands simultaneously (see the section titled "Executing Commands in the Background") or execute them conditionally, which means that the shell executes the next command only if the first command succeeds or fails (see the section titled "Executing Commands Conditionally").

Entering Commands Too Long for One Line

Sometimes command lines get quite lengthy. On some terminals, when you reach the edge of the display screen the input autowraps to the next line, but depending on terminal settings, some do not. It would be nice if you could type part of a command on one line and enter the remainder of the command on a second line. This can be accomplished by escaping the newline character.

Remember that the shell sees a line of input as a statement terminated with a newline character. But the newline character is also considered to be a white space character. If you end a line with a backslash (\), the next character—the newline character—will be treated literally, meaning that the shell will not interpret the newline character as the end of the line of input.

```
% echo Now is the time for all good men        \_
to come to the aid of the party.
Now is the time for all good men to come to the aid of the party.
```

Executing Commands in the Background

Normally when you execute commands, they are executed in the *foreground*. This means that the command has the system's undivided attention, and you can't do anything else until the command finishes executing. For commands that take a long time to execute, however, this can be a problem. To free your system without waiting for the command to finish, you can execute the command in the *background* by putting an ampersand (&) at the end of the command:

```
% who -H &
[1] +  Running    who -H &
%
```

You also can run multiple commands in the background simultaneously:

```
% who -H & df -v & ps -e &
```

A command executing in the background is referred to as a *job*, and each job is assigned a job number—the bracketed number in the preceding example. C shell provides you with several commands for managing background jobs; see the section later in this chapter titled "Job Control."

Repetitively Executing a Command—*repeat*

You can use the repeat command to execute some other command a specified number of times. While the repeat command doesn't see frequent use, it can on occasion be quite handy. For example, if you had stored some text in a model file, and wanted to make five copies of it, you could do so easily with the command

```
repeat 5 cat model.txt new.txt
```

Or, if you were writing a shell script to print a document, you might use the command

```
repeat 5 echo *******************************
```

to mark its first page clearly as the start of the document.

The syntax of the `repeat` command is as follows:

```
repeat count command
```

For *count*, specify a decimal integer number. A count of zero is valid and suppresses execution of the command.

For *command*, specify a simple command that is subject to the same restrictions as the first format of the `if` statement. The command is scanned for variable, command, and history substitutions, filename patterns, and quoting. It cannot be a compound command, a pipeline, a statement group (using `{}`), or a parenthesized command list.

Any I/O redirections are performed only once regardless of the value of *count*. For example, `repeat 10 echo Hello >hello.list` would result in ten lines of *Hello* in a file named `hello.list`.

Executing Commands in a Subshell—()

A command (or a list of commands separated with semicolons) enclosed in parentheses groups the command or commands for execution in a subshell. A subshell is a secondary invocation of the shell, so any change to shell variables, the current directory, or other such process information lasts only while executing the commands in the group. This is a handy way, for example, to switch to another directory, execute a command or two, and then switch back without having to restore your current directory:

```
% (cd /home/bill; cp *.txt /home/john)
```

Without the parentheses, you would have to write:

```
% cd /home/bill
% cp *.txt /home/john
% cd /home/john
```

The syntax for grouping commands is:

```
( commands )
```

Enclosing a list of commands in parentheses is a way to override the default precedence rules for the `&&`, `¦¦`, and `¦` operators, at the expense of invoking a subshell and losing any environmental effects of the commands' execution. For example, `(grep ¦¦ echo) ¦ pr` will pipe the output of the `grep` command, and possibly that of `echo` if `grep` sets a nonzero exit code, to the `pr` command.

I/O redirections can be appended to the subshell just as for a simple command; the redirections are in effect for all of the commands within the subshell. For example, (cat; echo; date) > out will write the output of the cat, echo, and date commands to a file named out without any breaks. If you look at the file afterward, first you'll see the lines written by cat, followed by the lines written by echo, and finally the lines written by date. Similarly, input redirections apply to all commands in the subshell, so that each command in turn reads lines from the redirected file, starting with the line following those read by any previously executed commands in the subshell.

Executing Commands Conditionally

Compound commands are actually two or more commands combined together so that the shell executes all of them before prompting (or, in the case of shell scripts, reading) more input.

Compound commands are not often needed for work at the keyboard, and you'll rarely feel the lack if you don't understand or don't use compound commands. However, compound commands form a very useful extension to the shell's syntax, especially in shell scripts. Some compound command formats, such as & (background job) and ¦ (the pipe operator) are essential to effective work with UNIX.

Conditional Execution on Success—&& (And)

The double ampersand operator (read *and*) is used to join two commands: *command1* && *command2*. It causes the shell to execute *command2* only if *command1* is successful (has a zero exit code).

For *command1* or *command2*, you can write a simple command or a compound command. The && operator has higher precedence than ¦¦ but lower precedence than ¦. For example,

```
grep '#include' *.c ¦ pr && echo OK
```

will echo *OK* only if the pipeline grep ¦ pr sets a zero exit code. (For pipelines, the exit code is the exit code of the last command in the pipeline.)

The compound command cp file1.c file1.bak && rm file1.c shows the possible benefit of using &&: The rm command will delete file1.c only if it is first successfully copied to file1.bak.

Conditional Execution on Failure —¦¦ (Or)

The *or* operator is used to join two commands: *command1* ¦¦ *command2*. It causes the shell to execute *command2* only if *command1* failed (set a nonzero exit code).

For *command1* or *command2*, you can write a simple command or a compound command. The ¦¦ operator has lower precedence than both the && and ¦ operators. For example, in the following command

```
grep '#include' *.c ¦¦ echo No files ¦ pr
```

either grep succeeds, or else the words *No files* are piped to the pr command. That is, the pipe is between the echo and pr commands, not between grep (or grep ¦¦ echo) and pr.

Use the ¦¦ operator to provide an alternative action. For example, in the following case, if the mkdir command fails, the exit command prevents further execution of the shell script:

```
mkdir $tmpfile ¦¦ exit
```

Shell Statements—A Closer Look

A command is either a *basic command*, or a basic command embellished with one or more *I/O redirections*.

A basic command is a series of words, each subject to *replacements*, which when fully resolved specifies an action to be executed and provides zero or more *options* and *arguments* to modify or control the action taken. The first word of a basic command, sometimes called the command *name*, must specify the required action.

In plainer terms, a statement is the smallest executable unit. When the shell is operating in interactive mode, it displays its prompt when it requires a statement. You must continue to enter shell statement components, using multiple lines if necessary, until you have completed a full statement. If the statement is not completed on one line, the shell will continue to prompt you, without executing the line or lines you have entered, until it has received a full statement.

Shell statements are formed from a number of *tokens*. A token is a basic syntactic element and can be any of the following:

- *Comments.* A comment begins with any word having a pound sign (#) as its first character, and extends to the end of the line. This interpretation can be avoided by enclosing the pound sign (or the entire word) in quotes. (See "Quoting and Escaping Special Characters" later in this chapter.)

- *White space.* White space consists of blanks and tabs, and sometimes the newline character. White space is used to separate other tokens which, if run together, would lose their separate identity. Units of text separated by white space are generically called *words*.

- *Statement delimiters.* Statement delimiters include the semicolon (;) and the newline character (generated when you press return). You can use the semicolon to run commands together on the same line. The shell treats the commands as if they had been entered on separate lines.

Normally every command or shell statement ends at the end of the line. The return (or Enter) key you press to end the line generates a character distinct from printable characters, blanks and tabs, which the shell sees as a *newline* character. Some statements require more than one line of input, such as the if and while commands. The syntax description for these commands shows how they should be split over lines; the line boundaries must be observed, and you must end each line at the indicated place or else you will get a syntax error.

■ *Operators.* An operator is a special character, or a combination of special characters, to which the shell attaches special syntactic significance. Operators shown as a combination of special characters must be written without white space between them, otherwise they will be seen as two single operators instead of the two-character operator.

Punctuation characters having special significance to the shell must be enclosed in quotes to avoid their special interpretation. For example, the command grep '#' *.c uses quotes to hide the pound sign from the shell so that the pound sign can be passed to grep as an argument. See the section later in this chapter titled "Quoting and Escaping from Special Characters" for details about using quotes.

■ *Words.* A word is any consecutive sequence of characters occurring between white space, statement delimiters, or operators. A word can be a single group of ordinary characters, a quoted string, a variable reference, a command substitution, a history substitution, or a filename pattern; it can also be any combination of these elements. The final form of the word is the result of all substitutions and replacements, together with all ordinary characters, run together to form a single string. The string is then used as the command name or command argument during command execution.

Filename Substitutions (Globbing)

Filename generation using patterns is an important facility of the Bourne shell. The C shell supports the filename patterns of the Bourne shell and adds the use of {} (braces) to allow greater flexibility.

Several shell commands and contexts allow the use of pattern-matching strings, such as the case statement of switch and the =~ and !~ expression operators. In these cases, pattern strings are formed using the same rules as for filename generation, except that the patterns are matched to another string.

When any of the pattern expressions described below are used as arguments of a command, the entire pattern string is replaced with the filenames or pathnames that match the pattern. By default, the shell searches the current directory for matching filenames, but if the pattern string contains slashes (/), it searches the specified directory or directories instead. Note that several directories can be searched for matching files in a single pattern string: a pattern of the form `dir/*/*.c` will search all the directories contained in `dir` for files ending with `.c`.

    *   The asterisk matches any string of characters, including a null string. Used by itself, it matches all filenames. Used at the beginning of a pattern string, it means that leading prefixes of the filename pattern are ignored: `*.c` matches any filename ending with `.c`. Used at the end of a pattern string, it means that trailing suffixes of the filename pattern are ignored: `s.*` will match `s.main`, `s.prog.c`, and any filename beginning with `s.`. Used in the middle of a pattern, it means that matching filenames must begin and end as shown but can contain any character sequences in the middle: `pay*.c` matches filenames beginning with pay and ending with `.c`, such as `payroll.c`, `paymast.c`, and `paycheck.c`.

    ?   The question mark matches any one character. For example, `?` as a complete word will match all filenames one character long in the current directory. The pattern `pay?.c` will match `pay1.c` and `pay2.c` but not `payroll.c`. Multiple question marks can be used to indicate a specific number of don't-care positions in the filename: `pay??.c` will match filenames beginning with pay and containing any two characters before `.c`, such as `pay01.c` and `paybb.c`, but will not match `payroll.c`.

    []   The square brackets enclose a list of characters. Matching filenames contain one of the indicated characters in the corresponding position of the filename. For example, `[abc]*` will match any filename beginning with the letter *a*, *b*, or *c*. Because of the asterisk, the first character can be followed by any sequence of characters.

              Use a hyphen (-) to indicate a range of characters. For example, `pay[1-3].c` will match filenames `pay1.c`, `pay2.c`, and `pay3.c`, but not `pay4.c` or `pay11.c`. Multiple ranges can be used in a single bracketed list. For example, `[A-Za-z0-9]*` will match any filename beginning with a letter or a digit. To match a hyphen, list the hyphen at the beginning or end of the character list: `[-abc]` or `[abc-]` will match an *a*, *b*, *c*, or hyphen.

              Use a circumflex (^) after `[` to negate the range of characters. The pattern `[^a-zA-Z0-9]*` will match all filenames that do not begin with a letter or digit—that is, filenames beginning with a punctuation character such as `.c` or `#myfile.txt`.

    {}   Braces enclose a list of patterns separated by commas. The brace expression matches filenames having any one of the listed patterns in the corresponding position of the name. For example, the pattern

`/usr/home/{kookla,fran,ollie}/.profile` expands to the path list `/usr/home/kookla/.profile /usr/home/fran/.profile /usr/home/ollie/.profile`. Unlike *, ?, and [ ], brace-enclosed lists are not matched against existing filenames; they are simply expanded into filenames regardless of whether the corresponding files exist. Brace-enclosed lists can be nested, for example `/usr/{bin,lib,home/{john,bill}}` refers to any of the directories `/usr/bin`, `/usr/lib`, `/usr/home/john`, and `/usr/home/bill`.

The tilde (~) can be used at the beginning of a word to invoke directory substitution. The tilde forms are as follows:

~	Substituted with the full pathname of your home directory. Also used in the form ~/*path* to refer to a file or directory under your home directory.
~*name*	Substituted with the full pathname of user *name*'s home directory. For example, `~ken/bin` refers to `/usr/ken/bin` if the home directory for user ken is `/usr/ken`. The password file `/etc/passwd` is searched for *name* to determine the directory pathname; if *name* is not found, the shell generates an error message and stops.

If the tilde does not appear by itself as a word, and is not followed by a letter or by a slash, or appears in any position other than the first, it is not replaced. Thus, `/usr/marta/~file.c` is a reference to the file `~file.c` in the directory `/usr/marta`.

It is important to realize that filename generation using pattern strings causes a replacement of one word with many. A filename pattern must be a single word. The ordinary characters and pattern-matching characters in the word describe a rule for choosing filenames from the current or specified directory. The word is replaced with each filename or pathname found that matches the pattern. Consider the following examples:

```
% echo Files: *.txt
Files: ch1.txt ch2.txt chlast.txt
% set files=(*.txt)
% echo Found $#files files
Found 3 files
% echo $files[2]
ch2.txt

mkdir $tmpfile || exit
```

Redirecting Input and Output

C shell provides several commands for redirecting the input and output of commands. You might already be familiar with the input (<) or output (>) redirection characters from earlier chapters. C shell provides you with these and more.

An I/O redirection is an instruction to the shell you append to a command. It causes one of the standard file descriptors to be assigned to a specific file. You might have previously encountered standard files in the discussion of the Bourne shell (Chapter 11). The UNIX operating system defines three standard file descriptors: *standard input, standard output, and standard error.* (These names are sometimes abbreviated to *stdin, stdout,* and *stderr.*)

> **NOTE:** The UNIX operating system actually provides at least twenty-five file descriptors for use by a command. It is only by convention that the first three are set aside for reading input, writing output, and printing error messages. Unless you instruct otherwise, the shell always opens these three file descriptors before executing a command, and assigns them all to your terminal.

A file descriptor is not the file itself. Rather, it is a *channel,* much like the phone jack on the back of your stereo: you can connect it to any audio source you like. Similarly, a file descriptor such as *standard input* must be connected to a file—your terminal by default, or the disk file or readable device of your choice.

You can change the location where a command reads data, writes output, and prints error messages, using one or more of the *I/O redirection operators.* The operators are shown in Table 13.2.

Table 13.2. I/O redirection operators.

Format	Effect
	Input Redirection
`< filename`	Use the contents of `filename` as input to a command.
`<< word`	Provide shell input lines as command input. Lines of the shell input which follow the line containing this redirection operator are read and saved by the shell in a temporary file. Reading stops when the shell finds a line beginning with *word.* The saved lines then become the input to the command. Of course, the lines read and saved are effectively deleted from the shell input, and will not be executed as commands; they are effectively "eaten" by the << operator. Shell execution continues with the line following the line beginning with *word.* If you use the << operator on a command you type at the terminal, be careful: lines you type afterward will be gobbled up by the shell—not executed—until you enter a line beginning with whatever you specified as *word.* The << operator is most often used in shell scripts.

Format	*Effect*
	Output Redirection
`> filename`	Write command output to `filename`
`>! filename`	Write command output to `filename`, and ignore the *noclobber* option. The *noclobber* option is fully explained in the section "Using Predefined Variables" later in this chapter. Briefly it causes the shell to disallow the > *filename* redirection when *filename* already exists; *noclobber* is therefore a safety you can use to prevent your accidentally destroying an existing file. Of course, sometimes you want to redirect output to a file even though it already exists. In such a case, you must use the >! operator to tell the shell you really want to proceed with the redirection. If you don't set the *noclobber* option, then you won't need to use the >! operator either.
`>& filename`	Open `filename` and write both the command output and error messages to it
`>&! filename`	Open `filename` and write both the command output and error messages to it, and ignore the *noclobber* option
`>> filename`	Open `filename` and write command output at the end of the file (append mode)
`>>! filename`	Open `filename` and write command output at the end of the file (append mode), and ignore the *noclobber* option
`>>& filename`	Open `filename` and write command output and error messages at the end of the file (append mode)
`>>&! filename`	Open `filename` and write command output and error messages at the end of the file (append mode), and ignore the *noclobber* option

In Table 13.2, `filename` represents any ordinary filename or pathname, or any filename or pathname resulting after variable substitution, command substitution, or filename generation.

I/O redirection operators are appended to a command; for example, `date >curdate` will write the current date to the file `curdate` instead of to your terminal. You can also use more than one redirection per command: simply list them one after another at the end of the command. The order doesn't matter: for example, both `cat <infile >outfile` and `cat >outfile <bigfile` will have the same effect.

Input Redirection

Some commands make no special use of the standard input file, such as the `date` and the `ls` system commands; others require an input file to function properly, such as the `cat` and `awk` commands. You can use the < redirection operator in the form *command* < *filename* to designate a file as the source of input for commands like `cat` and `awk`; if you do not, these commands will read data from your keyboard—sometimes useful, but usually not. If you provide an input redirection, but the command does not read data (such as `ls`), the I/O redirection is still performed by the shell, it is just ignored by the command.

It is an error to redirect standard input to a file that doesn't exist.

The redirection << *word* is a special form of the input redirection operator. Rather than taking input from a file, input to the command comes from the current shell input stream— your keyboard, if you append << to a command you type in, or your shell script if you use << on a command in a shell script.

For *word*, you choose an arbitrary string to delimit the lines of input. Then write the lines to be provided to the command as input immediately following the command line, and follow the last line with a line beginning with *word*. The shell reads the lines ahead, stores them in a temporary file, and sets up the temporary file as standard input for the command.

This form of input redirection is called a *here document*, because it is located here, in line with your shell commands. It is useful when you want to provide predefined data to a command, and it saves you from having to create a file to hold the data.

Unlike the *filename* part of other I/O redirection operators, *word* for the here document is not scanned for variable references, command substitutions, or filename patterns; it is used as is. Also, the following shell input lines are checked for the presence of *word* as the first word of the line before any substitutions or replacements are performed on the line.

Normally, lines of the here document are checked for variable references and command replacements; this allows you to encode variable information in the here document. If you quote any part of *word*, however, the lines are read and passed to the command without modification. For example, the redirection << STOP reads lines up to STOP, and performs substitutions on the lines it reads; the redirection << "STOP" reads lines up to the line beginning with STOP, and passes the lines directly to the command, as is, without substitutions or replacements of any kind.

The line beginning with *word* is discarded, and neither passed to the command in the here document, nor executed by the shell.

The following example shows the use of a here document to print a customized message:

```
pr << HERE ¦ lp
```

```
Hello, $user.
Your print job,
'lpstat'
has been scheduled for output at a later time.
Please contact Joe if you have any questions.
HERE
```

The line containing the word *HERE* will not appear in the output message; it is simply a mark to let the shell know where the redirected lines end.

Output Redirection

Output redirections have the general form > and >>. The first operator creates a new file of the specified name. The file is opened before command execution begins, so even if the command fails, or cannot be found, or if the shell finds an error on the command line and stops, the output file will still be created.

If you've set the *noclobber* option (with `set noclobber`), then the shell will refuse to create the named output file if it already exists; doing so would destroy its current contents. If you want to perform the output redirection even if the file *filename* already exists, use the redirection operator >! instead; it overrides the *noclobber* option.

The >> command arranges for command output to be added to the end of the named file. For this redirection operator, the *noclobber* option requires that the named file already exist. If you use the alternate form >>!, or if you use >> and the *noclobber* option is not set, the shell will create the named file if necessary.

The >& and >>& operators redirect both the standard output and standard error files to *filename*. The Bourne shell allows you to redirect the standard output and standard error files separately; the C shell does not. Actually, this is not much of a limitation in real life.

If you have the *noclobber* option set, you'll need to use >&! instead of >& to proceed even if the named file exists, or >>&! to proceed even if the named file doesn't exist.

> **NOTE:** For purposes of understanding shell syntax, it might be noted that appending an I/O redirection to a simple command yields a simple command. Except where specifically prohibited, a command with redirections appended can be used wherever a simple command is allowed, such as on the single-line `if` statement.

Quoting or Escaping from Special Characters

As you've seen from previous sections, certain characters have special meaning for the shell. That is, when the shell encounters a special character, it will perform the action that the special character calls for. The following punctuation characters available on the standard keyboard are special to the shell and disrupt the scanning of ordinary words:

```
~ ' ! @ # $ % ^ & * ( ) \ ¦ { } [ ] ; ' " < > ?
```

In some contexts, particularly within the switch statement, the : (colon) is also a special character. The colon is recognized as a special character only when expected, in a case or default statement, and as a statement label. It does not need to be quoted except to avoid these specific interpretations.

To use one of these characters as a part of a word without its special significance, you can *escape* the character by placing a backslash (\) immediately in front of the character. Note that a backslash intended as an ordinary character must be written as two backslashes in succession: \\. To escape a two-character operator such as >>, you must insert a backslash in front of each character: \>\>.

Alternatively, you can enclose the special character or any portion of the word containing the character in quotes. The shell recognizes three kinds of quotes: the apostrophe ('), the quote ("), and the backquote (`).

Use two apostrophes (also called *single quotes*) to enclose a character sequence and avoid all interpretation by the shell. I often call a string enclosed in apostrophes a *hard-quoted* string, because the shell performs absolutely no substitution, replacement, or special interpretation of anything appearing between the apostrophes. Even the backslash character is treated as an ordinary character, so there are no escapes within an apostrophe-enclosed string, and you cannot embed an apostrophe in such a string. That is, the string 'who's there' will cause a shell error: the shell will see this as *who* concatenated with an *s*, followed by a white space delimiter, followed by a word beginning with *there*, and then the starting apostrophe of another string. The third apostrophe starts a quoted string that the shell will follow over as many lines as necessary to find an ending apostrophe, probably eating up shell lines you intended as commands, and eventually yielding a shell syntax error or an erroneous command execution.

One of the uses of quoted strings is to specify a single word containing blanks, tabs, and newline characters. For example, the following shows the use of a single echo command to print two lines of output:

```
% echo -n 'Hello.
Please enter your name: '
Hello.
Please enter your name:
```

The double apostrophe or quote (") also provides a special bracket for character strings. Like the apostrophe, the quote hides most special characters from the shell's observation. Quoted strings, however, are subject to two kinds of scan and replacement: variable references and command substitutions.

Any of the reference forms for shell variables ($1, $*name*, ${name}, $*name*[*index*], $*, and others) are recognized inside quoted strings and are replaced with the corresponding string value. The replacement occurs inside the quoted string, leaving its unity as a single word intact (even if the substituted value includes blanks, tabs, or newline characters).

Command substitution occurs for strings enclosed in backquotes ('). The entire string enclosed between matching backquotes is extracted and executed by the shell as if it were an independent command. The command can be two or more commands separated with semicolons, or a pipeline, or any form of compound statement. Any data written to standard output by the command is captured by the shell and becomes the string value of the backquoted command. The string value is parsed into words, and the series of words replaces the entire backquoted string.

All forms of shell substitution will occur inside backquoted command strings, including variable replacement, nested command executions, history substitutions, and filename patterns. Nested command strings will work, but the backquotes introducing them must be escaped with \ to hide them from the shell's first scan of the backquoted string.

A backquoted command string (or any number of them) can appear inside a quoted string and will have its normal effect; this is the second form of substitution performed on "-quoted strings. A quoted command substitution ("*xxx*`commands`*xxx*") generates new words only at the end of each line, except at the end of the last line. If the executed command prints only one line of text, the text replaces the backquoted expression without introducing any word breaks.

Both quoting forms '...' and "..." suppress filename generation. For example, note the difference in the following echo commands:

```
% echo *.c
main.c io.c parse.c math.c
% echo "*.c"
*.c
```

Apostrophes and quotes can appear inside a double-quoted string. The double quote must be escaped with a backslash to prevent premature termination of the quoted string (for example "He said, \"John!\""). The apostrophe has no special significance when appearing inside a double-quoted string and does not need to be backslashed. The following example shows the use of quotes inside quoted strings:

```
% echo "He said, \"John!\""
He said, "John!"
% echo "Filename: '$1'"
Filename: '/usr/bin/ls'
```

A backslash appearing inside an apostrophe-quoted string is retained and appears in the string's value, because no substitutions occur inside an apostrophe-quoted string. Inside a double-quoted string or a command substitution using ', or in a normal unquoted word, a backslash has the effect of suppressing shell interpretation of the character that follows it; the backslash is then removed from the string. The following examples show the effect of a backslash in all these contexts:

```
% echo "Double \" quote"
Double " quote
% echo Double \" quote
Double " quote
% echo 'Single \' quote
Single \ quote
% echo Single \' quote
Single ' quote
```

Working with Directories and the Directory Stack

C shell provides you with several built-in commands for working with directories. The cd, chdir, pushd, and popd commands all change the current directory in one way or another.

The pushd and popd commands provide a pushdown stack mechanism for changing directories, and the dirs command displays the contents of the stack. If you switch to another directory using pushd instead of cd, the pathname of your previous directory is "saved" in the directory stack. A subsequent popd will then return you to the previous directory. Be aware that the cd command does not maintain the directory stack; you cannot use popd to return to a directory that you left using cd.

Changing Directories—*cd* and *chdir*

In C shell, you can choose from two commands for changing your current working directory: cd and chdir. The chdir command is equivalent to cd in every way. The syntax for these commands is as follows:

```
cd [ name ]
chdir [ name ]
```

If you omit the *name* argument, the command attempts to change to the directory whose pathname is given by the value of the C shell variable home; see the section later in this chapter titled "Using Predefined Variables" for more about home.

If you specify a *name*, the cd or chdir command uses a search hierarchy to attempt to locate the referenced directory, as follows:

1. If *name* begins with /, ./, or ../, the command attempts to switch to the named directory; failure terminates the command immediately. In other words, if you use a relative or absolute pathname, the specified directory must exist and must be accessible to you, otherwise the command fails.

2. The command searches your current directory. A partial pathname, of the form `name1/name2/.../namen` implies searching your current directory for the entire subtree.

3. If the directory path cannot be found in your current directory, the command checks to see if the variable *cdpath* exists and has a value. If it does, then each of the directories named in *cdpath* is checked to see if it contains *name*. If successful, the command changes to the *name* in that directory and prints the full pathname of the new current directory.

4. If no variable *cdpath* exists, or if *name* cannot be found in any of the directories listed in *cdpath*, the command checks to see if *name* is a variable name and has a value beginning with `/`. If so, the command changes to that directory.

5. If *name* still cannot be found, the command fails.

For more information about the *cdpath* variable, see the section titled "Using Predefined Variables" later in this chapter.

The `cd` and `chdir` commands as implemented by the C shell provide a great deal of flexibility in generating shortcuts for directory names. There is nothing more painful than having to repeatedly type long directory names on the `cd` command. The purpose of the cd command's search hierarchy is to provide some mechanisms you can use for shortening a reference to a directory name. The cdpath variable is your principal tool: if you set it to a list of directories you often reference, you can switch to one of those directories just by giving the base directory name. If *cdpath* is not sufficiently flexible to suit your needs, you can define a shell variable as an alias for a directory's full pathname, then `cd` *varname* will switch you to that directory for the price of a few keystrokes.

> **NOTE:** When using a shell variable as a pseudonym for a directory path, you do not need to write `$` in front of the variable name; doing so is permitted and also works because of the shell's variable substitution mechanism but is not required.

Listing the Directory Stack—*dirs*

The directory stack is a mechanism by which you can store and recall directories you have changed to using the special change-directory commands `pushd` and `popd`, discussed in the next two sections. The `dirs` command lists the directories in the directory stack:

```
% dirs
/usr/home/john/bin /usr/home/john /usr/home/john/docs
```

Three directories are on the directory stack in this example for user `john`. The first directory listed is the current directory (the one you would see if you entered the `pwd` command). Directories to the right are previous directories, the farthest to the right being the least recent. In this example, the directory `/usr/home/john/docs` was the first directory to be changed to—that is, "pushed" onto the pushdown directory stack, `/usr/home/john` was the next directory, and `/usr/home/john/bin` was the directory most recently changed to (the current directory).

Changing to a Directory Using the Directory Stack—*pushd*

To save the pathname of a directory on the directory stack, use the `pushd` command to change to another directory. Using `pushd` saves the pathname of your previous directory on the directory stack so that you can return to the previous directory quickly and easily using the `popd` command. Use `dirs` to display the directories currently saved on the pushdown stack.

There are three forms of the `pushd` command:

```
pushd
pushd name
pushd +n
```

Used in the form `pushd`, the command exchanges the top two directory stack elements, making your previous directory the current and your current directory the previous. Successive `pushd` commands used without an argument therefore switch you back and forth between the top two directories.

Used in the form `pushd name`, the command changes to directory *name* in the same way as `cd` would have; `pushd` uses the `cdpath` directory list to resolve *name*, and succeeds or fails in the same cases as `cd`. The pathname of the current directory is saved in a directory stack prior to the change. The directory stack is an implicit array variable maintained by the shell (which you cannot access directly) so that each `pushd` adds the current directory on the left and pushes all existing entries to the right; the top (or *first*) element is always your current directory, and subsequent entries are the pathnames of your previous directories in reverse order. The `popd` command discards the top stack entry and changes to the new top entry, reducing the total number of items stacked by one.

Use the form `pushd +n` to do a circular shift of the directory stack by *n* positions, changing to the new top directory. A circular shift treats the list of elements as if they were in a ring, with the first preceded by the last and the last followed by the first; the shift changes your position in the ring without deleting any of the elements. Consider the following example:

```
% dirs
/home/john /home/mary /home/doggie /home/witherspoon
% pushd +2
/home/doggie
% dirs
/home/doggie /home/witherspoon /home/john /home/mary
```

Note that both before and after the `pushd`, `/home/john` precedes `/home/mary`, and `/home/doggie` precedes `/home/witherspoon`. The example also shows that, for the purpose of the pushd +*n* command form, /home/witherspoon (the last entry) is effectively followed by /home/john (the first entry).

Returning to a Previous Directory Using the Directory Stack—*popd*

After you have saved directories on the directory stack with popd, you can use popd to return to a previous directory. The syntax for the popd command is as follows:

```
popd [ +n ]
```

The following example shows the use of pushd, dirs, and popd together:

```
% pwd
/usr/home/john
% pushd /usr/spool
% pushd uucppublic
% pushd receive
% dirs
/usr/spool/uucppublic/receive /usr/spool/uucppublic /usr/spool
➥/usr/home/john
% popd
/usr/spool/uucppublic
% dirs
/usr/spool/uucppublic /usr/spool /usr/home/john
% popd
/usr/spool
% dirs
/usr/spool /usr/home/john
% popd
/usr/home/john
% dirs
/usr/home/john
```

Used in the form popd +*n*, the command deletes the *n*th entry in the stack. Stack entries are numbered from 0, which is your current directory.

Changing the Active Shell

The C shell provides a number of commands for changing the active shell. Although your login shell may be the C shell, you are not limited to it; you can change your shell to Bourne shell or the Korn shell at any time using the exec command. The exit and logout commands also change the active shell, by returning you to the shell that was active before your current shell: issued from your login shell, they return you to the login screen, which is itself a kind of shell (of somewhat limited functionality).

Other commands, such as umask and nohup, change the manner in which UNIX treats the shell.

In order to make the best use of the information in this section, you should also read Part IV, Process Control, later in this book, which describes some of the UNIX mechanisms these commands are designed to manipulate.

Invoking a New Shell—exec

The exec command transfers control to the specified command, replacing the current shell. The command you specify becomes your new current shell. The syntax of the exec command is as follows:

```
exec command
```

Nearly always, *command* should be a shell invocation command such as csh, sh, or ksh. Control cannot be returned to the invoking environment because it is replaced by the new environment. Shell variables exported with the setenv command will be passed to the new shell in the usual manner; all other command contexts, including local variables and aliases, will be lost.

The exec command is equivalent to the Bourne shell exec.

Exiting from the Current Shell—exit

The exit command causes the current shell invocation to be exited. Its syntax is as follows:

```
exit [ (exp) ]
```

If issued from within a shell script, the shell script is terminated and control returns to the invoking shell. If issued from your login shell, the .logout script in your home directory will be executed before the shell exits. Normally, the UNIX operating system will redisplay a login screen after an exit from the login shell.

If you provide the optional *exp* argument (which must be enclosed in parentheses), the argument is evaluated as an arithmetic expression, and the resulting value is used as the shell's exit code; otherwise, the current value of the status variable is taken as the shell's exit code. The status variable is described in the section "Using Predefined Variables" later in this chapter.

Invoking the System Login Procedure—*login*

Use the login command to log out from your current shell and to immediately log in under the same or a different user ID. Its syntax is as follows:

```
login name [ arg ... ]
```

Using this shell built-in command is not quite equivalent to logging out in the normal manner and then logging in. If you use the login command from a remote terminal, the line connection will not be dropped, whereas logging out in the normal manner drops the line and requires you to re-establish the connection before you can log in again.

You cannot execute the `login` built-in command from a subshell; it is legal only for your login shell.

For *name*, specify the user name you want to log in with. Any arguments you specify after *name* are passed to the `/bin/login` command and are defined by `/bin/login`, not by the shell.

Exiting from a Login Shell—*logout*

Use the `logout` command to log out from your login shell.

```
logout
```

You can also terminate the login shell (or any subshell) with the `exit` command. If you have the `ignoreeof` option set, you cannot use the *EOF* key to exit from the shell; in such a case, use `logout` or `exit`. See the section "Using Predefined Variables" for a definition of the `ignoreeof` option.

Preventing a Command from Terminating Execution after Logout— *nohup*

Use the `nohup` command to run a command that is insensitive to the *Hangup* signal.

```
nohup [ command ]
```

The UNIX operating system always sends a *Hangup* signal (signal 1) to a process when its process group leader logs out. The net effect is that normally any command you are running when you log out is terminated. (Although you can't ordinarily issue the `logout` or `exit` command, or enter an *EOF* character, while you are running a command, you can always force a logout by turning off your terminal, or if using a remote terminal connection, by hanging up the line.)

When you invoke a command with `nohup`, the shell effectively disables the *Hangup* signal so that the command cannot receive it, thus allowing *command* to continue to execute after you log out.

You can disable the *Hangup* signal for your interactive shell or from within a shell script using the `trap` built-in command, and binary programs written in the C language can also disable or ignore the *Hangup* signal. However, not all commands do this. If you use `nohup` to invoke the command, you are assured that the *Hangup* signal will be ignored whether or not the command disables the signal.

Use `nohup` with no arguments from within a shell script to disable the *Hangup* signal for the duration of the script.

Use `nohup` *command* to run *command* with the signal disabled.

Displaying and Setting the Process File Creation Mask— umask

The process file creation mask (sometimes, for purposes of brevity, called the *umask*), is an attribute of the shell process, just like the current directory is a process attribute. The purpose of the file creation mask is to specify the default permissions assigned to new files you create, for example when redirecting the output of a command to a file with the > operator. It would be extremely inconvenient if the system prompted you for file permissions every time it created a file, especially since most of the time you would assign the same permissions to all new files.

If you're not familiar with file permissions, you may want to review the section "File Security" in Chapter 3, "The UNIX File System." Briefly, file permissions are little flags that UNIX associates which each file. The flags indicate whether the file can be read, written, or executed, and by whom.

The file creation mask is a device you use for indicating what permissions UNIX is to assign to a new file by default. If you want some other access permissions for a file, the usual approach is to first create the file, then change the file's permissions with the chmod command.

The file creation mask itself is a binary value consisting of nine bits, corresponding to each of the permission bits for a file. As a matter of convention, the nine bits are represented by three octal digits, with each digit representing three bits. The file creation mask is therefore a value expressed in octal as three octal digits. The use of octal number representation for the file creation mask is a matter of convention, not necessity, yet the umask command does not allow you to use any other number form for displaying or setting the file creation mask: you must use octal to set the mask, and you must interpret octal values to understand the mask when displayed.

As for the mask itself, each of the bits in the mask indicate whether the corresponding bit of the file permission should be set *off*, (set to zero). By default, virtually all UNIX commands attempt to set all reasonable permission bits to one when creating the file. A command that creates a data file (such as a text file), tries to create the file with permissions of 666. In octal, this would grant read and write permission to you the file's owner, to other members of your UNIX group, and to all other system users; it would however leave the execute permission unset. Commands which create executable files (such as cc and ld) attempt to set the file's permissions to 777, which in octal would set the read, write, and execute bits for all users.

Because of this default action by UNIX commands, it is the function of the file creation mask to specify permissions you *don't* want set. When you set a bit in the file creation mask, it causes the corresponding bit of the file's permissions to be forced to zero. Bits not set in the file creation mask are interpreted as *don't care*: the file permission bit stays unchanged.

Now, the bits of the file permissions, from left to write, are written *rwxrwxrwx*, where the first three bits represent read, write, and execute permissions for the file's owner; the second set of three bits represent read, write, and execute permissions for the file's group; and the third set of three bits are the permissions for other users. To grant read and write permissions to the file's owner, but only read access to other users, the appropriate file permissions setting would be the bits *110100100*. Writing this in octal, you arrive at the familiar permissions value of *644*, which you may already have seen in the output of the ls command.

Remember that UNIX commands try to create files with all reasonable permissions set. For a data file, these bits are 110110110, corresponding to rw-rw-rw-. To get the permissions switched to rw-r--r--, you need to set off the fifth and eight bits. A file creation mask of 000010010 (in octal 022) would do the trick. When the file is created, UNIX lines up the bits in the file permissions requested by the command, and your file creation mask, like this:

```
1 1 0 1 1 0 1 1 0      attempted file permissions
0 0 0 0 1 0 0 1 0      file creation mask
-----------------
1 1 0 1 0 0 1 0 0      actual file permissions
```

What you have to do when using the umask command, therefore, is first to decide what file permissions you would like assigned to your new files by default, and then write a bit mask as an octal number which sets the appropriate file permission bits to zero.

As it happens, most UNIX users want to reserve write permission for their files to themselves, but are willing to let other people look at the files. The appropriate file creation mask for this is *022* in octal. In many cases, the system administrator sets up the system so that the umask 022 command is automatically executed for you when you login in. If the administrator has not set up a default, or you wish to use another file creation mask, you can set a new mask in your login profile.

The actual syntax of the umask command is straightforward:

To display the current process file creation mask, use the umask command as follows:

```
% umask
022
```

You can also use umask to set the process file creation mask by specifying the *octal* argument as follows:

```
% umask octal
```

The process file creation mask is set to the bit pattern corresponding to the low-order nine bits of the octal number *octal*.

Echoing Arguments to Standard Output

C shell provides two commands for echoing arguments to standard output: echo and glob. The only difference between them is the delimiter used to separate words in the output line.

The echo command, though most often used when writing shell scripts, also comes in handy in a number of keyboard situations, for example when constructing a pipe to a non-interactive command. One of the best examples of the echo command is using it to display the value of a shell variable:

```
% echo $path
/usr/bin /usr/ucb/bin /usr/local/bin /home/jjv/bin
%
```

In this case, it is the variable substitution expression $path which does the real work; the echo command provides only the step of printing the value on the terminal. Nonetheless, without the echo command it would be cumbersome to check the value of a variable: the set command will also print variable variables, but it prints all variables, sometimes producing a lengthy list that takes time to search for the entry you want.

The glob command, on the other hand is rarely used in any context. It was originally intended to be called from a C program (not a shell script), to get the shell to expand a filename wildcard expression. However, most C programmers don't use this technique because it relies on the existence of the C shell.

Using the *echo* Command

The echo command prints a line containing its arguments to standard output. The syntax for the command is as follows:

```
echo [ -n ] wordlist
```

The arguments are printed with one intervening blank between them and a newline character after the last one. The echo command does not modify the words in *wordlist* in any way, but the arguments as seen by echo might differ from those on the original command because of variable, command, and history replacement and filename globbing. For example, the following command

```
echo Directory $dir contains these files: *.c
```

might generate the following line to standard output:

```
Directory /usr/lib1 contains these files: myprog.c bigprog.c
```

Specify option -n to suppress printing a newline character; this allows the next input or output to occur on the same line as the output of the echo command.

Using the *glob* Command

The `glob` command also prints a line containing its arguments to standard output. The syntax for the command is as follows:

```
glob [ wordlist ]
```

Use `glob` to print the words in *wordlist* to standard output. The words are printed with a null character between each (not white space as `echo` does). The last word is followed by a newline character.

The words in *wordlist* are subject to variable, command, and history substitution and filename expansion in the usual manner. After scanning for substitutions, the resulting strings are redivided into words, which are then written using the null character delimiter.

The `glob` command is similar to `echo`, differing only in the delimiter used to separate words in the output line. Because most terminals cannot print a null character, `glob` is not normally used to generate terminal output. It is intended to be called from a C language program, in the form `/bin/csh -c 'glob ...'`, to invoke the shell substitution and filename expansion mechanisms.

Rescanning a Line for Substitutions—*eval*

Use `eval` to rescan the arguments *arg* for variable, command, and history substitutions, filename expansion and quote removal, and then execute the resulting words as a command.

```
eval arg ...
```

With `eval`, you can essentially write shell script lines with a shell script and execute the resulting generated commands. Remember, however, that to embed variable symbols in a string, you must hide the leading dollar sign from earlier shell substitutions.

The `eval` command implemented by the C shell is equivalent to the Bourne shell `eval` command.

Changing Your Group ID—*newgrp*

The `newgrp` command is the same as the UNIX `newgrp` command:

```
newgrp groupname
```

When issued from your login shell (not to be confused with a login shell script, the login shell is simply that shell started up for you automatically when you log in), `newgrp` causes the current shell to be replaced by a new shell with the real and effective group IDs both changed to the specified group *groupname*. Because the shell is replaced, all context, including exported variables and aliases, is lost.

Use the `newgrp` command when you have been authorized by the system administrator for membership in two or more user groups, and you wish to change your group identification from your current or login group to another group. Your group identification is used by the system when determining whether to grant you access to files.

Timing the Execution of a Command—*time*

Use `time` with no argument to display the amount of CPU time in seconds used by the current shell and all commands and subshells invoked since its start. This form of the command is usually of interest only to folks who are being billed for the amount of machine time they use, as might be the case if you are renting time on a commercial machine. By entering the command with no arguments occasionally, you can monitor how much machine time you have used and limit your online time accordingly.

```
time [ command ]
```

Only for your login shell will this be the amount of machine time used since you logged-in. Also, note that this is not elapsed wall clock time—it is only machine time used.

Use the form `time` *command* to execute *command* and report the amount of CPU time used by the command's execution. The command must be a simple command, not a compound command, statement group, or parenthesized statement, and cannot be a pipeline.

You might be interested in timing the execution of a command if you are a production operations manager and you want to find out how much time a new application is adding to your daily workload. A development programmer would use the `time` command to determine whether a new program has a performance problem. The average interactive user, however, would have infrequent occasion to use the `time` command.

Aliases

One of the handier features of the C shell is the alias feature. An alias is a shorthand method of referring to a command or a part of a command. For example, if you have several favorite options that you always supply to the `ls` command, rather than having to type the whole command every time, you can create a two-character alias. Then you can type the two-character alias, and the shell will execute its definition.

An alias can represent not only a command name, but also leading options and arguments of the command line. Any words you type following the alias name are considered to follow options and arguments included in the alias definition, allowing you to customize the command with key options and arguments.

More complex processing can be achieved using shell scripts, where the function performed by the shell script file's name used as a command can be arbitrarily complex. The command alias feature was provided only for use as a keyboard shortcut, and anything that can be achieved using an alias can be done with shell scripts.

You should add command aliases that you use often to your `.login` file, so that the alias will be defined every time you log in. It is often handy, however, to define command aliases at the keyboard for special commands you'll be using during this session. Unless you incorporate the alias into your `.login` file, it will be lost when you log out.

Defining, Listing, and Changing Command Aliases—alias

The `alias` command allows you to list currently defined aliases, to define a new command alias, or to change an existing alias. The command format is

```
alias [ name [ definition ... ]]
```

For *name*, choose a word consisting of upper- and lowercase letters and digits. For *definition*, write any sequence of words that defines the command string you want *name* to stand for. For example, the following defines two aliases for the `ls` command, each providing a different set of options. It's shorter to type the alias name for the particular style of `ls` command output than it is to type the `ls` command and options.

```
alias lx /usr/bin/ls -FC
alias ll /usr/bin/ls -l
```

If you want to change the definition of an alias, you simply define it again.

Once you have defined aliases, you can display a list of their names and definitions by entering the `alias` command without arguments, as in the following example:

```
% alias
alias lx /usr/bin/ls -FC
alias ll /usr/bin/ls -l
```

You can also display the definition of a specific alias by specifying its name as an argument:

```
% alias lx
alias lx /usr/bin/ls -FC
```

Alias substitution occurs early in the shell's processing cycle for commands, thereby allowing you to use *globbing* (filename replacement), variable substitution, command substitution, and command history substitution in the wordlist. Because of this, you will often need to quote at least one of the words of *definition*, and perhaps the entire alias definition. Some people always enclose the alias definition in quotes to avoid surprises. Consider the following alias:

```
alias lc ls *.[ch]
```

For a C language programmer, the alias would be rather natural: by simply typing lc, you get a listing of all source program files in the current directory, devoid of any other file clutter.

> **NOTE:** Note that substitutions will occur when the alias command is processed, unless you quote all or part of the wordlist.

However, the preceding alias definition will not work as expected. The filename pattern *.[ch] will be substituted on the alias command itself, and the actual alias stored (depending on the actual directory contents when you enter the alias command) will be as you see here:

```
% alias lc
ls app.h io.c main.c prog.c sundry.h
```

Because the filename pattern was replaced before the alias definition was stored by the shell, the lc alias won't list all files ending in .c or .h; it will attempt to list the files app.h, io.c, main.c, prog.c, and sundry.h whether they exist in the current directory or not.

The alias should have been defined as follows:

```
% alias lc ls '*.c'
```

An alias definition can also use command aliases. During alias substitution, the alias definition is scanned repeatedly until no further substitutions can be made. An alias definition for *name*, however, cannot invoke the *name* alias within itself; a reference to *name* in the wordlist will be taken as a reference to the shell built-in command or executable file named *name*, not as a reference to the alias. This allows you to use an alias to redefine a system command or shell built-in command, for example:

```
% alias pg pg -cns -p"Page %d:"
```

You can refer to arguments of the original command line, before any substitutions were made, using the command history substitution syntax (see the section later in this chapter titled "Command History"). For example, the command

```
alias print 'pr \!* ¦ lp'
```

defines an alias named *print* that executes the pr command using all the arguments of the original command line (\!*), then pipes the output to lp for printing.

To properly understand and use the alias command, you must be clear about the way an alias is used. When you define an alias by entering the alias command, the only thing that happens at that time is that the system stores the alias in computer memory. Later, when you enter a command with the same name as the alias, the C shell does a little magic. The command you typed will not be executed in the form you typed it. Rather, the command name (which is an alias name) will be replaced by the *value* of the alias. The result is a new command text, the front part of which is the alias definition, and which ends with any other arguments you typed.

For example, suppose you define an alias for the 1s command as follows:

```
% alias lax ls -ax
```

If at some later time you enter this command:

```
% lax big*.txt
```

the command actually executed will be:

```
ls -ax big*.txt
```

The command alias (lax) is replaced by its definition (ls -ax). Remaining arguments on the command line (big*.txt) are simply tacked on after the alias substitution, to yield the command the computer will actually execute.

Using history substitutions in an alias provides additional flexibility, namely by allowing the executed command to employ arguments in a different order or a different form than entered, but require a little extra work from the shell. Consider the following alias definition:

```
alias lsp 'ls \!* ¦ lp'
```

Entering the command lsp *.c *.sh will result in alias substitution for lsp. The symbol !* will cause the arguments you entered on the line *.c *.sh to be inserted into the alias definition, rather than tacked on after. In other words, if an alias definition contains a history substitution, the shell suspends its normal action of tacking on command arguments after the alias value. The command actually executed will be ls *.c *.sh ¦ lp. Without this special mechanism, the executed command would have been ls *.c *.sh ¦ lp *.c *.sh, with the final *.c *.sh being tacked on in the usual manner, leading to an undesirable result: instead of printing a directory listing, the lp command would print the full contents of the files.

When writing an alias, you therefore need to visualize what will happen when the alias is substituted in later commands.

Deleting a Command Alias—*unalias*

Use unalias to delete one or more aliases. You can delete a specific alias by specifying its name as an argument, or you can delete multiple aliases by using pattern-matching:

```
unalias name
unalias pattern
```

If you specify a specific alias *name,* only that alias definition is deleted. If you specify a *pattern,* all those currently defined aliases whose names match the pattern are deleted. *pattern* can contain the pattern-matching characters *, ?, and [...]. In the following example, the first line deletes the lx alias, and the second line deletes all currently defined aliases:

```
unalias lx
unalias *
```

Shell Options

The C shell supports a number of command-line options to support special uses of the shell. These options are shown in Table 13.3.

Table 13.3. C shell options.

Option	Usage
-c	The shell executes the commands in the first argument string, then exits. Called from a C language program in the form csh -c "commands" to execute a shell command or list of commands (separated with semicolons or newline characters).
-e	If set, causes immediate termination of the shell if a command returns a nonzero exit code. This option is mainly used in shell scripts to abandon processing if a command sequence fails; it is simpler to use than individually checking the exit code of each command.
-f	If set, suppresses reading of the .cshrc initialization script. Use this option to speed up shell initialization and shell script execution. (See "Customizing Your Shell Environment" later in this chapter for more information about the .cshrc file.)
-i	Forces the shell to use interactive mode, even if its input is not a terminal. In interactive mode, the shell writes prompts to the standard error file prior to reading each command and ignores the *Intr* and *Quit* signals. The -i option is assumed when the shell is started with terminal input and output.
-n	If set, suppresses execution of commands. Command interpretation still occurs. Use the -n option to discover whether the shell script contains any syntax errors without actually executing commands it may contain.

Option	Usage
-s	If set, prevents interpretation of the first command-line argument of csh as a shell script filename. Used when you are executing a stream of commands from standard input and you wish to set one or more argv arguments on the shell command line—for example, csh -s /usr/bin < *file*. Command-line arguments can be referenced by the commands in *file*.
-t	Forces the shell to terminate after reading and executing one line from standard input. If the command must be continued onto more lines, append \ to all lines but the last. The shell does not buffer up input when this option is set; it can therefore be used to read and execute the next line from a currently open file.
-v	Sets the verbose variable. The verbose variable causes the shell to echo commands to the terminal before any substitutions are made and before the commands' execution. Sometimes used to assist with debugging a shell script, in the form csh -v *filename*.
-x	Sets the echo variable. Commands are echoed to the terminal after substitution and filename generation but before execution. Sometimes used to assist with debugging a shell script, in the form csh -x *filename*.
-V	Like -v but sets the verbose option before processing the .cshrc initialization script. Use this option to display lines from the .cshrc script as they are executed.
-X	Like -x but sets the echo option before processing the .cshrc initialization script.

Unless one of the -c, -i, -s, or -t options is set, the shell construes the first command-line argument as the name of a file to be executed. Remaining command-line arguments are assigned to the $1, $2, ... variables, and to the argv array variable. The -c option allows only one command-line argument and takes it as a list of commands to be executed; after execution of the argument string, csh exits. When the -i, -s, or -t option is set, the shell assigns all arguments including the first to the $1, $2,...variables and the argv array variable.

The shell supports additional options that you can switch on or off during shell operation. These options are controlled by variables; if the variable is set, the corresponding option is activated; if it is not, the option is off. These options are described in the section titled "Using Predefined Variables" later in this chapter. Briefly, their names are echo, ignoreeof, noclobber, noglob, nonmatch, notify, and verbose.

Additionally, the shell variables `cdpath`, `history`, `mail`, `path`, `prompt`, and `shell`, although not options as such, allow you to control certain shell behaviors such as searching for commands and checking for mail. See the section titled "Using Predefined Variables" for further information.

Command History

The shell's command history service maintains a list of previously executed commands. You can use command history for two purposes: as a reference to determine what you've already done, and, with history substitution, as a shorthand method to reuse all or part of a previous command in entering a new command.

Displaying the Command History

The `history` command enables you to print all or selected lines of the current command history.

```
history [ -r ] [ n ]
```

To display all the lines currently held in the history list, enter the `history` command (it takes no arguments):

```
% history
1  cd src
2  ls
3  vi foo.c
4  cc foo.c
5  grep '#include' foo.c
```

The shell displays each line preceded with a line number. You can use the line number to refer to commands with the history substitution mechanism. Line numbers start with *1* at the beginning of your session.

The amount of history a shell maintains is dependent on the amount of memory available to the shell. History is not saved in an external disk file, so capacity is somewhat limited. You can set the `history` variable to a value indicating the number of lines of history you want the shell to maintain; it will keep that number of lines and more if possible, but your specification is only advisory. The value of `history` must be a simple number to be effective. For example, `set history=25` retains at least twenty-five lines of history.

> **CAUTION:** The history service retains command *lines*, not *commands*. As the history area becomes full, the shell discards old lines. This might result in some lines containing incomplete, partial commands. You need to use caution with the

history substitution facility to avoid calling for the execution of an incomplete command.

To limit the number of lines displayed, specify an integer decimal for *n* to limit the number of lines displayed to the last *n* lines of history.

Specify the `-r` option to print history lines in reverse order, from the most recent to the oldest.

Using History Substitutions to Execute Commands

History substitutions are introduced into a command with the `!` (exclamation point, sometimes called the *bang* operator). You append one or more characters to `!` to define the particular kind of history substitution you want. If followed by a blank, tab, newline, equal sign (=), or open parenthesis (, the exclamation point is treated as an ordinary character.

NOTE: The exclamation point is an ordinary character to other shells, but it is special to the C shell: you must precede it with \ (backslash) to avoid its special meaning, even inside quoted strings. The shell will attempt a history substitution wherever it finds an exclamation point in the command line, without regard to any quoting; only the backslash can avoid interpretation of `!` as a history substitution mark.

You can write a history substitution anywhere in the current shell input line, as part or all of the command. When you enter a command containing one or more history substitutions, the shell echoes the command after performing the substitutions so that you can see the command that will actually be executed. (You do not have an opportunity to correct the command; it is executed immediately after being displayed.)

The simplest forms of history substitution are `!!` and `!number`. The `!!` symbol is replaced with the entire previous command line. The expression `!number` is replaced with line *number* from the command history list.

Suppose command history currently contains the following lines:

```
% history
1  cd src
2  ls
3  vi foo.c
4  cc foo.c
5  grep '#include' foo.c
```

If you now enter the command !!, the shell will repeat the grep command in its entirety. Press return to execute the grep command, or type additional words to add to the end of the grep command:

```
% !! sna.h
grep '#include' foo.c sna.h
```

Continuing the example, suppose after running grep you want to edit the foo.c file again. You could type the vi command as usual, but it already appears in command history as line 3. A history substitution provides a handy shortcut:

```
% !3
vi foo.c
```

That's almost all there is to basic history substitution. Actually, the shell supports any of the following forms for referring to command history lines:

!!	Replaced with the previous command line (the last line of command history).
!*number*	Replaced with line *number* of command history.
!-*number*	Replaced with the history line *number* lines back; !-1 is equivalent to !!.
!*string*	Replaced with the most recent history line having a command that begins with *string*. For example, use !v to refer to a previous vi command.
!?*string*?	Replaced with the most recent history line containing *string* anywhere in the line. For example, use !?foo? to repeat a previous vi foo.c command.

You can do more with history substitutions than merely reuse a previous command. The shell also provides extensions to the history operator that allow you to select individual words or a group of words from a history line, inserting the selected word or words into the current command. These extensions are in the form of a suffix beginning with : (colon). For example, !vi:1 is replaced not with the most recent vi command, but rather with its first argument word. Similarly, !3:3-4 is replaced with arguments 3 and 4 of history line 3. You can use any of the following expressions as word selectors by appending the expression to a line reference, preceded with a colon:

0	First word of the command (usually the command name).
n	*n*th argument of the command. Arguments are numbered from 1. Note that *0* refers to the command name, which is actually the first word of the line, whereas *1* refers to the second word of the line.
^	Same as :1, the first argument.
$	Last argument word of the command.

%	For the !?*string*? format, the word matched by *string*. Use this word selector only with the !?*string*? history reference. Its value is the entire word matching *string*, even though *string* might have matched only a part of the word.
m-n	Multiple word substitution. Replaced with words *m* through *n* of the history line. For *m* and *n*, specify an integer number, or one of the special symbols ^, $, or %.
m-	Substitutes words beginning with the *m*th word and extending up to but not including the last word.
-*n*	Same as 0-*n*; substitutes words beginning with the first word of the history line (the command name) through the *n*th word.
m*	Same as *m*-$; substitutes words beginning with the *m*th word and extending through the last word of the line.
*	Same as ^-$; substitutes all argument words of the line.

If the word selector expression you want to write begins with ^, $, *, -, or %, you can omit the colon between the line selector and the word selector. For example, !vi* refers to all the arguments of the previous vi command, and is the same as !vi:* or !vi:^-$.

You can use any number of word selectors in the same command line. By combining multiple word selectors, you can reuse arguments of a previous command in a different order and use arguments originally appearing on different commands. For example, the command rm !115^ !117^ removes files that were named on two earlier commands.

When counting words of a previous command line, the shell takes quoting into consideration but uses the line as it appears in the history list; words generated by variable or command substitution or filename generation are not accessible.

You can append modifiers to a word selector to alter the form of the word before insertion in the new command. A modifier is written in the form :*x*, where *x* is a letter specifying how the word should be modified. For example, !vi^:t will substitute the *tail* of the first argument of the vi command: for the argument /usr/X/lib/samples/xclock.c, the value of :t will be xclock.c.

The following modifiers can be appended to a word selector to alter the selected word before substitution:

:h	Removes a trailing path component. Successive :h modifiers remove path components one at a time, right to left. Thus for the argument /usr/X/lib/samples/xclock.c, :h will return /usr/X/lib/samples, whereas :h:h will return /usr/X/lib.
:r	Removes a filename suffix of the form .*string*. For example, for the argument foo.c, :r will return foo.

`:e`	Removes all but the filename suffix. For the argument `foo.sh`, `:e` will return `.sh`.
`:t`	Removes all leading components of a path, returning just the filename part. For the word `/usr/bin/ls`, the value of `:t` is `ls`.
`:s/x/y/`	Replaces the string *x* in the selected word with the string *y*. String *x* cannot be a regular expression. The symbol & appearing in *y* is replaced with the search string *x*, thus `:s/bill/&et/` will substitute `billet` for `bill`. Any character can be used in place of the slash, for example `:s?/usr?/user?`. The final `/` can be omitted if followed by a newline. The delimiter (`/` or your delimiter) or & can be used as a text character by escaping it with \ (backslash), for example `:s/\/usr/\/user/`. The search string *x* can be omitted, in which case the search string of the previous `:s` on the same line is used, or if no previous `:s` occurred, the string of `!?string?` is used.
`:&`	Reuses the previous string substitution modifier `:s` appearing in the same command line, thus `!grep:2:s/bill/marty/ !:3:&` is the same as `!grep:2:s/bill/marty/ !3:s/bill/marty/`.
`:p`	Used in any history substitution expression on the command line, causes the shell to print the command after substitutions, but not to execute it. Use `:p` to try the effect of a history substitution before executing it.
`:q`	Encloses the substituted word or words in quotes to prevent further substitutions.
`:x`	Breaks the selected word or words at blanks, tabs, and newlines.

Normally, a modifier affects only the first selected word. When selecting multiple words, such as with `!12:2*`, you can apply a modifier to all of the selected words by inserting a `g` in front of the modifier letter. For example, `!12:2*:gh` will apply the `:h` modifier to all of the words. The `g` is not valid with the `:p`, `:q`, and `:x` modifiers.

You can omit the command identifier from a history substitution when using two or more `!` expressions in the same line; successive history references then refer to the same command as the first. For example,

```
% vi %grep^:t %:3:t %:4:t
```

all refer to the same `grep` command but select the first, third, and fourth arguments.

The history mechanism supports a special abbreviation `^` useful for correcting a keying error in the previous line. The general form of the abbreviation is `^x^y`, where *x* and *y* are strings. The previous command line is selected and searched for string *x*; if found, it is replaced with *y*, then executed. For example, after the command `cd /usr/ban`, enter the line `^ban^bin` (or `^an^in`) to execute the command as `cd /usr/bin`. The caret `^` must be the first nonblank character of the line to be recognized as a line editing substitution. This abbreviation is available only for the immediately preceding command line; you must use the full history expression `!line:s/x/y/` to edit any line other than the last.

One final, important provision of the history substitution mechanism is that you can enclose any history reference in braces {} to isolate it from characters following it. Thus, `!{vi^:h}.c` forms a word beginning with the selected history reference and ending in `.c`.

Variables

You can use shell variables to hold temporary values, and shell scripts can use variables to manage changeable information. The shell itself also has variables of its own that you can use to customize features of the shell and your shell environment.

A variable is actually an area of the shell's memory set aside to hold a string of characters and given a name. You assign the name of a variable when you define it with `set`. You can change the value of a variable in several ways.

The shell provides a complex set of syntax for referring to the value of a variable. Any variable reference, when scanned in a command line, is replaced by the corresponding value of the reference before the command is executed. In its simplest form, a variable reference simply replaces the name of a variable with its string value.

This section looks at the kinds of variables the shell supports and the rules for naming them and referring to their value.

Variable Names

The shell imposes no set limit on the size of variable names. People commonly use variable names of six to eight characters, and names up to sixteen characters are not unusual.

A variable name can consist of only uppercase and lowercase letters and digits. The name cannot begin with a digit, because names beginning with a digit are reserved for use by the shell. General usage indicates the use of all capital letters for the names of environment variables, and all lowercase letters for local variables, although the shell imposes no such restriction.

You assign a value to a variable using the `set` or `setenv` built-in commands, depending on the type of variable you are setting.

NOTE: The C shell does not support the assignment statement *name=value*, which might be familiar to you from the Bourne and Korn shells.

Creating Shell Variables

Use the set statement to create new local variables and optionally to assign a value to them. *Local variables* are known only to the current shell and are not passed to shell scripts or invoked commands.

Use the setenv statement to create new environment variables. *Environment variables* are passed to shell scripts and invoked commands, which can reference the variables without first defining them (no setenv statement is required or should be used in a shell script for passed environment variables you wish to access). (See the section "Displaying and Setting Global Environment Variables" below for more about environment variables.)

A shell variable can contain any characters, including unprintable characters, as part of its value. A shell variable can also have a *null* value, which is a zero-length string containing no characters. A variable with a null value differs from an unset variable: a reference to the former has the effect of merely deleting the variable reference, because it is replaced with a zero-length string; a reference to an unset variable is an error, generates an error message, and causes the shell interpretation of commands to stop.

Displaying and Setting Local Shell Variables—*set*

The set command can be used to display or set local variables.

```
set
set name=word
set name=(wordlist)
set name[index]=word
```

Use set with no arguments to list the currently defined variables and their respective values. The listing includes exported variables as well as local variables.

Any of the operand formats can be combined on a single set statement; each assigns a value to a single shell variable or element of an array variable. Note that no white space should separate the variable name, equal sign, or value when writing an assignment; any white space appearing in *word* or *wordlist* must be hidden with quotes.

Use set *name* to define a variable *name* and to initialize it with a null string. This form can be used to set a number of shell options (such as set ignoreeof). A variable with a null value is not the same as an unset variable; the former exists but has no value, whereas the latter does not exist. A reference to an unset variable results in a shell error message; a reference to a null variable results in substitution of the null string.

Use set *name=word* to assign the string *word* as the current value of variable *name*. The string replaces the current value of *name* if the variable is already defined; otherwise, a new variable named *name* is created. If *word* contains characters special to the shell (including blanks or tabs), it must be enclosed in single or double quotes.

Use the form set *name*=(*wordlist*) to assign each word in *wordlist* to successive elements of the array variable *name*. After the assignment, the expression $name[1] refers to the first word in *wordlist*, $name[2] to the second word, and so on. Any word in *wordlist* must be quoted if it contains characters special to the shell (including blanks or tabs).

Use the form set *name*[*i*]=*word* to assign the string *word* as the current value of the *i*th element of the array variable *name*. For *i*, specify a decimal integer number not less than 1. Note that you do not have to assign a value to every element of an array. The number of elements in an array is effectively the highest-numbered element to which a value has been assigned. Elements to which no value has been assigned have an effective value of the null (zero-length) string. Also note that you cannot assign a (*wordlist*) to an array element; an array variable can have multiple values, but each element can represent only one string value.

Deleting Local Shell Variables—*unset*

Use the unset command to delete one or more shell variables from the shell's memory.

unset *pattern*

The unset command is effective for variables defined with the set command only; use the unsetenv command to delete variables defined with setenv.

For *pattern*, specify a string that might optionally contain one or more occurrences of the pattern-matching characters *, ?, or [...]. All local variables known to the shell whose names match the specified pattern are deleted. You will receive no warning message if nothing matches *pattern*, and no confirmation documenting the variables that were deleted.

Displaying and Setting Global Environment Variables—*setenv*

Use the setenv statement to create new environment variables. Environment variables are passed to shell scripts and invoked commands, which can reference the variables without first defining them (no setenv statement is required or should be used in a shell script for passed environment variables you wish to access). See the section later in this chapter titled "Customizing Your Shell Environment" for more about environment variables.

The format of the setenv command is: setenv [*name*=*value* ...]. Issued without arguments, the setenv command lists all global environment variables currently in effect, together with their values. Used in the form setenv *name*=*value* , the shell creates a new global variable with the specified name and assigns the *string* value as its initial value. If the value contains contains characters such as the space or tab, be sure to enclose the value string in quotes. (See the section "Quoting and Escaping Special Characters" in this chapter for information about shell special characters and the use of quoting techniques.)

UNIX also provides a command (env) for displaying the current list of environment variables and their values. The env command actually supports a number of options and arguments for modifying the current environment.

The section "Using Predefined Variables" below provides a list of all variables (local and environment) which are defined by the C shell. Environment variables defined by other UNIX components are defined in the documentation for those components. Unfortunately there is no comprehensive list of environment variables, because some are defined by non-shell programs. The mailx command, for example, defines some variables, and the vi command looks for some variables of its own. Altogether the environment variable pool is optional anyway: if you don't know of a variable some UNIX command uses, the command will still work without it. At any rate, be aware that the shell is not responsible for defining all environment variables; it merely provides a means for manipulating and accessing them.

Deleting Global Environment Variables—*unsetenv*

To delete global environment variables, you use the unsetenv command:

```
unsetenv variablename
unsetenv pattern
```

Use the unsetenv command to delete one or more environment variables from the shell's memory. The unsetenv command is effective only for variables defined with the setenv command; use the unset command to delete variables defined with set.

To delete a particular variable definition, specify its name as *variablename*. To delete multiple variable definitions, use *pattern* to specify a string that might optionally contain one or more occurrences of the pattern-matching characters *, ?, or [...]. All environment variables known to the shell whose names match the specified pattern are deleted. You will receive no warning message if nothing matches *pattern*, and no confirmation documenting the variables that were deleted.

Obtaining Variable Values with Reference Expressions

You obtain the value of a shell variable by writing a variable reference on the command line. A variable reference results in replacement of the entire reference expression, including the $ that introduces the reference, the variable's name, and any other characters that might adorn the reference, with a string value of the reference.

A variable reference does not itself define the start or end of a word: the reference can be a complete word or a part of a word. If a part of a word, the substituted string is combined with other characters in the word to yield the substituted word. However, if the reference value substitutes one or more blanks or tabs into the word, the word will be split into two or more words unless it is quoted. For example, if the value of *var* is "two words," then the reference expression $var will appear as two words after substitution, but the quoted string "$var" will appear as the one word "two words" afterward.

A variable reference can result in the substitution of the value of either a local or a global variable: a local variable is used if it exists, otherwise the value of an environment variable is taken. Remember, a variable reference refers to a variable by name: local and environment variables cannot have the same name, so a reference is to whatever variable has the specified name.

You can use any of the variable reference forms shown in Table 13.4 in a word.

Table 13.4. Shell variable references.

Syntax	Meaning
$name	Replaced with the value of *name*. It is an error if the ${name} variable *name* is not defined.
$name[n]	Replaced with the value of elements of array variable ${name[n]} *name*. For *n*, write an element number, or a range of element numbers in the form *m-n*. Use *-n* to substitute elements *1-n*, and *m-* to substitute elements *m* through the end of the array.
$#name	Replaced with the number of elements in array variable ${#name} *name*.
$?name	Replaced with 1 if variable *name* is set, otherwise 0. ${?name}

The reference forms using braces (for example, ${name} and ${#name}) are useful when the variable name would run onto the remainder of the current word, yielding an undefined variable name. For example, if the variable *dir* contains the path prefix /usr/bin/, then the word ${dir}name.c will form the full pathname /usr/bin/name.c upon expansion; however, the simpler form $dirname.c would be taken as a reference to variable *dirname*, not at all what was intended. In effect, the braces set off the variable reference from the remainder of the word.

A reference to an unset variable generates a shell error message and, if the reference occurs inside a shell script, causes reading of the shell script to terminate. You can use the $?name or ${?name} forms to handle the case where a variable might not be set. For example:

```
if ($?nfiles) echo "File count is $nfiles"
```

Using Array Variables

Unless you provide otherwise, a variable can have only one value. An array variable, on the other hand, can have any number of values (provided only that the shell has sufficient memory available to store the values). For example, the path variable, used by the shell as a list of directories to search for commands, is an array variable where each element is a directory path.

You assign values to an array variable in one of two ways—all at once, or one at a time. To assign many values at once, use a *wordlist* argument to the set command. A wordlist is a parenthesized list of words. For example, the following array contains four values:

```
set path=(/bin /usr/bin $home/bin .)
```

Each of the words in a wordlist is assigned to the next available element of the array variable. Assigning a wordlist to a variable automatically defines the variable as an array.

To assign values individually to elements of an array, you must use array subscript notation. Written in the form *name*[*index*], the *index* must be a number designating an array element; elements are numbered starting with 1, so $name[1] is a reference to the first element of an array. The following example assigns three values to the array *planets*, then prints one of them using an array reference:

```
% set planets[1]=Mercury
% set planets[2]=Venus
% set planets[3]=Earth
% echo Planet 3 is $planet[3]
Planet 3 is Earth
```

If you reference the array variable name without an index, the shell replaces the reference with a wordlist:

```
% echo The planets are $planets
The planets are (Mercury Venus Earth)
```

You can also use the reference $name[*] to obtain all the words of the array without the surrounding parentheses:

```
% echo The planets are: $planets[*]
The planets are: Mercury Venus Earth
```

You can reference a specific range of elements using the notation $name[m-n], where *m* and *n* are the beginning and ending index numbers of the elements you want. For example, the following lists only the earth-like planets:

```
% set planets=(Mercury Venus Earth Mars Jupiter Saturn Uranus Neptune Pluto)
% echo The terraform planets are: $planets[2-4]
The terraform planets are: Venus Earth Mars
```

The special form $name[-n] refers to elements of the array beginning with the first and extending through *n*:

```
% echo The inner planets are: $planets[-4]
The inner planets are: Mercury Venus Earth Mars
```

The special form $name[n-] refers to the elements of the array beginning with *n* and extending through the last:

```
% echo The outer planets are: $planets[5-]
The outer planets are: Jupiter Saturn Uranus Neptune Pluto
```

One of the primary reasons for using array variables is to permit looping through the array, inspecting and manipulating each of its elements in turn. This programming technique, often used in shell scripts, can be used at the keyboard as well:

```
% set files=(main io math dbase)
% foreach file ($files)
? cp $file.c $file.bak
? end
```

This example first assigns the root names of a list of files to an array variable, then uses the `foreach` shell statement to process each of the files in turn, by copying the file to a backup file, changing its filename in the process. (In the example, the question mark ? is the shell's prompt when it requires additional lines to complete an outstanding statement; it signals that you haven't finished the command yet.)

Using Special Read-Only Variables

In addition to ordinary variables that you define with the `set` and `setenv` commands, a number of variables are automatically defined by the shell and have preset values. Often the value of a special variable changes as the result of a command action. You can use these variables to acquire specific information that isn't available any other way. You cannot, however, use `set` or `setenv` to define these variables, and you can't assign new values to them.

The special variables can be referenced using the notation shown in Table 13.5.

Table 13.5. Shell special variables.

Variable	Meaning
$0	Replaced with the name of the current shell input file, if known. If unknown, this variable is unset, and a reference to it is an error.
$?0	Replaced with *1* if $0 is set, otherwise *0*.

continues

Table 13.5. continued

Variable	Meaning
$1, $2, ...	Replaced with the value of the shell command's first (second, third,...) argument. If used within a shell script invoked by name, these symbols refer to the command $9 arguments. Up to nine arguments can be referenced this way. To reference arguments beyond nine, you must use the reference notation $argv[n].
$*	Equivalent to $argv[*]. Replaced with all the shell's arguments.
$$	Replaced with the process number of the parent shell. Used within a shell script, refers to the process number of the invoking shell.
$<	Replaced with a line of text read from the standard input file.

The variables $1, $2, through $9 have special significance when used inside a shell script, because they refer to the arguments of the command line that invoked the shell script. The same command arguments are accessible via the array variable argv. Using the argv variable, you can refer to all command-line arguments, not just the first nine. For example, $argv[10] references the tenth argument, and $argv[$n] references whichever argument is designated by another variable $n.

The shift built-in command can be used to manipulate command arguments. See the section titled "Shell Programming" for details about the shift command.

Using Predefined Variables

The C shell also recognizes a number of conventionally named variables as having special meaning. Some are automatically initialized when the shell starts; others you set yourself. You can assign a value to most of these variables, but some variables are set automatically by the shell when a corresponding event occurs.

NOTE: Note that all predefined shell variables have lowercase names. This is to avoid conflicts with environment variables, which usually have uppercase names.

To set any predefined variable, use the set command. You need to specify a value only if the variable requires one; otherwise you can omit the value string. For example, use set noclobber to enable the noclobber option, but use set prompt='$cwd: ' to assign a new command-line prompt string. (See the set built-in command in the section titled "Displaying and Setting Local Shell Variables—set" for more information about set.)

You can use the unset built-in command to destroy the variable and any associated value, but be aware that an unset variable does not revert to its initial or default value and is not the same as a variable having a null value: an unset variable simply doesn't exist. (See the unset built-in command in the section titled "Deleting Local Shell Variables—unset" for more information about unset).

The following list describes the variables to which the shell is sensitive and indicates any initialization or assignment restrictions.

argv	An array variable containing the current shell parameters. A reference to argv[1] is equivalent to $1, argv[2] to $2, and so on. The value of argv is set by the shell at startup and just prior to the execution of each command.
cdpath	An array variable specifying a list of directories to be searched by the cd command. The shell does not provide an initial value for cdpath. If you do not provide a value, the cd command searches only the current directory to resolve unanchored pathnames.
cwd	Contains the full pathname of the current directory. On startup, the shell initializes cwd to the pathname of your home directory. Each cd command you execute changes the value of cwd.
echo	If set, the shell prints each command before execution. The echo variable is initialized to the null string if the -x option is present on the csh command line; otherwise the variable is left unset. You can activate command tracing at any time by executing the command set echo; to turn it off, use unset echo. Command tracing is effective only for the current shell invocation; it is not propagated into called shell scripts.
history	Specifies the number of commands to be maintained in the history list. The shell will retain at least this many lines of command history if sufficient memory is available. The history variable is not initialized and does not need to be assigned a value. If unset, the shell maintains an optimum amount of command history for the size of available memory. You can set the value of history at any time.
home	Initialized to the value of the *HOME* environment variable at shell startup. The value of home is used as the default directory for cd, and as the value substituted for ~. It is almost always improper for you to change the value of home, but you are not prevented from doing so.

ignoreeof	If set, the shell will ignore an end of file (*EOF*) character typed at the beginning of a line. If not set, an EOF character typed at the beginning of the line signals the shell to exit, which, for your login shell, also logs you out. The specific key corresponding to the EOF character can be displayed and changed using the stty (UNIX) command.
mail	An array variable listing the files to be monitored for change. If the first value is numeric, it specifies the frequency in seconds that the shell should check for new mail. If the last modification date of any one of the files is observed to change, the file issues the message *New mail in* name, where name is the name of the file that changed. (If mail lists only one file to be monitored, the notification message is *You have new mail.*) This command will monitor two mail files and specifies a give-minute interval for mail checking: set mail=(10 /usr/mail/jjv /usr/spool/mail/jjv).
noclobber	If set, the shell will not replace an existing file for the I/O redirection >. For >>, it will require that the target file already exists. You can activate the option with the command set noclobber, and turn it off with unset noclobber. When noclobber is set, you can use >! and >>! to perform the redirection anyway. The noclobber variable is initially unset.
noglob	If set, filename expansion using the pattern characters *, ?, and [...] is disabled. The noglob variable is initially unset.
nonomatch	If set, a filename pattern that matches no files will be passed through unchanged to the command. By default the shell issues an error message and ignores a command if no matching files can be found for a filename pattern argument. (Note that nonomatch is the default behavior of the Bourne shell.) Use set nonomatch to accept unmatched pattern arguments, and unset nonomatch to force a shell error message. The nonomatch variable is initially unset.
notify	If set, the shell writes a message to your terminal at once if the status of a background job changes. By default the shell does not notify you of status changes until just before issuing the next command-line prompt. Be aware that setting notify can cause messages to appear on your screen at inopportune times, such as when using a full-screen editor. The initial value of notify is unset.
path	An array variable listing the directories to be searched for commands. If the path variable is not set, you must use full, explicit pathnames to execute non-built-in commands, even those in your current directory (./mycmd, etc). The initial value of path is the same as the *PATH* environment variable.

The shell maintains a hash table of all the executable files in your search path. The hash table is initialized at startup time and is rebuilt whenever you change the value of path or *PATH*. Note, however, that if a new command is added to one of the files in your search path (including your current directory), the shell might not necessarily be aware of the addition and so might fail to find the command even though it exists. Similarly, removing an executable file from a directory early in your search path might not allow the execution of a like-named command in some other directory. In either of these cases, use the rehash built-in command to force rebuilding of the shell hash table.

Other than the cases mentioned earlier, the shell hash table is invisible to you. It exists to speed up the search for commands by skipping directories where a command is known not to exist.

prompt   Your prompt string. The value of prompt is printed at the start of each line when the shell is ready to read the next command. The value of prompt is scanned for variable and command substitutions before printing; history substitutions are allowed in the prompt string and refer to the command you last entered. The initial value of prompt is the string "% " (a percent sign followed by a blank) or, if you are the superuser, "# " (a pound sign followed by a blank).

shell   Because the C shell is capable of executing only shell scripts written in the C shell language, a mechanism is needed so that shell scripts written for the Bourne shell can be detected and passed to the proper program for execution. Any shell script where the first line begins with a nonexecutable command is considered to be a Bourne shell. To support this convention, Bourne shell scripts usually specify the : built-in command on the first line; there is no : command in the C shell. Similarly, scripts intended for the C shell usually begin with a command line and have the pound sign (#) in the first position.

When the shell recognizes that a shell script has been invoked but is not a valid C shell script, the value of shell is used as the initial part of a command to execute the script. The value of shell is initialized to the full pathname of the C shell using a system-dependent directory prefix (usually /bin/csh). However, any number of options and arguments can be specified along with the shell pathname; the filename of the shell script will be appended to the value of shell.

You should change the value of shell if you intend to execute Bourne shell scripts. (Note that many commands supplied with UNIX are implemented as Bourne shell scripts.)

status   Contains the exit code of the last command executed, as a decimal number. The value of status is changed after the execution of each command, so it is normally useless for you to assign a value to status.

time   If set, the value of time should specify a number of seconds. Any command you execute that exceeds this time limit will cause the shell to print a warning line giving the amount of time the command has used and the current CPU utilization level as a percentage. The initial value of time is unset.

verbose   If set, causes each command to be printed after history substitutions but before other substitutions. The verbose option is normally used within a shell script to echo the commands that follow. The initial value of verbose is unset.

Shell Programming

Although the C shell provides a number of useful extensions to the keyboard interface, such as the command history mechanism, job control, and additional filename wildcards, it would probably be fair to say that its most significant departure from the traditional Bourne shell is its syntax for programming constructs: array variables, variable reference forms in general, arithmetic expressions, and the if, while, foreach, and switch statements.

Array variables were previously discussed in the section titled "Using Array Variables." The syntax of variable references was discussed in "Obtaining Variable Values with Reference Expressions." The section titled "Using Expressions and Operators in Shell Statements," discusses the use of arithmetic expressions and the special @ command used for calculations. This section looks at the shell statements for flow control: the conditional statements if and switch and the loop control statements while and foreach.

What Is a Shell Script?

A shell script is simply a text file containing shell commands. What makes shell scripts especially handy is the ability to execute the commands in the file simply by typing the file's name as if it were a command. To put it another way, shell scripts provide a fairly painless way to add new commands to your UNIX system. A shell script can be as simple or as complicated to write as you choose. It can be designed to be used by yourself alone, or by many people as a general-purpose command.

Generally you'll want to write a shell script when you recognize either of two situations:

■ You find yourself repeating a lengthy series of commands over and over to accomplish one general task. Any time you need to accomplish a task on a fairly frequent basis (daily, weekly, or maybe several times a day), and the task requires more than one UNIX command, the task is a good candidate for packaging in a shell script.

■ A procedure needs to be established for a formal activity. For example, printing a weekly customer invoicing report might require a complex procedure, extracting billing information from a master file, computing the invoice data, setting up the printer, and actually generating the print file.

As a general rule, shell scripts written for the purpose tend to be straightforward to write, whereas the more formal procedures demand generalized shell scripts of greater complexity.

Writing Shell Scripts—An Overview

Writing a shell script is much like entering commands at the keyboard, with a few important differences:

■ You might want to support arguments on your command. The shell automatically sets any words entered on the command line following your script's name into a set of *parameters*: shell variables named $1 and $2. You don't need to take any special action to get arguments from the command line—they're already available in the parameter variables when your script begins its execution.

■ You might want to support one or more *options* with your new command. The shell passes options to your script the same as other arguments: each command-line word is set into the $1 variables (also accessible in the special shell array variable argv[*n*]). Options, however, can have a complicated structure, especially if you intend to support the standard UNIX convention for options. See the description of the getopt UNIX command for help with processing command-line option strings.

■ Keyboard commands are usually entered with all information customized to the command's use, whereas commands inside shell scripts are often parameterized and can be conditionally executed. You parameterize a command by providing variable references and filename substitutions as the command's arguments instead of literal text. To write alternative sets of commands to handle different situations, you need to use the shell's if, switch, while, and foreach commands. These commands are rarely used at the keyboard but occur heavily in shell scripts.

You use the same general procedure for writing shell scripts regardless of their purpose:

1. Develop a text file containing the required commands.
2. Mark the text file executable, using the chmod command: chmod +x *filename*.
3. Test the shell script.
4. Install the script in its permanent location.
5. Use it.

You probably already know how to prepare text files using a text editor. If not, see Chapter 7, "Editing Text Files." You can use any text editor you like, because the shell is interested in only the file's contents, not in how you created it. The text file cannot, however, contain the formatting characters generated by some word processors; it must contain lines identical in format and content to those you would enter at the keyboard. For this reason, you'll probably use a general text editor such as vi to prepare shell script files.

A text file must be marked executable to be invoked as a command by entering its filename. You can execute a file as a command even if it is not marked executable by naming it as the first argument of a csh command: csh payroll would cause the shell to search for a file named payroll using the standard search path (defined by the path variable), to open the file for reading, and to proceed to execute the commands in the file. But if you mark the payroll file executable, you don't have to type csh first: payroll becomes a new command.

The shell uses the same search path for locating script files as it does for locating the standard UNIX commands. To invoke a shell script by name, you must store it in a directory listed in your search path. Alternatively, you can add the directory in which the shell script resides to your search path, but naming too many directories in the search path can slow the shell down, so shell scripts are commonly gathered together into a few common directories.

You'll find that if you do any shell script writing at all, having a directory named bin under your home directory will be very handy. Place all the shell scripts you write for your own personal use in ~/bin, and include the directory ~/bin in your search path. Then, to add a new command to your personal environment, simply write a command script file, mark it executable, and store it in the ~/bin directory: it's ready for use.

Shell scripts intended for use by a community of users are usually installed in a general directory not owned by any specific user, such as /usr/bin or /usr/local/bin. Most system administrators prefer to store locally written script files in a separate directory from the standard UNIX commands; this makes system maintenance easier. If your installation practices this procedure, you probably already have the path of the local commands directory in your search path. You'll need the help of the system administrator to store a shell script file in such a directory though, because you won't have write access to the directory (unless you're the administrator).

There is generally nothing magical about testing shell scripts. As a rule, you'll develop a new shell script in a directory you set aside for the purpose. The directory might contain data files you use to test the shell script, and possibly several different versions of the script. You won't want to make the script file accessible to others until you finish testing it.

Sometimes, if you find the behavior of a shell script confusing and unexplainable, you might find it a help to see the commands the shell is actually executing when you run it. Simply invoke the script with the -x option (for example, csh -x payroll), or embed the command set echo in the script file while you are testing it. With the echo variable set, the shell prints each command just before executing it. You'll see variable substitutions, filename expansions, and other substitutions all expanded, so that you'll know exactly what the shell is doing while running your script. With this *trace* to look at, you'll probably have no difficulty finding errors in your script file.

If the output is especially voluminous, you can cut down the range of commands displayed by the shell by bracketing the commands you want to trace: put the command set echo in front of the range of commands to be traced, and the command unset echo at their end. The shell will print just the commands between the set and unset while running your script file. Don't forget to remove the set and unset commands after you finish testing and before putting the shell script into production usage.

A Simple Shell Script

Shell scripts can be very easy to write. For example, the following lines, if entered into a file named lld, implement a new command that lists only the directories contained in a directory:

```
# lld - long listing of directories only
if ($#argv < 1) set argv=(.)
find $argv[*] -type d -exec /bin/ls -ld \{\} \;
```

The script contains only three commands. The first, a line containing only a shell comment, serves as a heading and description of the file for anyone displaying it. Many shell script writers place one or more comment lines at the beginning of their script files to provide some documentation for others, in case anyone else ever needs to read, change, or enhance the script. Actually, a well-written script file contains many comment lines to help explain the script's operation. Scripts you write for your own use don't need to contain as many comments as scripts written for more public consumption.

The operative statements in the script do two things:

- Provide a default command-line argument if the user didn't provide any. In this case, if the user specifies no directory names, the lld command lists the current directory

- Execute the find UNIX command to locate just the directory files contained in the named directory. The -exec option invokes the ls command for each subdirectory located.

Even though the lld shell script is short, it serves the useful purpose of hiding the relatively complicated find command from its users. Even for users very familiar with the find command, it is much quicker to type lld than to type the complete find command.

Using Expressions and Operators in Shell Statements

There are a number of contexts where the shell requires you to write an *expression*. An expression is a combination of terms and operators which, when evaluated, yield an arithmetic or logical result. An arithmetic result is always represented as a string of decimal digits. A logical value is either *true* or *false*; in the C shell, a true condition is indicated by *1* and a false condition by *0*. An arithmetic value can be used where a logical value is expected: any nonzero value will be construed as *true* and a zero value as *false*.

A digit string beginning with *0* (for example, *0177*) is considered an octal number. The shell generates decimal numbers in all cases, but wherever a number is permitted, you can provide either a decimal or an octal value.

Expressions can be used in the @ (arithmetic evaluation), exit, if, and while commands. For these commands, most operators do not need to be quoted; only the < (less than), > (greater than), and ¦ (bitwise or) operators must be hidden from the shell. It is sufficient to enclose an expression or subexpression in parentheses to hide operators from the shell's normal interpretation. Note that the if and while command syntax requires the expression to be enclosed in parentheses.

When writing an expression, each term and operator in the expression must be a separate word. You usually accomplish this by inserting white space between terms and operators. For example, observe the shell's response to the following two commands. (The @ built-in command is described later in this chapter; it tells the shell to evaluate the expression appearing as its arguments.)

```
$ set x=2 y=3 sum
$ @ sum=$x*$y
2*3: no match
% @ sum=$x * $y
% echo $sum
6
```

In the first @ command, after substitution the shell saw the statement @ sum=2*3. Because *2*3* is a single word, the shell tries to interpret it as either a number or an operator: it is neither, so the shell complains because the word starts with a digit but contains non-digit characters.

Most operators have their normal interpretation familiar from the C programming language. Both unary and binary operators are supported. A complete list of the expression operators supported by the C shell appears later.

Operators combine *terms* to yield a result. A term can be any of the following:

A literal number, for example *125* (decimal) or *0177* (octal).

An expression enclosed in parentheses: (exp). Using a parenthesized expression hides the <, >, and ¦ operators from the shell's normal interpretation. The parenthesized expression is evaluated as a unit to yield a single numeric result, which is then used as the value of the expression. Parentheses override the normal operator precedence.

Any variable, command, or history substitution (or combination of these) that when evaluated yields a decimal or octal digit string. The usual shell replacement mechanisms are used when scanning an expression. The only requirement you must observe is that, after all substitutions, the resulting words must form decimal or octal digit strings or expressions.

Arithmetic and Logical Operators

The operators shown in Table 13.6 can be used to combine numeric terms. Arithmetic operators yield a word consisting of decimal digits. Logical operators yield the string "1" or "0".

Table 13.6. Arithmetic and logical shell operators.

Operator	Syntax	Operation
~	~a	Bitwise one's complement. The bits of *a* are inverted so that 1 yields 0, and 0 yields 1.
!	!a	Logical negation. If the value of *a* is zero, the value of the expression is 1; if the value of *a* is nonzero, the value of the expression is zero.
*	a*b	Multiplication. The value of the expression is the arithmetic product of *a* times *b*.

continues

Table 13.6. continued

Operator	Syntax	Operation
/	*a/b*	Division. The value of the expression is the integer quotient of *a* divided by *b*.
%	*a%b*	Remainder. The value of the expression is the remainder from the integer division of *a* by *b*.
+	*a+b*	Addition. Yields the sum of *a* and *b*.
-	*a-b*	Subtraction. Yields the sum of *a* and *-b*.
<<	*a << b*	Left shift. Shifts *a* left the number of bits specified by *b*. Equivalent to $a \times 2^b$.
>>	*a >> b*	Right shift. Shifts *a* right the number of bits specified by *b*. Equivalent to $a \div 2^b$.
<	*a < b*	Less than. Yields 1 if *a* is less than *b*, otherwise 0.
>	*a > b*	Greater than. Yields 1 if *a* is greater than *b*, otherwise 0.
<=	*a <= b*	Less than or equal to. Yields 1 if *a* is not greater than *b*, otherwise 0.
>=	*a >= b*	Greater than or equal to. Yields 1 if *a* is not less than *b*, otherwise 0.
=~	*a =~ b*	Pattern matching. Yields 1 if string *a* matches pattern *b*.
!~	*a !~ b*	Pattern matching. Yields 1 if string *a* does not match pattern *b*.
==	*a == b*	String comparison. Yields 1 if *a* is identical to *b*, compared as strings.
!=	*a != b*	String comparison. Yields 1 if string *a* is not identical to string *b*.
¦	*a ¦ b*	Bitwise or. Yields the inclusive-or of *a* and *b*.
^	*a ^ b*	Bitwise exclusive-or. Yields the exclusive-or of *a* and *b*.
&	*a & b*	Bitwise and. Yields the *and* of corresponding bits of *a* and *b*.
&&	*a && b*	Logical and. Yields 1 if *a* is true and *b* is true; otherwise 0 if either is false.
¦¦	*a ¦¦ b*	Logical or. Yields 1 if either *a* is true or *b* is true (or both are true); otherwise 0.

Assignment Operators—Evaluating Expressions and Assigning the Results to Variables

Use the @ command to evaluate an expression and assign the result to a variable, or to an element of an array variable. The special characters <, >, and ¦ must be quoted or enclosed in parentheses if part of the expression; other expression operators can be used without quoting.

```
@
@ name=expr
@ name[i]=expr
```

The assignment operators +=, -=, *=, /=, %=, <<=, >>=, ¦=, ^=, and &= are also supported. The format *name op= expr* is equivalent to writing *name = name op expr*; for example @ x=x+y can be written @ x += y.

The C operators ++ and -- are supported in both postfix and prefix forms within *expr*. This usage is allowed for the @ command, but not for *expr* generally.

Use the form @ *name[i]=* to assign the result to the *i*th element of array variable *name*.

The variable *name* (or array element *name[i]*) must exist prior to execution of the @ command; the @ command will not create it. A variable or array element is considered to exist even if it has a null value.

Operator Precedence for Arithmetic and Logical Operators

The shell uses *precedence* rules to resolve ambiguous expressions, which are expressions containing two or more operators, as in *a+b*c*. This expression could be interpreted either as *(a+b)*c* or as *a+(b*c)*. In fact, the latter interpretation applies. Using the values a=3, b=5, and c=7, the expression *a+b*c* will evaluate to *38*, not *56*.

> **NOTE:** To make life easier for everyone, the shell's rules are identical to those of the C language and a superset of the same precedence rules used by the common handheld calculator.

In Table 13.6, operators appear in decreasing order of precedence. Operators fall into eight precedence groups:

- Unary operators !, ~, and -. These operators have highest priority. In succession they associate right to left, thus !~a is equivalent to the parenthesized expression !(~a).
- Multiplicative operators *, /, and %.
- Additive operators + and -.

- Shift operators << and >>. The second argument (*b*) is used as a count and specifies the number of bits by which the first argument should be shifted left or right. Bits shifted out are discarded, for example *5 >> 1* yields *2*.

- Relational operators <, <=, >, and >=. These operators compare their operands as numbers and yield 1 *(true)* if the relation is true, or 0 *(false)* if it is not.

- Equality operators ==, !=, =~, and !~. Note that, unlike other operators, these treat their arguments as strings. This requires caution, because the strings " 10", "10 ", and " 10 " will all appear unequal even though they are numerically equivalent. To compare strings numerically, use an expression such as `$val == ($x + 0)`.

- Bitwise operators ¦, ^, and &. These operators combine the internal binary form of their operands, applying an *inclusive-or, exclusive-or,* or *and* function to corresponding bits. These operations are defined as follows:

  Inclusive-or: Generates a 1 if either of the arguments bits is 1, thus (in binary), `0110 ¦ 1010` yields `1110`.

  Exclusive-or: Generates a 1 if corresponding bits are different, thus (in binary), `0110 ^ 1010` yields `1100`.

  And: Generates a 1 if both source bits are 1, thus `0110 & 1010` yields `0010`.

- Logical operators && and ¦¦. These operators accept numeric values and yield 1 or 0.

Operators for Command Execution and File Testing

The shell also supports an additional, unconventional set of operators for command execution and file testing in expressions.

Within an expression, you can write a command enclosed in {} (braces). The value of a command execution is 1 if the command executes successfully, otherwise 0. In other words, a zero exit code yields a value of 1 (logical *true*) for the command expression {*command*}; a nonzero exit code yields a value of 0.

Operators for file testing allow you to determine whether a file exists and what its characteristics are. These operators have the form `-f` *filename* and are treated in expressions as complete subexpressions. For *filename*, specify the name or path of a file, optionally using pattern characters; the argument is subject to all forms of shell substitution, including filename expansion before testing.

Table 13.7 summarizes the file testing operations supported within expressions.

Table 13.7. File testing expressions.

Expression	Condition When True
-r *filename*	True if file exists and is readable
-w *filename*	True if file exists and is writable
-x *filename*	True if file exists and is executable
-e *filename*	True if file exists
-o *filename*	True if file exists and is owned by the current real user ID
-z *filename*	True if file exists and is zero length
-f *filename*	True if file exists and is a regular file
-d *filename*	True if file exists and is a directory

The following is an example of an expression that mixes file test operators with other operators. In this case, the expression tests whether the file is readable and not a directory:

```
if (-r $thisfile && ! -d $thisfile) echo Good file
```

Entering Comments in Shell Programs

Quite often when writing programs, program code that was quite logical six months ago might be fairly obscure today. Good programmers annotate their programs with comments. Comments are entered into shell programs by inserting the pound sign (#) special character. When the shell interpreter sees the pound sign, it considers all text to the end of the line as a comment.

Conditional Statements

A conditional statement provides a way to describe a choice between alternative actions to the shell. The choice is actually made by the shell while executing commands, based on decision criteria you specify. You write a conditional statement when you want your shell script to react properly to alternative real-world situations, for example to complain when the user omits required command-line arguments, or to create a directory when it is missing.

The shell supports two (well, three) commands for conditional execution: `if`, which evaluates an expression to decide which commands should be executed next; and `switch`, which chooses commands based on matching a string. The `if` statement is more appropriate for deciding whether or not to execute a command, or to choose between two commands.

The `switch` statement poses a multiple-choice question; it is designed to handle the situation where there are many different actions that could be taken, depending on the particular value of a string.

The `jump` command, although not strictly a conditional statement, because it makes no decision, is nonetheless usually used in conjunction with a conditional statement to move around to arbitrary places in a shell script. The `jump` command, although valuable in some limited contexts, generally leads to poorly structured shell scripts that are difficult to test and difficult to maintain. Experience with the Bourne and Korn shells, which have no `jump` command, show that its use is never necessary. You should try to avoid the use of the `jump` statement whenever possible.

The following sections look at the `if` and `switch` statements in more detail.

The *if* Statement

There are really two different forms of the `if` statement: a single-line command and a multiline command.

The single-line command has the general syntax `if (expr) command`. Use this form when you need to conditionally execute only one command. This form of the `if` statement provides the basic type of conditional execution: either you execute the command or you don't. The *expr* can be any valid expression as described in the section titled "Using Expressions and Operators in Shell Statements." If the expression evaluates to a nonzero value at runtime, the expression is considered to be *true*, and the shell executes *command*. But if the value of the expression, after evaluation, is zero, then the shell simply skips *command*, doing nothing. In either case, the shell continues to the next consecutive line of the script file.

> **CAUTION:** Some implementations of the C shell will perform an I/O redirection on *command* even if *expr* evaluates to *false*. Unless you have confirmed that your version of `csh` works otherwise, you should use redirections on the single-line `if` statement with this presumption in mind.

The multiline command has a more complex syntax:

```
if (expr) then
commands
else if (expr) then
commands
else
commands
endif
```

In this case, the if statement consists of all the lines beginning with if up to and including the endif line. The multiline form provides a way to tell the shell "either do this or do that." More precisely, the shell executes a multiline if statement as follows: Evaluate the *expr* expression. If the evaluated expression yields a nonzero result, execute the command group (*commands*) following then up to the next else or endif. If the evaluated expression yields a zero result, skip the command group following then. For else, skip the commands following it up to the next else or endif when the evaluated expression is true, and execute the commands following else when the evaluated expression is false. For endif, simply resume normal command execution. The endif clause performs no action itself; it merely marks the end of the if statement.

Notice that, in its basic form if...then...else, the multiline form of the if statement provides for choosing between two mutually exclusive actions based on a test. The *expr* expression provides the basis for the choice. The special words then and else serve to introduce command groups associated with the *true* and *false* outcomes, respectively.

Because both the single-line and multiline forms of the if statement form complete commands, and you can (indeed you must) embed commands within an if statement, you can *nest* if statements by writing one inside the other; programmers refer to this kind of construction as a *nested if statement*. Nested if statements are legal but can be potentially confusing if the nesting is carried too far. Generally one level of nesting (an if inside an if) is considered fair and reasonable; two levels deep (an if inside an if inside an if) is treading on thin ice, and three or more levels of nesting implies that you, as the writer, will forever be called upon to make any necessary changes to the script file (the *flypaper* theory of programmer management). Of course, you are helpless to a certain extent: the amount of nesting you use depends on the job you are trying to do, and not very much on your sense of esthetics.

In case you haven't got a clear idea of how if statements work, here's an example of a single-line statement:

```
if (-d ~/bin) mv newfile ~/bin
```

This simple if statement provides an expression that is true only if a file named bin exists in your home directory (~/bin) and is a directory. If the directory exists, the shell proceeds to execute the mv command in the normal fashion. If the directory ~/bin doesn't exist, then the entire expression (-d ~/bin) is false, and the shell goes on to the next line in the script file without executing the mv command: the mv command is skipped. The entire statement can be interpreted as the directive *move the file* newfile *to the directory* ~/ bin *if (and only if) the directory* ~/bin *exists; otherwise do nothing.*

Here's a more complex example, using the multiline `if` statement. In this example, the shell is directed to move the file `newfile` into the directory `~/bin` if it exists, otherwise to write an error message to the user's terminal and abandon execution of the shell script:

```
if (-d ~/bin) then
mv newfile ~/bin
else
echo ~/bin: directory not found
exit 1
endif
```

The longer, multiline `if` statement is the more appropriate of the two examples for many situations, because it provides the user with some feedback when the script can't perform an expected action. Here, the user is given a helpful hint when the `if` statement fails to move the file as expected: either create the missing directory or stop asking to move files there.

Even the dreaded *nested if statement* can arise from natural situations. For example, the following nests a single-line `if` statement inside a multiline `if` statement:

```
if (-f newfile) then
    if (! -d ~/bin) mkdir ~/bin
    mv newfile ~/bin
else
    echo newfile: file not found
    exit
endif
```

This last example uses a slightly different approach than the previous two: it begins by dealing with the basic choice between the case where the file to be moved exists or it doesn't. If `newfile` doesn't exist, then one can reasonably conclude that the user doesn't know what he's talking about: he should never have invoked the shell script containing these lines, so describe the problem to him and abandon the shell script (all done by the lines following `else`). However, if the file `newfile` exists, then the script moves the file as expected, creating the directory `~/bin` on the fly if it doesn't already exist.

As the preceding examples show, the `if` statement is often used in shell scripts as a safety mechanism, testing whether the expected environment actually exists, and warning the user of problems. At the keyboard, you would simply enter the `mv` command by itself and analyze any error message it reported. When used inside a shell script, the script must decide how to proceed when the `mv` statement fails, because the user didn't enter the `mv` command himself—in fact he might not even realize that invoking the shell script implies executing an `mv` command. The responsible shell script writer takes into account command failures and provides proper handling for all outcomes, producing scripts that behave in a predictable fashion and appear reliable to their users.

The *switch* Statement

The switch statement is like if but provides for many alternative actions to be taken. The general form of the statement follows:

```
switch (string)
case pattern:
    commands
default:
    commands
endsw
```

Literally, the shell searches among the patterns of the following case statements for a match with *string*. In actual usage, *string* is usually the outcome of variable and command substitution, filename generation, and possibly other forms of shell substitution. Each case statement between switch and endsw begins a different command group. The shell skips over command groups following case statements up to the first case statement that matches *string*. It then resumes normal command execution, ignoring any further case and default statements it might encounter. The default: statement introduces a statement group that should be executed if no preceding case statement matched the *string*. The required endsw statement provides an ending boundary to the switch statement in case the shell is still skipping over commands when it reaches that point: the shell then reverts to normal command execution.

In practice, you'll usually place a breaksw statement after each *commands* group, to prevent the shell from executing the commands in case groups after the one that matched. On rare occasions, you'll have two cases where one case requires some additional preliminary processing before the other case: you can then arrange the two case groups so that the shell can continue from one into the other, omitting a breaksw. Being able to arrange case groups to allow *fallthrough* (as it is called) is rare, however.

For a simple example, consider the situation where you want your shell script to prompt the user for a choice; the user should respond by typing *y* (for *yes*) to proceed, or else *n* (for *no*). The switch statement provides a natural implementation because of its string pattern-matching capability:

```
echo -n Do you want to proceed?
set reply=$<
switch ($reply)
case y*:
    mv newfile ~/bin
    breaksw
default:
    echo newfile not moved
endsw
```

The echo statement writes a prompt message to the terminal; the -n option causes the cursor to remain poised after the message so that the user can type a reply on the same line. The set statement uses the shell special variable $< to read a line from the terminal, which is then stored as the value of the `reply` variable. The `switch` statement tests the value of `reply`. Although the syntax of `switch` calls for a simple string between parentheses, variable substitution is performed before analysis of the `switch` statement, so by the time the shell executes `switch`, it sees the user's typed response as a string instead of a variable reference. In other words, if the user typed *yes*, after substitution the shell switch will see the `switch` statement as if it had been written `switch ("yes")`.

There is only one case in the switch, and a default case. If the user typed any line beginning with the letter *y*, the value of `$reply` will match the pattern string for the first case; the shell will then execute the lines that follow the `case` statement. When it reaches `breaksw`, the shell then skips forward to the next `endsw` statement.

If the user's typed reply does not begin with the letter *y*, it won't match any of the `case` statement patterns (there is only one). This will cause the shell to reach the `default:` case while still in skipping mode. The effect of `default` is to start executing statements if the shell is in skipping mode, so the effect is to provide a case where the user doesn't type a *y*; the shell script prints a little message to the terminal confirming that nothing was done. Normal execution then continues to and beyond the `endsw`.

Here's a slightly more advanced example, where the first command-line argument of the shell script could be an option beginning with - (dash). If the argument is an option, the script saves an indication of the option it found for later reference and discards the option. If it finds an unexpected option, it complains with an error message to the user and abandons execution.

```
if ($#argv >= 1) then
    switch ($argv[1])
        case -all:
            set flagall
            breaksw
        case -first:
            set flagfirst
            breaksw
        case -last:
            set flaglast
            breaksw
        default:
            echo Invalid option: $1
            exit 1
    endsw
    shift
else
    echo "Usage: [ -first ¦ -last ¦ -all ] filename ..."
    exit 1
endif
```

The example nests a `switch` statement inside a multiline `if` statement: if the user provides no command-line arguments, the script skips all the way down to the `else` statement, prints a brief description of the command's expected argument format, and exits the script. If the user provided at least one argument, a switch statement analyzes the first argument to see which option it is. If the argument matches any of the three strings `-first`, `-last`, or `-all`, it discards the argument after setting an indicator variable. If the argument doesn't match any of the strings, the `default:` case results in typing the error message `Invalid option` and terminating again.

Beginning a Case in *switch–case*

For *label*, specify a pattern-matching expression to be compared to the control expression of the enclosing `switch` command.

```
case label:
```

If, for a given execution of the `switch` command, the control expression of `switch` matches the pattern *label*, statements following `case` will be executed; otherwise, the case statement and statements up to the next `case`, `default`, or `endsw` statement will be skipped.

The pattern-matching expression *label* can consist of ordinary characters as well as the wildcard symbols `*`, `?`, and `[...]`. The pattern will be matched against the argument of `select` in the same manner as filenames are matched, except that the search here is for a `case` statement label that matches the `select` argument.

For additional information about `switch`, see the section titled "Conditional Statements" earlier in this chapter.

The `case` statement is intended primarily for use in shell scripts.

Using the Default Case in *switch–default*

Use `default` to designate a group of statements in the range of a `switch` statement that should be executed if no other `case` label matches the `switch` argument.

For consistent results, you should place the `default` statement group after the last `case` statement group in the `switch`.

For more information about the `default` statement, see the section titled "Conditional Statements" earlier in this chapter.

The `default` command is intended primarily for use in shell scripts.

Exiting from a *switch* Statement—*breaksw*

Use the `breaksw` command to exit from the immediately enclosing `switch` statement. The `breaksw` command causes transfer of control to the statement following the `endsw` statement. Note that `breaksw` can exit only from the immediately enclosing `switch`; any outer `switch` statements remain active.

For more information on `breaksw`, see the section titled "Conditional Statements" earlier in this chapter.

The `breaksw` command is intended primarily for use in shell scripts.

Iterative Statements

You use iterative statements to repeatedly execute a group of commands. The iterative statements are `while` and `foreach`.

The *while* Loop

Use the `while` statement to repeatedly execute a group of statements until a specified condition occurs. The `while` command is very generalized. It executes a group of commands repeatedly as long as a calculated expression yields a true result. Some care is needed when writing a `while` loop, because an improper design could cause the commands to be repeated forever in an unending loop, or never to be executed at all.

The general syntax of the `while` command is as follows:

```
while (expr)
commands...
end
```

For *expr*, write a shell expression (see the section titled "Using Expressions and Operators in Shell Statements"). For *commands*, write one or more commands to be executed on each iteration of the `while` loop. Simple and compound commands, pipelines, and parenthesized command lists are all valid.

The shell evaluates *expr* before the first iteration of the loop, and before each subsequent iteration. If the value of *expr* is nonzero (in other words, *true*), then *commands* is interpreted and executed. Any substitutions contained in *commands* are performed each time the command is encountered, allowing a different value to be substituted on each iteration.

When first encountered, the shell processes a `while` statement much like an `if`: it evaluates the expression *expr*: if it is true (nonzero), the shell proceeds with the next statement. Similarly, if *expr* is false when the shell first encounters the `while` statement, it skips forward to the `end` statement, effectively bypassing all the commands between `while` and `end`. When you write a `while` statement, you need to write the test expression *expr* carefully, realizing that the shell might entirely skip the `while` statement for certain cases of the expression.

Here is a simple example of a `while` statement:

```
while ($#argv > 0)
    if (! -f $1) echo $1: missing
```

```
    shift
end
```

The `while` statement evaluates the expression `$#argv > 0` on each repetition; that is, it tests to see if there are any command-line arguments. As long as the answer is *yes*, it executes the following `if` and `shift` commands. It stops when the number of command-line arguments has gone to zero, which after enough repetitions of `shift` it will eventually do. For each repetition, the `if` command simply tests whether a file exists with the same name as the command-line argument: if not, it writes a warning message. The effect of the `while` statement is that, invoked with a list of filenames, it lists those where the corresponding file is missing. A similar effect could be obtained by simply entering the command `ls` *name name name...*, with the difference that you'd have to pick out the filenames generating a *not found* message from among the normal `ls` output, whereas the `while` example simply lists the files that don't exist.

```
while (expr)
    commands ...
end
```

The `end` statement must be used to mark the end of the range of the `while` loop. It is a valid statement only within the range of the `foreach` and `while` statements; elsewhere, it generates a shell error message and the shell halts.

The foreach Loop

The `foreach` command is intended for processing lists. It executes a command group once for each word given as an argument to the `foreach` command. The shell sets a variable to indicate which argument word the iteration is for; you can use the variable in the repeated commands to take the same general action for each word in the list; hence the name of the command.

The general syntax of the `foreach` statement follows:

```
foreach name (wordlist)
commands
end
```

For *name*, specify the name of a shell variable to which the words of *wordlist* will be assigned in succession. The named variable does not need to be a new one; it can also be an existing variable. However, any current value of the variable will be lost. On exit from the loop, *name* contains the value of the last word in *wordlist*.

For *wordlist*, specify one or more words enclosed in parentheses. The words can be quoted strings, strings of ordinary characters, variable references, command substitution strings quoted with backquote ('), filename patterns, or history substitutions introduced with ! . All of the words are scanned and substitutions performed, and the resulting strings redivided into words (except where prevented by quoting) before the first loop iteration. You can omit the parenthesized wordlist, in which case the shell uses the command-line arguments as the list of words.

For *command,* specify one or more complete commands using the normal shell syntax. A *command* can be a simple or compound command and can be any of the legal command types, including aliases and shell built-in commands.

The last command must be followed with end as a separate command. It can appear on the same line as the last command, separated from it with the semicolon statement delimiter (;), or on a line by itself. Note that the end command is a valid shell command only when used as in a foreach or while statement; in other contexts it is considered an illegal command and causes a shell error.

The loop is executed once for each word in *wordlist.* The variable *name* is set to the current word before each iteration of the loop, in effect stepping through the wordlist word by word from left to right. It stops when the loop has been executed once for each word. In *commands,* you can use the value of $name to identify which word the repetition is for, or you can ignore its value. You can even change its value. The shell doesn't care. It simply sets *name* to each *word* in turn, stopping when it runs out of words.

The foreach statement is a very handy tool because it allows you to repeat an action for each item in a list. It is as useful at the keyboard as inside shell scripts. In the following example, it is used to change the suffix of a series of files, renaming them:

```
foreach file (main util parse io)
  mv $file.c $file.C
end
```

There are two additional, special shell commands you can use in the *command* list within the scope of foreach or while: these are the continue and break commands.

The continue command, which takes no arguments, can be used as part of a conditional statement to terminate execution of the current loop iteration, skip the remaining statements in the *command* list, and immediately begin the next loop iteration. The continue command is provided as a convenience, so that you don't have to use complex if statements to thread a path through the foreach loop; when you've executed all the commands that you want to for the current loop iteration, simply invoke continue to skip the remaining commands and start the next iteration with the first command following foreach.

The break command terminates the current and all subsequent iterations of the foreach loop; after break, the next statement to be executed will be the one following the end statement. Like continue, break skips all intervening commands between itself and the end statement; unlike continue, break also halts iteration of the loop.

You can nest foreach and while loop control statements within each other, constructing nested loops. If you do so, you will usually want to use a different control variable *name* on each inner foreach statement, although the shell doesn't enforce such a restriction.

Keep in mind, however, that after execution of an inner `foreach` loop, the control variable will be changed. Changing the value of the control variable in one of the *command* statements does not affect the behavior of the `foreach` statement; on the next iteration, it will be assigned the next word in *wordlist* in the usual manner.

When using `break` and `continue`, you must remember that they affect only the `foreach` statement on the same level; you cannot use `break` or `continue` to abandon an iteration of any outer loop. To break out of a `foreach` loop nested two or more levels deep, you would need to use conditional statements (such as `if`) to test some condition and execute another `break` or `continue` statement.

The following example shows the use of `foreach` to rename each of a set of files whose names end in `.c` to a filename ending in `.x`:

```
foreach file (main sub1 sub2)
   mv $file.c $file.x
   end
```

As shown by the example, it is customary when writing shell scripts to indent commands included in the scope of the `foreach` statement. The indentation helps to clarify the commands' subordination to the `foreach` statement and graphically highlights their inclusion in the loop.

Altering the Order of Command Execution—*goto*

Use `goto` to change the order of command execution.

`goto` *word*

Ordinarily, commands are executed one after another in succession. The looping statements `foreach` and `while` provide the ability to repeat a group of statements a fixed or variable number of times, and the `if` and `switch` conditional statements allow choosing between two or more alternative statement groups. Other than this, the general flow of control in statement execution is from the first to the last statement in a shell script or input command sequence. The `goto` command makes it possible to change the flow of control in an arbitrary way.

For *word*, specify an ordinary symbol (a string of characters not enclosed in quotes, not containing blanks or tabs, and not containing any punctuation characters having special meaning to the shell).

The shell searches the command input stream for a line beginning with *word* followed immediately by a colon (*word*:); this forms a *statement label*. If found, execution resumes with the first command following the label. If the statement label cannot be found, the shell writes an error message and stops.

The goto command is usually used inside a shell script, in which case the range of statements searched for the label is restricted to the contents of the script file. In any other context, the shell backspaces the input medium as far as possible, then searches forward to the statement label. Backspacing is not supported for the terminal, so the goto statement is limited to the current available command history lines when goto is issued from the keyboard.

Specifying the Response to a Signal—*onintr*

Use onintr to specify the action to be taken when the shell receives a signal.

```
onintr
onintr -
onintr label
```

The onintr command is roughly equivalent to the Bourne shell trap command but differs in syntax and usage.

Specified without arguments, the onintr command sets the default signal action for all signals. Used within a shell script, this will cause most signals to result in termination of the shell script. Used from the keyboard, this resets any special signal handling you might have established with previous onintr commands.

Use onintr - to disable and ignore all signals. This form is handy when used within a shell script to protect a sensitive series of commands, which if interrupted (abandoned because of shell script termination on receipt of a signal) might leave unwanted files or generate invalid results. Use onintr without arguments to restore the normal default signal actions.

Use onintr *label* to cause the shell to perform an implicit goto to the statement label *label* on receipt of a signal. The shell provides no indication of which signal was received. However, because most signals represent a request for termination, this form of onintr can be used to perform orderly cleanup before exiting from a shell script. You might use onintr *label* in a shell script, for example, to provide a cleanup routine if the user presses the *INTR* key, signaling his desire to cancel the shell script's execution. After performing any desired actions, exit the shell script with the exit command.

For more information about statement labels, see the goto command description in this section.

Processing an Arbitrary Number of Parameters—*shift*

Use shift to shift the shell parameters ($1, $2,...) to the left.

```
shift
shift name
```

After execution, the value of $2 is moved to $1, the value of $3 is moved to $2, and so on. The original value of $1 is discarded, and the total number of shell parameters (as indicated by $argv#) is reduced by one.

Use shift *name* to perform the same type of action on the named array variable.

Interpreting a Script in the Current Shell—*source*

Use source to read and interpret a script of shell commands within the current shell environment.

source *name*

No subshell is invoked, and any changes to the environment resulting from commands in the script remain in effect afterward. Possible changes that can result from execution of a script file with source include changing the current directory, creation or alteration of local and environment variables, and definition of command aliases.

An exit statement encountered in a script interpreted with source will result in exit from the current shell level; if this is your login shell, you will be logged out.

For *name*, provide the filename or pathname of a file containing shell commands and statements. The shell will search the current directory path (path variable) for the file if you do not specify a name beginning with /, ./, or ../.

Customizing Your Shell Environment

The C shell provides for two initialization scripts, the .cshrc and .login files, and one shutdown procedure, the .logout file.

The C shell always looks for a file in your home directory named .cshrc whenever it is invoked, whether as a login shell, as a command, implicitly by entering the filename of a shell script as a command, or by a subshell expression enclosed in parentheses.

The .cshrc script should perform only those initializations that you require for any C shell environment, including shells you invoke from other commands like vi and pg.

When invoked as a login shell, the .login script is executed to perform any one-time-only initializations you might require. These can include issuing the stty command to define your preferred *Erase, Kill,* and *Intr* keys, setting your cdpath, path, and mail variables, and printing the news of the day.

When you exit from a login shell by typing the *EOF* key at the start of a line or by entering the exit or logout command, the shell searches for a file named .logout in your home directory. If found, the shell executes it and then terminates. You could, for example, use the `.login` and `.logout` scripts to maintain a timesheet log recording your starting and ending times for terminal sessions.

What to Put in Your *.cshrc* Initialization File

You should define command aliases, variable settings, and shell options in your `~/.cshrc` file. It is always executed before the `.login` script, and by placing such definitions in `.cshrc`, you are assured of having the definitions available in subshells.

Typical items you will want to have in your `.cshrc` file include the following:

```
alias lx /usr/bin/ls -FC
```

You will probably want one or more aliases for the `ls` command. After developing some experience with UNIX, you'll find that there are certain options you prefer to use when listing directory contents. On some occasions you'll want the long listing given by the `-l` option, but more often a multicolumn listing of some form will provide the quick overview of directory contents that helps to orient yourself. You can have as many aliases for the `ls` command as you like, but only one named `ls`. If you define an alias for `ls`, remember that it will affect your use of the command in pipelines.

```
set ignoreeof
```

The `ignoreeof` option prevents you from logging out by accidentally typing the *EOF* character (usually *Ctrl+d*). When this option is set, you must explicitly invoke the `exit` or `logout` command to exit from the shell.

```
set noclobber
```

Some users prefer to use the *noclobber* option, some don't. If set, you can't accidentally destroy an existing file by redirecting a command's output to it with > `filename`. If you develop a feeling of frustration after destroying useful files too often with the > operator, by all means try *noclobber*. Note, however, that it provides no protection from accidentally deleting the wrong files with `rm`.

```
set path=(dirname dirname ...)
```

You might want to define your search path in `.cshrc` instead of `.login`. Defined in `.cshrc`, you are assured of always having the same search path available for all invocations of the shell. However, you also prevent inheriting an environment. Most people find that it is sufficient to define the search path in the `.login` script.

For further information about variables and how to set them, see the section titled "Variables" earlier in this chapter.

What to Put in Your *.login* Initialization File

The .login script is an excellent place to do the following things: Identify the kind of terminal you are using, perhaps by prompting the user to enter a code. Set the TERM environment variable to match the terminal type; TERM is used by the vi command to send the correct terminal control codes for full-screen operation; it can't work correctly with an incorrect TERM.

Issue the stty command to set your preferred control keys, for example

```
stty erase '^H' kill '^U' intr '^C'
```

Set global environment variables:

```
setenv TERM vt100
setenv EDITOR /usr/bin/vi
setenv PAGER /usr/bin/pg
```

Set local variables:

```
set path=(/usr/bin /usr/ucb /usr/X/bin $home/bin .)
set cdpath=(. .. $home)
set mail=(60 /usr/spool/mail/$logname)
```

Execute any system commands you find interesting:

```
news
df
```

For further information about variables and how to set them, see the section titled "Variables" earlier in this chapter.

What to Put in Your *.logout* File

There are no standard usages for the .logout file. If you don't have a use for the .logout file, you can omit it without incurring any shell error messages.

Job Control

When you type a command on the command-line and press return, the command executes in the *foreground*, which means that it has your system's undivided attention and ties up your system until it is finished executing. This means that you must wait until that command executes before you can do any other work. For commands or programs that execute quickly, this isn't usually a problem. It is a problem for commands or programs that take minutes or hours to execute, however. By executing commands or programs in the *background*, you can free up your system immediately to do other tasks.

C shell provides you with a *job control* mechanism for executing and managing background jobs.

> **NOTE:** When csh was implemented years ago, its job control mechanism was quite an advancement. In fact, when the Korn shell was implemented to provide C shell features in a Bourne shell style, the csh job control interface was carried virtually intact and without change. The description of job control in Chapter 12, "Korn Shell," is essentially accurate for the C shell as well.

The C shell commands provided for managing background processes started with & (called *jobs*) are as follows:

&	Execute a command in the background
jobs	List active background jobs
wait	Wait for specified (or all) jobs to finish
kill	Send a signal to specified jobs
bg	Resume execution of stopped jobs in the background
fg	Switch background jobs to foreground execution

Executing Jobs in the Background—&

Use & to execute a command in the background. A background process has no associated terminal.

```
command &
```

If the process attempts to read from your terminal, its execution is suspended until you bring the process into the foreground (with the fg command) or cancel it. A command executed in the background is called a *job* by the C shell.

For *command*, write a simple command or a compound command. The & operator must appear at the end of the command. The & operator also serves as a statement delimiter; any commands following & on the same line are treated as if they were written on the following line. The & operator also has lower precedence than any other compound operators. In the following example, all the commands are executed in the background as a single job:

```
grep '#include' *.c ¦ pr && echo Ok &
```

When you execute a command in the background by appending an &, the shell writes a notification message to your terminal identifying the job number assigned to the job. Use this job number, in the form %*number*, as the operand of kill, fg, bg, or wait to manipulate the job.

Listing Active Background Jobs—*jobs*

The jobs command simply lists the process group leaders you have active in background execution. The process group leader is the process that owns itself and zero or more additional subprocesses. A simple command appended with & launches one process and one process group leader (that is, one job with one process); a pipe of three commands all executed in the background (for example ls ¦ sed ¦ xargs &) launches three processes but is still one job. See Part IV for more information about processes.

Use the jobs statement to list the current set of background jobs.

```
jobs [ -l ]
```

The output of jobs has the following general format:

```
% jobs
[1] + Stopped      vi prog.c
[2]   Done         cc myprog.c
```

A plus sign (+) marks the shell's idea of the *current* job; a minus sign, if shown, marks the previous job. Various messages, including *Stopped* and *Done*, can be shown to indicate the job's current status.

Use option -l to print the process identifier of each job beside its job number.

fg and *bg*—Referring to Job Numbers

Both the bg and fg commands require you to specify a job number. A job number is any of the following:

%n
: A reference to job number *n*. When you start a job using the & operator, the shell prints a job number you can use to refer to the job later. For example
```
% cc myprog.c &
    [1] 27442
```
The number in brackets is the job number *n*. The other number is the process identifier of the job. (For more information about processes, see Part IV, "Process Control.")

%string
: A reference to the most recent background command you executed beginning with *string*. For *string*, you can specify only the first command name of the line, but you don't need to specify the entire command name: any unique prefix of the command name will be accepted. Thus, you can use %da to mean the date command, but you couldn't safely use %pr to refer to a print command if you have also used the pr command in the same login session.

%?*string*	A reference to the most recent background command containing *string* anywhere in the line. For example, %?myprog would be a valid reference to the job cc myprog.c.
%+	A reference to the current job: the job you last started, stopped, or referenced with the bg or fg command. In the listing produced by the jobs command, the current job is marked with + and can be referenced with the shorthand notation %+.
%%	Same as %+.
%-	A reference to the previous job. In the listing produced by the jobs command, the previous job is marked with - and can be referenced by the shorthand notation %-.

Moving Foreground Jobs into the Background—*bg*

Use the bg command to switch the specified jobs (or the current job, if no *job* arguments are given) to background execution. If any of the jobs are currently stopped, their execution resumes.

```
bg [ job ... ]
```

A job running in the background will be stopped automatically if it tries to read from your terminal; the terminal input will not be executed unless the job is switched to foreground execution. If you use the bg command to resume a job that has been stopped for terminal input, the job will immediately stop again when it repeats the pending terminal read request, making the bg command appear to have been ineffective. In such a case, you must either terminate the job (using the kill command) or switch the job to foreground execution and respond to its input request (see the fg command).

You must use the job number when referring to the job: for example fg %3 or fg %cc. The C shell also supports an abbreviation for the fg command: %10 in itself will switch job 10 to foreground execution, acting as an implied fg command. (The Korn shell doesn't exactly support this, although you can set up an alias to achieve the same effect.)

Pausing and Resuming Background Jobs

The *Ctrl+z* mechanism provides a handy way to stop doing one thing and temporarily do another, then switch back. Although some interactive commands like vi allow you to escape to the shell, not all do. Whether the command does or not, simply press *Ctrl+z* to temporarily stop the command; you'll immediately get a shell prompt. Now you can do whatever you want. To resume the interrupted command, enter fg %vi (or just %vi). You can get yourself quite confused this way, with three or four jobs stopped. The jobs command provides a quick summary to remind you of what commands you currently have stacked up.

Moving Background Jobs into the Foreground—*fg*

fg switches the specified jobs into foreground execution and restarts any that were stopped.

```
fg [ job ... ]
```

If you specify no *job* arguments, the current job is assumed; the current job is the last job you started, stopped, or referenced with the bg or fg command and is identified with a + in the listing produced by the jobs command.

For *job*, specify any percent expression as described in the section "fg and bg—Referring to Job Numbers." Note that %5 or %ex (or any of the allowable percent expressions), entered as a command, is equivalent to issuing the fg command with that argument; thus %5 would restart job 5 in the foreground, and %ex would restart the most recent ex command if it is one of your active jobs. (See also the bg, wait, and jobs related commands.)

Stopping a Background Job—*stop*

You can pause a job that is executing in the background with stop.

```
stop [ %job ]
```

This command sends a *STOP* signal to the named job, as if the *STOP* key were pressed (usually *Ctrl+z*). The job is stopped.

Use the bg command to resume execution of the stopped job, or fg to bring the job to the foreground and resume its execution.

To terminate the execution of a background job, use the kill command. See the section titled "Signaling a Process—kill" for details.

Stopping the Current Shell—*suspend*

The suspend command suspends execution of, or stops, the current shell; its effect is the same as pressing the *STOP* key (ordinarily *Ctrl+z*).

```
suspend
```

Waiting for Background Jobs to Finish—*wait*

Use the wait command to wait for all background jobs to finish.

```
wait
```

The shell simply stops prompting for command input until it has received notification of the termination of all background jobs.

To stop waiting, simply press the return (or Enter) key. The shell will print a summary of all background jobs, then resume prompting for commands in the normal fashion.

Requesting Notification of Background Job Status Changes—*notify*

Use the `notify` command to request that the shell always report any change in the status of a background job immediately.

```
notify [ %job ]
```

By default, the shell reports the completion, termination, stoppage, or other status change by writing a message to your terminal just before the command prompt.

Use `notify` with no arguments to request immediate notification of background job status changes. Be aware, however, that a notification message might be written to your terminal at inopportune times, such as when it is formatted for full-screen operation; the message could garble a formatted screen.

Use `notify` `%job` to request notification of status change for only the specified job. This form is handy when you run a background command and later decide you need its results before continuing. Rather than repeatedly executing `jobs` to find out when the background job is done, just issue `notify` `%job` to ask the shell to tell you when the job is done.

For `%job`, specify any of the job reference formats, as described for the `bg` command.

Controlling Background Process Dispatch Priority—*nice*

Use the `nice` command to change the default dispatch priority assigned to batch jobs.

```
nice [ +number ] [ command ]
```

The idea underlying the `nice` facility (and its unusual name) is that background jobs should demand less attention from the system than interactive processes. Background jobs execute without a terminal attached and are usually run in the background for two reasons: (1) the job is expected to take a relatively long time to finish, and (2) the job's results are not needed immediately. Interactive processes, however, are usually shells where the speed of execution is critical because it directly affects the system's apparent response time. It would therefore be nice for everyone (others as well as yourself) to let interactive processes have priority over background work.

UNIX provides a `nice` command that you can use to launch a background job and at the same time assign it a reduced execution priority. The `nice` built-in command replaces the UNIX command and adds automation. Whereas the UNIX `nice` command must be used explicitly to launch a reduced-priority background job, the shell always assigns a reduced execution priority to background jobs; you use the `nice` command to change the priority the shell assigns.

Invoked with no arguments, the `nice` built-in command sets the current `nice` value (execution priority) to 4. A login shell always assumes a `nice` value of 0 (same priority as interactive processes); you must execute `nice` or `nice +value` to change the `nice` value (until then you aren't being nice; all your background jobs compete with interactive processes at the same priority).

Use `nice +number` to change the default execution priority for background jobs to a positive or zero value: a zero value (`nice +0`) is the same as interactive priority; positive values correspond to reduced priority, so that `nice +5` is a lower priority than `nice +4`, and `nice +6` is a lower priority than `nice +5`, and so on.

If you specify `command`, the `nice` command launches the command using the default or specified execution priority but doesn't change the default execution priority. For example, `nice cc myprog.c` launches the compilation using the default priority, whereas `nice +7 cc myprog.c` launches the compilation with an explicit priority of seven.

Note that you do not need to append `&` to the `nice` command to run a command as a background job; when you specify `command`, the background operator is assumed.

Signaling a Process—*kill*

Use the `kill` built-in command to send a signal to one or more jobs or processes.

```
kill [ -signal ] job ...
kill -l
```

The built-in command hides the UNIX `kill` command; to invoke the UNIX `kill` command directory, use its full pathname (probably `/bin/kill` or `/usr/bin/kill`). The built-in command provides additional features that are not supported by `/bin/kill` and can be used in the same manner.

For `signal`, specify a number or a symbolic signal name. All UNIX implementations support signals 1 through 15; some implementations can support more. By convention, the signals listed in Table 13.8 are always defined.

Table 13.8. Signals.

Signal	Name	Effect or Meaning
1	HUP	*(Hangup.)* Sent to all processes in a process group when the terminal is disconnected by logout or, for a remote terminal, when the terminal connection is dropped.

continues

Table 13.8. continued

Signal	Name	Effect or Meaning
2	INT	*(Interrupt.)* Sent when the user presses the *INTR* key (defined by the `stty` command; usually *Ctrl+c,* sometimes *BREAK*).
3	QUIT	*(Quit.)* Sent when the user presses the *QUIT* KEY (defined by the `stty` command; there is no default).
9	KILL	*(Kill.)* Sent only by the `kill` command; it forces immediate termination of the designated process and cannot be ignored or trapped.
10	BUS	*(Bus error.)* Usually caused by a programming error, a bus error can be caused only by a hardware fault or a binary program file.
11	SEGV	*(Segment violation.)* Caused by a program reference to an invalid memory location; can be caused only by a binary program file.
13	PIPE	*(Pipe.)* Caused by writing to a pipe when no process is available to read the pipe; usually a user error.
15	TERM	*(Termination.)* Caused by the `kill` command or system function. This signal is a gentle request to a process to terminate in an orderly fashion; the process can ignore the signal.

If you omit `signal`, the TERM signal is sent by default (unless the `-l` option is specified, in which case no signal is sent at all).

For `job`, specify one or more jobs or process identifiers. A job reference can be any one of the following:

`%job`	Specify a job number (as shown by the `jobs` command).
`%string`	Specify a prefix of the job's command name. For example, after `cxref myprog.c&`, any of the references `%cxref`, `%cxre`, `%cxr`, or `%cx` can be used (`%c` is also legal but is probably too ambiguous).
`%?string`	Specify a string contained anywhere in the job's command. For example, after `cxref myprog.c&`, the reference `%?myprog` will identify the job by a portion of its argument.
`%+`	Specifies the current job. The current job can be identified using the `jobs` command: it is marked with +.

%-   Specifies the previous job. The previous job is marked with - in the output of the jobs command.

There is no default for *job*. You must specify at least one job or process to which the signal will be sent.

The command kill -l can be used to list the valid symbolic signal names. Always use the kill -l command to identify the exact signal names provided when using a new or unfamiliar version of csh.

Also see the bg, fg, wait, and jobs commands for more information about job control using the C shell.

Using the Shell's Hash Table

The C shell's hash table is used to expedite command searches by identifying the directory or directories where a command might be located. The hash table is created based on the directories specified in your path C shell variable. The order in which the directories are specified determines the search order as well as the efficiency of locating commands that you execute.

For each directory in the search path or hash table, the shell invokes the exec UNIX operating system function to search for the command to be executed. If unsuccessful, the search continues with other possible locations for the command; however, the exec operating system function entails considerable operating system overhead; its use increases system load levels and degrades system performance. Consequently, the effectiveness of the shell's hash table is a matter of concern. C shell provides you with three commands for working with the hash table: hashstat, rehash, and unhash.

Determining the Effectiveness of the Hash Table— hashstat

Use the hashstat command to determine the effectiveness of the shell's hash table mechanism.

```
$ hashstat
```

The statistics printed by hashstat indicate the number of trials needed on average to locate commands, and hence the number of exec function calls per shell command issued. Ideally, every command would be found with one trial. If the hit rate is too low, many directory searches (exec invocations) are occurring for each command executed. You need to reorder the directories in your search path and if possible eliminate directories from your path that don't contain any commands you use. In other words, poor hash table performance is caused by an improperly structured search path, as defined by the path C shell variable. The commands you use most frequently should be located in the directory named first in the path, and successive directories should be referenced less and less frequently. If you list directories in your path that don't contain any commands you use, the shell will waste time searching those directories for commands you do use.

Rebuilding the Hash Table—*rehash*

Use the rehash command to rebuild the shell's hash table. The hash table is used to expedite command execution by reducing the set of directories that need to be searched to locate a particular command.

```
rehash
```

The hash table is automatically updated when you change the value of the path variable, but no automatic update is possible when you change the name of an executable file or move executable files in or out of directories in your search path. Changes made by the system administrator to directories containing system commands will also go unnoticed. In such cases, use rehash to resynchronize the shell's hash table with the real world.

You need to execute the rehash command only when an attempt to execute a command that you know exists in your search path results in a *not found* message.

Disabling the Use of the Hash Table—*unhash*

Use the unhash command to discontinue the shell's use of a hash table to expedite directory searches for commands. The shell continues to search directories using the path variable for programs in the usual fashion, although with reduced efficiency. See the rehash command to resume usage of the hash table.

```
unhash
```

You might want to issue the unhash command while developing a new shell script, or when restructuring the contents of directories listed in your path variable.

Managing Resource Limits—*limit* and *unlimit*

UNIX imposes a number of limitations on the amount of resources any system user can commit. For each type of resource, there is a system-defined maximum. The system administrator can increase or reduce the size of a limitation, using the limit command, or restore the limitation to its normal value with unlimit. Normal users can also employ the limit and unlimit commands, but only to further restrict resource usage, not to increase it.

The specific types of resources you can control with the limit and unlimit commands are described below.

Unless you are the system administrator, changing a resource limit affects only the current process; it doesn't affect any other commands you may be running as background jobs at the same time, and it doesn't affect any other users.

Manipulating resource limits is not something you do very often: it is of interest mainly to programmers and system administrators involved in problem determination. However, you should be aware of the kinds of limits that exist and what their values are, because a resource limit can cause a command to fail for spurious or misleading reasons. For example, one of the resource limits sets an upper bound on the size of a disk file. If a command you execute tries to write a file bigger than the file size limit, the command may fail, reporting that it is out of disk space. This may lead you to ask the system administrator to give you more disk space. Getting more disk space won't solve the problem, however, because the file size limit won't allow your command to use the space even if it's available. The proper resolution is either to ask the system administrator to change the system's built-in file size limit, or to stop trying to write such large files.

Displaying or Setting Maximum Resource Limits—*limit*

Use the limit command to display or change system maximums that apply to the current invocation of the shell and all commands and jobs you launch from the shell.

```
limit [ resource [ maximum ] ]
```

UNIX provides a limit command you can use to change the maximum file size you can write with any command. The limit shell built-in command can be used for the same purpose, and to change a number of other limits as well.

If you specify no arguments, the limit command lists all settable limits currently in effect.

For *resource*, specify one of the following. (Note: The resource types you can specify depends on the particular implementation of csh and UNIX you are using.)

cputime	The maximum number of CPU seconds any process can run. A process exceeding this limit will be terminated.
filesize	The maximum number of bytes a file can contain. An attempt to create a new file or to append bytes to a file that would exceed this size will cause the operating system to signal an end-of-medium condition to the program. The UNIX system specifies

an upper limit for file size that you cannot change. You can use the `limit` command to display the limit or to reduce it; you cannot increase it, however, unless you have previously reduced the limit, in which case you can increase it up to the system-defined limit.

datasize   The maximum amount of memory that can be allocated to a program's data and stack area. The system defines a default upper limit for the amount of memory a program can use; you can reduce the limit, or if you previously reduced it you can increase it back up to the system-defined limit.

stacksize   The maximum amount of memory the system should allow for a program's stack area. The system defines a maximum size to which any program's stack area can grow. You can reduce the limit, or if you previously reduced it you can increase it back up to the system-defined limit.

coredumpsize   The maximum size of a coredump file that can be written. The system defines a maximum size for core files. You can reduce the limit or increase the limit up to the system-defined limit.

If you specify *resource* but omit *maximum*, the `limit` command displays the current limit value for the specified resource. Otherwise, specify a number of seconds (for `cputime`), or a number of kilobytes for any other resource (`limit filesize 32` sets the maximum filesize to 32 KB or 32,768 bytes). You can append *m* to the number to specify megabytes instead of kilobytes: `limit datasize 2m` sets the maximum program data area to 2,097,152 bytes (2048 KB).

Canceling a Previous *limit* Command—*unlimit*

Use `unlimit` to cancel the effect of a previous `limit` restriction.

```
unlimit [ resource ]
```

Because the `limit` command can be used only to reduce system-defined constraints even further (for other than the superuser), the `unlimit` command restores the named limit (or all limits) to their system-defined maximums.

See the previous section titled "Displaying or Setting Maximum Resource Limits—`limit`" for a description of the allowable values for *resource*.

Summary

When compared to the Bourne shell, facilities provided by the C shell include extensions for both the keyboard environment and the shell programming environment. Besides more filename wildcards, command history, history substitution, and job control, the C shell also provides array variables, arithmetic expressions, a somewhat more convenient if statement, and briefer forms of while and foreach (dropping the useless do of the Bourne shell).

Virtually all of the features of the C shell are also supported by the Korn shell, in a form more consistent with the syntax and usage of the Bourne shell. Because of its many extensions for both the keyboard user and shell script writer, the C shell is well worth your investigation: you might find that you like it.

This chapter has provided a quick overview of the C shell syntax and features. A more detailed, though turgid, presentation will also be found in the reference manuals for your particular version of UNIX; you should consult these for the last word on details of its operation. The C shell, being descended from BSD roots, has never been subjected to the same degree of standardization as the System V side of the UNIX family.

Which Shell Is Right for You? Shell Comparison

14

By John Valley

Most contemporary versions of UNIX provide all three shells—the Bourne shell, C shell, and Korn shell—as standard equipment. Choosing the right shell to use is an important decision because you will spend considerable time and effort learning to use a shell, and more time actually using it. The right choice will allow you to benefit from the many powerful features of UNIX with a minimum of effort. This chapter is intended to assist you in making that choice by drawing your attention to specific features of each shell.

Of course, no one shell is best for all purposes. If you have a choice of shells, then you need to learn how to choose the right shell for the job.

The shell has three main uses:

1. As a keyboard interface to the operating system
2. As a vehicle for writing scripts for your own personal use
3. As a programming language to develop new commands for others

Each of these three uses places different demands on you and on the shell you choose. Furthermore, each of the shells provides a different level of support for each use. This chapter describes the advantages and disadvantages each shell brings to the three kinds of tasks you can perform with it.

Interactive

The first point to keep in mind when choosing a shell for interactive use is that your decision affects no one but yourself. This gives you a great deal of freedom: you can choose any of the three shells without consideration for the needs and wishes of others. Only your own needs and preferences will matter.

The principal factors that will affect your choice of an interactive shell are as follows:

- *Learning.* It is a lamentable fact of life that as the power and flexibility of a tool increases, it becomes progressively more difficult to learn how to use it. The much-maligned VCR, with its proliferation of convenience features, often sits with its clock unset as silent testimony. So too it is with UNIX shells. There is a progression of complexity from the Bourne shell, to the C shell, to the Korn shell, with each adding features, shortcuts, bells and whistles to the previous. The cost of becoming a master is extra time spent learning and practicing. You'll have to judge whether you'll really use those extra features enough to justify the learning time. Keep in mind though that all three shells are relatively easy to learn at a basic level.

■ *Command editing.* The C shell and the Korn shell offer features to assist with redisplaying and reusing previous commands; the Bourne shell does not. The extra time savings you can realize from the C shell or the Korn shell command editing features depends greatly on how much you use the shell. Generations of UNIX users lived and worked before the C and Korn shells were invented, demonstrating that the Bourne shell is eminently usable, just not as convenient for the experienced, well-practiced C shell or Korn shell user.

■ *Wildcards and shortcuts.* Once again, your personal productivity (and general peace of mind) will be enhanced by a shell that provides you with fast ways to do common things. Wildcards and command aliases can save you a great deal of typing if you enter many UNIX commands in the course of a day.

■ *Portability.* If you will sit in front of the same terminal every day, use the same UNIX software and applications for all your work, and rarely if ever have to deal with an unfamiliar system, then, by all means choose the best tools that your system has available. If you need to work with many different computers running different versions of UNIX, as system and network administrators often must, you may need to build a repertoire of tools (shell, editor, and so on) that are available on most or all of the systems you'll use. Don't forget that being expert with a powerful shell won't buy you much if that shell isn't available. For some UNIX professionals, knowing a shell language that's supported on all UNIX systems is more important than any other consideration.

■ *Prior experience.* Prior experience can be either a plus or a minus when choosing a shell. For example, familiarity with the Bourne shell is an advantage when working with the Korn shell, which is very similar to the Bourne shell, but somewhat of a disadvantage when working with the C shell, which is very different. Don't let prior experience dissuade you from exploring the benefits of an unfamiliar shell.

Table 14.1 rates the three shells using the preceding criteria, assigning a rating of 1 for *best choice,* 2 for *acceptable alternative,* and 3 for *poor choice.*

Table 14.1. Ranking of shells for interactive use.

Shell	Learning	Editing	Shortcuts	Portability	Experience
Bourne	1	3	3	1	3
C	2	2	1	3	2
Korn	3	1	2	2	1

Bourne Shell

I rated the Bourne shell as your best choice for learning because it is the simplest of the three to use, with the fewest features to distract you and the fewest syntax nuances to confuse you. If you won't be spending a lot of time using a command shell with UNIX, then by all means develop some proficiency with the Bourne shell. You'll be able to do all you need to, and the productivity benefits of the other shells aren't important for a casual user. Even if you expect to use a UNIX command shell frequently, you might need to limit your study to the Bourne shell if you need to become effective quickly.

I rated the Bourne shell as lowest in the productivity categories because it has no command editor and only minimal shortcut facilities. If you have the time and expertise to invest in developing your own shell scripts, you can compensate for many of the Bourne shell deficiencies, as many shell power users did in the years before the C shell and the Korn shell were invented. Even so, the lack of command editing and command history facilities means you'll spend a lot of time retyping and repairing commands. For intensive keyboard use, the Bourne shell is the worst of the three. If you have any other shell, you'll prefer it over the Bourne shell.

The C shell and the Korn shell were invented precisely because of the Bourne shell's low productivity rating. They were both targeted specifically to creating a keyboard environment that would be friendlier and easier to use than the Bourne shell, and they are here today only because most people agree that they're better.

However, portability concerns might steer you toward the Bourne shell despite its poor productivity rating. Being the oldest of the three shells (it was written for the very earliest versions of UNIX), the Bourne shell is available virtually everywhere. If you can get your job done using the Bourne shell, you can do it at the terminal of virtually any machine anywhere. This is not the case for the C and Korn shells, which are available only with particular vendors' systems or with current UNIX releases.

I gave the Bourne shell a rating of 3 for prior experience because prior experience using the Bourne shell is no reason to continue using it. You can use the Korn shell immediately with no additional study and no surprises, and you can gradually enhance your keyboard skills as you pick up the Korn shell extensions. If you have access to the Korn shell, you have no reason not to use it.

C Shell

The C shell rates a 2 for learning difficulty, based simply on the total amount of material available to learn. The C shell falls between the Bourne shell and the Korn shell in the number and complexity of its facilities. Make no mistake—the C shell can be tricky to use, and some of its features are rather poorly documented. Becoming comfortable and proficient with the C shell takes time, practice, and a certain amount of inventive experimentation. Of course, when compared to the Bourne shell only on the basis of common features, the C shell is no more complex, just different.

The C shell rates a passing nod for command editing because it doesn't really have a command editing feature. Its history substitution mechanism is complicated to learn and clumsy to use, but it is better than nothing at all. Just having a command history and history substitution mechanism is an improvement over the Bourne shell, but the C Shell is a poor second in comparison to the simple and easy command editing of the Korn shell.

With the Korn shell, you can reuse a previously entered command, even modify it, just by recalling it (*Esc-k* if you're using the vi option) and overtyping the part you want to modify. With the C shell, you can also reuse a previous command, but you have five different forms for specifying the command name (!!, !11, !-5, !vi, or !?vi?), additional forms for selecting the command's arguments (:0, :^, :3-5, :-4, :*, to name a few), and additional modifiers for changing the selected argument (:h, :s/old/new/, and so forth). Even remembering the syntax of command substitution is difficult, not to speak of using it.

On the other hand, if you like to use wildcards, you'll find that the C shell wildcard extensions for filenames are easier to use—they require less typing and have a simpler syntax—than the Korn shell wildcard extensions. Also, its cd command is a little more flexible. The pushd, popd, and dirs commands are not directly supported by the Korn shell (although they can be implemented in the Korn shell by the use of aliases and command functions). Altogether, the C shell rates at the top of the heap in terms of keyboard shortcuts available, perhaps in compensation for its only moderately successful command editing. Depending on your personal mental bent, you might find the C shell the most productive of all three shells to use. We have seen that those already familiar with the C shell have not been drawn away in droves by the Korn shell in the past.

For portability considerations, the C shell ranks at the bottom, simply because it's a unique shell language. If you know only the C shell, and the particular system you're using doesn't have it, you're out of luck. A C shell user will almost always feel all thumbs when forced to work with the Bourne shell, unless she is bilingual and knows the vagaries and peculiarities of both.

The C shell gets a 2 for prior experience. If you already know it and want to continue using it, I see no compelling reason why you shouldn't. On the other hand, you may be missing a good bet if you decide to ignore the Korn shell. Unless you feel quite comfortable with the C shell's history substitution feature and use it extensively to repair and reuse commands, you might find the Korn shell's command editing capability well worth the time and effort to make the switch. Anyone accustomed to using the Korn shell's command editing capability feels unfairly treated when deprived of it—it's that good. If you haven't already experimented with the Korn shell and you have the chance, I would strongly recommend spending a modest amount of time gaining enough familiarity with it to make an informed choice. You might be surprised.

Altogether, the C shell is a creditable interactive environment with many advantages over its predecessor, the Bourne shell, and it is not clear that the Korn shell is a compelling improvement. Personal preference has to play a role in your choice here. However, if you're new to UNIX, the C shell is probably not the best place for you to start.

Korn Shell

In terms of time and effort required to master it, the Korn shell is probably the least attractive. That's not because it's poorly designed or poorly documented, but merely because it has more complex features than either of the other two shells. Of course, you don't have to learn everything before you can begin using it. The Korn shell can be much like good music and good art, always providing something new for you to learn and appreciate.

For productivity features, the Korn shell is arguably the best of the three shells. Its command editor interface enables the quick, effortless correction of typing errors, plus easy recall and reuse of command history. It's hard to imagine how the command line interface of the Korn shell could be improved without abandoning the command line altogether.

On the down side, the Korn shell provides equivalents for the C shell's wildcard extensions, but with a complicated syntax that makes the extensions hard to remember and hard to use. You can have the pushd, popd directory interface, but only if you or someone you know supplies the command aliases and functions to implement them. The ability to use a variable name as an argument to cd would have been nice, but you don't get it. The Korn shell's command aliasing and job control facilities are nearly identical to those of the C shell. From the point of view of keyboard use, the Korn shell stands out over the C shell only because of its command editing feature. In other respects, its main advantage is that it provides the C shell extensions in a shell environment compatible with the Bourne shell; if Bourne shell compatibility doesn't matter to you, then the Korn shell might not either.

Speaking of Bourne shell compatibility, the Korn shell rates a close second to the Bourne shell for portability. If you know the Korn shell language, you already know the Bourne shell, because ksh is really a superset of sh syntax. If you're familiar with the Korn shell, you can work reasonably effectively with any system having either the Bourne or Korn shells, which amounts to virtually one hundred percent of the existing UNIX computing environments.

Finally, in terms of the impact of prior experience, the Korn shell gets an ambiguous rating of 2. If you know the Bourne shell, you'll probably want to beef up your knowledge by adding the extensions of the Korn shell and switching your login shell to ksh. If you already know ksh, you'll probably stick with it. If you know csh, the advantages of ksh may not be enough to compel you to switch.

If you're a first-time UNIX user, the Korn shell is the best shell for you to start with. The complexities of the command editing feature will probably not slow you down much; you'll use the feature so heavily its syntax will become second nature to you before very long.

Shell Scripts for Personal Use

If you develop any shell scripts for your personal use, you'll probably want to write them in the same shell language you use for interactive commands. As for interactive use, the language you use for personal scripts is largely a matter of personal choice.

If you use either the C shell or the Korn shell at the keyboard, you might want to consider using the Bourne shell language for shell scripts, for a couple of reasons. First, personal shell scripts don't always stay personal; they have a way of evolving over time and gradually floating from one user to another until the good ones become de facto installation standards. As you'll learn in the section titled "Shell Scripts for Public Consumption," writing shell scripts in any language but the Bourne shell is somewhat risky because you limit the machine environments and users who can use your script. Of course, for the truly trivial scripts, containing just a few commands that you use principally as an extended command abbreviation, portability concerns are not an issue.

If you're not an experienced UNIX user and shell programmer, you probably know only one of the three shell languages. Writing short, simple shell scripts to automate common tasks is a good habit and a good UNIX skill. To get the full benefit of the UNIX shells, you almost have to develop some script writing capability. This will happen most naturally if you write personal scripts in the same language that you use at the keyboard.

For purposes of comparison, Table 14.2 describes the shell features that are available in only one or two of the three shells.

Table 14.2. Nonportable shell features.

Feature	sh	csh	ksh
Arithmetic expressions	-	X	X
Array variables	-	X	X
Assignment id=string	X	-	X
case statement	X	-	X
cdpath searches	SysV	X	X
clobber option	-	X	X
Command aliases	-	X	X

continues

Table 14.2. continued

Feature	sh	csh	ksh
echo -n option	-	X	-
export command	X	-	X
foreach statement	-	X	-
getopts built-in command	-	-	X
glob command	-	X	-
Hash table problems, rehash and unhash commands	-	X	-
Job control (bg, fg, ...)	-	X	X
let command	-	-	X
limit, unlimit commands	-	X	-
nice shell built-in	-	X	-
nohup shell built-in	-	X	-
notify shell built-in	-	X	-
onintr command	-	X	-
print command	-	-	X
pushd, popd commands	-	X	-
RANDOM shell variable	-	-	X
repeat shell built-in	-	X	-
select statement	-	-	X
setenv, unsetenv commands	-	X	-
SHELL variable specifies command to execute scripts	-	X	-
switch statement	-	X	-
until statement	X	-	X
set -x	X	-	X
set optionname	-	X	-
Set-uid scripts	-	-	X
Shell functions	SysV	-	X
Substring selectors :x	-	X	-
trap command	X	-	X
typeset command	-	-	X

Feature	sh	csh	ksh
ulimit command	X	-	X
Undefined variable is an error	-	X	-
! special character	-	X	-
@ command	-	X	-
*(...) wildcards	-	-	X
$(...) command expression	-	-	X
{...} wildcards	-	X	-
¦& coprocessing	-	-	X
>& redirection	-	X	-

NOTE: In the preceding table, sysV indicates the feature is available in the Bourne shell only for System V variants; it is not a feature of the Version 7 shell or the BSD implementation of sh. The Version 7 implementation of sh may entail restrictions not reflected in this table.

Shell Scripts for Public Consumption

Shell scripts developed for public consumption, whether as some or all the commands of a system, or as installation standard commands for using system facilities, should be designed for enduring portability.

Shell scripts developed for public use are almost always written in the Bourne shell language. Although there is a tendency today to write such scripts in the Korn shell language, people who do so realize they're taking a risk, albeit a modest one.

Some versions of UNIX allow you to specify the shell interpreter to use for a given script file by embedding a special command as the first line of the script: #! /bin/sh as the first line of a script would, on most modern UNIX systems, force the use of the Bourne shell to execute the script file. This is a handy device to allow you to develop scripts in the shell language of your choice, while also allowing users to avail themselves of the script regardless of their choice of an interactive shell. However, the #! device is not available on all versions of UNIX.

Shell scripts written in the C shell or the Korn shell language require that the operating system include the corresponding shell, either csh or ksh. Not all systems meet this requirement, and if portability among several platforms or between current and future platforms is a consideration (that is, if you're writing a script to be used by anyone anywhere, both now and years from now), common sense and reasonable prudence dictate that you avoid C shell and Korn shell syntax constructs in your script.

True portability also limits your use of UNIX commands and command options inside your shell script. Some versions of UNIX, especially the implementation by IBM, offer many new command options on many commands, leading the unwary into developing shell scripts that can run only under the IBM implementation of UNIX. Other versions of UNIX, such as ULTRIX and XENIX, support only the old-fashioned command library, along with some local peculiarities. If you're truly interested in developing portable programs and shell scripts, you should make use of the POSIX and X/Open compatibility guidelines, which describe only commands and command options that are generally available on most UNIX operating system implementations.

Even the dialect of the Bourne shell you use can be a portability consideration. For example, on ULTRIX systems, the command sh supplies only UNIX Version 7 functionality; you have to invoke the command sh5 to run a System V compatible Bourne shell.

Because perfect portability is, like Scotty's transporter, simply not obtainable in the twentieth century, a further application of common sense dictates that the level of effort you invest in portable programming be suitable to the job at hand. You might want to adopt guidelines somewhat like the following:

- For really important projects, choose any shell language (or other tool) you want—your choice simply becomes another requirement for installation and use of the system. (Don't forget to tell your user community of such requirements.)

- If your shell script might enter the public domain, restrict yourself to the Bourne shell language, and assume a System V Release 1 environment. This provides you with a great many tools but also suits your application to the vast majority of contemporary UNIX installations.

- If your shell script is targeted for use at your local installation, choose either the Bourne or the Korn shell language. Use the Korn shell if you feel you need its features, but do not use it gratuitously or casually. The odds are heavily in your favor that any future operating system releases or vendor changes will still support your shell script.

- If your project must meet certain stated compatibility goals (for example, you must support the XENIX machines running at three offices out in Podunk, Nebraska), then by all means adjust your project to meet those goals. There will still be aspects of your project where no stated goals apply. In those cases, choose the level of generality and portability that you (or your project timetable) can afford.

■ In all other cases, choose the tools and languages that you feel permit the most effective, trouble-free, user friendly implementation you can devise, and don't forget to maximize your own productivity and effectiveness.

Summary

Selecting a shell for use at the keyboard, as an interactive command line processor, is a relatively straightforward task, once you realize that your choice does not affect others. If you are new to UNIX, you should consider using the Korn shell because its built-in command editing feature can significantly increase productivity. Users accustomed to the C shell are also advised to investigate the Korn shell, for the same reason.

Familiarity with the Bourne shell and its capabilities and restrictions is essential for individuals who must work with a variety of UNIX systems or with the general UNIX public. It is the only shell that is universally available under all implementations of the UNIX operating system.

For daily keyboard use, both the C shell and the Korn shell appear to be viable alternatives. The Bourne shell is not a good choice when either of the other two shells is available because its lack of features, especially command history and command editing, degrade personal productivity.

Choosing a shell for writing scripts is, however, a different matter entirely.

Writing shell scripts is a difficult job because it is programming, and as everyone has learned by now, computer programming is not well suited to the human psyche or talents. The need for tools to make the job easier, to catch your mistakes, and to make the best use of your time draws you in the direction of using the most powerful, flexible tools available. If UNIX users had given in to this temptation in the past, seventy percent or more of all existing shell scripts would be written in the C shell language, and all new scripts being written today would be written in the Korn shell language. The temptation, however, is a siren song, and you should allow yourself the weakness of giving in to it only when the cost is small.

Both the C shell and Korn shell offer tools to the script writer that are hard to do without, such as simplified syntax for command substitutions, array variables, variable arithmetic and expressions, and better structured commands such as `select`. Because these tools are so helpful, they should be used for any work intended only for personal consumption.

They should also be preferred for location-specific projects, where the environment can be predicted reasonably accurately. However, for shell scripts claiming a wider audience, the Bourne shell still serves as the *lingua franca* of the UNIX world and will for some time to come.

The script writer who cannot anticipate the hardware and software environment must consider the choice of commands and command options used in the script as well as the shell language. A few environments offer a wider variety of commands and command options than most, and some UNIX versions omit some of the conventional UNIX runtime features. For most purposes, an implementation compatible with UNIX System V Release 1 can be considered as a minimum portability base. In situations where portability is especially important, the POSIX and X/Open standards should be consulted as guides to available operating system features and capabilities, rather than the vendor's manuals.

Shell programming can be as simple or as complex as you wish it to be. The C shell and the Korn shell are sufficiently sophisticated to permit the implementation of many programs as shell scripts that in the past would have been implemented in the C programming language. The use of shell scripts has also become popular as a prototyping and rapid development method. Indeed, a meaningful and significant amount of programming can be performed even on UNIX not having a compiled programming language.

It would seem that, while one shell can be chosen for customary use at the keyboard, the choice of a shell environment for writing shell scripts needs to be reconsidered for each project.

PART

3

Programming

Awk, Awk

By Ann M. Marshall

Overview

The UNIX utility awk is a pattern matching and processing language with considerably more power than you may realize. It searches one or more specified files, checking for records that match a specified pattern. If awk finds a match, the corresponding action is performed. A simple concept, but it results in a powerful tool. Often an awk program is only a few lines long, and because of this, an awk program is often written, used, and discarded. A traditional programming language, such as Pascal or C, would take more thought, more lines of code, and hence, more time. Short awk programs arise from two of its built-in features: the amount of predefined flexibility and the number of details that are handled by the language automatically. Together, these features allow the manipulation of large data files in short (often single-line) programs, and make awk stand apart from other programming languages. Certainly any time you spend learning awk will pay dividends in improved productivity and efficiency.

Uses

The uses for awk vary from the simple to the complex. Originally awk was intended for various kinds of data manipulation. Intentionally omitting parts of a file, counting occurrences in a file, and writing reports are naturals for awk.

Awk uses the syntax of the C programming language, so if you know C, you have an idea of awk syntax. If you are new to programming or don't know C, learning awk will familiarize you with many of the C constructs.

Examples of where awk can be helpful abound. Computer-aided manufacturing, for example, is plagued with nonstandardization, so the output of a computer that's running a particular tool is quite likely to be incompatible with the input required for a different tool. Rather than write any complex C program, this type of simple data transformation is a perfect awk task.

One real problem of computer-aided manufacturing today is that no standard format yet exists for the program running the machine. Therefore, the output from Computer A running Machine A probably is not the input needed for Computer B running Machine B. Although Machine A is finished with the material, Machine B is not ready to accept it. Production halts while someone edits the file so it meets Computer B's needed format. This is a perfect and simple awk task.

Due to the amount of built-in automation within awk, it is also useful for rapid prototyping or trying out an idea that could later be implemented in another language.

Features

Reflecting the UNIX environment, awk features resemble the structures of both C and shell scripts. Highlights include its being flexible, its predefined variables, automation, its standard program constructs, conventional variable types, its powerful output formatting borrowed from C, and its ease of use.

The flexibility means that most tasks may be done more than one way in awk. With the application in mind, the programmer chooses which method to use . The built-in variables already provide many of the tools to do what is needed. Awk is highly automated. For instance, awk automatically retrieves each record, separates it into fields, and does type conversion when needed without programmer request. Furthermore, there are no variable declarations. Awk includes the "usual" programming constructs for the control of program flow: an `if` statement for two way decisions and `do`, `for` and `while` statements for looping. Awk also includes its own notational shorthand to ease typing. (This is *UNIX* after all!) Awk borrows the `printf()` statement from C to allow "pretty" and versatile formats for output. These features combine to make awk user friendly.

Brief History

Alfred V. Aho, Peter J. Weinberger, and Brian W. Kernighan created awk in 1977. (The name is from the creators' last initials.) In 1985, more features were added, creating nawk (new awk). For quite a while, nawk remained exclusively the property of AT&T, Bell Labs. Although it became part of System V for Release 3.1, some versions of UNIX, like SunOS, keep both awk and nawk due to a syntax incompatibility. Others, like System V run nawk under the name awk (although System V. has nawk too). In The Free Software Foundation, GNU introduced their version of awk, gawk, based on the *IEEE POSIX* (Institute of Electrical and Electronics Engineers, Inc., IEEE Standard for Information Technology, Portable Operating System Interface, Part 2: Shell and Utilities Volume 2, ANSI approved 4/5/93), awk standard which is different from awk or nawk. Linux, PC shareware UNIX, uses gawk rather than awk or nawk. Throughout this chapter I have used the word awk when any of the three will do the concept. The versions are mostly upwardly compatible. Awk is the oldest, then nawk, then POSIX awk, then gawk as shown below. I have used the notation *version*++ to denote a concept that began in that version and continues through any later versions.

> **NOTE:** Due to different syntax, awk code can never be upgraded to nawk. However, except as noted, all the concepts of awk are implemented in nawk (and gawk). Where it matters, I have specified the version.

FIGURE 15.1.

The evolution of awk.

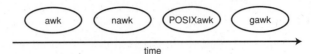

Refer to the end of the chapter for more information and further resources on awk and its derivatives.

Fundamentals

This section introduces the basics of the awk programming language. Although my discussion first skims the surface of each topic to familiarize you with how awk functions, later sections of the chapter go into greater detail. One feature of awk that almost continually holds true is this: you can do most tasks more than one way. The command line exemplifies this. First, I explain the variety of ways awk may be called from the command line—using files for input, the program file, and possibly an output file. Next, I introduce the main construct of awk, which is the pattern action statement. Then, I explain the fundamental ways awk can read and transform input. I conclude the section with a look at the format of an awk program.

Entering Awk from the Command Line

In its simplest form, awk takes the material you want to process from standard input and displays the results to standard output (the monitor). You write the awk program on the command line.

You can either specify explicit awk statements on the command line, or, with the -f flag, specify an awk program file that contains a series of awk commands. In addition to the standard UNIX design allowing for standard input and output, you can, of course, use file redirection in your shell, too, so awk < inputfile is functionally identical to awk inputfile. To save the output in a file, again use file redirection: awk > outputfile does the trick. Helpfully, awk can work with multiple input files at once if they are specified on the command line.

The most common way to see people use awk is as part of a command pipe, where it's filtering the output of a command. An example is ls -l ¦ awk {print $3} which would print just the third column of each line of the ls command. Awk scripts can become quite complex, so if you have a standard set of filter rules that you'd like to apply to a file, with the output sent directly to the printer, you could use something like awk -f myawkscript inputfile ¦ lp.

> **TIP:** If you opt to specify your awk script on the command line, you'll find it best to use single quotes around the program part of the awk command to let you use spaces and to ensure that the command shell doesn't falsely interpret any portion of the command.

Files for Input

These input and output places can be changed if desired. You can specify an input file by typing the name of the file after the program with a blank space between the two. The input file enters the awk environment from your workstation keyboard (standard input). To signal the end of the input file, type Ctl + d. The program on the command line executes on the input file you just entered and the results are displayed on the monitor (the standard output.)

Here's a simple little awk command that echoes all lines I type, prefacing each with the number of words (or fields, in awk parlance, hence the NF variable for number of fields) in the line. (Note that Ctrl+d means that while holding down the Control key you should press the d key).

```
$ awk '{print $NF : $0}'
I am testing my typing.
A quick brown fox jumps when vexed by lazy ducks.
Ctrl+d
5: I am testing my typing.
10: A quick brown fox jumps when vexed by lazy ducks.
$ _
```

You can also name more than one input file on the command line, causing the combined files to act as one input. This is one way of having multiple runs through one input file.

> **TIP:** Keep in mind that the correct ordering on the command line is crucial for your program to work correctly: files are read from left to right, so if you want to have file1 and file2 read in that order, you'll need to specify them as such on the command line.

The Program File

With awk's automatic type conversion, a file of names and a file of numbers entered in the reverse order at the command line generate strange-looking output rather than an error message. That is why for longer programs, it is simpler to put the program in a file and specify the name of the file on the command line. The -f option does this. Notice that this is an exception to the usual way UNIX handles options. Usually the options occur at the end of a command; however, here an input file is the last parameter.

> **NOTE:** Versions of awk that meet the POSIX awk specifications are allowed to have multiple -f options. You can use this for running multiple programs using the same input.

Specifying Output on the Command Line

Output from awk may be redirected to a file or piped to another program (see Chapter 4). The command awk /^5/ {print $0} ¦ grep 3, for example, will result in just those lines that start with the digit five (that's what the awk part does) and also contain the digit three (the grep command). If you wanted to save that output to a file, by contrast, you could use awk /^5/ {print $0} > results and the file results would contain all lines prefaced by the digit 5. If you opt for neither of these courses, the output of awk will be displayed on your screen directly, which can be quite useful in many instances, particularly when you're developing—or fine tuning—your awk script.

Patterns and Actions

Awk programs are divided into three main blocks; the BEGIN block, the per-statement processing block, and the END block. Unless explicitly stated, all statements to awk appear in the per-statement block (you'll see later where the other blocks can come in particularly handy for programming, though).

Statements within awk are divided into two parts: a *pattern*, telling awk what to match, and a corresponding *action*, telling awk what to do when a line matching the pattern is found. The action part of a pattern action statement is enclosed in curly braces ({}) and may be multiple statements. Either part of a pattern action statement may be omitted. An action with no specified pattern matches every record of the input file you want to search (that's how the earlier example of {print $0} worked). A pattern without an action indicates that you want input records to be copied to the output file as they are (i.e., printed).

The example of /^5/ {print $0} is an example of a two-part statement: the pattern here is *all lines that begin with the digit five* (the ^ indicates that it should appear at the beginning of the line: without it the pattern would say *any line that includes the digit five*) and the action is print the entire line verbatim. ($0 is shorthand for the entire line.)

Input

Awk automatically scans, in order, each record of the input file looking for each pattern action statement in the awk program. Unless otherwise set, awk assumes each record is a single line. (See the sections "Advanced Concepts", "Multi-line Records" for how to change this.) If the input file has blank lines in it, the blank lines count as a record too. Awk automatically retrieves each record for analysis; there is no *read* statement in awk.

A programmer may also disrupt the automatic input order in either of two ways: the next and exit statements. The next statement tells awk to retrieve the next record from the input file and continue without running the current input record through the remaining portion of pattern action statements in the program. For example, if you are doing a crossword puzzle and all the letters of a word are formed by previous words, most likely you wouldn't even bother to read that clue but simply skip to the clue below; this is how the next statement would work, if your list of clues were the input. The other method of disrupting the usual flow of input is through the exit statement. The exit statement transfers control to the END block—if one is specified—or quits the program, as if all the input has been read; suppose the arrival of a friend ends your interest in the crossword puzzle, but you still put the paper away. Within the END block, an exit statement causes the program to quit.

An input record refers to the entire line of a file including any characters, spaces, or Tabs. The spaces and tabs are called *whitespace*.

> **TIP:** If you think that your input file may include both spaces and tabs, you can save yourself a lot of confusion by ensuring that all tabs become spaces with the expand program. It works like this: `expand filename | awk { stuff }`.

The whitespace in the input file and the whitespace in the output file are not related and any whitespace you want in the output file, you must explicitly put there.

Fields

A group of characters in the input record or output file is called a field. Fields are predefined in awk: $1 is the first field, $2 is the second, $3 is the third, and so on. $0 indicates the entire line. Fields are separated by a *field separator* (any single character including Tab), held in the variable FS. Unless you change it, FS has a space as its value. FS may be changed by either starting the *programfile* with the following statement:

```
BEGIN {FS = "char" }
```

or by setting the `-Fchar` command line option where `char` is the selected field separator character you want to use.

One file that you might have viewed which demonstrates where changing the field separator could be helpful is the `/etc/passwd` file that defines all user accounts. Rather than having the different fields separated by spaces or tabs, the password file is structured with lines:

```
news:?:6:11:USENET News:/usr/spool/news:/bin/ksh
```

Each field is separated by a colon! You could change each colon to a space (with sed, for example), but that wouldn't work too well: notice that the fifth field, `USENET News`, contains a space already. Better to change the field separator. If you wanted to just have a list of the fifth fields in each line, therefore, you could use the simple awk command `awk -F: {print $5} /etc/passwd`.

Likewise, the built-in variable `OFS` holds the value of the output field separator. `OFS` also has a default value of a space. It, too, may be changed by placing the following line at the start of a program.

```
BEGIN {OFS = "char" }
```

If you want to automatically translate the `passwd` file so that it listed only the first and fifth fields, separated by a tab, you can therefore use the awk script:

```
BEGIN { FS=":" ; OFS="    " }
{ print $1, $5 }
```

Notice here that the script contains two blocks: the BEGIN block and the main per-input line block. Also notice that most of the work is done automatically.

Program Format

With a few noted exceptions, awk programs are free format. The interpreter ignores any blank lines in a *programfile*. Add them to improve the readability of your program whenever you wish. The same is true for Tabs and spaces between operators and the parts of a program. Therefore, these two lines are treated identically by the awk interpreter.

```
$4 == 2              {print "Two"}

$4     ==    2    {    print    "Two"    }
```

If more than one pattern action line appears on a line, you'll need to separate them with a semicolon, as shown above in the BEGIN block for the `passwd` file translator. If you stick with one-command-per-line then you won't need to worry too much about the semicolons. There are a couple of spots, however, where the semicolon must always be used:

before an else statement or when included in the syntax of a statement. (See the "Loops" or "The Conditional Statement" sections.) However, you may always put a semicolon at the end of a statement.

The other format restriction for awk programs is that at least the opening curly bracket of the action half of a pattern action statement must be on the same line as the accompanying pattern, if both pattern and action exist. Thus, the following examples all do the same thing.

The first shows all statements on one line:

```
$2==0     {print ""; print ""; print "";}
```

The second with the first statement on the same line as the pattern to match:

```
$2==0     {    print ""
          print ""
          print ""}
```

and finally as spread out as possible:

```
$2==0     {
          print ""
          print ""
          print ""
     }
```

When the second field of the input file is equal to 0, awk prints three blank lines to the output file.

> **NOTE:** Notice that `print ""` prints a blank line to the output file, whereas the statement `print` alone prints the current input line.

When you look at an awk program file, you may also find commentary within. Anything typed from a # to the end of the line is considered a comment and is ignored by awk. They are notes to anyone reading the program to explain what is going on in words, not computerese.

A Note on *awk* Error Messages

Awk error messages (when they appear) tend to be cryptic. Often, due to the brevity of the program, a typo is easily found. Not all errors are as obvious; I have scattered some examples of errors throughout this chapter.

Print Selected Fields

Awk includes three ways to specify printing. The first is implied. A pattern without an action assumes that the action is to print. The two ways of actively commanding awk to print are print and printf(). For now, I am going to stick to using only implied printing and the print statement. printf is discussed in a later section ("Input/Output") and is used mainly for precise output. This section demonstrates the first two types of printing through some step-by-step examples.

Program Components

If I want to be sure the System Administrator spelled my name correctly in the /etc/password file, I enter an awk command to find a match but omit an action. The following command line puts a list on-screen.

```
$ awk '/Ann/' /etc/passwd

amarshal:oPWwC9qVWI/ps:2005:12:Ann Marshall:/usr/grad/amarshal:/bin/csh
andhs26:0TFnZSVwcua3Y:2488:23:DeAnn O'Neal:/usr/lstudent/andhs26:/bin/csh
alewis:VYfz4EatT4OoA:2623:22:Annie Lewis:/usr/lteach/alewis:/bin/csh
cmcintyr:0FciKEDDMkauU:2630:22:Carol Ann McIntyre:/usr/lteach/cmcintyr:/bin/csh
jflanaga:ShrMnyDwLI/mM:2654:22:JoAnn Flanagan:/usr/lteach/jflanaga:/bin/csh
lschultz:mic35ZiFj9zWk:3060:22:Lee Ann Schultz, :/usr/lteach/lschultz:/bin/csh
akestle:job57Lb5/ofoE:3063:22:Ann Kestle.:/usr/lteach/akestle:/bin/csh
bakehs59:yRYV6BtcW7wFg:3075:23:DeAnna Adlington, Baker :/usr/bakehs59:/bin/csh
ahernan:AZZPQNCkw6ffs:3144:23:Ann Hernandez:/usr/lstudent/ahernan:/bin/csh
$ _
```

I look on the monitor and see the correct spelling.

> **ERROR NOTE:** For the sake of making a point, suppose I had chosen the pattern /Anne/. A quick glance above shows that there would be no matches. Entering awk '/Anne/' /etc/passwd will therefore produce nothing but another system prompt to the monitor. This can be confusing if you expect output. The same goes the other way; above, I wanted the name Ann, but the names LeAnn, Annie and DeAnna matched, too. Sometimes choosing a pattern too long or too short can cause an unneeded headache.

> **TIP:** If a pattern match is not found, look for a typo in the pattern you are trying to match.

Printing specified fields of an ASCII (plain text) file is a straightforward awk task. Because this program example is so short, only the input is in a file. The first input file, "sales", is a file of car sales by month. The file consists of each salesperson's name, followed by a monthly sales figure. The end field is a running total of that person's total sales.

The Input File and Program

```
$cat sales
John Anderson,12,23,7,42
Joe Turner,10,25,15,50
Susan Greco,15,13,18,46
Bob Burmeister,8,21,17,46
```

The following command line prints the salesperson's name and the total sales for the first quarter.

```
awk -F, '{print $1,$5}' sales

John Anderson 42
Joe Turner 50
Susan Greco 46
Bob Burmeister 46
```

A comma (,) between field variables indicates that I want OFS applied between output fields as shown in a previous example. Remember without the comma, no field separator will be used, and the displayed output fields (or output file) will all run together.

> **TIP:** Putting two field separators in a row inside a print statement creates a syntax error with the print statement; however, using the same field twice in a single print statement is valid syntax. For example:
>
> ```
> awk '{print($1,$1)'
> ```

Patterns

A pattern is the first half of an awk program statement. In awk there are six accepted pattern types. This section discusses each of the six in detail. You have already seen a couple of them, including BEGIN, and a specified, slash-delimited pattern, in use. Awk has many string matching capabilities arising from patterns, and the use of regular expressions in patterns. A range pattern locates a sequence. All patterns except range patterns may be combined in a compound pattern.

I began the chapter by saying awk was a pattern-match and process language. This section explores exactly what is meant by a pattern match. As you'll see, what kind pattern you can match depends on exactly how you're using the awk pattern specification notation.

BEGIN and END

The two special patterns BEGIN and END may be used to indicate a match, either before the first input record is read, or after the last input record is read, respectively. Some versions of awk require that, if used, BEGIN must be the first pattern of the program and, if used, END must be the last pattern of the program. While not necessarily a requirement, it is nonetheless an excellent habit to get into, so I encourage you to do so, as I do throughout this chapter. Using the BEGIN pattern for initializing variables is common (although variables can be passed from the command line to the program too; see "Command Line Arguments") The END pattern is used for things which are input-dependent such as totals.

If I want to know how many lines are in a given program, I type the following line:

```
$awk 'END {print _Total lines: _$NR}' myprogram
```

I see Total lines: 256 on the monitor and therefore know that the file myprogram has 256 lines. At any point while awk is processing the file, the variable NR counts the number of records read so far. NR at the end of a file has a value equal to the number of lines in the file.

How might you see a BEGIN block in use? Your first thought might be to initialize variables, but if it's a numeric value, it's automatically initialized to zero before its first use. Instead, perhaps you're building a table of data and want to have some columnar headings. With this in mind, here's a simple awk script that shows you all the accounts that people named Dave have on your computer:

```
BEGIN {
    FS=_:_      # remember that the passwd file uses colons
    OFS=_    _      # we_re setting the output to a TAB
    print _Account_,_Username_
    }
/Dav/    {print $1, $5}
```

Here's what it looks like in action (we've called this file _daves.awk_, though the program matches Dave and David, of course):

```
$ awk -f daves.awk /etc/passwd
Account     Username
andrews     Dave Andrews
d3          David Douglas Dunlap
daves       Dave Smith
taylor      Dave Taylor
```

Note that you could also easily have a summary of the total number of matched accounts by adding a variable that's incremented for each match, then in the END block output in some manner. Here's one way to do it:

```
BEGIN { FS=_:_ ; OFS=_    _ # input colon separated, output tab separated
    print _Account_,_Username_
    }
/Dav/    {print $1, $5 ; matches++ }
END     { print _A total of _matches_ matches._}
```

Here you can see how awk allows you to shorten the length of programs by having multiple items on a single line, particularly useful for initialization. Also notice the C increment notation: _matches++_ is functionally identical to _matches = matches + 1_. Finally, also notice that we didn't have to initialize the variable _matches_ to zero since it was done for us automatically by the awk system.

Expressions

Any expression may be used with any operator in awk. An expression consists of any operator in awk, and its corresponding operand in the form of a pattern-match statement. Type conversion—variables being interpreted as numbers at one point, but strings at another—is automatic. The type of operand needed is decided by the operator type. If a numeric operator is given a string operand, it is converted and vice versa.

> **TIP:** To force a conversion, if the desired change is string to number, add (+) 0. If you wish to explicitly convert a number to a string add " " (the null string) to the variable. Two quick examples: num=3; num=num __ creates a new numeric variable and sets it to the number three, then by appending a null string to it, translates it to a string (e.g., the string with the character 3 within). Adding zero to that string — num=num + 0 — forces it back to a numeric value.

Any expression can be a pattern. If the pattern, in this case the expression, evaluates to a nonzero or nonnull value, then the pattern matches that input record. Patterns often involve comparison. The following are the valid awk comparison operators:

Table 15.1. Comparison Operators in awk.

Operator	Meaning
==	is equal to
<	less than
>	greater than
<=	less than or equal to
>=	greater than or equal to
!=	not equal to
~	matched by
!~	not matched by

In awk, as in C, the logical equality operator is == rather than =. The single = compares memory location, whereas == compares values. When the pattern is a comparison, the pattern matches if the comparison is true (non-null or non-zero). Here's an example: what if you wanted to only print lines where the first field had a numeric value of less than twenty? No problem in awk:

```
$1 < 20 {print $0}
```

If the expression is arithmetic, it is matched when it evaluates to a nonzero number. For example, here's a small program that will print the first ten lines that have exactly seven words:

```
BEGIN  {i=0}
NF==7 { print $0 ; i++ }
/i==10/ {exit}
```

There's another way that you could use these comparisons too, since awk understands collation orders (that is, whether words are greater or lesser than other words in a standard dictionary ordering). Consider the situation where you have a phone directory—a sorted list of names—in a file and want to print all the names that would appear in the corporate phonebook before a certain person, say D. Hughes. You could do this quite succinctly:

```
$1 >= "Hughes,D" { exit }
```

When the pattern is a string, a match occurs if the expression is non-null. In the earlier example with the pattern /Ann/, it was assumed to be a string since it was enclosed in slashes. In a comparison expression, if both operands have a numeric value, the comparison is based on the numeric value. Otherwise, the comparison is made using string ordering, which is why this simple example works.

> **TIP:** You can write more than two comparisons to a line in awk.

The pattern $2 <= $1 could involve either a numeric comparison or a string comparison. Whichever it is, it will vary from file to file or even from record to record within the same file.

> **TIP:** Know your input file well when using such patterns, particularly since awk will often silently assume a type for the variable and work with it, without error messages or other warnings.

String Matching

There are three forms of string matching. The simplest is to surround a string by slashes (/). No quotation marks are used. Hence /"Ann"/ is actually the string ' *"Ann"* ' not the string *Ann*, and /"Ann"/ returns no input. The entire input record is returned if the expression within the slashes is anywhere in the record. The other two matching operators have a more specific scope. The operator ~ means "is matched by," and the pattern matches when the input field being tested for a match contains the substring on the right hand side.

```
$2 ~ /mm/
```

This example matches every input record containing mm somewhere in the second field. It could also be written as $2 ~ "mm".

The other operator !~ means "is not matched by."

```
$2 !~ /mm/
```

This example matches every input record not containing mm anywhere in the second field.

Armed with that explanation, you can now see that /Ann/ is really just shorthand for the more complex statement $0 ~ /Ann/.

Regular expressions are common to UNIX, and they come in two main flavors. You have probably used them unconsciously on the command line as wildcards, where * matches zero or more characters and ? matches any single character. For instance entering the first line below results in the command interpreter matching all files with the suffix abc and the rm command deleting them.

```
rm *abc
```

Awk works with regular expressions that are similar to those used with grep, sed, and other editors but subtly different than the wildcards used with the command shell. In particular, . matches a character and * matches zero or more of the previous character in the pattern (so a pattern of x*y will match anything that has any number of the letter x followed by a y. To force a single x to appear too, you'd need to use the regular expression xx*y instead). By default, patterns can appear anywhere on the line, so to have them tied to an edge, you need to use ^ to indicate the beginning of the word or line, and $ for the end. If you wanted to match all lines where the first word ends in abc, for example, you could use $1 ~ /abc$/. The following line matches all records where the fourth field begins with the letter a:

```
$4 ~ /^a.*/
```

Range Patterns

The pattern portion of a pattern/action pair may also consist of two patterns separated by a comma (,); the action is performed for all lines between the first occurrence of the first pattern and the next occurrence of the second.

At most companies, employees receive different benefits according to their respective hire dates. It so happens that I have a file listing all employees in my company, including hire date. If I wanted to write an awk program that just lists the employees hired between 1980 and 1987 I could use the following script, if the first field is the employee's name and the third field is the year hired. Here's how that data file might look (notice that I use : to separate fields so that we don't have to worry about the spaces in the employee names)

```
$ cat emp.data.
John Anderson:sales:1980
Joe Turner:marketing:1982
Susan Greco:sales:1985
Ike Turner:pr:1988
Bob Burmeister:accounting:1991
```

The program could then be invoked:

```
$ awk -F: '$3 > 1980,$3 < 1987 {print $1, $3}' emp.data
```

With the output:

```
John Anderson 1980
Joe Turner 1982
Susan Greco 1985
```

> **TIP:** The above example works because the input is already in order according to hire year. Range patterns often work best with pre-sorted input. This particular data file would be a bit tricky to sort within UNIX, but you could use the rather complex command `sort -c: +3 -4 -rn emp.data > new.emp.data` to sort things correctly. (See Chapter 6 for more details on using the powerful sort command.)

Notice range patterns are inclusive—they include both the first item matched and the end data indicated in the pattern. The range pattern matches all records from the first occurrence of the first pattern to the first occurrence of the second. This is a subtle point, but it has a major affect on how range patterns work. First, if the second pattern is never found, all remaining records match. So given the input file below:

```
$ cat sample.data
1
3
5
7
9
11
```

The following output appears on the monitor, totally disregarding that 9 and 11 are out of range.

```
$ awk '$1==3, $1==8' file1 sample.data
3
5
7
9
11
```

The end pattern of a range is not equivalent to a <= operand, though liberal use of these patterns can alleviate the problem, as shown in the employee hire date example above.

Secondly, as stated, the pattern matches the *first* range; others that might occur later in the data file are ignored. That's why you have to make sure that the data is sorted as you expect.

> **CAUTION:** Range patterns cannot be parts of a larger pattern.

A more useful example of the range pattern comes from awk's ability to handle multiple input files. I have a function finder program that finds code segments I know exist and tells me where they are. The code segments for a particular function X, for example, are bracketed by the phrase "function X" at the beginning and } /* end of X at the end. It can be expressed as the awk pattern range:

```
'/function functionname/,/} \/* end of functionname/'
```

Compound Patterns

Patterns can be combined using the following logical operators and parentheses as needed.

Table 15.2. The Logical Operators in awk.

Operator	Meaning
!	not
¦¦	or (you can also use ¦ in regular expressions)
&&	and

The pattern may be simple or quite complicated: (NF<3) ¦¦ (NF >4). This matches all input records not having exactly four fields. As is usual in awk, there are a wide variety of ways to do the same thing (specify a pattern). Regular expressions are allowed in string matching, but their use is not forced. To form a pattern that matches strings beginning with a or b or c or d, there are several pattern options:

```
/^[a-d].*/

/^a.*/ !! /^b.*/ ¦¦ /^c.*/ ¦¦ /^d.*/
```

> **NOTE:** When using range patterns: $1==2, $1==4 and $1>= 2 && $1 <=4 are not the same ranges at all. First, the range pattern depends on the occurrence of the second pattern as a stop marker, not on the value indicated in the range. Secondly, as I mentioned earlier, the first pattern only matches the first range, others are ignored.

For instance, consider the following simple input file:

```
$ cat mydata
1       0
3       1
4       1
5       1
7       0
4       2
5       2
1       0
4       3
```

The first range I try, '$1==3,$1==5, produces:

```
$ awk '$1==3,$1==5' mydata
3       1
4       1
5       1
```

Compare this to the following pattern and output.

```
$ awk '$1>=3 && $1<=5' mydata
3       1
4       1
5       1
4       2
5       2
4       3
```

Range patterns cannot be parts of a combined pattern.

Actions

The remainder of this chapter explores the action part of a pattern action statement. As the name suggests, the action part tells awk what to do when a pattern is found. Patterns are optional. An awk program built solely of actions looks like other iterative programming languages. But looks are deceptive—even without a pattern, awk matches every input record to the first pattern action statement before moving to the second.

Actions must be enclosed in curly braces ({}) whether accompanied by a pattern or alone. An action part may consist of multiple statements. When the statements have no pattern and are single statements (no compound loops or conditions), brackets for each individual action are optional provided the actions begin with a left curly brace and end with a right curly brace. Consider the following two action pieces:

```
{name = $1
print name}
```

and

```
{name = $1}
{print name},
```

These two produce identical output.

Variables

An integral part of any programming language are variables, the virtual boxes within which you can store values, count things, and more. In this section, I talk about variables in awk. Awk has three types of variables: user-defined variables, field variables, and predefined variables. The next section is devoted to a discussion of built-in variables. Awk doesn't have variable declarations. A variable comes to life the first time it is mentioned; in a twist on René Descarte's philosophical conundrum, you use it, therefore it is. The section concludes with an example of turning an awk program into a shell script.

> **CAUTION:** Since there are no declarations, be doubly careful to initialize all the variables you use, though you can always be sure that they automatically start with the value zero.

Naming

The rule for naming user-defined variables is that they can be any combination of letters, digits, and underscores, as long as the name starts with a letter. It is helpful to give a variable a name indicative of its purpose in the program. Variables already defined by awk are written in all uppercase. Since awk is case-sensitive, ofs is not the same variable as OFS and capitalization (or lack thereof) is a common error. You have already seen field variables—variables beginning with $, followed by a number, and indicating a specific input field.

A variable is a number or a string or both. There is no type declaration, and type conversion is automatic if needed. Recall the car sales file used earlier. For illustration suppose I enter the program **awk -F: { print $1 * 10} emp.data**, and awk obligingly provides the rest:

```
0
0
0
0
0
```

Of course, this makes no sense! The point is that awk did exactly what it was asked without complaint: it multiplied the name of the employee times ten, and when it tried to translate the name into a number for the mathematical operation it failed, resulting in a zero. Ten times zero, needless to say, is zero...

Awk in a Shell Script

Before examining the next example, review what you know about shell programming (Chapters 10-14). Remember, every file containing shell commands needs to be changed to an executable file before you can run it as a shell script. To do this you should enter `chmod +x` *filename* from the command line.

Sometimes awk's automatic type conversion benefits you. Imagine that I'm still trying to build an office system with awk scripts and this time I want to be able to maintain a running monthly sales total based on a data file that contains individual monthly sales. It looks like this:

```
cat monthly.sales
John Anderson,12,23,7
Joe Turner,10,25,15
Susan Greco,15,13,18
Bob Burmeister,8,21,17
```

These need to be added together to calculate the running totals for each person's sales. Let a program do it!

```
$cat total.awk
BEGIN     {OFS=,}      #change OFS to keep the file format the same.
{print $1, " monthly sales summary: " $2+$3+$4 }
```

That's the awk script, so let's see how it works:

```
$ awk -f total.awk monthly.sales
cat sales
John Anderson, monthly sales summary: 42
Joe Turner, monthly sales summary: 50
Susan Greco, monthly sales summary: 46
Bob Burmeister, monthly sales summary: 46
```

> **CAUTION:** *Always* run your program once to be sure it works before you make it part of a complicated shell script!

Your task has been reduced to entering the monthly sales figures in the sales file and editing the program file total to include the correct number of fields (if you put a for loop for(i=2;i<+NF;i++) the number of fields is correctly calculated, but printing is a hassle and needs an if statement with 12 else if clauses).

In this case, not having to wonder if a digit is part of a string or a number is helpful. Just keep an eye on the input data, since awk performs whatever actions you specify, regardless of the actual data type with which you're working.

Built-in Variables

This section discusses the built-in variables found in awk. Because there are many versions of awk, I included notes for those variables found in nawk, POSIX awk, and gawk since they all differ. As before, unless otherwise noted, the variables of earlier releases may be found in the later implementations. Awk was released first and contains the core set of built-in variables used by all updates. Nawk expands the set. The POSIX awk specification encompasses all variables defined in nawk plus one additional variable. Gawk applies the POSIX awk standards and then adds some built-in variables which are found in gawk alone; the built-in variables noted when discussing gawk are unique to gawk. This list is a guideline not a hard and fast rule. For instance, the built-in variable ENVIRON is formally introduced in the POSIX awk specifications; it exists in gawk; it is in also in the System V implementation of nawk, *but* SunOS nawk doesn't have the variable ENVIRON. Consult the man pages for the variables of your version on your system.

As I stated earlier, awk is case sensitive. In all implementations of awk, built-in variables are written entirely in upper case.

Built-in Variables for Awk

When awk first became a part of UNIX, the built-in variables were the bare essentials. As the name indicates, the variable FILENAME holds the name of the current input file. Recall the function finder code; type the new line below:

```
/function functionname/,/} \/* end of functionname/' {print $0}
END    {print ""; print "Found in the file " FILENAME}
```

This adds the finishing touch.

The value of the variable FS determines the input field separator. FS has a space as its default value. The built-in variable NF contains the number of fields in the current record (remember, fields are akin to words, and records are input lines). This value may change for each input record.

What happens if within an awk script I have the following statement?

```
$3 = "Third field"
```

It reassigns $3 and all other field variables, also reassigning NF to the new value. The total number of records read may be found in the variable NR. The variable OFS holds the value for the output field separator. The default value of OFS is a space. The value for the output format for numbers resides in the variable OFMT which has a default value of %.6g. This is the format specifier for the print statement, though its syntax comes from the C printf format string. ORS is the output record separator. Unless changed, the value of ORS is newline(\n).

Built-in Variables for Nawk

NOTE: When awk was expanded in 1985, part of the expansion included adding more built-in variables.

CAUTION: Some implementations of UNIX simply put the new code in the spot for the old code and didn't bother keeping both awk and nawk. System V and SunOS have both available. Linux has neither awk nor nawk but uses gawk. System V has both, but the awk uses nawk expansions. The book *"awk the programming language"* by the awk authors speaks of awk throughout the book, but the programming language it describes is called nawk on most systems.

The built-in variable ARGC holds the value for the number of command line arguments. The variable ARGV is an array containing the command line arguments. Subscripts for ARGV begin with 0 and continue through ARGC-1. ARGV[0] is always awk. The available UNIX options do not occupy ARGV. The variable FNR represents the number of the current record within that input file. Like NR, this value changes with each new record. FNR is always <= NR. The built-in variable RLENGTH holds the value of the length of string matched by the match function. The variable RS holds the value of the input record separator. The default value of RS is a newline. The start of the string matched by the match function resides in RSTART. Between RSTART and RLENGTH, it is possible to determine what was matched. The variable SUBSEP contains the value of the subscript separator. It has a default value of "\034".

Built-in Variables for POSIX Awk

The POSIX awk specification introduces one new built-in variable beyond those in nawk. The built-in variable ENVIRON is an array that holds the values of the current environment variables. (Environment variables are discussed more thoroughly later in this chapter.) The subscript values for ENVIRON are the names of the environment variables themselves, and each ENVIRON element is the value of that variable. For instance, ENVIRON["HOME"] on my PC under Linux is "/home". Notice that using ENVIRON can save much system dependence within awk source code in some cases but not others. ENVIRON["HOME"] at work is "/usr/anne" while my SunOS account doesn't have an ENVIRON variable because it's not POSIX compliant.

Here's an example of how you could work with the environment variables:

```
ENVIRON[EDITOR] == "vi"  {print NR,$0}
```

This program prints my program listings with line numbers if I am using *vi* as my default editor. More on this example later in the chapter.

Built-in Variables in Gawk

The GNU group further enhanced awk by adding four new variables to gawk, its public re-implementation of awk. Gawk does not differ between UNIX versions as much as awk and nawk do, fortunately. These built-in variables are in addition to those mentioned in the POSIX specification as described above. The variable CONVFMT contains the conversion format for numbers. The default value of CONVFMT is "%.6g" and is for internal use only. The variable FIELDWIDTHS allows a programmer the option of having fixed field widths rather than a single character field separator. The values of FIELDWIDTHS are numbers separated by a space or Tab (\t), so fields need not all be the same width. When the FIELDWIDTHS variable is set, each field is expected to have a fixed width. Gawk separates the input record using the FIELDWIDTHS values for field widths. If FIELDWIDTHS is set, the value of FS is disregarded. Assigning a new value to FS overrides the use of FIELDWIDTHS; it restores the default behavior.

To see where this could be useful, let's imagine that you've just received a datafile from accounting that indicates the different employees in your group and their ages. It might look like:

```
$ cat gawk.datasample
1Swensen, Tim   24
1Trinkle, Dan   22
0Mitchel, Carl 27
```

The very first character, you find out, indicates if they're hourly or salaried: a value of 1 means that they're salaried, and a value of 0 is hourly. How to split that character out from the rest of the data field? With the FIELDWIDTHS statement. Here's a simple gawk script that could attractively list the data:

```
BEGIN {FIELDWIDTHS = 1 8 1 4 1 2}
{ if ($1 == 1) print "Salaried employee "$2,$4" is "$6" years old.";
  else           print "Hourly   employee "$2,$4" is "$6" years old."
}
```

The output would look like:

```
Salaried employee Swensen, Tim  is 24 years old.
Salaried employee Trinkle, Dan  is 22 years old.
Hourly    employee Mitchel, Carl is 27 years old.
```

> **TIP:** When calculating the different FIELDWIDTH values, don't forget any field separators: the spaces between words do count in this case.

The variable IGNORECASE controls the case sensitivity of gawk regular expressions. If IGNORECASE has a nonzero value, pattern matching ignores case for regular expression operations. The default value of IGNORECASE is zero; all regular expression operations are normally case sensitive.

Conditions (No *IFs*, *&&s* or *buts*)

Awk program statements are, by their very nature, conditional; if a pattern matches, then a specified action or actions occurs. Actions, too, have a conditional form. This section discusses conditional flow. It focuses on the syntax of the if statement, but, as usual in awk, there are multiple ways to do something.

A conditional statement does a test before it performs the action. One test, the pattern match, has already happened; this test is an action. The last two sections introduced variables; now you can begin putting them to practical uses.

The *if* Statement

An if statement takes the form of a typical iterative programming language control structure where E_1 is an expression, as mentioned in the "Patterns" section earlier in this chapter:

if E_1 S_2; else S_3.

While E_1 is always a single expression, S_2 and S_3 may be either single- or multiple-action statements (that means conditions in conditions are legal syntax, but I am getting ahead of myself). Returns and indention are, as usual in awk, entirely up to you. However, if S_2 and the else statement are on the same line, and S_2 is a single statement, a semicolon must separate S_2 from the else statement. When awk encounters an if statement, evaluation occurs as follows: first E_1 is evaluated, and if E_1 is nonzero or nonnull(true), S_2 is executed;

if E_1 is zero or null(false) and there's an else clause, S_3 is executed. For instance, if you want to print a blank line when the third field has the value 25 and the entire line in all other cases, you could use a program snippet like this:

```
{ if $3 == 25
     print ""
else
     print $0 }
```

The portion of the if statement involving S is completely optional since sometimes your choice is limited to whether or not to have awk execute S_2:

```
{ if $3 == 25
     print "" }
```

Although the if statement is an action, E_1 can test for a pattern match using the pattern-match operator ~. As you have already seen, you can use it to look for my name in the password file another way. The first way is shorter, but they do the same thing.

```
$awk '/Ann/'/etc/passwd
$awk '{if ($0 ~ /Ann/) print $0}' /etc/passwd
```

One use of the if statement combined with a pattern match is to further filter the screen input. For example here I'm going to only print the lines in the password file that contain both Ann and a capital m character:

```
$ awk '/Ann/ { if ($0 ~ /M/) print}' /etc/passwd
amarshal:oPWwC9qVWI/ps:2005:12:Ann Marshall:/usr/grad/amarshal:/bin/csh
cmcintyr:0FciKEDDMkauU:2630:22:Carol Ann McIntyre:/usr/lteach/cmcintyr:/bin/csh
jflanaga:ShrMnyDwLI/mM:2654:22:JoAnn Flanagan:/usr/lteach/jflanaga:/bin/csh
```

Either S_2 or S_3 or both may consist of multiple-action statements. If any of them do, the group of statements is enclosed in curly braces. Curly braces may be put wherever you wish as long as they enclose the action. The rule of thumb: if it's one statement, the braces are optional. More than one and it's required.

You can also use multiple else clauses. The car sales example gets one field longer each month. The first two fields are always the salesperson's name and the last field is the accumulated annual total, so it is possible to calculate the month by the value of NF:

```
if(NF=4) month="Jan."
else if(NF=5) month="Feb"
else if(NF=6) month="March"
else if(NF=7) month="April"
else if(NF=8) month="May" # and so on
```

NOTE: Whatever the value of NF, the overall block of code will execute only once. It falls through the remaining else clauses.

The Conditional Statement

Nawk++ also has a conditional statement, really just shorthand for an if statement. It takes the format shown and uses the same conditional operator found in C:

```
E₁ ? S₂ : S₃
```

Here, E_1 is an expression, and S_2 and S_3 are single-action statements. When it encounters a conditional statement, awk evaluates it in the same order as an if statement: first E_1 is evaluated; if E_1 is nonzero or nonnull (true), S_2 is executed; if E_1 is zero or null (false), S_3 is executed. Only one statement, S_2 or S_3, is chosen, never both.

The conditional statement is a good place for the programmer to provide error messages. Return to the monthly sales example. When we wanted to differentiate between hourly and salaried employees, we had a big if-else statement:

```
{ if ($1 == 1) print "Salaried employee "$2,$4" is "$6" years old.";
  else         print "Hourly   employee "$2,$4" is "$6" years old."
}
```

In fact, there's an easier way to do this with conditional statements:

```
{ print ($1==1? "Salaried":"Hourly") "employee "$2,$4" is "$6" years old." }
```

> **CAUTION:** Remember the conditional statement is not part of original awk!

At first glance, and for short statements, the if statement appears identical to the conditional statement. On closer inspection, the statement you should use in a specific case differs. Either is fine for use when choosing between either of two single statements, but the if statement is required for more complicated situations, such as when E_2 and E_3 are multiple statements. Use if for multiple else statements (the first example), or for a condition inside a condition like the second example below:

```
{ if (NR == 100)
    { print \$(NF-1)\{""
    print "This is the 100th record"
    print $0
      print
    }
}
{ if($1==0)
    if(name~/Fred/
        print "Fred is broke" }
```

Patterns as Conditions

As if that does not provide ample choice, notice that the program relying on pattern-matching (had I chosen that method) produces the same output. Look at the program and its output.

```
$ cat lowsales.awk}
BEGIN       {OFS=\\t\{"\t"}}
$(NF-1) <= 7    {print $1, $(NF-1),\,\"Check \Attendance"\ {Sales"}      }
$(NF-1) > 7     {print $1, $(NF-1)     }      # Next to last field

{$ awk -f lowsales.awk emp.data}
John Anderson       7      \check attendance\ {Check Sales}
Joe Turner          15
Susan Greco         18
Bob Burmeister      17
```

Since the two patterns above are nonoverlapping and one immediately follows the other, the two programs accomplish the same thing. Which to use is a matter of programming style. I find the `conditional` statement or the `if` statement more readable than two patterns in a row. When you are choosing whether to use the nawk `conditional` statement or the `if` statement because you're concerned about printing two long messages, using the `if` statement is cleaner. Above all, if you chose to use the `conditional` statement, keep in mind you can't use awk; you must use nawk or gawk.

Loops

People often write programs to perform a repetitive task or several repeated tasks. These repetitions are called loops. Loops are the subject of this section. The loop structures of awk very much resemble those found in C. First, let's look at a shortcut in counting with 1 notation. Then I'll show you the ways to program loops in awk. The looping constructs of awk are the do(nawk), `for`, and `while` statements. As with multiple-action groups in an `if` statement, curly braces(`{}`) surround a group of action statements associated in a loop. Without curly braces, only the statement immediately following the keyword is considered part of the loop.

> **TIP:** Forgetting curly braces is a common looping error.

The section concludes with a discussion of how (and some examples of why) to interrupt a loop.

Increment and Decrement

As stated earlier, assignment statements take the form x = y, where the value y is being assigned to x. Awk has some shorthand methods of writing this. For example, to add a monthly sales total to the car sales file, you'll need to add a variable to keep a running total of the sales figures. Call it `total` . You need to start `total` at zero and add each `$(NF-1)` as read. In standard programming practice, that would be written `total = total + $(NF-1)`. This is okay in awk, too. However, a shortened format of `total += $(NF-1)` is also acceptable.

There are two ways to indicate `line+= 1` and `line -=1` (`line =line+1` and `line=line-1` in awk shorthand). They are called increment and decrement, respectively, and can be further shortened to the simpler `line++` and `line--`. At any reference to a variable, you can not only use this notation but even vary whether the action is performed immediately before or after the value is used in that statement. This is called prefix and postfix notation, and is represented by `++line` and `line++`.

For clarity's sake, focus on increment for a moment. Decrement functions the same way using subtraction. Using the `++line` notation tells awk to do the addition before doing the operation indicated in the line. Using the postfix form says to do the operation in the line, then do the addition. Sometimes the choice does not matter; keeping a counter of the number of sales people (to later calculate a sales average at the end of the month) requires a counter of names. The statements `totalpeople++` and `++totalpeople` do the same thing and are interchangeable when they occupy a line by themselves. But suppose I decide to print the person's number along with his or her name and sales. Adding either of the second two lines below to the previous example produces different results based on starting both at `totalpeople=1`.

```
$ cat awkscript.v1
BEGIN { totalpeople = 1 }
{print ++totalpeople, $1, $(NF-1)      }

$ cat awkscript.v2
BEGIN { totalpeople = 1 }
{print totalpeople++, $1, $(NF-1)      }
```

The first example will actually have the first employee listed as #2, since the `totalpeople` variable is incremented before it's used in the print statement. By contrast, the second version will do what we want because it'll use the variable value, then afterwards increment it to the next value.

> **TIP:** Be consistent. Either is fine, but stick with one numbering system or the other, and there is less likelihood that you will accidently enter a loop an unexpected number of times.

The *While* Statement

Awk provides the `while` statement for general looping. It has the following form:

```
while(E₁)
    S₁
```

Here, E_1 is an expression (a condition), and S_1 is either one action statement or a group of action statements enclosed in curly braces. When awk meets a `while` statement, E_1 is evaluated. If E_1 is true, S_1 executes from start to finish, then E_1 is again evaluated. If E_1 is true, S_1 again executes. The process continues until E_1 is evaluated to false. When it does, execution continues with the next action statement after the loop. Consider the program below:

```
{ while ($0~/M/)
    print
}
```

Typically the condition (E_1) tests a variable, and the variable is changed in the `while` loop.

```
{ i=1
  while (i<20)
    { print i
      i++
    }
}
```

This second code snippet will print the numbers from 1 to 19, then once the `while` loop tests with `i=20`, the condition of `i<20` will become false and the loop will be done.

The *Do* Statement

Nawk++ provides the `do` statement for looping in addition to the `while` statement. The `do` statement takes the following form:

```
do
    S
while (E).
```

Here, `S` is either a single statement or a group of action statements enclosed in curly braces, and `E` is the test condition. When awk comes to a `do` statement, `S` is executed once, and then condition `E` is tested. If `E` evaluates to nonzero or nonnull, `S` executes again, and so on until the condition `E` becomes false. The difference between the `do` and the `while` statement rests in their order of evaluation. The `while` statement checks the condition first and executes the body of the loop if the condition is true. Use the `while` statement to check conditions that may be initially false. For instance, `while (not end-of-file(input))` is a common example. The `do` statement executes the loop first and then checks the condition. Use the `do` statement when testing a condition which depends on the first execution to meet the condition.

The `do` statement can be initiated using the `while` statement. Put the code that is in the loop before the condition as well as in the body of the loop.

The *For* Statement

The `for` statement is a compacted `while` loop designed for counting. Use it when you know ahead of time that S is a repetitive task and the number of times it executes can be expressed as a single variable. The `for` loop has the following form:

```
for(pre-loop-statements;TEST:post-loop-statements)
```

Here, `pre-loop-statements` usually initialize the counting variable; `TEST` is the test condition; and `post-loop-statements` indicate any loop variable increments.

For example,

```
{ for(i=1; i<=30; i++) print i.}
```

This is a succinct way of saying initialize `i` to 1, then continue looping while `i<=30`, and incrementing `i` by one each time through. The statement executed each time simply prints the value of `i`. The result of this statement is a list of the numbers 1 through 30.

> **TIP:** The condition test should either be < 21 or <= 20 to execute the loop 20 times. The equality operator == is not a good test condition. Changing the loop to the line below illustrates why.
>
> ```
> { for (i=1;i==20;i+2) print i }
> ```
>
> Each iteration of the loop adds 2 to the value of i. i goes to 3 to 5 to 7... to 19 to 21—never having a value of 20. Consequently, you have an infinite loop; it never stops.

The `for` loop can also be used involving loops of unknown size:

```
for (i=1; i<=NF; i++)
    print $i
```

This prints each field on a unique line. True, you don't know what the number of fields will be, but you do know `NF` will contain that number.

The `for` loop does not have to be incremented; it could be decremented instead:

```
$awk -F: '{ for (i = NF; i > 0; --i) print $i }' sales.data
```

This prints the fields in reverse order, one per line.

Loop Control

The only restriction of the loop control value is that it must be an integer. Because of the desire to create easily readable code, most programmers try to avoid branching out of loops midway. Awk offers two ways to do this; however, if you need it: break and continue. Sometimes unexpected or invalid input leaves little choice but to exit the loop or have the program crash—something a programmer strives to avoid. Input errors are one accepted time to use the break statement. For instance, when reading the car sales data into the array name, I wrote the program expecting five fields on every line. If something happens and a line has the wrong number of fields, the program is in trouble. A way to protect your program from this is to have code like:

```
{ for(i=1; i<=NF; i++)
    if (NF != 5) {
        print "Error on line " NR invalid input...leaving loop."
        break  }
    else
        continue with program code...
```

The break statement terminates only the loop. It is not equivalent to the exit statement which transfers control to the END statement of the program. I handle the problem as shown on the CD-ROM in file LIST15_1.

TIP: The ideal error message depends, of course, on your application, the knowledge of the end users, and the likelihood they will be able to correct the error.

As another use for the break statement consider do S while (1). It is an infinite loop depending on another way out. Suppose your program begins by displaying a menu on screen. (See the LIST 15_2 file on the CD-ROM.)

The above example shows an infinite loop controlled with the break statement giving the end user a way out.

NOTE: The built-in nawk function getline does what it seems. For the point of the example take it on faith that it returns a character.

The `continue` statement causes execution to skip the current iteration remaining in both the `do` and the `while` statements. Control transfers to the evaluation of the test condition. In the `for` loop control goes to post-loop-instructions. When is this of use? Consider computing a true sales ratio by calculating the amount sold and dividing that number by hours worked.

Since this is all kept in separate files, the simplest way to handle the task is to read the first list into an array, calculate the figure for the report, and do whatever else is needed.

```
FILENAME=="total"          read each $(NF-1) into monthlytotal[i]
FILENAME=="per"            with each i
                              monthlytotal[i]/$2

whatever else
```

But what if `$2` is `0`? The program will crash because dividing by 0 is an illegal statement. While it is unlikely that an employee will miss an entire month of work, it is possible. So, it is good idea to allow for the possibility. This is one use for the `continue` statement. The above program segment expands to Listing 15.1.

Listing 15.1. Using the `continue` statement.

```
BEGIN          { star = 0

          other stuff...
}

FILENAME=="total"      { for(i=1;NF;i++)
                              monthlyttl[i]=$(NF-1)
               }

FILENAME=="per"        { for(i=1;NF;i++)
                            if($2 == 0)   {
                               print "*"
                               star++
                               continue }
                        else
                            print monthlyttl[i]/$2
                    whatever else
                        }

END    { if(star>=1)
           print "* indicates employee did not work all month."
         else
whatever
}
```

The above program makes some assumptions about the data in addition to assuming valid input data. What are these assumptions and more importantly, how do you fix them? The data in both files is assumed to be the same length, and the names are assumed to be in the same order.

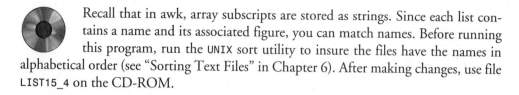 Recall that in awk, array subscripts are stored as strings. Since each list contains a name and its associated figure, you can match names. Before running this program, run the UNIX sort utility to insure the files have the names in alphabetical order (see "Sorting Text Files" in Chapter 6). After making changes, use file LIST15_4 on the CD-ROM.

Strings

There are two primary types of data that awk can work with—numeric values or sequences of characters and digits that comprise words, phrases or sentences. The latter are called strings within awk and most other programming languages. For instance, "now is the time for all good men" is a string. A string is always enclosed in double quotes(""). It can be almost any length (the exact number varies from UNIX version to version).

One of the important string operations is called concatenation. The word means putting together. When you concatenate two strings you are creating a third string that is the combination of string₁, followed immediately by string₂. To perform concatenation in awk simply leave a space between two strings.

```
print "My name is" "Ann."
```

This prints the line:

```
My name isAnn.
```

(To ensure that a space is included you can either use a comma in the `print` statement or simply add a space to one of the strings: `print "My name is " "Ann"`).

Built-In String Functions

As a rule, awk returns the leftmost, longest string in all its functions. This means that it will return the string occurring first (farthest to the left). Then, it collects the longest string possible. For instance, if the string you are looking for is `"y*"` in the string `"any of the guyys knew it"` then the match returns `"yy"` over `"y"` even though the single y appears earlier in the string.

Let's consider the different string functions available, organized by awk version.

Awk

The original awk contained few built-in functions for handling strings. The `length` function returns the length of the string. It has an optional argument. If you use the argument, it must follow the keyword and be enclosed in parentheses: `length(string)`. If there is no argument, the length of `$0` is the value. For example, it is difficult to determine from some screen editors if a line of text stops at 80 characters or wraps around. The following invocation of awk aids by listing just those lines that are longer than 80 characters in the specified file.

```
$ awk '{ if (length > 80)  { print NR ": " $0}' file-with-long-lines
```

The other string function available in the original awk is substring, which takes the form `substr(string,position,len)` and returns the `len` length substring of the string starting at `position`.

> **NOTE:** A disagreement exists over which functions originated in awk and which originated in nawk. Consult your system for the final word on awk string functions. The functions in nawk are fairly standard.

Nawk

When awk was expanded to nawk, many built-in functions were added for string manipulation. The function `gsub(r, s, t)` substitutes string s into target string t every time the regular expression r occurs and returns the number of substitutions. If t is not given `gsub()` uses `$0`. For instance, `gsub(/l/, "y","Randall")` turns `Randall` into `Randayy`. The g in gsub means global because all occurrences in the target string change.

The function `sub(r, s, t)` works like `gsub()`, except the substitution occurs only once. Thus `sub(/l/, "y","Randall")` returns `"Randayl"`. The place the substring t occurs in string s is returned with the function `index(s, t)`: `index("i", "Chris"))` returns 4. As you'd expect the return value is zero if substring t is not found. The function `match(s, r)` returns the position in s where the regular expression r occurs. It returns the index where the substring begins or 0 if there is no substring. It sets the values of RSTART and RLENGTH.

The `split` function separates a string into parts. For example, if your program reads in a date as 5-10-94, and later you want it written May 10, 1994 the first step is to divide the date appropriately. The built-in function `split` does this: `split("5-10-94", store, "-")` divides the date, and sets `store["1"] = "5"`, `store["2"] = "10"` and `store["3"] = 94`. Notice that here the subscripts start with "1" not "0".

POSIX Awk

The POSIX awk specification added two built-in functions for use with strings. They are `tolower(str)` and `toupper(str)`. Both functions return a copy of the string str with the alphabetic characters converted to the appropriate case. Non-alphabetic characters are left alone.

Gawk

Gawk provides two functions returning time-related information. The systime() function returns the current time of day in seconds since Midnight UTC (Universal Time Coordinated, the new name for Greenwich Mean Time), January 1970 on POSIX systems. The function strftime(f, t), where f is a format and t is a timestamp of the same form as returned by system(), returns a formatted timestamp similar to the ANSI C function strftime().

String Constants

String constants are the way awk identifies a non-keyboard, but essential, character. Since they are strings, when you use one, you must enclose it in double quotes (""). These constants may appear in printing or in patterns involving regular expressions. For instance, the following command prints all lines less than 80 characters long that don't begin with a tab. See Table 15.3.

```
awk 'length < 80 && /\t/' another-file-with-long-lines
```

Table 15.3. Awk string constants.

Expression	Meaning
\\	The way of indicating to print a backslash.
\a	The "alert" character; usually the ASCII BEL.
\b	A backspace character.
\f	A formfeed character.
\n	A newline character.
\r	Carriage return character.
\t	Horizontal tab character.
\v	Vertical tab character.
\x	Indicates the following value is a hexidecimal number.
\0	Indicates the following value is an octal number.

Arrays

An array is a method of storing pieces of similar data in the computer for later use. Suppose your boss asks for a program that reads in the name, social security number, and a bunch of personnel data to print check stubs and the detachable check. For three or four employees keeping name1, name2, etc. might be feasible, but at 20, it is tedious and at 200, impossible. This is a use for arrays! See file LIST15_5 on the CD-ROM.

> **NOTE:** Since the first input record is the checkdate, the total lines (NR) is not the number of checks to issue. I could have used NR-1, but I chose clarity over brevity.

Much easier, cleaner, and quicker! It also works for any number of employees without code changes. Awk only supports single-dimension arrays. (See the section "Advanced Concepts" for how to simulate multiple-dimensional arrays.) That and a few other things set awk arrays apart from the arrays of other programming languages. This section focuses on arrays; I will explain their use, then discuss their special property. I conclude by listing three features of awk (a built-in function, a built-in variable, and an operator) designed to help you work with arrays.

Arrays in awk, like variables, don't need to be declared. Further, no indication of size must be given ahead of time; in programming terms, you'd say arrays in awk are dynamic. To create an array, give it a name and put its subscript after the name in square brackets ([ ]), name[2] from above, for instance. Array subscripts are also called the *indices* of the array ; in name[2], 2 is the index to the array name, and it accesses the one name stored at location 2.

> **NOTE:** One peculiarity in awk is that elements are not stored in the order they are entered. This bug is fixed in nawk++.

Awk arrays are different from those of other programming languages because in awk, array subscripts are stored as strings, not numbers. Technically, the term is *associative arrays* and it's unusual in programming languages. Be aware that the use of strings as subscripts can confuse you if you think purely in numeric terms. Since "3" > "15", an array element with a subscript 15 is stored before one with subscript of "3", even though numerically 3 > 15.

Since subscripts are strings, a subscript can be a field value. grade[$1]=$2 is a valid statement, as is salary["John"].

Array Specialties

Nawk++ has additions specifically intended for use with arrays. The first is a test for membership. Suppose Mark Turner enrolled late in a class I teach, and I don't remember if I added his name to the list I keep on my computer. The following program checks the list for me.

```
BEGIN {i=1}

{ name [i++] = $1 }

END { if ("Mark Turner" in name)
      print "He's enrolled in the course!"
    }
```

The `delete` function is a built-in function to remove array elements from computer memory. To remove an element, for example, you could use the command `delete name[1]`.

> **CAUTION:** Once you remove an element from memory, it's gone, and it ain't coming back! When in doubt, keep it.

Although technology is advancing and memory is not the precious commodity it once was considered to be, it is still a good idea to clean up after yourself when you write a program. Think of the check printing program on the CD-ROM. Two hundred names won't fill the memory. But if your program controls personnel activity, it writes checks and checkstubs; adds and deletes employees; and charts sales. It's better to update each file to disk and remove the arrays not in use. For one thing, there is less chance of reading obsolete data. It also consumes less memory and minimizes the chance of using an array of old data for a new task. The clean-up can be most easily done:

```
END  {i= totalemps
     while(i>0) {
          delete name[i]
          delete data[i—] }
     }
```

Nawk++ creates another built-in variable for use when simulating multidimensional arrays. More on its use appears later, in the section "Advanced Concepts." It is called SUBSEP and has a default value of "\034". To add this variable to awk, just create it in your program:

```
BEGIN { SUBSEP = "\034" }
```

Recall that in awk, array subscripts are stored as strings. Since each list contains a name and its associated figure, you can match names and hence match files. Here are the answers to the question about using two files and assuring they have the same order (from the car sales example earlier). Before running this program, run the UNIX sort utility to insure the files have the names in alphabetical order. (See "Sorting Text Files" in Chapter 6.) After making changes, use the program in file LIST15_6 on the CD-ROM.

Arithmetic

Although awk is primarily a language for pattern matching, and hence, text and strings pop into mind more readily than math and numbers, awk also has a good set of math tools. In this section, first I show the basics, then we look at the math functions built into awk.

Operators

Awk supports the usual math operations. The expression x^y is x superscript y, that is, *x to the y power.* The % operator calculates remainders in awk: x%y is the remainder of x divided by y, and the result is machine-dependent. All math uses, floating point, and numbers are equivalent no matter which format they are expressed in so 100 = 1.00e+02.

The math operators in awk consist of the four basic functions: + (addition), - (subtraction), / (division), and * (multiplication), plus ^ and % for exponential and remainder.

As you saw earlier in the most recent sales example, fields can be used in arithmetic too. If, in the middle of the month, my boss asks for a list of the names and latest monthly sales totals, I don't need to panic over the discarded figures; I can just print a new list. My first shot seems simple enough (Listing 15.2).

Listing 15.2. Print sales totals for May.

```
BEGIN     {OFS="\t"}
{         print $1, $2, $6 }        # field #6 = May
```

Then a thought hits. What if my boss asks for the same thing next month? Sure, changing a field number each month is not a big deal but is it really necessary??

I look at the data. No matter what month it is, the current month's totals are always the next to last field. I start over with the program in Listing 15.3.

Listing 15.3. Printing the previous month's sales totals.

```
BEGIN     {OFS= _\t_}
{         print $1,$2, $(NF-1) }
```

> **TIP:** Again, watch yourself because awk lets you get away with murder. If I forgot the parentheses on the last statement above, rather than get a monthly total, I would print a list of the running total—1! Also, rather than generate an error, if I mistype `$(NF-1)` and get `$(NF+1)` (not hard to do using the number pad), awk assigns nonexistent variables (here the number of fields + 1) to the null string. In this case, it prints blank lines.

Another use for arithmetic concerns assignment. Field variables may be changed by assignment. Given the following file, the statement `$3 = 7` is a valid statement and produces the results below:

```
$ cat inputfile
1 2
3 4
5 6
7 8
9 10

$ awk '{$3 = 7}' inputfile
1 2 7
3 4 7
5 6 7
7 8 7
9 10 7
```

> **NOTE:** The above statement forces `$0` and `NF` values to change. Awk recalculates them as it runs.

If I run the following program, four lines appear on the monitor, showing the new values.

```
{   if(NR==1)
      print $0, NF  }
  { if (NR >= 2 && NR <= 4) { $3=7; print $0, NF } }
END {print $0, NF }
```

Now when we run the data file through awk here's what we see:

```
$awk -f newsample.awk inputfile
1 2 2
3 4 7 3
5 6 7 3
7 8 7 3
```

Numeric Functions

Awk has a well-rounded selection of built-in numeric functions. As before in the sections on "Built-in Variables" and "Strings," the functions build on each other beginning with those found in awk.

Awk

To start, awk has built-in functions exp(exp), log(exp), sqrt(exp), and int(exp) where int() truncates its argument to an integer.

Nawk

Nawk added further arithmetic functions to awk. It added atan2(y,x) which returns the arctangent of y/x. It also added two random number generator functions: rand() and srand(x). There is also some disagreement over which functions originated in awk and which in nawk. Most versions have all the trigonometric functions in nawk, regardless of where they first appeared.

Input and Output

This section takes a closer look at the way input and output function in awk. I examine input first and look briefly at the getline function of nawk++ . Next, I show how awk output works, and the two different print statements in awk: print and printf.

Input

Awk handles the majority of input automatically—there is no explicit read statement, unlike most programming languages. Each line of the program is applied to each input record in the order the records appear in the input file. If the input file has 20 records then the first pattern action statement in the program looks for a match 20 times. The next statement causes the input to skip to the next program statement without trying the rest of the input against that pattern action statement. The exit statement acts as if all input has been processed. When awk encounters an exit statement, if there is one, the control goes to the END pattern action statement.

The Getline Statement

One addition, when awk was expanded to nawk, was the built-in function getline. It is also supported by the POSIX awk specification. The function may take several forms. At its simplest, it's written getline. When written alone, getline retrieves the next input record and splits it into fields as usual, setting FNR, NF and NR. The function returns 1 if the operation is successful, 0 if it is at the end of the file (EOF), and -1 if the function encounters an error. Thus,

```
while (getline == 1)
```

simulates awk's automatic input.

Writing `getline` *variable* reads the next record into *variable* (`getline char` from the earlier menu example, for instance). Field splitting does not take place, and `NF` remains `0`; but `FNR` and `NR` are incremented. Either of the above two may be written using input from a file besides the one containing the input records by appending < "`filename`" on the end of the command. Furthermore, `getline char` < "`stdin`" takes the input from the keyboard. As you'd expect neither `FNR` nor `NR` are affected when the input is read from another file. You can also write either of the two above forms, taking the input from a command.

Output

There are two forms of printing in awk: the `print` statement and the `printf` statement. Until now, I have used the `print` statement. It is the fallback. There are two forms of the `print` statement. One has parentheses; one doesn't. So, `print $0` is the same as `print($0)`. In awk shorthand, the statement `print` by itself is equivalent to `print $0`. As shown in an earlier example, a blank line is printed with the statement `print ""`. Use the format you prefer.

> **NOTE:** `print()` is not accepted shorthand; it generates a syntax error.
>
> Nawk requires parentheses, if the `print` statement involves a relational operator.

For a simple example consider file1:

```
$cat file1
1       10
3       8
5       6
7       4
9       2
10      0
```

The command line

```
$ nawk 'BEGIN {FS="\t"}; {print($1>$2)}' file1
```

shows

```
0
0
0
1
1
1
```

on the monitor.

Knowing that 0 indicates false and 1 indicates true, the above is what you'd expect, but most programming languages won't print the result of a relation directly. Nawk will.

> **NOTE:** This requires nawk or later. Trying the above in awk results in a syntax error.

Nawk prints the results of relations with both `print` and `printf`. Both `print` and `printf` require the use of parentheses when a relation is involved, however, to distinguish between > meaning greater than and > meaning the redirection operator.

The *printf* Statement

`printf` is used when the use of formatted output is required. It closely resembles C's `printf`. Like the print statement, it comes in two forms: with and without parentheses. Either may be used, except the parentheses are required when using a relational operator. (See below.)

```
printf format-specifier, variable1,variable2, variable3,..variablen
```

```
printf(format-specifier, variable1,variable2, variable3,..variablen)
```

The format specifier is always required with `printf`. It contains both any literal text, and the specific format for displaying any variables you want to print. The format specifier always begins with a `%`. Any combination of three modifiers may occur: a - indicates the variable should be left justified within its field; a number indicates the total width of the field should be that number, if the number begins with a 0: %-05 means to make the variable 5 wide and pad with 0s as needed; the last modifier is *.number* the meaning depends on the type of variable; the number indicates either the maximum number string width, or the number of digits to follow to the right of the decimal point. After zero or more modifiers, the display format ends with a single character indicating the type of variable to display.

> **TIP:** And yes, numbers can be displayed as characters and nondigit strings can be displayed as a number. With `printf` anything goes!

Remember the format specifier has a string value and since it does, it must always be enclosed in double quotes("), whether it is a literal string such as

```
printf("This is an example of a string in the display format.")
```

or a combination,

```
printf("This is the %d example", occurrence)
```

or just a variable

```
printf("%d", occurrence).
```

> **NOTE:** The POSIX awk specification (and hence gawk) supports the dynamic field width and precision modifiers like ANSI C `printf()` routines do. To use this feature, place an * in place of either of the actual display modifiers and the value will be substituted from the argument list following the format string. Neither awk nor nawk have this feature.

Before I go into detail about display format modifiers, I will show the characters used for display types. The following list shows the format specifier types without any modifiers.

Table 15.8. The format specifiers in awk.

Format	Meaning
%c	An ASCII character
%d	A decimal number (an integer, no decimal point involved)
%i	Just like %d (Remember i for integer)
%e	A floating point number in scientific notation (1.00000E+01)
%f	A floating point number (10001010.434)
%g	awk chooses between %e or %f display format, the one producing a shorter string is selected. Nonsignificant zeros are not printed.
%o	An unsigned octal (base 8) number
%s	A string
%x	An unsigned hexadecimal (base 16) number
%X	Same as %x but letters are uppercase rather than lowercase.

> **NOTE:** If the argument used for %c is numeric, it is treated as a character and printed. Otherwise, the argument is assumed to be a string and only the first character of that string is printed.

Look at some examples without display modifiers. When the file `file1` looks like this:

```
$ cat file1
34
99
-17
2.5
-.3
```

the command line

```
awk '{printf("%c %d %e %f\n", $1, $1, $1, $1)}' file1
```

produces the following output:

```
" 34 3.400000e+01 34.000000
c 99 9.900000e+01 99.000000
_ -17 -1.700000e+01 -17.000000
_ 2 2.500000e+00 2.500000
 0 -3.000000e-01 -0.300000
```

By contrast, a slightly different format string produces dramatically different results with the same input:

```
$ awk '{printf("%g %o %x", $1, $1)}' file1
34 42 22
99 143 63
-17 37777777757 ffffffef
2.5 2 2
-0.3 0 0
```

Now let's change `file1` to contain just a single word:

```
$cat file1
Example
```

The string above has seven characters. For clarity, I have used * instead of a blank space so the total field width is visible on paper.

```
printf("%s\n", $1)
      Example
printf("%9s\n", $1)
    **Example
printf("%-9s\n", $1)
      Example**
printf("%.4s\n", $1)
      Exam
printf("%9.4s\n", $1)
    *****Exam
printf("%-9.4s\n", $1)
      Exam*****
```

One topic pertaining to `printf` remains. The function `printf` was written so that it writes exactly what you tell it to write—and how you want it written, no more and no less. That is acceptable until you realize that you can't enter every character you may want to use from the keyboard. Awk uses the same escape sequences found in C for nonprinting characters. The two most important to remember are \n for a carriage return and \t for a tab character.

> **TIP:** There are two ways to print a double quote; neither of which is that obvious. One way around this problem is to use the printf variable by its ASCII value:
>
> ```
>     doublequote = 34
> printf("%c", doublequote)
> ```
>
> The other strategy is to use a backslash to escape the default interpretation of the double quote as the end of the string:
>
> ```
>     printf("Joe said \"undoubtedly\" and hurried along.\n")
> ```
>
> This second approach doesn't always work, unfortunately.

Closing Files and Pipes

Unlike most programming languages there is no way to open a file in awk; opening files is implicit. However, you must close a file if you intend to read from it after writing to it. Suppose you enter the command cat file1 < file2 in your awk program. Before you can read file2 you must close the pipe. To do this, use the statement close(cat file1 < file2). You may also do the same for a file: close(file2).

Command Line Arguments

As you have probably noticed, awk presents a programmer with a variety of ways to accomplish the same thing. This section focuses on the command line. You will see how to pass command line arguments to your program from the command line and how to set the value of built-in variables on the command line. A summary of command line options concludes the section.

Passing Command Line Arguments

Command line arguments are available in awk through a built-in array called, as in C, ARGV. Again echoing C semantics, the value of the built-in ARGC is one more than the number of command line arguments. Given the command line awk -f *programfile infile1*, ARGC has a value of 2. ARGV[0] = awk and ARGV[1] = *infile1*.

> **NOTE:** The subscripts for ARGV start with 0 not 1.
>
> programfile is not considered an argument—no option argument is. Had -F been in the command line, ARGV would not contain a comma either. Note that this behavior is very different to how argv and argc are interpreted in C programs too.

Setting Variables on the Command Line

It is possible to pass variable values from the command line to your awk program just by stating the variable and its value. For example, for the command line, awk -f *programfile* *infile* x=1 FS=,. Normally, command line arguments are filenames, but the equal sign indicates an assignment. This lets variables change value before and after a file is read. For instance, when the input is from multiple files, the order they are listed on the command line becomes very important since the first named input file is the first input read. Consider the command line awk -f program file2 file1 and this program segment.

```
BEGIN { if ( FILENAME != "foo") {
             print 'Unexpected input...Abandon ship!"
             exit
        }
        }
```

The programmer has written this program to accept one file as first input and anything else causes the program to do nothing except print the error message.

```
awk -f program x=1 file1 x=2 file2
```

The change in variable values above can also be used to check the order of files. Since you (the programmer) know their correct order, you can check for the appropriate value of x.

Awk only allows two command line options. The -f option indicates the file containing the awk program. When no -f option is used, the program is expected to be a part of the command line. The POSIX awk specification adds the option of using more than one -f option. This is useful when running more than one awk program on the same input. The other option is the -Fchar option where char is the single character chosen as the input field separate. Without a specified -F option, the input field separator is a space, until the variable FS is otherwise set.

Functions

This section discusses user-defined functions, also known in some programming languages as *subroutines*. For a discussion of functions built into awk see either "Strings" or "Arithmetic" as appropriate.

The ability to add, define, and use functions was not originally part of awk. It was added in 1985 when awk was expanded. Technically, this means you must use either nawk or gawk, if you intend to write awk functions; but again, since some systems use the nawk implementation and call it awk, check your man pages before writing any code.

Function Definition

An awk function definition statement appears like the following:

```
function functionname(list of parameters) {
     the function body
}
```

A function can exist anywhere a pattern action statement can be. As most of awk is, functions are free format but must be separated with either a semicolon or a newline. Like the action part of a pattern action statement, newlines are optional anywhere after the opening curly brace. The list of parameters is a list of variables separated by commas that are used within the function. The function body consists of one or more pattern action statements.

A function is invoked with a function call from inside the action part of a regular pattern action statement. The left parenthesis of the function call must immediately follow the function name, without any space between them to avoid a syntactic ambiguity with the concatenation operator. This restriction does not apply to the built-in functions.

Parameters

Most function variables in awk are given to the function call by value. Actual parameters listed in the function call of the program are copied and passed to the formal parameters declared in the function. For instance, let's define a new function called isdigit, as shown:

```
function isdigit(x) {
     x=8
}
{  x=5
   print x
   isdigit(x)
   print x
}
```

Now let's use this simple program:

```
$ awk -f isdigit.awk
5
5
```

The call `isdigit(x)` copies the value of *x* into the local variable x within the function itself. The initial value of *x* here is five, as is shown in the first `print` statement, and is not reset to a higher value after the `isdigit` function is finished. Note that if there was a `print` statement at the end of the `isdigit` function itself, however, the value would be eight, as expected. Call by value ensures you don't accidentally clobber an important value.

Variables

Local variables in a function are possible. However, as functions were not a part of awk until awk was expanded, handling local variables in functions was not a concern. It shows: local variables must be listed in the parameter list and can't just be created as used within a routine. A space separates local variables from program parameters. For example, `function isdigit(x a,b)` indicates that x is a program parameter, while a and b are local variables; they have life and meaning only as long as `isdigit` is active.

Global variables are any variables used throughout the program, including inside functions. Any changes to global variables at any point in the program affect the variable for the entire program. In awk, to make a variable global, just exclude it from the parameter list entirely.

Let's see how this works with an example script:

```
function isdigit(x) {
     x=8
     a=3
 }
  { x=5 ; a = 2
  print "x = " x " and a = " a
  isdigit(x)
  print "now x = " x " and a = " a
 }
```

The output is:

```
x = 5 and a = 2
x = 8 and a = 3
```

Function Calls

Functions may call each other. A function may also be recursive (that is, a function may call itself multiple times). The best example of recursion is factorial numbers: factorial(*n*) is computed as n * factorial(n-1) down to n=1, which has a value of one. The value factorial(5) is 5 * 4 * 3 * 2 * 1 = 120 and could be written as an awk program:

```
function factorial(n) {
   if (n == 1) return 1;
   else return ( n * factorial(n-1) )
}
```

For a more in-depth look at the fascinating world of recursion I recommend you see either a programming or data structures book.

Gawk follows the POSIX awk specification in almost every aspect. There is a difference, though, in function declarations. In gawk, the word func may be used instead of the word function. The POSIX2 spec mentions that the original awk authors asked that this shorthand be omitted, and it is.

The Return Statement

A function body may (but doesn't have to) end with a return statement. A return statement has two forms. The statement may consist of the direction alone: return. The other form is return E, where E is some expression. In either case, the return statement gives control back to the calling function. The return E statement gives control back, and also gives a value to the function.

> **TIP:** Be careful: if the function is supposed to return a value and doesn't explicitly use the return statement, the results returned to the calling program are undefined.

Let's revisit the isdigit() function to see how to make it finally ascertain whether the given character is a digit or not:

```
function isdigit(x) {
     if (x >= "0" && x <= "9")
          return 1;
     else
          return 0
}
```

As with C programming, I use a value of zero to indicate false, and a value of 1 indicates true. A return statement often is used when a function cannot continue due to some error. Note also that with inline conditionals—as explained earlier—this routine can be shrunk down to a single line: function isdigit(x) { return (x >= "0" && x <= "9") }

Writing Reports

This section discusses writing reports. Before continuing with this section, it would be a good idea to be sure you are familiar with both the UNIX sort command (see section

"Sorting Text Files" in Chapter 6) and the use of pipes in UNIX (see section "Pipes" in Chapter 4). Generating a report in awk is a sequence of steps, with each step producing the input for the next step. Report writing is usually a three step process: pick the data, sort the data, make the output pretty.

BEGIN and END Revisited

The section on "Patterns" discussed the BEGIN and END patterns as pre- and post-input processing sections of a program. Along with initializing variables, the BEGIN pattern serves another purpose: BEGIN is awk's provided place to print headers for reports. Indeed, it is the only chance. Remember the way awk input works automatically. The lines:

```
{ print "                    Total Sales"
  print "  Salesperson       for the Month"
  print "  ----------------------------" }
```

would print a header for each input record rather than a single header at the top of the report! The same is true for the END pattern, only it follows the last input record. So,

```
{print "----------------------------"
 print "            Total sales",ttl" }
```

should only be in if you want one total line.

```
BEGIN { print "                    Total Sales"
        print "  Salesperson       for the Month"
        print "  ----------------------------" }
{ per person processing statements }
{print "----------------------------"
 print "            Total sales",ttl" }
```

The Built-in System Function

While awk allows you to accomplish quite a few tasks with a few lines of code, it's still helpful sometimes to be able to tie in the many other features of UNIX. Fortunately almost all versions of nawk++ have the built-in function system(value) where *value* is a string that you would enter from the UNIX command line.

> **NOTE:** The original awk does *NOT* have the system function.

The text is enclosed in double quotes and the variables are written using a space for concatenating. For example, if I am making a packet of files to e-mail to someone, and I create a list of the files I wish to send, I put a file list in a file called sendrick:

```
$cat sendrick
/usr/anne/ch1.doc
/usr/informix/program.4gl
/usr/anne/pics.txt
```

then awk can build the concatenated file with:

```
$ nawk '{system("cat" $1)}' sendrick > forrick
```

creates a file called forrick containing a full copy of each file. Yes, a shell script could be written to do the same thing, but shell scripts don't do the pattern matching that awk does, and they are not great at writing reports either.

UNIX users are split roughly in half over which text editor they use—vi or emacs. I began using UNIX and the vi editor, so I prefer vi. The vi editor has no way to set off a block of text and do some operation, such as move or delete, to the block, and so falls back on the common measure, the line; a specified number of lines are deleted or copied.

 When dealing with long programs, I don't like to guess about the line numbers in a block...or take the time to count them either! So I have a short script which adds line numbers to my printouts for me. It is centered around the following awk program. See file LST15_10 on the CD-ROM.

Advanced Concepts

As you spend more time with awk, you might yearn to explore some of the more complex facets of the programming language. I highlight some of the key ones below.

Multi-Line Records

By default, the input record separator RS recognizes a newline as the marker between records. As is the norm in awk, this can be changed to allow for multi-line records. When RS is set to the null string, then the newline character always acts as a field separator, in addition to whatever value FS may have.

Multidimensional Arrays

While awk does not directly support multidimensional arrays, it can simulate them using the single dimension array type awk does support. Why do this? An array may be compared to a bunch of books. Different people access them different ways. Someone who doesn't have many may keep them on a shelf in the room—consider this a single dimension array with each book at location[i]. Time passes and you buy a bookcase. Now each book is in location[shelf,i]. The comparison goes as far as you wish—consider the intercounty library with each book at location[branchnum, floor, room, bookcasenum, `shelf, i]`. The appropriate dimensions for the array depend very much on the type of problem you are solving. If the intercounty library keeps track of all their books by a catalog number rather than location; a single dimension of `book[catalog_num]` = title makes more sense than `location[branchnum, floor, room, bookcasenum, shelf, i]` = title. Awk allows either choice.

Awk stores array subscripts as strings rather than as numbers, so adding another dimension is actually only a matter of concatenating another subscript value to the existing subscript. Suppose you design a program to inventory jeans at Levi's. You could set up the inventory so that `item[inventorynum]=itemnum` or `item[style, size, color]` = itemnum. The built-in variable SUBSEP is put between subscripts when a comma appears between subscripts. SUBSEP defaults to the value \034, a value with little chance of being in a subscript. Since SUBSEP marks the end of each subscript, subscript names do not have to be the same length. For example,

```
item["501","12w","stone washed blue"],
```

```
item["dockers","32m","black"]
```

```
item["relaxed fit", "9j", "indigo"]
```

are all valid examples of the inventory. Determining the existence of an element is done just as it is for a single dimension array with the addition of parentheses around the subscript. Your program should reorder when a certain size gets low.

```
if (("501",,) in item) reorder.
```

> **NOTE:** The in keyword is nawk++ syntax.

The price increases on 501s, and your program is responsible for printing new price tags for the items which need a new tag:

```
for ("501" in item)
    print a new tag.
```

Recall the string function split; `split("501", ,SUBSEP)` will retrieve every element in the array with "501" as its first subscript.

Summary

In this chapter I have covered the fundamentals of awk as a programming language and as a tool. In the beginning of the chapter I gave an introduction to the key concepts, an overview of what you would need to know to get started writing and using awk. I spoke about patterns, a feature that sets awk apart from other programming languages. Two sections were devoted to variables, one on user defined variables and one on built-in variables.

The later part of the chapter talks about awk as a programming language. I discussed conditional statements, looping, arrays, input output, and user defined functions. I close with a brief section on writing reports.

The next chapter is about Perl, a language very related to awk.

Table 15.4. Built-in Variables in Awk
V is the first implementation using the variable.
A = awk G = gawk P = POSIX awk N = nawk

V Variable	Meaning	Default(if any)
N ARGC	The number of command line arguments	
N ARGV	An array of command line arguments	
A FS	The input field separator	space
A NF	The number of fields in the current record	
G CONVFMT	The conversion format for numbers	%.6g
G FIELDWIDTHS	A white-space separated	
G IGNORECASE	Controls the case sensitivity	zero (case sensitive)
P FNR	The current record number	
A FILENAME	The name of the current input file	
A NR	The number of records already read	
A OFS	The output field separator	space
A ORS	The output record separator	newline
A OFMT	The output format for numbers	%.6g
N RLENGTH	Length of string matched by match function	
A RS	Input record separator	newline
N RSTART	Start of string matched by match function	
N SUBSEP	Subscript separator	"\034"

Further Reading

For further reading:

Aho, Alfred V., Brian W. Kernighan and Peter J. Weinberger, *The awk Programming Language*. Reading, Mass.: Addison-Wesley,1988 (copyright AT&T Bell Lab.)

Dougherty, Dale, *sed & awk*. Sebastopol, CA: O'Reilly & Assoc., 1990. Reprint 1992.

IEEE Standard for Information Technology, *Portable Operating System Inferface (POSIX), Part 2: Shell and Utilities, Volume 2.* Std. 1003.2-1992. New York: IEEE, 1993.

See also the man pages for awk, nawk, or gawk on your system.

Obtaining Source Code

Awk comes in many varieties. I recommend either gawk or nawk. Nawk is the more standard whereas gawk has some non-POSIX extensions not found in nawk. Either version is a good choice.

To obtain nawk from AT&T: nawk is in the UNIX Toolkit. The dialup modem number in the United States is 908-522-6900, login as guest.

To obtain gawk: contact the Free Software Foundation, Inc. The phone number is 617-876-3296.

Perl

By David Till

16

Overview

The following sections tell you what Perl is and how you can get it, and provide a short example of a working Perl program.

What Is Perl?

Perl is a simple yet useful programming language that provides the convenience of shell scripts and the power and flexibility of high-level programming languages. Perl programs are interpreted and executed directly, just as shell scripts are; however, they also contain control structures and operators similar to those found in the C programming language. This gives you the ability to write useful programs in a very short time.

Where Can I Get Perl?

Perl is freeware: it can be obtained by file transfer (`ftp`) from the Free Software Foundation at `prep.ai.mit.edu` (in the directory `pub/gnu`). Perl is also available from several other sites on the Internet, including any site that archives the newsgroup `comp.sources.unix`.

The Free Software Foundation gives you the right to obtain Perl and its source, provided others have the right to obtain them from you. For more details on the Free Software Foundation licensing policy, refer to the file `GETTING.GNU.SOFTWARE`, also available from the foundation.

A Simple Sample Program

To show easy it is to use Perl, here is a simple program that echoes (writes out) a line of input typed in at a terminal.

Listing 16.1. A Sample Perl Program.

```
#!/usr/bin/perl
$inputline = <STDIN>;
print ("$inputline");
```

To run this program, do the following:

1. Type in the program and save it in a file (say, `foo`).
2. Tell the system that this file contains executable statements. To do this, enter the command `chmod +x foo`.
3. Run the program by entering the command `foo`.

If you receive the error message `foo not found` or some equivalent, either enter the command `./foo` or add the current directory `.` to your `PATH` environment variable.

At this point, the program waits for you to type in an input line. Once you have done so, it echoes your input line and exits.

The following sections describe each of the components of this simple program in a little more detail.

Using Comments

The first line of this program is an example of a Perl *comment.* In Perl, anytime a # character is recognized, the rest of the line is treated as a comment:

```
# this is a comment that takes up the whole line
$count = 0;     # this part of the line is a comment
```

A comment appearing as the first line of a program is special. This *header comment* indicates the location of the program interpreter to use. In this example, the string !/usr/bin/perl indicates that this file is a Perl program.

The Perl interpreter should be located in /usr/bin/perl on your system. If it is not, replace /usr/bin/perl in the header comment with the location of the Perl interpreter on your system.

Reading from Standard Input

Like C, Perl recognizes the existence of the UNIX standard input file, standard output file, and standard error file. In C, these files are called stdin, stdout and stderr; in Perl, they are called STDIN, STDOUT and STDERR.

The Perl construct <STDIN> refers to a line of text read in from the standard input file. This line of text includes the closing newline character.

Storing Values: The Scalar Variable

The construct $inputline is an example of a *scalar variable.* A scalar variable is a variable that holds exactly one value. This value can be a string, integer, or floating point number.

All scalar variables start with a dollar sign, $. This distinguishes them from other Perl variables. In a scalar variable, the character immediately following the dollar sign must be a letter. Subsequent characters can be letters, digits, or underscores. Scalar variable names can be as long as you like.

For more information on scalar variables and their values, see the section "Working with Scalar Variables" later in this chapter.

Assigning a Value to a Scalar Variable

The statement `$inputline = <STDIN>;` contains the = character, which is the Perl *assignment operator*. This statement tells Perl that the line of text read from standard input, represented by `<STDIN>`, is to become the new value of the scalar variable `$inputline`.

Perl provides a full set of useful arithmetic, logical, and string operators. For details, refer to the sections "Working with Scalar Variables" and "Using Lists and Array Variables" later in this chapter.

> **CAUTION:** All scalar variables are given an initial value of the null string, `""`. Therefore, a Perl program can be run even when a scalar variable is used before a value has been assigned to it. Consider the statement
>
> `$b = $a;`
>
> This statement assigns the value of the variable `$a` to `$b`. If `$a` has not been seen before, it is assumed to have the value `""`, and `""` is assigned to `$b`. Since this behavior is legal in Perl, you must check your programs for "undefined" variables yourself.

Scalar Variables Inside Character Strings

The final statement of the program, `print ("$inputline");`, contains a *character string*, which is a sequence of characters enclosed in double quotes. In this case, the character string is `"$inputline"`.

The string `"$inputline"` contains the name of a scalar variable, `$inputline`. When Perl sees a variable inside a character string, it replaces the variable with its value. In this example, the string `"$inputline"` is replaced with the line of text read from the standard input file.

Writing to Standard Output

The built-in function `print()` writes its *arguments* (the items enclosed in parentheses) to the standard output file. In this example, the statement `print ("$inputline");` sends the contents of the scalar variable `$inputline` to the standard output file.

The `print()` function can also be told to write to the standard error file or to any other specified file. See the section "Reading from and Writing to Files" later in this chapter for more details.

Working with Scalar Variables

Now that you know a little about Perl, it's time to describe the language in a little more detail. This section starts you off by discussing scalar variables and the values that can be stored in them.

Understanding Scalar Values

In Perl, a *scalar value* is any value that can be stored in a scalar variable. The following are scalar values:

- Integers
- Double and single-quoted character strings
- Floating-point values

The following assignments are all legal in Perl:

```
$variable = 1;
$variable = "this is a string";
$variable = 3.14159;
```

The following assignments are not legal:

```
$variable = 67M;
$variable = ^803;
$variable = $%$%!;
```

Using Octal and Hexadecimal Representation

Normally, integers are assumed to be in standard base 10 notation. Perl also supports base 8 (octal) and base 16 (hexadecimal) notation.

To indicate that a number is in base 8, put a zero in front of the number:

```
$a = 0151;        # 0151 octal is 105
```

To indicate base 16, put 0x (or 0X) in front of the number:

```
$a = 0x69;        # 69 hex is also 105
```

The letters A through F (in either upper- or lowercase) represent the values 10 through 15:

```
$a = 0xFE;        # equals 16 * 15 + 1 * 14, or 254
```

> **NOTE:** Strings containing a leading 0 or 0x are not treated as base 8 or base 16:
>
> ```
> $a = "0151";
> $a = "0x69";
> ```
>
> These strings are treated as character strings whose first character is "0."

Using Double- and Single-Quoted Strings

So far, all of the strings you have seen have been enclosed by the " (double quotation mark) characters:

```
$a = "This is a string in double quotes";
```

Perl also allows you to enclose strings using the ' (single quotation mark) character:

```
$a = 'This is a string in single quotes';
```

There are two differences between double-quoted strings and single-quoted strings. The first difference is that variables are replaced by their values in double-quoted strings, but not in single-quoted strings:

```
$x = "a string";
$y = "This is $x";  # becomes "This is a string"
$z = 'This is $x';  # remains 'This is $x'
```

Also, double-quoted strings recognize *escape sequences* for special characters. These escape sequences consist of a backslash (\) followed by one or more characters. The most common escape sequence is \n, representing the newline character:

```
$a = "This is a string terminated by a newline\n";
```

Table 16.1 lists the escape sequences recognized in double-quoted strings.

Table 16.1. Escape Sequences in Double-Quoted Strings.

\a	bell (beep)
\b	backspace
\cn	the control-n character
\e	escape
\f	form feed
\l	force next letter into lowercase
\L	all following letters are lowercase
\n	newline
\r	carriage return

\t   tab

\u   force next letter into uppercase

\U   all following letters are uppercase

\v   vertical tab

\L and \U can be turned off by \E:

```
$a = "T\LHIS IS A \ESTRING";  # same as "This is a STRING"
```

To include a backslash or double quote in a double-quoted string, precede it with another backslash:

```
$a = "A quote \" in a string";
$a = "A backslash \\ in a string";
```

You can specify the ASCII value for a character in base 8 or octal notation using \nnn, where each *n* is an octal digit:

```
$a = "\377";        # this is the character 255, or EOF
```

You can also use hexadecimal to specify the ASCII value for a character. To do this, use the sequence \xnn, where each *n* is a hexadecimal digit:

```
$a = "\xff";        # this is also 255
```

None of these escape sequences is supported in single-quoted strings, except for \' and \\, which represent the single quote character and the backslash, respectively:

```
$a = '\b is not a bell'
$a = 'a single quote \' in a string'
$a = 'a backslash \\ in a string'
```

> **NOTE:** In Perl, strings are not terminated by a null character (ASCII 0), as they are in C. In Perl, the null character can appear anywhere in a string:
>
> ```
> $a = "This string \000 has a null character in it";
> ```

Using Floating-Point Values

Perl supports floating-point numbers in both conventional and scientific notation. The letter E (or e) represents the power of ten to which a number in scientific notation is to be raised.

```
$a = 11.3;          # conventional notation
$a = 1.13E01;       # 11.3 in scientific notation
$a = -1.13e-01;     # the above divided by -10
```

> **CAUTION:** Note that Perl uses your machine's floating point representation. This means that only a certain number of digits (in mathematical terms, a certain *precision*) are supported. For example, consider the following very short program:
>
> ```
> #!/usr/bin/perl
> $pi = 3.14159265358979233;
> print ("pi is $pi\n");
> ```
>
> This program prints the following:
>
> ```
> pi = 3.1415926535897922
> ```
>
> This is because there just isn't room to keep track of all of the digits of pi specified by the program.
>
> This problem is made worse when arithmetic operations are performed on floating point numbers; see "Performing Comparisons" for more information on this problem.
>
> Note that most programming languages, including C, have this problem.

Interchangeability of Strings and Numeric Values

 In Perl, as you have seen, a scalar variable can be used to store a character string, an integer, or a floating point value. In scalar variables, a value that was assigned as a string can be used as an integer whenever it makes sense to do so, and vice versa. For example, consider the program in file LIST 16_2 on the CD-ROM, which converts distances from miles to kilometers and vice versa. In this example, the scalar variable `$originaldist` contains the character string read in from the standard input file. The contents of this string are then treated as a number, multiplied by the miles-to-kilometers and kilometers-to-miles conversion factors, and stored in `$miles` and `$kilometers`.

This program also contains a call to the function `chop()`. This function throws away the last character in the specified string. In this case, `chop()` gets rid of the newline character at the end of the input line.

If a string contains characters that are not digits, it is converted to 0:

```
# this assigns 0 to $a, since "hello" becomes 0
$a = "hello" * 5;
```

In cases like this, Perl does not tell you that anything has gone wrong, and your results may not be what you expect.

Also, strings containing misprints yield unexpected results:

```
$a = "12O34"+1      # the letter O, not the number 0
```

When Perl sees a string in the middle of an expression, it converts the string to an integer. To do this, it starts at the left of the string and continues until it sees a letter that is not a digit. In this case, `"12034"` is converted to the integer 12, not 12034.

Using Scalar Variable Operators

The statement `$miles = $originaldist * 0.6214;` uses two scalar variable operators: `=`, the assignment operator, which assigns a value to a variable, and `*`, the multiplication operator, which multiplies two values.

Perl provides the complete set of operators found in C, plus a few others. These operators are described in the following sections.

Performing Arithmetic

To do arithmetic in Perl, use the *arithmetic operators*.

Perl supports the following arithmetic operators:

```
$a = 15;           # assignment: $a now has the value 15
$a = 4 + 5.1;      # addition: $a is now 9.1
$a = 17 - 6.2;     # subtraction: $a is now 10.8
$a = 2.1 * 6;      # multiplication: $a is now 12.6
$a = 48 / 1.5;     # division: $a is now 32
$a = 2 ** 3;       # exponentiation: $a is now 8
$a = 21 % 5;       # remainder (modulo): $a is now 1
$a = - $b;         # arithmetic negation: $a is now $b * -1
```

Non-integral values are converted to integers before a remainder operation is performed:

```
$a = 21.4 % 5.1;   # identical to 21 % 5
```

Performing Comparisons

To compare two scalar values in Perl, use the *logical operators*.

Logical operators are divided into two classes: numeric and string. The following numeric logical operators are defined:

```
11.0 < 16          # less than
16 > 11            # greater than
15 == 15           # equals
11.0 <= 16         # less than or equal to
16 >= 11           # greater than or equal to
15 != 14           # not equal to
$a || $b           # logical OR:  true if either is non-zero
$a && $b           # logical AND:  true only if both are non-zero
! $a               # logical NOT:  true if $a is zero
```

In each case, the result of the operation performed by a logical operator is non-zero if true and zero if false, just like in C.

The expression on the left side of a `||` (logical or) operator is always tested before the expression on the right side, and the expression on the right side is only used when necessary. For example, consider the following expression:

```
$x == 0 || $y / $x > 5
```

Here, the expression on the left side of the `||`, `$x == 0`, is tested first. If `$x` is zero, the result is true regardless of the value of `$y / $x > 5`, so Perl doesn't bother to compute this value. `$y / $x > 5` is only evaluated if s is not zero. This ensures that division by zero can never occur.

Similarly, the expression on the right side of a `&&` operator is only tested if the expression on the left side is true:

```
$x != 0 && $y / $x > 5
```

Once again, a division by zero error is impossible, because `$y / $x > 5` is only evaluated if `$x` is non-zero.

Perl also defines the `<=>` operator, which returns `0` if the two values are equal, `-1` if the left value is larger, and `1` if the right value is larger:

```
4 <=> 1         # returns -1
3 <=> 3.0       # returns 0
1 <=> 4.0       # returns 1
```

> **CAUTION:** Be careful when you use floating point numbers in comparison operations, because the result may not be what you expect. Consider the following code fragment:
>
> ```
> $val1 = 14.3;
> $val2 = 100 + 14.3 - 100;
> print "val1 is $val1, val2 is $val2\n";
> ```
>
> On first examination, `$val1` and `$val2` appear to contain the same value, 14.3. However, the print statement produces the following:
>
> ```
> val1 is 14.300000000000001, val2 is 14.299999999999997
> ```
>
> Adding and subtracting 100 affects the value stored in `$val2` because of the way floating point values are calculated and stored on the machine. As a result, `$val1` and `$val2` are not the same, and `$val1 == $val2` is not true.
>
> This problem occurs in most programming languages (including C).

Besides the preceding numeric logical operators, Perl also provides logical operators that work with strings:

```
"aaa" lt "bbb"      # less than
"bbb" gt "aaa"      # greater than
"aaa" eq "aaa"      # equals
"aaa" le "bbb"      # less than or equal to
"bbb" ge "aaa"      # greater than or equal to
"aaa" ne "bbb"      # not equal to
```

Perl also defines the cmp operator, which, like the numeric operator <=>, returns -1, 0 or 1:

```
"aaa" cmp "bbb"     # returns -1
"aaa" cmp "aaa"     # returns 0
"bbb" cmp "aaa"     # returns 1
```

This behavior is identical to that of the C function strcmp().

Note that the logical string operators perform string comparisons, not numeric comparisons. For example, "40" lt "8" is true—if the two strings are sorted in ascending order, "40" appears before "8".

Manipulating Bits

Any integer can always be represented in binary or base-2 notation, of course. For example, the number 38 is equivalent to the binary value 100110: 32 plus 4 plus 2. Each 0 or 1 in this binary value is called a *bit*.

If a Perl scalar value happens to be an integer, Perl allows you to manipulate the bits that make up that integer. To do this, use the Perl *bitwise operators*.

The following bitwise operators are supported in Perl:

- The & (bitwise AND) operator
- The ¦ (bitwise OR) operator
- The ^ (bitwise EXOR, or exclusive OR) operator
- The ~ (bitwise NOT) operator
- The << (left shift) and >> (right shift) operators

If a scalar value is not an integer, it is converted to an integer before a bitwise operation is performed:

```
$a = 24.5 & 11.2    # identical to $a = 24 & 11
```

The & operator works as follows: first, it examines the values on either side of the &. (These values are also known as the *operands* of the & operator.) These values are examined in their binary representations. For example, consider the following bitwise operation:

```
$a = 29 & 11;
```

In this case, the 29 is converted to 11101, and the 11 is converted to 01011. (A binary representation can have as many leading zeroes as you like.)

Next, Perl compares each bit of the first operand with the corresponding bit in the second operand:

```
11101
01011
```

In this case, only the second and fifth bits (from the left) of the two operands are both 1; therefore, the binary representation of the result is 01001, or 9.

The ¦ operator works in much the same way. The bits of the two operands are compared one at a time; if a bit in the first operand is 1 or its corresponding bit in the second operand is 1, the bit in the result is set to 1. Consider this example:

```
$a = 25 ¦ 11;
```

Here, the binary representations are 11001 and 01011. In this case, only the third bits are both 0, and the result is 11011 or 27.

The ^ operator sets a result bit to 1 if exactly one of the corresponding bits in an operand is 1. If both bits are 1 or both are 0, the result bit is set to 0. In the example $a = 25 ^ 11; the binary representations of the operands are 11001 and 01011, and the result is 10010, or 18.

The ~ operator works on one operand. Every 0 bit in the operand is changed to a 1 and vice versa. For example, consider the following:

```
$a = ~ 25;
```

Here, the binary representation of 25 is 11001. The result, therefore, is 00110, or 6.

The << operator shifts the bits of the left operand the number of places specified by the right operand, and fills the vacated places with zeroes:

```
$a = 29 << 2;
```

Here the value 29, whose binary representation is 11101, is shifted left two positions. This produces the result 1110100, or 116.

Similarly, the >> operator shifts the bits rightward, with the rightmost bits being lost:

```
$a = 29 >> 2;
```

In this case, 29, or 11101, is shifted right two places. The 01 on the end is thrown away, and the result is 111, or 7.

Shifting left one bit is equivalent to multiplying by 2:

```
$a = 54 << 1;     # this result is 108
$a = 54 * 2;      # this result is also 108
```

Shifting right one bit is equivalent to dividing by 2:

```
$a = 54 >> 1;      # this result is 27
$a = 54 / 2;       # this result is also 27
```

Similarly, shifting left or right n bits is equivalent to multiplying or dividing by 2**n.

Using the Assignment Operators

The most common assignment operator is the = operator, which you've already seen:

```
$a = 9;
```

Here, the value 9 is assigned to the scalar variable $a.

Another common assignment operator is the += operator, which combines the operations of addition and assignment:

```
$a = $a + 1;       # this adds 1 to $a
$a += 1;           # this also adds 1 to $a
```

Other assignment operators exist that correspond to the other arithmetic and bitwise operators:

```
$a -= 1;           # same as $a = $a - 1
$a *= 2;           # same as $a = $a * 2
$a /= 2;           # same as $a = $a / 2
$a %= 2;           # same as $a = $a % 2
$a **= 2;          # same as $a = $a ** 2
$a &= 2;           # same as $a = $a & 2
$a |= 2;           # same as $a = $a ¦ 2
$a ^= 2;           # same as $a = $a ^ 2
```

Using Autoincrement and Autodecrement

Another way to add 1 to a scalar variable is with the ++, or autoincrement, operator:

```
++$a;              # same as $a += 1 or $a = $a + 1
```

This operator can appear either before or after its operand:

```
$a++;              # also equivalent to $a += 1 and $a = $a + 1
```

The ++ operator can also be part of a more complicated sequence of operations. (A code fragment consisting of a sequence of operations and their values is known as an *expression*.) Consider the following statements:

```
$b = ++$a;
$b = $a++;
```

In the first statement, the ++ operator appears before its operand. This tells Perl to add 1 to $a before assigning its value to $b:

```
$a = 7;
$b = ++$a;         # $a and $b are both 8
```

If the ++ operator appears after the operand, Perl adds 1 to $a after assigning its value to $b:

```
$a = 7;
$b = $a++;          # $a is now 8, and $b is now 7
```

Similarly, the --, or autodecrement, operator subtracts 1 from the value of a scalar variable either before or after assigning the value:

```
$a = 7;
$b = --$a;          # $a and $b are both 6
$a = 7;
$b = $a--;          # $a is now 6, and $b is now 7
```

The ++ and -- operators provide a great deal of flexibility, and are often used in loops and other control structures.

Do not use the ++ and -- operators on the same variable more than once in the same expression:

```
$b = ++$a + $a++;
```

The value assigned to $b depends on which of the operands of the + operator is evaluated first. On some systems, the first operand (++$a) is evaluated first. On others, the second operand ($a++) is evaluated first.

You can ensure that you get the result you want by using multiple statements and the appropriate assignment operator:

```
$b = ++$a;
$b += $a++;
```

Concatenating and Repeating Strings

Perl provides three operators that operate on strings: The . operator, which joins two strings together; the x operator, which repeats a string; and the .= operator, which joins and then assigns.

The . operator joins the second operand to the first operand:

```
$a = "be" . "witched";      # $a is now "bewitched"
```

This join operation is also known as *string concatenation.*

The x operator (the letter x) makes *n* copies of a string, where *n* is the value of the right operand:

```
$a = "t" x 5;                  # $a is now "ttttt"
```

The .= operator combines the operations of string concatenation and assignment:

```
$a = "be";
$a .= "witched";          # $a is now "bewitched"
```

Using Other C Operators

Perl also supports the following operators, found in the C programming language: The , (comma) operator, and the ? and : (conditional) operator combination.

The , operator ensures that one portion of an expression is evaluated first:

```
$x += 1, $y = $x;
```

The , operator breaks this expression into two parts:

```
$x += 1
$y = $x
```

The part before the comma is performed first. Thus, 1 is added to $x and then $x is assigned to $y.

The ? and : combination allows you to test the value of a variable and then perform one of two operations based on the result of the test. For example, in the expression $y = $x == 0 ? 15 : 8 the variable $x is compared with zero. If $x equals zero, $y is assigned 15; if $x is not zero, $y is assigned 8.

Matching Patterns

Perl allows you to examine scalar variables and test for the existence of a particular pattern in a string. To do this, use the =~ (pattern matching) operator:

```
$x =~ /jkl/
```

The character string enclosed by the / characters is the pattern to be matched, and the scalar variable on the left of the =~ operator is the variable to be examined. This example searches for the pattern jkl in the scalar variable $x. If $x contains jkl, the expression is true; if not, the expression is false. In the statement $y = $x =~ /jkl/;, $y is assigned a non-zero value if $x contains jkl, and is assigned zero if $x does not contain jkl.

The !~ operator is the negation of =~:

```
$y = $x !~ /jkl/;
```

Here, $y is assigned zero if $x contains jkl, and a non-zero value otherwise.

Using Special Characters in Patterns

You can use several special characters in your patterns. The * character matches zero or more of the character it follows:

`/jk*l/`

This matches jl, jkl, jkkl, jkkkl, and so on.

The + character matches one or more of the preceding character:

`/jk+l/`

This matches jkl, jkkl, jkkkl, and so on.

The ? character matches zero or one copies of the preceding character:

`/jk?l/`

This matches jl or jkl.

The character . matches any character except the newline character:

`/j.l/`

This matches any pattern consisting of a j, any character, and an l.

If a set of characters is enclosed in square brackets, any character in the set is an acceptable match:

```
/j[kK]l/        # matches jkl or jKl
```

Consecutive alphanumeric characters in the set can be represented by a dash (-):

```
/j[k1-3K]l/     # matches jkl, j1l, j2l, j3l or jKl
```

You can specify that a match must be at the start or end of a line by using ^ or $:

```
/^jkl/          # matches jkl at start of line
/jkl$/          # matches jkl at end of line
/^jkl$/         # matches line consisting of exactly jkl
```

You can specify that a match must be either on a word boundary or inside a word by including \b or \B in the pattern:

```
/\bjkl/         # matches jkl, but not ijkl
/\Bjkl/         # matches ijkl, but not jkl
```

Some sets are so common that special characters exist to represent them:

- ■ \d matches any digit, and is equivalent to [0-9].

- ■ \w matches any character that can appear in a variable name; it is equivalent to [A-Za-z_0-9].

■ \s matches any *whitespace* (any character not visible on the screen); it is equivalent to [\r\t\n\f]. (These backslash characters were explained in "Using Double- and Single-Quoted Strings" earlier in this chapter.)

To match all but a specified set of characters, specify ^ at the start of your set:

```
/j[^kK]l/
```

This matches any string containing j, any character but k or K, and l.

To use a special character as an ordinary character, precede it with a backslash (\):

```
/j\*l/            # this matches j*l
```

This matches j*l.

In patterns, the * and + special characters match as many characters in a string as possible. For example, consider the following:

```
$x = "abcde";
$y = $x =~ /a.*/;
```

The pattern /a.*/ can match a, ab, abc, abcd, or abcde. abcde is matched, since it is the longest. This becomes meaningful when patterns are used in substitution.

Substituting and Translating Using Patterns

You can use the =~ operator to substitute one string for another:

```
$val =~ s/abc/def/;    # replace abc with def
$val =~ s/a+/xyz/;      # replace a, aa, aaa, etc., with xyz
$val =~ s/a/b/g;        # replace all a's with b's
```

Here, the s prefix indicates that the pattern between the first / and the second is to be replaced by the string between the second / and the third.

You can also translate characters using the tr prefix:

```
$val =~ tr/a-z/A-Z/;   # translate lower case to upper
```

Here, any character matched by the first pattern is replaced by the corresponding character in the second pattern.

The Order of Operations

Consider the following statement:

```
$a = 21 * 2 + 3 << 1 << 2 ** 2;
```

The problem: Which operation should be performed first?

The following sections answer questions of this type.

Precedence

In standard grade-school arithmetic, certain operations are always performed before others. For example, multiplication is always performed before addition:

```
4 + 5 * 3
```

Because multiplication is performed before addition, it has higher *precedence* than addition.

Table 16.2 defines the precedence of the Perl operators described in these sections. The items at the top of the table have the highest precedence, and the items at the bottom have the lowest.

Table 16.2. Operator Precedence in Perl.

++, --	Autoincrement and autodecrement
-, ~, !	Operators with one operand
**	Exponentiation
=~, !~	Matching operators
*, /, %, x	Multiplication, division, remainder, repetition
+, -, .	Addition, subtraction, concatenation
<<, >>	Shifting operators
-e, -r, etc.	File status operators
<, <=, >, >=, lt, le, gt, ge	Inequality comparison operators
==, !=, <=>, eq, ne, cmp	Equality comparison operators
&	Bitwise AND
|, ^	Bitwise OR and exclusive OR
&&	Logical AND
||	Logical OR
..	List range operator
? and :	Conditional operator
=, +=, -=, *=, etc.	Assignment operators
,	Comma operator

For example, consider the following statement:

```
$x = 11 * 2 + 6 ** 2 << 2;
```

The operations in this statement are performed in the following order:

1. `6 ** 2`, yielding 36.

2. `11 * 2`, yielding 22.

3. `36 + 22`, yielding 58.

4. `58 << 2`, yielding 116.

Therefore, 116 is assigned to `$x`.

This operator precedence table contains some operators that are defined in later sections. The `..` (list range) operator is defined in "Using Lists and Array Variables." The file status operators are described in "Reading from and Writing to Files."

Associativity

Consider the following statement:

```
$x = 2 + 3 - 4;
```

In this case, it doesn't matter whether the addition (`2 + 3`) or the subtraction (`3 - 4`) is performed first, because the result is the same either way. However, for some operations, the order of evaluation makes a difference:

```
$x = 2 ** 3 ** 2;
```

Is `$x` assigned 64 (`8 ** 2`) or 512 (`2 ** 9`)?

To resolve these problems, Perl associates a specified *associativity* with each operator. If an operator is *right-associative*, the rightmost operator is performed first when two operators have the same precedence:

```
$x = 2 ** 3 ** 2;    # the same as $x = 2 ** 9, or $x = 512
```

If an operator is *left-associative*, the leftmost operator is performed first when two operators have the same precedence:

```
$x = 29 % 6 * 2;    # the same as $x = 5 * 2, or $x = 10
```

The following operators in Perl are right-associative:

■ The assignment operators (`=`, `+=`, and so on)

■ The `?` and `:` operator combination

■ The `**` operator (exponentiation)

■ The operators that have only one operand (`!`, `~` and `-`)

All other operators are left-associative.

Forcing Precedence Using Parentheses

Perl allows you to force the order of evaluation of operations in expressions. To do this, use parentheses:

```
$x = 4 * (5 + 3);
```

In this statement, 5 is added to 3 and then multiplied by 4, yielding 32.

You can use as many sets of parentheses as you like:

```
$x = 4 ** (5 % (8 - 6));
```

Here, the result is 4:

- 8 - 6 is performed, leaving 4 ** (5 % 2)
- 5 % 2 is performed, leaving 4 ** 1
- 4 ** 1 is 4

Using Lists and Array Variables

So far, the Perl programs you have seen have only used scalar data and scalar variables. In other words, they have only dealt with one value at a time.

Perl also allows you to manipulate groups of values, known as *lists* or *arrays*. These lists can be assigned to special variables known as *array variables*, which can be processed in a variety of ways.

This section describes lists and array variables, and how to use them. It also describes how to pass command-line arguments to your program using the special-purpose array @ARGV.

Introducing Lists

A list is a collection of scalar values enclosed in parentheses. The following is a simple example of a list:

```
(1, 5.3, "hello", 2)
```

This list contains four elements, each of which is a scalar value: the numbers 1 and 5.3, the string "hello", and the number 2. As always in Perl, numbers and character strings are interchangeable: each element of a list can be either a number or a string.

A list can contain as many elements as you like (or as many as your machine's memory can store at one time). To indicate a list with no elements, just specify the parentheses:

```
()              # this list is empty
```

Scalar Variables and Lists

Lists can also contain scalar variables:

```
(17, $var, "a string")
```

Here, the second element of the list is the scalar variable $var. When Perl sees a scalar variable in a list, it replaces the scalar variable with its current value.

A list element can also be an expression:

```
(17, $var1 + $var2, 26 << 2)
```

Here, the expression $var1 + $var2 is evaluated to become the second element, and the expression 26 << 2 is evaluated to become the third element.

Scalar variables can also be replaced in strings:

```
(17, "the answer is $var1")
```

In this case, the value of $var1 is placed into the string.

Using List Ranges

Suppose that you want to define a list consisting of the numbers 1 through 10, inclusive. You can do this by typing in each of the numbers in turn:

```
(1, 2, 3, 4, 5, 6, 7, 8, 9, 10)
```

However, there is a simpler way to do it: use the *list range operator*, which is .. (two consecutive periods). The following is a list created using the list range operator:

```
(1..10)
```

This tells Perl to define a list whose first value is 1, whose second value is 2, and so on up to 10.

The list range operator can be used to define part of a list:

```
(2, 5..7, 11)
```

This list consists of five elements: the numbers 2, 5, 6, 7 and 11.

List range operators can also be used with floating-point values:

```
(2.1..5.3)
```

This list consists of four elements: 2.1, 3.1, 4.1, and 5.1. Each element of the list is one greater than the previous element, and the last element of the list is the largest possible number less than or equal to the number to the right of the .. operator. (If the value to the left of the .. operator is greater than the value to the right, an empty list is created.)

Elements that define the range of a list range operator can be expressions, and these expressions can contain scalar variables:

```
($a..$b+5)
```

This list consists of all values between the current value of $a and the current value of the expression $b+5.

Storing Lists in Array Variables

Perl allows you to store lists in special variables designed for that purpose. These variables are called *array variables*.

The following is an example of a list being assigned to an array variable:

```
@array = (1, 2, 3);
```

Here, the list (1, 2, 3) is assigned to the array variable @array.

Note that the name of the array variable starts with the character @. This allows Perl to distinguish array variables from other kinds of variables, such as scalar variables, which start with the character $. As with scalar variables, the second character of the variable name must be a letter, and subsequent characters of the name can be letters, numbers, or underscores.

When an array variable is first created (seen for the first time), it is assumed to contain the empty list () unless something is assigned to it.

Because Perl uses @ and $ to distinguish array variables from string variables, the same name can be used in an array variable and in a string variable:

```
$var = 1;
@var = (11, 27.1, "a string");
```

Here, the name var is used in both the string variable $var and the array variable @var. These are two completely separate variables.

Assigning to Array Variables

As you have already seen, lists can be assigned to array variables with the assignment operator =:

```
@x = (11, "my string", 27.44);
```

You can also assign one array variable to another:

```
@y = @x;
```

A scalar value can be assigned to an array variable:

```
@x = 27.1;
@y = $x;
```

In this case, the scalar value (or value stored in a scalar variable) is converted into a list containing one element.

Using Array Variables in Lists

As you have already seen, lists can contain scalar variables:

```
@x = (1, $y, 3);
```

Here, the value of the scalar variable $y becomes the second element of the list assigned to @x.

You can also specify that the value of an array variable is to appear in a list:

```
@x = (2, 3, 4);
@y = (1, @x, 5);
```

Here, the list (2, 3, 4) is substituted for @x, and the resulting list (1, 2, 3, 4, 5) is assigned to @y.

Assigning to Scalar Variables from Array Variables

Consider the following assignment:

```
@x = ($a, $b);
```

Here, the values of the scalar variables $a and $b are used to form a two-element list that is assigned to the array variable @x.

Perl also allows you to take the current value of an array variable and assign its components to a group of scalar variables:

```
($a, $b) = @x;
```

Here, the first element of the list currently stored in @x is assigned to $a, and the second element is assigned to $b. Additional elements in @x, if they exist, are not assigned.

If there are more scalar variables than elements in an array variable, the excess scalar variables are given the value " " (the null string), which is equivalent to the numeric value 0:

```
@x = (1, 2);
($a, $b, $c) = @x;  # $a is now 1, $b is now 2, $c is now ""
```

Retrieving the Length of a List

As you have already seen, when a scalar value is assigned to an array variable, the value is assumed to be a list containing one element. For example, the following statements are equivalent:

```
@x = $y;
@x = ($y);
```

However, the converse is not true. In the statement `$y = @x;`, the value assigned to `$y` is the number of elements in the list currently stored in `@x`:

```
@x = ("string 1", "string 2", "string 3");
$y = @x;            # $y is now 3
```

To assign the value of the first element of a list to a scalar variable, enclose the scalar variable in a list:

```
@x = ("string 1", "string 2", "string 3");
($y) = @x;          # $y is now "string 1"
```

Using Array Slices

Perl allows you to specify what part of an array to use in an expression. The following example shows you how to do this:

```
@x = (1, 2, 3);
@y = @x[0,1];
```

Here, the list (1, 2, 3) is first assigned to the array variable `@x`. Then, the array slice [0,1] is assigned to `@y`: in other words, the first two elements of `@x` are assigned to `@y`. (Note that the first element of the array is specified by 0, not 1.)

You can assign to an array slice as well:

```
@x[0,1] = (11.5, "hello");
```

This statement assigns the value 11.5 to the first element of the array variable `@x`, and assigns the string `"hello"` to the second.

Array variables automatically grow when necessary, with null strings assigned to fill any gaps:

```
@x = (10, 20, 30);
@x[4,5] = (75, 85);
```

Here, the second assignment increases the size of the array variable `@x` from three elements to six, and assigns 75 to the fifth element and 85 to the sixth. The fourth element is set to be the null string.

Using Array Slices with Scalar Variables

An array slice can consist of a single element. In this case, the array slice is treated as if it is a scalar variable:

```
@x = (10, 20, 30);
$y = $x[1];        # $y now has the value 20
```

Note that the array slice is now preceded by the character $, not the character @. This tells Perl that the array slice is to be treated as a scalar variable.

Recall that array variables and scalar variables can have the same name:

```
$x = "Smith";
@x = (47, "hello");
```

Here, the scalar variable $x and the array variable @x are both defined, and are completely independent of one another. This can cause problems if you want to include a scalar variable inside a string:

```
$y = "Refer to $x[1] for more information.";
```

In this case, Perl assumes that you want to substitute the value of the array slice $x[1] into the string. This produces the following:

```
$y = "Refer to hello for more information.";
```

To specify the scalar variable and not the array slice, enclose the variable name in braces:

```
$y = "Refer to ${x}[1] for more information.";
```

This tells Perl to replace $x, not $x[1], and produces the following:

```
$y = "Refer to Smith[1] for more information.";
```

Using the Array Slice Notation as a Shorthand

So far, we have been using the array slice notation @x[0,1] to refer to a portion of an array variable. As it happens, in Perl the above is exactly equivalent to a list of single-element array slices:

```
@y = @x[0,1];
@y = ($x[0], $x[1]);   # these two statements are identical
```

This allows you to use the array slice notation whenever you want to refer to more than one element in an array:

```
@y = @x[4,1,5];
```

In this statement, the array variable @y is assigned the values of the fifth, second, and sixth elements of the array variable @x.

```
@y[0,1,2] = @x[1,1,1];
```

Here, the second element of @x is copied to the first three elements of @y.

In Perl, assignments in which the operands overlap are handled without difficulty. Consider this example:

```
@x[4,3] = @x[3,4];
```

Perl performs this assignment by creating a temporary array variable, copying @x[3,4] to it, and then copying it to @x[4,3]. Thus, this statement swaps the values in the fourth and fifth elements of @x.

Other Array Operations

Perl provides a number of built-in functions that work on lists and array variables. For example, you can sort array elements in alphabetic order, reverse the elements of an array, remove the last character from all elements of an array, and merge the elements of an array into a single string.

Sorting a List or Array Variable

The built-in function sort() sorts the elements of an array in alphabetic order and returns the sorted list:

```
@x = ("this", "is", "a", "test");
@x = sort (@x);     # @x is now ("a", "is", "test", "this")
```

Note that the sort is in alphabetic, not numeric, order:

```
@x = (70, 100, 8);
@x = sort (@x);     # @x is now ("100", "70", "8")
```

The number 100 appears first because the string "100" is alphabetically ahead of "70" (since "1" appears before "7").

Reversing a List or Array Variable

The function reverse() reverses the order of the elements in a list or array variable and returns the reversed list:

```
@x = ("backwards", "is", "array", "this");
@x = reverse(@x);   # @x is now ("this", "array", "is", "backwards")
```

You can sort and reverse the same list:

```
@x = reverse(sort(@x));
```

This produces a sort in reverse alphabetical order.

Using *chop()* on Array Variables

The chop() function can be used on array variables as well as scalar variables:

```
$a[0] = <STDIN>;
$a[1] = <STDIN>;
$a[2] = <STDIN>;
chop(@a);
```

Here, three input lines are read into the array variable @a—one in each of the first three elements. chop() then removes the last character (in this case, the terminating newline character) from all three elements.

Creating a Single String from a List

To create a single string from a list or array variable, use the function join():

```
$x = join(" ", "this", "is", "a", "sentence");
```

The first element of the list supplied to join() contains the characters that are to be used to glue the parts of the created string together. In this example, $x becomes "this is a sentence".

join() can specify other join strings besides " ":

```
@x = ("words","separated","by");
$y = join("::",@x,"colons");
```

Here, $y becomes "words::separated::by::colons".

To undo the effects of join(), call the function split():

```
$y = "words::separated::by::colons";
@x = split(/::/, $y);
```

The first element of the list supplied to split() is a pattern to be matched. When the pattern is matched, a new array element is started and the pattern is thrown away. In this case, the pattern to be matched is ::, which means that @x becomes ("words", "separated", "by", "colons").

Note that the syntax for the pattern is the same as that used in the =~ operator; see "Matching Patterns" for more information on possible patterns to match.

Example: Sorting Words in a String

The example in LIST 16_2 on the CD-ROM uses split(), join(), and sort() to sort the words in a string.

Using Command Line Arguments

The special array variable @ARGV is automatically defined to contain the strings entered on the command line when a Perl program is invoked. For example, if the program

```
#!/usr/bin/perl
print("The first argument is $ARGV[0]\n");
```

is called printfirstarg, entering the command

```
printfirstarg 1 2 3
```

produces the following output:

```
The first argument is 1
```

You can use join() to turn @ARGV into a single string, if you like:

```
#!/usr/bin/perl
$commandline = join(" ", @ARGV);
print("The command line arguments: $commandline\n");
```

If this program is called printallargs, entering

```
printallargs 1 2 3
```

produces

```
The command line arguments: 1 2 3
```

Note that $ARGV[0], the first element of the @ARGV array variable, does not contain the name of the program. For example, in the invocation

```
printallargs 1 2 3
```

$ARGV[0] is "1", not "printallargs". This is a difference between Perl and C: in C, argv[0] is "printallargs" and argv[1] is "1".

Standard Input and Array Variables

Since an array variable can contain as many elements as you like, you can assign an entire input file to a single array variable:

```
@infile = <STDIN>;
```

This works as long as you have enough memory to store the entire file.

Controlling Program Flow

Like all programming languages, Perl allows you to include statements that are only executed when specified conditions are true; these statements are called *conditional statements*.

The following is a simple example of a conditional statement:

```
if ($x == 14) {
        print("\$x is 14\n");
}
```

Here, the line if ($x == 14) { tells Perl that the following statements—those between the { and }—are only to be executed if $x is equal to 14.

Perl provides a full range of conditional statements; these statements are described in the following sections.

Conditional Execution: The *if* Statement

The if conditional statement has the following structure:

```
if (expr) {
        ...
}
```

When Perl sees the if, it evaluates the expression expr to be either true or false. If the value of the expression is the integer 0, the null string "", or the string "0", the value of the expression is false; otherwise, the value of the expression is true.

> **CAUTION:** The *only* string values that evaluate to false are "" and "0". Strings such as "00" and "0.0" return true, not false.

Two-Way Branching Using *if* and *else*

The else statement can be combined with the if statement to allow for a choice between two alternatives:

```
if ($x == 14) {
        print("\$x is 14\n");
} else {
        print("\$x is not 14\n");
}
```

Here, the expression following the if is evaluated. If it is true, the statements between the if and the else are executed. Otherwise, the statements between the else and the final } are executed. In either case, execution then proceeds to the statement after the final }.

Note that the `else` statement cannot appear by itself: it must follow an `if` statement.

Multi-Way Branching Using *elsif*

The `elsif` statement allows you to write a program that chooses between more than two alternatives:

```
if ($x == 14) {
        print("\$x is 14\n");
} elsif ($x == 15) {
        print("\$x is 15\n");
} elsif ($x == 16) {
        print("\$x is 16\n");
} else {
        print("\$x is not 14, 15 or 16\n");
}
```

Here, the expression `$x == 14` is evaluated. If it evaluates to true (if `$x` is equal to 14), the first `print()` statement is executed. Otherwise, the expression `$x == 15` is evaluated. If `$x == 15` is true, the second `print()` is executed; otherwise, the expression `$x == 16` is evaluated, and so on.

You can have as many `elsif` statements as you like; however, the first `elsif` statement of the group must be preceded by an `if` statement.

The `else` statement can be omitted:

```
if ($x == 14) {
        print("\$x is 14\n");
} elsif ($x == 15) {
        print("\$x is 15\n");
} elsif ($x == 16) {
        print("\$x is 16\n");
} # do nothing if $x is not 14, 15 or 16
```

If the `else` statement is included, it must follow the last `elsif`.

Conditional Branching Using *unless*

The `unless` statement is the opposite of the `if` statement:

```
unless ($x == 14) {
        print("\$x is not 14\n");
}
```

Here, the statements between the braces are executed unless the value of the expression evaluates to true.

You can use `elsif` and `else` with `unless`, if you like; however, an `if-elsif-else` structure is usually easier to follow than an `unless-elsif-else` one.

Repeating Statements Using *while* and *until*

In the examples above, each statement between braces is executed once, at most. To indicate that a group of statements between braces is to be executed until a certain condition is met, use the `while` statement:

```
#!/usr/bin/perl
$x = 1;
while ($x <= 5) {
        print("\$x is now $x\n");
        ++$x;
}
```

Here, the scalar variable $x is first assigned the value 1. The statements between the braces are then executed until the expression `$x <= 5` is false.

When you run the program shown above, you get the following output:

```
$x is now 1
$x is now 2
$x is now 3
$x is now 4
$x is now 5
```

As you can see, the statements between the braces have been executed five times.

The `until` statement is the opposite of `while`:

```
#!/usr/bin/perl
$x = 1;
until ($x <= 5) {
        print("\$x is now $x\n");
        ++$x;
}
```

Here, the statements between the braces are executed until the expression `$x <= 5` is true. In this case, the expression is true the first time it is evaluated, which means that the `print()` statement is never executed. To fix this, reverse the direction of the arithmetic comparison:

```
#!/usr/bin/perl
$x = 1;
until ($x > 5) {
        print("\$x is now $x\n");
        ++$x;
}
```

This now produces the same output as the program containing the `while` statement above.

> **CAUTION:** If you use `while`, `until`, or any other statement that repeats, you must make sure that the statement does not repeat forever:
>
> ```
> $x = 1;
> while ($x == 1) {
>         print("\$x is still $x\n");
> }
> ```
>
> Here, $x is always 1, $x == 1 is always true, and the `print()` statement is repeated an infinite number of times.
>
> Perl does not check for *infinite loops* such as this one above. It is your responsibility to make sure that infinite loops don't happen!

Using Single-Line Conditional Statements

If only one statement is to be executed when a particular condition is true, you can write your conditional statement using a *single-line conditional statement*. For example, instead of writing

```
if ($x == 14) {
        print("\$x is 14\n");
}
```

you can use the following single-line conditional statement:

```
print("\$x is 14\n") if ($x == 14);
```

In both cases, the `print()` statement is executed if $x is equal to 14.

You can also use `unless`, `while`, or `until` in a single-line conditional statement:

```
print("\$x is not 14\n") unless ($x == 14);
print("\$x is less than 14\n") while ($x++ < 14);
print("\$x is less than 14\n") until ($x++ > 14);
```

Note how useful the autoincrement operator ++ is in the last two statements: it allows you to compare $x and add one to it all at once. This ensures that the single-line conditional statement does not execute forever.

Looping with the *for* Statement

Most *loops*—segments of code that are executed more than once—use a counter to control and eventually terminate the execution of the loop. Here is an example similar to the ones you've seen so far:

```
$count = 1;                   # initialize the counter
while ($count <= 10) {        # terminate after ten repetitions
```

```
        print("the counter is now $count\n");
        $count += 1;        # increment the counter
}
```

As you can see, the looping process consists of three components:

- The initialization of the counter variable
- A test to determine whether to terminate the loop
- The updating of the counter variable after the execution of the statements in the loop

Because a loop so often contains these three components, Perl provides a quick way to do them all at once by using the for statement. The following example uses the for statement and behaves the same as the example you just saw:

```
for ($count = 1; $count <= 10; $count += 1) {
        print("the counter is now $count\n");
}
```

Here the three components of the loop all appear in the same line, separated by semicolons. Because the components are all together, it is easier to remember to supply all of them, which makes it more difficult to write code that goes into an infinite loop.

Looping Through a List: The *foreach* Statement

So far, all of the examples of loops that you've seen use a scalar variable as the counter. You can also use a list as a counter by using the foreach statement:

```
#!/usr/bin/perl
@list = ("This", "is", "a", "list", "of", "words");
print("Here are the words in the list: \n");
foreach $temp (@list) {
        print("$temp ");
}
print("\n");
```

Here, the loop defined by the foreach statement executes once for each element in the list @list. The resulting output is

```
Here are the words in the list:
    This is a list of words
```

The current element of the list being used as the counter is stored in a special scalar variable, which in this case is $temp. This variable is special because it is only defined for the statements inside the foreach loop:

```
#!/usr/bin/perl
$temp = 1;
@list = ("This", "is", "a", "list", "of", "words");
print("Here are the words in the list: \n");
foreach $temp (@list) {
```

```
        print("$temp ");
}
print("\n");
print("The value of temp is now $temp\n");
```

The output from this program is the following:

```
Here are the words in the list:
    This is a list of words
The value of temp is now 1
```

The original value of $temp is restored after the foreach statement is finished.

Variables that only exist inside a certain structure, such as $temp in the foreach statement in the preceding example, are called *local variables*. Variables that are defined throughout a Perl program are known as *global variables*. Most variables you use in Perl are global variables. To see other examples of local variables, refer to "Using Subroutines."

> **CAUTION:** Changing the value of the local variable inside a foreach statement also changes the value of the corresponding element of the list:
>
> ```
> @list = (1, 2, 3, 4, 5);
> foreach $temp (@list) {
>         if ($temp == 2) {
>                 $temp = 20;
>         }
> }
> ```
>
> In this loop, when $temp is equal to 2, $temp is reset to 20. Therefore, the contents of the array variable @list become (1, 20, 3, 4, 5).

Exiting a Loop with the *last* Statement

Normally, you exit a loop by testing the condition at the top of the loop and then jumping to the statement after it. However, you can also exit a loop in the middle. To do this, use the last statement.

File LIST 16_5 on the CD-ROM totals a set of receipts entered one at a time; execution is terminated when a null line is entered. If a value entered is less than zero, the program detects this and exits the loop.

Using *next* to Start the Next Iteration of a Loop

In Perl, the `last` statement terminates the execution of a loop. To terminate a particular pass through a loop (also known as an *iteration* of the loop), use the `next` statement.

 File LIST 16_4 on the CD-ROM sums up the numbers from 1 to a user-specified upper limit, and also produces a separate sum of the numbers divisible by two.

Be careful when you use `next` in a `while` or `until` loop. The following example goes into an infinite loop:

```
$count = 0;
while ($count <= 10) {
        if ($count == 5) {
                next;
        }
        $count++;
}
```

When `$count` is 5, the program tells Perl to start the next iteration of the loop. However, the value of `$count` is not changed, which means that the expression `$count == 5` is still true.

To get rid of this problem, you need to increment `$count` before using `next`, as in:

```
$count = 0;
while ($count <= 10) {
        if ($count == 5) {
                $count++;
                next;
        }
        $count++;
}
```

This, by the way, is why many programming purists dislike statements such as `next` and `last`: it's too easy to lose track of where you are and what needs to be updated.

Perl automatically assumes that variables are initialized to be the null string, which evaluates to 0 in arithmetic expressions. This means that in code fragments such as

```
$count = 0;
while ($count <= 10) {
        ...
        $count++;}
```

you don't really need the `$count = 0;` statement. However, it is a good idea to explicitly initialize everything, even when you don't need to. This makes it easier to spot misprints:

```
$count = $tot = 0;
while ($count <= 10) {
    $total += $count;  # misprint: you meant to type "$tot"
        $count += 1;
```

```
}
print ("the total is $tot\n");
```

If you've gotten into the habit of initializing everything, it's easy to spot that $total is a misprint. If you use variables without initializing them, you first have to determine whether $total is really a different variable than $tot. This may be difficult if your program is a large and complicated one.

Using Labelled Blocks for Multi-Level Jumps

In Perl, loops can be inside other loops: such loops are said to be nested. To get out of an outer loop from within an inner loop, label the outer loop and specify its label when using last or next:

```
$total = 0;
$firstcounter = 1;
DONE: while ($firstcounter <= 10) {
        $secondcounter = 1;
        while ($secondcounter <= 10) {
                $total += 1;
                if ($firstcounter == 4 && $secondcounter == 7) {
                        last DONE;
                }
                $secondcounter += 1;
        }
        $firstcounter += 1;
}
```

The statement

```
last DONE;
```

tells Perl to jump out of the loop labelled DONE and continue execution with the first statement after the outer loop. (By the way, this code fragment is just a rather complicated way of assigning 37 to $total.)

Loop labels must start with a letter, and can consist of as many letters, digits, and underscores as you like. The only restriction is that you can't use a label name that corresponds to a word that has a special meaning in Perl:

```
if: while ($x == 0) {    # this is an error in perl
...
}
```

When Perl sees the if, it doesn't know whether you mean the label if or the start of an if statement.

Words such as if that have special meanings in Perl are known as *reserved words* or *keywords*.

Terminating Execution Using *die*

As you have seen, the `last` statement terminates a loop. To terminate program execution entirely, use the `die()` function.

 To illustrate the use of `die()`, see File `LIST 16_6` on the CD-ROM, a simple program that divides two numbers supplied on a single line. `die()` writes its argument to the standard error file, `STDERR`, and then exits immediately. In this example, `die()` is called when there are not exactly two numbers in the input line, or if the second number is zero.

If you like, you can tell `die()` to print the name of the Perl program and the line number being executed when the program was terminated. To do this, leave the closing newline character off the message:

```
die("This prints the filename and line number");
```

If the closing newline character is included, the filename and line number are not included:

```
die("This does not print the filename and line number\n");
```

Reading from and Writing to Files

So far, all of the examples have read from the standard input file, `STDIN`, and have written to the standard output file, `STDOUT`, and the standard error file, `STDERR`. You can also read from and write to as many other files as you like.

To access a file on your UNIX file system from within your Perl program, you must perform the following steps:

1. First, your program must *open* the file. This tells the system that your Perl program wants to access the file.

2. Then, the program can either read from or write to the file, depending on how you have opened the file.

3. Finally, the program can *close* the file. This tells the system that your program no longer needs access to the file.

The following sections describe these operations, tell you how you can read from files specified in the command line, and describe the built-in file test operations.

Opening a File

To open a file, call the built-in function `open()`:

```
open(MYFILE, "/u/jqpublic/myfile");
```

The second argument is the name of the file you want to open. You can supply either the full UNIX pathname, as in `/u/jqpublic/myfile`, or just the filename, as in `myfile`. If only the filename is supplied, the file is assumed to be in the current working directory.

The first argument is an example of a *file variable*. Once the file has been opened, your Perl program accesses the file by referring to this variable. Your file variable name must start with a letter, and can then contain as many letters and digits as you like. (You must ensure, however, that your file variable name is not the same as a reserved word, such as `if`. See the note in "Using Labelled Blocks for Multi-Level Jumps" for more information on reserved words.)

By default, Perl assumes that you want to read any file that you open. To open a file for writing, put a > (greater than) character in front of your filename:

```
open(MYFILE, ">/u/jqpublic/myfile");
```

When you open a file for writing, any existing contents are destroyed. You cannot read from and write to the same file at the same time.

To append to an existing file, put two > characters in front of the filename:

```
open(MYFILE, ">>/u/jqpublic/myfile");
```

You still cannot read from a file you are appending to, but the existing contents are not destroyed.

Checking Whether the Open Succeeded

The `open()` function returns one of two values:

- `open()` returns true (a non-zero value) if the open succeeds
- `open()` returns false (zero) if an error occurs (that is, the file does not exist or you don't have permission to access the file)

You can use the return value from `open()` to test whether the file is actually available, and call `die()` if it is not:

```
unless (open(MYFILE, "/u/jqpublic/myfile")) {
        die("unable to open /u/jqpublic/myfile for reading\n");
}
```

This ensures that your program does not try to read from a nonexistent file.

You can also use the `||` (logical or) operator in place of `unless`:

```
open(MYFILE, "/u/jqpublic/myfile") ||
    die("unable to open /u/jqpublic/myfile for reading\n");
```

This works because the right side of the `||` operator is only executed if the left side is false. See "Performing Comparisons" for more information on the `||` operator.

Reading from a File

To read from a file, enclose the name of the file in angle brackets:

```
$line = <MYFILE>;
```

This statement reads a line of input from the file specified by the file variable MYFILE, and stores the line of input in the scalar variable $line. As you can see, you read from files in exactly the same way you read from the standard input file, STDIN.

Writing to a File

To write to a file, specify the file variable when you call the function print():

```
print MYFILE ("This is a line of text to write \n",
     "This is another line to write\n");
```

The file variable must appear before the first line of text to be written to the file.

This method works both when you are writing a new file and when you are appending to an existing one.

Closing a File

When you are finished reading from or writing to a file, you can tell the system that you are finished by calling close():

```
close(MYFILE);
```

Note that close() is not required: Perl automatically closes the file when the program terminates or when you open another file using a previously defined file variable.

Determining the Status of a File

As you have seen, when you open a file for writing, the existing contents of the file are destroyed. If you only want to open the file for writing if the file does not already exist, you can first test to see if a file exists. To do this, use the -e operator:

```
if (-e "/u/jqpublic/filename") {
        die ("file /u/jqpublic/filename already exists");
}
open (MYFILE, "/u/jqpublic/filename");
```

The -e operator assumes that its operand—a scalar value—is the name of a file. It checks to see if a file with that name already exists. If the file exists, the -e operator returns true; otherwise, it returns false.

Similar tests exist to test other file conditions. The most commonly used file status operators are listed in Table 16.3.

Table 16.3. File Status Operators.

-d	Is this file really a directory?
-e	Does this file exist?
-f	Is this actually a file?
-l	Is this file really a symbolic link?
-o	Is this file owned by the person running the program?
-r	Is this file readable by the person running the program?
-s	Is this a non-empty file?
-w	Is this file writeable by the person running the program?
-x	Is this file executable by the person running the program?
-z	Is this file empty?
-B	Is this a binary file?
-T	Is this a text file?

Reading from a Sequence of Files

Many UNIX commands have the form

```
command file1 file2 file3 ...
```

These commands operate on all of the files specified on the command line, starting with `file1` and continuing on from there.

You can simulate this behavior in Perl. To do this, use the <> operator.

File LIST 16_7 on the CD-ROM counts all the times the word "the" appears in a set of files.

Suppose that this example is stored in a file named `thecount`. If the command `thecount myfile1 myfile2 myfile3` is entered from the command line, the program starts by reading a line of input from the file `myfile1` into the scalar variable `$inputline`. This input line is then split into words, and each word is tested to see if it is "the." Once this line is processed, the program reads another line from myfile1.

When myfile1 is exhausted, the program then begins reading lines from myfile2, and then from myfile3. When myfile3 is exhausted, the program prints the total number of occurrences of "the" in the three files.

Using Subroutines

Some programs perform the same task repeatedly. If you are writing such a program, you may soon get tired of writing the same lines of code over and over again. Perl provides a way around this problem: frequently used segments of code can be stored in separate sections, known as *subroutines*.

The following sections describe how subroutines work, how to pass values to subroutines and receive values from them, and how to define variables that only exist inside subroutines.

Defining a Subroutine

A common Perl task is to read a line of input from a file and break it into words. Here is an example of a subroutine that performs this task. Note that it uses the <> operator described in "Reading from a Sequence of Files."

```
sub getwords {
        $inputline = <>;
        @words = split(/\s+/, $inputline);
}
```

All subroutines follow this simple format: The reserved word sub, followed by the name of the subroutine (in this case, getwords), a { (open brace) character, one or more Perl statements (also known as the *body* of the subroutine), and a closing } (close brace) character.

The subroutine name must start with a letter, and can then consist of any number of letters, digits, and underscores. (As always, you must ensure that your variable name is not a reserved word. See the note in "Using Labelled Blocks for Multi-Level Jumps" for more information on reserved words.)

A subroutine can appear anywhere in a Perl program—even right in the middle, if you like. However, programs are usually easier to understand if the subroutines are all placed at the end.

Using a Subroutine

Once you have written your subroutine, you can use it by specifying its name. Here is a simple example that uses the subroutine getwords to count the number of occurrences of the word "the":

```
#!/usr/bin/perl
$thecount = 0;
&getwords;
while ($words[0] ne "") {      # stop when line is empty
        for ($index = 0; $words[$index] ne ""; $index += 1) {
                $thecount += 1 if $words[$index] eq "the";
        }
        &getwords;
}
print ("Total number of occurrences of the: $thecount\n");
```

The statement &getwords; tells Perl to call the subroutine getwords. When Perl calls the subroutine getwords, it executes the statements contained in the subroutine, namely

```
$inputline = <>;
@words = split(/\s+/, $inputline);
```

Once these statements have been executed, Perl then executes the statement immediately following the &getwords statement.

Returning a Value from a Subroutine

The getwords subroutine defined above is useful, but it suffers from one serious limitation: it assumes that the words from the input line are always going to be stored in the array variable @words. This may lead to problems:

```
@words = ("These", "are", "some", "words");
&getwords;
```

Here, calling getwords destroys the existing contents of @words.

To solve this problem, consider the subroutine getwords you saw earlier:

```
sub getwords {
        $inputline = <>;
        @words = split(/\s+/, $inputline);
}
```

In Perl subroutines, the last value seen by the subroutine becomes the subroutine's *return value*. In this example, the last value seen is the list of words assigned to @words. In the call to getwords, this value can be assigned to an array variable:

```
@words2 = &getwords;
```

Note that this hasn't yet solved the problem, since @words is still overwritten by the getwords subroutine. However, now you don't need to use @words in getwords, because you are assigning the list of words by using the return value. You can now change getwords to use a different array variable:

```
sub getwords {
        $inputline = <>;
        @subwords = split(/ s+/, $inputline);
}
```

Now, the statements

```
@words = ("These", "are", "some", "words");
@words2 = &getwords;
```

work properly: @words is not destroyed when getwords is called. (For a better solution to this problem, see the following section, "Using Local Variables.")

Since the return value of a subroutine is the last value seen, the return value may not always be what you expect.

Consider the following simple program that adds numbers supplied on an input line:

```
#!/usr/bin/perl
$total = &get_total;
print("The total is $total\n");
sub get_total {
        $value = 0;
        $inputline = <STDIN>;
        @subwords = split(/\s+/, $inputline);
        $index = 0;
        while ($subwords[$index] ne "") {
                $value += $subwords[$index++];
        }
}
```

At first glance, you might think that the return value of the subroutine get_total is the value stored in $value. However, this is not the last value seen in the subroutine!

Note that the loop exits when $subwords[index] is the null string. Since no statements are processed after the loop exits, the last value seen in the subroutine is, in fact, the null string. Thus, the null string is the return value of get_total, and is assigned to $total.

To get around this problem, always have the last statement of the subroutine refer to the value you want to use as the return value:

```
sub get_total {
        $value = 0;
        $inputline = <STDIN>;
        @subwords = split(/\s+/, $inputline);
        $index = 0;
        while ($subwords[$index] ne "") {
                $value += $subwords[$index++];
        }
        $value;     # $value is now the return value
}
```

Now, get_total actually returns what you want it to.

Using Local Variables

As you saw in "Returning a Value from a Subroutine," defining variables that appear only in a subroutine ensures that the subroutine doesn't accidentally overwrite anything:

```
sub getwords {
        $inputline = <>;
        @subwords = split(/s+/, $inputline);
}
```

Note, however, that the variables $inputline and @subwords could conceivably be added to your program at a later time. Then, a call to getwords would once again accidentally destroy values that your program needs to keep.

You can ensure that the variables used in a subroutine are known only inside that subroutine by defining them as *local variables*. Here is the subroutine getwords with $inputline and @subwords defined as local variables:

```
sub getwords {
        local($inputline, @subwords);
        $inputline = <>;
        @subwords = split(/s+/, $inputline);
}
```

The local() statement tells Perl that versions of the variables $inputline and @subwords are to be defined for use inside the subroutine. Once a variable has been defined with local(), it cannot accidentally destroy values in your program:

```
@subwords = ("Some", "more", "words");
@words = getwords;
```

Here, @subwords is not destroyed, because the @subwords used in getwords is known only inside the subroutine.

Passing Values to a Subroutine

You can make your subroutines more flexible by allowing them to accept values.

As an example, here is the getwords subroutine modified to split the input line using a pattern that is passed to it:

```
sub getwords {
        local($pattern) = @_;
        local($inputline, @subwords);
        $inputline = <>;
        @subwords = split($pattern, $inputline);
}
```

The array variable @_ is a special system variable that contains a copy of the values passed to the subroutine. The statement local($pattern) = @_; creates a local scalar variable named $pattern and assigns the first value of the array, @_, to it.

Now, to call getwords you must supply the pattern you want it to use when splitting words. To split on white space, as before, call getwords as follows:

```
@words = getwords(/\s+/);
```

If your input line consists of words separated by colons, you can split it using getwords by calling it as follows:

```
@words = getwords(/:/);
```

If you like, you can even break your line into single characters:

```
@words = getwords(//);
```

For more information on patterns you can use, see "Matching Patterns."

The array variable @_ behaves like any other array variable. In particular, its components can be used as scalar values:

```
$x = $_[0];
```

Here, the first element of @_—the first value passed to the subroutine—is assigned to $x.

Usually, assigning @_ to local variables is the best approach, because your subroutine becomes easier to understand.

Calling Subroutines from Other Subroutines

If you like, you can have a subroutine call another subroutine you have written. For example, here is a subroutine that counts the number of words in an input line:

```
sub countline {
        local(@words, $count);
        $count = 0;
        @words = getwords(/\s+/);
        foreach $word (@words) {
                $count += 1;
        }
        $count;         # make sure the count is the return value
}
```

The subroutine countline first calls the subroutine getwords to split the input line into words. Then it counts the number of words in the array returned by getwords and returns that value.

Once you have written countline, it is easy to write a program called wordcount that counts the number of words in one or more files:

```
#!/usr/bin/perl
$totalwordcount = 0;
while (($wordcount = &countline) != 0) {
        $totalwordcount += $wordcount;
}
```

```
print("The total word count is $totalwordcount\n");
# include the subroutines getwords and countline here
```

This program reads lines until an empty line—a line with zero words—is read in. (It assumes that the files contain no blank lines. You can get around this problem by having getwords test whether $inputline is empty before breaking it into words, returning a special "end of file" value in this case. This value could then be passed from getwords to countline, and then to the main program.)

Because getwords uses the <> operator to read input, the files whose words are counted are those listed on the command line:

```
wordcount file1 file2 file3
```

This counts the words in the files file1, file2, and file3.

The variable @_ is a local variable whose value is only defined in the subroutine in which it appears. This allows subroutines to pass values to other subroutines: each subroutine has its own copy of @_ and none of the copies can destroy each other's values.

Associative Arrays

A common programming task is to keep counts of several different things at once. You can, of course, use scalar variables or array variables to solve this problem, but this requires a rather messy if-elsif structure:

```
if ($fruit eq "apple") {
        $apple += 1;
} elsif ($letter eq "banana") {
        $banana += 1;
} elsif ($letter eq "cherry") {
        $cherry += 1;
...
```

This takes up a lot of space, and is rather boring to write.

Fortunately, Perl provides an easier way to solve problems like these—*associative arrays.* The following sections describe associative arrays and how to manipulate them.

Defining Associative Arrays

In ordinary arrays, you access an array element by specifying an integer as the index:

```
@fruits = (9, 23, 11);
$count = $fruits[0];     # $count is now 9
```

In associative arrays, you do not have to use numbers such as 0, 1, and 2 to access array elements. When you define an associative array, you specify the scalar values you want to use to access the elements of the array. For example, here is a definition of a simple associative array:

```
%fruits = ("apple", 9,
           "banana", 23,
           "cherry", 11);
$count = $fruits{"apple"};   # $count is now 9
```

Here, the scalar value `"apple"` accesses the first element of the array `%fruits`, `"banana"` accesses the second element, and `"cherry"` accesses the third. You can use any scalar value you like as an array index, or any scalar value as the value of the array element:

```
%myarray = ("first index", 0,
            98.6, "second value",
            76, "last value");
$value = $myarray{98.6};   # $value is now "second value"
```

Associative arrays eliminate the need for messy `if-elsif` structures. To add 1 to an element of the `%fruits` array, for example, you just need to do the following:

```
$fruits{$fruit} += 1;
```

Better still, if you decide to add other fruits to the list, you do not need to add more code, because the preceding statement also works on the new elements.

The character `%` tells Perl that a variable is an associative array. As with scalar variables and array variables, the remaining characters of the associative array variable name must consist of a letter followed by one or more letters, digits, or underscores.

Accessing Associative Arrays

Since an associative array value is a scalar value, it can be used wherever a scalar value can be used:

```
$redfruits = $fruits{"apple"} + $fruits{"cherry"};
print("yes, we have no bananas\n") if ($fruits{"banana"} == 0);
```

Note that Perl uses braces (the `{` and `}` characters) to enclose the index of an associative array element. This makes it possible for Perl to distinguish between ordinary array elements and associative array elements.

Copying to and from Associative Arrays

Consider the following assignment, which initializes an associative array:

```
%fruits = ("apple", 9,
           "banana", 23,
           "cherry", 11);
```

The value on the right of this assignment is actually just the ordinary list, (`"apple"`, `9`, `"banana"`, `23`, `"cherry"`, `11`), grouped into pairs for readability. You can assign any list, including the contents of an array variable, to an associative array:

```
@numlist[0,1] = ("one", 1);
@numlist[2,3] = ("two", 2);
%numbers = @numlist;
$first = $numbers{"one"};    # $first is now 1
```

Whenever a list or an array variable is assigned to an associative array, the odd-numbered elements (the first, third, fifth, and so on) become the array indexes, and the even-numbered elements (the second, fourth, sixth, etc.) become the array values.

You can also assign an associative array to an array variable:

```
%numbers = ("one", 1,
            "two", 2);
@numlist = %numbers;
$first = $numlist[3];        # first is now 2
```

Here, the array indexes and array values both become elements of the array.

Adding and Deleting Array Elements

To add a new element to an associative array, just create a new array index and assign a value to its element. For example, to create a fourth element for the %fruits array, use the following:

```
$fruits{"orange"} = 1;
```

This statement creates a fourth element with index "orange" and gives it the value 1.

To delete an element, use the delete() function:

```
delete($fruits{"orange"});
```

This deletes the element indexed by "orange" from the array %fruits.

Listing Array Indexes and Values

The keys() function retrieves a list of the array indexes used in an associative array:

```
%fruits = ("apple", 9,
           "banana", 23,
           "cherry", 11);
@fruitindexes = keys(%fruits);
```

Here, @fruitindexes is assigned the list consisting of the elements "apple", "banana", and "cherry". Note that this list is in no particular order. To retrieve the list in alphabetic order, use sort() on the list:

```
@fruitindexes = sort(keys(%fruits));
```

This produces the list ("apple", "banana", "cherry").

To retrieve a list of the values stored in an associative array, use the function `values()`:

```
%fruits = ("apple", 9,
           "banana", 23,
           "cherry", 11);
@fruitvalues = values(%fruits);
```

`@fruitvalues` now contains a list consisting of the elements 9, 23, and 11 (again, in no particular order).

Looping with an Associative Array

Perl provides a convenient way to use an associative array in a loop:

```
%fruits = ("apple", 9,
           "banana", 23,
           "cherry", 11);
while (($fruitname, $fruitvalue) == each(%fruitnames) {
    ...
}
```

The `each()` function returns each element of the array in turn. Each element is returned as a two-element list (array index, then array value). Again, the elements are returned in no particular order.

Formatting Your Output

So far, the only output produced has been raw, unformatted output produced using the `print()` function. However, you can control how your output appears on the screen or on the printed page. To do this, define *print formats* and use the `write()` function to print output using these formats.

The following sections describe print formats and how to use them.

Defining a Print Format

Here is an example of a simple print format:

```
format MYFORMAT =
====================================
Here is the text I want to display.
====================================
.
```

Here, `MYFORMAT` is the name of the print format. This name must start with a letter, and can consist of any sequence of letters, digits, or underscores.

The subsequent lines define what is to appear on the screen. Here, the lines to be displayed are a line of = characters followed by a line of text and ending with another line of = characters. A line consisting of a period indicates the end of the print format definition.

Like subroutines, print formats can appear anywhere in a Perl program.

Displaying a Print Format

To print using a print format, use the `write()` function. For example, to print the text in `MYFORMAT`, use

```
$~ = "MYFORMAT";
write();
```

This sends

```
==================================
Here is the text I want to display.
==================================
```

to the standard output file.

`$~` is a special scalar variable used by Perl; it tells Perl which print format to use.

Displaying Values in a Print Format

To specify a value to be printed in your print format, add a *value field* to your print format. Here is an example of a print format that uses value fields:

```
format VOWELFORMAT =
=========================================================
Number of vowels found in text file:
        a: @<<<<< e: @<<<<< i: @<<<<< o: @<<<<< u: @<<<<<
$letter{"a"}, $letter{"e"}, $letter{"i"}, $letter{"o"}, $letter{"u"}
=========================================================
.
```

The line

```
a: @<<<<< e: @<<<<< i: @<<<<< o: @<<<<< u: @<<<<<
```

contains five value fields. Each value field contains special characters that provide information on how the value is to be displayed. (These special characters are described in the following section, "Choosing a Value Field Format.")

Any line that contains value fields must be followed by a line listing the scalar values (or variables containing scalar values) to be displayed in these value fields:

```
$letter{"a"}, $letter{"e"}, $letter{"i"}, $letter{"o"}, $letter{"u"}
```

The number of value fields must equal the number of scalar values.

Choosing a Value Field Format

The following value field formats are supported:

@<<<<	Left-justified output: width equals the number of characters supplied
@>>>>	Right-justified output: width equals the number of characters supplied
@||||	Centered output: width equals the number of characters supplied
@##.##	Fixed-precision numeric: . indicates location of decimal point
@*	Multi-line text

In all cases, the @ character is included when the number of characters in the field are counted. For example, the field @>>>> is five characters wide. Similarly, the field @###.## is seven characters wide: four before the decimal point, two after the decimal point, and the decimal point itself.

Writing to Other Output Files

You can also write to other files by using print formats and write(). For example, to write to the file represented by file variable MYFILE using print format MYFORMAT, use the following statements:

```
select(MYFILE);
$~ = "MYFORMAT";
write(MYFILE);
```

The select() statement indicates which file is to be written to, and the $~ = "MYFORMAT"; statement selects the print format to use.

Once an output file has been selected using select(), it stays selected until another select() is seen. This means that if you select an output file other than the standard output file, as in select(MYFILE);, output from write() won't go to the standard output file until Perl sees the statement select (MYFILE);.

There are two ways of making sure you don't get tripped up by this:

Always use STDOUT as the default output file. If you change the output file, change it back when you're done:

```
select(MYFILE);
$~ = "MYFORMAT";
write(MYFILE);
select(STDOUT);
```

Always specify the output file with select() before calling write():

```
select(STDOUT);
$~ = "MYFORMAT";
write();    # STDOUT is assumed
```

It doesn't really matter which solution you use, as long as you're consistent.

If you are writing a subroutine that writes to a particular output file, you can save the current selected output file in a temporary variable and restore it later:

```
$temp = select(MYFILE);    # select the output file
$~ = "MYFORMAT";
write(MYFILE);
select($temp); # restore the original selected output file
```

This method is also useful if you're in the middle of a large program and you don't remember which output file is currently selected.

Specifying a Page Header

You can specify a header to print when you start a new page. To do this, define a print format with the name filename_TOP, where filename is the name of the file variable corresponding to the file you are writing to. For example, to define a header for writing to standard output, define a print format named STDOUT_TOP:

```
format STDOUT_TOP =
page @<
$%
```

The system variable $% contains the current page number (starting with 1).

Setting the Page Length

If a page header is defined for a particular output file, write() automatically paginates the output to that file. When the number of lines printed is greater than the length of a page, it starts a new page.

By default, the page length is 60 lines. To specify a different page length, change the value stored in the system variable $=:

```
$= = 66;    # set the page length to 66 lines
```

This assignment must appear before the first write() statement.

Formatting Long Character Strings

A scalar variable containing a long character string can be printed out using multiple value fields:

```
format QUOTATION =
Quotation for the day:
------------------------------------------------------------
  ^<<<<<<<<<<<<<<<<<<<<<<<<<<<<<<<<<<<<<<<<<<<<<<<<
  $quotation
  ^<<<<<<<<<<<<<<<<<<<<<<<<<<<<<<<<<<<<<<<<<<<<<<<<
  $quotation
  ^<<<<<<<<<<<<<<<<<<<<<<<<<<<<<<<<<<<<<<<<<<<<<<<<
  $quotation
```

Here the value of $quotation is written on three lines. The @ character in the value fields is replaced by ^: this tells Perl to fill the lines as full as possible (cutting the string on a space or tab). Any of the value fields defined in "Choosing a Value Field Format" can be used.

If the quotation is too short to require all of the lines, the last line or lines are left blank. To define a line that is only used when necessary, put a ~ character in the first column:

```
~   ^<<<<<<<<<<<<<<<<<<<<<<<<<<<<<<<<<<<<<<<<<<<<<<<<<
```

To repeat a line as many times as necessary, put two ~ characters at the front:

```
~~  ^<<<<<<<<<<<<<<<<<<<<<<<<<<<<<<<<<<<<<<<<<<<<<<<<
```

> **CAUTION:** The contents of the scalar variable are destroyed by this write operation. To preserve the contents, make a copy before calling write().

Using Built-In Functions

The examples you have seen so far use some of the many built-in functions provided with Perl. The following table provides a more complete list.

For more details on these functions and others, see the online manual page for Perl.

Table 16.4. Built-In Functions.

alarm($scalar)	Deliver SIGALRM in $scalar seconds
atan2($v1, $v2)	Return arctangent of $v1/$v2
caller($scalar)	Return context of current subroutine
chdir($scalar)	Change working directory to $scalar
chmod(@array)	Change permissions of file list
chop($scalar)	Remove the last character of a string
chown(@array)	Change owner and group of file list
close(FILE)	Close a file
cos($scalar)	Return cosine of $scalar in radians
crypt($v1, $v2)	Encrypt a string
defined($scalar)	Determine whether $scalar is defined
delete($array{$val})	Delete value from associative array

continues

`die(@array)`	Print @array to STDERR and exit
`each(%array)`	Iterate through an associative array
`eof(FILE)`	Check whether FILE is at end of file
`eval($scalar)`	Treat $scalar as a subprogram
`exec(@array)`	Send @array to system as command
`exit($scalar)`	Exit program with status $scalar
`exp($scalar)`	Compute e ** $scalar
`fileno(FILE)`	Return file descriptor for FILE
`fork()`	Create parent and child processes
`getc(FILE)`	Get next character from FILE
`getlogin()`	Get current login from /etc/utmp
`gmtime($scalar)`	Convert time to GMT array
`grep($scalar, @array)`	Find $scalar in @array
`hex($scalar)`	Convert value to hexadecimal
`index($v1, $v2, $v3)`	Find $v2 in $v1 after position $v3
`int($scalar)`	Return integer portion of $scalar
`join($scalar, @array)`	Join array into single string
`keys(%array)`	Retrieve indexes of associative array
`length($scalar)`	Return length of $scalar
`link(FILE1, FILE2)`	Hard link FILE1 to FILE2
`localtime($scalar)`	Convert time to local array
`log($scalar)`	Get natural logarithm of $scalar
`mkdir(DIR, $scalar)`	Create directory
`oct($string)`	Convert value to octal
`open(FILE, $scalar)`	Open file
`ord($scalar)`	Return ASCII value of character
`pack($scalar, @array)`	Pack array into binary structure
`pipe(FILE1, FILE2)`	Open pair of pipes
`pop(@array)`	Pop last value of array
`print(FILE, @array)`	Print string, list or array
`push(@array, @array2)`	Push @array2 onto @array
`rand($scalar)`	Return random value
`readlink($scalar)`	Return value of symbolic link

`require($scalar)`	include library file $scalar
`reverse(@list)`	Reverse order of @list
`rindex($v1, $v2)`	Return last occurrence of $v2 in $v1
`scalar($val)`	Interpret $val as scalar
`shift(@array)`	Shift off first value of @array
`sin($scalar)`	Return sine of $scalar in radians
`sleep($scalar)`	Sleep for $scalar seconds
`sort(@array)`	Sort @array in alphabetical order
`splice(@a1, $v1, $v2, @a2)`	Replace elements in array
`split($v1, $v2)`	Split scalar into array
`sprintf($scalar, @array)`	Create formatted string
`sqrt($expr)`	Return square root of $expr
`srand($expr)`	Set random number seed
`stat(FILE)`	Retrieve file statistics
`substr($v1, $v2)`	Retrieve substring
`symlink(FILE1, FILE2)`	Create symbolic link
`system(@array)`	Execute system command
`time()`	Get current time
`undef($scalar)`	Mark $scalar as undefined
`unlink(@array)`	Unlink a list of files
`unpack($v1, $v2)`	Unpack array from binary structure
`unshift(@a1, @a2)`	Add @a2 to the front of @a1
`utime(@array)`	Change date stamp on files
`values(%array)`	Return values of associative array
`vec($v1, $v2, $v3)`	Treat string as vector array
`wait()`	Wait for child process to terminate
`write(FILE)`	Write formatted output

The $_ Variable

By default, any function that accepts a scalar variable can have its argument omitted. In this case, Perl uses $_, which is the default scalar variable.

$_ is also the default variable when reading from a file. So, for example, instead of writing

```
$var = <STDIN>;
chop($var);
```

you can write

```
chop(<STDIN>);
```

Summary

Perl is a programming language that allows you to write programs that manipulate files, strings, integers, and arrays quickly and easily. The features of Perl include:

- String and integer interchangeability
- Arithmetic, logical, bitwise, and string operators
- List, array, and associative array manipulation
- Control structures for handling program flow
- File input and output capability
- Subroutines
- Formatted output
- A wide range of built-in functions

The C Programming Language

17

By James Armstrong

C is the programming language most frequently associated with UNIX. Since the 1970s, the bulk of the operating system and applications have been written in C. This is one of the major reasons why UNIX is a portable operating system.

The History of C

C was first designed by Dennis Ritchie for use with UNIX on DEC PDP-11 computers. The language evolved from Martin Richard's BCPL, and one of its earlier forms was the B language, which was written by Ken Thompson for the DEC PDP-7. The first book on C was *The C Programming Language* by Brian Kernighan and Dennis Ritchie, published in 1978.

In 1983, the American National Standards Institute established a committee to standardize the definition of C. Termed *ANSI C,* it is the recognized standard for the language grammar and a core set of libraries. The syntax is slightly different from the original C language, which is frequently called *K&R*—for Kernighan and Ritchie.

Creating, Compiling, and Executing Your First Program

The development of a C program is an iterative procedure. Many UNIX tools are involved in this four-step process. They are familiar to software developers:

1. Using an editor, write the code into a text file.
2. Compile the program.
3. Execute the program.
4. Debug the program.

The first two steps are repeated until the program compiles successfully. Then the execution and debugging begin. Many of the concepts presented may seem strange to non-programmers. This chapter endeavors to introduce C as a programming language.

The typical first C program is almost a cliché. It is the "Hello, World" program, and it prints the simple line `Hello, World`. Listing 17.1 is the source of the program.

Listing 17.1. Source of `Hello World`.

```
main()
{
printf("Hello, World\n");
}
```

This program can be compiled and executed as follows:

```
$ cc hello.c
$ a.out
Hello, World
$
```

The program is compiled with the `cc` command, which creates a program `a.out` if the code is correct. Just typing `a.out` will run the program. The program includes only one function, `main`. Every C program must have a `main` function; it is where the program's execution begins. The only statement is a call to the `printf` library function, which passes the string `Hello, World\n`. (Functions are described in detail later in this chapter.) The last two characters of the string, `\n`, represent the carriage return-line feed character.

An Overview of the C Language

As with all programming languages, C programs must follow rules. These rules describe how a program should appear, and what those words and symbols mean. This is the syntax of a programming language. Think of a program as a story. Each sentence must have a noun and a verb. Sentences form paragraphs, and the paragraphs tell the story. Similarly, C statements can build into functions and programs.

For more information about programming in C, I recommend the following books from Sams Publishing:

- *Teach Yourself C in 21 Days* by Peter Aitken and Bradley Jones
- *Programming in ANSI C* by Stephen G. Kochan

Elementary C Syntax

Like all languages, C deals primarily with the manipulation and presentation of data. BCPL deals with data as data. C, however, goes one step further to use the concept of data types. The basic data types are character, integer, and floating point numbers. Other data types are built from these three basic types.

Integers are the basic mathematical data type. They can be classified as `long` and `short` integers, and the size is implementation-dependent. With a few exceptions, integers are four bytes in length, and they can range from 2,147,483,648 to 2,147,483,647. In ANSI C, these values are defined in a header—`limit.h`—as `INT_MIN` and `INT_MAX`. The qualifier `unsigned` moves the range one bit higher, to the equivalent of `INT_MAX-INT_MIN`.

Floating point numbers are used for more complicated mathematics. Integer mathematics is limited to integer results. With integers, 3/2 equals 1. Floating point numbers give a greater amount of precision to mathematical calculations: 3/2 equals 1.5. Floating point numbers can be represented by a decimal number, such as 687.534, or with scientific notation: 8.87534E+2. For larger numbers, scientific notation is preferred. For even greater precision, the type `double` provides a greater range. Again, specific ranges are implementation-dependent.

Characters are usually implemented as single bytes, although some international character sets require two bytes. One common set of character representations is ASCII, and is found on most U.S. computers.

An array is used for a sequence of values that are often position-dependent. An array is useful when a range of values of a given type is needed. Related to the array is the pointer. Variables are stored in memory, and a pointer is the physical address of that memory. In a sense, a pointer and an array are similar, except when a program is invoked. The space needed for the data of an array is allocated when the routine that needs the space is invoked. For a pointer, the space must be allocated by the programmer, or the variable must be assigned by dereferencing a variable. The ampersand is used to indicate dereferencing, and an asterisk is used to when the value pointed at is required. Here are some sample declarations:

`int i;`	Declares an integer
`char c;`	Declares a character
`char *ptr;`	Declares a pointer to a character
`double temp[16];`	Declares an array of double-precision floating point numbers with 16 values

Listing 17.2 shows an example of a program with pointers.

Listing 17.2. An example of a program with pointers.

```
int i;
int *ptr;

i=5;
ptr = &i;
printf("%d %x %d\n", i,ptr,*ptr);

output is: 5 f7fffa6c 5
```

NOTE: A pointer is just a memory address and will tell you the address of any variable.

There is no specific type for a string. An array of characters is used to represent strings. They can be printed using an `%s` flag, instead of `%c`.

Simple output is created by the printf function. printf takes a format string and the list of arguments to be printed. A complete set of format options is presented in Table 17.1. Format options can be modified with sizes. Check the documentation for the full specification.

Table 17.1. Format conversions for printf.

Conversion	Meaning
%%	Percentage sign
%E	Double (scientific notation)
%G	Double (format depends on value)
%X	Hexadecimal (letters are capitalized)
%c	Single character
%d	Integer
%e	Double (scientific notation)
%f	Double of the form mmm.ddd
%g	Double (format depends on value)
%i	Integer
%ld	Long integer
%n	Count of characters written in current printf
%o	Octal
%p	Print as a pointer
%s	Character pointer (string)
%u	Unsigned integer
%x	Hexadecimal

Some characters cannot be included easily in a program. New lines, for example, require a special escape sequence, because there cannot be an unescaped newline in a string. Table 17.2 contains a complete list of escape sequences.

Table 17.2. Escape characters for strings.

Escape Sequence	Meaning
\"	Double quote
\'	Single quote
\?	Question mark

continues

Table 17.2. Continued.

Escape Sequence	Meaning
\\	Backslash
\a	Audible bell
\b	Backspace
\f	Form feed (new page)
\n	New line
\ooo	Octal number
\r	Carriage return
\t	Horizontal tab
\v	Vertical tab
\xhh	Hexadecimal number

A full program is compilation of statements. Statements are separated by semicolons. They can be grouped in blocks of statements surrounded by curly braces. The simplest statement is an assignment. A variable on the left side is assigned the value of an expression on the right.

Expressions

At the heart of the C programming language are expressions. These are techniques to combine simple values into new values. There are three basic types of expressions: comparison, numerical, and bitwise expressions.

Comparison Expressions

The simplest expression is a comparison. A comparison evaluates to a TRUE or a FALSE value. In C, TRUE is a non-zero value, and FALSE is a zero value. Table 17.3 contains a list of comparison operators.

Table 17.3. Comparison operators.

Operator	Meaning	Operator	Meaning
<	Less than	>=	Greater than or equal to
>	Greater than	||	Or
==	Equal to	&&	And
<=	Less than or equal to		

Expressions can be built by combining simple comparisons with ANDs and ORs to make complex expressions. Consider the definition of a leap year. In words, it is any year divisible by 4, except a year divisible by 100 unless that year is divisible by 400. If year is the variable, a leap year can be defined with this expression.

```
((((year%4)==0)&&((year%100)!=0))||((year%400)==0))
```

On first inspection, this code might look complicated, but it isn't. The parentheses group the simple expressions with the ANDs and ORs to make a complex expression.

Mathematical Expressions

One convenient aspect of C is that expressions can be treated as mathematical values, and mathematical statements can be used in expressions. In fact, any statement—even a simple assignment—has values that can be used in other places as an expression.

The mathematics of C is straightforward. Barring parenthetical groupings, multiplication and division have higher precedence than addition and subtraction. The operators are standard. They are listed in Table 17.4.

Table 17.4. Mathematical operators.

Operator	Meaning	Operator	Meaning
+	Addition	/	Division
-	Subtraction	%	Integer remainder
*	Multiplication	^	Exponentiation

There are also unary operators, which effect a single variable. These are ++ (increment by one) and — (decrement by one). These shorthand versions are quite useful.

There are also shorthands for situations in which you want to change the value of a variable. For example, if you want to add an expression to a variable called a and assign the new value to a, the shorthand a+=expr is the same as a=a+expr. The expression can be as complex or as simple as required.

> **NOTE:** Most UNIX functions take advantage of the truth values and return 0 for success. This enables a programmer to write code such as
>
> ```
> if (function())
>        {
> ```

```
     error condition
     }
```
The return value of a function determines whether the function worked.

Bitwise Operations

Because a variable is just a string of bits, many operations work on those bit patterns. Table 17.5 lists the bit operators.

Table 17.5. Bit operators.

Operator	Meaning	Operator	Meaning
&	Logical AND	<<	Bit shift left
¦	Logical OR	>>	Bit shift right

A logical AND compares the individual bits in place. If both are 1, the value 1 is assigned to the expression. Otherwise, 0 is assigned. For a logical OR, 1 is assigned if either value is a 1. Bit shift operations move the bits a number of positions to the right or left. Mathematically, this is the same as multiplying or dividing by 2, but circumstances exist where the bit shift is preferred.

Bit operations are often used for masking values and for comparisons. A simple way to determine whether a value is odd or even is to perform a logical AND with the integer value 1. If it is TRUE, the number is odd.

Statement Controls

With what you've seen so far, you can create a list of statements that are executed only once, after which the program terminates. To control the flow of commands, three types of loops exist in C. The simplest is the `while` loop. The syntax is

```
while (expression)
      statement
```

So long as the expression between parentheses evaluates as non-zero—or TRUE in C—the statement is executed. The statement actually can be a list of statements blocked off with curly braces. If the expression evaluates to zero the first time it is reached, the statement is never executed. To force at least one execution of the statement, use a `do` loop. The syntax for a `do` loop is

```
do
      statement
      while (expression);
```

The third type of control flow is the `for` loop. This is more complicated. The syntax is

```
for(expr1;expr2;expr3) statement
```

When the expression is reached for the first time, `expr1` is evaluated. Next, `expr2` is evaluated. If `expr2` is non-zero, the statement is executed, followed by `expr3`. Then, `expr2` is tested again, followed by the statement and `expr3`, until `expr2` evaluates to zero. Strictly speaking, this is a notational convenience, for a `while` loop can be structured to perform the same actions. For example,

```
expr1;
while (expr2) {
      statement;
      expr3
      }
```

Loops can be interrupted in three ways. A `break` statement terminates execution in a loop and exits it. `continue` terminates the current iteration and retests the loop before possibly re-executing the statement. For an unconventional exit, you can use `goto`. `goto` changes the program's execution to a labelled statement. According to many programmers, `goto` is poor programming practice, and you should avoid using it.

Statements can also be executed conditionally. Again, there are three different formats for statement execution. The simplest is an `if` statement. The syntax is

```
if (expr) statement
```

If the expression `expr` evaluates to non-zero, the statement is executed. You can expand this with an `else`, the second type of conditional execution. The syntax for `else` is

```
if (expr) statement else statement
```

If the expression evaluates to zero, the second statement is executed.

NOTE: The second statement in an `else` condition can be another `if` statement. This situation might cause the grammar to be indeterminant if the structure

```
if (expr) if (expr) statment else statement
```

is not parsed cleanly.

As the code is written, the `else` is considered applicable to the second `if`. To make it applicable with the first `if`, surround the second `if` statement with curly braces. For example:

```
$ if (expr) {if (expr) statement} else statement
```

The third type of conditional execution is more complicated. The `switch` statement first evaluates an expression. Then it looks down a series of `case` statements to find a label that matches the expression's value and executes the statements following the label. A special label `default` exists if no other conditions are met. If you want only a set of statements executed for each label, you must use the `break` statement to leave the `switch` statement.

This covers the simplest building blocks of a C program. You can add more power by using functions and by declaring complex data types.

If your program requires different pieces of data to be grouped on a consistent basis, you can group them into structures. Listing 17.3 shows a structure for a California driver's license. Note that it includes integer, character, and character array (string) types.

Listing 17.3. An example of a structure.

```
struct license {
        char name[128];
        char address[3][128];
        int zipcode;
        int height, weight,month, day, year;
        char license_letter;
        int license_number;
        };

struct license licensee;
struct license *user;
```

Since California driver's license numbers consist of a single character followed by a seven digit number, the license ID is broken into two components. Similarly, the licensee's address is broken into three lines, represented by three arrays of 128 characters.

Accessing individual fields of a structure requires two different techniques. To read a member of a locally defined structure, you append a dot to the variable, then the field name. For example:

```
licensee.zipcode=94404;
```

To use a pointer, to the structure, you need `->` to point to the member:

```
user->zipcode=94404;
```

Interestingly, if the structure pointer is incremented, the address is increased not by 1, but by the size of the structure.

Functions are an easy way to group statements and to give them a name. These are usually related statements that perform repetitive tasks such as I/O. `printf`, described above, is a function. It is provided with the standard C library. Listing 17.4 illustrates a function definition, a function call, and a function.

> **NOTE:** The three-dot ellipsis simply means that some lines of sample code are not shown here, in order to save space.

Listing 17.4. An example of a function.

```
int swapandmin( int *, int *);      /* Function declaration */

...

int i,j,lower;

i=2; j=4;
lower=swapandmin(&i, &j);           /* Function call */

...

int swapandmin(int *a,int *b)       /* Function definition */
{
int tmp;

tmp=(*a);
(*a)=(*b);
(*b)=tmp;
if ((*a)<(*b)) return(*a);
return(*b);
}
```

ANSI C and K&R differ most in function declarations and calls. ANSI requires that function arguments be prototyped when the function is declared. K&R required only the name and the type of the returned value. The declaration in Listing 17.4 states that a function swapandmin will take two pointers to integers as arguments and that it will return an integer. The function call takes the addresses of two integers and sets the variable named lower with the return value of the function.

When a function is called from a C program, the values of the arguments are passed to the function. Therefore, if any of the arguments will be changed for the calling function, you can't pass only the variable—you must pass the address, too. Likewise, to change the value of the argument in the calling routine of the function, you must assign the new value to the address.

In the function in Listing 17.4, the value pointed to by a is assigned to the tmp variable. b is assigned to a, and tmp is assigned to b. *a is used instead of a to ensure that the change is reflected in the calling routine. Finally, the values of *a and *b are compared, and the lower of the two is returned.

If you included the line

```
printf("%d %d %d",lower,i,j);
```

after the function call, you would see 2 4 2 on the output.

This sample function is quite simple, and it is ideal for a macro. A macro is a technique used to replace a token with different text. You can use macros to make code more readable. For example, you might use EOF instead of (-1) to indicate the end of a file. You can also use macros to replace code. Listing 17.5 is the same as Listing 17.4 except that it uses macros.

Listing 17.5. An example of macros.

```
#define SWAP(X,Y) {int tmp; tmp=X; X=Y; Y=tmp; }
#define MIN(X,Y) ((X<Y) ? X : Y )

...

int i,j,lower;

i=2; j=4;
SWAP(i,j);
lower=MIN(i,j);
```

When a C program is compiled, macro replacement is one of the first steps performed. Listing 17.6 illustrates the result of the replacement.

Listing 17.6. An example of macro replacement.

```
int i,j,lower;

i=2; j=4;
{int tmp; tmp=i; i=j; j=tmp; };
lower= ((i<j) ? i : j );
```

The macros make the code easier to read and understand.

Creating a Simple Program

For your first program, write a program that prints a chart of the first ten integers and their squares, cubes, and square roots.

Writing the Code

Using the text editor of your choice, enter all the code in Listing 17.7 and save it in a file called `sample.c`.

Listing 17.7. Source code for `sample.c`.

```c
#include <stdio.h>
#include <math.h>

main()
{
int i;
double a;

for(i=1;i<11;i++)
        {
        a=i*1.0;
        printf("%2d. %3d %4d %7.5f\n",i,i*i,i*i*i,sqrt(a));
        }
}
```

The first two lines are header files. The `stdio.h` file provides the function definitions and structures associated with the C input and output libraries. The `math.h` file includes the definitions of mathematical library functions. You need it for the square root function.

The `main` loop is the only function that you need to write for this example. It takes no arguments. You define two variables. One is the integer `i`, and the other is a double-precision floating point number called a. You wouldn't have to use a, but you can for the sake of convenience.

The program is a simple `for` loop that starts at 1 and ends at 11. It increments `i` by 1 each time through. When `i` equals 11, the `for` loop stops executing. You could have also written `i<=10`, because the expressions have the same meaning.

First, you multiply `i` by 1.0 and assign the product to a. A simple assignment would also work, but the multiplication reminds you that you are converting the value to a double-precision floating point number.

Next, you call the `print` function. The format string includes three integers of widths 2, 3, and 4. After the first integer is printed, you print a period. After the first integer is printed, you print a floating point number that is seven characters wide with five digits following the decimal point. The arguments after the format string show that you print the integer, the square of the integer, the cube of the integer, and the square root of the integer.

Compiling the Program

To compile this program using the C compiler, enter the following command:

```
cc sample.c -lm
```

This command produces an output file called a.out. This is the simplest use of the C compiler. It is one of the most powerful and flexible commands on a UNIX system.

A number of different flags can change the compiler's output. These flags are often dependent on the system or compiler. Some flags are common to all C compilers. These are described in the following paragraphs.

The -o flag tells the compiler to write the output to the file named after the flag. The cc -o sample sample.c command would put the program in a file named sample.

> **NOTE:** The output discussed here is the compiler's output, not the sample program. Compiler output is usually the program, and in every example here, it is an executable program.

The -g flag tells the compiler to keep the symbol table (the data used by a program to associate variable names with memory locations), which is necessary for debuggers. Its opposite is the -O flag, which tells the compiler to optimize the code—that is, to make it more efficient. You can change the search path for header files with the -I flag, and you can add libraries with the -l and -L flags.

The compilation process takes place in several steps.

1. First, the C preprocessor parses the file. To parse the file, it sequentially reads the lines, includes header files, and performs macro replacement.

2. The compiler parses the modified code for correct syntax. This builds a symbol table and creates an intermediate object format. Most symbols have specific memory addresses assigned, although symbols defined in other modules, such as external variables, do not.

3. The last compilation stage, linking, ties together different files and libraries and links the files by resolving the symbols that have not been resolved yet.

Executing the Program

The output from this program appears in Listing 17.8.

Listing 17.8. Output from the `sample.c` program.

```
$ sample.c
 1.    1     1 1.00000
 2.    4     8 1.41421
 3.    9    27 1.73205
 4.   16    64 2.00000
 5.   25   125 2.23607
 6.   36   216 2.44949
 7.   49   343 2.64575
 8.   64   512 2.82843
 9.   81   729 3.00000
10.  100  1000 3.16228
```

NOTE: To execute a program, just type its name at a shell prompt. The output will immediately follow.

Building Large Applications

C programs can be broken into any number of files, so long as no function spans more than one file. To compile this program, you compile each source file into an intermediate object before you link all the objects into a single executable. The -c flag tells the compiler to stop at this stage. During the link stage, all the object files should be listed on the command line. Object files are identified by the .o suffix.

Making Libraries with *ar*

If several different programs use the same functions, they can be combined in a single library archive. The ar command is used to build a library. When this library is included on the compile line, the archive is searched to resolve any external symbols. Listing 17.9 shows an example of building and using a library.

Listing 17.9. Building a large application.

```
cc -c sine.c
cc -c cosine.c
cc -c tangent.c
ar c libtrig.a sine.o cosine.o tangent.o

cc -c mainprog.c
cc -o mainprog mainprog.o libtrig.a
```

Building Large Applications with *make*

Of course, managing the process of compiling large applications can be difficult. UNIX provides a tool that takes care of this for you. make looks for a makefile, which includes directions for building the application.

You can think of the makefile as being its own programming language. The syntax is

```
target: dependencies
        Commandlist
```

Dependencies can be targets declared elsewhere in the makefile, and they can have their own dependencies. When a make command is issued, the target on the command line is checked; if no targets are specified on the command line, the first target listed in the file is checked.

When make tries to build a target, first the dependencies list is checked. If any of them requires rebuilding, it is rebuilt. Then, the command list specified for the target itself is executed.

make has its own set of default rules, which are executed if no other rules are specified. One rule specifies that an object is created from a C source file using $(cc) $(CFLAGS) -c (source file). CFLAGS is a special variable; a list of flags that will be used with each compilation can be stored there. These flags can be specified in the makefile, on the make command line, or in an environment variable. make checks the dependencies to determine whether a file needs to be made. It uses the mtime field of a file's status. If the file has been modified more recently than the target, the target is remade.

Listing 17.10 shows an example of a makefile.

Listing 17.10. An example of a makefile.

```
CFLAGS= -g

igfl: igfl.o igflsubs.o
        cc -g -o igfl igfl.o igflsubs.o -lm

igflsubs.o: igfl.h

clean:
        rm -f *.o
```

Listing 17.10 uses several targets to make a single executable called igfl. The two C files are compiled into objects by implicit rules. Only igflsubs.o is dependent on a file, igfl.h. If igfl.h has been modified more recently than igflsubs.o, a new igfl.o is compiled.

Note that there is a target called `clean`. Because there are no dependencies, the command is always executed when `clean` is specified. This command removes all the intermediate files. Listing 17.11 shows the output of `make` when it is executed for the first time.

Listing 17.11. Output of `make`.

```
cc -g  -target sun4 -c  igfl.c
cc -g  -target sun4 -c  igflsubs.c
cc -g -o igfl igfl.o igflsubs.o -lm
```

Debugging Tools

Debugging is a science and an art unto itself. Sometimes, the simplest tool—the code listing—is best. At other times, however, you need to use other tools. Three of these tools are `lint`, `prof`, and `sdb`. Other available tools include `escape`, `cxref`, and `cb`. Many UNIX commands have debugging uses.

`lint` is a command that examines source code for possible problems. The code might meet the standards for C and compile cleanly, but it might not execute correctly. Two things checked by `lint` are type mismatches and incorrect argument counts on function calls. `lint` uses the C preprocessor, so you can use similar command-like options as you would use for `cc`.

The `prof` command is used to study where a program is spending its time. If a program is compiled and linked with `-p` as a flag, when it executes, a `mon.out` file is created with data on how often each function is called and how much time is spent in each function. This data is parsed and displayed with `prof`. An analysis of the output generated by `prof` helps you determine where performance bottlenecks occur. Although optimizing compilers can speed your programs, this analysis significantly improves program performance.

The third tool is `sdb`—a symbolic debugger. When a program is compiled with `-g`, the symbol tables are retained, and a symbolic debugger can be used to track program bugs. The basic technique is to invoke `sdb` after a core dump and get a stack trace. This indicates the source line where the core dump occurred and the functions that were called to reach that line. Often, this is enough to identify the problem. It is not the limit of `sdb`, though.

`sdb` also provides an environment for debugging programs interactively. Invoking `sdb` with a program enables you to set breakpoints, examine variable values, and monitor variables. If you suspect a problem near a line of code, you can set a breakpoint at that line and run the program. When the line is reached, execution is interrupted. You can check variable values, examine the stack trace, and observe the program's environment. You can single-step through the program, checking values. You can resume execution at any point. By using breakpoints, you can discover many of the bugs in your code that you've missed.

cpp is another tool that can be used to debug programs. It will perform macro replacements, include headers, and parse the code. The output is the actual module to be compiled. Normally, though, cpp is never executed by the programmer directly. Instead it is invoked through cc with either a -E or -P option. -E will put the output directly to the terminal; -P will make a file with a .i suffix.

Summary

In this chapter, we've discussed the basics of the C language: building C programs, running them, and debugging them. While this overview isn't enough to make you an expert C programmer, you can now understand how programmers develop their products. You should also be able to read a C program and know what the program is doing.

PART

4

Process Control

What Is a Process?

18

By Rachel and
Robert Sartin

IN THIS CHAPTER

This chapter introduces the concept of processes and how you use UNIX to interact with them.

What Happens When You Execute a Command?

When you execute a program on your UNIX system, the system creates a special environment for that program. This environment contains everything needed for the system to run the program as if no other program were running on the system.

Forking a Process

Each process has *process context*, which is everything that is unique about the state of the program you are currently running. The process context includes then following:

- The *text* (program instructions) being run
- The memory used by the program being run
- The current working directory
- The files that are open and positions in the files
- Resource limits
- Access control information
- Others—various low-level information

Every time you execute a program the UNIX system does a *fork*, which performs a series of operations to create a process context and then execute your program in that context. The steps include the following:

1. Allocate a slot in the *process table*, a list of currently running programs kept by UNIX. UNIX creates the illusion of multiple programs running simultaneously by switching quickly between active processes in the process table. This allocation can fail for a number of reasons, including these:

   - You have exceeded your *per user* process limit, the maximum number of processes your UNIX system will allow you to run.
   - The system runs out of open *process slots*. The UNIX kernel stores information about currently running processes in a table of processes. When this table runs out of room for new entries, you are unable to fork a new process.
   - UNIX has run out of memory and does not have room for the text and data of the new process.

2. Assign a unique *process identifier* (PID) to the process. This identifier can be used to examine and control the process later.

3. Copy the context of the *parent*, the process that requested the spawning of the new process.

4. Return the new PID to the parent process. This enables the parent process to examine or control the process directly.

After the fork is complete, UNIX runs your program. One of the differences between UNIX and many other operating systems is that UNIX performs this two-step procedure to run a program. The first step is to create a new process that's just like the parent. The second is to execute a different program. This procedure allows interesting variations. (See the section "A Special Process Called Daemon.")

Running a Command

When you enter `ls` to look at the contents of your current working directory, UNIX does a series of things to create an environment for `ls` and the run it:

1. The shell has UNIX perform a fork. This creates a new process that the shell will use to run the `ls` program.

2. The shell has UNIX perform an *exec* of the `ls` program. This replaces the shell program and data with the program and data for `ls` and then starts running that new program.

3. The `ls` program is loaded into the new process context, replacing the text and data of the shell.

4. The `ls` program performs its task, listing the contents of the current directory.

Looking at Processes

Because processes are so important to getting things done, UNIX has several commands that enable you to examine processes and modify their state. The most frequently used command is `ps`, which prints out the process status for processes running on your system. Each system has a slightly different version of the `ps` command, but there are two main variants, the System V version and the Berkeley version, covered in this section. Different versions of `ps` do similar things, but have somewhat different output and are controlled using different options. The X/Open Portability Guide makes an attempt to standardize somewhat on output of the `ps` command. The `ps` command is covered in more detail in chapter 19, "Administrative Processes."

On a System V or XPG-compliant system, you can examine all the processes you are running by entering `ps -f` and you will get output such as the following:

```
$ ps -f
     UID   PID  PPID  C    STIME TTY       TIME COMMAND
    root 14931   136  0 08:37:48 ttys0     0:00 rlogind
  sartin 14932 14931  0 08:37:50 ttys0     0:00 -sh
  sartin 15339 14932  7 16:32:29 ttys0     0:00 ps -f
$
```

> **NOTE:** After the first line, which is the header, each line of output tells about the status of a single process. The UID column tells the owner of the process. The PID column tells the process ID. The PPID tells the process ID of the parent process (the process that executed the fork). The STIME is the time the process began executing. The TIME is the amount of computer time the process has used. The COMMAND field tells what command line was executed.

Look at this example and you can see that *root* (the system administration user) is running rlogind as process 14931. This process is a special kind of administrative program, called a daemon (daemons are described in the section "A Special Process Called Daemon"). This particular daemon is responsible for managing a connection from rlogin, which is described in Chapter 8, "Getting Around the Network." As you can see from the next line, there is a process called -sh, which is a Bourne shell. The shell has rlogind as its parent because the daemon did a fork to run the login shell. Similarly, there is a ps -f command that has the shell as its parent.

> **TIP:** The leading hyphen on the -sh in the output of ps means that the shell is executing as a *login shell*, which does certain special processing that other instances of the shell do not. See the chapter on your shell for more information on login shells.

Visiting the Shell Again

Earlier in this chapter you learned that the shell creates a new process for each command you execute. This section covers in a bit more detail how the shell creates and manages processes.

Processing a Command

When you type a command to your shell user interface, the shell performs a series of tasks to process the command. Although the steps may seem a bit cumbersome at first, they create an environment that is highly flexible.

Checking the Aliases and Built-Ins

The first thing the shell does is alias and built-in processing to see if your command is one of the shell's internally implemented functions. Each shell implements a number of functions internally either because external implementation would be difficult (for example, while loops) or because internal implementation is a big performance win (for example, echo in some shells). One reason the built-in commands are easier is that they can operate directly in the shell process rather than forcing the shell to create a new process to run a different command. That new command would not have access to the shell's memory.

Make a New Process with *fork*

If the command you typed is not a built-in command (for example, if you entered ps), the shell performs a fork to create a new process. Your UNIX system allocates the necessary resources. The shell modifies the process environment to configure correctly for the command to be executed. This includes any input or output redirect you may have requested (including command pipelines) and creating a new background process group if you executed the command in the background.

Start a New Command with *exec*

Finally, the shell performs an exec to execute the program that you requested. The program will replace the shell with a forked shell, but your shell will still be running.

An Example

The following happens when you enter ps -f > t1 followed by cat t1:

```
$ ps -f > t1
$ cat t1
     UID   PID  PPID  C    STIME TTY     TIME COMMAND
    root 14931   136  0 08:37:48 ttys0   0:00 rlogind
  sartin 14932 14931  0 08:37:50 ttys0   0:00 -sh
  sartin 15339 14932  7 16:32:29 ttys0   0:00 ps -f
$
```

UNIX performs the following steps to execute ps -f> t1:

1. **Shell command processing.** The login shell (PID 14932 in this example) performs variable substitution and examines the command line to determine that ps is not a built-in or an alias.

2. **fork/wait.** The login shell (PID 14932) forks a new process (PID 15339). This new process is an exact copy of the login shell. It has the same open files, the same user ID, and a copy of the memory, and it is executing the same code. Because the command was not executed in the background, the login shell (14932) will execute a wait to wait for the new child (15339) to complete.

3. **setup.** The new shell (PID 15339) performs the operations it needs to do in order to prepare for the new program. In this case, it redirects the standard output to a file (if it existed) in the current directory named t1, overwriting the file.

4. **exec.** The new shell (PID 15339) asks the UNIX system to exec the ps command with -f as its argument. UNIX throws away the memory from the shell and loads the ps command code and data into the process memory. The ps command will run and write its output to the standard output, which has been redirected to the file t1.

5. **wait ends.** When the ps command is done executing, the login shell (PID 14932) receives notification and will prompt the user for more input.

Executing in the Background

You can tell your shell to execute commands in the *background*, which tells the shell not to wait for the command to complete. This enables you to run programs without having to wait for them to complete.

> **TIP:** For long-running commands that are not interactive, you can run the command in the background and continue to do work while it executes. Use the nohup command to make sure the process will not get interrupted; nohup will redirect the command output to a file called nohup.out. For example, to run a make in the background enter nohup make all. When the make terminates, you can read nohup.out to check the output.

An Example

This example is almost the same as the previous example. The only difference is that the ps command is executed in the background. The following happens when you are using the Bourne shell and enter ps -f > t1 & followed by cat t1:

```
$ ps -f > t1 &
15445
$ cat t1
       UID  PID  PPID  C    STIME TTY       TIME COMMAND
     root 14931   136  1 08:37:48 ttys0     0:00 rlogind
   sartin 14932 14931  0 08:37:50 ttys0     0:00 -sh
   sartin 15445 14932  8 17:31:14 ttys0     0:00 ps -f
$
```

> **WARNING:** Do not depend on the output of a background process until you know the process has completed. If the command is still running when you examine the output, you may see incomplete output.

UNIX performs the following steps to execute `ps -f > t1 &`:

1. **Shell command processing.** The login shell (PID 14932 in this example) performs variable substitution and examines the command line to determine that `ps` is not a built-in or an alias.

2. **fork.** The login shell (PID 14932) forks a new process (PID 15445). This new process is an exact copy of the login shell. It has the same open files, the same user ID, and a copy of the memory, and it is executing the same code. Because the command was executed in the background, the login shell (14932) will immediately prompt you for input. Because your background command may still be running, you should not depend on its output until you know the process completed. You will be able to run a new command immediately.

3. **setup.** The new shell (PID 15445) performs the operations it needs to do in order to prepare for the new program. In this case, it redirects the standard output to a file in the current directory named `t1`, overwriting the file (if it existed).

4. **exec.** The new shell (PID 15445) asks the UNIX system to exec the `ps` command with `-f` as its argument. UNIX throws away the memory from the shell and loads the `ps` command code and data into the process memory. The `ps` command will run and write its output to the standard output, which has been redirected to the file `t1`.

Kinks in Your Pipeline

One of the things the fork/exec model enables is creating command *pipelines*, a series of commands with the output of one command as the input for the next. This powerful notion is one of the major advantages of UNIX over some other systems. See Chapter 1, "Operating Systems."

Creating a pipeline is similar to creating an ordinary command. The difference is in how output is redirected. In the ordinary case, the shell performs some simple I/O redirection before executing the program. In the pipeline case, the shell will instead connect the standard output of one command as the standard input of another.

If you enter ps -f ¦ grep sartin you might get output such as the following:

```
$ ps -f ¦ grep sartin
  sartin 14932 14931  1 08:37:50 ttys0   0:00 -sh
  sartin 15424 14932  1 17:15:02 ttys0   0:00 grep sartin
  sartin 15425 15424  7 17:15:02 ttys0   0:00 ps -f
$
```

> **NOTE:** Some shells perform these tasks in slightly different orders. This example illustrates what one version of the Bourne shell does. Variations are relatively minor and involve the details of which process does the extra fork calls.

In order to get this output, the shell went through the following series of steps:

1. **fork (1).**   The login shell (PID 14932) forks a new process (15424) to execute the pipeline. This subprocess (15424) redirects input, or creates a pipe, so that standard input is from a pipe. The login shell (14932) then waits for the pipeline execution to complete.

2. **fork (2).**   The shell subprocess (15424) forks another new process (15425) to help execute the pipeline. This new subprocess (15425) connects its standard output to the pipe that its parent (15424) is using for input.

3. **exec (1).**   The first subprocess (15424) executes the grep program.

4. **exec (2).**   The second subprocess (15425) executes the ps program.

> ### Avoiding the Background with GUI
>
> With the advent of graphical user interfaces (GUIs) on UNIX, you do not need to use background processes to be able to run multiple programs at once. Instead, you can run each command either from a graphical interface or from its own terminal window. This can be very resource intensive, so don't try to do too many things at once.

A Special Process Called Daemon

As you learned in Chapter 1, many of the features that are sometimes implemented as part of the *kernel,* the core of the operating system, are not in the UNIX kernel. Instead, many of these features are implemented using special processes called daemons. A *daemon* is a process that detaches itself from the terminal and runs, disconnected, in the background, waiting for requests and responding to them. Many system functions are commonly performed by daemons, including the sendmail daemon, which handles mail, and the NNTP daemon, which handles USENET news. Many other daemons may exist on your system; check the documentation for more information.

Generally only system administrators need to know about most daemons, but there are three daemons that are important and widespread enough that you should probably have a minimal understanding of what they do; they are init, inetd, and cron.

init

In a way the init program is the "super daemon." It takes over the basic running of the system when the kernel has finished the boot process. It is responsible for the following:

- **Running scripts that change state.**   Every time the system administrator switches the system to a new state, init runs any programs needed to update the system to the new state.

- **Managing terminals.**   Each physical terminal is monitored by a program called getty; it is the job of init to keep getty properly running and shut it down when the system administrator disables logins. On systems with GUI consoles, init may be responsible for keeping the graphical login program running.

- *Reaping* **processes.**   When a process terminates, UNIX keeps some status information around until the parent process reads that information. Sometimes the parent process terminates before the child. Sometimes the parent process terminates without reading the status of the child. Any time either of these happens, UNIX makes init the parent process of the resulting *zombie* process, and init must read the process status so that UNIX can reuse the process slot. Sometimes, init isn't able to do the job of releasing zombies, too. However, this is unusual in most of the recent UNIX-based systems.

For further information on init, see Chapter 34, "Starting Up and Shutting Down."

inetd

A second powerful daemon is the inetd program common to many UNIX machines (including those based on BSD and many that are based on System V). The inetd process is the network "super server" daemon. It is responsible for starting network services that do not have their own stand-alone daemons. For example, inetd usually takes care of incoming rlogin, telnet, and ftp connections. (See Chapter 9, "Getting Around the Network.")

For further information on inetd, see Chapter 37, "Networking."

cron

Another common daemon is the cron program, which is responsible for running repetitive tasks on a regular schedule. It is a perfect tool for running system administration tasks such as backup and system logfile maintenance. It can also be useful for ordinary users to schedule regular tasks including calendar reminders and report generation. For more information, see Chapter 20, "Scheduling Processes."

Summary

In this chapter you have learned what a UNIX process is, how your interaction with UNIX starts and stops processes, and a little bit about a few special processes called daemons. A process is an entire execution environment for your computer program; it is almost like having a separate computer that executes your program. UNIX switches quickly between processes to give the illusion that they are all running simultaneously. You start a process any time you run a command or pipeline in the shell. You can even start a process in the background and perform other tasks while it is executing. Several processes called daemons run on your system to perform special tasks and supply services that some operating systems supply in the kernel.

Administering Processes

19

*By Rachel
and Robert Sartin*

IN THIS CHAPTER

You use processes on UNIX every time you want to get something done. Each command (that isn't built into your shell) you run will start one or more new processes to perform your desired task. To get the most benefit out of your UNIX machine you need to learn how to monitor and control the processes that are running on it. You will need to know how to make large, but not time-critical, tasks take less of your CPU time. You will need to learn how to shut down programs that have gone astray. You will need to learn how to improve the performance of your machine.

Monitoring Processes—*ps* and *time*

The first step in controlling processes in UNIX is to learn how to monitor them. By using the process-monitoring commands in UNIX, you will be able to find what programs are using your CPU time, find jobs that are not completing, and generally explore what is happening to your machine.

What Is *ps*?

The first command you should learn about is the ps command, which prints out the process status for some or all of the processes running on your UNIX machine.

There are two distinctly different versions of ps: the SYSV version and the BSD version. Your machine might have either one or both of the ps commands. If you are running on a machine that is mostly based on Berkeley UNIX, try looking in /usr/5bin for the SYSV version of ps. If you are running on a machine that is mostly based on System V UNIX, try looking in /usr/ucb for the BSD version of ps. Check your manuals and the output of your ps program to figure out which one you have. You may want to read the introductions to both SYSV and BSD ps output since some systems either combine features of both (for example, AIX) or have both versions (for example, Solaris 2.3, which has SYSV /usr/bin/ps and BSD /usr/ucb/ps).

Introduction to SYSV *ps* Output

If you are using SYSV, you should read this section to learn about the meaning of the various fields output by ps.

Look at what happens when you enter ps:

```
$ ps
   PID TTY       TIME COMD
  1400 pts/5     0:01 sh
  1405 pts/5     0:00 ps
$
```

The PID field gives you the *process identifier,* which uniquely identifies a particular process. The TTY fields tell what terminal the process is using. It will have ? if the process has no controlling terminal. It may say console if the process is on the system console. The terminal listed may be a *pseudo terminal,* which is how UNIX handles terminal-like connections from a GUI or over the network. Pseudo terminal names often begin with *pt* (or just *p,* if your system uses very short names). The TIME field tells how much CPU time the process has used. The COMD field (sometimes labelled CMD or COMMAND) tells what command the process is running.

Now look at what happens when you enter ps -f:

```
$ ps -f
    UID   PID  PPID  C   STIME TTY    TIME COMD
  sartin 1400  1398 80 18:31:32 pts/5  0:01 -sh
  sartin 1406  1400 25 18:34:33 pts/5  0:00 ps -f
$
```

The UID field tells which user ID owns the process. Your login name should appear here. The PPID field tells the process identifier of the parent of the process; notice that the PPID of ps -f is the same as the PID of -sh. The C field is process-utilization information used by the scheduler. The STIME is the time the process started.

Next, look at what happens when you enter ps -l:

```
$ ps -l
 F S  UID   PID  PPID  C PRI NI    ADDR    SZ   WCHAN TTY    TIME COMD
 8 S  343  1400  1398 80   1 20 fc315000  125 fc491870 pts/5  0:01 sh
 8 O  343  1407  1400 11   1 20 fc491800  114          pts/5  0:00 ps
$
```

Note that the UID is printed out numerically this time. The PRI field is the priority of the process; a lower number means more priority to the scheduler. The NI field is the nice value. See the section "Prioritizing Processes" for more information on the scheduler and nice values. The SZ field shows the process size. The WCHAN field tells what event, if any, the process is waiting for. Interpretation of the WCHAN field is specific to your system.

On some SYSV systems with real-time scheduling additions, you may see output such as the following if you enter ps -c:

```
$ ps -c
  PID CLS PRI TTY    TIME COMD
 1400  TS  62 pts/5  0:01 sh
 1409  TS  62 pts/5  0:00 ps
$
```

The CLS field tells the scheduling class of the process; TS means *time sharing* and is what you will usually see. You may also see SYS for system processes and RT for real-time processes.

On some SYSV systems running the Fair Share Scheduler, you may see output such as the following if you enter ps -f:

```
$ ps -f
     UID     FSID   PID  PPID  C    STIME TTY      TIME COMMAND
  sartin rddiver 18735 18734  1  Mar 12 ttys0    0:01 -ksh
  sartin rddiver 19021 18735  1 18:47:37 ttys0   0:01 xdivesim
  sartin rddiver 19037 18735  4 18:52:58 ttys0   0:00 ps -f
    root default 18734   136  0  Mar 12 ttys0    0:01 rlogind
$
```

The extra FSID field tells the fair share group for the process.

Introduction to BSD *ps* Output

If you are using BSD, you should read this section to learn about the meaning of the various fields output by ps.

Look at what happens when you enter ps:

```
$ ps
  PID TT STAT  TIME COMMAND
22711 c0 T     0:00 rlogin brat
22712 c0 T     0:00 rlogin brat
23121 c0 R     0:00 ps
$
```

The PID field gives you the process identifier, which uniquely identifies a particular process. The TT fields tell what terminal the process is using. It will have ? if the process has no controlling terminal. It may say co if the process is on the system console. The terminal listed may be a pseudo terminal. The STAT field shows the process state. Check your manual entry for ps to learn more about state. The TIME field tells how much CPU time the process has used. The COMMAND field tells what command the process is running. Normally, the COMMAND field lists the command arguments stored in the process itself. On some systems, these arguments can be overwritten by the process. If you use the c option, the real command name will be given, but not the arguments.

> **NOTE:** The BSD ps command predates standard UNIX option processing. It does not take hyphens to introduce options. On systems where one ps acts like either SYSV or BSD (e.g., AIX ps), the absence of the hyphen is what makes it run in BSD mode.

Look at what happens when you enter ps l:

```
$ ps l
    F UID   PID  PPID CP PRI NI  SZ  RSS WCHAN    STAT TT  TIME COMMAND
```

```
20408020 343 22711 22631  0  25  0  48    0           TW  c0  0:00 rlogin brat
    8000 343 22712 22711  0   1  0  48    0 socket    TW  c0  0:00 rlogin brat
20000001 343 23122 22631 19  29  0 200  400           R   c0  0:00 ps l
$
```

The F field gives a series of flags that tell you about the current state of the process. Check your system manuals for information on interpreting this field. The UID field tells the user ID that owns the process. Your login name should appear here. The PPID field tells the process identifier of the parent of the process; notice that the PPID of the second rlogin is the same as the PID of the other, its parent process. The CP is process utilization information used by the scheduler. The PRI field is the priority of the process; a lower number means more priority to the scheduler. See the section "Prioritizing Processes" for more information on the scheduler. The SZ field shows the process size. The RSS field shows the *resident set size*, which is the actual amount of computer memory occupied by the process. The WCHAN field tells what event, if any, the process is waiting for. Interpretation of the WCHAN field is specific to your system.

Look at what happens when you enter ps u:

```
$ ps u
USER       PID %CPU %MEM  SZ  RSS TT STAT START  TIME COMMAND
sartin   23127  0.0  1.6 200  416 c0 R    19:25  0:00 ps u
sartin   22712  0.0  0.0  48    0 c0 TW   18:40  0:00 rlogin brat
sartin   22711  0.0  0.0  48    0 c0 TW   18:40  0:00 rlogin brat
$
```

The %CPU and %MEM fields tell the percentage of CPU time and system memory the process is using. The START field tells when the process started.

```
$ ps v
  PID TT STAT   TIME SL RE PAGEIN SIZE  RSS  LIM %CPU %MEM COMMAND
23126 c0 R      0:00  0  0      0  200  420   xx  0.0  1.6 ps
$
```

The SL field tells how long the process has been sleeping, waiting for an event to occur. The RE field tells how long the process has been resident in memory. The PAGEIN field tells the number of disk input operations caused by the process, to read in pages that were not already resident in memory. The LIM field tells the soft limit on memory used.

Checking on Your Processes with *ps*

This section gives a few handy ways to examine the states of certain processes you might care about. Short examples are given using the SYSV and BSD versions of ps.

Everything You Own

Viewing all processes that you own can be useful in looking for jobs that you accidentally left running or to see everything you are doing so you can control it. On SYSV, you type ps -u *userid* to see everything owned by a particular user. Try ps -u $LOGNAME to see everything you own:

```
$ ps -u $LOGNAME
   PID TTY       TIME COMMAND
 18743 ttys0    0:01 ksh
 19250 ttys0    0:00 ps
$
```

On BSD, the default is for ps to show everything you own:

```
$ ps l
         F UID   PID  PPID CP PRI NI  SZ  RSS WCHAN     STAT TT  TIME COMMAND
20088201 343   835   834  1  15  0   32  176 kernelma  S    p0  0:00 -ksh TERM=vt
20000001 343   861   835 25  31  0  204  440           R    p0  0:00 ps l
20088001 343   857   856  0   3  0   32  344 Heapbase  S    p1  0:00 -ksh HOME=/t
$
```

Specific Processes

Looking at the current status of a particular process can be useful to track the progress (or lack thereof) of a single command you have running. On SYSV you type ps -p*PID* ... to see a specific process:

```
$ ps -p19057
   PID TTY       TIME COMMAND
 19057 ttys3    0:00 ksh
$
```

On BSD, if the last argument to ps is a number, it is used as a PID:

```
$ ps 122712
         F UID   PID  PPID CP PRI NI  SZ  RSS WCHAN     STAT TT  TIME COMMAND
    8000 343 22712 22711  0   1  0   48    0 socket    TW   c0  0:00 rlogin brat
$
```

Specific Process Groups

Looking at the status of a process group (See the section "Job Control and Process Groups.") can be useful in tracking a particular job you run. On SYSV you can use ps -g*PGID* to see a particular process group:

```
$ ps -lg19080
  F S  UID   PID  PPID  C PRI NI    ADDR   SZ   WCHAN TTY     TIME COMD
  1 S  343 19080 19057  0 158 24  710340   51  39f040 ttys3   0:58 fin_analysis
  1 S  343 19100 19080  0 168 24  71f2c0   87 7ffe6000 ttys3  2:16 fin_marketval
$
```

On BSD, there is no standard way to see a particular process group, but the output of ps j gives much useful information:

```
$ ps j
  PPID   PID  PGID   SID TT TPGID  STAT  UID  TIME COMMAND
   834   835   835   835 p0   904  SOE   198  0:00 -ksh TERM=vt100 HOME=/u/sart
   835   880   880   835 p0   904  TWE   198  0:00 vi
```

```
  835   881   881   835 p0   904   TWE   198   0:00 vi t1.sh
  835   896   896   835 p0   904   IWE   198   0:00 ksh t2.sh _ /usr/local/bin/k
  896   897   896   835 p0   904   IWE   198   0:00 task_a
  896   898   896   835 p0   904   IWE   198   0:00 task_b
  835   904   904   835 p0   904   RE    198   0:00 ps j
$
```

Note the PGID field for PIDs 896–898, which are all part of one shell script. Note the TPGID field, which is the same for all processes and identifies the current owner of the terminal.

Specific Terminal

Looking at the status of a particular terminal can be a useful way to filter processes started from a particular login, either from a terminal or over the network. On SYSV use ps -t *termid* to see processes running from a particular terminal or pseudo terminal. (See your system documentation to determine the correct values for *termid*.)

```
$ ps -fts3
     UID   PID  PPID  C    STIME TTY       TIME COMMAND
    root 19056   136  0 19:21:00 ttys3    0:00 rlogind
  sartin 19080 19057  0 19:23:53 ttys3    1:01 fin_analysis
  sartin 19057 19056  0 19:21:01 ttys3    0:00 -ksh
  sartin 19100 19080  0 19:33:53 ttys3    3:43 fin_marketval
  sartin 19082 19057  0 19:23:58 ttys3    0:00 vi 19unxor.adj
$
```

On BSD use ps t *termid* to see processes running from a particular terminal or pseudo terminal (See your system documentation to determine the correct values for *termid*.):

```
$ ps utp5
USER       PID  %CPU %MEM   SZ  RSS TT STAT  TIME COMMAND
sartin    2058   0.0  0.9  286      p5 R     0:00 -sh (sh)
sartin    2060   0.0  2.7   53      p5 R     0:00 vi 19unxor.adj
$
```

Specific User

Looking at processes run by a particular user can be useful for the system administrator to track what is being run by others and to deal with "runaway" processes. On SYSV enter ps -u *userid* to see everything owned by a particular user:

```
$ ps -fusartin
     UID   PID  PPID  C    STIME TTY       TIME COMMAND
  sartin 18743 18735  0    Mar 12 ttys0    0:31 collect_stats
  sartin 19065 19057  1 19:21:04 ttys3    0:00 vi 19unxor.adj
  sartin 19057 19056  0 19:21:01 ttys3    0:00 -ksh
  sartin 18735 18734  0    Mar 12 ttys0    0:00 -ksh
  sartin 19066 18743  8 19:21:12 ttys0    0:00 ps -fusartin
$
```

On BSD, there is no simple, standard way to see processes owned by a particular user other than yourself.

Checking on a Process with *time*

The time command prints out the *real, system,* and *user* time spent by a command (in ksh, the built-in time command will time a pipeline as well). The real time is the amount of clock time it took from starting the command until it completed. This will include time spent waiting for input, output, or other events. The user time is the amount of CPU time used by the code of the process. The system time is the amount of time the UNIX kernel spent doing things for the process. The time command prints real, user, and sys times on separate lines (BSD time may print them all on one line). Both csh and ksh have built-in versions of time that have slightly different output formats. The csh built-in time command prints user time, system time, clock time, percent usage, and some I/O statistics all on one line. The ksh time built-in time command prints real, user, and sys time on separate lines, but uses a slightly different format for the times than does time:

```
% time ./doio
9.470u 0.160s 0:09.56 100.7% 0+99k 0+0io 0pf+0w
% ksh
$ time ./doio

real    0m9.73s
user    0m9.63s
sys     0m0.10s
$ sh
$ time ./doio
real       9.8
user       9.5
sys        0.1
$
```

Background and Foreground Processes

So far, you have seen examples and descriptions of a user typing a command, watching as it executes, possibly interacting during its execution, and eventually completing. This is the default way your interactive shell executes processes. Using only this order of events means your shell executes a single process at a time. This single process is running in the foreground. Shells are able to keep track of more than one process at a time. In this type of environment, one process at most can be in the foreground; all the other processes are running in the backgound. This allows you to do multiple things at once from a single screen or window. You can think of the foreground and the background as two separate places where your interactive shell keeps processes. The foreground holds a single process, and you may interact with this process. The background holds many processes, but you cannot interact with these processes.

Foreground Processing

Running a process in the foreground is very common—it is the default way your shell executes a process. If you want to write a letter using the vi editor, you enter the command vi *letter* and type away. After you enter the vi command, your shell starts the vi process in the foreground so you can write your letter. In order for you to enter information interactively, your process must be in the foreground. When you exit the editor, you are terminating the process. After your foreground process terminates, but not before, the shell prompts you for the next command.

This mode of execution is necessary for all processes that need your interactions. It would be impossible for the computer to write the letter you want without your input. Mind reading is not currently a means of input, so you commonly type, use your mouse, and even sometimes speak the words. But not all processes need your input—they are designed to be able to get all the necessary input via other ways. They may be designed to get input from the computer system, from other processes, or from the file system.

Still, such processes may be designed to give you information. Status information could be reported periodically, and usually the process results are displayed at a certain point. If you wish to see this information as it is reported, the process must be running in the foreground.

Where Is the Background and Why Should You Go There?

Sometimes a program you run doesn't need you to enter any information or view any results. If this is the case, there is no reason you need to wait for it to complete before doing something else. UNIX shells provide a way for you to execute more than one process at a time from a single terminal. The way you do this is to run one or more processes in the background. The background is where your shell keeps all processes other than the one you are interacting with (your foreground process). You cannot give input to a process via standard input while it is in the background—you can give input via standard input only to a process in the foreground.

The most common reason to put a process in the background is to allow you to do something else interactively without waiting for the process to complete. For example, you may need to run a calculation program that goes through a very large database, computing a complicated financial analysis of your data and then printing a report; this may take several minutes (or hours). You don't need to input any data because your database has all the necessary information. You don't need to see the report on your screen since it is so big you would rather have it saved in a file and/or printed on your laser printer. So when you execute this program, you specify that the input should come from your database (redirection of standard input) and the report should be sent to a file (redirection of standard output). At the end of the command you add the special background symbol, &. This symbol tells your shell to execute the given command in the background. Refer to the following example scenario.

```
$ fin_analysis < fin_database > fin_report &
[1]   123
$ date
Sat Mar 12 13:25:17 CST 1994
$ tetris
$ date
Sat Mar 12 15:44:21 CST 1994
[1] + Done            fin_analysis < fin_database > fin_report &
$
```

After starting your program on its way (in the background), the shell prints a prompt and awaits your next command. You may continue doing work (executing commands) while the calculation program runs in the background. When the background process terminates (all your calculations are complete), your shell may print a termination message on your screen, followed by a prompt.

Job Control

Some shells (C shell, csh, and Korn shell, ksh, are two) have increased ability to manipulate multiple processes from a single interactive shell. Although graphical interfaces have since added the ability to use multiple windows (each with it's own interactive shell) from one display, job control still provides a useful function.

First you need to understand the shell's concept of a job. A *job* is an executed command line. Recall the discussion of processes created during execution of a command. For many command lines (for example, pipelines of several commands), several processes are created in order to carry out the execution. The whole collection of processes that are created to carry out this command line belong to the same process group. By grouping the processes together into an identifiable unit, the shell allows you to perform operations on the entire job, giving you job control.

Job control allows you to do the following:

- Move processes back and forth between the foreground and background
- Suspend and resume process execution

Each job or process group has a controlling terminal. This is the terminal (or window) from which you executed the command. Your terminal can only have one foreground process (group) at a time. A shell that implements job control will move processes between the foreground and the background.

The details of job control use are covered in the section "Job Control and Process Groups."

Signaling Processes

When a process is executing, UNIX provides a way to send a limited set of messages to this process: It sends a signal. UNIX defines a set of signals, each of which has a special meaning. Then the user, or other processes that are also executing, can send a specific signal to a process. This process may ignore some signals, and it may pay attention to others. As a nonprogramming user, you should know about the following subset of signals. The first group is important for processes, no matter what shell you are using. The second group applies if your shell supports job control.

General Process Control Signals

HUP	Detection of terminal hangup or controlling process death
INT	Interactive attention signal—INTR control character generates this
KILL	Termination—process cannot ignore or block this
QUIT	Interactive termination—QUIT control character generates this
TERM	Termination—process may ignore or block this

Job Control Process Control Signals

CONT	Continue a stopped process—process cannot ignore or block this
STOP	Stop a process—process cannot ignore or block this
TSTP	Interactive stop—SUSP control character generates this
TTIN	Background job attempted a read—process group is suspended
TTOU	Background job attempted a write—process group is suspended

The default action for all the general process control signals is abnormal process termination. A process can choose to ignore all signals except the KILL signal. There is no way for you to tell what processes are ignoring what signals. But if you need to terminate a process, the KILL signal cannot be ignored and can be used as a last resort when attempting to terminate a process.

The default action for the job control process control signals is suspending process execution, except for the CONT signal which defaults to resuming process execution. Once again, a process may choose to ignore most of these signals. The CONT signal cannot be ignored, so you can always continue a suspended process. The STOP signal will always suspend a process because it cannot be ignored.

Except for KILL and STOP, a process may *catch* a signal. This means that it can accept the signal and do something other than the default action. For example, a process may choose to catch a TERM signal, do some special processing, and finally either terminate or continue as it wishes. Catching a signal allows the process to decide which action to take. If the process does not catch a signal and is not ignoring the signal, the default action results.

Killing Processes

At some time or other, you will run a command and subsequently find out that you need to terminate it. You may have entered the wrong command, you may have entered the right command but at the wrong time, or you may be stuck in a program and can't figure out how to exit.

If you want to terminate your foreground process, the quickest thing to try is your interrupt control character. This is usually set to Ctrl+C, but make sure by looking at your stty -a output. The interrupt control character sends an INT signal to the process. It is possible for a program to ignore the INT signal, so this does not always terminate the process. A second alternative is to use your quit character (often Ctrl +\, set using stty quit *char*), which will send a QUIT signal. A process can ignore the QUIT signal. If your shell supports job control (C or Korn shells), you can suspend the process and then use the kill command. Once again, your process can ignore the suspend request. If you don't have job control or if none of these attempts work, you need to find another window, terminal, or screen where you can access your computer. From this other shell you can use the ps command along with the kill command to terminate the process. To terminate a process that is executing in the background, you can use the shell that is in the foreground on your terminal.

The *kill* Command

The kill command is not as nasty as it sounds. It is the way that you can send a signal to an executing process (see the section "Signaling a Process"). A common use of the kill command is to terminate a process, but it can also be used to suspend or continue a process.

To send a signal to a process, you must either be the owner of the process (that is, it was started via one of your shells) or you must be logged in as root.

See the section "Job Control and Process Groups" for information on how to use special features of the kill command for managing jobs.

Finding What to Kill Using *ps*

To send a signal to a process via the kill command, you need to somehow identify the particular process. Two commands can help you with this: the ps command and the jobs command. All UNIX systems support some version of the ps command, but the jobs command is found in job control shells only. (See the section "Job Control and Process Groups" for details on job control and the jobs command.)

The ps command shows system process information for your computer. The processes listed can be owned by you or other users, depending on the options you specify on the ps command. Normally, if you want to terminate a process, you are the owner. It is possible for the superuser (root) to terminate any processes, but non-root users may only terminate their own processes. This helps secure a system from mistakes as well as from abuse.

Terminating a process can be a three-step process: first you should check the list of processes with ps. See the section "Monitoring Processes" if you're not sure how to do this. The output of ps should contain the process identifier of each process. Make sure you look for the PID column and not the PPID column. The PPID is the process ID for the parent process. Terminating the parent process could cause many other processes to terminate as well.

Second, you can send a signal to the process via the kill command. The kill command takes the PID as one argument; this identifies which process you want to terminate. The kill command also takes an optional argument, which is the signal you wish to send. The default signal (if you do not specify one) is the TERM signal. There are several signals that all attempt to terminate a process. Whichever one you choose, you may specify it by its name (for example, TERM) or by a number. The name is preferable because the signal names are standardized. The numbers may vary from system to system. To terminate a process with PID 2345, you might try kill -HUP 2345. This sends the HUP signal to process 2345.

Third, you should check the process list to see if the process terminated. Remember that processes can ignore most signals. If you specified a signal that the process ignored, the process will continue to execute. If this happens, try again with a different signal.

> **TIP:** If you have a CPU-intensive job running in the background and you want to get some work done without killing the job, try using kill -STOP *PID*. This will force the job to be suspended, freeing up CPU time for your more immediate tasks. When you are ready for the job to run again, try kill -CONT *PID*.

Determining Which Signal to Send

The sure way to make a process terminate is to send it the KILL signal. So why not just send this signal and be done with it? Well, the KILL signal is important as a last resort, but it is not a very clean way to cause process termination. A process cannot ignore or catch the KILL signal, so it has no chance to terminate gracefully. If a process is allowed to catch the incoming signal, it has an opportunity to do some cleaning up or other processing prior to termination.

Try starting with the TERM signal. If your interrupt control character did not work, the INT signal probably won't either, but it is probably a reasonable thing to try next anyway. A common signal that many processes catch and then cleanly terminate is the HUP signal, so trying HUP next is a good idea. If you would like a core image of the process (for use with a debugging tool), the QUIT signal causes this to happen. If your process isn't exiting at this point, it might be nice to have the core image for the application developer to do debugging. If none of these signals caused the process to terminate, you can fall back on the KILL signal; the process cannot catch or ignore this signal.

> **NOTE:** If your process is hung up waiting for certain events (such as a network file server that is not responding), not even kill will have any visible effect immediately. As long as your process isn't using CPU time, you can probably stop worrying about it. The hung process will abort if the event ever occurs (for example, the file server responds or the request times out), but it might not go away until the next time you reboot.

If you need a list of the available signals, the -1 option to the kill command will display this list. You can also check the kill and signalf man pages for descriptions of each signal. The signals described in this section are the standard signals, but some systems may have additional supported signals. Always check the manual for your system to be sure.

The *dokill* Script: An Example

Look at the dokill script as an example of how to kill a process reasonably and reliably:

```
#!/bin/sh
# TERM, HUP and INT could possibly come in a different order
# TERM is first because it is what kill does by default
# INT is next since it is a typical way to let users quit a program
# HUP is next since many programs will make a recovery file
# QUIT is next since it can be caught and often generates a core dump
# KILL is the last resort since it can't be caught, blocked or ignored
for sig in TERM INT HUP QUIT KILL
do
        dosleep=0
        for pid in $*
        do
                # kill -0 checks if the process still exists
                if kill -0 $pid
                then
                        # Attempt to kill the process using the current signal
                        kill -$sig $pid
                        dosleep=1
                fi
        done
        # Here we sleep if we tried to kill anything.
        # This gives the process(es) a chance to gracefully exit
```

```
        # before dokill escalates to the next signal
        if [ $dosleep -eq 1 ]
        then
                sleep 1
        fi
done
```

This script uses the list of signals suggested in the section "Determining Which Signal to Send." For each signal in the suggested list, dokill sends the signal to any processes remaining in its list of processes to kill. After sending a signal, dokill sleeps for one second to give the other processes a chance to catch the signal and shut down cleanly. The last signal in the list is KILL and will shut down any process that is not blocked, waiting for a high-priority kernel event. If kill -KILL does not shut down your process, you may have a kernel problem. Check your system documentation and the WCHAN field of ps to find out which event blocked the process.

Logging Out with Background Processes

After you start using executing processes in the background, you may forget or lose track of what processes you have running. You can always check on your processes by using the ps command (see the section "Monitoring Processes"). Occasionally, you will try to exit from your shell when you have processes running in the background. By default, UNIX tries to terminate any background or stopped jobs you have when you log out. UNIX does this by sending a HUP signal to all of your child processes.

> **NOTE:** As a safeguard, job control shells (such as csh and ksh) issue a warning instead of allowing you to log out. The message will be similar to "You have stopped (running) jobs." If you immediately enter exit again, the shell will allow you to log out without warning. But, beware! The background processes are terminated immediately. If you don't want these background processes to be terminated, you must wait until they have completed before exiting. There is no way to log out while keeping the processes alive unless you plan ahead.

Using *nohup*

Some of the commands you use may take so long to complete that you may not be able to (or want to) stay logged in until they complete. To change this behavior, you can use the nohup command. The word nohup simply precedes your normal command on the command line. Using nohup runs the command, ignoring certain signals. This allows you to log out, leaving the process running. As you log out, all your existing processes (those processes with your terminal as the controlling terminal) are sent the HUP signal. Since the process on which nohup is used ignores this signal, you can log out and the process will not terminate. If you have a nohup process in the background as you attempt to log out, your shell may warn you on your first exit command and require an immediate second exit in order to actually log out. (If yours is a shell that does job control, such as ksh or csh, see the section "Job Control and Process Groups.")

> **NOTE:** There are several varieties of the nohup command. The SYSV nohup executable arranges for the command to ignore NOHUP and QUIT signals but does nothing regarding the TERM signal. If the output is going to standard out, it is redirected to the file nohup.out (or alternately to $HOME/nohup.out if you can't write to the first).
>
> The C shell has a built-in nohup command. It arranges for the command to ignore TERM signals. (In C shell, background commands automatically ignore the HUP signal.) It does not redirect output to the file nohup.out.
>
> Your system or shell may have a slight variation on the exact signals ignored and whether the nice value is changed when you use nohup.

Prioritizing Processes

Part of administering your processes is controlling how much CPU time they use and how important each process is relative to the others. UNIX supplies some fairly simple ways to monitor and control CPU usage of your process. This section describes how to use UNIX *nice values* to control your process CPU usage. By setting nice values for large jobs that aren't time critical, you can make your system more usable for other jobs that need to be done now.

What Is a Priority?

The UNIX kernel manages the scheduling of all processes on the system in an attempt to share the limited CPU resource fairly. Because UNIX has grown as a general purpose time-sharing system, the mechanism the scheduler uses tries to favor interactive processes over long-running, CPU-intensive processes so that users perceive good system response. UNIX always schedules the process that is ready to run (not waiting for I/O or an event) with the lowest numerical priority (that is, lower numbers are more important). If two processes with the same priority are ready, the scheduler will schedule the process that has been waiting the longest. If your process is CPU intensive, the kernel will automatically change your process priority based on how much CPU time your process is using. This gives preference to interactive applications that don't use lots of CPU time.

> **NOTE:** Low PRI means high priority. You may find it a bit confusing that lower numbers for priority mean "higher" priority. Try thinking of the scheduler starting out at priority zero and seeing if any processes at that priority are ready. If not, the scheduler tries priority 1, and so on.

To see how the UNIX scheduler works, look at the example in Table 19.1. In this example, three processes are each running long computations, and no other processes are trying to run. Each of the three processes will execute for a time slice and then let one of the other processes execute. Note that each process gets an equal share of the CPU. If you run an interactive process, such as a ps, while these three processes are running, you will get priority to run.

Table 19.1. Scheduling three CPU-intensive processes.

Process 1	*Process 2*	*Process 3*
Running	Waiting	Waiting
Waiting	Running	Waiting
Waiting	Waiting	Running
Running	Waiting	Waiting
Waiting	Running	Waiting
Waiting	Waiting	Running

Being Nice

One of the factors the kernel uses in determining a process priority is the *nice value,* a user-controlled value that indicates how "nice" you want a process to be to other processes. Traditionally, nice values range from 0 to 39 and default to 20. Only root can lower a nice value. All other users can only make processes more nice than they were.

To see how the UNIX scheduler works with nice, look at the example in Table 19.2. In this example, three processes are each running long computations and no other processes are trying to run. This time, Process 1 was run with a nice value of 30. Each of the three processes will execute for a time slice and then let one of the other processes execute. However, in this case, Process 1 gets a smaller share of the CPU because the kernel uses the nice value in calculating the priority. Once again, if you run an interactive process, like a ps, while these three processes are running, you will get priority to run.

Table 19.2. Scheduling three CPU-intensive processes, one nicely.

Process 1	Process 2	Process 3, Nice Process
Running	Waiting	Waiting
Waiting	Running	Waiting
Waiting	Waiting	Running
Running	Waiting	Waiting
Waiting	Running	Waiting
Running	Waiting	Waiting
Waiting	Waiting	Running
Waiting	Running	Waiting
Running	Waiting	Waiting
Waiting	Running	Waiting

Using *renice* on a Running Process

BSD introduced the ability to change the nice value of other processes that are owned by you. The renice command gives you access to this capability. If you run a job and then decide it should be running with lower priority, you can use renice to do that.

> **CAUTION:** Not all systems have the renice command. Most systems based on BSD have it. Some systems, which are not based on BSD have added renice. The renice command on your system may take slightly different arguments than in the examples here. Check your system documentation to see if you have renice and what arguments it takes.

On BSD-based systems, the renice command takes arguments in this manner:

```
renice priority [ [-p] pid ... ] [ -g pgrp ... ] [ -u userid ... ]
```

The priority is the new nice value desired for the processes to be changed. The -p option (the default) allows a list of process identifiers; you should get these from ps or by saving the PID of each background task you start. The -g option allows a list of process groups; if you are using a shell that does job control you should get this from the PID of each background task you start or by using ps and using the PID of the process that has a PPID that is your shell's PID. The -u option outputs a list of user IDs; unless you have appropriate privileges (usually only if you are root), you will be able to change only your own processes. If you want to make all of your current processes nicer, you can use renice -u *yourusername*. Remember that this will affect your login shell! This means that any command you start after renice will have lower priority.

Here is an example of using renice on a single process. You start a long job (called longjob) and then realize you have an important job (called impjob) to run. After you start impjob, you can do a ps to see that longjob is PID 27662. Then you run renice 20 27662 to make longjob have a lower priority. If you immediately run ps 1 (try ps -1 on a SYSV system that has renice), you will see that longjob has a higher nice value (see the NI column). If you wait a bit and do another ps 1, you should notice that impjob is getting more CPU time (see the TIME column).

```
$ longjob &
27662
$ impjob &
28687
$ ps 1
     F S UID   PID  PPID   C PRI NI ADDR   SZ  RSS  WCHAN   TTY   TIME CMD
240801 S 343 24076 29195   0  60 20 4231   88  268          pts/4 0:00 -sh
240001 R 343 26398 24076   4  62 20 4e52  108  204          pts/4 0:00 ps 1
241001 R 343 27662 24076  52  86 20 49d0   32   40          pts/4 0:03 longjob
241001 R 343 28687 24076  52  86 20 256b   32   40          pts/4 0:00 impjob
$ renice 20 27662
27662: old priority 0, new priority 20
$ ps 1
     F S UID   PID  PPID   C PRI NI ADDR   SZ  RSS  WCHAN   TTY   TIME CMD
240001 R 343 18017 24076   3  61 20 60b8  108  204          pts/4 0:00 ps 1
240801 S 343 24076 29195   0  60 20 4231   88  268          pts/4 0:00 -sh
241001 R 343 27662 24076  32  96 40 49d0   32   40          pts/4 0:09 longjob
241001 R 343 28687 24076  52  86 20 256b   32   40          pts/4 0:07 impjob
$ # Wait a bit
$ ps 1
     F S UID   PID  PPID   C PRI NI ADDR   SZ  RSS  WCHAN   TTY   TIME CMD
240801 S 343 24076 29195   0  60 20 4231   88  268          pts/4 0:00 -sh
241001 R 343 27662 24076  74 117 40 49d0   32   40          pts/4 0:31 longjob
241001 R 343 28687 24076 115 117 20 256b   32   40          pts/4 0:41 impjob
240001 R 343 29821 24076   4  62 20 4ff2  108  204          pts/4 0:00 ps 1
$
```

Some jobs you run may start multiple processes, but renice -p will affect only one of them. One way to get around this is to use ps to find all of the processes and list each one to renice -p. If you are using a job control shell (for example, Korn shell or C shell), you may be able to use renice -g. In the following example, longjob spawns several subprocesses to help do more work (see the output of the first ps 1). Notice that if you use renice -p you affect only the parent process's nice value (see the output of the second ps 1). If you are using a shell that does job control, your background process should have been put in its own process group with a process group ID the same as its process ID. Try renice 20 -g *PID* and see if it works. Notice in the output of the third ps 1 that all of the children of longjob have had their nice values changed.

```
$ longjob &
[1]      27823
$ ps l
      F S UID   PID   PPID   C PRI NI ADDR   SZ   RSS   WCHAN   TTY   TIME CMD
   1001 R 343 21938 27823  27  77 24 328e   56    20           pts/5 0:01 longjob
   1001 R 343 26545 27823  26  77 24 601a   48    20           pts/5 0:01 longjob
 201001 R 343 27823 27973  26  77 24 1647   56    20           pts/5 0:01 longjob
 200801 S 343 27973 24078   0  60 20 6838  104   384           pts/5 0:00 -ksh
   1001 R 343 28336 27823  26  77 24 7f1e   40    20           pts/5 0:01 longjob
 200001 R 343 29877 27973   4  62 20 4ff2  108   204           pts/5 0:00 ps l
$ renice 20 -p 27823
27823: old priority 4, new priority 20
$ ps l
      F S UID   PID   PPID   C PRI NI ADDR   SZ   RSS   WCHAN   TTY   TIME CMD
   1001 R 343 21938 27823  24  76 24 328e   56    20           pts/5 0:04 longjob
   1001 R 343 26545 27823  24  76 24 601a   48    20           pts/5 0:04 longjob
 201001 R 343 27823 27973  11  85 40 1647   56    20           pts/5 0:04 longjob
 200801 S 343 27973 24078   0  60 20 6838  104   384           pts/5 0:00 -ksh
   1001 R 343 28336 27823  24  76 24 7f1e   40    20           pts/5 0:04 longjob
 200001 R 343 29699 27973   4  62 20 4ff2  108   204           pts/5 0:00 ps l
$ renice 20 -g 27823
27823: old priority 4, new priority 20
$ ps l
      F S UID   PID   PPID   C PRI NI ADDR   SZ   RSS   WCHAN   TTY   TIME CMD
   1001 R 343 21938 27823  39  99 40 328e   56    20           pts/5 0:06 longjob
   1001 R 343 26545 27823  38  99 40 601a   48    20           pts/5 0:06 longjob
 201001 R 343 27823 27973  38  99 40 1647   56    20           pts/5 0:05 longjob
 200801 S 343 27973 24078   0  60 20 6838  104   384           pts/5 0:00 -ksh
   1001 R 343 28336 27823  38  99 40 7f1e   40    20           pts/5 0:06 longjob
 200001 R 343 29719 27973   4  62 20 705d  108   204           pts/5 0:00 ps l
$
```

Job Control and Process Groups

Job control is a BSD UNIX addition that is used by some shells. Both C shell and Korn shell support job control. In order to support job control, these shells use the concept of process groups. Each time you enter a command or pipeline from the command line, your shell creates a process group. The process group is simply the collection of all the processes that are executed as a result of that command. For simple commands, this could be a single process. For pipelines, the process group could contain many processes. Either way, the shell keeps track of the processes as one unit by identifying a process group ID. This ID will be the PID of one of the processes in the group.

If you run a process group in the background or suspend its execution, it is referred to as a *job*. A small integer value, the *job number*, is associated with this process group. The shell prints out a message with these two identifiers at the time when you perform the background operation. A process group and a job are almost the same thing. The one distinction you might care about is that every command line results in a process group (and therefore a process group identifier); a job identifier is assigned only when a process group is suspended or put into the background.

Given process groups and job IDs, the shells have added new commands that operate on the job (or process group) as a whole. Further, existing commands (such as `kill`) are modified to take advantage of this concept. The two shells (C shell and Korn shell) have very minor differences from one another, but for the most part the job control commands in each are the same.

Using the *jobs* Command

The `jobs` command will show you the list of all of your shell's jobs that are either suspended or executing in the background. The list of jobs will look similar to this:

```
[1]   Stopped                  vi mydoc.txt
[2] - Running                  fin_analysis < fin_database > fin_report &
[3] + Stopped (tty output) summararize_log &
```

Each line corresponds to a single process group, and the integer at the start is its job number. You can use the job number as an argument to the `kill` command by prefixing the job number with a percent (%) sign. To send a signal to the process `vi mydoc.txt`, you could enter `kill %1`. Since you did not specify the signal you wanted to send to the process, the default signal, `TERM`, is sent. This notation is just a convenience for you since you can do the same thing via `kill` and the PID. The real power of job control comes with the ability to manipulate jobs between the foreground and the background.

The shell also keeps the concept of current and previous jobs. On the output of the `jobs` command you will notice a + next to the current job and a - next to the previous job. If you have more than two jobs, the remaining jobs have no particular distinction. Again, this notation is mainly a convenience for you. In some job control commands, if you do not specify a job (or PID) number, the current job is taken by default. Keep in mind that your current job is different from your foreground process group. A job is either suspended or in the background.

The following are various ways to reference a job:

`%n`	Where *n* is the job number reported by jobs
`%+`	Your current job
`%%`	Your current job
`%-`	Your previous job
`%string`	Job whose command line begins with *string*
`%?string`	Job whose command line contains *string*

Putting Jobs in the Foreground

After executing a process group in the background, you may decide for some reason that you would like it to execute in the foreground. With non-job control shells, after executing a command line in the background (via the & symbol), it stays in the background until it completes or is terminated (for example, if you send a terminate signal to it via kill). With a job control shell, the fg command will move the specified job into the foreground. The fg command will take either a job number preceded by a percent (%) sign or a PID as an argument. If neither is given, the current job is taken as the default.

The result of the fg command is that the specified job executes as your foreground process. Remember that you can have only one foreground process at a time. To move the vi mydoc.txt job into the foreground, you could enter fg %1.

Suspending Process Groups

To suspend an executing process group, you need to send a suspend signal to the process. There are two ways to do this: (1) use the suspend control character on your foreground process, or (2) send a suspend signal via the kill command.

The suspend control character, commonly Ctrl+Z, is used to send a suspend signal to the foreground process. Your shell may be configured with a different suspend control character, so be sure to find out your own configuration by running the stty -a command. (Refer to the section "Working on the System" for information on control characters.) After you have executed a command in the foreground, you simply press Ctrl+Z (or whatever your suspend control character is) to suspend the running process. The result is that the process is suspended from execution. When this happens, your shell prints a message giving the job number and process group ID for that job. You can subsequently use the fg or bg commands to manipulate this process.

Putting Jobs in the Background

The bg command puts the specified jobs into the background and resumes their execution. The common way to use this command is following a suspend control character. After a job is put in the background, it will continue executing until it completes (or attempts input or output from the terminal). You manipulate it via fg or kill.

An example may help you see the power of these commands when used together:

```
$ long_job\
^Z[1] + Stopped              long_job
$ important_job 1
$ jobs
[1] + Stopped                sleep 400
$ bg
[1]      long_job&
$ important_job 2
$ kill -STOP %1
```

```
[1] + Stopped (signal)      long_job
$ important_job 3
$ fg %1
long_job
```

If you don't have a `long_job`, try using `sleep 100`. If you don't have an `important_job`, try using `echo`. This example shows how you can use job control to move jobs between the foreground and background and suspend, then later resume, jobs that might be taking computer resources that you need.

Using *wait* to Wait for Background Jobs

The `wait` command built into most shells (including all the shells discussed in this book) will wait for completion of all background processes or a specific background process. Usually, `wait` is used in scripts, but occasionally you may want to use it interactively to wait for a particularly important background job or to pause until all of your current background jobs complete so you will not load the system with your next job. The command `wait` will wait for all background jobs. The command `wait` *pid* will wait for a particular PID. If you are using a job control shell, you can use a job identifier instead of a PID:

```
$ job1 &
[1]      20233
$ job2 &
[2]      20234
$ job3 &
[3]      20235
$ job4 %
[4]      20237
$ wait %1
$ wait 20234
$ wait
[4] +  Done              job4 &
[3] +  Done              job3 &
$ jobs
$
```

Using *csh notify* to Learn About Changes Sooner

Most interactive use of `wait` in `csh` can be replaced by `notify`. The `notify` command tells `csh` not to wait until issuing a new prompt before telling you about the completion of all or some background jobs. The command `notify` will tell `csh` to give asynchronous notification of job completion. The command `notify` *jobid* will tell `csh` to give asynchronous notification for a particular job. For example:

```
% sleep 30 &
[1] 20237
% sleep 10 &
[2] 20238
% notify %2
%
```

```
[2]   Done              sleep 10
jobs
[1]  +Running           sleep 30
%
```

When you do this example, don't type anything after hitting return to enter `notify %2`. The notification appears as soon as job 2 finishes.

My System Is Slow—Performance Tuning

UNIX offers several tools that can be useful in finding performance problem areas. This section covers using `ps` and `sar` to look for processes which are causing problems and system bottlenecks which need to be resolved. Your system may have more performance analysis tools; check your system documentation.

Monitoring the System with *ps*

If your system is having performance problems, you may want to terminate or suspend some of the large or CPU-intensive processes to let your system run more effectively. You can use `ps` to locate some of these processes.

> **NOTE:** Many UNIX systems have or can run a program called `top`, which displays the current heavy users of system CPU resources.

On a SYSV system, you can use `ps -fe` or `ps -le` to look at all processes and examine the list to look for those processes which are using lots of CPU or memory. Try running `ps` twice in a row to look for processes with rapidly increasing `TIME`:

```
$ ps -le
 F S   UID   PID  PPID  C PRI NI   ADDR      SZ  WCHAN TTY      TIME COMD
19 T     0     0     0 80   0 SY f808c4bc     0         ?       0:20 sched
 8 S     0     1     0241  1  20 fc1c2000    43 fc1c21c4 ?      0:02 init
19 S     0     2     0  1   0 SY fc13c800     0 f80897a0 ?      0:00 pageout
19 S     0     3     0 80   0 SY fc13c000     0 f8089e4e ?      0:06 fsflush
 8 S     0   204   120 35   1  20 fc311000   265 f808fb60 ?     0:00 in.rlogi
 8 S     0   179     1 29   1  20 fc3b2800   196 fc16554e ?     0:00 sac
 8 S     0   136     1 29   1  20 fc36d000   353 f808fb60 ?     0:00 automoun
 8 S     0   103     1 80   1  20 fc32e800   326 f808fb60 ?     0:01 rpcbind
 8 S     0   109     1 52   1  20 fc333800   294 f808fb60 ?     0:01 ypbind
 8 S     0   120  1154  1  20 fc349800   289 f808fb60 ?        0:01 inetd
 8 S     0   111     1 20   1  20 fc34b800   294 f808fb60 ?     0:00 kerbd
 8 S     0   105     1  3   1  20 fc335800   223 f808fb60 ?     0:00 keyserv
 8 S     0   123     1 80   1  20 fc348000   332 f808fb60 ?     0:19 statd
 8 S     0   125     1 65   1  20 fc353800   395 f808fb60 ?     0:01 lockd
 8 S     0   159   151 15   1  20 fc39d000   239 f808fb60 ?     0:00 lpNet
 8 S   343   151     1 61   1  20 fc399000   891 f808fb60 ?     0:00 bigproc
 8 S     0   143     1 18   1  20 fc30c000   259 fc308b4e ?     0:00 cron
 8 S     0   160     1 17   1  20 fc3a0800   329 fc22de4e ?     0:00 sendmail
```

```
8 0    343   210   206   9   1 20 fc314000   114            pts/0    0:00 ps
8 S      0   167     1  80   1 20 fc3b4800   310 f808fb60 ?        0:12 syslogd
8 S      0   181     1  29   1 20 fc3b8800   213 f808fb60 console  0:00 ttymon
8 S    343   206   204  80   1 20 fc30e800   125 fc314070 pts/0    0:00 sh
8 S    343   208   204  80   1 20 fc30e800   212            pts/0    0:46 busyproc
8 S      0   184   179  44   1 20 fc3b6800   208 f808fb60 ?        0:00 listen
8 S      0   185   179  38   1 20 fc3b3000   221 fc3b31c4 ?        0:00 ttymon
$
```

Note that `bigproc` has a rather large value for SZ and that `busyproc` has a lot of TIME.

On a BSD system, you can use ps xau to look at all processes and examine the %CPU and %MEM field for processes with high CPU and memory usage:

```
% ps xau
USER       PID %CPU %MEM   SZ  RSS TT STAT START  TIME COMMAND
sartin    1014 88.7  0.9   32  192 p0 R    15:46  0:19 busyproc
root         1  0.0  0.0   52    0 ?  IW   Mar 12 0:00 /sbin/init -
root         2  0.0  0.0    0    0 ?  D    Mar 12 0:00 pagedaemon
root        93  0.0  0.0  100    0 ?  IW   Mar 12 0:00 /usr/lib/sendmail -bd -q
root        54  0.0  0.0   68    0 ?  IW   Mar 12 0:02 portmap
root       300  0.0  0.0   48    0 ?  IW   Mar 12 0:00 rpc.rquotad
root        59  0.0  0.0   40    0 ?  IW   Mar 12 0:00 keyserv
sartin     980  0.0  1.5  268  336 p0 S    15:33  0:00 -sh (tcsh)
root        74  0.0  0.0   16    0 ?  I    Mar 12 0:00 (biod)
root        85  0.0  0.0   60    0 ?  IW   Mar 12 0:00 syslogd
root       111  0.0  0.0   28    0 ?  I    Mar 12 0:00 (nfsd)
root       117  0.0  0.1   16   28 ?  S    Mar 12 17:03 /usr/bin/screenblank
root       127  0.0  0.0   12    8 ?  S    Mar 12 11:07 update
root       130  0.0  0.0   56    0 ?  IW   Mar 12 0:00 cron
root       122  0.0  3.3  740  748 ?  S    Mar 12 0:05 bigproc
root       136  0.0  0.0   56    0 ?  IW   Mar 12 0:00 inetd
sartin    1016  0.0  2.0  204  444 p0 R    15:46  0:00 ps xau
root       140  0.0  0.0   52    0 ?  IW   Mar 12 0:00 /usr/lib/lpd
root       834  0.0  0.2   44   44 ?  S    15:03  0:03 in.telnetd
root       146  0.0  0.0   40    0 co IW   Mar 12 0:00 - std.9600 console (gett
sartin     835  0.0  0.0   32    0 p0 IW   15:03  0:01 -ksh TERM=vt100 HOME=/ti
root      1011  0.0  0.9   24  204 ?  S    15:45  0:00 in.comsat
root         0  0.0  0.0    0    0 ?  D    Mar 12 0:01 swapper
%
```

Note that `busyproc` has 88.7 percent CPU usage and that `bigproc` has higher than average memory usage, but still only 3.3 percent.

By using ps to examine the running processes, you can keep track of what is happening on your system and catch runaway processes or memory hogs.

Monitoring the System with *sar*

The sar command can be used to generate a System Activity Report covering things such as CPU usage, buffer activity, disk usage, TTY activity, system calls, swapping activity, file access calls, queue length, and system table and message/semaphore activity. If you run sar [-ubdycwaqvmA] [-o *file*] *interval* [*num_samples*], sar will print summaries a total of *num_samples* times every *interval* seconds and then stop. If *num_samples* is not supplied, sar will run until interrupted. With sar -o *file* the output will go in binary format to *file* and can be read using sar -f *file*. If you run sar [-ubdycwaqvmA] [-s *time*] [-s *time*] [-i *sec*] [-f *file*], the input will be read from a binary *file* (default is where the system command sa1 puts its output).

> **NOTE:** The sar command is the user interface to the System Activity Report. Your system administrator can configure your system to do continual activity reporting (using sa1 and other commands). See your system documentation on sar for more information.

> **CAUTION:** If you are on a BSD system, you may not have sar. Try checking out the vmstat and iostat commands for some similar information.

The command sar -u 5 5 will print CPU usage statistics:

```
$ sar -u 5 5

HP-UX cnidaria A.09.00 C 9000/837    03/14/94

16:18:53   %usr    %sys    %wio    %idle
16:18:58      0       0       0      100
16:19:03     58      28       1       13
16:19:08     84      16       0        0
16:19:13     57      11      31        0
16:19:18      0       6      94        0

Average      40      12      25       23
$
```

The column headings %usr, %sys, %wio, and %idle report the percentage of time spent respectively on user processes, system mode, waiting for I/O, and idling (doing nothing). The command sar -b will print buffer activity:

```
$ sar -b 5 5

HP-UX cnidaria A.09.00 C 9000/837    03/14/94

16:19:34 bread/s lread/s %rcache bwrit/s lwrit/s %wcache pread/s pwrit/s
16:19:39       0       5      96       0       0       0       0       0
16:19:44       2    2809     100     174    2081      92       0       0
16:19:49       1    1456     100      83     950      91       0       0
16:19:54       4    1598     100      71    1267      94       0       0
16:19:59       3    1374     100      92    1055      91       0       0

Average        2    1449     100      84    1071      92       0       0
$
```

The bread/s and bwrit/s columns report transfers between the system buffers and disk (or other block) devices. The lread/s and lwrit/s columns report accesses of system buffers. The %rcache and %wcache columns report cache hit ratios. The UNIX kernel attempts to keep copies of buffers around in memory so that it can satisfy a disk read request without having to read the disk. For example, if one process writes block 5 of your disk and shortly after that another process writes different data to block 5, your system will save one write if it kept the data cached rather than writing to disk. High cache:hit ratios are good because they mean your system is able to avoid reading from or writing to the disk when it isn't necessary. The pread/s and pwrit/s columns report raw transfers. Raw transfers are transfers that don't use the file system at all. You will usually see raw transfers when using tar to read or write a tape or when using fsck to repair a file system. The command sar -d will print buffer activity for each block device (disk or tape drive):

```
$ sar -d 5 2

HP-UX cnidaria A.09.00 C 9000/837    03/14/94

16:41:16  device    %busy   avque   r+w/s  blks/s  avwait  avserv

16:41:21  disc3-0       3     1.4       2      14     8.8    21.2

16:41:26  disc3-0      70   105.8      55     867  1328.6    12.7

Average   disc3-0      37   101.0      28     441  1291.5    12.9
$
```

The device column will report your system-specific disk name. The %busy and avque columns report the percentage of time the device was busy servicing requests and the average number of requests outstanding. The r+w/s and blks/s columns report the number of transfers per second and number of 512 byte blocks transferred per second. The avwait and avserv columns report the average time in milliseconds that transfer requests wait in the queue and the average time for a request to be serviced. The command sar -y will report TTY activity

```
$ sar -y 10 4

HP-UX cnidaria A.09.00 C 9000/837    03/14/94

16:43:12 rawch/s canch/s outch/s rcvin/s xmtin/s mdmin/s
16:43:22     424     420     458       0       0       0
16:43:32     595     596    1469       0       0       0
16:43:42     678     674    1542       0       0       0
16:43:52     736     743     755       0       0       0

Average      608     608    1056       0       0       0
$
```

The rawch/s, canch/s, and outch/s columns report the input rate, input rate for characters with canonical processing, and output rate. The rcvin/s, xmtin/s, and mdmin/s columns report the modem receive rate, transmit rate, and interrupt rate. The command sar -c will report system call activity:

```
$ sar -c 5 5

HP-UX cnidaria A.09.00 C 9000/837    03/14/94

16:50:33 scall/s  sread/s  swrit/s  fork/s  exec/s  rchar/s   wchar/s
16:50:38   1094       15     1016     0.60    0.60  16938189  1047142
16:50:43    592        8      540     0.20    0.20   9033318   590234
16:50:48    641        9      602     0.00    0.00  10007142   613376
16:50:53    735       14      766     0.20    0.20  11245978   507494
16:50:58    547       16      359     0.00    0.00   7215923   605594

Average     722       12      657     0.20    0.20  10887960   672768
$
```

The scall/s column reports the total number of system calls per second. The sread/s, swrit/s, fork/s, and exec/s columns report the number of read, write, fork, and exec system calls. The rchar/s, and wchar/s columns report the number of characters read and written by system calls. The command sar -w reports system-swapping activity:

```
$ sar -w 5 5

HP-UX cnidaria A.09.00 C 9000/837    03/14/94

16:51:40 swpin/s  bswin/s  swpot/s  bswot/s  pswch/s
16:51:45   0.00     0.0     0.00     0.0       24
16:51:50   0.00     0.0     0.00     0.0       49
16:51:55   0.00     0.0     0.00     0.0        5
16:52:00   0.00     0.0     0.00     0.0       67
16:52:05   0.00     0.0     0.00     0.0       42

Average    0.00     0.0     0.00     0.0       37
$
```

The swpin/s, bswin/s, swpot/s, and bswot/s columns report the number of transfers and 512 byte blocks for swapins and swapouts. The pswch/s column reports the number of process context switches per second. The command sar -a reports system file access activity:

```
$ sar -a 5 5

HP-UX cnidaria A.09.00 C 9000/837    03/14/94

16:52:31  iget/s  namei/s  dirbk/s
16:52:36     0        1       0
16:52:41    65       79       4
16:52:46   495      561      23
16:52:51   487      572      30
16:52:56   726      828      36

Average    354      408      18
$
```

The columns report the number of calls to the system function named. The command sar -q reports run queue activity:

```
$ sar -q 5 5
```

```
HP-UX cnidaria A.09.00 C 9000/837    03/14/94

16:53:15 runq-sz %runocc swpq-sz %swpocc
16:53:20    1.0      80
16:53:25    1.5      80
16:53:30    2.0     100
16:53:35    1.4     100
16:53:40    1.6     100

Average     1.5      92
$
```

The runq-sz and %runocc columns report the average length of the run queue when occupied and the percentage of time it was occupied. The run queue is the list of processes that are ready to use the CPU (not waiting for I/O or other events). The swpq-sz and %swpocc columns report the average length of the swap queue when occupied and the percentage of time it was occupied. The swap queue is the list of processes that are ready to use the CPU, but are completely swapped out of memory and can't use the CPU until they are swapped into memory. This column may not appear (or may be empty or appear with 0 values) for systems without swapping. The command sar -v reports status of various system tables:

```
$ sar -v

HP-UX cnidaria A.09.00 C 9000/837    03/14/94

13:12:54 text-sz  ov  proc-sz  ov  inod-sz  ov  file-sz  ov
13:13:02   N/A    N/A  48/276   0  114/356   0  121/600   0
13:20:00   N/A    N/A  51/276   0  111/356   0  128/600   0
13:40:00   N/A    N/A  51/276   0   95/356   0  128/600   0
14:00:01   N/A    N/A  51/276   0  108/356   0  128/600   0
14:20:01   N/A    N/A  51/276   0   94/356   0  128/600   0
14:40:01   N/A    N/A  51/276   0   94/356   0  128/600   0
15:00:01   N/A    N/A  48/276   0  106/356   0  124/600   0
15:20:01   N/A    N/A  48/276   0   91/356   0  124/600   0
15:40:01   N/A    N/A  48/276   0   91/356   0  124/600   0
16:00:00   N/A    N/A  54/276   0  213/356   0  135/600   0
16:20:00   N/A    N/A  49/276   0  113/356   0  119/600   0
16:40:00   N/A    N/A  47/276   0   84/356   0  118/600   0
17:00:01   N/A    N/A  47/276   0   99/356   0  118/600   0

$
```

The column table-sz reports the entries/size of a particular system table. The tables for SYSV (from SVID3) are proc, inod, file, and lock. UNIX SVR4 (SVID3) includes a program synchronization mechanism using *semaphores*, which are critical resource controls. A process generally acquires a semaphore, performs a critical action, and releases the semaphore. No other process can acquire a semaphore already in use. The command sar -m reports message and semaphore activity:

```
$ sar -m 6 5

HP-UX cnidaria A.09.00 C 9000/837    03/14/94
```

```
17:00:22   msg/s   sema/s
17:00:28    4.50    0.00
17:00:34    4.50    0.00
17:00:40    4.50    0.00
17:00:46    4.50    0.00
17:00:52    4.50    0.00

Average     4.50    0.00
$
```

The columns msg/s and sema/s report message and semaphore primitives per second.

Summary

In this chapter, you have learned how to use the UNIX commands ps, time, and sar to examine the state of your processes and your system. You have learned about foreground and background jobs and how to use the job control features of UNIX and your shell (csh or ksh) to control foreground and background jobs. You have learned to use the nice and renice commands to limit the CPU impact of your jobs. You have learned to use the kill command to suspend or terminate jobs that are using too much of the available system resources. Applying this knowledge to your daily use of UNIX will help you and your system be efficient at getting tasks completed.

Scheduling Processes

By Rachel and Robert Sartin

IN THIS CHAPTER

Typically, UNIX machines are left running all day and all night. UNIX offers several commands that let you take extra advantage of your existing computer resources. This chapter covers key concepts needed to schedule processes to run when you are not present to start them manually. This chapter introduces the at command, which is used to schedule a command to run once later, and the cron command, which is used to schedule commands that need to be run regularly. Using these two commands can help you manage your computer more effectively.

Using *at* to Schedule Delayed Commands

The at command is used to schedule a single command for execution at a later time. It is a tool that reads a series of commands from the standard input and schedules them for execution at a later time. Using at allows you to schedule system-intensive jobs for off hours.

Introduction to *at*

In its most basic form, you run at *time* and then type in a series of commands (followed by EOF) to be executed at the time you specify. The time can be one, two, or four digits (different versions of at support somewhat different time specifications; check your online manual by typing man at or check your hardcopy manuals to learn more about your version of at). If you use one or two digits, the time is in hours. If you use four digits, the time is in minutes. The time is in twenty-four hour clock time. The output of a job submitted to at is sent to you by electronic mail.

> **NOTE:** Some systems allow specifying an AM (or even just A) or PM (or just P) suffix to use twelve-hour time. Some systems allow more detailed specification of time and date. Check your system manuals to be sure what your system allows. This introduction covers the lowest common denominator of at features from BSD, POSIX, and System V.

For example, to schedule a job to read the message of the day file and mail it to yourself at 5:30 p.m. today:

```
% # This example is from Solaris 2.3, which is SVR4
% at 1730
cat /etc/motd ¦ mail myself
<ctrl><d>
warning: commands will be executed using /usr/bin/sh
job 763169400.a at Tue Mar  8 17:30:00 1994
%
```

NOTE: In this example, at printed out a warning. The warning was because the shell used by at on that system was different from the shell being used by the user. On most systems, at defaults to using /bin/sh, which is usually the Bourne Shell.

TIP: Some versions of at allow you to specify that commands should be run with the csh. This is implemented in the -c option introduced in BSD. Check your system manual to see whether your version of at supports this.

Scheduling Personal Reminders

One important use of the at command is to schedule personal reminders. For example, if you have a meeting at 10:00 a.m. (and you run X11 and have the xmessage command), you might try the following command:

```
$ # This example is from HP-UX
$ at 10
xmessage -display \fIhostname\fB:0.0 "You have a meeting!!!"
<ctrl><d>
job 763056000.a at Mon Mar 07 10:00:00 1994
$
```

This command schedules an at job that will run the xmessage program at 10 a.m. to display the message "You have a meeting!!!" on your X display.

Scheduling Big Jobs for Later

Often, when you are using a computer, you will have large jobs that take up lots of computer time, memory, or do lots of input and output. You may want to run these jobs when you are away from your machine so that the machine won't be heavily loaded when you need it for other tasks.

For example, if you want to run a large make that compiles many C files to build a tool you are working on, you might try:

```
$ #This example is from a BSD system
$ cd make_directory
$ at 1930
at> make -k all > /dev/null
at> <ctrl><d>
$
```

> **TIP:** This example introduces an interesting technique for using at. It redirects the standard output, which will contain all the messages from make and the tools run by make, to /dev/null, which is the bit bucket. This means that you will get only mail notification about errors encountered during the job. This is a particularly useful technique for jobs that might have lots of "normal" output that you don't care about. Look at the examples in the sections on cron for more information.

Using Batch to Manage Big Jobs

> **CAUTION:** The batch command is part of System V but is not available on all versions of UNIX. Check your system to make sure that you can use this.

The batch command is very similar to the at command, with some useful differences. Rather than specify a time for your job to execute, the batch command schedules it to run as soon as possible with the restriction that only one or two batch jobs run at a time. Jobs submitted with batch also run with a higher nice value so that they won't interfere with CPU usage. These two differences make batch a useful tool for scheduling large jobs that need to finish as soon as possible. The example of the make job shown previously is easily modified to work with batch:

```
$ #This example is from a Solaris system
$ cd make_directory;
$ batch
make -k all > /dev/null
<ctrl><d>
warning: commands will be executed using /usr/bin/sh
job 763072415.b at Mon Mar  7 14:33:35 1994
at: this job may not be executed at the proper time.
$
```

This job will run immediately and all error output will be mailed to you when it completes. Normal output is discarded.

Queue Levels in *at*

> **CAUTION:** The implementation of queue levels is in the System V version of at, but is not available in all versions of UNIX. Check your system to make sure that you can do this.

The at and batch commands as they have been introduced are two different interfaces to a single job-queuing system on SYSV-based UNIX (and other versions of UNIX that have added these features). The queuing system is implemented in the SYSV cron program (see "Chronologically Speaking—cron" later in this chapter). There are 25 queues available: a, b, and d-z ("c" is used internally to implement crontab). By default, there are two queues that are implemented. Queue "a" is used for jobs submitted by at; it allows a larger number of jobs (typically 4) to run with a small nice value (typically 1). Queue "b" is used for jobs submitted by batch; it allows a smaller number of jobs (typically 2) to run with a larger nice value (typically 2).

On systems that use this version of cron, you may be able to add new queue levels by editing the queuedefs file (typically in /usr/lib/cron/queuedefs).

The template for a queuedefs entry is:

```
q.[jobj][nicen][nwaitw]
```

in which:

> q is the queue designation: "a", "b" or c-z
> job is the maximum number of simultaneous jobs
> nice is the nice value for each job
> nwait is the number of seconds to wait between attempts to reschedule a job delayed because of njob limits

A typical queuedefs file looks like the following:

```
a.4j1n
b.2j2n90w
m.1j10n600w
```

Queue "a" can have a maximum of four jobs running with nice value of one and a (default) reschedule delay of sixty seconds. Queue "b" can have a maximum of two jobs running with nice value of two and a reschedule delay of ninety seconds. Queue "m" can have a maximum of one job running with nice value of ten and a reschedule delay of ten minutes.

Listing Your *at* Jobs

Both the SYSV and BSD versions of at allow you to examine the list of jobs you have in the queues. The method of getting the list and the appearance of the output are slightly different.

On SYSV, you can list at jobs using at -1, which lists all jobs that you have in any of the at queues. For example, with several batch jobs submitted and a couple of jobs waiting to run in queue "m" (as specified in the example in the preceding section, "Queue levels in at") and a single regular at job scheduled for 5:30 p.m., your output might look like the following:

```
$ date
Wed Mar  9 15:13:56 CST 1994
$ at -l
763247633.m     Wed Mar 09 15:13:53 1994
763255800.a     Wed Mar 09 17:30:00 1994
763247641.m     Wed Mar 09 15:14:01 1994
763247595.b     Wed Mar 09 15:13:15 1994
763247599.b     Wed Mar 09 15:13:19 1994
763247602.b     Wed Mar 09 15:13:22 1994
$
```

On BSD, you can list at jobs using atq, which lists all jobs that you have in the single queue. With a single job scheduled, your output might look like the following:

```
$ at

LAST EXECUTION TIME: Mar 9, 1994 at 15:00

Rank      Execution Date    Owner    Job #    Job Name
  1st   Mar 10, 1994 12:00  sartin   66588    stdin
$
```

Removing *at* Jobs

If you make a mistake or change your mind about running a job, you can remove it from the queue. If you didn't save the job ID that is printed by some versions of at when they add your job to the queue, you can get the job ID by listing at jobs and removing the job. On SYSV, you remove the job using at -r *jobid*:

```
$ at -l
763250700.a     Wed Mar  9 16:05:00 1994
$ at -r 763250700.a
$ at -l
$
```

On a BSD system, you remove the job using atrm *jobid*:

```
$ atq

LAST EXECUTION TIME: Mar 9, 1994 at 15:00

Rank      Execution Date    Owner    Job #    Job Name
  1st   Mar 10, 1994 12:00  sartin   66588    stdin
$ atrm 66588
 66588: removed
$ atq
no files in queue.
$
```

TIP: If you submit many jobs using at, you should save the job ID somewhere. The output of atq or at -1 isn't very helpful if you have lots of jobs scheduled for approximately the same time. On some systems, you will be able to edit the job file in /usr/spool/cron/atjobs/*jobid* or /var/spool/cron/atjobs/*jobid*, but it's best not to depend on this behavior.

Chronologically Speaking—*cron*

Although the at command is very useful for one-time jobs, it is somewhat difficult to use for scheduling repetitive tasks (see the note on using at to replace cron). UNIX also includes a program called cron that is responsible for running repetitively scheduled jobs in a flexible fashion.

Historically, cron was introduced as a tool for system administrators and originally only allowed scheduling of tasks by "root" using a file /etc/crontab that the cron program would read for information on what jobs to run at what times. Since that time, newer versions of cron have been introduced that allow individual users to have their own crontab, which specifies what jobs to run for that particular user.

NOTE: The use of cron by non "root" users is not available on all versions of UNIX (for example, BSD 4.2 and 4.3). The CD-ROM contains a version of cron that includes support for user-level crontabs.

Using at to Replace cron

On systems that don't have cron access for normal users, you can duplicate some of the features of cron by writing at jobs that reschedule themselves. For example, to write a script that runs weekly, you could add to the end of the script:

```
echo "sh this_script" | at 1900 thursday week
```

to reschedule *this_script* to run at 7 p.m. next Thursday. When *this_script* runs next Thursday, it will reschedule itself for the Thursday after that. Take great care when using scripts to reschedule themselves so that you don't lose control of your creations.

When cron runs a job for you, it executes using your user ID and privileges, but with a more sparse environment. A job executed by cron will run with sh (usually the Bourne shell) in your home directory, but will not execute .profile. The environment variables HOME, LOGNAME, PATH, and SHELL will be set. Your job should make minimal assumptions about its environment. For example, your PATH may only include /bin, /usr/bin and possibly your current working directory (which should be your home directory at the start of the job).

> **TIP:** To run scripts from cron using a different shell, use the #! construct at the start of your script. For example:
>
> ```
> #!/bin/ksh
> # This script uses Korn shell extensions
> typeset -i count=0
> while [ $count -lt 5 ]
> do
>       echo $count
>       (( count = count + 1 ))
> done
> ```

The output of each job you run is saved and sent to you by electronic mail.

> **TIP:** Write your cron jobs so that they produce output only if there is an error. Scripts that are going to produce statistics or summary information should probably be written to explicitly send mail with an informative subject line. That way, you know something has gone wrong when you receive a message from the cron daemon.

Manipulating Your *crontab*

There are several different operations available from the crontab command that are used to view, modify, or remove your crontab. To see your current crontab, use crontab -l. This will list your current crontab on the standard output. For an example, see Listing 20.1.

To replace your crontab with a new crontab, use the command crontab *new_crontab_file*. This will replace your crontab completely, so make sure that *new_crontab_file* has any old crontab entries you want to keep. A good way to do this is to use crontab -l first:

```
$ crontab -l > new_crontab_file
$ vi new_crontab_file
[edit the file to update your crontab]
$ crontab new_crontab_file
$
```

Some versions of crontab support a special option for editing and replacing your crontab. If your system supports this, you can edit your crontab by executing crontab -e.

To make it so that cron will not execute any jobs for you, you could execute crontab / dev/null, which would give you an empty crontab. A better way to do this is to execute crontab -r, which will remove your crontab completely.

Decoding a *crontab*

A crontab has six fields:

> minute (0-59)
> hour (0-23)
> day of month (1-31)
> month of year (1-12)
> day of week (0-6, 0 is Sunday)
> Command (rest of line)

The first five fields are numeric patterns, which can be an asterisk (which means to use all legal values) or a list of elements. An element is either a single number or two numbers separated by a hyphen (which specifies an allowed range). Note that both a day of month and day of week are specified. If both fields are used, they are both honored. For example:

```
0 17 1 * 0   date ¦ mail user
```

will execute at 5 p.m. on the first of each month as well as at 5 p.m. on every Sunday.

Now look at Listing 20.1 in detail. Each line in the sample crontab illustrates a technique for using cron.

See LIST20_1 on the CD-ROM for a not-so-typical crontab.

Look at the line in Listing 20.1 that runs a program called hourly. Notice that both day fields, the month field, and the hour field are wild cards, whereas the minute field is "0." This means that the job will run on all days of all months at all hours at 0 minutes into the hour. This job runs every hour on the hour.

Look at line 2 in Listing 20.1 that runs a program called quarter_hourly. Note the change. Note the use of a list in the minute field. The minute field is now a list of "0,15,30,45." This means that the job will run on all days of all months at all hours at 0, 15, 30, and 45 minutes into the hour. This job runs every quarter hour.

The business_hourly script runs every hour during business hours. Note the use of ranges in the hour field (to limit the job to run between 8 a.m. and 6 p.m.) and the day of week field (to limit the job to run Monday through Friday).

Look at the line in Listing 20.1 that runs a program called `daily`. Notice that both day fields and the month field are wild cards, whereas the hour field is "8" and the minute field is "0." This means that the job will run every day at 8 a.m. The `weekly` script will run every Monday at 8 a.m. The `monthly` script will run just after midnight on the morning of the first of each month.

The two executions of the `birthday` script will each run once per year, one on April 20, with the argument `rachel`, and one on October 7, with the argument `rob`.

See Listing 20.2 for an example of a Korn shell script intended to be run as a `cron` job. This script sends a status summary based on the contents of two files in `~/status`: a file named `todo`, which is a "to do" list, and a file named `done`, which is a list of tasks completed. During the week, you can move items from the `todo` file to the `done`. At the end of the week, this script can be run from `cron` and it will mail a weekly summary, add your `done` items to the file `log`, and mail a summary to you. Note that the script redirects all expected output either to a file or to the *mail_command*. Note that it tries to configure using only the environment variables `LOGNAME` and `HOME`. It uses only standard commands that are available in the default `PATH`.

Here is a `cron` entry to run this script every Monday morning at 8:00:

```
0     8     *     *     /u/sartin/bin/status_report
```

 See `LIST 20_2` on the CD-ROM for a sample `cron` script.

> **WARNING:** Twice a year, users of `cron` get to experience the potential of having some jobs run twice or not at all when they were expected to run exactly once. The problem is that once a year (when you set your clocks back) some local clock times occur twice, and once a year (when you set your clocks ahead) some local clock times don't occur at all. Most versions of `cron` attempt to deal with this by making jobs that are scheduled for ambiguous times (those that occur twice in one day) run exactly once, and those that are scheduled for nonexistent times (the ones that were skipped when the clock was set ahead) run once, but at a different time than requested in the `crontab`. Historically, different versions of `cron` have run some jobs twice or not at all near the time change.

> **TIP:** Schedule daily, weekly, and monthly jobs to avoid ambiguous and nonexistent times due to daylight savings time changes. For example, instead of scheduling a weekly backup to run at 2 a.m., schedule it for 0055 (55 0 ...) or 0303 (3 3 ...). This will ensure that your job runs once even if your `cron` doesn't do what you expect.

cron for the System Administrator

As a system administrator, you will either control cron and at access using cron.allow or cron.deny and at.allow and at.deny (Check your system's documentation to determine the locations of these files. They are typically in /usr/spool/cron or /var/spool/cron.) You will need to make a basic policy decision on whether users should be granted access to these tools. One possible policy is that all users are granted access and are denied access only if they abuse the facility; in this case, use the cron.deny file to list those users who should not use cron, and at.deny to list those who should not use at. Another possible policy is that users must request permission to use these tools; in this case, use cron.allow and at.allow to list users who have been granted permission.

> **TIP:** Choose your policy right away so that you can get your configuration set up correctly. Don't try to mix cron.allow and cron.deny. Similarly, don't attempt to mix at.allow and at.deny.

> **NOTE:** If your system runs a cron that supports a crontab only for "root," you may want to consider installing the vixie-cron package from the CD-ROM. This will give your users access to the crontab command. You will need a separate atrun command if you wish to continue using at, because this package doesn't implement at queues.

Using *cron* to Schedule Administrative Tasks

You should use one or more crontabs to schedule all of your repetitive administrative tasks, such as backups, log file administration, news expiration, and file archival. See Listing 20.3 for a sample script that does simple log file pruning. Run this from your crontab as prunelog *path_to_log_file* . . . . It will keep the 10 most recent days (or weeks or hours) of log files available for review, and throw out older data to prevent running out of disk space.

If your system uses a cron like the SYSV one, you should take advantage of the user-specific crontabs to split administrative tasks. For example, all Usenet cron jobs should be in the crontab for user netnews (or whatever user ID you use for the news software). Only those jobs that need "root" privileges should be in the crontab for "root."

Here is a crontab entry that will execute this job to prune /usr/spool/mqueue/syslog:

```
0    1    *    *    *    /usr/adm/prunelog    /usr/spool/mqueue/syslog
```

See LIST20_3 on the CD-ROM for a program that prunes log delete files with cron.

Summary

In this chapter, you have learned how to use at to schedule one-time jobs; how to use batch (and at -q) to run large jobs without loading your system badly; and how to use cron to schedule recurring jobs. These techniques should help you to get maximum benefit out of your computer even when you are not around to use it.

Text Formatting and Printing

5

PART

Basic Formatting with troff/nroff

21

By James C. Armstrong

One of the most common uses for any computer is text processing, and in this respect machines running UNIX are no different than any others.

Many products exist for UNIX machines, including WordPerfect, Microsoft Word, IslandWrite, and FrameMaker. Although very powerful, these text processors might not be available on every machine. The best solution for almost every platform is the `troff` text processor and its cousin, `nroff`. `troff` is short for "text run-off" and was originally developed by Joseph Ossanna in the early 1970s, for use with the Graphics Systems CAT typesetter. This was the typesetter in use at the Murray Hill Computer Center of Bell Labs, where UNIX was first developed. In 1979, in response to the need to support more type-setters, Brian Kernighan rewrote `troff`. Although alternatives were investigated, UNIX had already invested a large amount of effort in `troff`, including macro packages and pre-processors for the utility. You have already learned about manual pages, which are written in `troff` using a specialized macro package.

Closely associated with `troff` is `nroff`. They both use the same set of commands to format text, the biggest exception being that `nroff` does not support commands for changing point sizes and supports only a limited number of character set changes. `nroff` also provides ASCII output, so you can see the results of your `nroff` command on your screen. Although third-party products can show the results of your `troff` command on screen if they have graphics capabilities, on a standard UNIX system, the only way to see the `troff` output is to send it to a printer.

Formatting with *nroff/troff*: An Overview

Many word processors such as Microsoft Word and WordPerfect are *WYSIWYG* processors (what you see is what you get). With those word processors, you choose menu items or press key combinations that cause the formatting to occur right on the screen, but the formatting codes do not appear in your document. Text processors like `nroff` and `troff` are called *descriptive markup languages,* which means that you enter the formatting codes into your document like any other text, and you don't see the effects of those instructions until you print the file.

Several building blocks are available for formatting files using `nroff` and `troff`, including the following:

> *Primitive requests*   The standard command in `troff` is called a primitive request and has the form of a period followed by two lowercase letters. The period must appear in the first column, and any text after the request is an argument. Primi-tives are used to do all kinds of formatting, such as indenting paragraphs, adding space between paragraphs, changing fonts, and centering text. This chapter provides examples of using the more common primitives and a quick reference

that briefly describes all primitives. If you are new to nroff/troff, you might want to try using a macro package before you dive into primitives.

Macros   Most UNIX systems provide standard macro packages, which enable you to format documents more easily than with primitives. Macros perform operations more or less automatically, such as formatting bulleted lists, headings, and indented paragraphs. Four macro packages, mm, ms, me, and man are described in detail in Chapter 22, "Formatting with Macro Packages." Chapter 27, "Writing Your Own Macros," shows you the ins and outs of creating macros. You can create a file using only macro package commands, or you can mix macros and primitives in the same file.

Preprocessors   Most UNIX systems provide standard preprocessors. Each preprocessor is a set of commands devoted to a special task. You can format tables with the tbl preprocessor (Chapter 23), equations with eqn (Chapter 24), line drawings with pic (Chapter 25), and graphs with grap (Chapter 26). You can create a file containing only preprocessor commands, and you can embed preprocessor commands in regular documents formatted with primitives, a macro package, or both.

Strings   Strings can be defined, just as macros can. For example, if you were writing about a new product whose name hadn't been decided yet, you could define a string for the temporary name "Hot New Product." When the name was finally chosen, you wouldn't have to do a global search and replace for "Hot New Product." You could just redefine the string to produce "XYZZY Thingo." Specific instructions for defining strings are in the section titled "Strings and Macros" later in this chapter, and in Chapter 26, "Writing Your Own Macros."

Number registers   Number registers are used to keep track of values like your current font and point size, your current indentation, and the current list item. They are really nothing more than storage locations. Some are read-only; others can be manipulated. You can define your own number registers and use them in macros. Specific examples are given in the section titled "Number Registers" later in this chapter, and in Chapter 26, "Writing Your Own Macros."

NOTE: troff insists on calling these registers "number registers," but in fact they don't need to contain numbers; they can—and often do—contain alphabetic characters.

Escape sequences   Escape sequences (backslash-character or backslash-open-parenthesis-character-character) can be used to change fonts and point sizes and for many other tasks. Some escape sequences enable you to enter troff primitives in-line with the text they affect rather than on lines by themselves. Specific examples are given in the section titled "In-Line Escape Sequences" later in this chapter and in other chapters where they apply.

Special characters   Although these are system-dependent, there are a number of special characters that are usually available on all systems, such as a long dash, a degree symbol, and a copyright symbol. Specific examples are given in the section titled "Special Characters" later in this chapter and in other chapters where they apply.

Processing `troff` and `nroff` files for printing is discussed in Chapter 29, "Processing, Printing, and Troubleshooting Formatted Files."

Chapters 21 through 29 give you a good start on using the `nroff/troff` family of text processing tools, but there is much more that you can do with them. For additional information, you can consult the `nroff` and `troff` man pages online or your local bookstore for books dedicated to this subject.

Printing *nroff* and *troff* Files

UNIX offers a selection of commands and utilities for printing. Printing `nroff` and `troff` output files is covered in detail in Chapter 29. It describes the role of the preprocessors, `nroff` and `troff`, the role of the postprocessors, and introduces you to PostScript. It also reviews raw printing (just dumping the contents of your file with no formatting at all) because sometimes you'll want to print a file without formatting it.

Text Filling and Adjusting

The cleanest look to any document is when the text looks symmetric, with one or two smooth margins, and spread across the page—like this paragraph. The default settings for `nroff` and `troff` are to "fill" each line with text, and to "adjust" the position of the text so that all lines begin at the left margin, and the right margin is *justified*. In the simplest case, the input file does not need any `troff` requests to format a basic document. Listing 21.1 illustrates a basic input file, and Figure 21.1 illustrates the output produced by `nroff`.

Listing 21.1. Basic `nroff/troff` source with no requests.

```
We, the people of the United States, in order
to form a more perfect Union, establish justice, insure
domestic tranquility, provide for the common defense, promote
the general welfare,
and secure the blessing of liberty to ourselves and our posterity do
ordain and establish this Constitution for the United States of
America.
```

FIGURE 21.1.

nroff output with no requests.

```
We, the people of the United States, in order to form a more per-
fect  Union, establish  justice, insure domestic  tranquility, pro-
vide for the common defense, promote  the  general  welfare,  and
secure  the blessing of liberty to ourselves and our posterity do
ordain  and establish this Constitution for the United  States  of
America.
```

The raw text file has a ragged right margin, with some lines very short, and one line longer than desired. By putting the text through nroff, the lines are set to an even length, and the margins are smooth. Two words were broken across lines. If you look closely at the output, you'll see that nroff justifies the right margin by inserting extra spaces between words, at alternating ends of each line. The first line needed no extra spaces, but to even the margin on the second line, an extra space was included between "perfect" and "Union," and the third line needed four extra spaces.

troff output of the same text, shown in Figure 21.2, shows that the lines are expanded to justify the margins by changing the spacing of letters across the entire line.

FIGURE 21.2.

troff output of Figure 21.1.

We, the people of the United States, in order to form a more perfect Union, establish justice, insure domestic tranquility, provide for the common defense, promote the general welfare, and secure the blessing of liberty to ourselves and our posterity do ordain and establish this Constitution for the United States of America.

The ability to fill the text can be set with two requests. The first, .fi, tells troff that you want the text to be filled with input. This is the default setting. The request .nf tells troff that you don't want text filled, that you want the right margin to be *ragged*. This is useful for cases where a block of text is inappropriate, such as a return address or poetry. Listing 21.2 shows a sample input file for a letter, with no fill in places, and fill in places. Figure 21.3 shows the output.

Listing 21.2. troff **source illustrating the fill requests.**

```
.nf
101 Main Street
Morristown, NJ  07960
15 March, 1994

Dear Sir,

.fi
I just wanted to drop you a note to thank you for spending the
time to give me a tour of your facilities. I found the experience
both educational and enjoyable. I hope that we can work together
to produce a product we can sell.
```

FIGURE 21.3.

troff output showing filled and nonfilled text.

101 Main Street
Morristown, NJ 07960
15 March, 1994

Dear Sir,

I just wanted to drop you a note to thank you for spending the time to give me a tour of your facilities. I found the experience both educational and enjoyable. I hope that we can work together to produce a product we can sell.

Note that a blank line is used to separate blocks of text. On a longer document, these blank lines can be used to separate paragraphs. Another way to separate blocks is to use .br. This interrupts the filling of the current line and starts a new block of text. The same can be done by starting a line of text with a space. Figure 21.4 shows the output of Listing 21.1, but includes a break after "the general welfare."

FIGURE 21.4.

troff output showing the effect of a break in midsentence.

We, the people of the United States, in order to form a more perfect Union, establish justice, insure domestic tranquility, provide for the common defense, promote the general welfare,
and secure the blessing of liberty to ourselves and our posterity do ordain and establish this Constitution for the United States of America.

Although smooth margins are the default, this is also something under the control of the writer. The .ad command controls adjustment. It can take the following as arguments: l means to adjust the left margin only; r is to adjust the right margin only; c is to center each line; and b or n means to adjust both margins. Figure 21.5 shows the effects of .ad l, .ad r, and .ad c on the first text sample. .ad b is the default starting value and is effectively demonstrated in the first example.

FIGURE 21.5.

troff output showing the effects of different line adjustments.

We, the people of the United States, in order to form a more perfect Union, establish justice, insure domestic tranquility, provide for the common defense, promote the general welfare, and secure the blessing of liberty to ourselves and our posterity do ordain and establish this Constitution for the United States of America.

We, the people of the United States, in order to form a more perfect Union, establish justice, insure domestic tranquility, provide for the common defense, promote the general welfare, and secure the blessing of liberty to ourselves and our posterity do ordain and establish this Constitution for the United States of America.

We, the people of the United States, in order to form a more perfect Union, establish justice, insure domestic tranquility, provide for the common defense, promote the general welfare, and secure the blessing of liberty to ourselves and our posterity do ordain and establish this Constitution for the United States of America.

Obviously, adjustment makes no sense if the text is not filled. Right margin adjustment can also be turned off with .na. The adjustment mode is not changed.

The last type of text adjustment is centering. This is a bit different than .ad c, which continues to fill lines before centering the text, but only if .fi is specified. The centering request is .ce and can be followed by a number. This centers the next line or lines, without filling text. If the text is being filled, each input line is treated as if it is followed by a break. Non-filled lines would be treated the same as .ce. Chapter titles are an example of text centering. Listing 21.3 is the source for a centering command, and the output is illustrated in Figure 21.6.

Listing 21.3. `troff` **source for the centering command.**

```
.ce 3
Scientific Methods of Computing
A Simulation
by John Smith
```

FIGURE 21.6.

The effects of the centering request.

Scientific Methods of Computing
A Simulation
by John Smith

Vertical Spacing

There are three types of vertical space controls in `troff`. Baseline spacing controls the basic spacing between consecutive lines of text. The next type is extra line spacing; this is the ability to double-space text, or more, both on a regular basis, and on a per case basis. The last is a block of vertical space.

Space measurements have different scales. When a request needs a distance, you can use the default type or modify the number with an indicator. The measurement types are inches, centimeters, Picas, Ems, Ens, points, units, and vertical line spaces. A Pica is 1/6 of an inch. An em is the width of the letter *m* and is dependent on the font used in `troff`. An en is half an em. The modifiers are listed in Table 21.1.

Table 21.1. `troff` **space measurement modifiers.**

Measurement Option	Description
i	inch
c	centimeter
p	Pica
m	Em
n	En
p	point
u	unit
v	vertical space

The default vertical spacing between lines of text is dependent on the text processor used. For `nroff`, it is 1/6 of an inch. For `troff`, it is 12 points. This can be changed with `.vs`. For `nroff`, the command argument is rounded to Picas, so if extra space is needed regularly, `.ls` is clearer. With `troff`, the default space measurement is points, although any measurement type can be used. An example of different spacings is given in Figure 21.7, using the initial text sample.

FIGURE 21.7.

Different vertical spacing using `troff`.

We, the people of the United States, in order to form a more perfect Union, establish justice, insure domestic tranquility, provide for the common defense, promote the general welfare, and secure the blessing of liberty to ourselves and our posterity do ordain and establish this Constitution for the United States of America.

We, the people of the United States, in order to form a more perfect Union, establish justice, insure domestic tranquility, provide for the common defense, promote the general welfare, and secure the blessing of liberty to ourselves and our posterity do ordain and establish this Constitution for the United States of America.

We, the people of the United States, in order to form a more perfect Union, establish justice, insure domestic tranquility, provide for the common defense, promote the general welfare, and secure the blessing of liberty to ourselves and our posterity do ordain and establish this Constitution for the United States of America.

FIGURE 21.8.

Different line spacing using `troff`.

We, the people of the United States, in order to form a more perfect Union, establish justice, insure domestic tranquility, provide for the common defense, promote the general welfare, and secure the blessing of liberty to ourselves and our posterity do ordain and establish this Constitution for the United States of America.

The `.ls` request, mentioned previously, is used to indicate the number of blank lines between each line of text. The default value is 1, for single spacing. Double-spacing text is accomplished with `.ls 2`. Figure 21.8 shows the first text sample, but with `.ls 2`.

Block spacing can be achieved with the `.sp` request. With no arguments, this gives a single blank line. It can take arguments of any size, with the default unit being the vertical spacing. Negative numbers space back up the page; positive numbers head down the page. Spacing changes requested here will not leave the page—if the requested space is beyond the bottom of the page, the text will start at the top of the next page. Using the sample letter, you can leave an inch of space between the date and the salutation. The source is changed in Listing 21.4, with the output in Figure 21.9.

Listing 21.4. `troff` source for block spacing.

```
.nf
101 Main Street
Morristown, NJ  07960
15 March, 1994
.sp 1i
Dear Sir,

.fi
I just wanted to drop you a note to thank you for spending the
time to give me a tour of your facilities. I found the experience
both educational and enjoyable. I hope that we can work together
to produce a product we can sell.
```

FIGURE 21.9.

troff output with a block of space.

```
101 Main Street
Morristown, NJ  07960
15 March, 1994




Dear Sir,

I just wanted to drop you a note to thank you for spending the time to give me a tour of your facilities.  I found
the experience both educational and enjoyable.  I hope that we can work together to produce a product we can
sell.
```

Another method to grab a block of vertical space is the .sv request. It takes the same arguments as .sp but has some different behaviors. You cannot request space at the top of a page with .sp, for example. Also, if a space request exceeds the size of the page, it is truncated at the bottom of the page with .sp. With .sv, the space is not generated unless there is room on the page for the space. In this case, the space requested is remembered and can be released on a new page with .os. Normally, .os appears only in complicated macro definitions, which are discussed later.

For the sample letter, save a half inch of space at the top of the page. The source is Listing 21.5, and the output is Figure 21.10.

Listing 21.5. `troff` source using .sv.

```
.sv 0.5i
.nf
101 Main Street
Morristown, NJ   07960
15 March, 1994
.sp 1i
Dear Sir,

.fi
I just wanted to drop you a note to thank you for spending the
time to give me a tour of your facilities. I found the experience
both educational and enjoyable. I hope that we can work together
to produce a product we can sell.
```

FIGURE 21.10.

troff output with requested space using .sv.

```
101 Main Street
Morristown, NJ  07960
15 March, 1994




Dear Sir,

         I just wanted to drop you a note to thank you for spending the time to give
    me a tour of your facilities.  I found the experience both educational and enjoyable.  I
    hope that we can work together to produce a product we can sell.
```

Two other spacing controls are also available. The request `.ns` turns off spacing mode, effectively disabling the `.sp` command. To restore spacing, `.rs` is used. These commands are more likely to be found in macros.

Line Controls

So far, I have examined `troff` requests to fill and adjust lines of text and to move your location on a page. I will now examine how to alter the line itself.

By default, the length of a line of text is 6.5 inches in `nroff`, and 7.54 inches in `troff`. This can be changed with the `.ll` request. The default space measurement is in ems, but I find using inches a bit easier. Listing 21.6 shows the source, changing the line length to 4 inches; its effect on the output is shown in Figure 21.11.

Lines of text can also be indented, both for a single line and for all text. The `.in` request indents all lines of text a common distance. This is illustrated by indenting the return address in Listing 21.6. A temporary indent can be requested with `.ti`, such as might lead a paragraph. This is also illustrated in Listing 21.6 and Figure 21.11.

Listing 21.6. `troff` source illustrating line indents and lengths.

```
.nf
.ll 4.0i
.in 2.0i
101 Main Street
Morristown, NJ  07960
15 March, 1994
.sp 1i
.in 0
Dear Sir,

.fi
.ti 0.25i
I just wanted to drop you a note to thank you for spending the
time to give me a tour of your facilities. I found the experience
both educational and enjoyable. I hope that we can work together
to produce a product we can sell.
```

Using text indents can help organize a document.

FIGURE 21.11.

troff output with line indents and lengths.

101 Main Street
Morristown, NJ 07960
15 March, 1994

Dear Sir,

    I just wanted to drop you a note to thank you for spending the time to give me a tour of your facilities. I found the experience both educational and enjoyable. I hope that we can work together to produce a product we can sell.

Page Control

So far, this chapter has examined how to format text independent of the page, but for most documents, page controls are necessary. Both nroff and troff default to an 11-inch page. troff has a one-inch left margin, and nroff has no left margin. Pages start at page one and are sequentially numbered. Each of these details can be changed by the document writer.

The .pl request sets the length of a page; the default space measurement is in vertical spaces. Again, inches can be better used here. For the sample letter, assume a page length of 8 inches. (Some other normal page lengths are 12 inches for A4 paper and 14 inches for legal-sized paper. troff can support pages up to 75 inches in length, and nroff up to 136 inches.)

You can force new pages with the .bp request. An argument can affect the number of pages output. The .ns request, mentioned earlier, disables the .bp request, unless a specific number of pages is requested.

The .pn request assigns a page number to the next page printed. This does not affect the present page, only subsequent pages. These three requests are illustrated in Listing 21.7 and Figure 21.12, an extended form of the letter.

Listing 21.7. troff source illustrating page controls.

```
.nf
.ll 5.0i
.pl 8.0i
.in 2.5i
101 Main Street
Morristown, NJ  07960
```

continues

Listing 21.7. continued

```
15 March, 1994
.in 0
.sp 1i
Dear Sir,

.fi
.ti 0.5i
I just wanted to drop you a note to thank you for spending the
time to give me a tour of your facilities. I found the experience
both educational and enjoyable. I hope that we can work together
to produce a product we can sell.
.pn 4
I am sending a copy of our proposal on the next page. I look forward
to hearing from you.
.sp 2
.in 2.5i
Yours,
.sp 0.5i
Joe Smith, President Any Corp.
.bp
.in 0
We propose to build our widget tools with your widget makers.
```

Note that the page number is not printed. Page numbers are printed only if explicitly requested by the programmer. These techniques are discussed later in this chapter in Section 21.19 "Flotsam and Jetsam," where I discuss page titling.

The text can be offset on the page using the .po request. This is different from the .in request. .po sets the 0 value for indents and temporary indents. This is illustrated in Figure 21.13, which has a page offset of two inches to the preamble of the Constitution.

Two very powerful page controls are the .mk and the .rt requests. The .mk request saves the current vertical location in an internal register (which can be specified in the argument). This sets a flag at the current location. The .rt request returns to that previous location. One good use for these requests is to establish multiple column output. The programmer can set the mark at the top of the page, and at the bottom of the page return to the mark. This is illustrated in Listing 21.8 and Figure 21.14. Note that the simple multiple column approach also requires the use of the .ll and .po requests.

FIGURE 21.12.

troff output with page controls.

101 Main Street
Morristown, NJ 07960
15 March, 1994

Dear Sir,

    I just wanted to drop you a note to thank you for spending the time to give me a tour of your facilities. I found the experience both educational and enjoyable. I hope that we can work together to produce a product we can sell.
 I am sending a copy of our proposal on the next page. I look forward to hearing from you.

        Yours,

        Joe Smith, President Fu-Bar Corp.

We propose to build our widget tools with your widget makers.

FIGURE 21.13.

troff output with a two-inch page offset.

We, the people of the United States, in order to form a more perfect Union, establish justice, insure domestic tranquility, provide for the common defense, promote the general welfare, and secure the blessing of liberty to ourselves and our posterity do ordain and establish this Constitution for the United States of America.

Listing 21.8. `troff` source using `.mk` and `.rt` requests.

```
.ll 3i
.mk a
.ce
Preamble
.sp
We, the people of the United States, in order
to form a more perfect Union, establish justice, insure
domestic tranquility, provide for the common defense, promote
the general welfare,
and secure the blessing of liberty to ourselves and our posterity do
ordain and establish this Constitution for the United States of
America.
.sp
.ce
Article I
.sp
Section 1  Legislative powers; in whom vested:
.sp
All legislative powers herein granted shall be vested in a
Congress of the United States, which shall consist of a Senate
and a House of Representatives.
.sp
Section 2  House of Representatives, how and by whom chosen,
Qualifications of a Representative. Representatives and direct
taxes, how apportioned. Enumeration. Vacancies to be filled.
Power of choosing officers and of impeachment.
.sp
1. The House of Representatives shall be composed of members
chosen every second year by the people of the several states,
and the electors in each State shall have the qualifications
requisite for electors of the most numerous branch of the
State Legislature.
.sp
2. No person shall be a Representative who shall not have
attained to the age of twenty-five years, and been seven years
a citizen of the United States, and who shall not, when elected,
be an inhabitant of that State in which he shall be chosen.
.sp
.rt
.po 4.5i
3. Representatives and direct taxes shall be apportioned among
the several States which maybe included within this Union,
according to their respective numbers, which shall be determined
by adding to the whole number of free persons, including those
bound for service for a term of years, and excluding Indians not
taxed, three-fifths of all other persons. The actual enumeration
shall be made within three years after the first meeting of the
Congress of the United States, and within every subsequent term
of ten years, in such manner as they shall by law direct. The
number of Representatives shall not exceed one for every thirty
thousand, but each State shall have at least one Representative;
and until such enumeration shall be made, the State of New
Hampshire shall be entitled to choose three, Massachusetts eight,
Rhode Island and Providence Plantations one, Connecticut five,
New York six, New Jersey four, Pennsylvania eight, Delaware one,
Maryland six, Virginia ten, North Carolina five, South Carolina
five, and Georgia three.
```

```
.sp
4. When vacancies happen in the representation from any State,
the Executive Authority thereof shall issue writs of election
to fill such vacancies.
.sp
5. The House of Representatives shall choose their Speaker and
other officers; and shall have the sole power of impeachment.
```

FIGURE 21.14.

troff output showing the work of .mk and .rt.

Preamble

We, the people of the United States, in order to form a more perfect Union, establish justice, insure domestic tranquility, provide for the common defense, promote the general welfare, and secure the blessing of liberty to ourselves and our posterity do ordain and establish this Constitution for the United States of America.

Article I

Section 1 Legislative powers; in whom vested:

All legislative powers herein granted shall be vested in a Congress of the United States, which shall consist of a Senate and a House of Representatives.

Section 2 House of Representatives, how and by whom chosen, Qualifications of a Representative. Representatives and direct taxes, how apportioned. Enumeration. Vacancies to be filled. Power of choosin officers and of impeachment.

1. The House of Representatives shall be composed of members chosen every second year by the people of the several states, and the electors in each State shall have the qualifications requisite for electors of the most numerous branch of the State Legislature.

2. No person shall be a Representative who shall not have attained to the age of twenty-five years, and been seven years a citizen of the United States, and who shall not, when elected, be an inhabitant of that State in which he shall be chosen.

3. Representatives and direct taxes shall be apportioned among the several States which maybe included within this Union, according to their respective numbers, which shall be determined by adding to the whole number of free persons, including those bound for service for a term of years, and excluding Indians not taxed, three-fifths of all other persons. The actual enumeration shall be made within three years after the first meeting of the Congress of the United States, and within every subsequent term of ten years, in such manner as they shall by law direct. The number of Representatives shall not excede one for every thirty thousand, but each State shall have at least one Representative; and until such enumeration shall be made, the State of New Hampshire shall be entitled to choose three, Massachusetts eight, Rhode Island and Providence Plantations one, Connecticut five, New York six, New Jersey four, Pennsylvania eight, Delaware one, Maryland six, Virginia ten, North Carolina five, South Carolina five, and Georgia three.

4. When vacancies happen in the representation from any State, the Executive Authority thereof shall issue writs of election to fill such vacancies.

5. The House of Representatives shall choose their Speaker and other officers; and shall have the sole power of impeachment.

The last page control is .ne. This is used to indicate that a certain amount of space is needed before the end of a page. Using this request, you can avoid starting paragraphs at the bottom of a page. Normally, .ne would be included in a macro. If the space requested is available, nothing happens. If the space is not available, the end of page processing is triggered.

Fonts and Style Controls

The previous sections have dealt with the positioning of text on the page and have ignored the actual modification of the text itself. This section handles different fonts and point sizes.

The standard font is a Times Roman font. Italic, Bold, and Special fonts are also available on all systems. Some sites may also include Helvetica, Bold-Helvetica, Italic-Helvetica, and Constant-Width fonts. Check your local system for which fonts are available.

The request .ft sets the appropriate font. Mounting and unmounting fonts is performed automatically with this request. The requested font must be specified in the argument; if no argument is present, the previous font is restored. The arguments are shown in Table 21.2.

Table 21.2. Standard `troff` and `nroff` fonts.

Identifier	Font
B	Bold
I	Italic
R	Roman
P	Previous
H	Helvetica
CW	Constant Width
HB	Helvetica Bold
HI	Helvetica Italic

Fonts have limited meaning in nroff. The font used is a constant-width font. By specifying bold, characters are overstruck in printing. Italic is interpreted as an underline. Other fonts have no meaning.

By setting fonts, you can italicize the preamble to the Constitution and print each section header in bold. The source is in Listing 21.9, and the output is in Figure 21.15.

Listing 21.9. Font selection in `troff`.

```
.ce
.ft B
Preamble
.sp
.ft I
We, the people of the United States, in order
to form a more perfect Union, establish justice, insure
domestic tranquility, provide for the common defense, promote
the general welfare,
and secure the blessing of liberty to ourselves and our
posterity do ordain and establish this Constitution for the
United States of America.
.sp
.ce
.ft B
Article I
.sp
.ft R
```

```
Section 1  Legislative powers; in whom vested:
.sp
All legislative powers herein granted shall be vested in a
Congress of the United States, which shall consist of a Senate
and a House of Representatives.
```

FIGURE 21.15.

*troff output using
multiple fonts.*

Preamble

*We, the people of the United States, in order to form a more perfect Union, establish justice, insure domestic
tranquility, provide for the common defense, promote the general welfare, and secure the blessing of liberty to
ourselves and our posterity do ordain and establish this Constitution for the United States of America.*

Article I

Section 1 Legislative powers; in whom vested:

All legislative powers herein granted shall be vested in a Congress of the United States, which shall consist of a
Senate and a House of Representatives.

The .bd request sets an artificial bold capability by offsetting a second printing of the character by a number of points. This can be used to make the italic font appear to be bold, with .bd I 3. There is no effect in nroff.

Different sizes of text can be created using the .ps request. You can specify either a relative change or an absolute point size. Closely related is the .ss request, which sets the width of the space character. Similarly, when the point size is changed, the vertical spacing may also need to be changed, or parts of consecutive lines may overlap. Using these requests, you can increase the size of the section headers in the Constitution and increase the size of the words "We the people." This is illustrated in Listing 21.10 and Figure 21.16.

Listing 21.10. troff **source showing multiple point sizes.**

```
.ce
.ft B
.ps 24
.ss 28
.vs 28
Preamble
.sp
.ft I
We, the people
.ps 12
.ss 14
.vs 14
of the United States, in order
to form a more perfect Union, establish justice, insure
domestic tranquility, provide for the common defense, promote
the general welfare,
and secure the blessing of liberty to ourselves and our
posterity do ordain and establish this Constitution for the
United States of America.
.sp
.ce
.ft B
```

continues

Listing 21.10. continued

```
Article I
.sp
.ft R
Section 1  Legislative powers; in whom vested:
.sp
All legislative powers herein granted shall be vested in a
Congress of the United States, which shall consist of a Senate
and a House of Representatives.
```

FIGURE 21.16.

Multiple point sizes in troff output.

Preamble

We, the people of the United States, in order to form a more perfect Union, establish justice, insure domestic tranquility, provide for the common defense, promote the general welfare, and secure the blessing of liberty to ourselves and our posterity do ordain and establish this Constitution for the United States of America.

Article I

Section 1 Legislative powers; in whom vested:

All legislative powers herein granted shall be vested in a Congress of the United States, which shall consist of a Senate and a House of Representatives.

The last text request is .cs, which sets a constant character width for a given font in troff. This takes three arguments. The first is a font, the second is the width of the space, and the last is the character point size. If the third argument is absent, the default is the current character width. If the second argument is also absent, that turns off the constant width.

Listing 21.11 shows this for the default Times Roman font in the preamble, and turns it off for the remainder of the Constitution. Figure 21.17 shows the output.

Listing 21.11. troff source illustrating the .cs request.

```
.ce
.ft B
.ps 24
.ss 28
.vs 28
Preamble
.sp
.ft I
We, the people
.ps 12
.ss 14
.vs 14
.ft R
.cs R 15
of the United States, in order
to form a more perfect Union, establish justice, insure
```

```
domestic tranquility, provide for the common defense, promote
the general welfare,
and secure the blessing of liberty to ourselves and our
posterity do ordain and establish this Constitution for the
United States of America.
.sp
.cs R
.ce
.ft B
Article I
.sp
.ft R
Section 1  Legislative powers; in whom vested:
.sp
All legislative powers herein granted shall be vested in a
Congress of the United States, which shall consist of a Senate
and a House of Representatives.
```

FIGURE 21.17.

troff output using .cs.

Preamble

We, the people of the United States, in order to form a more perfect Union, establish justice, insure domestic tranquility, provide for the common defense, promote the general welfare, and secure the blessing of liberty to ourselves and our posterity do ordain and establish this Constitution for the United States of America.

Article I

Section 1 Legislative powers; in whom vested:

All legislative powers herein granted shall be vested in a Congress of the United States, which shall consist of a Senate and a House of Representatives.

Fonts can also be specified by position—font 1, font 2, font 3, and so on. In the olden days of troff, before device-independent troff (ditroff), only four positions were available. Quite naturally, 1 was the body type (Times Roman), 2 was the italic version of 1, and 3 was the bold version of 1. You got one elective—position 4—but it was almost always used for the Special font (the one with Greek letters and mathematical symbols). As a consequence, specifying fonts by position is not done frequently.

The following examples all change the word "very" to italics (in nroff, the words are underlined):

```
This is \f2very\fP easy.
This is
.fp 2
very
.fp 1
easy.
```

Notice that in the first line, \fP is used to turn off italics. The P stands for Previous and resets the font to what it was before the italic font was requested (in this case, Times Roman). The second example resets the font to Times Roman by specifying its font position.

You can count on finding your default body type in position 1, italics in 2, and bold in 3. Beyond that, you have no idea. It depends on your system installation, and they're all different.

TIP: Don't specify font changes by position for any position other than 1, 2, or 3. If someone at another branch of your company prints your file, you don't know what font 4 might be, and you can't control the results.

What Does \f4 Look Like?

If you want to know what font is loaded in what position on your printers, create a test file that looks something like this:

```
When I ask for \ef4, I get \f4This Font\fP.
When I ask for \ef5, I get \f5This Font\fP.
When I ask for \ef6, I get \f6This Font\fP.
  .
  .
  .
```

Print the file, and you'll have a wall decoration that's attractive and useful.

In-Line Escape Sequences

The basics of document building are now passed. All the requests I have examined have been of the form *.xx* and stand alone on each line. Although any document can be produced using these requests, an in-line request may be easier to use in many cases. These can generate special characters, change fonts, change point sizes, and produce local motions.

Escape sequences (backslash-character or backslash-open-parenthesis-character-character) can be used to change fonts and point size and for many other tasks. Table 21.3 lists troff escape sequences.

Table 21.3. troff **escape sequences.**

Sequence	Description
\	Prevents the next character from being processed by troff
\e	Prints the escape character; default is the backslash (\)

Sequence	Description
\'	Prints acute accent
\'	Prints grave accent
\-	Prints a minus sign in the current font
\[space]	Creates an unpaddable 1-en space
\0	Prints a space the width of a digit
\¦	Prints a 1/6-em width space
\^	Prints a 1/12-em width space
\&	Nonprinting zero-width character
\!	Transparent line indicator
\"	Begins a comment
\\$n	Interpolates argument
\%	Before word, prevents hyphenation; in middle of word, indicates where word can be hyphenated
\(xx	Specifies character named *xx*
*x , *(xx	Specifies string named *x* or *xx*
\a	Specifies leader character used in macros
\b'abc...'	Bracket-building function
\c	Interrupts text processing
\d	Moves down half a line space
\D	Draws line, circle, ellipse, arc, or spline
\fx, \f(xx, \fn	Requests a font change; font with 1-character name is specified as \fH; font with 2-character name is specified as \f(HB.
\h'n'	Moves horizontally to the right; to move left, specify negative number
\H'n'	Sets character height to *n* points
\jx	Marks horizontal place on output line in register *x*
\kx	Marks horizontal place on input line in register *x*
\l	Draws horizontal line
\L	Draws vertical line
\nx, \n(xx	Interpolates number register *x* or *xx*
\o	Overstrikes specified characters
\p	Breaks output line

continues

Table 21.3. continued

Sequence	Description
\r	Reverse 1-em vertical motion
\s	Requests a change in point size; can be specified as an absolute value or with ±
\S'n'	Slants output *n* degrees to the right
\t	Horizontal tab
\u	Moves up half a line space
\v'n'	Moves vertically down; to move up the page, specify negative number
\w	Interpolates width of specified string
\x	Extra line-space function
\zc	Prints *c* with zero width (without spacing)
\{	Begins conditional input
\}	Ends conditional input
\[newline]	Concealed (ignored) newline
\X	*X*, any character not listed above

Listing 21.12 shows troff input with in-line font and size changes, and Figure 21.18 shows the output.

Listing 21.12. troff source with in-line font changes.

```
\fB\s+4We, the people\s-4\fP of the United States, in order
to form a more perfect Union, establish justice, insure
domestic tranquility, provide for the common defense, promote
the general welfare,
and secure the blessing of liberty to ourselves and our
posterity do ordain and establish this Constitution for the
United States of America.
```

FIGURE 21.18.

troff output with in-line font changes.

$2\pi r$

$\int \sin \tau d\tau = \cos \tau$

$\Sigma(\alpha \times \beta) \rightarrow \infty$

Two other in-line escapes are \& and \p. The \& escape is a zero-length control character and can be used to enable the printing of a control character (.) at the start of a line. The \p escape generates a break, but also requests that the line be spread to the current input line length.

Similarly, if a word requires extra vertical space, the in-line escape \x is used to request the additional vertical space. The amount of space needed must be enclosed in single quotes.

The next in-line escape deals with unfilled text only. If a line of unfilled text is terminated with a \c, the next text present will be treated as a continuation of that line. This allows the document writer to include a sequence of requests in the middle of a line, even if those requests do not have associated in-line escapes. The .cs request is an example of a case where \c may be used.

Fonts may be changed in-line by using the \f escape. Single character font identifiers can be designated with \fB, but two-character identifiers need a (to group the letters. An example would be \f(HI for a change to Helvetica-Italic. Point sizes can similarly be changed with \s. Here, two-digit fonts are acceptable. Relative changes can be made, too. Figure 21.18 shows a case where the words "We the people" are bold and four points larger than surrounding text.

Special Characters

Although special characters are system-dependent, there are several special characters that you can expect to have in your system. Table 21.4 lists these.

ASCII is limited to a small number of printable characters; fortunately, troff provides access to many more characters and symbols needed for mathematics and other applications. A few are escape sequences, but most are two-character escapes. Several two-character printing symbols are available, some on the default font, and some on a special font. These include Greek characters, mathematical characters, and editing symbols. An example of this is the mathematical expressions in Listing 21.13 and Figure 21.19.

Listing 21.13. In-line character requests for troff.

```
2\(*pr

\(issin\(*td\(*t\(eqcos\(*t

\(*S(\(*a\(mu\(*b)⌠(->\(if
```

FIGURE 21.19.

troff output of special characters.

We, the people of the United States, in order to form a more perfect Union, establish justice, insure domestic tranquility, provide for the common defense, promote the general welfare, and secure the blessing of liberty to ourselves and our posterity do ordain and establish this Constitution for the United States of America.

Other characters that can come in handy are bullets, \(bu, the copyright symbol, \(co, and daggers, \(dg. Four characters have their own commands. To print a backslash, use \\. A minus sign is \-, an open quote is \', and a close quote is \'.

Table 21.4 list the special characters typically available for the standard fonts.

Table 21.4. Special characters.

In-line Request	Character Produced
\\	backslash
\'	close quote
\'	open quote
-	hyphen
\-	current font minus sign
\(bu	bullet
\(co	copyright
\(ct	cent sign
\(de	degree
\(dg	dagger
\(em	3/4 em dash
\(ff	ff ligature
\(fi	fi ligature
\(Fi	ffi ligature
\(fl	fl ligature
\(Fl	ffl ligature
\(fm	foot mark
\(hy	hyphen
\(rg	registered trademark
\(ru	rule
\(sq	square
\(14	1/4
\(12	1/2
\(34	3/4

Strings and Macros

troff and nroff provide the ability to specify strings that can be used repeatedly. The strings can be given one- or two-character identifiers, and those identifiers can be referenced later. Strings can be defined with the .ds request. The next argument must be the identifier, and the string that follows is assigned to the identifier. The .as request appends additional text to the string. Accessing the string is accomplished with the in-line escape *. Our Constitution provides an example in Listing 21.14 and Figure 21.20.

Listing 21.14. troff source defining a string.

```
.ce
.ds us United States
Preamble
.sp
We, the people
of the \*(us, in order
to form a more perfect Union, establish justice, insure
domestic tranquility, provide for the common defense, promote
the general welfare,
and secure the blessing of liberty to ourselves and our
posterity do ordain and establish this Constitution for the
\*(us of America.
.sp
.ce
Article I
.sp
Section 1  Legislative powers; in whom vested:
.sp
All legislative powers herein granted shall be vested in a
Congress of the \*(us, which shall consist of a Senate and a
House of Representatives.
```

FIGURE 21.20.

troff output with a defined string.

Preamble

We, the people of the United States, in order to form a more perfect Union, establish justice, insure domestic tranquility, provide for the common defense, promote the general welfare, and secure the blessing of liberty to ourselves and our posterity do ordain and establish this Constitution for the United States of America.

Article I

Section 1 Legislative powers; in whom vested:

All legislative powers herein granted shall be vested in a Congress of the United States, which shall consist of a Senate and a House of Representatives.

TIP: Using a defined string for repeated text ensures a consistent look to the document.

Macros provide a technique for the document writer to group repeated requests into a single `troff` request. If the document writer notices that groups of requests are being repeated, those are ideal candidates for making a macro. Examples include quotations, paragraphs, and section headers. Chapter 26 goes into greater detail on macro writing; however, I will show you the basics here.

Macros are defined with the `.de` request. A one- or two-character label should follow the request. By convention, macro names are often uppercase, although this is not a requirement. The `troff` requests then follow the `.de` until the `..` request is present. These requests are then executed whenever the macro is called. You call the macro by starting the line with a `.` followed by the macro name, without a space.

Macros can be designed to take arguments. Up to nine arguments can be passed to a macro and are accessed as `\$N`, where N is the argument position from 1 to 9. These can be treated as ordinary variables and can be used anywhere in the macro. When a macro is defined, the contents of the commands are interpreted. This means that the presence of strings, variables, and comments are translated when the macro is read. To insure that the argument is not interpreted until the macro is used, the argument should be listed in the definition as `\\$N`. The `\\` will be interpreted as `\`. This `\\` can be used whenever the writer wants the escape to be interpreted when the macro is invoked.

Two examples are illustrated in Listing 21.15 and Figure 21.21. The first macro defined, `PP`, is used to signal a new paragraph. You first request a space, then you temporarily indent the first line by a quarter-inch. You also insure that the font is Times Roman. The second macro defined is for a header, `HD`. Give it two arguments: the first is the point size desired for the header and the second is the text of the header. First request a space, then change the point size to the requested size. Next, request that the text be centered and made bold. Then issue the text, reset the point size and font, and request an additional space.

Listing 21.15. `troff` source defining macros.

```
.de PP
.sp
.ti +0.25i
.ft R
..
.de HD
.sp
.ps \\$1
.ce
.ft B
\\$2
.ps
.ft P
.sp
..
```

```
.HD 14 "A sample header"
.PP
We begin the text of the first paragraph here. This is indented
and formatted. We continue with the text of the first paragraph
until we want the second paragraph.
.PP
We re-issue the macro, and get the space and indent.
```

FIGURE 21.21.

troff output with a defined macro.

A sample header

We begin the text of the first paragraph here. This is indented and formatted. We continue with the text of the first paragraph until we want the second paragraph.

We re-issue the macro, and get the space and indent.

Macros can be changed after creation using the .am request. This appends troff requests to the already existing macro, given in the first argument. In the preceding example, assume you wanted the second and subsequent paragraphs to have a point size of ten for the text. You could do this by including the following commands after the first call to PP:

```
.am PP
.ss 10
..
```

You could have redefined the macro with .de, but the .am request is quicker. You can also rename macros with .rn. This can be used even with standard troff requests and strings. The original name is the first argument, and the new name is the second argument. The old name is not retained.

Lastly, macros, strings, and other requests can be removed with .rm. Any subsequent commands to the macro will be ignored.

Number Registers

troff provides number registers for the tracking of parameters for troff. These can be accessed with the escape sequence \n. For single character names, like x, use \nx. For multiple character names, like xx, use \n(xx. Number registers are used for items such as page numbers and line length. The predefined registers include % for page number, dw for the day of the week, dy for the day, mo for the month, and yr for the year. nl also shows the position of the last printed line. Listing 21.16 shows how some of these registers can be used. Figure 21.22 is the output.

Listing 21.16. Using number registers.

```
.nf
.ll 5.0i
```

continues

Listing 21.16. continued

```
.in 2.5i
101 Main Street
Morristown, NJ  07960
\n(mo/\n(dy/\n(yr
.in 0
.sp
Dear Sir,
```

FIGURE 21.22.

*troff number registers
in output.*

101 Main Street
Morristown, NJ 07960
3/7/94

Dear Sir,

Many read-only registers contain configuration parameters. Some of these are listed in Table 21.5.

Table 21.5. Common number registers in `troff`.

Register	Description
.$	Number of arguments to a macro
.A	Set to 1 if -a is used on troff command line; always 1 for nroff
.T	Set to 1 if -T is used on nroff command line; always 1 for troff
.a	Value of extra space most recently used
.c	Number of lines read from current input file
.f	Current font
.h	Text high water mark for current page
.i	Current indent
.l	Current line length
.n	Length of text on previous output line
.o	Current page offset
.p	Current page length
.s	Current point size
.u	Fill more flag (1 for on, 0 for off)
.v	Current vertical line spacing

A short script to list default values is shown in Listing 21.17, with Figure 21.23 showing the output.

Listing 21.17. `troff` **source to identify register values.**

```
.nf
The current font is \n(.f
The current point size is \n(.s
The line length is \n(.l
The page length is \n(.p
The page offset is \n(.o
```

FIGURE 21.23.

troff output with register values.

The current font is 1
The current point size is 10
The line length is 2808
The page length is 4752
The page offset is 416

Of course, these registers are useful; however, the real benefit of registers comes from the user's ability to define their own registers. These can be used to track headers, paragraph numbers, and section numbers. The `.nr` request initializes and modifies user-specified registers. It takes two or three arguments: the first is the register name, and the second is the register modification. When first created, a register is assigned the value of zero. A positive number is added to the value; a negative number is subtracted. An optional third argument sets a default increment and decrement value. The automatic increment can be used in escape sequences: `\n+(xx` adds the increment to register `xx`, and `\n-(xx` subtracts the decrement.

The appearance of the number is set with the `.af` request. The first argument is the register, the second is one of six formats. `1` is for an Arabic number sequence, `001` is for a zero-filled Arabic number sequence. `i` and `I` are for Times Roman numbers, upper- and lowercase, and `a` and `A` are for alphabetic sequences.

Lastly, the `.rr` request removes a number register. There are a limited number of registers available, identified by the read-only register `.R`. The document writer may need to remove registers if space becomes a problem.

Listing 21.18 illustrates the source of a macro that numbers sections of the Constitution. The output is in Figure 21.24. The section header macros are for Articles, sections, and paragraphs of the constitution. First define the `aR` number register to count the articles, and set its display format to Times Roman numerals. You first define the `AR` macro. It centers a 16-point bold text, with the word "Article" and the number register. Note that you increment the number register every time you print the value. You also set the `sE` number register to zero, as an Arabic number. You then reset the point size and font. The SE macro is similar, printing the section and number, and setting pP to zero. The PP macro increments pP.

Listing 21.18. `troff` source using number registers.

```
.ce
Preamble
.sp
We, the people of the United States, in order
to form a more perfect Union, establish justice, insure
domestic tranquility, provide for the common defense, promote
the general welfare,
and secure the blessing of liberty to ourselves and our
posterity do ordain and establish this Constitution for the
United States of America.
.sp
.nr aR 0 1
.af aR I
.de AR
.ce
.ps 16
.ft B
Article \\n+(aR
.nr sE 0 1
.af sE 1
.ps 12
.ft P
..
.de SE
.sp
.ft B
\\s-2SECTION \\n+(sE:\\s+2
.ft P
.nr pP 0 1
.af pP 1
..
.de PP
.sp
.ft I
\\s-3Paragraph \\n+(pP:\\s+3
.ft P
..
.AR
.SE
Legislative powers; in whom vested:
.PP
All legislative powers herein granted shall be vested in a
Congress of the United States, which shall consist of a Senate
and a House of Representatives.
.SE
House of Representatives, how and by whom chosen, Qualifications
of a Representative. Representatives and direct taxes, how
apportioned. Enumeration. Vacancies to be filled. Power of
choosing officers and of impeachment.
.PP
```

The House of Representatives shall be composed of members chosen
every second year by the people of the several states, and the
electors in each State shall have the qualifications requisite
for electors of the most numerous branch of the State Legislature.
.PP
No person shall be a Representative who shall not have attained
to the age of twenty-five years, and been seven years a citizen
of the United States, and who shall not, when elected, be an
inhabitant of that State in which he shall be chosen.
.PP
Representatives and direct taxes shall be apportioned among the
several States which maybe included within this Union, according
to their respective numbers, which shall be determined by adding
to the whole number of free persons, including those bound for
service for a term of years, and excluding Indians not taxed,
three-fifths of all other persons. The actual enumeration shall
be made within three years after the first meeting of the
Congress of the United States, and within every subsequent term
of ten years, in such manner as they shall by law direct. The
number of Representatives shall not exceed one for every thirty
thousand, but each State shall have at least one Representative;
and until such enumeration shall be made, the State of New
Hampshire shall be entitled to choose three, Massachusetts eight,
Rhode Island and Providence Plantations one, Connecticut
five, New York six, New Jersey four, Pennsylvania eight,
Delaware one, Maryland six, Virginia ten, North Carolina five,
South Carolina five, and Georgia three.
.PP
When vacancies happen in the representation from any State, the
Executive Authority thereof shall issue writs of election to fill
such vacancies.
.PP
The House of Representatives shall choose their Speaker and other
officers; and shall have the sole power of impeachment.

FIGURE 21.24.

troff output with number registers.

Preamble

We, the people of the United States, in order to form a more perfect Union, establish justice, insure domestic tranquility, provide for the common defense, promote the general welfare, and secure the blessing of liberty to ourselves and our posterity do ordain and establish this Constitution for the United States of America.

Article I

SECTION 1: Legislative powers; in whom vested:

Paragraph 1: All legislative powers herein granted shall be vested in a Congress of the United States, which shall consist of a Senate and a House of Representatives.

SECTION 2: House of Representatives, how and by whom chosen, Qualifications of a Representative. Representatives and direct taxes, how apportioned. ·Enumeration. Vacancies to be filled. Power of choosin officers and of impeachment.

Paragraph 1: The House of Representatives shall be composed of members chosen every second year by the people of the several states, and the electors in each State shall have the qualifications requisite for electors of the most numerous branch of the State Legislature.

Paragraph 2: No person shall be a Representative who shall not have attained to the age of twenty-five years, and been seven years a citizen of the United States, and who shall not, when elected, be an inhabitant of that State in which he shall be chosen.

Paragraph 3: Representatives and direct taxes shall be apportioned among the several States which maybe included within this Union, according to their respective numbers, which shall be determined by adding to the whole number of free persons, including those bound for service for a term of years, and excluding Indians not taxed, three-fifths of all other persons. The actual enumeration shall be made within three years after the first meeting of the Congress of the United States, and within every subsequent term of ten years, in such manner as they shall by law direct. The number of Representatives shall not excede one for every thirty thousand, but each State shall have at least one Representative; and until such enumeration shall be made, the State of New Hampshire shall be entitled to choose three, Massachusetts eight, Rhode Island and Providence Plantations one, Connecticut five, New York six, New Jersey four, Pennsylvania eight, Delaware one, Maryland six, Virginia ten, North Carolina five, South Carolina five, and Georgia three.

Paragraph 4: When vacancies happen in the representation from any State, the Executive Authority thereof shall issue writs of election to fill such vacancies.

Paragraph 5: The House of Representatives shall choose their Speaker and other officers; and shall have the sole power of impeachment.

Traps and Diversions

So far, I have examined the results of invoking troff requests where you place them in your document. These are not the only examples of executing troff requests. You can specify macros to be executed at any given physical position on a document. These are called traps, and they can be triggered by page position, diversions, and input line count. A common use for page traps is to place headers or footers on pages. Diversion traps can be used to create footnotes in text, or to create a reference list for the end of a chapter. Input line traps count the number of lines since the request. These are useful for when macros are meant to be a single line.

Diversions are used to direct output to a macro, instead of to the page. The diversion requests are usually in macros, and traps must be set to produce the diversion output. Diversions are created with the .di request, the call followed by the name of the diversion macro. If no argument is present, the diversion ends, and output resumes on the page. Text can be added to the diversion with the .da request. Diversions can also be requested by page position with .dt, followed by the position and diversion macro name.

Traps are set with the `.wh` request. This is followed by a position and a macro name. If a macro had previously been set at that position, then that trap is removed. If no macro is passed as an argument, then any traps at that position are removed. The position of a macro trap can be changed with the `.ch` request, followed by the macro name and position. If a position is missing, the macro is removed. Input traps are set with the `.it` request, followed by a text position and macro name. Finally, a trailing macro can be set with `.em`. This sets a macro to be run at the end of input.

The use of diversions and traps is illustrated in Chapter 26, "Writing Your Own Macros."

Tabs, Character Conversions, and Controls

Tabs and tab spacing can be set by the document writer in troff. This gives the writer the ability to create simple tables by lining up columns and using tabs. The `.ta` request sets the tab stops, and if a stop value is preceded by a +, then the stop is relative to the previous tab stop. The tab repetition character (the character that fills the space between text and tab stops) can be specified with the `.tc` request. The nature of the tab stop can also be specified right after the tab stop distance. The text left-adjusts within the tab space by default. To center the text, use a `C` after the distance (no space), and use an `R` to right-adjust.

A simple table is illustrated in Listing 21.19, with the output in Figure 21.25.

Listing 21.19. Formatting a table using tabs.

```
.nf
.ta 3i 4.5i
Name            Birthday   Telephone

John Smith      1/1/70     (410) 555-1111
Dave Jones      2/2/63     (311) 800-0000
.tc -
Bob Williams    3/3/56     (999) 555-2222
```

FIGURE 21.25.

A formatted table with tabs.

Name	Birthday	Telephone
John Smith	1/1/70	(410) 555-1111
Dave Jones	2/2/63	(311) 800-0000
Bob Williams --3/3/56 ----------------------(999) 555-2222		

Some characters are considered control characters. These are the . used to signal a troff request, \ to indicate an in-line escape, and ' to indicate a breakless command. The escape character can be reset with the .ec request and can be turned off with the .eo request. .ec takes an argument, which is the new escape character. If no argument is present, it returns to the default. The .cc request changes the basic control character, ., to whatever is specified. This is particularly useful if a writer wishes to show a sample of troff input in a document, as shown in Listing 21.20 and Figure 21.26. Finally, .c2 changes the no-break control character from ' to the specified argument.

Underlining in nroff and italics in troff can also be invoked with the .ul and .cu requests. This turns on underline mode. In troff, the two requests have an identical effect; in nroff, .cu is for continuous underlining, and .ul underlines characters. The underlining font can be changed with the .uf request.

Character translations are also possible with troff. The .tr request is analogous to the tr UNIX command. Instead of two groups of characters, though, the from-to pairs of characters are side by side in a single character string argument. This is also illustrated in Listing 21.20 and Figure 21.26.

Listing 21.20. troff source illustrating character translations.

```
.nf
A sample of troff input:
.sp
.cc ,
.de PP
.br
.sp
.it +0.5i
..
,sp
,cc
And another sample:
.tr ,.
.sp
,de PP
,br
,sp
,it +0.5i
,,
```

Input can be made transparent to troff by prepending the input line with \!. This can be used to pass information to a post processor. Comments can also be embedded in the troff source document with \. This must come after the requests. It can appear at the start of a line if prepended with the control character.

FIGURE 21.26.

troff *output with*
character translations.

A sample of *troff* input:

```
.de PP
.br
.sp
.it +0.5i
..
```

And another sample:

```
.de PP
.br
.sp
.it +0.5i
..
```

Local Motions

Besides the .sp and related requests, there are in-line techniques to move the current output location in troff. These are called local motions and can be vertical or horizontal.

There are four types of vertical motions. All are in-line escapes. The first, \r, moves up single line. \d is used to move down half a line, for subscripts, and \u is used to move up half a line, for superscripts. Finally, \v'N' is used to make a local motion of vertical distance N. A negative number moves up the page, and a positive number moves down the page. You cannot leave the page with a local motion. An example is in Listing 21.21, with output in Figure 21.27.

There are five types of horizontal motions. Two simple space functions are \ , which is an unpadded space-sized space (as defined by .ss). The \0 request is a digit-sized space. \¦ produces one-sixth of a character width, and \^ produces one-twelfth. Finally, generic local motion is produced by \h'N'. The rules for vertical motions also apply to horizontal motions.

Listing 21.21. troff **source with local motions.**

```
Jan 26\u\s-2th\s+2\d is a sample.
.sp 2
We can move up \r easily.
.sp 2
Here is some space \0\0\0for us.
```

FIGURE 21.27.
*troff output with local
motions.*

Jan 26th is a sample.

                            easily.
We can move up

Here is some space   for us.

The width of a string can be determined with the \w escape. The string follows in single quotes. This width can be used in local motions and for other times when space measures are needed. Listing 21.22 illustrates how you can use this to place paragraph numbers outside the left margin of some text.

You can also mark the horizontal space with the \k request. Listing 21.22 also shows a primitive use of this to embolden a word, and Figure 21.28 shows its output.

Listing 21.22. `troff` source with width.

```
.sp 0.5i
.in 1i
.ti -\w'1.\0'u
1.\0This is a paragraph with a number indented out the
\kxleft\h'¦'\nxu+2u'left margin. We continue with the text to prove
the indent.
```

FIGURE 21.28.
*troff output with local
motions and width
calculations.*

1. This is a paragraph with a number indented out the left margin. We continue with th text to prove the indent.

Overstrikes, Lines, and Arcs

Characters can be overstruck with the \o escape. Up to nine characters can be overstruck, each appearing in the string following the escape.

Both vertical and horizontal lines can be drawn in troff. These are done by escape sequences \l, \L, and \D. The first draws a line of length specified in quotes after the escape. An optional character after the length can be used, and that will be used instead of the line. The second escape draws a horizontal line. The \D escape is the drawing escape, and it draws lines, circles, ellipses, and arcs. The specific format is the first character, followed by one to four arguments. These escapes are generated by calls to preprocessors like pic, described in Chapter 25, "Drawing Pictures with pic."

A line is drawn with two arguments, and the line is drawn from the present location to the specified location. The first character argument is l.

A circle of a fixed diameter is drawn with c. The single argument is the diameter.

An ellipse is drawn with e, and the two arguments are the two diameters of the ellipse.

An arc is drawn with a. There are four arguments, in two pairs. The arc is drawn from the present position to the first argument, assuming that the second argument is the center of the circle.

A spline can be drawn with the character ~. This can take an unlimited group of pairings, drawing the spline from the current position through the pairs of points.

Conditional Text

Like a programming language, troff and nroff provide for a conditional execution of requests. There are two forms of the if request: .if followed by a condition and then requests, and an if-else construct, .ie and .el. There are six conditional formats, and there is a format for grouping requests after an if: \{-requests-\}.

The six conditional forms are shown in the following.

```
.if c           .if !N

.if !c          .if 'string1'string2'

.if N           .if !'string1'string2'
```

In each of the six conditional forms, the ! represents the negation of the basic form. In the first two cases, c represents one of four special condition flags: o for an odd-numbered page, e for an even-numbered page, t for troff, and n for nroff. The middle two cases are for a numerical value N. The third case is for N>0, and the fourth case is for N<=0. In the last two cases, the strings are compared: if they are identical, the fifth is true; if not, the sixth is true.

if requests are rarely included in a normal document but are essential tools of macro writers. Macro writing is explored in greater depth in Chapter 26. Despite this, there are occasional circumstances where you might use the conditional. Listing 21.23 and Figure 21.30 show a simple case.

Listing 21.23. troff source with conditional input.

```
This text is formatted with the
.if n nroff
.if t troff
text processor.
```

File Switching and Environments

These text processors also provide the ability to change input files, and to modify output files. There are three ways to modify input.

Input can be requested with the .rd request. A prompt can be provided as an argument, and the input is read from the terminal until two consecutive newlines are input. This is often used for insertion into form letter type documents.

An entire file can be interpreted with the .so command. If a document writer has created his own macro set, he may wish to keep this in a separate file and include that file in sub-

FIGURE 21.29.

troff conditional output.

This text is formatted with the troff text processor.

sequent documentation using this request. Once the file has been read and interpreted, the text processor continues to read from the current file.

The .nx request is similar to the .so request, except that when the file is completed, the text processor is considered to have finished its input.

An example of these three requests is shown in Listing 21.24. Listing 21.25 shows the contents of the header file, which defines a few macros. Listing 21.26 shows the terminal session.

Listing 21.24. troff source with file requests.

```
.so headers
.in 3i
.nf
1 Main Street
Myhometown, ST  98765
\n(mo/\n(dy/\n(yr
.sp 2
.in 0
.rd Please_enter_the_company_address
.sp
Dear Sir,
.PP
I read your add in the \fISan Jose Mercury News\fP advertising
positions with
.rd Please_enter_the_company_name
for software engineers. I'd like to express my interest in
a position. My resume is enclosed.
.sp
.in 3i
Yours sincerely,
.sp 3
```

```
Joe Smith
.in 0
.bp
.nx resume
```

Listing 21.25. Contents of the header file.

```
.de PP
.sp
.ti +0.5i
.fi
.ad b
..
```

Listing 21.26. Terminal session with terminal input.

```
$ troff -t fig21.58src
Please_enter_the_company_address:The Fixture Company
1001 Main Street
Anytown, USA  77777

Please_enter_the_company_name:The Fixture Company

$
```

Note that the .rd request needed the underbars between words. The space would normally end the argument, even with surrounding double quotes. Also, note that the text read in is processed based on the fill and adjustment settings.

A fourth type of file input is .cf. This copies a file directly onto the output, without interpolation.

Output from nroff and troff can be piped automatically through a program. The .pi request must be placed before any output is generated, and it can receive no arguments.

The current settings for troff are considered the troff environment. These settings include indentation, page length, line length, fonts, and other values that describe the page. There are occasions when this environment may need to be saved. Three environments are allowed, and the specific environment can be set with the .ev request. The environments are numbered 0, 1, and 2. Environments are usually included in macro calls that include diversions, such as for footnotes.

Two other controls are for aborts and exits. The .ex request terminates input processing as if the file were complete. This is often used for debugging macros. The .ab request aborts all processing. Any arguments are printed on the diagnostic output, usually the terminal, and the program exits without terminal processing.

A last control is for system calls. The `.sy` request executes a UNIX command. The output is not captured anywhere, and there is no input.

Flotsam and Jetsam

There are a few requests I have not covered, which do not conveniently fit into any of the previous categories. These include hyphenation requests, three-part titles, and line numbering.

Four requests affect word hyphenation. The `.nh` request turns off all hyphenation, except for input with hyphens, such as "sister-in-law." The `.hy` request provides a greater control over hyphenation. It accepts a numeric argument. If 0, hyphenation is turned off. If 2, lines that will trigger a trap are not hyphenated. If 4, the first two characters of a word are not split off, and if 8, the last two are not split off. The values can be added to create a single hyphenation request. The `.hw` request enables the writer to specify hyphenation points within words, by using an embedded minus sign. An example might be `.hw fish-head`. The buffer for these words is only 128 characters in length.

Lastly, word hyphenation can be specified with an embedded character with a word. By default, this is `\%`, although the character can be changed with the `.hc` request.

A three-part title can be specified with the `.tl` request. This takes three strings as arguments, separated by a single quote and surrounded by single quotes: `.tl 'left'center'right'`. Any string can be empty. The title length is set with `.lt` and is separate from the `.ll` request. The page character, initially `%`, can be changed with `.pc`.

Output lines can be numbered with the `.nm` request. It takes up to four arguments: a start number, a multiplier, a spacing value, and an indent value. If a multiplier is present, only those lines that are even multiples will have numbers attached. The `.nn` request is used to ignore a number of lines for line numbering.

A margin character can be specified for the right margin using the `.mc` request. It takes two arguments: the margin character and a distance to the right for the character. This is often used to highlight changed sections of text between document revisions.

The `.tm` request is used to print a line to the invoking terminal.

The `.ig` request ignores all subsequent lines until the terminating request is issued, usually ...

The `.pm` request prints all the macros defined, and their associated sizes. The sizes are in

128-character blocks.

The .fl request flushes the output buffer.

The .lf request sets the current line number and file name.

Character heights can be changed in troff using the \H'*n*' in-line request. This can result in a disproportionate font. The value *n* is the point size height of the text.

Also illustrated is the ability to put the text at a slant, using the \S'*n*' request. The value *n* is the degree of slant.

Quick Reference of *nroff/troff* Requests

Table 21.6 presents all the nroff/troff requests along with their syntax. Arguments not in brackets are arguments that you must specify for the request. Arguments in brackets are optional arguments that you can specify for the request. Italicized arguments indicate that you need to substitute something specific; for example, .so *file* means that you need to provide a real filename as an argument to the .so request.

Table 21.6. nroff/troff **requests.**

Request	Description
.ab [text]	Abort and print message
.ad [c]	Adjust text margins
.af r c	Assign format c to register r
.am xx yy	Append following commands to macro xx, terminated with yy
.as xx string	Append string to defined string xx
.bd f n	Embolden font f with ^ overstrikes
.bd f s n	Embolden special font when current font is s, with ^ overstrikes
.bp [n]	Begin a page and set page number to n
.br	Break—stop filling text
.c2 c	Set no break control character
.cc c	Set control character
.cf filename	Copy file
.ce [n]	Center text
.ch xx [n]	Change trap position for macro xx to n

continues

Table 21.6. continued

Request	Description
.cs *f n m*	Use constant character spacing for font *f*
.cu [*n*]	Constant underlining
.da [*xx*]	Direct and append text to macro *xx*
.de xx [*yy*]	Define macro
.di [*xx*]	Direct text to macro *xx*
.ds *xx string*	Define string
.dt *n xx*	Install division trap
.ec [*c*]	Set escape character
.el *action*	Else portion of *if-else*
.em *xx*	Set macro to run at the end of the document
.eo	Turn off in-line escapes
.ev [*n*]	Change environment to *n* or restore environment
.ex	Exit formatter
.fc *a b*	Set field character and padding character
.fi	Fill text
.fl	Flush output buffer
.fp *n f*	Change font positions
.ft *f*	Change font in output
.hc [*c*]	Set hyphenation character
.hw *words*	Set hyphenation exception list
.hy *n*	Set hyphenation mode
.ie *c action*	If else
.if *c action*	If *c* is true, perform *action*
.if !*c action*	If condition is false, perform *action*
.if *n action*	If n>0, perform *action*
.if !*n action*	If n>=0, perform *action*
.if !'*string1*'*string2*' *action*	If strings are equal, perform *action*
.if !'*string1*'*string2*' *action*	If strings are different, perform *action*
.ig *yy*	Ignore subsequent text to *yy*
.in ±[*n*]	Set indent

Request	*Description*
`.it` *n* *xx*	Set input trap
`.lc` *c*	Set leader repetition character
`.lg` *n*	Set ligature mode
`.ll` ±[*n*]	Set line length
`.ls` *n*	Set line spacing
`.lt` *n*	Set title length
`.mc` [*c*] [*m*]	Set margin character
`.mk` [*r*]	Mark vertical place in register
`.na`	Do not adjust text
`.ne` *n*	If *n* lines do not remain on the page, get a new page
`.nf`	Turn off filling
`.nh`	Turn off hyphenation
`.nm` [*n* *m* s i]	Number output lines
`.nn` *n*	Disable numbering output but track line numbers
`.nr` *r* *n* [*m*]	Assign number register
`.ns`	Turn on no-space mode
`.nx` *file*	Go to the next file
`.os`	Output saved space
`.pc` *c*	Set page number character
`.pi` *command*	Pipe output of troff to *command*
`.pl` ±[*n*]	Set page length
`.pm`	Print names and sizes of macros
`.pn` ±[*n*]	Set next page number
`.po` ±[*n*]	Set page offset
`.ps` *n*	Set font point size
`.rd` [*prompt*]	Read input from #y
`.rm` *xx*	Remove macro or string
`.rn` *xx* *yy*	Rename macro, request, or string
`.rr` *r*	Remove register
`.rs` *xx* *yy*	Restore spacing
`.rt` ±[*n*]	Return back to marked place

continues

Table 21.6. continued

Request	Description
.so *file*	Include file
.sp *n*	Leave *n* blank lines
.ss *n*	Set character size
.sv *n*	Save *n* lines of space
.sy *command* [*arguments*]	Execute *command*
.ta *n*[*t*] *m*[*t*]	Set tab stops
.tc *c*	Set tab character
.ti ±*[n]*	Set temporary indent
.tl '*l*'*c*'*r*'	Three part title
.tm *message*	Display *message* on terminal
.tr *ab*	Translate characters
.uf *f*	Set underline font
.ul [*n*]	Underline lines
.vs [*n*]	Set vertical space
.wh *n* *xx*	Set trap locations

Summary

The essentials of troff allow a user to format a document. The real value of troff, though, comes when incorporated with a standard macro package, such as ms or me, which are described in the next chapter.

Formatting with Macro Packages

22

By Susan Peppard

IN THIS CHAPTER

This chapter is about macros and macro packages. Starting with a sample macro, you'll see how and why it works, and you'll see it evolve from simple to complex.

Macro packages are made of macros. By way of analogy, a macro package is to a macro as a macro is to a troff primitive. In the chapter, we will examine how to use the man macro package.

What Is a Macro?

With embedded troff primitives, you can format a page just about any way you want. The trouble is that you have to reinvent the wheel every time you write a new document. For example, every time you format a first-level heading, you have to remember the sequence of primitives you used to produce a centered 14-point Helvetica bold heading. Then you have to type three or four troff requests, the heading itself, and another three or four requests to return to the normal body style. (This is practical only if you're being paid by the line.) It's a laborious process and one that makes it difficult—perhaps impossible—to maintain consistency over a set of files.

Good news: You can use *macros* to simplify formatting and ensure consistency. Macros take advantage of one of the UNIX system's distinguishing characteristics: the ability to build complex processes from basic—primitive—units. A macro is nothing more than a series of troff requests, specified and named, that perform a special formatting task.

The *man* Macro Package

The man macro package produces a specialized format: the format used for UNIX system documentation manual pages—*manpages*, for short. In addition, information entered with the man macros is used to create the formidable permuted indexes so dear to the hearts of UNIX users.

There are only a few macros in this package. If you're familiar with ms, you already know most of them.

> **NOTE:** If you use mm, man's paragraph style macros and the way they're used to produce lists will dismay you.

The man macros produce an 8.5- by -11 inches page with a text area of 6.5- by-10 inches. There is a troff—but not an nroff—option for producing a smaller page—6-by-9 inches with a text area of 4.75- by-8.375 inches. If you choose this option, point size and leading are reduced from 10/12 to 9/10.

Page Layout

The `.IN` macro sets the indent relative to subheads. The default setting is 7.2 ens in `troff` and 5 ens in `nroff`.

The `.LL` macro sets the line length, which includes the value of `IN`.

The footer produced by the `man` macros is an example of making the best of a bad deal. The date is hard coded into the macro package. (This is usually a sign that you're not supposed to change it.) It's not the current date. It's whatever date your local macromancer deems appropriate. The reason for this eccentricity has been lost over time. Perhaps people used to be smarter and used to like playing with number registers. Perhaps this was a way of controlling updates to reference manuals. I don't know. I do know how to change the date, though.

In the definition of the `.TH` macro (table heading), there is a string definition for a string called `[5`. That's the date. All you have to do is redefine `[5` at the top of your file. For example,

```
.ds [5 "January 1, 2001
```

TIP: When you define strings, use an opening quotation mark, but no closing mark. If you forget and put that closing quotation mark, the closing quotation mark will be printed.

Now, what about that "Page 1"? Manpages are not numbered like ordinary document pages. The reason is that reference manuals are lengthy and are updated frequently. Furthermore, Bell Laboratories decided many years ago never to number replacement pages with letters, such as 101a, 101b, and so on. Because it was impractical to reprint a 2000-page manual just because you had inserted two pages at the beginning, Bell Labs came up with another solution: Number the pages consecutively only for each entry; then start again with "Page 1."

You can change this, but you'll face the same dilemma that Bell Labs faced: What do you do about updates? Assuming this isn't a problem, how do you number reference manual pages consecutively?

You can achieve consecutive page numbering by using the register (`-r`) option when you print your file:

```
troff -rc1 filename
```

Headings

The man macros fall into two basic categories: headings and paragraph styles. Using these macros correctly is an art, whereas once it was a science. Fonts are no longer as rigidly defined. For example, earlier UNIX reference manuals did not use a monospace—or constant width—font. Today, monospace is routinely used for file and directory names and for "computer voice"—that is, anything you see on the screen. Sometimes a distinction is made between monospace (\f(CW) and bold monospace (\f(CB). Bold monospace is used to indicate what the user types; it appears in the syntax section of a manpage.

The example in Figure 22.1 represents one way of using the man macros. Type styles are a matter of individual or company preference.

man recognizes three types of headings:

- Title headings are produced with the .TH macro
- Subheadings are produced with .SH
- Sub-subheadings are produced with .SS

.TH and .SH are mandatory. A manpage must have a .TH and at least one .SH.

.TH takes up to four arguments. These are positional arguments. Therefore, if you don't use the third (and least common) argument but you want the fourth, you must insert a null argument ("") before the fourth argument. The syntax for .TH is

```
.TH <title> <section number> <commentary> <manual name>
```

title specifies the title of the manpage. This appears in the page header on the left and the right. It can be more than one word, so enclose it in quotation marks. The title of the manpage shown in Figure 22.1 is namehim.

> **CAUTION:** Failure to enclose arguments to the .TH macro in quotation marks produces random unsightly dots on the printed page.

section number is a number from 1 through 5 that indicates the section of the reference manual to which the entry belongs. (Refer to Chapter 5, "Popular Tools," for information about UNIX reference manuals.) This number appears in the header in parentheses after the title. Don't include parentheses; they are supplied automatically. The manpage shown in Figure 22.1 has 0 as the section number. (Note: 0 is not really a permissible section number.)

commentary is an extra comment, such as Local. The argument appears in the header. It must be enclosed in quotation marks if there are embedded blanks. The manpage shown in Figure 22.1 doesn't have any commentary.

> **NOTE:** *Local* means that the command described by the manual page is not a standard SVR4 command. It might be a brand new command created for your particular UNIX system, or it might be a standard SVR4 command that has been modified for your system.

manual name is the name of the manual—for example, UNIX System V or Documenter's Workbench. The name of the manual shown in Figure 22.1 is Novelist's Workbench.

.TH is a shared macro name. The tbl preprocessor, identified by its starting and ending macros—.TS and .TE—relies on a .TH macro to specify column headings on a multipage table. This presents a potential problem. (tbl is discussed fully in Chapter 23, "Formatting Tables with tbl.")

The .TH table heading macro can appear only within a .TS and .TE pair. Supposedly, this insulates the macro and alerts the macromancer to rename the .TH man title macro whenever a .TS is encountered. Don't bet on it.

> **NOTE:** The troff primitive .rn renames macros.

> **CAUTION:** Don't use the .TH table heading macro on a manpage. The results are unpredictable and depend on your individual system. If you have a multipage table, you can always create the column headings manually. It isn't an elegant solution, but it doesn't break anything.

The .SH macro is a crucial one. With .TH it is mandatory for manpages. It is customarily followed by a keyword, although you can specify any word or words you want. The most common .SH keywords are

```
NAME
SYNTAX or SYNOPSIS
DESCRIPTION
EXAMPLE or EXAMPLES
FILES
DIAGNOSTICS
BUGS
SEE ALSO
```

The .SH macros are used like this:

```
.SH NAME
namehim - brief description of entry
```

Text following .SH is indented, as shown in Figure 22.1.

.SH keywords are always printed in all caps, and you don't need to put quotation marks around a two-word keyword. If you do use quotation marks, they won't be printed.

The most crucial .SH is .SH NAME. .SH NAME is mandatory. It is used to produce the permuted index, and its arguments must be entered on a single line—no matter how long that line is. No period is used at the end of the line. Naturally, it's a good idea to be as terse as possible.

The manpage shown in Figure 22.1 uses .SH OPTIONS after .SH SYNTAX. An alternate style sometimes seen in the reference manuals is the *where* form, which puts the word where on a line by itself and lists the options and arguments shown in the syntax section.

If a manpage needs headings under the .SHs, use .SS. Text following .SS is indented further.

Paragraph Styles

Almost all the man paragraph styles will be familiar to ms users. There are four ordinary paragraph macros:

.PP Begins a paragraph with an indented first line
.P Synonym for .PP. The only thing it does is call .PP
.LP Begins left-blocked paragraphs (no indent)
.PD Specifies interparagraph spacing

To set the indentation for .PP (and .P), use number register PI. The default unit is ens, but you can use any unit you want as long as you specify it. Unlike ms, man provides a macro to change the spacing between paragraphs: .PD.

NOTE: This section ("The man Macro Package") shows you how to use number registers that are useful with man macros. If you want to find out what other registers are available in troff, refer to the "Number Registers" section in Chapter 21, "Basic Formatting with troff and nroff."

The .PD macro is nothing more than ms's PD number register turned into a macro. Because the format of manpages is so exacting, writers need more control over spacing. The argument to .PD specifies interparagraph spacing. (Note that for nroff this argument is interpreted as whole lines; for troff you can specify .3v or something similar.) .PD is most often used to suppress spacing between list items, which are paragraphs in man. This is done very simply: .PD 0. The default spacing for .PD is .4r in troff, one line in nroff.

man has two hanging paragraph styles that will be new to ms users. They are .HP and .TP. .HP is a simple hanging paragraph. The first line is flush with the margin. All subsequent lines in the paragraph are indented by the amount specified in the argument to .HP. .TP is more complex. It is described below, following the discussion of .IP.

In addition to these more or less straightforward paragraph styles, man has the same indented paragraph as ms, also initiated by the .IP macro. The .IP macro is useful for formatting lists.

.IP can take two arguments. The first argument is a label, or tag. It can be a word, a number, or even the troff code for a bullet. The second argument specifies how far in from the left margin to indent the rest of the first line and all the rest of the paragraph. For a detailed description of this technique, refer to "Paragraph Styles" in the "Using the ms Macro Package" section earlier in this chapter.

The .RS and .RE pair is used to create relative indents. .RS (relative start) starts a 5-en indent from whatever the current indent is. .RE returns to the indent whatever it was before .RS was called. For every .RS in your file, you need a .RE to undo it. You can use this pair of macros to build nested lists. This technique is described under "Paragraph Styles" in the "Using the ms Macro Package" section earlier in this chapter.

.TP is similar to .IP. In fact, .TP produces virtually the same output. However, you specify it a little differently. Whereas .IP takes two arguments, .TP takes only one—the indentation. The line following the .TP macro call is called the tag. If the tag is wider than the specified indentation, the text following the tag starts on the next line. Therefore, although you can use .IP without a tag—or, more accurately, with a null tag—.TP requires a tag.

These codes that produces uses .IP, .RS., and .RE. Here are some lines of that code:

```
.TH namehim 0 "Novelist's Work Bench"
.SH NAME
\f3namehim \fP - supplies one or more names (first, last, or both) for fictional
character
.SH SYNTAX
\f5namehim\f1[ \f5F ¦ L\f1 ] [ \f5-a\f2age\f1 ] [ \f5-y\f2year\f1 ] ...
.SH OPTIONS
.IP "\f5-F ¦ -L\fP" 3m
specifies first or last nam; if neither \fF\fP nor \f5L\fP
is specified, both are produced.
.IP \f5-t\fP 3m
Specifies type of name:
select from the following (may be combined):
```

```
.RS
.IP \f5a\fP 3m
all
.IP \f5f\fP 3m
fancy
.IP \f5h\fP 3m
hero
.IP \f5l\fP 3m
.RE
```

Fonts and Point Size

man recognizes the .R (roman), .I (italics), and .B (bold) macros, all of which operate exactly as they do in ms and mm. Because man was originally designed to produce output using only those fonts—no monospace—it also has some macros that specify alternating fonts. At first glance, these seem superfluous. Take another look, though, at the code. Formatted without monospace, the first part of the syntax line would have alternated bold and roman:

```
.BR
namehim [ F ¦ L ] [ -a ...
```

man permits all six permutations of alternating roman, italic, and bold fonts:

```
.RI
.RB
.IR
.IB
.BR
.BI
```

You may never have occasion to use these macros, but it's nice to know that they're available.

In addition to the font change macros, there is one macro for changing point size: .SM. (Users of ms might wonder what became of .LG and .NL.) man needs .SM more than the other macro packages because manual pages contain terms with long names that must be written in capital letters. To make these terms more readable and to conserve space, man includes a macro that produces a smaller point size—two points smaller.

.SM has another special use: printing the word UNIX in capital or small cap letters. Because UNIX is a registered trademark, it should be printed in a way that distinguishes it from ordinary text. Sometimes it appears in all capital letters. Another acceptable way is with a capital U and small capital N, I, and X, as in UNIX.

Preprocessor Macros

The only preprocessor macros recognized by man are the `.TS` and `.TE` table macros. Remember not to use the table macro `.TH`.

Predefined Strings

The man package has three predefined strings. They are

`\*R`	Produces the registered trademark symbol
`\*(Tm`	Produces the trademark symbol
`\*S`	Returns to the default point size and vertical spacing

Miscellaneous Macros

`.TH` resets tab stops whenever it is called. The default settings are every 7.2 ens in `troff` and every 5 ens in `nroff`. However, experimenting with various customized indents might affect tab settings. If you want to restore the tab settings and you can't wait for the next `.TH`, use the `.DT` macro.

The `.PM` (proprietary marking) macro is interesting for its history, but unless you change its text, it isn't really useful. It takes two arguments. The first argument identifies the type of marking, such as Proprietary or Restricted. The second argument is the year. If you omit the year, the default is the current year.

Using *man* Macros with *troff* and *nroff*

You can invoke the man macros with the `troff` or `nroff` command. Printing man files is covered in detail in the "Printing Files Formatted with man Macros" section in Chapter 29, "Processing and Printing Formatted Files."

man Macro Summary

Table 22.1 lists the man macros and describes their functions.

Table 22.1. Summary of the man macros.

Macro	Description	Comments
`.B`	Bold	With text, sets text in bold. On a line by itself, changes to bold font.
`.BI`	Bold italic	Alternates bold and italic fonts.

continues

Table 22.1. continued

Macro	Description	Comments
.BR	Bold roman	Alternates bold and roman fonts.
.DT	Defines tabs and sets and tab stops	The default is 7.2 ens in `troff` 5 ens in `nroff`.
.HP	Hanging paragraph	
.I	Italics	With text, sets text in italics. On a line by itself, changes to italic font.
.IB	Italic bold	Alternates italic and bold fonts.
.IP	Indented paragraph	
.IR	Italic roman	Alternates italic and roman fonts.
.LP	Block-style paragraph	
.P	Paragraph	Synonym for `.PP`. `.P` actually calls `.PP`.
.PD	Sets the distance between paragraphs 1v	The default is `.4v` in `troff` and in `nroff`.
.PM	Proprietary marking	This is an AT&T macro for placing different types of Proprietary notices at the bottom of each page.
.PP	Paragraph	
.R	Roman	With text, sets text in roman type. On a line by itself, changes to roman type.
.RB	Roman bold	Alternates roman and bold fonts.
.RE	Ends a relative indent begun by `.RS`	
.RI	Roman italic	Alternates roman and italic fonts.
.RS	Begins a relative indent	
.SH	Subhead	`.SN NAME` is the crucial macro for producing the permuted index .
.SM	Reduces point size by 2 points	Stands for small.
.SS	Sub-subhead	

Macro	Description	Comments
.TE	Table end	
.TH	Title head	
.TP	Indented paragraph with hanging tag.	
.TS	Table start	Supposedly, the H argument with the .TH macro for continuing table column heads works with the man macros. It's safer, though, to avoid the issue.

Summary

Macro packages take the guesswork out of formatting. Your document has a defined "look and feel"—no surprises. And it's easier than you think to use a macro package. As you work with a package, you learn more about it, but you can start with only the basics and produce good-looking documents.

Formatting Tables with *tbl*

23

By Susan Peppard

IN THIS CHAPTER

Meet tbl, the troff and nroff table preprocessor.

tbl is not a popular troff tool. It is cursed and vilified and mocked, but it is *used.* The people who hate tbl rarely take the time to learn even the basics of formatting a table. Instead, they have two or three reliable samples that they just keep copying over and over, changing the data each time. When something goes wrong, they ask a friend or a colleague—maybe even an enemy—for help.

You don't have to do that. tbl isn't that hard to learn. As with all UNIX utilities and programs, you can learn as much or as little as you like. You can learn the rudiments of tbl in an hour. This chapter includes some sample tables to enlarge your collection.

tbl Requirements

tbl is a troff preprocessor. This means that the tbl code you write is processed by tbl before troff gets anywhere near it. Typically, you send a file through tbl and pipe the output to troff. The syntax is

```
tbl filename ¦ troff options
```

tbl Macros

troff recognizes tbl output by the macros that begin and end a table: .TS and .TE. (The .TS H and .TH macros are discussed in the "Column Headings" section later in this chapter.)

The code that produces a simple table is

```
.TS
box;
cB cB cB
l l l.
Days[TAB]Months[TAB]Years
Monday[TAB]January[TAB]1990
Tuesday[TAB]February[TAB]1991
Wednesday[TAB]March[TAB]1992
.TE
```

Minimal Format Options

In addition to the macros, a table must include at least one line of format options. These options tell tbl whether you want your columns left-justified, centered, or right-justified—in short, how you want each column to look. The rule is one option per column. Therefore, a three-column table with all columns left-justified has the following format options:

```
l l l.
```

The last line of format options must end with a period.

These are the minimum options you need for a three-column table. With these options, every row in your table has left-justified columns. If you want centered column headings with left-justified data, then you need two rows of format options:

```
c c c
l l l.
```

tbl uses the first format line to format the first row of your table. It uses the second format line to format the second row of your table. When it runs out of format lines, as it does in row 3 in this example, tbl formats the rest of your table according to the last format line.

You can't format a complex table with the bare minimum; you need to use more of the options that tbl provides.

Table Data

Table data is entered with a tab between each column. If a line is too long for your terminal and, therefore, wraps, you can use the continuation character (\). Each new line starts a new row in the table.

To leave a cell empty, use a tab. For example, to enter a row that contains no entries in the first, second, and fourth columns but contains an entry in the third column, do this:

```
[TAB][TAB]entry
```

You don't need to enter the last tab—the one for the fourth column. tbl doesn't mind if you specify too little data. It complains only if you specify too much.

tbl Options

In addition to format options, tbl enables you to use global options. Global options affect the appearance of your table as a whole. tbl provides a wide range of format and global options.

Format Options

Format options include more than just instructions on how to justify columns. The tbl format options include

l (or L)	Left-justifies the column.
r (or R)	Right-justifies the column.
c (or C)	Centers the column.

n (or N)	Specifies a numeric column. It lines up the column on decimal points—or units digits if there are no decimal points.
a (or A)	Specifies an alphabetic column. It indents text one em.
s (or S)	Spans the column horizontally.
^	Spans the column vertically.

Spanning is explained in the "Horizontal and Vertical Spanning" section later in this chapter.

TIP: The a option doesn't work properly in older versions of `tbl`. Use `\0\0` instead.

Two more format options enable you to adjust the width of your columns. You can use them in conjunction with any of the options listed above.

| e | Equalizes the width of the indicated columns. |
| w | Enables you to specify a width for a column. |

`lw(1i)`, for example, creates a left-justified column that is one inch wide.

NOTE: Be sure to specify a unit with the w (width) option. The default unit is ens. The width you specify does not include the gap between columns. To set the column gap, refer to the "Spacing and Lines" section later in this chapter.

Other format options enable you to change the font and the point size. You can also change vertical spacing.

f (or F)	Changes the font. The font is specified immediately after f, as in fCW.
b (or B)	Changes to bold font.
i (or I)	Changes to italic font.
p (or P)	Changes the point size. The size is specified immediately after p, as in p9.
v (or V)	Changes vertical spacing. The spacing is specified immediately after v, as in v10.

Global Options

`tbl`'s global options affect the placement of your table on the page and its appearance. They are specified on a single line that ends with a semicolon (;). The options must be separated by spaces, tabs, or commas.

One global option, for example, enables you to change the default column separator, the tab, to another character. The exclamation point is typically used in technical writing. Because there's nothing to get excited about in the text, `tbl` doesn't get confused.

The global options are

`expand`	Expands the table to the full width of the page. It cannot be used with `center`.
`box`	Puts a box around the table.
`doublebox`	Puts a double box—a box drawn with two lines—around the table.
`allbox`	Puts each item in the table in a box.
`tab(x)`	Changes the column separation character to *x*.
`linesize(n)`	Sets the point size of lines under column heads or of lines that make up boxes to *n* points.
`delim(xy)`	Uses *x* and *y* as `eqn` delimiters. (`eqn` is discussed in Chapter 24, "Formatting Equations with `eqn`.")

The `center` and `expand` options are straightforward and do exactly what you would expect.

By default, tables are left-justified. The `center` option centers your table with respect to the defined line length. The table might not always look centered. It depends on what indents are used before the table and after it. You can use `.in` with a positive or negative value to adjust the horizontal placement of the table. Remember, though, to reset the indent that comes after the table.

The reasons for using `expand` are less obvious. `expand` makes the width of your table equal to the defined line length. You might want to do this for a special effect. It also comes in handy if you're working with a custom macro package that has outdented headings with text indented an inch or more. `expand` enables you to take advantage of the unused left margin.

NOTE: Occasionally, you get an error message from `tbl` that reads `table too wide`. Processing doesn't stop, though. The table is printed. Chances are, though, that it will be too wide. `tbl` does not respect margins. You can often use this feature to your advantage, however.

`tbl` provides three global options that you you can use to draw boxes around tables. Figure 23.1 shows an example of each option.

FIGURE 23.1.

The box *options.*

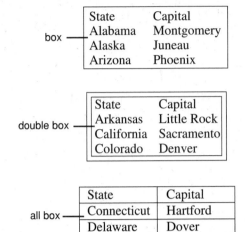

allbox is useful when you have many narrow columns (perhaps with numeric data). The lines make the table easier to read. In most other situations, the lines are distracting and unattractive.

The tab option enables you to specify a different character as the column separator. Many people do this routinely. Just be careful to choose a character that doesn't appear in your table.

There is a benefit to changing the tab character to a single character such as # or !. If your input line is long, you might exceed the wrap margin, and your input line will become two lines. If you then join the two lines, your tab turns into a space. If you change the space to a tab, the line might split again. This is annoying. It is also less likely to happen if you are using # or !. # and ! are single characters, not 4 to 8 characters like the tab.

The linesize option affects all the lines in your table. If you use it to draw a heavy box around the whole table, you must adjust the point size for internal lines.

If your table contains equations, you can set the eqn delimiters in a tbl global option. These delimiters must not appear elsewhere in the table, except as eqn delimiters. They also can't be the same as the tab character. (Refer to Chapter 24, "Formatting Equations with eqn," for more information.)

Advanced *tbl* Formatting

tbl gives you control over almost every aspect of table formatting, including column headings, horizontal and vertical spanning, text blocks, spacing options and lines, and changing format options.

Column Headings

To make column headings stand out, underline them. tbl provides several styles to choose from.

_	Draws a continuous single underscore the width of the table. When it used with allbox, it draws a double underscore under the column headings. The code line containing _ must have no other entries.
=	Draws a continuous double underscore the width of the table. The code line containing = must have no other entries.
[TAB]	Two or more underscores separated by tabs. _[TAB]_ draws a single underscore the width of the contents of each column.
=[TAB]=	Two or more equals signs separated by tabs. =[TAB]= draws a double underscore the width of the contents of each column.
[TAB]	Backslash underscores separated by tabs. _ draws a single underscore the width of each column. (Does not work with newer versions of tbl.)
\=[TAB]\=	Backslash equals signs separated by tabs. \= draws a double underscore the width of each column. (Does not work with newer versions of tbl.)

To specify column headings that will appear on every page of a multipage table, use the .TS H and .TH macros.

Use .TS H to start your table if you are going to specify a column heading. Then use .TH after the lines that constitute the heading. Be sure to include underscores and spaces if they are part of the heading.

Horizontal and Vertical Spanning

tbl accommodates both horizontal and vertical spanning. Use horizontal spanning to center a column heading over more than one column, as in

c s s

Figure 23.2 illustrates horizontal spanning.

You can code vertical spanning in the tbl format options or in the table data. Vertical spanning in the column headings is produced by using ^ in the format specifications. Vertical spanning in the table data is produced by using \^.

FIGURE 23.2.

A table with horizontal spanning.

State Statistics		
State	**Capital**	**Population**
Missouri	Jefferson City	5,192,632
Montana	Helena	823,697
Nebraska	Lincoln	1,605,603

Text Blocks

A text block is a block of text—a paragraph—used as a table entry. Figure 23.3 shows a table with text blocks.

FIGURE 23.3.

A table with text blocks.

1990-1991	Writer. *Jurassic Park II, Daughter of the Firm, The Cat in the Hat Spends a Year in Provence*. Took best-selling ideas and capitalized on them. Increased my income by 576% in just one year.
1991-date	Law Student. Attending Harvard Law School (by correspondence); expect to receive degree this year and also get out of prison.

The text block is coded as part of the table entry:

```
1990-1991[TAB]T{
.na
Writer. \f2Jurassic Park II\fP, \f2Daughter of the Firm\fP, \f2The
Cat in the Hat Spends a Year in Provence\fP. Took best-selling ideas
and capitalized on them. Raised my income 576% in just one year.
T}
.sp .5
1991-date[TAB]T{
.na
Law Student. Attending Harvard Law School; expect to receive degree
this year.
T}
```

Because `tbl` right-justifies text blocks, you might want to turn off adjustment inside the text blocks, as in the previous example. Use `.na` to do this.

The number of text blocks that can be used within a single table varies, depending on the `tbl` version. If you're using a recent version, don't worry about this. Even if you're using an old version, don't worry. `tbl` will complain loudly if you use too many text blocks. Your only remedy is to break the table into smaller tables.

> **NOTE:** Text blocks affect vertical spacing. There's a little more space between text block rows than there is between ordinary rows. If you notice this in a table, you might have to make even your short columns into text blocks.

Text blocks complicate a table. The first time you use them, you're almost certain to leave out the beginning or ending T-brace or to use an opening brace instead of a closing one. If you do this, tbl assumes your unmatched T-brace is data and prints it, so the error is easy to find.

Spacing and Lines

The default gap between columns is 3 ens. You can adjust this gap by putting a number between your format options, as in

```
cB 2 lB 2 lB 1 cB
```

You can even set the gap to 0.

You can use .sp to put more space between table rows. (Don't use macros; use the troff primitive.) Using .sp .25 before and after an underscore and with column headings usually improves the appearance of the table.

If you have some two-line column heads and some one-line column heads, the allbox global option looks really awful. Similarly, if you've spanned any column, allbox doesn't work correctly. You can insert vertical lines between columns by using the pipe character (¦). You can even combine vertical lines with changes in the column gap.

Changing Format Options

You can change format options in the middle of a table. You can't change the number of columns, but you can change anything else. Use spanning to change the *apparent* number of columns.

To change tbl format options, use the .T& macro and insert a line (or several lines) of format options.

A Fancy Table

The following code illustrates the advanced formatting techniques described in the previous sections. It produces the table shown in Figure 23.4.

```
.TS
center;
c s s s
lB cB cB cB
l l l l.
\fb\s14Old Garden Roses\s0\fP
.sp .25
Type[TAB]Examples[TAB]Color[TAB]Date
.sp .25
\_[TAB]\_[TAB]\_[TAB]\_
```

```
.sp .25
Alba[TAB]Celestial[TAB]milky peach[TAB]before1848
\^[TAB]Felicite Parmentier[TAB]pale pink[TAB]before 1834
.sp .5
Bourbon[TAB]La Reine Victoria[TAB]rich pink[TAB]1872
\^[TAB]Louise Odier[TAB]deep pink[TAB]1851
\^[TAB]Souvenir de la Malmaison[TAB]soft pink[TAB]1843
.sp .5
.Centifolia[TAB]Fantin-Latour[TAB]rich pink[TAB]unknown
.sp .5
China[TAB]Mutabilis[TAB]warm pink[TAB]unknown
.sp .5
Damask[TAB]Celsiana[TAB]soft pink[TAB]before 1750
\^[TAB]Mme. Hardy[TAB]white[TAB]1832
.sp .5
Gallica[TAB]Cardinal de Richelieu[TAB]rosy violet[TAB]1840
\^[TAB]Rosa Mundi[TAB]striped crimson[TAB]before 1581
[TAB][TAB][TAB]\0\0and pale pink
.TE
```

FIGURE 23.4.

A fancy table.

Old Garden Roses

Type	Examples	Color	Date
Alba	Celestial	milky pink	before 1848
	Felicite Parmentier	pale pink	before 1834
Bourbon	La Reine Victoria	rich pink	1872
	Louise Odier	deep pink	1851
	Souvenir de la Malmaison	soft pink	1843
Centifolia	Fantin-Latour	rich pink	unknown
China	Mutabilis	warm pink	unknown
Damask	Celsiana	soft pink	before 1750
	Mme. Hardy	white	1832
Gallica	Cardinal de Richelieu	rosy violet	1840
	Rosa Mundi	striped crimson and pale pink	before 1851

Troubleshooting

When you use tbl, keep the following points in mind:

- *Don't use macros in tables.* They don't get digested properly. It's tempting to put in a .P. You do it without thinking, but often a single .P can wreck your table. Don't try to embed lists in tables. At the very least, don't try it when you're on a tight deadline. Macros and tables don't mix.

■ *Don't mix your font changes.* If you use `B` in a format option line to get bold text, don't use `f2` for italics. However, escape sequences in your table data are fine. Likewise, don't use macros.

■ If you can't get the a format option to work, indent with `\0`. `\0` inserts a space the width of a numeral.

■ A common source of error in tables is a space after a T-brace. For some reason, it really makes tables crazy. The space is invisible, too, so you don't see it.

TIP: Use the ex command `:se list` (from `vi`). `list` turns each tab into a Ctrl-I, which shows up as `^I` in your file but is actually a single character. You can count them to see whether you've put in too many. `list` also puts the line end symbol (`$`) at the end of each line in the file. A space between `T{` and `$` is easy to see. To turn `list` off, use `:se nolist`.

■ If you specify a column width and the contents of that column are longer than the specified width, your width setting is ignored. Think of it as a minimum width, not a maximum.

■ If you omit a T-brace, `tbl` gets confused about your columns and might, for example, put column 2 in column 1. This plays havoc with your column width. You might not even see column 2 if this happens. Don't worry; column 2 isn't lost. It simply printed somewhere out in the middle of the Atlantic Ocean. When you fix your table, it will come back and behave.

Summary

`tbl` is one of the most used, yet least liked programs, offered by the UNIX system. It is well worth the effort to learn at least the rudiments of `tbl`, because you can use tables to your advantage in unexpected situations. You can also make friends and influence supervisors if you take the time to learn `tbl` thoroughly. A good `tbl` debugger is hard to find.

Formatting Equations with *eqn*

24

By Susan Peppard

IN THIS CHAPTER

Suppose that you had to format an expression like this:

$$\sum_{i=0}^{n} \frac{4a^2}{b^2} x_i^2 \nabla x_i$$

You could format it with `troff` primitives, but it would take some time—probably a great deal of time. If you're writing a calculus text, you don't want to spend half of your day moving tiny numbers and letters up and down. You want to get on with your writing.

There's good news. UNIX provides a tool, called `eqn`, that does all the formatting for you. There's more good news, too. Because the focus of `eqn` is limited—all it does is format equations—it is easier to learn and use than `tbl` or `pic`.

`eqn` is a `troff` preprocessor—like `tbl`, `pic`, and `grap`—that you use to format mathematical expressions. There is an `nroff` version. But let's face it: Formatting a complex equation with `nroff` is a bit like wearing double-bladed skates to the Olympic trials.

Like the other preprocessor files, `eqn` files can't be sourced in (with `.so`). If you try this, `troff` formats your code neatly, but your code is left untouched by `eqn`. To source in code that has already been processed by `eqn`, run `eqn` on a file that contains only your equation. First write the output to a file (`eqn *filename* > *outputfile*`), and then source in the output file. You can also read in the output file.

> **NOTE:** You can't source in an in-line equation.

The devisers of `eqn` make a point of telling you that you don't have to know anything about mathematics (or typesetting) to use `eqn`. This is a bit misleading. If you don't know anything about math, you'll be surprised by the output of `eqn`: all the letters are in italics. (If you don't know anything about typesetting you may not know what italics are, but I'm assuming you do.)

The italics are a mathematical convention. Letters representing constants or variables (a, b, c, x, y, z, etc.) are always set in italics. Numbers and special words (like "sin" and "cos") are set in roman type.

Besides selecting fonts for the characters in your equations, `eqn` provides you with a wide range of mathematical symbols, including the integral sign, upper- and lower-case Greek letters, plus, minus, equal sign, greater than, and less than.

eqn Macros and Delimiters

eqn processes your code before troff sees it. This means that you must send your file through eqn and pipe the output to troff. troff needs to know that you've used eqn. You tell it so by using two macros and one or two delimiters. A *delimiter* is a character used to signal the beginning or the end—or both—of an equation. For example, # is a delimiter. To tell troff that you are using eqn with # as the beginning and ending delimiters, put these lines before the start of your equation:

```
.EQ
delim ##
.EN
```

> **TIP:** It's usually a good idea to put delimiter identification lines near the top of your file.

The eqn delimiters are used for in-line equations. (Even if you're sure you won't need in-line equations, it's a good idea to provide the delimiters. You never know.)

To define the delimiter, include the following lines in your file:

```
.EQ
delim ##
.EN
```

To turn the delimiters off:

```
.EQ
delim off
.EN
```

To use the delimiters, just surround your eqn code with them:

```
# a + b = c #
```

Don't worry about the height of your in-line equation. troff automatically adjusts line spacings.

Choosing Delimiters and Placing the Definition

The books suggest $$ and warn you to stay away from eqn symbols like { and (and ~ and ^ and ". There is no default delimiter. They also suggest you put your delimiter definition at the top of your file. This is fine until you have to say that the widget costs $5000.

```
.EQ
delim $$
.EN
```

```
The widget costs $5000.
.P
The enhanced widget costs $7500.
.P
Here's a formula for the cost of the widget:
$x sup 2 + x sup 2 =$ cost of widget.
```

The result is:

```
The widget costs 5000. . PTheenhancedwidgetcosts7500.
Here's a formula for the cost of the widget:x²+x²=cost of widget.
```

Not quite what you wanted. You can, of course, turn the delimiters off before you use the dollar sign as dollar sign.

Or you can choose a different delimiter. (There are drawbacks to all of them.) I prefer ##, but this choice can't be used with the other preprocessors. (See "eqn and the Preprocessors" later in the chapter.) Exclamation points are usually safe, especially if you're doing technical writing. (Technical writing rarely rises to the level of excitement needed to justify exclamation points.)

The same might be said for placing the delimiter definition: There are drawbacks to any location. The traditional place for eqn delimiters is at the top of your file. That's where someone else would look for it. That's where you look for it six months from now. If you're juggling text that's full of dollar signs and pound signs and exclamation points, then turn the delimiters off at the top of your file and invoke them as needed. Turn the delimiters off as soon as you're done with them.

If you really want to wreak havoc on a file, try this:

```
.EQ
delim ee
.EN
```

This is a *wonderful* April Fool's joke to play on your boss, if you have access to her files, and if you've already found another job.

eqn Keywords

eqn was designed to be easy for mathematicians to learn and use. It uses familiar words and abbreviations. For example, if you read $a_1 = b_2$ aloud, you would say, "*a* sub one equals *b* sub two." That's what eqn says. The spaces here are important. They are discussed later in this chapter.

```
#a sub 1 = b sub 2#
```

The opposite of sub is sup, for superscript. For example,

```
#a sup 2 > b sup 2
```

The eqn keywords are

above	back	bar	bold	ccol
copy	cpile	define	delim	dot
dotdot	down	dyad	fat	font
from	fwd	gfont	gsize	hat
highbar	ifdef	include	int	integral
inter	italic	lcol	left	lineup
lowbar	lpile	mark	matrix	over
pile	prod	rcol	right	roman
rpile	size	space	sqrt	sub
sumsup	tilde	to	under	union
uputilde	vec			

Table 24.1 lists the keywords for Greek letters.

Table 24.1. Keywords for Greek letters.

Keyword	Letter	Keyword	Letter
Upper-Case Letters			
GAMMA	Γ	DELTA	Δ
THETA	Θ	LAMBDA	Λ
XI	Ξ	PI	Π
SIGMA	Σ	UPSILON	Υ
PHI	Φ	PSI	Ψ
OMEGA	Ω		
Lower-Case Letters			
alpha	α	beta	β
gamma	γ	delta	δ
epsilon	ε	zeta	ζ
eta	η	theta	θ
iota	ι	kappa	κ
lambda	λ	mu	μ
nu	ν	xi	ξ
omicron	o	pi	π
rho	ρ	sigma	σ
tau	τ	upsilon	υ
phi	ϕ	chi	χ
psi	ψ	omega	ω

Note that there is no provision for the upper-case letters that are identical to their roman cousins (*A, B, E, H, I, K, M, N, O, P, T, X,* and *Z*). If you want an upper-case alpha, just type A.

> **NOTE:** If you want an upper-case alpha that is not italicized, you have to specify `roman A`.

eqn also includes the following terms, which are printed in roman, not italic, type:

```
and      arc      cos      cosh
det      exp      for      if
Im       lim      ln       log
max      min      Re       sin
sinh     tan      tanh
```

eqn Operators

You've already met some of the eqn operators—+, -, =, and >. Table 24.2 lists the other eqn operators.

Table 24.2. Some eqn operators.

Keyword	Operator	Keyword	Operator
>=	[AS242]	<=	[AS243]
==	[AS240]	!=	≠
+-	[AS241]	->	→
<-	←	<<	<<
>>	>>	approx	[AS247]
inf	[AS236]	sum	Σ
prod	Π	int	
union		inter	
nothing		partial	
half		prime	
cdot		times	×
del		grad	
...		,...,	
dollar	$		

In addition, eqn offers nine diacritical marks, which are listed in Table 24.3.

Table 24.3. Diacritical marks.

Keyword	Diacritical Mark	Keyword	Diacritical Mark
dot	.	dotdot	..
hat	^	tilde	~
vec	→	dyad	↔
bar	-	under	_
utilde	~		

If you need to use a bar with one of the other diacritical marks, use highbar to place the bar correctly. There is also a lowbar. For example, the following code

```
.EQ
delim ##
.EN
#X highbar#
.sp .5
#x highbar#
.sp .5
#x bar#
.sp .5
#x lowbar#
.sp .5
#x dotdot highbar#
.sp .5
#{x tilde} highbar#
```

produces this output:

$$\overline{x}$$
$$\overline{X}$$
$$\overline{x}$$
$$\overline{\ddot{x}}$$
$$\overline{x}$$

To draw a bar over an entire expression, use braces. For example:

```
{ ( alpha - beta ) * gamma } bar
```

Spaces and Braces

Like most UNIX programs, eqn has to be able to recognize keywords. And, like UNIX, eqn understands that spaces delimit keywords, as do certain operators. For example, UNIX understands

```
who¦grep sally
```

or

```
who ¦ grep sally
```

The pipe acts as a delimiter, so UNIX can parse your command. Similarly, UNIX understands both the following:

```
mail sally<myletter
```

```
mail sally < myletter
```

In this example, the redirect (less than) sign acts as a delimiter. UNIX does not recognize the hyphen (minus sign) as a delimiter, despite the fact that many options must be preceded by this character. If you type `ls-1`, UNIX politely responds: `ls-1:  not found`.

eqn behaves the same way. If you write

```
.EQ
a+b=c
.EN
```

eqn will process this easily because it recognizes + and = as delimiters. The output of this code will be identical to the output from

```
.EQ
a + b = c
.EN
```

or even

```
.EQ
a+ b
        =
    c
.EN
```

All of these are output as $a+b=c$.

eqn pays no attention to spaces or newlines except as delimiters. Once eqn has determined what you mean (or what it thinks you mean), it throws away spaces and newlines.

To obtain spaces in your output, use a tilde (~) for a 1-character space, or a circumflex (^) for a half-character space:

```
.EQ
a~+~b~=~c
a^+^b~=~c
.EN
```

This produces

$a+b=c$

Grouping

If you say, "3 plus 2 times 5" your listener doesn't know whether you mean 25 or 13. eqn has the same problem. Like your listener, eqn makes an assumption about # a + b * c #. If you provide no more information, eqn groups according to the order in which you enter information. In other words, it assumes parentheses.

Although computers do this, mathematicians don't. They believe in precedence, which holds that multiplication always precedes addition. Therefore, $3 + 2 \times 5$ is 13. Period. Even mathematicians, though, sometimes need parentheses.

Because parentheses are used so often in mathematical expressions, eqn wants you to use curly braces—{ and }—to indicate grouping in your expressions. Therefore, if you really meant 13, you would write

```
# a + {b * c} #
```

The spaces here are important.

Because eqn's treatment of spaces is its hardest aspect to get used to, here is a list of rules to memorize. You could have them printed on a tee-shirt or tattooed on your hand if that seems easier.

1. eqn throws away all internal spaces once it has used them.
2. eqn uses internal spaces to recognize special words and symbols.
3. You can use circumflexes (^)—eqn calls them hats—or tildes (~) to set off special words and symbols. eqn replaces each tilde with a space in the output. It replaces each circumflex with a half space.

> **NOTE:** Earlier versions of eqn may not replace the circumflex with a half space. They may simply throw the circumflex away.

4. You can use braces or quotation marks to set off parts of an equation, but they have special meanings.

    Braces are used for grouping. They force eqn to treat the enclosed term (or terms) as a unit. Braces can be nested.

    Quotation marks force eqn to treat the enclosed term literally. For example, to print a brace, enclose it in quotation marks.

5. When in doubt, use a space.
6. eqn ignores newlines, so you can spread your equation over several lines to make it more readable.

Table 24.4 contains some examples that may help:

Table 24.4. Using spaces and brackets in eqn.

Desired Output	Code	Actual Output
$a + b = c$	a~+~b~=~c	(as desired)
$a + b = c$	a + b = c	$a+b=c$
$a=(x^2)+1$	a=(x sup 2) + 1	(as desired)
$a=(x^2)+1$	a=(x sup 2)+ 1	$a=(x^{2)+1}$
x_2	x sub 2	(as desired)
x_2	x sub2	$xsub2$
x_i^2	x sub i sup 2	(as desired)
x_i^2	x sup 2 sub i	x^2i

Fractions

Fractions are produced in a straightforward way. Simply use the word over. For example, the code

```
# a over b #
```

produces

$$\frac{a}{b}$$

More complex fractions present additional problems. Think about the following equation for a moment:

```
a + b over c
```

This code line could mean # {a+b} over c # or # a + {b over c} #. The most important thing to remember about fractions is to use braces.

You can, of course, produce an expression with a fraction like this:

$$rate = \frac{distance}{time}$$

Square Roots

The keyword `sqrt` produces the root sign. Consider these expressions:

$$\sqrt{a} + b = x$$

$$\sqrt{\overline{X}}$$

$$y = \sqrt{a-b}$$

$$y = \frac{\sigma}{\sqrt{N}}$$

They are produced with the following code:

```
sqrt a+b=x
sqrt {X bar}
y= sqrt {a-b}
y = sigma over {sqrt N}
```

You can also produce large root signs. For example,

```
sqrt {{a sup x} over b sub y}
```

When you do this, however, the root sign doesn't just get bigger; it gets thicker—and uglier. In cases like this, you're better off using a fractional power. For example,

```
{( a sup x /b sub y ) } sup half
```

produces

$$x = \sqrt{\frac{a^2}{b^2}}$$

Sums, Integrals, and Limits

In their simplest form, sums, integrals, and limits are produced by `sum`, `int`, and `lim`. Of course, you never see them in their simplest form. Usually included is a `from` or even a `from` and a `to`. For example,

```
sum from 1=0 to {i=inf} x sup i
int from a to b
lim from {n -> inf} sum from i=0 to m c sup i
```

produces

$$\sum_{i=0}^{1=\infty} x^i$$

$$\int_{a}^{b}$$

$$\lim_{n\to\infty} \sum_{i=0}^{n} mc^i$$

In addition, you can use `prod`, `union`, and `inter` to produce the symbols used with sets.

Brackets, Braces, and Piles

You can create big braces and brackets by enclosing expressions that require them. Consider the following code:

```
#left [ {a over b} + {c over d} right ]#
#left { {s over t} - {r over q} right }#
```

The expression that this code produces is

$$\left[\frac{a}{b} + \frac{c}{d} \right]$$

$$\left\{ \frac{s}{t} - \frac{r}{q} \right\}$$

You can specify `floor` and `ceiling` characters. For example,

```
left floor a over b right floor =>
left ceiling x over y right ceiling
```

produces

$$\left\lfloor \frac{a}{b} \right\rfloor => \left\lceil \frac{x}{y} \right\rceil$$

Although piles look like big brackets, they are actually different. Piles line up in three ways: left, right, and centered. For example,

```
A= left [
pile { a above b above c }
pile { x above y above z }
right ]
```

produces

$$A = \begin{bmatrix} a & x \\ b & y \\ c & z \end{bmatrix}$$

If you require only one brace, you must include a null argument for the missing side. Consider

```
left ""
lpile
{SIGMA X sub 3 above SIGMA X sub 1
X sub 3 above SIGMA X sub 2 X sub 3}
right )
```

which produces

$$\left. \begin{matrix} \Sigma X_3 \\ \Sigma X_1 X_3 \\ \Sigma X_2 X_3 \end{matrix} \right]$$

Arrays and Matrices

To create an array or a matrix, use the keyword `matrix`, as in

```
matrix {
lcol { 0 above {x over y} }
rcol { 1 above {x sup 2} }
}
```

This code produces

$$\begin{matrix} 0 & 1 \\ \dfrac{x}{y} & x^2 \end{matrix}$$

You could use `ccol` to center columns. The main advantage of using the `matrix` keyword, though, is that the elements align themselves horizontally better.

Defines

If you use a complex term over and over again, you can define it as something short. A good choice, for example, is &. Then, instead of typing

```
x= sqrt {SIGMA {x sup 2}} over N
```

you can type

```
x= &
```

`define` works like this:

```
.EQ
define &   'sqrt {SIGMA {x sup 2}} over N'
x = &
.EN
```

You can select any characters you want—fg, xy, and so on—but be sensible. Don't choose ^ or ~. Don't choose your eqn delimiters. And don't choose an eqn keyword, even though it is permitted.

Precedence

Without braces to force it to look at terms as groups, eqn recognizes the following orders of precedence:

```
dyad vec under bar tilde hat dot dotdot
left right
fwd back down up
fat roman italic bold size
sub sup
sqrt over
from to
```

All operations group to the right, except for sqrt, left, and right, which group to the left.

Finishing Touches

eqn offers several ways for you to beautify your output. You can line up several equations, change fonts and point sizes, and insert vertical and horizontal movement.

To line up several equations, use mark and lineup. mark, which can be used only once in an equation, marks the horizontal position where lineup aligns the other equations. For example,

```
.EQ
a mark = b
.EN

.EQ
lineup = b+1
.EN

.EQ
lineup = b+c+1
.EN
```

produces

$$a = b$$
$$= b + 1$$
$$= b + c + 1$$

You can also change fonts and point sizes in an equation. Table 24.5 describes the keywords used.

Table 24.5. Keywords used to change fonts and point sizes.

Keyword	Description
bold	Prints the next character or term in bold type
fat	Prints the next character or term in pseudo-bold, by overstriking
font *f*	Changes to font *f* any font that troff recognizes (such as R, B, I, CW, and HB)
italic	Prints the next character or term in italic type
roman	Prints the next character or term in roman type
size *n*	Changes to point size *n*, which can be specified as a number or as a relative quantity (such as size -2 or size +3)

There is a gsize option for setting a global point size. Similarly, there is a gfont. You should put these options near the top of your file; otherwise, eqn uses the default point size (usually 10).

Unconventional Uses for *eqn*

You can use eqn to put diacritical marks on foreign words. Just remember that eqn prints words in italics. So you need to specify roman. Consider the following code:

```
No# roman e dotdot #l Coward
Georg H# roman a dotdot #ndel
malague# roman n tilde #a
```

It produces

Noël Coward

Georg Händel

malagueña

You can also use eqn to produce the service mark symbol if it isn't available as a troff special character. The service mark is like the trademark except that it reads SM. For example,

```
XYZZY-Box# sup roman SM #
```

produces

XYZZY-Box^{SM}

Okay, it's not as neat as XYZZY-BOX\(SM, but it's a whole lot better than XYZZY-Box\v' -3p'\s-3SM\s+3\v' +3p'!

Troubleshooting

Sometimes, despite your best efforts, your equations just don't come out right. Here are some suggestions for detecting and correcting faulty code, and for dealing with some of eqn's more arcane characteristics.

Using *checkeq*

At its best, eqn is quirky. So, before you print a 50-page chapter containing 70 equations, check your equations. This pinpoints syntax errors such as unmatched delimiters. The checkeq program is a good place to start. Use checkeq like this:

```
checkeq myeqnfile
```

If checkeq finds no errors, it displays the following:

```
myeqnfile
```

or

```
myeqnfile:
    New delims: ##, line 2
```

If you have an odd number of delimiters, you'll see something like this:

```
myeqnfile:
myeqnfile:
     New delims: ##, line 2
     3 line ##, lines 7-9
     3 line ##, lines 9-11
     3 line ##, lines 11-13
     3 line ##, lines 13-15
     3 line ##, lines 15-17
     Unfinished ##
```

If, for some reason, you've specified bad delimiters (#$, for example, or #), checkeq announces:

```
myeqnfile
     Strange delims at Line 2
```

or

```
myeqnfile
     Unfinished
```

checkeq isn't good for much more than this.

Processing to /dev/null

Because checkeq lets a lot of mistakes slip by, you can also process your equation and send output to /dev/null (so you don't clutter your directory with a lot of troff output).

To do this:

```
eqn myeqnfile > /dev/null
```

When errors are found, you see a message like the following:

```
eqn: syntax error near line 19, file nyeqnfile
     context is
     !a = (x >>> {sup <<<< 2}) + 1!
```

The line number is not guaranteed, but it should be close.

Again, this is not foolproof because, if eqn *can* process your code, it will. You'll get no error message, even if your output is garbled or nonexistent.

Additional Suggestions

If you get no output at all:

If your file contains nothing but an equation, try inserting a line of text before the equation. If you don't want text, use translated tildes:

```
.tr ~
~ ~ ~
.EQ
x sup 2 + y sup 2 = z sup 2
.EN
```

Oddly enough, this does not seem to affect eqn code—even code with tildes in it.

If the vertical spacing is wrong: Try printing your file with a different macro package— or with no macro package. (If you're using a home-grown package, you may have to pipe your file through eqn before you send it through troff.) Try processing the eqn code and replacing the code with the processed code in your file. Try using space 0 as the first line of your eqn code:

```
.EQ
space 0
code
.
.
.
.EN
```

If you're using the .EQ/.EN macros to delimit your equation, try using delimiters (## or !!)—and, of course, vice versa.

If your equation is garbled: Check for omitted spaces and braces. (Use them, even if you don't really need them.) Count braces and parentheses to make sure you have an even number of each. checkeq—and eqn itself—doesn't always find this problem. If your equation contains a sup, make sure you use spaces around its argument, even if there's a brace. Make sure you have keywords in the right order. For example, #x highbar tilde# produces no error message, but it prints the bar right on the tilde. (The correct order is #x tilde highbar#.) If your equation is long or complicated, use lots of spaces and newlines to make it easy to read.

eqn and the Preprocessors

You can use eqn with any of the other preprocessors (pic, grap, and tbl), but only with delimiters—not with .EQ/.EN macros. Before you do this, however, ask yourself if it's really necessary. You could always get another job, or move to a tiny island with no electricity and no telephone lines.

The sections that follow provide some help if you can't face life without grap.

eqn and *pic*

You cannot use ## as eqn delimiters with pic code. You *can* use $$ and !! and %%. I wouldn't experiment with anything else.

Complicated equations inside pic pictures will come out wrong if eqn has to provide extra vertical space—for example, for an integral sign. Use space 0 to (try to) prevent this, as follows:

```
.EQ
delim !!
.
.
.
pic code "!space 0 eqn code!"
```

You need the quotation marks for pic.

A simple example of pic and eqn is

$$a^2 + b^2 = c^2$$

The code is as follows:

```
.EQ
delim !!
.EN
.PS
box ht .75i wid i.5i "!a sup 2 + b sup 2 = c sup 2!"
.PE
```

eqn and grap

Because grap is built on pic, you can expect similar problems if you use eqn with grap. You can use the same delimiters, and you can expect to have to use space 0 to correct vertical spacing problems. eqn tries to override grap's spacing unless you do. Do just as you did for pic; here's an example:

```
.EQ
delim !!
.EN
.G1
label left "!y= sqrt { (2x sup 3 + 1)/3}!"
.G2
```

You must use quotation marks, as with pic.

eqn and tbl

There are a few simple rules for using eqn in tables. (tbl is discussed in detail in Chapter 23.)

- If you have equations and tables in your file, run the file through `tbl` first.
- Do not use pound signs (##) as delimiters. (I tried it and got several indignant screenfulls of complaints. I'm not sure what the conflict is.)
- Do not use the same characters for eqn delimiters and `tbl` tab characters.
- Avoid using T braces with equations.
- Don't put an equation in an `n`-style column. `tbl` cannot process the equation properly.

To put an equation in a table, do the following:

1. Define your eqn delimiters (use exclamation points).
2. Start your table.
3. Insert your eqn code between exclamations points.

With me and ms, you can use arguments to the `.EQ` macro to position your equation horizontally. Both packages accept the following:

```
.EQ C      \centers the equation
.EQ I      \indents the equation
.EQ L      \left justifies the equation
```

Summary

eqn is a limited use program, but a very useful one. It's easy to learn, easy to use (except for the spaces), and it does an excellent job of setting mathematical expressions.

Drawing Pictures with *pic*

25

By Susan Peppard

IN THIS CHAPTER

pic is rarely your first choice as a drawing tool. With pic you can draw lines and a limited variety of shapes—no color, no shading—but you can create a complex and detailed picture, if you're willing to work at it. pic was developed before everyone had personal computers with sophisticated, mouse-based drawing packages. Today, troff users with graphics terminals can use mouse-based programs such as xcip. These programs provide many of the capabilities—except for color—of the sophisticated packages, and they don't require a knowledge of pic. xcip produces pic code, which—and here's the point—you can edit if you know pic.

pic is no substitute for a sophisticated drawing tool. It doesn't have color. It provides shading only inside boxes, circles, and ellipses. It doesn't even let you draw a randomly wiggly line.

The Basics

To draw a box, type

```
.PS
box ht 1 wid 1.25
.PE
```

The result is

This example specifies a height and a width. If you don't specify them—you're not required to—the box will be three-quarters inch high and one-half inch wide.

You can draw circles. For example,

```
.PS
circle rad .5
.PE
```

produces

You can draw ellipses, too. For example,

```
.PS
ellipse ht .5 wid 1.25
.PE
```

produces

The default pic unit is inches. pic has default sizes for boxes, circles, and ellipses. The pic default sizes are listed in the "Controlling Size" section later in this chapter.

Required Macros and Primitives

troff recognizes pic code by its opening and closing macros: .PS and .PE. ms includes a .PF macro for picture flyback. This macro restores you to your last position on the page (vertically and horizontally) before the picture—where you were before you invoked pic. This feature is rarely used; some pic users surround their pic code with display macros and specify no-fill mode. For example,

```
.DS
.nf
.PS
.box ht 1 wid 1.25
.

.
.PE
.DE
```

This might look like overkill, but mm likes it.

The .PS macro also can be used to do the following:

.PS < filename	Sources in a pic file; imports an external file called filename and allows it to be processed as if filename were part of your text file.
.PS *wid ht*	Enables you to specify the width or the height—or both—of the final picture

CAUTION: If you have a space after the .PS and no measurements, your figure will be enlarged proportionally so that its width is the current width (line length) of your pages.

To insert comments in `pic` code, begin a line with #.

Forbidden Macros and Primitives

Whatever you do, don't include any spacing requests—`.sp`, `.ls`, `.vs`, `.SP`, and `.P`—inside your `pic` code. `pic` does its own spacing, and it gets really annoyed if you interfere. Use the `move` command instead.

Adding Text

You can put labels in these basic `pic` shapes. Consider the following code:

```
.PS
box ht .75 wid .75 "A Square"
move
box ht .75 wid .75 "Another" "Square"
.PE
```

It produces

Each line of text is enclosed in its own set of quotation marks.

`pic` attempts to center your text, both vertically and horizontally, which isn't helpful if you want to label a line. For example,

```
.PS
line right 1i "line"
.PE
```

comes out looking like

Fortunately, `pic` recognizes the words `above` and `below`, so you can position your text so that it is more readable. If you have two lines of text, `pic` puts one above the line and one below it. For example,

```
.PS
line right 1i "over" "under"
.PE
```

produces

$$\frac{\text{over}}{\text{under}}$$

pic doesn't object if you want to specify the font and point size for your text, so long as you keep the specifications inside the quotation marks. For example,

```
.PS
line right 1i "\f(HB\s12over" "under\fP\s0"
.PE
```

produces

$$\frac{\textbf{over}}{\textbf{under}}$$

> **NOTE:** To right or left justify text, use `rjust` or `ljust`.

The preceding examples are troff escape sequences and are discussed further in Chapter 21, "Basic Formatting with `troff/nroff`."

Default Placement of Objects

pic assumes that all objects it draws should touch one another. Therefore, if you specify

```
.PS
box ht .5 wid 1 "Box 1"
box ht .5 wid 1 "Box 2"
.PE
```

you will get

Box 1	Box 2

Fortunately, pic has a move command, which you can use to separate the boxes. For example,

```
.PS
box ht .5 wid 1 "Box 1"
move
box ht .5 wid 1 "Box 2"
.PE
```

produces

Box 1   Box 2

The move command's default direction is to the right. Its default distance is one-half inch. You can change these defaults by specifying a direction and a distance, as in

```
.PS
box ht .5 wid 1 "Box 1"
move left 2i
box ht .5 wid 1 "Box 2"
.PE
```

Now the boxes look like

Box 2   Box 1

Note that the distance between the two boxes is actually one inch, not the two inches you specified in the move command. The reason is that pic measures from center to center, not from edge to edge.

Connecting Objects

pic is especially suited for charts and flow diagrams. Consider the following code:

```
.PS
box; line; box
move right 1i
box; arrow; box
.PE
```

It produces

> **NOTE:** When you write pic code, you specify one command per line, or you can separate commands with semicolons. Long lines require the continuation symbol (\).

As you can see from the code and the figure, arrow is a synonym for line.

The following commands are useful as well:

`line ->`	Draws an arrowhead at the end of the arrow. It doesn't necessarily point to the right.
`line <-`	Draws an arrowhead at the beginning of the arrow. It doesn't necessarily point to the left.
`line <->`	Draws arrowheads on both ends of the arrow.

> **TIP:** To draw a line with an arrow at both ends, use `line <->` or `arrow <->`. This might seem obvious, but for seven years I drew two-headed arrows using the `arrow` command twice—drawing a right-pointing arrow over a left-pointing arrow—because nobody told me about `<->`.

Suppose that you want Box 2 directly under Box 1. Consider the following code:

```
.PS
box "Box 1"
move down
box "Box 2"
.PE
```

It produces

```
┌──────────┐
│          │
│  Box 1   │
│          │
└──────────┘


      ┌──────────┐
      │  Box 2   │
      └──────────┘
```

The problem with this code is that `pic` moves half an inch from wherever it left off drawing the first box, which in this case is the middle of the box top. To place Box 2 correctly, you have to move down another one-half inch and to the left:

```
.PS
box "Box 1"
move left .375i
move down .75i
box "Box 2"
.PE
```

Figure 25.1 shows you the result.

FIGURE 25.1.

Two boxes positioned correctly.

Box 1

Box 2

This is a nuisance, to say the least, because in a complicated drawing you quickly lose track of where pic begins and ends each element of the drawing. You can use reference points with pic so that you know where each element of your drawing will be placed. They are discussed in the next section.

More about Placement

To avoid having to think like pic—an exercise that can be dangerous to your mental health—you can refer to parts of objects that you've drawn. pic recognizes all of the following:

.l left	.ne northeast
.r right	.nw northwest
upper	bottom
lower	start
.t top	end
.n north	1st
.e east	2nd
.w west	3rd (and so on)
.s south	last
.nw northwest	2nd last
.sw southwest	3rd last (and so on)

pic also understands compass points. Figure 25.2 shows the parts of a pic element to which you can refer.

FIGURE 25.2.

pic *reference points.*

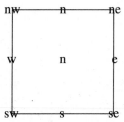

The position notation words and the compass points enable you to specify positions like these:

```
line from upper right of 2nd last box to upper left of last box
arrow from 1st circle.e to 2nd circle.w
box at end of last line
move left 1i from start of last box
line from Box.c to Box.s
move down 1i from bottom of 2nd last ellipse
```

> **NOTE:** You can use terms like `upper left` and `lower right`, but not `top left` and `lower bottom`.

Now you have several ways of specifying the two boxes shown in Figure 25.1. You could write

```
.PS
box "Box 1"
move to last box.s down .5
box "Box 2"
.PE
```

or you could write

```
.PS
box "Box 1"
move to bottom of last box down .5
box "Box 2"
.PE
```

If you want to avoid the wordiness of `bottom of last box`, you can label your construct

```
B1: box "Box 1"
```

Labels must begin with a capital letter.

Using labels enables you to specify the two boxes as follows:

```
.PS
B1:box "Box 1"
B2:box  with .c down 1i from B1.c "Box 2"
.PE
```

> **TIP:** If you reference objects by their centers, you don't have to worry about where `pic` starts a new object or in which direction the new object is drawn.

These notations—`left`, `right`, `.ne`, `.sw`, and so on—assume that you can tell left from right and east from west. If you are directionally challenged like me, you should allow extra debugging time for your `pic`s. I've tried sticking scraps of paper labelled *left/west* and *right/east* on the sides of my monitor. It helps a little.

`pic` comes to your rescue with a solution. It understands Cartesian coordinates, as shown in Figure 25.3.

FIGURE 25.3.

x,y coordinates.

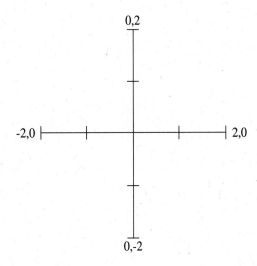

Again, the unit is inches. The important thing to remember is that your first object starts at 0,0. In other words, the coordinates are relative. There is no specific location on a page or in a drawing that is always 0,0. It depends on where you start.

Cartesian coordinates enable you to specify the two boxes shown in Figure 25.1 as

```
.PS
box at 0,0 "Box 1"
box at 0,-1 "Box 2"
.PE
```

You'll probably find this easier.

`pic` also has an `invis` command. At first glance, it doesn't seem very useful. How often do you expect to draw a page full of invisible boxes? The real advantage of `invis` is in placing text. Consider Figure 25.4.

FIGURE 25.4.

Using invisible lines.

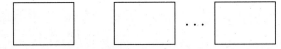

Placing those pesky dots could be a problem. Using `invis`, though, makes it easy. The code that produces Figure 25.4 is

```
.PS
box; move; box
line invis .75 "\s12 . . . \s0"
box
.PE
```

There are other uses for invis. You can use it, for example, to define a large area in which you will be drawing several smaller objects and to provide compass points outside a smaller object.

Additional Shapes and Functions

pic includes two more shapes in addition to the ones you've already seen. They are the arc and the spline.

To pic, an arc is a quarter of a circle. You can use the arc command to draw a circle, as in

```
.PS
arc; arc; arc; arc
.PE
```

A more sensible use of arc is to draw a rectangle with rounded corners. For example,

```
.PS
line left; arc; line down; arc
line right; arc; line up; arc
.PE
```

To make a spiral like the one shown in Figure 25.5, combine a series of arcs. For example,

```
.PS
arc rad .04
arc rad .08
arc rad .12
arc rad .16
arc rad .20
arc rad .24
arc rad .28
arc rad .32
arc rad .36
arc rad .40
arc rad .44
arc rad .48
.PE
```

produces the following:

FIGURE 25.5.

A spiral made of arcs.

pic also recognizes trigonometric and other mathematical functions:

| atan2 | (e_1, e_2) | the arctangent of e_1, e_2 |
| cos | (e) | cosine of *e* (*e* must be in radians) |

exp	(e)	10^e
int	(e)	integer part (by truncation)
log	(e)	logarithm base 10 of e
max	(e_1, e_2)	maximum of e_1 and e_2
min	(e_1, e_2)	minimum of e_1 and e_2
rand	(n)	random number between 1 and n
sin	(e)	sine of e (e must be in radians)
sqrt	(e)	square root of e

These functions must be followed by an expression in parentheses. In the case of atan2, max, and min, two expressions must follow. rand is followed by empty parentheses and produces a random number between 0 and 1.

Lines and shapes don't have to be solid. You can draw dotted and dashed objects. Consider the following code.

```
.PS
B1: box
move to B1.n up .05 right .05
B2: box dashed
move to B2.n up .05 right .05
B3: box dotted
.PE
```

Controlling Size

pic variables include several that specify the default size of pic objects. Table 25.1 lists these variables and their default values.

Table 25.1. Default values of pic variables.

Variable	Default Value	Variable	Default Value
arcrad	.25i	ellipsewid	.75i
arrowhead	2i	lineht	.5i
arrowht	.1i	linewid	.75i
arrowwid	.05i	moveht	.5i
boxht	.5i	movewid	.75i
boxwid	.75i	scale	1i
circlerad	.25i	texht	0i
dashwid	.5i	textwid	0i
ellipseht	.5i		

`arrowwid` and `arriowht` refer to the arrowhead. The `arrowhead` variable specifies the fill style of the arrowhead.

It's easy to change the value of a variable. For example,

```
boxht = .75; boxwid = .5
```

Remember: The default unit for pic is inches.

There are other ways of controlling the size of a picture. You can specify a height or a width—or both—on the .PS line. Usually it's better to specify only the width. If you specify both dimensions, your picture may be distorted.

> **NOTE:** For some reason, you must specify the width first. For example, .PS 2 4 produces a picture 2 inches wide and 4 inches long. This is the opposite of the order in which you specify the dimensions of a box or ellipse. The width and height you specify refer to the whole picture.

You can also set the variable `scale`. By default, `scale` is set at 100 or 1, depending on your version of pic. (You can test this by scaling a drawing to 1.5. If you get an error message or a garbled result, use 150.) All the dimensions in a pic drawing are divided by the scaling factor. Therefore, if the scale is normally 1 and you set it to 4, your 1-inch lines will be a quarter-inch long. For example,

```
.PS
scale = 2
box ht 2i wid 2i
.PE
```

This code produces a box scaled down to half the size of its specifications, that is, a 1-inch square.

> **CAUTION:** Text is not scaled. If your text needs resizing, you must do it with \s, and it's usually a matter of trial and error to find out what will fit in your scaled figure.

Object Blocks

You can define any sequence of objects or moves as a block, which you can manipulate almost as if it were a simple box. You need to name the block. The name must begin with an uppercase letter. Although pic places no specific restrictions on the length of the name, shorter is better.

Object blocks are useful when you are placing text.

You can also position an object block easily, as in

```
.PS
C1: circle rad .125
Spiral [
arc rad .04
arc rad .08
arc rad .12
arc rad .16
arc rad .20
arc rad .24
arc rad .28
arc rad .32
arc rad .36
arc rad .40
arc rad .44
arc rad .48
] with .s at C1.n
.PE
```

Macros and Variables

If you want to reuse an object, you can put it in a file by itself and use the copy function:

```
.PS
<pic code>
copy filename
<pic code>
.PE
```

You can also define a pic macro. Don't confuse pic macros with troff macros. In the broadest sense, a macro is a short way of referring to a complex process. In other words, a pic macro is just a collection of pic commands that have been given a name.

Unlike object blocks, which merely give you a convenient way of referring to positions in and around the object, macros can be used to draw objects. The first three lines of the following code sequence enable you to draw the defined object by invoking its name, as shown in the last line.

```
.PS
define SQ %
box ht .5 wid .5
%
SQ; move; SQ
.PE
```

This code produces

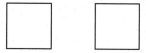

To create a macro, use the word define followed by a name for your macro and a delimeter. Next come all your pic instructions and finally, another delimeter. In the first example, I used % for delimeters. In the second example, I used curly braces. There is no default. The choice is yours.

Macros can have up to nine arguments, specified $1 through $9. For example, you can define a square and supply the dimensions as arguments when you invoke the macro, as shown in the first three lines of the following code. The last line produces the 1/2 inches square shown in Figure 25.6.

```
.PS
define SQ }
box ht $1 wid $1 "$2"
{
SQ(.5, square)
.PE
```

produces

FIGURE 25.6.

Squares Created with a Macro

Macro definitions require delimiters. As you can see, though, the choice is up to you. Percent signs (%) are usual choices. When you invoke the macro, the arguments go in parentheses.

Macro definitions persist throughout a file. If you ever have to get rid of a macro, use undef SQ—or whatever you've named your macro.

Debugging

When you're dealing with pic, you aren't troubleshooting—you're debugging. It's much easier to do this as you code. Draw the first element of your picture. Before you print it, send the file through pic to see whether any error messages are generated. If your file contains only pic, you can do this:

```
pic filename
```

If your file contains text, just use your normal `troff` command line. However, instead of sending the file to a printer, redirect your output to `/dev/null`. See Chapter 28, "Tools for Writers," for more information on directing output to `/dev/null`.

`pic` tries to help you pinpoint your errors with messages similar to the following:

```
pic: syntax error near line 26
context is
        >>> linr <<< left 1i
```

Occasionally, `pic` tells you that it has reduced the size of your picture. This is almost always because you've made a mistake. Most often, you've left out a decimal point, and `pic` is trying to fit a line 1625 inches long—you meant 1.625 inches—on an 8.5-inch page. When this happens, your picture naturally is mangled out of all recognition.

Usually, your debugging involves the placement of objects and the placement or size of text.

pic Tips and Tricks

If you can't get an object placed correctly by moving down and left (or up and right) from an object, try referring to both objects by their centers, as in `box.c`.

If your drawing involves a number of objects and placement is crucial, use *x,y* coordinates.

If you're having trouble placing text, remember `over` and `under`.

Using a `box invis` or a `line invis` to place your text usually works well.

Make yourself a library of `pic` drawings so that you don't have to keep reinventing the spiral.

Summary

`pic` is a `troff` preprocessor for drawing lines, arrows, boxes, circles, ellipses, arcs, and splines. Output tends to vary from system to system, so be prepared to spend some time debugging. `pic` is well worth the trouble if you frequently include simple graphics in text files. It is especially useful for organization charts, flow charts, state diagrams, and the like.

Creating Graphs with *grap*

26

By Susan Peppard

What Is *grap*?

grap is a `troff` preprocessor that uses `pic` to construct different types of graphs. Its use in data analysis is limited. For example, you can use grap to determine whether a population is growing exponentially. grap, then, is used primarily to include graphs in `troff` documents. Like the other `troff` preprocessors, it is fussy about syntax. You can't simply sit down and toss off three or four complicated graphs. You have to read the documentation. grap, like `pic`, faces stiff competition from the PC-based packages.

> **NOTE:** grap does not provide color or shading.

The Basics

One of the more endearing qualities of UNIX is its inconsistency. You would expect the grap macros to be `.GS` and `.GE`, and you would be wrong. The grap macros are `.G1` and `.G2`. In addition to these macros, all that grap requires for a primitive graph is some data. Take, for example, the grades on a test:

```
.G1
75
78
81
52
63
61
70
71
84
58
.G2
```

These dismal grades, after sorting, produce a scatter point graph.

Because grap has a copy facility similar to that of `pic`, you can simplify your code even more by putting the data in a separate file. (See Chapter 25.) For example,

```
.G1
copy "test.scores"
.G2
```

If you want the graph to have a solid line instead of scatter points, simply add a line of code that says `draw solid` immediately after the `.G1` macro.

Adding Bells, Whistles, and Ticks

You can make your graph much more attractive by drawing a frame, adding labels, and specifying ticks. The following code, for example, produces a more sophisticated graph.

```
frame invis ht 2 wid 3 left solid bot solid
label left "1990" "Dollars" left .5
label bot "Grand Total:  $210,000"
ticks left out at 6000 "6,000", 9000 "9,000", 12000 "12,000", 15000 "15,000",\
18000 "18,000", 21000 "21,000"
ticks bot at 1990 "1990", 1995 "1995", 2000 "2000", 2005 "2005", \
2010 "2010"
draw solid
copy "cost.child"
.G2
```

Here, the frame is shown only on the bottom and left side. The *x* and *y* coordinates have labels. Also, the ticks have been specified explicitly; they are not determined by grap.

TIP: You can save yourself hours of debugging if you remember that grap doesn't understand commas in large numbers. The ticks left line above specifies 9000 "9,000". The commas are safely isolated in labels specified in quotation marks. The grap specifications themselves contain no commas.

The data file—in this case, cost.child—also must contain no commas.

NOTE: Earlier versions of grap may not recognize the abbreviation bot for bottom.

You can specify ticks as out. This means that the ticks themselves, but not their labels, appear outside the grap frame. You can also specify ticks as in, in which case they appear inside the frame.

If there are too many dates to fit across the bottom of a graph, you might want to use apostrophes in the labels, as in '10, '20, and '30. To do this, you must tell grap that your label is a literal. (This is what C programmers have to do all the time.) If you want to specify the first and last dates in full, you need to use two tick lines. The following code, for example, produces bottom labels of 1900, '05, '10, '15, and so on, up to 1950:

```
ticks bottom out at 0 "1900", 50 "1950"
ticks bottom out from 05 to 45 by 5 "'%g"
```

NOTE: To suppress tick labels, use a null argument (" ").

Notice the words at 0 in the previous example. grap recognizes *x,y* coordinates, and un-like pic, it understands that 0,0 is the intersection of the *x* and *y* axes. To use coordinates, you use the coord command, as in

```
coord x first-value, y last-value
```

Without the coord command, grap automatically pads your first and last values, giving you blank space at the beginning and at the end of your graph. coord suppresses padding.

Likewise, use coord if you want an exponential graph rather than a linear graph.

You can plot the figures for low-income and high-income families on the graph shown in Figure 26.1.

FIGURE 26.1.

The cost of raising a child, by income level.

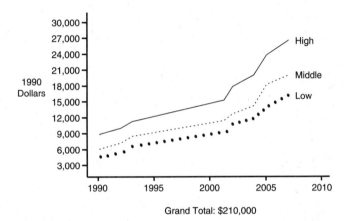

The following code produced Figure 26.1.

```
.G1
frame invis ht 2 wid 3 left solid bottom solid
label left "1990" " Dollars" left .4
"High" ljust at 2008,27000
"Middle" ljust at 2008,20000
"Low" ljust at 2008,14000
ticks left out at 3000 "3,000", 6000 "6,000",\
9000 "9,000", 12000 "12,000", 15000 "15,000",\
18000 "18,000", 21000 "21,000", 24000 "24,000",\27000 "27,000", 30000 "30,000"
ticks bottom at 1990 "1990", 1995 "1995", 2000 "2000", 2005 "2005", 2010 "2010"
copy "cost2.child"
draw dotted
copy "cost.child"
new solid
copy "cost3.child"
new dashed
.G2
```

The data file is formatted like this:

```
1990     4330
1991     4590
1992     4870
1993     5510
1994     5850
1995     6200
1996     6550
1997     6859
1998     7360
1999     7570
2000     8020
2001     8500
2002     10360
2003     10980
2004     11640
2005     13160
2006     13950
2007     14780
```

NOTE: grap doesn't care whether you separate data columns with a space or a tab so long as you're consistent.

Adding Shapes and Other Features

grap does more than just draw lines. It can print a grid. It can draw a circle, ellipse, or arrow. In fact, grap can draw just about anything that pic can.

grap has a macro facility just like that of pic:

```
define name X commands X
```

For the delimiter, you can use any character that isn't in the command text. You can also use braces. grap permits up to nine arguments, just as pic does.

In addition to data explicitly specified in a file, grap works with functions that more or less describe the data. The following code, for example, produces a sine curve:

```
frame ht 1 wid 3
draw solid
pi=atan2(0,-1)
for i from 0 to 2*pi by .1 do { next at i, sin(i) }
```

Summary of *grap* Commands

Table 26.1 summarizes the grap commands. Square brackets indicate that an argument is optional. A pipe between arguments means that you must use only one of the arguments.

Table 26.1. Summary of grap commands.

Command	Syntax	Description
frame	frame [ht *expr*] [wid *expr*] [[*side*] [*descr*]]	Specifies the dimensions for the frame drawn around the graph
side	top¦bot¦right¦left	Refers to the frame
descr	solid¦invis¦dotted¦dashed	Describes the lines used to draw the frame. You can control dotting and dashing by specifying the distance between dots or the length of and distance between dashes.
label	side list	Specifies the placement of and the text for labels
shift	left¦right¦up¦down *expr*	Specifies the shift
list	rjust¦ljust, above¦below, size *expr*	Encloses items in quotation marks. You can modify the placement. size *expr* reduces the point size. This is useful for labels or for putting words or symbols in the graph itself.
coord	coord [*name*] [x *expr,expr*] [y *expr,expr*] [log x¦log y¦log log]	Specifies points on a graph and suppresses padding
ticks	ticks [*side*] in¦out	Specifies ticks on the side(s) of graph. The ticks can be inside or outside the frame.
grid	grid side [descr]	Draws a grid with solid, dotted, dashed lines
point	[*name*] expr, expr	Identify a point in a graph
line	line¦arrow from *point* to *point* [descr]	Draws a line (solid, dashed, dotted, and so on)

Command	Syntax	Description
circle	circle at *point* [radius *expr*]	Draws a circle
draw	draw [*name*] descr	Draws a graph (solid, dotted, dashed, and so on)
new	new [*name*]	Draws a new graph in the same frame
next	next *name* at *point*	Continues plot of data in *name* at *point*. Default is current position.
for	for *var* from *expr* to *expr* [by *expr*]	Looping function for grap
if	if *expr* then X *anything* X else X *anything* X	Conditional statement for grap
graph	graph *Picname*	Labels a graph. The label must start with an uppercase letter.
define	define *name* X *commands* X	Defines a macro
copy	copy "*filename*"	Copies the specified file into the graph file. copy is used for data files.
sh	sh X *anything* X	Executes a shell command from within grap
pic	pic *anything*	Draws a pic construct from within grap
assignment	*var* = *expr*	Assigns a value to a variable

In addition to the commands listed in Table 26.1, grap provides for predefined strings and built-in functions.

Predefined strings include bullet, plus, box, star, dot, times, htick, vtick, square, and delta.

Built-in functions include log (base 10), exp (base 10), int, sin, cos, atan2, sqrt, min, max, and rand.

Summary

grap gives you a quick and relatively easy way of inserting graphs into memos or other text files. It can produce line and bar graphs, but no pie charts, no color, and no shading. Nevertheless, grap can be a useful tool. Like pic, grap is system-sensitive, so allow time for debugging.

Writing Your Own Macros

27

By Susan Peppard

IN THIS CHAPTER

Why Would Anyone Write a Macro?

If you work with macros every day, sooner or later you'll get the urge to write one. Sometimes it's a mild case of the disease: You're creating a document with mm, but you want paragraphs with a first-line indent and no extra space between paragraphs. Occasionally you want to do something more elaborate—like create a macro package for formatting that screen play.

Before you start, make sure you're familiar with the building blocks. troff provides you with the following: troff primitives (discussed in detail in Chapter 21, "Basic Formatting with troff/nroff"); escape sequences, such as \e and \^ (also discussed in detail in Chapter 21); other macros, either from a standard macro package, or ones you've written; number registers; and defined strings.

The next section reviews just what a macro is made of and introduces you to concepts that will be explained in detail later in the chapter.

Macro Review and Overview

With embedded troff primitives, you can format a page just about any way you want. The trouble is you have to reinvent the wheel every time you write a new document. And every time you format a first-level heading, you have to remember just what sequence of primitives you used to produce that centered 14-point Helvetica Bold heading. Then you have to type three or four troff requests, the heading itself, and another three or four requests to return to your normal body style. (This is practical only if you're being paid by the line.) It's a laborious process and one that makes it difficult—perhaps impossible—to maintain consistency over a set of files.

Good news: You can use macros to simplify formatting and ensure consistency.

Macros take advantage of one of the UNIX system's distinguishing characteristics—the ability to build complex processes from basic (primitive) units. A macro is nothing more than a series of troff requests, specified and named, that perform a special formatting task.

> **NOTE:** The expression "troff request" is often used as a synonym for troff primitive. When I say "troff request," I mean any or all of the facilities provided by troff: primitives, escape sequences, strings, registers, and special characters.

Macros can be simple or complex, short or long, straightforward or cryptic. For example, a new paragraph macro might entail

```
.sp .5
.ti .5i
```

This produces spacing of half a line space (nroff) or half an em (troff) between paragraphs, and indents the first line of each paragraph half an inch.

> **NOTE:** You can use just about any unit of measurement you want—inches, centimeters, points, picas—as long as you specify the units.

Macro names consist of a period followed by one or two characters. Traditionally, these characters are uppercase, to distinguish them from primitives. (The me package is the exception to this rule.) The paragraph macro above could be called .P or .PP or .XX.

> **NOTE:** In general, macro names, like primitive names, are mnemonic; there's some relationship, however farfetched, between the macro name and its function. Thus .P or .PP would be reasonable names for a paragraph macro, and .XX wouldn't.

Macros are invoked in a text file by typing their names. (The period must be in the first position on the line.) Macros can also be invoked with an apostrophe (single quote) instead of a period as the first character. This delays processing of the macro until the current line has been filled.

A Heading Macro, Dissected and Explained

A fairly straightforward example of a macro is that centered heading I mentioned earlier. To create it, you need to provide spacing information before and after the heading, font information, size information, and position information (centering).

You could do this as follows:

```
.sp 2    \"space before the heading
.ce 99   \"turns on centering for the next 99 lines
.        \"to accommodate headings that might start
.        \"out as 1 line and then get longer
.ft HB   \"changes the font to Helvetica Bold
.ps 14   \changes the point size to 14 points
.vs 16   \"changes vertical spacing to 16 points
first line of heading
second line of heading (optional)
third line of heading (optional)
.sp      \"space after the heading
.ce 0    \turns off centering
.ft      \"returns to default font
.ps      \returns to default point size
.vs      \"returns to default vertical space
```

That simple series of troff primitives illustrates several important points.

Most important, it is full of comments. Comments are identified by the sequence.\"

Note, however, that you can have as many spaces as you want between the initial period and the backslash. In this way, you can put a comment on a line by itself or you can add a comment at the end of a line of `troff` requests. You can use spaces to line up your comments so they're easy to read.

Another useful technique, illustrated in the sample above might be called generalization or thinking ahead. Instead of providing for a 1-line heading with a simple `.ce`, which centers the next line of text, the sample code turns centering on by requesting `.ce 99` (which centers the next 99 lines of text). Most headings are not much longer than that. After the heading lines are specified, the code turns centering off with a `.ce 0`.

All of that code could be combined into a single pair of macros, called `.H1` (for first-level heading) and `.HE` (for heading end), so that all you need type is

```
.H1
heading
.HE
```

A big improvement!

But wait. What if the heading came near the bottom of the page? There's nothing in the `.H1` macro to prevent the heading from printing all by itself just before a page break. You need at least three lines of text after the heading. Fortunately there's a `troff` primitive trained for just this job—`.ne`.

`.ne` (for need) says "I need the number of lines specified right after me or else I'm going to start a new page." (This is similar to the "Keep with Next" feature of the better word processors and desktop publishing software.) Perfect. How many lines do you need? Three (so there will be at least three lines of text after the heading), plus one for the heading itself, two more for the spaces before the heading, and one last line for the space after the heading. So a real working version of the sample heading macro might have `.ne 7` at the top.

This may seem like a lot of detail. (It gets worse.) If all you want to do is use a macro package to format documents, you may not want to learn how macros work. But, even if you have no intention of writing a macro yourself, it can be useful to understand how they work. (It can save you a lot of debugging time.) The more you know about the way macros are written, the easier it is to format a document.

What else might be done with a heading macro like `.H1`? Well, most often it would be combined with the `.HE` macro, so all you must type is

```
.H1 "heading"
```

Simple for the user, a bit harder for the macro writer.

To provide this kind of service, the .H1 macro would have to allow an argument. (An argument provides additional information for the macro or primitive—like the 7 specified for the .ne primitive. The section "Arguments," later in this chapter goes into more detail.)

An argument is coded in a special way. troff recognizes $1 as the first argument following the invocation of the macro. (This is a common UNIX convention.) There can be several (up to nine) arguments to a single macro (again, a common UNIX convention).

The code would look something like this:

```
.ne 7      \"need 7 spaces on page or start new page
.sp 2      \"space down 2 spaces before the heading
.ce 99     \"turn centering on
\f(HB\s+2\\$1\fP\s0
.          \"the font is Helvetica Bold, 2 points larger than
.          \"the body type, the heading itself - $1 -and then return to
.          \"previous font and default point size
.ce 0      \"turn centering off
.sp        \"space down after the heading
```

> **NOTE:** Don't worry about all the backslashes just yet. They are explained in the section "Arguments," too. For now, just concentrate on the code and the comments.

This macro is beginning to get complicated. (That means it's beginning to look like the kind of macro you'll see in a macro package.) But all it really says is the same old thing in a different way. UNIX is famous for providing 75 ways to do everything. troff code is no exception to this rule.

In the example above, the font change is accomplished by an escape sequence (\f(HB), instead of the .ft primitive. The point size is accomplished the same way (\s+2 instead of .ps), but note that a relative point size—the current point size plus 2—is specified. Next comes the heading itself, the first argument to .H1, specified as $1.

To return to the previous font, use the escape sequence \fP. In many cases, \f1 works just as well. \f1 returns you to the default body type. To return to your original point size, use \s0 (or \s-2). \s0 returns you to the default point size. Since you don't always know what this is, \s0 can be very useful.

> **TIP:** When you use a heading macro, make a habit of surrounding the heading with quotation marks, even if it's a one-word heading. If you forget the quotes, your heading will be exactly one word long. troff simply disregards the rest of the line.

There's just one more concept you need: conditional execution (`if` statements). Details on conditional statements can be found later in this chapter in the section, "Conditional Statements." How would that work with the heading macro?

For one thing, you could change the macro name to plain `.H` and then use an argument to specify the heading level.

```
.H 1 "first-level heading"
.H 2 "second-level heading"
.
.
.
.H 7 "seventh-level heading"
```

And this is just what most macro packages do. They provide a general heading macro, and you supply the level and the text for the heading.

What would the code look like?

```
if \\$1 1 {      \"if the heading level is 1, do everything within the
.                \"curly braces; otherwise skip everything within them
.
.
.
\f(HB\s+2\\$fP\s0
.
.
.
}
```

Similarly,

```
if \\$1 2 {
```

for a second-level heading, and so on.

Number Registers

Number registers are locations that store values. They store only whole numbers which can, but need not, have units attached to them. There are three things you can do with a number register:

- set (or define or initialize) it
- interpolate it (that is, examine the contents and, optionally, compare the contents to a specified number or even to the contents of a different number register)
- remove it

Number registers are used very frequently in macro definitions. They contain such information as line length, page offset, current font number, previous font number, current indent, current list item number, and so on.

For example, if you're formatting an automatic list (with mm), you would find the following information in number registers: current indent; current nesting level (That is, is the list a list-within-a-list?); item number; format of item number (that is, Arabic, uppercase roman numeral, lowercase roman numeral, uppercase alphabetic, or lowercase alphabetic).

Every time troff processes a .LI, the number registers that control these characteristics are interpolated. Some of them (the list item number, for example) are also incremented.

This information can be useful if you are formatting what I call a "discontinuous list" (a list that has ordinary text between two of the list items).

Before you insert the ordinary text, you must end the current list. When you want to continue the list, another .AL and .LI will start the list at 1. However, you want it to start at 5. If you know which number register stores this information, you can reset it.

To set a number register:

```
.nr a 0
.nr aa 0
.nr AA 1i
.nr b +1i
```

The units are optional—and very tricky. If you specify a unit of measurement (called a scaling factor) with a number register, the value is stored by troff in *troff units* (*u*), no matter what unit you specify. Thus, (for a 300dpi device) 1i is stored as 300u. When you add 1 to the register, you are adding 1 troff unit—unless you specify units. Note the following:

```
.nr x 21    \"has a value of 600u
.nr x +1    \"now has a value of 601u

.nr x 2i    \"has a value of 600u
.nr x +1    \"now has a value of 900u
```

You also have the option of specifying the increment/decrement to the register when you define it:

```
.nr b 10 1
.nr bb 0 2
```

Note that you do not specify whether 1 (in the first instance) or 2 (in the second instance) is to be an increment or a decrement. That is done when you interpolate the register.

To interpolate the contents of a number register:

```
\\na       \"one-character name
\\n(aa     \"two-character name
\\n+a      \"increments register b
\\n-(bb    \"decrements register bb
```

Number registers contain numbers. They are often used in arithmetic expressions:

```
.if \\na<1
```

```
.if \\na=\\nb
.if \\na+\\nb<\\nc
```

There is another arithmetic expression, common in troff, that looks unfinished:

```
.if \\na          \"if a is greater than 0
.if \\na-\\nb      \"if a minus b is greater than 0
.if !\\na          \"if a is not greater than 0
```

To increment or decrement a number register, use

```
.nr a \\na+1
.nr a \\na-1
```

(Note that you don't use an equal sign when you set a register.)

You can define a number register in terms of another number register (or two):

```
.nr z (\\nx+\\ny)
```

Toward the end of this chapter there are two tables of number registers predefined by troff. You will not want to use those names for your own number registers. If you are working with a macro package like ms or mm, however, you must also check the number registers used by your macro package because you don't want to overwrite the contents of the number register that numbers lists or stores indents.

Using Number Registers for Automatic Numbering

Every now and then you work on a document that cries out for automatic numbering. The examples that come to mind (because they're documents I've worked on) are storyboards for training materials. Each "board" represents a screen (in computer-based tutorials) or a viewgraph (in ordinary courses). Each board consists of graphics, text, and possibly animation or sound instructions.

I've found that you need to number the boards, both for your own convenience and to make things simple for your reviewers. I've also found that the order of the boards changes with depressing frequency.

If you explicitly number the boards, you have to explicitly change the numbers every time you switch 7 and 8 or 30 and 54. This is not fun and not an efficient way to spend your time.

You can use number registers to provide automatic numbers for the boards. (You can also write an awk program, but, if you don't know awk, this isn't an efficient solution either.)

To use number registers for automatic numbering, do the following:

1. Select a number register that is not being used by troff or by your macro package. (For this example, I'm using vv.)

2. Initialize the register at the top of your file: .nr vv 0.

3. Whenever you want a number, interpolate vv : \n(vv+1. (Remember, you're doing this in your text file. You don't have to hide the register from troff.)

You can do this even more elegantly by defining an autoincrementing/decrementing number register:

```
.nr vv 0 1
```

The initial value in vv is 0; the autoincrement/decrement is 1. At this point, troff doesn't know whether you want the register contents to be incremented or decremented. You specify that when you interpolate the register.

```
\n+(vv
```

(The plus sign tells troff to increment the register.)

You can refine this to include a unit number, giving you compound folios, but this is practical only if you're using a macro package with chapter numbers (or some similar device like section or unit numbers) and you're using these numbers in your files.

Assuming you're using chapter numbers and the register for chapter numbers is cn, you can specify your board numbers like this:

```
.\n(cn-\n+(vv
```

If your chapter numbers are stored in a string called cn, do this:

```
\*(cn-\n+(vv
```

There is one disadvantage to using automatic numbering in this way. It's the same disadvantage you may have experienced with mm's automatic lists. When you look at your file, you have no idea what your current step (or board) is. And, if you have to refer to a previous step or board, you probably end up writing "Repeat Steps 1 through ???," printing your file, and inserting the correct numbers later.

Sometimes you need to remove registers. This is especially necessary if your macros use a large number of registers. It's a good idea to get into the habit of removing temporary registers as soon as you're done with them. To remove a register, use the .rr primitive:

```
.rr a     \"remove register a
```

Defined Strings

A defined string is a set of characters to which you assign a name. The string is always treated as a literal, and you cannot perform any arithmetic operation on it. You can, however, compare it to another string, or even compare the string "2" to the contents of a number register.

A string definition looks a lot like a macro definition:

```
.ds name value
.ds name "value that has a lot of separate words in it
.dsU U\s-1NIX\s0
.dsUU "UNIX Unleashed
```

String names consist of one or two characters. The names come from the same pool as macro names, so be careful to choose a unique name for your string. In the examples above, note that the .ds can (but does not have to be) followed by a space. Note also that you use only the opening quotation marks when your string consists of multiple words. (If you forget and include a closing quotation mark, it will be printed as part of the string).

To invoke the string:

```
\\*a      \"one-character name
\\*(aa    \"two-character name
```

Sometimes a string is a better choice than a number register. If you're dealing with alphabetic characters, a string may be your only choice.

Consider the following: You want to define something to hold the number of your current chapter. If you use a number register, you can increment these numbers very easily. You'll only have to set the value once, at the beginning of the book. Unless you have appendixes. If you have appendixes, you'll have to reset to 1 when you reach Appendix A, and then you'll have to translate that number into a letter.

> **NOTE:** To use a number register for chapter numbers, use `.af` (alter format) to produce uppercase letters for your appendixes. `.af` recognizes the following formats:
>
> | | |
> |---|---|
> | 1 | Arabic numerals |
> | i | lowercase roman numerals |
> | I | uppercase roman numerals |
> | a | lowercase alphabetic characters |
> | A | uppercase alphabetic characters |
>
> To use the letter A in a compound page number (where the number register storing chapter numbers is cn), specify the following: `.af cn A`.

Perhaps a string would be simpler. You'll have to redefine the string at the beginning of each chapter, but you won't have to do any diddling.

Strings can be used as general purpose abbreviations, although this is not their primary purpose, nor even the best use of strings. A better use is to define a string containing the preliminary name of the product you are documenting. Then, when the marketing people finally decide to call their new brainchild "XYZZY Universal Widget," you don't have to do any searching or grepping to replace the temporary name. You can just redefine the string.

Define a string near the top of your file as the preliminary name of the product:

```
.ds Pn "Buzzy      \"code name for product
```

Remember that strings cannot share names with macros.

When the ugly duckling "Buzzy" becomes the swan "XYZZY Universal Widget," just change the definition:

```
.ds Pn "XYZZY Universal Widget      \"official name for product
```

Like macros, strings can have information appended. To add to a string, use the troff primitive .as. Although it's hard to imagine a use for this primitive, consider the following:

You are documenting three versions of the XYZZY Universal Widget in three separate documents. For the first document, you could add "Version 1.0" to the string:

```
.as Pn "(Version 1.0)
```

The other versions can be similarly identified in their documents as "Version 2.0" and "Version 3.0."

Listing Names of Existing Macros, Strings, and Number Registers

If you are using mm or ms and adding macros to either of these packages, you need to know what names (for macros, strings, and number registers) are available and what names have already been used.

To create a file called sortmac containing the macro names used in mm (assuming mm to be where it ought—namely in /usr/lib/tmac/tmac.m):

```
grep "^\.de" /usr/lib/tmac/tmac.m ¦ sort ¦ uniq > sortmac
```

(That code also assumes that you are executing grep from the directory in which you want sortmac to end up.)

Strings are listed pretty much the same way:

```
grep "^\.ds" /usr/lib/tmac/tmac.m ¦ sort ¦ uniq > sortstr
```

To list number registers defined in the mm macro package, execute the following sed script in the directory with the macros (/usr/lib/tmac):

```
sed -n -e 's/.*.nr *\(..\).*/\1/p' tmac.m ¦ sort ¦uniq > $HOME/sortnum
```

The standard macro packages should all be in /usr/lib/tmac. The macro filenames are as follows:

tmac.m	mm macros
tmac.s	ms macros
tmac.e	me macros (don't hold your breath looking for this one)
tmac.an	man macros

Remember that troff and nroff—and each macro package—use predefined number registers, and these may not be set within the package.

Getting Started

To define a macro, you use the .de primitive and end the definition with two periods. A macro to indent the first line of a paragraph could be defined like this:

```
.dePX      \"macro to create indented paragraphs, no space between
.ti 3P
..
```

This is a very simple example. A "real" paragraph macro would check to make sure there was room for two or three lines and, if not, go to the next page. Nevertheless, this simple definition illustrates some important points. The macro name can consist of one or two characters. If you use a name that's already assigned to a macro, the definition in your text file overrides the definition in a macro package. The macro name follows the .de. It can be separated from the .de by a space, but a space is not necessary.

TIP: Although the space following the .de doesn't matter, consistency does. Someday, you'll want to list and sort your macro definitions, and you can't sort them as easily unless you can rely on a space (or no space) between the .de and the macro name.

A macro definition can include troff primitives and other macros. A brief description of the macro is included on the definition line. This is crucial. You can forget more about macros in two weeks that you can learn in two years. Comment lavishly. And make sure you include a comment on the definition line to identify the macro. This helps when you grep for macro definitions and then sort them.

There is one more constraint on macro names: A macro cannot have the same name as a defined string. (Macros are perfectly happy sharing names with number registers, however.)

> **NOTE:** By the way, there's no law against giving a macro the same names as a primitive. In fact, it sounds like an excellent April Fool. If you should be foolish enough to try this, bear in mind that the primitive will, for all intents and purposes, cease to exist. All that will remain will be your macro. So make it a good one.

If, instead of defining a new macro, you want to redefine an existing one, then you use the existing macro's name:

```
.deP
.ti 3P
..
```

If you redefine the .P macro, the old definition is no longer used (although it's still sitting there in the mm macro package). To return to the old definition, you must get rid of your new definition (delete it from the top of your file or delete the file containing the definition).

The benefit to writing a new macro with a new name is that the old definition is still usable. The drawback is that you're used to typing .P, so you'll probably forget to type .PX when you want to use your new macro.

In addition to defining a new macro and redefining an existing macro, you can remove a macro, and you can add to an existing macro.

Defining a Macro

To define a macro, use .de. You can end the definition, as shown above, with .., or you can use the delimiters of your choice, like this:

```
,deP!!
.ti 3P
!!
```

(I've never actually known anyone who used this form of the definition primitive, but it's there, if you want it. You know how UNIX always provides you with many roads to the same end.)

Once you have written your macro definition, you can add it to an existing macro package, add it to your own file of new macros, and source the file into your text files with `.so`, or just put the macro definition in your text file.

> **TIP:** Creating an add-on file of macros is the least desirable way of incorporating your macros. If your current macro package needs that much help, someone should rewrite the package. The purpose of a macro package is to ensure a consistent look to documents prepared with the package. If everyone defines her or his own set of paragraph macros, this purpose is defeated.

Removing a Macro

To remove a macro, use the `.rm` primitive:

```
.rmP
```

Again, the space between the `.rm` and the macro name is optional.

This is not something that you do on a whim. Removing a macro requires serious, mature consideration. You might do it if you were experimenting with a better version of an existing macro—a list end macro (`.LE`) that left the right amount of space after it, for example. Your new, improved macro might be called `.1E`, or `.Le`. You could encourage people to use your new macro by removing `.LE`. (This is unlikely to be wise; you always forget to tell your department head who is working on a weekend on a crucial document, and—well, you can imagine the rest.) A safer way to use your new `.Le` might be to substitute the definition of `.Le` for `.LE` (after it's been tested and found to be truly superior), but to leave the `.LE` macro definition in the package and remove it at the end of the macro package file. (Even better, you could comment it out.)

Unless you are very knowledgeable about macros and are in charge of maintaining one or more macro packages, you will never remove a macro.

Renaming a Macro

To rename a macro, use the `.rn` primitive:

```
.rnP Pp
```

As usual, the space between the `.rn` and the macro name is optional. The space between the old name and the new name is not optional.

Renaming a macro is almost as serious as removing it. And it can be a great deal more complicated. For example, you might want to fix mm's list macro by adding some space after the `.LE`. You can do this by renaming. Here's what you do:

1. Rename the `.LE` macro. (`.rn LE Le`)

2. Define a new `.LE`.

   ```
   .deLE      \"This is a new improved version of LE - adds space
   .Le
   .sp .5
   ..
   ```

3. Invoke `.LE` as usual.

The new `.LE` (which is the old `.LE` plus a half-line space) takes the place of the old `.LE`.

You might think of using `.rn` so that you could include the `.TH` (table column heading) macro in a man file. (`.TH` is the basic title heading macro used in all man files.)

This seems to be a reasonable idea. If this sort of thing interests you, you can think through the process with me. (Otherwise, skip to "Adding to a Macro.")

The first thing to establish is the conditions for each of the `.TH` macros: When should `.TH` mean table heading, and when should it mean title?

That's easy to answer. You want the normal `.TH` to mean title all the time except following a `.TS H`. So when do you rename `.TH`—and which `.TH` do you rename? And, if you boldly put `.rnTH Th` in your file, to which `.TH` does it refer?

Think about that, and you'll begin to see that maybe `.TH` is not the ideal candidate for renaming.

Adding to a Macro

To add to a macro definition, use `.am`:

```
.amP
.ne 2      \"of course this isn't the right place for this request
..
```

(Yes, the space after the `.am` is optional.)

Adding to a macro, while not a task for beginners, is a lot more straightforward. `.am` is often used to collect information for a table of contents. Whenever the file has a `.H` (of any level, or of specified levels) you want to write that information into a data file which will be processed and turned into a TOC.

A Simple Example

Suppose you've found yourself in the unenviable position of typing a term paper for your child, spouse, or self. It's easy enough to double space the paper—just use `.ls 2`. But, if you're not using ms, you don't have an easy way of handling long quotes (which are supposed to be single spaced and indented from the left and right). What do you have to do every time you type a long quotation?

```
.in +1i
.ll -2i
.ls 1
```

And at the end of the quotation, you have to reverse that coding:

```
.in -1i
.ll +2i
.ls 2
```

Instead of typing those three lines, you could define a `.Qb` and a `.Qe` macro. Those two sets of three lines are the definitions. All you need to add is a `.deQb` (or `.deQe`) to start the macro definition and two dots to end it. If you want to refine the definition, you can add some space before and after the quotation and a `.ne 2` so you don't get one line of the quotation at the bottom of page 5 and the other six lines on page 6:

```
.deQb
.sp
.ls 1
.ne 2
.in +1i
.ll -2i
..

.deQe
.br
.ls 2
.sp
.ne 2
.in -1i
.ll +2i
..
```

NOTE: There's no rule that says user-defined macros have to consist of an upper-case character followed by a lowercase character. It just makes things easier when you have guidelines.

troff **Copy Mode**

`troff` processes each file twice. The first time, called "copy mode," consists of copying without much interpretation. There is some interpretation, however. In copy mode, `troff` interprets the following immediately: the contents of number registers (`\n`); strings (`\*`); and arguments (`\$1`).

You do not want this to happen. `troff` will find `\ns` and `\*s` and `\$1s` in your macro package file—before the number register or string or argument has any meaningful contents. Fortunately, troff also interprets \\ as \, so you can "hide" these constructs by preceding them with an extra backslash. \\n copies as \n— which is what you want when the macro using that number register is invoked.

Note, however, that this rule does not apply to number registers invoked in your text file. When you invoke a number register in your text file, you want it interpreted then and there. So you don't use the extra backslash.

This seems simple. In fact, it is simple in theory. In practice, it's a horrible nuisance. A glance at a macro package like ms or mm will show you triple, even quadruple, backslashes. If you don't enjoy thinking through processes step by painful step, you will not enjoy this aspect of macro writing.

troff does not interpret ordinary escape sequences in copy mode. \h, \&, \d are all safe and do not have to be hidden.

During copy mode, troff eliminates comments following \".

Arguments

Macros, like other UNIX constructs, can take arguments. You specify an argument every time you type a heading after a .H 1 or a .NH. You specify arguments to primitives, too, like .sp .5 or .in +3P. In a macro definition, arguments are represented by \$1 through \$9. (Yes, you are limited to nine arguments.)

A couple of examples of arguments are:

```
.deCo      \"computer output (CW) font
\f(CW\\$1\fP
..
```

```
.dePi      \"paragraph indented amount specified by $1
.br
.ne 2
.ti \\$1
..
```

(Note that you must hide the argument (with the extra backslash) in order to survive copy mode.)

If you omit an argument, troff treats it as a null argument. In the case of the .Co macro, nothing at all would happen. In the case of the .Pi macro, the paragraph would not be indented. If you specify too many arguments (which would happen if you had .Co Press Enter in your file), troff merrily throws away the extras. You'd get "Press" in CW font; "Enter" would disappear. Use double quotation marks (.Co "Press Enter") to hide spaces from troff.

Conditional Statements

A conditional statement says, "Do this under certain (specified) conditions." It may add, "and under any other conditions, do that." You know the conditional statement as an "if" or an "if-else." The troff versions are .if (if) and .ie (if-else). The troff if has a different syntax from the shell if, but the principle is the same.

A simple if is coded like this:

```
.if condition simple-action

.if condition \{
complex-action
\}
```

The backslash-brace combinations delimit the actions to be taken when the condition is true.

The if-else works like this:

```
.ie condition simple-action
.el simple-action

.ie condition \{
complex-action
\}
.el \{
complex-action
\}
```

You use the conditional statement whenever you want to test for a condition. Is this an even page? Okay, then use the even-page footer. Are these files being nroffed (as opposed to troffed)? Okay, then make the next few lines bold instead of increasing the point size.

Believe it or not, troff has four built-in conditions to test for just those conditions:

o	current page is odd
e	current page is even
t	file is being formatted by troff
n	file is being formatted by nroff

The odd-even conditions simplify writing page header and footer macros. You can simply say:

```
.if o .tl '''%'     \"if odd - page no. on right
.if e .tl '%'''     \"if even - page no. on left
```

The single quotation marks delimit fields (left, center, and right). Thus, '''%' places the page number on the right side of the page and '%''' places it on the left side.

You could do the same thing with `.ie`:

```
.ie o .tl '''%'      \"if odd - page no. on right
.el .tl '%'''        \"else if even - page no. on left
```

The `.if`, even when it requires a seemingly endless list of conditions, is easier to use.

Suppose you are writing that heading macro discussed earlier in this chapter. You want to specify different spacing and different point sizes, depending on the level of the heading. You might start like this:

```
.deH
.if \\$1=1 \{
.bp
\s14\f(HB\\$1\fP\s0
.sp
\}
.if \\$1=2 \{
.sp 2
\s12\f(HB\\$1\fP\s0
.sp
¦}
.
.
.
```

You can compare strings, but you use delimiters instead of an equal sign:

```
.if "\\$1"A"
.if '\\$2'Index'
```

> **TIP:** The bell character, made by pressing Ctrl+G, is often used as a delimiter because it's not much use in a text file. It looks like ^G in a file, but don't be fooled. This is a non-printing character. Before you print out every macro file on your system, check them for ^Gs. Unless you want to spend a lot of time drawing little bells or printing ^G, try substituting another character for the bell before you print. (Try this on small portions of the file at a time.)

In addition to comparing numbers and strings, you can also test for inverse conditions. `troff` recognizes the exclamation mark (!) as the reverse of an expression, for example:

```
.if !o       \"same as .if e
.if !\\$1=0  \"if $1 is not equal to 0
.if !"\\$1"" 
```

(The last example above tests for a null argument.)

Be careful when you use `!`. It must precede the expression being reversed. For example, to check for an unequal condition, you must write `.if !\\na=\\nb`. You cannot write `.if \\na!=\\nb`.

Units of Measurement

troff allows you to use just about any units you want (except rods and kilometers):

i—inch	p—point	u—troff unit
c—centimeter	m—em	v—verticaspace
P—Pica	n—en	

Unfortunately, it is impossible to be 100 percent certain of the default units for any given primitive. For the most part, the troff default for horizontal measurements is the em and for vertical measurements is the line space. The nroff default for horizontal measurement is device-dependent, but it's usually ¹⁄₁₀ or ¹⁄₁₂ of an inch.

If you use arithmetic expressions, you will soon find that none of those defaults work the way they are supposed to. The culprit is the troff unit (u). A troff unit is about ¹⁄₃₀₀ of an inch (for a 300 dpi printer). Because this is a very much smaller unit than any of the others troff accepts, you can expect loony output from time to time. (Your text will print, but not on the paper.)

Always specify units.

If you want to divide 37 inches by 2, you are far safer doing the arithmetic in your head and specifying 18.5P than letting troff decide how to process 37P/2. troff will not do what you expect. troff will divide 37 picas by 2 ems. You will not like the result. If, in desperation, you try 37/2P, you will still not like the result because troff will divide 37 ems by 2 picas. You have to specify 37P/2u. The u acts as a sort of pacifier and lets troff perform the arithmetic correctly.

When you're unsure of the units, use troff units. It's sort of like adding backslashes. A few more will probably fix the problem.

Arithmetic and Logical Expressions

As you see, conditional statements are often combined with arithmetic expressions. You can also use logical expressions. troff understands all of the following:

+ - * /	plus, minus, multiplied by, divided by
%	modulo
> <	greater than, less than

>= <=	greater than or equal to, less than or equal to
=	equal (== is a synonym)
&	AND
:	OR

Unlike other UNIX programs, troff has no notion of precedence. An expression like \\$1+\\$2*\\$3-\\$4 is evaluated strictly from left to right. Thus, to troff, 2+3*5-10\2 equals 7.5. This is hard to get used to and easy to forget.

Always specify units.

Diversions

Diversions let you store text in a particular location (actually a macro that you define), from which the text can be retrieved when you need it. Diversions are used in the "keep" macros and in footnotes.

The diversion command is .di followed by the name of the macro in which the ensuing text is to be stored. A diversion is ended by .di on a line by itself.

Diverted text is processed (formatted) before it is stored, so when you want to print the stored text, all you have to do is specify the macro name. Since there is virtually no limit either to the number of diversions you can have in a file or to the length of any diversion, you can use diversions to store repeated text.

> **NOTE:** Storing repeated text in a diversion isn't necessarily a good idea. You can avoid typing the repeated text just as easily by putting it in a file and reading that file into your text file.

For example, suppose the following text is repeated many, many times in your document:

```
.AL 1
,LI
Log in as root.
.LI
Invoke the UNIX system administrative menu by
typing \f(CWsysadm\fP and pressing Enter.
.P
The system administrative menu is displayed.
.LI
Select \f(CWEquine Systems\fP by highlighting
the line and pressing Enter.
.P
The Equine Systems menu is displayed
```

You could store this text in `.Em` (for Equine Menu) by prefacing it with `.diEm` and ending it with `.di`.

Note that your diversion contains an unterminated list. If this is likely to cause problems, add `.LE` to the diverted text.

To print the `Equine Systems` text, just put `.Em` in your file.

In addition to `.di`, there is a `.da` (diversion append) primitive that works like `.am`. `.da` is used to add text to an existing diversion. It can be used over and over, each time adding more text to the diversion. (To overwrite the text in a given diversion, just define it again with a `.diEm`.) The `.am` primitive can be used, like `.am`, to create TOC data.

You can even have a diversion within a diversion. The "inside" diversion can be used on its own, as well.

Traps

`troff` provides several kinds of traps: page traps (`.wh` and `.ch`); diversion traps (`.dt`); and input line traps (`.it`).

Page traps usually invoke macros. For example, when `troff` gets near the bottom of a page, the trap that produces the page footer is sprung. A simple illustration of this is the following.

Suppose you wanted to print the current date one inch from the bottom of every page in your document. Use the `.wh` primitive:

```
.deDa                  \"define date macro
\\n(mo/\\n(dy/18\\n(yr  \"set date
..
.wh 1i Da              \"set the trap
```

The order of the arguments is important.

To remove this kind of trap, invoke it with the position, but without the macro name:
`.wh 1i`.

The `.ch` primitive changes a trap. If you wanted the date an inch from the bottom of the page on page 1 of your document, but an inch and a half from the bottom of the page on all subsequent pages, you could use `.ch Da 1.5i`.

(Note that the argument order is different.)

Diversion traps are set with the `.dt` primitive, for example:

```
.dt 1i Xx
```

This diversion trap, set within the diversion, invokes the `.Xx` macro when (if) the diversion comes within one inch of the bottom of the page.

Input text traps are set with the `.it` primitive. This trap is activated after a specified number of lines in your text file.

There is a fourth kind of trap, though it isn't usually thought of as a trap. This is the end macro (`.em`) primitive. `.em` is activated automatically at the end of your text file. It can be used to print overflow footnotes, TOCs, bibliographies, etc.

Environments

The `.ev` (environment) primitive gives you the ability to switch to a completely new and independent set of parameters, such as line length, point size, font, and so forth. It lets you return to your original set of parameters just as easily. This process is known as environment switching. The concept is used in page headers, for example, where the font and point size are always the same—and always different from the font and point size in the rest of the document.

Three environments are available: ev 0 (the normal, or default, environment); ev 1; and ev 2.

To switch from the normal environment, just enter `.ev 1` or `.ev 2` on a line by itself and specify the new parameters. These new parameters will be in effect until you specify a different environment. To return to your normal environment, use `.ev` or `.ev 0`.

You could use environment switching instead of writing the `.Qb` and `.Qe` macros. Here's how it would work:

```
.ev 1       \"long quote begins
.sp
.ls 1
.in +1i
.ll -2i
text of quotation
.sp
.ev
```

Environments are often used with diversions or with footnotes where the text is set in a smaller point size than body type. It is to accommodate diversions within diversions that the third environment is provided.

Debugging

Debugging macros is slow and often painful. If you have a version of `troff` that includes a trace option, use it—but be warned: It produces miles of paper. If you don't have a trace option, you can use the `.tm` primitive (for terminal message) to print the value of a number register at certain points in your file. The value is sent to standard error, which is probably your screen. Use `.tm` like this:

```
.tm Before calling the Xx macro, the value of xX is \n(xX.
.Xx
.tm After calling the Xx macro, the value of xX is \n(xX.
```

(Note that you don't hide the number register from copy mode because you put these lines right in your text file. Remember to delete them before the document goes to the printer.)

troff Output

Sometimes you have to look at `troff` output. It's not a pretty sight, but after the first few files, it begins to make sense. Here's the `troff` code produced by a file with two words in it: UNIX Unleashed.

(By the way, use `troff -o > outputfile` to produce this output.)

```
x T post
x res 720 1 1
x init
v0
p1
x font 1 R
x font 2 I
x font 3 B
x font 4 BI
x font 5 CW
x font 6 H
x font 7 HI
x font 8 HB
x font 9 S1
x font 10 S
s10
f1
H720
V120
cU
72N72I33Xw97U72n50128e44as39h50e44dn120 0
x trailer
v7920
x stop
```

If you look hard, you can pick out the text in the long line. The numbers are horizontal motions reflecting the width of the letters. You can also see where the font positions are defined. The `s10` on a line by itself is the point size. `f1` is the font in position 1 (in this case, Times-Roman). The `H` and `V` numbers following the font definition specify the starting horizontal and vertical position on the page.

PostScript Output

PostScript output is a little easier to read, but the set-up lines are endless. Where UNIX Unleashed generates 24 lines of troff code, the same two words generate more than 800 lines of PostScript code. The significant lines are at the beginning and the end. The last 17 lines of the PostScript file are as follows:

```
setup
2 setdecoding
%%EndSetUp
%%Page: 1 1
/saveobj save def
mark
1 pagesetup
10 R f
(\255 1 \255)2 166 1 2797 490 t
(UNIX Uleashed) 1 695 1 720 960 t
cleartomark
showpage
saveobj restore
%%EndPage: 1 1\%%Trailer
done
%%Pages: 1
%%DocumentFonts: Times-Roman
```

Font and point size are specified as 10 R f (10 point Roman). Text is enclosed in parentheses (which makes it easy to find). The showpage is crucial. Every page in your document needs a showpage in the PostScript file. Occasionally, PostScript output is truncated and the last showpage is lost. No showpage means no printed page.

Hints for Creating a Macro Package

The following suggestions may be helpful. Most of them are very obvious, but, since I've made all these mistakes myself at one time or another, I pass on this advice:

Starting from scratch is necessary if you intend to sell your macro package. If you just want to provide a nice format for your group, use ms or mm as a basis. Remove all the macros you don't need and add the ones you do need (lists from mm, if you're using ms, boxes from ms, if you're using mm). Don't reinvent the wheel. Copy, steal, and plagiarize.

Make sure to include autoindexing and automatic generation of master and chapter TOCs.

Write a format script for your users to send their files to the printer, preferably one that will prompt for options if they aren't given on the command line.

Write—and use—a test file that includes all the difficult macros you can think of (lists, tables, headers and footers, etc.).

Try to enlist one or two reliable friends to pre-test your package.

You'll never be able to anticipate all the weird things users do to macro packages. Start with a reasonable selection. Save lists within tables within diversions within lists for later.

Don't replace your current macro package with the new one while people are working. Do it at night or after sufficient warning.

Make sure the old macro package is accessible to your users (but not easily accessible, or they won't use your new one).

Don't use PostScript shading if most of your documents are Xeroxed rather than typeset. Copiers wreak havoc on shading. Also, there's always one person in your group who doesn't use a PostScript printer.

Beyond Macro Packages

If you've gone to the trouble of creating an entire macro package, you want it to be easy to use, and you want it to do everything your users could possible desire. This means that you should provide users with a format script. Although actual programs for these tools are beyond the scope of this chapter, the following hints should get you started:

- ■ The command `format`, entered with no arguments, should prompt users for each option; a version for experienced users should allow options to be entered on the command line.

- ■ Your `format` program should invoke all the preprocessors (`tbl`, `eqn`, `pic`, and `grap`). If the file to be formatted has no `pic`s or `grap`s, no harm is done and very little time is wasted.

- ■ Your program should allow users to specify the standard macro packages as well as your shiny new one. (But make your shiny new one the default.)

- ■ Users should be able to specify a destination printer (assuming you have more than one printer available). Useful additional destinations are null and postscript.

- ■ Users should not have to specify anything (or know anything) about a postprocessor.

- ■ Users should see a message when their file is done processing (`file sent to printer` is adequate).

- ■ Users should be able to select portrait or landscape page orientation—and possibly page size.

- ■ Your `format` command should be documented, and all your users should have a copy of the documentation. (If you can arrange to have your documentation added to UNIX's online manual, accessed with the `man` command, so much the better.)

Predefined Number Registers (*nroff/troff*)

Table 26.1 lists the number registers that are predefined by `troff`. You can change the contents of these registers, but, whatever you do, don't use these names for your own number registers.

Table 26.1. Predefined Number Registers

Register Name	Description
%	current page number
ct	character type (set by \w)
dl	(maximum) width of last completed
dn	height (vertical size) of last completed diversion
dw	current day of the week (1-7)
dy	current day of the month (1-31)
ln	output line number
mo	current month (1-12)
nl	vertical position of last printed baseline
sb	depth of string below baseline (generated by \w)
st	height of string above baseline (generated by \w)
yr	last 2 digits of current year

Predefined Read-Only Number Registers (*nroff/troff*)

Table 26.2 lists the read-only number registers that are predefined by `troff`. You cannot change the contents of these registers, but you can inspect them and use their contents in condition statements and arithmetic expressions.

Table 26.2. Predefined Read-Only Number Registers

Register Name	Description
$$	process id of `troff` or `nroff`
.$	number of arguments available at the current macro level

Table 26.2. continued

Register Name	Description
.a	post-line extra line-space most recently used in \x'N'
.A	set to 1 in troff if -a option used; always 1 in nroff
.b	emboldening level
.c	number of lines read from current input file
.d	current vertical place in current diversion; equal to n1 if no diversion
.f	current font number
.F	current input filename
.h	text baseline high-water mark on current page or diversion
.H	available horizontal resolution in basic (troff) units
.I	current indent
.j	current ad mode
.k	current output horizontal position
.l	current line length
.L	current ls value
.n	length of text portion on previous output line
.o	current page offset
.p	current page length
.R	number of unused number registers
.T	set to 1 in nroff, if -T option used; always 0 in troff
.s	current point size
.t	distance to the next trap
.u	equal to 1 in fill mode and 0 in no-fill mode
.v	current vertical line spacing
.V	available vertical resolution in basic (troff) units
.w	width of previous character
.x	reserved version-dependent register
.y	reserved version-dependent register
.z	name of current diversion

Summary

Writing one or two macros can be fun and can greatly simplify your life. Start small and easy—no number registers defined by other number registers, no renaming, and (if you can manage it) no traps or diversions. Writing macros helps to understand macro processing, which makes you a more valuable employee.

Writing an entire macro package is a long, difficult process, one that continues for months, even years, after you write that last macro, because someday some user will combine a couple of macros in ways you never dreamed of. Don't write a macro package unless you're prepared to maintain it, provide documentation and user support, and modify it.

Tools for Writers

28

By Susan Peppard

IN THIS CHAPTER

Using *spell*

You've gone to a lot of trouble to prepare a document that looks splendid and you don't want it to be marred by spelling mistakes. The spell program will catch most of your typos. An interactive version of spell, called ispell, also is available on some systems.

> **NOTE:** spell will not find errors such as is for in or affect for effect. You still have to proofread your document carefully.

spell uses a standard dictionary. It checks the words in your file against this dictionary and outputs a list of words not found in the dictionary. You can create a personal dictionary to make spell more useful, as you'll learn in the next section.

If your file includes .sos or .nxs, spell searches the sourced in files.

To invoke spell, type spell and your filename. All the words that spell doesn't recognize are displayed on your screen, one word per line. This list of unrecognized words is arranged in ASCII order. That is, special characters and numbers come first, uppercase letters come next, and then lowercase letters. In other words, the words are not in the order in which they occur in your file. Each unrecognized word appears only once. Therefore, if you typed teh for the 15 times, teh appears only once in the spell output.

The list of unrecognized words can be very long, especially if your text is full of acronyms or proper names or if you don't type well. The first few screens will speed by at what seems like 1,000 miles per hour, and you won't be able to read them at all. To read all the screens, redirect the output of spell to a file:

```
$ spell filename > outputfilename
```

> **TIP:** Use a short name for this output file. w—for wrong—works well. You can open a file with a short name more quickly, and delete it more quickly, too. It's also less embarrassing to have a file called w in all your directories instead of one called misspelled_words.

After you create the file of unrecognized words, you can handle it in several ways:

- ■ You can print the file.
- ■ You can vi the file and try to remember the misspellings—or scribble them on a slip of paper.
- ■ You can vi the file in another window if you are using a window-like environment.

Now correct your mistakes. The list probably contains a number of words that are perfectly legitimate. For example, spell refuses to recognize the words diskette and detail. There is no good reason for this, but it may spur you to create a personal dictionary.

To correct your mistakes, first vi your file. Next, do one of the following:

- Search for the misspelling—/teh—and correct it—cw the. Then search for the next occurrence of teh—n—and correct it with the . command. Continue doing this until the search produces pattern not found.

- Globally change all occurrences of teh to the—:1, $ s/teh/the/g.

There's a risk associated with the global method. For example, if I ran spell on this chapter, teh would appear on the list of unrecognized words. Then if I globally changed all occurrences of teh to the, this chapter, or at least this section, would be virtually incomprehensible. The moral is, use global substitutions wisely, and *never* use them on someone else's files.

After you correct your file, run it through spell once more just to be sure. The new output overwrites the old file.

> **TIP:** If you're a less-than-perfect typist—or if you have fat fingertips—unwanted characters can sneak into words—for example, p[rint. When this happens, rint appears on spell's list of unrecognized words. Just search for rint. However, if you type p[lace, spell won't help you, because lace is a perfectly good word.

Occasionally, spell finds something like ne. Searching for all instances of ne isn't fun, especially in a file with 2,000 lines. You can embed spaces in your search—s/[space]ne[space]. However, this is rarely helpful, because spell ignores punctuation marks and special characters. If you typed This must be the o ne, s/[space]ne[space], it won't find it. You can try searching with one embedded space—s/[space]ne and s/ne[space]—, but you still may not find the offender. Try /\<ne\>. This will find ne as a complete word, that is, surrounded by spaces; at the beginning or end of a line; or followed by punctuation.

> **TIP:** Even if you added only half a line, run spell once more after you've edited a chapter. You *always* find a mistake.

Creating a Personal Dictionary

If your name is Leee—with three *e*s—and you get tired of seeing it in the list of unrecognized words, you can add `Leee` to a personal dictionary.

To create a personalized dictionary, follow these steps:

1. Create a file called `mydict`. Of course, you may call it anything you like.

2. Invoke `spell` with `$ spell+mydict inputfile > w`.

Your personal dictionary doesn't have to be in the same directory as your input files. If it isn't, however, you must specify a path on the command line, as in

```
$ spell+/dict/mydict inputfile > w
```

Creating Specialized Dictionaries

Personalized dictionaries are a great help if you're working on several writing projects, each of which has a specialized vocabulary. For example, if you're working on the XYZZY project, and the same words keep turning up in your `w` file—words that are perfectly O.K. in the context of the XYZZY system but not O.K. in any other files—you can create an `xyzzy.dict`.

An easy way to automate some of the steps necessary for creating a specialized dictionary is to run `spell` on your first file. For example,

```
$ spell ch01 > w
```

Then run it on all the rest of your files. Append the output to `w`, instead of replacing `w`. For example,

```
$ spell ch02 >> w
```

At this point, you'll have a long file that contains all the words that `spell` doesn't recognize. First, you need to sort the file and get rid of the duplicates. (Refer to the `sort` command in Chapter 6, "Popular File Tools.")

```
$ sort w -u>sorted.w
```

Here, the `-u` option stands for *unique*. `sort` drops all the duplicates from the list.

Now edit `sorted.w`, deleting all the misspelled words and all words not specific to your XYZZY project. The words that remain form the basis of `xyzzy.dict`. Change the name of `sorted.w` to `xyzzy.dict` by using `mv sorted.w xyzzy.dict`. You can add words to or delete words from this file as necessary.

Repeat this process to create additional specialized dictionaries. And if you're a nice person, you'll share your specialized dictionaries with your colleagues.

Using *ispell*

`ispell` is an interactive version of `spell`. It works like the spell checkers that come with word processing applications. That is, it locates the first word in your file that it doesn't recognize—`ispell` uses the same dictionary as `spell`—and stops there. Then you can correct the word or press Enter to continue.

To invoke `ispell`, do one of the following:

- Enter `ispell ch01`.
- `vi` your first chapter. Then from within `vi`, escape to the shell and invoke `ispell` with `:!ispell`.

Although some people prefer `ispell`, unadorned, ordinary `spell` is more useful if you want to create personal or specialized dictionaries or if you want make global changes to your input file.

/dev/null: The Path to UNIX Limbo

As you're surely tired of hearing, UNIX views everything as a file, including devices (such as your terminal or the printer you use). Device files are stored neatly in the `/dev` directory.

Occasionally, you specify devices by their filenames (for example, when you're reading a tape or mounting a disk drive), but most often you don't bother to think about device files.

There's one device file, however, that you may want to use: `/dev/null`.

The null file in the `/dev` directory is just what it sounds like: nothing. It's the equivalent of the fifth dimension or the incinerator chute. If you send something there, you can't get it back—ever.

Why would you want to send output to `/dev/null`? If you've just created a complex table (or picture, graph, or equation), you can process your creation without wasting paper. Just direct the output to `/dev/null`:

```
tbl filename> /dev/null
eqn filename> /dev/null
pic filename > /dev/null
```

You'll see any error messages on your screen. This is usually more reliable than `checkeq`. And you can use it for text files.

Counting Words with wc

Sometimes you need to count the words in a document. UNIX has the tool for you. The `wc` shell command counts lines, words, and characters. It can give you a total if you specify more than one file as input.

To count the words in `ch01`, enter `wc -w ch01`.

You can count lines by using the `-l` option, or characters by using the `-c` option. Bear in mind, however, that `wc` counts all your macros as words. (Refer to Chapter 6 for more details on `wc`.)

Using grep

The `grep` command is an invaluable aid to writers. It is used primarily for checking the organization of a file or collection of files, and for finding occurrences of a character string.

Checking the Organization of a Document

If you're writing a long, complex document—especially one that uses three or more levels of headings—you can make sure that your heading levels are correct and also produce a rough outline of your document at the same time.

> **NOTE:** This technique is useful only if you are using a macro package—a reasonable assumption for a long, complex document. If you've formatted your document with embedded `troff` commands, this technique won't work.

For example, if your heading macros take the form

```
.H n "heading"
```

a first-level heading might be

```
H 1 "Introduction to the XYZZY System"
```

If your chapters are named ch01, ch02, and so on through ch*n*, the following command will search all your chapter files for all instances of the .H macros. It will also print the filename and the line that contains the .H macro in a file called outline.

```
$ grep "\.H " ch* > outline
```

The backslash is needed to escape the special meaning of the period. The space after H is needed so that you don't inadvertently include another macro or macros with names such as .HK or .HA. The quotation marks are used to include that space.

You can view your outline file with vi, or you can print it. At a glance, you're able to see whether you've mislabeled a heading in Chapter 1, omitted a third-level heading in Chapter 4, and so forth. You also have an outline of your entire document. Of course, you can edit the outline file to produce a more polished version.

Finding Character Strings

If you've just finished a 1,000-page novel and suddenly decide—or are told by your editor—to change a minor character's name from Pansy to Scarlett, you might vi every one of your 63 files, search for Pansy, and change it to Scarlett. But Scarlett isn't in every chapter—unless you've written *Scarlett II*. So why aggravate yourself by viing 63 files when you need to vi only six? grep can help you.

To use grep to find out which files contain the string Pansy, enter the following:

```
$ grep "Pansy" ch* > pansylist
```

Here, the quotation marks aren't strictly necessary, but it's a good idea to get into the habit of using them. In other situations, such as the previous example, you need them.

This command creates a file called pansylist, which looks something like this:

```
ch01:no longer sure that Pansy was
ch01:said Pansy.
ch07:wouldn't dream of wearing the same color as Pansy O'Hara.
ch43:Pansy's dead. Pansy O'Hara is dead.
ch57:in memory of Pansy. The flowers were deep purple and yellow
```

Now you know which chapters have to be edited: 1, 7, 43, and 57. To change Pansy to Scarlett globally, vi one of the files that contains the string Pansy and enter the following command. Make sure that you're in Command mode, not Insert mode.

```
:/,$ s/Pansy/Scarlett/g
```

The g at the end of this code line is important. If the string Pansy occurs more than once in a line, as it does in Chapter 43, g ensures that all instances be changed to Scarlett.

> **NOTE:** The same cautions about making global changes apply here. You might be referring to the flower, not the character; therefore, you'll want to retain Pansy. grep usually gives you enough context to alert you to potential problems.

Using *sed*

The UNIX stream editor, sed, provides another method of making global changes to one or more files. sed is described in Chapter 7, "Editing Text Files."

> **CAUTION:** Don't use sed unless you understand the perils of overwriting your original file with an empty file.

There are two ways to use sed: on the command line or with a sed script. (The example given here uses the command line form, not because it is preferable, but because it is easier to see what is going on.) The script, called substitute, changes all occurrences of the first argument to the second argument. You wouldn't want to go to all this trouble just to change Pansy to Scarlett. However, because you can specify more than one command with sed—in the command line form and in the sed script form—sed is a useful and powerful tool.

Using *diffmk*

diffmk comes from the many diff commands offered by the UNIX system. Its purpose is to diffmark text—that is, to mark text that has changed from one version of a file to another. The text is marked with a vertical bar in the right margin. Sometimes, other characters creep in, especially with tables.

Use diffmk like this:

```
$ diffmk oldfile newfile difffile
```

The order is important. If you get it wrong, `diffmk` blithely prints your old file with diffmarks on it. That's probably not what you want.

Often your files are in two different directories—possibly because the files have the same names. Suppose that you have a `ch01` in the `draft2` directory and in the `draft3` directory. You can specify a pathname for `diffmk`, and you can even write the diffmarked files into a third directory. The third directory must already exist; `diffmk` won't create it for you. The following command diffmarks files in two directories and writes them into a third directory. It assumes that your current directory is `draft3`.

```
$ diffmk ../draft2/file1 file1 ../diffdir/dfile1
```

If you have many chapters, you might want to consider a shell script. To create a shell script that diffmarks all the files in the `draft3` directory against the files in the `draft2` directory, follow these steps:

1. Make sure that you're in the `draft3` directory—that is, the directory for the new file.

2. List the files in `draft3`:

   ```
   $ ls > difflist
   ```

3. Create the following shell script:

   ```
   for i in 'cat difflist'
   do
   diffmk ../draft2/$i $i ../diffdir/d$i
   done
   ```

4. Make the script executable:

   ```
   $ chmod +x diffscript
   ```

5. Put `diffscript` in your `bin`:

   ```
   $ mv diffscript $HOME/bin
   ```

6. Execute `diffscript`:

   ```
   $ diffscript
   ```

The *man* Command

The man command consults a database of stored UNIX system commands—basically everything that is in the system reference manuals—and nroffs it to your screen. If you don't have all that documentation on a shelf in your office, the man command can save the day.

man is simple to use:

```
man commandname
```

The output is far from beautiful, and it's slow. It's paged to your screen, so you press Enter when you're ready to go on to the next page. You can't backtrack, though. Once you leave the first screen—that is, the one with the command syntax on it—the only way you can see it again is to run the man command a second time.

If your terminal has windowing or layering capabilities, man can is more useful, because you can look at it and type on your command line at the same time.

You can also print the output from man, but you may not know which printer the output is going to. If you work in a multi-printer environment, this can be a nuisance. Check with your system administrator.

Using SCCS to Control Documentation

Although the Source Code Control System—SCCS for short—was written to keep track of program code, it also makes a good archiving tool for documentation. It saves each version of a text file—code, troff input, and so on—and essentially enables only the owner to change the contents of the file. SCCS is described in detail in Chapter 30, "SCCS Version Control." You can use SCCS to control versions of a document that you often revise. You can also use SCCS on drafts of a document. If you work with a publications group and your group doesn't have a good archiving and document control system, look into SCCS.

Processing and Printing Formatted Files

29

By Susan Peppard

UNIX offers a selection of commands and utilities for printing. In addition, your system probably has a number of home-grown commands. Be guided by your colleagues and system administrator. If they always use a weird little shell script called `prinnumup` to send their files to the printer, you'd better use `prinnumup` too.

This chapter attempts to find a safe ground somewhere between no information at all and a lot of information that won't work on your system. If you get tired of reading "ask your system administrator," think how tired I got of typing it.

The truth is that systems differ. Printers differ. And new models as well as entirely new printers are popping up all over the place. This chapter should guide you through the basics and give you an understanding of what happens to your file from the time you type `troff` until the neat, white pages emerge from your printer.

Basic Printing with *nroff* and *troff*

This section covers the basics of printing with `nroff` and `troff`. As it explains the ins and outs of how `nroff` and `troff` work, it shows the command lines for printing files that contain only `troff` primitives.

Displaying and Printing *nroff* Files

`nroff` enables you to format your file on the screen instead of (or before) you format it on a printer. (You can do this with `troff`, too, if you have a graphics terminal with windowing or layering capabilities, and if your local system provides this option.)

To `nroff` a file containing only `troff` primitives to the standard output device (screen), use one of these commands:

```
nroff filename¦pg
nroff filename¦more
```

The choice between piping to `pg` or to `more` really depends on your system. Sometimes `more` produces just a single line of additional text rather than a new screenful.

Differences between *nroff* Output and *troff* Output

Printed files will look different, depending on whether they are formatted with `nroff` or `troff`. In general, `nroff`ed files exhibit the following characteristics: All values are treated as a number of character positions (spaces) or line spaces. Vertical space is in multiples of a full linespace. Tabs are set every 8 characters by default. Certain `troff` requests are not available (for example, `.fp`, `.lg`, `.ss`). Text in italic font is underlined; text in bold font is emboldened by overstriking. Point size and vertical space requests (`.ps` and `.vs`) are ignored. Right-margin justification is turned off for the `mm` macros.

Options for the *nroff* and *troff* Commands

The options shown in Table 29.1 are available with current versions of `nroff` and (device-independent) `troff`:

Table 29.1. `nroff`/`troff` **Options**

Option	Effect
-e	(`nroff` only) produces equally spaced words in adjusted lines instead of using multiples of space character
-h	(`nroff` only) uses output tabs (instead of spaces) during horizontal spacing to spread output and reduce output character count; tab settings are assumed to be every 8 characters
-i	reads from standard input after files are exhausted
-mname	prepends the macro file `/usr/lib/tmac.name` to the input file—in other words, uses the macros in filename
-nN	numbers the first output page N
-olist	prints only the pages specified in list; use commas to separate page numbers; use hyphens (-) to indicate page range; -12 prints all the pages up to and including page 12; 12- prints page 12 and all subsequent pages in the file (example: `-o1,3,7,12-20,35,40-`)
-q	invokes the simultaneous input/output of the `.rd` primitive; that is, the file to be processed contains at least one `.rd` primitive
-ran	sets register a to value N; DWB (version 3.1) documentation states that register name can be no more than 1 character
-sN	(`nroff` only) stops printing every *N* pages (default is N=1); this lets you add or change paper; to resume printing, use a linefeed (a newline also works if no pipeline is involved)

continues

Table 29.1. continued

Option	Effect
`-Tname`	(`troff` only) prepares output for typesetter/printer specified as name; default is post
`-Ttype`	(`nroff` only) prepares output for terminal (printer) specified as type; the following types should be known to any system:

2631	Hewlett-Packard 2631 printer in regular mode
2631-c	Hewlett-Packard 2631 printer in compressed mode
2631-e	Hewlett-Packard 2631 printer in expanded mode
300	DASI-300 printer
300-12	DASI-300 terminal set to 12 pitch (12 cpi)
300s	DASI 300s printer
300s-12	DASI-300s printer set to 12 pitch
37	Teletype Model 37 terminal (default)
382	DTC-382
4000a	Trendata 4000a terminal
450	DASI-450 (Diablo Hyterm) printer
450-12	DASI-450 terminal set to 12 pitch
832	Anderson Jacobson 832 terminal
8510	C.Itoh printer
lp	generic name for printers that can underline and tab; all text using reverse line feeds (such as files having tables) that is sent to lp must be processed with col.
tn300	GE Terminet 300 terminal

Option	Effect
`-uN`	(`nroff` only) sets the emboldening factor (number of character overstrikes) to N, or to 0 if N is not specified
`-z`	prints only messages generated by the `.tm` primitive; useful for debugging or, if you are using `.tm`, to generate a list of some kind

Printing Files Formatted with Macro Packages

You can use either `nroff` or `troff` to process files formatted with the standard macro packages, `mm`, `ms`, `me`, and `man`.

> **CAUTION:** You cannot use two macro packages to format one file. The urge to do so usually arises when you want to put a `manpage` in a text file. It can't be done. Make separate files; better yet, put the `manpage` in an appendix and refer to it in your text.

Both `nroff` and `troff` expect to find a pointer to the appropriate macro package in the `/usr/lib/tmac` directory and to find the macro file in the `/usr/lib./macro` directory.

Printing Files Formatted with *mm*

Files that use the `mm` macros can be printed by using `nroff` or `troff`, or by using either of two commands developed specifically for the `mm` macros. These are `mm` (which `nroff`s your file) and `mmt` (which `troff`s your file).

Using the *nroff* or *troff* Command

When you use `nroff` or `troff` to print files formatted with `mm`, your command line takes this form:

```
nroff -mm options filenames
troff -mm options filenames
```

The options must precede the filename(s).

A complete listing of `nroff` and `troff` options can be found in Table 29.1.

`mm` uses number registers to keep track of indents, list item numbers and letters, and a host of information related to page layout (page offset, line length, paragraph style, and so forth).

The `-r` option to `nroff`/`troff` lets you set certain number registers on the command line. This initializes the registers because it is done before the macro package is called. Only registers with one-character names can be initialized this way.

> **NOTE:** To initialize a number register, you must set it before the macro package is called. You can initialize registers with two-character names by doing the following:
>
> 1. Set the registers in the first lines of your text file:
>
> ```
> .nr XX 0
> .nr YY 1
> .nr ZZ 3
> ```
>
> 2. Source in the mm macros right after you initialize the number registers:
>
> ```
> .so /usr/lib/tmac/tmac.m
> ```
>
> 3. Invoke nroff or troff without the -m option:
>
> ```
> troff file
> ```

Table 29.2 lists the registers that can be initialized with the -r option to nroff/troff.

Table 29.2. Registers That Can Be Initialized on the nroff/troff Command Line

Register	Effect
A	Modifies the first page for memos and letters. If A is set to any nonzero number, the letterhead block is suppressed to accommodate personal stationery.
C	Sets the type of copy as follows:
	0 none (default)
	1 OFFICIAL FILE COPY
	2 DATE FILE COPY
	3 DRAFT with single spacing, default paragraph style
	4 DRAFT with double spacing, 10 en paragraph indent
	5 double spacing with 10 en paragraph indent
D	Sets debug mode. (Formatter will continue processing even if mm detects errors that would otherwise cause processing to stop.)
E	Controls the font of the subject/date/from fields on memos and letters. If D is 1, these fields are emboldened; if D is 0, the fields are printed in normal font.

continues

Table 29.2. continued

Register	Effect
L	Sets the length of the physical page to N (default 11 inches). Specify units with this option since N is scaled.
N	Specifies page numbering style as follows:

	0	All pages include header
	1	Header replaces footer on page 1; all other pages have a header
	2	Page 1 has no header; all other pages have a header
	3	All pages use section-page as footer
	4	No header on page 1; header on other pages only if .PH is defined
	5	Same as 3, but section-figure

Register	Effect
O	Sets page offset (left margin) to N where N is a scaled value.
P	Specifies that pages are to be numbered starting with N.
S	Sets point size and vertical spacing for document. By default point size is 10, vertical spacing is 12.
W	Sets page width to N where N is a scaled value (default 6i).

The -r option is useful if you have a file that will be printed somewhat differently over the course of its life. As an example, assume the first draft of your document has to be double spaced and have the word "DRAFT" at the bottom of every page. Set the C register to 4 on your command line:

```
troff -mm -rC4 docname
```

As the document nears completion, you have to print it single spaced, but you still want the word "DRAFT" at the bottom of every page:

```
troff -mm -rC3 docname
```

When the document is complete, you can use -rC1 to print "OFFICIAL FILE COPY" at the bottom of each page, or you can use -rC0 to omit that line entirely.

Using the *mm* or *mmt* Command

The mm macros are the macros of choice throughout much of AT&T. This may explain why mm has been singled out for special treatment. Only mm has its own set of processing commands: mm, to process files with nroff, and mmt, to process files with troff.

> **NOTE:** If your system users always use troff and never use nroff, your system administrator may not have mounted the mm (for nroff) command and may have named the troff version mm (instead of mmt). I know this sounds loony, but I've seen it happen.

To format a file with mm or mmt, use a command of this form:

```
mm options filenames
mmt options filenames
```

> **NOTE:** If you specify a hyphen (-) instead of a filename or filenames on the command line, mm and mmt read standard input instead of files.

As is the case with the nroff and troff commands, the options must precede the filename(s).

The mm and mmt commands have their own set of options; however, they can pass arguments to nroff and troff, so you can use any nroff/troff option as an option to mm/mmt.

mm and mmt can initialize the number registers that can be initialized by the nroff and troff commands. (See Table 29.2.)

Printing Files Formatted with *ms, me,* and *man*

You can use either nroff or troff to process files that use the me, ms, or man macros. All of the options shown in Table 29.1 can be used; however, the -r option has limited use because all predefined number registers in me and ms have two-character names.

Most of man's predefined number registers also have two-character names. You can set register s to 1 to reduce the page size from 8 1/2 by 11 to 5 1/2 by 8.

Printing Files Formatted with Your Own Macro Package

To substitute your own macro package for mm, ms, me, or man, you have a choice of two methods:

- Use nroff or troff without the -m option and source in your own macro file at the top of your text file (right after you initialize registers).
- Use the -m option to nroff or troff and specify your macro file. Remember to specify the full pathname.

All other options to nroff and troff can be used just as you use them for mm, ms, me, or man. Remember that the -r option can be used only to initialize registers with one-character names.

Error Messages

Error messages are largely self explanatory. They can be generated by the system (if you type torff instead of troff), by nroff or troff, by the macro package, or by the preprocessors. (Chapter 23, Formatting Tables with tbl," Chapter 24, "Formatting Equations with eqn," Chapter 25, "Drawing Pictures with pic," and Chapter 26, "Creating Graphs with grap" contain information about error messages generated by the proprocessors.

It doesn't really matter whether troff or mm generates a message; you have to correct the error. Errors usually fall into one of the following categories:

- Order: Memo type macros for mm or ms are in the wrong order.
- Missing one of bracketed pair: You have a .TS but no .TE (or vice versa).
- (mm only) No list active: You have a .LI, but no .BL.
- Bad or no argument: You've omitted an argument after a .VL or you've specified an impossible number as an argument (5 for .SA, for example).

The one thing to remember is that the line number, helpfully supplied by troff, is the troff output line number. So it's not uncommon to be told that you have an error in line 1500 when your text file is 600 lines long. mm attempts to give you the source file line number. Don't wager a large amount on its accuracy.

Deroffing, or Removing All Traces of nroff/troff

Sometimes documentation customers want electronic files as well as hard copy. If they can't handle troff, they may request ASCII files from you. There's a simple way of complying with this request—use deroff.

deroff removes all troff requests, macros, and backslash constructs. It also removes tbl commands (that is, everything between the .TS and the .TE), equation commands (everything between the .EQ and the .EN or between the defined eqn delimiters). It can follow a chain of included files, so if you've sourced in a file with .so or .nx, deroff operates on those files, too. This feature can be suppressed with the -i option, which simply removes the .so and .nx lines from your file.

Other options are -mm and -ml. -mm completely deletes any line that starts with a macro. This means all your headings will be gone. The -ml option invokes -mm *and* removes all lists.

This may be just as well. deroff doesn't do well with nested lists.

deroff, like nroff and troff, can process multiple files.

To use deroff, enter the following:

```
$ deroff options inputfilename > outputfilename
```

Don't forget to redirect the output to a file. You don't really want to see your denuded, deroffed file streaking across your screen, do you?

Summary

Printing is no easier than anything else within the UNIX system, but there are powerful tools to enable you to print just about anything you can imagine. From the simplest print command (lp) to the complexities of preprocessors, troff, and postprocessors, you can control the process and achieve outstanding results.

PART

Advanced File Utilities

Source Control with SCCS and RCS

*By Rachel and
Robert Startin*

This chapter covers the basic concepts of source control. These concepts apply to almost any system that does source control and should help you even if you use a system for source control other than the ones described here. You will learn the specific structure and commands used by two widely available source control systems: Revision Control System (RCS) and Source Code Control System (SCCS).

You will also learn, through examples, how source control can be used. One example covers the use of source control on a simple software project that has only a single active version. Another covers the complexity added when you continue to make revisions to a prior release while still doing development. Yet another example covers how you can use source control to work on documents. Finally, you will learn how to use source control to perform simple backups of critical files.

What Is Source Control?

Source control refers to controlling the process of modifying software by mediating changes. It lets you control who can make changes and when. It helps to prevent conflict that could arise when many people edit the same file. It lets you save multiple versions of a file and choose the one you would like to use. It lets you review the history of changes made to a file. It lets you save *configurations*, or *baselines*, which are lists of collections of files and revisions that are part of a common release.

This section introduces some of the functions of source control and the need for those functions. It helps answer the question What are the advantages of source control?

Normally, you want to use the most recent version of a file, but using source control gives you flexibility and the ability to examine the history of changes that went into a file. There are some important advantages to this.

If you are using UNIX to do software development, you may need to support older releases of your product. Using source control, you can recall the exact sources that were used to build the older release and use those files to track down and fix the problem. After you fix the problem in the old release, you can merge the changes, as appropriate, into the current release.

Source control also gives you the ability to review the history of changes to a file. This is useful for almost any evolving file, be it source code or the files used to create a book.

You can also use source control to perform a limited personalized backup of critical files. If your system is backed up once a week and you write daily progress notes, you can check the notes into a source control system and have a safe copy in case you accidentally erase or damage the file. This is not a replacement for doing system backups because you will still be vulnerable to system or disk problems, but it does give you finer control over recovering from your own mistakes.

By saving the history of revisions to a file, you give yourself the ability to analyze that history later. This can be invaluable for software projects because it gives you the ability to see the logic of each incremental change that led from the original source to the current source.

The ability to recreate old versions of a single file or a group of files allows you to use source control as a simple backup system and to recover and modify earlier releases of a product or document.

Source control systems usually allow some form of branching (see the section "Basic Source Control Concepts") that gives you the ability to produce variants of a file. This gives you the capability to perform parallel development of two different variants of the same file. For example, while working on the 2.0 release of your product you can produce a maintenance update to the 1.0 release of your product by modifying one or more of the source files from the 1.0 release. You can merge the changes to the 1.0 release into the 2.0 release if you desire.

Source control systems are good tools for controlling all sorts of files, not just source code. This chapter was edited and produced using source control with one file containing each section. The final copy of the chapter was produced using make to merge the sections together and reformat them to meet the publisher's submission guidelines. This allowed both authors to work independently to a certain extent and to merge changes after reviews.

Basic Source Control Concepts

Source control systems store files as a series of *revisions* (in SCCS they're called *deltas*), a set of documents that evolved from each other, as a tree. See Figure 30.1 for a generic example. Refer to this figure as you read this section on source control concepts. Each node in the tree represents a revision of the same file.

> **NOTE:** RCS uses the term *revision* and SCCS uses the term *delta*. The two terms can be used interchangeably. This chapter uses the RCS terms except when explicitly discussing SCCS. Definitions of terms used in RCS include the SCCS term in parenthetic comments.

The tree has a *root*, which is the original text of the file. In Figure 30.1, the node labeled root is the root. The *trunk* of the revision tree is the main sequence of revisions of the file that were derived from the root. In Figure 30.1, the node root and all of the nodes in a straight line above it (branch_start, a_revision, and head) are the trunk of the tree. The simplest form of revision control will have only a root and a trunk. For example, if you are developing a single document and want to save the development history, you are likely to only use the trunk for storing edits.

FIGURE 30.1.

A tree of revisions.

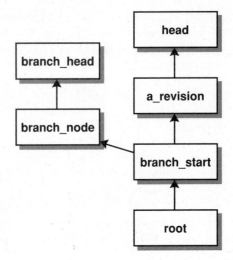

A *branch* occurs where a single revision has two or more revisions derived from it. In Figure 30.1, the node labeled branch_start is a trunk node that has a descendent on the trunk and a branch starting at node branch_node. Each branch and the trunk have a head, which is the latest revision on the branch. In Figure 30.1, the nodes head and branch_head are the respective heads of the trunk and a branch. Branches are useful when you need to split into parallel development paths for your file. You will learn more about branches in the section "Branches—Complicating the Tree."

Interacting with Source Control

There are several common interactions with a source control system that everyone who uses source control needs to understand.

In order to use a copy of a file, you need to *check out* (in SCCS, *get*) the file, or ask the source control system for a copy of a particular revision of a file. You will need to check out a file if you want to read its contents, print it out, or use it as part of a make.

In order to modify a copy of a file, you need to check out with a *lock* (in SCCS, *get for edit*) to tell the source control system that you intend to make a modification to the file. See the section "Locks—Mediating Conflict" for more information on how and why locks are useful.

In order to register your changes with the source control system, you need to *check in* (in SCCS, *delta*) the file. This registers your changes with the source control system and makes them available for anyone else using the source control system.

Locks—Mediating Conflict

Source control systems enable you to place a lock on a revision, which indicates that you intend to modify the file. This helps to prevent loss of changes when two people attempt to modify a file at the same time. For other possible solutions to this problem, see the sections "Branches—Complicating the Tree" and "Merges—Controlling Parallel Changes."

Although both RCS and SCCS use locks, some source control systems do not explicitly use locks. Notably (and perhaps confusingly), the free CVS, which uses RCS for managing revisions, does not use locks; many commercial source control or configuration management systems also do not use locks. Instead they include tools that allow you to deal with problems after the fact. This usually includes some form of automatic merging with a manual review of conflicts. The section "Merges—Controlling Parallel Changes" describes this alternative in greater detail.

See Figures 30.2 and Figure 30.3 for the progression of a typical conflict.

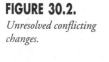

FIGURE 30.2.

Unresolved conflicting changes.

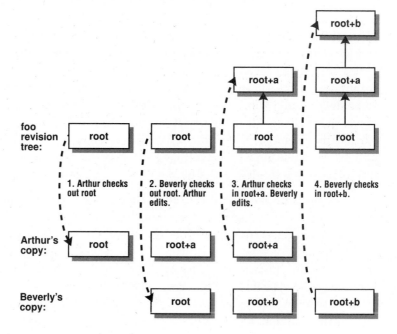

FIGURE 30.3.

Using locks to prevent conflicts.

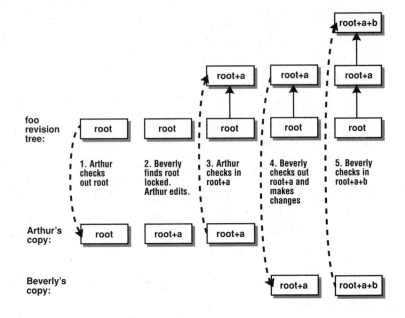

In the first time line (Figure 30.2) there is no revision locking. Arthur grabs a copy of revision root of foo and begins editing it. While he is making changes, Beverly also grabs a copy of revision root of foo and begins making her changes, independently of Arthur. Arthur checks in his changes as revision root+a, reports to his manager that the changes are complete, and confidently flies to Belize for his two-week scuba diving vacation. Beverly checks in her changes as revision root+b, which now contains none of Arthur's changes! Charlie, their manager, discovers that Arthur's changes are not in the weekly release and calls Arthur to find out why, completely ruining Arthur's vacation. Note that even though revision root+b is the descendent of root+a, it doesn't contain the changes Arthur made.

Compare this with the second time line (Figure 30.3). Arthur grabs a copy of revision root of foo, setting a lock on that revision, and begins editing it. While he is making changes, Beverly tries to grab a copy of revision root of foo, but the source control system informs her that the revision is locked and that she is not allowed to check it out. Beverly waits for Arthur to finish, or if her changes are urgent, she contacts Arthur to work out a way to get her changes done quickly. Arthur checks in his changes as revision root+a, reports to his manager that the changes are complete, and blissfully flies to Australia for his four-week scuba diving vacation, on which he is spending the bonus he received for implementing a source control system for the company. Beverly learns that foo is no longer locked and checks out revision root+a with lock. Beverly checks in her changes as revision root+a+b, which contains both her modifications and Arthur's. Charlie notices that Arthur's changes are in the weekly release and remembers what a great thing it was that they finally implemented that source control system after Arthur's previous vacation.

Revising the Trunk—Straight up the Tree

Many efforts that use source control require only the use of modifications to the trunk. If your needs do not require parallel efforts (see the section "Branches—Complicating the Tree") you should be able to manage your revisions without any of the complications introduced by branches. If you develop on the trunk, you will create an initial root revision of your file and then each time you change the file, you will check in a new trunk revision of the file.

See Figure 30.4 for a sample tree that uses modifications to the trunk only. In the sample tree, each revision was created by modifying the previous revision, and all modifications were done serially; there was no overlap between edits on the file.

FIGURE 30.4.

Straight up the tree.

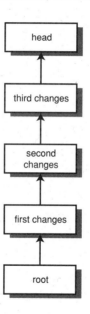

Branches—Complicating the Tree

As you have learned, branches are used when you need to split into parallel modification paths for your file. Often this happens when you need to produce patches for a released version of the file (or product built using the file). It can also happen when you wish to create a parallel track for doing a major long-term effort. For example, if you are creating an internationalized version of your application while doing development on the application itself, you might want to make the internationalization changes on a stable base and check them in as branches. You would then merge them into the trunk development. See the section on "Merges—Controlling Parallel Changes" for information on how to merge changes from branches back into the main trunk.

See Figure 30.5 for an example of a revision tree that has branches. For this project, there is a main line of development that is targeting the next product release and a branch on product development that is producing patches to the previous release. The previous release patches are made as a branch based on the revision of the file that was released. Often, you will want to merge changes from a branch back into the trunk. See the section "Merges—Controlling Parallel Changes" for more information on how this works. (This example will be given in greater detail in the section "A Complex Example.")

FIGURE 30.5.

A revision tree with branches.

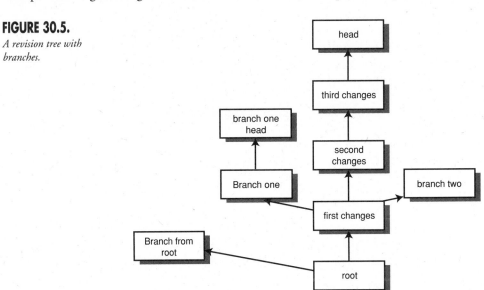

RCS actually supports an even more flexible branching scheme. See "Introduction to RCS" for more information.

Revision Numbers

Most source control systems, including both RCS and SCCS, name revisions using *revision numbers,* which describe where the revision is in the tree of revisions. See Figure 30.6 for an example of how both RCS and SCCS number a revision tree. Notice that this figure is the same tree as Figure 30.5, with revision numbers replacing the earlier names. A revision on the main trunk is identified by a pair of numbers. The *release number* is often used to specify an internal release number for the product. The *level number* specifies which revision within a release is being referenced. The release and level numbers are there to allow a structure that has the release number incremented each time the product is released.

Branches extend this naming structure using the same release and level as the *branchpoint,* the revision on which the branch is based (nodes 1.1 and 1.2 in the figure). Branches add a *branch number* to identify the particular branch and a *sequence number* to identify the revision within the branch. The first branch from revision R.L is numbered R.L.1.1.

FIGURE 30.6.

Revision numbers.

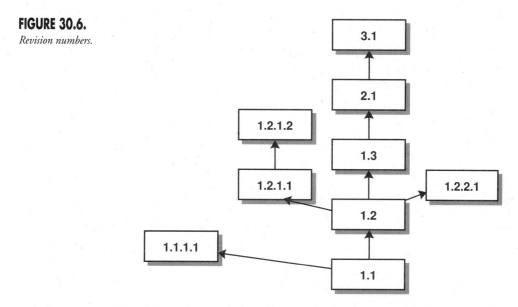

> **NOTE:** The terms branch and sequence for revision numbers in branches are actually from SCCS. The RCS documentation does not use specific terms here. Because RCS largely uses the same revision model as SCCS, this chapter uses the SCCS terms.

Merges—Controlling Parallel Changes

You may also be effectively performing parallel development by releasing your files (rather than access to the source control system) to other people. This can happen when you send out preliminary versions of a document for review or when you do a release of the source code for a project or product. After you have made your own postrelease changes, you may find that people with access to the released files suggest changes to you. One way to deal with this is to use *merge facilities* of your source control system, which support merging sets of changes that have a common base.

See Figure 30.7 for an example of parallel revisions and merging them. In this example, instead of using a source control system you use the merge command. Many source control systems use merge or a similar program to perform the merging task. If your source control system does not explicitly support merges, you can use the merge command to perform merges manually.

> **NOTE:** The source for merge is included in the RCS package on the CD-ROM. If your system doesn't have merge, you may want to install merge even if you don't plan to use RCS.

FIGURE 30.7.

Merging parallel changes.

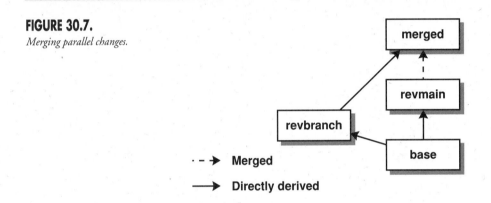

For this example, you should create three files, called base, revmain, and revbranch. The first is the base from which both of the others are created. The common ancestor revision is needed so the merge program can determine the changes from base to revbase and from base to revmain and merge the changes together. The file base should contain the following:

```
A line in the base file
Another line in the base file
A third line in the base file
The final line of the base file
```

The file revmain should contain the following:

```
A line in the base file
A line added in revmain
Another line in the base file
A third line in the base file
The final line of the base file
```

The file revbranch should contain the following:

```
A line in the base file
Another line in the base file
A third line in the base file
A line added in revbranch
The final line of the base file
```

After you create these three files, type `merge -p revmain base revbranch > merged`. When you look at the resulting file `merged`, you should see the following:

```
A line in the base file
A line added in revmain
Another line in the base file
A third line in the base file
A line added in revbranch
The final line of the base file
```

Because the merge process is automated and not intelligent, it can run into problems trying to merge changes that are in conflict. Try rerunning the `merge` command after changing the contents of revbranch to the following:

```
A line in the base file
A line added in revbranch
Another line in the base file
A third line in the base file
The final line of the base file
```

This time you should wind up with significantly different results. First, you should get a warning message from `merge` that says something like this: `merge warning: overlaps or other problems during merge`. Second, the file `merged` should look something like this:

```
A line in the base file
<<<<<<< revmain
A line added in revmain
=======
A line added in revbranch
>>>>>>> revbranch
Another line in the base file
A third line in the base file
The final line of the base file
```

When you try to merge files that have overlaps of the changed areas of the file, you will need to resolve the conflicts. You will need to manually review the merged file for all of the conflict areas marked. Some commercial source control systems and other products include graphical tools to help perform and verify merges.

Symbolic Names, Baselines, and Releases

A *symbolic name* is a name that is attached to a particular revision of a file and that you can use to check out the desired revision of a file without having to know the exact revision number. For example, if you send out for review copies of your great American novel, you might want to attach symbolic names to the revisions of the chapters you sent out so you can effectively use any editorial comments you get back.

SCCS does not support symbolic names. Some uses of symbolic names can be replaced by using SCCS release numbers. For other uses it is possible to replicate the behavior of symbolic names by keeping the correspondence between names, files, and revision numbers in an outside file or database and implementing scripts that will perform SCCS operations based on that configuration information.

See Figure 30.8 for an example of how you might use symbolic names to record reviews of your novel. Your novel in this example has three chapters. For the first review, you sent revision 1.3 of Chapter 1 and only had the original outlines for Chapters 2 and 3 (both revision 1.1). You used the name REVIEW1 for this review. For the second review, you had made minor changes to Chapter 1 (in revision 1.4) and had written Chapter 2 (revision 1.3) and drafted Chapter 3 (revision 1.2). This review was marked REVIEW2. You can now use the REVIEW1 and REVIEW2 names to refer to the correct versions of the novel to remember which revision of which chapter that meant. Revision names are a powerful tool for performing baselines and releases.

FIGURE 30.8.

Symbolic names.

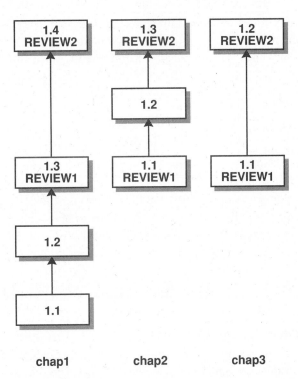

A *baseline* is a captured set of revisions that have some special property. That property might be "sent out for review," "compiles successfully," "passes lint successfully," "released for alpha testing," or anything that you find useful. In the example on symbolic names, the files of REVIEW1 and REVIEW2 were baselines. A *release* is really a special kind of baseline with the property "released," and you can decide exactly what you mean by released. Often, when you declare a release, you will check in new trunk revisions of all of your files so that you can use release numbers on source control commands.

Using Releases to Replace Symbolic Names

Without symbolic names you can achieve a similar effect using release numbers. Every time you ship out your novel for review, you increase the revision number of all files after the release. This allows you to use checkout commands that name the release, which in both RCS and SCCS check out the highest level within a release. In this example, after shipping release, you check in the next revision of the file as release 2, level 1. Therefore, instead of REVIEW1, you use release 1, which includes chap1 revision 1.3, chap2 revision 1.1, and chap3 revision 1.1. When you make you minor revisions to chap1, you check them in as revision 2.1. When you write and then rewrite chap2, you check it in as revision 2.1 and then as 2.2. When you draft chap3 you check it in as revision 2.1. Instead of REVIEW2, you use release 2, which includes chap1 revision 2.1, chap2 revision 2.2, and chap3 revision 2.1. This achieves the same effect (but with slightly more effort) as using symbolic names. Unfortunately, this approach is not always able to replace symbolic names. If you have checked in a new revision of a file using the old release number before deciding that you want to release the files, you may face some difficulties using this method.

Introduction to RCS

RCS was originally designed and developed by Walter Tichy of Purdue University as a version control system intended primarily for source code, documents, and test cases. Since its original release, the system has evolved somewhat over the years, but it maintains a great deal of backward compatibility with the initial release. The most popular current version is probably GNU RCS 5.6. RCS addresses several areas that are not well covered by SCCS, such as merging branches and marking baselines and configurations.

RCS is not available by default on all platforms, and only old versions are available on others. The 5.6.0.1 version of GNU RCS is included on the CD-ROM in case you need (a newer version of) RCS on your system.

Interacting with RCS

The basics of RCS are simply checking in a version of your file (ci), and checking out a version of your file (co). If you are a first-time user working alone, you may never need to do more. Viewing the history (rlog) and comparing changes from one revision to another (rcsdiff) may be useful to you. As your needs grow, you can start using branches and merging. If you are in a multiperson project, you should start using locking. Depending on the level of detail you need, RCS can be peripheral or central to your development environment.

Initial Revisions

In order to start using RCS to control revisions of a particular file, you need to create an *initial revision*, which is the root of the revision tree for this file. Maybe you have already created and edited a file. Now you realize that your development will be enhanced by using RCS. Or you may be planning ahead, just trying to get a project started, and you have no file contents yet. You would like to create an RCS file and you will check in an initial revision later.

In the first case, you have a file with contents. In RCS terminology, this is your *working file*. You can create an initial revision by using the RCS check-in command, `ci`. RCS will save the working file as the initial revision and prompt for a description of the revision group. Your working file is then removed from your directory.

In the second case, you have a file name but no contents. You can create an RCS file with the command `rcs -i`. RCS will prompt for the revision group description. Later, when you have some file contents, you can do an initial check in using `ci`. For now, there is no initial revision.

RCS files

RCS views your file as a pair of files. The file that you have named and to which you make changes is called the *working file*. You create this file in a directory of your choosing. When you check in this file, RCS creates an RCS file (if this is the first check in) or adds to an existing RCS file. The RCS filename is simply your working filename with a suffix added to the end. The default suffix on UNIX systems is usually v. You can control the suffix of a file via the -x option during check in. This option lets you specify a list of possible suffixes that will be tried, in order, during check in and check out.

RCS commands enable you to specify one of or both the working file and the RCS file. It is common to specify only the working file and let RCS handle the placement of the RCS file. If the RCS file is not specified, RCS first tries to deposit the revision in a subdirectory, RCS. If no such directory exists, the revision is placed in the current working directory. Creating a directory called RCS in your working directory helps to organize your work. All the RCS files are kept in this directory, out of sight.

Checking Out a File

To use a file you have under RCS control, you must check it out via the RCS command co, which causes RCS to copy the revision of the specified file into a working file. Then you can use the file, for example, for printing or compiling. But if you want to make changes to this file, you must obtain a lock for the file. You can check out a file with a lock via co -l. See the section "Locks—Mediating Conflict" for details of using locks.

Checking In a File

To save a version of your working file after making changes, use the ci command. If you want to keep a copy of the working file around to use, you can add the -u option. This is just like doing a ci, followed by a co. Whenever you do a ci, you will be asked to enter a *log message*, a description of the changes you have made. This is for your (and your co-workers') use. Keep in mind that a short phrase might be very meaningful now, but these *logs* may be perused down the road. The more specific you are now, the easier it will be to figure out revision contents later.

It is common to check in several files at once, perhaps ones that are related to one another. For example, you are fixing a defect in your product, and several files must be modified to solve the problem. You check out the files as needed and work in your working directory until the product defect is fixed. You test your solution. When you are convinced that everything works, you want to check in the changes. It could be tedious to enter a log message for each file as it's checked in. When you check in more than one file at once, after the first file, RCS asks if you want to use the same log as the previous file. This speeds things up a bit. To totally automate the check in, you can specify the log message via the check in command's -m option. So if the log message is to be the same for each file, using the -m option to specify the log message, along with shell metacharacters to specify all the working files, can shorten a huge job so that it takes only a single command.

> **TIP:** If you have a lengthy log message that is common to more than one file, enter the text of the message into a file. Then on the check in command line, use -m'cat filename' to specify that the contents of the file filename should be used as the log message

Examining Revision Details and History

If you need to examine the history and status of an RCS file, you can use the rlog command. This displays each revision log, ordered from highest number to lowest. This can help you see the progress of changes that have been made during development history. These logs can be very helpful for locating a specific revision of the file that you want to examine in complete detail.

The `rlog` command shows you other details besides just the log messages. The first several lines are called the *header* and contain details about the revision group. Included in this header is the RCS pathname, the working pathname, the head revision, the default branch, the access list, locks, symbolic names, the suffix, and a few other items. If you are interested in header information only, and no log messages, use the `-h` option to limit the output to only the header. `rlog` has other useful options to limit the data it displays. Refer to the man page for details.

If you do find a particular revision that you would like to examine or use, you can check out the revision by specifying the revision number on the `co` command line. Keep in mind, though, that performing `co` will overwrite your existing working file. This may be okay with you. If not, you can ask RCS to check out a file to standard out. Then you can use UNIX redirection of standard output to place the old revision contents wherever you would like. Using the command

```
co -r2.4 -p the_file > the_file.2.4
```

will put (old) revision 2.4 into a file called `the_file.2.4`.

rcsdiff

If you are familiar with the UNIX `diff` command, the RCS command `rcsdiff` will be familiar to you. `rcsdiff` compares two revisions of the same file and displays the differences between the two versions. RCS manages the retrieval of the versions while `rcsdiff` uses the UNIX `diff` to perform the actual comparison. The two versions are compared line-by-line, and if any character in the line is different between the two files, a message is displayed to standard out describing the place where the difference occurs.

To use the `rcsdiff` command, you need to specify the two revisions that are to be compared. You can explicitly specify each with two instances of the `-r` option. If you specify only one revision on the command line, this revision is compared against your working file. If you omit both revisions from the command line, your working file is compared against the head revision on the default branch (usually the trunk). Here are some examples:

```
rcsdiff -r2.3 -r2.6 the_file
```

compares revisions 2.3 and 2.6 of `the_file`.

```
rcsdiff -r2.3 the_file
```

compares revision 2.3 of `the_file` with the working file `the_file`.

```
rcsdiff the_file
```

compares the head of the default branch of `the_file` with the working file `the_file`.

Keywords

RCS allows the user to imbed certain words into the working file. These words, *keywords*, have special meaning to RCS. Each keyword is initially inserted into the working file, then later the current value is placed after the keyword, with a colon separator. When keywords are in the file during a check out, the co command updates the value of each keyword.

There are many keywords available. You should check which will be most useful to you by examining the co man page. The $Header:$ 30unxor2.adj,v 1.7 94/04/05 18:24:08 sartin Exp $ keyword contains a composite of most of the individual keywords. If you include the $Header:$ 30unxor2.adj,v 1.7 94/04/05 18:24:08 sartin Exp $ keyword, the value that is inserted will contain the RCS file, the revision number, the date, the author, the state, and the locker (if the file is locked).

> **TIP:** If you are using the $Revision:$ keyword to identify revisions distributed to other people, make sure you do a clean check out (co) of all files before distributing (or that you build source code). If you fail to check out a file, the revision number will not be up-to-date because only co updates the keyword values.

Locks—Mediating Conflict

RCS has two kinds of locking mechanisms: strict and nonstrict. If you are the only person who will be modifying this file, you can turn off strict locking via rcs -U. This will allow you, the file owner, to make changes without obtaining a lock. Anyone else must obtain a lock in order to modify the file.

If you are one of several people who can modify this file, you should set the locking to strict. This is done via rcs -L. In this case, anyone wanting to modify the file should obtain a lock before making changes. This should be done during the check out with the -l option. This way, the revision is copied to your working file and the revision is locked, all at the same time.

Sometimes you will find yourself in the situation of modifying a file without first obtaining a lock. You usually find this out when you go to check in your changes and you get a ci error message saying that your user name does not have a lock set. If this happens, all is not lost, but you need to do a little investigation before you can resolve the situation.

First, you need to find out if anyone else has checked in any revisions since you last checked out this file. Look at the revision number at the top of your working file to find the revision that is the basis of your changes. If you have the keyword $Revision:$ in your file, RCS will substitute the revision number after this keyword. If you do not have this keyword in your file, it is much more difficult to figure out what revision you started editing.

You can try looking at the RCS logs, using the `rcsdiff` command to examine changes between revisions, or use the `rcs -P` command to obtain temporary copies of old revisions. Hopefully you will be able to recognize the revision you started with! If someone has made changes and checked them in since the version you started with, you should check in your changes as a branch off your basis revision. Then do a merge of your file at the top of the other changes. See the sections "Merges—Controlling Parallel Changes" and "Branches—Complicating the Tree" for details.

If nobody has checked in any changes since your version was checked out, all you need to do is lock the file and check it in. Be careful here. Do not use `co -l` to obtain the lock. This will overwrite your working file and you'll lose all your changes. Instead, use the `rcs -l` command. This simply manipulates the file lock—no copying is involved. After obtaining the lock, check in the file as usual.

In either of these possible scenarios, someone else could have the file locked. You can always check on the status of a file lock with the `rlog -h` command. This shows the header information for the specified file. If someone holds the lock, the header will contain a message stating which user has it locked. If this is the case, you can work out with that person a strategy to deal with the conflict. Once again, using the RCS merging facility can help this resolution. In an emergency, or if the user holding the lock is no longer available, you may break the lock with the `rcs` command. You first use the `rcs -u` command to unlock the revision. When you unlock someone else's lock, you are asked to enter a comment about breaking the lock that is forwarded to the user via electronic mail. After breaking the lock, you can then obtain the lock for yourself via `rcs -l`.

Branches—Complicating the Tree

RCS has a very flexible branching scheme. It allows you to make branches off the main trunk. You can also make branches that branch off an existing branch. For example, main trunk file revision 2.3 has a branch. This branch is 2.3.1 and has revisions 2.3.1.1, 2.3.1.2, and so on. At some point during this branch's development, say at 2.3.1.7, you need to branch off again. You create branch 2.3.1.7.1, which has revisions 2.3.1.7.1.1, 2.3.1.7.1.2, and so on. You get the idea. As you can see, the revision numbers get long quite quickly. For this reason it is probably good to limit the branching as much as is reasonable.

In order to create and refer to files on a branch, you need to explicitly reference the revision of the file. Look at how this works. Start with trunk revisions including 2.3 already checked in. Now you want to create branch 2.3.1. First check out with a lock revision 2.3. Next do your edits. Now when you go to check in your changes, specify the branch revision number. This creates revision number 2.3.1.1. Similar commands will create the next branch.

Merges—Controlling Parallel Changes

If you have parallel development of a single file, for whatever reason, and you need to roll all the changes together into a single revision, you should use the rcsmerge command. Say you have branched off the main trunk of development at revision 2.3. Revisions 2.4 through 2.7 represent your main development efforts, whereas 2.3.1.1 through 2.3.1.4 represent defect fixes to your released (2.3) product. Now you would like to merge your changes together and check them in as revision 2.8.

Using rcsmerge to do this, you must specify the common base revision, in this case 2.3, via option -r. One set of the changes can be specified with a second -r option. If you do not specify this option, the default revision (usually the top of the main trunk) is assumed. In this example, 2.7 is one of the revisions that holds changes. You can either let this be the default or explicitly specify -r2.7. Alternatively, you could specify -r2.3.1.4 to denote the branch revision. The other set of changes that should be merged in are taken from the working file specified. Therefore, you must be aware of the contents of this file. It is also important to remember that this file is overwritten with the merged file. Use the -p option to make the output go to standard out, which you can redirect to a file if you don't want your working file modified.

Now look at a couple of ways to put together all the options with rcsmerge. If you are developing on the main branch, check out revision 2.7 with a lock:

```
co -12.7 the_file
```

merge together the changes:

```
rcsmerge -r2.3 -r2.3.1.4 the_file
```

and check in the changes to the main trunk:

```
ci -u the_file
```

The command in step 2 could be changed to

```
rcsmerge -p -r2.3 -r2.3.1.4 the_file > the_file.merged
```

to preserve the contents of file the_file. If you are working on the branched releases obtain a lock on the main trunk (to check in the merge results):

```
rcs -12.7 the_file
```

check out a copy of revision 2.3.1.4 without a lock:

```
co -u2.3.1.4 the_file
```

merge together the changes:

```
rcsmerge -p -r2.3 -r2.7 the_file > the_file.merged
```

when you wish to check in the changes, move the merged file into the working file:

```
mv the_file.merged the_file
```

and check in your changes as revision 2.8:

```
ci -u the_file
```

These are only two variations of many possible ways to use the rcsmerge command to merge together two set of changes. These are the basic things you need to remember: The first revision specified is the common base. The second revision specified is one setof changes and can be implied. The working file specified includes the other changes. The working file will be overwritten with the merged file unless -p is specified.

There is a second way to merge together changes. The co command has an option, -j, that specifies pairs of files whose changes should be merged (*joined*) to the specified revision during the check out. Repeating the merge example with the co command gives the following possible solution:

```
co -12.7 -j2.3:2.3.1.4 the_file
```

The first revision specified (-12.7) is checked out. The changes that occurred between the two revisions specified in the join list, 2.3 and 2.3.1.4, are merged into revision 2.7. The resulting merged file is placed in the working file the_file. Then you may check in the changes using the following command:

```
ci -u the_file
```

The merging/joining abilities of RCS are quite flexible. You have seen several possible methods of combining your parallel development using the rcsmerge command and the co command. Each of these commands may not be able to resolve all types of merges. During the merge process, if RCS has conflicts you will be notified and must examine the resulting file. The conflicts will be denoted and you must choose the desired solution. See the man page for merge for details on conflicts.

Symbolic Names, Baselines, and Releases

So far, this section on RCS has used numeric revision numbers. However, RCS enables you to use symbolic revision numbers as well as symbolic branches. Two commands, rcs and ci, allow you to set these symbolic names. After you have created these names, you can use them in place of numeric revision numbers in all of the RCS commands. First look at how you set up symbolic names.

During check in, you can set or change the symbolic name associated with that revision number. If you have just added a new bit of functionality to your product, you may want to associate a symbolic name that you can advertise to your co-workers. Say you call it ERR-MUSIC, because your product plays a little music when the user makes an error. When you check in your changes, use the -n option to add this symbolic name:

```
ci -u -nERR-MUSIC the_file
```

If you later need to fix a defect in your new music routines, make the change and check it in. However, this time you must use a capital -N as the option. This will override the previous value of the ERR-MUSIC symbol.

The rcs command can also be used to manipulate symbolic names. To add a symbolic name initially, use -n followed by : and then a revision number. The revision number is optional, and if left unspecified, the default revision will be used. Be careful, because if you omit the : the symbolic name will be deleted. The -N option has the same behavior except that it will override an existing symbol.

The rcs command is also used to create and manipulate the symbolic branch names. Say you are using a branch off revision 3.4 to do patches for an internal release. You have created branch 3.4.1 and checked in revision 3.4.1.1 as the first patch changes. To make interacting with this branch easier, you can name the branch (not a particular revision, but the branch as a whole) via rcs -nPATCH:3.4.1. Now when you want to check in and out off the head of the PATCH branch, simply use the symbolic name PATCH.

Here are some specific examples:

rcs -nERR-MUSIC: the_file creates a new symbolic name, ERR-MUSIC, for the default revision of the_file.

rcs -NERR-MUSIC: the_file moves the symbolic name, ERR-MUSIC, to the default revision of the_file.

rcs -nERR-MUSIC:2.3 the_file creates a new symbolic name, ERR-MUSIC, for the 2.3 revision of the_file.

rcs -NERR-MUSIC:2.5 the_file moves the symbolic name, ERR-MUSIC, to the 2.5 revision of the_file.

rcs -NERR-MUSIC:RELEASE1 the_file moves the symbolic name, ERR-MUSIC, to the RELEASE1 revision of the_file.

rcs -nERR-MUSIC the_file deletes the symbolic name, ERR-MUSIC, from the_file.

co -lPATCH the_file checks out and locks the head of branch PATCH.

Now that you have created symbolic version numbers and branches, you can use these names in any places where you would use their numeric equivalents.

Introduction to SCCS

SCCS was developed by AT&T as a system to control source code development. It has features in it that help support a production environment, including freezing of released code and hooks for integration of a problem-tracking system. This section includes a brief introduction to SCCS, primarily as a contrast to RCS. Refer to the sections "A Simple Example" and "A Complex Example" for detailed samples of SCCS command usage.

Some systems ship with SCCS, but without the sccs command that was introduced by BSD. This book's CD-ROM includes a version of the sccs command as available on the free source from BSD.

Interacting with SCCS

SCCS includes the admin command for interacting with the source control system. It can be used to create source control files, control availability of revisions, and change the rules about requirements for submitting a revision. SCCS also uses several temporary files to indicate internal state and temporary locks. SCCS files are named s.*filename*. All SCCS commands take the name of the SCCS file itself rather than allowing a working filename as RCS commands do. It also has get and delta, which are similar in function to the RCS commands co and ci.

Initial Revisions

SCCS files require explicit initialization using the admin command before you can perform any other action. There are two different ways to initialize an SCCS file. First, you can create an SCCS file with an empty initial revision by executing admin -n s.*filename*. This will create s.*filename* with the appropriate SCCS file structure and an empty revision 1.1. You can then use the get and delta commands to add text; unlike in RCS, the empty revision 1.1 will always remain. Second, you can create an SCCS file with initial contents from another file using admin -i *filename* s.*filename*. The two occurrences of *filename* are not required to be the same, but it is generally useful to do so because other SCCS commands assume that the working file for s.*filename* is *filename*.

SCCS files

Like RCS, SCCS has an implicit notion of working files, but SCCS always requires the command line to use the s-file, which is the s.*filename* source control file. SCCS uses a file format completely different from that of RCS.

NOTE: It is a common misconception that SCCS uses *forward deltas* that save the root revision and build all later revisions using deltas from there. This leads to the incorrect conclusion that SCCS checks out new revisions more slowly than it checks out old ones. In truth, SCCS uses a technique called *interleaved deltas*, which stores blocks of delta changes in such a way that a single pass over the entire SCCS file can produce any revision using fairly straightforward techniques. The result is that SCCS get performance slows as the SCCS file gets large, but has similar performance regardless of which revision is retrieved. In a study by Walter F. Tichy, the original author of RCS, the RCS command co is faster than the SCCS command get unless 10 or more deltas are being applied to derive a revision.

This note is brought to you courtesy of *RCS—A System for Version Control* by Tichy, which includes descriptions of RCS and the algorithms used by RCS and SCCS. A postscript version of this paper is on this book's CD-ROM.

Checking Out a File

SCCS enables you to get a read-only copy of a revision with the get command. Using get -p will output the revision contents to the standard output. You can also supply a revision number using the -r option. Partial revision numbers for the -r option will usually do what is desired. See the get man page entry for more details. You can specify a cutoff date (get the last delta before the cutoff) with -cYY[MM[DD[HH[MM[SS]]]]].

You can use the get command to set a lock, by doing a get for edit, or get -e, which locks the SCCS file and disables keyword expansion.

Checking In a File

SCCS uses the delta command to submit changed revisions, which is also called *creating a delta*.

TIP: If you have a lengthy log message that is common to more than one file, enter the text of the message into a file. Then on the check in command line, use -y'cat *filename*' to specify that the contents of the file *filename* should be used as the log message.

Examining Revision Details and History

The `prs` command enables you to print reports on the SCCS file. It has somewhat more flexibility than the `rlog` command in RCS. It enables you to supply a format specification using the `-d` option that will control the printing of information about the SCCS file. This can be used to created customized reports. `prs` shows you other details besides just the log messages.

Keywords

SCCS has a keyword substitution method that's different from that of RCS. SCCS keywords are of the form %x% and are expanded when you do a `get` with the `-k` (or `-e`) option. See the `get` man page entry for a full list of keywords. Expanded keyboards have advantages and disadvantages. Expanded keywords need no processing to be easily human readable (for example, `printf("Revision %I%\n");` in C code will print out as `Revision 1.1` for revision 1.1 checked out with the keywords expanded). Expanded keywords are difficult to recover. If someone sends you a modified version of one of your sources, you will need to find all of the expanded keywords and replace them with the actual keyword (for example, replace `printf("Revision 1.1\n");` with `printf("Revision %I%\n");` in C code); this can be very difficult if you don't localize keyword usage.

> **TIP:** You can embed SCCS keywords that identify your program executable by using this:
>
> ```
> char sccsid[] = "%W%";
> ```
>
> To take advantage of this, make sure you perform your build with no files out for editing (remember that when you perform `get -e` the keyword is not expanded). If you do this, you will be able to use the `what` command to identify what revision(s) of what file(s) went into creating the executable.
>
> You can also use the `%I%` keyword to identify your revision(s) for printing version messages.

Locks—Mediating Conflict

SCCS locks are *strict* in that they will not allow a `delta` without a `get -e`. You can use the `admin -fj` command to allow concurrent `get -e` commands on the same revision.

Branches—Complicating the Tree

SCCS supports branches as described in the section "Basic Source Control Concepts." Using get -b -e will cause SCCS to create a branch from the specified revision. SCCS does not support branches on branches the way RCS does.

Merges—Controlling Parallel Changes

SCCS has no built-in support for performing merges. You can use the merge program as described in "Basic Source Control Concepts" to merge revisions of SCCS files if your version of UNIX has it.

Extra SCCS Features

SCCS includes extra software configuration management support hooks that are not in RCS. The admin -f x and admin -d x commands can be used to do the following:

x	Action
v[pgm]	Require modification request numbers for delta.
cceil	Limit the releases that can be retrieved using get.
ffloor	Limit the releases that can be retrieved using get.
llist	Limit the releases that can be submitted using delta.
j	Enable/disable concurrent locks.
b	Enable/disable branching.
dSID	Set default revision for get.
n	Create null deltas for skipped releases. This can be used to create a base revision for branches in releases that had no source modifications.
[qtm]	Control expansion of some keywords.

See the admin man page entry for more details on these options.

Using Source Control for Backups

Both RCS and SCCS can also be used as a simple personal backup system. To do this, you periodically check in copies of the files that are to be backed up. This will give you a revision history of the files, and you can use this history to recover from errors you may make (for example, accidentally removing a file or deleting some text you meant to keep).

> **CAUTION:** Because it is likely that your source control files will be on the same disk (and same computer) as the original files, using source control systems to perform backup is not a perfect solution. If catastrophic damages occur on the computer or disk on which the source control files are stored, both the original file and the backup source control files may be destroyed. Despite this, backup using source control can be useful.

Do not use source control as your only backup system. Use it to enhance an existing system. For example, if your system is backed up weekly, but you would like to protect your daily edits, you may want to run a cron job that performs your source control backups. (See Chapter 20, "Scheduling Processes" for more information on adding cron jobs.) Your script might look something like this:

```ksh
#!/bin/ksh
# (/usr/bin/ksh on some systems)
# This script will use RCS to do a checkpoint of
# all files listed in the file BACKUP_LIST.
# Make sure non-strict locking (rcs -U) is set on
# the RCS files.
#
# Algorithm
# For each file in the backup list
#   if the file has changed
#     check it in to RCS
#
# Assumptions:
# This script assumes that strict locking has been turned
# off in the corresponding RCS file since the purpose of
# the script is for personal backup. This script assumes
# the head is the right place to put the new revision.
# This script assumes the RCS file is in one of the default
# locations for RCS. For GNU RCS, use the RCSINIT variable
# to change this.
BACKUP_LIST=${HOME:-/u/sartin}/backup/rcs_backup_list
# Uses POSIX mktemp!!!
ERR_FILE='mktemp -p rcsbk'
# Remove the scratch error file on exit
trap "rm -f ${ERR_FILE}" 0
exit_code=0
# For each file in the backup list
for file in 'cat ${BACKUP_LIST}'
do
    # Check if the file has changed (old rcsdiff doesn't take -q)
    rcsdiff -q ${file} >/dev/null 2>${ERR_FILE}
    rcs_res=$?
# WARNING: Some versions of rcsdiff don't return error code
# that match these. These error codes agree with GNU RCS 5.6.0.1
    if [ ${rcs_res} -eq 0 ]
    then
        # no change in file
        # echo "No changes to $file"
        # The ":" is an empty command.
        :
```

```
        elif [ ${rcs_res} -eq 1 ]
        then
                # rcsdiff found differences, checkpoint the file
                # echo "Backing up changes to $file"
                ci -m"Backup on 'date'" -q -u $file 2>${ERR_FILE} </dev/null
                if [ $? -ne 0 ]
                then
                        echo "Could not check in changes for $file"
                        echo "Contents of stderr from ci -u $file:"
                        cat ${ERR_FILE}
                        echo "End of stderr from ci -u $file."
                        exit_code=1
                fi
        else
                # Got an error, log it for mail
                echo "Could not get RCS differences for $file"
                echo "Contents of stderr from rcsdiff $file:"
                        cat ${ERR_FILE}
                echo "End of stderr from rcsdiff $file."
                exit_code=1
        fi
        {ERR_FILE}
done
# Exit code should be 0 or 1, exit 2 if it's not set
exit ${exit_code:-2}
```

The example script will use the file named in the BACKUP_LIST shell variable. For each file in the list, it uses rcsdiff to check for differences. Note that it currently depends on the GNU RCS 5.6.0.1 rcsdiff exit codes, which agree well with most implementations (however, this script does not work on HP-UX 9.0 RCS, where rcsdiff appears to return 0 unless there is an error). If you need to replace the exit code check, you might try saving the stdout of rcsdiff and checking the sizes or contents of the stdout and the ERR_FILE. If there was an error in performing the rcsdiff, the script prints an error message and sets the shell variable exit_code so that on exit it will indicate an error. If the rcsdiff indicated changes, the script attempts a ci and logs an error and sets exit_code if the ci fails. Here it is assuming nonstrict locking. You could add rcs -l to lock the file if strict locking is enabled, but this is potentially error prone (for example, if the file is locked). This backup system is intended for personal use only, which is where nonstrict locking is usually safe.

For specific needs you might develop a more complex system. Here are some suggested directions for improvement:

- **Allow strict locking.** This would make the backup workable with strict locks and possibly even allow it to be used for project checkpoints rather than just for personal checkpoints.

- **Keep all the RCS files in a different location.** This might require listing pairs of names in the BACKUP_LIST or creating a directory tree especially for RCS files. This could help make a project-style backup work better (one set of RCS files only for backup). This could also be used to put the RCS files on a file system different from the original files, which would improve your protection from a disaster.

■ **Perform a check in only if the changes exceed a certain minimum size.**   This will decrease the number of revisions at some cost in backup currency.

■ **Use** `rcs -o` **automatically to make obsolete old backups at some point.**   This will decrease the size of the RCS files and improve performance.

Although performing backup using a source control system is certainly not a panacea, it can be used as additional protection for your personal files. It allows a finer grain of control of the backup than most system backups give.

A Simple Example

This section and the next section give a rather simple example of source control in action. The example shows how either RCS or SCCS can be used to solve a source control problem. To keep the example simple, it involved only three files—enough to show some of the benefits of source control, but not so many that the example becomes buried in detail. To prepare for this example, you should create a new directory for the example. In that new directory, create three files: `file1`, `file2`, and `file3`. If you like, you may create a directory named RCS for storing the RCS files. You should be able to perform this example using RCS and SCCS simultaneously.

The contents of `file1` should be

```
This is file1
```

The contents of `file2` should be

```
This is file2
```

The contents of `file3` should be

```
This is file3
```

Starting to Use Source Control

Both RCS and SCCS have several ways to initialize the source control files. You will use three different methods here to illustrate the possibilities. Normally, you would choose one method for an entire project. In the first method you will initialize an empty source control file and then manually check in the current version of the file. In the second method you will initialize the source control file to contain the current contents of the source file and manually enter descriptive information. In the third method you will initialize the source control file to contain the current contents of the source file, and all descriptive information and comments will be supplied on the command line. The third method is probably the most desirable for starting a large project.

> **NOTE:** To see what is happening with the source control files, you may want to run rlog (for RCS examples) or prs (for SCCS examples) to observe the changes in the source control files.
>
> If you are truly adventurous, you might even want to view the source control files themselves (*file*,v for RCS and s.*file* for SCCS) to see how they change. Check your online documentation (rcsfile or sccsfile man page entries might be on your system) for information on the file formats.

Creating an Empty Source Control File and Adding the Initial Revision

First, initialize an empty RCS file for file1 and check in the initial revision:

```
$ Brcs -i file1
RCS file: RCS/file1,v
enter description, terminated with single '.' or end of file:
NOTE: This is NOT the log message!
>> Contents of file1 for source control example
>> .
done
$ ci -u file1
RCS/file1,v  <--  file1
initial revision: 1.1
done
$ co -l file1
RCS/file1,v  -->  file1
revision 1.1 (locked)
done
$ ci -f -q file1
enter log message, terminated with single '.' or end of file:
>> To keep revision numbers in sync with SCCS.
>> .
$
```

The rcs -i file1 command creates RCS/file1,v with your description, with no revisions. When you do ci -u file1, RCS automatically creates revision 1.1 with the comment initial revision. The last two commands are there simply to keep the revision numbers in sync with the numbers you will have in the SCCS files.

Next initialize an empty SCCS file and check in file1:

```
$ admin -n s.file1
$ get -e -p s.file1
Retrieved:
1.1
new delta 1.2
0 lines
```

```
$ delta s.file1
comments? Initial revision
No id keywords (cm7)
1.2
1 inserted
0 deleted
0 unchanged
$ get s.file1
Retrieved:
1.2
1 lines
No id keywords (cm7)
$
```

The admin command creates an empty initial revision. To lock the SCCS file, you need to perform a get for edit using get -e. In this example, you use get -e -p s.file1, which prints the file to standard output and locks it. Because you already have the contents of file1 you do not need and do not want to overwrite file1 with the empty revision 1.1. The delta command checks in the initial revision of the file as revision 1.2, leaving an empty revision 1.1 as an artifact. The final get command ensures that you have a current, read-only copy of file1.

Creating a Full Source Control File with Manually Supplied Comments

Now create the source control file with all of the correct original text. In RCS, you can do this using ci:

```
$ ci -u file2
RCS/file2,v  <--  file2
enter description, terminated with single '.' or end of file:
NOTE: This is NOT the log message!
>> Contents of file2 for source control example
>> .
initial revision: 1.1
done
$
```

This command causes a check in of the initial revision. RCS requests a description of the file, which you type after seeing the request. The -u option causes RCS to leave a read-only copy of file2 in your directory. Notice that RCS can initialize the RCS file without use of the rcs command. It can be very convenient (and is necessary for this example) to keep available a current copy of the head revision.

To initialize an SCCS file with the current contents of file2 use the admin command:

```
$ admin -ifile2 s.file2
No id keywords (cm7)
$ get s.file2
Retrieved:
1.1
1 lines
No id keywords (cm7)
$
```

> **NOTE:** For some versions of SCCS, after $ *admin -ifile2 s.file2*, you may need to *rm file2*.

The admin command creates s.file2 with the current contents of file2 as revision 1.1. The get command is to keep available a current copy of the head revision of file2.

Creating a Full Source Control File with Command Line Comments

This method supplies all the possible descriptive comments on the command line used to create the full source control file. In RCS, it takes extra commands to do this completely:

```
$ echo "Contents of file3 for source control example" > desc
$ ci -u -m"Original source for file3" -tdesc file3
RCS/file3,v <-- file3
initial revision: 1.1
done
$
```

The echo command saves the description to a file. The ci command supplies the initial revision but replaces the default message Initial revision that RCS normally uses for the first revision with the message Original source for file3. It also uses the -t option to supply a description from the desc file. Although this method may seem more awkward when you use it interactively for a single file, it can be much more efficient if you are checking in many files and can write a script to generate descriptions and messages.

> **TIP:** If you are creating a source-controlled copy of files you got elsewhere (for example, from an ftp site), you may want the initial revision comment to indicate the origin of the source. This can be of great assistance later, when you need to know something about the source (for example, to whom you should send comments or questions).

For SCCS, the command sequence to create the following:

```
$ echo "Contents of file3 for source control example" > desc
$ admin -tdesc -ifile3 -y"Original source for file3" s.file3
No id keywords (cm7)
$ get s.file3
Retrieved:
1.1
1 lines
No id keywords (cm7)
$
```

The `admin` command sets up the SCCS file completely using the source from `file3`, the description from `desc`, and the comment supplied with the `-y` option. Once again, this presents a good opportunity for writing scripts to do large initializations of source control hierarchies.

Modifying Files

In RCS and SCCS, you need to set a lock to edit a file. The normal way to do that is to set the lock before you begin editing. You will now make changes to `file2` and `file3` to prepare for the alpha test. An alpha test is a preliminary release of a possibly incomplete software product that is likely to have new features added and many defects repaired before it is released. These changes will be simple and will involve locking the file, editing the file, and checking in the change to source control. You will perform these in two different ways so you can see what to do when you forget to set a lock on a source control file.

A common area of contention in source control systems is the subject of when a revised version of a file should be checked in to source control. The two extreme positions are these:

■ Whenever the file is edited, it should be checked in to source control. Check in as early and as often as possible.

■ Whenever the product is released, the files should be checked in to source control. Check in as late and as infrequently as possible.

Of course, neither of these is particularly appealing in practice. The first is unappealing because it results in large source control files, many versions that have had no review or testing (if they are source code, they may not even compile!), and revision logs that are difficult to follow because the changes are all so small. The second is unappealing because it results in little, if any, log of the logic behind the series of changes made to a file and gives no alternative for phased review and release of project files.

The best alternative is somewhere in the middle, and you should think carefully about the correct balance for your projects.

Lock, Modify, Check In

First you will make changes in the most desirable way. You will lock the file, then modify it, and finally check it back in to source control. For this example, you will change `file2` to have the following text:

```
This is file2
Added line 1
Added line 2
Added line 3
Added line 4
```

```
Added line 5
Added line 6
Added line 7
```

In RCS, you should run this:

```
$ co -l file2
RCS/file2,v  —>  file2
revision 1.1 (locked)
done
$ # Edit file2
$ ci -u -m"Changes for alpha" file2
RCS/file2,v  <—  file2
new revision: 1.2; previous revision: 1.1
done
$
```

This will create revision 1.2 with the changes you made. For SCCS, you should run this:

```
$ get -e s.file2
Retrieved:
1.1
new delta 1.2
1 lines
$ # Edit file2 (cheaters using RCS and SCCS can run co -p file2 > file2)
$ delta -y"Changes for alpha" s.file2
No id keywords (cm7)
1.2
7 inserted
0 deleted
1 unchanged
$ get s.file2
Retrieved:
1.2
8 lines
No id keywords (cm7)
$
```

This creates revision 1.2 with the changes you made. Notice that the delta command tells you how many lines were inserted, deleted, and unchanged. You can get the same information from RCS using rlog. The final get keeps a read-only copy of the head.

Modify (Oops!), Lock, Check In—Recovering from a Mistake

If you change a file without locking the source control file, it is still possible to lock the source control file and check in the changes.

> **TIP:** If you have RCS set to nonstrict locks (rcs -U *file*) and you own the source control file (*file*,v) you don't need a lock. This is probably safe for personal files, but can create problems in multiperson projects.

For this example, you will change the text of file3 to the following:

```
This is file3
A line called A
A line called B
A line called C
A line called D
```

> **CAUTION:** In a multiperson project, making modifications to a file without checking it out can be a very risky proposition. By not locking the file, you create a situation just like the one in the example in Figure 30.2. Be very careful about this practice in real life. Make sure that the file didn't get locked or modified by anyone else. Review future revisions to make sure all the old changes made it to the head.

Using RCS, execute these commands:

```
$ co file3
RCS/file3,v  —>  file3
revision 1.1
done
$ chmod u+w file3
$ # Edit file3
$ rcs -l file3
RCS file: RCS/file3,v
1.1 locked
done
$ ci -u -m"Dangerous changes to file3" file3
RCS/file3,v  <—  file3
new revision: 1.2; previous revision: 1.1
done
$
```

The co command makes sure you have the contents of file3, but it does not set a lock. The chmod should be a red flag that you are doing something dangerous; RCS and SCCS both leave files with write enabled when they have set a lock for you. The rcs -l command sets a lock on the head revision of file3. The ci command checks the changes into RCS.

Using SCCS, execute these commands:

```
$ get s.file3
Retrieved:
1.1
1 lines
No id keywords (cm7)
$ chmod u+w file3
$ # Edit file3 (cheaters using RCS and SCCS can run co -p file3 > file3)
$ get -e -p s.file3 >/dev/null
Retrieved:
1.1
new delta 1.2
```

```
1 lines
$ delta -y"Dangerous changes to file3" s.file3
No id keywords (cm7)
1.2
4 inserted
0 deleted
1 unchanged
$ get s.file3
Retrieved:
1.2
5 lines
No id keywords (cm7)
$
```

The first get command is to make sure you have the correct contents for file3, but does not set a lock. The chmod should be a red flag that you are doing something dangerous; RCS and SCCS both leave files with write enabled when they have set a lock for you. The get -e -p command sets a lock on the head revision of file3 (and copies the text of the head revision of file3 to /dev/null). This trick does the same as rcs -l in RCS. The delta command checks the changes into SCCS. The final get command is to get a read-only copy of the head.

> **CAUTION:** Because of the way SCCS performs keyword expansion, you may lose keywords by using this approach. If you use any of the SCCS keywords, they will be expanded on a get that is not for editing. When the keywords are expanded, SCCS no longer recognizes them as keywords.

To see the risk of losing SCCS keywords, try this example. First create a file called badsccskw with the following text:

```
This is %F% revision %I%, created on %D%, %T%
```

Load SCCS with the contents of the file, using admin -ibadsccskw s.badsccskw. Next do a get s.badsccskw and chmod u+w badsccskw to get the current contents of the file (notice that if you use cat badsccskw the keywords are expanded. Now do get -e -p s.badsccskw; notice how the keywords look when you request an editable copy. Now do delta -y"Lose keywords" s.badsccskw; notice the warning No id keywords (cm7). Now look at what happened to the file, using get -e s.badsccskw, and then cat badsccskw and notice the lack of keywords. By performing the "modify, lock, check in" style of modification, you have lost the SCCS keywords completely. Look at what happens:

```
$ admin -ibadsccskw s.badsccskw
$ rm badsccskw
$ get s.badsccskw
Retrieved:
1.1
1 lines
$ chmod u+w badsccskw
```

```
$ cat badsccskw
This is s.badsccskw revision 1.1, created on 94/04/04, 12:26:47
$ get -e -p s.badsccskw
Retrieved:
1.1
new delta 1.2
This is %F% revision %I%, created on %D%, %T%
1 lines
$ delta -y"Lose keywords" s.badsccskw
No id keywords (cm7)
1.2
1 inserted
1 deleted
0 unchanged
$ get -e s.badsccskw
Retrieved:
1.2
new delta 1.3
1 lines
$ cat badsccskw
This is s.badsccskw revision 1.1, created on 94/04/04, 12:26:47
$
```

Shipping a Prerelease

After all of your hard work, it's time to ship a prerelease alpha version of your files for testing and review. Ideally you would like to collect a list of which revisions of which files you sent out for the alpha. This will give you the ability to look at the correct revisions anytime there is an error to be fixed or a question to be answered.

Recording a Configuration with RCS

RCS offers a number of ways to recall files:

- By head of trunk (default)
- By exact revision number (`-r rel.level[.branch.seq]`)
- By author (`-w author`)
- By highest revision in a release (`-r rel`)
- By highest revision in a branch (`-r rel.level.branch`)\
- By date (`-ddate`)
- By state (`-sstate`)
- By symbolic name (`-rNAME`)

The fist three alternatives are not very useful for recalling a particular release. The second two can be useful, but you need to arrange to increment the release number of all RCS files each time you ship out a release and keep all release numbers in all RCS files synchronized. Retrieving by date can be reasonably appealing if you know the date of the release and on what branch it occurred, but it will break down if you wish to save and retrieve patches for a release (because the patch dates will be different from the release date). For example, if your release occurred on April 3, 1994, you might try this:

```
$ co -d"1994/04/03 23:59" RCS/*,v
RCS/file1,v  —>  file1
revision 1.2
done
RCS/file2,v  —>  file2
revision 1.2
done
RCS/file3,v  —>  file3
revision 1.2
done
$
```

> **NOTE:** You will need to use different dates to perform these actions yourself. The dates here are correct for the example RCS and SCCS files on the CD-ROM.

Notice that the correct revisions for the alpha release are retrieved.

Retrieving by state can be useful for release. Call the alpha release stable and set the RCS state of the head revisions to `stab`.

```
$ rcs -sStab RCS/*,v
RCS file: RCS/file1,v
done
RCS file: RCS/file2,v
done
RCS file: RCS/file3,v
done
$ rlog file1
RCS file: RCS/file1,v
Working file: file1
head: 1.2
branch:
locks: strict
access list:
symbolic names:
comment leader: "# "
keyword substitution: kv
total revisions: 2;    selected revisions: 2
description:
Contents of file1 for source control example.
----------------------------
revision 1.2
date: 1994/04/04 03:04:47;  author: sartin;  state: Stab;  lines: +0 -0
To keep revision numbers in sync with SCCS.
----------------------------
revision 1.1
date: 1994/04/04 02:05:47;  author: sartin;  state: Exp;
Initial revision
=====================================================================
```

```
$ co -sStab RCS/*,v
RCS/file1,v  —>  file1
revision 1.2
done
RCS/file2,v  —>  file2
revision 1.2
done
RCS/file3,v  —>  file3
revision 1.2
done
$
```

Notice that the state field for revision 1.2 of file1 is Stab and that the co command gets the correct revisions.

The best alternative is probably to use a symbolic name to mark all the revisions used in the release. Use rcs to apply a symbolic name to the release:

```
$ rcs -nRel_1_Alpha: RCS/*,v
RCS file: RCS/file1,v
done
RCS file: RCS/file2,v
done
RCS file: RCS/file3,v
done
$ rlog file1

RCS file: RCS/file1,v
Working file: file1
head: 1.2
branch:
locks: strict
access list:
symbolic names:
        Rel_1_Alpha: 1.2
comment leader: "# "
keyword substitution: kv
total revisions: 2;     selected revisions: 2
description:
Contents of file1 for source control example.
----------------------------
revision 1.2
date: 1994/04/04 03:04:47;  author: sartin;  state: Stab;  lines: +0 -0
To keep revision numbers in sync with SCCS.
----------------------------
revision 1.1
date: 1994/04/04 02:05:47;  author: sartin;  state: Exp;
Initial revision
=============================================================================
$
```

The command rcs -nRel_1_Alpha: RCS/*,v associates the current head revision (use -n*name*:*revision_number* to choose a different revision) with the name Rel_1_Alpha. Notice the symbolic names list in the rlog output. You can use symbolic names for revisions in any RCS command or option that takes a revision number. GNU RCS includes a script called rcsfreeze to help do this:

```
$ rcsfreeze Rel_1_Alpha
rcsfreeze: symbolic revision number computed: "C_1"
rcsfreeze: symbolic revision number used:     "Rel_1_Alpha"
rcsfreeze: the two differ only when rcsfreeze invoked with argument
rcsfreeze: give log message, summarizing changes (end with EOF or single '.')
Alpha release to partners and QA
.
rcsfreeze: 1.2 RCS/file1,v
rcsfreeze: 1.2 RCS/file2,v
rcsfreeze: 1.2 RCS/file3,v
$ cat RCS/.rcsfreeze.log
Version: Rel_1_Alpha(C_1), Date: Mon Apr 04 13:55:01 1994
----------
        Alpha release to partners and QA
----------

$ rcs -q -nRel_1_Alpha_Orig:Rel_1_Alpha RCS/*,v
$
```

The rcsfreeze command works on all RCS files for the current directory (either in the current directory or in a directory called RCS). It saves the log message in a file called .rcsfreeze.log (in the RCS directory, if there is one), which allows you to read the description of the frozen configurations. If you do not supply a symbolic name on the rcsfreeze command line, rcsfreeze uses C_*number*, where *number* is decided by rcsfreeze from the .rcsfreeze.ver file (in the RCS directory if there is one). The final rcs command is to assign an extra symbolic name Rel_1_Alpha_Orig to the alpha revisions. This name will be useful later in performing merges.

Using SCCS for a Prerelease

Unlike RCS, SCCS does not offer symbolic names. It does offer several similar options for getting particular revisions, highest delta in a release, or head of a branch or the trunk. See the get man page entry for more details. SCCS can use a cutoff date for a get; it will get the most recent delta before the cutoff date. For this example, you would use the release date and time as the cutoff (the cutoff time you use will be different!). The following shows how to retrieve an SCCS file by date:

```
$ get -c9404032359 s.*

s.file1:
Retrieved:
1.2
1 lines
No id keywords (cm7)

s.file2:
Retrieved:
1.2
8 lines
No id keywords (cm7)

s.file3:
Retrieved:
```

```
1.2
5 lines
No id keywords (cm7)
$
```

Release 1

After the alpha release, make some changes to the system before release 1. Change `file2` to contain the following:

```
This is file2
Added line 1
Added line 2
Added line 3
A change added after the alpha release
Added line 4
Added line 5
Added line 6
Added line 7
```

To edit `file2` and update it in RCS, do the following:

```
$ co -l -q file2
$ # Edit file2
$ ci -u -m"Post alpha changes" -q file2
$
```

Note the use of -q to eliminate the RCS output. With -q only errors are reported.

To edit `file2` and update it in SCCS, do the following:

```
$ get -e -s s.file2
$ # Edit file2 (cheaters using RCS and SCCS can run co -p file2 > file2)
$ delta -s -y"Post alpha changes" s.file2
$
```

Note the use of -q to eliminate the RCS output. With -*q* only errors are reported.

Performing release 1 is just like performing the alpha release, with one exception. It may be a good idea to increase the release number of future file revisions to 2. This will make release tracking much easier in SCCS and may help in RCS (although symbolic name gives you most of the advantages).

RCS doesn't offer an easy way to set the release for the next change checked in, but you can force a revision 2.1 even without changes by running a co -l and then ci -r2 -f. You will not do this in this example, but keep it in mind for the future. Run the command rcs -q -nRel_1: -nRel_1_orig: RCS/*,v to set the symbolic names Rel_1 and Rel_1_orig for the head revision of all files. The first name will be used to track release 1 and any patches. The second name will be used to save the original release 1 source and will help in performing merges. Remember to use release 2 for future revisions.

SCCS offers a simple way to set the release for the next delta. To perform your release in SCCS, run the command admin -fd2 s.*. This sets the default SID to 2 for all of your SCCS files. Because of the way get works for nonexistent releases, get will retrieve the highest revision from release 1 and delta will submit the change as revision 2.1.

A Complex Example

Now it's time to make the example a bit more complicated. This section includes making changes for release 2, creating patches for release 1, merging the patches into the trunk, receiving patches from others (and merging them) and (for SCCS only) requiring proper authorization to make changes.

Beginning Changes for Release 2

After release 1, make changes to all three files that add a single line at the end of the file that says Line added for release 2. Check the changes in at release 2 (this will be the default for SCCS). After changes, the files should look like this:

```
$ cat file1
This is file1
Line added for release 2
$ cat file2
This is file2
Added line 1
Added line 2
Added line 3
A change added after the alpha release
Added line 4
Added line 5
Added line 6
Added line 7
Line added for release 2
$ cat file3
This is file3
A line called A
A line called B
A line called C
A line called D
Line added for release 2
```

To create changes for release 2 in RCS, do the following:

```
$ co -l -q file1 file2 file3
$ # Edit the files
$ ci -u -m"Line added for release 2" -r2 file1 file2 file3
RCS/file1,v  <—  file1
new revision: 2.1; previous revision: 1.2
done
RCS/file2,v  <—  file2
new revision: 2.1; previous revision: 1.3
done
```

```
RCS/file3,v  <—  file3
new revision: 2.1; previous revision: 1.2
done
$
```

Notice that for RCS to increment the release number, you need to tell it on the `ci` command line.

For SCCS, you already ran `admin -fd2 s.*`, so the change to release 2 will occur automatically:

```
$ get -e s.*

s.file1:
Retrieved:
1.2
new delta 2.1
1 lines

s.file2:
Retrieved:
1.3
new delta 2.1
9 lines

s.file3:
Retrieved:
1.2
new delta 2.1
5 lines
$ # Edit files
$ delta -s -y"Line added for release 2" s.*
$ get -s s.*
$
```

Notice that the `get -e` command retrieves the proper revisions and informs you that the delta will be submitted as revision 2.1.

Creating Patches for Release 1 and Alpha

After release 1, you discover some errors. To fix these in the release 1 source code you will need to check out the correct source and create a branch in the source control system for the change. You will now change the text of `file2` to add a new first line:

```
Line added for patch to release 1
This is file2
Added line 1
Added line 2
Added line 3
A change added after the alpha release
Added line 4
Added line 5
Added line 6
Added line 7
```

For the RCS example, you will move the Rel_1 symbolic name to track the release with all patches. To do this in RCS, you check out the revision by the symbolic name Rel_1 (should be revision 1.3), perform the edit, and check in the new branch (changing the symbolic name Rel_1 with the -N option, which replaces an existing symbolic name):

```
$ co -q -lRel_1 file2
$ # Edit file
$ ci -u -m"Patch to release 1" -NRel_1 file2
RCS/file2,v  <—  file2
new revision: 1.3.1.1; previous revision: 1.3
done
$
```

Notice that ci automatically creates the branch for you. If you do rlog file2 you will see that the name Rel_1 now refers to revision 1.3.1.1.

To do this in SCCS, you use get -e -b with a cutoff date, perform the edit, and then check in the delta:

```
$ get -e -b -c9404041430 s.file2
Retrieved:
1.3
new delta 1.3.1.1
9 lines
$ delta -y"Patch to release 1" s.file2
No id keywords (cm7)
1.3.1.1
1 inserted
0 deleted
9 unchanged
$
```

Note that the -b option causes get to set up a branch, and that delta automatically uses the branch. The cutoff time you use will be different from the example because you will be executing the example and creating new revisions at a different time than we did! You will need to remember that branch 1.3.1 is the branch for release 1 patches.

Now do the same thing for file3, changing the contents to the following:

```
Line added for patch to release 1
This is file3
A line called A
A line called B
A line called C
A line called D
```

To create the patch in RCS, do the following:

```
$ co -q -lRel_1 file3
$ # Edit file
$ ci -q -NRel_1 -m"Patch to release 1" -u file3
$
```

The use of the -n and -N options in RCS might be confusing. The two options do the same thing, except that -N will replace an existing symbol and -n will not.

In addition, the -n (and -N) option to ci always assigns the new revision number to the symbol. The -n (and -N) option to rcs has three forms. First, -n *symbol* will delete an existing *symbol* completely. Second, -n *symbol*: will assign the head revision to *symbol*. Finally, -n *symbol*:revision will assign the specific revision to *symbol*.

This will create revision 1.2.1.1 with the changed contents, and change the Rel_1 name to be revision 1.2.1.1.

To create the patch in SCCS, do the following:

```
$ get -s -b -e -c9404041430 s.file3
$ # Edit file
$ delta -s -y"Patch to release 1" s.file3
$
```

This will create revision 1.2.1.1 with the changed contents. You will need to remember that branch 1.2.1 is the branch for release 1 patches.

Merging Patches into the Trunk

It's all well and good to use branches to create patches to the old release 1, but what do you do if you want to add those patches to the next release? The answer is to use some sort of merging facility to combine the changes for the patch with the changes since the release. You will now merge the patch to file2 into the trunk.

Merging with *rcsmerge*

RCS includes a program called rcsmerge, which performs some merging. When you assigned symbolic names for Rel_1_orig, you laid the groundwork for making merges easy. The Rel_1_orig name gives a common ancestor for performing merges (remember that merges require a common ancestor and two variants).

```
$ co -rRel_1 file2
RCS/file2,v   ->  file2
revision 1.3.1.1
done
$ chmod u+w file2
$ rcs -l -q file2
$ rcsmerge -rRel_1_orig file2
RCS file: RCS/file2,v
retrieving revision 1.3
retrieving revision 2.1
Merging differences between 1.3 and 2.1 into file2
$ cat file2
```

```
Line added for patch to release 1
This is file2
Added line 1
Added line 2
Added line 3
A change added after the alpha release
Added line 4
Added line 5
Added line 6
Added line 7
Line added for release 2
$ ci -u -q -m"Merge changes from release 1 patch" file2
$
```

The key command is the rcsmerge command, which tells RCS to merge changes between revision Rel_1_orig (1.3) and the current head (2.1) into the current contents of file2 (which contains the patch to release 1).

Merging with SCCS and *merge*

SCCS has no built-in merge facility, but if you have the merge program you can perform merges by hand and check in the results. Notice that getting the correct revisions checked out of SCCS is a little bit more challenging.

```
$ rm -f file2
$ get -s -p -r1.3 s.file2 > base
$ get -s -p -r1.3.1.1 s.file2 > branch
$ get -s -e -p s.file2 > head
$ merge -p head base branch > file2
$ cat file2
Line added for patch to release 1
This is file2
Added line 1
Added line 2
Added line 3
A change added after the alpha release
Added line 4
Added line 5
Added line 6
Added line 7
Line added for release 2
$ delta -s -y"Merge changes from release 1 patch" s.file2
$
```

The use of merge is similar to that in the example in the section "Merges—Controlling Parallel Changes" and performs the same task as the rcsmerge in the previous example, but uses manual setup from source control of the files to be merged.

Receiving Patches from Others and Merging Them

You may be faced with situations in which you receive suggested patches from outside sources. In this example, you receive a suggested patch based on the source of release 1. The submitter suggests that file3 should read as follows:

```
This is file3
A line called A
A line called B
Outside patch to release 1
A line called C
A line called D
```

This is the same as the release 1 version of `file3`, with a line added in the middle. The best way to handle such a patch is to check it in as a branch from the released version of the file and then merge the change into the head of the trunk. You have not yet merged the release 1 patch to `file3` to the trunk head, so you will perform that merge as well.

Merging with co

The RCS `co` command includes merging capability. To use it you will need to check in the modified version of `file3` as a branch to the `Rel_1_orig` revision and then use `co -l` `-j` to merge the changes. Most of this example should be familiar. First, you set a lock on revision `Rel_1_orig` of `file3` (you could use `co` to check out the lock, but you would just overwrite `file3` right away with the patched version you received). Next, you put the text you received into `file3` and then check in the changes, which will automatically create a new branch 1.2.2.1. Now comes the new part: Execute `co -l -` `jRel_1_orig:Rel_1,Rel_1_orig:1.2.2.1 file3`. The `-l` tells RCS to lock the head revision. The `-jRel_1_orig:Rel_1,Rel_1_orig:1.2.2.1` tells RCS to merge two sets of changes into `file3`; first the changes made between `Rel_1_orig` (revision 1.2) and `Rel_1` (revision 1.2.1.1) will be merged; next the changes made between `Rel_1_orig` (revision 1.2) and revision 1.2.2.1 will be made. This will merge all of the patch changes into `file3`. Finally, perform a `ci` to create revision 2.2 with the merged changes:

```
$ rcs -lRel_1_orig file3
RCS file: RCS/file3,v
1.2 locked
done
$ # Edit file3
$ ci -m"Patch from outside" file3
RCS/file3,v  <—  file3
new revision: 1.2.2.1; previous revision: 1.2
done
$ co -l -jRel_1_orig:Rel_1,Rel_1_orig:1.2.2.1 file3
RCS/file3,v  —>  file3
revision 2.1 (locked)
revision 1.2
revision 1.2.1.1
merging...
revision 1.2
revision 1.2.2.1
merging...
done
$ cat file3
Line added for patch to release 1
This is file3
A line called A
A line called B
```

```
Outside patch to release 1
A line called C
A line called D
Line added for release 2
$ ci -q -u -m"Merge patches to release 1 (internal and outside)" file3
$
```

Notice that both sets of patches were merged. In real life, you might find that the merges encountered an overlap. In that case, you would need to edit the resulting file before performing a check in.

Using SCCS and *merge*

SCCS does not include a merge facility, so you will use the merge program repeatedly to perform the merges for this example if your version of UNIX has it. First, you do a get -e of the released file and add the changes. Then you use delta to submit the changes.

> **CAUTION:** Remember that the file you received as a patch might have any SCCS keywords expanded. This will create problems when you attempt the merge because you may lose the keywords. Before implementing this sort of merge strategy for a real project, you should develop some method for recovering the keywords.

After the changes are submitted, you will use a series of get commands to retrieve the various revisions to be merged. Copy revision 1.2 of file3 into file3_base (get -p -s -r1.2 s.file3 > file3_base). Copy revision 1.2.1.1 of file3 into file3_p1. Copy revision 1.2.2.1 of file3 into file3_p2. Get the head revision of file3 for edit into file3_head (get -p -s -e s.file3 > file3_head). Then execute a pair of merge commands, first merging the changes from the first patch (merge -p file3_p1 file3_base file3_head > file3_tmp) and then merging the result of that with the changes from the second patch (merge -p file3_p2 file3_base file3_tmp > file3). Finally, use delta to commit the change.

Perform the SCCS merge by executing the commands:

```
$ get -e -b -r1.2 -s s.file3
$ delta -s -y"Patch from outside" s.file3
$ get -p -s -r1.2 s.file3 > file3_base
$ get -p -s -r1.2.1.1 s.file3 > file3_p1
$ get -p -s -r1.2.2.1 s.file3 > file3_p2
$ get -p -s -e s.file3 > file3_head
$ merge -p file3_p1 file3_base file3_head > file3_tmp
$ cat file3_tmp
Line added for patch to release 1
This is file3
A line called A
```

```
A line called B
A line called C
A line called D
Line added for release 2
$ merge -p file3_p2 file3_base file3_tmp > file3
$ cat file3
Line added for patch to release 1
This is file3
A line called A
A line called B
Outside patch to release 1
A line called C
A line called D
Line added for release 2
$ delta -s -y"Merge patches to release 1 (internal and outside)" s.file3
$
```

You may want to review these examples several times to be sure you understand what is happening. The RCS example performed the same series of merging, but the co command handled all of the temporary files and extra bookkeeping work.

Requiring Proper Authorization for Changes (SCCS Only)

SCCS offers the option of having delta require verified *modification request* numbers, which identifies a particular report or enhancement request that required a change. This can be useful if you need a more completely controlled configuration-management environment. SCCS implements this by allowing you to set the name of a verification program using admin. If you set the verification program, it will be used by delta to verify that the modification request number(s) supplied on the command line (with -m) or interactively (with verification enabled, delta will ask for modification requests if none were given on the command line). Modification requests are separated by blanks, tabs, or new lines.

> **NOTE:** Remember to quote blanks, tabs, and new lines on the command line. For example:
>
> ```
> delta -m'01011 01012 01014' s.file2.
> ```

If the verification script exits successfully (exit code 0), then delta will allow the change and record the modification requests in the SCCS file. Here is a sample script that verifies that the modification request is a five-digit number:

```
#!/bin/ksh
exit_code=0
filename=$1
shift
for mr in $*
do
```

```
        case $mr in
        [0-9][0-9][0-9][0-9][0-9])
                ;;
        *)
                echo Invalid MR: $mr
                exit_code=1
                ;;
        esac
done
exit ${exit_code}
```

To try out this script, put the script in `mr_verify` and make it executable:

```
$ touch foo
$ admin -mxyzzy -ifoo -fv./mr_verify s.foo
Invalid MR: xyzzy
ERROR [s.foo]: invalid MRs (de9)
$ admin -m00000 -ifoo -fv./mr_verify s.foo
No id keywords (cm7)
$
```

For a production system, you could write the verification script to check with the problem-tracking database to make sure the modification requests are current and open. You could also have the script log the `delta` with the problem-tracking system.

Shutting Down Development on Release 1 (SCCS Only)

SCCS allows you to disable further `delta` changes to a list of releases or to prohibit `get` `-e` on a range of releases.

To disable `delta` change to release 1 of this example, run `admin -fl1 s.file1 s.file2` `s.file3`. If you then attempt to perform an action that would cause a release 1 delta, you will get an error message:

```
$ admin -fl1 s.file1 s.file2 s.file3
$ get -e -r1.2 s.file1
Retrieved:
1.2
ERROR [s.file1]: release '1' locked against editing (co23)
$
```

The example given in this and the preceding sections is quite long and complex. You may want to review parts of the example several times to help your understanding.

> **NOTE:** The RCS and SCCS files for these examples are included on the CD-ROM. One version (`example_1`) has the state of the source control system as of release 1. Another version (`example_2`) has the state of the source control system after all patches have been merged and the system is ready for a second release.

Using *make* with Source Control

To create an integrated development environment, you may want make to perform automatic check outs from the source control system. This can be very useful as a default rule for make so that it attempts to get from source control any file it is unable to find or create using existing rules. You may also want to write make rules that will perform time stamp–based check outs.

Default Rules

The easiest way to use source control with make is as a fallback. By setting the default target in make so that it attempts to get the head revision from a source control system, you will usually get the desired behavior for development. Try adding this rule to your Makefile:

```
.DEFAULT:
    co -q $<
```

For SCCS, try adding this rule to Makefile:

```
.DEFAULT:
    get -s s.$<
```

Both of these rules will be activated only if make has no explicit or implicit rules on how to construct the file, so the rule will not interfere with modifications to your Makefile.

Rules Using Time Stamps

There are some pitfalls to using make rules that check out files based on time stamps. The first problem is the difficulty in creating reliable rules that will work with anything other than head revision (or at least the top of a branch). It is possible to write a rule that does a check out based on an RCS tag or an SCCS cutoff date, but getting it to work in practice is fairly difficult. The second problem is one of false execution of the rule. Because make bases its update rules entirely on time stamps, it can be fooled by certain kinds of changes to a source control file. If you use the rcs or admin command to change a source control file without changing the head revision, your rule will detect that the working file is out of date with the source control file and check out the latest copy from source control. The third, and most serious, problem is one of false failure to execute a make rule. This can happen if you are not careful about what is in the working file. This is best illustrated by an example. Say you have an RCS-controlled file named file1 that has two revisions, 1.1 and 1.2, and you check out revision 1.1. If you then run your make (which is intended to build from the head revision), make will decide that file1 is up-to-date (because you wrote to file1, not to file1,v, the working file is newer) and will not replace revision 1.1 with revision 1.2.

Knowing that lengthy warning, you can write simple rules that will perform time stamp–based check out. Review this `Makefile`:

```
catfile:  file1 file2
    cat file1 file2 > catfile

file1:    file1,v
    co -q file1

file2:    s.file2
    get -s s.file2
```

These rules will get the head revision from the source control system any time the working file is older than the source control file. If you only use the directory for builds this should work rather reliably (with occasional false builds when you use `admin` or `rcs` to modify the source control file).

Summary

In this chapter you have learned basic principles of source control and how to apply them to using RCS and SCCS.

Concepts covered include the following:

Revisions	Symbolic names
Locks	SCCS
Merges	RCS
Baselines	Using source control for backup
Releases	Using source control with `make`

These topics give a good foundation in the basics of UNIX source control and how to use it to be more effective at using UNIX to develop any controlled document or product. Remember that source control isn't just for source code.

Archiving

By S. Lee Henry

The very worst thing about using computers is how easily you can throw away weeks of work. Even with fast, sophisticated file systems and almost countless options for how you store your files, you can easily make big mistakes. Human error is recognized as the biggest cause of data loss. Disk crashes and deranged controllers trail far behind as contenders for this honor. Yet, as easy as it is to remove files you might need, it is also far too easy to fill up disks with files you don't need. Electronic pack rats are so common that management of disk space is at the top among the concerns of system administrators everywhere.

Archiving important files is, therefore, a very good thing to do. Preserving your work at important times—such as when you've just completed a large proposal or debugged a major program—may save hours and weeks of your important time, not to mention the frustration of re-creating something you have just finished. In addition, reliable archiving of important files that you want to save makes it easier for you to be comfortable removing the electronic clutter that would otherwise fill your disk and complicate your view of your electronic "holdings." Once you know you've got the good stuff tucked away, you don't have to be so careful getting rid of the clutter.

You might also want to create archives of your work when you are moving to another site within your company or simply as a way to reorganize files you want to preserve during spring-cleaning.

Archives give you a reliable point to return to when subsequent changes, deliberate or unintentional, make it necessary to revert to previous copies of single files or restore entire directories.

An equally important use of archives is to organize and store software and documents for public or limited access, often over the Internet. Given a limited set of popularly used formats, creating, retrieving, and using archives is fairly easy for you and everyone else. Exchange of archive files between ftp sites on the Internet, for example, is a thriving activity.

There are a number of popular formats that you can use for archives and, of course, various commands to create and extract data from these formats. In addition, used in conjunction with other UNIX commands, archiving commands provide many ways to select what you store. You also may have a wide variety of choices over what media to use for your archives, including hard disk, tape, diskette, and optical drives.

The *tar* Command

One of the simplest and most versatile commands for creating archives is the tar command. Although you may have used this command only to read and write tapes in the past, tar offers advantages that make it an excellent utility for reading and writing disk-based archives as well. It is also a good command for copying directories between systems and between locations on a single system.

The `tar` command can specify a list of files or directories and can include name substitution characters. The filenames always follow any arguments corresponding to specified options, as shown in Figure 31.1.

FIGURE 31.1.

Anatomy of the tar *command.*

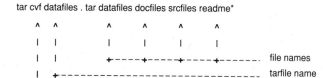

Most often, the `tar` command for creating a tar archive uses a string of options as well as a list of what files are to be included and names the device to be written to. The default device, `/dev/rmt0`, is seldom used today. Most sites have higher density devices available to them. Since it is the nature of UNIX to treat devices and files identically, you can archive to a file as easily as to a tape device. The two commands

```
boson% tar cvf /dev/rst0 datafiles
boson% tar cvf datafiles.tar datafiles
```

archive the same files. The first command writes to a tape device and the second creates a disk-based file called `datafiles.tar`.

The `cvf` argument string specifies that you are writing files (*c* for create), providing feedback to the user (*v* for verbose), and specifying the device rather than using the default (*f* for file).

Archives created with the `tar` command will almost always have the file extension `.tar`. Naming conventions such as this make it obvious to you and to anyone else who needs to use these files just what they are. Further, unless an archive is to be used immediately, and almost always if it is to be available for access using `ftp`, it is a good idea to compress the file. This significantly reduces the space required to store the file and the time required to transfer it. Most often, compressed `tar` files will end with `.tar.Z`. However, you will likely encounter compressed files with other extensions, such as `.gz`, which signify that a different compression routine was used; in this case, the public domain utility `gzip` was used.

To compress the `tar` file using the standard compress utility, use the command `compress <filename>`, as shown in this example:

```
boson% compress datafiles.tar
boson% ls datafiles.*
datafiles.tar.Z
```

The tar command on most UNIX systems also enables you to create lists of files that should be included or excluded from the archive. The options -I and X represent include and exclude. Both are accomplished through lists of files to either include in or exclude from the directory. If you had an exclude file containing its own name and two other files, such as

```
eta% cat exclude
exclude
foo
SAMS.tar
```

these files would not be included in a tar file that references the file exclude through the X option. It's a good idea to exclude the exclude file itself, as well as the tar file that you are creating in your exclude file. Notice that this has been done in the following example:

```
eta# tar cvfX SAMS.tar exclude *
a Archiving 21 blocks
a Backups 37 blocks
a dickens 1 blocks
a Flavors 0 blocks
a SAMS.tar excluded
a dickens.shar 1 blocks
a exclude excluded
a tmp0 1 blocks
a tmp1 1 blocks
a update_motd 2 blocks
```

Similarly, the include file can be used to specify which files should be included. In the next example, both an include and an exclude file are used. Any file that appears in both files, by the way, will be included.

```
boson% tar cvfX tar.tar exclude -I include
```

Notice that the -I option stands apart from the rest of the tar options. This is because it is a substitute for the list of filenames that normally occupies this position at the end of the command.

Keep in mind that the include and exclude files can have any name you want. The files in the example are called include or exclude simply to be obvious.

Combining tar with the find utility, you can archive files based on many criteria, including such things as how old the files are, how big, and how recently used. The following sequence of commands locates files that are newer than a particular file and creates an include file of files to be backed up.

```
boson% find -newer lastproject -print >> include
boson% tar cvf myfiles.tar -I include
```

GNU tar has some features that enable it to mimic the behavior of find and tar in a single command. Some of the most impressive options of GNU tar include appending to an existing archive, looking for differences between an archive and a "live" file system, deleting files from an archive (not for tapes), only archiving files created or modified since a given date, and compressing during creation of a tar file using either `compress` or `gzip`.

If you're moving files from one location on a UNIX system to another, or even between systems, you can use `tar` without ever creating a tar file by piping one `tar` command to another.

```
boson% (cd mydata; tar cvf - *) ¦ tar xvpBf -
```

What this command does is move to a subdirectory and read files, which it then pipes to an extract at the current working directory. The parentheses group the `cd` and `tar` commands so that you can be working in two directories at the same time. The two `-` characters in this command represent standard output and standard input, informing the respective `tar` commands where to write and read data. The `-` designator thereby allows `tar` commands to be chained in this way. The following command is similar, but it reads the files from the local system and extracts them on a remote host:

```
boson% tar cvf - mydata ¦ rsh boson "cd /pub/data; tar xvpBf -"
```

Archives created with `tar` can include executables. This is an important consideration when you are determining what style of archiving you want to do. Text files, source code, and binary data can all be included in the same tar file without any particular thought given to the file types. The file ownership, file permissions, and access and creation dates of the files all remain intact as well. Once the files are extracted from a tar file they look the same in content and description as they did when archived. The `p` (preserve) option will restore file permissions to the original state. This is usually good since you'll ordinarily want to preserve permissions as well as dates so that executables will execute and you can determine how old they are. In some situations, you might not like that original owners are retrieved, since the original owners may be people at some other organization altogether. The `tar` command will set up ownership according to the numeric UID of the original owner. If someone in your local `passwd` file or network information service has the same UID, that person will become the owner; otherwise the owner will display numerically. Obviously, ownership can be altered later.

To list the contents of a tar file without extracting, use the `t` option as shown below. Including the `v` option as well results in a long listing.

```
boson% tar tf myfiles.tar
boson% tar tvf myfiles.tar
```

Tar archives can be transferred with remote copy commands `rcp`, `ftp`, `kermit`, and `uucp`. These utilities know how to deal with binary data. You will generally not use `tar` when mailing archived files, but you can first encode the files to make it work. The `uuencode` command turns the contents of files into printable characters using a fixed-width format that allows them to be mailed and subsequently decoded easily. The resultant file will be larger than the file before uuencoding; after all, `uuencode` must map a larger character set of printable and nonprintable characters to a smaller one of printable characters, so it uses extra bits to do this, and the file will be about a third larger than the original.

To get an idea of what uuencode does to a file, try this simple example:

```
boson%  uuencode dickens dickens > dickens.uu
```

This command uses uuencode on the file `dickens`. The filename to be used upon extraction is also included in this command as well as the filename resulting from this use of uuencode (see Figure 31.2).

FIGURE 31.2.

Syntax of the uuencode command.

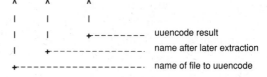

boson% uuencode dickens dickens > dickens . uu

When you take the file `dickens`, which has the following contents:

```
"Buried how long?"
The answer was always the same: "Almost eighteen years."
"You had abandoned all hope of being dug out?"
"Long ago."
"You know that you are recalled to life?"
"They tell me so."
"I hope that you care to live?"
"I can't say."

Charles Dickens, A Tale of Two Cities
```

and use uuencode on it, it looks like this:

```
begin 644 dickens
M(D)U<FEE9"!H;W<@;&]N9S\B"E1H92!A;G-W97(@=V%S(&%L=V%Y<R!T:&4@
M<V%M93H@(D%L;6]S="!E:6=H=&5E;B!Y96%R<RXB"B)9;W4@:&%D(&%B86YD
M;VYE9"!A;&P@:&]P92!O9B!B96EN9R!D=6<@;W5T/R(*(DQO;F<@86=O+B(*
M(EEO=2!K;F]W('1H870@>6]U(&%R92!R96-A;&QE9"!T;R!L:69E/R(*(E1H
M97D@=&5L;"!M92!S;RXB"B))(&AO<&4@=&AA="!Y;W4@8V%R92!T;R!L:79E
M/R(*(DD@8V%N)W0@<V%Y+B(*"D-H87)L97,@1&EC:V5N<RP@02!486QE(&]F
,(%1W;R!#:71I97,*
,(%1W;R!#:71I97,*
, (%1W;R!#:71I97,*
```

```
end
```

The first line of the uuencode file lists the permissions that the file will have and the name it will have once it's extracted (see Figure 31.3).

If you receive in the mail a file on which uudecode has been used, you can retrieve the original file using the reverse process of what has been described. Strip the mail header off until you get to just the file on which uudecode has been used (so that it looks like what is shown in the example). Then use the uudecode file to extract the original file.

FIGURE 31.3.

First line of file created by uuencode.

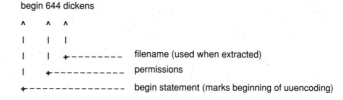

```
boson% uudecode dickens.uu
boson% ls dickens*
dickens
dickens.uu
```

Notice that the file on which uuencode was used will still be there. The uudecode command does not decode "in place" the way uncompress decompresses in place. Instead, it extracts to whatever filename you included in the uuencode process.

Shell Archives

Another common format for archives is the shell archive. Shell archives are also called *shar files* and have, by convention, the extension .shar. They are very different from tar archives in that they do not allow inclusion of executables. They also do not include any of the file descriptive information, such as permissions and ownership. Shar files are just text files with the shell commands for extracting the original files embedded between the text of the files themselves.

Shar files are extracted using the Bourne shell command, sh. It is easy to create a shar file and it is easy to extract from one. It is likewise easy to create a script that creates shell archives.

The basic "trick" in creating shar files is knowing how to use what is known as the "here" document. In the Bourne shell, the operator << instructs the shell to accept input until it encounters a given string (which you provide) and uses this input as input to a command.

Type these commands on your system:

```
echo Extracting File from Shell Archive
cat > dickens << TheEnd
"Buried how long?"
The answer was always the same: "Almost eighteen years."
"You had abandoned all hope of being dug out?"
"Long ago."
"You know that you are recalled to life?"
"They tell me so."
"I hope that you care to live?"
"I can't say."

Charles Dickens, A Tale of Two Cities
TheEnd
```

You get a file `dickens` with the content specified between the `cat` command and the `TheEnd` marker. If you imbed these same commands in an executable file and invoke it, you get the same thing. You can, therefore, create files including such sequences and provide them to other people so that they can extract your original files using a command like this:

```
myhost% /bin/sh anyname.shar
```

Better still, you can create a script which takes any file you want to share and wraps it in the appropriate here document commands. To create such a script, you first need to include the here document commands. You can easily modify the commands you entered above to read:

```
echo "echo Extracting File from Shell Archive"
echo "cat > dickens << TheEnd"
cat dickens
echo TheEnd
```

You can then insert them into your shell script.

This command sequence looks a little peculiar, but you need to examine it closely to understand what it is doing. First, it creates the line `echo Extracting File from Shell Archive`. Next it adds the line `cat > dickens << 'TheEnd'` to the file. This is the command that is going to create the file `dickens` when the extraction is done. It will cause data following this line to be read until the line `TheEnd` is encountered. Then you actually use `cat` to add the file to the archive, followed by the end marker you selected, `'TheEnd'`.

To make this script general-purpose, you should replace the specified filename with an argument.

```
echo "echo Extracting File from Shell Archive"
echo "cat > $1 << TheEnd"
cat $1
echo TheEnd
```

You can then use this script like this to create a `shar` archive from any file. Make sure that your script is executable and redirect its output to the file that you will share.

```
mk_shar dickens > dickens.shar
```

So, here's what the archive, `dickens.shar`, will look like when you're done:

```
echo Extracting File from Shell Archive
cat > dickens << 'TheEnd'
"Buried how long?"
The answer was always the same: "Almost eighteen years."
"You had abandoned all hope of being dug out?"
"Long ago."
"You know that you are recalled to life?"
"They tell me so."
"I hope that you care to live?"
"I can't say."
```

```
Charles Dickens, A Tale of Two Cities
TheEnd
```

When you extract this file, you will get a file `dickens`.

```
boson% sh dickens.shar
```

Notice that you can include multiple files in the same shar archive by using the append operator, >>.

```
mk_shar dickens2 >> dickens.shar
```

Clearly, you can string together multiple files in this way, creating a very useful archiving method since you can group together related files in a text-only format that clearly remembers the filenames and marks their beginnings and endings. Shell archives can also be read on just about any UNIX system. It would be surprising if you found any UNIX system without the Bourne shell.

Shar files, obviously, do not save any space. Since you have the original files plus some overhead for packing them in the simple structure of extract commands, text, and end-of-file markers, the resultant archive is somewhat larger than the original files. Generally, the extra length is considerably less than the extra space taken by using uuencode.

Shar files are nice because it is obvious what you're getting. You can easily examine them before extracting from them to be sure that this is what you want. You can check out the filenames and look for extraneous commands that you might not want to execute. Keep in mind that "stray" commands included in an archive when you extract from it will also be executed, provided that they are not within the beginning and end markers of a here document.

In any case, you should always examine shar files before extracting them, even if they're from someone you trust (that person may have gotten them from somewhere else). The following simple awk script could be used to quickly scan through a shell archive, looking for commands that are extraneous and possibly sinister. It looks for the beginning and the end of each here document and prints anything not enclosed within these documents. If used against the `dickens.shar` file presented in this chapter, it would print the string `echo Extracting File from Shell Archive`.

> **NOTE:** Note that this particular awk script expects the filenames of the extracted files to contain only alphabetic and numeric characters. You can expand this expression if necessary.

```
#
BEGIN {OK = "OFF"}
$0 ~ /^cat > [A-Za-z0-9]+ <</ { OK = "ON";TERMINATOR = $5 }
```

```
{
if (OK == "OFF")
    print $0
if ($0 == TERMINATOR) {
    OK = "OFF"
}
}
```

Summary

The commands that UNIX provides for archiving your files allow you to recover from disastrous mistakes, as well as conveniently share files with strangers who will not need to know anything about your systems (except how to access them) to make use of them.

Almost no one archives files too often. Regular use of the commands described in this chapter will help you manage your systems.

Backups

By S. Lee Henry

IN THIS CHAPTER

The only thing wrong with backups is that you have to do them, and that is often a big problem. Necessary safeguards against disaster, backups take time and are generally not used. As a result, the motivation for doing them is often lacking, except immediately following a disaster, and the recognition you get for all the time and effort that backups require is almost always nonexistent. At the same time, no responsible system administrator or user would fail to see that backups are done on a regular basis.

Routinely storing entire file systems or individual directories and files to protect the integrity of your system and your work can be very time-consuming or it can be fairly well automated.

Whether caused by human error (most likely), by media failure, or by acts of God, loss of important files warrants the time and attention that goes into planning and executing a good backup scheme.

After reading this chapter, you will be able to back up and restore file systems or individual files, design a backup schedule that is right for your site, and evaluate the advantages of commercial backup software.

Backups and Archives

The last chapter discussed archiving. Very similarly to backups, archives are usually created by individual users interested in storing "snapshots" of their work when they reach important milestones. Archives are usually the result of an individual's interest in making a safe copy of his own work.

Backups, on the other hand, are most often the responsibility of system administrators and represent the state of entire file systems rather than the work of specific individuals. Usually periodic in nature, backups are an attempt to preserve the state of a system so that any type of loss, whether through human error or catastrophe, can be averted.

Another important distinction between archives and backups is the issue of completeness. Archives will include files that may subsequently be deleted from the system. These archives may be kept indefinitely, or at least as long as the project or effort being archived has some relevance. Backups, on the other hand, are generally cycled. Files that are removed from file systems will eventually disappear from the backups as well. There is usually a fixed window of a couple weeks or a couple months within which a file that is removed can be recovered.

Backups should be automated. Most people will not reliably back up their systems if it is a boring and painful task. The best backups happen "by themselves." This doesn't mean that a good deal of insight isn't required to configure the process.

One of the most important distinctions to be made regarding backups is whether you back up an entire file system or only those files that have been created or modified since some earlier time. A combination of full and incremental backups is usually the best strategy for getting the greatest reliability while minimizing the work of retrieving files and the number of backup tapes (or other media) that must be maintained.

The *dump* Command

The dump command is the command most commonly used for backups. Typically used to dump entire file systems to tape, whether fully or incrementally, the dump command can also be used to dump specified files and directories. The dump command creates backups in a format that includes directory information as well as a notation of where the file system was last mounted. The directory index precedes the actual files.

The dump command can access remote or local drives. To use the remote dump command, all you need to do is precede the name of the tape device with the name of the remote host (for example, boson:/dev/rst0). On some UNIX systems, there is a second dump command, rdump, which specifies a remote dump. When rdump is used, the system will look for a host named dumphost in your host file and attempt to dump to dumphost:/dev/rmt0. To perform a remote dump (that is, dump to another host's tape drive or hard disk), the other host needs to trust the one you are dumping from. Including the local host in the remote host's /.rhosts file is the simplest way to do this, but this gives the local host considerable access to the remote one and may not be a good strategy for security reasons. It is often possible to dump to the remote host as a specific user rather than as root. In this case, the syntax user@remotehost:device is used instead of remotehost:device, and the user must have an .rhosts file in his home directory.

The following is some typical dump command output. It provides a lot of information about the file system being dumped, including the dates of the last dumps at this level and the lower level, the partition name and the mount point, the passes dump makes as it dumps the directory information and the contents of the files themselves, and an estimate of how much tape will be used in the process.

The command

```
boson% /usr/etc/dump 7cusdtf 590 1200 18 /dev/nrst0 /dev/sd0h
```

produces the following output:

```
DUMP: Date of this level 7 dump: Tue Mar  8 00:20:01 1994
DUMP: Date of last level 5 dump: Sat Mar  5 02:22:11 1994
DUMP: Dumping /dev/rsd0h (/export/data1) to /dev/nrst0
DUMP: mapping (Pass I) [regular files]
DUMP: mapping (Pass II) [directories]
DUMP: mapping (Pass II) [directories]
DUMP: estimated 520 blocks (260KB) on 0.00 tape(s).
DUMP: dumping (Pass III) [directories]
DUMP: dumping (Pass IV) [regular files]
DUMP: level 7 dump on Tue Mar  8 00:20:01 1994
DUMP: Tape rewinding
DUMP: 546 blocks (273KB) on 1 volume
DUMP: DUMP IS DONE
```

In SVR4 systems, the dump command is called ufsdump. The format of the dump files, however, is the same so that you can almost always read dumps from one UNIX system on another.

The dump command uses dump levels to indicate whether full or incremental dumps should be made. A level 0 dump is a full dump. Levels 1–9 create incremental dumps. The level of an incremental dump has significance only in relationship to other dumps. If John Doe made a level 0 dump once a month and a level 9 once a week, while Jane Doe ran a level 0 dump once a month and a level 5 once a week, they would both have the same dump result (we are assuming that they are dumping different systems). Both the level 9 and the level 5 dumps will include all files that have been modified since the earlier dump, at a lower level (that is, the level 0 dump). If John dumped at levels 0, 5, and 8, on the other hand, his level 8 dumps would include files modified only since the most recent level, 0 or 5 (whichever most closely preceded it).

The dump command keeps track of the date and level of the prior dumps through use of a file called /etc/dumpdates. Unsuccessful backups will not update this file, which includes a record for each file system and dump level used, along with the date and time of the backup. Here is an example:

```
/dev/rsd0g      0 Sat Jul 12 03:45:00 1994
/dev/rsd0g      5 Fri Jul  4 03:45:01 1994
/dev/rsd2a      0 Tue Jul  1 03:52:49 1994
/dev/rsd2a      5 Fri Jul  4 03:55:49 1994
```

Each of these records will be updated the next time a backup is done of the same file system at the same level.

One useful way to employ this information is to extract the dates of the latest backups and include them in your /etc/motd file. This will reassure users that their files are being backed up routinely and give them an idea of how current the latest backups are.

Here's a script that will do this:

```
#!/bin/csh
#
# remove old dump dates (if there)
/bin/cat /etc/motd | /usr/local/bin/grep -v "^Last" > /tmp/motd.$$
# determine home partition
#set PART='grep /export/home /etc/fstab | awk -F/ '{print $3}''
# get dates for last level 0 and 5 backups
set FULL='grep "/dev/rusr        0" /etc/dumpdates | awk '{print $3,$4,$5,$6}''
set INCR='grep "/dev/rusr        5" /etc/dumpdates | awk '{print $3,$4,$5,$6}''
# create new motd file w this info
echo "Last full backup:        " $FULL >> /tmp/motd.$$
echo "Last incremental backup:        " $INCR >> /tmp/motd.$$
# put new motd file in place
mv /tmp/motd.$$ /etc/motd
```

Here's a typical /etc/motd updated by such a script:

```
SunOS Release 4.1.3 (boson) #2: Wed Aug 11 13:54:26 EDT 1994

     Dial-in.......123-4567
     ExaByte........./dev/rst0
     9-Track......../dev/rmt0
     9-Track......../dev/rmt8 (1600/6250)

***********************************************************************
*                                                                     *
*          Don't forget tea and cookies at 3 PM this afternoon        *
*                                                                     *
***********************************************************************

Last full backup:         Sat Mar 12 03:45:00
Last incremental backup:      Fri Mar 4 03:45:01
```

Similar to the tar command described in the previous chapter, the dump command is usually used to back up file systems to tape. Given the nature of UNIX, however, dump files can also be created on hard disk or on less expensive media, such as read-write optical disks. Like the tar command, the dump command can create a file in a specific format that can be used later to extract files. The benefit of disk-based dumps is that they are always available, and the process can be automated so that there is practically no human intervention needed. With tape-based backups, it is often the manual procedures of inserting, removing, and labelling the tapes that cause the most problems. With disk-based dump, you can rely on file naming conventions to "cycle" your backups. It is also possible to get a similar effect using a multitape backup device. In any case, the more you can automate your backups, the more likely it is that you will be able to recover when the need arises.

You should be familiar with the optional parameters of the dump command. These can very significantly affect how efficiently your backups are, in terms of both space and speed. Density and length parameters that are proper for a 1/2-inch tape are not at all correct for an 8 mm Exabyte drive. Even if you are backing up to hard disk, the parameters you provide will determine whether the dump is successful or not because dump will use these parameters to calculate the space available for the disk-based dump. Most UNIX systems will include suggestions about dump parameters in the man page for the dump command. Here are some suggestions:

60 MB cartridge:	cdst 1000 425 9
150 MB cartridge:	cdst 1000 700 18
1/2-inch tape:	dsb 1600 2300 126
2.3-GByte 8mm tape:	dsb 54000 6000 126

The dump options in these specifications represent the following:

c = cartridge tape
d = density
s = size (that is, length)
t = tracks
b = block size

The dump command can also be used to dump specific files rather than entire file systems. In this mode, the command always works at a level 0; that is, it fully backs up every file that you include, regardless of when that file was last backed up or modified. In addition, the /etc/dumpdates file will not be updated even if you include the -u option; it is used only when you back up complete file systems. Records in the /etc/dumpdates file, after all, are kept by file system for each dump level used, not by individual files.

If you wanted to back up two files in the dump format, you might use a command like this one. This command dumps the files chapter1 and chapter2 to an 8mm Exabyte drive using the dump parameters described earlier:

```
eta# dump fdsb /dev/rst0 54000 6000 126 chapter1 chapter2
```

As mentioned earlier, the output from the dump command includes a lot of information about the dump process. As shown in the following paragraphs, this includes the date and level of the backup, the partition and file system mount point, the approximate size of the data being dumped, and the amount of tape expected to be used. The dump command makes a number of passes through the file system it is dumping. The first two passes are for *mapping*, or creating a list of those files to be included in a directory structure. In the second two passes, it dumps the files. The directory structure of the file system being dumped is included within the dump.

The following dump output is for a level 0 (that is, complete) dump of the /var partition on a Sun workstation:

```
DUMP: Date of this level 0 dump: Sun Mar 13 13:22:39 1994
DUMP: Date of last level 0 dump: the epoch
DUMP: Dumping /dev/rsd2f (/var) to /dev/nrst0
DUMP: mapping (Pass I) [regular files]
DUMP: mapping (Pass II) [directories]
DUMP: estimated 66208 blocks (32.33MB) on 0.02 tape(s).
DUMP: dumping (Pass III) [directories]
DUMP: dumping (Pass IV) [regular files]
DUMP: level 0 dump on Sun Mar 13 13:22:39 1994
DUMP: Tape rewinding
DUMP: 66178 blocks (32.31MB) on 1 volume
DUMP: DUMP IS DONE
```

The output of the dump command is written to standard error (rather than standard out). Still, it is possible to redirect this output and mail it to someone responsible for ensuring that backups are completing properly. For example, in this excerpt from a crontab file (the dump commands themselves are in the referenced scripts) the output of the dump command is mailed to root:

```
# backups to 8mm each night
# NOTE:  Dates looks "off" but Mon backups, eg, really run Tues at 1:30 AM
45 3 * * 2 /etc/Monday.backups ¦ mail root 2>&1
45 3 * * 3 /etc/Tuesday.backups ¦ mail root 2>&1
45 3 * * 4 /etc/Wednesday.backups ¦ mail root
45 3 * * 5 /etc/Thursday.backups ¦ mail root
45 3 * * 6 /etc/Friday.backups ¦ mail root 2>&1
```

The dump command creates a file with considerable overhead. If you use the dump command, for example, to dump a single file to disk, the resulting file will be considerably larger than the original. In the following example, a fairly small file has been dumped to a disk-based dump file. The dump file is more than 14 times the size of the original file. As with the tar command, the dump command stores information about each file, including its ownership and permissions. The pathnames of each file relative to the base of the directory being dumped are also contained in the dump file.

```
eta# dump f Archiving.dump Archiving
eta# ls -l Arch*
-rw-r--r--  1 slee       10068 Mar  8 18:29 Archiving
-rw-r--r--  1 slee      143360 Mar 13 14:02 Archiving.dump
```

When restoring from a dump, you should first move to the base of the file system where the recovered file belongs, unless you want to examine the files before moving them into the correct locations (for example, to overwrite other files). Using restore will restore a file from the current working directory and will create whatever directory structures are needed to retrieve the file. For example, if you are restoring a mail file from a dump of / var, you could restore the file from /tmp. The extracted file might be called /tmp/spool/ mail/slee after restoration, although it was clearly /var/spool/mail/slee before the dump. After ensuring that this is the correct file, you might choose to overwrite or append it to the current mail file.

The *restore* Command

Entire file systems can be restored with the `restore` command if they were dumped with the `dump` command. If you specified a block size during the dump, you must specify it for the restore as well. Density and length parameters, on the other hand, are required only during the dump.

The interactive mode of the `restore` command is useful when you want to restore selected files. It provides commands such as `cd` and `ls` so that you can examine the files included within the dump, `add` to select files, and `extract` to start the extraction process.

The following example illustrates an interactive restore from a disk-based `dump` file:

```
boson# restore ivbf 126 sor.usr.Sun
Verify volume and initialize maps
Dump    date: Sun Mar 13 15:22:47 1994
Dumped from: Wed Feb 16 05:06:59 1994
Level 5 dump of /usr on sor:/dev/usr
Label: none
Extract directories from tape
Initialize symbol table.
restore > ls
.:
    2 *./          2294  bsd/        2724  mail/        3189  sysgen/
    2 *../          2394  include/    2721  people/     28724  tmp/
 2121  adm/           12  lib/        3006  preserve/   28713  tmp_rex/
 2152  bin/        29413  local/      3111  spool/

restore > cd people/slee
restore > ls
./people/slee:
 2759  ./           2806  .login      7730  check        2912  mycron
 2721  ../         13266  .plan       2857  incr2boson

restore > add mycron
Make node ./people
Make node ./people/slee
restore > extract
Extract requested files
You have not read any volumes yet.
Unless you know which volume your file(s) are on you should start
with the last volume and work towards the first.
Specify next volume #: 1
extract file ./people/slee/mycron
Add links
Set directory mode, owner, and times.
set owner/mode for '.'? [yn] y
restore> quit
boson#
```

Dump Schedules

System administrators develop a schedule of dumps at various levels to provide a compromise between redundancy (to ensure that dumps will be available even if some of the media become unusable) and the number of tapes that need to be cycled through when looking for a file that needs to be restored. Most system administrators design their backup strategy so that they will not have to look through more than a few tapes to get any file they need to restore.

Suggested schedules for backup at various levels look something like what is shown here. Such schedules provide a good balance between redundancy and duplication.

```
                Sun   Mon   Tue   Wed   Thu   Fri
    Week 1:     Full  5     5     5     5     3
    Week 2:           5     5     5     5     3
    Week 3:           5     5     5     5     3
    Week 4:           5     5     5     5     3
```

Because all system administrators have better things to do than stand by a tape drive for hours at a time, they generally have available high-density tape drives, such as 8 mm or DAT drives. These hold from a couple gigabytes to a couple dozen gigabytes (with compression). With multiple tape devices, it is sometimes possible to dump entire networks to a single device with extremely little human intervention.

Backups are often initiated through cron so that the system administrator does not have to manually invoke them. Conducting unattended backups is always the best strategy. Doing backups is boring work, and boring work means a high probability of error.

The dump command is best used when the file system being dumped is not in use. This is because certain changes that might occur during the dump can cause the resultant dump to be unrestorable (for example, if inodes are between the writing of directory information and the dumping of the files themselves). Reuse of an inode, for example, can result in a bad dump. Such changes are not likely. Many system administrators dump live files without ever encountering such problems. On the other hand, some have been bitten. It is best to avoid this error if at all possible.

The *tar* Command

The tar command (described in the previous chapter) can also be used for backups, although it is more appropriate for creating archives of selected files. There is no interactive mode for reading files from a tar file. It is possible, however, to list the files contained in a tar file and then issue a second command to extract specific files, but this is not as convenient. For this and other reasons, the tar command is generally used when you might want to restore all the files from the backup.

Unlike the dump command, the tar command dumps files with a pathname beginning with the current working directory, rather than with the base of the file system. This makes it a useful tool for recreating directories in another location on the same or another system.

Commercial Software

Fortunately, for those who can afford it, there are many software products that provide sophisticated front ends for backup commands. Some of these provide an interface that is so understandable that even casual users can restore files for themselves.

When considering commercial backup software, there are a number of very important issues to keep in mind. Chiefly, commercial backup software ought to provide some level of functionality significantly better than what you can provide using dump and cron. It can do this by providing any or all of the following features:

A classy user interface—We're not necessarily talking "pretty" here. The user interface needs to be clearly understandable and very usable.

Little or no operator intervention—Operator intervention should always be minimized. Some initial setup should be expected, but afterwards backups should be fairly automatic.

Multitape and multifile system control—You need some method of using multiple tapes for large backups or backing up multiple file systems without operator-assisted positioning.

Labeling support—Mislabeling and failing to label backup media can cause big problems when the need to restore arises. It is easy to reuse the wrong tape and overwrite an important backup. Commercial software should assist the operator in labeling media so as to minimize this kind of error. Software labeling and verification of the backup media is even better; if your backup software rejects a tape because it isn't the proper one to overwrite, you have an important safeguard against ruining backups you might still need. On the other hand, you should always have access to a fresh tape, because the expected tape might have "gone south."

Revision control—Keep track of versions of a file and which appears on which backup. If casual users can determine which version of a file they need, this is ideal.

High-Reliability Technology

Some technology that has been developed in response to the need for high reliability has reduced the requirement for more traditional backup. Disk mirroring, for example, in which two or more disks are updated at the same time and therefore are replicas of each other, provides protection against data loss resulting from certain types of catastrophe—such as a single disk crash—but not others. Replication of disk images does not help recover files that are intentionally erased from the disk (and the removal is replicated as well) and does not prevent data loss due to failing disk controllers (which is likely to trash files on both the original and replication disks).

Technology that periodically provides a snapshot of one disk onto another provides some protection. The utility of this protection, however, is tightly tied to the frequency of the replication and the method used to detect the loss in the first place.

Replication technology can guard against certain types of data loss but is seldom a complete replacement for traditional backup.

Summary

With a well-planned backup schedule and a modest degree of automation, you can take most of the drudgery out of backing up your systems and make it possible to recover from most inadvertent or catastrophic file losses.

7

PART

System Administration

UNIX Installation Basics

33

By Syd Weinstein

Installing a UNIX system requires a bit more planning than does installing a PC. You need to decide whether the system is autonomous (able to run without any other systems being present on a network) or how dependent it would be on the other systems on its network. You also have to decide which parts of the UNIX system and its various utilities and application programs each user of this system will need.

Why? MS-DOS is a system that takes less than 10 MB of disk space. MS-Windows takes a bit more, but it's still a rather small amount. UNIX is a large system. The complete installation of just the operating system and all that comes with it for Sun's Solaris 2.3 release, as an example, is about 300 MB. With that much disk space in use, it's often wise to share it across several systems. In addition, there are few options in installing DOS or Windows that can be made by the installer. UNIX splits the install into many different sections, called packages. Each package consists of files that provide a specific set of features. Many packages can be installed locally, remotely on a server, or not at all, depending on your needs.

Whereas DOS and Windows are not designed to easily share large sections of the installation, UNIX (especially because of its disk needs) almost expects that some sharing will occur. The degree of disk space sharing leads to the definition of stand-alone, server, dataless, and diskless systems.

A stand-alone system is one that is capable of operating without a connection to a local area network (LAN) and other UNIX systems. It's not that it cannot be connected; it's capable of booting and operating without any connection. This means that it does not need to access any other UNIX system's disk for boot or operating system files and for swap space.

A server is also a stand-alone system. It is capable of operating without a connection to other systems. But it also generally contains some extra files, which are used by its clients.

The clients may only have part of the operating system installed—just enough to boot the system—and depend on the server for the remainder of the commands, utilities, and library files. Such a client is called a dataless system. It has a boot disk and local swap space, and it is missing the remainder of the utilities and operating system.

If the client system has no disk drive at all, it is considered diskless. It depends on its server for booting, for the entire operating system, and for swap space.

In addition to sharing the operating system, UNIX systems can share other disks, such as drives containing databases or user files. Sharing these disks does not make a system a server in the "install" sense. The "server" name is reserved for serving the operating system or its utilities. A system might be an NFS server (sharing via Network File System user files) and still be considered a stand-alone system for the installation of the UNIX operating system.

As an example, Sun's Solaris 2.3 requires either 27 MB, 101 MB, 158 MB, or 213 MB just to install the operating system and its utilities and documentation.

A diskless system does not require that any of these files be installed, as it uses them from the server. A dataless system requires that the core system support files be installed. A stand-alone system could be set up with either end-user packages or with developer packages, whereas a server traditionally needs the entire distribution.

So far this chapter just touches on the disk installation. There is much more to it: planning for users, the network and its traffic, applications, printers, remote access, and much more.

Thus, planning for a UNIX installation requires planning not only for this one system, but for all the systems in this segment of the network.

What Do I Need to Know from the Start?

The first think you need to do is decide what you are going to install on this system. You decide this by looking not only at this system, but at all the systems on this segment of the network.

NOTE: A network segment is a group of machines all plugged into the same EtherNet, a type of LAN which uses a bus topology. Because the EtherNet uses a bus topology, each of the machines sees all the traffic on the network. Each is local to each other and is immediately accessible via the network. Since the EtherNet LAN is only able to handle a finite amount of traffic, the network is broken into segments connected by routers or bridges. Traffic to systems within the segment is not repeated, or retransmitted, into the other segments. Only traffic that is for systems outside the segment is repeated. With proper planning, almost all of the traffic will be internal to the segment, and more systems can be placed on the overall network before everyone bogs down from trying to put more bytes out over the LAN than it can handle.

You base your decision about what to install on the intended usage of the system, what systems it can be served by, and for which systems it will have to provide services.

Who Is Going to Use This System?

Just as a PC for a user to run a spreadsheet and a word processor needs a much smaller disk and less of UNIX and its applications installed, such a UNIX system will also require less to be installed. However a power user or application developer needs much more to be installed, perhaps including compilers and development libraries. To decide what to install on this segment of the LAN, let alone on this system, you need to determine which type of users are going to be using this system.

> **TIP:** Not only will the type of user dictate what gets installed, it will also dictate how many systems can be put on this segment of the LAN, server capacity (sizing), and swap space requirements.

Which Type of Users

UNIX users generally fall into one or more of several categories:

- *Application users*

    These users run commercial or locally developed applications. They rarely interact with the shell directly and do not write their own applications. These users might be running a database application, a word processor or desktop publishing system, a spreadsheet, or some in-house developed set of applications. They spend most of their time in "think" mode, where they are deciding what to do with the results the application has presented them, or in data entry mode, typing responses or data into the system. Their need for large amounts of local disk access is minimal, and they do not change applications frequently, nor are they running many applications simultaneously. (They might have them open, but they are generally interacting with only a couple of them at a time—the rest are waiting for the user to provide input.) Although application users might put a large load on their database servers, they do not normally put large disk loads on their own systems.

- *Power users*

    These users run applications, just like the application users, but they also run shell scripts and interact more closely with the system. They are likely to be running multiple applications at once, with all these applications processing in parallel. These users keep several applications busy and access the disk more frequently and use more CPU resources than does the normal application user.

- *Developers*

    Developers not only run applications, they also run compilers, access different applications than do users, require access to the development libraries, and generally use more components of the operating system than do users. Furthermore, they tend to use debugging tools that require more swap space and access to more disk resources than the application user generally needs. The UNIX operating system has packages that are only needed by developers, and if a developer is on this segment of the LAN, these files must be installed and accessible to the systems used by these developers.

> **TIP:** You must not only consider who will use the system right away, but because you only install UNIX once, consider who might use the system over the next six months to a year.

For What Purpose?

UNIX systems that are being used as shared development machines, or are going be placed in a common user area, will need a lot of swap space, a large section of the disk for temporary files, and more of the packages from the operating system than systems that are just being used on a single user's desk. In addition, if the system is going to be used as a computation or database server, it will need increased swap space.

What Other Systems Are Located on This Segment of the LAN?

As stated in the section "What Do I Need to Know from the Start?," you have to consider all of the systems on this segment of the LAN. You are looking for systems that provide access to sections of the operating system, provide access to application disk areas, have sufficient disk and memory resources to handle your diskless clients, and make suitable servers for the other systems on the segment.

In UNIX it is a good idea to remotely serve systems with most of the operating system packages. Dataless systems are a good idea. Sharing the operating system not only saves disk space, it also makes the future task of upgrading the operating system easier. You only have to upgrade the server system with the full distribution, a process that can take an hour or more. For the Dataless clients, a small, few-minute procedure will update the small amount of the system that is located on their private disks.

If a little disk sharing is good, isn't a lot better? If you are running diskless clients, they need no upgrade at all. All of the upgrade is done on the server. However, there is a downside to diskless systems: excessive network traffic. A diskless system depends on its server not only for the operating system, but also for its swap and temporary disk space. The network is not as fast as a local disk, especially if it is getting overloaded by too many diskless clients. A reasonable trade-off is to use diskless clients for small systems that are used by application users, and dataless clients for the rest.

When you make a system a diskless or dataless client, you reduce redundancy in the segment. These systems are totally dependent on their servers to function. If the server is down for any reason, these systems are also down. This causes many systems to go down if a server is down. (This includes while upgrading the server with a new revision of the operating system.) You should not place mission-critical applications on systems that are clients of other systems. Having a mission-critical system freeze due to NFS Server Unreachable is not good.

Determining Suitable Servers

It's usually easier to determine suitable servers than suitable clients, so start there. To make a good server system, you need the following:

Plenty of RAM—A server must not only cache files for its own use, but also for the demands of its clients. Having plenty of RAM so the in-memory disk cache managed by UNIX can be large really helps on servers. With the rapid drop in memory prices, what used to be a good-sized buffer might not be any more, but as a minimum, consider 32 MB of RAM in the system.

Fast Disks—The client sees the delay to read a disk block as the time to ask the server for the block, the time the server takes to read the block, and the time to transmit the block over the network back to the client. If the server has a fast disk, this time might be no longer, and is often shorter, than reading the same number of blocks locally.

Since a server is handling multiple clients, including itself, it is more likely that a disk block is already in the server's disk cache. This is especially true for program files and the operating system utilities, as they are used often. Access is then very fast, as the disk read time is not needed at all. This helps make servers as responsive as if they were reading the disk block locally on the client server.

Sufficient disk space—A server will hold not only its own files and a copy of the UNIX operating system, but also the swap and temporary space for its diskless clients. A suitable server should have some spare disk space for adding not only the current clients, but some extra to account for growth.

Dataless clients do not use space on the server for swap and temporary files.

Spare CPU resources—A server needs to have enough CPU cycles to serve its local users and still provide disk and network access services to its clients. But that does not mean to make the fastest system the server. Often you should do just the opposite.

It does not take much CPU power to be a server. File access in UNIX is very efficient, as is network traffic. A system that is heavily loaded will delay the response of disk block requests for its clients. To keep response time up for the clients, leave your power users on the faster systems and use a system with sufficient other resources and a light user load for the server, even if this system has a slower-model CPU.

Determining Suitable Clients

Once the server is determined, choosing suitable clients is a balancing act. You need to mix performance, ease of administration, network traffic, and available resources.

Diskless clients—These are the easiest to determine. If the system does not have a disk, it must have a diskless client. Choose a server for this system that is going to be relatively lightly loaded. Diskless clients make larger demands on their servers than do dataless clients.

Make sure the server for diskless clients is on the same segment of the network as the client. Although NFS requests for disk blocks will cross out of a segment and across a router to a different LAN segment, the boot request will not. It is a local broadcast packet. The diskless client needs its `bootp` server, the system that holds its boot files and responds to its diskless request, to be local to the segment on which it resides. Even if the system that holds its boot files responds to its diskless boot request, the segments are not connected by routers today. Follow this rule: when the segments are converted to using routers to reduce backbone traffic, the system will be unbootable without a local `bootp` server.

Dataless clients—Since a dataless client accesses the utility portions of the UNIX operating system only from its server, it makes relatively small demand on its server. Almost any system that is not critical that it operates if the server is down makes a good choice for use as a dataless client.

If a system will have a large number of disk accesses to user files, such as for a local database, it still can be a dataless client. It can keep on its local disk a file system for those heavily used files, and still access the server for the portions of the system that are not on its local disk. This will free more of the space on its local disk for the local file system.

For those systems that support a newer type of NFS remote mount, called a Cached File System, consider its use for the read-only mounting of the shared portions of the UNIX installation. It provides the remote access desired and can greatly reduce the amount of network traffic. It is ideal for these partitions because they are read-only anyway.

If you have a very reliable server, such as a redundant system, consider placing the UNIX OS server on the backbone with multiple LAN connections on it, servicing each of the local LANs. This can greatly reduce the overhead in maintaining the server and keeping it up to the latest release. This is only practical if the server can provide sufficient I/O band width to support all its clients.

Managing Network Traffic

Before you can decide how to install the new system, you need to check on the amount of traffic on the network. Sources of this traffic include the following:

- Traffic from the systems in Department A to its local server for the following:

  Remote file systems, including accessing shared UNIX OS partitions and user files.

  Access to client/server applications hosted on the Department A server.

  Diskless client access to swap, temporary, and spool partitions.

- Traffic between the systems in Department A, including the following:

  Client/server application traffic.

  Remote display updates (a window on one system showing output from a process on a different system).

  Sharing of local file systems that are not on the server.

- Traffic between the systems in Department A and the backbone server, including the following:

  Remote file access to company-wide files.

  Access to client/server applications running on the backbone, such as a master database.

- Traffic between the systems in Department A and those in Department B, including the following:

  Access to files located locally at Department B.

  Access to client/server applications running on the systems in Department B.

  Remote file access to local disks on Department B systems.

The additional traffic generated by the installation of this new system must be compared to the existing traffic on the network. Adding a diskless client on a network segment running at 80% utilization is asking for trouble.

You don't need sophisticated tools to monitor network traffic. Just take one of the workstations and use the tools provided by your vendor to count the packets it sees on the network. A simple approach is to use a tool such as etherfind or snoop to place the EtherNet interface into promiscuous mode, where it listens to all the packets on the network, not just those addressed to itself. Then count the number of packets received by the system over a period of time and their respective length. Most UNIX systems can drive an EtherNet segment up to about 800 KB/second in bursts and over 500 KB/second sustained. If the traffic is anything close to this, consider splitting the segment into two segments to reduce the traffic.

There is a mistake in the silicon of many EtherNet chips, causing them not to be able to reach the numbers described before having excessive collisions. If the netstat -i command is consistently showing a significant number of collisions, say over 1 percent, even though the traffic levels are well below those numbers, you should consider the segment overloaded. You might have several systems on your network with chips with that problem.

When splitting the network into segments, if you can place a server and its systems into each of the split segments, often you can use a less expensive bridge to reduce the traffic on each segment rather than using a router.

Summarizing What You Need to Know Before Starting

In summary, before starting to plan for the actual installation of the new system, you need to determine who is going to use the system. You need to determine how much disk access they will be performing and how much they will contribute to the overall network traffic; whether this system is going to be a client or a server; and whether the network can tolerate another system on this segment before the segment has to be split because of overloading.

Planning for the Installation

You now have to determine on which segment to install this new system, decide what type of user it's for, and decide where to place it. What more do you need to plan for other than where to plug in the power cord and network connection?

This section guides you through a short pre-installation checklist to make the installation process go smoothly. It will have you answer the following questions:

- From where am I going to install?
- Is this to be a diskless, dataless, stand-alone, or server system?
- What is its name?
- What is its address?
- Which packages should be installed?
- How should the disk be partitioned?
- Should you use a network database?

These are some of the questions the system will ask as you install UNIX. Most of the rest have obvious answers, such as what time zone are you in.

From Where Am I Going to Install?

Traditionally one installed a system by placing the medium in a drive and booting from that medium, such as floppy, tape, or CD-ROM. With the advent of networking, things are no longer so simple, but they actually can be a lot more convenient.

You have two choices for installing: locally and remotely. A local installation is the traditional case, where the media is inserted into some drive attached to the computer being installed, and the software is copied onto the system. A remote installation further falls into two types.

You might use the remote systems's CD-ROM or tape drive to read the media because the system you are installing does not have one. But if there is a large number of systems to install you would access an install server, which already has all of the installable files and boot images on its local disks. Since the local disks are faster than CD-ROM or tape, this is faster. It's only worthwhile to set up the install server, however, when you have a lot of systems to install.

Media Distribution Type

With 300 MB of software to install, floppies are no longer practical. UNIX software vendors have switched from floppies to either a tape or CD-ROM as the install media. Currently, different UNIX vendors use different tape formats, some offering more than one. You need to make sure you know which format your vendor is supplying, and that you will have access to a drive capable of reading the data.

If you have a choice, choose the CD-ROM media. It has several advantages over tape. Although it is slower than tape, it is random access. This makes the install process easier, as it is no longer necessary for the install to proceed in the order of the data written on the tape.

Another advantage is that the media is read-only. It is impossible to overwrite it by mistake or by hardware malfunction. In addition, a CD-ROM is much less expensive to produce and holds more than the tape or floppies it replaces. Usually with a CD-ROM there is no need to change media part way through the installation.

If your computer is unable to boot off the tape or CD-ROM, the vendor also supplies what is called a mini-root on floppy. This is a minimal RAM-based system that is loaded off the floppy and is used to read the tape or CD-ROM. Most workstations have boot roms that are capable of booting directly off the tape or CD-ROM. Most PC-based systems do not, and they require boot floppies.

> **CAUTION:** If you need boot floppies, be sure you order the proper boot floppies for your system. Many vendors of System V Releases 3 and 4 provide different boot floppies for systems that use SCSI-based tape drives than for those that use dedicated controllers for the tape drive. Also some provide different floppies for CD-ROM than for tape and for different versions of disk controllers.

> **CAUTION:** Read the release notes carefully. Most PC-based UNIX systems support only a limited set of hardware. Be sure your display adapter card, network card, and disk controller are supported. Check to see if any special device drivers are required and that you have those drivers for your version of the operating system.

If not, before you start the installation be sure to acquire current drivers for those cards from the manufacturer of the cards or from your UNIX vendor. Be sure the driver is specific to the version of UNIX you will be installing.

If the installation procedure does not ask you to install these drivers, be sure to install them before rebooting from the mini-root used to install the system to the operating system just installed. Otherwise the system will not boot.

Using a Local Device or a Remote Device for Installation

Since most UNIX vendors have decided to switch to CD-ROM as the distribution media of choice, most likely you will have a CD-ROM drive somewhere in the network. At this time you have two choices:

■ Unplug the drive from where it is currently and add it to the new system to perform the install. Then you have a local CD-ROM drive and can follow the instructions in the installation notes for using a local CD-ROM drive.

■ Use the networking abilities of UNIX to access the drive remotely from the system on which it currently resides.

Since the network is so much faster than the CD-ROM drive, either choice will work. You just have to be sure that the drive remains available to you for the entire installation process. If someone else is going to need the CD-ROM drive, you will not be able to relinquish it to them until the entire install procedure is complete.

CAUTION: If the system must boot off the CD-ROM drive, it is not always possible to plug any CD-ROM drive into the system. Many UNIX workstation vendors have placed special roms in their CD-ROM drives to modify their behavior to look more like a disk drive during the boot process. When in doubt, it is best to have available a model of that workstation vendor's CD-ROM drive for the installation.

Diskless, Dataless, or Stand-Alone Server System?

Now is the time to decide whether this system is going to be a diskless client of some server, a dataless system, or a stand-alone system or server. You need to make this decision to make sure that the system ends up in the same domain as its server and in the same segment of the network if it's diskless.

In addition you need to make this decision now so you can decide how to partition the disk.

In general, price determines whether a system is totally diskless. If you can afford a disk drive, you should purchase one and make the system a dataless system. Reserve your use of diskless clients times when it is impractical to place a disk locally with the system because of environmental or power concerns; or where access to the system to upgrade the local disk is going to be difficult or impossible. Then it will be necessary to perform all the administration and upgrades on the server system.

You should see the release notes of your system for specifics, but use the following disk space requirements as a guideline:

Diskless—Since there is no local disk, all disk space resides on the server. Each diskless client must mount its root, swap, temp and spool partitions from the server. Expect to allocate the following from the server:

> root: 10–20 MB
> swap: Varies by memory size, but 16–256 MB is the normal range.
> spool: 10–20 MB
> tmp: 10–40 MB

Dataless—Dataless clients use the local disk for each of the partitions listed above for the diskless client.

Stand-alone—If system is for an application user, the same sizes as those for the dataless clients are appropriate.

In addition, a /usr partition will be needed with an additional 100 MB to hold the remainder of the operating system. If X window system is also to be stored locally, it can require up to an additional 70 MB, depending on the number of tools and fonts that are installed. A minimal X installation requires about 30 MB.

If the user is a developer, the /usr partition will need to be about 150–200 MB to hold the compilers, libraries, additional tools, and local tools the user will need.

Server—Server systems generally need the entire operating system installed. Here is a guideline for overall sizes:

> root: 20 MB
> swap: varies by memory size, but 64–512 MB is normal range.
> spool: 20–80 MB
> tmp: 20–80 MB
> usr: 200 MB
> x: 70 MB

Per diskless client: 50–200 MB (more if large swap areas are needed for the client)

In addition, a server may have more than one network interface installed. This is so it can serve multiple segments.

TIP: Consider making one or two systems on the segment servers. Split the remaining systems between those that must stay up regardless of the server and those that are not as critical. Make the critical ones stand-alone and the remainder dataless. The performance improvement gained from placing a small disk (even 200 MB) in a system is worthwhile.

Naming the System

Each UNIX system is given a set of names:

- *Host name*—a short name it is known by locally.
- *UUCP name*—usually the same as the host name. Used for modem-based communications between UNIX systems.
- *Domain name*—a name that identifies which set of systems this system is a part of for electronic mail and routing.
- *NIS domain*—a name that identifies which set of systems this system is grouped with for systems administration purposes. The set of systems share common password and other systems administration files. See Chapter 37, "Networking," for further details on the NIS system.

This chapter deals with the systems host and domain names. Using a UUCP name that is different from the host name is covered in Chapter 43, "UUCP Administration." The NIS Domain is covered in Chapter 37.

Host Name

A host name is typed often, so it should be relatively short. While it can be up to 256 characters long in System V Release 4 systems, no one wants to type a name that long all the time. A short word usually is desired. If this name is to be shared as the UUCP name as well, it should be no longer than 8 characters.

TIP: At any organization, people generally come and go, and when they go, the system they were using gets reassigned. Hardware also gets replaced. It's not a good idea to name a system for its current user or for its current hardware.

These are some poor name choices:

- sun1051—Today it might be a Sun Sparc 10/51. Tomorrow it might be a Dec Alpha or something else. Choose a name that will retain its meaning regardless of the changes in hardware.

- ■ jerry—It was Jerry's system, but who has it now? The name should help identify the system for the user and the administrators. You will be referring to the system by this name in many contexts.

- ■ mis1—Systems migrate, even from department to department. When this system ends up in engineering, calling it mis anything could be confusing.

Instead, consider using some name that allows for a selection of one of a group of names.

These are some popular choices:

- ■ The names of the seven dwarves—This gives the systems some personality, and at least allows for seven. You could expand to use the names of other characters in stories besides Snow White when more names are needed.

- ■ Street names—Be careful, though. If you name the aisles of your cubical system for streets, don't use the same street names for your systems. Moving them around could get confusing.

Don't take this tip too literally. If functional names, such as mis1 or database make sense, use them. It isn't that difficult to retire the old name and change the system's name to a new one in the future.

Domain Name (DNS/Mail)

If you want to uniquely address every UNIX system by name, and you try to use short names for local convenience, you quickly run into the problem bemoaned often on the Internet: "All the good ones are taken." One way around this problem is the same way people resolve it with their own names. You can give systems first, middle, and last names.

One of the results of UNIX and the Internet growing up together is the domain name system. This allows every machine to be uniquely addressed by giving its fully qualified domain name, which is comprised of its host name and its domain name, separated by dots, as in the following:

```
hostname.localdomain.masterdomain.topdomain
```

As an example, the mail gateway at my company, Myxa Corporation, uses this fully qualified domain name:

```
dsinc.hv.myxa.com
```

You read this name from right to left as follows:

`com:` This is the top-level or root domain in the United States for commercial organizations. Other choices include `edu`, for educational institutions; `gov`, for governmental bodies; `net`, for network providers; `org`, for charitable organizations; and `us`, used mostly for individuals. Outside of the United States, the International Standards Organization (ISO) country code is the top-level domain.

`myxa:` This is the chosen domain name for the entire organization. Since the company is connected to the Internet, `myxa.com` had to be unique before it could be assigned.

`hv:` The company is split into more than one office. This level splits the domains logically and distributes the responsibility for maintaining the local host names. This third level of the domain name is optional and is used only by larger organizations to split the administrative responsibility. See Chapter 37 for more details on maintaining a domain name service.

`dsinc:` This is the actual host name of this system.

The system is then referred to as `dsinc` within the local office, `dsinc.hv` within the company, and `dsinc.hv.myxa.com` from outside the company.

If this is an installation of a system into an existing network, you should already have an existing domain name to use. Then you have to choose only a host name. If this is the first system to install in a local group of systems, consider choosing a local domain name as well.

> **TIP:** Why use a local domain name? In networked systems, a central administration group is responsible for assigning and maintaining all host names and their corresponding addresses. When the number of systems gets large, there is too much burden on this one group. It can cause delays while you wait for the administration group to get around to adding your new information to their master files. If they delegate this responsibility for a set of systems to a local group, they only need to add the local domain to their files and then you can add systems and make changes as needed.
>
> See Chapter 37 for more details on administering a local domain.

Only if this is the first system in the organization will you have to choose the remaining levels of the domain name. They should be the same for all systems within the organization.

Choosing Which Packages to Install Locally

When you made the choice of being a server, stand-alone system, dataless client, or diskless client, you made the base choice of what portions of the operating system to install. You can fine-tune this choice if you need to conserve disk space. Sun's Solaris 2.3 gives you a large choice of packages to install. Some of those packages are specific to hardware you may not have installed. You can choose to omit those packages now, and if you change the configuration later, you can always add them to the existing installation.

Sun is not the only vendor that gives choices of packages. System V Release 4.0, which is provided from many vendors, splits the operating system into the major groups of packages:

V4 Runtime System
V4 Software Development
V4 Networking System
V4 X-Windowing System
V4 Real-Time Extensions

You can choose which of these you need to install locally. In addition, each of these is broken down further into individual packages. While every system needs the runtime group of packages, not all individual packages within it are required. The Runtime System is further broken down into the following:

compat	BSD compatibility package
crypt	Security administration utilities
ed	Editing package
face	AT&T Framed Access Command Environment
fmli	AT&T Form and Menu Language Interpreter
lpLP	print service
manbase	Online manual pages, base system
mouse	Mouse driver package
oam	Operations, administration, and maintenance
pci	PC-interface utilities and RS-232 service
pts	Pseudo-tty support
qt	Cartridge tape utilities
rpc	Remote procedure call utilities
termcap	AT&T Termcap Compatibility Package
terminf	Terminal information utilities
xcp	XENIX compatibility package
xl	Archive XL floppy tape utilities

If disk space is not critical, make the installation easy by choosing to install everything for the overall set of packages. If space is critical, you can choose not to install those items that correspond to hardware or options you do not intend to use.

Once you have chosen the packages you intend to install, sum their sizes as specified in the release notes for that version and you will be ready to lay out the disk slices.

Laying Out the Disk Slices

Rather than use an entire disk drive for one file system, which leads to inefficiencies and other problems, UNIX systems have the ability to split a single drive into sections. These sections are called slices, as each is a slice of the disk's capacity.

If your system is based on a PC, the master disk will first be split into partitions, using a program that emulates the MS-DOS fdisk layout. Once the UNIX partition has been allocated, this partition becomes the logical disk drive. This chapter refers to this partition as if it were the entire disk drive. Non–PC-based systems do not have this step and allocate space on the disk drive directly.

Generally a disk can be split into eight subdisks or slices, each of which the operating system treats independently as a logical disk drive. This splitting of the disk is often called partitioning or labeling the disk.

Why split the disk? UNIX can only place one file system per logical disk. It is advantageous to split the files across multiple file systems. You can always buy multiple disk drives, one for each file system, and one for the swap space, but placing six or more disk drives on a system tends to up the cost a bit. Instead, this method of subdividing the disk is used.

Why Multiple File Systems?

Damage control—If the system were to crash due to software error, hardware failure, or power problems, some of the disk blocks might still be in the file system cache and not have been written to disk yet. This causes damage to the file system structure. While the methods used try to reduce this damage, and the `fsck` UNIX utility can repair most damage, spreading the files across multiple file systems reduces the possibility of damage, especially to critical files needed to boot the system. When you split the files across disk slices, these critical files end up on slices that rarely change or are mounted read-only and never change. Their chances of being damaged and preventing you from recovering the remainder of the system are greatly reduced.

Access control—Only a complete slice can be marked as read-only or read-write. If you desire to mount the shared operating system sections as read-only to prevent changes, they have to be on their own slice.

Space management—Files are allocated from a pool of free space on a per-file system basis. If a user allocated a large amount of space, depleting the free space, and the entire system were a single file system, there would be no free space left for critical system files. The entire system would freeze when it ran out of space.

Using separate file systems, especially for user files, allows only that single user, or group of users, to be delayed when a file system becomes full. The system will continue to operate, allowing you to handle the problem.

Performance—The larger the file system, within limits, the larger its tables that have to be managed. As the disk fragments and space become scarce, the further apart the fragments of a file might be placed on the disk. Using multiple smaller partitions reduces the absolute distance and keeps the sizes of the tables manageable. Although the UFS file system does not suffer from table size and fragmentation problems as much as System V file systems, this is still a concern.

Backups—Many of the backup utilities work on a complete file system basis. If the file system is very big, it could take longer than you want to allocate to back up. Multiple smaller backups are easier to handle and recover from.

> **NOTE:** Just because you are doing multiple backups does not necessarily mean you need multiple tapes. UNIX can place more than one backup on a single tape, provided there is space on the tape to hold them.

The following slices are required on all UNIX installations: root and swap.

The recommended additional slices are these: usr, var, opt, home, and tmp.

As you read the sections on each slice, make a map of your disk space and allocate each slice on the map. You will use this map when you enter the disk partitioning information as you install the system.

> **TIP:** For optimum performance, it's best to start each slice on an even cylinder boundary.
>
> This is easy enough to do for non-scsi disks. However, many scsi disks use zone bit recording. This means there is a different number of sectors per cylinder on the inside tracks than on the outside tracks of the disk. This means that the cylinder boundaries are not computable, as they vary track to track.
>
> However, in either case, the disk is normally described to the operating system as a combination of heads, sectors, and tracks. A cylinder boundary occurs at an even combination of heads multiplied by sectors. The operating systems tables work out more efficiently if the partitions occur on what it thinks by your description of the disk is a cylinder boundary.

The *root* Slice

The root slice is mounted at the top of the file system hierarchy. It is mounted automatically as the system boots, and it cannot be unmounted. All other file systems are mounted below the root.

The root needs to be large enough to hold the following:

- The boot information and the bootable UNIX kernel, and a backup copy of the kernel in case the main one gets damaged
- Any local system configuration files, which are typically in the /etc directory
- Any stand-alone programs, such as diagnostics, that might be run instead of the OS

This partition typically runs on between 10 and 20 MB. It is also usually placed on the first slice of the disk, often called slice 0 or the a slice.

> **TIP:** In System V–based UNIX systems the recommended size from the vendor is probably sufficient for this slice. In BSD-based UNIX systems, consider increasing the size of this slice to allow for a few extra kernels. BSD uses prelinked kernels instead of runtime driver loading, and you will need to keep more UNIX kernels around.

The *swap* Slice

The note in the section "For What Purpose" describes how UNIX uses the swap slice. The default rule is that there's twice as much swap space as there is RAM installed on the system. If you have 16 MB of ram, the swap space needs to be a minimum of 32 MB. If you have 256 MB of RAM, the minimum swap is 512 MB.

This is just a starting point. If the users of this system run big applications that use large amounts of data, such as desktop publishing or CAD, this might not be enough swap. If you are unsure as to the swap needs of your users, start with the rule of twice RAM. Monitor the amount of swap space used via the pstat or swap commands. If you did not allocate enough, most UNIX systems support adding additional swap at runtime via the swapon or swap commands.

The *usr* Slice

The usr slice holds the remainder of the UNIX operating system and utilities. It needs to be large enough to hold all the packages you chose to install when you made the list earlier.

If you intend to install local applications or third-party applications in this slice, it needs to be large enough to hold them as well. However, it is generally better, for ease of performing upgrades, if the usr slice contains the operating system and only symbolic links, if necessary, to the applications.

This file system is often mounted read-only to prevent accidental changes.

The *var* Slice

The var slice holds the spool directories used to queue printer files and electronic mail, as well as log files unique to this system. It also holds the /var/tmp directory, which is used for larger temporary files. It is the read-write counterpart to the usr slice. Every system, even a diskless client, needs its own var file system. It cannot be shared with other systems.

> **NOTE:** Although the var file system cannot be shared, subdirectories under it can (for example, /var/mail).
>
> These would be mounted on top of the var file system after it is already mounted.

If you do not print very large files, accept the size the release notes suggest for this slice. If you do print a large number of files or large files, or if your site will be performing a large volume of UUCP traffic, consider increasing the size of this slice to accommodate your needs.

> **TIP:** For print files, a good starting point is adding 10 times the size of the largest print file to the size recommended. Add more if there are a large number of users or multiple printers attached to this system.
>
> For UUCP files, have enough space to hold at least a day's worth of traffic for every site.

The *opt* Slice

In the newer UNIX systems based on System V Release 4 (Solaris 2.x, UnixWare, and so on), many sections of the operating system are considered optional and are no longer installed on the /usr file system. They are now installed into the /opt file system. In addition, they place add-on packages in this file system.

To size this partition, take the suggested size from the release notes, and add to that the size of any add-on packages you plan to install.

> **TIP:** Don't worry too much about getting it right. If you need to install an add-on package later and there is not enough room left in opt, install the package elsewhere and create a symbolic link from where you did install it back into /opt.

The *home* Slice

This is where the user's login directories are placed. Making home its own slice prevents users from hurting anything else if they run this file system out of space.

A good starting point for this slice is 1 MB per application user plus 5 MB per power user and 10 MB per developer you intend to support on this system.

> **TIP:** Don't worry too much about getting it exactly right. If you need more space for a particular user, just move that user's directory to a different file system that does have room and create a symbolic link in /home to point to its new location. The user may never know you moved the directory.

The *tmp* Slice

Large temporary files are placed in /var/tmp but sufficient temporary files are placed in /tmp that you don't want it to run your root file system out of space. If your users are mostly application users, 5–10 MB is sufficient for this slice. If they are power users or developers, 10-20 MB is better. If there are more than 10 users on the system at once, consider doubling the size of this slice.

> **TIP:** The files in the /tmp directory are very short-lived. Use the file system type TMPFS (Tmp file system, a ram based file system) for /tmp if your version of UNIX offers it. It can improve performance by placing this file system in RAM instead of on the disk. Losing the files on each reboot is not a concern, as UNIX clears the /tmp directory on each reboot anyway.

The disk label that contains the disk layout is held in block 0 of the disk. UNIX does not use this block in file systems, so there is no danger of overwriting it if a file system is located as the first slice on a disk. However, if a raw slice is the first slice, the application that uses the slice may overwrite block 0. Doing so will lose the label and make the disk inaccessible.

To prevent this, do the following: Make a file system the first slice (the one that contains block 0 of the disk drive). Skip cylinder 0 in assigning the space on the disk drive. It may waste one cylinder, but you won't lose your data.

Assigning Slices to Disk Drives

If you have more than one disk drive, a second decision you have is on which drive to place the slices. The goal is to balance the disk accesses between all of the drives. If you have two drives, consider the following split:

Drive 1	Drive 2
root	var
swap	opt
usr	home

The remaining slices split over the drives as space allows.

Assigning IP (network) Addresses

If the system has a network connection, it will need to be assigned an IP address. IP addresses are explained in Chapter 37. An IP address is a set of four numbers separated by dots, called a dotted quad. Each network connection has its own IP address. Within a LAN segment, usually the first three octets of the dotted quad will be the same. The fourth must be unique for each interface. The addresses 0 and 255 (all zeros and all ones) are reserved for broadcast addresses. The remaining 254 addresses may be assigned to any system.

> **NOTE:** The IP address is not the EtherNet address. An EtherNet address is a hardware-level address assigned by the manufacturer. It is six octets long (48 bits). The first three represent the manufacturer of the network interface board. The remaining three octets are unique to the system. An IP address is a software level address. Part of the IP protocol, also called ARP or Address Resolution Protocol, is used to match the software IP address with the physical EtherNet address.

If this is your first system, you must decide on the first three octets as well. See Chapter 37 for applying for a network number. The number should be unique within the world and is obtainable at no cost.

If this is not the first system, then any unused value for the fourth octet can be used for this system.

Do You Have the Needed Network Connections?

Now is the time to check that you have a network connection for each network interface. Now is the time to check that you have the proper cables, transceivers (if needed), and connectors.

EtherNet comes in three varieties: thick (10Base5), thin (10Base2), and twisted pair (10BaseT). UNIX Systems come with some combination of three types of EtherNet connections: AUI, BNC, or RJ45. If your system has multiple connector types, they are all for the same network interface, unless you purchased an add-on interface that uses a connector type different from that of the main system. Using the matrix below, you can see which parts you need:

Connector		Network Type		
Type	10Base5	10Base2	10BaseT	
AUI	AUI cable and transceiver	AUI to BNC transceiver	AUI to RJ45 transceiver	
BNC	10Base2 Hub	BNC Tee	10Base2 Hub	
RJ45	10BaseT Hub with AUI port and RJ45 Cable	10BaseT Hub with BNC port and RJ45 Cable	RJ45 Cable and free slot on BaseT Hub	

Using NIS/NIS+

Administering a UNIX system requires dealing with many files, such as the password, group, network, and EtherNet address control files. Having to maintain each one of these files on multiple systems can be time-consuming. Discrepancies in the files can lead to problems logging in to systems or to security issues.

One solution to this problem is the Network Information Service, or NIS. NIS is a network-wide set of databases for the common administrative files. This allows for centralized administration, even by using multiple servers having a redundant system in case the master is down.

When installing a system into an NIS environment, you have to answer the install questions with the name of the NIS domain for this system. This is the name that is placed in the file `/etc/defaultdomain` by the install program.

The NIS domain does not unnecessarily match the mail domain entered earlier. Generally it is for security reasons or to further subdivide the administrative responsibilities when they do not match.

Performing the Installation

By now, if you've been following along, you should have an installation checklist. It should contain the following:

■ The name of the system holding the drive for the installation, and its device name

> **TIP:** Check your release notes—you might have to enter the name of the new system into the root user's `.rhost` file temporarily during the installation or load the CD-ROM and mount the partition prior to running the remote installation.

■ Diskless, dataless, stand-alone, or server system

The name of the server for the new client, if it's a dataless or diskless system, should be on your sheet along with its IP address.

- The name of the host and domain
- The IP address
- The packages to install
- How to partition the disk (This is the map of the disk drive or drives you made earlier.)
- Whether to use a network database (This is the name of the NIS domain, if you intend to run NIS.)

Now you should be all set.

> **CAUTION:** You are about to do things that will change the information on the disks. If this is not a brand new system, be sure you have readable backups in case something goes wrong.

Booting the Installation Media

The first step in installing a UNIX system is to load the mini-root into RAM. UNIX uses the UNIX operating system to perform its installation. It needs a version of UNIX it can run, and to do this the install loader uses RAM to hold a small version of the UNIX file system. When you boot the installation media, it builds a root file system and copies the files it needs to control the installation to this RAM-based file system. This is the reason it takes a while to boot the media.

If the system is PC based, boot floppies are generally provided. Workstation and server systems use the tape or CD-ROM media as a boot device.

Booting from Floppies

If your system is PC based, take the first boot floppy and place it in what MS-DOS would call drive A. Boot the system in the normal manner, by pressing the Ctrl+Alt+Del keys at the same time.

The system will load the boot loader off the first floppy and then use that to create the RAM-based file systems and load the UNIX image into RAM. It will ask for additional floppies as needed and then ask for the install media. Answer tape or CD-ROM, as appropriate, and the system will then load the remainder of the mini-root from the installation media.

Booting Directly from the CD-ROM

Workstations and servers boot from the CD-ROM. They have the commands necessary built directly into the ROM monitor. Entering the command, **b cdrom**, or the command, boot cdrom, is normally sufficient to boot the CD-ROM. Sun's, SGI's, and HP's systems all use this form of boot command. If your system does not boot with this command, refer to the release notes for the exact boot command for your system.

Installing the Master System

Once the mini-root is loaded, you are generally presented with the install options. Some systems leave you at a shell prompt. If this happens, enter install to start the installation procedure.

UNIX contains a set of install procedures that walk you through the installation. They are almost identical to one another in concept, but they are slightly different in implementation. Given the information on the checklist produced as you followed this chapter, answer the questions as presented by the installation screens.

> **TIP:** On Sun systems, to install a system with custom disk layouts or to install any server requires selecting the Custom Install menu option on the opening installation screen. This will walk you through all the questions, setting everything up for you automatically.

Expect it to take over an hour to read all the information off the install media to the local disks if you are installing more than just a dataless client. Each system gives you a progress meter to show you how much it has done and how much further it has to proceed.

> **CAUTION:** If you are installing from a nonstandard disk controller, be sure to select the option to add the custom driver for this controller and provide the floppy with the driver when requested. If you exit install and attempt to reboot without providing this driver, you will be unable to boot the system and you will have to start the installation from the beginning.

> **CAUTION:** If you are installing from a nonstandard tape controller, be sure to select the option to add the custom driver for this controller and provide the floppy with the driver when requested. If you exit install and attempt to reboot without providing this driver, you will be unable to access the tape drive to install additional components and you will have to start the installation from the beginning.

Provided you plan ahead and fill out an installation checklist, installing a UNIX system is a simple and automatic process.

Installing Optional or Additional Packages

Once the system is installed and rebooted, you are running UNIX. Congratulations. Of course, you will still need to perform installations from time to time to add packages and applications. All UNIX packages and most standard applications for System V Release 4 use the `pkgadd` format. Installation of these packages and applications is automatic using the `pkgadd` utility.

Other applications use their own installation format or tar format. Follow the release notes for these applications.

Using *pkgadd* and *pkgrm*

Packages are added to System V Release 4 systems such as Solaris 2 and UnixWare by using the `pkgadd` command. This command automatically installs the software from the release media and updates a database of what is currently installed on the system. Packages are deleted just as easily with the `pkgrm` command.

> **CAUTION:** Many packages must be deleted before being reinstalled. If `pkgadd` is asked to install a package that is already installed, it will attempt to overwrite the existing package. Some packages work with this overwrite and some do not. If the installation is an upgrade to a newer version of a package, it is safer to first remove the old copy with the `pkgrm` program and then install the new one.

> **TIP:** To determine which packages are currently installed UNIX provides the `pkginfo` command. This command has two forms. The first form, when run with no path name as an argument, lists which packages are currently installed. When run as `pkginfo -l`, it will also list when the package was installed, the version currently installed, if any patches installed affect this version, and how much disk space it is currently consuming.
>
> When run with a pathname, `pkginfo` tells you which packages reside on the installation media. Note that the `-l` argument also works in this mode and can tell you how much space each package will take to install.

To run `pkgadd` on the install media, place the media in the drive and enter the command

```
pkgadd -d path-name-to-device
```

`pkgadd` will then prompt you for which packages to install and give you progress messages as it installs the package. Different packages may also ask you questions prior to installation. These questions usually relate to where to install the package and any other installation options.

> **NOTE:** pkgadd also checks to make sure that other packages this new package requires are already installed. It will warn you or not let you install a package if the prerequisites are not already installed.

Using *swmtool*

Sun's Solaris system provides an X application to guide you through running pkgadd. It displays the contents of the CD-ROM and provides point-and-click installation and removal of the entire media or selected packages.

To install new packages using swmtool, click on the Properties button to pop up the menu for where the packages are located. Select the local or remote CD-ROM drive if the installation media is not already mounted. If it is already mounted, select Mounted File System, and then type the pathname of the directory containing the packages.

swmtool then displays the contents of the disk. It can provide details on sizes required and versions on the media. To start the installation, select each of the packages to install and press the Begin Installation button. swmtool runs pkgadd for you. You will still have to answer pkgadd's questions just as if you had run pkgadd by hand.

To remove software with swmtool, just select the Remove button from the top of the screen. Select the packages to remove and press the Begin Removal button. swmtool runs pkgrm for you.

Adding a Diskless Client to a Server

You take two steps to add a diskless client to a server: Add the common files to support any client. Add the specific files for this client. The first needs to be done only if this is the first client of this type and revision of the operating system to be installed.

Installing the Diskless Client Operating System Support Files

Traditionally diskless client support files are installed in the /export file system on the server. With System V Release 4, the common executable files are placed under the /export/exec directory. Each architecture will have its own subdirectory under /export/exec.

Each UNIX vendor that supports diskless clients has an install procedure for loading support files from the installation media for each supported architecture. In Solaris 2, the swmtool edit menu contains the pull-down item Add client software.... This configures the server to support clients of each of the available architecture types.

Adding the Diskless Client

Once the client support is available on the server, the client must be added to the server. Since the client has no disk, all installation occurs on the server. A shell script or window command is run to add the `/export/root/hostname` directory tree and the `/export/swap/hostname` swap file.

Under Solaris 2, this is performed under `admintool`'s host manager. Select the host manager icon from the `admintool` and then select Add Host from the Edit pull-down menu. Select diskless from the Client Type pull-down menu, and enter the host name, IP address, and EtherNet address onto the menu and select the time zone from the pull-down menu. The remainder of the parameters should be correct except for the `swap` size. Adjust that to the proper `swap` size for this client and click on the Add button.

Other UNIX systems provide shell scripts or administrative pull-down menus for adding diskless clients.

Summary

The key to a trouble-free installation of your UNIX system is advance planning, using the guideline in this chapter and the release notes that came with your software. These are the things you should plan:

- The type of system you are installing: server, stand-alone, dataless, or diskless
- Who will act as server for this system, if necessary
- What size and on what disk each slice will be located

  `root`, `usr`, `var`, `home`, and `tmp` file systems

  `swap` slice

- The name and address for this system: host name, domain name, IP address, and NIS domain name, if applicable
- Which packages you are going to install
- From where you are going to install

With the answers to these questions you can answer the UNIX install procedures questions. From there the installation is automatic.

Starting Up and Shutting Down

34

By Chris Negus

Booting the System

Before you can use your computer, you must start up the operating system. Starting the operating system is referred to as booting. When the system has been booted, the devices, applications, and services on your computer are available to be used.

Because UNIX is a powerful multitasking and multiuser operating system, many processes are set in motion when you start it up. First, UNIX runs system initialization processes to do things such as set the system clock from hardware, configure devices, and build a new UNIX kernel (if necessary). Then the system begins running processes associated with the particular initialization state (or `init` state) assigned to your system.

When the UnixWare version of the UNIX system is delivered, the default run state for your system is state 3. This state makes your UNIX system available for multiuser use in a networked environment (including file sharing). What this means is that all file systems are connected (mounted) on your system, daemon processes are started to let users log in, and processes to handle incoming and outgoing networking traffic are started.

You can achieve different levels of activity and access to your system by setting it to boot to other states or by changing system states while your system is running. These states range from the full network/multiuser state (state 3) to single-user/limited access states (states 1 and 2).

This chapter describes the processing that occurs when you start up and shut down your UNIX system. It also describes how you can change your system to different system states while it is running. Examples in this chapter are based on the UnixWare version of UNIX, as implemented on an IBM PC or compatible (that is, Intel 386 technology).

Turning On the Computer

When you turn on a computer that has the UNIX system installed, starting up UNIX is managed by a process called `init`. The `init` process sets many processes in motion, based on the initialization state defined in the `/etc/inittab` file.

> **NOTE:** A computer's hard disk can have several operating systems installed. The description in this system assumes that UNIX is the active operating system configured on your computer. See the description of `fdisk` for information on assigning different operating systems to boot on your computer.

This section describes what happens when you start up the UnixWare 1.1 version of the UNIX system on your personal computer, as it is delivered from Novell, Inc.

The init process starts up and checks the /etc/inittab file. The first thing init does is run processes that are marked in the inittab file as sysinit processes. sysinit processes are those that make sure the system is set up properly.

init finds the following sysinit lines in the /etc/inittab file:

```
cr::sysinit:/sbin/ckroot >/dev/sysmsg 2>&1
ck::sysinit:/sbin/setclk  >/dev/sysmsg 2>&1
mm::sysinit:/etc/conf/bin/idmodreg >/dev/sysmsg 2>&1
ldmd::sysinit:/etc/conf/bin/idmodload >/dev/sysmsg 2>&1
ap::sysinit:/sbin/autopush -f /etc/ap/chan.ap
bchk::sysinit:/sbin/bcheckrc </dev/console >/dev/sysmsg 2>&1
bu::sysinit:/etc/conf/bin/idrebuild reboot </dev/console >/dev/sysmsg 2>&1
ia::sysinit:/sbin/creatiadb </dev/console >/dev/sysmsg 2>&1
```

NOTE: See the description of the inittab file later in this chapter for a complete description of the entries in the inittab file.

Here's a quick rundown of what the system initialization (sysinit) processes do when you start the system:

- ckroot—This reads the mount options for the root file system from the /etc/vfstab file. These options, including the file system type, are needed to make the root file system available (that is, to mount it). ckroot also checks the file system (fsck command) if it determines that there are any problems in the file system. For example, if you turn off the system instead of doing a shutdown, the system sends you the message "Please wait while the system is examined" while it resolves any inconsistencies it finds.

- setclk—This sets the UNIX system clock from the hardware clock.

- idmodreg—This registers the loadable kernel modules listed in the /etc/mod_register file.

- idmodload—This loads the loadable kernel modules listed in the /etc/loadmods file.

- autopush—This configures a list of modules to be automatically pushed on a Streams device when the device is opened. In this case, modules listed in the /etc/ap/chan.ap file are pushed on top of the console monitor device to provide line discipline information.

- bcheckrc—This does several start-up tasks, including setting your system name, mounting /proc (processes) and /dev/fd (floppy disk) devices, and checking and linking additional devices related to floppy disks.

- idrebuild—This checks whether the kernel has to be rebuilt, and if so runs the idbuild command to rebuild it. The kernel needs to be rebuilt after you add devices or change tunable parameters.

- creatiadb—This sets up security tables.

Once system initialization functions are set up, init checks the initdefault entry in the inittab to determine the run level that the system is supposed to start up in. It finds the following initdefault line:

```
is:3:initdefault:
```

This tells init to start up UNIX in run level, or system state, 3. System state 3 is defined as the remote file-sharing state. With that information stored away, init proceeds to run all commands set in the /etc/inittab file that are designated as belonging to run state 3. Here is a list:

```
r2:23:wait:/sbin/rc2 1> /dev/sysmsg 2>&1 </dev/console
r3:3:wait:/sbin/rc3  1> /dev/sysmsg 2>&1 </dev/console
li:23:wait:/usr/bin/ln /dev/systty /dev/syscon >/dev/null 2>&1\
     [cc]sc:234:respawn:/usr/lib/saf/sac -t 300
co:12345:respawn:/usr/lib/saf/ttymon -g -v -p "Console Login: " \
     [cc]-d /dev/console -l console
d2:23:wait:/sbin/dinit 1> /dev/sysmsg 2>&1 </dev/console
co:12345:once:/usr/bin/mapchan -f /usr/lib/mapchan/88591.dk \
     [cc]console
```

The r2 and r3 lines set the most processes in action. The r2 line runs the /etc/rc2 command, which in turn starts up all scripts contained in the /etc/rc2.d directory that begin with the letter *S*. These include the following:

```
S01MOUNTFSYS S02mse      S18setuname   S50merge
S75rpc       S01tzsetclk S05RMTMPFILES S21perf
S55merge     S02PRESERVE S11uname      S27nuc
S69inet      S15mkdtab   S42els        S73snmp
```

You can list these files to see what they do. On the whole, however, the scripts start networking and other add-on features. For example, S27nuc starts NetWare connectivity, S69inet starts TCP/IP, and S50merge starts DOS merge features.

The processes specific to state 3, file-sharing state, are started by the /etc/rc3 command. This command runs all scripts in the /etc/rc3.d directory that begin with the letter *S*. The file-sharing state was originally created to start the remote file sharing (RFS) application. RFS has since been overshadowed by its more popular counterpart network file system (NFS). So the /etc/rc3.d directory is usually empty unless you have purchased the NFS add-on software.

When the system is operational, you will see the login screen or a console login prompt:

```
Console Login:
```

To get an idea of what's happening on a running UNIX system, the following list describes some of the processes that are running. (You can list the active processes by typing `ps -ef` from the shell.)

- ■ `init`—This runs, waiting for changes to the run state that you request with the `init` or `telinit` commands.

- ■ `sac`—This manages the port monitors on your system. Port monitors are processes that listen to ports for login requests or other networking requests.

- ■ `mousemgr`—This handles your mouse activities.

- ■ `in.routed`—This manages your TCP/IP routing tables, keeping your system up-to-date with routes to other systems on the Internet.

- ■ `nfs*`—The NFS software starts up a bunch of processes that run, waiting for requests relating to sharing NFS resources.

- ■ `cron`—This checks spool directories for commands that were set up to run later. It then starts those commands when they are scheduled to run.

- ■ `lpNet`—This handles remote printing requests between your system and other UNIX systems.

- ■ `lpsched`—This manages the printing queue for print requests on your system.

If you have logged and started up the graphical interface, you will see other processes as well. For example, the X process is the X windowing system server, and Desktop Manager (dtm) manages the windows and icons on your desktop.

Booting Multiple Operating Systems (Intel)

If you are running UNIX on a PC, it is possible to have several different operating systems installed on different partitions of your hard disk.

When you install UnixWare, you are allowed to create several partitions and are asked which partitions you want to use for UnixWare and which you want to use for other operating systems. Other operating systems can be DOS, OS/2, or NT. Once you have partitioned the disk and installed the operating systems, you can manage which system you boot from (that is, which is the active partition) with the `fdisk` utility.

Versions of the `fdisk` command are available in DOS, UNIX, and other operating systems. To run `fdisk`, open a shell, type su (followed by the root password, when requested), and type `/usr/sbin/fdisk`. You'll see the following:

```
          Total disk size is 683 cylinders (202.8 MB)

                          Cylinders          Approx
Partition  Status    Type    Start  End Length  %    MB\
    [ic:cc]=========  ======  =========== =====  === ====== === ======
```

```
1                  pre-5.0DOS    0   101   102   15   30.3
2        Active UNIX System    103   681   579   85   171.9

SELECT ONE OF THE FOLLOWING:

    0.    Overwrite system master boot code
    1.    Create a partition
    2.    Change Active (Boot from) partition
    3.    Delete a partition
    4.    Update (Update disk configuration and exit)
    5.    Exit (Exit without updating disk configuration)
Enter Selection:
```

This example shows the partitions for two operating systems (DOS and UnixWare) on a 202.8 MB hard disk. UNIX is the active operating system and consumes 85 percent of the hard disk (171.9 MB). DOS is on the first partition, consuming 15 percent, or 30.3 MB, of the hard disk.

To change the active partition from UNIX to DOS in the example, enter 2, then 1, then 4. The next time you reboot your system, DOS will start.

Understanding System States

The early UNIX systems ran on minicomputers and mainframes. The concept of system states grew from the need to have different levels of activity occurring on the system, depending on whether the system was in full use, undergoing system maintenance, or transitioning between those states.

An administrator could start up a large computing system in single-user mode, with no networking running or terminals logged in (other than the console terminal). In this way, the administrator could debug any problems with the system before being bombarded with requests from the outside world.

Over the years, some system states have become outdated. If you're the only UNIX user on a PC, you will rarely need to use any system states other than those that bring the system up and bring it down.

The following list describes the UNIX system states:

- 0—This is the shutdown state. When you change to state 0, all processes, including the UNIX system itself, are stopped.

- 1 (s or S)—This is the single-user state. Actually, there are three states to change to that are single-user states: 1, s, and S. Put the system in single-user state if you want to keep other users off the system while you do administrative tasks. Differences between 1, s, and S are as follows:

1—All file systems are mounted, all networking is turned off, all terminal processes are turned off (so no other users can log in).

s or S—This is the state the system enters if there is no /etc/inittab file. If you change to this state, your terminal becomes the system console, other terminals are logged off, and all file systems remain mounted. When the system comes up in this state, only the following file systems are mounted: /, /var, /stand, /proc, and /dev/fd.

■ 2—This is the multiuser state. Actually, this state starts all scripts in the /etc/rc2.d directory, which includes networking as well as multiuser processes such as those that allow other users to log in. So, even if you are the only person using your system, you need to come up in a multiuser state (2 or 3) to run networking effectively. (In fact, the graphical user interface won't even run in single-user state.)

■ 3—This is the remote file-sharing state. If NFS is installed, your system automatically advertises local file systems and mounts remote file systems associated with NFS. The reason there is a whole state for file sharing is that one of the developers at AT&T who was given the job of doing the start-up scripts for RFS rewrote the entire way changing system states was done and added the RFS state. This method is still used today (as described in this chapter).

■ 6—This is the reboot state. When you change to init 6, the system shuts down and starts back up.

Other initialization states include the following:

■ 4—An alternate system state. You can add your own state 4 entries to the /etc/inittab file to create your own run state.

■ 5—This is the firmware state. On a PC, this simply does a shutdown and reboot (the same as state 6). Historically, firmware mode was used on the old AT&T 3B2 computers to enter firmware mode to do hardware maintenance tasks.

■ a, b, or c—These are states you can define if you want to start additional processes. These states just start commands without changing the run level.

■ Q or q—These options simply tell init to re-read the /etc/inittab file. Use this if you have made changes to the /etc/inittab file and you want new commands run for the current run level.

You can set initdefault to run levels 1, s, S, 2, or 3. You will almost always set the run level to level 2 or 3 on a small system. Other states are states that you change to on a running system. To change system states, you can use the init command.

Understanding the Initialization Table (*inittab*)

The /etc/inittab file contains the processes that are started when init brings up the system or changes to another state. Some of the entries in inittab are daemons (processes that run continuously in the background) and others, such as the /etc/rc2 entry, are used to start up other processes for particular run states.

Each entry in the inittab file consists of the following four-item, colon-separated field:

idtag:*runstate*:*action*:*process*

The *idtag* is any tag (from one to four characters) that identifies the entry. The *runstate* is the system state in which this entry should be run. You can have several system states assigned to an entry.

The *action* is a keyword that corresponds to one of the following: respawn (if the process goes away, start it again), wait (wait for the process to finish before continuing to the next process), once (run the process once, wait for it to finish, then don't start it again), boot (run the process the first time you go into a multiuser state, without waiting for it to finish), bootwait (run the process the first time you go into a multiuser state, waiting for it to finish before proceeding), and sysinit (run the process when the system first comes up). There is one initdefault action in the inittab file to indicate the state that the system starts in.

The *process* is the command that is actually run when the criteria in the first two fields are met (that is, the correct *runstate* and *action*).

The following is an example of an inittab entry:

```
co:12345:respawn:ttymon -g -v -p "Console Login: " -d \
    [cc]/dev/console -l console
```

Here the entry is tagged co. The entry is run in system states 1, 2, 3, 4, and 5. If the process dies, it is started again (respawn). The actual process runs in the ttymon command (terminal monitor), which gives you the ability to log in from the system console.

Understanding Run State Directories (*rc?.d*)

Applications that have daemon processes (that is, processes that must run continuously for the application to process properly), or that require that something be initialized when the system starts, often have scripts in a run state directory to do these functions. There are different directories for each of the run states you could change to.

The following is a list of the run state directories:

- ■ /etc/rc0.d—Contains start-up scripts relating to the shutdown (0) and reboot (5 and 6) run states.
- ■ /etc/rc1.d—Contains start-up scripts relating to the single-user (1, s, and S) run states.
- ■ /etc/rc2.d—Contains start-up scripts related to multiuser (2 and 3) run states.
- ■ /etc/rc3.d—Contains start-up scripts related to the file-sharing (3) run state.
- ■ /etc/shutdown—Included for backward compatibility for pre-System V, Release 3 systems to include scripts that are run when the system is shut down. This directory is empty unless an application adds a script there.
- ■ /etc/rc.d—Included for backward compatibility for pre-System V, Release 3 systems to include scripts that are run when the system is started. This directory is empty unless an application adds a script there.
- ■ /etc/init.d—Acts as a holding place for all start-up scripts. Scripts are not actually run from this directory, but are linked to their appropriate rc?.d directories. This concept is a bit strange. Read the section "Understanding Startup Scripts" for information on how start-up scripts are set up and run.

Understanding Startup Scripts

A startup script is a command that is run when you start the system, shut down the system, or change to a different run state. If you list a startup script, using cat or pg, you will see that it is a series of shell commands that are run when the script is executed with either a start or stop option.

When an application adds a startup script to UNIX, it adds that script to the /etc/init.d directory. It then links that script to one or more directories to filenames that begin with either the letter *S* (for start) or the letter *K* (for kill).

Startup scripts are run when you go into a new run state. When you enter a run state relating to one of the directories described in the section "Run State Directories," the rc? command runs all startup scripts in that directory that begin with the letters *S* and *K*. It runs the S scripts with the start option and K scripts with the stop option, in the ASCII order.

Now that you are completely confused, look at the example in the next section. It steps you through how a particular startup script, for the mouse manager, is installed, started, and stopped.

Example: The Mouse Startup Script

When you install the UnixWare version of UNIX, a shell script for starting and stopping the process that manages your mouse on the graphical user interface is installed as the `/etc/init.d/mse` file. Also, this file is linked to two other files: `/etc/rc2.d/S02mse` and `/etc/rc0.d/K02mse`.

That script contains the following:

```
case "$1" in

'start')
    /usr/lib/mousemgr &
    ;;

'stop')
    pid='/usr/bin/ps -e ¦ /usr/bin/grep mousemgr ¦\
        [cc]/usr/bin/sed -e 's/^ *//' -e 's/ .*//''
    if [ "${pid}" != "" ]
    then
        /usr/bin/kill ${pid}
    fi
    ;;

*)
    echo "Usage: /etc/init.d/mse { start ¦ stop }"
    ;;
esac
```

When you boot your system, the `init` process checks the `/etc/inittab` file for entries that match the default run state (`initdefault`), which is usually run state 3. It finds the `r2` entry, among others, which runs the `/sbin/rc2` command and which checks all scripts in the `/etc/rc2.d` directory. Next, it runs all files that begin with *K* with the stop option and all that begin with *S* with the start option. So, for example, the `S02mse` script is run as this:

```
S02mse start
```

Notice from the listing of the script that the start option causes the `/usr/lib/mousemgr` command to be run. From this point on, the `mousemgr` runs continuously until you change system states again.

When you shut down the system (that is, change to a shutdown state), `init` goes through the same process for state 0 as it did for state 3. This time it runs the `r0` entry, which runs the `/etc/rc0` command, which check scripts in the `/etc/rc0.d` directory. All the scripts in this directory begin with K, to kill processes that were started in other states. The mouse script, `K02mse`, is run, but this time with the stop option, as follows:

```
K02mse stop
```

As you can see from the script shown above, the stop option finds the running mouse process, determines its process ID, and kills it. After all other startup processes are stopped, the system can shut down.

> **NOTE:** The convention for naming these start-up scripts is a letter (K or S), followed by a number (00 through 99), followed by the name of the script as it exists in the /etc/init.d directory. The number determines the order in which the script is run.

Changing States with *init* or *telinit*

While your UNIX system is running, you can change the system state or the level of activity using the init or the telinit commands. If you are shutting down the system or moving to a lower state (especially one that will kick users off your system) you can use the shutdown command.

The init command is the easiest way of changing system states. To use init, you simply type init followed by a system state letter or number (from a shell in which you have root permission). For example, the command

init 2

could be used to change your system from state 3 to state 2, effectively turning off file-sharing features. You could also change to user configurable states, such as state 4, a, b, or c. Or you can change to q or Q to simply re-read the /etc/inittab file.

The telinit command is simply a link to the init command. The telinit command was created for users who might be afraid to use a command as potentially drastic as the init command to simply re-read the /etc/inittab file. So telinit was recommended for rechecking the /etc/inittab file and running any new commands (telinit Q). In reality, however, you can use init and telinit interchangeably.

Instead of using the init or telinit commands, UnixWare offers more friendly ways to shut down your system.

Shutting Down the System

There are several ways to shut down your UnixWare system: double-clicking the Shutdown icon from the graphical user interface, using shutdown from the command line, or by simply turning off your computer. The merits of each are discussed in the following sections.

Using the Shutdown Icon

If you are using the GUI and you have ownership permissions to do system shutdown, you can stop your system using the Shutdown icon. To use the Shutdown icon, simply double-click on the Shutdown icon in the UnixWare Desktop window. When you see a Shutdown confirmation window, click on Shutdown. The graphical interface closes and the system shuts down.

Using the *shutdown* Command

The shutdown command can be used instead of the init command to move to lower system states, in particular shutdown (0) and reboot (6) states. The init command can be a bit abrupt if you are working with a multiuser system. When you enter init 0, the system simply goes down. The shutdown command lets you warn users and give them a grace period to log off.

The following is an example of the shutdown command (used as the root user from a shell):

```
# cd /
# shutdown -y -g60 -i0
```

The -y option lets you skip the shutdown confirmation question. The -g60 assigns a 60 second grace period to users in which they can log off before the system comes down. The -i0 assigns the init state to state 0 (shutdown state).

Once you run the command, all users logged in to the system are warned about the impending system shutdown. They have the length of the grace period to close whatever work they are doing before the system comes down.

Turning Off the Computer

Because UnixWare uses a hardened file system, vfxs from Veritas, you can turn off your computer without losing data. As a rule, however, it is safer to do an orderly shutdown with either the shutdown command or the Shutdown icon.

Those who have used UNIX systems for years often feel uncomfortable simply turning off their computers with UNIX running. In the old days, the next time you booted your UNIX system after turning it off you would have to wait for a massive file system check to take place. This would often take a half hour or more, occasionally resulting in some data loss.

Even though this author has never lost any data when turning off UnixWare, it does take a little longer the next time the system is booted. On the whole, it is best to close your applications and do an orderly shutdown.

Miscellaneous Start-up and Shutdown Notes

Here are a few tips relating to starting and shutting down your system:

- When you start your Intel-based computer, the computer checks your floppy disk drive before it checks your hard disk to find the operating system. If you have mistakenly left in a floppy disk that is not a bootable floppy, your computer won't boot. If your hard disk is corrupted or damaged, booting from a bootable floppy disk is one way you might be able to salvage your system. Call your UNIX support representative for help.

- Some administrators like to run the `sync` command before running the `init` command to shut down their computers. This takes information that is stored in memory waiting to be written to hard disk and writes it to hard disk.

- If you are ever curious about what your current system state is, run the `who -r` command. This tells you the current and previous run levels.

- You can modify start-up scripts to change their behavior. The most common thing you might do is add a debugging option to a networking start-up script to try to find more information about why a particular feature isn't starting. Be sure, however, that you make a copy of the script before changing it. If you make an error, you could break an entire system feature.

Summary

When you start up UNIX, a complex set of processes is run. These processes initialize the system, connect system resources, and allow access by multiple users and networks.

As a UNIX system administrator, you can change the state of your system to do administrative tasks or to limit access to the system. You can also modify the processes that are run when you change system states.

When you are done using your UNIX system for the moment, UNIX can be shut down in several ways. With the latest releases of UNIX, an orderly shutdown (with the `shutdown` or `init` commands) is no longer necessary. Hardened file systems let you just turn off your computer with little risk of losing data.

File System Administration

35

By Sydney Weinstein

IN THIS CHAPTER

In DOS, the primary division of file storage space is disk drives. These are further broken down into directories. UNIX uses a slightly different system that is also a bit more flexible. The primary division of file storage space is the file system. File systems can be placed anywhere in the directory hierarchy, enabling the tree to be expanded wherever space is needed.

In DOS, a disk drive is divided into partitions, each of which is a logical drive letter. In UNIX, a disk drive is divided into slices, each one of which can be a file system. Both are dividing the disk into logical disks for use by their respective operating systems.

This chapter walks you through adding, administering, checking, and backing up UNIX file systems. From a basic review of where UNIX places things, to how to install, configure, and use disk drives, you will see how UNIX deals with disk devices. The file system section describes how to administer and maintain the files and free space. Finally, I cover protecting your data from destruction from hardware failure, software failure, and pilot error by performing regular backups using the backup tools built into each UNIX system.

How UNIX Uses Disks

UNIX views all disks as a continuous hierarchy starting at /, the root. It doesn't matter whether they are on the same disk drive, of the same file system type, or even on the same computer. What makes this possible is the file system. Each file system is independent of the others and allows UNIX to make them all look the same. Before I delve into creating and administering the disk space, some definitions and introduction are in order.

The Pathname

A UNIX file is addressed by its pathname. This is the collection of directories starting in one of two places:

- From the top of the tree (/), showing each directory from the root to the file, called an absolute pathname

  `/usr/bin/cat`

- From the current directory, going up or down the hierarchy to the file, called a relative pathname

  `bin/cat`

Each element between the pathname delimiters (/) is a directory, and the last element is the item being addressed, which in this case is a file.

Some Definitions

- **File.** A collection of bytes on the disk. Its characteristics are specified by the inode in the file system that describes it. Its name is specified by the directory entries that point to that inode. It has no structure but is just a collection of bytes.

- **Directory.** A file with a special meaning overlaid on top of the collection of bytes. The contents of the file are a list of filenames and inode numbers. These are the files in this directory. Although there is a one-to-one mapping of inode to disk blocks, there can be a many-to-one mapping from directory entry to inode. Thus, the directory contains the list of items in this directory, but those items might also appear in a different directory.

- **Device.** A device is a special type of inode entry. It describes a driver in the UNIX kernel. Using this entry, the system performs the I/O via the device driver. These types of entries are used to access the raw underlying disk drive. The UNIX device driver makes a device pointed to by these entries appear as a stream of bytes, just like any other file.

- **Link (Hard Link).** A link is the name given to a directory entry. It links the directory entry to the inode that describes the actual item (file, device, and so on). This physical linking is a map directly to the inode, and the inode describes space on this file system. Thus, the link can be a file only on this file system. Each file has one or more links. (When a file is removed from a directory, the link count is decremented. When it reaches zero, the inode and the disk space it points to are freed, causing the data to be deleted.) The number of links to a given inode is shown in the `ls -l` output.

I created a directory, t, and made three empty directories underneath it to show how UNIX makes use of links to tie the file system hierarchy together. The empty directories are a, b, and c. Here is an `ls -liR` output of the tree, starting at t:

```
total 40
   23 drwxr-xr-x   5 syd      users    91 Feb 26 10:18 .
    2 drwxrwxrwx   5 root     root    408 Feb 26 10:18 ..
   27 drwxr-xr-x   2 syd      users    37 Feb 26 10:18 a
   31 drwxr-xr-x   2 syd      users    37 Feb 26 10:18 b
   33 drwxr-xr-x   2 syd      users    37 Feb 26 10:18 c
./a:
total 16
   27 drwxr-xr-x   2 syd      users    37 Feb 26 10:18 .
   23 drwxr-xr-x   5 syd      users    91 Feb 26 10:18 ..
./b:
total 16
   31 drwxr-xr-x   2 syd      users    37 Feb 26 10:18 .
   23 drwxr-xr-x   5 syd      users    91 Feb 26 10:18 ..
./c:
total 16
   33 drwxr-xr-x   2 syd      users    37 Feb 26 10:18 .
   23 drwxr-xr-x   5 syd      users    91 Feb 26 10:18 ..
```

The first number on each line is the inode number, followed by the permission mask. The next number is the hard link count. This is the number of times that this inode appears in a directory entry. The last column is the filename (remember, directories are just files with special characteristics). The file . is the current directory, which is pointed to by inode 23. The file .. is the parent of this directory, and for the directory t, it is inode 2, the root of this file system. Notice how in directories a, b, and c, the .. entries are also inode 23. By mapping the name .. to the same inode as the parent directory, UNIX has built the reverse link in the file system. This listing shows four entries with the inode number 23, yet the link count on each is 5. The fifth link is the entry in the root directory for t, this directory itself.

```
23 drwxr-xr-x   5 syd      users      91 Feb 26 10:18 t
```

- **Symlink (Soft Link).** A symlink or symbolic link is a file whose contents are treated as a pathname. This pathname is used whenever the symlink is referenced. Because it is just a pathname (relative or absolute), it can cross file system boundaries. Unlike links, creating a symlink does not require the existence of the file it points to, and removing the symlink does not remove the file. It is merely a pointer to the file to be used whenever this symlink is referenced.

NOTE: Symbolic links were developed in the Berkeley derivatives of UNIX. They are available on any derivative of the Berkeley fast file system, such as ufs file systems. They are not available on the older UNIX s5 type file system.

TIP: Because symbolic links can point anywhere, they are a wonderful tool to remap directories to other file systems when space is a problem, or to make multiple links into the same directory (something UNIX does not allow with hard links because it would mess up the meaning of ..). Just move the files to the new file system, then create a symlink in the old directory pointing to the new location. It will cause a problem, however, in traversing back up the chain using .. unless the shell you use is aware of symlinks and compensates for the problem. The Korn Shell under SVR4 does handle this correctly.

- **Mount Point.** This is the directory entry in the file system hierarchy where the root directory of a different file system is overlaid over the directory entry. UNIX keeps track of mount points and accesses the root directory of the mounted file system instead of the underlying directory. A file system can be mounted at any point in the hierarchy, and any type of file system can be mounted—it doesn't have to be the same type as its parent.

CAUTION: Because the new file system is mounted on top of a directory of its parent, its parent must be mounted first. Also, this hides the underlying directory entry and any contents it had. See the section titled "Mounting File Systems" later in this chapter.

■ **Inode.** This is the building block of the UNIX file system. Each file system contains an array of inodes. They contain a complete description of the directory entry, including the following:

mode	Permission mask and type of file. The bit mask in this field defines whether the file is an ordinary file, directory, device, symlink, or other special type of entry. It also describes the permissions. This is the field that is decoded into the `drwxr-xr-x` string by the `ls` command.
link count	The number of links to this file (the number of directories that contain an entry with this inode number).
user ID	User ID of the owner of the file.
group ID	Group ID of the owner of the file, used to map the group access permissions in `mode`.
size	Number of bytes in the file.
access time	Time (in UNIX time format) that the file was last accessed.
mod time	Time (in UNIX time format) that the file was last modified.
inode time	Time (in UNIX time format) that the inode entry was last modified. This does not include changes to the size or time fields.
block list	A list of the disk block numbers of the first few blocks in the file. Only the first few (10–12, it varies depending on file system type) are kept directly in the inode.
indirect list	A list of the disk block numbers holding the single, double, and triple indirect blocks.

NOTE: A trade-off of size versus speed was made in the design of the original UNIX file system; it was effective and has remained. Most files in UNIX are small. By placing only the first 10–12 block numbers in the inode, the space used by the inode table can be kept small. Yet for normal files that are small (less than 96 KB on `ufs` file systems), all of the block numbers are immediately accessible in the inode. For larger files, a disk block is used to hold a list of block numbers. This is called the single indirect block. Still larger files use a block containing a list of blocks containing the block numbers or a double indirect block. The largest files can use triple indirect blocks. (See Figure 35.1.) The largest file that can be described is a ufs file system with

no indirects	12×8192 = 96 KB or 98,304 bytes
only single	no indirect + 2048×8192 = 16,480 KB or 16,875,520 bytes
only double	single indirect + 2048×2048×8192 = 32,784 MB or 34,376,613,888 bytes
with triple	double indirect + 2048×2048×2048×8192 = 67,141,648 MB or 70,403,120,791,552 bytes (if you could find a disk that large)

FIGURE 35.1.

ufs disk allocation block layout.

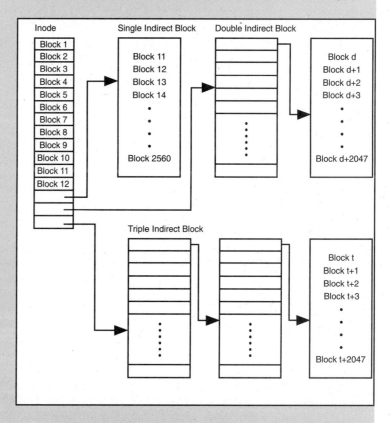

In UNIX, the inode, not the directory entry, contains all the information about the file. The only information in the directory is the filename and its inode number. This indirection from the filename to inode entry is what allows for links.

■ **Super-block.** The controlling block of a file system. It contains the information about the file system and the heads of several lists, including the inode list, the free inode list, and the free block list. This block is cached in memory for all mounted file systems and is periodically also written to the disk.

The System V Release 4 File System Layout

As installed in Chapter 33, the files in a UNIX installation are split into several file systems. One typical layout is shown in Figure 35.2.

FIGURE 35.2.

Typical UNIX System V Release 4 file system layout.

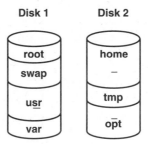

> **TIP:** Note that in Figure 35.2, the file systems have been split across the two disks in an attempt to allow for parallel access to the file systems. Files are accessed from usr and opt quite often. Files are written to var and home frequently. These are split across the two disk drives.

Formatting a Disk

Adding a disk to a UNIX system requires the following three steps:

■ Low level formatting—Writing the sector addresses to the disk
■ Labeling—Writing the slice information to the disk
■ Making file systems—Writing the file system header information to a slice

The first two are covered in this section and making file systems is covered in the next section.

Low-Level Format

Before any operating system can use a disk, it must be initialized. This low-level format writes the head, track, and sector numbers in a sector preamble and a checksum in the postamble to every sector on the disk. At the same time, any sectors that are unusable due to flaws in the disk surface are so marked and, depending on the disk format, an alternate sector might be mapped in place to replace the flawed sector.

Low-level disk formatting is performed differently for the three types of disk drives used by UNIX systems.

Formatting ESDI, MFM, or SMD Drives

UNIX cannot format these drives while it is running. Instead, a stand-alone format program is used. It is usually provided by the manufacturer of the computer or the disk controller board. On PC hardware, this formatter runs either in 'Debug' mode (before the operating system is loaded) or as an MS-DOS utility. Follow the manufacturer's directions for formatting these drives and be sure to have the drive mark the flawed sectors into the flaw map. UNIX will make use of this flaw map when creating its alternate track list.

> **TIP:** All three of these disk types are obsolete and slow. UNIX performance is very dependent on disk access times and transfer rate. It would be best to consider replacing these disks as soon as practical with SCSI disks.

> **CAUTION:** When adding this disk to your UNIX system, UNIX will insist on scanning the disk for flawed sectors, destroying any information on the disk. It needs to do this because UNIX file systems expect the disk to be flawless. The operating system or the disk drive itself is expected to map out bad sectors. For performance reasons, it often flaws entire tracks when any sector is bad. This can cause the actual disk space to be less than the drive indicates.

IDE

These drives are found on PC systems and extend the PC's ISA bus directly into the disk drive. They were designed to reduce the cost of MS-DOS PCs, and they come preformatted from the factory. Most format utilities are unable to low-level format these drives.

> **CAUTION:** Do not attempt to format an IDE drive without a specialized format utility approved for the specific IDE drive you are using. Normally there is no need to low-level format these drives, because they come from the factory preformatted.

SCSI

Most current UNIX systems are designed for SCSI disks. These disks come preformatted from the factory and normally do not need to be reformatted in the field. They also handle bad sector remapping internally. There is no reason to scan these disks for flawed sectors.

If you do need to reformat these disks, you generally have three options:

- Use the UNIX vendor's format utility. Most workstation vendors include such a utility. SCSI disks do their own formatting when sent a format command. Just select the format menu option, and the SCSI disk will do the rest. Because the disk does its own formatting, there is normally no progress indication. Low-level formatting can take from several minutes to an hour or so.

- Use a third-party disk management utility. These applications, such as SpeedStor for UNIX, provide a button on their window to directly format the SCSI disk.

- Use the disk controller's MS-DOS utility. For PCs, where most UNIX vendors have not provided a utility to format the disk, boot MS-DOS and use the disk controller vendor's format utility to format the disk.

> **TIP:** Unlike MFM, ESDI, and SMD disks, where it matters what controller did the formatting, SCSI disks can be formatted on any system. If you don't want to take down the UNIX system for an hour or more to format the disk, use some other system or PC to do the format. Then just add the disk to the SCSI chain on the UNIX system.

> **CAUTION:** Unless your disk enclosure came with a Hot Swap tray, do not plug it in while power is applied. SCSI uses a fuse on the terminator power line, and plugging and unplugging the cable while the system and drives are powered up can blow this fuse, making the controller, and thus the computer system, unusable until it is repaired.

Dealing with Flawed Sectors

As I mentioned, UNIX expects the disks to be flawless. However, this is rarely true. It is too expensive to build large disks with no flaws. By allowing for a relatively small number of flaws, the price of drives can be much lower. UNIX can deal with flawed sectors in several ways:

- Alternate sectors per track. In this scheme, one or two sectors per track are reserved for use in remapping flawed sectors. If a sector is flawed, its sector ID is instead written to the mapped sector. This reduces the overall storage capacity of the drive by some fixed percentage, to allow for flaws. This method has a problem if the track has more than the reserved number of bad sectors. This method is used mostly on SMD disks.

■ Alternate tracks. In this scheme, several tracks are set aside, and whenever a track has a flawed sector, the operating system substitutes one of these tracks for the flawed track. Again, the storage space on all of the alternate tracks is lost. This method has a problem in that a single flaw wastes an entire track.

■ Letting the disk controller map out bad blocks. In this scheme, the disk controller handles remapping the blocks, and the disk appears flawless. This is the method used by SCSI disks, where the disk controller is actually on the disk itself and the controller in the computer is really a SCSI bus controller.

Factory Flaw Map

In either of the first two cases, the factory performs tests on the disk and writes to a special location on the disk the list of sectors found to be flawed or weak. This is referred to as the factory flaw map. Every sector on this map should be entered as flawed, even if it passes the UNIX bad sector test. This is because some of them might be weak and intermittently change over time. SCSI disks automatically access the factory flaw map when they perform their internal format. For non-SCSI disks, you will either access the factory flaw map with the formatting utility or enter it by hand from a table that is either attached to the top of the drive or enclosed with it when it is shipped.

Newly Developed Flaws After Formatting

Disk sectors can also go bad for several reasons after formatting. Sometimes there is a hardware problem and the formatting information for that sector is ruined. Other times the sector was weak to begin with or gets physically damaged. Either way, the disk is no longer flawless. This causes a problem because UNIX expects flawless disks.

You will see this problem when UNIX reports to the console log that it had an Unrecoverable Read or Unrecoverable Write error on a disk block. A warning about an upcoming problem would be a set of recoverable errors. You will need to map this block number to an absolute disk block. UNIX reports the block number, starting with block 0 at the beginning of each logical device. To convert the block number to absolute, you need to add the starting block number to the number reported in the log. To perform this conversion, you must meet the following requirements:

1. logical disk starting sector = starting cylinder of the logical slice × number of heads × number of sectors/track

2. logical disk starting block = logical disk starting sector / number of sectors per block

3. absolute block = logical disk starting block + reported block number from error message

You will then need to repair or map the flawed sector.

> **CAUTION:** Most repair methods will destroy the data on the block. In addition, the flaw makes the file under the block damaged. Either way, recovery of that file will be necessary. However, if you make a mistake, you could damage the data on the entire disk. Therefore, always perform and verify a backup before attempting to repair a disk block.

Non-SCSI Disks

To repair a formatting problem, if your format utility allows it, just reformat the sectors that were damaged. Perform a nondestructive scan for unflawed defective sectors and re-format only those sectors.

If your format utility does not support repairing a single sector, you can flaw the sector, causing it to remap. Most formatting utilities provide an option to perform this automatically on the nondestructive scan.

Lastly, you can reformat the entire disk. Of course, this will lose all the data on the disk. You will have to re-install UNIX or restore from backup after this kind of repair.

SCSI Disks

Older SCSI disks required reformatting to add flaws. Newer disks fall into two categories:

- Automatic repair: Most newer SCSI disks automatically detect the problem and remap the sector on the fly. These generally do not even report a problem.
- Manual Repair: There is a SCSI command to ask the disk to repair the sector. This command is activated by the vendor's disk utility.

Your last resort is to reformat the entire disk. Of course, this will lose all the data on the disk. You will have to re-install UNIX or restore from backup after this kind of repair.

Labeling the Disk

Once the disk is formatted, it needs to have a special block, called the label, written to it. This block describes the geometry of the disk (heads, tracks, sectors) and how to split the disk into multiple logical disks (virtual table of contents).

On UNIX, it is often convenient to use multiple file systems. These provide protection from overruns and changes and can increase performance. However, it is expensive to place each file system on its own disk drive. Some are too small to warrant a drive, and requiring eight or ten disk drives would be too expensive. UNIX works around this by splitting the disk into logical disks. The label records how the disk is split.

PC Partitions Versus UNIX Slices

On a PC-based system, to be compatible with DOS, disks 0 and 1 are first labeled with the DOS `fdisk` partition table. The UNIX partition is marked NON-DOS and active. The `fdisk` partition table can be written by the DOS utility `fdisk`, by the disk controller vendor's formatting utility, or during the UNIX disk add sequence (by the UNIX command `fdisk`).

> **TIP:** Because PCs often require DOS programs to format disks and use the DOS utility to access the ESDI configuration utility, placing a small DOS partition on the hard disk is very useful. In addition, most UNIX systems let you boot from that DOS partition by typing the command DOS during the boot cycle.

The UNIX label is not the same thing as the DOS `fdisk` partition table. Instead, it is written to the first block of the UNIX partition along with the UNIX boot block.

On non-PC systems, the label is written directly to the first block of the disk along with the UNIX boot block.

UNIX Slices

The virtual table of contents in the label is used to split the disk into 8 or 16 logical disks. (Some UNIX vendors allow for 8, some for 16—you don't make the choice yourself.) Once the system boots, each of these logical disks looks like a complete disk to UNIX. By convention, one of the slices is used to refer to the entire physical disk drive, and the remaining slices are left for you to configure.

Configuring the Slices

When you installed the system (see Chapter 33), you were prompted to enter the configuration information for each slice. When adding a disk, you will have to do the same thing. SVR4 will walk you through this using the `adddisk` option of the System Administrator shell (sysadm). Other systems require you to run a command to define the virtual table of contents (`format` on Solaris or SunOS, `disksetup` on Unixware).

Adding a Disk Using the Solaris *format* Command

By convention, disk drives on Solaris are set at SCSI target addresses 0–3. Targets 4 and 5 are for tape drives, and target 6 is for the CD-ROM drive. Configure the disk to an unused SCSI, target it, and add it to the SCSI chain. Then reboot the system. Once booted, log in and become root. Then run the format command and select the new disk from the list of available disks, as follows:

```
# format
Searching for disks...done


AVAILABLE DISK SELECTIONS:
       0. c0t1d0 <SUN1.05 cyl 2036 alt 2 hd 14 sec 72>
/iommu@f,e0000000/sbus@f,e0001000/espdma@f,400000/esp@f,800000/sd@1,0
       1. c0t2d0 <DEC DSP5350 cyl 2343 alt 2 hd 25 sec 119>
/iommu@f,e0000000/sbus@f,e0001000/espdma@f,400000/esp@f,800000/sd@2,0
       2. c0t3d0 <SUN1.05 cyl 2036 alt 2 hd 14 sec 72>
/iommu@f,e0000000/sbus@f,e0001000/espdma@f,400000/esp@f,800000/sd@3,0
Specify disk (enter its number): 0
selecting c0t1d0
[disk formatted]


FORMAT MENU:
          disk        - select a disk
          type        - select (define) a disk type
          partition   - select (define) a partition table
          current     - describe the current disk
          format      - format and analyze the disk
          repair      - repair a defective sector
          label       - write label to the disk
          analyze     - surface analysis
          defect      - defect list management
          backup      - search for backup labels
          verify      - read and display labels
          save        - save new disk/partition definitions
          inquiry     - show vendor, product and revision
          volname     - set 8-character volume name
          quit
```

If the disk is already labeled, its label type will be show on the selection list. Otherwise, the disk will be shown with the type unknown.

```
format> type

AVAILABLE DRIVE TYPES:
        0. Auto configure
        1. Quantum ProDrive 80S
        2. Quantum ProDrive 105S
        3. CDC Wren IV 94171-344
        . . .
       16. other
Specify disk type (enter its number)[12]: 16
Enter number of data cylinders: 2034
```

The number of data cylinders is set to the number of cylinders minus the number of alternate cylinders for bad block mapping. The default number of cylinders for bad block mapping in Solaris is 2, so set this to the number of cylinders reported by the drive minus 2 cylinders.

> **TIP:** Many SCSI drives use a variable number of sectors per cylinder. In this case, map the drive to provide an even number of heads and sectors per track. The allocation of data to cylinders works best if a cylinder is an integral number of disk blocks. Try to make `sectors` * `heads` a multiple of 16 (for 8 KB file systems). Then just divide the number of blocks by this product to get the number of cylinders. However, most disk drive vendors can provide you with a Sun `format.dat` entry for your drive. This will have all of these parameters already listed for you.

```
Enter number of alternate cylinders[2]:
Enter number of physical cylinders[2036]:
Enter number of heads: 14
Enter physical number of heads[default]:
Enter number of data sectors/track: 72
Enter number of physical sectors/track[default]:
Enter rpm of drive[3600]:
Enter format time[default]:
Enter cylinder skew[default]:
Enter track skew[default]:
Enter tracks per zone[default]:
Enter alternate tracks[default]:
Enter alternate sectors[default]:
Enter cache control[default]:
Enter prefetch threshold[default]:
Enter minimum prefetch[default]:
Enter maximum prefetch[default]:
Enter disk type name (remember quotes): "New Disk Type"
```

Assign the drive a name that matches the manufacturer and model of the drive. Use the other drive names shown in the selection list as examples. It is best to take the default values for the SCSI parameters—the system will fetch them from the SCSI pages in the drive.

Next you have to define the slices (partitions). This is performed from the partition menu, as follows:

```
format>  par

PARTITION MENU:
        0      - change '0' partition
        1      - change '1' partition
        2      - change '2' partition
        3      - change '3' partition
        4      - change '4' partition
        5      - change '5' partition
        6      - change '6' partition
        7      - change '7' partition
        select - select a predefined table
        modify - modify a predefined partition table
        name   - name the current table
        print  - display the current table
        label  - write partition map and label to the disk
        quit
```

Partition 2 is the Sun convention for the entire disk. The remaining partitions on a non-boot disk can be used for any section of the disk.

```
partition> 0
Part      Tag     Flag    Cylinders       Size       Blocks
0    unassigned   wm      0               0          (0/0/0)

Enter partition id tag[unassigned]: ?
Expecting one of the following: (abbreviations ok):
        unassigned    boot           root           swap
        usr           backup         var            home
```

If you are unsure of an answer, you can type ?, and the system will prompt you for the choices. The types of partition IDs are as follows:

unassigned	This partition entry will not be used; the starting cylinder and size should be 0
boot	Stand-alone boot images
backup	The entire disk, used to back up the disk in image format
root	The root file system
swap	Swap partition
var	System partition for local data
usr	System partition for system files
home	Any partition for user files

```
Enter partition id tag[unassigned]: home
Enter partition permission flags[wm]: ?
Expecting one of the following: (abbreviations ok):
    wm    - read-write, mountable
    wu    - read-write, unmountable
    rm    - read-only, mountable
    ru    - read-only, unmountable
```

Mountable partitions hold file systems; unmountable ones are for raw data, such as databases.

```
Enter partition permission flags[wm]:
Enter new starting cyl[0]:
```

Although partitions can sometimes overlap, if they are to be used at the same time, they cannot overlap. Normally, set the starting cylinder for each new partition to the starting cylinder + the number of cylinders in the prior partition.

```
Enter partition size[0b, 0c, 0.00mb]: ?
Expecting up to 2052288 blocks, 2036 cylinders, or 1002.09 megabytes
Enter partition size[0b, 0c, 0.00mb]: 1024c
```

Repeat the prior step until all the partitions are completed. Then use the p (print) command to check that it is correct. No partitions should overlap, except where you intend to use one or the other of them. Of course, partition 2, being the entire disk, will overlap everything.

When you are satisfied that the information is correct, label the disk

```
partition> label
```

and quit the format program.

Adding a Disk Using the Unixware *disksetup* Command

Configure the disk to an unused SCSI target that is higher than the target ID of the boot disk and add it to the SCSI chain. Then reboot the system. Unixware will detect the new device on boot and automatically create all the device entries. Once booted, log in and become root. Then run the `fdisk` command to add a partition table to the new disk drive. The argument to `fdisk` is the raw device entry for slice 0 on the disk. This is determined by taking the string `/dev/rdsk/` and entering the controller and target numbers as `cNtM`. Slice 0 is always `d0s0`.

```
# fdisk /dev/rdsk/c0t1d0s0
The recommended default partitioning for your disk is:

    a 100% "UNIX System" partition.

To select this, please type "y".  To partition your disk differently,
type "n" and the "fdisk" program will let you select other partitions. y
```

Unless you intend to place a DOS partition onto the drive, answer yes and let Unixware default the entire disk to UNIX. Then run `disksetup`, which takes the same argument as `fdisk`.

```
# disksetup -I /dev/rdsk/c0t1d0s0
Surface analysis of your disk is recommended
but not required.
Do you wish to skip surface analysis? (y/n) y
```

> **TIP:** If the disk is a SCSI disk that handles bad block mapping itself, you can safely skip the surface analysis. For ESDI, MFM, and SMD disks, always run the surface analysis.

```
You will now be queried on the setup of your disk. After you
have determined which slices will be created, you will be
queried to designate the sizes of the various slices.

How many slices/filesystems do you want created on the disk (1 - 13)? 2
```

Unixware supports 16 slices per disk. However, it reserves three of them for its own use to hold the boot track, the bad track map, and the alternate sector tracks.

```
Please enter the absolute pathname (e.g., /usr3) for
slice/filesystem 1 (1 - 32 chars)? /opt
```

This is the mount point for the file system. Non-file-system partitions can have an identifier entered here to remind you of the usage of this partition, because it won't be used in a mount command.

```
Enter the filesystem type for this slice (vxfs,ufs,s5,sfs),
type 'na' if no filesystem is needed, or press
<ENTER> to use the default (vxfs):

Specify the block size from the following list
(1024, 2048, 4096, 8192), or press <ENTER> to use the first one:

Should /opt be automatically mounted during a reboot?
Type "no" to override auto-mount or press enter to enable the option:

Please enter the absolute pathname (e.g., /usr3) for
slice/filesystem 2 (1 - 32 chars)? /home
```

> **CAUTION:** Be sure to save any files at the new mount point before running the disksetup command. Remove those files so there are no files or directories in the mount directory. The mount will hide any files in the parent file system at and below the mount point. After the disksetup command is completed, restore the saved files onto the new disk partition.

```
Enter the filesystem type for this slice (vxfs,ufs,s5,sfs),
type 'na' if no filesystem is needed, or press
<ENTER> to use the default (vxfs):

Specify the block size from the following list
(1024, 2048, 4096, 8192), or press <ENTER> to use the first one:

Should /home be automatically mounted during a reboot?
Type "no" to override auto-mount or press enter to enable the option:

You will now specify the size in cylinders of each slice.
(One megabyte of disk space is approximately 1 cylinder.)
How many cylinders would you like for /opt (0 - 638)?
Hit <ENTER> for 0 cylinders: 320

How many cylinders would you like for /home (0 - 318)?
Hit <ENTER> for 0 cylinders: 318

You have specified the following disk configuration:
A /opt filesystem with 320 cylinders (320.0 MB)
A /home filesystem with 318 cylinders (318.0 MB)

Is this allocation acceptable to you (y/n)? y

Filesystems will now be created on the needed slices

Creating the /opt filesystem on /dev/rdsk/c0t1d0s1
Allocated approximately 81888 inodes for this file system.
Specify a new value or press <Enter> to use the default:
```

```
WARNING: This file system will be able to support more than 65,536 files. Some older
applications (written for UNIX System V Release 3.2 or before) may not work correctly on
such a file system, even if fewer than 65,536 files are actually present. If you wish to
run such applications (without recompiling them), you should restrict the maximum number
of files that may be created to fewer than 65,536.
```

> **TIP:** In System V Release 4, the inode number was increased from a 16-bit to a 32-bit field. If the pre-4.0 application performs a stat call, it might not be capable of understanding the inode number that is returned. This is a problem for only a small number of applications. Normally you can safely ignore this message and allow the increased number of inodes.

```
Your choices are:

1. Restrict this file system to fewer than 65,536 files.
2. Allow this file system to contain more than 65,536 files
   (not compatible with some older applications).


Press '1' or '2' followed by 'ENTER': 2

Creating the /home filesystem on /dev/rdsk/c0t1d0s2
Allocated approximately 81376 inodes for this file system.
Specify a new value or press <Enter> to use the default:

WARNING: This file system will be able to support more than 65,536 files. Some older
applications (written for UNIX System V Release 3.2 or before) may not work correctly on
such a file system, even if fewer than 65,536 files are actually present. If you wish to
run such applications (without recompiling them), you should restrict the maximum number
of files that may be created to fewer than 65,536.

Your choices are:

1. Restrict this file system to fewer than 65,536 files.
2. Allow this file system to contain more than 65,536 files
   (not compatible with some older applications).


Press '1' or '2' followed by 'ENTER': 1
```

Other systems are similar to either the Solaris or Unixware examples.

Partition Uses

Partitions can be used for file systems or as raw data areas. Uses of raw data areas include the following:

- **Swap space.** Swap space can be split across several drives. This is normally done if the system grows and RAM is added, making more swap space necessary.

- **Backup staging area.** Perform your backups to disk and then copy them to tape at high speed after they complete. Then the backup is also available online for immediate access.

■ **Database devices.** Many UNIX databases perform faster and more reliably if
they do not have to use the UNIX file system cache.

> **CAUTION:** The label for a disk is stored in block 0. UNIX file systems skip block 0,
> reserving it for the boot block and label. If you create a non-file-system slice at the
> front of a disk, do not include block 0 in the slice. This will prevent the raw slice
> from overwriting the label and losing the partition layout of the disk.

Preparing a File System

Once the disk is partitioned and labeled with its slices, you are ready to make a file system. The Unixware `disksetup` utility combined this with the labeling step, but it allowed
only the default values for most of the parameters, allowing you a choice only of file system type and number of inodes. In addition, it does not help you build a file system after
the disk is already labeled. For that you still have to use the traditional methods of building a file system.

UNIX supports several file system types, and each of them has several tuning options. The
steps in preparing a file system follow:

1. Choose the type of file system.
2. Select the proper cluster size, block size, and number of inodes.
3. Use `mkfs` or `newfs` to build the file system.

Choosing a File System Type

Of the many types of file systems supported under UNIX, the first three listed here are
normally used:

■ `s5`   The older System V file system. A low overhead file system useful for
removable media.

■ `ufs`   The new name for the Berkeley Fast File System.

■ `vxfs`   The Veritas Extent-Based File System.

■ `pcfs`   MS-DOS FAT-based File System. Used to access DOS floppies and hard
disk partitions. Although this file system type is compatible with DOS, it is not as
robust as the UNIX formats and should be used only for exchange media with
DOS systems.

■ `hsfs`   High Sierra File System. Used by ISO-9660 CD-ROMs. Often used with
the Rock Ridge extensions to map UNIX filenaming conventions to the ISO-
9660 standard layout.

■ `cfs` Cached File System. A local storage area for caching an NFS file system. See Chapter 37 for further information on Network File Systems.

■ `bfs` A very simplistic file system used to hold stand-alone boot images. It supports only contiguous files and is not intended for use beyond the system boot images.

■ `tmpfs` A RAM-based file system used for the `/tmp` directory. It shares paging space with the swap partition. It is available on only a small number of UNIX systems.

s5—The System V File System

Before System V Release 4 adopted the `ufs` file system, this was the de facto standard for UNIX. It is a low overhead file system that supports only 14-character filenames and a restricted number of inodes (65536). In addition, it is prone to fragmentation, which can slow down access to the disk. It is currently used when sharing removable media between older systems and current ones is desired, and for floppies where the overhead of `ufs` wastes too much space. Except for backward compatibility uses, it should be limited to file systems of 2 MB or less.

ufs—The UNIX File System (Formerly the Berkeley Fast File System)

This file system is based on cylinder groups. It groups files together to reduce access times and reduce fragmentation. To achieve this, it extracts a 10–20 percent space overhead on the drive. It supports long filenames and is not restricted as to the number of inodes. This is the default file system type on Solaris. The `ufs` file system is the only one that supports disk quotas, restricting the amount of disk space a user can use.

vxfs—The Veritas Extent-Based File System

`s5` and `ufs` file systems rely on the full structural verification check in the `fsck` utility to recover from system failures. This takes several minutes per disk after a system crash. Normally not much is lost, usually just what was still in the file system cache in RAM, but the delay on boot can be large. On a file server it can add over an hour to the boot time.

The `vxfs` file system provides recovery in seconds after a system failure by using a tracking feature called intent logging. The `fsck` utility scans this log and needs to check only those intents that were not yet completed. In addition, the `vxfs` uses extent-based allocation to further reduce fragmentation.

TIP: If the `vxfs` file system type is available, it is the file system type of choice except for some special conditions. Use a `ufs` file system in the following circumstances:

The file system is going to consist of many small short-lived files.

You are going to have a set of files that will be growing, causing many extents to be needed.

You need to enforce quotas.

The file system is static and read-only.

Use an s5 file system in the following circumstances:

Backward compatibility is required.

The removable media is small and the overhead of vxfs and ufs use too much of the available space.

Choosing File System Parameters

Most of the time the default parameters chosen by disksetup or newfs are sufficient. This section will explain the meaning of these parameters in case you ever have to tune them. The most common ones to tune are

- ■ Number of inodes
- ■ Number of cylinders per group (ufs only)

Number of Inodes

Each file takes one inode. Each inode also takes space: 128 bytes. There is a trade-off between the number of inodes and the size of the partition. If your average file is many megabytes long, the default of 1 inode per 4 KB will generate many more inodes than needed, wasting space on the file system. On the other hand, if the partition is full of small files, such as a USENET Network News partition, you might run out of inodes before you run out of space. If you know how many files to expect, you can tune this parameter to wring more space out of the slice.

Block Size

For ufs file systems, this should be the same as the page size of the memory management system: either 4 KB or 8 KB. There is little reason to change this. However, if a disk will be moved between systems with 4 KB and 8 KB page sizes, it is best to use 4 KB for the partition. The larger the block size, the large the amount of data per I/O. However, small files will also need more fragmentation space.

For s5 file systems, this is both the I/O block size and the file allocation increment. If the media is small, consider making this 512 bytes to squeeze as much as you can on the disk. The default value is tuned more toward performance at 2 KB.

Expected Fragmentation/Fragment Size

On ufs file systems, the last block of the file is usually not full. Rather than wasting 4 KB or 8 KB for the last block, it places multiple fragments of files into one block. If you have a large number of very small files, make this parameter small to avoid wasting so much space. It defaults to 1 KB but can be set as low as 512 bytes. The default of 1 KB is sufficient in almost all cases.

Cylinder Size

In ufs file systems, files are grouped together into cylinder groups to reduce seeks. A cylinder group consists of 1 to 32 cylinders. If you set it to 1 cylinder, the file systems do very little seeking while reading a single file. The trade-off is space overhead. Each cylinder group has a set of structures including a backup copy of the super-block in case the main one gets damaged. Increasing the number of cylinders reduces overhead but also increases seeks. It is the classic trade-off of space versus performance. The default of 16 is normally adequate. It is usually changed only to wring the last bit of space out of a file system.

Rotational Delay

To optimize disk performance, the system tries to slip the sector usage from cylinder to cylinder to compensate for the track-to-track seek time of the disk. By starting each cylinder on a different sector number, it can try to avoid a complete rotation after a seek to an adjacent track. On modern SCSI disks, there is little or no correlation between block number and the actual layout of the disk. This is due to using a variable number of sectors per track to increase the storage capacity of the drive. For SCSI disks, this parameter should be 0. For ESDI, MFM, and SMD disks, vary this parameter while writing a large file to try to achieve the optimum performance from the drive.

Making File Systems with *newfs*

So you have decided on an appropriate file system type for the slice and have determined approximately what order of magnitude of inodes will be required. Now it is time to actually make the file systems. This task is controlled by the newfs utility on Solaris. newfs uses the information in the label to choose appropriate defaults for the file system.

> **TIP:** Use the -Nv option of newfs to display what it is going to do first. Then you can tune the parameters. Once you like the results, just edit the command line and delete the N flag, and newfs will make the file system, showing you what it did.

```
# newfs -Nv /dev/rdsk/c0t3d0s7
/dev/rdsk/c0t3d0s7:
```

newfs reports the name of the partition you passed to it and its size from the label. It then passes the arguments to `mkfs`. Because it is computing all of the arguments, it passes them as a direct vector in a compact format. `mkfs` does allow a simpler argument format if you have to run it yourself.

```
mkfs -F ufs -o N /dev/rdsk/c0t3d0s7 228816 72 14 8192 1024 16 10 90 2048 t 0 -1 8 -1
228816 sectors in 227 cylinders of 14 tracks, 72 sectors
    111.7MB in 15 cyl groups (16 c/g, 7.88MB/g, 3776 i/g)
super-block backups (for fsck -F ufs -o b=#) at:
 32, 16240, 32448, 48656, 64864, 81072, 97280, 113488, 129696,
 145904, 162112, 178320, 194528, 210736, 226944,
```

See the next section on `mkfs` for the meaning of the output from `mkfs`.

> **CAUTION:** Keep a hard copy of the output from the `newfs` command in a safe place. One of the times you run it with the -N flag, redirect the output to the printer. You will need the information if you ever have a disk failure or severe system crash where you need to use the alternate super-block list for recovery. In addition, you will have a record of the parameters you used if you decide to rebuild the file system later to tune the number of inodes.

> **TIP:** To tune the number of inodes, you cannot directly enter the number but must vary the number of bytes per inode using the -i parameter. The default value is 2048. This is a good value for file systems with many small files and a few big ones. If the file system has a large number of symbolic links or very small files, you might want to drop this a bit. If it has mostly larger files, increase it.

Making File Systems with *mkfs*

Unixware does not use the `newfs` command; it was a Berkeley-derived command. It requires you to directly invoke `mkfs`. This isn't as bad as it seems because most of the parameters shown in the prior section on `newfs` would have been computed by default by `mkfs` anyway.

Making *ufs* File Systems

The only required options to `mkfs` are the file system type, character special device name, and the size in sectors of the file system to be built. The remaining options will all default. However, these defaults do not come from the label. Running the same partition through `mkfs` with default values yields the following:

```
# mkfs -F ufs -o N /dev/rdsk/c0t3d0s7 228816
Warning: 48 sector(s) in last cylinder unallocated
/dev/rdsk/c0t3d0s7:
228816 sectors in 447 cylinders of 16 tracks, 32 sectors
    111.7MB in 28 cyl groups (16 c/g, 4.00MB/g, 1920 i/g)
```

Notice that it chose the default values of 16 tracks per cylinder (heads) and 32 sectors per track. To make the layout optimum for the disk, use the parameters `nsect` and `ntrack`.

```
# mkfs -F ufs -o N,nsect=72,ntrack=14 /dev/rdsk/c0t3d0s7 228816
/dev/rdsk/c0t3d0s7:
228816 sectors in 227 cylinders of 14 tracks, 72 sectors
    111.7MB in 15 cyl groups (16 c/g, 7.88MB/g, 3776 i/g)
super-block backups (for fsck -F ufs -o b=#) at:
 32, 16240, 32448, 48656, 64864, 81072, 97280, 113488, 129696,
 145904, 162112, 178320, 194528, 210736, 226944,
```

This produces the same output as the `newfs` command.

> **CAUTION:** As mentioned earlier under `newfs`, keep a hard copy of the output from the `mkfs` command in a safe place. One of the times you run it with the -N flag, redirect the output to the printer. You will need the information if you ever have a disk failure or severe system crash where you need to use the alternate super-block list for recovery. In addition, you will have a record of the parameters you used if you decide to rebuild the file system later to tune the number of inodes.

As the caution states, one of the important pieces of output produced by `mkfs` is the list of backup super-blocks. If some disk error destroys or corrupts the primary super-block, the file system would be totally lost without backup copies. To avoid this catastrophe, `ufs` file systems place backup copies of the super-block in every cylinder group header. The file system check utility, `fsck`, can use these backup copies to restore the master super-block and recover the file system if needed. The reason for saving a paper copy is that if the master super-block is destroyed, it will not be possible to get the system to print out the block numbers of the backup super-block. Of course, one backup is always available at block number 32, but if you overwrite the front of the disk slice, you will probably lose the primary super-block and that backup copy as well, so store the paper copy for safe keeping.

Making *vxfs* File Systems

The `vxfs` file system requires less tuning from the default values than `ufs` file systems. There is little reason to change the block size or allocation unit parameters. The only two parameters worth tuning are as follows:

- ninode. Number of inodes to allocate. `vxfs` file systems allow direct entry of the number of inodes. The default value is computed using the formula

```
ninode = number of sectors / (block size * 4)
```

The L option can be used to prevent being asked the question about having more than 65536 inodes. The C option can be used to force no more that 65536 inodes when the default formula is used.

> **NOTE:** The actual number of inodes could be slightly less than the number specified. The `mkfs` command computes the number of allocation blocks required to hold the inode list and rounds down the number of inodes to fit an integral number of blocks.

- logsize. The number of blocks of size *blocksize* to use for the log region. Large, actively changing file systems might want to increase this parameter by a factor of 2 from its default value. For most file systems, the default value is sufficient.

The `mkfs` command for vxfs file systems reads

```
# mkfs -F vxfs -o N,L,ninode=128000 /dev/rdsk/c0t3d0s7 228816
```

The *lost+found* Directory

When you make a new file system, `mkfs` automatically creates a directory in it called *lost+found*. The `lost+found` directory is a placeholder. It is space that you set aside to hold pointers to inodes whose directory entries are corrupted. When the file system checks utility, `fsck` runs and detects a problem with an inode; if it cannot patch up the directory entries pointing to that inode, it clears them and makes a new directory entry in the `lost+found` directory. Because it doesn't know the proper name for the file, it calls it *#inode-number*.

Rather than lose the files entirely, when `fsck` detects some problems, it reconnects the inode into the `lost+found` directory. If this directory does not exist, `fsck` does not want to risk writing over blocks that might mistakenly be on the free list to create it. Then the files would be lost instead of reconnected.

The name comes from those files that have been disconnected from all directories (lost) and still have data blocks allocated to them. They are found and returned to the `lost+found` department in that directory.

> **TIP:** You should periodically peruse the `lost+found` directory of every file system to see if any automatic reboots after crashes have placed any files in them. If the file is a plain file, you can look at the contents to try to guess the filename. Because all the information about a file except its filename is kept in the inode, the remaining

information, including its owner, can help you determine what the file is and what its name used to be.

If the file is a directory, all of the files in the directory will still have their proper names. The owner of the directory can usually tell you what its name should have been. Then just remake the directory and move its contents back to where they belong and delete the directory entry in `lost+found`. Although you could do a `mvdir` command to move the entry back where it belongs, remaking it will also reorder and compact the directory.

Mounting File Systems

You've now built the file system, but no one can use it until it is made part of the file hierarchy. This is called mounting the file system. The new file system is placed on top of an existing directory in the hierarchy and replaces that directory. Thus file systems can be seamlessly grafted anywhere in the hierarchy.

Where to Mount

The first decision is where to place the new file system. Sometimes this decision is very simple. If you create a file system to hold the X11 utilities, the logical mount point is /usr/X. But if it is a general-purpose file system, to be shared by many projects and users, where do you mount it?

A file system can be mounted anywhere in the hierarchy. However, it does hide the directory it replaces. Mounting a new file system at the root (/) would be useless because the entire system would then be hidden.

> **CAUTION:** The files in the directory of an underlying mount point, for example, /usr/X when a file system is being mounted on /usr/X, are no longer accessible while the new file system is mounted. The root directory of the new file system replaces the mount point's directory in the hierarchy. If you intend to permanently mount a file system, be sure the mount point's directory is empty. Otherwise the space consumed by the files in and under the underlying mount point will be wasted.

There is no single correct place to mount file systems. However, just using them to extend directories in the hierarchy that run out of space can needlessly fragment the hierarchy. Instead, consider placing several large file systems near the top of the hierarchy, perhaps in the root directory, and then using symbolic links to link them into places in the hierarchy that need additional space. For example:

```
/home/users/john -> /files1/john
/home/users/tim  -> /files1/tim
/home/users/bob  -> /files2/bob
/proj/development -> /files2/development
```

In this example, two file systems are created and mounted as /files1 and /files2. Rather than mount them as /home/users or /proj, they are mounted in the root directory. Then symbolic links are created from the home/users and /proj directories to these file systems as space is needed. This way, if development outgrew the space available on /files2, it could easily be moved to a new file system, /files3, just by copying the files and changing the symlink to

```
/proj/development -> /files3/development
```

Everyone would still refer to the files as /proj/development.

How Permissions of the Underlying Mount Point Affect the Mounted File System

Every directory on UNIX has a permission mask. This indicates who is allowed to create and remove files in the directory (the w bits), see which files are in the directory (the r bits), and use this directory as part of a pathname (the x bits). This is just as true for the root directory of a file system. However, the UNIX system adds one more restriction. It ands the two permission bit masks. Thus, if the underlying mount point directory is

```
drwxrwxr-x (775)
```

allowing all access but file creation or destruction to the public, and the permissions of the root directory of the file system is

```
drwxrwx-wx (773)
```

allowing all access but seeing what files are in the directory to the public, the permission when mounted would be

```
drwxrwxr-x & drwxrwx-wx or (775 & 773) = drwxrwx—x (771)
```

This would allow the public to use this directory only in a search path and not create or destroy files or see what is in the directory.

> **CAUTION:** Although UNIX enforces this anding of the permission masks, the `ls` command displays the contents of the inode of the root of the mounted file system. This is just one part of the and. If you are having permission problems with the root directory of a mounted file system, unmount it and check the permissions of the underlying mount point.

TIP: Should all mount points have their permissions wide open (`drwxrwxrwx (777)`)? Not necessarily. If the mount point is for a file system where the root directory would normally have its permissions restricted, changing the underlying mount point's permission mask is a safeguard to prevent someone else from creating new files in the root of the mount point. I generally keep the mount points of my file systems at `drwxr-xr-x (755)` and do not allow users to create files in the root of a mounted file system.

Mounting a File System One Time

You decided where to mount it, created the mount point's directory if it didn't already exist, and are now ready to mount the file system. It is time to use the `mount` command. There are two ways to use mount: one specifies everything, the other uses the file `/etc/vfstab` to determine how to mount the file system.

■ Doing the mount manually

If you are just checking the mount point, or mounting a file system in a different place temporarily, perhaps to copy the files to a new disk, you enter three parameters to the mount command: type of file system, block special device of the slice, and the mount point

```
mount -F vxfs /dev/dsk/c0t3d0s7 /opt
```

If you wish only to look and want to prevent changes to the file system, you can mount it in read-only mode by adding an -r option

```
mount -F vxfs -r /dev/dsk/c0t3d0s7 /opt
```

■ Using `/etc/vfstab`

If the file system is already defined in `/etc/vfstab`, then the mount command can be shortened to just the mount point.

```
mount /opt
```

Likewise, for read-only mounting it would be

```
mount -r /opt
```

To add a manually mounted file system to `/etc/vfstab`, see the next section, but set the mount at boot time column to no.

Mounting a File System Every Time at Boot

The system will mount at boot time all file systems specified in the *virtual file system table*, or `/etc/vfstab`. This file specifies all the parameters it needs for mounting local and remote file systems. (See Chapter 37 for more information on remote file systems.) The file is just a text file and can be edited with any text editor. The Unixware command `disksetup` automatically adds the slices it creates to this file if you specify boot time mounting.

The file consists of seven columns of data separated by white space (usually tabs).

```
#device              device              mount    FS    fsck  mount    mount
#to mount            to fsck             point    type  pass  at boot  options
#
/dev/dsk/c0t3d0s0    /dev/rdsk/c0t3d0s0  /        ufs   1     no       -
/dev/dsk/c0t3d0s6    /dev/rdsk/c0t3d0s6  /usr     ufs   2     no       -
/dev/dsk/c0t3d0s7    /dev/rdsk/c0t3d0s7  /var     ufs   4     no       -
/dev/dsk/c0t2d0s6    /dev/rdsk/c0t2d0s6  /files   ufs   5     yes      -
/dev/dsk/c0t2d0s7    /dev/rdsk/c0t2d0s7  /files4  ufs   6     yes      -
/dev/dsk/c0t1d0s2    /dev/rdsk/c0t1d0s2  /opt     ufs   11    yes      -
/dev/dsk/c0t3d0s5    /dev/rdsk/c0t3d0s5  /usr/openwin ufs 12  yes      -
/dev/dsk/c0t3d0s1    -                   -        swap  -     no       -
```

The preceding comment lines explain pretty well all of the columns except `fsck` pass and mount options.

`fsck` pass is designed for allowing `fsck` to run on multiple disk drives in parallel. The `fsck` passes are executed in order, and any file systems with the same pass number are allowed to be executed in parallel.

CAUTION: Never place two file systems on the same spindle or RAID device in the same pass. It will dramatically slow the check down because it tries to seek over both file systems simultaneously.

Running in parallel might not be any faster if the SCSI channel is close to saturation or the system does not have enough RAM to buffer all the structures. It can cause slowdowns as it pages the structures out to swap space on the disk.

Mount options are passed to the mount command as part of the -o option and are entered here exactly as they would be entered in the -o option list of the mount command. Mark read-only file systems as ro, not -r, because the -o flag for read-only is -o ro.

NOTE: Note that /, /usr, and /var are not marked mount at boot time. It's not that they are not mounted all the time, but they are mounted by the startup scripts prior to mounting the rest of the file systems. Because they are already mounted, there is no need to mount them again.

Unmounting a File System

A file system must be unmounted to check it, and if it is a removable media, it must be unmounted before it is removed. The umount command is used to unmount file systems, as in

```
umount /opt
```

No options are needed on the umount command.

> **CAUTION:** Do not eject any removable media that is still mounted. UNIX caches in memory important information about the file system and writes that back when you use the umount command.

> **NOTE:** If you get
>
> ```
> /opt: busy
> ```
>
> back from the umount command, it means that some processes are still using the file system. The first thing to check is that you don't have your current directory set to somewhere within that file system. If you do, change back to the root file system and try again. If it still reports as busy, use the fuser command to determine which processes are still using the file system.
>
> ```
> # fuser -cu /opt
> /opt:    1189t(syd)    1105t(syd)    871to(syd)    838t(syd)
>          229to(root)    164t(root)
> ```
>
> The number is the process ID that is using the file system; the letter is as follows:
>
> - c—has a current directory on the file system
> - o—has an open file on the file system
> - r—has its root directory on the file system
> - t—has a program running from the file system (needs access to the file system to handle page faults)
>
> The name in parentheses is the owner of the process.
>
> If necessary, you can then send the kill signal to any processes that are using the file system to get it unmounted.

Checking File Systems

Sooner or later it happens. Someone turns off the power switch. The power outage lasts longer than your UPS's batteries and you didn't shut down the system. Someone presses the reset button. Someone overwrites part of your disk. A critical sector on the disk develops a flaw. If you run UNIX long enough, eventually a halt occurs where the system did not write the remaining cached information (sync'ed) to the disks.

When this happens, you need to verify the integrity of each of the file systems. This is necessary because if the structure is not correct, using them could quickly damage them beyond repair. Over the years, UNIX has developed a very sophisticated file system integrity check that can usually recover the problem. It's called `fsck`. Of course, if it cannot handle the problem, the gurus out there can always try `fsdb`, the file system debugger.

The *fsck* Utility

The `fsck` utility takes its understanding of the internals of the various UNIX file systems and attempts to verify that all the links and blocks are correctly tied together. It runs in five passes, each of which checks a different part of the linkage and each of which builds on the verifications and corrections of the prior passes.

`fsck` walks the file system, starting with the super-block. It then deals with the allocated disk blocks, pathnames, directory connectivity, link reference counts, and the free list of blocks and inodes.

The Super-Block

Every change to the file system affects the super-block, which is why it is cached in RAM. Periodically, at the sync interval, it is written to disk. If it is corrupted, `fsck` will check and correct it. If it is so badly corrupted that `fsck` cannot do its work, find the paper you saved when you built the file system and use the -b option to `fsck` to give it an alternate super-block to use. The super-block is the head of each of the lists that make up the file system and maintains counts of free blocks and inodes.

Inodes

`fsck` validates each of the inodes. It makes sure that each block in the block allocation list is not on the block allocation list in any other inode, that the size is correct, and that the link count is correct. If the inodes are correct, then the data is accessible. All that's left is to verify the pathnames.

What Is a Clean (Stable) File System?

Some times `fsck` responds

```
/opt: stable                          (ufs file systems)
file system is clean - log replay not required (vxfs file systems)
```

This means that the super-block is marked clean and that no changes have been made to the file system since it was marked clean. What the system does is first mark the super-block dirty, then it starts modifying the rest of the file system. When the buffer cache is empty and all pending writes are complete, it goes back and marks the super-block as clean. If it is marked clean, there is normally no reason to run `fsck`, so unless `fsck` is told to ignore the clean flag, it just prints this notice and skips over this file system.

Where Is *fsck*?

When you run `fsck`, you are running an executable in the `/usr/sbin` directory called `/usr/sbin/fsck`, but this is not the real `fsck`. It is just a dispatcher that invokes a file system type-specific `fsck` utility. In the directory `/usr/lib/fs` resides a directory for each supported file system type. There are specific programs in this directory for dealing with a particular file system type.

When Should I Run *fsck*?

Normally you do not have to run `fsck`. The system runs it automatically when you try to mount a file system that is dirty. However, problems can creep up on you. Software and hardware glitches do occur from time to time. It wouldn't hurt to run `fsck` just after performing the monthly backups.

> **CAUTION:** It is better to run `fsck` after the backups rather than before. If `fsck` finds major problems, it could leave the file system in worse shape than it was prior to running. Then you can just build an empty file system and reread your backup, which will also clean up the file system. If you did it in the other order, you would be left with no backup and no file system.

How Do I Run *fsck*?

Because the system normally runs it for you, running `fsck` is not an everyday occurrence for you to remember. However, it is quite simple and mostly automatic.

First, to run `fsck`, the file system you intend to check must not be mounted. This is a bit hard to do if you are in multiuser mode most of the time, so to run a full system `fsck` you should shut the system down to single user mode. For System V type systems, such as Unixware or Solaris, use

```
shutdown -i s
```

to transition the system to state s, or single user. For older Berkeley style systems, such as SunOS, shut down the system entirely and reboot into single user mode using

```
boot -s
```

In single user mode you need to invoke `fsck`, giving it the options to force a check of all file systems, even if they are already stable.

```
fsck -o f                      (ufs file systems)
fsck -o full                   (vxfs file systems)
```

If you wish to check a single specific file system, type its character special device name

```
fsck -o full /dev/rdsk/c0t1d0s1
```

Checking s5 File Systems

For s5 file systems, `fsck` is a 5- or 6-phase process, depending on what errors were found, if any. `fsck` can automatically correct most of these errors and will do so if invoked by the mount command to automatically check a dirty file system. However, when it is run manually you will be asked to answer the questions that the system would automatically answer.

Phase 1: Blocks and Sizes

During this phase, `fsck` checks that a file has an appropriate number of blocks allocated for its size and begins to scan for blocks being allocated to more than one file.

You may have to approve (answer yes or no) for clearing inode entries for

```
UNKNOWN FILE TYPE I=inode number (CLEAR?)
PARTIALLY ALLOCATED INODE I=inode number (CLEAR?)
```

In both of these cases, the entire file is lost. Other errors you may be asked to handle include

```
SIZE ERROR I=inode number
DELETE OR RECOVER EXCESS DATA
```

If the file appears to be of a different size than allocated, you can either delete the excess data or extend the inode to cover the excess data.

> **CAUTION:** If you get the error
>
> ```
> WARNING: SUPER BLOCK, ROOT INODE, OR ROOT DIRECTORY ON fs MAY BE COR-
> RUPTED. fsck CAN'T DETERMINE LOGICAL BLOCK SIZE OF fs BLOCK SIZE COULD
> BE 512, 1024, OR 2048 BYTES. ENTER LOGICAL BLOCK SIZE OF fs IN BYTES
> (NOTE: INCORRECT RESPONSE COULD DAMAGE FILE SYSTEM BEYOND REPAIR!) ENTER
> 512, 1024, OR 2048 OR ENTER s TO SKIP THIS FILE SYSTEM:
> ENTER 512, 1024, 2048, OR s:
> ```
>
> be very careful what you answer. Be sure you have a backup before proceeding.
> Find the sheet you saved when you built the file system, and retrieve the value
> from that sheet. If you do enter the correct value, fsck has a good chance of
> recovering the file system, unless something else was really written over it.

```
BAD BLK blocknum I=inode number
EXCESSIVE BAD BLKS I=inode number
```

fsck will ask you if you want to clear (erase) this file. One of the files with the duplicate
blocks will have to be erased.

```
DUP BLK blocknum I=inode number
EXCESSIVE DUP BLKS I=inode number
```

If duplicate blocks are found, a phase 1b will be run to scan for the original file that has
the duplicate blocks.

Phase 2: Pathnames

This phase removes directory entries from bad inodes found in phase 1 and 1b and checks
for directories with inode pointers that are out of range or pointing to bad inodes. You
might have to handle

```
ROOT INODE NOT DIRECTORY (FIX?)
```

You can convert inode 2, the root directory, back into a directory, but this usually means
there is major damage to the inode table.

```
I OUT OF RANGE I=inode number NAME=file name (REMOVE?)
UNALLOCATED I=inode number OWNER=O MODE=M SIZE=S MTIME=T NAME=file name (REMOVE?)
BAD/DUP I=inode number OWNER=O MODE=M SIZE=S MTIME=T DIR=file name (REMOVE?)
BAD/DUP I=inode number OWNER=O MODE=M SIZE=S MTIME=T FILE=file name (REMOVE?)
```

A bad inode number was found, an unallocated inode was used in a directory, or an inode
that had a bad or duplicate block number in it is referenced. You are given the choice to
remove the file, losing the data, or to leave the error. If you leave the error, the file system
is still damaged, but you have the chance to try to dump the file first and salvage part of
the data before rerunning fsck to remove the entry.

Phase 3: Connectivity

This phase checks for unreferenced directories and connects them into the lost+found directory. Errors occur only if there isn't enough room in lost+found or if the lost+found directory does not exist. Status messages are printed for each reconnection.

Phase 4: Reference Counts

This phase uses the information from phases 2 and 3 to check for unreferenced files and incorrect link counts on files, directories, or special files.

```
UNREF FILE I=inode number OWNER=O MODE=M SIZE=S MTIME=T (RECONNECT?)
```

The filename is not known (it is an unreferenced file), so it is reconnected into the lost+found directory with the inode number as its name. If you clear the file, its contents are lost. Unreferenced files that are empty are cleared automatically.

```
LINK COUNT FILE I=inode number OWNER=O MODE=M SIZE=S MTIME=T COUNT=X (ADJUST?)
LINK COUNT DIR I=inode number OWNER=O MODE=M SIZE=S MTIME=T COUNT=X (ADJUST?)
```

In both cases, an entry was found with a different number of references than what was listed in the inode. You should let `fsck` adjust the count.

Phase 5: Free List

The list of free-blocks is checked for duplicates, bad blocks (block number is invalid), and blocks that are in use. If there is a problem, you will be asked to salvage the free list. This will run a sixth phase to reconstruct the free list.

Checking *ufs* File Systems

For `ufs` file systems, `fsck` is a 5-phase process. `fsck` can automatically correct most of these errors and will do so if invoked by the mount command to automatically check a dirty file system. However, when run manually you will be asked to answer the questions that the system would automatically answer.

> **CAUTION:** Serious errors reported by `ufs`'s `fsck` at the very beginning, especially before reporting the start of phase 1, indicate an invalid super-block. `fsck` should be terminated and restarted with the -b option specifying one of the alternate super-blocks. Block 32 is always an alternate and can be tried first, but if the front of the file system was overwritten, it also may be damaged. Use the hard copy you saved from the `mkfs` to find an alternate from later in the file system.

Phase 1: Check Blocks and Sizes

This phase checks the inode list, looking for invalid inode entries. Errors requiring answers include

`UNKNOWN FILE TYPE I=`*inode number* `(CLEAR)`

The file type bits are invalid in the inode. Options are to leave the problem and attempt to recover the data by hand later or to erase the entry and its data by clearing the inode.

`PARTIALLY TRUNCATED INODE I=`*inode number* `(SALVAGE)`

The inode appears to point to less data than the file does. This is safely salvaged, because it indicates a crash while truncating the file to shorten it.

block `BAD I=`*inode number*
block `DUP I=`*inode number*

The disk block pointed to by the inode is either out of range for this inode or already in use by another file. This is an informational message. If a duplicate block is found, phase 1b will be run to report the inode number of the file that originally used this block.

Phase 2: Check Pathnames

This phase removes directory entries from bad inodes found in phase 1 and 1b and checks for directories with inode pointers that are out of range or pointing to bad inodes. You may have to handle

`ROOT INODE NOT DIRECTORY (FIX?)`

You can convert inode 2, the root directory, back into a directory, but this usually means there is major damage to the inode table.

`I=OUT OF RANGE I=`*inode number* `NAME=`*file name* `(REMOVE?)`
`UNALLOCATED I=`*inode number* `OWNER=O MODE=M SIZE=S MTIME=T TYPE=F (REMOVE?)`
`BAD/DUP I=`*inode number* `OWNER=O MODE=M SIZE=S MTIME=T TYPE=F (REMOVE?)`

A bad inode number was found, an unallocated inode was used in a directory, or an inode that had a bad or duplicate block number in it is referenced. You are given the choice to remove the file, losing the data, or to leave the error. If you leave the error, the file system is still damaged, but you have the chance to try to dump the file first and salvage part of the data before rerunning fsck to remove the entry.

`Various Directory Length Errors: zero length, too short, not multiple of block size,`
`corrupted`

You will be given the chance to have fsck fix or remove the directory as appropriate. These errors are all correctable with little chance of subsequent damage.

Phase 3: Check Connectivity

This phase will detect errors in unreferenced directories. It will create or expand the lost+found directory if needed and connect these directories into the lost+found directory. It prints status messages for all directories placed in lost+found.

Phase 4: Check Reference Counts

This phase uses the information from phases 2 and 3 to check for unreferenced files and incorrect link counts on files, directories, or special files.

```
UNREF FILE I=inode number OWNER=O MODE=M SIZE=S MTIME=T (RECONNECT?)
```

The filename is not known (it is an unreferenced file), so it is reconnected into the lost+found directory with the inode number as its name. If you clear the file, its contents are lost. Unreferenced files that are empty are cleared automatically.

```
LINK COUNT FILE I=inode number OWNER=O MODE=M SIZE=S MTIME=T COUNT=X (ADJUST?)
LINK COUNT DIR  I=inode number OWNER=O MODE=M SIZE=S MTIME=T COUNT=X (ADJUST?)
```

In both cases, an entry was found with a different number of references than what was listed in the inode. You should let fsck adjust the count.

```
BAD/DUP FILE I=inode number OWNER=O MODE=M SIZE=S MTIME=T (CLEAR)
```

A file or directory has a bad or duplicate block in it. If you clear it now, the data is lost. You can leave the error and attempt to recover the data, and rerun fsck later to clear the file.

Phase 5: Check Cylinder Groups

This phase checks the free block and unused inode maps. It will automatically correct the free lists if necessary, although in manual mode it will ask permission first.

Checking vxfs File Systems

Although s5 and ufs file systems are not all that different in their fsck, vxfs is totally different. It first runs a sanity check on the file system recovering the super-block from the first allocation unit if needed or any allocation unit headers from the super-block if needed. Then, unless a full fsck was requested, it replays the intent log and exits in a few seconds. No intervention is needed.

If a full fsck is requested—this should be needed only in cases of hardware failure—you should run it in interactive mode (no -p, -y or -n options on the fsck command line) and answer yes to the questions. Errors in connecting files or directories will clear those files or directories. It will then be necessary to recover them from backups.

What Do I Do After *fsck* Finishes?

First relax, because fsck rarely finds anything serious wrong, except in cases of hardware failure where the disk drive is failing or where you copied something on top of the file system. UNIX file systems really are very robust.

However, if fsck did find major problems or made a large number of corrections, rerun it to be sure the disk isn't undergoing hardware failure. It shouldn't find more errors in a second run. Then recover any files that it may have deleted. If you keep a log of the inodes it clears, you can go to a backup tape and dump the list of inodes on the tape. Recover just those inodes to restore the files.

Back up the system again, because there is no reason to have to do this all over again.

Dealing with What Is in *lost+found*

If fsck reconnected unreferenced entries, it placed them in the lost+found directory. They are safe there, and the system should be backed up in case you lose them while trying to move them back to where they belong. Items in lost+found can be of any type: files, directories, special files (devices), or fifos. If it is a fifo, you can safely delete it: the process that opened it is long since gone and will open a new one when it runs again.

For files, use the owner name to contact the owner and have him look at the contents and see if the file is worth keeping. Often it is a file that was deleted and is no longer needed, but the system crashed before it could be fully removed.

For directories, the files in the directory should help you and the owner determine where they belong. You can look on the backup tape lists for a directory with those contents if necessary. Then just remake the directory and move the files back. Then remove the directory entry in lost+found. This re-creation and move has the added benefit of cleaning up the directory.

Finding and Reclaiming Space

One of the banes of system administrators is that users always use 100 percent of the disk space available to them on a system. It always falls on the systems administrator to prod users into removing files and directory trees they no longer need. It helps if you can attack the portion of the problem that will yield the greatest reward: the users with large files and the users tying up the most space.

What Takes Space

Besides users leaving around files they no longer need, two types of files are often blamed for taking up a lot of wasted space: core files and backup images.

Whenever a user program aborts on a programming error, a copy of the data space is made to a file named core. Core files are very useful for debugging but if left around can take up large amounts of space.

Backup images are made whenever a program automatically saves a backup copy before modifying a file. Many UNIX programs have this behavior. Often old backups remain long after the file has stopped being modified. Some examples of this are .orig files from patch, .backup files from frame, and name% files from emacs.

Developers also often make backup copies of directories before working on them, and they may forget to remove these when completed. It all adds up to large amounts of disk being used for nonproductive files.

Determining Who Is Using Up the Disk

UNIX provides several tools for determining disk utilization. These include the accounting system, which can track the ownership of disk storage on a daily basis, du for determining where storage is being used, and the diskusg family of utilities for determining totals per user ID. For information on du, see Chapter 38, "Accounting System."

The System Administrator's Friend: The *find* Utility

One of the most useful tools for a system administrator is the find utility. It traverses all or sections of the UNIX file system hierarchy and can perform tests and execute commands on the files it visits, including the following:

- Finding core files

  Many sites run the script findcores from cron each night to find and remove old core files. It contains one line:

  ```
  find / -local -name core -mtime +7 -print ¦ xargs rm -f
  ```

  This use of find starts at the root. It traverses only local file systems, avoiding ones on other machines on the network. If the file is named core and has not been modified for at least seven days, it prints its name. Then the xargs utility is used to remove these core files.

- Finding files not accessed recently

  Files that are on the disk but never read are prime candidates for removal when space is at a premium. The find statement

  ```
  find / -local -atime +60 -a -mtime +60 -print ¦ sort
  ```

  will produce a useful list of files that have not been accessed or modified in the past 60 days. Because find traverses the file system tree in the order of the directory entries (the order in which they were created, not the alphabetical order shown by ls), the sort utility is a handy way of making the output of the list appear in a more human readable order.

■ Finding large files

Of course, large files are the easiest targets. Finding them is just as easy.

```
find / -local -size +500 -print ¦ sort ¦ xargs ls -lsd
```

will produce a listing of all files larger than 500 blocks. The use of the xargs command will produce a listing showing the owner and size in both blocks and bytes for each file. The sort step will place files in the same directory together in the listing; otherwise, the quantization effects of the xargs command could separate these files in the listing.

Reorganizing the File System Hierarchy

Sooner or later, you'll have to add space to the system. The only way to make more space on a disk drive without deleting the files is to move the files on part of that drive somewhere else. Using the move command to move the files one at a time is tedious and prone to mistakes. The cp -r command will move a directory and its descendents, but it changes the owner and time stamps, which is sort of intrusive. However, all is not lost. UNIX does provide utilities to make moving files around simple.

Using Symbolic Links to Hide Actual Disk Locations

One of the goals in moving the files was to make space, but that conflicts with the goal of not disturbing the user. It would be best if the user could still think the files were in the old directory even though you have moved them. Symbolic links are the answer. Using a symbolic link from the old location to the new location makes the files appear to still be in the old location.

All that is left is to move the files and create the symbolic link.

Moving Trees via *cpio*

cpio, or cp in/out, has one more mode that when combined with the find utility lets you easily move entire directory trees. This is the pass mode. In this mode, it takes entire hierarchies from one place on the disk and makes a perfect replica of them in another. To move the files in /home/bob to /disks/bob, all you do is

```
cd /home
find bob -print ¦ cpio -pdluam /disks
rm -rf bob
ln -s /disks/bob bob
```

and you are done. The `find` command prints a list of all the files in and below bob in the tree. `cpio` then re-creates these files under the /disks directory. The arguments used for `cpio` are as follows:

- `p`—Pass mode; create a replica of the pathnames read on standard input
- `d`—Create directories as needed
- `l`—Create links if possible (hard links)
- `u`—Unconditional; overwrite the file if it already exists and is newer than the copy
- `a`—Reset the access time of the original and replica file to what it was prior to `cpio` running
- `m`—Reset the modification time of the replica file to match the modification time of the original

`cpio` copies everything about the file. It even copies special files.

The `rm` command removes the original files after the copy is complete, and the `ln` creates the symbolic link.

See Chapters 31, "Archiving" and 32, "Backups," for information on the other archiving methods, `dump` and `tar`.

Summary

In UNIX, the following is true:

- Disks are a sequence of bytes.
- Disks are split into sections called slices.
- After a disk is formatted and partitioned, a label is written to the disk to define the slices in a virtual table of contents.
- The slices appear as disk drives.
- Each slice can hold one file system. Some slices are used as raw data areas for swap space or application-specific data such as for databases.
- The file system hierarchy is a tree.
- New file systems can be mounted onto that tree at any place.
- Mounted file systems obscure the mount point directory.
- The basis of a file system is the inode list. It contains all the information about a file.
- Support is provided for multiple types of file systems.
- Multiple methods are provided for backing up these file systems.

As a Systems Administrator, the following are your responsibilities:

- Monitor the available space on the file systems.

  The tools provided in this chapter will help you keep track of usage.
- Perform regular checks on file system integrity.

  UNIX file systems are very stable, but it doesn't hurt to check them out once a month.
- Perform and verify the readability of backups.

  Perform them daily. UNIX's tools make full and incremental backups easy to interleave.

User Administration

36

By Sydney S. Weinstein

Although users may be the reason for the existence of your UNIX system, they also can be the sysadmin's worst nightmare. Users are always making demands and changing things. The one thing that remains constant is that users come and go, but the system remains.

As system administrator, you will have to add and remove users from the system. It is also your task to provide the default environment so users can get their jobs done. This chapter shows what makes up a user's account, how to create new user accounts, and what to do when a user leaves and his account must be removed.

What Makes Up a User Account

Users see UNIX as a home directory and a shell. Behind the scenes are many other files and parameters that affect the user. This section explains each part of the user's account and how it affects the user.

The User's Home Directory

Every process in UNIX has a current directory. This is no different for the login shell for a user. The initial current directory for a login shell is called its home directory. The login program sets the HOME environment variable to the full pathname to this directory. It is in this directory that the login shell looks for its start-up files. It is also in this directory that system daemons look for the following:

- .Xauthority—the processes that are allowed to access the *X* screen being used by this user.

- .Xdefaults—*X* programs keep default values for their options in this file.

- .cshrc—csh/tcsh start-up script.

- .exrc—vi/ex start-up script.

- .forward—mail redirection file. In this file you place the address or addresses to forward your mail. It allows you to receive mail from many accounts on a single account, or to pass your mail through a program to filter it before reading it.

- .history—holds the last set of commands you executed in the shell for use in the history shell command.

- .ksh_env—ksh start-up script.

- .login—csh login script, which is executed once at login after .cshrc.

- .mailrc—mail start-up script.

- .mwmrc—motif window manager start-up script.

- .openwin-init—openlook window manager start-up script.

- `.openwin-menu`—openlook window manager root menu.
- `.profile`—sh/ksh login script, which is executed once at login, after `/etc/profile`.
- `.rhosts`—the remote hosts and users that are equivalent to this user. Equivalent means can log in as this user from a remote system without specifying a password and can access files and perform commands as this user on this system without being challenged for a password. (Used by the networking commands `rsh`, `rexec`, `rcp`, and `rlogin`.)
- `.xinitrc`—*X* start-up file.
- `.xmodmaprc`—*X* keyboard remapping file.

Many other programs also look for special start-up files in the user's home directory.

The User's Mail File

Each user on a UNIX system is eligible to receive electronic mail. Normally, this file is in one of these systemwide spool directories:

- `/var/mail`—System V–derived systems (obsolete name `/usr/mail`)
- `/var/spool/mail`—Berkeley-derived systems (obsolete name `/usr/spool/mail`)

Some systems now place this mail file in the user's home directory. No matter where it's located, this file will hold the mail this user has yet to read, delete, or move into other folders.

Mail Alias File Entries

In addition to the mail file, the user name might be listed in the systemwide mail alias file. This file resides in one of several places:

- `/etc/aliases`
- `/etc/mail/aliases`
- `/usr/lib/aliases`
- `/usr/lib/mail/aliases`

Regardless of where the alias file resides, it consists of lines containing the alias and the mail address to use for mail received for that alias. Aliases are checked before local user names when mail is being delivered, so you can even alias a local user name to a different machine or user. Listing 36.1 is a small excerpt from a mail alias file. It has the required postmaster alias and some local aliases.

Listing 36.1. Excerpt from a sample mail alias file.

```
##
#  Aliases can have any mix of upper and lower case on the
#    left-hand side,     but the right-hand side should be proper
#    case (usually lower)
#
#    >>>>>>>>>     The program "newaliases" will need to be run
#    >> NOTE >> after    this file is updated for any changes to
#    >>>>>>>>>     show through to sendmail.
##

# Following alias is required by the mail protocol, RFC 822
# Set it to the address of a HUMAN who deals with this system's

Postmaster: root
nobody: /dev/null

# Sample aliases:
# Alias for distribution list, members specified here:
#staff:wnj,mosher,sam,ecc,mckusick,sklower,olson,rwh@ernie

# Alias for distribution list, members specified elsewhere:
#keyboards: :include:/usr/jfarrell/keyboards.list

# Alias for a person, so they can receive mail by several names:
#epa:eric

#######################
# Local aliases below #
#######################

Syd.Weinstein:      syd
Sydney.Weinstein:   syd
```

> **TIP:** As demonstrated in the end of Listing 36.1, it is wise to create full-name aliases. These aliases let someone be addressed by their full name, without the sender knowing the user name. Since aliases are case insensitive, it doesn't matter how you list the full name. Remember, however, that delivery addresses (the part after the colon) are case sensitive.

An alias can point to another alias. Aliases listed in this file are systemwide, and are addresses to which another user can reply. This is not true of private aliases users might enter into their mail reader's start-up files.

The Shell Start-up Files

Each user interacts with UNIX via a command shell. The command shells use a file in the user's home directory to customize themselves for each user. As administrator, it is your responsibility to provide a default shell customization file. There are two different sets of customization files—the one you use depends on the shell family being used. For shells that are derived from /bin/sh the initialization file is .profile, with the Korn shell using an additional file whose name is user definable, but is often called .ksh_env. Shells derived from Berkeley's C-shell use .login and .cshrc. A short explanation of the purpose and contents of these 4 files is as follows:

■ .profile

This is the start-up file executed by Bourne (/bin/sh) and Korn (/bin/ksh) shells at login. This is the file where you place changes to environment variables and global settings. This file is executed after /etc/profile is executed.

■ .ksh_env

The Bourne shell does not have a start-up file for non–login-level shells. The Korn shell does, as it supports aliases and functions that are not exported from the login shell to subshells. If the login shell, via the .profile file, exports the variable ENV, each Korn shell will read the file named in that environment variable on start-up. This file should not include changes to environment variables, but should include function and alias definitions. For login shells, this file is run after /etc/profile and .profile. For subshells, it is the only file executed.

■ .login

This file is run only at login by the C-shell. It should contain environment variable and global settings. It is executed after /etc/cshrc and .cshrc are executed.

■ .cshrc

This file is run by all C-shells at start-up. It is used to initialize aliases and local variables. Changes to environment variables should not be made in this file. For login shells, this file is run after /etc/cshrc and before .login. For subshells, it is the only file executed.

The User's *passwd* File Entry or NIS/NIS+ Database Entry

The system keeps track of users via an entry in the password database. This databases is maintained in the following ways:

■ traditionally—in /etc/passwd

■ SVR4 style—in /etc/passwd and /etc/shadow

■ NIS/NIS+—in a networkwide database, and on the NIS/NIS+ master in files specified at the time that NIS/NIS+ is configured.

It really doesn't matter which method is used because all of them track the same information. It is this information that defines the user to the UNIX system.

> **CAUTION:** In a networked environment, it is very important that every system on the network use the same user ID for the same user. Although NIS and other methods share the password information to achieve this, that is not required. All that is required is that any systems that share files via NFS also share user IDs.

The passwd file, as shown in Listing 36.2, is composed of single-line entries. Each must appear on a single line and cannot be continued. All the lines must have seven fields, delimited by colons. No comments or blank lines are allowed in this file. This file is world readable, so it does not contain plain-text passwords.

Listing 36.2. Excerpts from a sample `/etc/passwd` file from an SVR4 system.

```
root:x:0:1:0000-Admin(0000):/:/sbin/sh
daemon:x:1:1:0000-Admin(0000):/:
bin:x:2:2:0000-Admin(0000):/usr/bin:
sys:x:3:3:0000-Admin(0000):/:
adm:x:4:4:0000-Admin(0000):/var/adm:
lp:x:71:8:0000-lp(0000):/usr/spool/lp:
smtp:x:0:0:mail daemon user:/:
uucp:x:5:5:0000-uucp(0000):/usr/lib/uucp:
nuucp:x:9:9:0000-uucp(0000):/var/spool/uucppublic:/usr/lib/uucp/uucico
listen:x:37:4:Network Admin:/usr/net/nls:
syd:x:201:200:Syd Weinstein:/home/syd:/usr/bin/ksh
Pwcsite:x:9001:9:PPP from wc:/:/usr/sbin/aspppls
nobody:x:60001:60001:uid no body:/:
noaccess:x:60002:60002:uid no access:/:
```

> **CAUTION:** Be very careful that all the lines have six colons separating the seven fields. A blank line will be taken as an alternate entry for the root user with no password.

The seven fields, in order, in the passwd file are described in the following sections.

User Name

This is a one- to eight-character alphanumeric field that represents the user's login name. Traditionally the name is all lowercase characters. Any value may be used for this field. To make it easy to tell a user name from a user ID, the name should not start with a number.

TIP: Accounts fall into two basic categories: human users and computer users. UUCP accounts are an example of the latter. To make it easy to spot accounts that are used by other computers to log in for uucp transfers, a convention is to start all those user names with an uppercase *U*.

Password (if Not Using a Shadow Password Scheme)

The users password, encrypted with a one-way cipher is stored in the second field. Only the first 8 characters of the password are used. These are mixed with a 2-character salt to produce a 13-character encrypted password. When it is necessary to compare a password, the plain text is encrypted with the salt, and a comparison is made against the encrypted version. If the passwd field is empty, this account has no password, and none is required to log in.

On systems that support password aging and place the password in the passwd file, the password data can be followed by a comma and four characters that describe the aging information. Each of these characters is drawn from the following character set:

- `. = 0`
- `/ = 1`
- `0-9 = 2–11`
- `A-Z = 12–37`
- `a-z = 38–63`

The first character after the comma denotes the maximum number of weeks the password is valid. The second character is the minimum number of weeks required between password changes. If both of these characters are zero (`..`), the user is forced to change his password the next time he logs in. If the change interval is larger than the valid interval, only the root user can change the password.

The remaining two characters are the number of weeks since the epoch when the password was last changed. In UNIX, the current epoch, or beginning of time, is January 1, 1970, 00:00 GMT.

NOTE: You must manually edit the passwd file to set the aging characters the first time. They are not created automatically by the system. Be sure to use vipw when editing the passwd file to be sure it is locked while you are in it.

On systems that do not use the passwd file to hold the password, such as those using /etc/shadow or some password adjunct scheme, this field contains a fixed string that has fewer than 13 characters.

> **TIP:** If you need to temporarily lock out a user, insert the string *LK* on the front of that user's encrypted password string. It now will never match any valid password, as the encryption string uses the same character set as the aging characters, and * is not in the set. You can delete *LK* from the front when you need to re-enable the account, and the original password is intact.

> **NOTE:** To lock an account against being used for logins, use a fixed string that contains an invalid password character to prevent logins. The convention is to use *LK* for accounts that are locked against login.

User ID

UNIX internally uses a numeric ID to refer to a user. This is the user ID field of the passwd file. It is a number in the range 0—32767 on older systems, 0—65535 on some systems, and 0—2147483648 on SVR4 systems. The number 0 is reserved for the root user, the user with special privileges. Many networked systems save -1 for no access and -2 for nobody.

> **CAUTION:** These two values, -1 and -2, have been known to be a security hole. On systems that did not handle sign extension correctly in the user ID, any user ID that mapped to a negative value caused a security hole due to other assumptions those systems made about checking. They have been replaced by positive values for noaccess and nobody.
>
> noaccess is the value to use when a file is to be made so that it is not owned by root, but no one will be able to access it. nobody is used by NFS. Remote users with the ID 0 (root) are mapped to the nobody ID on NFS accesses unless the file system is exported with root access permission. See Chapter 37, "Networking," for more details.

TIP: Although you have total control over the user IDs, it is best to follow a convention that will make it easier to determine which IDs are being used for which purpose.

UNIX has several accounts that are required. These all have low numbered IDs. It's wise to reserve all the IDs below 100 for these reserved system accounts.

In addition, there are several accounts that are for nonhuman use. These include UUCP access accounts and file ownership accounts. (A *file ownership account* is one that has no person associated with it, but is designed to hold the ownership of a set of files for a department. Then when changes to those files need to be made, any member of the department can su to that user to make the changes.

Consider breaking the numbering space apart into the following:

- Restricted accounts—system use: 0–99
- Networkwide user accounts—100–19999
- System restricted user accounts—20000–29999 (These are still unique on the network, but the account is valid only on one system.)
- UUCP access accounts—30000–30999
- File ownership accounts—31000–31999
- nobody—32000
- noaccess—32001

Of course, if you need more accounts than this scheme supports, and if your system supports extended user IDs, move the regions around to make them bigger.

Default Group ID

UNIX file permissions have three fields: owner (user ID), group (group ID), and world. The default group for files created by this user is the ID listed for this field. Groups are listed in the file /etc/group or in the file specified by the NIS/NIS+ configuration.

NOTE: As with user IDs, consider breaking up this numbering space as well. A numbering scheme similar to the one proposed for user IDs is just as valid.

Full Name (GCOS Field)

In the original versions of UNIX at Bell Laboratories, UNIX was also used as a front end computer to submit jobs to the GE/Honeywell mainframe. This system ran GECOS/GCOS, and this field was used to store the mainframe account information for this user.

This is obsolete and of little use outside the labs, so this field was usurped and used to hold the full name of the user. It is used for placing the full name on printouts and on electronic mail. It is stored in one of two formats:

- System V Format: nnnn-Name(nnnn)

  The first four digits are the GCOS account number. The name is everything after the - and before the (. The number in the parentheses is the GCOS box number.

- Berkeley Format: Name, comments

  Everything in the field up to the comma is the name. After the comma can go comments about the account that are not part of the name.

Initial Home Directory

The login program changes to this directory before starting the shell, and sets the HOME environment variable to its value. The user's login scripts can change this value and define a different home directory, which is why this is called the initial home directory.

Shell

This field contains the full pathname of which script or program is started by the login program as the shell. If this field is empty, the Bourne shell is used by default. For UUCP accounts, the full pathname to the uucico program is the program to be run by login, and it appears in this field.

Shadow File Entry (NIS/NIS+ database entry)

Since the passwd file is world readable, as an added measure of security, SVR4 UNIX systems use a shadow file to hold the password information. It is readable only by root. It contains the password field data in an expanded format.

The shadow file, as shown in Listing 36.3, is not designed to be edited directly, but instead is modified by the passwd command automatically as needed. The passwd command has the ability to convert dates from standard format to the number of days since January 1, 1970, as needed in the date fields in this file.

Listing 36.3. Excerpts from a sample /etc/shadow file from an SVR4 system.

```
root:03de466J423f5:6445::::::
daemon:NP:6445::::::
```

```
bin:NP:6445::::::
sys:NP:6445::::::
adm:NP:6445::::::
lp:NP:6445::::::
smtp:NP:6445::::::
uucp:NP:6445::::::
nuucp:NP:6445::::::
listen:*LK*::::::::
Pwcsite:x3d5dtyfetonK:8774::::::
syd:43ASxete436h.:8776:0:168:7:::
nobody:NP:6445::::::
noaccess:NP:6445::::::
```

The shadow file consists of the following fields:

User Name

This name is used to match against the name in the passwd file.

Password

The user's password, encrypted with a one-way cipher, is stored in the second field. Only the first 8 characters of the password are used. These are mixed with a 2-character salt to produce a 13-character encrypted password. When it is necessary to compare a password, the plain text is encrypted with the salt, and a comparison is made against the encrypted version. If the passwd field is empty, the account has no password, and none is required to log in.

Password Last Changed Date

The number of days between January 1, 1970, and the date that the password was last modified. It is stored as an integer value. All the remaining day fields are relative to this date.

Minimum Number of Days Between Password Changes

The user is not allowed to change his password until the number of days specified in this field after the last password change. The number of days is specified by the system administrator. 0 means that no limit is enforced, and the user may change his password at anytime.

Maximum Number of Days a Password Is Valid

The user is required to change his password when the number of days specified in this field has passed since the last change. An empty field means the password never expires.

> **TIP:** Do not enable password aging (leave this field blank) for UUCP accounts. The UUCP chat script cannot handle requests to change an expired password.

Number of Days to Warn User to Change *passwd*

Beginning this many days before password expiration, on login the user is warned that his password is about to expire and will need to be changed.

Number of Days the Login May Be Inactive

If the account is inactive for more than this number of days, the login is considered locked and requires administrative action to reset a new date.

Date When the Login Is No Longer Valid

After this date, again specified as the number of days since January 1, 1970, the account is locked and may not be used for login.

The */etc/group* File

A user can belong to more than one group. He has access rights to files in every group of which he is a member. The groups file, like the passwd file, is delimited by colons as shown in Listing 36.4.

Listing 36.4. A sample /etc/group file from an SVR4 system.

```
root::0:root
other::1:
bin::2:root,bin,daemon
sys::3:root,bin,sys,adm
adm::4:root,adm,daemon
uucp::5:root,uucp
mail::6:root
tty::7:root,tty,adm
lp::8:root,lp,adm
nuucp::9:root,nuucp
staff::10:
daemon::12:root,daemon
nobody::60001:
noaccess::60002:
```

The following are the fields in the group file:

- Group name—text name of the group, up to eight alphanumeric characters. Again, to avoid confusion with IDs it's best to begin with a letter.

- Group password—a password that users can use with the `newgrp` command to make this group their current default group ID.

- Group ID—the numeric representation of the group name.

- Members—names of users who are members of this group. It is this section that is scanned to determine the other groups to which a user belongs.

> **CAUTION:** Many systems have a limit as to the number of groups to which a user can belong. The most common limit is 16. Placing a user in more than this number of groups prevents the user from being able to log in at all.

Building the Skeleton

Rather than building all of the configuration files by hand for each user as you create the user, UNIX provides the concept of a skeleton user. The files created for the skeleton are copied automatically to the home directory of the newly created user. The skeleton is located in `/etc/skel`. Any files found in this directory are copied by the `useradd` command to the newly created home directory. Note that the `useradd` command allows using alternate skeletons via the `-k` argument.

Creating Skeleton Shell Files

In the `/etc/skel` directory there are the following files:

- `.login, .cshrc, .profile`

  These are in the SVR4 version of the directory. They are the default files provided by the vendor. You can use a text editor to customize them as necessary.

- `local.login, local.cshrc, local.profile`

  This is the Solaris version of the directory. These files must be edited and renamed `.login`, `.cshrc`, and `.profile`.

Edit these files to alter the path lines for local conventions, and to add any local start-up options desired.

Samples named `.login`, `.cshrc`, and `.profile` can be found on the CD-ROM, along with a file named `.ksh_env`.

Additional Files You May Wish to Create

In addition to the default shell files, a user skeleton should consider adding the following:

- ■ .mailrc—mailx start-up script—In this file it is helpful to set some local mail options, such as when to use an external pager (set crt=22). See the Mail or mailx command page.

- ■ .mwmrc—motif window manager start-up script—You might want to provide a localized main menu for motif.

- ■ .openwin-menu—openlook window manager root menu—You might want to provide a localized main menu for openlook window manager.

You add these files not just to change the defaults but to show the users what files they can customize and what the current values are.

Adding a User

There are three ways to add a user:

- ■ Edit the passwd, shadow, and associated files yourself by hand.
- ■ Use the useradd command.
- ■ Use the specialized Graphical User Interface (GUI) interface provided by your UNIX vendor, such as admintool under Solaris or LoginMgr under UnixWare.

It is no longer recommended using the first option to prevent errors. The useradd command is very easy to use, and can handle all the internal security files directly. The GUI interfaces are also very easy to use and will guide you through the steps.

Before Adding the User

In any case, before actually adding the user you need to do the following:

- ■ *Choose a user name*—Often used are the first name, the first name with the first letter of the last name, the last name, the first letter of the first name and the last name. It really doesn't matter. Each name must be unique in the network and consistent on all machines the user is valid to log into.

- ■ *Assign a user ID*—Use the grouping of user ID values previously described and choose a user ID that has never been used. It is not a good idea to recycle user IDs, as a file in the system might still be owned by the old user of that ID, and would then belong to the new user of that ID.

- ■ *Choose group memberships*—Determine which groups best fit this user as the primary group and as supplemental groups.

■ *Choose the location for the user's home directory*—Using symbolic links you can later move the home directory to any disk drive that has storage. Consider using a common /home directory and symlinks to where space is available, on an as-needed basis.

Running *useradd*

The useradd command takes many arguments that specify the answers to the questions you asked yourself in the previous section. From the man page, the command line arguments are these:

```
useradd [ -c comment ] [ -d dir ] [ -e expire ] [ -f inactive ]
[ -g group ] [ -G group [, group...]]  [ -m [ -k skel_dir ]]
[   - u uid [ -o]] [ -s shell ] login
```

The following list goes over where each of these arguments ends up in the files:

■ -c comment—This is the GCOS field of the /etc/passwd file. Put the full information for this field here. Use the Berkeley format if you do not need the GCOS features. Here is an example of a - c argument:

-c "Syd Weinstein, Room 101"

■ -d dir—This is the home directory field of the /etc/passwd file:

■ -e expire—This is the ending date for this login. This field is not required, and if omitted no expiration date will be used. The date is converted from the input format to the days since January 1, 1970, and placed in the /etc/shadow file. Any input date format except a Julian date can be used. For example:

-e "January 1, 1995" or -e 1/1/95

■ -f inactive—This is the maximum number of days this login can be inactive before being invalidated. It is stored in the number of days inactive field of the /etc/shadow file. If this argument is omitted, no checking for inactivity is performed.

■ -g group—This is the primary group ID field of the /etc/passwd file. Either a group name or a numeric ID may be supplied.

■ -G group [, group .\x11.\x11.   ]—These are the secondary groups. The user's name is added to each of these group entries in the /etc/group file. Again, either a name or a numeric ID may be supplied.

■ -m [-k skel_dir]—If no -k argument is given, create a home directory for this user and copy the files from:

/etc/skel

If the `-k` argument is given, create a home directory and copy the files from the specified directory instead of the default `/etc/skel` directory.

- `-u uid [ -o]`—This is the user ID field of the `/etc/passwd` file. If the `-o` flag is given, the `uid` does not have to be unique. It is not recommended for more than one user to share a user ID.

- `-s shell`—This is the full pathname of the login shell and is the shell field of the `/etc/passwd` file.

- `login`—This is the login name you have assigned this user.

Creating Mail Alias Entries

After the user is added you should update the mail alias file. Add an alias for this user for the full spelling of his name to map to his user name. After the aliases are added, run the `newaliases` command to compile the alias hash table.

NIS Effects

If you are running NIS, most of this doesn't apply to you, although understanding it will help you do what NIS needs. NIS uses a different set of configuration files that parallel the `/etc/passwd` file. The files used are totally under your control, but a common convention is to use `/etc/passwd` for accounts local to this machine and `/etc/yppasswd` for the remainder of the accounts. See Chapter 37 for more information on NIS.

Removing a User

The first thing to understand about removing a user is *don't*. When a user must be denied access to the UNIX system, disable him instead. You don't want to remove him for the following reasons:

- *By not deleting, you prevent reuse of user IDs*

  You need to track which user IDs have been used to avoid reuse. One way of knowing this is to keep an entry in the password file with the deleted user's ID.

- *You may need to recover old files*

  When you recover files from an old tape, some of them might belong to the deleted user's ID. If the entry still exists, `ls` will be able to tell you who they belonged to so you can reassign them. This is another reason not to reuse user IDs.

Disabling the User's Login

It is very easy to disable the user's login. An option to the `passwd` command, when run by `root`, will mark the login as locked. Once locked, the user will not be able to log in. The command to lock a user is:

```
passwd -l user
```

> **CAUTION:** Just locking the account is not enough. You need to do the following:
>
> - Make sure the user is not logged on anywhere in the network. If so, he could use the `passwd` command to re-enable his login.
> - Remove or move to another name the `.rhosts` file in his home directory to prevent him from logging in as himself from another system.
> - Check the system to make sure there are no `setuid` programs with his user ID. This can be done with the command
>
> ```
> find / -user user_name -perm -04000 -print
> ```
>
> Any of these files should be modified to clear the `setuid` bit. If a production application requires these files to have this bit set, have someone verify that these files are not a security risk.
>
> Remember to run the `find` command on every system in the network.

Cleaning Up Disk Space Assigned to This User

After the user's login has been disabled, you need to clean up after him. This takes four steps:

1. Find files owned by this user.

   The `find` command traverses the file systems and prints the names of all files owned by this user. The ones in the user's home directory tree may be obvious, but there often are others elsewhere in the hierarchy. For example

   ```
   find / -user user_name -print
   ```

   prints a listing of the names of all the files owned by the user `user_name`. This should be run on each system in the network.

2. Back up the files to tape.

   In case you make a mistake, or there is a question later, make a tape backup of all of this user's files.

3. Reassign the ownership of files you desire to retain.

This is performed with the chown command.

4. Remove the remaining files you wish to discard.

You can use the xargs command with the files left on the list after you have deleted all the ones you reassigned ownership with the command

```
xargs rm < remaining_list
```

Final User Removal After All Files Are Handled

When you are sure you no longer need to access this user ID, because all the files have been handled and the home directory is removed, it's time to make the remaining password entry totally unusable by any shell program.

> **CAUTION:** After you do this you will be unable to su to this user ID, so be sure you really do not need to be this user anymore before clearing the entry.

To make sure that the password entry is only used as a uid placeholder, four fields in the entry should be changed:

- *User name*—While the user name is available, it can still receive mail. This can cause any mail being received for this now-deleted user to clutter up your mail spool directory. Changing the user name will cause any mail received for this user to bounce back to the sender.

  So that you know the entry is now a placeholder, use a pattern for the login name, perhaps d_uid, to indicate that this is a deleted entry for *uid uid*.

- *GCOS (comment/full name)*—Update the full name field to show when this entry was deleted. Leave the old user's name in there so you know who it belonged to when files are recovered that have this owner ID.

- *Home directory*—To prevent logging in to this user, set the login directory to a known nonexistent directory. This will prevent others from using su to use this user ID.

- *Login shell*—Finally, change the shell to /usr/bin/false. This will also prevent any accesses by remote commands for this user. This is accomplished with the usermod command:

```
usermod -l d_100 -c "Syd Weinstein, deleted 4/1/94 by ssw"\
 -d /nodir -s /usr/bin/false syd
```

The last step is to remove this user from any mail aliases to which he was a member. This is done by editing the alias file and searching for all occurrences of the user name. Remember also to remove occurrences of alternatives to his name listed in the alias file.

When the backups have rolled around, such that there are no longer any tapes from when this user was around, and you are sure you will never need the ID again, you can remove the placeholder from the /etc/passwd file to reduce the clutter in that file.

Summary

Dealing with user accounts is much easier once you know where everything is located. This chapter shows you where the UNIX system keeps the information on the user's account. With this information you can decide which options to the useradd, usermod, groupadd, and groupmod commands you need to use. You can even decide if you need to directly edit the files and go around these commands (but be cautious if you do so!).

The new user's account starts with the skeleton. It's from the skeleton that the initial contents of his home directory are created. You have to create the skeleton to meet your local needs. A simple default is delivered with the UNIX system, but it is up to you to modify that to fit local conventions.

Finally, eventually you need to remove users. This chapter gives a set of steps you can follow when that becomes necessary.

Networking

37

By Sydney S. Weinstein

UNIX is a network operating system. It is tightly integrated with the TCP/IP networking protocols. Most of the original work on networking and UNIX was done at the University of California at Berkeley in the late 1970s and early 1980s. Thus, UNIX has a well-developed and rich set of networking utilities available to both the user and the system administrator.

This chapter explains the basics of networking with TCP/IP and introduces you to how the network is administered. Then it goes into using the network, via the Network File System (NFS) and the Network Information Service (NIS). Because things don't always go right, the last part of this chapter is on troubleshooting UNIX networks.

TCP/IP Basics

The primary protocol used by UNIX is the Internet Protocol, or IP. Often called TCP/IP, it actually is composed of several parts, including the following:

- **Internet Protocol (IP)**   The underlying layer that provides the transfer of information from computer to computer.

- **Transmission Control Protocol (TCP)**   A protocol layer on top of IP that provides reliable connection-oriented communications between two processes. The TCP layer adds flow control, error detection and recovery, and connection services.

- **User Datagram Protocol (UDP)**   A protocol layer on top of IP that provides a low-overhead, unnumbered datagram protocol. It is connectionless and does not provide error checking or flow control.

- **Serial Line IP (SLIP)**   An adaptation of the normal EtherNet-based IP that runs over asynchronous serial lines. It is considered obsolete and has been replaced by PPP.

- **Point to Point Protocol (PPP)**   An adaptation of the normal EtherNet-based IP that runs over asynchronous and synchronous serial lines. It supports dial-up and dedicated circuits and compression to improve bandwidth utilization.

- **Internet Control Message Protocol (ICMP)**   A protocol layer on top of IP that provides control messages to control the IP protocol, such as Host or Network Unreachable, or "reroute this message." The most common use of it is for the ping packet to see if a computer is alive.

The basis of communications in IP is the packet. All communications over any medium IP supports are in integral units of packets. Packets are exchanged between nodes. Every node has an address. From the user's point of view, every IP node can communicate with every other node in the network. However, underneath, the IP software may route the packet via many store and forward hops before the packet gets to the final destination.

Addressing

IP addresses are 32-bit quantities. Every computer has one or more addresses assigned to it. Each network interface (EtherNet adapter, token ring, FDDI, serial line, and so on) has its own 32-bit address. With 32 bits there are 2^{32} addresses available, or a maximum of 4,294,967,296 network interfaces. However, to make routing (sending the packets for each address to the proper computer, or *network node*) easier, not all the addresses are used. Instead, the addressing space is broken up to make it easier to route to networks of different sizes.

In IP each network is given a network number. Each computer on the network is given a node number within that network. Thus the address is split into two parts separated by a dot (`network.node`). Routing decisions are made on the `network` part. Reception decisions within a network are made on the entire address.

For ease of reference, the addresses are not normally written as `network.node`, but as dotted quads, where each section refers to the value of 8 bits of the 32-bit address, as in this:

`192.65.202.1`

which is the address of our gateway host at MYXA Corporation.

Class A, B, and C Addresses

Networks come in different sizes. Really big organizations have thousands of locations and thousands of computers. Middle-sized organizations have hundreds of locations and thousands of computers. Small organizations are, well, small. To make it easy to handle routing decisions, which are made on a network basis and not on the full address, the addressing space is split into several classes.

Class A Addresses

The 32 bits are split into 1 bit of 0, 7 bits of network number, and 24 bits of node number. (See Figure 37.1.) There could have been a maximum of 127 Class A addresses. However, net 0 is reserved, because at one time it was used as a global broadcast, and net 127 is reserved to mean loop back, or stay within my own computer. This leaves 126 possible Class A addresses. Each Class A address can have 2^{24}—or 16,777,214—nodes (the addresses with all 0s and all 1s are reserved to mean "broadcast to all nodes in this network"). In reality, the organization that uses a Class A address internally splits it up to route to their many internal networks, called *subnets*, and it really supports many fewer systems. Class A addresses are very rarely handed out. An example of a Class A address is net 16, Digital Equipment Corporation.

FIGURE 37.1.

A Class A network address layout.

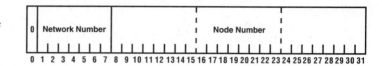

Class B Addresses

In a Class B address the 32 bits are split into 2 bits of 10, 14 bits of network number, and 16 bits of node number. (See Figure 37.2.) Allowing the address of 128 to equal a Class B broadcast, this leaves 16,383 Class B addresses with up to 65,534 nodes per network. Again, an address that is all 0s or all 1s is a broadcast address. Class B addresses, like Class A addresses, are normally split by their owners into many networks of fewer nodes per network. Even so, Class B addresses are running out and are hard to obtain. Most major universities have one or more Class B addresses.

FIGURE 37.2.

A Class B network address layout.

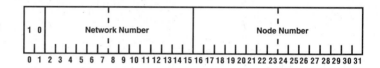

Class C Addresses

In a Class C address the 32 bits are split into 3 bits of 110, 21 bits of network number, and 8 bits of node number. (See Figure 37.3.) This provides 2,097,150 Class C addresses, with up to 254 nodes per network. Again, an address that is all 0s or all 1s is a broadcast address. Class C addresses are often handed out in blocks of 4 or 8 to allow for more than 254 nodes in the same network. MYXA Corporation has several Class C networks and a block of 8 Class C's.

FIGURE 37.3.

A Class C network address layout.

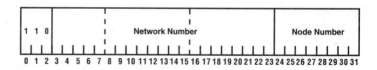

NOTE: Notice that bit 2 of a Class C address has a forced 0 in the network portion of the address. There are Class D and Class E addresses, but those are labeled as experimental and are not in current use. Class D addresses are now being considered for use as multicast addresses.

Acquiring a Network Number

Every network, whether connected to the Internet or not, should apply for a network number. If you are connected to the Internet, you will have to do this. Routing is based on the network number, and if you don't want your packets going to some other network, you have to have a unique network number.

 Even if your network is not connected to the Internet, you still should apply for the network number. It's a lot easier to set up your network now, with a unique network number, than to decide later that you want to connect to a public TCP/IP network, such as the Internet, and have to reassign the network numbers and IP addresses for all your nodes. Besides, the network number is free—all it takes is a small amount of effort to get one. You simply need to fill in a network address request template and send it in to the Network Information Center, known as NIC. (The CD-ROM for this book contains a complete copy of the application template in a file called `NET-ADDR.TXT`.)

Here is how to provide information for the nine items in the application found on the disk:

Item 1

If you are a connected network, you will get your network number from your Internet provider, who will file this form with the NIC on your behalf. Therefore, let the Internet provider answer this question (you can leave it blank).

If you are a nonconnected network, you don't need to answer it, so leave it blank.

Item 2

Who is the person responsible for this network number? This should be your network administrator or some such person. If this person has already filed information with the NIC, he or she will have a NIC handle. If not, don't worry. The first time you send an application in, the NIC will assign you a net handle.

If you do not have an Internet-reachable electronic mail address, leave the `Net Mailbox` field blank.

Item 3

This shows how NIC will list this network in its database. Just make up some short name so you can recognize that it's yours.

Item 4

This is the name and address of the site of this network—usually it's your name and address.

Item 5

You can skip this question because the military's network known as MILNET uses its own forms and files them with the NIC.

Items 6 and 7

This is very important, because it determines what type of network number you get (and if you get a Class C number(s), it determines how many you get). The NIC expects the five year number to be a guess.

You will be assigned a Class C number unless your answer in Item 7 explicitly shows that because the number of networks and nodes you have that you really cannot fit into a set of Class C numbers and you require a Class B number. How you answer this question, however, also indicates how many Class C numbers you can get. It helps to document your entire network and show how the net numbers will be used. Since address space is getting short, NIC is getting particular on how you answer this question.

Item 8

This should not be a problem. If you are a commercial organization, your net is most likely commercial.

Item 9

This needs only a short response on how you plan to use the network. The big justification is in Item 7 on the class of network required.

Filing the application is simple enough. If you are requesting a connected network number, send your application via electronic mail to your Internet service provider, who will file it with the NIC on your behalf or assign you a number from their pool of addresses. If the application is for a nonconnected network, and you have access to electronic mail, that is the preferred method of filing. If this is not the case, print out the application and mail it to the address on the form.

Broadcast Address

In IP messages are addressed to a single node, to all nodes on the subnet, or to all nodes on the network. The last two are called broadcast addresses. When IP was first implemented, the address of all 0s for the node number was used for the broadcast address. This was later changed to all 1s. To retain backward-compatibility, IP implementations will accept either all 0s or all 1s as the broadcast address. In addition, if the network number is all 0s or all 1s it is considered a networkwide broadcast address. This makes the following broadcast addresses:

- `x.y.z.255`   Subnet broadcast on subnet `x.y.z`
- `x.y.255.255`   Subnet broadcast on subnet `x.y`
- `x.255.255.255`   Subnet broadcast on subnet `x`
- `255.255.255.255`   Global broadcast

To prevent a broadcast address in one network from leaking to other networks by accident, most routers are configured not to propagate a broadcast across network boundaries.

Net Mask

Since the IP address is broken into two parts, the network number and the node number, some way must be used to split the address into these two parts. This is the netmask. It is a bit mask that when bit-wise anded with the full 32-bit address results in the network number portion of the address. Although the specifications of IP do not require this mask to be a consecutive set of 1s followed by all 0s, most implementations of IP do require this. The default netmask for IP addresses is the following:

- For Class A: `255.0.0.0`
- For Class B: `255.255.0.0`
- For Class C: `255.255.255.0`

The net mask is heavily involved in routing. Packets with a network number matching your network number are considered local and are not routed. Packets with a network number different from your network number are routed. The netmask is used to make this distinction.

As an example, you have a Class B address of `190.109.252.6` for your workstation. This could be configured as one of the following:

- One big network with many thousands of possible addresses, with a netmask of `255.255.0.0` and a network number of `190.109.0.0` and a node address of `252.6`.
- A subnet allowing only a few nodes under the big network, with a netmask of `255.255.255.0` and a network number of `190.109.252` and a node address of `6`.
- A larger subnet allowing more nodes under the big network, with a netmask of `255.255.240.0` and a network number of `190.109.240.0` and a node address of `12.6`.

Routing

A network by it self is not as much use as one that can connect to other networks. To get a message off your network and onto the others requires knowing where and how to deliver the packets. This is known as *routing*.

In IP each network keeps track of only the first hop on the route to all other networks. It keeps track of which gateway to use for each other network to which it wants to communicate. Those nodes know the next hop for the packet, and so on. Eventually the packet reaches its destination. This is called *store and forward routing*, because each node in the chain receives the packet and then forwards it to the next destination. However, it is networks that have routes to gateway nodes, not nodes that have routes.

There are several types of routes:

- **Default**   All packets for networks you don't explicitly list elsewhere are sent to this node for forwarding. If your network has only one gateway, this is all you need.

- **Static**   A command is used to add a route for one or more networks, and it never changes. This is used when there are a few gateways to fixed networks, and normally a default route is used for the remaining networks.

- **Dynamic**   The system listens to broadcasts of routes from the gateways and adjusts automatically. Many Internet nodes use this method.

Routing is transparent and automatic by the system. You can turn it off by performing a modification to the TCP parameters in the operating system. Firewall gateways, which are used to protect networks from security breaches, turn off this automatic forwarding.

Naming

Although you can refer to anything via its dotted quad, you may have difficulty remembering the dotted quad. So the developers of the Internet and IP invented a scheme to assign names to the numbers. A name can be used to map to dotted quad network node address. Thus, the node `190.109.252.6` could be referred to as `fasthost`. A table of translations between the names and the dotted quads is kept on UNIX systems in `/etc/hosts`. Not only hosts, but also dotted quad values, can have names, as in:

- `190.109.252.0`   The network on which `fastnode` resides could be fastnet.

- `190.109.252.255`   The broadcast address for that network could be `fastnet-broadcast`.

- `255.255.255.0`   The netmask for `fastnet` could be `fastnet-netmask`.

- `190.109.0.0`   The Class B overall net could be `backbone-net`.

These names are interchangeable in UNIX commands with dotted quads wherever a node address or network number is needed.

Port Number

In addition to the IP address, some of the IP protocols use a port number. This is a 16-bit quantity that allows for more than one connection to the node. Each concurrent connection is to a port, and with 16 bits this limits any node to 65535 connections simultaneously. Port numbers lower than 1024 are considered privileged and require root access to open.

UDP Versus TCP

The two major protocols in IP are UCP and TDP. These two are used by most other services and protocols to transfer the data.

UDP is the simpler of the two and is an unnumbered message sent to a particular IP address and port. UNIX buffers the request and provides the message to any process that reads that port. It is a connectionless service and no acknowledgment of reception is sent to the sending system. It is only possible to read complete messages. The messages may be of any size less than the buffer size of the UDP queue (usually less than 24 KB).

TCP is a connection-oriented protocol. It guarantees delivery of the data, in order and error free. A TCP connection is a unique combination of four values:

- The sending IP address
- The sending port number
- The receiving IP address
- The receiving port number

This allows multiple connections at the same time to the same receiving port, as all four values uniquely identify a connection. The connection is bidirectional, and what is written at one end is read by the other, and vice versa.

TCP connections work just like stream I/0 in that any number of bytes at a time can be read or written. When the connection is broken, a write receives a broken pipe error and a read receives EOF (End of File).

ARP

Behind the scenes, the IP protocol still needs to converse over the EtherNet. In doing so, it has to address the message to an EtherNet address, not just an IP address. This is necessary so that the EtherNet hardware receives the message and passes it on for further processing. This conversion from IP address to EtherNet address is handled by the Address Resolution Protocol (ARP).

A node needing to convert an IP address to an EtherNet address for the first time broadcasts a message using the ARP protocol, asking what is the EtherNet address for a particular IP address. When a node running ARP hears its IP address, it responds with its EtherNet address directly (not via broadcast) to the requesting node. That node then caches the result for later reuse. If an address is not used in a while, it is timed out and flushed from the cache.

RARP

The opposite translation—converting an EtherNet address to an IP address—is performed by the Reverse Address Resolution Protocol (RARP). In any network, several nodes are usually set up to run rarp daemons. (*Daemons* are processes that run in the background—they are discussed later in this chapter.) These programs listen for rarp requests, and using a data table provided in a disk file, respond with the IP address that is mapped to that EtherNet address.

RARP can be used by nodes when they boot. Instead of configuring the node with its IP address in a system configuration file, it can ask the network, and therefore some central mapping server, what IP address it is to use. Once it has the IP address, it can use the naming service or the host's file to determine its hostname. Diskless workstations have no local configuration and rely on RARP for boot time setup.

ICMP

When something goes wrong, someone has to act as traffic cop. That role belongs to the Internet Control Message Protocol (ICMP). ICMP is used to transparently control the network and for diagnostic purposes. If too much traffic is being generated by a connection, the system can send it an ICMP source quench message and ask it to slow down. If a packet is being sent to a host that a gateway knows does not exist, an ICMP host unreachable message is returned. If a gateway receives a packet, but doesn't know how to route it to its final destination, a ICMP network unreachable message is returned. If the wrong gateway is used for a packet, an ICMP redirect message is used to instruct the connection about the proper route. But the most well-known ICMP message is echo. It just echoes what it receives and is how the ping command works. (ping is covered later in this chapter.)

Well-Known Services

Many daemons listen for connections on pre-agreed on ports. These are the well-known services. The port numbers are specified in the file /etc/services. Many of these services are controlled by the Internet dispatch daemon, inetd.

> **NOTE:** Daemons are special processes that run exclusively in the background. Most of the time you can tell that a process or command that has run or is running is a daemon because it ends in the letter *d* (for example, `inetd`, `nfsd`, and `lockd`). Some daemons allow to run multiple copies of themselves in memory (for example, `nfsd`, which is one of the network file system daemons discussed later in the chapter).

Telnet

Remote serial communication via IP is performed via telnet. The receiving UNIX system listens either via a `telnetd` daemon or via `inetd` for telnet connection requests on TCP port 23. A connection request is made using the `telnet` program. Once a connection is established, `telnetd` establishes a connection to the login program, and a remote login session is started.

FTP

If an interactive session isn't needed, but file transfer is desired, the file transfer protocol (ftp) is used. ftp is actually run under the TCP protocol, but is called a protocol itself because it uses specific commands to transfer the information. Again, as with telnet, an `ftpd` or `inetd` listens for a connection on TCP port 20. Using the `ftp` program a UNIX user establishes a connection. The `ftpd` program accepts login information and provides file transfer capabilities both to and from each system.

ftp is one of the original four-letter command and three-digit response protocols that are common in TCP/IP. Commands sent from `ftp` to `ftpd` include USER to log in and PASS to provide the password. Responses are three-digit numeric codes with a human-readable explanation following. The number codes are divided into response groups:

- ■ `1xx` Informative message.
- ■ `2xx` Command succeeded.
- ■ `3xx` Command ok so far, send the rest of it.
- ■ `4xx` Command was correct, but couldn't be performed for some reason. This error group generally means try again later.
- ■ `5xx` Command unimplemented, or incorrect, or a serious problem has occurred. Abort this command and do not retry it later.

This same protocol style is used by almost all protocols run on top of TCP/IP.

DNS

Whereas telnet and ftp are examples of TCP-based services, the domain name service (DNS) is an example of a UDP-based service. The DNS daemon, named, listens on UDP port 53. When it receives a request to look up a name or number, it searches in memory tables for the answer. If it has seen the answer recently, it can respond immediately from its in-memory tables. If not, it asks a higher-level server whom to ask for this query and then requests the information from that server. This provides a very fast-responding, totally distributed naming service.

Haste Makes Waste, So Plan!

Providing a reliable, responsive network takes planning. Except in the smallest of networks, you can't just connect all the systems together, slap on any address, and then expect everything to work perfectly. This section contains some guidelines to help you plan your network so that it works not only reliably but also responsively for your UNIX system.

Segmenting the Network

Depending on how you plan to use the network, UNIX systems can place much more traffic on a network than can a comparable number of PCs or Macs. If you intend to share disk resources across the network using NFS, UNIX can saturate a network very quickly.

In designing a UNIX network, you need to keep in mind the following goals:

- Diskless and dataless clients should be on the same segment as their servers.
- File servers can be on the same segment, or if they serve multiple segments, on a backbone segment.
- Don't overload any segment. Depending on the amount of file sharing, 12 to 24 nodes per segment should be considered full.
- Place servers for broadcast services, such as RARP and BOOTP, on each segment and do not transmit broadcasts between segments.
- Use bridging routers or routers to connect the segments to the backbone.

Although each segment as well as the backbone needs its own network address, you do not need to use a Class C address for each network. With only 24 nodes per network being considered full load, using 5 bits for the node address will allow 30 nodes. This give 3 bits for subnetting, allowing 6 networks to share the same Class C address.

TIP: If you use a hierarchy of networks for routing purposes, and you split a Class C network as described, place the 0 net (the one with the 3 bits, 001) on the backbone, and then place the others on segments below the backbone. This will allow other nets that are outside the backbone to route using the 24-bit netmask to the backbone and let it use a 27-bit netmask to route to the segments connected to it. In the external gateway, the netmask for the 190.109.252 net, which is used to reach all 8 subnets, is 255.255.255.0, or 24 bits. However, each router would be using a 27-bit netmask of 255.255.255.224 to reach the other subnets, and a default route of the address of the external gateway, 190.109.252.33. Hosts on each of the subnets would use a 27-bit netmask and a default route of the router on their network (in the case of 190.109.252.64 net, the default route would be 190.109.252.65).

CAUTION: Be careful. Not all software supports non–byte-aligned netmasks. While all UNIX systems do, many PCs and Macs do not follow the specifications for TCP/IP and allow for non–byte-aligned netmasks.

Draw a Map

It really helps when planning a network to draw a logical connection map such as the one in Figure 37.4. This map does not show the geography of the net, but it does show its logical topology. Note how I listed the node addresses of each gateway to the network on the map. You use these to make up your routing tables.

Draw several maps, at different level of details. It's not necessary, nor even desirable, to show which nodes are connected to each of the networks in the map. But each of the subnets would also have its own map showing every node connected and their addresses. Having and keeping these maps up-to-date might take a small amount of time, but it's worthwhile when you have to figure out configurations or troubleshoot the network.

Down to the Wire

So far this chapter has dealt with the network as a virtual entity. It's time to give the network some identity. Most UNIX systems connect to an EtherNet-type local area network. EtherNet was invented by Xerox to act as a network for their printers and it was perfected by a cooperative effort of DEC, Intel, and Xerox. EtherNet is a bus-based network in which all nodes on the network can hear all other nodes. All EtherNets share some common features:

■ A 10 MB-per-second transfer rate.

■ Limited distance for the network cable. The actual limit is based on the cable type and it ranges from 250 meters (10BASE2) to about 750 meters (10BASE5).

■ A limit on the number of nodes possible on a segment.

■ Uses the Carrier Sense Multi-Access with Collision Detection protocol for transmission on the cable.

■ Uses a 48-bit Media Access Control (MAC) address that is unique. The first 24 bits are the vendor and model of the EtherNet adapter, the last 24 bits are a serial number. No two EtherNet adapters are supposed to have the same MAC-level address.

Specialized chips now handle the mechanics of listening to the network, deciding when to transmit, transmitting, receiving, and filtering packets.

Types of EtherNets

EtherNet comes in three main connection types, which describe the type of cable used.

10BASE5, or Thicknet

This is the original EtherNet. It is a triaxial cable, usually yellow or orange in color, with black bands every 2 meters. The nodes are connected to the cable using taps at those black bands. While rarely used for new installations any longer, many backbones have used this connection method.

Thicknet networks require external transceivers to connect the EtherNet board to the cable. A drop cable called an AUI (Attachment Unit Interface) cable is used to connect the transceiver to the network board. The AUI cable has 15 pin connectors on each end and uses a special variant of the DB-15 connector with an unusual slide-locking mechanism.

Thicknet is the most expensive method of connecting nodes, but can also connect the most nodes over the longest distances.

10BASE2, or Thinnet

In an effort to reduce costs, the next development was to place the transceiver directly on the board and drop the expensive triaxial cable for inexpensive RG-58/U cable and BNC connectors. This led to Thinnet, or as it is often called, Cheapernet. In 10BASE5 the transceivers tap onto the cable and an AUI stub cable allows the node to be up to 30 meters from the network backbone cable. In 10BASE2 the cable is looped through each node and a BNC T-connector is used to connect directly to the network board.

10BASE2 networks are limited in distance to several hundred meters, and a fault at any point in the network usually takes down the entire network. However, 10BASE2 networks are very reliable.

10BASET, or Twisted Pair

The newest type of EtherNet simulates the bus topology, using a star configuration and a central repeating hub. It uses two twisted-pair cables running directly from each node to a central hub. At the node end, these cables are usually terminated in an RJ-45 connector that looks like a telephone plug but is 8 pins wide instead of the usual 6 for the RJ-11.

At the hub end many different connection types are used, including RJ-45 for single lines and 25 pair Amphenol connectors for multiple terminations. Hubs are available with from 4 to hundreds of ports and many even have sophisticated monitoring abilities.

This method was developed to allow EtherNet to use existing twisted-pair telephone cabling. However, it works better if type 3 network cabling is used. It is also the least expensive method of wiring a new network.

What Is a Hub?

10BASET networks need a central device to repeat the signals from each leg of the star onto all other legs. This is performed by a hub. It converts the star back into a logical bus topology. It also provides signal conditioning and regeneration to allow the twisted-pair cable to be used at EtherNet speeds.

Hubs are content-passive devices in that anything received on one port is retransmitted on all other ports of the hub.

What Is a Repeater?

Because EtherNets are limited in length due to signal timings and attenuation, a device was needed to regenerate the signals to extend the network. This is the repeater. It is connected between two segments of an EtherNet network and repeats whatever it hears on one segment onto the other segment.

Repeaters are also content-passive devices in that anything received from one segment is repeated on the other one.

What Is a Bridge?

A bridge is also used to connect two segments of a network. However, its not content passive. It is a link-level filtering device. It reads the EtherNet MAC header, looking for the MAC-level address. If the address is for another node it recognizes as being on the same segment on which it received the packet, it discards the packet. If it is a broadcast packet, or one it does not recognize, it repeats the packet onto the other network.

Bridges have to read the packet to determine the address, so there is a delay inherent in going through a bridge. This delay could be just long enough to read the MAC header and determine whether to forward the packet. Other bridges store the entire packet and then retransmit it. This type of bridge has a longer delay because it must read not just the header but the entire packet.

Bridges are rated by the number of packets per second they can forward.

What Is a Router?

Whereas a bridge makes its decision based on the link level or MAC address, a router makes its forwarding decisions based on the network level or IP address. Routers read the entire packet into memory, and then decide what to do with the packet, based on its contents.

Whereas bridges work at the EtherNet level and do not need to understand the protocol being used in the messages, routers work at the network level and need special software to understand every network protocol being used (IP, IPX, DECNET, and so on).

Routers are very configurable and can be used to filter packets and isolate networks from other network problems. Some configurations can also be used as security filters to keep out unwanted traffic.

However, for all this flexibility and protection you pay a price. Routers are more expensive and slower than bridges. They must read in the entire packet, and this causes a delay at least equal to the time it takes to read in the entire packet. This delay is called *latency*, and although it has little effect on throughput, it does effect response time.

What Is Switched EtherNet?

With the growth in networking and multimedia software, the old 10 MB/s EtherNet is showing its age. One stop gap measure on the way to faster networks is switched EtherNet. Using a special computer as a switch, a private EtherNet is created between the switch and each node. Then the switch forwards the packets onto the desired node on its private EtherNet connection.

This breaks the bus and sends only broadcast and addressed traffic to each node. The overall traffic can be higher when each node talks to many other nodes. It works well, but introduces latency. The switch must delay the packet at least long enough to read the MAC-level address. Often switches are implemented as a store and forward bridge.

In addition, the use of switched Ethernet makes it more difficult to diagnose problems on the network because you can no longer listen in to the bus from any node to determine where problems are occurring.

How to Segment and Expand an EtherNet Network

When a segment is getting too full, the first thing to do is to split it into two segments connected by a bridge. This reduces the traffic on each segment, but does not require you to readdress all of the IP addresses on the network.

Place all diskless systems on the same segment as their servers and try to split the groups of servers and workstations across both segments. Then split the network and place a bridge between the two segments.

If this is insufficient for the growth, it will be necessary to split the network into two or more subnets and use routing instead of bridging to reduce the traffic load.

Configuring TCP/IP

When you first hook a UNIX system to the network there are many files that need to be populated with the data describing the IP network. Several of these files have default contents provided by the vendor. These may be sufficient, but often there are additions needed. This section describes the contents of the UNIX TCP/IP configuration files found in the /etc directory.

NOTE: If you are running Network Information Service (NIS), most of these files are not used past boot and starting NIS. NIS provides networkwide access to the same information, allowing you to enter it only once. NIS is covered later in this chapter.

NOTE: On some UNIX systems the files actually reside in /etc/inet. There are symbolic links from the /etc/inet directory to the names in the /etc directory. This should not affect you when you're editing the files.

Assigning Addresses—/etc/hosts

The hosts file is used for translating names into IP addresses and IP addresses back into names. A sample file consists of:

```
#
# Internet host table
#
127.0.0.1          localhost loghost
190.109.252.1      gateway
190.109.252.2      sn1-router
190.109.252.33     sn1-gateway
190.109.252.34     sn1-host sn1-boothost
```

The # is the common character, which means that the system ignores all the characters that appear on a line following the #.

Entries are individual lines. Each entry starts with the dotted quad for the IP address, followed by white space, blanks, and/or tabs, and a list of names for this host. Any one of the names listed will be translated into the IP address. Looking up the hostname for an IP address will return the first name listed. All the rest of the names are considered aliases.

> **CAUTION:** The same IP address cannot appear on more than one line in the file. Although this will not normally hurt, it can confuse NIS and cause the entire host file information not to be made available via NIS.

Naming Networks—/etc/networks

Just as it is easier to refer to hosts by name rather than by number, it's also easiest to refer to networks by name. A file is provided to separate network numbers from host numbers. This file differs from the hosts file in that only the network number portion is listed in the file as seen in this example:

```
#
# The networks file associates Internet Protocol (IP) network
# numbers with network names.  The format of this file is:
#
#      network-name     network-number     nicnames . . .
#

#
# The loopback network is used only for intra-machine communication
#
loopback     127

#
# Internet networks
#
arpanet          10                arpa      # Historical
subnet           190.109.252
subnet-seg1      190.109.252.32
subnet-seg2      190.109.252.64
```

Choosing the Netmask for a Network—/etc/netmasks

Normally when a netmask is needed, the IP system looks at the address class and chooses a netmask that matches the class of the address. However, as in the subnetting example, often a different netmask is needed. These exceptions to the rule are listed in the `netmasks` file as shown in this example:

```
#
# The netmasks file associates Internet Protocol (IP) address
# masks with IP network numbers.
#
#       network-number      netmask
#
# Both the network-number and the netmasks are specified in
# "decimal dot" notation, e.g:
#
#                           128.32.0.0 255.255.255.0
#
190.109.252.0       255.255.255.0
190.109.252.32      255.255.255.224
190.109.252.64      255.255.255.224
```

A command that needs a netmask can either take the netmask as an override on the command line or consult the `netmasks` file to determine if there is a specific netmask before resorting to calculating one based on the class of the address.

Mapping Names to Machines—/etc/ethers

BOOTP and RARP need a file to map EtherNet addresses into IP numbers. This is provided by the `ethers` file, which maps the EtherNet MAC address into a hostname. Then the `hosts` file is used to map this into an IP address.

```
#
# The ethers file associates ethernet addresses with hostnames
#
08:00:20:0e:b9:d3       gateway
08:00:20:11:30:d0       sn1-router
08:00:20:0e:1d:0b       sn1-gateway
08:00:20:0b:de:0d       sn1-host
```

By placing the IP address in only the `hosts` file and making use of RARP for assigning network numbers, it is possible to readdress an entire network just by changing the `hosts` file and rebooting the machines. This makes changes very convenient.

Mapping Names to Interfaces—/etc/hostname.??n

Many UNIX systems have more than one network interface. Each network interface on a host has its own IP address. Because a node name can appear only once in the `/etc/hosts` file, each interface also has its own node name. So the node, on boot, still needs to know which name, and therefore which IP address, to use on which network interface.

This is provided by the file /etc/hostname.*??n* where *??* is the name of the interface type, and *n* is a digit referring to the interface number. On Suns this is usually /etc/hostname.le0 for the first interface, /etc/hostname.le1 for the second, and so on.

This file contains just one line with one word on that line, the hostname to use for that particular interface:

```
fasthost
```

Naming Supported Protocols—/etc/protocols

To enable the diagnostic output of the utilities to list the protocols by name rather than by protocol number, a mapping is kept in the file /etc/protocols. This file is provided by the vendor and should not need changing. Not all the protocols listed in this file are necessarily supported on your system. An example of the contents of /etc/protocols is as follows:

```
#
# Internet (IP) protocols
#
ip        0       IP        # internet protocol, pseudo protocol number
icmp      1       ICMP      # internet control message protocol
ggp       3       GGP       # gateway-gateway protocol
tcp       6       TCP       # transmission control protocol
egp       8       EGP       # exterior gateway protocol
pup       12      PUP       # PARC universal packet protocol
udp       17      UDP       # user datagram protocol
hmp       20      HMP       # host monitoring protocol
xns-idp   22      XNS-IDP   # Xerox NS IDP
rdp       27      RDP       # "reliable datagram" protocol
```

Naming Supported Services—/etc/services

Programs that wish to connect to a specific port use the services file to map the service name to the port number. This file is shipped from your vendor with all the default services in it. Local services can be added to support databases or any local extensions desired. The file is large, so the following example is only a small extract. Remember that ports smaller than 1024 are privileged and can only be listened on by processes owned by root.

```
#
# Network services, Internet style
# This file is never consulted when the NIS are running
#
tcpmux      1/tcp                       # rfc-1078
echo        7/tcp
echo        7/udp
discard     9/tcp       sink null
discard     9/udp       sink null
systat      11/tcp      users
daytime     13/tcp
```

```
daytime      13/udp
netstat      15/tcp
chargen      19/tcp      ttytst source
chargen      19/udp      ttytst source
ftp-data     20/tcp
ftp          21/tcp
telnet       23/tcp
smtp         25/tcp      mail
time         37/tcp      timserver
time         37/udp      timserver
name         42/udp      nameserver
whois        43/tcp      nicname         # usually to sri-nic
domain       53/udp
domain       53/tcp
hostnames    101/tcp     hostname        # usually to sri-nic
sunrpc       111/udp
sunrpc       111/tcp
ident        113/tcp     auth tap
#
# Host specific functions
#
bootps       67/udp                      # bootp server
bootpc       68/udp                      # bootp client
tftp         69/udp
rje          77/tcp
finger       79/tcp
link         87/tcp      ttylink
supdup       95/tcp
iso-tsap     102/tcp
x400         103/tcp                     # ISO Mail
x400-snd     104/tcp
csnet-ns     105/tcp
pop-2        109/tcp                     # Post Office
auth         113/tcp
uucp-path    117/tcp
nntp         119/tcp     usenet          # Network News Transfer
ntp          123/tcp                     # Network Time Protocol
ntp          123/udp                     # Network Time Protocol
snmp         161/udp
#
# UNIX specific services
#
# these are NOT officially assigned
#
exec         512/tcp
login        513/tcp
shell        514/tcp     cmd             # no passwords used
printer      515/tcp     spooler         # line printer spooler
courier      530/tcp     rpc             # experimental
uucp         540/tcp     uucpd           # uucp daemon
biff         512/udp     comsat
who          513/udp     whod
syslog       514/udp
talk         517/udp
ntalk        518/udp
route        520/udp     router routed
timed        525/udp     timeserver
new-rwho     550/udp     new-who         # experimental
rmonitor     560/udp     rmonitord       # experimental
```

```
monitor     561/udp                      # experimental
pcserver    600/tcp                      # ECD Integrated PC board srvr
kerberos    750/udp     kdc              # Kerberos key server
kerberos    750/tcp     kdc              # Kerberos key server
```

The format of the file is the name of the service followed by white space, then the port number, followed by a / and the protocol (either TCP or UDP). This is optionally followed by nicknames for the service. If a service is available both under UDP and TCP it must be listed twice in the file, once for UDP and once for TCP.

Binding Daemons to Services—/etc/inetd.conf

Rather than having each task listen for connections on its own ports, UNIX uses a common daemon to listen on many ports at once. This is the Internet services daemon or `inetd`. It listens on every port listed in its configuration file. When it receives a connection it forks off and starts the appropriate service daemon. Some services are handled internally by `inetd`, including `daytime` and `echo`.

When you change the `inetd.conf` file you need to signal the daemon to reread the file. Sending `inetd` the HUP signal causes it to reread the file. HUP is the signal 1 so you can use the following commands to have `inetd` reread the `/etc/inetd.conf` file:

```
kill -HUP pid
```

Alternatively, you can enter this:

```
kill -1 pid
```

In these commands *pid* is replaced by the *pid* of the `inetd` process, which will cause `inetd` to reread its configuration file. The following is a small sample of the file to show the format:

```
#
# Configuration file for inetd(1M).  See inetd.conf(4).
#
# To re-configure the running inetd process, edit this file, then
# send the inetd process a SIGHUP.
#
# Syntax for socket-based Internet services:
#  <service_name> <socket_type> <proto> <flags> <user> <server_pathname> <args>
#
# Syntax for TLI-based Internet services:
#
#  <service_name> tli <proto> <flags> <user> <server_pathname> <args>
#
# Ftp and telnet are standard Internet services.
#
ftp         stream      tcp     nowait      root    /etc/in.tcpd    in.ftpd
telnet      stream      tcp     nowait      root    /etc/in.tcpd    in.telnetd
#
# Shell, login, exec, comsat and talk are BSD protocols.
#
shell       stream      tcp     nowait      root    /etc/in.tcpd    in.rshd
```

```
login     stream    tcp     nowait     root     /etc/in.tcpd     in.rlogind
#
#
# RPC services syntax:
#  <rpc_prog>/<vers> <endpoint-type> rpc/<proto> <flags> <user> \
#  <pathname> <args>
#
# <endpoint-type> can be either "tli" or "stream" or "dgram".
# For "stream" and "dgram" assume that the endpoint is a socket descriptor.
# <proto> can be either a nettype or a netid or a "*". The value is
# first treated as a nettype. If it is not a valid nettype then it is
# treated as a netid. The "*" is a short-hand way of saying all the
# transports supported by this system, ie. it equates to the "visible"
# nettype. The syntax for <proto> is:
#      *¦<nettype¦netid>¦<nettype¦netid>{[,<nettype¦netid>]}
# For example:
# dummy/1   tli    rpc/circuit_v,udp    wait    root    /tmp/test_svc    test_svc
#
# System and network administration class agent server
#
# This is referenced by number because the admind agent is needed for the
# initial installation of the system. However, on some preinstalled systems
# the SNAG packages may not be present. Referencing the service by number
# prevents error messages in this case.
#
100087/10    tli     rpc/udp     wait     root     /usr/sbin/admind     admind
```

Dealing with Naming

There are three methods of translating names and IP addresses commonly in use in UNIX networking:

- **/etc files**   The C library routines will use the files in the /etc directory to perform the translations.

- **NIS**   The Network Information Service will be used. Calls are made by the C library routines to the NIS server for translation of the names and numbers.

- **DNS**   The Internet Domain Name Service is used. Calls are made by the C library routines to the DNS server for translation of the names and numbers.

This choice is controlled by a combination of methods:

- **The presence of the file /etc/resolv.conf**   On some systems, providing this file automatically enables the use of DNS. This file is required for DNS and lists the default domain name and the IP address of your DNS servers as in:

  ```
  domain conglomerate.com

  nameserver 190.109.252.17

  nameserver 190.109.252.37
  ```

- **Installation of a special shared library**   Some systems have the choice of naming service compiled directly into the shared library. This was true for older

BSD systems such as SunOS 4. In these systems you need to build a new shared library to change the method.

- **Specifying the method in `/etc/nsswitch.conf`** Newer operating systems provide a control file to specify how to perform naming lookup. The contents of this file specify which method to use. The sample below uses NIS and DNS, but not the files in `/etc`:

```
#
# /etc/nsswitch:
#
# An example file that could be copied over to
# /etc/nsswitch.conf
# It uses NIS (YP) in conjunction with files and DNS for hosts.
#
# "hosts:" and "services:" in this file are used only if the
transports.

# the following two lines obviate the "+" entry in /etc/passwd and
/etc/group.
passwd:     files nis
group:      files nis

# consult /etc "files" only if nis is down.
hosts:      nis dns [NOTFOUND=return] files
networks:   nis [NOTFOUND=return] files
protocols:  nis [NOTFOUND=return] files
rpc:        nis [NOTFOUND=return] files
ethers:     nis [NOTFOUND=return] files
netmasks:   nis [NOTFOUND=return] files
bootparams: nis [NOTFOUND=return] files
publickey:  nis [NOTFOUND=return] files

netgroup:   nis

automount:  files nis
aliases:    files nis

# for efficient getservbyname() avoid nis
services:   files nis
sendmailvars:   files
```

- **System V Release 4 (SRV4) uses the `/etc/netconfig`** This file specifies which shared libraries are to be used to perform name lookups as well as other TCP services. The sample below uses the file first and DNS second:

```
##
#     The Network Configuration File.
#
# Each entry is of the form:
#
# network_id semantics flags protofamily protoname device nametoaddr_libs
#
ticlts      tpi_clts      v    loopback   -    /dev/ticlts     /usr/lib/straddr.so
ticots      tpi_cots      v    loopback   -    /dev/ticots     /usr/lib/straddr.so
ticotsord   tpi_cots_ord  v    loopback   -    /dev/ticotsord  /usr/lib/straddr.so
tcp         tpi_cots_ord  v    inet       tcp  /dev/tcp        /usr/lib/tcpip.so,/
```

```
➥usr/lib/resolv.so
 udp         tpi_clts     v      inet      udp   /dev/udp       /usr/lib/tcpip.so,/
➥usr/lib/resolv.so
 icmp        tpi_raw      -      inet      icmp  /dev/icmp      /usr/lib/tcpip.so,/
 usr/lib/resolv.so
rawip        tpi_raw      -      inet      -     /dev/rawip     /usr/lib/tcpip.so,/usr/
➥lib/resolv.so
```

Starting TCP/IP at Boot Time

TCP/IP doesn't just magically start when UNIX is booted. The interfaces, addresses, and routes all need to be configured. In addition, daemons need to be started. This is performed automatically at boot time by the start-up scripts. On BSD-derived systems, this is in /etc/rc.boot to set up the protocol and /etc/rc.local to start the rest. On SVR4, it's /etc/init.d/inetinit, which also runs /etc/inet/rc.inet. On Solaris 2, it's /etc/init.d/rootusr to set the hostname, /etc/init.d/inetinit for the main configuration, and /etc/init.d/inetsvc for the services that need NIS to be running before they can be started.

In all three cases it's necessary to configure the protocol, set the parameters for the hostname and address, and start the daemons.

Starting TCP/IP

The TCP/IP protocol stack is implemented differently in BSD and SVR4 operating systems. On BSD it's part of the kernel. On SVR4 it's a streams driver and is configured at run time. This leads to different start-up scripts.

BSD Start-Up

Starting TCP/IP on SunOS and other BSD systems requires initializing the network interface with its address and then enabling it. This is performed in /etc/rc.boot. Using the relevant portions of the rc.boot file, here are the steps in configuring a BSD system:

```
##! /bin/sh -
#
#       @(#)rc.boot 1.44 90/11/02 SMI
#
# Executed once at boot time
#
PATH=/sbin:/single:/usr/bin:/usr/etc; export PATH
HOME=/; export HOME


                         . . .


#
# Set hostname from /etc/hostname.xx0 file, if none exists no harm done
```

```
#
hostname="'shcat /etc/hostname.??0     2>/dev/null'"
if [ ! -f /etc/.UNCONFIGURED -a ! -z "$hostname" -a "$hostname" != "noname" ];
then
        hostname $hostname
fi


#
# Get the list of ether devices to ifconfig by breaking /etc/hostname.* into
# separate args by using "." as a shell separator character, then step
# through args and ifconfig every other arg.
#
interface_names="'shcat /etc/hostname.*2>/dev/null'"
if test -n "$interface_names"
then
      (
      IFS="$IFS."
      set 'echo /etc/hostname\.*'
      while test $# -ge 2
      do
          shift
          if [ "$1" != "xx0" ]; then
                ifconfig $1 "`shcat /etc/hostname\.$1`" netmask + -trailers up
          fi
          shift
      done
      )
fi


#
# configure the rest of the interfaces automatically, quietly.
#
ifconfig -ad auto-revarp up


              . . .


ifconfig lo0 127.0.0.1 up


#
# If "/usr" is going to be NFS mounted from a host on a different
# network, we must have a routing table entry before the mount is
# attempted.  One may be added by the diskless kernel or by the
# "hostconfig" program above.  Setting a default router here is a problem
# because the default system configuration does not include the
# "route" program in "/sbin".  Thus we only try to add a default route
# at this point if someone managed to place a static version of "route" into
# "/sbin".  Otherwise, we add the route in "/etc/rc.local" after "/usr"
# has been mounted and NIS is running.
#
# Note that since NIS is not running at this point, the router's name
# must be in "/etc/hosts" or its numeric IP address must be used in the file.
#
if [ -f /sbin/route -a -f /etc/defaultrouter ]; then
      route -f add default 'cat /etc/defaultrouter' 1
fi
```

The first block of code accessing `hostname.xx0` sets the overall hostname for this system. It is the name that the `hostname` command will return. A loop is then run on each of the `hostname.` files to configure their interfaces using `ifconfig`. It uses the default netmask computed or residing in the `/etc/netmasks` file and the host address as listed in the `/etc/hosts` file. It cannot use DNS or NIS at this point because the network is not yet able to ask someone else. Then it configures the loopback interface, which is always at address `127.0.0.1`. Finally, it tries to set up a default route to allow the `/usr` file system to be NFS mounted if it's shared.

> **CAUTION:** If the boot script cannot set up a route, the server for this host must be on the same network segment as this machine. This is normally the case anyway, so this is not a problem.

The `rc.local` file is used to finalize the configuration once NIS is running. It sets the final address, netmask, and routes. This code excerpt shows the relevant sections that control this initialization:

```
#
# @(#)rc.local 1.116 91/05/10 SMI; from UCB 4.27 83/07/06
#

        . . .

# set the netmask from NIS if running
# or /etc/netmasks for all ether interfaces

ifconfig -a netmask + broadcast + > /dev/null

#
# Try to add a default route again, now that "/usr" is mounted and NIS
# is running.
#
if [ ! -f /sbin/route -a -f /etc/defaultrouter ]; then
    route -f add default 'cat /etc/defaultrouter' 1
fi

        . . .

# If we are a diskless client, synchronize time-of-day with the server.
#
server='grep ":.*[        ][        ]*/[        ]" /etc/fstab ¦
        sed -e "/^#/d" -e "s/:.*//"`
if [ "$server" ]; then
    intr -a rdate $server
fi

#
# Run routed only if we don't already have a default route installed.
#
defroute="'netstat -n -r ¦ grep default'"
```

```
if [ -z "$defroute" ]; then
    if [ -f /usr/etc/in.routed ]; then
        in.routed;     echo 'running routing daemon.'
    fi
fi
```

Only if there is no default route does the `rc.local` script automatically start the routing daemon to listen for route broadcasts.

SVR4 Start-Up

If you use SVR4 you must first load the streams modules into the system. It then performs the interface configuration. `/etc/inetd.inet` runs the file `/etc/confnet.d/inet/config.boot.sh`. The file is not as straightforward as the BSD `rc.boot` and is very large, so it is not listed here. However, it completes the following steps:

■ It determines from the system configuration information (`/etc/confnet.d/inet/interfaces`) which network devices exist.

■ It loops over those devices performing the following:

  Address determination for the interface from the `interfaces` file

  Installation of the protocol stack onto the stream head for the interface device

  `ifconfig` of the interface to set its address, netmask, and broadcast address

The loopback devices is listed in the interfaces file and is handled as part of the loop.

When the interfaces are up, the `/etc/inet/rc.inet` file is used to start the daemons. As the following excerpt shows, if you need to start other daemons or set up static routes, you will have to edit this file yourself to add the commands. Just place them were indicated in the comments.

```
#       @(#)rc.inet     1.5 STREAMWare TCP/IP SVR4.2  source
# Inet startup script run from /etc/init.d/inetinit
                         . . .
#
# Add lines here to set up routes to gateways, start other daemons, etc.
#

#
# Run the ppp daemon if /etc/inet/ppphosts is present
#
if [ -f /etc/inet/ppphosts -a -x /usr/sbin/in.pppd ]
then
    /usr/sbin/in.pppd
fi

# This runs in.gated if its configuration file (/etc/inet/gated.conf) is
# present.  Otherwise, in.routed is run.
#
if [ -f /etc/inet/gated.conf -a -x /usr/sbin/in.gated ]
```

```
then
     /usr/sbin/in.gated
else
     #
     # if running, kill the route demon
     #
     kill 'ps -ef¦grep in[.]routed¦awk '{print $2}'' 2>/dev/null
     /usr/sbin/in.routed -q
fi
#
# /usr/sbin/route add default your_nearest_gateway hops_to_gateway
# if [ $? -ne 0 ]
# then
#       exitcode=1
# fi


#
#  Run the DNS server if a configuration file is present
#
if [ -f /etc/inet/named.boot -a -x /usr/sbin/in.named ]
then
     /usr/sbin/in.named
fi


#
#  Run the NTP server if a configuration file is present
#
if [ -f /etc/inet/ntp.conf -a -x /usr/local/etc/xntpd ]
then
     /usr/local/etc/xntpd
fi
```

Solaris 2 Start-Up Code

Solaris 2 uses a slightly different configuration. It splits the task into three parts, which are listed in the following sections.

/etc/init.d/rootusr

You need to configure enough of the network to be able to NFS mount /usr if needed. Except for the pathnames, this code is almost identical to the code in the BSD /etc/rc.boot.

```
#
# Configure the software loopback driver. The network initialization is
# done early to support diskless and dataless configurations.
#
/sbin/ifconfig lo0 127.0.0.1 up 2>&1 >/dev/null


#
# For interfaces that were configured by the kernel (e.g. those
# on diskless machines), reset the netmask using the local
# "/etc/netmasks" file, if one exists.
#
/sbin/ifconfig -au netmask + broadcast + 2>&1 >/dev/null
```

```
#
# Get the list of network interfaces to configure by breaking
# /etc/hostname.* into separate args by using "." as a shell
# separator character, then step through args and ifconfig
# every other arg. Set the netmask along the way using local
# "/etc/netmasks" file. This also sets up the streams plumbing
# for the interface. With an empty /etc/hostname.* file this
# only sets up the streams plumbing allowing the ifconfig
# auto-revarp command will attempt to set the address.
#
interface_names="'echo /etc/hostname.*[0-9]2>/dev/null'"
if test "$interface_names" != "/etc/hostname.*[0-9]"
then
      (
      echo "configuring network interfaces:\c"
      IFS="$IFS."
      set 'echo /etc/hostname\.*[0-9]'
      while test $# -ge 2
      do
         shift
         if [ "$1" != "xx0" ]; then
                addr='shcat /etc/hostname\.$1'
                /sbin/ifconfig $1 plumb
                if test -n "$addr"
                then
                      /sbin/ifconfig $1 "$addr" netmask + \
                      broadcast + - trailers up \
                      2>&1 > /dev/null
                fi
                echo " $1\c"
         fi
         shift
      done
      echo "."
      )
fi


#
# configure the rest of the interfaces automatically, quietly.
#
/sbin/ifconfig -ad auto-revarp netmask + broadcast + -trailers up \
      2>&1 >/dev/null


#
# Set the hostname from a local config file, if one exists.
#
hostname="'shcat /etc/nodename 2>/dev/null'"
if [ ! -z "$hostname" ]; \
then
      /sbin/uname -S $hostname
fi


#
# Otherwise, set host information from bootparams RPC protocol.
#
if [ -z "'/sbin/uname -n'" ]; then
      /sbin/hostconfig -p bootparams
fi


#
```

```
# If local and network configuration failed, re-try network
# configuration until we get an answer.  We want this loop to be
# interruptable so that the machine can still be brought up manually
# when the servers are not cooperating.
#

trap 'intr=1' 2 3
while [ -z "`/sbin/uname -n`" -a ! -f /etc/.UNCONFIGURED -a -z "${intr}" ];
do
    echo "re-trying host configuration..."
    /sbin/ifconfig -ad auto-revarp up 2>&1 >/dev/null
    /sbin/hostconfig -p bootparams 2>&1 >/dev/null
done
trap 2 3

echo "Hostname: `/sbin/uname -n`" >&2


#
# If "/usr" is going to be NFS mounted from a host on a different
# network, we must have a routing table entry before the mount is
# attempted. One may be added by the diskless kernel or by the
# "hostconfig" program above. Setting a default router here is a
# problem because the default system configuration does not include the
# "route" program in "/sbin". Thus we only try to add a default route
# at this point if someone managed to place a static version of
# "route" into "/sbin".  Otherwise, we may add the route at run
# level 2 after "/usr" has been mounted and NIS is running.
#
# Note that since NIS is not running at this point, the router's name
# must be in "/etc/hosts" or its numeric IP address must be used in
the file.
#
if [ -f /sbin/route -a -f /etc/defaultrouter ]; then
     /sbin/route -f add default 'cat /etc/defaultrouter' 1
fi
```

When this script is completed, each interface has its IP address configured and is available for use.

/etc/init.d/inetinit

This is the configuration of the network before NIS is started. Because the name-mapping abilities provided by NIS are not yet available, all this code does is to initialize the routes, as shown below:

```
#
# This is the second phase of TCP/IP configuration. The first
# part, run in the "/etc/rcS.d/S30rootusr.sh" script, does all
# configuration necessary to mount the "/usr" filesystem via NFS.
# This includes configuring the interfaces and setting the
# machine's hostname. The second part, run in this script, does all
# configuration that can be done before NIS or NIS+ is started.
# This includes configuring IP routing, setting the NIS domainname
# and seting any tunable paramaters. The third part, run in a
# subsequent startup script, does all configuration that may be
# dependent on NIS/NIS+ maps. This includes a final re-configuration
# of the interfaces and starting all internet services.
```

```
#

#
# Set configurable parameters.
#
ndd -set /dev/tcp tcp_old_urp_interpretation 1

#
# Configure a default router, if there is one.  An empty
# /etc/defaultrouter file means that any default router added by the
# kernel during diskless boot is deleted.
#
if [ -f /etc/defaultrouter ]; then
     defroute="'cat /etc/defaultrouter'"
     if [ -n "$defroute" ]; then
          /usr/sbin/route -f add default $defroute 1
     else
          /usr/sbin/route -f
     fi
fi


#
# Set NIS domainname if locally configured.
#
if [ -f /etc/defaultdomain ]; then
     /usr/bin/domainname 'cat /etc/defaultdomain'
     echo "NIS domainname is `/usr/bin/domainname`"
fi


#
# Run routed/router discovery only if we don't already have a default
# route installed.
#
if [ -z "$defroute" ]; then
     #
     # No default route was setup by "route" command above -
     # check the kernel routing table for any other default route.
     #
     defroute="'netstat -rn ¦ grep default'"
fi

if [ -z "$defroute" ]; then
     #
     # Determine how many active interfaces there are and how many
     # pt-pt interfaces. Act as a router if there are more than 2
     # interfaces (including the loopback interface) or one or
     # more point- point interface. Also act as a router if
     # /etc/gateways exists.
     #
     numifs='ifconfig -au ¦ grep inet ¦ wc -l'
     numptptifs='ifconfig -au ¦ grep inet ¦ egrep -e '-->' ¦ wc -l'
     if [ $numifs -gt 2 -o $numptptifs -gt 0 -o -f /etc/gateways ];
     then
          # Machine is a router: turn on ip_forwarding, run routed,
          # and advertise ourselves as a router using router discovery.
          echo "machine is a router."
          ndd -set /dev/ip ip_forwarding 1
          if [ -f /usr/sbin/in.routed ]; then
               /usr/sbin/in.routed -s
```

```
          fi
          if [ -f /usr/sbin/in.rdisc ]; then
               /usr/sbin/in.rdisc -r
          fi
     else
          # Machine is a host: if router discovery finds a router then
          # we rely on router discovery. If there are not routers
          # advertising themselves through router discovery
          # run routed in space-saving mode.
          # Turn off ip_forwarding
          ndd -set /dev/ip ip_forwarding 0
          if [ -f /usr/sbin/in.rdisc ] && /usr/sbin/in.rdisc -s; then
               echo "starting router discovery."
          elif [   -f /usr/sbin/in.routed ]; then
               /usr/sbin/in.routed -q;
               echo "starting routing daemon."
          fi
     fi
fi
```

/etc/init.d/inetsvc

After NIS has started, the rest of the network configuration daemons are started by the execution of the /etc/init.d/inetsrv file. This script is very much like the remainder of the SVR4 rc.inet script. It starts the daemons in the same manner and is not listed here.

The Configuration Tools

Several tools are used by the configuration scripts. These same tools can be used directly by you to manually affect the configuration.

ifconfig

Interface configuration, or ifconfig, sets the IP address, broadcast address, and netmask used by a network interface. It also is used to mark the interface UP (enabled) or DOWN (disabled). ifconfig can also be used to report on the status of the network interfaces. Use the ifconfig with the -a option at the shell prompt:

```
# ifconfig -a <ENTER>
lo0: flags=849<UP,LOOPBACK,RUNNING,MULTICAST> mtu 8232
     inet 127.0.0.1 netmask ff000000
le0: flags=863<UP,BROADCAST,NOTRAILERS,RUNNING,MULTICAST> mtu 1500
     inet 190.109.252.33 netmask ffffff00 broadcast 190.109.252.63
#
```

It reports on the interfaces by name, listing the current parameters (flags) both numerically and by their meaning. In addition, it prints the maximum transfer unit (largest packet allowed on the network interface) and the addresses. ifconfig is covered in greater detail later in this chapter.

route

The next hop in a route is set with the `route` command. It can set static and default routes. The following could be entered at the shell prompt:

```
# route add default gateway 1
#
```

The `route` command has four arguments:

- `command`   Add, delete.
- `network`   What network to add. The network name is either numeric or it's converted by a lookup in `/etc/networks`. The keyword default is a special token to mean the default route.
- `address`   The address of the node that is the next hop. It is looked up in `/etc/hosts` if not a dotted quad.
- `metric`   How expensive (how slow) this route is. Any route off the current network must have a metric of at least 1. Higher metrics are used to prevent usage of slow links when faster links are available.

Alternatively, the daemon `routed` will listen for routing broadcasts and add the routes automatically.

The routing table is printed using the `netstat` command.

rdate/ntpdate

When systems share files with NFS, it's best that they agree on the time of day. This allows makefiles to be reliable among others. You can set the clock automatically from other systems by using either the `rdate` or the `ntpdate` command.

> **TIP:** `rdate` is provided as part of the Berkeley package and is rarely configured except for diskless clients. You should add it to your start-up scripts.
>
> If you intend to run the Network Time Protocol to synchronize clocks continuously, use the `ntpdate` command from that package instead of `rdate`. It's more accurate and will start the clocks closer to each other, leaving less for `xntpd` to adjust.

Network Daemons

Most of the work done by the networking system is not handled by the UNIX operating system itself, but by programs that run automatically. These are called daemons. There are many helper programs used by the networking system, and understanding which one does which functions will help you manage the system.

Three of the daemons can be considered the controllers. There's one for each of the communication service types: For sockets it's `inetd`, for RPC it's `rpcbind`, and for SAF it's `listen`.

The Master Daemon—*inetd*

`inetd` handles both TCP and UDP servers. For TCP `inetd` listens for connection requests on many ports at once. When it receives a connection request it starts the appropriate server and then goes back to listening. For UDP `inetd` listens for packets and when they are received it starts the server. When the server exits it goes back to listening on the UDP port.

In this chapter, you have seen the control file for `inetd`, which is called `/etc/inetd.conf`. It consists of several fields separated by white space. The seventh field continues until the end of the line or the first # character. The fields are the following:

- **Service**   The name of the service as listed in the `/etc/services` file.
- **Socket type**   `stream` or `dgram`. For TCP services it's almost always `stream`. For UDP services it has to be `dgram`.
- **Protocol**   `tcp` and `udp` are the only two supported.
- **Wait**   Tells whether `inetd` should wait until the server exists before listening again, or listen right away. Servers that once started listen for their own connections should use `wait`. Any service that must allow only one server at a time should use `wait`. Most TCP services use `nowait`.
- **User ID**   Tells what user ID `inetd` should use when starting the server. Only those services that need root access, such as `telnetd` to run login, should be started as `root`. All others should be started as `nobody`.
- **Process to Run**   The file name to run.
- **Command String**   The remainder of the line is passed in as the command string.

If the wait parameter is `nowait`, the connection is accepted and the socket is connected to standard input and output before the server is started. The server does not need to be aware that it is being run from the network.

> **TIP:** Notice in the example that the program to be started is not the same as the command to be run. For security you can run a wrapper program that first checks that the requestor (remote site) is approved to connect to the service. Only then

does it allow the server to be started. If the connection is not authorized, the security program logs it for future investigation. You can use the comp.sources.unix program tcp_wrapper for this checking. This program, as a shell archive, is included on the book's CD-ROM.

The Remote Procedure Call Master Daemon—*rpcbind*

Another client/server system is the remote procedure call. This is used by network file system (NFS), NIS, and the lock manager daemon. It is also used by many application programs. The controlling daemon for RPC is rpcbind. It is started at boot time by the system start-up scripts.

When RPC services are started they register themselves with rpcbind. Then when a call comes in it is dispatched by rpcbind to the appropriate server. No user configuration is necessary.

The Service Access Facility Master Daemon—*listen*

System V Release 4 introduced the Service Access Facility (SAF) to networking and added the listen process. SAF has its own configuration mechanism, which uses the port monitor facility. It is used by the System V line printer daemon. Most network services use Berkeley's inetd instead of saf.

listen requires no direct configuration. It is managed automatically by the port monitor system, pmadm. To list which services are currently using listen use pmadm -l. Most SAF facilities are managed via sysadm.

Other Daemons That Can Be Started at Boot Time

Typically servers that run continuously and listen for messages are started at boot time and are not run from inetd. Most servers are not started until needed and do run from inetd.

routed

TCP/IP has a protocol called Router Interchange Protocol, or RIP. routed listens for RIP packets on the network interfaces, and when it hears them adds the routes they contain to the current routing tables. It also expires routes it has not heard for a while. This allows the system to adapt dynamically.

> **TIP:** If your network has only one gateway, there is no reason to run routed. A default route to the gateway is much more efficient.

If a system is itself connected to more than one network, routed will by default broadcast on each network on which routes are available on the other networks of this system. If another node is supposed to act as a router and this node is not, routed can be started in -q, or quiet mode. Then it will only listen and not broadcast any routes.

gated

For external network gateways, a multi–protocol-routing daemon, gated, is available. It handles RIP, External Gateway Protocol (EGP) , Boundary Gateway Protocol (BGP), and HELLO. Unless you are the external gateway of a large network you will not need gated.

> **TIP:** One use of gated on internal networks is to prevent RIP broadcasts from bringing up dial-on-demand PPP links. routed broadcasts RIP information every 30 seconds to 3 minutes. routed would sense the PPP network as an interface and send the packet on that link. This would cause the PPP software to dial the remote system and establish the connection every 3 minutes or so.
>
> gated reports only changes. Therefore, it will not periodically bring up the link. See the documentation on gated for how to configure it. There is a good note on configuring gated for use with PPP links in the dp-2.3 installation tips. dp-2.3 is a USENET-contributed PPP protocol package.

syslogd

UNIX includes a very flexible message logger called syslog. The server daemon, syslogd, listens for messages and when it receives them it forwards them to other processes, files, and devices via the specifications in the /etc/syslog.conf file. Messages are classified as to who generated them and at what severity they were generated. Logging includes the time the message was generated, which host it came from, and the facility (who) and level (severity) at which it was issued.

Logging options include writing the message to a file or to a device (such as the console), starting a program and feeding it the message, or mailing the message. Zero or more actions are possible on any message. If a message matches no criteria in the configuration file it is silently discarded.

To reread the configuration file once `syslogd` is started, send it the HUP (-1) signal with the `kill` command.

NFS

UNIX shares disk via NFS. NFS is an extension to the UNIX virtual file system and becomes just another file system type. NFS is split into four server daemons.

nfsd

This daemon listens for requests for I/O operations on NFS files by the operating system. It then contacts remote systems to read or write data blocks, set or read status information, or delete files. A system generally runs many `nfsd` daemons at the same time. This allows for transactions to occur in parallel. Small systems generally run 4 `nfsd` daemons. Large servers can run 32 or more.

> **TIP:** If the network is not overloaded, the system is not CPU bound, and NFS file performance is poor, try increasing the number of `nfsd` daemons started at boot time. If performance improves, leave it that way. If it degrades or remains the same, drop back to the smaller number.

biod

The other end of a server to the `nfsd` client is a `biod` daemon. This listens to requests by `nfsd` daemons from remote systems and performs the local I/O required. Multiple `biod` daemons are normally run to allow multiple requests to be served in parallel.

> **TIP:** Just as adding more `nfsd` daemons improves performance, so can adding `biod` daemons. However, because `biod` daemons run locally and are not affected by network delays, generally the need for more `biod`'s does not increase as quickly. Consult your systems documentation for recommendation on the number of `biod` daemons to run.

> **CAUTION:** As `threads` is implemented, the use of multiple `nfsd` daemons and `biod` daemons is being changed to use a single `nfsd` daemon that runs multiple threads. On systems that support `threads`, only one `nfsd` daemon is run. It supports multiple threads internally. Tuning the number of threads can improve performance.

lockd

Remote and local file locking is handled via the locking daemon. A single copy of lockd is run and it keeps track of all lock requests. These are advisory locks. No configuration of lockd is required.

statd

statd works with lockd to handle fault recovery for systems that have locks outstanding and then are no longer reachable due to network problems or having crashed. A single statd is also run.

> **TIP:** When a system is removed from a network, and it had locks remaining when it was taken down, the other systems will continuously complain about not being able to reach the statd on that system.
>
> This message, and check, can be suppressed by removing the files in /etc/.sm.bak for that system and then rebooting the system that is complaining.

NIS

The Network Information Service (NIS), or as it used to be called, Yellow Pages, provides a networkwide directory lookup service for many of the system configuration files. It is described in more detail later in this chapter.

sendmail

UNIX exchanges electronic mail between networked systems via the Simple Mail Transport Protocol (SMTP). SMTP is a TCP service that is provided by the Mail Transport Agent (MTA). The most common network MTA is sendmail. sendmail handles listening for SMTP connections, processing the mail received, rewriting headers for further delivery, and handing off the message for final delivery.

sendmail uses a very complicated file, sendmail.cf, for configuration. Describing this file is beyond the scope of this chapter.

xntpd

Synchronizing the clocks across the network is very important. Tools such as make depend on it. However, clocks in computers drift. You can place calls to rdate in your cron scripts to force all systems to reset their clocks periodically to a single system, but this jumps the clock and the clock might still drift.

Therefore, the Network Time Protocol was developed. This server checks with several other servers and determines not only the correct time, but how far off the current system is. It then uses a feature of the operating system to redefine how many microseconds to add to the current time on each clock tick. It adjusts the length of a second, causing the system to slew its idea of the correct time slowly back to the correct time. It does this continuously, adapting to the changes in the system clock. xntpd can keep a system to within several milliseconds of all other systems on the network.

In addition, xtnpd has the ability to synchronize to an external clock source. Using a radio clock tuned to a government time service, your network can be kept within milliseconds of the correct time.

xntpd is configured via the /etc/ntp.conf file, as shown in the following code:

```
server clock.big-stateu.edu version 2
server ntp-2.cs.university.edu
server fuzz.network.net
#
requestkey 65535
controlkey 65534
keys /etc/ntp.keys
authdelay 0.000017
#
driftfile /etc/ntp.drift
```

The server lines list which servers this system will sync to. Your master systems should list external reference systems. The remainder of the systems should list your own master systems.

Daemons Started from *inetd*

Most servers are started from inetd. These servers transparently provide the network services to which UNIX users have grown accustomed.

ftpd

The file transfer protocol daemon is used to transfer files between any two systems, not just trusted ones.

CAUTION: If you are going to run a public ftp archive service or are going to support anonymous ftp, do not use your system's ftpd. Instead, acquire one of the more configurable logging ftp daemons, such as the wuarchive ftp daemon. Security is much better in these and you can control how many users log in to your server and how much they can transfer to and from your system.

The wuarchive ftp daemon is available via ftp from wuarchive.wustl.edu.

telnetd

The terminal sessions daemon is used to provide the basic remote login service. Telnet is a commonly used utility on many UNIX systems and now on non-UNIX systems.

shell

This is the server daemon for the Berkeley `rsh` command. `rsh` stands for *remote shell* and is used to execute a command on another system.

> **CAUTION:** This daemon is easily spoofed. Do not allow connections to this daemon from untrusted networks. Use a firewall gateway and TCP wrapper software to protect your network if you are connected to public or untrusted networks.

login

This is the server daemon for the Berkeley `rlogin` command. `rlogin` stands for *remote login* and is used to log in to a remote system. The caution for the shell service applies equally to this service.

exec

This is the server daemon for the `rexec` C subroutine. `rexec` stand for *remote execute* and is used to execute processes on a remote system. The caution for the shell service applies to this service as well.

comsat

The mail notification server daemon listens for incoming notifications of mail reception and informs processes that request it. It is used by the `biff` program.

talk, ntalk

`talk` and its newer cousin, `ntalk` (often just called `talk`), provide a keystroke-by-keystroke chat facility between two users anywhere on the network.

uucpd

The `uucpd` daemon transfers UUCP packets over the network. UUCP is used to transfer files from one UNIX system to another. See Chapter 43, "UUCP Administration," for more details on UUCP.

tftp

The Trivial File Transfer Protocol daemon is used for booting diskless systems and by some X terminals. See Chapter 33, "UNIX Installation Basics," and Chapter 40, "Device Administration," for more details. Again, the caution for the shell service applies to this service.

finger

The `finger` daemon determines what a user is currently doing.

systat

The `systat` daemon performs a process status on a remote system. `inetd` forks off a `ps` command and returns the output to the remote system.

netstat

`inetd` forks off a `netstat` command and returns the output to the remote system.

time

Return the current system time in internal format. This service is provided internally by `inetd` as both a UDP and a TCP service. It returns a `time-t` consisting of the current system time. This is expressed as the number of seconds since the epoch, January 1, 1970, at 0:00 GMT.

daytime

This is a human-readable equivalent of time. It is also internally provided both as a TCP and a UDP service and returns the time in the format `Day Mmm dd hh:mm:ss yyyy`.

echo

`echo` replies back what it receives. This service is provided internally by `inetd` as both a UDP and a TCP service. It returns whatever is sent to it. The UDP port echoes the packet back to the sender. The TCP service is line-oriented and echoes lines of text back to the sender.

discard

This service is provided internally by `inetd` as both a UDP and a TCP service. It discards whatever it receives.

chargen

The character generator service is provided internally by `inetd` as both a UDP and a TCP service. On UDP it returns one copy of the printable characters of the ASCII character set. As a TCP service it repeats this, 72 characters per line, starting one character later in the sequence on each line.

RPC Services Started from *inetd*

The following are RPC servers that are registered via `inetd` and are started when `inetd` receives a connection from `rpcbind`.

> **CAUTION:** All of these services can tell outsiders more than you want them to know or they can pose security risks. It is best to limit these services to internal systems via a firewall gateway.

admind

This is the distributed system administration tool server daemon.

rquotad

This is the disk quota server daemon, which returns the disk quota for a specific user.

rusersd

This daemon returns a list of users on the host.

sprayd

This daemon sprays packets on a network to test for loss.

walld

This daemon will write a message to all users on a system.

rstatd

This daemon returns performance statistics about this system.

cmsd

This is the calendar manager server daemon.

ttdbserverd

This is the tool talk server daemon.

Sharing Files and Directories—NFS

One of the advantages of UNIX is how seamlessly the network is built in to everything else. This extends to the file system as well. Any part of the file system hierarchy can exist on any computer in the network. That computer doesn't even have to be running UNIX. This is accomplished with the network file system, which is a very simple extension to the file system that transparently extends your disk over the network.

NFS is so effective that a fast disk on a server can be accessed faster than a medium-speed local disk on a workstation. This is partly due to caching effects of having many systems access the server, but it does show that using NFS is not necessarily going to slow down your system.

How NFS Works

UNIX supports many file system types. The kernel accesses files via the virtual file system (VFS). This makes every file system type appear the same to the operating system. One VFS type is the network file system. When the kernel I/O routines access an inode that is on a file system of the type NFS and the data is not in the memory cache of the system, the request is shunted to the next available nfsd task (or thread).

When the nfsd task receives the request it figures out on which system the partition resides and forwards the request to a biod (or nfsd thread) on the remote system using UDP. That system accesses the file using the normal I/O procedures just as in any other process and returns the requested information via UDP. Since the biod just uses the normal I/O procedures the data will be cached in the RAM of the server for use by other local or biod tasks. If the block was recently accessed, the I/O request will be satisfied out of the cache and no disk activity will be needed.

NFS uses UDP to allow multiple transactions to occur in parallel. But with UDP the requests are unverified. nfsd has a time-out mechanism to make sure it gets the data it asks for. When it cannot retrieve the data within its time-outs, it reports via a logging message that it is waiting for the server to respond.

To increase performance the client systems add to their local file system caches disk blocks read via NFS. They also cache attribute lookups (inodes). However, to ensure that the disk writes complete correctly, NFS does those synchronously. This means that the process doing the writing is blocked until the remote system acknowledges that the disk write is complete. It is possible to change this to asynchronous writes, where the disk write is acknowledged back to the process immediately and then the write occurs later. The problem occurs when the write fails due either to the server being unreachable or a disk error. The local process was already told that the write succeeded and can no longer handle the error status. Although using asynchronous writes is faster, it can lead to data corruption.

Exporting Hierarchies

Each server—and any system that exports its local disk via NFS is a server—must grant its permission to allow remote systems to access its disks. It does this by exporting part of its file system hierarchy. When you enable a system to access your disks you provide a list of points in your file system hierarchy where you will allow access to that point and all places below that point. You cannot allow only single directories or files-only sections of the hierarchy at and below the export point.

Export points are listed in a file, and a command is run on that file to make the NFS aware of the list. BSD-derived UNIX systems and SVR4 use different mechanisms for this file.

/etc/exports—BSD-Derived UNIX Systems

The original NFS, as developed on BSD UNIX systems, used the `exports` file to hold the list of exportable points. This file is processed by the `exportfs` command to make NFS aware of the list. A sample `exports` file contains:

```
/files1 -access=ws1:ws2:gateway
/files2 -access=ws1:ws2
/export
/usr
/cdrom -ro
```

Each line consists of a pathname for the export point and a list of export options. The list of options is not required.

When `root` runs the `exportfs` command with the `-a` argument, it will read the `exports` file and process it. The `exportfs` command can also be used by any user to print the current export list and by root to unexport a specific file system.

/etc/dfs/dfstab—SVR4

To allow for more than just NFS sharing, SVR4 extended the concept of an `exports` file and created the distributed file system directory. In this directory the file `dfstab` lists the shell commands to export any shared file systems, regardless of the method of sharing. The share exports as a `dfstab` file is:

```
#  place share(1M) commands here for automatic execution
#  on entering init state 3.
#
#  share [-F fstype] [ -o options] [-d "<text>"] <pathname> [resource]
```

```
# .e.g,
# share -F nfs -o rw=engineering -d "home dirs" /export/home2
share -F nfs -o rw=ws1,root=ws2 -d "home dirs" /files
share -F nfs -o r0=ws1:ws2 -d "frame 4" /opt/Xframe4
share -F nfs -o ro -d "cdrom drive" /cdrom
```

The share command is very similar to the export lines. It adds two options. The first is the -F nfs option to specify that this is an NFS export. The second is the -d option to specify a descriptive text string about this export. The remainder of the options are the same as those possible in the exports file.

Export Options

There are many options to control the access allowed by remote systems. Most of the options reduce the access rights allowed.

rw[=client[:client]...]

The list of client hosts will be allowed read-write access to the hierarchy. If no hostnames are listed, any host can access the files read-write. If the ro option is given with no hostnames forcing read-only export, the hosts listed on the rw list are considered exceptions to the ro list and are allowed read-write access.

ro[=client[:client]...]

The list of client hosts will be allowed read-only access to the hierarchy. If no hostnames are listed, any host can access the files read-only. If the rw option is given with no hostnames, forcing read-write export, the hosts listed on the ro list are considered exceptions to the ro list and are allowed only read-only access.

anon=uid

Some systems cannot authenticate their users. Map any unauthenticated users to this user ID, which is normally set to nobody. Setting it to -1 (or 65535 on BSD) will deny access to unauthenticated users.

root=host[:host]...

Normally the root user ID from remote hosts is mapped to nobody. This option overrides this mapping and allows remote root users to have root access to this hierarchy.

> **CAUTION:** Be very careful with this option. Anyone at a workstation console can acquire root access without too much difficulty, so let only secure systems have root access rights.

secure

You should use a secure authentication scheme to authenticate users. Any unauthenticated requests are mapped as per the anon option previously described. Not all NFSs support this feature.

kerberos (SVR4 only)

Use `kerberos` instead of DES as the secure authentication method.

Export Security

Because your files are the key to your system you need to exercise some caution in exporting. The following are some simple rules:

- Avoid blanket read-write exports. List the valid systems for the export. Use netgroups if a large list of systems is being exported.
- Be very restrictive in providing root access.
- Block access from public networks to port 111, the RPC port, and port 2049, the NFS port, to prevent spoofed mount requests from systems outside your network. Use the port filtering ability of routers to block this access.

Mounting Remote Hierarchies

Accessing remote disks is a two-step process. The remote system must export it and the local system must mount it. An NFS mount is like any other mount in that it grafts a new file system onto the mount point in the hierarchy. However, NFS is also different. Not only is the disk remote but any place in the export hierarchy can be mounted, not just the export point itself. This allows for small sections of the export tree, such as a single home directory, to be mounted.

Mounting is accomplished via the `mount` command, using the remote system name and export path as the disk device and the local mount point, as in the following:

```
mount server:/files/home/syd /home/syd
mount -F nfs server:/files/home/syd /home/syd
```

The first line is for BSD systems and the second is for SVR4 and includes the file system type. In addition, NFS mounts support many options. These are specified with the `-o` argument before the server name.

If the entry is listed in `/etc/fstab` (`/etc/vfstab` on SVR4), the `mount` command needs to specify only the mount point. It will read the remainder of the data directly from the file.

NFS Mount Options

NFS mounts are tuned via the mount options. These options not only control mount time behavior but also access behavior. Options are separated by commas.

rw

Mount the file system for read-write access. This is the default mount method if no other option overrides it. Must be exported as read-write to succeed.

ro

Mount the file system read-only. You can mount a read-write exported file system as read only.

suid, nosuid

Honor or ignore the `setuid` bit. The default is `setuid`.

Since you have no control over which files are created on a remote file system, if you cannot trust the system you can instruct NFS to ignore the `setuid` bit on executable files.

remount

Change the mount options on an existing mount point.

fg, bg

Retry mount failures in the foreground or background. The default is `fg`.

If the first mount attempt fails because it could not reach, the server mount will retry the mount for *retry* times. With the default `fg` option the `mount` process will block until the mount succeeds. If you are mounting a partition at boot time this will cause your boot to freeze until the partition can be mounted. Using `bg` will allow the mount to return. The file system is not mounted, but retry attempts occur in the background.

retry=n

This refers to the number of times to retry the mount operation. The default is `10000`.

port=n

This is the server IP port number. The default is `NFS_PORT`, which is `2049`.

rsize=n

Set the read buffer size to *n* bytes. The default is `8192`.

If you are using older PCs on the network that cannot keep up with 8 KB worth of data in back-to-back packets, use this option to reduce the read size to a size they can handle. This will reduce performance slightly compared to if they could handle the large `rsize`.

> **TIP:** For slow serial links, such as dial-up PPP links, reduce the `rsize` to reduce the amount of traffic on the link if only a few bytes are needed.

wsize=n

Set the `write` buffer size to *n* bytes.

> **CAUTION:** The only reason to change this parameter is for slow serial links. If your UNIX system cannot keep up with the back-to-back packets, replace the network board. Not being able to handle back to back packets will greatly affect performance.

timeo=n

Set the NFS time-out to *n* tenths of a second. This is the time the `nfsd` daemons wait for a response before retrying. On a local EtherNet the default value will be sufficient.

> **CAUTION:** On slow links to remote systems the daemon could time-out while the request is being transferred and rerequest it. This will cause a second response. The daemon will eventually hear the first response and use that one, discarding the second response. However, the second request and response will tie up needed bandwidth on the slow link, causing it to be even slower. Be sure to set this parameter to at least the time required to send and receive the packets across the link.
>
> As an example, using V.32bis modems with V.42bis compression you can expect to achieve about 2000 bytes per second on normal files and a bit more on `ascii` ones. Using the 2000 byte speed, transferring 8 KB takes 4 seconds. Using a time-out of less than 4 seconds will cause re-requests and will further slow down the link.

retrans=n

Set the number of NFS retransmissions to *n*. If the request takes a time-out, it is retried *n* number of times. Each time it is retried the time-out is multiplied by 2. If after the number of retransmissions is exceeded it still fails, an error is returned for soft mounts or a message is logged, indicating that the server is unreachable and the retries continue for hard mounts.

hard, soft

Retry an operation until the server responds or returns an error if the server takes more time-outs than *retrans* times. The default is hard.

All partitions mounted rw should be mounted hard to prevent corruption. This will hang processes waiting for response if the server becomes unreachable.

> **CAUTION:** Normally you should mount a partition soft only if you are sure that the application correctly handles the error return from a time-out. Otherwise, the behavior of the system could be unpredictable.

intr, nointr

This allows (or prevents) SIGINT to kill a process that is hung while waiting for a response on a hard-mounted file system. The default is intr.

> **TIP:** Rather than mounting the partition soft, use the intr attribute. This will allow you to kill processes that are hung in NFS wait when the server becomes unreachable.

secure

Use DES authentication for NFS transactions.

kerberos

Use kerberos authentication for NFS transactions.

noac

Suppress attribute caching.

> **TIP:** This option forces the client to always ask the server for the status of a file. This is extremely useful on remote mounting the mail spool. It will allow the `.lock` files to be detected immediately. If your mail transport software does not use the `lockd`-based locks and you intend to mount the mail spool via `nfs` on the clients, set the `noac` option.

acregmin=n

Hold cached attributes for at least *n* seconds after file modification. This option is useful for slow links to reduce the number of lookups, but is normally not tuned by system administrators.

acregmax=n

Hold cached attributes for no more than *n* seconds after file modification. On fast-changing file systems this will increase the responsiveness to updates made by other systems. If you have a file system that you are mounting on multiple clients which frequently updates the same files from each of those clients, you might want to shorten this interval. The default is fine for most usage.

acdirmin=n

Hold cached attributes for at least *n* seconds after directory update. This option is useful for slow links to reduce the number of lookups, but is normally not tuned by system administrators.

acdirmax=n

Hold cached attributes for no more than *n* seconds after directory update. See the note under the explanation of `acregmax`.

actimeo=n

Set `min` and `max` times for regular files and directories to *n* seconds. This is a combined option that sets all four of the prior options to the same value.

Using the Cache File System

One of the newer concepts in NFS is the cache file system. On heavily loaded networks using the cache file system can reduce delays by substituting local disk space for network accesses. It also can be used to substitute a fast disk for slow CD-ROM.

It works by using part of or all of a local file system to cache recently used files. It caches both read and writes (optionally it can write directly back and cache only reads) and automatically handles refreshing the cache when the backing store file is changed.

It is really simple to set up. You first create the cache and then mount the file system as type `cachefs`. One cache can handle multiple back end file systems.

Setting Up the Cache

If you want to let the cache take over an entire file system, then the default parameters of

```
cfsadmin -c /pathname
```

will create a cache on the file system at *pathname*. This will allow the cache to grow to the full size of the file system.

If you want the cache to be limited in size to a percentage of the file system you can use the `maxblocks` and `maxfiles` options to specify what percentage of the file system is allowed to be used by the cache.

Mounting as a *cachefs* File System

When the cache has been initialized there are two options for mounting it. In the first, when no special NFS mount options are used, the `-F nfs` in the mount command is replaced by two options: `-F cachefs` and `-o backtype=nfs,cachedir=/pathname`, as in the following:

```
mount -F cachefs -o backtype=nfs,cachedir=/local/cache1 gateway:/sharedfiles /
sharedfiles
```

Options to specify write-around and nonshared gateless options, `suid/nosuid` cache consistency-checking intervals, and suppressing the checking for changes (when used for read only file systems) are also available. See the chapter on the cache file system in the *Administering File Systems* manual.

Backing Up on a Network

One advantage of a network is that you can share resources. One expensive resource that is easy to share is a high-speed tape drive such as DAT or 8mm. With all the disk in a network, something with a jukebox or autochanger is also handy. But it's useless unless you can back up the systems over the network. There are commercial products that can make all of this point-and-shoot from the GUI, but the standard UNIX tools can also handle the backups.

There are three sets of utilities that can be used to perform backups:

- dump/restore
- tar
- cpio

Chapter 35, "File System Administration," presents the merits and drawbacks of each of these utilities. dump/restore, tar, and cpio are covered in more detail in Chapter 32, "Backing Up."

dump/restore has a direct network counterpart, rdump/rrestore. The others require using a connection via the rsh command to a program to access the drive on the server.

Using *rdump/rrestore*

Under the older BSD operating systems, using the command rdump instead of dump enabled you to specify the device name for the dump as *hostname:device*. The dump would then be pushed from the system running rdump onto the *device* at *hostname*. This requires that the remote system have the dumping system in its .rhosts file for the operator or whatever user was doing the dump. Restores are performed using rrestore. Again, the device is referred to as *hostname:device*.

SVR4's ufsdump directly supports using the remote system and *hostname:device* so no special command is needed. Likewise, ufsrestore supports remote access.

Using *tar* over a Network

To use tar over the network you need to simulate the process that dump uses internally. You need to have it write to standard output and redirect that output across the network to a process that will read standard input and write it to the tape drive. Unfortunately, doing so will preclude handling tape changes. The simplest way is to combine tar and dd, as in the following:

```
tar vcf pathname ¦ rsh remote dd of=/dev/rst1
```

Alternatively, you can use this:

```
rsh client tar vcf - pathname ¦ dd of=/dev/rst1
```

The first example uses a push to create the backup from the client to the remote system with the tape drive. The second is a pull to run the backup from the client remotely to the local system with the tape drive.

Using *cpio* over a Network

cpio can just as easily be used as tar, with the same method. Again, redirecting the output across the network is performed by the rsh command as in the following:

```
find / -print ¦ cpio -oacv ¦ rsh remote dd of=/dev/rst1
```

Alternatively, you can use this:

```
rsh client "find / -print ¦ cpio -oacv" ¦ dd of=/dev/rst1
```

Again, the first example uses a push to create the backup from the remote to the server. The second is a pull backup from the client to the system with the tape drive.

Introduction to NIS

NIS provides a networkwide management of the UNIX configuration and system administration files. It also can be used to manage any local administrative files. This section introduces you to NIS, showing what it does and a little of how it works.

What Is NIS?

Without NIS each UNIX process that needs access to the passwd, hosts, group, or other UNIX system administration files must open a local file on the host on which it is executing and read the information. This is performed via a standard set of C library calls, but the system administrator must replicate this configuration information on every host in the network.

NIS replaces these local files with a central database containing the same information. Instead of making the changes on every host, you make the changes in one place and then let NIS make the data available to everyone.

NIS works by assigning hosts to domains via the domainname call. All hosts in the same domain share a common set of database files called *maps*. Within a domain one host is designated as the NIS master server. This host holds the configuration files (passwd, group, hosts) that are used to build the maps. In addition to a master server there can be one or more slave servers. These servers get their updates from the master server. This pool of servers will answer NIS lookup requests for the all of the systems in the domain.

When an NIS system starts up, it starts the NIS lookup daemon, ypbind. This daemon broadcasts a request asking who is a server for its domain. All the servers respond, and the first server it hears becomes the server for this NIS client. If a server is heavily loaded, it will take a while to respond and a server that is less loaded usually will respond faster. This helps balance the NIS load. You can check which server is serving this client with the ypwhich command.

> **NOTE:** Although only a few systems are NIS servers, every system including the servers is an NIS client. Thus, it is not uncommon for an NIS server, when it starts, to receive a response from a different server before it receives the response from itself. This means that this server will actually ask a different server for its runtime lookups. This is perfectly normal and is not a problem.
>
> It is even common for the master server to bind to one of the slave servers as its NIS client. The master still controls the distribution of maps to each of the servers. It is only the lookup routines that will access the slave server.
>
> You can determine who is the master with the ypwhich -m command.

If your NIS server becomes unreachable, the NIS system will take a time-out after about 90 seconds and then rebroadcast, asking for another server. If it finds one it continues as if nothing except the delay has happened. If it cannot find one, it will freeze that process until it can find a server. Of course, as more processes need lookup services, those will also be frozen. The overall effect is for the entire system to appear to lock up.

> **CAUTION:** To prevent just such lockups, it is advisable to have two NIS servers per network segment. Then if a network segment gets isolated due to network problems the systems will still have NIS servers. The overhead of having many slave servers is very small.

The NIS Components

NIS provides a set of components that make up the NIS management. These include database administration, distribution, and lookup utilities, plus a number of daemons.

Database Administration Utilities

These build the database and receive update requests to some of the database files from remote processes. These utilities are located in the /usr/etc/yp directory and include the following:

- ■ makedbm   Converts the flat files into dbm database files
- ■ mkalias   Builds the sendmail aliases
- ■ mknetid   Builds the information used by the RPC system
- ■ revnetgroup   Builds the user-to-netgroup–mapping file
- ■ stdethers   Builds the ethers-to-name–mapping file

- ◼ `stdhosts`   Builds the IP address-to-name–mapping file
- ◼ `ypinit`   Creates a new NIS domain

Each of these is used in `/var/yp/Makefile`, which controls the build.

NIS Daemons

NIS daemons provide the lookup service at runtime. This includes:

- ◼ `ypserv`   An NIS server—can be either a slave or a master server
- ◼ `ypxfrd`   Handles transferring updated maps to the slave servers on request from the slaves
- ◼ `rpc.yppasswdd`   Handles remote requests by users to change their own passwords
- ◼ `ypbind`   An NIS database lookup daemon, run by both clients and servers
- ◼ `rpc.ypupdated`   Runs on the master server to update the slave servers when the database is updated

Database Distribution Utilities

Database distribution utilities will cause the database to be updated or transferred on request. These include:

- ◼ `yppoll`   Requests an update of a slave server from another server
- ◼ `yppush`   Pushes the maps from the master to its slave servers
- ◼ `ypset`   Forces a particular host to be the server for this host's `ypbind`
- ◼ `ypxfr`   Transfers (copies) an individual map from one server to another

Database Lookup Utilities

Database lookup utilities are replacements for the C runtime library routines that automatically use the NIS database lookup methods instead of accessing the flat files. Some of the utilities access the flat files first and then when they hit a line with a + in the first character, they switch to using the NIS database. This allows for overriding the NIS information on a single host by placing the override information before the line with the + in the appropriate file. The `passwd` and `group` files are examples of files whose lookup routines use this method.

DB Files

The NIS database files reside in the directory `/var/yp/'domainname'` on every server. On the master server there is also a set of files that control the rebuilding of the database in the `/var/yp` directory, including a `Makefile`. Each of the files is a DBM database that makes the lookups very efficient.

You rebuild the database by becoming root on the master server, changing to the /var/yp directory, and entering make.

To avoid having to change directories just enter make, build a shell script, which I like to call ypmake, and place it in the /etc directory with execute permission. Have it do the cd and make calls. Mine reads as follows:

```
#!/bin/sh
# Rebuild the YP Database
cd /var/yp
make
```

This will allow you to stay in the same directory where the configuration file resides and still rebuild the database.

What Files Does NIS Control?

Each NIS installation controls all the maps found in the /var/yp/'*domainname*' directory. The default configuration includes the following:

- passwd   Account and password information
- group   UNIX group table
- hosts   IP addresses
- ethers   EtherNet-to-hostname mapping
- networks   IP network number-to-name mapping
- rpc   A bound RPC program
- services   IP port names
- protocols   IP protocol names
- netgroup   User-to-netgroup mappings
- bootparams   bootp parameters for each host
- aliases   MTA (sendmail) aliases
- publickey   RPC publickey security database
- netid   The version number of the NIS maps (This is used by the servers to be sure they have the latest maps.)
- netmasks   IP network number-to-netmask override file
- c2secure   An optional C2 security database
- timezone   Time zone name-to-time conversions
- auto.master   Automounter configuration information
- auto.home   Automounter indirect map for home directories

To add new maps you need to perform three steps:

1. Modify the Makefile to add the commands to build the map.
2. Build the map on the master server with the -DNOPUSH option.
3. On each slave use ypxfr to request the map for the first time from the master.

From that point on the new map will be transferred automatically.

Automounting File Systems

Having NFS mounts always mounted has led to some problems. Since most NFS mounts are hard mounts when the server is unreachable it can cause client systems to freeze waiting for the server to become available again. Furthermore, every time you move files around and change the layout, every fstab on every client needs to be redone. There is an easier way to handle both problems. Let UNIX automatically mount any needed directory.

The automounter also lets you specify multiple servers for a mount point. This allows the closest server handle the request. Of course this is most useful for read-only file systems, but many shared file systems via NFS fit this category (bin directories, libraries, and so on). Then when the closest server is not available, a backup server is used automatically.

NFS includes a special daemon called automount. This daemon intercepts NFS requests for file systems that aren't mounted, sidesteps them for a moment, and requests that they be mounted, and then resubmits the request after the file system is mounted. It then mounts the file system after there is no activity for a period of time.

The automount daemon mounts the file system in /tmp_mnt and creates a symbolic link to the desired access directory. When the directory is unmounted the daemon removes the link.

An additional feature of the automounter is that it can perform variable substitution on the mount commands, allowing different directories to be mounted in differing circumstances, while referencing the same path. As an example, if the path /usr/local/bin were referenced, the actual mounted file system count be /usr/local/bin.'arch', where *arch* is replaced by the output of the arch command. This would allow different directories to be automatically mounted for different architecture computers.

The Automounter Configuration File—*/etc/auto.master*

The automount daemon uses a map file to control its operations. This file can be distributed by NIS or it can be on a local file. The normal local configuration file is /etc/auto.master. However, this file often refers to other files, which allows for segmenting the configuration.

Although there are many options available via the automounter, a simple `auto.master` looks like:

```
#Mount-point    Map                     Mount-options
/ -             /etc/auto.direct        -ro,intr
/home/users     /etc/auto.home          -rw,intr,secure
```

There are three columns. The first is the mount point to listen for. Any requests for files under /home/users, in this example, are managed by the automounter via the map /etc/ auto.home. The mount commands generated will be performed with the options listed in the third column.

The / - line specifies a direct map. Entries in this map file specify the full pathname of the mount point and are not relative to the mount point listed. Each entry in a direct map is a separate mount.

Indirect Map Files

The map file /etc/auto.home is considered an indirect map file because it is relative to / home/users. A sample auto.home includes:

```
#key            mount-options      location
syd                           server:/home/server/syd
```

This specifies that the directory syd under /home/users should be mounted from the server's /home/server/syd directory. Any specific mount options to add to the options in the master map file can be listed between the key and the location.

Analyzing and Troubleshooting Utilities

Like in all aspects of a computer system, things can go wrong on the network. However, the network can be a bit harder to troubleshoot than other aspects because things happen across multiple computers. But there is a basic set of questions you can start with:

- Is the network configured properly? Using `ifconfig` you can check to see if the interfaces are configured and up.

- Are the routes configured properly? Using `netstat` you can check routing.

- Can I talk to the other nodes? Using `ping` and `traceroute` you can verify connectivity.

- Is the process listening? Using `netstat` you can check the connections.

- Am I sending the right data and is it responding? Using `etherfind` or `snoop` you can listen in to the network and see what is being sent.

ifconfig

You configure and report on the configuration of the interfaces using `ifconfig`. It can set the IP address, netmask, broadcast address, MTU, a routing metric, and whether the interface is up and should be used or down and should be ignored. It also reports on the current configuration of the interface and its EtherNet address. Running `ifconfig -a` from the shell yields:

```
# ifconfig -a
lo0: flags=849<UP,LOOPBACK,RUNNING,MULTICAST> mtu 8232
        inet 127.0.0.1 netmask ff000000
le0: flags=863<UP,BROADCAST,NOTRAILERS,RUNNING,MULTICAST> mtu 1500
        inet 190.109.252.34 netmask ffffffe0 broadcast 192.65.202.224
        ether 8:0:20:1d:4e:1b
#
```

`flags` is a bitmask, and the meaning of each bit is explained in the words following the flag value. The important one is UP or DOWN. The interface should always be RUNNING. It's with the second line for each interface that you are most concerned. The `inet` (IP) address should be correct for this interface for this host. The `netmask` must match, and the broadcast address should be all 1s in all the 0 bits of the `netmask` and it should match the IP address in the 1 bits.

A common mistake in initializing an interface is to get the order of the arguments to `ifconfig` incorrect. `ifconfig` processes its arguments left to right, and this matters if a + is used.

`ifconfig` can automatically determine the default netmask and broadcast address, but it does it for the current values at the time it sees the +. This leads to a different result, depending on the order of the arguments. As an example, the `ifconfig` command

```
ifconfig le0 190.109.252.34 broadcast + netmask + up
```

would set the IP address correctly, the broadcast address to the default for `190.109`, which is `190.109.255.255`, and the netmask, using an override in the /etc/netmasks file, to `255.255.255.0`. This is not what you wanted. Even specifying

```
ifconfig le0 190.109.252.34 broadcast + netmask 255.255.255.224 up
```

won't do what you want because the broadcast address will be controlled by the default netmask value. It is important that the order be

```
ifconfig le0 190.109.252.34 netmask 255.255.255.224 broadcast + up
```

netstat

The main reporting command for the network is `netstat`. The interface report will show you if the network is being used and if there are too many collisions. The route report will show you not only if the route is configured but also if it is being used. The connection report will show what is using the network, and the various statistics show how much is being used.

netstat -i—Interfaces

The following is the interface status report:

```
# netstat -i
Name  Mtu  Net/Dest    Address     Ipkts   Ierrs Opkts   Oerrs Collis Queue
lo0   8232 loopback    localhost   527854  0     527854  0     0      0
le0   1500 subnet1     ws1         965484  1     979543  1     6672   0
#
```

This report can be run showing the cumulative counts since boot, or with a repeat interval in seconds on the end of the command, which will show the delta in the counts every *interval* seconds.

When troubleshooting you are looking for three things in the output of netstat:

- The input and output counts are incrementing. This shows that the network is being accessed.

- The error counts are not incrementing. This shows that there is not likely to be a hardware error in wiring or the equipment.

- The collision count is staying small relative to the packet counts. No single node is hogging the network and the network is not overloaded. If the collisions are more than 1 to 2 percent of the delta in packet counts, you should be concerned.

netstat -r—Routes

The route is listed with netstat -r as in:

```
# netstat -r
Routing Table:
  Destination          Gateway         Flags Ref   Use    Interface
-------------------- -------------------- ---- ---- ------ --------
localhost            localhost            UH    0  109761  lo0
rmtnet               ws2                  UG    0   20086
rmtppp               ws2                  UG    0    1096
subnet1              ws1                  U     3    1955  le0
224.0.0.0            ws1                  U     3       0  le0
default              gateway              UG    0   16100
#
```

In the routing table you are looking for the existence of the proper routes and their flags. In addition, you should run the command more than once while traffic is supposed to be flowing to the sites you are looking at to see that the use count is incrementing.

The flags show the status and how the route was created:

- ■ U **(up)**   The route is up and available.

- ■ G **(gateway)**   This route is not to a final destination, but to a host that will forward it. The gateway field should contain the address (name) of the next hop. If there is no G flag, the Gateway field should show your address (name).

- ■ D **(redirect)**   This route was created by a redirect. This is a cautionary note. Your routes were not correct and the TCP/IP code received an ICMP redirect message with the proper route. Things will work, but eventually you should fix your configuration files with the proper route.

- ■ H **(host)**   Internal to the host. This should appear only on the loopback interface.

netstat -a—Connections

There are two formats of the connection list output. The first is from BSD and SVR4 UNIX's and the second is from Solaris 2. On BSD or SVR4, running the netstart connection report shows:

```
# netstat -a -f inet (BSD, SVR4)
Active Internet connections
Proto Recv-Q Send-Q  Local Address      Foreign Address       (state)
tcp        0      0  gateway.smtp       cunyvm.cuny.edu.60634  SYN_RCVD
tcp        0  14336  gateway.1314       qms860.qmspr          ESTABLISHED
tcp        0      0  gateway.1313       qms860.qmspr          TIME_WAIT
tcp        0      0  gateway.1312       qms860.qmspr          TIME_WAIT
tcp        0      0  gateway.1295       NETNEWS.UPENN.ED.nntp  ESTABLISHED
tcp        0      0  gateway.nntp       NETNEWS.UPENN.ED.2930  ESTABLISHED
tcp        0      0  gateway.1242       eerie.acsu.buffa.nntp  ESTABLISHED
tcp        0      0  gateway.login      dsiss2.1020           ESTABLISHED
tcp        0      0  gateway.telnet     xterm.1206            ESTABLISHED
tcp        0      0  gateway.telnet     xterm.1205            ESTABLISHED
tcp        0      0  gateway.login      photo.1022            ESTABLISHED
tcp        0     80  gateway.login      photo.1023            ESTABLISHED
tcp        0      0  gateway.printer    *.*                   LISTEN
tcp        0      0  gateway.listen     *.*                   LISTEN
udp        0      0  gateway.nameserv   *.*
udp        0      0  localhost.nameserv *.*
#
```

Under Solaris 2, running the netstat connection report shows:

```
# netstat -a -f inet (Solaris)

UDP
   Local Address       State
--------------------  ------
      *.sunrpc        Idle
      *.*             Unbound
      *.talk          Idle
      *.time          Idle
      *.echo          Idle
      *.discard       Idle
      *.daytime       Idle
```

```
        *.chargen      Idle
ws1.syslog             Idle
        *.ntalk        Idle
        *.ntp          Idle
localhost.ntp          Idle
ws1.ntp                Idle
        *.nfsd         Idle

TCP
   Local Address        Remote Address      Swind Send-Q Rwind Recv-Q  State
 -------------------  -------------------  ----- ------ ----- ------  ------
        *.*                  *.*               0      0  8576      0  IDLE
        *.sunrpc             *.*               0      0  8576      0  LISTEN
        *.ftp                *.*               0      0  8576      0  LISTEN
        *.telnet             *.*               0      0  8576      0  LISTEN
        *.shell              *.*               0      0  8576      0  LISTEN
        *.login              *.*               0      0  8576      0  LISTEN
        *.systat             *.*               0      0  8576      0  LISTEN
        *.netstat            *.*               0      0  8576      0  LISTEN
        *.time               *.*               0      0  8576      0  LISTEN
        *.echo               *.*               0      0  8576      0  LISTEN
        *.discard            *.*               0      0  8576      0  LISTEN
        *.daytime            *.*               0      0  8576      0  LISTEN
        *.chargen            *.*               0      0  8576      0  LISTEN
        *.chalklog           *.*               0      0  8576      0  LISTEN
        *.lockd              *.*               0      0  8576      0  BOUND
ws1.1019             gateway.login          4096      0  9216      0  FIN_WAIT_2
ws1.1023             gateway.login          4096      0  9216      0  ESTABLISHED
        *.6000               *.*               0      0  8576      0  LISTEN
        *.*                  *.*               0      0  8576      0  IDLE
ws1.34125            xterm.6000             8192      0 10164      0  ESTABLISHED
ws1.1018             pppgate.login          4096      0  9112      0  ESTABLISHED
        *.ident              *.*               0      0  8576      0  LISTEN
        *.smtp               *.*               0      0  8576      0  LISTEN
ws1.1022             gateway.login          4096      0  9216      0  ESTABLISHED
        *.printer            *.*               0      0  8576      0  LISTEN
        *.listen             *.*               0      0  8576      0  LISTEN
localhost.32793      localhost.32787       16340      0 16384      0  FIN_WAIT_2
localhost.32787      localhost.32793       16384      0 16340      0  CLOSE_WAIT
#
```

These listings provide similar information. In troubleshooting you are looking for three things:

- A process should be listening or connected on that port. You want to see a `*.port` with a LISTEN status for daemons or a `host.port` for TCP connections.

- Send-Q shouldn't be staying stable at any value other than 0. You want the system and the remote process to be reading the data. Seeing a non-zero send queue entry indicates that data is waiting to be sent and the remote TCP code has not acknowledged enough prior packets to allow the sending of more data. That in itself is not a problem—it happens all the time on sockets that are continuously sending data and is a method of flow control. What should raise your concern is seeing it stay stable at the same number all the time.

■ `Recv-Q` should have a non-zero value. This nonzero value means that your local task is not reading the data from the socket. Your local task might be hung.

In addition, the state of the connection if it's not `ESTABLISHED` or `LISTEN` is worth noting. If a connection stays in `FIN_WAIT` or `FIN_WAIT2` for long periods of time, the remote end is not acknowledging the close window packet. Being in `CLOSE_WAIT` is not a problem. `CLOSE_WAIT` is a time-out–based state that waits to be sure all data is drained by tasks from the socket before allowing the port address to be reused. Controlling the use of a `CLOSE_WAIT` state is handled by an option when opening the socket in the C code of programs.

netstat -s—Statistics

The format of the statistic output varies by the vendors of the TCP/IP driver stack. However, it always contains similar data. Here is a sample output:

```
# netstat -s
UDP

        udpInDatagrams      =6035056    udpInErrors        =      0
        udpOutDatagrams     =10353333

TCP     tcpRtoAlgorithm     =       4   tcpRtoMin          =    200
        tcpRtoMax           =   60000   tcpMaxConn         =     -1
        tcpActiveOpens      =    1749   tcpPassiveOpens    =    722
        tcpAttemptFails     =      96   tcpEstabResets     =   1964
        tcpCurrEstab        =      27   tcpOutSegs         =2442096
        tcpOutDataSegs      =1817357    tcpOutDataBytes    =1688841836
        tcpRetransSegs      =    6986   tcpRetransBytes    =904977
        tcpOutAck           =624749     tcpOutAckDelayed   =563849
        tcpOutUrg           =      25   tcpOutWinUpdate    =    133
        tcpOutWinProbe      =      31   tcpOutControl      =   5282
        tcpOutRsts          =     423   tcpOutFastRetrans  =     11
        tcpInSegs           =2064776
        tcpInAckSegs        =1522447    tcpInAckBytes      =1688826786
        tcpInDupAck         =    6299   tcpInAckUnsent     =      0
        tcpInInorderSegs    =856268     tcpInInorderBytes  =280335873
        tcpInUnorderSegs    =     564   tcpInUnorderBytes  =293287
        tcpInDupSegs        =      15   tcpInDupBytes      =   2314
        tcpInPartDupSegs    =       5   tcpInPartDupBytes  =   1572
        tcpInPastWinSegs    =       0   tcpInPastWinBytes  =      0
        tcpInWinProbe       =       3   tcpInWinUpdate     =532122
        tcpInClosed         =     121   tcpRttNoUpdate     =   6162
        tcpRttUpdate        =1514447    tcpTimRetrans      =  24065
        tcpTimRetransDrop   =       1   tcpTimKeepalive    =    369
        tcpTimKeepaliveProbe=     193   tcpTimKeepaliveDrop =     0

IP      ipForwarding        =       2   ipDefaultTTL       =    255
        ipInReceives        =7873752    ipInHdrErrors      =      0
        ipInAddrErrors      =       0   ipInCksumErrs      =     12
        ipForwDatagrams     =       0   ipForwProhibits    =      0
        ipInUnknownProtos   =       0   ipInDiscards       =      0
        ipInDelivers        =8098783    ipOutRequests      =11669260
        ipOutDiscards       =       0   ipOutNoRoutes      =      0
        ipReasmTimeout      =      60   ipReasmReqds       =137309
```

```
        ipReasmOKs          =137309     ipReasmFails       =     0
        ipReasmDuplicates   =      0     ipReasmPartDups    =     0
        ipFragOKs           =211618     ipFragFails        =     0
        ipFragCreates       =1062582     ipRoutingDiscards  =     0
        tcpInErrs           =     15     udpNoPorts         =496673
        udpInCksumErrs      =      0     udpInOverflows     =     0
        rawipInOverflows    =      0

ICMP  icmpInMsgs            =   8555     icmpInErrors       =     0
        icmpInCksumErrs     =      0     icmpInUnknowns     =     0
        icmpInDestUnreachs  =   8516     icmpInTimeExcds    =    22
        icmpInParmProbs     =      0     icmpInSrcQuenchs   =     0
        icmpInRedirects     =      0     icmpInBadRedirects =     0
        icmpInEchos         =      6     icmpInEchoReps     =     0
        icmpInTimestamps    =      0     icmpInTimestampReps =    0
        icmpInAddrMasks     =     11     icmpInAddrMaskReps =     0
        icmpInFragNeeded    =     44     icmpOutMsgs        =   492
        icmpOutDrops        =      5     icmpOutErrors      =     0
        icmpOutDestUnreachs =    486     icmpOutTimeExcds   =     0
        icmpOutParmProbs    =      0     icmpOutSrcQuenchs  =     0
        icmpOutRedirects    =      0     icmpOutEchos       =     0
        icmpOutEchoReps     =      6     icmpOutTimestamps  =     0
        icmpOutTimestampReps=      0     icmpOutAddrMasks   =     0
        icmpOutAddrMaskReps =      0     icmpOutFragNeeded  =     0
        icmpInOverflows     =      0

 IGMP:
        0 messages received
        0 messages received with too few bytes
        0 messages received with bad checksum
        0 membership queries received
        0 membership queries received with invalid field(s)
        0 membership reports received
        0 membership reports received with invalid field(s)
        0 membership reports received for groups to which we belong
        0 membership reports sent
 #
```

Of particular interest are any error counts. A large number of errors can indicate a hardware or wiring problem. In addition, comparing two outputs over time gives an indication of the overall loading on the network.

Seeing redirects in the ICMP section is a sign of a routing problem. However, time exceededs are most likely just the result of someone running a traceroute command.

nfsstat

NFS keeps many statistics that aid in checking the overall performance of the NFS system and in troubleshooting problems. They are reported via the nfsstat command. The two most useful options are -n and -m, shown in the following:

```
# nfsstat -m
/files3 from ws2:/files3
 Flags:   hard,intr,dynamic read size=8192, write size=8192,  retrans = 5
 Lookups: srtt=7 (17ms), dev=3 (15ms), cur=2 (40ms)
```

```
Reads:   srtt=15 (37ms), dev=3 (15ms), cur=3 (60ms)
Writes:  srtt=28 (70ms), dev=6 (30ms), cur=6 (120ms)
All:     srtt=12 (30ms), dev=3 (15ms), cur=3 (60ms)

/files2 from ws2:/files2
 Flags:   hard,intr,dynamic read size=8192, write size=8192,  retrans = 5
 Lookups: srtt=11 (27ms), dev=4 (20ms), cur=3 (60ms)
 All:     srtt=11 (27ms), dev=4 (20ms), cur=3 (60ms)

/files1 from ws2:/files1
 Flags:   hard,intr,dynamic read size=8192, write size=8192,  retrans = 5
 Lookups: srtt=8 (20ms), dev=4 (20ms), cur=3 (60ms)
 All:     srtt=8 (20ms), dev=4 (20ms), cur=3 (60ms)

# nfsstat -n
Server nfs:
calls       badcalls
4162132     0
null        getattr     setattr     root         lookup      readlink    read
14  0%      694625 17%  33302  1%   0   0%      2579204 62% 12561  0%   167293   4%
wrcache     write       create      remove       rename      link        symlink
0   0%      154051  4%  6310   0%   4870  0%     709   0%    1665   0%   0   0%
mkdir       rmdir       readdir     statfs
368  0%     367   0%    505799 12%  994   0%

Client nfs:
calls       badcalls    nclget       nclcreate
26512       0           26512        0
null        getattr     setattr      root         lookup      readlink    read
0   0%      3771  14%   169   1%     0   0%      3775  14%   4   0%     6495  24%
wrcache     write       create       remove       rename      link        symlink
0   0%      11643 44%   182   1%     74   0%     133   1%    0   0%     0   0%
mkdir       rmdir       readdir      statfs
0   0%      0   0%      124   0%     142   1%
#
```

In the first set of output, note the srtt times. This is the smoothed round trip time or how responsive the server has been to NFS requests. Of course, the smaller the better, but the times shown in the example are pretty typical.

In the second set of output you can see what kinds of calls are being made. This will help you tune the system. Comparing periodic output of this second set of numbers can show you the load on your NFS servers.

arp

The correct arp table can be printed with the command:

```
# arp -a
Net to Media Table
Device   IP Address              Mask          Flags   Phys Addr
------   --------------          ------------  ----    --------------
le0      xterm                   255.255.255.255       00:80:96:00:0c:bd
le0      gateway                 255.255.255.255       00:00:c0:c7:f4:14
le0      ws2                     255.255.255.255       08:00:20:0e:b9:d3
le0      ws4                     255.255.255.255       00:00:c0:51:6f:5b
```

```
le0     ws1                 255.255.255.255 SP    08:00:20:1d:4e:1b
le0     224.0.0.0           240.0.0.0       SM    01:00:5e:00:00:00
#
```

The arp command prints the current contents of the address resolution protocol cache. This is the table that maps IP addresses to EtherNet addresses. In troubleshooting you are looking to see that the proper EtherNet address is listed for the IP address in question. If a second node is masquerading with an incorrect EtherNet address, the ARP table will show this. You can use the -d option to arp to delete an entry from the cache to see which system responds to that IP address translation request.

ping

ping has two uses. The first is to see if a host is reachable. It's not enough to say it sees if the host is up; ping also checks that you have a valid and operational route to the node. Both versions produce output as follows:

```
# ping gateway
gateway is alive
#
# ping -s gateway
64 bytes from gateway (190.109.252.34): icmp_seq=0. time=3. ms
64 bytes from gateway (190.109.252.34): icmp_seq=1. time=1. ms
64 bytes from gateway (190.109.252.34): icmp_seq=2. time=3. ms
64 bytes from gateway (190.109.252.34): icmp_seq=3. time=1. ms

----gateway PING Statistics----
4 packets transmitted, 4 packets received, 0% packet loss
round-trip (ms)  min/avg/max = 1/2/3
#
```

In the first case, ping was just used to check whether the host was reachable. This gives you confidence that the rest of the configuration is usable. The second output shows you whether packets are getting lost and the roundtrip time for the ICMP echo ping uses.

If you see packet losses where sequence numbers are missing, look for hardware problems and overloaded networks.

> **CAUTION:** Not every system responds to ICMP echoes. Some PCs, Macs, and routers do not. If you can telnet or otherwise communicate, consider that the host may not respond to ping.

traceroute

Packets can get lost from anywhere. Getting a host unreachable or network unreachable error really doesn't tell you much. You need to know how far the packets are getting before things go awry. Using the ICMP echo command along with a time-out field in the packet, the traceroute command can cause each hop in the route to identify itself. Running trace route from your gateway to uunet's ftp host yields:

```
# /etc/traceroute ftp.uu.net
traceroute to ftp.uu.net (192.48.96.9), 30 hops max, 40 byte packets
 1  gateway (190.109.252.1)  5 ms  2 ms  2 ms
 2  phl3-gw.PREPNET.COM (129.250.26.1)  6 ms  7 ms  6 ms
 3  pgh4-gw.PREPNET.COM (129.250.3.2)  32 ms  28 ms  24 ms
 4  psc-gw.PREPNET.COM (129.250.10.2)  68 ms  27 ms  25 ms
 5  enss-e.psc.edu (192.5.146.253)  48 ms  48 ms  52 ms
 6  t3-0.Cleveland-cnss41.t3.ans.net (140.222.41.1)  60 ms  53 ms  *
 7  mf-0.Cleveland-cnss40.t3.ans.net (140.222.40.222)  34 ms  29 ms  36 ms
 8  t3-1.New-York-cnss32.t3.ans.net (140.222.32.2)  41 ms  39 ms  516 ms
 9  * t3-1.Washington-DC-cnss56.t3.ans.net (140.222.56.2)  65 ms  72 ms
10  mf-0.Washington-DC-cnss58.t3.ans.net (140.222.56.194)  82 ms  85 ms  *
11  t3-0.enss136.t3.ans.net (140.222.136.1)  89 ms  *  *
12  Washington.DC.ALTER.NET (192.41.177.248)  88 ms  87 ms  72 ms
13  Falls-Church1.VA.ALTER.NET (137.39.43.97)  106 ms  67 ms  77 ms
14  IBMpc01.UU.NET (137.39.43.34)  79 ms  97 ms  74 ms
15  ftp.UU.NET (192.48.96.9)  83 ms  75 ms  72 ms
#
```

Just to send a packet to UUnet in Virginia from Philadelphia took 15 hops. Wherever you see a * is where no packet was received before the time-out. However, if the list stopped part way down and just listed each * from then on, or listed !H (host unreachable) or !N (network unreachable), you know where to start looking for the problem.

snoop

When all else fails and you need to see exactly what is being transmitted over the network, it's snoop to the rescue. snoop places the EtherNet interface in promiscuous mode and listens to all traffic on the network. Then it uses its filtering abilities to produce listings of the relevant traffic. It also can decode the data in the traffic for many of the IP subprotocols.

snoop has the ability to record and later analyze traffic capture files. Its arguments are too complex to cover here, but it is a good tool to use when everyone is claiming that a packet never did get sent.

Summary

UNIX and TCP/IP networking are very tightly bound together. A UNIX system can be run standalone, and it also seamlessly runs over a network. This chapter introduces the basics of UNIX networking. If you intend to program UNIX systems in C using the networking calls, there is still much more to learn. However, what is presented here should provide a system administrator what he or she needs to know to understand how to configure and run the network.

The most important task of administering a network is to plan. Many of the problems you will run into later can easily be avoided by planning server placement, traffic flows, routers, and gateways, and especially security controls. The network is a back door to every one of your systems. Your overall security is as secure or as weak as the weakest of all your systems. Don't let this scare you—it is quite possible to plan and install a secure network of systems. You need to plan where the firewalls have to be placed and what access you are going to allow each system.

NFS will allow you to balance your disk requirements and your disk space availability across the entire network. Use of the automounter will allow this to be transparent to your users. Make generous use of both.

NIS will make your life easier by allowing you to maintain a single copy of the system administration files.

Finally, realize that others have also had to troubleshoot the network when things go wrong, so the tools are already there. Make use of them to find the problems.

UNIX System Accounting

38

By Scott Allen Parker

As you have learned by now, UNIX is a very complex operating system with many types of files, utilities, and programs. Your users are logging in and out, storing files, and running programs. One of the problems you may run into is keeping track of usage of the system. UNIX system accounting was created to assist you in keeping track of your users and processes. UNIX system accounting can help you troubleshoot and tune your system performance. You can even give a value to the resources on your system. This means that you can charge your users money or a fee for storing files and running processes. In this chapter, you will learn:

- What is UNIX system accounting?
- How do I set up and turn on the system accounting option?
- How to generate report?

How Does System Accounting Work?

The moment the UNIX system is up and running, the system accounting is tracking information about the system. Information is tracked until the system shutdown. The information that is tracked is as follows:

- Users logging in and out of the system
- How much and many resources a user processes has taken
- How much disk space has been used by the users' files

Several processes and the UNIX kernel help the system track this usage. Several of these daemons have been covered in previous chapters.

At the Start

When you boot the UNIX system into multiuser mode, UNIX runs a program called `/usr/lib/acct/startup`. `startup` is a shell script that runs other accounting programs and sets flags in the system to make the kernel and other processes to start recording information. Some of the accounting programs that are run by the `startup` shell script are as follows:

```
acctwtmp
turnacct
remove
```

These programs are discussed in the following sections.

acctwtmp

The `/usr/lib/acct/acctwtmp` program writes a record into the file called `/var/adm/wtmp`. wtmp is a key file of the accounting system, containing records about users connecting to the system, date changes, reboots, and system startup and shutdowns. Specifically, `/var/adm/wtmp` has information about the following:

- A user's login name
- The device the user is logging in on
- The user's process id (PID)
- How the user is logging in
- The date and time the login was made

The record created by `acctwtmp` is a "boot" record containing the name of the system and the date and time the accounting system was started. You might see this information referred to as *reasons* in your man pages. In the startup and shutdown script, you could see:

```
/usr/lib/acct/acctwtmp "Accounting System ON" >> /var/adm/wtmp
```

or

```
/usr/lib/acct/acctwtmp "Accounting System OFF" >> /var/adm/wtmp
```

If you were to list the `/var/adm/wtmp` file you would find entries for the two examples above. The wording might be slightly different depending upon your Operating System.

turnacct

The `/usr/lib/acct/turnacct` program turns on the accounting system. If you look inside the startup shell script, you will see the line containing:

```
/usr/lib/acct/turnacct on
```

This program will run a special process called `accton`.

```
/usr/lib/acct/accton /var/adm/pacct
```

`/var/adm/pacct` has information about processes that are running the system. Specifically, `/var/adm/pacct` has information about the following:

- Who is using the process
- Group ID's of users using the process
- The start and elapsed time of the process
- The CPU timed used
- The memory used
- The commands run
- The `tty` used to run or use the process.

> **NOTE:** You will find a number of `/var/adm/pacct` files on your system over a period time. The reason for this is that UNIX runs a program called `/usr/lib/acct/ckpacct`. ckpacct will be discussed later in this chapter, but for now suffice it to say that ckpacct checks the `/var/adm/pacct` for its size. If the `/var/adm/pacct` file is more than 500 blocks, ckpacct runs turnacct to move the current pacct file to `/var/adm/pacct` with an incremented version number attached. For instance, `/var/adm/pacct` would be moved to the free name in `/var/adm/pacct#` (where # starts with the number 1 and is incremented by one every time an additional `/var/adm/pacct` is needed). The next time ckpacct runs turnacct, it will move the `/var/adm/pacct` file to `/var/adm/pacct1`, and so on. This increment insures that the `/var/adm/pacct` file is kept in sequence and never overwritten.

remove

`/usr/lib/acct/remove` will wipe out the `/var/adm/acct/sum/pacct` and `/var/adm/acct/sum/wtmp` files. The `/var/adm/acct/sum` directory contains accumulated summary files for most of the daily files tracked by the accounting system. You wouldn't want the file to remain between "reboots" of the accounting system or even the operating system. These files are relevant only from one boot of the accounting system to the next. We will discuss the `/var/adm/acct` directory later in this chapter.

Login, Run What You Will, and Logout

In a matter of minutes after the system comes up in multiuser mode, someone logs onto the system. No need to fear: the `login` and `init` programs are ready for them. `login` and `init` record the user's session by adding a record to the `/var/adm/wtmp` file. Next, the user runs a process, and the UNIX kernel monitors the process and writes a record about this to the `/var/adm/pacct file`.

There are other programs that help the accounting periodically. The `/usr/lib/acct/ckpacct` file, which checks `/var/adm/pacct` for its size, is run every hour. The ckpacct shell script runs

`/usr/lib/acct/turnacct switch`

to switch the current `/var/adm/pacct` to an archived file with a version number such as `/var/adm/pacct1`, `/var/adm/pacct2`, and so on. These archives will become important when you are recovering from a failure to process these files.

On a daily basis, the `/usr/lib/acct/runacct` program is run to create daily and cumulative totals for connections, fees, disk storage, and processes. You will learn more about runacct later in this chapter.

System Shutdown

When the UNIX system is shut down, the shutdown utility invokes several shell scripts found in the /sbin/rc0.d directory. One of the shells, called k22acct, runs the utility

/usr/lib/acct/shutacct

which will write a record into /var/adm/wtmp. The record is called the "reason" record. After this reason is written, the accounting system is then shutdown. Then the shutdown program finishes the system shutdown. See Chapter 34, "Starting Up and Shutting Down," for more information about the shutdown program.

Setting Up and Turning On the System Accounting Option

There are several things that you need to brush up on before starting the accounting system. The /sbin contains directories that the boot and the shutdown program use. We are concerned with only three of these directories.

/etc/rc0.d	Contains the scripts that are executed during the shutdown process
/etc/rc2.d	Contains the scripts that are executed during the boot process to multiuser mode
/sbin/init.d/acct	Contains the programs (links to shell scripts) that are executed as the UNIX system is being initialized

The /etc/rc0.d/K22acct is a shell script that shuts the accounting system down when the system is shutting down. The /etc/rc2.d/S22acct is the shell script that turns on the accounting system. Here is what you do to set up these files:

1. Link the /sbin/init.d/acct file to the /etc/rc0.d/K22acct.

   ```
   $ link /etc/rc0.d/K22acct /sbin/init.d/acct
   $
   ```

2. Link the /sbin/init.d/acct file to the /etc/rc2.d/S22acct.

   ```
   $ link /etc/rc2.d/S22acct /sbin/init.d/acct
   $
   ```

When the system is booted, the init process will run these scripts to start the system accounting option. The last thing you need to do is add entries in the crontab file. The crontab file is used by cron to run programs at predetermined times. See Chapter 20, "Scheduling Processes," for more details on cron. We need to add ckpacct, runacct, monacct, and dodisk to the crontab file to finish the accounting system setup.

3. Edit the `crontab` file to add these utilities.

```
$ crontab -e
```

4. Add `/usr/lib/acct/ckpacct` to check `/var/adm/pacct` every hour to archive the pacct file after its size is more than 500 blocks.

```
0 * * * *    /usr/lib/acct/ckpacct
```

5. Add `/usr/lib/acct/runacct` to run daily to process the accounting files to prepare daily and cumulative summary files. It is recommended that you run this file at off-hours of the morning. You can pick any time. For this example, we will use 1:30 a.m.

```
30 1 * * *    /usr/lib/acct/runacct 2> /var/adm/acct/nite/fd2log
```

`/var/adm/acct/nite/fd2log` is a log file that you look at to verify that `runacct` is running cleanly.

6. Add `/usr/lib/acct/monacct` to run monthly. The `monacct` file takes data stored in the `/var/adm/acct/sum` directory and creates a monthly report of all daily totals.

```
30 3 * 1 *    /usr/lib/acct/monacct
```

7. Add `/usr/lib/acct/dodisk` program to do disk usage accounting. It is recommended that you run this program once a week and before `runacct` is executed daily.

```
00 22 * * 4   /usr/lib/acct/dodisk
```

8. Shutdown and reboot your system to activate the accounting system.

The Accounting System Programs

Remember the processes that you add to the `crontab` file. Those processes are essential to keep track of your system usage.

runacct

`/usr/lib/acct/runacct` is a shell program that is executed every day to process system usage. It will create daily summary files for the `/usr/lib/acct/prdaily` and `/usr/lib/acct/monacct` programs. `prdaily` is run by `runacct` to write daily accounting information to the `/var/adm/acct/sum/rprtMMDD` file. `MMDD` is the month and day the file was created. `monacct` is the month usage report, which will be covered later in this chapter. There can be one of these files for every day of the week. `runacct` actually writes information to several files.

`/var/adm/pacct?`	Contains process information. `?` represents the incremented `/var/adm/pacct` file.

/var/adm/wtmp	Contains user information
/var/adm/fee	Contains fees accessed for usage
/var/adm/acct/nite/disktacct	Contains the disk space usage

You can find the output of the runacct program in the /var/adm/acct/nite directory. Other files in the /var/adm/acct/nite directory are as follows:

lock and lock1	These files may or may not exist. If they do exist, runacct will not run. It will "think" that it is already running. If you get an error concerning these files during an attempted execute of runacct, remove them with rm (remove command).
lastdate	This file records the last date that runacct was executed. This file is checked to prevent runacct from being executed more than once daily.
fd2log	This file contains the message generated by runacct. It will contain important error information in case runacct fails to run.

NOTE: If runacct does have an error, root will be notified by mail. It will write information to /var/adm/acct/nite/fd2log and remove the lock files.

dodisk

The /usr/lib/acct/dodisk shell script cumulates disk usage information. This shell script program runs three programs.

diskusg	Collects file data by reading the file INODES
acctdusg	Collects file statistics in the file system
acctdisk	Formats the data from diskusg or acctdusg

NOTE: Only one of the file data accounting programs needs to run. /usr/lib/acct/diskusg and /usr/lib/acct/acctdusg output the same information, but how they approach the information differs. diskusg is much faster than acctdusg because it looks at the lowest level of file information in the INODE. To toggle between the two, the dodisk can invoke the -o option. The following script:

```
/usr/lib/acct/dodisk /dev/dsk/c1t0d0s2
```

will run the diskusg method against the device file name of /dev/dsk/c1t0d0s2. If the device name is not specified, then diskusg will look in the /etc/vfstab file and process all the devices. This is very similar to the fsck command that looks at the file system's INODE's when it checks the file system at boot time. This is much faster. The following script:

```
/usr/lib/acct/dodisk -o /user
```

will run the `acctdusg` method against the /user file system mounting point. If the mount point is not specified, the root mounting point is used.

Remember, if you want to use `acctdusg`, add the `-o` option to the `dodisk` line in the `crontab` file.

`acctdisk` will write the formatted output to the `/var/adm/acct/nite/disktacct` file. This file will have the following information about users' files on the system:

- The user's login name
- The user's id number
- The number of blocks in use in the user's files

WARNING: `dodisk` stores all this information in `/var/adm/acct/nite/disktacct`. Each and every time `dodisk` is executed, it overwrites the `/var/adm/acct/nite/disktacct` file. Executing `dodisk` more than once daily should be avoided.

chargefee

If you are in a Computer Services department or part of a service provider, you may elect to charge other departments or users for the resource they use. UNIX has provided a program called `chargefee` that will charge your user for a number of services. The charges that are generated by `chargefee` are stored in `/var/adm/fee`. Say that `carolynp` sends me a message to mount a tape for her on my system and I charge $1.50 for every mount.

```
$ chargefee carolynp 1.50
$
```

An entry in `/var/adm/fee` would be made having `carolynp`, her user id number, and 1.50. Later in my monthly accounting report charges for mounting tapes, restoring files, etc. can be polled into an invoice billed to the user. Most places will normally charge for processor time and disk space on a monthly basis. The `monacct` program, which you can read about next, will generate a nice report to run charge-back scripts against the invoice users.

monacct

`monacct` runs monthly, or you can run it whenever your fiscal period ends, to generate files that summarize the statistic files created by `dodisk` and `runacct`. These files are stored in the `/var/adm/acct/fiscal` directory. After the `monacct` program is run, the files created by `dodisk` and `runacct` removed and reset for the next fiscal period.

acctcom

The `acctcom` utility allows you to see the accounting system at any given time. You can execute this command from the command line with several different options.

```
$ acctmon -a
```

This will show the average statistics about processes.

```
$ acctmon -r
```

This will show the amount of user time per total time (system time plus user time).

```
$ acctmon -u zachp
```

This will show all the processes belonging to the user `zachp`.

```
$ acctmon -O 20
```

This will show all the processes running longer than 20 seconds.

To see more options for the `acctcom` command, please refer to your man pages. `acctcom` will look in the `/var/adm/pacct?` files for these little records.

Daily Reports

`runacct` generates a number of reports.

The Daily	Shows the usage of ports on your system.
The Daily Usage	Shows the system resource used by your users during the daily period.
The Daily Command Summary	Shows the commands run on your system and resources those commands used. This report can be essential in helping you determine the process that might bottleneck your system.
The Last Login	Tells you the last time a login id was used by a user. This report can help you remove unused login id's and directories associated with those id's.

Daily Report

The Daily Report can be found in the `/var/adm/acct/nite/lineuse` file.

```
$ cat /var/adm/acct/nite/lineuse
Apr 06 01:33 1994  DAILY REPORT FOR excelsior Page 1


from Tue Apr 05 05:10:41 1994
to   Wed Apr 06 01:31:20 1994
1          runacct
1          accton

TOTAL DURATION IS 5155 MINUTES
LINE      MINUTES   PERCENT   # SESS   # ON    #OFF
ttyp01    1541      30        4        9       5
ttyp10    2564      50        25       8       6
ttyp13    1050      20        15       3       4
TOTALS    5155      100       44       20      10

$
```

The detail of this report column by column are as follows:

LINE	The port that was accessing the system.
MINUTES	The number of minutes the line was in usage during the daily period.
PERCENT	The number of minutes in use divided by TOTAL DURATION. TOTAL DURATION is the number of minutes the system was in multiuser mode.
# SESS	The number of times the port was accessed to log in to the system.
# ON	The number of times the port was used to log in the user into the system. Hey, if you see that the # SESS is very large compared to the # ON, then you have a problem. There might be someone hacking your system on that port.
# OFF	The number of logoffs that occurred at that port and the number of interrupts like Ctrl-c, EOF, etc.

Daily Usage Report

The Daily Usage Report can be found in the /var/adm/acct/nite/daytacct file.

```
$ cat /var/adm/acct/nite/daytacct
Apr 06 01:33 1994  DAILY USAGE REPORT FOR excelsior Page 1
```

	LOGIN	CPU (MINS)		KCORE-MINS		CONNECT (MINS)		DISK	# OF	# OF	# DISK	FEE
UID	NAME	PRIME	NPRIME	PRIME	NPRIME	PRIME	NPRIME	BLOCKS	PROCS	SESS	SAMPLES	
0	TOTAL	6	13	7	14	165	67	0	1020	6	0	0
0	root	3	7	1	8	0	0	0	400	0	0	0
3	sys	0	3	0	1	0	0	0	51	0	0	0
4	adm	0	1	0	1	0	0	0	251	0	0	0
5	uucp	0	0	0	0	0	0	0	60	0	0	0

```
1091 carolyn 2     1    4    3    140    47    0    249    2    0    0
2155 zach    1     1    2    1     25    20    0      9    4    0    0
$
```

Here it is column by column:

UID	The user's identification number.
LOGIN NAME	The user's name.
CPU (MINS)	The amount of time the user's program required the use of CPU. This is rounded up to the nearest minute.
KCORE-MINS	The amount of memory per minute used to run the programs. This is rounded up to the nearest kilobyte.
CONNECT (MINS)	Total time the user was actually connected to the system.
DISK BLOCKS	The number of disk blocks used. This sum is placed by dodisk.
# OF PROCS	The number of processes the user executed.
# OF SESS	The number of sessions the user incurred by logging in to the system.
# DISK SAMPLES	The number of times acctdusg or diskusg was run to cumulate the average number of DISK BLOCKS.
FEE	The total amount of usage charges accessed to the user for this given period.

NOTE: You might have noticed that I didn't mention PRIME and NPRIME in the above list. PRIME is the prime-time hours for processing, and NPRIME is the non-prime hours for processing. For instance, holidays would not be considered prime-time hours. You would expect that a majority of your users would not be on the system during the holiday. The file /etc/acct/holidays allows you to tailor the non-prime times for your company. Why would this be important? I want to bill my customer a premium rate for using my system during the days or during the heavy processing hours. I will charge a lower rate at non-prime hours. For example, my prime-time hours are from 8:00 a.m. (800 hours) to 6:30 p.m. (1830 hours) for 1994. I would add the following entry in the /etc/acct/holidays file.

```
# Prime Time Hours for 1994
1994  0800  1830
```

Here is a sampling of my /etc/acct/holidays file:

```
$ cat /etc/acct/holidays
#
# Holidays
#
```

```
0101  New Year's Day
0528  Memorial Day
0704  Independence Day
#
# Prime Time Hours for 1994
#
1994  0800  1830
$
```

Daily Command Summary Report and Total Command Summary Report

The Daily Command Summary Report can be found in the /var/adm/acct/nite/daycms file.

```
$ cat /var/adm/acct/nite/daycms
Apr 06 01:32 1994  DAILY COMMAND SUMMARY REPORT FOR excelsior Page 1



                                TOTAL COMMAND SUMMARY
COMMAND  NUMBER   TOTAL  TOTAL    TOTAL   MEAN   MEAN    HOG    CHARS  BLOCKS
NAME      CMDS  KCOREMIN CPU-MIN REAL-MIN SIZE-K CPU-MIN FACTOR TRNSFD  READ

TOTALS   2050     3.57   21.59   157.57   0.21   0.02   0.14  6570519  2726

csh       171     2.50    2.56    10.71   0.45   0.02   0.05   257429   212
grep       14     0.10     .56     2.71   0.40   0.01   0.34    17537    42
more        5     0.04    0.09     1.01   0.59   0.01   0.45    25414     2
awk         2     0.01    0.12     1.71   0.15   0.01   0.55      529     5
  .
  .
  .

$
```

The Total Command Summary Report looks like the preceding report with one exception. It is a monthly summary showing total accumulated since last month or execution of monacct. This report can be seen in the /var/adm/acct/sum/cms file. Here are the column-by-column details.

COMMAND NAME	The name of the command.
NUMBER COMMANDS	The total number of times the command has been executed.
KCOREMIN	The total cumulative kilobytes segments used by the command.

TOTAL CPU-MIN	The total processing time in minutes.
REAL-MIN	The actual processing time in minutes.
MEAN SIZE-K	The mean of TOTAL KCOREMIN divided by execution.
MENU CPU-MIN	The mean of executions divided by total processing time in minutes.
HOG FACTOR	The total processing time divided by elapsed time. This is the utilization ratio of the system.
CHARS TRNSFD	The total number of reads and writes to the file system.
BLOCKS READ	The total number of physical block reads and writes.

NOTE: For purposes of illustration, I have deleted the PRIME and NPRIME column from this report. On your system, these will be there for you to view. See the previous note box about what PRIME and NPRIME represent.

Last Login Report

The Last Login Report can be found in the /var/adm/acct/sum/loginlog file. This report has the last login that your users have made on your system. Any entry that you find that is several months old could be a candidate to purge from your system.

```
$ cat /var/adm/acct/nite/daycms
Apr 06 01:32 1994  LAST LOGIN Page 1

   ...


93-01-05 briano    94-01-11 philp     94-02-21 deanm     94-03-01 stacyh
93-01-13 jordang   94-01-11 kittyw    94-02-21 richards  94-03-01 zachp
93-10-03 bradj     94-01-11 cindym    94-02-21 davidb    94-03-01 jimg
93-10-07 deborahf  94-01-11 franh     94-02-21 seanm     94-03-11 mitzig
93-11-05 gaylej    94-01-21 gregc     94-02-21 maryi     94-03-12 chrisd
93-12-05 keithd    94-01-21 wayneb    94-02-24 kristih   94-03-17 lynetteq
93-12-11 markt     94-01-21 matthewu  94-02-24 sandrad   94-03-20 sharonc
93-12-13 robh      94-01-21 philk     94-02-24 gregb     94-03-21 margaret
93-12-25 cindyk    94-01-21 dianah    94-02-24 daniels   94-03-21 paulas
94-01-05 deniseo   94-01-21 richc     94-02-24 lauric    94-03-22 mikes
94-01-05 gingera   94-02-05 carolynp  94-02-24 keitho    94-03-25 scottp
94-01-05 greggb    94-02-13 jimg      94-02-24 joew      94-04-01 kathye
94-01-05 katyo     94-02-15 matthewh  94-02-24 virgilp   94-04-05 daveh
94-01-05 viginiap  94-02-15 douga     94-03-01 briant    94-04-08 stepht
94-01-05 mollyp    94-02-15 cameront  94-03-01 sneakerp  94-04-10 sugerp
94-01-05 bwhitmer  94-02-17 beths     94-03-01 carola    94-04-11 rosemari

   .
   .
   .

$
```

Summary

In this chapter, you learned how to set up the accounting system to track your users and the processes they run. UNIX System Accounting can be a useful tool to help you tune your system and to plan for future expansion of hard disks, memory, and processors. This is the most common usage of the accounting system. If you are a provider for UNIX resource, such as connections to the Internet, the accounting system allows you to bill those users for the use of your system.

Performance Monitoring

By Ronald Rose

39

IN THIS CHAPTER

Chapter 38, "Accounting System," teaches about the UNIX accounting system, and the tools that the accounting system provides. Some of these utilities and reports give you information about system utilization and performance. In Chapter 18, "What Is a Process," you learned that the sadc command, in combination with the shell scripts sa1 and sa2, enables you to automatically collect activity data. These automatic reports can create a documented history of how the system behaves, which can be a valuable reference in times of performance problems. Requesting similar reports in an ad hoc manner is demonstrated in this chapter, as this method is usually most appropriate when investigating performance problems that are in progress.

In this portion of the book, you will learn all about performance monitoring. There are a series of commands that enable system administrators, programmers, and users to examine each of the resources that a UNIX system uses. By examining these resources you can determine if the system is operating properly or poorly. More important than the commands themselves, you will also learn strategies and procedures that can be used to search for performance problems. Armed with both the commands and the overall methodologies with which to use them, you will understand the factors that are affecting system performance, and what can be done to optimize them so that the system performs at its best.

Although this chapter is helpful for users, it is particularly directed at new system administrators that are actively involved in keeping the system they depend on healthy, or trying to diagnose what has caused its performance to deteriorate.

This chapter introduces several new tools to use in your system investigations and revisits several commands that were introduced in Chapter 19, "Administrative Processes."

The sequence of the chapter is not based on particular commands. It is instead based on the steps and the strategies that you will use during your performance investigations. In other words, the chapter is organized to mirror the logical progression that a system administrator uses to determine the state of the overall system and the status of each of its subsystems.

You will frequently start your investigations by quickly looking at the overall state of the system load, as described in the section "Monitoring the Overall System Status." To do this you see how the commands uptime and sar can be used to examine the system load and the general level of Central Processing Unit (CPU) loading. You also see how tools such as SunOS's perfmeter can be helpful in gaining a graphic, high-level view of several components at once.

Next, in the section "Monitoring Processes with ps," you learn how ps can be used to determine the characteristics of the processes that are running on your system. This is a natural next step after you have determined that the overall system status reflects a heavier-than-normal loading. You will learn how to use ps to look for processes that are consuming inordinate amounts of resources and the steps to take after you have located them.

After you have looked at the snapshot of system utilization that ps gives you, you may well have questions about how to use the memory or disk subsystems. So, in the next section, "Monitoring Memory Utilization," you learn how to monitor memory performance with tools such as vmstat and sar, and how to detect when paging and swapping have become excessive (thus indicating that memory must be added to the system).

In the section "Monitoring Disk Subsystem Performance," you see how tools such as iostat, sar, and df can be used to monitor disk Input/Output (I/O) performance. You will see how to determine when your disk subsystem is unbalanced and what to do to alleviate disk performance problems.

After the section on disk I/O performance is a related section on network performance. (It is related to the disk I/O discussion because of the prevalent use of networks to provide extensions of local disk service through such facilities as NFS.) Here you learn to use netstat, nfsstat, and spray to determine the condition of your network.

This is followed by a brief discussion of CPU performance monitoring, and finally a section on kernel tuning. In this final section, you will learn about the underlying tables that reside within the UNIX operating system and how they can be tuned to customize your system's UNIX kernel and optimize its use of resources.

You have seen before in this book that the diversity of UNIX systems make it important to check each vendor's documentation for specific details about their particular implementation. The same thing applies here as well. Furthermore, modern developments such as symmetric multiprocessor support and relational databases add new characteristics and problems to the challenge of performance monitoring. These are touched on briefly in the discussions that follow.

Performance and Its Impact on Users

Before you get into the technical side of UNIX performance monitoring, there are a few guidelines that can help system administrators avoid performance problems and maximize their overall effectiveness.

All too typically, the UNIX system administrator learns about performance when there is a critical problem with the system. Perhaps the system is taking too long to process jobs or is far behind on the number of jobs that it normally processes. Perhaps the response times for users have deteriorated to the point where users are becoming distracted and unproductive (which is a polite way of saying frustrated and angry!). In any case, if the system isn't actually failing to help its users attain their particular goals, it is at least failing to meet their expectations.

It may seem obvious that when user productivity is being affected, money and time, and sometimes a great deal of both, are being lost. Simple measurements of the amount of time lost can often provide the cost justification for upgrades to the system. In this chapter you learn how to identify which components of the system are the best candidates for such an upgrade. (If you think people were unhappy to begin with, try talking to them after an expensive upgrade has produced no discernible improvement in performance!)

Often, it is only when users begin complaining that people begin to examine the variables that are affecting performance. This in itself is somewhat of a problem. The system administrator should have a thorough understanding of the activities on the system before users are affected by a crisis. He should know the characteristics of each group of users on the system. This includes the type of work that they submit while they are present during the day, as well as the jobs that are to be processed during the evening. What is the size of the CPU requirement, the I/O requirement, and the memory requirement of the most frequently occurring and/or the most important jobs? What impact do these jobs have on the networks connected to the machine? Also important is the time-sensitivity of the jobs, the classic example being payrolls that must be completed by a given time and date.

These profiles of system activity and user requirements can help the system administrator acquire a holistic understanding of the activity on the system. That knowledge will not only be of assistance if there is a sudden crisis in performance, but also if there is a gradual erosion of it. Conversely, if the system administrator has not compiled a profile of his various user groups, and examined the underlying loads that they impose on the system, he will be at a serious disadvantage in an emergency when it comes to figuring out where all the CPU cycles, or memory, have gone. This chapter examines the tools that can be used to gain this knowledge, and demonstrates their value.

Finally, although all users may have been created equal, the work of some users inevitably will have more impact on corporate profitability than the work of other users. Perhaps, given UNIX's academic heritage, running the system in a completely democratic manner should be the goal of the system administrator. However, the system administrator will sooner or later find out, either politely or painfully, who the most important and the most influential groups are. This set of characteristics should also somehow be factored into the user profiles the system administrator develops before the onset of crises, which by their nature obscure the reasoning process of all involved.

Introduction to UNIX Performance

While the system is running, UNIX maintains several counters to keep track of critical system resources. The relevant resources that are tracked are the following:

CPU utilization	Buffer usage
Disk I/O activity	Tape I/O activity
Terminal activity	System call activity

Context switching activity	File access utilization
Queue activity	Interprocess communication (IPC)
Paging activity	Free memory and swap space
Kernel memory allocation (KMA)	Kernel tables
Remote file sharing (RFS)	

By looking at reports based on these counters you can determine how the three major subsystems are performing. These subsystems are the following:

CPU
: The CPU processes instructions and programs. Each time you submit a job to the system, it makes demands on the CPU. Usually, the CPU can service all demands in a timely manner. However, there is only so much available processing power, which must be shared by all users and the internal programs of the operating system, too.

Memory
: Every program that runs on the system makes some demand on the physical memory on the machine. Like the CPU, it is a finite resource. When the active processes and programs that are running on the system request more memory than the machine actually has, *paging* is used to move parts of the processes to disk and reclaim their memory pages for use by other processes. If further shortages occur, the system may also have to resort to *swapping*, which moves entire processes to disk to make room.

I/O
: The I/O subsystem(s) transfers data into and out of the machine. I/O subsystems comprise devices such as disks, printers, terminals/keyboards, and other relatively slow devices, and are a common source of resource contention problems. In addition, there is a rapidly increasing use of network I/O devices. When programs are doing a lot of I/O, they can get bogged down waiting for data from these devices. Each subsystem has its own limitations with respect to the bandwidth that it can effectively use for I/O operations, as well as its own peculiar problems.

Performance monitoring and tuning is not always an exact science. In the displays that follow, there is a great deal of variety in the system/subsystem loadings, even for the small sample of systems used here. In addition, different user groups have widely differing requirements. Some users will put a strain on the I/O resources, some on the CPU, and some will stress the network. Performance tuning is always a series of trade-offs. As you will see, increasing the kernel size to alleviate one problem may aggravate memory utilization. Increasing NFS performance to satisfy one set of users may reduce performance in another area and thereby aggravate another set of users. The goal of the task is often to find an optimal compromise that will satisfy the majority of user and system resource needs.

Monitoring the Overall System Status

The examination of specific UNIX performance monitoring techniques begins with a look at three basic tools that give you a snapshot of the overall performance of the system. After getting this high-level view, you will normally proceed to examine each of the subsystems in detail.

Monitoring System Status Using *uptime*

One of the simplest reports that you use to monitor UNIX system performance measures the number of processes in the UNIX run queue during given intervals. It comes from the command uptime. It is both a high-level view of the system's workload and a handy starting place when the system seems to be performing slowly. In general, processes in the run queue are active programs (that is, not sleeping or waiting) that require system resources. Here is an example:

```
% uptime
   2:07pm  up 11 day(s),  4:54,  15 users,  load average: 1.90, 1.98, 2.01
```

The useful parts of the display are the three load-average figures. The 1.90 load average was measured over the last minute. The 1.98 average was measured over the last 5 minutes. The 2.01 load average was measured over the last 15 minutes.

> **TIP:** What you are usually looking for is the trend of the averages. This particular example shows a system that is under a fairly consistent load. However, if a system is having problems, but the load averages seem to be declining steadily, then you may want to wait a while before you take any action that might affect the system and possibly inconvenience users. While you are doing some ps commands to determine what caused the problem, the imbalance may correct itself.

> **NOTE:** uptime has certain limitations. For example, high-priority jobs are not distinguished from low-priority jobs although their impact on the system can be much greater.

Run uptime periodically and observe both the numbers and the trend. When there is a problem it will often show up here, and tip you off to begin serious investigations. As system loads increase, more demands will be made on your memory and I/O subsystems, so keep an eye out for paging, swapping, and disk inefficiencies. System loads of 2 or 3 usually indicate light loads. System loads of 5 or 6 are usually medium-grade loads. Loads above 10 are often heavy loads on large UNIX machines. However, there is wide variation among types of machines as to what constitutes a heavy load. Therefore, the mentioned technique of sampling your system regularly until you have your own reference for light, medium, and heavy loads is the best technique.

Monitoring System Status Using *perfmeter*

Because the goal of this first section is to give you the tools to view your overall system performance, a brief discussion of graphical performance meters is appropriate. SUN Solaris users are provided with an OpenWindows XView tool called `perfmeter`, which summarizes overall system performance values in multiple dials or strip charts. Strip charts are the default. Not all UNIX systems come with such a handy tool. That's too bad because in this case a picture is worth, if not a thousand words, at least 30 or 40 man pages. In this concise format, you get information about the system resources shown in Table 39.1:

Table 39.1. System resources and their descriptions.

Resources	*Description*
cpu	Percent of CPU being utilized
pkts	EtherNet activity, in packets per second
page	Paging, in pages per second
swap	Jobs swapped per second
intr	Number of device interrupts per second
disk	Disk traffic, in transfers per second
cntxt	Number of context switches per second
load	Average number of runnable processes over the last minute
colls	Collisions per second detected on the EtherNet
errs	Errors per second on receiving packets

The charts of the `perfmeter` are not a source for precise measurements of subsystem performance, but they are graphic representations of them. However, the chart can be very useful for monitoring several aspects of the system at the same time. When you start a particular job, the graphics can demonstrate the impact of that job on the CPU, on disk transfers, and on paging. Many developers like to use the tool to assess the efficiency of their work for this very reason. Likewise, system administrators use the tool to get valuable clues about where to start their investigations. As an example, when faced with intermittent and transitory problems, glancing at a perfmeter and then going directly to the proper display may increase the odds that you can catch in the act the process that is degrading the system.

The scale value for the strip chart changes automatically when the chart refreshes to accommodate increasing or decreasing values on the system. You add values to be monitored by clicking the right mouse button and selecting from the menu. From the same menu you can select properties, which will let you modify what the perfmeter is monitoring, the format (dials/graphs, direction of the displays, and solid/lined display), remote/local machine choice, and the frequency of the display.

You can also set a ceiling value for a particular strip chart. If the value goes beyond the ceiling value, this portion of the chart will be displayed in red. Thus, a system administrator who knows that someone is periodically running a job that eats up all the CPU memory can set a signal that the job may be run again. The system administrator can also use this to monitor the condition of critical values from several feet away from his monitor. If he or she sees red, other users may be seeing red, too.

The perfmeter is a utility provided with SunOS. You should check your own particular UNIX operating system to determine if similar performance tools are provided.

Monitoring System Status Using *sar -q*

If your machine does not support uptime, there is an option for sar that can provide the same type of quick, high-level snapshot of the system. The -q option reports the average queue length and the percentage of time that the queue is occupied.

```
% sar -q 5 5

07:28:37 runq-sz %runocc swpq-sz %swpocc
07:28:42    5.0      100                 _
07:28:47    5.0      100                 _
07:28:52    4.8      100                 _
07:28:57    4.8      100                 _
07:29:02    4.6      100                 _

Average     4.8      100                 _
```

The fields in this report are the following:

runq-sz	This is the length of the run queue during the interval. The run queue list doesn't include jobs that are sleeping or waiting for I/O, but does include jobs that are in memory and ready to run.
%runocc	This is the percentage of time that the run queue is occupied.
swpq-sz	This is the average length of the swap queue during the interval. Jobs or threads that have been swapped out and are therefore unavailable to run are shown here.
%swpocc	This is the percentage of time that there are swapped jobs or threads.

The run queue length is used in a similar way to the load averages of uptime. Typically the number is less than 2 if the system is operating properly. Consistently higher values indicate that the system is under heavier loads, and is quite possibly CPU bound. When the run queue length is high and the run queue percentage is occupied 100% of the time, as it is in this example, the system's idle time is minimized, and it is good to be on the lookout for performance-related problems in the memory and disk subsystems. However, there is still no activity indicated in the swapping columns in the example. You will learn about swapping in the next section, and see that although this system is obviously busy, the lack of swapping is a partial vote of confidence that it may still be functioning properly.

Monitoring System Status Using *sar -u*

Another quick and easy tool to use to determine overall system utilization is sar with the -u option. CPU utilization is shown by -u, and sar without any options defaults on most versions of UNIX to this option. The CPU is either busy or idle. When it is busy, it is either working on user work or system work. When it is not busy, it is either waiting on I/O or it is idle.

```
% sar -u 5 5

13:16:58    %usr    %sys    %wio    %idle
13:17:03      40      10      13      38
13:17:08      31       6      48      14
13:17:13      42      15       9      34
13:17:18      41      15      10      35
13:17:23      41      15      11      33

Average       39      12      18      31
```

The fields in the report are the following:

%usr	This is the percentage of time that the processor is in user mode (that is, executing code requested by a user).
%sys	This is the percentage of time that the processor is in system mode, servicing system calls. Users can cause this percentage to increase above normal levels by using system calls inefficiently.
%wio	This is the percentage of time that the processor is waiting on completion of I/O, from disk, NFS, or RFS. If the percentage is regularly high, check the I/O systems for inefficiencies.
%idle	This is the percentage of time the processor is idle. If the percentage is high and the system is heavily loaded, there is probably a memory or an I/O problem.

In this example, you see a system with ample CPU capacity left (that is, the average idle percentage is 31%). The system is spending most of its time on user tasks, so user programs are probably not too inefficient with their use of system calls. The I/O wait percentage indicates an application that is making a fair amount of demands on the I/O subsystem.

Most administrators would argue that `%idle` should be in the low 'teens rather than 0, at least when the system is under load. If it is 0 it doesn't necessarily mean that the machine is operating poorly. However, it is usually a good bet that the machine is out of spare computational capacity and should be upgraded to the next level of CPU speed. The reason to upgrade the CPU is in anticipation of future growth of user processing requirements. If the system work load is increasing, even if the users haven't yet encountered the problem, why not anticipate the requirement? On the other hand, if the CPU idle time is high under heavy load, a CPU upgrade will probably not help improve performance much.

Idle time will generally be higher when the load average is low.

A high load average and idle time is a symptom of potential problems. Either the memory or the I/O subsystems, or both, are hindering the swift dispatch and completion of the jobs. You should review the following sections that show how to look for paging, swapping, disk, or network-related problems.

Monitoring Processes with *ps*

You have probably noticed that, while throughout the rest of this chapter the commands are listed under the topic in which they are used (for example, `nfsstat` is listed in the section "Monitoring Network Performance"), this section is dedicated to just one command. What's so special about ps? It is singled out in this manner because of the way that it is used in the performance monitoring process. It is a starting point for generating theories (for example, processes are using up so much memory that you are paging and that is slowing down the system). Conversely, it is an ending point for confirming theories (for example, here is a burst of network activity—I wonder if it is caused by that communications test job that the programmers keep running?). Since it is so pivotal, and provides a unique snapshot of the processes on the system, ps is given its own section.

One of the most valuable commands for performance monitoring is the ps command. It enables you to monitor the status of the active processes on the system. Remember the words from the movie *Casablanca*, "round up the usual suspects"? Well, ps helps to identify the usual suspects (that is, suspect processes that could be using inordinate resources). Then you can proceed to determine which of the suspects is actually guilty of causing the performance degradation. It is at once a powerful tool and a source of overhead for the system itself. Using various options, the following information is shown:

Current status of the process	Process ID
Parent process ID	User ID
Scheduling class	Priority

Address of process	Memory used
CPU time used	

Using ps provides you a snapshot of the system's active processes. It is used in conjunction with other commands throughout this section. Frequently, you will look at a report from a command, for example vmstat, and then look to ps either to confirm or to deny a theory you have come up with about the nature of your system's problem. The particular performance problem that motivated you to look at ps in the first place may have been caused by a process that is already off the list. It provides a series of clues to use in generating theories that can then be tested by detailed analysis of the particular subsystem.

The ps command is described in detail in Chapter 19, "Administrating Processes." The following are the fields that are important in terms of performance tuning:

Field		Description
F		Flags that indicate the process's current state and are calculated by adding each of the hexadecimal values:
	00	Process has terminated
	01	System process, always in memory
	02	Process is being traced by its parent
	04	Process is being traced by parent, and is stopped
	08	Process cannot be awakened by a signal
	10	Process is in memory and locked, pending an event
	20	Process cannot be swapped
S		The current state of the process, as indicated by one of the following letters:
	O	Process is currently running on the processor
	S	Process is sleeping, waiting for an I/O event (including terminal I/O) to complete
	R	Process is ready to run
	I	Process is idle
	Z	Process is a zombie process (it has terminated, and the parent is not waiting but is still in the process table)
	T	Process is stopped because of parent tracing it
	X	Process is waiting for more memory
UID		User ID of the process's owner
PID		Process ID number
PPID		Parent process ID number
C		CPU utilization for scheduling (not shown when -c is used)
CLS		Scheduling class, real-time, time sharing, or system (only shown when the -c option is used)

PRI	Process scheduling priority (higher numbers mean lower priorities).
NI	Process `nice` number (used in scheduling priorities—raising the number lowers the priority so the process gets less CPU time)
SZ	The amount of virtual memory required by the process (This is a good indication of the memory load the process places on the systems memory.)
TTY	The terminal that started the process, or its parent (A ? indicates that no terminal exists.)
TIME	The total amount of CPU time used by the process since it began
COMD	The command that generated the process

If your problem is immediate performance, you can disregard processes that are sleeping, stopped, or waiting on terminal I/O, as these will probably not be the source of the degradation. Look instead for the jobs that are ready to run, blocked for disk I/O, or paging.

```
% ps -el
```

F	S	UID	PID	PPID	C	PRI	NI	ADDR	SZ	WCHAN	TTY	TIME	COMD
19	T	0	0	0	80	0	SY	e00ec978	0		?	0:01	sched
19	S	0	2	0	80	0	SY	f5735000	0	e00eacdc	?	0:05	pageout
8	S	1001	1382	1	80	40	20	f5c6a000	1227	e00f887c	console	0:02	mailtool
8	S	1001	1386	1	80	40	20	f60ed000	819	e00f887c	console	0:28	perfmete
8	S	1001	28380	28377	80	40	20	f67c0000	5804	f5cfd146	?	85:02	sqlturbo
8	S	1001	28373	1	80	40	20	f63c6000	1035	f63c61c8	?	0:07	cdrl_mai
8	S	1001	28392	1	80	40	20	f67ce800	1035	f67ce9c8	?	0:07	cdrl_mai
8	S	1001	28391	28388	80	40	20	f690a800	5804	f60dce46	?	166:39	sqlturbo
8	S	1001	28361	1	80	60	20	f67e1000	30580	e00f887c	?	379:35	mhdms
8	S	1001	28360	1	80	40	20	f68e1000	12565	e00f887c	?	182:22	mhharris
8	O	1001	10566	10512	19	70	20	f6abb800	152		pts/14	0:00	ps
8	S	1001	28388	1	80	40	20	f6384800	216	f60a0346	?	67:51	db_write
8	S	1000	7750	7749	80	40	20	f6344800	5393	f5dad02c	pts/2	31:47	tbinit
8	O	1001	9538	9537	80	81	22	f6978000	5816		?	646:57	sqlturbo
8	S	1033	3735	3734	164	40	20	f63b8800	305	f60e0d46	pts/9	0:00	ksh
8	S	1033	5228	5227	80	50	20	f68a8800	305	f60dca46	pts/7	0:00	ksh
8	S	1001	28337	1	80	99	20	f6375000	47412	f63751c8	?	1135:50	velox_ga

The following are tips for using `ps` to determine why system performance is suffering.

Look at the UID (user ID) fields for a number of identical jobs that are being submitted by the same user. This is often caused by a user who runs a script that starts a lot of background jobs without waiting for any of the jobs to complete. Sometimes you can safely use `kill` to terminate some of the jobs. Whenever you can, you should discuss this with the user before you take action. In any case, be sure the user is educated in the proper use of the system to avoid a replication of the problem. In the example, User ID 1001 has multiple instances of the same process running. In this case, it is a normal situation, in which multiple processes are spawned at the same time for searching through database tables to increase interactive performance.

Look at the TIME fields for a process that has accumulated a large amount of CPU time. In the example, you can see the large amount of time acquired by the processes whose command is shown as velox_ga. This may indicate that the process is in an infinite loop, or that something else is wrong with its logic. Check with the user to determine whether it is appropriate to terminate the job. If something is wrong, ask the user if a dump of the process would assist in debugging it (check your UNIX system's reference material for commands, such as gcore, that can dump a process).

Request the -l option and look at the SZ fields for processes that are consuming too much memory. In the example you can see the large amount of memory acquired by the processes whose command is shown as velox_ga. You could check with the user of this process to try to determine why it behaves this way. Attempting to renice the process may simply prolong the problem that it is causing, so you may have to kill the job instead. SZ fields may also give you a clue as to memory shortage problems caused by this particular combination of jobs. You can use vmstat or sar -wpgr to check the paging and swapping statistics that are examined.

Look for processes that are consuming inordinate CPU resources. Request the -c option and look at the CLS fields for processes that are running at inappropriately high priorities. Use the nice command to adjust the nice value of the process. Beware in particular of any real-time (RT) process, which can often dominate the system. If the priority is higher than you expected, you should check with the user to determine how it was set. If he is resetting the priority because he has figured out the superuser password, dissuade him from doing this. (See Chapter 19 to find out more about using the nice command to modify the priorities of processes.)

If the processes that are running are simply long-running, CPU-intensive jobs, ask the users if you can nice them to a lower priority or if they can run them at night, when other users will not be affected by them.

Look for processes that are blocking on I/O. Many of the example processes are in this state. When that is the case, the disk subsystem probably requires tuning. The section "Monitoring Disk Performance Using vmstat" examines how to investigate problems with your disk I/O. If the processes are trying to read/write over NFS, this may be a symptom that the NFS server to which they are attached is down, or that the network itself is hung.

Monitoring Memory Utilization

You could say that one can never have too much money, be too thin, or have too much system memory. Memory sometimes becomes a problematic resource when programs that are running require more physical memory than is available. When this occurs UNIX systems begin a process called paging. During paging the system copies pages of physical memory to disk, and then allows the now-vacated memory to be used by the process that required the extra space. Occasional paging can be tolerated by most systems, but frequent and excessive paging is usually accompanied by poor system performance and unhappy users.

UNIX Memory Management

Paging uses an algorithm that selects portions, or pages, of memory that are not being used frequently and displaces them to disk. The more frequently used portions of memory, which may be the most active parts of a process, thus remain in memory, while other portions of the process that are idle get paged out.

In addition to paging, there is a similar technique used by the memory management system called *swapping*. Swapping moves entire processes, rather than just pages, to disk in order to free up memory resources. Some swapping may occur under normal conditions. That is, some processes may just be idle enough (for example, due to sleeping) to warrant their return to disk until they become active once more. Swapping can become excessive, however, when severe memory shortages develop. Interactive performance can degrade quickly when swapping increases since it often depends on keyboard-dependent processes (for example, editors) that are likely to be considered idle as they wait for you to start typing again.

As the condition of your system deteriorates, paging and swapping make increasing demands on disk I/O. This, in turn, may further slow down the execution of jobs submitted to the system. Thus, memory resource inadequacies may result in I/O resource problems.

By now, it should be apparent that it is important to be able to know if the system has enough memory for the applications that are being used on it.

> **TIP:** A rule of thumb is to allocate twice the swap space as you have physical memory. For example, if you have 32 MB of physical Random Access Memory (RAM) installed upon your system, you would set up 64 MB of swap space when configuring the system. The system would then use this diskspace for its memory management when displacing pages or processes to disk.

Both vmstat and sar provide information about the paging and swapping characteristics of a system. Let's start with vmstat. On the vmstat reports you will see information about page-ins, or pages moved from disk to memory, and page-outs, or pages moved from memory to disk. Further, you will see information about swap-ins, or processes moved from disk to memory, and swap-outs, or processes moved from memory to disk.

Monitoring Memory Performance Using *vmstat*

The vmstat command is used to examine virtual memory statistics, and present data on process status, free and swap memory, paging activity, disk reports, CPU load, swapping, cache flushing, and interrupts. The format of the command is:

```
vmstat  t [n]
```

This command takes *n* samples, at *t* second intervals. For example, the following frequently used version of the command takes samples at 5-second intervals without stopping until canceled:

```
vmstat 5
```

The following screen shows the output from the SunOS variant of the command

```
vmstat -S 5
```

which provides extra information regarding swapping.

```
procs     memory            page            disk          faults         cpu
r b w   swap  free  si so pi po fr de sr s0 s3 s5 s5   in   sy   cs us sy id
0 2 0  16516  9144   0  0  0  0  0  0  0  1  4 34 12  366  1396  675 14  9 76
0 3 0 869384 29660   0  0  0  0  0  0  0  0  4 63 15  514 10759 2070 19 17 64
0 2 0 869432 29704   0  0  0  0  0  0  0  4  3 64 11  490  2458 2035 16 13 72
0 3 0 869448 29696   0  0  0  0  0  0  0  0  3 65 13  464  2528 2034 17 12 71
0 3 0 869384 29684   0  0  0  0  0  0  0  1  3 68 18  551  2555 2136 16 14 70
0 2 0 869188 29644   0  0  0  2  2  0  0  2  3 65 10  432  2495 2013 18  9 73
0 3 0 869176 29612   0  0  0  0  0  0  0  0  3 61 16  504  2527 2053 17 11 71
0 2 0 869156 29600   0  0  0  0  0  0  0  0  3 69  8  438 15820 2027 20 18 62
```

The fields in the vmstat report are the following:

procs	Reports the number of processes in each of the following states
r	In the Run queue
b	Blocked, waiting for resources
w	Swapped, waiting for processing resources
memory	Reports on real and virtual memory
swap	Available swap space
free	Size of free list
page	Reports on page faults and paging, averaged over an interval (typically 5 seconds) and provided in units per second
re	Pages reclaimed from the free list (not shown when the -S option is requested)
mf	Minor faults (not shown when -S option is requested)
si	Number of pages swapped in (only shown with the -S option)
so	Number of pages swapped out (only shown with the -S option)
pi	Kilobytes paged in
po	Kilobytes paged out

fr	Kilobytes freed
de	Anticipated short-term memory shortfall
sr	Pages scanned by clock algorithm, per second
disk	Shows the number of disk operations per second
faults	Shows the per-second trap/interrupt rates
in	Device interrupts
sy	System faults per second
cs	CPU context switches
cpu	Shows the use of CPU time
us	User time
sy	System time
id	Idle time

NOTE: The vmstat command's first line is rarely of any use. When reviewing the output from the command, always start at the second line and go forward for pertinent data.

Let's look at some of these fields for clues about system performance. As far as memory performance goes, po and w are very important. For people using the -S option so is similarly important. These fields all clearly show when a system is paging and swapping. If w is non-zero and so continually indicates swapping, the system probably has a serious memory problem. If, likewise, po consistently has large numbers present, the system probably has a significant memory resource problem.

TIP: If your version of vmstat doesn't specifically provide swapping information, you can infer the swapping by watching the relationship between the w and the fre fields. An increase in w, the swapped-out processes, followed by an increase in fre, the number of pages on the free list, can provide the same information in a different manner.

Other fields from the vmstat output are helpful, as well. The number of runnable and blocked processes can provide a good indication of the flow of processes, or lack thereof, through the system. Similarly, comparing each percentage CPU idle versus CPU in system state, and versus CPU in user state, can provide information about the overall composition of the workload. As the load increases on the system, it is a good sign if the CPU is spending the majority of the time in the user state. Loads of 60 or 70 percent for CPU user state are ok. Idle CPU should drop as the user load picks up, and under heavy load may well fall to 0.

If paging and swapping are occurring at an unusually high rate, it may be due to the number and types of jobs that are running. Usually you can turn to ps to determine what those jobs are.

Imagine that ps shows a large number of jobs that require significant memory resources. (You saw how to determine this in the ps discussion in the previous section.) That would confirm the vmstat report. To resolve the problem, you would have to restrict memory-intensive jobs, or the use of memory, or add more memory physically.

> **TIP:** You can see that having a history of several vmstat and ps reports during normal system operation can be extremely helpful in determining what the usual conditions are, and, subsequently, what the unusual ones are. Also, one or two vmstat reports may indicate a temporary condition, rather than a permanent problem. Sample the system multiple times before deciding that you have the answer to your system's performance problems.

Monitoring Memory Performance with *sar -wpgr*

More information about the system's utilization of memory resources can be obtained by using sar -wpgr.

```
% sar -wpgr 5 5

07:42:30 swpin/s pswin/s swpot/s bswot/s pswch/s
         atch/s  pgin/s  ppgin/s pflt/s  vflt/s slock/s
         pgout/s ppgout/s pgfree/s pgscan/s %s5ipf
         freemem freeswp

07:42:35   0.00    0.0    0.00    0.0    504
           0.00    0.00   0.00    0.00   6.20   11.78
           0.00    0.00   0.00    0.00   0.00
          33139  183023

...

Average    0.00    0.0    0.00    0.0    515
Average    0.00    0.32   0.40    2.54   5.56   16.83
Average    0.00    0.00   0.00    0.00   0.00
Average   32926  183015
```

The fields in the report are the following:

swpin/s   Number of transfers into memory per second.

bswin/s   Number of blocks transferred for swap-ins per second.

swpot/s   Number of transfers from memory to swap area per second. (More memory may be needed if the value is greater than 1.)

bswot/s	Number of blocks transferred for swap-outs per second.
pswch/s	Number of process switches per second.
atch/s	Number of attaches per second (that is, page faults where the page is reclaimed from memory).
pgin/s	Number of times per second that file systems get page-in requests.
ppgin/s	Number of pages paged in per second.
pflt/s	Number of page faults from protection errors per second.
vflt/s	Number of address translation page (validity) faults per second.
slock/s	Number of faults per second caused by software lock requests requiring I/O.
pgout/s	Number of times per second that file systems get page-out requests.
ppgout/s	Number of pages paged out per second.
pgfree/s daemon.	Number of pages that are put on the free list by the page-stealing daemon. (More memory may be needed if this is a large value.)
pgscan/s	Number of pages scanned by the page-stealing daemon. (More memory may be needed if this is a large value, because it shows that the daemon is checking for free memory more than it should need to.)
%ufs_ipf	Percentage of the ufs inodes that were taken off the free list that had reusable pages associated with them. (Large values indicate that ufs inodes should be increased, so that the free list of inodes will not be page bound.) This will be %s5ipf for System V file systems, like in the example.
freemem	The average number of pages, over this interval, of memory available to user processes.
freeswp	The number of disk blocks available for page swapping.

You should use the report to examine each of the following conditions. Any one of them would imply that you may have a memory problem. Combinations of them increase the likelihood all the more.

Check for page-outs, and watch for their consistent occurrence. Look for a high incidence of address translation faults. Check for swap-outs. If they are occasional, it may not be a cause for concern as some number of them is normal (for example, inactive jobs). However, consistent swap-outs are usually bad news, indicating that the system is very low on memory and is probably sacrificing active jobs. If you find memory shortage evidence in any of these, you can use ps to look for memory-intensive jobs, as you saw in the section on ps.

Multiprocessor Implications of *vmstat*

In the CPU columns of the report, the vmstat command summarizes the performance of multiprocessor systems. If you have a two-processor system and the CPU load is reflected as 50 percent, it doesn't necessarily mean that both processors are equally busy. Rather, depending on the multiprocessor implementation it can indicate that one processor is almost completely busy and the next is almost idle.

The first column of vmstat output also has implications for multiprocessor systems. If the number of runnable processes is not consistently greater than the number of processors, it is less likely that you can get significant performance increases from adding more CPUs to your system.

Monitoring Disk Subsystem Performance

Disk operations are the slowest of all operations that must be completed to enable most programs to complete. Furthermore, as more and more UNIX systems are being used for commercial applications, and particularly those that utilize relational database systems, the subject of disk performance has become increasingly significant with regard to overall system performance. Therefore, probably more than ever before, UNIX system tuning activities often turn out to be searches for unnecessary and inefficient disk I/O. Before you learn about the commands that can help you monitor your disk I/O performance, some background is appropriate.

Some of the major disk performance variables are the hard disk activities themselves (that is, rotation and arm movement), the I/O controller card, the I/O firmware and software, and the I/O backplane of the system.

For example, for a given disk operation to be completed successfully, the disk controller must be directed to access the information from the proper part of the disk. This results in a delay known as a *queuing delay*. When it has located the proper part of the disk, the disk arm must begin to position itself over the correct cylinder. This results in a delay called *seek latency*. The read/write head must then wait for the relevant data to happen as the disk rotates underneath it. This is known as *rotational latency*. The data must then be transferred to the controller. Finally, the data must be transferred over the I/O backplane of the system to be used by the application that requested the information.

If you think about your use of a compact disk, many of the operations are similar in nature. The CD platter contains information, and is spinning all the time. When you push 5 to request the fifth track of the CD, a controller positions the head that reads the information at the correct area of the disk (similar to the queuing delay and seek latency of disk drives). The rotational latency occurs as the CD spins around until the start of your music passes under the reading head. The data—in this case your favorite song—is then transferred to a controller and then to some digital to analog converters that transform it into amplified musical information that is playable by your stereo.

Seek time is the time required to move the head of the disk from one location of data, or track, to another. Moving from one track to another track that is adjacent to it takes very little time and is called *minimum seek time*. Moving the head between the two furthest tracks on a disk is measured as the *maximum seek time*. The *average seek time* approximates the average amount of time a seek takes.

As data access becomes more random in nature, seek time can become more important. In most commercial database applications that feature relational databases, for example, the data is often being accessed in a random manner, at a high rate, and in relatively small packets (for example, 512 bytes). Therefore, the disk heads are moving back and forth all the time looking for the pertinent data. Therefore, choosing disks that have small seek times for those systems can increase I/O performance.

Many drives have roughly the same rotational speed, measured as revolutions per minute, or RPMs. However, some manufacturers are stepping up the RPM rates of their drives. This can have a positive influence on performance by reducing the rotational delay, which is the time that the disk head has to wait for the information to get to it (that is, on average one-half of a rotation). It also reduces the amount of time required to transfer the read/write information.

Disk I/O Performance Optimization

While reviewing the use of the commands to monitor disk performance, you will see how these clearly show which disks and disk subsystems are being the most heavily used. However, before examining those commands, there are some basic hardware-oriented approaches to this problem that can help increase performance significantly. The main idea is to put the hardware where the biggest disk problem is, and to evenly spread the disk work load over available I/O controllers and disk drives.

If your I/O work load is heavy (for example, with many users constantly accessing large volumes of data from the same set of files), you can probably get significant performance increases by reducing the number of disk drives that are daisy chained off one I/O controller from five or six to two or three. Perhaps doing this will force another daisy chain to increase in size past a total of four or five, but if the disks on that I/O controller are only used intermittently, system performance will be increased overall.

Another example of this type of technique is if you had one group of users that are pounding one set of files all day long, you could locate the most frequently used data on the fastest disks.

Notice that, once again, the more thorough your knowledge of the characteristics of the work being done on your system, the greater the chance that your disk architecture will answer those needs.

NOTE: Remember, distributing a work load evenly across all disks and controllers is *not* the same thing as distributing the disks evenly across all controllers, or the files evenly across all disks. You must know which applications make the heaviest I/O demands, and understand the work load itself, to distribute it effectively.

TIP: As you build file systems for user groups, remember to factor in the I/O work load. Make sure your high-disk I/O groups are put on their own physical disks and preferably their own I/O controllers as well. If possible, keep them, and /usr, off the root disk as well.

Disk-striping software frequently can help in cases where the majority of disk access goes to a handful of disks. Where a large amount of data is making heavy demands on one disk or one controller, striping distributes the data across multiple disks and/or controllers. When the data is striped across multiple disks, the accesses to it are averaged over all the I/O controllers and disks, thus optimizing overall disk throughput. Some disk-striping software also provides Redundant Array of Inexpensive Disks (RAID) support and the ability to keep one disk in reserve as a hot standby (that is, a disk that can be automatically rebuilt and used when one of the production disks fails). When thought of in this manner, this can be a very useful feature in terms of performance because a system that has been crippled by the failure of a hard drive will be viewed by your user community as having pretty bad performance.

This information may seem obvious, but it is important to the overall performance of a system. Frequently, the answer to disk performance simply rests on matching the disk architecture to the use of the system.

Relational Databases

With the increasing use of relational database technologies on UNIX systems, I/O subsystem performance is more important than ever. While analyzing all the relational database systems and making recommendations is beyond the scope of this chapter, some basic concepts are in order.

More and more often these days an application based on a relational database product is the fundamental reason for the procurement of the UNIX system itself. If that is the case in your installation, and if you have relatively little experience in terms of database analysis, you should seek professional assistance. In particular, insist on a database analyst that has had experience tuning your database system on your operating system. Operating systems and relational databases are both complex systems, and the performance interactions between them is difficult for the inexperienced to understand.

The database expert will spend a great deal of time looking at the effectiveness of your allocation of indexes. Large improvements in performance due to the addition or adjustment of a few indexes are quite common.

You should use raw disks versus the file systems for greatest performance. File systems incur more overhead (for example, inode and update block overhead on writes) than do raw devices. Most relational databases clearly reflect this performance advantage in their documentation.

If the database system is extremely active, or if the activity is unbalanced, you should try to distribute the load more evenly across all the I/O controllers and disks that you can. You will see how to determine this in the following section.

Checking Disk Performance with *iostat* and *sar*

The *iostat* Command

The `iostat` command is used to examine disk input and output, and produces throughput, utilization, queue length, transaction rate, and service time data. It is similar both in format and in use to `vmstat`. The format of the command is:

```
iostat  t [n]
```

This command takes *n* samples, at *t* second intervals. For example, the following frequently used version of the command takes samples at 5-second intervals without stopping, until canceled:

```
iostat 5
```

For example, the following shows disk statistics sampled at 5-second intervals.

tty			sd0			sd30			sd53			sd55			cpu			
tin	tout	Kps	tps	serv	Kps	tps	serv	Kps	tps	serv	Kps	tps	serv	us	sy	wt	id
0	26	8	1	57	36	4	20	77	34	24	31	12	30	14	9	47	30
0	51	0	0	0	0	0	0	108	54	36	0	0	0	14	7	78	0
0	47	72	10	258	0	0	0	102	51	38	0	0	0	15	9	76	0
0	58	5	1	9	1	1	23	112	54	33	0	0	0	14	8	77	1
0	38	0	0	0	25	0	90	139	70	17	9	4	25	14	8	73	6
0	43	0	0	0	227	10	23	127	62	32	45	21	20	20	15	65	0

The first line of the report shows the statistics since the last reboot. The subsequent lines show the interval data that is gathered. The default format of the command shows statistics for terminals (`tty`), for disks (`fd` and `sd`), and CPU.

For each terminal, `iostat` shows the following:

`tin`	Characters in the terminal input queue
`tout`	Characters in the terminal output queue
	For each disk, iostat shows the following:
`bps`	Blocks per second
`tps`	Transfers per second
`serv`	Average service time, in milliseconds
	For the CPU, iostat displays the CPU time spent in the follow ing modes:
`us`	User mode
`sy`	System mode
`wt`	Waiting for I/O
`id`	Idle mode

The first two fields, `tin` and `tout`, have no relevance to disk subsystem performance, as these fields describe the number of characters waiting in the input and output terminal buffers. The next fields are relevant to disk subsystem performance over the preceding interval. The `bps` field indicates the size of the data transferred (read or written) to the drive. The `tps` field describes the transfers (that is, I/O requests) per second that were issued to the physical disk. Note that one transfer can combine multiple logical requests. The `serv` field is for the length of time, in milliseconds, that the I/O subsystem required to service the transfer. In the last set of fields, note that I/O waiting is displayed under the `wt` heading.

You can look at the data within the report for information about system performance. As with `vmstat`, the first line of data is usually irrelevant to your immediate investigation. Looking at the first disk, `sd0`, you see that it is not being utilized as the other three disks are. Disk 0 is the root disk, and often will show the greatest activity. This system is a commercial relational database implementation, however, and the activity that is shown here is often typical of online transaction processing, or OLTP, requirements. Notice that the activity is mainly on disks `sd53` and `sd55`. The database is being exercised by a high volume of transactions that are updating it (in this case over 100 updates per second).

Disks 30, 53, and 55 are three database disks that are being pounded with updates from the application through the relational database system. Notice that the transfers per second, the kilobytes per second, and the service times are all reflecting a heavier load on disk 53 than on disks 30 and 55. Notice that disk 30's use is more intermittent but can be quite heavy at times, while 53's is more consistent. Ideally, over longer sample periods, the three disks should have roughly equivalent utilization rates. If they continue to show disparities in use like these, you may be able to get a performance increase by determining why the load is unbalanced and taking corrective action.

You can use `iostat -xtc` to show the measurements across all of the drives in the system.

```
% iostat -xtc 10 5 _
```

					extended	disk	statistics			tty			cpu		
disk	r/s	w/s	Kr/s	Kw/s	wait	actv	svc_t	%w	%b	tin	tout	us	sy	wt	id
sd0	0.0	0.9	0.1	6.3	0.0	0.0	64.4	0	1	0	26	12	11	21	56
sd30	0.2	1.4	0.4	20.4	0.0	0.0	21.5	0	3 _						
sd53	2.6	2.3	5.5	4.6	0.0	0.1	23.6	0	9 _						
sd55	2.7	2.4	5.6	4.7	0.0	0.1	24.2	0	10 _						

...

					extended	disk	statistics			tty			cpu		
disk	r/s	w/s	Kr/s	Kw/s	wait	actv	svc_t	%w	%b	tin	tout	us	sy	wt	id
sd0	0.0	0.3	0.0	3.1	0.0	0.0	20.4	0	1	0	3557	5	8	14	72
sd30	0.0	0.2	0.1	0.9	0.0	0.0	32.2	0	0 _						
sd53	0.1	0.2	0.4	0.5	0.0	0.0	14.6	0	0 _						
sd55	0.1	0.2	0.3	0.4	0.0	0.0	14.7	0	0 _						

This example shows five samples of all disks at 10-second intervals.

Each line shows the following:

r/s	Reads per second
w/s	Writes per second
Kr/s	KB read per second
Kw/s	KB written per second
wait	Average transactions waiting for service (that is, queue length)
actv	Average active transactions being serviced
svc_t	Average time, in milliseconds, of service
%w	Percentage of time that the queue isn't empty
%b	Percentage of time that the disk is busy

Once again, you can check to make sure that all disks are sharing the load equally, or if this is not the case, that the most active disk is also the fastest.

The *sar -d* Command

The sar `-d` option reports on the disk I/O activity of a system, as well.

```
% sar -d 5 5
```

20:44:26	device	%busy	avque	r+w/s	blks/s	avwait	avserv
...							
20:44:46	sd0	1	0.0	1	5	0.0	20.1
	sd1	0	0.0	0	0	0.0	0.0
	sd15	0	0.0	0	0	0.0	0.0

	sd16	1	0.0	0	1	0.0	27.1
	sd17	1	0.0	0	1	0.0	26.8
	sd3	0	0.0	0	0	0.0	0.0
Average	sd0	1	0.0	0	3	0.0	20.0
	sd1	0	0.0	0	2	0.0	32.6
	sd15	0	0.0	0	1	0.0	13.6
	sd16	0	0.0	0	0	0.0	27.6
	sd17	0	0.0	0	0	0.0	26.1
	sd3	2	0.1	1	14	0.0	102.6

Information about each disk is shown as follows:

device	Names the disk device that is measured
%busy	Percentage of time that the device is busy servicing transfers
avque	Average number of requests outstanding during the period
r+w/s	Read/write transfers to the device per second
blks/s	Number of blocks transferred to the device per second
avwait	Average number of milliseconds that a transfer request spends waiting in the queue for service
avserv	Average number of milliseconds for a transfer to be completed, including seek, rotational delay, and data transfer time.

You can see from the example that this system is lightly loaded, since %busy is a small number and the queue lengths and wait times are small as well. The average service times for most of the disks is consistent; however, notice that SCSI disk 3, sd3, has a larger service time than the other disks. Perhaps the arrangement of data on the disk is not organized properly (a condition known as *fragmentation*) or perhaps the organization is fine but the disproportionate access of sd3 (see the blks/s column) is bogging it down in comparison to the other drives.

> **TIP:** You should double-check vmstat before you draw any conclusions based on these reports. If your system is paging or swapping with any consistency, you have a memory problem, and you need to address that first because it is surely aggravating your I/O performance.

As this chapter has shown, you should distribute the disk load over I/O controllers and drives, and you should use your fastest drive to support your most frequently accessed data. You should also try to increase the size of your buffer cache if your system has sufficient memory. You can eliminate fragmentation by rebuilding your file systems. Also, make sure that the file system that you are using is the fastest type supported with your UNIX system (for example, UFS) and that the block size is the appropriate size.

Monitoring File System Use with *df*

One of the biggest and most frequent problems that systems have is running out of disk space, particularly in /tmp or /usr. There is no magic answer to the question How much space should be allocated to these? but a good rule of thumb is between 1500KB and 3000KB for /tmp and roughly twice that for /usr. Other file systems should have about 5 or 10 percent of the system's available capacity.

The *df* Command

The df command shows the free disk space on each disk that is mounted. The -k option displays the information about each file system in columns, with the allocations in KB.

```
% df -k
```

Filesystem	kbytes	used	avail	capacity	Mounted on
/dev/dsk/c0t0d0s0	38111	21173	13128	62%	/
/dev/dsk/c0t0d0s6	246167	171869	49688	78%	/usr
/proc	0	0	0	0%	/proc
fd	0	0	0	0%	/dev/fd
swap	860848	632	860216	0%	/tmp
/dev/dsk/c0t0d0s7	188247	90189	79238	53%	/home
/dev/dsk/c0t0d0s5	492351	179384	263737	40%	/opt
gs:/home/prog/met	77863	47127	22956	67%	/home/met

From this display you can see the following information (all entries are in KB):

kbytes	Total size of usable space in file system (size is adjusted by allotted head room)
used	Space used
avail	Space available for use
capacity	Percentage of total capacity used
mounted on	mount point

The usable space has been adjusted to take into account a 10 percent reserve head room adjustment, and thus reflects only 90 percent of the actual capacity. The percentage shown under capacity is therefore used space divided by the adjusted usable space.

> **TIP:** For best performance, file systems should be cleansed to protect the 10 percent head room allocation. Remove excess files with rm, or archive/move files that are older and no longer used to tapes with tar or cpio, or to less-frequently-used disks.

Monitoring Network Performance

"The network is the computer" is an appropriate saying these days. What used to be simple ASCII terminals connected over serial ports have been replaced by networks of workstations, Xterminals, and PCs, connected, for example, over 10 BASE-T EtherNet networks. Networks are impressive information transmission media when they work properly. However, troubleshooting is not always as straightforward as it should be. In other words, he who lives by the network can die by the network without the proper procedures.

The two most prevalent standards that you will have to contend with in the UNIX world are TCP/IP, (a communications protocol) and NFS, (a popular network file system). Each can be a source of problems. In addition, you need to keep an eye on the implementation of the network, which can also can be a problem area. Each network topology has different capacities, and each implementation (for example, using thin-net instead of 10 BASE-T twisted pair, or using intelligent hubs, and so on) has advantages and problems inherent in its design. The good news is that even a simple EtherNet network has a large amount of bandwidth for transporting data. The bad news is that with every day that passes users and programmers are coming up with new methods of using up as much of that bandwidth as possible.

Most networks are still based on EtherNet technologies. Ethernet is referred to as a 10 Mps medium, but the throughput that can be used effectively by users and applications is usually significantly less than 10 MB. Often, for various reasons, the effective capacity falls to 4 Mps. That may still seem like a lot of capacity, but as the network grows it can disappear fast. When the capacity is used up, EtherNet is very democratic. If it has a capacity problem, all users suffer equally. Furthermore, one person can bring an EtherNet network to its knees with relative ease. Accessing and transferring large files across the network, running programs that test transfer rates between two machines, or running a program that has a loop in it that happens to be dumping data to another machine, and so on, can affect all the users on the network. Like other resources (that is, CPU, disk capacity, and so on), the network is a finite resource.

If given the proper instruction, users can quite easily detect capacity problems on the network by which they are supported. A quick comparison of a simple command executed on the local machine versus the same command executed on a remote machine (for example, `login` and `rlogin`) can indicate that the network has a problem.

A little education can help your users and your network at the same time. NFS is a powerful tool, in both the good and the bad sense. Users should be taught that it will be slower to access the file over the network using NFS, particularly if the file is sizable, than it will be to read or write the data directly on the remote machine by using a remote login. However, if the files are of reasonable size, and the use is reasonable (editing, browsing, moving files back and forth), it is a fine tool to use. Users should understand when they are using NFS appropriately or not.

Monitoring Network Performance with *netstat -i*

One of the most straightforward checks you can make of the network's operation is with `netstat -i`. This command can give you some insight into the integrity of the network. All the workstations and the computers on a given network share it. When more than one of these entities try to use the network at the same time, the data from one machine "collides" with that of the other. (Despite the sound of the term, in moderation this is actually a normal occurrence, but too many collisions can be a problem.) In addition, various technical problems can cause errors in the transmission and reception of the data. As the errors and the collisions increase in frequency, the performance of the network degrades because the sender of the data retransmits the garbled data, thus further increasing the activity on the network.

Using `netstat -i` you can find out how many packets the computer has sent and received, and you can examine the levels of errors and collisions that it has detected on the network. Here is an example of the use of `netstat`:

```
% netstat -i

Name  Mtu   Net/Dest   Address     Ipkts    Ierrs  Opkts   Oerrs  Collis Queue _
lo0   8232  loopback   localhost   1031780  0      1031780  0      0      0
le0   1500  100.0.0.0  SCAT        13091430 6      12221526 4      174250 0
```

The fields in the report are the following:

Name	The name of the network interface. The names show what the type of interface is (for example, an en followed by a digit indicates an EtherNet card, the `lo0` shown here is a loopback interface used for testing networks).
Mtu	The maximum transfer unit, also known as the packet size, of the interface.
Net/Dest	The network to which the interface is connected.
Address	The Internet address of the interface. (The Internet address for this name may be referenced in `/etc/hosts`.)
Ipkts	The number of packets the system has received since the last boot.
Ierrs	The number of input errors that have occurred since the last boot. This should be a very low number relative to the `Ipkts` field (that is, less than 0.25 percent, or there is probably a significant network problem).

Opkts	Same as Ipkts, but for sent packets.
Oerrs	Same as Ierrs, but for output errors.
Collis	The number of collisions that have been detected. This number should not be more than 5 or 10 percent of the output packets (Opkts) number or the network is having too many collisions and capacity is reduced.

In this example you see that the collision ratio shows a network without too many collisions (approximately 1 percent). If collisions are constantly averaging 10 percent or more, the network is probably being over utilized.

The example also shows that input and output error ratios are negligible. Input errors usually mean that the network is feeding the system bad input packets, and the internal calculations that verify the integrity of the data (called checksums) are failing. In other words, this normally indicates that the problem is somewhere out on the network, not on your machine. Conversely, rapidly increasing output errors probably indicates a local problem with your computer's network adapters, connectors, interface, and so on.

If you suspect network problems you should repeat this command several times. An active machine should show Ipkts and Opkts consistently incrementing. If Ipkts changes and Opkts doesn't, the host is not responding to the client requesting data. You should check the addressing in the hosts database. If Ipkts doesn't change, the machine is not receiving the network data at all.

Monitoring Network Performance Using *spray*

It is quite possible that you will not detect collisions and errors when you use netstat -i, and yet will still have slow access across the network. Perhaps the other machine that you are trying to use is bogged down and cannot respond quickly enough. Use spray to send a burst of packets to the other machine and record how many of them actually made the trip successfully. The results will tell you if the other machine is failing to keep up. Here is an example of a frequently used test:

```
% spray SCAT

sending 1162 packets of length 86 to SCAT ...
        no packets dropped by SCAT
        3321 packets/sec, 285623 bytes/sec
```

This shows a test burst sent from the source machine to the destination machine called SCAT. No packets were dropped. If SCAT were badly overloaded some probably would have been dropped. The example defaulted to sending 1162 packets of 86 bytes each. Another example of the same command uses the -c option to specify the number of packets to send, the -d option to specify the delay so that you don't overrun your buffers, and the -1 option to specify the length of the packet. This example of the command is a more realistic test of the network:

```
% spray -c 100 -d 20 0 -1 2048 SCAT

sending 100 packets of length 2048 to SCAT ...
        no packets dropped by SCAT
        572 packets/sec, 1172308 bytes/sec
```

Had you seen significant numbers (for example, 5 to 10 percent or more) of packets dropped in these displays, you would next try looking at the remote system. For example, using commands such as uptime, vmstat, sar, and ps as described earlier in this section, you would check on the status of the remote machine. Does it have memory or CPU problems, or is there some other problem that is degrading its performance so it can't keep up with its network traffic?

Monitoring Network Performance with *nfsstat -c*

Systems running NFS can skip spray and instead use nfsstat -c. The -c option specifies the client statistics, and -s can be used for server statistics. As the name implies, *client statistics* summarize this system's use of another machine as a server. The NFS service uses synchronous procedures called RPCs (remote procedure calls). This means that the client waits for the server to complete the file activity before it proceeds. If the server fails to respond, the client retransmits the request. Just as with collisions, the worse the condition of the communication, the more traffic that is generated. The more traffic that is generated, the slower the network and the greater the possibility of collisions. So if the retransmission rate is large, you should look for servers that are under heavy loads, high collision rates that are delaying the packets en route, or EtherNet interfaces that are dropping packets.

```
% nfsstat -c

Client rpc:
calls      badcalls retrans  badxid   timeout  wait      newcred  timers
74107      0        72       0        72       0         0        82        _

Client nfs:
calls      badcalls nclget   nclcreate
73690      0        73690    0          _
null       getattr  setattr  root      lookup    readlink  read
0   0%     4881 7%  1   0%    0   0%    130  0%   0   0%    465  1%    _
wrcache    write    create   remove    rename    link      symlink
0   0%     68161 92% 16  0%   1   0%    0   0%    0   0%    0   0%     _
mkdir      rmdir    readdir  statfs    _
0   0%     0   0%   32  0%    3   0%    _
```

The report shows the following fields:

calls	The number of calls sent
badcalls	The number of calls rejected by the RPC
retrans	The number of retransmissions
badxid	The number of duplicated acknowledgments received
timeout	The number of time-outs
wait	The number of times no available client handles caused waiting

```
newcred    The number of refreshed authentications
timers     The number of times the time-out value is reached or exceeded
readlink   The number of reads made to a symbolic link
```

If the `timeout` ratio is high, the problem can be unresponsive NFS servers or slow networks that are impeding the timely delivery and response of the packets. In the example, there are relatively few time-outs compared to the number of calls (72/74107 or about 1/10 of 1 percent) that do retransmissions. As the percentage grows toward 5 percent, system administrators begin to take a closer look at it. If `badxid` is roughly the same as `retrans`, the problem is probably an NFS server that is falling behind in servicing NFS requests, since duplicate acknowledgments are being received for NFS requests in roughly the same amounts as the retransmissions that are required. (The same thing is true if `badxid` is roughly the same as `timeout`.) However, if `badxid` is a much smaller number than `retrans` and `timeout`, then it follows that the network is more likely to be the problem.

> **TIP:** `nfsstat` enables you to reset the applicable counters to 0 by using the `-z` option (executed as root). This can be particularly handy when trying to determine if something has caused a problem in the immediate time frame, rather than looking at the numbers collected since the last reboot.

Monitoring Network Performance with *netstat*

One way to check for network loading is to use `netstat` without any parameters:

```
% netstat

TCP
   Local Address       Remote Address    Swind Send-Q Rwind Recv-Q  State
-------------------  ----------------    ----- ------ ----- ------  -------
AAA1.1023            bbb2.login           8760      0  8760      0  ESTABLISHED
AAA1.listen          Cccc.32980           8760      0  8760      0  ESTABLISHED
AAA1.login           Dddd.1019            8760      0  8760      0  ESTABLISHED
AAA1.32782           AAA1.32774          16384      0 16384      0  ESTABLISHED
...
```

In the report, the important field is the `Send-Q` field, which indicates the depth of the send queue for packets. If the numbers in `Send-Q` are large and increasing in size across several of the connections, the network is probably bogged down.

Looking for Network Data Corruption with *netstat -s*

The `netstat -s` command displays statistics for each of several protocols supported on the system (that is, UDP, IP, TCP, and ICMP). The information can be used to locate problems for the protocol. Here is an example:

```
% netstat -s

UDP
      udpInDatagrams      =2152316  udpInErrors        =       0
      udpOutDatagrams     =2151810


TCP   tcpRtoAlgorithm     =       4  tcpRtoMin          =     200
      tcpRtoMax           =   60000  tcpMaxConn         =      -1
      tcpActiveOpens      =1924360  tcpPassiveOpens    =      81
      tcpAttemptFails     =584963   tcpEstabResets     =1339431
      tcpCurrEstab        =      25  tcpOutSegs         =7814776
      tcpOutDataSegs      =1176484  tcpOutDataBytes    =501907781
      tcpRetransSegs      =1925164  tcpRetransBytes    =444395
      tcpOutAck           =6767853  tcpOutAckDelayed   =1121866
      tcpOutUrg           =     363  tcpOutWinUpdate    =129604
      tcpOutWinProbe      =      25  tcpOutControl      =3263985
      tcpOutRsts          =      47  tcpOutFastRetrans  =      23
      tcpInSegs           =11769363
      tcpInAckSegs        =2419522  tcpInAckBytes      =503241539
      tcpInDupAck         =3589621  tcpInAckUnsent     =       0
      tcpInInorderSegs    =4871078  tcpInInorderBytes  =-477578953
      tcpInUnorderSegs    =910597   tcpInUnorderBytes  =826772340
      tcpInDupSegs        =  60545  tcpInDupBytes      =46037645
      tcpInPartDupSegs    =  44879  tcpInPartDupBytes  =10057185
      tcpInPastWinSegs    =       0  tcpInPastWinBytes  =       0
      tcpInWinProbe       =704105   tcpInWinUpdate     =4470040
      tcpInClosed         =      11  tcpRttNoUpdate     =     907
      tcpRttUpdate        =1079220  tcpTimRetrans      =    1974
      tcpTimRetransDrop   =       2  tcpTimKeepalive    =     577
      tcpTimKeepaliveProbe=     343  tcpTimKeepaliveDrop =      2


IP    ipForwarding        =       2  ipDefaultTTL       =     255
      ipInReceives        =12954953 ipInHdrErrors      =       0
      ipInAddrErrors      =       0  ipInCksumErrs      =       0
      ipForwDatagrams     =       0  ipForwProhibits    =       0
      ipInUnknownProtos   =       0  ipInDiscards       =       0
      ipInDelivers        =13921597 ipOutRequests      =12199190
      ipOutDiscards       =       0  ipOutNoRoutes      =       0
      ipReasmTimeout      =      60  ipReasmReqds       =       0
      ipReasmOKs          =       0  ipReasmFails       =       0
      ipReasmDuplicates   =       0  ipReasmPartDups    =       0
      ipFragOKs           =    3267  ipFragFails        =       0
      ipFragCreates       =   19052  ipRoutingDiscards  =       0
      tcpInErrs           =       0  udpNoPorts         =   64760
      udpInCksumErrs      =       0  udpInOverflows     =       0
      rawipInOverflows    =       0


ICMP  icmpInMsgs          =     216  icmpInErrors       =       0
      icmpInCksumErrs     =       0  icmpInUnknowns     =       0
      icmpInDestUnreachs  =     216  icmpInTimeExcds    =       0
      icmpInParmProbs     =       0  icmpInSrcQuenchs   =       0
      icmpInRedirects     =       0  icmpInBadRedirects =       0
      icmpInEchos         =       0  icmpInEchoReps     =       0
      icmpInTimestamps    =       0  icmpInTimestampReps =      0
      icmpInAddrMasks     =       0  icmpInAddrMaskReps =       0
      icmpInFragNeeded    =       0  icmpOutMsgs        =     230
      icmpOutDrops        =       0  icmpOutErrors      =       0
      icmpOutDestUnreachs =     230  icmpOutTimeExcds   =       0
      icmpOutParmProbs    =       0  icmpOutSrcQuenchs  =       0
```

```
      icmpOutRedirects    =     0    icmpOutEchos        =     0
      icmpOutEchoReps     =     0    icmpOutTimestamps   =     0
      icmpOutTimestampReps=     0    icmpOutAddrMasks    =     0
      icmpOutAddrMaskReps =     0    icmpOutFragNeeded   =     0
      icmpInOverflows     =     0
IGMP:
          0 messages received
          0 messages received with too few bytes
          0 messages received with bad checksum
          0 membership queries received
          0 membership queries received with invalid field(s)
          0 membership reports received
          0 membership reports received with invalid field(s)
          0 membership reports received for groups to which we belong
          0 membership reports sent
```

The checksum fields should always show extremely small values, as they are a percentage of total traffic sent along the interface.

By using netstat -s on the remote system in combination with spray on your own, you can determine whether data corruption (as opposed to network corruption) is impeding the movement of your network data. Alternate between the two displays, observing the differences, if any, between the reports. If the two reports agree on the number of dropped packets, the file server is probably not keeping up. If they don't, suspect network integrity problems. Use netstat -i on the remote machine to confirm this.

Corrective Network Actions

If you suspect that there are problems with the integrity of the network itself, you must try to determine where the faulty piece of equipment is. Hire network consultants, who will use network diagnostic scopes to locate and correct the problems.

If the problem is that the network is extremely busy, thus increasing collisions, time-outs, retransmissions, and so on, you may need to redistribute the work load more appropriately. This is a good example of the "divide and conquer" concept as it applies to computers. By partitioning and segmenting the network nodes into subnetworks that more clearly reflect the underlying work loads, you can maximize the overall performance of the network. This can be accomplished by installing additional network interfaces in your gateway and adjusting the addressing on the gateway to reflect the new subnetworks. Altering your cabling and implementing some of the more advanced intelligent hubs may be needed as well. By reorganizing your network, you will maximize the amount of bandwidth that is available for access to the local subnetwork. Make sure that systems that regularly perform NFS mounts of each other are on the same subnetwork.

If you have an older network and are having to rework your network topology, consider replacing the older coax-based networks with the more modern twisted-pair types, which are generally more reliable and flexible.

Make sure that the work load is on the appropriate machine(s). Use the machine with the best network performance to do its proper share of network file service tasks.

Check your network for diskless workstations. These require large amounts of network resources to boot up, swap, page, etc. With the cost of local storage descending constantly, it is getting harder to believe that diskless workstations are still cost-effective when compared to regular workstations. Consider upgrading the workstations so that they support their users locally, or at least to minimize their use of the network.

If your network server has been acquiring more clients, check its memory and its kernel buffer allocations for proper sizing.

If the problem is that I/O-intensive programs are being run over the network, work with the users to determine what can be done to make that requirement a local, rather than a network, one. Educate your users to make sure they understand when they are using the network appropriately and when they are being wasteful with this valuable resource.

Monitoring CPU Performance

The biggest problem a system administrator faces when examining performance is sorting through all the relevant information to determine which subsystem is really in trouble. Frequently, users complain about the need to upgrade a processor that is assumed to be causing slow execution, when in fact it is the I/O subsystem or memory that is the problem. To make matters even more difficult, all of the subsystems interact with one another, thus complicating the analysis.

You already looked at the three most handy tools for assessing CPU load in the section "Monitoring the Overall System Status." As stated in that section, processor idle time can, under certain conditions, imply that I/O or memory subsystems are degrading the system. It can also, under other conditions, imply that a processor upgrade is appropriate. Using the tools that have been reviewed in this chapter, you can by now piece together a competent picture of the overall activities of your system and its subsystems. You should use the tools to make absolutely sure that the I/O and the memory subsystems are indeed optimized properly before you spend the money to upgrade your CPU.

If you have determined that your CPU has just run out of gas, and you cannot upgrade your system, all is not lost. CPUs are extremely powerful machines that are frequently underutilized for long spans of time in any 24 hour period. If you can rearrange the schedule of the work that must be done to use the CPU as efficiently as possible, you can often overcome most problems. This can be done by getting users to run all appropriate jobs at off-hours (off work load hours, that is, not necessarily 9 to 5). You can also get your users to run selected jobs at lower priorities. You can educate some of your less efficient users and programmers. Finally, you can carefully examine the work load and eliminate some jobs, daemons, and so on, that are not needed.

The following is a brief list of jobs and daemons that deserve review, and possibly elimination, based on the severity of the problem and their use, or lack thereof, on the system. Check each of the following and ask yourself whether you use it or need them: accounting services, printer daemons, mountd remote mount daemon, sendmail daemon, talk daemon, remote who daemon, NIS server, and database daemons.

Monitoring Multiprocessor Performance with *mpstat*

One of the most recent developments of significance in the UNIX server world is the rapid deployment of symmetric multiprocessor (SMP) servers. Of course, having multiple CPUs can mean that you may desire a more discrete picture of what is actually happening on the system than `sar -u` can provide.

You learned about some multiprocessor issues in the examination of `vmstat`, but there are other tools for examining multiprocessor utilization. The `mpstat` command reports the per-processor statistics for the machine. Each row of the report shows the activity of one processor.

```
% mpstat

CPU minf mjf xcal  intr ithr  csw icsw migr smtx  srw syscl  usr sys  wt idl
  0    1   0    0   201   71  164   22   34  147    0   942   10  10  23  57
  1    1   0    0    57   37  171   23   34  144    1   975   10  11  23  56
  2    1   0    0    77   56  158   22   33  146    0   996   11  11  21  56
  3    1   0    0    54   33  169   23   34  156    0  1139   12  11  21  56
  4    1   0    0    21    0  180   23   33  159    0  1336   14  10  20  56
  5    1   0    0    21    0  195   23   31  163    0  1544   17  10  18  55
```

All values are in terms of events per second, unless otherwise noted. You may specify a sample interval, and a number of samples, with the command, just as you would with sar. The fields of the report are the following:

CPU	CPU processor ID
minf	Minor faults
mjf	Major faults
xcal	Interprocessor cross-calls
intr	Interrupts
ithr	Interrupts as threads (not counting clock interrupt)
csw	Context switches
icsw	Involuntary context switches
migr	Thread migrations (to another processor)

smtx	Spins on mutexes (lock not acquired on first try)
srw	Spins on reader/writer locks (lock not acquired on first try)
syscl	System calls
usr	Percentage of user time
sys	Percentage of system time
wt	Percentage of wait time
idl	Percentage of idle time

Don't be intimidated by the technical nature of the display. It is included here just as an indication that multiprocessor systems can be more complex than uniprocessor systems to examine for their performance. Some multiprocessor systems actually can bias work to be done to a particular CPU. That is not done here, as you can see. The user, system, wait, and idle times are all relatively evenly distributed across all the available CPUs.

Kernel Tuning

Kernel tuning is a complex topic, and the space that can be devoted to it in this section is limited. In order to fit this discussion into the space allowed, the focus is on kernel tuning for SunOS in general, and Solaris 2.x in particular. In addition, the section focuses mostly on memory tuning. Your version of UNIX may differ in several respects from the version described here, and you may be involved in other subsystems, but you should get a good idea of the overall concepts and generally how the parameters are tuned.

The most fundamental component of the UNIX operating system is the kernel. It manages all the major subsystems, including memory, disk I/O, utilization of the CPU, process scheduling, and so on. In short, it is the controlling agent that enables the system to perform work for you.

As you can imagine from that introduction, the configuration of the kernel can dramatically affect system performance either positively or negatively. There are parameters that you can tune for various kernel modules that you can tune. A couple reasons could motivate you to do this. First, by tuning the kernel you can reduce the amount of memory required for the kernel, thus increasing the efficiency of the use of memory, and increasing the throughput of the system. Second, you can increase the capacity of the system to accommodate new requirements (users, processing, or both).

This is a classic case of software compromise. It would be nice to increase the capacity of the system to accommodate all users that would ever be put on the system, but that would have a deleterious effect on performance. Likewise, it would be nice to tune the kernel down to its smallest possible size, but that would have negative side-effects as well. As in most software, the optimal solution is somewhere between the extremes.

Some people think that you only need to change the kernel when the number of people on the system increases. This is not true. You may need to alter the kernel when the nature of your processing changes. If your users are increasing their use of X Windows, or increasing their utilization of file systems, running more memory-intensive jobs, and so on, you may need to adjust some of these parameters to optimize the throughput of the system.

Two trends are changing the nature of kernel tuning. First, in an effort to make UNIX a commercially viable product in terms of administration and deployment, most manufacturers are trying to minimize the complexity of the kernel configuration process. As a result, many of the tables that were once allocated in a fixed manner are now allocated dynamically, or else are linked to the value of a handful of fields. Solaris 2.x takes this approach by calculating many kernel values based on the maxusers field. Second, as memory is dropping in price and CPU power is increasing dramatically, the relative importance of precise kernel tuning for most systems is gradually diminishing. However, for high-performance systems, or systems with limited memory, it is still a pertinent topic.

Your instruction in UNIX kernel tuning begins with an overview of the kernel tables that are changed by it, and how to display them. It continues with some examples of kernel parameters that are modified to adjust the kernel to current system demands, and it concludes with a detailed example of paging and swapping parameters under SunOS.

CAUTION: Kernel tuning can actually adversely affect memory subsystem performance. As you adjust the parameters upward, the kernel often expands in size. This can affect memory performance, particularly if your system is already beginning to experience a memory shortage problem under normal utilization. As the kernel tables grow, the internal processing related to them may take longer, too, so there may be some minor degradation related to the greater time required for internal operating system activities. Once again, with a healthy system this may be transparent, but with a marginal system the problems may become apparent or more pronounced.

CAUTION: In general you should be very careful with kernel tuning. People that don't understand what they are doing can cripple their systems. Many UNIX versions come with utility programs that help simplify configuration. It's best to use them. It also helps to read the manual, and to procure the assistance of an experienced system administrator, before you begin.

> **CAUTION:** Finally, always make sure that you have a copy of your working kernel before you begin altering it. Some experienced system administrators actually make backup copies even if the utility automatically makes one. And it is always a good idea to do a complete backup before installing a new kernel. Don't assume that your disk drives are safe because you are "just making a few minor adjustments," or that the upgrade that you are installing "doesn't seem to change much with respect to the I/O subsystem." Make sure you can get back to your original system state if things go wrong.

Kernel Tables

When should you consider modifying the kernel tables? You should review your kernel parameters in several cases, such as before you add new users, before you increase your X Window activity significantly, or before you increase your NFS utilization markedly. Also review them before the makeup of the programs that are running is altered in a way that will significantly increase the number of processes that are run or the demands they will make on the system

Some people believe that you always increase kernel parameters when you add more memory, but this is not necessarily so. If you have a thorough knowledge of your system's parameters and know that they are already adjusted to take into account both current loads and some future growth, then adding more memory, in itself, is not necessarily a reason to increase kernel parameters.

Some of the tables are described as follows:

- **Process table**   The process table sets the number of processes that the system can run at a time. These processes include daemon processes, processes that local users are running, and processes that remote users are running. It also includes forked or spawned processes of users—it may be a little more trouble for you to accurately estimate the number of these. If the system is trying to start system daemon processes and is prevented from doing so because the process table has reached its limit, you may experience intermittent problems (possibly without any direct notification of the error).

- **User process table**   The user process table controls the number of processes per user that the system can run.

- **Inode table**   The inode table lists entries for such things as the following:
  Each open pipe

Each current user directory

Mount points on each file system

Each active I/O device

When the table is full, performance will degrade. The console will have error messages written to it regarding the error when it occurs. This table is also relevant to the open file table, since they are both concerned with the same subsystem.

- **Open file table**   This table determines the number of files that can be open on the system at the same time. When the system call is made and the table is full, the program will get an error indication and the console will have an error logged to it.

- **Quota table**   If your system is configured to support disk quotas, this table contains the number of structures that have been set aside for that use. The quota table will have an entry for each user who has a file system that has quotas turned on. As with the inode table, performance suffers when the table fills up, and errors are written to the console.

- **Callout table**   This table controls the number of timers that can be active concurrently. Timers are critical to many kernel-related and I/O activities. If the callout table overflows, the system is likely to crash.

Checking System Tables with *sar -v*

The -v option enables you to see the current process table, inode table, open file table, and shared memory record table.

The fields in the report are as follows:

proc-sz	The number of process table entries in use/the number allocated
inod-sz	The number of inode table entries in use/the number allocated
file-sz	The number of file table entries currently in use/the number 0 designating that space is allocated dynamically for this entry
lock-sz	The number of shared memory record table entries in use/the number 0 designating that space is allocated dynamically for this entry
ov	The overflow field, showing the number of times the field to the immediate left has had to overflow

Any non-zero entry in the ov field is an obvious indication that you need to adjust your kernel parameters relevant to that field. This is one performance report where you can request historical information, for the last day, the last week, or since last reboot, and actually get meaningful data out of it.

This is also another good report to use intermittently during the day to sample how much reserve capacity you have.

Here is an example:

```
% sar -v 5 5

18:51:12  proc-sz    ov  inod-sz    ov  file-sz  ov  lock-sz
18:51:17  122/4058    0  3205/4000   0  488/0     0   11/0  _
18:51:22  122/4058    0  3205/4000   0  488/0     0   11/0  _
18:51:27  122/4058    0  3205/4000   0  488/0     0   11/0  _
18:51:32  122/4058    0  3205/4000   0  488/0     0   11/0  _
18:51:37  122/4058    0  3205/4000   0  488/0     0   11/0  _
```

Since all the ov fields are 0, you can see that the system tables are healthy for this interval. In this display, for example, there are 122 process table entries in use, and there are 4058 process table entries allocated.

Displaying Tunable Kernel Parameters

To display a comprehensive list of tunable kernel parameters, you can use the nm command. For example, applying the command to the appropriate module, the name list of the file will be reported:

```
% nm /kernel/unix

Symbols from /kernel/unix:

[Index]   Value    Size  Type  Bind  Other Shndx   Name

... _
[15]|         0|      0|FILE |LOCL |0   |ABS   |unix.o
[16]|3758124752|      0|NOTY |LOCL |0   |1     |vhwb_nextset
[17]|3758121512|      0|NOTY |LOCL |0   |1     |_intr_flag_table
[18]|3758124096|      0|NOTY |LOCL |0   |1     |trap_mon
[19]|3758121436|      0|NOTY |LOCL |0   |1     |intr_set_spl
[20]|3758121040|      0|NOTY |LOCL |0   |1     |intr_mutex_panic
[21]|3758121340|      0|NOTY |LOCL |0   |1     |intr_thread_exit
[22]|3758124768|      0|NOTY |LOCL |0   |1     |vhwb_nextline
[23]|3758124144|      0|NOTY |LOCL |0   |1     |trap_kadb
[24]|3758124796|      0|NOTY |LOCL |0   |1     |vhwb_nextdword
[25]|3758116924|      0|NOTY |LOCL |0   |1     |firsthighinstr
[26]|3758121100|    132|NOTY |LOCL |0   |1     |intr_thread
[27]|3758118696|      0|NOTY |LOCL |0   |1     |fixfault
[28]|         0|      0|FILE |LOCL |0   |ABS   |confunix.c
...
       (Portions of display deleted for brevity)
```

The relevant fields in the report are the following:

Index	The index of the symbol (appears in brackets).
Value	The value of the symbol.
Size	The size, in bytes, of the associated object.

Type	A symbol is one of the following types: NOTYPE (no type was specified), OBJECT (a data object such as an array or variable), FUNC (a function or other executable code), SECTION (a section symbol), or FILE (name of the source file).
Bind	The symbol's binding attributes. LOCAL symbols have a scope limited to the object file containing their definition; GLOBAL symbols are visible to all object files being combined; and WEAK symbols are essentially global symbols with a lower precedence than GLOBAL.
Shndx	Except for three special values, this is the section header table index in relation to which the symbol is defined. The following special values exist: ABS indicates that the symbol's value will not change through relocation; COMMON indicates an allocated block and the value provides alignment constraints; and UNDEF indicates an undefined symbol.
Name	The name of the symbol.

Displaying Current Values of Tunable Parameters

To display a list of the current values assigned to the tunable kernel parameters, you can use the sysdef -i command:

```
% sysdef -i

... (portions of display are deleted for brevity)
*
* System Configuration
*
swapfile              dev  swaplo blocks    free
/dev/dsk/c0t3d0s1    32,25      8 547112   96936
*
* Tunable Parameters
*
 5316608   maximum memory allowed in buffer cache (bufhwm)
    4058   maximum number of processes (v.v_proc)
      99   maximum global priority in sys class (MAXCLSYSPRI)
    4053   maximum processes per user id (v.v_maxup)
      30   auto update time limit in seconds (NAUTOUP)
      25   page stealing low water mark (GPGSLO)
       5   fsflush run rate (FSFLUSHR)
      25   minimum resident memory for avoiding deadlock (MINARMEM)
      25   minimum swapable memory for avoiding deadlock (MINASMEM)
*
* Utsname Tunables
*
     5.3   release (REL)
    DDDD   node name (NODE)
   SunOS   system name (SYS)
Generic_101318-31   version (VER)
```

```
*
* Process Resource Limit Tunables (Current:Maximum)
*
Infinity:Infinity    cpu time
Infinity:Infinity    file size
7ffff000:7ffff000    heap size
  800000:7ffff000    stack size
Infinity:Infinity    core file size
      40:     400    file descriptors
Infinity:Infinity    mapped memory
*
* Streams Tunables
*
       9    maximum number of pushes allowed (NSTRPUSH)
   65536    maximum stream message size (STRMSGSZ)
    1024    max size of ctl part of message (STRCTLSZ)
*
* IPC Messages
*
     200    entries in msg map (MSGMAP)
    2048    max message size (MSGMAX)
   65535    max bytes on queue (MSGMNB)
      25    message queue identifiers (MSGMNI)
     128    message segment size (MSGSSZ)
     400    system message headers (MSGTQL)
    1024    message segments (MSGSEG)
     SYS    system class name (SYS_NAME)
```

As stated earlier, over the years there have been many enhancements that have tried to minimize the complexity of the kernel configuration process. As a result, many of the tables that were once allocated in a fixed manner are now allocated dynamically, or else linked to the value of the maxusers field. The next step in understanding the nature of kernel tables is to look at the maxusers parameter and its impact on UNIX system configuration.

Modifying the Configuration Information File

SunOS uses the /etc/system file for modification of kernel-tunable variables. The basic format is this:

```
set parameter = value
```

It can also have this format:

```
set [module:]variablename = value
```

The /etc/system file can also be used for other purposes (for example, to force modules to be loaded at boot time, to specify a root device, and so on). The /etc/system file is used for permanent changes to the operating system values. Temporary changes can be made using adb kernel debugging tools. The system must be rebooted for the changes made for them to become active using /etc/system. With adb the changes take place when applied.

CAUTION: Be very careful with set commands in the /etc/system file! They basically cause patches to be performed on the kernel itself, and there is a great deal of potential for dire consequences from misunderstood settings. Make sure you have handy the relevant system administrators' manuals for your system, as well as a reliable and experienced system administrator for guidance.

The *maxusers* Parameter

Many of the tables are dynamically updated either upward or downward by the operating system, based on the value assigned to the maxusers parameter, which is an approximation of the number of users the system will have to support. The quickest and, more importantly, safest way to modify the table sizes is by modifying maxusers, and letting the system perform the adjustments to the tables for you.

The maxusers parameter can be adjusted by placing commands in the /etc/system file of your UNIX system:

```
set maxusers=24
```

A number of kernel parameters adjust their values according to the setting of the maxusers parameter. For example, Table 39.2 lists the settings for various kernel parameters, where maxusers is utilized in their calculation.

Table 39.2. Kernel parameters affected by *maxusers*.

Table	Parameter	Setting
Process	max_nprocs	10 + 16 * maxusers (sets the size of the process table)
User process	maxuprc	max_nprocs-5 (sets the number of user processes)
Callout	ncallout	16 + max_nprocs (sets the size of the callout table)
Name cache	ncsize	max_nprocs + 16 + maxusers + 64 (sets size of the directory lookup cache)
Inode	ufs_ninode	max_nprocs + 16 + maxusers + 64 (sets the size of the inode table)
Quota table	ndquot	(maxusers * NMOUNT) / 4 + max_nprocs (sets the number of disk quota structures)

The directory name lookup cache (dnlc) is also based on maxusers in SunOS systems. With the increasing usage of NFS, this can be an important performance tuning parameter. Networks that have many clients can be helped by an increased name cache parameter ncsize (that is, a greater amount of cache). By using vmstat with the -s option, you can determine the directory name lookup cache hit rate. A cache miss indicates that disk I/O was probably needed to access the directory when traversing the path components to get to a file. If the hit rate falls below 70 percent, this parameter should be checked.

```
% vmstat -s

         0 swap ins
         0 swap outs
         0 pages swapped in
         0 pages swapped out
   1530750 total address trans. faults taken
     39351 page ins
     22369 page outs
     45565 pages paged in
    114923 pages paged out
     73786 total reclaims
     65945 reclaims from free list
         0 micro (hat) faults
   1530750 minor (as) faults
     38916 major faults
     88376 copy-on-write faults
    120412 zero fill page faults
    634336 pages examined by the clock daemon
        10 revolutions of the clock hand
    122233 pages freed by the clock daemon
      4466 forks
       471 vforks
      6416 execs
  45913303 cpu context switches
  28556694 device interrupts
   1885547 traps
 665339442 system calls
    622350 total name lookups (cache hits 94%)
         4 toolong
   2281992 user    cpu
   3172652 system  cpu
  62275344 idle    cpu
    967604 wait    cpu
```

In this example, you can see that the cache hits are 94 percent, and therefore enough directory name lookup cache is allocated on the system.

By the way, if your NFS traffic is heavy and irregular in nature, you should increase the number of nfsd NFS daemons. Some system administrators recommend that this should be set between 40 and 60 on dedicated NFS servers. This will increase the speed with which the nfsd daemons take the requests off the network and pass them on to the I/O subsystem. Conversely, decreasing this value can throttle the NFS load on a server when that is appropriate.

Parameters That Influence Paging and Swapping

The section isn't large enough to review in detail how tuning can affect each of the kernel tables. However, for illustration purposes, this section describes how kernel parameters influence paging and swapping activities in a SunOS system. Other tables affecting other subsystems can be tuned in much the same manner as these.

As processes make demands on memory, pages are allocated from the free list. When the UNIX system decides that there is no longer enough free memory—less than the `lotsfree` parameter—it searches for pages that haven't been used lately to add them to the free list. The page daemon will be scheduled to run. It begins at a slow rate, based on the `slowscan` parameter, and increases to a faster rate, based on the `fastscan` parameter, as free memory continues toward depletion. If there is less memory than `desfree`, and there are two or more processes in the run queue, and the system stays in that condition for more than 30 seconds, the system will begin to swap. If the system gets to a minimum level of required memory, specified by the `minfree` parameter, swapping will begin without delay. When swapping begins, entire processes will be swapped out as described earlier.

> **NOTE:** If you have your swapping spread over several disks, increasing the `maxpgio` parameter may be beneficial. This parameter limits the number of pages scheduled to be paged out, and is based on single-disk swapping. Increasing it may improve paging performance. You can use the `po` field from `vmstat`, as described earlier, which checks against `maxpgio` and `pagesize` to examine the volumes involved.

The kernel swaps out the oldest and the largest processes when it begins to swap. The `maxslp` parameter is used in determining which processes have exceeded the maximum sleeping period, and can thus be swapped out as well. The smallest higher-priority processes that have been sleeping the longest will then be swapped back in.

The most pertinent kernel parameters for paging and swapping are the following:

- ■ `minfree` This is the absolute minimum memory level that the system will tolerate. Once past `minfree`, the system immediately resorts to swapping.
- ■ `desfree` This is the desperation level. After 30 seconds at this level, paging is abandoned and swapping is begun.
- ■ `lotsfree` Once below this memory limit, the page daemon is activated to begin freeing memory.
- ■ `fastscan` This is the number of pages scanned per second.
- ■ `slowscan` This is the number of pages scanned per second when there is less memory than `lotsfree` available. As memory decreases from `lotsfree` the scanning speed increases from `slowscan` to `fastscan`.

■ `maxpgio`   This is the maximum number of page out I/O operations per second that the system will schedule. This is normally set at approximately 40 under SunOS, which is appropriate for a single 3600 RPM disk. It can be increased with more or faster disks.

Newer versions of UNIX, such as Solaris 2.x, do such a good job of setting paging parameters that tuning is usually not required.

Increasing `lotsfree` will help on systems on which there is a continuing need to allocate new processes. Heavily used interactive systems with many Windows users often force this condition as users open multiple windows and start processes. By increasing `lotsfree` you create a large enough pool of free memory that you will not run out when most of the processes are initially starting up.

For servers that have a defined set of users and a more steady-state condition to their underlying processes, the normal default values are usually appropriate.

However, for servers such as this with large, stable work loads, but that are short of memory, increasing `lotsfree` is the wrong idea. This is because more pages will be taken from the application and put on the free list.

Some system administrators recommend that you disable the `maxslp` parameter on systems where the overhead of swapping normally sleeping processes (such as clock icons and update processes) isn't offset by any measurable gain due to forcing the processes out. This parameter is no longer used in Solaris 2.x releases, but is used on older versions of UNIX.

Conclusion of Kernel Tuning

You have now seen how to optimize memory subsystem performance by tuning a system's kernel parameters. Other subsystems can be tuned by similar modifications to the relevant kernel parameters. When such changes correct existing kernel configurations that have become obsolete and inefficient due to new requirements, the result can sometimes dramatically increase performance even without a hardware upgrade. It's not quite the same as getting a hardware upgrade for free, but it's about as close as you're likely to get in today's computer industry.

Summary

With a little practice using the methodology described in this chapter, you should be able to determine what the performance characteristics, positive or negative, are for your system. You have seen how to use the commands that enable you to examine each of the resources a UNIX system uses. In addition to the commands themselves, you have learned procedures that can be utilized to analyze and solve many performance problems.

Device Administration

By Salim Douba

Central to the system administrator's responsibilities is the provision to users of access to the distributed and shared resources belonging to their environment. Some of the resources are software (for example, applications, the file system, and so on), whereas others are hardware such as terminals, modems, printers, and so on. Other chapters will address the issues and concerns pertaining to the administration of software resources; this chapter addresses issues pertaining to the administration and management of hardware resources (that is, devices). Namely, you will be presented with the skills necessary to set up, configure, and maintain the performance of modems, terminals, printers, x terminals, and PCs.

For the purposes of terminal, modem, and printer setup UNIX comes with a very powerful and central access facility known as Service Access Facility (SAF). No treatment of device administration is complete without covering SAF. Neither is it possible for the system administrator to complete the aforementioned tasks successfully without a rigorous understanding of what SAF is all about, and the skillful use of its associated commands. This chapter starts by explaining SAF.

Understanding Service Access Facility (SAF)

Prior to System V release 4 of UNIX, administrators were provided with different processes and interfaces, along with their associated tools, to manage different physical resources on the system. Local port access used to be administered and controlled by interfaces that are different from those needed to set up for network access, or those pertaining to printer setup and so on. Administrators were therefore confronted with the challenge of learning and mastering the many different skills and interfaces needed to get the job done. To alleviate this challenge, SAF was introduced with SVR4. SAF provides a commonly applicable interface for the purpose of comprehensive and uniform management of all system resources. Upon mastering the concepts and associated commands that SAF provides, the administrator will be able to install, configure, monitor, and maintain information relevant to the local and network access to physical port services in SAF database files.

SAF consists primarily of port services, port monitors, the service access controller (sac) process, and SAF Administrative Files and Commands

A description of each of these components will be provided. Then the SAF initialization process will be detailed.

Port Services

SAF defines a hierarchy of port control processes, of which port service is the lowest and the most "intimate" to the actual physical services. A port service is defined as a process that controls and monitors access to applications and other services, through physical ports such as ttys and TCP/IP. A tty service may provide users with dial-in/dial-out capabilities, thus allowing them to utilize high-level applications such as uucp, cu, and login. A TCP/IP port-related service may be required to provide printing, rlogin, or nfs services across the network.

There is a one-to-one association between physical ports (the actual physical service) and port services (the controlling process). It is not possible, for example, for two ttys to share the same port service; neither is it possible for one tty port to be controlled by more than one port service.

Upon creation of a port service, the system administrator assigns it a service name, which is referred to as the service tag. Service tags are used to conveniently distinguish between the port services running on the system. Port services are supported and controlled by intermediate-level processes called port monitors, which are described next.

Port Monitors

A port monitor is an intermediate level process that controls a set of related services. SAF currently recognizes two types of port monitors: ttymon and listen. However SAF is not limited to those two types. Vendors and system programmers are provided with a well-defined network programming interface, to enable them to write their own monitor types.

Port monitor type ttymon controls and monitors tty-related port services, thus replacing pre-SVR4 getty and uugetty programs. Although maintaining support to uugetty and getty processes in SVR4 for reasons of backward compatibility, ttymon is the preferred method of installing, configuring, and monitoring tty port services in SVR4. Port monitor type listen, on the other hand, takes advantage of TCP/IP communications protocols (see Chapter 37 for more on TCP/IP) to provide across-the-network services mentioned earlier, such as network printing and remote file-sharing capabilities. Both port monitor types will be comprehensively explained in the upcoming sections.

System administrators are allowed the flexibility to create as many port monitors of any type as they deem necessary. Upon creation of a port monitor, a so-called port monitor tag has to be assigned to it. As in the case of port services, port monitor tags are names that help in distinguishing between port monitors. They can be given convenient names that may describe the nature of the service they support. Being a mid-level process, port monitors themselves are invoked, controlled, and monitored by the service access controller (sac) process.

Service Access Controller

The service access controller process is the highest in SAF hierarchy. There is only one sac per system. It invokes and controls all port monitors, irrespective of type, which have been created and configured by the system administrator. sac is a program that is spawned by init upon system startup when multiuser mode is entered. When SVR4 is installed, an entry supporting sac is automatically included in the /etc/inittab file. A depiction of how this entry should look is as follows:

```
sc:234:respawn:/usr/lib/saf/sac -t 300
```

Due to the -t 300 option, sac routinely checks port monitors every 300 seconds for services. In order to change it to any other different value, enter

```
#sacadm -t <seconds>
```

> **NOTE:** Do not be surprised, upon checking the /etc/inittab file, if you see entries pertaining to ttymon port monitor. There is no contradiction between what you see and what has already been explained. Simply put, SVR4 allows a so-called "express mode" invocation of ttymon by init. This particularly applies to the case of the console port. You will still be able, however, to create instances of ttymon that are controlled and administered by sac.

SAF Administrative Commands and Files

SAF distinguishes between sac-specific, port monitor-specific, and port service-specific administrative and configuration files as well as administrative commands. In this section, administrative and configuration files and SAF-related commands will be described. The emphasis will be on their nature and the job they do. Command syntax and utilization for the purposes of creating, configuring, or checking the status of port monitors and port services will be left until later sections where they'll be discussed at length in the context of tasks to accomplish.

Service Access Controller Specific Files and Commands

Once brought up, sac fetches two files. Those files are as follows: 1) /etc/saf/_sactab, which is the administrative database that contains entries pertaining to port monitors defined by the system administrator, and 2) the /etc/saf/_sysconfig file, which is a sac-specific configuration file. Whereas sac uses the first file to identify the port monitors to invoke, it uses the second one in order to self-customize its own environment. Contents of /etc/saf/_sactab can be modified by the sacadm command, which is sac's administrative command. Using sacadm allows administrators to create port monitors, check their status, and enable or disable them as well as remove them. Also, each port monitor provides an administrative command that can be used with sacadm in command substitution mode. The listen port monitor administrative command is nlsadmin, whereas ttymon's is ttyadm.

/etc/saf/_sysconfig file, on the other hand, is a file that would be used by sac to specify the environment governing all the services controlled by it. The sac program, once started by init, reads and interprets this file prior to the invocation of any service defined by /etc/saf/_sactab. There can optionally be one _sysconfig file per system, and it can be edited using vi or any other UNIX editor.

Port Monitor Specific Files and Commands

When a port monitor is created using sacadm, an /etc/saf/*<pmtag>* directory will be created where port-specific files are maintained. Of prime interest are 1) /etc/saf/*<pmtag>*/ _pmtab, and 2) /etc/saf/*<pmtag>*/_config. If, for example, you create a port monitor, which you assign a tag called ttyserv, the directory called /etc/saf/ttyserv will be created in which the administrative file called /etc/saf/ttyserv/_config will be maintained. This file is similar to the /etc/saf/_sactab in its functionality, as it is used by the port monitor to determine and bring up the port services as defined by the system administrator. /etc/saf/*<pmtag>*/_pmtab is a one-per-port monitor file and is modified using the pmadm command whether creating, deleting, or modifying the status of any of the associated port services. The /etc/saf/*<pmtag>*/_config is an optional port monitor specific configuration file that can be created by the system administrator using vi. Commands in this file can add to, or override, those found in the system configuration file _sysconfig. Before starting a port monitor defined in /etc/saf/_sactab file, sac checks the port monitors' respective directory, described previously, for the _config file. If found, _config is read and interpreted by sac to customize the port monitor's environment, and then the port monitor is started.

Port Service-Specific Files and Commands

Being at the bottom of the SAF hierarchy, port services have no administrative files associated with it. The system administrator, however, has the option to create a port service-specific configuration script named after the service tag and kept in the associated port monitor's directory. So if, for example, a port service was created under port monitor ttyserv and was given the service tag ttylogin1, then the port service configuration file is named ttylogin1 and is kept in the /etc/saf/ttyserv directory. The complete filename thus becomes /etc/saf/ttyserv/ttylogin1. This file is read and interpreted by the controlling port monitor before starting the port service. Configuration commands included in the file may override or add to those found in the _config port monitor's file or _sysconfig that are associated with this service.

Table 40.1 summarizes what has been discussed so far and provides you with a quick way to narrow down the files and commands associated with each SAF component.

Table 40.1. Administrative files and commands associated with each of the SAF components.

Process Filename	Invoked by Admin Command	Admin Filename	config
sac	init	/etc/saf/_sactab	/etc/saf/ _sysconfig sacadm
port monitor	sac pmadm	/etc/saf/<pmtag>/_pmtab	/etc/saf/ <pmtag>/ _config
port service	port monitor	optional pmadm	

SAF Initialization Process

Figure 40.1 shows a flow chart summarizing the SAF initialization process. Note how it all starts with init invoking sac after reading a sac-associated entry in the /etc/inittab file. Once sac is started, it proceeds as follows:

sac checks for the /etc/saf/_sysconfig configuration file. If found, it reads the file in order to self-customize its environment. This environment is a global one that, unless otherwise modified or overridden, will govern all defined SAF services.

sac determines which port monitors to invoke by reading the /etc/saf/_sactab file. For each port monitor, sac checks for the associated /etc/saf/<pmtag>/ _config file. If one exists, the sac process reads, interprets, and implements the contents and customizes the port monitor's environment, irrespective of any earlier associated settings defined in _sysconfig files. The port monitor is then invoked.

Once invoked, the port monitor determines which port services to start by reading its /etc/saf/<pmtag>/_pmtab file. Next, the port monitor checks for the optional /etc/saf/<pmtag>/<svctag> corresponding to each port service. If one exists, it is read and interpreted to customize the port service environment. The port service is then invoked.

After the initialization process is completed, sac continues to poll the port monitors at regular intervals as defined by the -t option in the corresponding entry in the /etc/inittab file. Port monitors failing to respond to this polling process prompt sac into respawning them.

FIGURE 40.1.

Flow chart illustration of SAF initialization process.

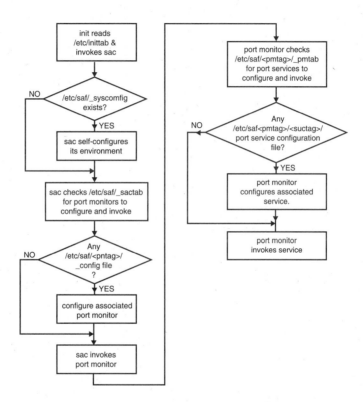

SAF Administration and Management

This section introduces some of the concepts and skills pertaining to SAF management and administration. Because those skills commonly apply to all types of port monitors and their associated port services, the discussion will focus on how to accomplish each of the following tasks described, with little emphasis on the nature of the service being rendered to the user. SAF management and administration is a two-level system: one level applies to port monitors, whereas the other applies to port services. This section is therefore presented in two parts.

Port Monitor Administration and Management

As explained earlier in this chapter, for an administrator to offer port services, be it across the network or local to the system, he or she must first create the port monitor supporting it. Only then can port services be created and released to the user community. There are also troubleshooting instances when the administrator may need to check on the status of suspect port monitors or even temporarily disable them.

Creating a Port Monitor

Port monitors are administered and managed using the sacadm administrative command. In addition to sacadm, each port monitor type provides for an administrative command that is commonly used with sacadm in "command substitution mode." ttyadm is ttymon's command, whereas nlsadmin is listen's. To create a port monitor, sacadm must be entered along with the following options:

```
#sacadm -a -p<pmtag> -t<type> -c"<pm_cmd>" -v ver [-fd¦x] \
[-n <count>] [-y"comment"]
```

where:

-a stands for add or create a port monitor.

-p *<pmtag>* assigns the port monitor being created a name, which can be conveniently used to distinguish it from other port monitors. Although the name can be anything you choose, it should be descriptive of the type of service with which it is associated.

-t *<type>* specifies the type of monitor to create (that is, ttymon versus listen).

-c "*<pm_cmd>*" specifies the command to invoke when the port monitor is later spawned by sac: /usr/lib/saf/ttymon to invoke a ttymon port monitor, or /usr/lib/saf/listen to invoke a listen port monitor.

-v *ver* specifies the version of the port monitor. The version may more conveniently be provided by invoking the port monitor's specific administrative command (ttyadm or nlsadmin) with the -V option in command substitution form (that is, as an argument to -v). In this case, the -V option would be typed as follows:

```
# sacadm -a ... -v'ttyadm -V' ...
```

-f [d¦x] specifies the status of the port monitor upon invocation, with d meaning to start the port monitor in disabled state and x meaning not to start it. If flagged x, the port monitor can only be started by the system administrator. There onward, sac takes over in controlling the port monitor.

-n*<count>* specifies the retry count used by the port monitor in restarting a failing port monitor. If not included, the default that applies is zero.

-y "*comment*" can be any comment that you may want to include in the /etc/ saf/_sactab file. For your convenience, you may want to include a comment describing what this port monitor is for.

When a port monitor is created, the following happens: 1) An entry in sac's administrative file /etc/saf/_sactab is added pertaining to the port monitor, including all of the arguments provided on the command line. 2) The port monitor's supporting directory /etc/saf/<*pmtag*> is also created. As a matter of fact, another directory, /var/saf/<*pmtag*>, will also be created where a port monitor log file is maintained. The filename is /var/saf/ <*pmtag*/log. It is used by sac to log all messages pertaining to the port monitor.

For a better feel for what has been said so far, take a look at an example of creating a port monitor. This example will be carried over to upcoming sections to demonstrate aspects of managing the port monitor. In this example it is assumed that the system administrator wants to allow users local logins to the system, using serial communications. Hence, the first task is to create the port monitor in preparation for creating the necessary associated port services.

Due to the nature of the service (that is, serial communication), the port monitor has to be of a ttymon type. The system administrator has chosen to assign the port monitor the tag ttyserv, start it in the disabled state, and include a comment saying "only two logins." Upon failure, sac should attempt restarting the monitor twice. The sacadm command should therefore look like this:

```
#sacadm -a -p serial -t ttymon -v 'ttyadm -V' \
 -c"/usr/lib/saf/ttymon" -fd -n 2 -y "only two logins"
```

Next, you'll be learning how to check on the status of the port monitor. For the time being, however, we can carry a check using cat to look up the contents of sac's /etc/saf/_sactab file. cat /etc/saf/_sactab should reveal the following entry:

```
ttyserv:ttymon:d:2:/usr/lib/saf/ttymon          #only two logins
```

and if you enter ls -l /etc/saf, you will be able to verify that the subdirectory is ttyserv. ttyserv (the subdirectory) is created among others existing at /etc/saf level. Reflecting back on the _sactab entry shown previously, you should have guessed how each field in /etc/saf/_sactab file maps to arguments you enter on the command line. The first field refers to the pmtag, the second to the port monitor type, the third to the state in which the port monitor is started (disable state, in this example). The fourth mandates that two restarts be attempted should the port monitor fail, and the fifth specifies the complete pathname of the command to invoke. Note also that the comment is included as well.

Checking the Status of the Port Monitor

To check on the status of the port monitor, use the sacadm command with -l option among the others as follows:

1. `# sacadm -t<type> -l` to obtain a listing of all port monitors of same type, or

2. `# sacadm -p<pmtag> -l` to obtain information about a specific port monitor.

If you enter `sacadm -pttyserv -l` to check on the port monitor just created in the preceding example, you get the following output:

```
PMTAG     PMTYPE    FLGS RCNT STATUS     COMMAND
ttyserv   ttymon    d    2    DISABLED   /usr/lib/saf/ttymon #only two logins
```

Note that the status field indicates that the port monitor is in a disabled state. If you check the status immediately after the port monitor is created, the status field may indicate that it is STARTING.

The port monitor can be in one of the following states:

STARTING: sac is in the process of starting it. This is a transitional state between NOTRUNNING and ENABLED or DISABLED.

ENABLED: The port monitor is running and is accepting connection requests.

DISABLED: The port monitor is running but refusing connection service requests.

STOPPED: The port monitor is undergoing the shutdown process. This state is transitional from ENABLED or DISABLED and NOTRUNNING.

NOTRUNNING: The port monitor is not running. None of the port services associated with it is currently accessible.

Enabling, Disabling, and Removing a Port Monitor

To enable, disable, or remove a port monitor, use `sacadm -e`, `sacadm -d`, or `sacadm -r`, respectively. To enable the ttyserv port monitor, enter

```
# sacadm -pttyserv -e
```

whereas to disable it, enter

```
# sacadm -pttyserv -d
```

and to remove it, enter

```
# sacadm -pttyserv -r
```

> **NOTE:** When a port monitor is removed, its associated directories are not cleaned up and deleted. To avoid confusion in the future, you may have to take care of that yourself.

Port Service Administration and Management

Only after the port monitor is created is the system administrator in a position to create and manage the associated port services. Port creation and administration is achievable via the `pmadm` command.

Creating a Port Service

To create a port service, `pmadm` should be used with the `-a` option, among the others as follows:

```
# pmadm -a -p<pmtag> -s<svctag> -m"pmspecific" \
-v ver [-fx|u] -y"comment"
```

in which

> `-a` stands for create a port service.
>
> `-p<pmtag>` specifies the tag of the port monitor to which the port service belongs.
>
> `-s<svctag>` specifies the service tag assigned to the port service.
>
> `-m"<pmspecific>"` specifies port-specific information to be passed as an argument to the `pmadm` command. Normally, this information is generated by employing either `ttyadm` or `nlsadmin` in command substitution mode, depending on the type of the port monitor specified with the `-p` option.
>
> `-v <ver>` passes the version of the port monitor. Depending on the type of the port monitor, either `ttymon -V` or `nlsadmin -V` can be used in command substitution mode.
>
> `-f` specifies the state with which the port service should be started, and whether a utmp entry is to be created. Both or any of the flags can be specified, where d specifies that the port should be started in disabled state, and u specifies that a utmp entry be created for the service.

The following example adds a `ttymon` port service to the `ttyserv` port monitor created earlier in this section:

```
#pmadm -a -pttyserv -s s01 -v 'ttyadm -C' -fd \
-m "`ttyadm -d /dev/term/01 -l 9600 -s/usr/bin/login \
-p"Welcome To UNIX, Please Login:"'"
```

The port service thus created is assigned service tag s01 and added to a port monitor called `ttyserv` (the one created in the earlier section). s01 port is associated with `/dev/term/01` device file (that is, COM2 on an Intel 386/486 machine. `-l 9600` refers to a record in a terminal line setting database file (`/etc/ttydefs`), which, when used by the port, sets the line speed. The other settings are described in a subsequent section. When s01 port is invoked by the `ttyserv` port monitor, it is going to write a prompt ("Welcome to UNIX, Please Login:" according to the preceding example) to the terminal connected to the COM2 port. It starts monitoring the port until it receives a request to connect. Upon receiving the prompt, it invokes /usr/bin/login to take care of the request.

When a port service is created, the /etc/saf/<*pmtag*>/_pmtab is modified to include an entry pertaining to the service. Hence, in the preceding example, an entry pertaining to s01 must be present in the /etc/saf/ttyserv/_pmtab. You can display it either by using cat or the pmadm command as described in the next section.

Listing and Checking the Status of a Port Service

To list and check on the status of a port monitor, enter

```
#pmadm -l -p<pmtag> -s<svctag>
```

To list or check on the status of all port services associated with a specific port monitor, enter

```
#pmadm -l -p<pmtag>
```

whereas to list, or check, the status of all port monitor services, enter

```
PMTAG        PMTYPE        SVCTAG       FLGS ID      <PMSPECIFIC>
ttymon3      ttymon        00s          u    root    /dev/term/00s - - /usr/bin/
                                                    ➡login - 2400 - login:  -  #
ttymon3      ttymon        01s          u    uucp    /dev/term/01s b - /usr/bin/
                                                    ➡login - 2400 - login:  -  #
ttymon3      ttymon        00h          u    root    /dev/term/00h - - /usr/bin/
                                                    ➡login - 9600 - login:  -  #
tcp          listen        0            x    root   \x02000ACE64000001 - c - /
                                                    ➡usr/lib/saf/nlps_server
                                                    ➡#NLPS SERVER
tcp          listen        lp           -    root    - - - - /var/spool/lp/fifos/
                                                    ➡listenS5 #NLPS SERVER
tcp          listen        105          -    root    - - c - /usr/net/servers/rfs/
                                                    ➡rfsetup #RFS server
```

The following two examples demonstrate the first two commands.

```
#pmadm -l -pttyserv -s s01
PMTAG     PMTYPE    SVCTAG     FLGS ID    PMSPECIFIC
ttyserv   ttymon    s01        d    root /dev/term/01 --
/usr/bin/login - 9600 - Welcome to UNIX, Please Login: - #

#pmadm -l -pttyserv
PMTAG     PMTYPE    SVCTAG FLGS ID       <PMSPECIFIC>
ttyyserv     ttymon      00s           u       root    /dev/term/00s - -
/usr/bin/login - 2400 - login:  -  #
ttyserv      ttymon      01s           u       uucp   /dev/term/01s b -
/usr/bin/login - 9600 - login:  -  #
```

Enabling, Disabling, and Removing a Port Service

To enable, disable, or remove a port service, use pmadm -e, pmadm -d, or pmadm -r, respectively. Hence, to enable s01 port monitor, enter

```
#pmadm -pttyserv -s s01 -e
```

whereas to disable it, enter

```
#pmadm -pttyserv -s s01 -d
```

and to remove it, enter

```
#pmadm -pttyserv -s s01 -r
```

The *ttymon* port monitor

As its name implies, the `ttymon` port monitor is responsible for invoking and monitoring port services associated with your system's tty ports. When invoked, `ttymon` looks up its `/etc/saf/<pmtag>/_pmtab` file to determine: which port services to invoke; which `tty` port associates with which service; how the port services are configured (for example, startup in an enabled state, what line speed to configure `tty` port to, and so on); and which application, or process, to invoke upon user request (for example, `login` service, `uucp`, and so on).

`ttymon` replaces both `getty` and `uugetty`. Though `getty` and `uugetty` are still supported by SVR4 for backward compatibility reasons, system administrators are strongly recommended to use `ttymon`. This recommendation stems from the following comparison:

1. `ttymon` administration conforms with SAF's generic interface. This brings managing `ttymon` port monitors into line with management concepts applied to other port monitors, providing the benefit of convenience.

2. By using SAF management commands, the administrator has the choice of managing `ttymon` port services collectively or selectively. When using `getty`, the administrator can manage only one port at a time.

3. One invocation of the `ttymon` port monitor by `sac` can take care of multiple `tty`s, whereas `getty`/`uugetty` requires an entry per supported `tty` in the `/etc/inittab` file.

4. As will be discussed later, `ttymon` comes with support of a new feature, namely the AUTOBAUD feature. This feature allows `ttymon` to automatically determine the line speed suitable to the connected terminal.

5. `ttymon` can optionally be invoked directly by `init`, in "express" mode. This may be done by including an entry in the `/etc/inittab` file. As a matter of fact, if you examine the contents of the `/etc/inittab` file, you will notice the existence of a similar entry taking care of the UNIX system console in express mode. The entry should look similar to the following:

```
co:12345:respawn:/usr/lib/saf/ttymon -g -v -p "Console Login: "-d /dev/
console -l console
```

Upon reading this entry, `init` starts a `ttymon` port monitor to take care of console login needs. This particular invocation of `ttymon` falls beyond `sac`'s control.

Special Device Files and the Terminal Line Settings Database

Among the arguments that the system administrator must pass to `pmadm` to create a port service, two will be described: the device special filename corresponding to the `tty` serial interface undergoing configuration and a label identifying an entry in a terminal line settings database.

Device Special Filenames under SAF

Special filenames underwent some changes under SVR4. In earlier releases of UNIX, `getty` and `uugetty` referred to the special files in the `/dev` directory as `tty##`, where `##` refers to the actual port number. With SAF under SVR4, `tty` port special files are maintained in a subdirectory called `/dev/term` and the special files are named `##` in that directory. `com1` port on a 386 machine is now referred to as `/dev/term/00`, whereas under `getty` it is referred to as `/dev/tty00`. Due to the ongoing support to `uugetty` and `getty`, both conventions are currently supported. It is the administrator's responsibility, however, to make sure that the right convention is applied with his or her preferred way of invoking a port service.

The Terminal Line Settings Database

As mentioned earlier, this database is the `ttymon` administrative file, which defines the line settings applying to the `tty` port being invoked. The database filename is `/etc/ttydefs`, whereas `getty`'s is `/etc/gettydefs`. Both files remain supported by SVR4 and both are maintained using the `/etc/sbin/sttydefs` command. A good understanding of these databases helps you to provide the level of support that matches the users' terminal emulation need. In the following discussion, however, only `/etc/ttydefs`' file data structure is examined and explained. The use of the `sttydefs` command to add, modify, or delete entries in the database also is described.

The discussion begins with a close look at the contents of the `/etc/ttydefs` file. To list its contents, enter

```
#/usr/sbin/sttydefs -l
-----------------------------------------------------------------------------------------------
19200: 19200 opost onlcr tab3 ignpar ixon ixany parenb istrip echo echoe echok isig cs7
cread : 19200 opost onlcr sane tab3 ignpar ixon ixany parenb istrip echo echoe echok
isig cs7 cread ::9600
-----------------------------------------------------------------------------------------------
```

```
ttylabel:    19200
initial flags:    19200 opost onlcr tab3 ignpar ixon ixany parenb istrip echo echoe
echok isig cs7 cread
final flags:    19200 opost onlcr sane tab3 ignpar ixon ixany parenb istrip echo echoe
echok isig cs7 cread
autobaud:    no
nextlabel:    9600


-------------------------------------------------------------------------------------------------------------

9600: 9600 opost onlcr tab3 ignpar ixon ixany parenb istrip echo echoe echok isig cs7
cread : 9600 opost onlcr sane tab3 ignpar ixon ixany parenb istrip echo echoe echok isig
cs7 cread ::4800

-------------------------------------------------------------------------------------------------------------

ttylabel:    9600
initial flags:    9600 opost onlcr tab3 ignpar ixon ixany parenb istrip echo echoe
echok isig cs7 cread
final flags:    9600 opost onlcr sane tab3 ignpar ixon ixany parenb istrip echo echoe
echok isig cs7 cread
autobaud:    no
nextlabel:    4800


-------------------------------------------------------------------------------------------------------------

4800: 4800 opost onlcr tab3 ignpar ixon ixany parenb istrip echo echoe echok isig cs7
cread : 4800 opost onlcr sane tab3 ignpar ixon ixany parenb istrip echo echoe echok isig
cs7 cread ::2400

-------------------------------------------------------------------------------------------------------------

ttylabel:    4800
initial flags:    4800 opost onlcr tab3 ignpar ixon ixany parenb istrip echo echoe
echok isig cs7 cread
final flags:    4800 opost onlcr sane tab3 ignpar ixon ixany parenb istrip echo echoe
echok isig cs7 cread
autobaud:    no
nextlabel:     2400
.
.
.
```

As you see, `sttydefs` formats the listing into a user-friendly format. If you want the actual data structure of the command, enter

```
#cat /etc/ttydefs
.
.
.
onlcr sane tab3 ignpar istrip ixon ixany echo echoe echok isig cs8 cread ::console5
console5: 19200 opost onlcr tab3 ignpar istrip ixon ixany echo echoe echok isig cs8
cread : 19200 opost onlcr sane tab3 ignpar istrip ixon ixany echo echoe echok isig cs8
cread ::console

4800H: 4800 : 4800 ixany parenb sane tab3 hupcl ::9600H
9600H: 9600 : 9600 ixany parenb sane tab3 hupcl ::19200H
19200H: 19200 : 19200 ixany parenb sane tab3 hupcl ::2400H
2400H: 2400 : 2400 ixany parenb sane tab3 hupcl ::1200H
1200H: 1200 : 1200 ixany parenb sane tab3 hupcl ::300H
300H: 300 : 300 ixany parenb sane tab3 hupcl ::4800H
```

```
19200NP: 19200 opost onlcr tab3 ignpar ixon ixany istrip echo echoe echok isig cs8 cread
: 19200
.
.
```

The following is a description of each field:

Label: It is unique and is used in identifying the record. You will be passing this label to `ttymon`, using `pmadm`, when creating the port service. Every time `ttymon` attempts invoking the port service, it searches for that label in the `ttydefs` file.

Initial flags: This field describes the initial terminal line settings. They allow users to provide login information upon initial contact.

Final flags: They define the terminal line settings after a connection request is detected, and right before the associated port service is invoked.

Autobaud: This field can contain either A or null. By including A in this field, you are prompting `ttymon` to automatically determine the line speed upon receiving a carriage return from the user's terminal.

Next label: This field includes the label of the next record to fetch should the line settings specified in the current label fail to meet the user's terminal needs. `ttymon` recognizes the failure upon receiving a BREAK sent by the user. This technique allows `ttymon` to fall back on any number of alternate configurations in search of the desired line speed. Records linked together in this fashion are said to form a hunt sequence, with the last one normally linked to the first record. The sample partial listing shown previously includes a hunt sequence that starts with label 4800H and ends with 300H.

An example record in `ttydefs` follows, along with an explanation of its field contents.

```
9600NP: 9600  tab3 ignpar ixon ixany  echo echoe  cs8 : 9600 sane tab3 ignpar ixon ixany
echo echoe  cs8::4800NP
```

This record is labelled `9600NP`. Both the initial and final flags set the port to 9600 bps, no parity (`ignpar`), enable XON/OFF flow control(`ixon`), any character should restart output (`ixany`), echo back every character typed (`echo`), echo erase character (`echoe`), and to set the character size to 8 bits. The `autobaud` field is null, which means that no autobaud support is required. The last field points to the next record labelled 4800N.

To find more about the valid initial and final flag settings, consult your vendor's manuals, or simply enter "man stty" on the command line.

What if you don't find what you want in `ttydefs`? As noted earlier, SVR4 provides you with the `/etc/sbin/sttydefs` command to make changes to the `/etc/ttydefs` database. Among the changes you are allowed to make is adding the record of your liking. The command syntax to do that follows:

```
#sttydefs -a<ttylabel> [-b] [-n<nextlabel>] [-i<initialflags>]\
[-f <finalflags>]
```

in which

-a *<ttylabel>* adds an entry to ttydefs with label specified (first field)

-i *<initialflags>* specifies initial speed among other line settings (second field)

-f *<finalflags>* specifies final line settings (third field)

-b enables autobaud (fourth field in which case A will be included in this field)

-n describes the next record's label

For example, the sttydefs that follows adds a new record, labelled 4800, with initial flags set to support 4800 bps line speed:

```
#sttydefs -a4800 -i"4800 hupcl tab3 erase ^b" \
-f"4800 sane ixany tab3 erase ^h echoe" -n2400np
```

To remove an entry, simply enter sttydefs -r *<ttylabel>*.

For example: to delete the 4800 label, enter

```
#sttydefs -r 4800
```

CAUTION: A record that you delete may belong to a hunt sequence, in which case it is your responsibility to restore integrity to the affected sequence.

The *ttymon* Port Monitor Administrative Command *ttyadm*

ttyadm is ttymon's administrative command. Its prime function is to pass information to both sacadm and pmadm in the formats they require. The following are the ttyadm options:

-V specifies the version of ttymon

-d device specifies the /dev/term/## tty with which the port service will be associated

-b if included, will configure the port service for bidirectional flow of data

-r *<count>* specifies the number of times ttymon should try to start the service before a failure is declared

-p *"prompt"* is the string used to prompt users when a port service request is detected.

-i *"message"* is the message to be displayed if the port is in a disabled state

-t <*timeout*> is the number of seconds that ttymon must wait for input data before closing the port

-l <*ttylabel*> specifies the label of the desired record in the /etc/ttydefs file described earlier in this section

-s specifies the name of the service provider program on the tty port (for example, login, cu, and so on)

At this point, all of the necessary elements that you will need to implement terminal and modem connections have been covered. If you are anxious to try implementing, you may jump right ahead to the section titled "Connecting Terminals and Modems." Otherwise, continue reading the next section, which explains the listen port monitor.

The *listen* Port Monitor

listen is a network port monitoring process that is invoked and controlled by sac. It runs on any transport provider (most commonly TCP), and supports two classes of service: a class of general services, such as RFS and network printing; and terminal login services for terminals trying to access the system by connecting directly to the network. Like ttymon, listen can support and monitor multiple ports, with each assigned a network service to take care of. Once invoked, the listen port monitor initializes port services as defined in its /etc/saf/<*pmtag*>/_pmtab file. It then monitors the ports for service connection requests. Once a request is received on a listen port, the associated service (for example, printing) is invoked and the user is connected to it.

Port Service Addressing

During TCP/IP setup (refer to Chapter 37 for more on TCP/IP), your system will have been assigned an Internet address that is 8 hexadecimal digits long, with each pair of digits represented by one octet. Stations shipping requests across the network to your system use this address to reach your machine's doorstep only. Because your machine is more likely to be configured to respond to a variety of service requests, there arises the requirement to assign unique addresses to port services. This allows the listen port monitor to support multiple port services. Upon adding a listen port service, you are required to provide the applicable address to nlsadmin (the listen port monitor administrative command). For this reason, you are provided with the address format shown in Figure 40.2.

FIGURE 40.2.

listen's port service address format.

The listener port service address format

Family Address (4 digits)	Port Address (4 digits)	Internet Address (8 digits)	Reserved (16 digits)

The elements of the address format are as follows:

Family address: This is four digits long. It is always set to 0020.

Port address: This is four digits long and is the port service-specific address. For example, listenS5 print server is assigned x0ACE, whereas listenBSD print server is assigned x0203.

Internet address: This is the IP address you assigned to the system upon installing TCP/IP. It is eight digits long.

Reserved: This is 16 digits long and is reserved for future use. Currently, it is set to 16 zeros.

As an example, assume that the IP address of your system is 100.0.0.1 and that you want to set up a listen port to take care of print service requests sent across the network by BSD systems. The port address in hexadecimal notation then becomes

000202036400000100000000000000000

> **TIP:** To avoid dealing with decimal-to-hex conversions to figure out the hexadecimal equivalent to your host IP address, you can use the lpsystem -A. Figure 40.3 demonstrates the use of lpsystem -A output in order to figure out the host's IP address in hexadecimal notation.

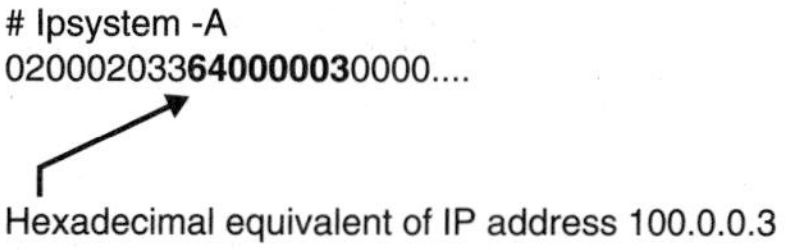

FIGURE 40.3.

Using lpsystem -A
*to find the hexadecimal
equivalent of the host's
IP address.*

```
# lpsystem -A
02000203364000030000....
```
Hexadecimal equivalent of IP address 100.0.0.3

It will be shown later in this section how to pass this address to pmadm when creating the port service.

The *listen* Port Monitor Administrative Command *nlsamdin*

nlsadmin is the administrative command specific to the listen port monitor. nlsadmin can be used to add, configure, and change the status of a port monitor. Also, it can be used to start or kill the listener process. Mostly it will be used in command substitution mode, in order to supply some of the required arguments to both sacadm (the sac administrative command) and pmadm. Options that you specify on the command line will determine which arguments to pass, and in what format.

Creating a *listen* Port Monitor

To create a `ttymon` port monitor, you use the `sacadm` command. The same applies to creating a `listen` port monitor. Instead of using `ttyadm`, however, you must use `nlsadmin` in command substitution mode in order to pass some of the required information to `sacadm`. The use of `sacadm` in creating a listen port monitor is as follows:

```
#sacadm -a -p<pmtag> -t listen -c<"command"> -v`nlsadmin -V` \
[-n<count>] [-fd¦x] [-y<"comment">]
```

All options bear the same significance described in earlier sections (refer back to the "Creating a Port Monitor" section for a review). Note in particular, the use of `nlsadmin -V` in order to pass the port monitor's version to `sacadm`. Also note that the `-c` option specifies the program invoked to bring up the `listen` port monitor. The program is `/usr/lib/saf/listen`. Once a port monitor is created, an entry pertaining to it is added to `sac`'s administrative file `/etc/saf/_sactab`.

As an example, the following `sacadm` command creates a `listen` port monitor with `pmtag` `tcp`. Note that the program filename to invoke is `/usr/lib/saf/listen`, and `sac` is required to try up to three times to bring up the port monitor, should it ever fail respond to `sac`'s polls.

```
sacadm -a -t listen -p tcp -c "/usr/lib/saf/listen" \
-v`nlsadmin - V` -n3
```

Managing *listen* Port Monitors

To check on the availability of `listen` port monitors, enter

```
#sacadm -l -t listen
```

As a result, you see a listing of all `listen` port monitors currently controlled by `sac` on your system. The listing looks like the following:

```
PMTAG    PMTYPE    FLGS    RCNT    STATUS     COMMAND
tcp       listen     -      3      ENABLED    /usr/lib/saf/listen -m inet/tcp0 tcp
```

For a review of the interpretation of the preceding listing, refer to the "Checking the Status of the Port Monitor" section.

In order to enable, disable, or remove a port monitor, enter `sacadm` with `-e`, `-d`, or `-r` respectively, as described earlier in this chapter.

Creating a *listen* Port Service

To create a `listen` port service, use the `pmadm` command. The syntax follows.

```
#pmadm -a -p<pmtag> -s<svctag> [-i id] -v 'nlsadmin -V' \
 -m"'nlsadmin options'" -y"comment"
```

The following command adds a new port service to a port monitor with `pmtag tcp`:

```
#pmadm -a -p tcp -s lpd -i root -v 'nlsadmin -V'\
 -m"'nlsadmin -o /var/spool/lp/fifos/listenBSD -A \
\x000202036400000200000000000000000'"
```

The preceding command demonstrates the use of the port address discussed earlier. The port address described in the preceding example configures the port to accept printing requests sent by BSD clients across the network.

Managing Port Services

To check on the status of a port service, enter

```
#pmadm -p<pmtag> -s<svctag> -l
```

To enable it, enter

```
#pmadm -p<pmtag> -s<svctag> -e
```

whereas to disable it, enter

```
#pmadm -p<pmtag> -s<svctag> -d
```

and to remove it, enter

```
#pmadm -p<pmtag> -s<svctag> -r
```

Connecting Terminals and Modems

UNIX has very powerful built-in serial communications capabilities. Administrators can make use of them in order to offer local terminal connection services, as well as across-the-telephone wire services. Services across the wire include remote terminal login, file transfer capabilities, and electronic mail exchange. Those services are provided by utilities such as uucp and cu, which are part of the Basic Networking Utilities (BNU) that comes with your UNIX operating system. A full treatment of UUCP utilities is provided in Chapter 43.

In this section, the concepts and steps to set up for both modem and terminal connections are presented. A properly wired and configured serial interface is a basic requirement that is common to both types of services. Once this requirement is fulfilled, you can proceed to implementing the necessary additional steps to take care of modem and terminal connections.

Making the Connection

To make the serial connection, prepare for the physical connection, determine the availability of associated resources, and create the port service.

Preparing for the Physical Connection

In this step, you are primarily involved in readying the cable that will connect the modem, or the user's terminal to the UNIX system. RS232C/D is the standard interface that most hardware platforms use to connect devices. So that you can understand the how and why of different cable arrangements, a brief examination of the standard is provided.

RS232D/C defines the interface between so-called data circuit-terminating equipment (DTE) and data circuit communication equipment (DCE). In practical terms, and for the purposes of this section, this means that it defines the physical interface between a computer (the DTE) and the modem (the DCE). The interface defines four aspects of the physical layer. These are electrical, mechanical, functional, and procedural.

The electrical specification defines how data is electrically represented on the wire. Because computer data is binary in its raw form, the specification describes what voltage level represents which logical level.

The mechanical specification describes the mechanics of the connection, including the connector type and the number of pins supported. A DB-25 connector is specified for the RS232C/D interface. The industry introduced another de facto standard, however. This is the DB-9 connector most commonly found on PC workstations.

The functional specification defines the pinout of the connector (that is, what each pin stands for).

The procedural specification defines the handshake mechanism that should precede, accompany, and terminate the exchange of data between the DTE and DCE.

Figure 40.4 shows the wiring diagram and corresponding pin definition of the DB25-to-DB25 cable, which is normally used to connect a DTE to a DCE. Figure 40.5 shows the wiring diagram of a DB9-to-DB25 cable. Following is a description of the most commonly used circuits. Because pin definitions are not the same for both types of connectors, the description refers to the circuit name rather than the pin number.

SG provides the common return path for both the transmit (TD) and receive (RD) circuits.

DTR and DSR are asserted by both the computer and modem, respectively, to indicate readiness to exchange data. Both circuits must be asserted before any other activity can occur across the interface. At this point, the computer may attempt to dial another computer by passing the dialing command string to the modem.

FIGURE 40.4.

Wiring diagram and corresponding pin definition of a DB25-to-DB25 RS232C/D straight-through cable.

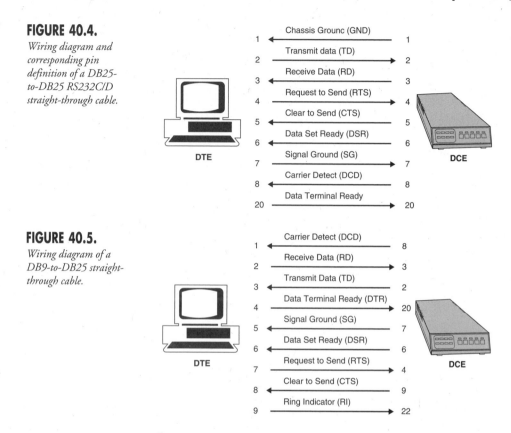

FIGURE 40.5.

Wiring diagram of a DB9-to-DB25 straight-through cable.

DCD is asserted by the modem if it successfully connects at the remote end. It is interpreted by the computer as an indication of a successful connection. This circuit has to remain asserted for the duration of the call.

TD and RD are the transmit and receive circuits, respectively.

Any time the computer wants to transmit it asserts the RTS circuit and waits for permission to do so from the modem, by virtue of asserting the CTS circuit. This usage of the RTS/CTS circuit pair applies to the half-duplex mode of communications. In full-duplex communications, RTS and CTS circuits are used to control the flow of data between the DTE and the DCE devices. The DTE drops its RTS circuit in order to request the DCE to stop sending data on DTE's receive circuit. Likewise, the CTS is dropped by the DCE in order to request the DTE to stop sending data on the transmit circuit.

CAUTION: In cases in which one end of the cable is a DB-25 connector, whereas the opposite end is a DB-9, the cable must be wired as shown in Figure 40.6.

Connecting a computer directly to a terminal (that is, a DTE-to-DTE type of connection) is a tricky business, but easy to understand. Because RS232C/D defines the interface strictly between a DTE and DCE, many vendors and users have developed variations on a cabling trick that allows DTE-to-DTE connection. This trick is called the null modem cable. The underlying idea is to convince both ends of the connection that they are indeed talking to modems directly connected to them. Figure 40.6 shows two diagrams depicting the same cabling trick corresponding to different combinations of connectors.

FIGURE 40.6.

Null modem wiring arrangements corresponding to different combinations of connectors.

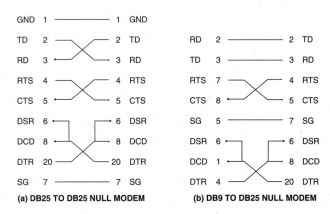

(a) DB25 TO DB25 NULL MODEM   (b) DB9 TO DB25 NULL MODEM

When the interface pinout was described, it was done from the DTE perspective. This means that if you look at the interface from the DCE perspective, some pins bear quite the opposite significance. For example, DTEs send and receive pins are DCEs receive and send, respectively. It is not, therefore, hard to imagine what would happen if you were to attempt connecting two DTEs using a direct cable. Data emerging from both devices on directly connected transmit circuits would be endlessly colliding, while they are hopelessly waiting for an impulse to occur on the wire connecting their receiving circuits. To remedy this situation, the send and receive circuits are cross-wired. Also, recall that whenever the computer asserts its RTS circuit, it is asking for clearance to transmit. This clearance is indicated by having the CTS asserted (normally by the modem), which explains why this circuit pair is also cross-wired. Finally, note how DSR, DTR, and DCD are wired. When DTR is asserted by any DTE, the other one detects a DCD and DSR, which are interpreted as both modem-ready and connection-established indicators, just as though they were sent by the receiving DTE's local modem. If the DTE is prepared to engage in data communications, it asserts its DTR and both sides can now talk to each other.

There are variations on the theme of the null modem. Although the preceding variation caters to the most general cases, it is advisable that you check with your vendor to determine your exact cabling needs.

Determine the Availability of Resources

Before you can proceed to creating the port service, there are two resources that you need to check: 1) availability of tty ports, and 2) availability of a suitable record in the /etc/ttydefs file.

To obtain a list of all tty ports that are currently in use, enter the command pmadm -1 -t ttymon. The listing will look like the following:

```
PMTAG      PMTYPE    SVCTAG    FLGS    ID      <PMSPECIFIC>
ttymon3    ttymon    00s       ux      root    /dev/term/00 ...
ttymon3    ttymon    11s       -       uucp    /dev/term/11 ...
```

The device special filenames under the <PMSPECIFIC> column indicate which ttys to avoid in your subsequent steps. Depending on availability of extra free tty ports, choose the one you want.

Next, list the contents of the /etc/ttydefs file by entering the command sttydefs -1, and examine its contents for the record and label that match your terminal needs. If you do not find one, then you ought to add the desired entry to the database yourself, by using the sttydefs command. For this, you are referred back to the "Special Device Files and the Terminal Line Setting Database" section.

Creating the Port Service

Now that you have all the pieces (that is, the cable, the tty port, and the label of the record in /etc/ttydefs file), you can proceed with putting them together to create the port service. To do so, you ought to use pmadm with the -a option. The example that follows demonstrates the use of pmadm to create a bidirectional port service, with *svctag* 04s, which invokes the service login, restarts the port three times upon failure, and prompts the terminal with a friendly message. Also note the use of ttyadm in command substitution mode in order to pass some of the arguments to pmadm.

```
#pmadm -a -pttyserv -s04s -i root -v 'ttyadm -V' \
-m "`ttyadm -b -r3 -p"Welcome Home! LOGIN:" -d/dev/term/04 \
-l 9600 -s /usr/bin/login'"
```

Use pmadm -1 to check on the state of the service. If the new service is not enabled, use pmadm -p<pmtag> -s<svctag> -e to do so.

Connecting the Modem

As noted earlier, you connect a modem to the serial port (for example, COM2) using a straight-through cable. To configure the modem properly, you must read the documentation supplied with it. The things you ought to pay attention to are the DIP switch settings and the AT commands that are necessary for proper modem initialization and dialing. Because the majority of modems today are Hayes compatible, the list in Table 40.2 can act as the configuration guidelines that apply to them.

Hayes modems have an 8-bit DIP switch. Table 40.2 summarizes the meanings associated with each bit switch position.

Table 40.2. Hayes modem switch settings; the * denotes the default setting of each switch.

Switch	Position	Function
1	Up	If the computer asserts its DTR low, the modem reacts by hanging up the line.
	Down*	Forces the DTR permanently high, which means the modem will no longer have to worry about this signal.
2	Up*	Forces the modem to respond to modem dialing and initialization commands in English.
	Down	Forces the modem to respond using numerical messages.
3	Up	Suppresses result codes, thus overriding switch 2.
	Down*	Enables result codes.
4	Up*	AT commands are echoes as they are entered.
	Down	AT commands are not echoed.
5	Up*	Modem answers the phone.
	Down	Modem does not answer the phone.
6	Up	CD is asserted when a carrier is detected; this allows the computer to know when a call is received.
	Down*	CD and DSR are forced permanently high.
7	Up*	Modem is attached to single-line phone.
	Down	Modem is attached to multiline phone.
8	Up	Disables the modem from recognizing and executing modem commands.
	Down*	Modem's intelligence is enabled; modem recognizes and executes modem commands.

On ports configured for dial-in, UNIX responds to asserted DSR and CD by writing a login prompt to the modem. This, therefore, requires turning off echoing as well as result codes on the modem. Failing to do so leads the login process into interpreting locally echoed login prompt characters as a sequence of responses, which leads into a vicious cycle of login denials and subsequent reattempts. To turn local echo and result codes off, set switch positions 3, 4, and 6 to up, down, and up, respectively.

What if you do not have switches on your modem? You can use the AT modem control command set instead! AT commands let you configure the modem to initialize and manage a connection in ways deemed suitable to your applications. Table 40.3 lists some of the AT commands commonly supported by Hayes compatible modems. For a complete command list, consult your modem's manuals.

Table 40.3. Partial list of some of the most commonly supported AT commands.

Command	Significance
AT&F	Reset modem to factory settings
ATDP	Dial using **P**ulse tone
ATDT	Dial using **T**ouch tone
ATE0	Enable local echoing of commands
ATE1	Disable local echoing of commands
ATQ0	Enable result codes
ATQ1	Disable result codes (that is, known as the quiet mode)
AT&W	Write settings to nonvolatile memory

To issue AT commands, you need to have some sort of direct access to the modem. The following steps show you how you can do it using the cu command (more on cu in Chapter 43).

After you login to UNIX, switch user, using the su command, to uucp:

```
#su uucp
password:
$
```

Edit the /etc/uucp/Devices file (see Chapter 43 for more details) to include the following entry:

```
Direct term/##    -    <speed> direct
```

where ## corresponds to the tty port number, and <speed> refers to the speed to which you want to initialize the modem. If, for example, you have a 2400 bps Hayes-compatible modem connected to COM2, the entry would look like this:

```
Direct     term/01    -    2400 direct
```

I am assuming here that there is no other reference to term/01. If there is one, disable the entry by inserting the # sign at the beginning of the line. Make sure to save the file before quitting.

At the command line, enter

```
#cu -l term/##
```

This command directly connects you to the modem and is confirmed by displaying the message "Connected" on your screen. Table 40.4 is an illustration of a sequence pertaining to a sample modem session, during which the modem is configured for proper dial-in support.

Table 40.4. An illustrated modem configuration session along with supporting explanation.

Command/Response	Explanation
`#cu -l term/01`	A command: I want to talk to the modem.
`Connected`	A response: Go ahead.
`AT`	A command: Do I have your attention?
`OK`	A response: Yes you do!
`AT&F`	A command: Reset to factory settings.
`OK`	A response: Done!
`AT&C1`	A command: Use CD to indicate carrier detection.
`OK`	A response: Done!
`AT&D2`	A command: Drop the connection when DTR drops.
`OK`	A response: Done!
`ATE0Q1`	A command: Disable local echo, and keep quiet (that is, disable result codes).
`OK`	A response: Done!
`AT&W`	A command: Save settings into nonvolatile RAM.
`OK`	A response: Done!
`~.`	A command to shell out to UNIX requesting disconnection, and going back to the UNIX shell.
`Disconnected`	A response: Granted!
`#`	

Note in particular the use of the ~. character sequence to disconnect from the modem and go back to the shell. In fact, ~ allows you to issue UNIX commands without having to quit the direct modem session.

For dial-out, it is more convenient to enable local echo and result codes. In any case, it is imperative that you carefully read and follow the modem's manual for proper operation.

Here is a checklist to which you may refer whenever you install, or troubleshoot, a modem.

1. Ensure that your modem is not conflicting with any other device over the chosen serial port. Conflicts normally arise when an internal modem is installed and configured to either COM1 or COM2.

2. Make sure that you have the proper RS232C/D cable. Consult your modem documentation, and follow its recommendations religiously.

3. If you intend to use the modem for dial-out, change the ownership of the tty port over to uucp (see Chapter 43 for more on this).

4. Set the modem DIP switches according to what has been discussed already. This is especially critical if the intended use of the modem is for dial-out.

5. For dial-in, check and make sure that a port monitor and a properly associated port service are created to take care of incoming service requests.

6. Verify and add entries to UUCP files as deemed necessary. In particular, to be able to configure the modem using cu, you should have the following entry in the /etc/uucp/Devices file:

```
Direct term/## - <speed>    direct
```

7. Using cu, establish a direct session with the modem and issue the AT commands to configure the modem properly. To establish the session, enter

```
#cu -l term/##
```

If the system fails to connect, use the -d option with cu. This option prompts cu to report the progress of the dial-out process. Depending on the nature of what is displayed on the screen, refer to the appropriate documentation for help.

8. While in session with the modem, you should be able to dial out by entering

```
ATDT <phone_number>
```

Remember to exit just enter the ~. character sequence.

9. If the modem is intended for dial-out use, test it by dialing into it. If it fails to respond properly, try the following troubleshooting tips: Verify that the modem is set to Autoanswer mode. Verify that echo is turned off. Verify that result codes are disabled (that is, the modem is set for quiet mode). Make sure that you always write modem settings to the modem's nonvolatile memory using the AT&W command.

Connecting Terminals

Many of the preparatory steps that are required to connect terminals have already been described in the last two sections. To summarize, these steps are as follows:

Depending on whether the terminal is connected directly or remotely to the system, you have to prepare either a cross-wired RS232C/D cable or a straight-through cable.

In the case of remote connection, you ought to configure the modem connecting to the UNIX system for dial-in in the manner depicted in the "Connecting the Modem" section.

A port service should have been created, which, upon detection of a service request (by virtue of having both DSR and CD asserted), will write a login prompt to the port and transfer port control to the login process itself. This is achieved by entering the following `pmadm` command:

```
#pmadm -a -p<pmtag> -s<svctag> -i root -v'ttyadm -V' \
-m"'ttyadm -b -rn -p"login prompt message" -d/dev/term/## \
-l<label> -s /usr/bin/login'"
```

The use of the `pmadm` command to create port services was described earlier in this section.

One more step, which will be discussed now, is to set the shell environment for proper support to the user's terminal.

UNIX is designed to shield programs from concerns pertaining to the physical terminal specifics. Instead of talking directly to the terminal, programs interface with a virtual terminal by making calls to a standard library of screen routines. Those calls invoke, on behalf of programs, the desired behavior on the physical screen.

In doing so, two advantages are derived: Developers are relieved of the laborious and needless (if not impossible) task of writing and maintaining programs in a way that keeps them compatible with all kinds of terminal types, those existing now and those that will emerge in the future. Also, users continue to benefit, without any modifications or the associated cost of upgrades, from programs deployed on their UNIX platforms irrespective of changes that may be introduced to their terminal types in the future.

Proper support to the actual terminal is conditional upon setting the environment variable TERM to the correct type. This is normally done from the user's login script. The user may as well set it by entering:

```
$TERM=<terminal_type>
$export TERM
```

An example of terminal type would be vt220.

UNIX uses the value assigned to TERM to reference a binary file, which exclusively defines that terminal's capabilities. The file is named after the terminal type (for example, if the terminal is vt220, then the file must have been named vt220) and is part of a large terminal information database maintained in the /usr/lib/terminfo directory.

If you list the contents of the /usr/lib/terminfo directory, you obtain a listing similar to the following:

```
#ls /usr/lib/terminfo
1 3 5 7 9 B H P V b d f h j l n p r t v x z
2 4 6 8 A C M S a c e g i k m o q s u w y
```

Each letter or numeric is the directory name where terminal capabilities definition files, pertaining to types starting with that letter or numeric, are saved. For example, if TERM is set to vt220, UNIX fetches the file /usr/lib/terminfo/v/vt220 for the terminal information capabilities (also referred to as terminfo entry).

> **NOTE:** TERMCAP is another shell environment variable that should be set to the name of the directory where the database is maintained.

After having gone through all of the steps required to connect the terminal, you should proceed to connect it, bring it up, and attempt login. It would be a good idea to try a direct connection first, if the terminal is intended for modem access. In any case, if you fail to get the login prompt and fail to login, you may have to carry the following checks:

Make sure that the port service is configured properly, and that it is enabled. Use pmadm to do that.

Check the cable to verify that it is the correct one. Do not rely only on the wiring diagram provided in this chapter; you are better off relying on your terminal and/or your modem vendor's documentation.

Verify that the modem is configured to Autoanswer.

Check the modem lights, and verify that the sequence of events depicted by the flashing lights conforms to what you expect to see. In particular, check DSR and CD during the connection establishment phase because, unless they are both asserted, the login prompt won't be written to the tty port. Check the modem's hard and soft settings to address any observed anomalies.

Make sure that the speed, parity, and number of stop bits match on both the terminal and the UNIX system.

Connecting Printers

Printing services in UNIX are supported by the LP spooler. The LP spooler offers administrators comprehensive capabilities that allow them to address varied scenarios in order to meet different user needs and requirements. To name a few, print services can be physically set up to allow users to print on printers connected to the host they are logged in to or, alternatively, to printers connected to other hosts on the network. LP printing service includes a library of filters from which administrators can choose to support their user needs. By implementing them, users' print jobs will be processed, making them more "compatible" with the target printer. Administrators are provided with management capabilities allowing them to use global management as well as selective management of print services. Because this chapter is about "Device Administration," the objectives of this section will be limited to include the following topics:

- A conceptual overview of the LP printing service
- Local printing services setup
- Network print servers setup
- Printer management
- Print user management

How Does the LP Printing Service Work?

Print services are invoked by `init` upon start-up when the system enters the multiuser state run level 2. The services are brought up by the `/etc/rc2.d/S80lp` script and are killed whenever the system is shut down by `/etc/rc2.d/K20lp` script.

When users address printers to handle their print jobs, the files they send for printing are not handled immediately by the printers. Instead, the files are queued in directories, by a process known as the spooler, for subsequent handling by a printing daemon known as `lpsched` (an acronym and program name for the lp scheduler daemon). To understand how this works, imagine yourself as part of a community of users sharing one or two printers, among other UNIX resources. Ask yourself what would happen should you be able to address the printer directly for a print request while someone else is doing exactly the same thing. You are right! The output will be more of a character soup than presentable piece of work. This is due to the fact that the printer will be handling characters as they arrive, thus mixing the ones that belong to your file with those belonging to other users.

To alleviate this problem, the spooler takes over as you send print jobs to printers. It simply stops them on their way to their destination and diverts them to a waiting area on your system disk. This area is a subdirectory known as the print queue. Files destined for the same printer are queued in the same directory until the printer becomes available. The aforementioned process is known as spooling. You may be wondering whether this means that the terminal will be tied up for as long as it takes for the print job to materialize. The answer is no. This is because once a print job is queued, another background process known as the printing scheduler daemon (lpsched) takes over and supervises the ongoing printing services, making sure that every request, including yours, is honored.

In addition to the basic service, LP printing services allow administrators to aggregate printers of similar type into a printer class. This provides for the optimal utilization of printing resources, as users target a class of printers instead of targeting a specific one. When this happens, lpsched sends the print job to the first printer to become available in the requested class. Other printing services include tasks pertaining to starting interface programs that are suitable to the printer, applying the filters to user files whenever necessary, notifying users, if desired, of the status of printing jobs, and, in the case of network printing, the LP printing service has the additional job of sending print jobs to the hosts to which requested printers are connected.

Setting Up Local Printing Services

In this section, the setup and configuration of local printing services are presented. Local printing services provide users with the capability to print to printers connected directly to the host they are logged in to. The following are the required steps to set up printers, irrespective of whether they are parallel, serial, or network printers.

1. Verify availability of resources.
2. Use lpadmin to create the printer.
3. Change ownership and permissions to device special file.
4. If this is your first printer, make it the default printer.
5. Release the printer to the user community.

The resources for which you want to check are lp login id, lpsched, and an available port (serial or parallel). The lp login id is normally created during initial system installation. If the lp account does not exist in the /etc/passwd directory, then you ought to create one. It will be required at a later step in the setup process. Second, verify that lpsched is running by checking the output of the command

```
#ps -ef ¦ grep "lpsched"
```

If not enabled, you may do so by entering the following command:

```
#/usr/lib/lp/lpsched
```

The next step is to create a print destination by using the lpadmin command. The syntax of lpadmin follows.

```
/usr/lib/lpadmin -p<name> -v<pathname> -m<interface> \
[-h¦l] - c<class>
```

In wjocj

-p<*name*> is the name you want to assign to the printer. It can be anything you like. It is more convenient, however, to assign it a name that makes sense to the user community.

-v<*pathname*> is the special device file *pathname*. Depending on whether the printer is parallel or serial, the *pathname* is /dev/lp# or /dev/term/##, respectively (# and ## represent decimal digits represetative of the parallel and serial ports on your system).

-m<*interface*> is a program that is invoked by lp as it sends print jobs to the printer port. <*interface*> is responsible for printer port and physical printer initialization, and performs functions pertaining to printing a banner if desired, producing the right number of copies, and setting the page length and width. You have the freedom to write and use your own interface programs (in which case you must specify its name using the -i<*interface*> option). If you do not specify one, the standard and generic interface supplied with the system will be used by default. When installing the printer for the first time, it is advisable to start with the standard interface. If all goes well, you can always change over to the interface of your choice. Printer interfaces are usually maintained in the /usr/lib/lp/model directory.

[-h¦l]: h indicates that the printer is hardwired, whereas l indicates that the device associated with the printer is a login terminal. h and l are mutually exclusive. In the event that none is specified, h is assumed.

-c<*class*> specifies the class to which the printer belongs. Users will subsequently be able to specify the class using lp with -d option.

Assuming that you want to create a printer destination for a parallel printer that is to be connected to your parallel port, the lpadmin command would look like this:

```
#lpadmin -d dotmatrix -v /dev/lp1 -m standard
#lpadmin
```

Because the printer port device special file can be written to directly, as with any other file, you ought to make sure that users have no direct access to it. This involves changing the port ownership to login lp, as well as changing the file permissions to 600. The following two commands demonstrate how to do this to /dev/lp1.

```
#chown lp  /dev/lp1
#chmod 600 /dev/lp1
```

Before you release the printer to the user community, you may want to make it the default destination. A user failing to specify the printer destination when using the lp command will have his or her print job sent to the default printer. To make a printer the default destination, enter the following command:

```
#lpadmin -d <printer_name>
```

The `lpadmin` command to make dot matrix the default printer therefore becomes

```
#lpadmin -d dotmatrix
```

Finally, to make the printer accessible to users, you must allow the printer destination to accept print jobs as well as logically turn on the printer. To allow printer dotmatrix to accept print jobs, enter

```
#accept dotmatrix
```

and to logically turn it on (that is, allow it to do the printing), enter

```
#enable dotmatrix
```

Setting Up Network Print Servers

Sometimes in a multisystem, multiplatform environment users find themselves in need of printers that are attached to a different system than what they are currently logged in to. Figure 40.7 depicts a scenario whereby the user wants his or her print job sent to printer odie, attached to system engg, while logged in to system arts.

FIGURE 40.7.

Concept of print servers illustrated.

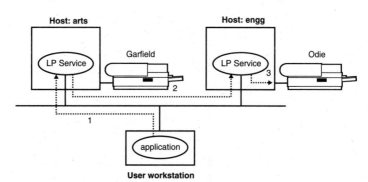

To provide this level of service, UNIX comes with enough support that, if implemented properly, allows users to print to any printer on the network. While doing so, users do not even have to be concerned with any additional detail on how to address those printers than they already know about addressing their own. Figure 40.8 demonstrates the governing principles of network print services. In the depicted scenario, system engg becomes the so-called print server, whereas system arts is the client. The setup procedure calls on having print destinations (that is, queues) created on both systems (say, odie and garfield on engg and arts, respectively). Whereas odie is associated with the printer attached to engg, garfield has to be logically associated with odie (not with any printer that may happen to be attached to system arts). A user logged in to arts has to address the local printer destination—in this case garfield—to be able to print to odie as shown. The lp print request then becomes

```
#lp -p garfield <file_name>
```

In doing so, the user is in fact addressing the local LP print service running on system arts. Next, LP on system arts checks the actual resource with which printer destination garfield is associated, to find that it actually maps to a print service resource (odie) supported on system engg. As a consequence, LP on system arts routes the request, along with the print job, to engg for subsequent handling.

The steps involved in setting up the service are not as complex as they may sound. For the most part, they are similar to those listed in the previous section with some subtle variations. Because this level of service involves both the client and server systems, both of them need to be configured.

Configuring the Print Server

Print server configuration requires two additional steps to those listed and described in the section on local printing. The two steps are creating a listen port service and registering client systems with the print service.

Because the print service under description is a network service (that is, runs on a connection-oriented transport service), then there is a requirement to create a listen port service with which it associates. Before doing that, however, it might be worth your while to check on readily available ones. When UNIX is first installed, your system is automatically configured to support a listen port monitor with port monitor tag tcp. Also, tcp is configured to support two print server-associated port services, with one taking care of System V clients whereas the other one takes care of BSD clients. To verify their existence, enter

```
#pmadm -l -t listen
PMTAG           PMTYPE          SVCTAG          FLGS ID         <PMSPECIFIC>
.
.
.
tcp             listen          0                           x       root
\x02000ACE64000001 -
 c - /usr/lib/saf/nlps_server #NLPS SERVER
tcp             listen          lp                       -       root    - - -
- /var/spool/lp
/fifos/listenS5 #NLPS SERVER
.
.
```

If the listing you get on your screen includes the two entries shown in the preceding partial listing, you do not need to create the port services and you may skip the next step. If they do not exist, then use pmadm to create them. To create a port service to listen to print requests sent by System V clients, enter

```
#pmadm -a -p<pmtag> -s lp -i root -v 'nlsadmin -V' \
-m 'nlsadmin -o /var/spool/lp/fifos/listenS5'
```

where `pmtag` is the name assigned to the port monitor. To create a port service to respond to BSD clients, however, you must enter `lpsystem -A`. The output displays the port address that you ought to use as an argument with `nlsadmin` upon using `pmadm` to create the port service. Following is an example output of `lpsystem -A`, as it appears on my monitor:

```
#lpsystem -A
020002036400000100000000000000000
```

Next, to create the port service under `tcp` port monitor, enter the following command:

```
#pmadm -a -p tcp -s lpd -i root -v 'nlsadmin -V' \
-m'nlsadmin -o /var/spool/lp/fifos/listenBSD \
-A'\x020002036400000100000000000000000''
```

To force the port monitor to recognize the changes you made, use the command

```
#sacadm -x -p tcp
```

The next step is to register the client with the server, using the `lpsystem` command. In addition to registering the client, `lpsystem` allows you to define the communications parameters that you want to enforce on the connection maintained between both the server and the client after it is invoked. Defined parameters are saved in the `/etc/lp/Systems` file. Though you can edit it directly using `vi`, it is recommended that you avoid doing that. The syntax of the `lpsystem` command is

```
lpsystem [-t<type>] [-T<timeout>] [-R <retry>] \
[-y"comment"] systemname
```

in which

> `-t<type>` specifies whether the client is System V or BSD.
>
> `-T<timeout>` specifies the idle time after which the connection should be terminated. The `<timeout>` can be n, 0, and N, where N is the number of minutes the connection idles before the connection is dropped. If 0 is specified, the connection will be dropped as soon as it idles, whereas n means never time-out. Depending on your environment, you should configure the connection to the one that suits you best. If users occasionally print across the network, you may be better off with the 0 option. This frees up the resources reserved on both systems to service the request as soon as it is honored. If, on the other hand, the frequency of service utilization is high, you may consider configuring the connection to n (never time-out). This way, you save both systems the repeated tasks of establishing, maintaining, and relinquishing the connection every time they ought to respond to a print service request. Added to the saving in CPU utilization on both systems is the saving on bandwidth utilization due to packet exchange pertaining to link establishment and disconnection.

-R*<retry>* specifies in minutes the duration of time to wait before link reestablishment is attempted, when it was abnormally disrupted.

-y*"comment"* can be any convenient comment.

systemname specifies the remote system's name to which the communications parameters apply.

Applying the preceding to the example in Figure 40.8, in order to register arts with the print server host engg, you should enter

```
#lpsystem -t s5 -T n arts
```

Configuring the Client

As in the case of server setup, here too you ought to make sure that you have a port monitor that is properly configured to support network printing services. To do that, enter

```
#pmadm -l -p tcp
```

The output should include the following three entries (the first two pertaining to System V support, whereas the third one pertains to BSD client support):

```
PMTAG  PMTYPE  SVCTAG FLGS  ID  <PMSPECIFIC>
tcp    listen  0      -     root \x00200ACE64000001 -c -
/usr/lib/sac/nlps_server #NLPS SERVER

tcp    listen  lp     -     root ....

tcp    listen  lpd    -     root \x0020020364000001 -c -
/var/spool/lp/fifos/listenBSD
```

If any of the preceding entries is missing, then you must create the associated port services yourself using pmadm. Depending on what is missing, use one or more of the following commands:

```
#pmadm -a -p tcp -s lp -i root -v'nlsadmin -V' \
-m 'nlsadmin -o /var/spool/lp/fifos/listen5'

#pmadm -a -p tcp -s 0 -i root -v 'nlsadmin -V' \
-m 'nlsadmin -o /usr/lib/saf/nlps_server \
-A "\x02000ACE6400000010000000000000000"` -y "NLPS SERVER"

#pmadm -a -p tcp -s lpd -i root -v 'nlsadmin -V' \
-m 'nlsadmin -o /var/spool/lp/fifos/listenBSD \
-A "\x002020364000000010000000000000000"`
```

The last pmadm command would be required only if you are setting up for BSD support as well.

Next, register the remote server with the client using the lpsystem command, as discussed in the preceding section.

Now, you have only to create the printer destination; instead of associating it with any particular port, you will associate it with the printer destination that you created on the print server host. To do that, enter the following command

```
#lpadmin -p<client_printer> \
-s<remote_printer>!<print_server_host>
```

in which

client_printer specifies the printer destination undergoing creation on the local machine.

remote_printer specifies the print server's printer destination, with which the *client_printer* is associated.

print_server_host specifies the host name of the system where the **remote_printer** destination is.

Applying the preceding to the scenario of Figure 40.7, the following is the command to enter at host arts:

```
#lpadmin -p odie -s garfield!engg
```

The remaining steps, as you should know by now, are to enable the printer and make it accept print jobs. Hence the commands,

```
#enable odie
#accept odie
```

To send a print job down the wire to garfield to print, the user must address odie while logged in to arts. For example, to print file monalisa, the user must enter

```
#lp -p odie monalisa
```

LP print service on host arts will redirect the print job to garfield destination on host engg.

Managing Printers

In addition to the tools required to set up, enable, and disable printers, the LP print service presents the system administrator with a comprehensive set of management tools. Those tools can be applied to change printer configuration, as well to assist in maintenance and troubleshooting situations. The following subsections describe aspects of printing management and associated tools.

Enabling and Disabling LP Print Service

lpsched is the program to start LP print service, whereas lpshut is the program to shut it down. Only login root or lp can start and shut down printing services. All printers that were printing at the time of invoking lpshut will stop printing. Whenever lpsched is restarted, print requests that were disrupted at the time LP service was shut down will print from the very beginning.

Managing Print Requests

lpmove is a command that lets you move print jobs from one printer to another. There are, primarily, two scenarios that may prompt you to do that. In one, you may want to disable printing to a printer in order to disconnect it for routine maintenance or trouble-shooting. Instead of leaving your users in the cold waiting for their print jobs to material-ize, you would move their print jobs to some other printer of equivalent quality. In the second scenario, you may use lpmove for load balancing purposes in case you encounter situations in which one printer is heavily used while another one is sitting idle. The syntax of the lpmove command is

```
#lpmove <requests> <dest>. Or,
```

where *requests* presents lpmove with a list of request id's to move to the printer specified in *dest*. To obtain the print request id's, use the lpstat command. Its output should look like the following:

```
#lpstat
garfield-4 root 112 March 24 06:20
garfield-5 root 567 March 24 06:22
```

where the first column is the print request id and is made of two components: the name of the printer to which the print job was submitted, and the order in which it is received. The second column displays the name of the user who submitted the print job, followed by the date and time of submission columns.

Assuming that acctlp is an idling printer to which you want to move the print job garfield-5, the lpmove command then becomes

```
#lpmove garfield-5 acctlp
```

To move the entire printing load from one printer to another, enter

```
#lpmove <dest1> <dest2>
```

> **NOTE:** Upon moving print requests, request IDs remain intact to allow users to track their print jobs.

> **CAUTION:** lpmove does not check on the acceptance status of print jobs that it moves. It is therefore your responsibility to do the check using the lpstat com-mand, and to take any corrective measure should a print job fail to be moved.

To cancel undesirable print requests, use the `cancel` command. The syntax is

```
#cancel <request-ID>
```

To cancel, for example, `garfield-5`, enter

```
#cancel garfield-ID
```

Printer Configuration Management

Printer configuration management includes tasks such as changing printer class, changing printer port, removing printers, and removing classes. All these tasks can be achieved using the `lpadmin` command.

To change a printer class, enter

```
#lpadmin -p<dest> -c<class>
```

If the specified class does not exist, the class will be created and the specified destination will be inserted into it. To remove the printer from a certain class, enter

```
#lpadmin -p<dest> -r <class>
```

If the printer is the last one of its class, then the class itself will be removed as well.

To change the printer port, enter

```
#lpadmin -p<dest> -v <special_file_pathname>
```

You may need to do this on occasions when you suspect something went wrong with the original port to which the printer was connected. This reconfiguration will allow you to continue offering print services while troubleshooting the defective port.

Finally, to check the configuration of a particular printer, enter

```
#lpstat -p<printer> -l
```

In the example that follows, `lpstat` is entered to check on the configuration of `garfield` destination.

```
#lpstat -pgarfield -l
printer garfield (login terminal) is idle. enabled since Thu Mar 24 18:20:01 EST 1994.
available.
    Form mounted:
    Content types: simple
    Printer types: unknown
    Description:
    Connection: direct
    Interface: /usr/lib/lp/model/standard
    On fault: mail to root once
    After fault: continue
```

```
Users allowed:
    (all)
Forms allowed:
    (none)
Banner required
Character sets:
    (none)
Default pitch:
Default page size:
Default port settings:
```

whereas to check the configuration of all printers, enter

```
#lpstat -l
```

Print Service User Management

User access to LP print service on UNIX systems can be managed and restricted for reasons that may pertain to security or resource allocation and management.

If you carefully examine the sample output of the `lpstat -p garfield -l` command in the last example, you will see the names of the users allowed access in the "Users allowed" entry. According to the preceding example, no one is either on the allowed or the denied lists. This corresponds to the default security configuration and implies that any logged-in user can send print jobs to printer `garfield`. If you do not like that, however, you can use `lpadmin` with the `-u` option to restrict access to the printer. The syntax of the `lpadmin -u` command to list users on the allow list is the following:

```
#lpadmin -p<printer> -u allow:<login-ID-list>
```

To prevent users from accessing the printer, enter

```
#lpadmin -p<printer> -u deny:<login-ID-list>
```

> **NOTE:** `login-ID-list` is a comma- or space-separated list of users' login IDs.

Following is a list of legal arguments that you can include in the `login-ID-list`:

`login-ID`	Denotes a user on the local system
`system_name!login-ID`	Denotes a user on a client system
`system_name!all`	Denotes all users on a client system
`all!login-ID`	Denotes a user on all systems
`all`	Denotes all users on the local system
`all!all`	Denotes all users on all systems

For each printer, the LP print service maintains deny and allow lists. The way they are used is summarized in the following paragraphs.

If the allow list is not empty, only users on that list are allowed access to the printer. If the allow list is empty but deny list is not, then all users except those on the deny list will be allowed access to the printer.

A user cannot exist on both lists simultaneously. When a user is added to either list, the user's login-ID will be checked and removed from the other one.

For example, to allow users Nadeem, Andrea, and May access to the printer `garfield`, you enter

```
#lpadmin -p garfield -u allow:Nadeem Andrea May
```

Next, you should check that this indeed took place by entering the command

```
#lpadmin -p garfield -l
```

```
printer garfield (login terminal) is idle. enabled since Tue Apr 12 05:18:07 EDT 1994.
not available.
    Form mounted:
    Content types: simple
    Printer types: unknown
    Description:
    Connection: direct
    Interface: /usr/lib/lp/model/standard
    On fault: mail to root once
    After fault: continue
    Users allowed:
        nadeem
        andrea
        may
    Forms allowed:
        (none)
    Banner required
    Character sets:
        (none)
    Default pitch:
    Default page size:
    Default port settings:
```

Users educated about the use of the `-q` option with the `lp` command can assign print queue priority levels to print jobs that they submit to the LP service. Although this can sometimes be a useful feature, it may well prove to be a cause of concern to some of the user community as they find that their print jobs are constantly delayed in favor of those belonging to others of equal or less functional status. Fortunately, the LP print service allows you to set limits on how high a priority can be a assigned to print jobs submitted by users. Using the `lpusers` different priority limit assignments can be made to apply to different users. The syntax of `lpusers` is as follows:

```
#lpusers -q<priority_level> -u<login-ID-list>
```

in which

-q<*priority_level*> is an integer ranging between 0 and 39, with 0 representing the highest priority level.

-u<*login-ID-list*> is a comma- or space-separated list of user IDs to whom the restriction applies. The login-ID list argument can have any of the following values:

login-ID	Denotes a user
system_name!login-ID	Denotes a user on a particular system
system_name!all	Denotes all users on a particular system
all	Denotes all users
all!*login-ID*	Denotes a user on all systems

Users submitting print jobs can assign them priorities as high as they are allowed to assign as set with the -q option.

Connecting a PC to UNIX Systems

Rather than purchase terminals, many users prefer to run UNIX sessions right from their desktop DOS-based PCs. This is mainly attributable to the low cost of the PC, its increased processing power, and the additional flexibility of being able to easily toggle back and forth between DOS applications and a UNIX session. This section describes two methods by which you can establish a connection with the UNIX system using the DOS platform. The two methods are as follows:

- Establishing a session via a serial port
- Establishing a session via TCP/IP

Connecting the PC Using COM Ports

Depending on how you are going to do it, configuring a PC to connect to a UNIX host via a COM port is the easier and less costly of the two methods. If both systems belong to the same site, where there is no requirement for a telephone wire to connect both machines, then a cross-wired cable is all the additional hardware you will need along with the COM port that is commonly readily available on your PC. Any communications software with decent terminal emulation capabilities can be used to emulate some the terminals that UNIX recognizes. I used to use Procomm Plus and I was satisfied with it until I decided to go the TCP/IP way for reasons that will be discussed later.

Configuring a PC to serially connect to a UNIX host involves some preparation on both systems. Before making any move, however, you must check on the availability of the following resources:

- On the PC: Verify that you have a free COM port, and that its use of the IRQ interrupt number and I/O port address is not conflicting with any other interface cards on the machine.

- On the UNIX hosts: Verify the availability of a `tty` port and a suitable terminal line setting record in the `/etc/ttydefs` file (refer to the section, "Determine the Availability of Resources," in this chapter).

Additional requirements include two modems and two straight-through cables, if you are configuring a connection over a telephone wire, or a cross-wired cable, as discussed earlier in this chapter, to directly connect the PC to the UNIX system.

Configuring the UNIX system for support to `tty` port services was discussed earlier in this chapter.

Configuring the PC is a very simple matter that basically involves configuring the communication software to the same communication parameters implemented on the UNIX side of the connection. The parameters include baud rate, number of bits per character, parity, and number of stop bits.

Configuring the Modems

The following are general guidelines that you should observe when configuring the modems:

Make sure that the modem you are installing at the UNIX end supports quiet mode. This mode is required in order to stop the modem from sending response codes to the port. Also, echo should be disabled. Failure to observe both of these rules may result in having the UNIX system "believe" that the echoed characters are in partial response to the login prompt it sent to the PC. This may lead to an endless sequence of login and password prompts, and so on.

Should you run into the problem of having user sessions unexpectedly suspending, try to re-create the problem. If, upon sending manually an XON (press Ctrl+Q), character communications resume, then you may need to disable XON/OFF flow control to rely only on RTS/CTS.

Set the modem connected to the UNIX system to autoanswer mode.

Connecting to UNIX via TCP/IP

TCP/IP is another way by which you can connect PCs in your environment to the UNIX system. This solution, however, is a bit more expensive than using COM ports. This is due to the investment in the network interface card (NIC) and the necessary software for implementing the TCP/IP suite of protocols in addition to the cabling cost incurred per workstation. Given the advantages of this solution, and depending on the intended use of the connection, you may find it worth the money and effort to take this route. Using TCP/IP, you will not only be able to establish a `telnet` session with the host, but you also will be able to use `ftp` for file transfers between the PC and UNIX, and `rsh` to remotely execute a UNIX command without having to necessarily log in to the system. Also, if you are using something like Novell's Lan Workplace for DOS version 4.1, you will be able to invoke multiple UNIX and Microsoft Windows applications simultaneously. You also will be able to cut and paste (to your heart's desire) between applications.

As in the COM port option, here too you have to set up both ends of the connection properly in order for them to communicate. Refer to Chapter 37 for a discussion on the installation and configuration of TCP/IP on the UNIX side. The discussion will highlight the steps required to install TCP/IP on the PC/DOS machine.

The method that you will be using to install TCP/IP on the PC depends to a large degree on the vendor from whom you purchased the software. You are required, however, to do the following:

1. You need to assign the PC an IP address in conformance with the rules discussed in Chapter 37.

2. Assign the PC a host name.

3. Create a hosts file on the PC. Include in the file the name to address mappings corresponding to all UNIX hosts to which the user has enough access rights. If domain name services are implemented on your site, then you can ignore this step.

4. Beware that some TCP/IP solutions impose a default upper limit on the allowed number of connections that a PC can handle. Check on that and reconfigure if need be to the desired number.

   Depending on whether DNS and/or RARP services are part of your environment, you may need to go farther:

5. Provide the name server's address to the PC.

6. Edit the `ethers` and the `hosts` file on the RARP server.

Depending on the vendor, the TCP/IP software comes with ranging tools to help you troubleshoot and manage your PC on the network. What I found particularly impressive about LAN WorkPlace for DOS V4.1 is the extensive support it provides to the network manager. Among the things you get with this product is an SNMP compliant management console that helps in troubleshooting your TCP/IP installation and configuration. It also lets you target other machines on the network for subsequent management and troubleshooting. For a minimum, any decent implementation of TCP/IP should provide tools such as the `ping` and `netstat` commands. Use these tools in case things fail to work properly. For more on troubleshooting TCP/IP networks, refer to Chapter 37.

Connecting X Terminals

Until X terminals emerged a few years ago, ASCII dumb terminals were almost exclusively the machines that users had at their disposal for accessing UNIX systems. Due to their nature, these terminals fell short of meeting the ever-increasing demands of engineering and scientific applications for graphical output. With X terminals, a new era of computer-to-human interface began. These terminals not only met the craving need of engineering and science applications for graphics, but they also presented UNIX users with a far more superior, and elegant, user interface.

An X terminal is a component of the X Window System technology (hereafter referred to as X, or X11) that was developed at the Massachusetts Institute of Technology, and is currently maintained by a consortium of universities and vendors.

One of X's greatest attributes is that it can be brought up on any platform. Though it was initially implemented in UNIX environments, X is now equally available to other platforms ranging from mainframes to DOS workstations. This platform independence is due to the mechanism and model that were put together to make X work: the X protocol and client/server model. As you will see later on, this has far-reaching implications as to how users will be able to work in multiplatfom/multivendor environments.

To setup X terminals, it is essential that you understand the governing concepts that drive this technology. This section will therefore start with an examination of its various components, including the client/server model that X follows. Some terms will be introduced and defined to make you more familiar with the associated jargon. Setting up X and X servers will be discussed next. The focus of the discussion will preclude the many different kinds of GUI interfaces that are currently available to run on top of X, concentrating more on how to bring the engine (X platform) and its associated gear to life.

The Architecture of X

X's architecture is based on two components: the client/server model and the X protocol.

The Client/Server Model of X

A client server/model follows a mechanism by which an application is split into two components: the so-called *backend* and *frontend*. In the database client/server technology, for example, the frontend runs at the user's workstation and is termed the *client*, whereas the backend runs on a remote host that is shared by all authorized users, and is called the *server*. The database server acts as the main repository of data that clients need. Instead of having an entire file transferred to its machine from the server, the client uses scope-and-filter techniques while requesting only the data relevant to its needs for subsequent processing. From what has just been said, the client/server model components could be expressed as a matter of which is managing access to a resource, versus which is requesting use of the resource. The server component is the access-resource manager, whereas the client component is the one requesting access to and use of the resource.

The application is split into the following components: X client and an X display server.

An X client handles all data processing aspects of an application, except for the I/O interaction, which it delegates to a server process. The server process could be running on the same machine or a terminal located elsewhere in the environment. This implies that, unlike database and other familiar server technologies, the X display server belongs to the user's machine where actual I/O and user interface capabilities are provided. Clients, therefore, become the shared resource that all users can access and run remotely.

The X Protocol

Rather than base the X client/server model on a particular set of software and hardware resources, which could restrict its portability across platforms, X architects chose to base it on a protocol mechanism called X protocol. In doing so, vendors and developers of X applications were insulated from platform-related concerns and specifics. Applications complying with X specifications can be easily ported to any environment, while having X servers mediate the I/O interaction with the physical display units. Having said that, this clearly implies that an X server presents applications with a virtual display unit that they can manage. The display server maps I/O primitives, passed to it by applications to physical actions on the actual display unit.

Another aspect of X protocol worth mentioning is that it builds on some of the most commonly deployed transport protocols, including TCP/IP, IPX/SPX, and DECnet to enable clients and servers to talk to each other. A user on an X terminal, with multiprotocol support, can invoke one session with a mainframe while maintaining another with a UNIX system, and yet another one across a dial-up line.

From what has already been said about X, it can be concluded that X is a network-based graphics engine. It allows users to connect to, and run applications on, remote systems while handling I/O interaction using locally available graphical terminals. Being an engine implies that readily available GUI interfaces are built on top of X, rather than being part of it.

X Resources

Central to X functionality is the concept of resources. A resource is a configurable attribute of an application. Examples of resource attributes are the font the application uses, background color, initial location, and size of an application window.

The fact that the same X client may have to deal with different servers means that it must be supported with a configuration mechanism that is flexible enough to deal with ranging hardware capabilities and user preferences. Examples of hardware differences are monitor color and resolution capabilities. Also, one user's preferred color, font, and window location and size may not agree with someone else's. It can be concluded that X applications cannot be developed with built-in support for any hardware type or for the developer's perception of how the user interface and preferences should look. Users should be allowed to have a choice of hardware and be able to configure an application's output however they feel is best for them.

X provides for this capability using one of two methods: command-line options and resource definition files.

Independent of the method you are using, when an application is invoked, an X display manager will autoload the associated attributes onto your server (more on this later). This provides the I/O capability and interface you have defined.

Setting X Resources with Command-Line Options

In this method, users define resources upon invoking an application using command-line options. Most X applications allow users to define resources using the same command option names. The following are examples of the most commonly used arguments:

Table 40.5. Most common user-definable X resources.

X Resource	Description
`-display <display>`	Specifies the name of the X server, display, and screen to use (that is, to send output to)
`-geometry <specs>`	Specifies the initial size and location of application's window
`-bg <colour>`	Specifies the background color
`-bd <colour>`	Specifies the border color

continues

Table 40.5. continued

X Resource	Description
`-fg <colour>`	Specifies the foreground color
`-fn <font>`	Specifies the font
`-title <title>`	Specifies the window title

For example, say that a user wants to invoke `xterm` (an X terminal emulation client) titled "X Terminal" with a blue background color, gray border, and the window initially located at the upper-left corner of the monitor. The user then has to enter the following command:

```
% xterm -display arts:0 -title "X Terminal" -bg blue -bd grey -g +1+1
```

Given the number of clients that a user may have to invoke simultaneously, this method of loading resources can be tedious and is prone to errors.

Defining Resources Using Resource Definition Files

To alleviate the tedium of defining resources using command-line options, X provides the following two resource definition files: `Xresources` and `$HOME/.Xresources`. Both of these files contain per-application lists of attribute assignments. `Xresources` contains global definitions applying to all X servers, whereas `$HOME/.Xresources` may contain user-specific definitions. Both sets of resources are loaded by the `xrdb` program whenever a connection is established with an X server. Sample `$HOME/.Xresources` file contents are as follows:

```
!xclock resource definitions:
xclock*update:      1
xclock*analog:      false
xclock*chime:       false
xclock*geometry:    -0+0
!xterm resource definitions:

xterm*title:        XTerminal
xterm*background:   grey
xterm*foreground:   black
xterm*geometry:     40x24+1+1
xterm*scrollBar:    true
```

The first set of resources pertains to `xclock`. According to what is shown, the clock is to be updated at the rate of once a second, displayed in digital format, and the chime is disabled. The second set of resources pertains to `xterm`, and that set specifies a window title XTerminal, a yellow background color, black text, scroll bar enabled, and a window size of 40x24 displayed at the upper-left corner of the monitor.

Window Managers

A window manager is an X client that normally is invoked during start-up on an X session, from the user's start-up $HOME/.xsession script file. It can also be invoked on the command line.

Window managers allow users to manage their applications' windows whether moving, resizing, or reducing them to icons.

There are many different flavors of window managers. Tab Window Manager (twm) is the one that comes with MIT's distribution of X. Open Look provides olwm, whereas OSF/Motif provides mwm. In this chapter, reference will be made to twm only.

twm behavior is governed by the system.twmrc configuration file in the /usr/X/lib/twm directory. You can edit this file, changing its default behavior to anything that suits your users' needs.

Because the default configuration is adequate for the purposes of this section (that is, setting up an X terminal), no further details will be provided on how to edit this file.

Setting the Shell Environment Variables

Two shell environment variables need to be taken care of, in order to successfully start an X session. These are PATH and DISPLAY.

PATH should be modified to include the path to X client programs. This can be done in the user's start-up script $HOME/.xsession. The script should include:

```
PATH=$PATH:/usr/X/bin
export PATH
```

DISPLAY X environment variable specifies to the client the name of the host, and display number, to send its output to.

X distinguishes between displays and screens. Figure 40.8 tries to make the distinction clear. In X, a display is a collection of monitors that share a common keyboard and mouse. Shown in Figure 40.8 is an X server that has one display and two monitors. The monitors are referred to as screens and are numbered starting with 0. In Figure 40.12b the X server has one display with one screen.

Hence an appropriate setup of the DISPLAY variable should take care of both the display and monitor to which the output is sent. The DISPLAY variable can be specified using the following format:

```
display=[iphost¦ipaddress]:displaynumber.screennumber
```

in which

[*iphost|ipaddress*]	Specifies the X server host name or its IP address.
displaynumber	This is the display number, normally 0 because most workstations have only one display.
screennumber	Designates the monitor to which the output should be sent. If not specified, screen number 0 will be assumed.

FIGURE 40.8.

X displays and screens.

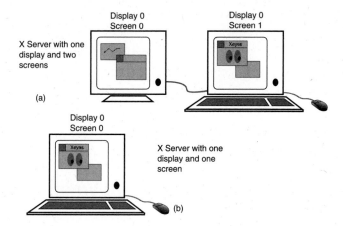

DISPLAY can be set in the user's login script. It can also be set manually as a command-line argument, using the -display option, when a client is being invoked:

```
% xterm -display arts:0
```

The X Display Manager

The X Display Manager (xdm) is the preferred way of starting up an X session. xinit is another option. This discussion is restricted to xdm only.

In SVR4, xdm is started as a daemon when the system is booted. It is invoked by one of the /etc/rc2.d scripts. On my system the startup script is S69xdm.

Once invoked, xdm provides users with a graphical login window where they must enter their user IDs and passwords. Once authenticated and logged in, xdm automatically loads resources to X servers and starts X clients as specified in the user's $HOME/.xsession startup script.

xdm is a customizable X client. Its behavior depends to a large degree on what is in its configuration files. All xdm configuration files are in the /usr/X/lib/xdm directory. They are as follows:

```
*xdm-config
*Xresources
*Xsession
*Xservers
*Xaccess
*Xsetup_0
*GiveConsole
*TakeConsole
```

Some of these files pertain to different versions of X. In the following subsections, the purpose of each file is described in the context of starting X server sessions. User-specific files (that is, $HOME/.xsession, $HOME/.Xresources, and $HOME/.xsession-errors) are described as well.

xdm-config

xdm-config is the first file that is read by xdm when spawned. This file primarily defines where the rest of the configuration files listed previously belong. Following is an example of the its contents:

```
DisplayManager*session:        /usr/X/lib/xdm/Xsession
DisplayManager*resources:             /usr/X/lib/xdm/Xresources
DisplayManager.errorLogFile:          /dev/X/xdm-errors
DisplayManager.pidFile:        /dev/X/xdm-pid
DisplayManager.keyFile:        /usr/X/lib/xdm/xdm-keys
DisplayManager.servers:        /usr/X/lib/xdm/Xservers
DisplayManager._0. authorize:    true
DisplayManager._0.setup:             /usr/X/lib/xdm/Xsetup_0
DisplayManager*authComplain:    false
```

It can be seen that the preceding xdm-config file contains some self-customizing resource definitions.

Xservers and Xaccess

There are two methods by which xdm knows which X servers to connect to. One method pertaining to release 3 of X (also referred to as X11R3) relies on the Xservers file. In Xservers, the administrator has to maintain a list of names of X servers to be managed by xdm. This was the only way available to xdm to connect to X servers. Following is a sample of the contents of an Xservers file:

```
0: local /usr/X/bin/X
engg:0 foreign May's X terminal
arts:0 foreign Andrea's X terminal
```

Note how, in all entries, the host's name and display number (colon separated) are followed by one of two terms, local or foreign. *local* means the X server is running on the console, whereas *foreign* means it is on the network.

Because Xservers was read only when xdm was started, however, this posed serious problems as X terminals were brought up later on and as others were temporarily turned off.

The only way the administrator could force xdm to recognize a newly brought up X server was by restarting. This involves sending xdm a SIGHUP signal using the following command:

```
#kill -HUP <pid_of_xdm>
```

where the process id can be found by entering

```
#cat /usr/X/lib/xdm/xdm-pid
```

To remedy this problem, X Display Manager Control Protocol (XDMCP) was introduced in X11R4. XDMCP is a protocol that is implemented at both ends of the connection: the X server and the xdm client. An X server with XDMCP support is responsible for requesting xdm for a connection and should not require an entry in the Xservers file.

To request a connection, an XDMCP-compatible server issues one of three types of queries, depending on how it is configured. The three types are as follows:

> *Direct query.* This is a directed query addressed to a specific host.
> *Broadcast query.* The server sends out a general query addressed to all xdm clients requesting a connection. In this case, the X server connects to the first xdm client responding to the query.
> *Indirect query.* The X server addresses the XDMCP query to an xdm client for "help." The latter forwards the request to other xdm clients on the network for a response.

Xaccess is an XDMCP-related file. As the name implies, it provides for a degree of access control at the machine level. This means that only hosts with their names listed in Xaccess will have their request to connect honored, receiving a login window. A user still has to undergo the authentication process by providing the login ID and the password.

The *Xresources* File

The Xresources file contains resource definitions that ought to be loaded to X servers upon establishing the connection. All X servers are subject to the same treatment. The first thing that xdm does upon connecting is send a login window, which requires that associated resources be loaded. As for user-specific resources, they are loaded by the server after the user logs in, based on either $HOME/.Xresources and/or $HOME/.xsession files.

Xsession and *$HOME/.xsession* files

Xsession and .xsession files are start-up scripts that execute upon user login. Xsession is a system-wide script that executes every time a user logs in to the system. .xsession is the user's personal script, which is executed by xdm only if Xsession (the system script) calls for it. It is mainly responsible for setting up the user's environment properly and the subsequent invocation of some of the user's applications. Following is a sample `.xsession` file.

```
#!/bin/sh
#Update the user's PATH variable to include /usr/X/bin where all the #X clients can be
found.
PATH=$PATH:/usr/X/bin
export PATH

#load and merge user resources as defined in $HOME/.Xresources
xrdb -merge $HOME/.Xresources

#start user's applications
xclock &
xterm &
xcalc &

#start the window manager
twm
```

The preceding `.xsession` file starts by modifying the PATH variable to include the directory where all the X binaries are stored in the file system. Next, `xdm` calls and executes `xrdb` to load and merge the X client resources with those already loaded from `Xresources` at the X server. This suggests that the user is maintaining a `.Xresources` file in the home directory. A `.Xresources` file may have the following contents:

```
!xclock resource definitions:
xclock*update:        1
xclock*analog:        false
xclock*chime:         false
xclock*geometry:      -0+0
!xterm resource definitions:

xterm*title:          XTerminal
xterm*background:     grey
xterm*foreground:     black
xterm*geometry:       40x24+1+1
xterm*scrollBar:      true

!xcalc resource definitions:
xcalc*title:          XCalculator
xcalc*geometry:       +0+0
```

It is important that resources are loaded first, explaining why `xrdb` is called first and running in the foreground.

After resources are loaded, application clients are called next. Note how they are made to run in the background. Otherwise (that is, if applications are run in the foreground), the script will hang pending the completion of the application.

Finally, `twm` (Tab Window Manager) is loaded in the foreground. Unless this is done, execution of the script completes and exits, which may reset your X server. Hence, the last application to load should always be running in the foreground.

> **CAUTION:** The `.xsession` file must be flagged x in order to execute. Failure to do so results in having the xdm login window bouncing back to you without error messages. To flag `.xsession` executable, enter
>
> `%chmod x .xsession`

Now that you have a feel for how the user-specific files (that is, `.Xresources` and `.xsession`) are used to set up the user's X server session, take one more look at the Xsession that made it all happen. As noted before, `.xsession` is called and executed from the system-wide `/usr/X/lib/xdm/Xsession`. Following is a listing of the `Xsession` file that comes within X11R5 distribution of X:

```sh
#!/bin/sh
exec > $HOME/.xsession-errors 2>&1

case $# in
1)
    case $1 in
    failsafe)
        exec xterm -geometry 80x24-0-0
        ;;
    esac
esac

startup=$HOME/.xsession
resources=$HOME/.Xresources

if [-f $startup]; then
    exec $startup
else
    if [ -f$resources]; then
        xrdb -load $resources
    fi
    twm &
    exec xterm -geometry 80x24+10+10 -ls
fi
```

Note the following points about the script:

■ It first directs xsession error messages to `.xsession-errors` file. It is a good idea to keep one error file per user, as it conveniently helps you troubleshoot user sessions.

■ Next, it checks whether the script was called with a failsafe argument. If so, `.xsession` is not executed and the user is sent a single xterm. This option is mainly used to assist users and administrators in troubleshooting a failing session. The user invokes a failsafe session by pressing the F1 key or Ctrl+Return. Some preparation must have been made in the Xresources file, however, for this trick to work. For more on this topic, you are referred to your vendor's X Windows user manuals.

■ In the last part of the script, Xsession tests for the existence of the $HOME/
.xsession script. If it exists, control is transferred to .xsession. Note how
.Xresources is avoided altogether in this case, and it is left to .xsession to handle
the user's resource definition file instead. In case .xsession does not exist,
Xsession establishes a minimal session by loading .Xresources and invoking a
single xterm session after spawning twm in the background.

GiveConsole and *TakeConsole* Configuration Files

GiveConsole and TakeConsole are scripts that, as their names imply, change the ownership of the system console to the user, and back to root, respectively. Both files are relatively new to X11R5.

To summarize the X startup and user session establishment process, xdm is invoked as
daemon by the /etc/rc2.d/S69xdm script when the system enters the multiuser state. Upon
starting up, xdm fetches its /usr/X/lib/xdm/xdm-config file to determine the names and
locations of its configuration files. It starts by loading Xresources file into the X servers
listed in its Xservers file, or into those who successfully queried it using the XDMCP protocol. A login window is subsequently sent. When a user requests a login by entering a
valid login ID and password, xdm fetches the /usr/X/lib/xdm/Xsession script for execution. Subsequent actions are determined depending on what was included in this script.
It is recommended that user session handling and configuration be dealt with using
.Xresources and .xsession in the manner discussed previously. xsession is equivalent to
a personal login script in that, if it exists, it invokes the xrdb client to load user resource
definitions in the .Xresources file, and to load user applications that are included in the
.xsession script.

X Server Access Security

The basic premise of the X Window System is that it allows an X client to send its output
to the X server specified using the -display option. This being the case, you should be
able to predict the security hazard that is associated with this mechanism. Unless your X
display server is properly secured against unwelcome X clients, hackers can maliciously
connect to it and crash your session. In the following few paragraphs, one security control
method is described, along with its advantages and disadvantages. For more on X security, refer to X Window System reference manuals that ship with UNIX.

xhost Access Control Method

Using this method of protection involves the use of xhost client and the /etc/Xn.hosts
file, where n refers to the display number to which the access control file applies. Because
most systems have one display, reference will be made only to the /etc/X0.hosts file. The
X0.hosts file must be created on the X server and edited by the system administrator to

include the names of hosts from which clients are allowed access to the X server. So, if the `/etc/X0.hosts` file contains the following host names:

```
arts
engg
fin
```

then clients on `arts`, `engg`, and `fin` can establish X sessions with the X server and have their outputs sent to it.

`xhost` is a command that also can be used to add hosts to the server's access control list. The syntax of `xhost` is as follows:

```
#xhost [+¦-] [hostname]
```

To authorize a host, enter

```
#xhost + hostname
```

whereas to remove a host from the server's access control list, enter

```
#xhost - hostname
```

In the following example, host `sam` is allowed access, whereas host `view` is not:

```
#xhost + sam - view
```

> **CAUTION:** `xhost` client can be invoked only from an X window displaying on the server undergoing security configuration.

If you want to allow all hosts access to the server, enter

```
#xhost +
```

and to disable access, enter

```
#xhost -
```

It must be kept in mind, however, that currently established sessions will not be affected by the "`xhost -`" commands. Only future connections will be refused.

A question that may have occurred in your mind by now is, what if you want to invoke clients on host `view`, or any other host, which is denied access to your server? The answer to that is tough. You simply cannot do it! X Windows System provides a few other alternatives to the `xhost` control method. An example is the MIT-MAGIC-COOKIE-1, which is more of a user-based authentication process in which restrictions are enforced on users rather than on hosts.

Types of X Servers

No discussion of X is complete without a degree of exposure to the different types of X servers and their ranging capabilities.

Originally, a few years ago, X servers and X terminals were synonyms. Talking of one used to imply the other. This is because X servers used to be supplied on terminals tailored to handle X services, thus providing users with GUI capabilities, as opposed to the ASCII terminals, which handled characters only. Today, in addition to X terminals, an X server can be brought up and delivered to users on a variety of platforms, thanks to X protocol design, which provided for X's independence from operating systems as well as hardware. Among the relative newcomers to the X market are PC-based implementations of X servers. An example is eXceed series of X servers for DOS, OS/2, and Windows by Hummingbird Communications Ltd.

X terminals are what the name implies: dumb terminals with X Windows support. They are therefore better suited to support graphical applications including arts, science, and engineering. X terminals come with different features and capabilities, some of which are as follows:

- The X server program loading method varies from one X terminal to another. One commonly used method is to have the terminal resort to TFTP protocol (see Chapter 37 for more on TFTP) to download X server software and fonts on boot time from a remote host. Other terminals would have the X server software available locally on ROM. Yet a third category would provide a combination of both: ROM-based and TFTP-based methods. Some models such as WYSE WX-Series include an extra PCMCIA slot to use with an optional FLASH ROM. With this support the terminal needs to contact a host for a download of X server software once, during which a permanent copy of it will be transferred to the FLASH ROM to be used for subsequent reboots.

- The most commonly supported transport protocol among vendors of X terminals is TCP/IP. Some of the vendors provide you with serial communications capabilities as well. In this case, you should carefully examine how the server is optimized to operate over the limited bandwidth that is normally associated with serial facilities. If you are administering a multiprotocol environment, you may even have to go farther to shop around for ones that support your transport requirements.

- Recently, due to the explosion in the demand for multimedia support, some vendors such as Hewlett-Packard introduced multimedia X servers. An example model is the HP XEnvizex X station.

PC X Servers

As mentioned earlier, PC-based X servers are relative newcomers to the X Windows market. The broad install base of PCs, the improved performance of Intel CPUs, and the continuing drop of PC hardware cost inspired vendors to develop X server software that nears the performance of dedicated X terminals. Some vendors went farther by implementing the X server software as an MS Windows application. This made them more attractive by allowing the user the luxury and flexibility of maintaining DOS, Windows, and UNIX sessions. And by supporting the Inter Client Communications Conventions Manual (ICCCM), X servers allow users to interchangeably cut and paste between those environments. Figure 40.16 illustrates how eXceed/W, a high-end X server by Hummingbird Communications Ltd., provides this support. It illustrates the use of the X server software to establish multiple X sessions with clients running on different host platforms including IBM, HP, and an MS Windows application.

There are some performance-related factors that need to be considered before trying to install PC X servers. These are as follows:

- CPU power
- Amount of Random Access Memory (RAM)
- Graphic interface card and monitor
- The network interface card (NIC)

Obviously, the more CPU power and RAM memory, the better the X server will run. For optimal performance, however, you need no less than a 386 CPU with clock rates starting from 16 Mhz. Though most vendors require memory sizes in the four-megabyte range, you will find that this range delivers the service but not the performance. Therefore, you may still need more memory. Of all the factors, the video graphic interface may prove to be the single most important factor on your PC. Remember that the idea of X is to provide users with the elegance and capabilities of the associated GUI interfaces. No matter how fast X is on the PC, there is nothing as annoying as poor, if not disgusting, graphics. There are many implementations of X, with each supporting a variety of graphical interfaces with ranging capabilities. Depending on the nature of what you intend to do on the PC X server, you ought to budget for the suitable interface and monitor. Finally, a 16-bit interface card provides better performance on the wire, and consequently contributes to the improved overall performance of the X server.

Not all PC X servers are born equal. Some currently available implementations are more compatible with the latest distribution of X than others. Some even may have more capabilities built into them, or they may be easier to install and configure. Following is a list of features and capabilities to help you better assess the PC X options that you may have at your disposal.

X compliance X11R5: Make sure that the PC X server you choose is 100 percent compatible with X11R5. Non- or partial compliance may even prevent some of the application from displaying on your PC. Lack of compatibility with ICCCMP protocol may impair your ability to cut and paste across application windows.

XDMCP full compliance: Though users will always be able to login and start an X session using protocols such as telnet, rlogin, and sh, today XDMCP is the preferred method of logging in to X hosts. It also relieves you of the headaches associated with the older way of administering connections using the Xservers configuration file.

MS Windows support: With the user community moving closer by the day to MS Windows, you may consider an implementation that integrates both environments. This is particularly useful if the PC X server you choose is ICCCMP compatible, which allows you to freely cut and paste across application windows.

Transport support: The PC X server of choice should provide the same level of transport support that is compatible with already deployed protocols supporting your X clients. Most PC X servers support TCP/IP, but not as many support additional protocols. To access, for example, X clients running on UnixWare using IPX/SPX transport, you will need a PC X server such as eXceed/W. Another aspect of transport support is the maximum number of connections the X server can simultaneously allow.

X traces capability: This is a diagnostic capability that may prove extremely helpful in troubleshooting X connections.

Summary

Among the resources that UNIX system administrators are required to manage are ASCII terminals, modems, printers, and X servers. To manage these resources more easily, UNIX SVR4 presents system administrators with a cohesive set of concepts and tools that come under the hood of Service Access Facility (SAF). SAF recognizes a three-level hierarchy of processes: sac (service access controller), port monitors, and port services. sac is at the top of the hierarchy, and is responsible for invoking and managing the port monitors, which are mid-level processes. Port monitors are responsible for invoking and managing port services, which run at the bottom of the SAF hierarchy. There are two types of port monitors: ttymon and listen. Whereas ttymon takes care of service requests received via the serial (or tty) ports, listen takes care of across-the-network services.

Once SAF is setup appropriately, the administrator can provide all kinds of services, including dial-in access, print services access, and access to X clients running on the UNIX host. Enough details for setting up these services were presented in this chapter to allow the administrator to successfully bring up a similar environment in his or her workplace.

Mail Administration

41

By Jeff Smith

Introduction

So, they've gone and made you postmaster, have they? Perhaps you're approaching this new job with a little trepidation—and you should. Electronic mail administration is one of the most complex system administration tasks and one of the most visible. If you break an obscure program that few people use, your mistake may go unnoticed. If you break the mail system, all the users on your system will be affected, and most people consider electronic mail to be one of UNIX's most valuable services. Even worse, if your site is connected to the Internet, your mistakes may be visible at remote sites, and those sites' postmasters will not hesitate to inform you that while your mother may love you, they consider you and your broken mail system to be little better than pond scum. (Those are the moderates—others may not be so kind.)

Still with me? Good. Despite the potential for making mistakes on a grand scale, mail administration at many sites is routine. You probably won't have to fuss with the e-mail system much once you manage to get it up and running, and this chapter helps you do just that. First, you get a broad overview of how e-mail works, an explanation of some of the terminology you'll see in this and other books, and pointers on where to get more information. Finally, you'll see a step-by-step example of how to set up the sendmail program and its configuration file, sendmail.cf.

What this chapter *won't* do is cover complex configurations like a multiprotocol mail hub that routes mail from the Internet to UUCP or a DECnet network. You won't learn how to set up the Domain Name System (DNS), although a properly working DNS is essential to the e-mail system. Coverage of UUCP is minimal, and you only learn about one of the many variants of sendmail (version 8, or just V8). Finally, this chapter won't make you into a sendmail guru, but if you're lucky you'll never need to be one.

Overview & Terminology—E-mail from Point A to Point B

An electronic mail message begins its life as a file on your computer's disk, created by a Mail User Agent (MUA). After you compose the letter, the MUA gives it to a *mail router* like sendmail. The mail router gives it to a Mail Transport Agent (MTA). The message traverses one or more hosts and networks and is given to a *final delivery agent*, which appends it to the recipient's mailbox, another disk file. Each of these terms is explained in detail later in this chapter.

An MUA is just a fancy name for a mail-reading and -sending program, such as the SVR4 `mailx`. Other examples of MUAs are `elm` and the Rand corporation's `Mail Handler` (MH) programs. An MUA is the only part of the mail system with which users usually interact, since a good MUA hides the complexity of the rest of the system from them (but not from the postmaster)!

A *mail router* is a program that takes a piece of mail and decides where it should go and how to get it there. For instance, depending on the recipient, a letter might need to travel over a TCP/IP network using the Simple Mail Transfer Protocol (SMTP), or via a dial-up connection using the UNIX to UNIX Copy (UUCP) protocol, or even to an office fax machine. The mail router uses the recipient address and its own internal configuration information to decide the best MTA, and then hands the letter to the MTA.

An MTA is a transport program that understands the e-mail protocols of a particular network and can transport a letter over that network. For instance, the UUCP transport agents understand UUCP protocols but know nothing about SMTP. If the mail router were to mistakenly route an SMTP letter to a UUCP transport agent, it wouldn't know how to deliver it.

The *final delivery agent* does nothing but take a mail message and append it to the recipient's mailbox, following whatever local conventions are used to separate messages within a mailbox. The program `/bin/mail` is the usual final delivery agent on SVR4 systems.

In real life the distinctions between MTAs and MUAs and mail routers are sometimes blurred. For instance, `sendmail`, although primarily a mail router, can also function as an MTA because it understands the SMTP protocol and can transport mail over a TCP/IP network. Therefore, in Figure 41.1 the separate functions of mail router and MTA are really a single program. Further, the SMTP-server part of the remote end of the MTA is often another `sendmail` program, which may do additional routing and forwarding of the mail before it reaches its final delivery agent. Some MUAs even do their own mail routing, and some, like MH, can be configured to speak SMTP, an MTA function. Despite this real-world blurring of function, the conceptual framework outlined above is a good one to keep in mind.

Background Material and Other Sources

E-mail administration is a complex endeavor. This chapter gives you enough background to get you out of the gate and running, but you must carefully study the following materials to really understand what you're doing. It's a lot better to learn it now—with a warm cup of cocoa in hand—than to wait until you've got a dozen angry users in your office demanding that you fix the mail system immediately. Trust me on this one.

Don't worry if some of the documents mentioned below don't make sense on a first reading; you don't have to understand every little clause of RFC 822 (described in the next section) to be a successful postmaster, and if you persevere you'll understand as much as you need to know at first. After you gain some experience, you'll re-read them and understand them even better.

Request for Comments Documents (RFCs)

RFCs are issued by working groups of the Internet Engineering Task Force (IETF). They are known initially as a *request for comments,* but as they are adopted as Internet standards, you should think of them as *requirements for compliance.* So if you want to exchange e-mail with another site on the Internet, you must comply with the provisions of both RFCs 821 and 822. RFCs are available for anonymous ftp on the host ftp.internic.net. The RFCs mentioned below are also on the *UNIX Unleashed* CD-ROM.

- RFC 821 Simple Mail Transfer Protocol (SMTP). RFC 821 defines the commands by which Internet mailers exchange e-mail. It is explained later in more detail.

- RFC 822 Standard for the format of ARPA Internet text messages. RFC 822 defines the proper form of an e-mail message. E-mail is divided into two parts, the *headers* and the *body,* which are separated by a blank line. The headers contain essential information such as the return address of the sender, and the body is the message you want to send.

- RFC 1425 SMTP Service Extensions. RFC 1425 extends the SMTP protocol to what is commonly known as ESMTP.

- RFC1123 Requirements for Internet Hosts—Application and Support. RFC1123 is commonly known as the *host requirements* RFC. It clarifies requirements that all hosts on the Internet must meet and corrects some errors in earlier RFCs.

- RFC 976 UUCP Mail Interchange Format Standard. RFC 976 explains the UUCP mail protocol, which is a *store-and-forward* mechanism. Instead of making a direct connection like a phone circuit, host A makes a temporary connection to send mail to host B, which stores it temporarily and forwards it to host C, the final recipient. UUCP is a pain in the neck; avoid it if you can.

Sendmail Documentation

V8 sendmail comes with three important documents:

- Sendmail Installation and Operation Guide (SIOG)
- SENDMAIL—An Internetwork Mail Router
- Mail Systems and Addressing in 4.2bsd

All three were written by Eric Allman, the author of the `sendmail` program. The SIOG is an essential reference manual that explains the guts of `sendmail`. The other documents are more general overviews of mail router design. All are worth reading, but the SIOG is your essential guide to sendmail. You'll want to read it several times and highlight parts relevant to your site's configuration.

sendmail, The Book

The book `sendmail` by Bryan Costales, Eric Allman and Neil Rickert (O'Reilly & Associates, Inc., 1993) is the most comprehensive treatment of the care and feeding of V8 `sendmail`. If you manage a complex site or must write custom configuration files, it is invaluable. If your site is fairly simple or you find that you can get most of what you need from this chapter, the standard V8 `sendmail` documentation, `comp.mail.sendmail` and the RFCs, save your money.

Comp.mail.sendmail

If your site receives USENET news, don't pass go, don't collect $200, just add the newsgroup `comp.mail.sendmail` to your newsreader's subscription list. Eric Allman, the author of `sendmail`, contributes regularly along with other `sendmail` wizards. You can get more quality, free advice here than anywhere else on the USENET.

However, as with any newsgroup, read it for a few weeks *before* you make your first posting, and save yourself the embarrassment of asking a question that has already been answered a hundred times by first reading the V8 `sendmail` Frequently Asked Questions (FAQ) document and the other documentation mentioned in this chapter. It may take a little longer to get your burning question answered, but you'll still respect yourself in the morning.

Internet Mail Protocols

In order to understand the different jobs that `sendmail` does, you need to know a little about Internet protocols. Protocols are simply agreed-upon standards that software and hardware use to communicate.

Protocols are usually layered, with higher levels using the lower ones as building blocks. For instance, the Internet Protocol (IP) sends packets of data back and forth without building an end-to-end connection such as-used by SMTP and other higher-level protocols. The Transmission Control Protocol (TCP) is built on top of IP and provides for connection-oriented services like those used by programs such as `telnet` and the Simple Mail Transfer Protocol (SMTP). Together, TCP/IP provide the basic network services for the Internet. Higher-level protocols like the File Transfer Protocol (FTP) and SMTP are built on top of TCP/IP. The advantage of such layering is that programs which implement the SMTP or FTP protocols don't have to know anything about transporting packets on the network and making connections to other hosts. They can use the services provided by TCP/IP for that.

SMTP defines how programs exchange e-mail on the Internet. It doesn't matter whether the program exchanging the e-mail is `sendmail` running on an HP workstation or an SMTP client written for an Apple Macintosh. As long as both programs implement the SMTP protocol correctly, they will be able to exchange mail.

The following example of the SMTP protocol in action may help demystify it a little. The user `betty` at `gonzo.gov` is sending mail to `joe` at `whizzer.com`:

```
$ sendmail -v joe@whizzer.com < letter
joe@whizzer.com... Connecting to whizzer.com via tcp...
Trying 123.45.67.1...  connected.
220-whizzer.com SMTP ready at Mon, 6 Jun 1994 18:56:22 -0500
220 ESMTP spoken here
>>> HELO gonzo.gov
250 whizzer.com Hello gonzo.gov [123.45.67.2], pleased to meet you
>>> MAIL From:<betty@gonzo.gov>
250 <betty@gonzo.gov>... Sender ok
>>> RCPT To:<joe@whizzer.com>
250 <joe@whizzer.com>... Recipient ok
>>> DATA
354 Enter mail, end with "." on a line by itself
>>> .
250 SAA08680 Message accepted for delivery
>>> QUIT
221 whizzer.com closing connection
joe@whizzer.com... Sent
$
```

The first line shows one way to invoke `sendmail` directly rather than letting your favorite MUA do it for you. The `-v` option tells `sendmail` to be verbose and shows you the SMTP dialogue. The other lines show an SMTP client and server carrying on a conversation. Lines prefaced with `>>>` are the client (or *sender)* on `gonzo.gov`, and the lines that immediately follow are the replies of the server (or *receiver)* on `whizzer.com`. The first line beginning with `220` is the SMTP server announcing itself after the initial connection, giving its hostname and the date and time, and the second line informs the client that this server understands the Extended SMTP protocol (ESMTP) in case the client wants to use it. Numbers such as `220` are reply codes that the SMTP client uses to communicate with the SMTP server. The text following the reply codes is only for human consumption.

Although this dialogue may still look a little mysterious, it will soon be old hat if you take the time to read RFC 821. Running `sendmail` with its `-v` option also helps you understand how an SMTP dialogue works.

The Domain Name System (DNS) and E-Mail

Names like `whizzer.com` are convenient for humans, but computers insist on using numeric IP addresses like `123.45.67.1`. The Domain Name System (DNS) provides this hostname to IP address translation and other important information.

In the olden days when most of us walked several miles to school through deep snow, there were only a few thousand hosts on the Internet. All hosts were registered with the Network Information Center (NIC), which distributed a *host table* listing the host names and IP addresses of all the hosts on the Internet. Those simple times are gone forever. No one really knows how many hosts are connected to the Internet now, but they number in the millions, and an administrative entity like the NIC can't keep their names straight. Thus was born the DNS.

The DNS distributes authority for naming and numbering hosts to autonomous administrative domains. For instance, a company `whizzer.com` could maintain all the information about the hosts in its own domain. When the host `a.whizzer.com` wished to send mail or `telnet` to the host `b.whizzer.com`, it would send an inquiry over the network to the `whizzer.com` *name server,* which might run on a host named `ns.whizzer.com`. The `ns.whizzer.com` name server would reply to `a.whizzer.com` with the IP address of `b.whizzer.com` (and possibly other information), and the mail would be sent or the `telnet` connection made. Because `ns.whizzer.com` is authoritative for the `whizzer.com` *domain,* it can answer any inquiries about `whizzer.com` hosts regardless of where they originate; the authority for naming hosts in this domain has been *delegated.*

Now, what if someone on `a.whizzer.com` wants to send mail to `joe@gonzo.gov`? `Ns.whizzer.com` has no information about hosts in the `gonzo.gov` domain, but it knows how to find out. When a name server receives a request for a host in a domain for which it has no information, it asks the *root* name servers for the names and IP addresses of servers authoritative for that domain, in this case `gonzo.gov`. The root name server gives the `ns.whizzer.com` name server the names and IP addresses of hosts running name servers with authority for `gonzo.gov`. The `ns.whizzer.com` name server enquires of them and forwards the reply back to `a.whizzer.com`.

From the description above you can see that the DNS is a large, distributed database containing mappings between hostnames and IP addresses, but it contains other information as well. When a program like `sendmail` delivers mail, it must translate the recipient's host name into an IP address. This bit of DNS data is known as an A (Address) record, and it is the most fundamental data about a host. A second piece of host data is the Mail eXchanger (MX) record. An MX record for a host like `a.whizzer.com` lists one or more hosts that are willing to receive mail for it.

What's the point? Why shouldn't `a.whizzer.com` simply receive its own mail and be done with it? Isn't a postmaster's life complicated enough without having to worry about mail exchangers? Well, while it's true that the postmaster's life is often overly complicated, MX records serve useful purposes:

- Hosts not on the Internet (e.g., UUCP-only hosts) may designate an Internet host to receive their mail and so appear to have an Internet address. For instance, suppose that `a.whizzer.com` is only connected to `ns.whizzer.com` once a day via a UUCP link. If `ns.whizzer.com` publishes an MX record for it, other Internet hosts can still send it mail. When `ns.whizzer.com` receives the mail, it saves it until `a.whizzer.com` connects. This use of MX records allows non-Internet hosts to appear to be on the Internet (but only to receive e-mail).

- Imagine a UNIX host `pcserv.whizzer.com` that acts as a file server for a cluster of personal computers. The PC clones have MUAs with built-in SMTP clients that allow them to send mail, but not receive mail. If return addresses on the outbound mail look like `someone@pc1.whizzer.com`, how can people reply to the mail? MX records come to the rescue again — `pcserv.whizzer.com` publishes itself as the MX host for all the PC clones, and mail addressed to them is sent there.

- Hosts may be off the Internet for extended times because of unpredictable reasons ranging from lightning strikes to the propensity of backhoe operators to unexpectedly unearth, fiber-optic cables. While your host is off the Internet, its mail queues on other hosts, and after a while it bounces back to the sender. If your host has MX hosts willing to hold its mail in the interim, the mail will be delivered when your host is available again. The hosts can be either on-site (i.e., in your domain) or off-site, or both. The last option is best, since backhoe operator disasters usually take your entire site off the net, in which case an on-site backup does no good.

- MX records hide information and allow you more flexibility to reconfigure your local network. If all your correspondents know that your e-mail address is `joe@whizzer.com`, it doesn't matter whether the host that receives mail for `whizzer.com` is named `zippy.whizzer.com` or `pinhead.whizzer.com`. It also doesn't matter if you decide to change it to `white-whale.whizzer.com`; your correspondents will never know the difference.

Mail Delivery and MX Records

When an SMTP client delivers mail to a host, it must do more than translate the hostname into an IP address. First, it asks for MX records. If any exist, it sorts them according to the priority given in the record. For instance, `whizzer.com` might have MX records listing the hosts `mailhub.whizzer.com`, `walrus.whizzer.com`, and `mailer.gonzo.gov` as the hosts willing to receive mail for it (and the "host" `whizzer.com` might not exist except as an MX record, meaning that there might be no IP address for it). Although *any* of these hosts will accept mail for `whizzer.com`, the MX priorities specify which of those hosts the SMTP client should try first, and properly behaved SMTP clients will do so. In this case the system administrator has set up a primary mail relay `mailhub.whizzer.com`, an on-site backup `walrus.whizzer.com`, and arranged with the system administrator at `mailer.gonzo.gov` for an off-site backup. They have set the MX priorities so that SMTP clients will try the primary mail relay first, the on-site backup second, and the off-site backup third. This setup takes care of the problems with the vendor who doesn't ship your parts on time as well as the wayward backhoe operator, who severs the fiber optic cable that provides your site's Internet connection.

After collecting and sorting the MX records, the SMTP client gathers the IP addresses for the MX hosts and attempts delivery to them in order of MX preference. You should keep this in mind when debugging mail problems. Just because a letter is addressed to `joe@whizzer.com`, it doesn't necessarily mean that a host named `whizzer.com` exists. Even if it does, it might not be the host that is supposed to receive the mail.

Header and Envelope Addresses

The distinction between *header* and *envelope* addresses is important because mail routers may process them differently. An example will help explain the difference between the two.

Suppose you have a paper memo that you want to send to your colleagues Mary and Bill at the Gonzo corporation, and Ted and Ben at the Whizzer company. You give a copy of the memo to your trusty mail clerk Alphonse, who notes the multiple recipients. Since he's a clever fellow who wants to save your company 29 cents, he makes two copies of the memo and puts each in an envelope addressed to the respective companies (rather than sending a copy to each recipient). On the cover of the `Gonzo` envelope he writes `Mary` and `Bill`, and on the cover of the `Whizzer` envelope he writes `Ted` and `Ben`. When his counterparts at `Gonzo` and `Whizzer` receive the envelopes, they make copies of the memo and send them to Mary, Bill, Ted and Ben, *without inspecting the addresses in the memo itself.* As far as the `Gonzo` and `Whizzer` mail clerks are concerned, the memo itself might be addressed to the pope; they only care about the *envelope addresses.*

SMTP clients and servers work in much the same way. Suppose that `joe@gonzo.gov` sends mail to his colleagues `betty@zippy.gov` and `fred@whizzer.com`. The recipient list in the letter's headers may look like this:

```
To: betty@zippy.gov, fred@whizzer.com
```

The SMTP client at `gonzo.gov` connects to the `whizzer.com` mailer to deliver Fred's copy. When it's ready to list the recipients (the *envelope* address), what should it say? If it gives both recipients as they are listed in the `To:` line above (the `header` address), Betty will get two copies of the letter because the `whizzer.com` mailer will forward a copy to `zippy.gov`. The same problem occurs if the `gonzo.gov` SMTP client connects to `zippy.gov` and lists both Betty and Fred as recipients. The `zippy.gov` mailer will forward a second copy of Fred's letter.

The solution is the same one that Alphonse and his fellow mail clerks used. The `gonzo.gov` SMTP client puts an *envelope* around the letter that contains only the names of the recipients on each host. The complete recipient list is still in the letter's headers, but those are inside the envelope, and the SMTP servers at `gonzo.gov` and `whizzer.com` don't look at them. In this example, the envelope for the `whizzer.com` mailer would list only `fred`, and the envelope for `zippy.gov` would only list `betty`.

Aliases illustrate another reason why header and envelope addresses differ. Suppose you send mail to the alias `homeboys`, which includes the names `alphonse`, `joe`, `betty`, and `george`. In your letter you write To: `homeboys`. However, `sendmail` expands the alias and constructs an envelope that includes all of the recipients. Depending on whether those names are also aliases, perhaps on other hosts, the original message might be put into as many as four different envelopes and delivered to four different hosts. In each case the envelope will contain only the name of the recipients, but the original message will contain the alias `homeboys` (expanded to `homeboys@your.host.domain` so replies will work).

A final example shows another way in which envelope addresses may differ from header addresses. `sendmail` allows you to specify recipients on the command line. Suppose you have a file named `letter` that looks like this:

```
$ cat letter
To: null recipient <>
Subject: header and envelope addresses

testing
```

and you send it with the following command (substituting your own login name for *yourlogin*):

```
$ sendmail yourlogin < letter
```

You will receive the letter even though your login name doesn't appear in the letter's headers because your address was on the envelope. Unless told otherwise (with the `-t` flag), `sendmail` constructs envelope addresses from the recipients you specify on the command line, and there isn't necessarily a correspondence between the header addresses and the envelope addresses.

sendmail's Jobs

To better understand how to set up `sendmail`, you need to know what different jobs it does and how those jobs fit into the scheme of MUAs, MTAs, mail routers, final delivery agents, and SMTP clients and servers. `sendmail` can act as a mail router, an SMTP client and an SMTP server. However, it does not do final delivery of mail.

sendmail as Mail Router

`sendmail` is primarily a mail router, meaning it takes a letter, inspects the recipient addresses, and decides the best way to send it. How does `sendmail` do this?

`sendmail` determines some of the information it needs on its own, like the current time and the name of the host on which it's running, but most of its brains are supplied by you, the postmaster, in the form of a configuration file, `sendmail.cf`. This somewhat cryptic file tells `sendmail` exactly how you want various kinds of mail handled. It is extremely flexible and powerful, and at first glance seemingly inscrutable. However, one of the strengths of V8 `sendmail` is its set of modular configuration file building blocks. Most sites can easily construct their configuration files from these modules, and many examples are included. Writing a configuration file from scratch is a daunting task and you should avoid it if you can.

sendmail as MTA—Client (Sender) and Server (Receiver) SMTP

As mentioned before, `sendmail` can function as an MTA since it understands the SMTP protocol (V8 `sendmail` also understands ESMTP). Because SMTP is a connection-oriented protocol, there is always a client and a server (also known as a *sender* and a *receiver*). The SMTP client delivers a letter to an SMTP server, which listens continuously on its computer's SMTP *port*. `sendmail` can be an SMTP client or an SMTP server. When run by an MUA, it becomes an SMTP client and speaks client-side SMTP to an SMTP server (not necessarily another `sendmail` program). When your system boots and it starts in *daemon* mode, it runs continuously, listening on the SMTP port for incoming mail.

sendmail as a Final Delivery Agent (NOT!)

One thing `sendmail` *doesn't* do is final delivery. `sendmail`'s author wisely chose to leave this task to other programs. `sendmail` is a big, complicated program that runs with super-user privileges, an almost guaranteed recipe for security problems, and there have been quite a few in `sendmail`'s past. The additional complexity of final mail delivery is the last thing `sendmail` needs.

sendmail's Auxiliary Files

`sendmail` depends on a number of auxiliary files to do its job. The most important are the *aliases* file and the configuration file, `sendmail.cf`. The statistics file, `sendmail.st`, can be created or not depending on whether you want the statistics. `sendmail.hf` is the SMTP help file, and should be installed if you intend to run `sendmail` as an SMTP server (most sites do). That's all that needs to be said about `sendmail.st` and `sendmail.hf` (there are other auxilary files that are covered in the SIOG), but the *aliases* and `sendmail.cf` files are important enough to be covered in their own sections.

The Aliases File

`sendmail` always checks recipient addresses for *aliases,* which are alternate names for a recipient. For instance, each Internet site is required to have a valid address *postmaster* to which mail problems may be reported. Most sites don't have an actual account of that name but divert the postmaster's mail to the person or persons responsible for e-mail administration. For instance, at the mythical site `gonzo.gov`, the users `joe` and `betty` are jointly responsible for e-mail administration, and the aliases file has the following entry:

```
postmaster: joe, betty
```

This line tells `sendmail` that mail to `postmaster` should instead be delivered to the login names `joe` and `betty`. In fact, those names could also be aliases:

```
postmaster: firstshiftops, secondshiftops, thirdshiftops
firstshiftops: joe, betty
secondshiftops: lou, emma
thirdshiftops: ben, mark, clara
```

In all of these examples, the alias name is the part on the left side of the colon, and the aliases for those names are on the right side. `sendmail` repeatedly evaluates aliases until they resolve to a real user or a remote address. In the previous example, to resolve the alias `post-master`, `sendmail` first expands it into the list of recipients `firstshiftops`, `secondshiftops`, and `thirdshiftops` and then expands each of these into the final list, `joe`, `betty`, `lou`, `emma`, `ben`, `mark`, and `clara`.

Although the right side of an alias may refer to a remote host, the left side may not. The alias `joe: joe@whizzer.com` is legal, but `joe@gonzo.gov: joe@whizzer.com` is not.

Reading Aliases from a File—the *:include:* Directive

Aliases may be used to create mailing lists (in the example above, the alias `postmaster` is in effect a mailing list for the local postmasters). For big or frequently changing lists, you can use the `:include:` alias form to direct `sendmail` to read the list members from a file. If the aliases file contains the line:

```
homeboys:  :include:/home/alphonse/homeboys.aliases
```

and the file `/home/alphonse/homeboys.aliases` contains:

```
alphonse
joe
betty
george
```

The effect is the same as the alias:

```
homeboys: alphonse, joe, betty, george
```

This is handy for mailing lists that change frequently, or those managed by users other than the postmaster. If you find a user is asking for frequent changes to a mail alias, you may want to put it under her control.

Mail to Programs

The aliases file also may be used to send the contents of e-mail to a program. For instance, many mailing lists are set up so that you can get information about the list or subscribe to it by sending a letter to a special address, `list-request`. The letter usually contains a single word in its body, such as `help` or `subscribe`, which causes a program to mail an information file to the sender. Suppose that the `gonzo` mailing list has such an address called `gonzo-request`:

```
gonzo-request: |/usr/local/lib/auto-gonzo-reply
```

In this form of alias, the pipe sign (¦) tells `sendmail` to use the *program mailer*, which is usually defined as `/bin/sh` (see "The M command—defining mailers" below). `sendmail` feeds the message to the standard input of `/usr/local/lib/auto-gonzo-reply`, and if it exits normally, `sendmail` considers the letter to be delivered.

Mail to Files

You can also create an alias that causes `sendmail` to send mail to files. An example of this is the alias `nobody`, which is common on systems running the Network File System (NFS):

```
nobody: /dev/null
```

Aliases that specify files cause `sendmail` to append its message to the named file. Because the special file `/dev/null` is the UNIX bit-bucket, this alias simply throws mail away.

Setting up *sendmail*

The easiest way to show you how to set up `sendmail` is to use a concrete example. However, because `sendmail` runs under many different versions of UNIX, your system may vary from the examples shown below. For the sake of concreteness, these examples assume that you're setting up sendmail on a Solaris 2.3 system, Sun Microsystem's version of SVR4 UNIX.

First you must obtain the source and compile sendmail. Next you must choose a sendmail.cf file that closely models your site's requirements and tinker with it as necessary. Then you must test sendmail and its configuration file. Finally, you must install sendmail, sendmail.cf, and other auxiliary files.

Those are the basic steps, but depending on where you install sendmail, you may also have to modify a file in the directory /etc/init.d so that sendmail will be started correctly when the system boots. In addition, if your system doesn't already have one, you must create an *aliases* file, often named /usr/lib/aliases or /etc/mail/aliases (the location of the aliases file is given in sendmail.cf, so you can put it wherever you want). You may also have to make changes to your system's DNS database, but that won't be covered here.

Obtaining the Source

sendmail version 8.6.9 is on the UNIX Unleashed CD. This is the most recent version available as this book goes to press, and it is the version documented in the O'Reilly book sendmail. However, if your site is on the Internet and you want to obtain the absolutely latest version, ftp to the host ftp.cs.berkeley.edu and look in the directory ~ftp/pub/ucb/ sendmail. Use the following steps to download it:

```
$ ftp ftp.cs.berkeley.edu
Connected to ftp.cs.berkeley.edu.
220 kohler FTP server (Version wu-2.4(4) Fri May 6 16:09:33 PDT 1994) ready.
Name (ftp.cs.berkeley.edu:yourname): anonymous
331 Guest login ok, send your complete e-mail address as password.
Password: (Type your e-mail address)
230 Guest login ok, access restrictions apply.
ftp> cd ucb/sendmail
250-This directory contains sendmail source distributions, currently for
250-Release 8. The latest version is in four files:
250-
250-    sendmail.${VER}.base.tar.Z -- the base system source & documentation.
250-    sendmail.${VER}.cf.tar.Z -- configuration files.
250-    sendmail.${VER}.misc.tar.Z -- miscellaneous support programs.
250-    sendmail.${VER}.xdoc.tar.Z -- extended documentation, with postscript.
250-
250-The status of various ${VER}s is:
250-8.6.9  This is the version documented in the O'Reilly sendmail book.
250-       and which will be on the 4.4BSD-Lite tape. The files
250-       sendmail.8.6.[123456789].patch will upgrade an 8.6 source to
250-       this version (apply all of them).
250-8.6.8  The previous version. It fixes some significant security
250-       problems; you should be running at least this version.
250-
250 CWD command successful.
ftp> binary
200 Type set to I.
```

```
ftp> mget sendmail.8.6.9.base.tar.Z sendmail.8.6.9.cf.tar.Z
mget sendmail.8.6.9.base.tar.Z? y
200 PORT command successful.
150 Opening BINARY mode data connection for sendmail.8.6.9.base.tar.Z (500945 bytes).
226 Transfer complete.
local: sendmail.8.6.9.base.tar.Z remote: sendmail.8.6.9.base.tar.Z
500945 bytes received in 14 seconds (34 Kbytes/s)
mget sendmail.8.6.9.cf.tar.Z? y
200 PORT command successful.
150 Opening BINARY mode data connection for sendmail.8.6.9.cf.tar.Z (199863 bytes).
226 Transfer complete.
local: sendmail.8.6.9.cf.tar.Z remote: sendmail.8.6.9.cf.tar.Z
199863 bytes received in 3.3 seconds (59 Kbytes/s)
ftp> quit
221 Goodbye.
```

Note that the exact name of the files to download differs depending on the current version of V8 sendmail, in this case version 8.6.9. Also, because the files are compressed, you *must* give ftp the binary command before transferring them. Note too that you should include your complete e-mail address as the password, for instance, mylogin@gonzo.gov. You may also wish to download the extended documentation and the support programs, which in this example would have been contained in the files sendmail.8.6.9.xdoc.tar.Z and sendmail.8.6.9.misc.tar.Z.

Unpacking the Source and Compiling *sendmail*

Now that you've got the source, you need to unpack it. Because it's a compressed tar image, you must first decompress it and then extract the individual files from the tar archive. If you're using the version from the CD-ROM, these steps are not necessary.

```
$ mkdir /usr/src/local/sendmail
$ mv sendmail.8.6.9.* /usr/src/local/sendmail
$ cd /usr/src/local/sendmail
$ uncompress *Z
$ ls
sendmail.8.6.9.base.tar sendmail.8.6.9.cf.tar
$ tar xf sendmail.8.6.9.base.tar; tar xf sendmail.8.6.9.cf.tar
$ ls -CF
FAQ                     cf/                     sendmail.8.6.9.cf.tar
KNOWNBUGS               doc/                    src/
Makefile                mailstats/              test/
READ_ME                 makemap/
RELEASE_NOTES           sendmail.8.6.9.base.tar
$ rm *tar
```

Now you're almost ready to compile sendmail, but first read the following files, which contain the latest news pertinent to the specific release of sendmail you've downloaded:

```
FAQ
RELEASE_NOTES
KNOWNBUGS
READ_ME
```

Now run `cd` and `ls` to see what files are in the source directory:

```
$ cd src
$ ls
Makefile             Makefile.SunOS.5.1   mailq.1
Makefile.386BSD      Makefile.SunOS.5.2   mailstats.h
Makefile.AIX         Makefile.SunOS.5.x   main.c
Makefile.AUX         Makefile.Titan       makesendmail
Makefile.BSD43       Makefile.ULTRIX      map.c
Makefile.BSDI        Makefile.UMAX        mci.c
Makefile.CLIX        Makefile.Utah        newaliases.1
Makefile.ConvexOS    Makefile.dist        parseaddr.c
Makefile.DGUX        READ_ME              pathnames.h
Makefile.Dell        TRACEFLAGS           queue.c
Makefile.DomainOS    alias.c              readcf.c
Makefile.Dynix       aliases              recipient.c
Makefile.FreeBSD     aliases.5            savemail.c
Makefile.HP-UX       arpadate.c           sendmail.8
Makefile.IRIX        cdefs.h              sendmail.h
Makefile.Linux       clock.c              sendmail.hf
Makefile.Mach386     collect.c            srvrsmtp.c
Makefile.NCR3000     conf.c               stab.c
Makefile.NeXT        conf.h               stats.c
Makefile.NetBSD      convtime.c           sysexits.c
Makefile.OSF1        daemon.c             trace.c
Makefile.RISCos      deliver.c            udb.c
Makefile.SCO         domain.c             useful.h
Makefile.SVR4        envelope.c           usersmtp.c
Makefile.Solaris     err.c                util.c
Makefile.SunOS       headers.c            version.c
Makefile.SunOS.4.0.3 macro.c
```

As you can see, because `sendmail` runs on a variety of hosts and operating systems, a Makefile is provided for many UNIX variants. Since in this example we're assuming a Sun Microsystems Solaris system, we'll use `Makefile.Solaris` to compile `sendmail`. But before we type `make`, we should look at the files `conf.h` and `Makefile.Solaris`.

You probably won't want to change much in `conf.h`, but `Makefile.Solaris` is a different story. At the very least you should make sure that the correct version of the Solaris operating system is defined. In this case, since we're compiling for Solaris 2.3, we must replace the line `ENV=-DSOLARIS` with the line `ENV=-DSOLARIS_2_3` (`Makefile.Solaris` tells us to do so). If you've purchased the SunPro `cc` compiler, you may want to change the definition of the `cc` macro to use that instead of `gcc`. You may want to make other changes; for example, you may not want to install `sendmail` in the default location. Read the Makefile carefully and make changes as needed.

Remember, when in doubt, you can always type `make -n` *arguments* to see what *would* happen *before* it happens. This is always an especially good idea when you're working as the super-user.

Now you're ready to compile. Type:

```
$ make -f Makefile.Solaris sendmail
gcc -I.  -I/usr/sww/include/db -DNDBM -DNIS -DSOLARIS_2_3 -c  alias.c
[...]
gcc -I.  -I/usr/sww/include/db -DNDBM -DNIS -DSOLARIS_2_3 -c  util.c
gcc -I.  -I/usr/sww/include/db -DNDBM -DNIS -DSOLARIS_2_3 -c version.c
gcc -o sendmail alias.o arpadate.o clock.o collect.o conf.o convtime.o daemon.o
deliver.o domain.o envelope.o err.o headers.o macro.o main.o  map.o mci.o
parseaddr.o queue.o readcf.o recipient.o  savemail.o srvrsmtp.o stab.o stats.o
sysexits.o  trace.o udb.o usersmtp.o util.o version.o
-L/usr/sww/lib -lresolv -lsocket -lnsl -lelf
```

The *[...]* above covers many deleted lines of output, as well as some warning messages from the compiler. Carefully inspect the output and determine whether the compiler warnings are pertinent. If necessary (and it should only be necessary if you're porting sendmail to a new architecture), correct any problems and compile again.

sendmail.cf—the Configuration File

Now you've got a working sendmail, but like the *Wizard of Oz's* Scarecrow, it's brainless. The sendmail.cf file provides sendmail with its brains, and because it's so important, we're going to cover it in fairly excruciating detail. Don't worry if you don't understand everything in this section the first time through. It will make more sense upon rereading, and after you've had a chance to play with some configuration files of your own.

sendmail's power lies in its flexibility, which comes from its configuration file, sendmail.cf. sendmail.cf statements comprise a cryptic programming language that at first glance doesn't inspire much confidence (but C language code probably didn't either the first time you saw it). However, learning the sendmail.cf language isn't that hard, and you won't have to learn the nitty-gritty details unless you plan to write a sendmail.cf from scratch—a bad idea at best. You *do* need to learn enough to understand and adapt the V8 sendmail configuration file templates to your site's needs.

General Form of the Configuration File

Each line of the configuration file begins with a single *command character* that tells the function and syntax of that line. Lines beginning with a # are comments, and blank lines are ignored. Lines beginning with a space or tab are a continuation of the previous line, although you should usually avoid continuations.

Table 41.1 shows the command characters and their functions. It is split into three parts corresponding to the three main functions of a configuration file, which are covered later in "A Functional Description of the Configuration File."

Table 41.1. `sendmail.cf` command characters.

Command Character	Command Syntax and Example	Function
#	# comments are ignored	A comment line. Always use lots of comments.
	# Standard RFC822 parsing	
D	D*X string*	Define a macro *X* to have the string value *string*.
	DMmailhub.gonzo.gov	
C	C*X word1 word2 ...*	Define a class *X* as *word1 word2 ...*
	Cwlocalhost myuucpname	
F	F*X/path/to/a/file*	Define a class *X* by reading it from a file.
	Fw/etc/mail/host_aliases	
H	H*?mailerflag?name:template*	Define a mail *header*.
	H?F?From: $q	
O	O*X option arguments*	Set option *X*. Most command-line options may be set in `sendmail.cf`.
	OL9 # set log level to 9	
P	P*class=nn*	Set mail delivery precedence based on the class of the mail.
	Pjunk=-100	
V	V*n*	Tell V8 `sendmail` the version level of the configuration file.
	V3	
K	K*name class arguments*	Define a *key file* (database map).
	Kuucphosts dbm /etc/mail/uucphsts	
M	M*name,field_1=value_1,...*	Define a *mailer*.
	Mprog,P=/bin/sh,F=lsD,A=sh -c $u	

Command Character	Command Syntax and Example	Function
S	S*nn* **S22**	Begin a new rule-set.
R	R*lhs rhs comment* **R$+ $:$>22 call ruleset 22**	Define a matching/ rewriting rule.

A Functional Description of the Configuration File

A configuration file does three things. First, it sets the environment for sendmail by telling it what options you want set and the locations of the files and databases it uses.

Second, it defines the characteristics of the *mailers* (delivery agents or MTAs) that sendmail uses after it decides where to route a letter. All configuration files *must* define *local* and *program* mailers to handle delivery to users on the local host; most also define one or more SMTP mailers; and sites that must handle UUCP mail define UUCP mailers.

Third, the configuration file specifies *rulesets* that rewrite sender and recipient addresses and select mailers. All rulesets are user-defined, but some have special meaning to sendmail. Ruleset 0, for instance, is used to select a mailer. Rulesets 0, 1, 2, 3, and 4 all have special meaning to sendmail and are processed in a particular order (see "The s and R Operators—Rulesets and Rewriting Rules") later in this chapter.

In the following sections we'll cover the operators in more detail, in the order in which they appear in Table 41.1.

The *D* Operator—Macros

Macros are like shell variables. Once you define a macro's value you can refer to it later in the configuration file and its value will be substituted for the macro. For instance, a configuration file might have many lines that mention our hypothetical mail hub, mailer.gonzo.gov. Rather than typing that name over and over, you can define a macro R (for *relay mailer):*

```
DRmailer.gonzo.gov
```

When sendmail encounters a $R in sendmail.cf, it substitutes the string mailer.gonzo.gov.

Macro names are always a single character. Quite a few macros are defined by sendmail and shouldn't be redefined except to work around broken software[1]. sendmail uses lower-case letters for its predefined macros. Uppercase letters may be used freely. V8 sendmail's predefined macros are fully documented in section 5.1.2 of the SIOG.

The *C* and *F* Operators—Classes

Classes are similar to macros but are used for different purposes in rewriting rules (see below, "The s and R operators—rulesets and rewriting rules"). As with macros, classes are named by a single character. Lowercase letters are reserved to sendmail, and uppercase letters for user-defined classes. A class contains one or more words. For instance, you could define a class H containing all the hosts in the local domain:

```
CH larry moe curly
```

For convenience, large classes may be continued on subsequent lines. The following definition of the class H is exactly the same as the previous one:

```
CH larry
CH moe
CH curly
```

You can also define a class by reading its words from a file:

```
CF/usr/local/lib/localhosts
```

If the file /usr/local/lib/localhosts contains the words larry, moe, and curly, one per line, this definition is equivalent to the previous two.

Why use macros and classes? The best reason is that they centralize information in the configuration file. In the example above, if you decide to change the name of the mail hub from mailer.gonzo.gov to mailhub.gonzo.gov, you only have to change the definition of the $R macro remedyand the configuration file will work as before. If the name mailer.gonzo.gov is scattered throughout the file, you might forget to change it in some places. Also, if important information is centralized, you can comment it extensively in a single place. Because configuration files tend to be obscure at best, a liberal dose of comments is a good antidote to that sinking feeling you get when, six months later, you wonder why you made a change.

The *H* Operator—Header Definitions

You probably won't want to change the header definitions given in the V8 sendmail configuration files because they already follow accepted standards. Here are some sample headers:

```
H?D?Date: $a
H?F?Resent-From: $q
H?F?From: $q
H?x?Full-Name: $x
```

Note that header definitions can use macros, which are expanded, when inserted into a letter. For instance, the $x macro used in the Full-Name: header definition above expands to the full name of the sender.

The optional *?mailerflag?* construct tells `sendmail` to insert a header only if the chosen mailer has that *mailer flag* set. (See "The M Operator—Mailer Definitions" later in this chapter.)

Suppose that the definition of your *local* mailer has a flag Q, and `sendmail` selects that mailer to deliver a letter. If your configuration file contains a header definition like the following one, `sendmail` will insert that header into letters delivered through the local mailer, substituting the value of the macro $F:

```
H?Q?X-Fruit-of-the-day: $F
```

Why would you use the *?mailerflag?* feature? Different protocols may require different mail headers. Since they also need different mailers, you can define appropriate mailer flags for each in the mailer definition, and use the *?mailerflag?* construct in the header definition to tell `sendmail` whether to insert the header.

The *O* Operator—Setting Options

`sendmail` has many options that change its operation or tell it the location of files it uses. Most of them may be given either on the command line or in the configuration file. For instance, the location of the *aliases* file may be specified in either place. To specify the aliases file on the command line, you use the -o option:

```
$ sendmail -oA/etc/mail/aliases [other arguments...]
```

To do the same thing in the configuration file, you include a line like this:

```
OA/etc/mail/aliases
```

Either use is equivalent, but options such as the location of the aliases file rarely change and most people set them in `sendmail.cf`. The V8 `sendmail` options are fully described in section 5.1.6 of the SIOG.

The *P* Operator—Mail Precedence

Users can include mail headers indicating the relative importance of their mail, and `sendmail` can use those headers to decide the priority of competing letters. Precedences for V8 `sendmail` are given as:

```
Pspecial-delivery=100
Pfirst-class=0
Plist=-30
Pbulk=-60
Pjunk=-100
```

If a user who runs a large mailing list includes the header `Precedence: bulk` in his letters, `sendmail` gives it a lower priority than a letter with the header `Precedence: first-class`.

The *V* Operator—*sendmail.cf* Version Levels

As V8 sendmail evolves its author adds new features. The v operator lets V8 sendmail know what features it should expect to find in your configuration file. Older versions of sendmail don't understand this command. Section 5.1.8 of the SIOG explains the different configuration file version levels in detail.

> **NOTE:** The configuration file version level does *not* correspond to the sendmail version level. V8 sendmail understands versions 1 through 5 of configuration files, and there is no such thing as a version 8 configuration file.

The *K* Operator—Key Files

sendmail has always used keyed databases, for instance, the aliases databases. Given the key postmaster, sendmail looks up the data associated with that key and returns the names of the accounts to which the postmaster's mail should be delivered. V8 sendmail extends this concept to arbitrary databases, including NIS maps (Sun's *Network Information Service,* formerly known as *Yellow Pages* or *YP).* The k operator tells sendmail the location of the database, its *class,* and how to access it. V8 sendmail supports the following classes of user-defined databases: *dbm, btree, hash,* and *NIS.* Depending on which of these databases you use, you must compile sendmail with different options. See section 5.1.9 of the SIOG for the lowdown on key files.

The *M* Operator—Mailer Definitions

Mailers are either MTAs or final delivery agents. Recall that the aliases file allows you to send mail to a login name (which might be aliased to a remote user), a program, or a file. A special mailer may be defined for each purpose. And even though the SMTP MTA is built-in, it must have a mailer definition to tailor sendmail's SMTP operations.

Mailer definitions are important because all recipient addresses must *resolve* to a mailer in ruleset 0. *Resolving to a mailer* is just another name for sendmail's main function, mail routing. For instance, resolving to the *local* mailer routes the letter to a local user via the final delivery agent defined in that mailer (usually /bin/mail), and resolving to the SMTP mailer routes the letter to another host via sendmail's built-in SMTP transport, as defined in the SMTP mailer. A concrete example of a mailer definition will make this clearer. Since sendmail requires a local mailer definition, let's look at that:

```
Mlocal, P=/bin/mail, F=lsDFMfSn, S=10, R=20, A=mail -d $u
```

All mailer definitions begin with the M operator and the name of the mailer, in this case local. Other fields follow, separated by commas. Each field consists of a field name and its value, separated by an equals sign (=). The allowable fields are explained in section 5.1.4 of the SIOG.

In the local mailer definition above, the P= equivalence gives the pathname of the program to run to deliver the mail, /bin/mail. The F= field gives the sendmail *flags* for the local mailer. (See also "The H Operator—Defining Headers" earlier in the chapter.) These flags are not passed to the command mentioned in the P= field but are used by sendmail to modify its operation depending on the mailer it chooses. For instance, sendmail usually drops its super-user status before invoking mailers, but you can use the S mailer flag to tell sendmail to retain it for certain mailers.

The S= and R= fields specify rulesets for sendmail to use in rewriting sender and recipient addresses. Since you can give different R= and S= flags for each mailer you define, you can rewrite addresses differently for each mailer. For instance, if one of your UUCP neighbors runs obsolete software that doesn't understand domain addressing, you might declare a special mailer just for that site and write mailer-specific rulesets to convert addresses into a form its mailer could understand.

The S= and R= fields can also specify different rulesets to rewrite the envelope and header addresses. (See "Header and Envelope Addresses".) A specification like S=21/31 tells sendmail to use ruleset 21 to rewrite sender envelope addresses and ruleset 31 to rewrite sender header addresses. This comes in handy for mailers that require addresses to be presented differently in the envelope and the headers.

The A= field gives the *argument vector* (command line) for the program that will be run, in this case /bin/mail. In this example, sendmail runs the command as mail -d $u, expanding the $u macro to the name of the user to which the mail should be delivered, for instance:

```
/bin/mail -d joe
```

This is exactly the same command that you could type to your shell at a command prompt.

There are many other mailer flags you may want to use to tune mailers, for instance to limit the maximum message size on a per-mailer basis. These flags are all documented in section 5.1.4 of the SIOG.

The *S* and *R* Operators—Rulesets and Rewriting Rules

A configuration file is composed of a series of rulesets, which are somewhat like subroutines in a program. Rulesets are used to detect bad addresses, to rewrite addresses into forms that remote mailers can understand, and to route mail to one of sendmail's internal mailers. (See the previous section, "The M Operator—Mailer Definitions".)

`sendmail` passes addresses to rulesets according to a built-in order. Rulesets may also call other rulesets not in the built-in order. The built-in order varies depending on whether the address being handled is a sender or receiver address, and what mailer has been chosen to deliver the letter.

Rulesets are announced by the s command, which is followed by a number to identify the ruleset. `sendmail` collects subsequent R (rule) lines until it finds another s operator, or the end of the configuration file. The following example defines ruleset 11:

```
# Ruleset 11
S11
R$+      $: $>22 $1     call ruleset 22
```

This ruleset doesn't do much that is useful. The important thing to note is that `sendmail` collects ruleset number 11, composed of a single rule.

sendmail's Built-In Ruleset Processing Rules

`sendmail` uses a three-track approach to processing addresses, one to choose a delivery agent, another to process sender addresses, and one for receiver addresses.

All addresses are first sent through ruleset 3 for preprocessing into a *canonical* form that makes them easy for other rulesets to handle. Regardless of the complexity of the address, ruleset 3's job is to decide the next host to which a letter should be sent. Ruleset 3 tries to locate that host in the address and mark it within angle brackets. In the simplest case, an address like `joe@gonzo.gov` becomes `joe<@gonzo.gov>`.

Ruleset 0 then determines the correct delivery agent (mailer) to use for each recipient. For instance, a letter from `betty@whizzer.com` to `joe@gonzo.gov` (an Internet site) and `pinhead!zippy` (an *old-style* UUCP site) will require two different mailers: an SMTP mailer for `gonzo.gov` and an old-style UUCP mailer for `pinhead`. Mailer selection determines later processing of sender and recipient addresses because the rulesets given in the s= and R= mailer flags vary from mailer to mailer.

Addresses sent through ruleset 0 must resolve to a mailer. This means that when an address matches the *lhs*, the *rhs* gives a triple[2] of *mailer, user, host*. The following line shows the syntax for a rule that resolves to a mailer:

```
Rlhs     $#mailer $@host $:user   your comment here...
```

The *mailer* is the name of one of the mailers you've defined in an M command, for instance `smtp`. The *host* and *user* are usually positional macros taken from the *lhs* match. (See "The Righthand Side *(rhs)* of Rules," later in the chapter.)

After `sendmail` selects a mailer in ruleset 0, it processes sender addresses through ruleset 1 (often empty), and then sends them to the ruleset given in the s= flag for that mailer.

Similarly, it sends recipient addresses through ruleset 2 (also often empty), and then to the ruleset mentioned in the R= mailer flag.

Finally, `sendmail` post-processes *all* addresses in ruleset 4, which among other things removes the angle brackets inserted by ruleset 3.

Why do mailers have different s= and R= flags? Consider the example above of the letter sent to `joe@gonzo.gov` and `pinhead!zippy`. If `betty@whizzer.com` sends the mail, her address must appear in a different form to each recipient. For Joe, it should be a domain address, `betty@whizzer.com`. For Zippy, since `whizzer.com` expects old-style UUCP addresses (and assuming it has a UUCP link to `pinhead` and `whizzer.com`'s UUCP hostname is `whizzer`), the return address should be `whizzer!betty`. Joe's address must also be rewritten for the `pinhead` UUCP mailer, and Joe's copy must include an address for Zippy that his mailer can handle.

Processing Rules Within Rulesets

`sendmail` passes an address to a ruleset, and then processes it through each rule line by line. If the *lhs* of a rule matches the address, it is rewritten by the *rhs*. If it doesn't match, `sendmail` continues to the next rule until it reaches the end of the ruleset[3]. At the end of the ruleset, `sendmail` returns the rewritten address to the calling ruleset or to the next ruleset in its built-in execution sequence.

If an address matches the *lhs* and is rewritten by the *rhs*, the rule is tried again—an implicit loop (but see the $@ and $: modifiers below for exceptions).

As shown in Table 41.1, each rewriting rule is introduced by the R command and has three fields, the lefthand side *(lhs,* or matching side), the righthand side *(rhs,* or rewriting side) and an optional comment, each of which *must* be separated by tab characters:

```
Rlhs      rhs        comment
```

Parsing—Turning Addresses into Tokens

`sendmail` *parses* addresses and the *lhs* of rules into tokens and then matches the address and the *lhs,* token by token. The macro $o contains the characters that `sendmail` uses to separate an address into tokens. It's often defined like this:

```
# address delimiter characters
Do.:%@!^/[]
```

All of the characters in $o are both token separators and tokens. `sendmail` takes an address such as `rae@rainbow.org` and breaks it into tokens according to the characters in the o macro, like this:

```
"rae"     "@"      "rainbow"    "."      "org"
```

`sendmail` also parses the *lhs* of rewriting rules into tokens so they can be compared one by one with the input address to see if they match. For instance, the *lhs* `$-@rainbow.org` gets parsed as:

```
"$-"       "@"       "rainbow"       "."       "org"
```

(Don't worry about the `$-` just yet. It's a *pattern-matching operator* similar to shell wild cards that matches any single token, and is covered below in "The Lefthand Side (lhs) of Rules.") Now we can put the two together to show how `sendmail` decides whether an address matches the *lhs* of a rule:

```
"rae"      "@"       "rainbow"       "."       "org"
"$-"       "@"       "rainbow"       "."       "org"
```

In this case, each token from the address matches a constant string (e.g., `rainbow`) or a pattern-matching operator (`$-`), so the address matches and `sendmail` would use the *rhs* to rewrite the address.

Consider the effect (usually bad!) of changing the value of `$o`. As shown above, `sendmail` breaks the address `rae@rainbow.org` into five tokens. However, if the `@` character were not in `$o`, the address would be parsed quite differently, into only *three* tokens:

```
"rae@rainbow"       "."       "org"
```

You can see that changing `$o` has a drastic effect on `sendmail`'s address parsing, and you should leave it alone until you really know what you're doing. Even then you probably won't want to change it since the V8 `sendmail` configuration files already have it correctly defined for standard RFC 822 and RFC 976 address interpretation.

The Lefthand Side (*lhs*) of Rules

The *lhs* is a pattern against which `sendmail` matches the input address. The *lhs* may contain ordinary text or any of the pattern-matching operators shown in Table 41.2:

Table 41.2. `lhs` pattern-matching operators.

$-	Match *exactly one* token[4]
$+	Match *one or more* tokens
$*	Match *zero or more* tokens
$@	Match the *null input* (used to call the error mailer)

The values of macros and classes are matched in the *lhs* with the operators shown in Table 41.3:

Table 41.3. lhs **macro and class matching operators.**

$X	Match the value of macro X
$=C	Match *any word* in class C
$-C	Match if token *is not* in class C

The pattern-matching operators and macro- and class-matching operators are necessary because most rules must match many different input addresses. For instance, a rule might need to match all addresses that end with gonzo.gov and begin with one or more of anything.

The Righthand Side (rhs) of Rules

The *rhs* of a rewriting rule tells sendmail how to rewrite an address that matches the *lhs*. The *rhs* may include text, macros, and positional references to matches in the *lhs*. When a pattern-matching operator from Table 41.2 matches the input, sendmail assigns it to a numeric macro *$n*, corresponding to the position it matches in the *lhs*. For instance, suppose the address joe@pc1.gonzo.gov is passed to the following rule:

```
R$+ @ $+        $: $1 < @ $2 >          focus on domain
```

In this example, joe matches $+ (one or more of anything), so sendmail assigns the string joe to $1. The @ in the address matches the @ in the *lhs*, but constant strings are not assigned to positional macros. The tokens in the string pc1.gonzo.gov match the second $+ and are assigned to $2. The address is rewritten as $1<@$2>, or joe<@pc1.gonzo.gov>.

$: and $@—Altering a Ruleset's Evaluation

Consider the following rule:

```
R$*   $: $1 < @ $j > add local domain
```

After rewriting an address in the *rhs*, sendmail tries to match the rewritten address with the *lhs* of the current rule. Since $* matches zero or more of anything, what prevents sendmail from going into an infinite loop on this rule? After all, no matter how the *rhs* rewrites the address, it will always match $*.

The $: preface to the *rhs* comes to the rescue; it tells sendmail to evaluate the rule only once.

There are also times when you want a ruleset to terminate immediately and return the address to the calling ruleset or the next ruleset in sendmail's built-in sequence. Prefacing a rule's *rhs* with $@ causes sendmail to exit the ruleset immediately after rewriting the address in the *rhs*.

$>—Calling Another Ruleset

A ruleset can pass an address to another ruleset by using the `$>` preface to the *rhs*. Consider the following rule:

```
R$*     $: $>66 $1          call ruleset 66
```

The *lhs* `$*` matches zero or more of anything, so `sendmail` always does the *rhs*. As we saw in the previous section, the `$:` prevents the rule from being evaluated more than once. The `$>66 $1` calls ruleset 66 with `$1` as its input address. Since the `$1` matches whatever was in the *lhs*, this rule simply passes the entirety of the current input address to ruleset 66. Whatever ruleset 66 returns is passed to the next rule in the ruleset.

Testing Rules and Rulesets—the *-bt, -d* and *-C* Options

Debugging a `sendmail.cf` can be a tricky business. Fortunately, `sendmail` provides several ways to test rulesets before you install them.

> **NOTE:** The examples in this section assume that you have a working `sendmail`. If your system doesn't, try running them again after you've installed V8 `sendmail`.

The `-bt` option tells `sendmail` to enter its rule-testing mode:

```
$ sendmail -bt
ADDRESS TEST MODE (ruleset 3 NOT automatically invoked)
Enter <ruleset> <address>
>
```

> **NOTE:** Notice the warning `ruleset 3 NOT automatically invoked`. Older versions of sendmail ran ruleset 3 automatically when in address test mode, which made sense since `sendmail` sends all addresses through ruleset 3 anyway. V8 `sendmail` does not, but it's a good idea to invoke ruleset 3 manually since later rulesets expect the address to be in canonical form.

The `>` prompt means `sendmail` is waiting for you to enter one or more ruleset numbers, separated by commas, and an address. Try your login name with rulesets 3 and 0. The result should look something like this:

```
> 3,0 joe
rewrite: ruleset  3   input: joe
rewrite: ruleset  3 returns: joe
rewrite: ruleset  0   input: joe
rewrite: ruleset  3   input: joe
rewrite: ruleset  3 returns: joe
rewrite: ruleset  6   input: joe
```

```
rewrite: ruleset  6 returns: joe
rewrite: ruleset  0 returns: $# local $: joe
>
```

The output shows how sendmail processes the input address joe in each ruleset. Each line of output is identified with the number of the ruleset processing it, the input address, and the address that the ruleset returns. The > is a second prompt indicating that sendmail is waiting for another line of input. When you're done testing, just type **Ctrl+D.**

Indentation and blank lines better show the flow of processing in this example:

```
rewrite: ruleset  3   input: joe
rewrite: ruleset  3 returns: joe

rewrite: ruleset  0   input: joe

    rewrite: ruleset  3   input: joe
    rewrite: ruleset  3 returns: joe

    rewrite: ruleset  6   input: joe
    rewrite: ruleset  6 returns: joe

rewrite: ruleset  0 returns: $# local $: joe
```

The rulesets called were 3 and 0, in that order. Ruleset 3 was processed and returned the value joe, and then sendmail called ruleset 0. Ruleset 0 called ruleset 3 again, and then ruleset 6, an example of how a ruleset can call another one by using $>. Neither ruleset 3 nor ruleset 6 rewrote the input address. Finally, ruleset 0 resolved to a mailer, as it must.

Often you need more detail than -bt provides—usually just before you tear out a large handful of hair because you don't understand why an address doesn't match the *lhs* of a rule. You may remain hirsute because sendmail has verbose debugging built-in to most of its code.

You use the -d option to turn on sendmail's verbose debugging. This option is followed by a numeric code that tells which section of debugging code to turn on, and at what level. The following example shows how to run sendmail in one of its debugging modes and the output it produces:

```
$ sendmail -bt -d21.12
Version 8.6.7
ADDRESS TEST MODE (ruleset 3 NOT automatically invoked)
Enter <ruleset> <address>
> 3,0 joe
rewrite: ruleset  3   input: joe
-----trying rule: $* < > $*
----- rule fails
-----trying rule: $* < $* < $* < $+ > $* > $* > $*
------ rule fails
[etc.]
```

The -d21.12 in the example above tells sendmail to turn on level 12 debugging in section 21 of its code. The same command with the option -d21.36 gives more verbose output (debug level 36 instead of 12).

> **NOTE:** You can combine one or more debugging specifications separated by commas, as in `-d21.12,14.2`, which turns on level 12 debugging in section 21 and level 2 debugging in section 14. You can also give a range of debugging sections, as in `-d1-10.35`, which turns on debugging in sections 1 through 10 at level 35. The specification `-d0-91.104` turns on all sections of V8 `sendmail`'s debugging code at the highest levels and produces thousands of lines of output for a single address.

The `-d` option is not limited to use with `sendmail`'s address testing mode (`-bt`); you can also use it to see how `sendmail` processes rulesets while sending a letter, as the following example shows:

```
$ sendmail -d21.36 joe@gonzo.gov < /tmp/letter
[lots and lots of output...]
```

Unfortunately, the SIOG doesn't tell you which numbers correspond to which sections of code. Instead, the author suggests that it's a lot of work to keep such documentation current (which it is), and that you should look at the code itself to discover the correct debugging formulas.

The function `tTd()` is the one to look for. For example, suppose you wanted to turn on debugging in `sendmail`'s address-parsing code. The source file `parseaddr.c` contains most of this code, and the following command finds the allowable debugging levels:

```
$ egrep tTd parseaddr.c
        if (tTd(20, 1))
[...]
        if (tTd(24, 4))
        if (tTd(22, 11))
[etc.]
```

The `egrep` output shows that debugging specifications like `-d20.1`,   `-d24.4`, and `-d22.11` (and others) will make sense to `sendmail`.

If perusing thousands of lines of C code doesn't appeal to you, the book `sendmail` documents the debugging flags for `sendmail` version 8.6.9.

The `-c` option allows you to test new configuration files *before* you install them, which is always a good idea. If you want to test a different file, use `-C/path/to/the/file`. This can be combined with the `-bt` and `-d` flags. For instance, a common invocation for testing new configuration files is:

```
sendmail -Ctest.cf -bt -d21.12
```

> **WARNING:** For security, `sendmail` drops its super-user permissions when you use the `-c` option. Final testing of configuration files should be done as the super-user to ensure that your testing is compatible with `sendmail`'s normal operating mode.

Conclusion

Now you know a lot about the `sendmail.cf` language as well as some useful debugging techniques. However, configuration files will be easier to grasp when you look at some real ones. The section below shows you how to create one from the `m4` templates included with V8 `sendmail`.

Creating a *sendmail.cf*

In this section, we'll develop a `sendmail.cf` for a Solaris 2.3 system, using the templates supplied with V8 `sendmail`. However, because every site is different, even if you're developing a `sendmail.cf` for another Solaris 2.3 system, yours will probably differ from the one below.

Previous versions of `sendmail` included complete, sample configuration files to adapt for your site. By contrast, the V8 `sendmail` configuration files are supplied as `m4` templates that you use like building blocks to create a custom configuration file. This is a big advantage for most people. In previous versions, if your site did not want UUCP support, you had to pick through hundreds of lines of a configuration file and remove it line by line. In this version, you simply insert the statement FEATURE(nouucp) into your configuration file template and you are done.

`M4` is a programming language that reads a file of macro definitions and commands and creates an output file from it. As a trivial example, suppose you create a document and find yourself repeatedly typing the phrase `sendmail Installation and Operation Guide`. To avoid the extra typing, you could define a macro `siog` and enter that instead:

```
$ cat > test.m4
define('siog','Sendmail Installation and Operation Guide')dnl
Testing: siog
Ctrl+D
$ m4 test.m4
Testing: Sendmail Installation and Operation Guide
```

Running `m4` on the file `test.m4` converts all occurrences of `siog` to `sendmail Installation and Operation Guide`. This example only hints at `m4`'s capabilities. The V8 `sendmail.cf` templates make full use of them.

The `sendmail.cf` templates and `m4` support files are in the `cf` directory you created earlier when you unpacked V8 `sendmail`:

```
$ cd cf
$ ls -CF
README      domain/     hack/       mailer/     sh/
cf/         feature/    m4/         ostype/     siteconfig/
```

Please note the file README. If you don't read it, you have little hope of making a working configuration file.

The `cf` subdirectory is the main one of interest. It contains `m4` templates for configuration files used at the University of California at Berkeley (UCB). You should look at them all; one of them may be very close to what you need, and all of them provide good examples for you to adapt to your own site.

The other subdirectories contain `m4` support files, the building blocks that are included based on the template you define in the cf subdirectory. You probably won't have to change any of these, although you may need to create site-specific files in the `domain` and `siteconfig` subdirectories.

The `cf` subdirectory contains the following configuration file templates:

```
$ cd cf
$ ls -CF
Makefile                knecht.mc               sunos4.1-cs-exposed.mc
Makefile.dist           mail.cs.mc              sunos4.1-cs-hidden.mc
alpha.mc                mail.eecs.mc            tcpproto.mc
auspex.mc               obj/                    ucbarpa.mc
chez.mc                 osf1-cs-exposed.mc      ucbvax.mc
clientproto.mc          osf1-cs-hidden.mc       udb.mc
cogsci.mc               python.mc               ultrix4.1-cs-exposed.mc
cs-exposed.mc           riscos-cs-exposed.mc    ultrix4.1-cs-hidden.mc
cs-hidden.mc            s2k.mc                  uucpproto.mc
hpux-cs-exposed.mc      sunos3.5-cs-exposed.mc  vangogh.mc
hpux-cs-hidden.mc       sunos3.5-cs-hidden.m
```

The template `tcpproto.mc` is intended for a generic Internet site without UUCP connections. We'll use that as a starting point to develop our own. Since we don't want to modify the original file, we'll make a copy called `test.mc` and modify that. Although we won't show this in the examples below, it's a good idea to use a version control system like SCCS or RCS, or some other version control system to track changes you make to your configuration file template.

Stripped of its comments (a copyright notice), blank lines, and an `m4` directive, `test.mc` looks like this:

```
include('../m4/cf.m4')
VERSIONID('@(#)tcpproto.mc     8.2 (Berkeley) 8/21/93')
FEATURE(nouucp)
MAILER(local)
MAILER(smtp)
```

This doesn't look like much, but m4 expands it to almost 600 lines. We'll look at this template line-by-line to show what it does.

The line `include('../m4/cf.m4')` *must* come first in all configuration file templates, immediately after any comments. It contains the macro definitions that m4 uses to build your configuration file, and if you don't include it here, nothing else will work.

The `VERSIONID()` macro provides a place to put version information for the edification of humans—sendmail ignores it. If you use RCS or SCCS, you can include their version information here. For instance, for RCS you can include the `$Id$` keyword:

```
VERSIONID('$Id$')
```

and the RCS `co` (check-out) command expands this to:

```
VERSIONID('$Id: test.mc,v 1.1 1994/03/26 21:46:12 joe Exp joe $')
```

The `FEATURE()` macro is used to specify which features you want (or don't want). The line `FEATURE(nouucp)` in this configuration file template removes UUCP support from the resulting configuration file. Other features are documented in the README file mentioned above. Some features of particular interest are `redirect`, which provides a clever way to notify senders when someone leaves your site; and `nullclient`, which creates a bare-bones configuration file that knows just enough to forward mail to a relay. (See the template `nullclient.mc` for an example of its use.)

The next two lines are `MAILER()` macros to specify the mailers included in this `sendmail.cf`. The `MAILER()` macro takes a single argument, the name of the mailer when m4 expands the `MAILER()` macro into one or more ruleset definitions, rules to select them in ruleset 0, and the rulesets given in the R= and S= flags. Selecting the `smtp` mailer actually causes three SMTP mailers to be included. The V8 templates also provide mailer definitions for UUCP mailers, a FAX mailer, and a POP (Post Office Protocol) mailer. See the README file for details.

This is almost enough of a specification to create a working `sendmail.cf` for an SMTP-only site, but you'll want to tune it a little first with additional macros.

The `OSTYPE()` macro also takes a single argument, the name of a file in `../ostype`. This file should contain definitions particular to your operating system, for instance, the location of the aliases file. A wide variety of operating system definitions are included with the V8 configuration files:

```
$ cd ../ostype
$ ls
aix3.m4      bsdi1.0.m4     hpux.m4       osf1.m4        sunos3.5.m4
aux.m4       dgux.m4        irix.m4       riscos4.5.m4   sunos4.1.m4
bsd4.3.m4    domainos.m4    linux.m4      sco3.2.m4      svr4.m4
bsd4.4.m4    dynix3.2.m4    nextstep.m4   solaris2.m4    ultrix4.1.m4
```

Since we're developing a configuration file for a Solaris 2.3 system, we'll look at that file:

```
$ cat solaris2.m4
define('ALIAS_FILE', /etc/mail/aliases)
define('HELP_FILE', /etc/mail/sendmail.hf)
define('STATUS_FILE', /etc/mail/sendmail.st)
define('LOCAL_MAILER_FLAGS', 'fSn')
```

This is pretty straightforward—the file gives the location of sendmail's auxiliary files on that system and specifies local mailer flags appropriate for the Solaris version of /bin/mail. We'll include an OSTYPE() macro just after the VERSIONID() macro, dropping the .m4 filename extension.

The other things you may define in an OSTYPE file are documented in the README.

You may also want to create a *domain* file and use the DOMAIN() macro to collect site-wide definitions such as your site's UUCP or BITNET relay hosts. You should only put things in this file that are true for all the hosts in your domain. If you only have a single host, you may want to forego creating a domain file and keep this information in your m4 template.

The DOMAIN() macro takes a single argument, the name of a file in ../domain. For instance, DOMAIN(gonzo) would cause m4 to look for a file named ../domain/gonzo.m4. (Note that the .m4 extension is not included in the macro argument.)

> **WARNING:** If you copy one of the UCB templates that includes a DOMAIN() macro, make sure you change that line to use your own domain file, or delete it.

A common feature to include in a domain file is the MASQUERADE_AS() macro, which causes all hosts using that sendmail.cf to masquerade as your mail hub. For example, if the Solaris 2.3 host we're building this configuration file for is one of many, all named sunX.gonzo.gov, the following line would cause all their outbound mail to be addressed as login@gonzo.gov, regardless of which workstation sent it:

```
MASQUERADE_AS(gonzo.gov)dnl
```

This line could also be included in the m4 template if you don't want to create a domain file. Now the template looks like this, with the lines we've added or changed in boldface type:

```
include('../m4/cf.m4')
VERSIONID('$Id$')
OSTYPE(solaris2)
MASQUERADE_AS(gonzo.gov)
FEATURE(nouucp)
MAILER(local)
MAILER(smtp)
```

To create the working sendmail.cf, run m4 on the template:

```
$ m4 test.mc > test.cf
```

This creates a 600 line configuration file, which should be tested thoroughly before you install it. We will do just that in the next section, "Testing sendmail and sendmail.cf."

But first, considering that building a sendmail.cf file from the V8 macros is so easy, you may be wondering why I went on at such length about the guts of it. After all, if including an SMTP mailer is as easy as typing MAILER(smtp), why bother to learn the grungy details? The first answer is that someday you'll probably need them; something will go wrong and you'll have to figure out exactly why your sendmail isn't working the way it should. You can't do that unless you understand the details. A second answer is that you can't properly test your sendmail.cf unless you know what's going on under the simplified m4 gloss. Finally, although the V8 configuration file templates are easy to work with compared to those included with previous versions of sendmail, they're still not exactly on a par with plugging in a new toaster and shoving in a couple of slices of rye. If sendmail were a toaster, instead of a single lever it would have hundreds of complicated knobs and dials, a thick instruction manual, and despite your best efforts, would periodically burst into flames.

Testing *sendmail* and *sendmail.cf*

Before installing a new or modified sendmail.cf you must test it thoroughly. Even small, apparently innocuous changes can lead to disaster, and as mentioned in the introduction to this chapter, people get really irate when you mess up the mail system.

The first step in testing is to create a list of addresses that you know should work at your site. For instance, at gonzo.gov, an Internet site without UUCP connections, they know that the following addresses must work:

```
joe
joe@pc1.gonzo.gov
joe@gonzo.gov
```

If gonzo.gov has a UUCP link, those addresses must also be tested. Other addresses to consider include the various kinds of aliases (e.g., postmaster, a :include: list, an alias that mails to a file and one that mails to a program), nonlocal addresses, source-routed addresses, and so on. If you want to be thorough, you can create a test address for each legal address format in RFC822.

Now that you've got your list of test addresses, you can use the -c and -bt options to see what happens. At a minimum you'll want to run the addresses through rulesets 3 and 0 to make sure they are routed to the correct mailer. An easy way to do this is to create a file containing the ruleset invocations and test addresses, and run sendmail on that. For instance, if the file addr.test contains the following lines:

```
3,0 joe
3,0 joe@pc1.gonzo.gov
3,0 joe@gonzo.gov
```

you can test your configuration file `test.cf` by typing:

```
$ sendmail -Ctest.cf -bt < addr.test
rewrite: ruleset  3   input: joe
rewrite: ruleset  3 returns: joe
[etc.]
```

You may also want to follow one or more addresses through the complete rewriting process. For instance, if an address resolves to the `smtp` mailer and that mailer specifies `R=21`, you can test recipient address rewriting with `3,2,21,4 test_address`.

If the `sendmail.cf` appears to work correctly so far, it's time to move on to sending some real letters. You can do so with a command like this:

```
$ sendmail -v -oQ/tmp -Ctest.cf recipient < /dev/null
```

The `-v` option tells `sendmail` to be verbose so you can see what's happening. Depending on whether the delivery is local or remote, you may see something as simple as `joe... Sent`, or an entire SMTP dialogue.

The `-oQ/tmp` tells `sendmail` to use `/tmp` as its queue directory. This is necessary because `sendmail` drops its super-user permissions when run with the `-C` option and can't write queue files into the normal mail queue directory. Because you are using the `-C` and `-oQ` options, `sendmail` also includes the following warning headers in the letter to help alert the recipient of possible mail forgery:

```
X-Authentication-Warning: gonzo.gov: Processed from queue /tmp
X-Authentication-Warning: gonzo.gov: Processed by joe with -C srvr.cf
```

`sendmail` also inserts the header `Apparently-to: joe` because although you specified a recipient on the command line, there was none in the body of the letter. In this case the letter's body was taken from the empty file `/dev/null`, so there was no `To:` header. If you do your testing as the super-user, you can skip the `-oQ` argument, and `sendmail` won't insert the warning headers. You can avoid the `Apparently-to:` header by creating a file like this:

```
To: recipient

testing
```

and using it as input instead of `/dev/null`.

The *recipient* should be you so you can inspect the headers of the letter for correctness. In particular, return address lines must include an FQDN for SMTP mail. That is, a header like `From: joe@gonzo` is incorrect since it doesn't include the domain part of the name, but a header like `From: joe@gonzo.gov` is fine.

You should repeat this testing for the same variety of addresses you used in the first tests. You may have to create special aliases that point to you for some of the testing.

The amount of testing you do depends on the complexity of your site and the amount of experience you have, but a beginning system administrator should test things very thoroughly, even for apparently simple installations. Remember the flaming toaster.

Installing *sendmail* and Friends

Once you're satisfied that your `sendmail` and `sendmail.cf` work, you must decide where to install them. The most popular approach is to put `sendmail` and its other files in the same place that your vendor puts its distributed `sendmail` files. The advantage of this approach is conformity; if someone else familiar with your operating system tries to diagnose a mail problem, he will know where to look.

However, some people prefer to install local programs separately from vendor programs, for several good reasons. First, operating system upgrades are usually easier when local modifications are clearly segregated from vendor programs. Second, some vendors, notably Sun Microsystems, release operating system patches that bundle together everything including the kitchen sink. If you naively install such a patch, you may inadvertently overwrite your V8 `sendmail` with your vendor's version, and it probably won't understand your V8 `sendmail.cf`.

Therefore, you may want to install `sendmail` in a subdirectory of `/usr/local`, the traditional directory for local enhancements to the vendor's operating system. The locations of `sendmail`'s auxiliary files are given in `sendmail.cf`, so you can either leave them in the vendor's usual locations or install them in `/usr/local` and modify the `sendmail.cf` to match. If you want to change the compiled-in location of the configuration file, redefine the C preprocessor macro `_PATH_SENDMAILCF` in `src/Makefile` and recompile `sendmail`. For example, add the definition:

```
-D_PATH_SENDMAILCF=\"/usr/local/lib/sendmail.cf\"
```

to the `CFLAGS` macro in the `Makefile`.

Once you've decided where the files should go, look at the Makefile you used to compile `sendmail` and see if it agrees. The easiest way is to use `make`'s `-n` option to see what *would* have happened. The results look like this for the V8 distribution's `Makefile.Solaris`:

```
$ make -n install
/usr/ucb/install -o root -g sys -m 6555 sendmail /usr/lib
for i in /usr/ucb/newaliases /usr/ucb/mailq; do rm -f $i; ln -s /usr/lib/sendmai
l $i; done
/usr/ucb/install -c -o root -g sys -m 644 /dev/null \
    /var/log/sendmail.st
/usr/ucb/install -c -o root -g sys -m 444 sendmail.hf /etc/mail
nroff -h -mandoc aliases.5 > aliases.0
nroff -h -mandoc mailq.1 > mailq.0
nroff -h -mandoc newaliases.1 > newaliases.0
nroff -h -mandoc sendmail.8 > sendmail.0
```

If this isn't what you want, modify the Makefile as necessary.

Note that the sendmail manual pages use the 4.4BSD mandoc macros, which your system probably doesn't have. You can ftp the mandoc macros from the host ftp.uu.net, in the directory /systems/unix/bsd-sources/share/tmac.

If your system doesn't have the /usr/ucb/install program, you can copy the new files instead, and use chown, chgrp and chmod to set the correct owner, group, and mode. However, if you're installing on top of your vendor's files, it's a good idea to first copy or rename them in case you ever need them again.

After you install sendmail and its auxiliary files, rebuild the aliases database by running sendmail -bi. You'll also need to kill and restart your sendmail daemon. If your vendor's system uses a *frozen configuration* file (sendmail.fc), remove it; V8 sendmail doesn't use one.

Modifying *sendmail's* Boot-Time Startup

In its SMTP server role, sendmail starts when the system boots and runs continuously. If you install it in a non-standard location like /usr/local, you'll have to modify your system's startup scripts. Even if you install it in the standard location, you should ensure that the default system startup is correct for V8 sendmail.

When SVR4 UNIX systems boot, they run a series of short shell scripts in the directories /etc/rc*x*.d, where the *x* corresponds to the system run level. For instance, shell scripts that bring the system to run level 2 are found in /etc/rc2.d.

However, SVR4 systems have many run levels and some software subsystems should be started in each of them. Therefore, the shell scripts in /etc/rc*x*.d are located in /etc/init.d and linked to the files in the /etc/rc*x*.d directories. The /etc/init.d directory is therefore the best place to look for your sendmail startup script.

The following example shows how to find how sendmail starts on a Solaris 2.3 system. Other SVR4 systems are similar:

```
$ cd /etc/init.d
$ grep sendmail *
sendmail:#ident "@(#)sendmail   1.4   92/07/14 SMI"   /* SVr4.0 1.5 */
sendmail:# /etc/init.d/sendmail - Start/Stop the sendmail daemon
sendmail:# If sendmail is already executing, don't re-execute it.
sendmail:if [ -f /usr/lib/sendmail -a -f /etc/mail/sendmail.cf ]; then
sendmail:               /usr/lib/sendmail -bd -q1h;
sendmail:pid='/usr/bin/ps -e ¦ /usr/bin/grep sendmail ¦ [...]
sendmail:echo "usage: /etc/rc2.d/S88sendmail {start¦stop}"
$
```

NOTE: Some of the lines above are truncated and shown as *[...]* due to page-width limitations.

In this case the grep output shows that the vendor starts sendmail with a script named sendmail because each line of the grep output is prefixed with that filename. Examine the script sendmail to see if any changes are necessary. This script expects sendmail to be located in /usr/lib. If you install V8 sendmail somewhere else, you'll have to modify the script to match, changing paths like /usr/lib/sendmail to /usr/local/lib/sendmail. If the command-line flags in the script aren't what you want, change those too.

Summary

It's not possible in a single chapter to tell you all you must know about e-mail administration, but as Yogi Berra (or maybe that was Casey Stengal) once said, "You could look it up," and you should. There are a lot of things you'll only learn by reading the documentation mentioned previously in "Background Material and Other Sources." However, this chapter should give you a good basis for understanding the theory behind Internet e-mail delivery and enough of the specifics of V8 sendmail to get your e-mail system up and running.

1. For instance, sendmail sets $j to your system's fully qualified domain name (FQDN, e.g., acme.com). If your system's gethostbyname() function returns something other than the FQDN, you must define $j in sendmail.cf.

2. The local mailer omits the $@*host*.

3. Ruleset 0 is an exception to this rule. sendmail stops evaluating rules in ruleset 0 as soon as a rule resolves to a mailer.

4. Tokens are explained in "Tokens—How sendmail Interprets Input Patterns."

News Administration

By Jeff Smith

Introduction

USENET is the name of what is almost certainly the world's largest electronic bulletin board system (BBS). It's a loose conglomeration of computers that run operating systems ranging from MS-DOS to UNIX and VM/CMS, and that exchange articles through UUCP, the Internet, and other networks. USENET is also probably the largest experiment to date with creative anarchy—there is no central authority or control, and anyone can join who runs the appropriate software and who can find a host already on the network with which to exchange news.

The lenient requirements for membership, the wide variety of computers able to run USENET software, and the tremendous growth of the Internet have combined to make USENET big. How big? No one really knows how many hosts and users participate, but the volume of news will give you some idea. A recent estimate (March 1994) in the "How to become a USENET site" Frequently Asked Questions (FAQ) document suggests 3,500 MB of news per month, which works out to an average of more than 100 MB per day. (See Table 42.1.) The same FAQ goes on to point out that a full newsfeed over a 14.4KB modem takes about 15 hours a day, and that's when data compression is used. To make matters worse, some people estimate that news volume is doubling every 12 months.

This huge volume can cause problems if you're the system administrator, because the amount of disk space used for news may vary a lot, and quickly. You might think you've got plenty of space in your news system when you leave on Friday night, but then you get a call in the wee hours of Sunday morning telling you that the news file system is full. If you've planned poorly, it might take more important things with it—such as e-mail, system logging, or accounting (see "Isolating the News Spool" later in this chapter to avoid that problem). This chapter (and good planning) will help you avoid some (but not all) of the late-night calls.

The chapter begins with some pointers on finding additional sources of information. Some information is included on the *UNIX Unleashed* CD-ROM, some is available on the Internet, and some (from the technical newsgroups) you'll be able to apply only *after* you get your news system running.

The examples in this chapter assume you have an Internet site running the Network News Transfer Protocol (NNTP). If your networking capabilities are limited to the UNIX-to-UNIX Copy Program (UUCP), you're mostly on your own. Although some of the general information given here will still apply, UUCP is a pain and the economics of a full news feed make Internet access more and more attractive every day. If your site isn't on the Internet but you want to receive news, it might be time to talk to your local Internet service provider. You may find it cheaper to pay Internet access fees than 15-hour-per-day phone bills. If your site's news needs aren't too great, it may even be more economical to buy USENET access from an Internet service provider. (See the section "Do You Really Want to Be a USENET Site?" later in this chapter.)

Additional Sources of Information

News software is inherently complex. This chapter can only begin to give you the information you need to successfully maintain a USENET site. The following sources of additional information will help you fill in the gaps.

Frequently Asked Questions (FAQ) Documents

In many USENET newsgroups, especially the technical ones, similar questions are repeated as new participants join the group. To avoid answering the same questions over and over, volunteers collect these prototypical questions (and the answers) into FAQs. The FAQs are posted periodically to that newsgroup and to the newsgroup news.answers. Many FAQs are also available through the Internet file transfer protocol (ftp), through e-mail servers, or through other information services such as Gopher, Wide Area Information Service (WAIS) and World Wide Web (WWW).

You should read the FAQs in the following list after you've read this chapter and *before* you install your news system. All of them are available on the host rtfm.mit.edu in subdirectories of the directory pub/usenet/news.answers.

usenet-software/part1	History of USENET; a gloss on software for transporting, reading, and posting news, including packages for non-UNIX operating systems (such as, VMS, MS-DOS).
site-setup	Guidance on how to join USENET.
news/software/b/intro	A short introduction to the newsgroup news.software.b.
news/software/b/faq	The news.software.b FAQ. Read this *before* you post to that newsgroup. Read it even if you don't plan to post.
INN FAQs	There is a four-part FAQ for INN. You can get it from any host that has the INN software, including ftp.uu.net in the directory ~ftp/networking/news/nntp/inn.

News Transport Software Documentation

The only currently recommended news-transport software systems are C-news and InterNetworkNews (INN). Both come with extensive documentation to help you install and maintain them and a good set of UNIX manual pages. Whichever you choose, read the documentation and then read it again. This chapter is no substitute for the software author's documentation, which is updated to match each release of the software and which contains details that a chapter of this size can't cover.

Request for Comments (RFC) Documents

RFCs are issued by working groups of the Internet Engineering Task Force (IETF). They were known initially as *requests for comments*, but as they become adopted as Internet standards you should think of them as *requirements for compliance*—if you want to exchange news with another Internet NNTP site, you must both comply with the provisions of RFCs 977 and 1036. RFCs are available for anonymous ftp on the host ftp.internic.net and others. The RFCs mentioned here are also included on the *UNIX Unleashed* CD-ROM.

- ■ RFC 977 (Network News Transfer Protocol) defines the commands by which Internet news servers exchange news articles with other news servers, newsreaders, and news-posting programs. The protocol is fairly simple, and this RFC will give you a better idea of what your newsreaders, news-posting programs, and news-transport software are doing behind your back.

- ■ RFC 1036 (Standard for Interchange of USENET Messages) explains the format of USENET news articles, which is based on the format of Internet e-mail messages. You don't need to memorize it, but a quick read will help you understand the functions and formats of the various news articles.

USENET Newsgroups

Once you get your news system running, there are several technical and policy newsgroups you'll want to read. These newsgroups will keep you abreast of new releases of your news-transport software, bug fixes, and security problems. You'll also see postings of common problems experienced at other sites, so if you encounter the same problems you'll have the solutions. Many knowledgeable people contribute to these newsgroups, including the authors of C-news and INN.

However, remember that the people answering your questions are volunteers doing so in their spare time, so be polite. The first step toward politeness is to read the newsgroup's FAQ (if there is one) and so avoid being the 1,001st lucky person to ask how to make a round wheel. You should also read the "Emily Postnews" guide to USENET etiquette and other introductory articles in the newsgroup news.announce.newusers. Listed below are a few of the newsgroups you may want to read. You may want to subscribe to all of the news.* groups for a few weeks and then cancel the subscriptions for the ones you don't need.

news.announce.newusers	Information for new users. You should subscribe all of your users to this group.
news.announce.newgroups	Announcements of newsgroup vote results and which newsgroups are about to be created.
news.software.readers	Information and discussion of news-reading software (also known as "newsreaders").
news.admin.policy	Discussions pertaining to site's news policies.
news.software.b	Discussions of software systems compatible with B-news (for example, C-news and INN).
news.software.nntp	Discussions of implementations of NNTP (for example, the so-called "reference implementation" and INN).

A Functional Overview of News Systems and Their Software

The following sections give a general idea of what a news system must do. Different news systems accomplish these tasks in different ways, but they all do basically the same thing.

Format of News Articles

Netnews articles are very similar to e-mail messages. An article consists of a *header*, which contains information such as the person who posted the article and the date, followed by a blank line and the *body* of the article. The body is mostly irrelevant as far as news-transport software is concerned—the content of the article's header tells it all it must know.

Newsgroup Hierarchies

Articles are posted to one or more *newsgroups*, whose names are separated by periods to categorize them into hierarchies. For instance, the newsgroups comp.unix.solaris and comp.risks are both in the comp hierarchy, which contains articles having to do with computers. The comp.unix.solaris newsgroup is further categorized by inclusion in the unix subhierarchy, which has to do with various vendors' versions of UNIX.

Some of the current USENET newsgroup hierarchies are shown below. There are others—this is by no means a definitive list. Some Internet mailing lists are fed into newsgroups in their own hierarchies. For instance, the GNU (GNU is a self-referential acronym for "GNU is not UNIX") project's mailing lists are fed to the gnu newsgroup hierarchy.

alt	The alternative newsgroup hierarchy. There is even less control here than in most of USENET, with new newsgroups created at the whim of anyone who knows how to send a newgroup control message. It is mostly a swamp, but you can often find something useful. Examples: alt.activism, alt.spam.
comp	Computer-related newsgroups. Example: comp.risks.
misc	Things that don't seem to fit anywhere else. Examples: misc.invest.stocks, misc.kids.vacation.
rec	Recreational newsgroups. Example: rec.woodworking.
soc	Social newsgroups. Examples: soc.college.grad, soc.culture.africa.
talk	Talk newsgroups. Intended for people who like to argue in public about mostly unresolvable and controversial issues. The talk hierarchy is a great waste of time and users love it. Examples: talk.politics.mideast, talk.abortion.

Newsgroup Distributions

Certain newsgroups and news postings are only relevant to certain geographical regions. For instance, it makes little sense to post an Indiana car-for-sale advertisement to the entire world, and Hungarian USENET sites won't appreciate the resources you waste in doing so—it costs thousands of dollars to send an article to all of USENET. Distributions allow you to control how far your article travels. For instance, typically you can post an article to your local site, your state, your continent, or to the entire world. News-posting programs usually offer users a choice of distributions as they construct their news postings. The news system administrator controls which distributions are presented to users, which distributions are accepted by the news system when articles are brought in by its newsfeeds, and which distributions are offered to outside hosts. The latter is important for sites that want to keep their local distributions private.

Where News Articles Live

News articles are stored in subdirectories of the *news spool*, which is usually named /var/spool/news or /usr/spool/news. The files that contain articles are given serial numbers as they are received, with the periods in the newsgroup names replaced by the slash character (/). For instance, article number 1047 of the newsgroup `comp.unix.solaris` would be stored in the file `/var/spool/news/comp/unix/solaris/1047`. Articles in the news spool directory can be read with newsreaders and shared with other hosts in your domain by using a network file system or the Network News Transfer Protocol (NNTP).

The User Interface—Newsreaders and Posting Programs

Newsreaders are the user interface to reading news. Since news articles are stored as ordinary files, you could use a program such as `cat` or `more` for your newsreading, but most users want something more sophisticated. Many newsgroups receive more than a hundred articles a day, and most users don't have time to read them all. They want a program that helps them quickly reject the junk so they can read only articles of interest to them. A good newsreader enables users to select and reject articles based on their `Subject` header; several provide even more sophisticated filtering capabilities. Some of the more popular newsreaders are `rn` (and its variant `trn`), `nn`, and `tin`. The GNU Emacs editor also has several packages (GNUS and Gnews) available for newsreading from within Emacs. These newsreaders are available for anonymous ftp from the host `ftp.uu.net` and others.

Newsreaders usually have built-in news-posting programs or the capability to call a posting program from within the newsreader. Most of them also let you respond to articles by e-mail.

Newsreaders are like religions and text editors—there are lots of them and no one agrees on which is best. Your users will probably want you to install them all, as well as whatever wonderful new one was posted to `comp.sources.unix` last week. If you don't have much time for news administration, you may want to resist or suggest the users get their own sources and install private copies. Otherwise you can spend a lot of time maintaining newsreaders.

News-posting programs enable you to post your own articles. A news-posting program prepares an article template with properly formatted headers, and then calls the text editor of your choice (usually whatever is named in the `EDITOR` environment variable) so you can type in your article. When you exit the editor, you're usually given the choice to post the article, edit it again, or quit without posting anything. If you choose to post the article, the news-posting program hands it to another news system program, which injects it into the news-transport system and puts a copy in the news spool directory.

Newsreaders and news-posting programs are usually both included in the same package of software. For instance, if you install the `rn` package you will also install `Pnews`, its news-posting program.

The News Overview Database (NOV)

Newsreaders (and users) have a difficult job. Remember that more than 100 MB of news is posted to USENET per day. That's about the same as a fairly thick novel every day of the year, without any holidays. Most people want to have their favorite newsreader sift the wheat from the chaff and present them with only the articles they want to see, in some rational order.

To do this, newsreaders must keep a database of information about the articles in the news spool; for instance, an index of `Subject` headers and article cross-references. These are commonly known as *threads databases*. The authors of newsreaders have independently developed different threads databases for their newsreaders, and naturally they're all incompatible with each other. For instance, if you install `trn`, `nn`, and `tin`, you must install each of their threads database maintenance programs and databases, which can take a lot of CPU cycles to generate and may become quite large.

Geoff Collyer, one of the authors of C-news, saw that this was not good and created the News Overview Database (NOV), a standard database of information for fancy newsreaders. The main advantage of NOV is that just one database must be created and maintained for all newsreaders. The main disadvantage is that it hasn't yet caught on with all the authors of news software.

If you're interested in NOV support, you must install news-transport software that has the NOV NNTP extensions (INN does) and newsreaders that can take advantage of it. According to the NOV FAQ, `trn3.3` and `tin-1.21` have built-in NOV support, and there is an unofficial version (not supported by the author) of `nn` for anonymous ftp on the host `agate.berkeley.edu` in the directory `~ftp/pub/usenet/NN-6.4P18+xover.tar.Z`.

Sharing News Over the Network

If you have several hosts on a local area network (LAN), you'll want to share news among them to conserve disk space. As mentioned previously, if you carry all possible newsgroups your news spool will need about a gigabyte of disk space, more or less depending on how long you keep articles online. A year from now, who knows how much you'll need? It makes more sense to add disk capacity to a single host than to add it to all your hosts.

There are two ways to share news over a LAN. If all of your hosts run a network file system such as Sun Microsystem's NFS or Transarc's AFS (Andrew File System), you can export the news host's spool directory to them and your newsreaders will probably never know the difference. (News-posting programs may need special support.) However, this approach assumes that all of your hosts can run a network file system, which may not be true.

A second way is to use NNTP to transfer news from a single server host to client newsreaders and news-posting programs. The only requirements for the client hosts are that they be able to open up a TCP/IP connection over the network and have client software that understands NNTP. Most common UNIX-based newsreaders and news-posting programs have built-in NNTP support, and there are many NNTP clients for non-UNIX operating systems such as DOS, VMS, VM/CMS, and others.

An NNTP daemon runs continuously on the news server host listening on a well-known port, just as the Simple Mail Transfer Protocol (SMTP) server listens on a well-known port for incoming e-mail connections. NNTP client programs connect to the NNTP server and issue commands for reading and posting news articles. For instance, there are commands to ask for all the articles that have arrived since a certain date and time. A client newsreader can ask for those articles and display them to the user as the NNTP server ships them over the network. Hosts with which you exchange news connect to the NNTP server's port and transfer articles to your host.

NNTP servers usually have some form of built-in access control so that only authorized hosts can connect to them—after all, you don't want all the hosts on the Internet to be able to connect to your news server.

Transferring News to Other Hosts

When a posting program hands an article to the news system, it expects a copy of the article to be deposited in the local news spool (or the news spool of the local NNTP server), sent to other hosts, and eventually sent to the rest of USENET. Similarly, articles posted on other USENET hosts should eventually find their way into the local (or NNTP server's) spool directory.

Figure 42.1 illustrates a simple set of connections between hosts transferring news. The incoming and outgoing lines emphasize that news is both sent and received between each set of hosts.

FIGURE 42.1

The USENET Flooding Algorithm.

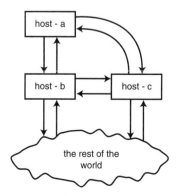

USENET news is transferred by a *flooding* algorithm, which means that when a host receives an article it sends it to all other hosts with which it exchanges news, and those hosts do the same. Now suppose that someone on host-b in Figure 42.1 posts a news article.

Because of the flooding algorithm, host-b sends the article to host-a, host-c, and any other hosts with which it exchanges news. Host-c gets the article and does the same, which means it gives the same article to host-a, which may try to give it back to host-b, which already has a copy of the article in its news spool. Further, since host-b gave host-a the article, it will try to give it to host-c, which already got it from host-b. It's also possible that host-a got a copy of the article from host-b before host-c offered it and will want to give it to host-c. Just to keep the news administrator's life interesting, no one can say whether any other hosts will ship the same article back to host-b or host-c. (Well-behaved hosts should avoid transferring articles back to the hosts from which they originally received them, but on USENET it's best to plan for worst-case behavior from another site's software.) How do these hosts know when articles are duplicates and should be rejected? Obviously they can't compare a new article with every article currently in the spool directory.

The news system software uses two different methods to avoid duplicate articles. The first is the Path header, which is a record of all the hosts through which a news article has passed. The Path header is just a list of hosts separated by punctuation marks other than periods, which are considered part of a hostname. A Path such as hst.gonzo.com,host-c.big.org!host-b.shark.com means that an article has been processed by each of the sites hst.gonzo.com, host-c.big.org and host-b.shark.com. Any of those hosts can reject the article because their names are already in the path.

RFC 1036 says that the Path header should *not* be used to generate e-mail reply addresses. However, some obsolete software might try to use it for that. INN discourages this use by inserting the pseudo-host not-for-mail into the Path.

The second way in which news systems avoid duplicate articles is the message-identifier header, Message-ID. Here is a sample Message-ID header:

```
Message-ID: <CsuM4v.3u9@hst.gonzo.com>
```

When a news article is created, the posting program or some other part of the news system generates this unique header. Since no two articles have the same Message-ID header, the news system can keep track of the message identifiers of all recent articles and reject those that it has already seen. The news history file keeps this record, and news-transport programs consult the history file when they're offered news articles. Because the volume of news is so large, history files get big pretty fast and are usually kept in some database format that allows quick access.

The history mechanism is not perfect. If you configure your news system to remember the message identifiers of all articles received in the past month, your history files may become inconveniently large. On the other hand, if a news system somewhere malfunctions and injects two-month-old articles into USENET, you won't have enough of a history to reject those articles. Inevitably, no matter how long a history you keep, it won't be long enough and you'll get a batch of old, bogus articles. Your users will complain. Such is life.

Host-to-host News-Transport Protocols

As with electronic mail, in order to transfer news from host to host, both hosts much speak the same language. Most USENET news is transferred either with the UUCP (UNIX to UNIX Copy Protocol) or NNTP. UUCP is used by hosts that connect with modems over ordinary phone lines, and NNTP is the method of choice for hosts on the Internet. As mentioned above, you should avoid UUCP if you can.

News-Transport System Configuration Files

The news-transport system needs a lot of information about your site. Minimally, it must know with which hosts you exchange news, at what times you do so, and what transport protocol you use for each site. It has to know which newsgroups and distributions your site should accept and which it should reject. NNTP sites must know which hosts are authorized to connect with them to read, post, and transfer news.

The news-transport system's configuration files provide this information. The news administrator must set up these files when installing the news system and must modify them in response to changes, such as a new newsfeed. The format of news-transport system control files varies, but all current systems provide detailed configuration documentation. Read it.

Planning a News System

You can see from the preceding discussion that there are many different strategies you can use to set up a news system. Because sites' needs vary, there is no single right way to do it. You must evaluate your site's needs and choose a strategy that fits. The questions in this section are intended to make you think about some of the issues you should consider.

Do You *Really* Want to Be a USENET Site?

As pointed out in the "how to join USENET" FAQ, you may not want to join at all. A news feed consumes significant CPU cycles, disk space, network (or modem) bandwidth, and staff time. Many Internet service providers will give your site access to USENET news over the network through NNTP client newsreaders, and if your site is small this may be more economical than a news feed. Do yourself a favor and do the math *before* you jump in. You can always join USENET at a later date if you find that your site's needs require a real feed.

Shared News versus One News Spool Per Host

A basic decision is whether you will maintain separate news spools and news systems on all of your hosts, or designate a single host to act as a news server and let other hosts access news through the network. If you have more than one host to administer, there are definite advantages to the latter approach.

If you have a single news host, your job as news administrator is much easier. Most news problems are confined to that host and you only have to maintain the (fairly complex) news transport software on that host. Software on client hosts is limited to newsreaders and news-posting software—no news-transport software is necessary. If there are problems, you know where to go to solve them, and once you solve them on the news host they will be solved for all the hosts in your domain.

USENET volume helps make a single-host strategy attractive. As mentioned previously, a full news feed can easily require a gigabyte of disk space, and the volume of USENET news continues to grow seemingly without bound. It's a lot easier to convince your boss to buy a bigger disk drive for a single host than for twenty. Since many users don't read news every day, the longer you can retain articles the happier they will be, and you can retain them longer on a single, dedicated news host than you can on multiple hosts.

Economics point to using a single news host both to minimize expensive staff time and to conserve disk space. The only reason you might want to store news on multiple hosts is if your network isn't up to par—if your only network connections are through UUCP, you can't use NNTP or a network file system to share news.

Isolating the News Spool

Most UNIX systems use the file system /var to contain files that grow unpredictably. For instance, /var/mail contains user mailboxes and /var/log contains system log files. Since the news spool is usually located in `/var/spool/news`, news articles may compete for space with potentially more important data such as e-mail. Having your e-mail system grind to a halt because someone posts his 10 MB collection of Madonna erotica will not endear you to your users or your boss.

The best way around this problem is to isolate the news spool in its own disk partition. If `/var/spool/news` is mounted on its own disk partition and it fills up, only the news system is affected.

The disadvantage of this approach is that it forces you to pre-allocate disk space. If you allocate too little to the news spool, you'll have to either expire articles sooner than you'd like or spend a lot of time fixing things by hand when the spool directory fills. If you allocate too much, it can't be used by other file systems, so you waste space. (However, it's better to guess too big than too little. Remember that the volume of USENET news constantly increases.)

Depending on how flexible your UNIX is, if you guess wrong and have to resize your partitions, it may be painful. You will have to resize at least two adjoining disk partitions to shrink or enlarge the news spool, which means dumping all the data in the partitions, creating new ones, and restoring the data. (A safer approach is to dump all the data on the disk and verify that you can read the backup tapes before you resize the partitions.) During this operation, the news system (and probably the computer) will be unavailable.

Configuring Your News Spool's File System

Before you can use a disk partition you must create a UNIX file system on it, using `newfs`, a front-end to the harder-to-user `mkfs` program. (Some versions of UNIX use `mkdev fs` to create file systems. Consult your system's administration manual.) Unless you tell it otherwise, `newfs` uses its built-in default for the ratio of *i-nodes* (index-nodes) to disk blocks. I-nodes are pre-allocated, and when you run out of them no new files can be created, even if you have disk space available in the file system. The `newfs` default for i-nodes is usually about right for most file systems but may not be for the news spool. News articles tend to be small, so you may run out of i-nodes in your news spool before you run out of disk space. On the other hand, since each pre-allocated i-node takes some disk space, if you allocate too many you'll waste disk space.

Most likely you'll want to tell `newfs` to create additional i-nodes when you create your news spool. The hard question is how many additional i-nodes to allocate. If your news system is already running, you can use the `df` command to find out. Simply compare the percentage of i-nodes in use to the percentage of disk blocks in use. If they are about the same, you're doing OK. If the disk block usage is a lot greater than the i-nodes in use, you've allocated too many i-nodes. What is more likely is that you'll find the i-nodes in use greatly outnumber the available disk blocks. The solution is to shut down your news system, dump the news spool to tape, run `newfs` to make a file system with more i-nodes, and restore the news spool from tape.

Where Will You Get Your News?

Some organizations use USENET for internal communications—for instance, a corporate BBS—and don't need or want to connect to USENET. However, if you want a USENET connection, you'll have to find one or more hosts willing to exchange news with you. Note that they are doing you a big favor—a full news feed consumes a lot of CPU cycles, network bandwidth, and staff time. However, the spirit of USENET is altruistic, and you may find a host willing to supply you with a news feed for free. In turn, you may someday be asked to supply a feed to someone else.

Finding a host willing to give you a news feed is easier if you're already on USENET, but if you were, you wouldn't need one. Your Internet service provider may be able to give you contact information, and as mentioned above, many service providers supply newsfeeds either as part of their basic service or at additional cost. Personal contacts with other system administrators who are already connected to USENET may help, even if they can't supply you a feed themselves. The "how to join USENET" FAQ mentioned previously contains other good ideas for finding a news feed.

It's a good idea to try to find a news feed that is topographically close on your network. If your site is in Indiana you don't want a transatlantic feed from Finland, even if you manage to find a host there willing to do it.

Site Policies

Your users' USENET articles reflect on your site, and new users often make mistakes. Unfortunately, the kinds of mistakes you can make on a world-wide network are the really bad ones. You should develop organizational USENET access policies and educate your users on proper USENET etiquette.

Policy questions tend toward the ethical and legal. For instance, if you carry the `alt` hierarchy, what will be your site's response when someone creates the newsgroup `alt.child-molesting.advocacy`? This is not beyond the pale of what you may expect in the `alt` hierarchy, and even within the traditional hierarchies where newsgroups are voted into existence you may find newsgroups your site may not wish to carry. What will you do when you receive a letter from joe@remote.site.edu, whining that one of your users is polluting his favorite newsgroup with "inappropriate" (in his opinion) postings. Do you want to get involved in USENET squabbles like that?

What will you do when you get 2,843 letters complaining that one of your users posted a pyramid-scheme come-on to 300 different newsgroups? Shoot him? Or maybe wish you'd done a more careful job of setting policy in the first place?

And what will you do when someone complains that the postings in alt.binaries.pictures.erotica.blondes are a form of sexual harassment and demands that the newsgroup be removed? Will you put yourself in the position of censor and drop that newsgroup, or drop the entire alt hierarchy to avoid having to judge the worth of a single newsgroup?

If you put yourself in the position of picking and choosing newsgroups, you will find that while it may be completely obvious to you that comp.risks has merit and alt.spam doesn't, your users may disagree, vehemently. If you propose to locally delete alt.spam to conserve computing resources, some users will refer to their right to free speech and accuse you of censorship and fascism. (Are you *sure* you wanted this job?)

Most news administrators don't want to be censors or arbiters of taste. Therefore, answers to policy questions should be worked out in advance, codified as site policy, and signed off on by management. You need to hammer away at your boss until you get a written policy telling you what you should and should not do with respect to news administration, and you need to do this *before* you join USENET. As implied above, such a policy should provide for user education and set bounds for proper user behavior.

Without taking a position on the merits of alt.spam, USENET access is not one of the fundamental rights enumerated in the United States Constitution. It's more like a driver's license—if you're willing to follow your site's rules, you can drive, and if you're not, you can't. It's management's job to provide those rules, with guidance from you.

Expiration Policies

News system software is flexible enough to selectively purge old articles. In other words, if your site doesn't care much about the alt hierarchy but considers the comp hierarchy to be important, it can retain comp articles longer than alt articles. From the proceeding discussion, you can see that this might be contentious. If Joe thinks that alt.spam is the greatest thing since indoor plumbing, he will cry foul if you expire spam articles in one day but retain comp articles for seven. You can see that article expiration is not just a technical issue but a policy issue and should be covered in the same written policies mentioned previously.

Automatic Response to newgroup/rmgroup Control Messages

Newsgroups are created and removed by special news articles called *control messages.* Anyone bright enough to understand RFCs 1036 and 977 can easily forge control messages to create and remove newsgroups. (That is, just about anyone.) This is a particular problem in the `alt` hierarchy, which for some reason attracts people with too much time on their hands, who enjoy creating newsgroups such as `alt.swedish-chef.bork.bork.bork`. The `alt` hierarchy also is used by people who don't want to go to the trouble of creating a new newsgroup through a USENET-wide vote, or who (usually correctly) guess that their hare-brained proposal wouldn't pass even the fairly easy USENET newsgroup creation process.

Another problem, somewhat less frequent, occurs when a novice news administrator posts *newgroup* messages with incorrect distributions and floods the net with requests to create his local groups.

You can configure your news system software to create and delete groups automatically upon receiving control messages, or to send e-mail to the news administrator saying that the group should be created or removed. If you like living dangerously, you can enable automatic creation *and* deletion, but most people don't. You don't want someone to delete all your newsgroups just to see if he can, and you don't want two or three hundred created because a news system administrator made a distribution mistake. Many sites allow automatic creation but do deletions manually. More cautious sites create and delete all groups by hand, and only if they have reason to believe the control message is valid. I recommend the latter approach. The only disadvantage is that you may miss the first few articles posted to a new newsgroup if you don't stay on top of things.

The ABCs of News-Transport Software

USENET began with A-news, a prototype news-transport system that was killed by its own success and was supplanted by B-news. B-news sufficed for quite a while but became another victim of USENET growth and was supplanted by C-news, a much more efficient system written by Henry Spencer and Geoff Collyer of the University of Toronto. C-news was followed by INN (InterNetworkNews), written by Rich Salz of the Open Software Foundation, who apparently hadn't heard of the letter "D."

Depending on your site's requirements, either C-news or INN make good news-transport systems, but this chapter has space for only one, INN. You may also want to consider C-news, which is fairly easy to install and will work well for most sites, but if you do you're on your own. Note too that if you install C-news and your site plans to use NNTP, you'll also have to obtain and install the NNTP "reference implementation," available by anonymous ftp from the host `ftp.uu.net` in the directory `~ftp/networking/news/nntp`. This isn't necessary for INN, which has a slightly modified version of NNTP built in.

INN is the news-transport system of choice for Internet sites that use NNTP to exchange news and provide newsreaders and news-posting services. It was designed specifically for efficiency in an Internet/NNTP environment, for hosts with many news feeds and lots of NNTP client newsreaders. Although its installation isn't as automated as C-news, it's not all that difficult, and it's well-documented. The following sections give an overview of how to build and install INN.

Getting Your Hands on the Sources

The latest version of INN available as this book goes to press is included on the *UNIX Unleashed* CD-ROM. This version is called `INN 1.4sec`. It was released on December 22, 1993, so it's had some time to mature. The *sec* stands for security—the `1.4sec` release corrects a security problem in INN 1.4. If you like to live on the bleeding edge (as opposed to the cutting edge), you can look for a later release of INN on the host `ftp.uu.net` in the directory `~ftp/networking/news/nntp/inn`. See Chapter 41, "Mail Administration," for more detailed instructions on obtaining software through ftp.

An INN Distribution Roadmap

Most of the important directories and programs in the INN distribution are summarized in the list below. Some are covered in more detail in the sections "Configuring INN— The config.data File," "Building INN," and "Site Configuration."

BUILD	A shell script for building and installing INN.
Install.ms.*	The `nroff` sources to INN's installation documentation.
README	What you might think. Read it.
backends	Programs for transferring news to your USENET neighbors.
config	Contains the file `config.dist`, with which you create `config.data`. `Config.data` controls the compilation of the rest of INN.
dbz	Sources for the database routines used by INN. `dbz` is a faster version of the `dbm` database programs included with many versions of UNIX.
doc	INN's manual pages.

expire	Contains programs that handle news expiration, or the purging of articles from your news spool. They also selectively purge old Message-IDs from the history file so it doesn't grow boundlessly.
frontends	Contains programs that control innd's operation or offer it news articles
include	C language header files for the INN programs.
innd	The heart of INN, innd is the daemon that listens on the NNTP port for incoming news transfers and newsreader connections. When newsreaders connect to this port, innd creates nnrpd processes and connects them to the newsreader.
lib	The sources for the C language function library used by other INN programs.
nnrpd	Communicates with NNTP newsreader clients, which frees innd to do its main job, transferring news.
samples	Sample configuration files that are copied into the site directory.
site	This directory contains shell scripts and site configuration files. The site configuration files must be edited to tell INN with which sites you exchange news, which hosts are allowed to connect to read and post news, and so on.
syslog	A replacement for older versions of the standard system logging program. You may not need this.

Learning About INN

The first step in setting up INN is to format and read its documentation. cd into the top of the INN source tree and type the following to create a formatted copy of the INN documentation named Install.txt:

```
$ make Install.ms
cat Install.ms.1 Install.ms.2 >Install.ms
chmod 444 Install.ms
$ nroff -ms Install.ms > Install.txt
```

If the make command doesn't work for you (and if it doesn't, your make is defective and will cause you problems later), type cat Install.ms.? > Install.ms and then the preceding nroff command. These two commands create a file named Install.txt, which you can view with your preferred editor or pager. Read it. Print it. Highlight it with your favorite color of fluorescent marker. Sleep with it under your pillow. Take it into the shower. Share it with your friends. Read it again. You won't be sorry.

The `Install.ms` document tells you just about everything you need to know to set up a news system based on INN. The only problem with it is that many people fail to read it carefully and think that there's something missing. There isn't. If you think there is, read it again. Buy a new fluorescent marker, print off a copy of the file, and sit down with a nice glass of your favorite tea. Put it back under your pillow. Discuss it at dinner parties until your hosts ask you to leave, and ask your spouse what she or he thinks about it. You may destroy your social life, but in the process you'll discover that you missed a few crucial bits of information the first time around. (Don't feel bad, nearly everyone does.)

Configuring INN—The *config.data* File

Once you've absorbed the INN documentation, you're ready to configure INN's compilation environment. Like C-news, INN can run on many different versions of UNIX. The programs that build INN need information about your version of UNIX so they can build INN correctly. This configuration is one of the most difficult parts of installing INN, and you must make sure that you get it right. The `Install.ms` documentation is essential because it contains sample configurations for many different versions of UNIX.

The directory `config` holds the INN master configuration file, `config.data`. INN uses the C-news `subst` program to modify its sources before compilation, and `config.data` provides the information `subst` needs to do its job. `Subst` uses the definitions in `config.data` to modify the INN source files before they are compiled.

INN supplies a prototype version of `config.data` named `config.dist`. `Config.dist` is almost undoubtedly wrong for your UNIX. You must create your own version of `config.data`:

```
$ cd config
$ cp config.dist config.data
```

Now edit `config.data` to match your site's version of UNIX. As mentioned above, this is one of the hardest parts of installing INN. `Config.data` is about 700 lines long, and there's nothing for it but to go through it line by line and make the appropriate changes. Depending on how experienced you are, you may have to set aside several hours for this task. `Install.ms` devotes about 18 pages to `config.data`, and you should refer to it as you edit.

Unless you know off the top of your head the answers to questions such as, "How does your UNIX set non-blocking I/O?", you'll need to keep your programmer's manuals handy. If you have a workstation, you can edit `config.data` in one window and use another to inspect your system's on-line documentation. As mentioned above, `Install.ms` gives sample configurations for many popular versions of UNIX. If your version is listed, use its values. (However, that doesn't relieve you of the chore of inspecting the entire file.)

> **TIP:** The subst program, originally supplied with C-news and used in INN by the kind permission of Geoff Collyer and Henry Spencer, is a clever shell script that relies on the sed program to do much of its work. The INN config.dist file is large enough to break some vendor's versions of sed. To see whether your vendor's sed will work with INN, cd into the config directory and type the following:
>
> ```
> $ cp config.dist config.data
> $ make sedtest
> ```
>
> If this test fails, the simplest workaround is to type **make c quiet** to create a C language version of the subst program. You should also gripe at your UNIX vendor for foisting a substandard sed onto you, an unsuspecting customer.

Once you've edited config.data, you're ready to let subst configure the INN sources. From within the config directory, type the following:

```
$ make quiet
```

Building INN

Now that INN is configured, you're ready to build the system. Install.ms gives several ways to do this, depending on how trusting you are and your general philosophy of life. If you're the kind of person who likes cars with automatic transmission, you can **cd** to the top of the INN source tree, type **./BUILD**, and answer its questions. The BUILD shell script compiles and installs INN without much input from you.

If you prefer to shift gears yourself, from the same directory you can type the following:

```
$ make world
$ cat */lint ¦ more
```

Carefully inspect the lint output for errors. (See the following Tip.)

> **TIP:** The lint program detects errors in C language programs. Because C is a fairly permissive language, it lets you do things you probably shouldn't, and lint helps you find these bits of fluff in your programs and correct them. For instance, lint can tell you if you're passing the wrong number (or type) of arguments to a C language function. Remember, just because a program compiles doesn't mean it will work correctly when you run it. If lint finds errors in your INN configuration after you've run subst, there may be a problem you need to correct by editing

config.data and rebuilding your system. Unfortunately, lint sometimes reports spurious errors. You'll have to consult the programmers's section of your system's manual pages to be sure which errors are real and which are not.

However, you'll learn the most about INN if you compile it bit by bit with Install.ms by your side. You may think that if INN is so simple to install you should take the easy road and use BUILD. But news systems are complex, and no matter how good they are you will inevitably have some problems to solve. When you do you'll need all the clues you can muster, and building INN step by step helps you learn more about it. Someday, when the weasels are at the door, you'll be glad you did.

The step-by-step compilation procedure is fairly simple. First build the INN library:

```
$ cd lib
$ make libinn.a lint 2>&1 | tee errs
$ cd ..
```

The tee command prints the output of the make command to your terminal and also saves it to the file errs. If you use an ugly shell such as csh or one of its variants, type sh or ksh before executing the command above, or read your shell's manual page for the correct syntax to save the standard output and standard error of a command into a file.

The make command creates a library of C language functions used by the other INN programs and a lint library to help detect possible problems with it. Since the other INN programs depend on the INN library, it's crucial that you compile it correctly. Check the output in the file errs and assure yourself that any errors detected by your C compiler or lint are innocuous. If you find errors (especially compiler warnings), it's probably due to a mistake you've made in config.data. The only solution is to correct config.data, run subst again, and recompile libinn.a.

Once you've successfully built the INN library, you can build the rest of INN. Cd into each of the following directories in turn: frontends, innd, nnrpd, backends, and expire. In each directory, type the following:

```
$ make all 2>&1 | tee errs
```

Check the output in the file errs. If there are compiler warnings or lint errors, do not pass go and do not collect $200. Consult your system's on-line documentation, edit config.data to correct the problems, rerun subst, and recompile the system beginning with libinn.a.

WARNING: The disadvantage of using subst to configure INN is that most of the system depends on the config.data file. If at any stage in building the system you discover errors that require you to change config.data, you *must* rerun subst and recompile *all* of INN, beginning with libinn.a.

Installing INN

Now you're ready to install INN. Assuming that everything has gone well so far, `cd` to the root of the INN source tree, type **su** to become the superuser, and type this:

```
$ sh makedirs.sh 2>&1 | tee errs
$ make update 2>&1 | tee -a errs
```

This runs the commands to install INN and saves the output in the file `errs`, which you should carefully inspect for errors. Note the `-a` argument to `tee` in the second command line, which makes `tee` append to the file `errs`.

The `makedirs.sh` shell script creates the directories for the INN system and must be run *before* you type **make update**. The latter command installs INN in the directories created by `makedirs.sh`. Now you've installed the INN programs and are ready to configure your news system.

Site Configuration

`Cd` into the `site` directory and type **make all 2>&1 | tee errs**. This command copies files from the `samples` and `backends` directories and runs `subst` over them. Some of these files must be edited before you install INN. They give INN information it can't figure out on its own; for instance, with which hosts you exchange news.

The `site` directory also contains some utility shell scripts. You probably won't have to change these, but you should look at them to see what they do and ensure that paths to programs in them are correct.

Modifying the files in the `site` directory is the second most difficult part of configuring INN, especially if you haven't configured a news system before. However, INN won't work if these files aren't configured correctly, so you'll want to spend some time here. The files you must edit are shown below, each with a brief explanation of its function. There are manual pages for each of these files in the `doc` directory, and you'll need to read them carefully in order to understand their function and syntax.

`expire.ctl` controls article expiration policy. In it you list a series of patterns to match newsgroup names and what actions `expire` should take for groups that match. This means that you can expire newsgroups selectively. The `expire.ctl` file is also where you tell `expire` how long you want it to remember Message-IDs. You can't keep a record of Message-IDs forever because your history file would grow without bound. `Expire` not only removes articles from the news spool but controls how long their Message-IDs are kept in the history file.

`hosts.nntp` lists the hosts that feed you news through NNTP. The main news daemon `innd` reads this file when it starts. If a host not listed in this file connects to `innd`, it assumes it's a newsreader and creates an `nnrpd` process to service it. If the host is in the file, `innd` accepts incoming news articles from it.

`inn.conf` contains some site configuration defaults, such as the names put in an article's `Organization` and `From` headers. For instance, your organization might want all `From` headers to appear as `From: someone@mailhub.corp.com`, regardless of which host posted the article. Some of these defaults may be overridden by environment variables. For instance, if the user sets the ORGANIZATION environment variable, it overrides the default in `inn.conf`.

Articles posted to a *moderated* newsgroup are first mailed to the newsgroup's moderator, who approves (or disapproves) the article. If it's approved, the moderator posts it with an `Approved` header containing his e-mail address. The `moderators` file tells INN where to mail these articles.

The `newsfeeds` file describes the sites to which you feed news, and how you feed them. This is something you will already have arranged with the administrator of the sites which you feed. The important thing is for both sites to agree. For instance, if you feed the `alt.binaries` groups to a site that doesn't want them, it discards the articles, and you both waste a lot of CPU time and network bandwidth in the process. The `newsfeeds` file allows you to construct specific lists of newsgroups for each site you feed. For instance, one site might not want to receive any of the `alt` groups, and another might want all of the `alt` newsgroups except for the `alt.binaries` newsgroups. The `newsfeeds` file is also where you specify INN's behavior with respect to an article's `Distribution` headers. There are other parameters you can set here to determine whether articles are transmitted, such as maximum message size.

`nnrp.access` controls which hosts (and optionally, users) can access your NNTP server. When a newsreader connects to the NNTP port, `innd` hooks it up with an `nnrpd` process so it can read and post news. The `nnrpd` program reads the `nnrp.access` file to see whether that host is allowed to read or post. The hosts may be specified as patterns, so it's easy to allow access to all the hosts in your organization. Reading and posting may also be controlled on a per-user basis if your newsreader knows how to use the `authinfo` command, a common extension to NNTP.

`passwd.nntp` contains `hostname:user:password` triplets for an NNTP client (for example, a newsreader) to use in authenticating itself to an NNTP server.

Once you've edited the files in `site`, install them:

```
$ make install 2>&1 ¦ tee errs
```

As usual, carefully inspect the `make` command's output for any problems.

System Startup Scripts and *news cron Jobs*

A news system doesn't run on its own. You must modify your system's boot sequence to start parts of it and create `cron` jobs for the `news` user to perform other tasks.

INN supplies the file `rc.news` to start the news system when your computer boots. For most SVR4 hosts, you should install it as `/etc/init.d/news` and make a hard link to it named `/etc/rc2.d/S99news`. (See the section "Modifying `sendmail`'s Boot-time Startup" in Chapter 41 for more information on how SVR4 systems boot.)

The shell script `news.daily` should be run as a `cron` job from the news user's *crontab*. `News.daily` handles article expiration and calls the `scanlogs` shell script to process news log files. You should probably schedule this for a time when most people aren't using the news system, such as after midnight.

You'll also need to add a `news` user `cron` entry to transmit news to your USENET neighbors. INN supplies sample shell scripts that show several different ways to do this for both NNTP and UUCP neighbors. The scripts are copied into the `site` directory. The shell scripts `nntpsend` (and its control file `nntpsend.ctl`), `send-ihave`, and `send-nntp` are various ways to transfer news through NNTP. The scripts `send-uucp` and `sendbatch` are for sites using UUCP. Pick the one that most closely suits your site's needs and add its invocation to the `news` user's crontab.

If you use `sendbatch`, edit it to ensure that the output of the `df` command on your system matches what the script expects. Unfortunately, the output of `df` varies a lot between vendors, and if `sendbatch` misinterprets it you may have problems with your news spool filling up.

How often you should run the shell script depends on the needs of the site you're feeding. If it's an NNTP site and it wants to receive your articles as soon as they are posted, you could run one of the NNTP submission scripts every five minutes. If it's an UUCP site or an NNTP site on the end of a slow link, it might want news much less often. You have to work this out with the remote site and make sure that your setup matches what it wants.

Miscellaneous Final Tasks

The *active* file shows what newsgroups are valid on your system. If you're converting to INN from another news system, you can convert your existing active file. Otherwise, you may want to get a copy of your feed site's active file and edit it to remove newsgroups you don't want and add local groups.

You must also create a history file or convert your existing one. Appendix II of Install.ms gives information for converting an existing news installation to INN.

Even if you didn't run the BUILD shell script to build and install INN, you can save the last 71 lines of it into a file and run that file to build a minimal active file and history database. You can then add whatever lines you want to the active file.

Some vendors' versions of sed, awk, and grep are deficient and may need to be replaced with better versions before INN can function correctly. The GNU project's versions of these commands work well with INN. They are available for anonymous ftp from the host prep.ai.mit.edu in the directory ~ftp/pub/gnu.

You may also have to modify your syslog.conf file to match the logging levels used by INN. These logging levels are defined in config/config.data, and the file syslog/syslog.conf shows sample changes you may need to make to your syslog.conf.

Checking Your Installation and Problem Solving

If you have perl installed on your system, you can run the inncheck program to check your installation. You should also try posting articles, first to the local group test and then to groups with wider distributions. Make sure that articles are being transmitted to your USENET neighbors.

If you have problems, many of the INN programs are shell scripts and you can see what they're doing by typing **sh -x *scriptname***. You might also temporarily modify a script to invoke its programs with their verbose options turned on. For instance, the nntpsend article submission shell script calls the innxmit program to do the work. If nntpsend wasn't working for you, you could edit it to turn on innxmit's verbose option (-v), run it by hand as **sh -x nntpsend**, and save the results to a file.

Some simple NNTP server problems can be checked with the `telnet` command. If you know the NNTP protocol, you can simply `telnet` to a host's NNTP port and type commands to the NNTP server. For instance:

```
$ telnet some.host.edu nntp
Trying 123.45.67.8 ...
Connected to some.host.edu.
Escape character is '^]'.
200 somehost NNTP server version 1.5.11 (10 February 1991) ready at Sun Jul 17 19:32:15
1994 (posting ok).
quit
```

(If your `telnet` command doesn't support the mnemonic name for the port, substitute `119` for `nntp` in the command above.) In this example no NNTP commands were given other than `quit`, but at least you can see that the NNTP server on `some.host.edu` is willing to let you read and post news.

Getting Help

If your news system develops problems you can't solve on your own, `comp.news.software.b` and `comp.news.software.nntp` are good resources. However, you'll get much better advice if you do two things. First, read the INN FAQ and other INN documentation and see if the problem is listed there. Imagine your embarrassment when you ask your burning question and the collective answer is, "It's in the FAQ. Read it." Second, make sure you include enough information for people to help you. A surprising number of problem posts don't even tell what version of UNIX the person uses. Your article should include the following:

A specific description of your operating system version and hardware. (For example, "A Sun4c running Solaris 2.3 with the following patches applied…")

The version of news software you're running and any patches you may have applied to it ("I'm running the Dec 22 release of INN 1.4sec"), as well an any configuration information that seems relevant, such as the contents of `config/config.data` or the configuration files installed from the `site` directory.

A detailed description of the problem you're having, what you've done to try to solve it, and what the results were. (For example, "I get a permission denied message when I try to post news. I've tried changing the `nnrp.access` file, but I still can't post.")

If you do a good job of researching your posting, you may even figure out the problem on your own. If you don't, you'll get much better advice for having done the work to include the necessary details.

Summary

This chapter gives you a good start on becoming a news administrator, but installing the software is only the beginning of what you'll need to know to keep your news system running. Most of your additional learning will probably be in the form of on-the-job training, solving the little (and big) crises your news system will create. Your best defense against this mid-crisis style of training is to read the INN manual pages, the INN and news.software.b FAQs, and the news.software.* newsgroups. The more information you pick up before something goes wrong, the better prepared you will be to handle it.

UUCP Administration

43

By James C.
Armstrong, Jr.

Long before the days of Networking, TCP/IP, NFS, and the like, there was still the need for UNIX machines to communicate with each other, to pass data, and to transfer files. Modern networks make this task easy, but if your machine is not attached to one of these networks, or if there is no direct network connection between your machine's network and the target machine's network, then there must be a technique for this communication. The package that handles these transfers is UUCP.

UUCP was originally written by Mike Lesk at Bell Labs in the mid-1970s, to facilitate communication between the growing network of UNIX machines. It has been modified several times since then, with the most fundamental changes occurring in 1983, when UUCP was rewritten by Peter Honeyman, David A. Nowitz, and Brian E. Redman. This is the standard UUCP distributed with System V Release 4, and sometimes goes by the moniker HoneyDanBer. It is this version of UUCP that this chapter covers.

What Is UUCP?

UUCP is the package of commands that allows a user to transfer data from one machine to another across a serial port, usually via a modem. Probably the most common uses of UUCP are the transfer of network e-mail and netnews, as described in Chapter 41, "Mail Administration", and Chapter 42 "News Administration". In both cases, the underlying UUCP commands are hidden from the regular user.

Transferring Files

The most likely contact a regular UNIX user has with UUCP is the command uucp. This is just an expansion of the cp command, with a special format to indicate the transfer to a new machine. The target machine and path are illustrated with an exclamation point. Assume that I have a file named data on a local machine named duke. I want to transfer that file to my home directory, /usr/james, on a machine named unc. This is the command I'd use:

```
uucp data unc!/usr/james/data
```

I do not need to specify the machine I am on, so I indicate just the current file. I then indicate that I want to send the file to the machine unc, with the file name there as /usr/james/data. This is an example of pushing a file to a new machine via uucp.

> **CAUTION:** Most systems set up permissions on data transfers that make the uucp command invalid, unless copied to one specific directory on the remote machine. Furthermore, setting permissions to allow transfers to and from any directory is very risky and is not secure. Permissions are discussed later in the chapter.

Files may also be pulled from machines. Suppose I have successfully copied `data` to `unc`, and now I need a copy back. I can do this with this command:

```
uucp unc!/usr/james/data .
```

In this case, the source file is on the `unc` machine, and I pull over a copy. If `unc` has the correct permissions, I can pull the needed file over to my machine and place it in my current directory.

Files can be transferred from one remote machine to another. In the first example, if I were on machine `ncsu` when I wanted to transfer a file from `duke` to `unc`, I could do it with this command:

```
uucp duke!/usr/james/data unc!/usr/james/data 2
```

The syntax of the command says "Go to machine duke and find the file `/usr/james/data`, then send it to machine unc to the destination `/usr/james/data 2`." Finally, if I want to send the file from `duke` to `wake`, but `wake` only has a link with `unc`, I can specify a path like this:

```
uucp duke!/usr/james/data unc!wake!/usr/james/data
```

If the permissions at `unc` allow the transfer, the file is first sent to `unc`, then sent from `unc` to `wake`.

> **NOTE:** You may have attempted these commands and received an error message such as `/usr/james/data: Event not found`. This is because the `!` is significant to the C shell—it implies history substitution. To avoid this problem, you should escape the `!` with a backslash (`\`), making the command `uucp duke\!/usr/james/data unc\!/usr/james/data`. This will also work with the Bourne and Korn shells and is a practice I find useful.

> **TIP:** A much easier technique for transferring files from the local machine to a remote machine is using `uuto` and `uupick`. These commands are simply shell scripts that change their arguments into a well-constructed `uucp` command for you. Their usage is described in more detail in the section "UUCP Utilities."

Running Remote Commands

UUCP also provides a command that allows the user to run commands remotely. The `uux` command enables a user to request that a remote machine run a command. It will accept redirection of standard input and output, and options can be used to indicate that the redirection should apply to the remote command's execution. For example, this command will return the output of the date command as run on unc:

```
uux unc!date
```

uux is normally hidden from the user, but it is the backbone for mail and news transfer. On my machine, I transfer news to a remote machine by piping the article into the command uux - -r -gd netcomsv!rnews. While this may look complicated, all it really says is that the standard input of this command will be fed to the remote machine netcomsv, and there the command rnews will be run. The -r option says to queue the request, and -gd sets a system priority on the request. Both options could easily be omitted.

The command for transferring mail is even simpler. When my mailer gets the request to send mail to a remote system, it executes uux - -r netcomsv!rmail. This is simplicity itself—it just pipes the mail message to rmail on netcomsv.

> **NOTE:** For security reasons, most sites have cut off remote execution of commands other than rmail and rnews. If you plan on needing to execute commands other than rnews and rmail, you should consult with the administrator of the remote machine.

Under It All

Beneath all the UUCP commands is the uucico command. This is the process that implements the actual communication between UNIX machines. Most users will never need to use this command, and its use by administrators is also rare.

uucico examines a series of data files to make its connection. These files include information such as which tty is used as a port, what modem commands are needed to use the attached modem, what is the phone number of the remote system, and what is the login protocol. Attached to both the modem commands and the login commands are what is called a "chat script." These chat scripts are the essence of UUCP communications.

Chat Scripts

Chat scripts are simply pairs of expect/send sequences. When all the criteria are met for communications, the uucico process waits on the port until it sees the next expect sequence. After that sequence is seen, the next send sequence is sent down the line. If the expect sequence is not seen in a certain period of time, a time-out occurs, and a different send sequence can be sent. If all expect/send sequences are completed, the connection starts to transfer data. If the send sequences are exhausted and no connection is made, the command fails.

The following is an example of a chat script for logging in to a machine:

```
"" \n in:—in: mylogin word: mypassword
```

Interpreted, this means that I first expect nothing and send a carriage return. When I see the sequence in: I send the sequence mylogin. If I don't see in:, then I wait for a time-out and send a new carriage return and continue to look for in:. Once I send mylogin, I wait for word:. Once I see that, I send mypassword and expect to start the data transfer.

The — in the expect sequence indicates that I might get a time-out and I might need to send more data. Any character sequence can be between the two dashes, and these are sent, along with a carriage return, and then a time-out occurs. Any number of these time-out sequences can occur in an expect pattern. If a line is known to be slow to acknowledge the connection, one may see the sequence in:—in:—in:—in:, which means to try four times to get the login: prompt before timing out. Some experimentation may be necessary to determine the exact chat script to connect to a machine. This is described in the section "Setting Up UUCP."

> **CAUTION:** Permissions to see the UUCP chat scripts should be restricted. One of the limitations of UUCP is that the remote machine passwords must be listed in the chat script and must be clear ASCII text. Anyone with the correct permissions can look at the file and steal the passwords for UUCP. None of the passwords indicated in this chapter are real.

Connection Files

The first task of uucico is to determine the target machine for the connection. When it determines the machine name, it examines the Systems file. This includes the system name, the connect times, devices, and speeds, the connection address, and the chat script to make the connection. This is not enough to make the connection.

Given the device type and speed, uucico must next examine the Devices file. This provides a list of devices and speeds, and associates them with actual ports and dialers to connect with those ports.

The dialers to connect to the port need to be looked up in the Dialers file, where a specific dialer can be associated with a chat script. That chat script should set up the modem in the proper format, and then dial the address provided by the Systems file. Sometimes, this address may need further expanding. The Dialcodes file provides some expansion for the address.

Addresses need not be telephone numbers. UUCP is capable of handling telephone calls via modems, as well as connections via local area networks such as Starlan, and even direct connections between machines. Each one requires different devices and dialer chat scripts to make the connection.

Setting Up UUCP

UUCP requires two sites willing to set up a connection. In the early days of UNIX, this was simply a matter of calling local UNIX sites and asking if they would be willing to transfer data for you. In those days, often the answer was yes, and you'd set up a link. With the development of the Internet, these connections are becoming less frequent, and many main sites no longer even use UUCP.

For my home machine, I sought a service provider. The local provider with a decent reputation was Netcom, based in the San Francisco Bay area. Netcom offers a UUCP service for a reasonable amount each month, including registering a domain name for Internet addressing. Netcom is not the only provider, but it's local for me.

When you've found a partner for exchanging UUCP, you'll need to determine how the connections will be made. There are three options: Your site could make all the calls to the provider's site (this is fairly standard with paid service providers), your site could receive calls only from the remote site, or the calls could go both ways. This results in two different administrative tasks for UUCP: setting up your system to receive calls and setting up your system to place calls.

Receiving UUCP Calls

Since UUCP accesses a system in the same way as a user—by logging in—you'll need to set up your system to allow UUCP to log in. One of your serial ports will need a modem attached. One action you'll need to take is to establish an account for UUCP to use. You'll need to use your administrative tools to edit the /etc/passwd file. You'll need root permissions to create the account. Some UNIX systems come with a default entry, nuucp, for UUCP connections. I prefer to set up a different account for each machine, prefixing the machine name with a U. That way I know just by using the who command who is logging in to transfer data at what times.

> **TIP:** Prefixing UUCP accounts with U also increases the administrative trail of user logins; although UUCP does give excellent logs, by keeping different login names the /etc/wtmp file will also keep a record that can identify call times and durations.

The /etc/passwd entry should have the same owner and group as your uucp account. This way, the remote site will be able to write correctly to the designated files; UUCP does not run in any privileged mode—it is just another user on the system. You should also make the home directory /var/spool/uucppublic. This directory is a standard UNIX directory, designated for file transfers. It should be owned by uucp, it should be of group uucp, and it should have permissions set to 777. That way, any user desiring to transfer files can write to the directory.

The unique aspect of the /etc/passwd entry is the default shell. Most users will have something like /bin/sh, /bin/csh, or some other command shell. Your UUCP entry should have /usr/lib/uucp/uucico, which is the command for data transfer. This means that when your UUCP successfully logs in, it will immediately start to transfer files.

> **NOTE:** You may have noticed that the same transfer command is used both for sending and receiving data. So how do you know which is which? It's simple—you don't. The same uucico command will both send and receive files during a single phone call. The two commands stay synchronized because of the master/ slave role. The command that is sending is considered the master, the command receiving is the slave. The slave role is the default. To be the master uucico, the uucico command must receive the flag -r1. Master and slave roles can switch during a phone call, and there is no limit to the number of times this switch happens.

You will also need to set a password for the UUCP account. To do this, you need to be root. Run the passwd command on the account and enter a password. After you have done this, you can notify the other site of its UUCP account and password.

> **TIP:** For the password you can use any combination of characters that are valid, and because this is not one you'll need to keep memorized, it can be any random sequence desired.

This is not all that's needed to set up the connection, however. You'll need to run the command that gives the UNIX prompt, /etc/getty. This command is kept in the file /etc/inittab. You'll need to include an entry that looks like this:

```
ucp:23:respawn:/etc/getty ttya 9600
```

Each field is separated by colons, so this has four fields. The first is a unique identifier in the inittab and can be anything. The second field specifies run states, the third is an action, and the fourth is a command. This file is monitored by the init daemon. The respawn action indicates that when a command is finished, a new getty command should be run. The run states indicate that the command should be run only in multiuser mode.

getty is the standard UNIX command for providing a login prompt. The two arguments indicate which port is used and the expected speed. Here the modem is on ttya and is 9600 baud. Your port and numbers may be different. For more details on the inittab and getty, see the section "Boot States."

There is a problem with getty: It can only receive calls. If you intend for your modem to have two-way traffic, you'll need to use the uugetty command. This command will know not to put up a login prompt when you are using the port to make outgoing calls. To use it, replace /etc/getty with /usr/lib/uucp/uugetty -r. The -r option tells uugetty not to put up a login prompt until it gets a character, which is usually a carriage return.

Permissions also need to be set, restricting what the calling system can do to your system. These will be covered later in the chapter, but for starters, consider restricting read and write access to /var/spool/uucppublic, and allow only the execution of rmail, and if you want netnews, rnews.

Initiating UUCP Calls

Initiating UUCP connections is a proactive job. The simplest way to set up a system to make UUCP calls is for the administrator to modify a single file, the Systems file. This file contains the specific information needed to contact a remote system. Each line is a separate entry, and each line must have six entries. The first entry on a line is the remote system's name. UUCP expects the first seven letters to be unique, so the system names newyorkcity and newyorkstate would be considered the same. Each system can have any number of entries—they are tried in the order found in the file, until one is successful.

The second field is a schedule field. Normally, the word Any will be here, meaning that the connection can be made at any time. Never means don't call; this entry is usually made when a system is polled; this means that a remote system will call to get what it wants. The schedule field Wk means weekdays only. A schedule field can be quite complicated. The schedule field can have an unlimited number of comma-separated schedule descriptions. Each description has a day code, an optional time code, and an option grade code. The day codes are easy to understand—Su, Mo, Tu, We, Th, Fr, and Sa. Any number and combination can be present. So if you only want to call a site on Fridays, Saturdays, and Sundays, you'd have FrSaSu as the schedule field. The start time can be after the end time, which would seem to include midnight, but that is not true. Instead, it means from midnight on the specified days to the end time, and the start time to midnight on the same day. So Wk1900-0700 means any weekday before 7 AM or after 7 PM.

Finally, the grade is a restriction on priority of transfers. By limiting the grade, only transfers of that grade or higher are made during that time. The grade is identified by a slash followed by a number or letter.

A full schedule specification may look like this:

```
SaSu,Wk0900-1700/C,Wk1700-0900
```

This means that transfers may occur at any time on Saturdays and Sundays, between 9 AM and 5 PM weekdays, only items grade C and above, and any time between 5 PM and 9 AM. This effectively says it's possible to transfer anything at any time except during work hours, when you move only priority material.

Finally, if a comma and number follow the schedule, this sets a minimum retry time. UUCP will make retry attempts based on its own internal formula, but that formula can be overridden in the schedule field.

The third field is the device field. This field is a lot simpler than the schedule field. It consists of a pointer to a device type. The devices are kept in the file Devices, usually in the same directory as Systems. UUCP will look up the device name in the Devices file and use the first free device found. The only option is that protocols may be specified after the device, preceded by a comma. Supported protocols include UUCP's g protocol for communication on a telephone line, as well as an x and an e protocol for devices that support those protocols.

The fourth field is the speed, or baud rate, of the connection. This is usually your modem's top speed, but different values may be present for different numbers, and different speeds also apply for direct connections.

The fifth field is the connection number. Usually it is a telephone number, but for UUCP connections over direct lines or for data switches, it is a connection address or path. For telephone numbers, it is the sequence of numbers needed to dial the remote modem. Note that an optional alphanumeric string can precede the phone number (this will be interpreted in the Dialcodes file).

The last field is the chat script. These are a sequence of text patterns that are expect/send pairs. The uucp command will read the data coming in from the remote site and attempt to match the expected text with the incoming text. When a match is found, the send text is transmitted with a new line, and a new expect pattern is found, until the entire chat script is completed. If successfully completed, the UUCP process starts; otherwise, an error is recorded and the connection is terminated.

Chat scripts can be filled with special character escapes. Table 43.1 shows Chat script escape sequences.

Table 43.1. Chat Script Escape Sequences.

Escape Sequence	Meaning
" "	Expect a null string
EOT	End of transmission
BREAK	Cause a break signal
\b	Backspace
\c	Suppress a new line at the end of the send string
\d	Delay for one second
\K	Insert a Break
\n	Send a new line
\N	Send a null
\p	Pause for a fraction of a second
\r	Carriage return
\s	Send a space
\t	Send a tab
\\	Send a backslash
\xxx	Send the ASCII character with the octal value *xxx*

A complete sample of Systems file entries is included here. Note that the sensitive data is changed, but reflects accurately my Systems file on sagarmatha.com:

```
machine1 Any ACU 9600 9899685 in:—in: uduke word: mypass
mach Never ACU 9600 9895690 in:—in: jca
tyler Any ACU 9600 5565935 "" \K\d\r :—: mygate "" \d\d >-\r->\
  mylog > rlogin\styler in:—in: uduke word: Strange1
```

I have three machines registered. All are within my local area code. I have set the machine to never call mach. Instead, I use that as an entry for the cu command. Also note that both machine1 and tyler have given me the UUCP account name uduke.

The machine tyler is an interesting case. I have to go through a switch to reach that machine. The first expect says that I don't expect anything, so the machine immediately sends the control characters \K\d\r. This means send a break, wait a second, and send a carriage return. UUCP then expects a colon, and to access this switch, I enter mygate. I then need to wait two seconds, with \d\d, to get the > character. I send mylog. I expect another >, and I send rlogin tyler. Here, I begin a more recognizable login session.

> **NOTE:** In the early days of UNIX networking, the need for unique system names was great, as this was the only way to identify a machine for electronic mail and network news. As there was no registry, conflicts sometimes did occur. In the mid-1980s, I administered a machine named `terminus` while working for AT&T. At one point, I started receiving some very odd mail to the administrative accounts; it turns out that somebody else, in Colorado, had named a system `terminus`. Once the problem was identified, the name conflict was resolved.
>
> Currently, the Internet has fully qualified domains, which separate our machines and networks. These domains are registered to prevent conflicts. My home machine is registered in the domain `sagarmatha.com`, but its UUCP name is `duke`. Because my service provider does not connect to Duke University or anyone else by this name, there is no name conflict.
>
> Interestingly, this is not the hostname. My UUCP machine at home has a hostname of `krzyzewski`, after Duke University's head basketball coach. Other machines at home have names of assistant coaches, `amaker`, `gaudet`, and `brey`. Because of the seven-character restriction on the UUCP name, I opted for `duke`, rather than abbreviating the hostname.

Testing the Connection

Once the Systems file is complete, you have to test the entry to see if the connection is actually being made, and if not, you need to figure out what is wrong. For this you use the command `Uutry`.

`Uutry` is a shell script that calls `uucico` with a debugging flag set, and then performs a tail on the output. You can press the Delete key any time to terminate `Uutry`. The default debug level is 5, but this can be changed with the `-x` option.

The example in Listing 43.2 shows what happens when the password is incorrect.

Listing 43.1. A failed UUCP call.

```
$ /usr/lib/uucp/Uutry machine1
/usr/lib/uucp/uucico -r1 -smachine1 -x5 >/tmp/machine1 2>&1&
tmp=/tmp/machine1
mchFind called (machine1)
conn(machine1)
Device Type ACU wanted
mlock ttya succeeded
processdev: calling setdevcfg(uucico, ACU)
```

continues

Listing 43.1. continued

```
gdial(tb9600) called
expect: ("")
got it
sendthem (????????)
expect: (OK)
AT^M^M^JOKgot it
sendthem (DELAY
????????PAUSE
????????PAUSE
????????PAUSE
<NO CR>????????)
expect: (OK^M)
^M^JAAATE1V1X1Q0S2=255S12=255S50=6S58=2S68=2S7=80^M^M^JOK^Mgot it
sendthem (ECHO CHECK ON
<NO CR>????????????????????????)
expect: (CONNECT 9600)
^M^JCONNECT 9600got it
getto ret 6
expect: (in:)
^M^Jsendthem (????????)
expect: (in:)
^M^Jmachine1 login:got it
sendthem (????????)
expect: (word:)
 uduke^M^JPassword:got it
sendthem (????????)
LOGIN FAILED - failed
exit code 101
Conversation Complete: Status FAILED
```

> **NOTE:** Please note that a lot of what is sent is not visible to the user. This is not the case if Uutry is run as root. In that case, the send information, including the password, would be echoed in the parentheses. Because Uutry leaves files in /tmp, I prefer to use it with my own account and just use root to edit the administrative files.

You can only see what is echoed back to you—your commands that are not echoed, such as your password, are not visible. By correcting the password in the Systems file and re-running Uutry, you get the output in Listing 43.2.

Listing 43.2. A successful UUCP call.

```
$ /usr/lib/uucp/Uutry machine1
mchFind called (machine1)
conn(machine1)
Device Type ACU wanted
```

```
mlock ttya succeeded
processdev: calling setdevcfg(uucico, ACU)
gdial(tb9600) called
expect: ("")
got it
sendthem (????????)
expect: (OK)
AT^M^M^JOKgot it
sendthem (DELAY
????????PAUSE
????????PAUSE
????????PAUSE
<NO CR>????????)
expect: (OK^M)
^M^JAAATE1V1X1Q0S2=255S12=255S50=6S58=2S68=2S7=80^M^M^JOK^Mgot it
sendthem (ECHO CHECK ON
<NO CR>???????????????????????????)
expect: (CONNECT 9600)
^M^JCONNECT 9600got it
getto ret 6
expect: (in:)
^M^J^M^Jmachine1 login:got it
sendthem (????????)
expect: (word:)
 uduke^M^JPassword:got it
sendthem (????????)
Login Successful: System=machine1
msg-ROK
 Rmtname machine1, Role MASTER, Ifn - 6, Loginuser - james
rmesg - 'P' got Pgetxf
wmesg 'U'g
Proto started g
*** TOP *** - role=1, setline - X
Request: duke!D.dukeb2ee40e —> machine1!D.dukeb2ee40e (james)
wrktype - S
 wmesg 'S' D.dukeb2ee40e D.dukeb2ee40e james - D.dukeb2ee40e 0666 james
rmesg - 'S' got SY
 PROCESS: msg - SY
SNDFILE:
-> 835 / 0.972 secs, 859 bytes/sec
rmesg - 'C' got CY
 PROCESS: msg - CY
RQSTCMPT:
mailopt 0, statfopt 0
```

Another debugging tool is cu. This command also uses the UUCP files to try to connect to the remote machine, but when you are connected to the remote machine, cu terminates and you must complete the login yourself. This is very useful for debugging telephone numbers and Dialer scripts. Also, by using cu to connect to the modem itself, you can alter the modem parameters that may have been set incorrectly.

Another debugging tool is uucico. By calling uucico with the option -x and a single number, you will get output showing the steps for the UUCP call. This, however, cannot be interrupted, so you should use it sparingly.

More on Chat Scripts

Chat scripts are the heart of UUCP communication. The concept of a chat script is phenomenally simple—read a port until you match a string, then send a response. It is found in two UUCP-related files, the Systems file and the Dialers file. The concept is rather portable, although it could have supported regular expressions for pattern matching.

Any number of expect/send pairs could be present. When attempting to navigate UUCP through a network of data switches to reach a destination, you may need a large number of pairs before you reach the login prompt.

The longer the chat script, the greater the chance that an error may occur. Normally, an error in the chat will result in the call failing; however, there are some error correction techniques. The uucico command will take a time-out after 30 seconds if an expected pattern is not seen. At that time, an alternate send sequence can be issued, and a new pattern expected. This alternate send is enclosed in dashes, with the new expect pattern following the second dash. There can be no spaces in this pattern, or UUCP will see it as a new member of an expect/send pair.

Often, this is seen with the login prompt and looks like this:

```
in:-in:
```

This pattern means, wait for in:, and if it is not found, send a carriage return and wait again for in:. (Remember that each send pattern is followed by a carriage return, even if it is an alternate send.)

Another frequent alternate sequence is \K. Sometimes, when calling a modem that operates at multiple speeds, sending a break down the line will allow the modem to change its speed to match yours. When you see a sequence like this:

```
in:-\K-in:-in:-\K-in:
```

there are four separate instances of an expected login prompt. If not found the first time, send a break, then a carriage return, then another break. Although this may look excessive, it is sometimes necessary.

Administering the Files

Besides the files already mentioned, there are six important UUCP files that need regular administration. They are the Devices, Dialers, Dialcodes, Permissions, Sysfiles, and Poll files. Each has its own format and usage.

Devices

The `Devices` file is just a list of the devices found on the system, with an identification of their use. The purpose of this file is to tie the device specification in the Systems file to a physical device with a known means of access. Each entry in the Devices file is a single line long, must start in the first column, and has five fields. The file permits comments, identified by the # character in the first column. It ignores lines with no entry in that column.

The first field is the device type. It must match exactly the device specified in the Systems file. Devices will be tried in order down the file until one is found to be available. This way, a system with multiple modems can have one entry in the Systems file. Some devices have standard identifiers. An *ACU* is an "automated call unit," better known as a modem. `direct` signifies that the link to the device is a direct link.

> **NOTE:** For you to use `cu -l`, the line specified must have a `direct` entry in the Devices file.

The second field is the data port. This is the filename of the special file in the `/dev` directory that matches the physical device, and will be the port through which the data communication is made.

The third field is the dialer port. This is a bit of an anachronism, but in the past, some modems required a separate dialer device to make the phone call. This was the special file that pointed to the dialer for that modem. If the modem is capable of dialing, this field is marked with a dash.

The fourth field is the speed of the device. This is also used for matching the Systems file. That way a site can indicate multiple speeds for connections through multiple devices.

The last field is the dialer token pairs. This specifies a specific dialer pattern, found in the Dialers file, and any arguments passed thereto. Normally, only a single pair (or single entry, if it gets no arguments) is found; however, if the system needs to go through a switch to reach the modem, a chat script may be expected.

My Devices file is rather small, and it looks like this:

```
ACU ttya - 9600 tb9600
Direct ttya - 9600 direct
```

I have only the single modem, a Telebit QBlazer at 9600 baud. It is attached to /dev/ttya and uses the tb9600 dialer script when I connect via UUCP. It is configured to allow me to use cu to talk to the modem.

Dialers

The Dialers file is used to initiate conversation with the modem. It ties the dialer specified in the Devices file to a chat script. It consists of three fields. The first is the name of the dialer script. This must match exactly with the dialer specified in the Devices file. Like with devices, all dialers are one line and are started in the first column. The #, or white space, in the first column indicates a comment.

The second field is a translation table for older communication devices.

The third field is the chat script needed to talk with the modem and to place the call. My machine came with several dialers already installed, including dialers for penril, ventel, micom, hayes, and telebit modems. I looked over my set of telebit dialers, listed below, and selected tbfast for my first dialer for my ACU.

```
tb1200    =W-, ""  \dA\pA\pA\pTE1V1X1Q0S2=255S12=255S50=2\r\c\
 OK\r \EATDT\T\r\c CONNECT\s1200
tb2400    =W-, ""  \dA\pA\pA\pTE1V1X1Q0S2=255S12=255S50=3\r\c\
 OK\r \EATDT\T\r\c CONNECT\s2400
tbfast    =W-, ""  \dA\pA\pA\pTE1V1X1Q0S2=255S12=255S50=255\r\c\
 OK\r \EATDT\T\r\c CONNECT\sFAST
```

I knew I wasn't connecting at 1200 or 2400 baud, so it seemed that the fast connection was the way to go. I quickly learned that this was wrong! By using cu to mimic the dialing of the UUCP number, I saw that the final message was not CONNECT FAST, but CONNECT 9600. I first considered altering tbfast, but instead opted to write my own dialer, tb9600, in case I need to make other changes.

Note that each of these dialers has a long, confusing list of numbers and characters as the first send sequence. These are the parameters that need to be set in the modem for the UUCP call to take place, in a language the modem understands. Although the hayes modem syntax is fairly common, some modems do not use it, so you'll need to check your modem's documentation to determine the correct settings.

In my efforts, I found that by sending just the string to the modem, I'd get an error, because I didn't yet have the modem's attention. To get its attention, I'd need to send AT to the modem and receive back OK. I placed this at the beginning of my chat script. Testing also revealed that the best modem settings were different from those above, so I added them to the chat script, as well. It ended up looking like this:

```
tb9600    =W-, "" AT OK-AT-OK \dA\pA\pA\pTE1V1X1Q0S2=255S12=255S50=6S58=2S68=2S7=80\r\c\
  OK\r \EATDT\T\r\c CONNECT\s9600-\c-CONNECT\s9600
```

Basically, I am setting modem registers to match what I need. I also wait for CONNECT 9600 a bit longer than the time-out, so if I don't get it, I just sit a little while longer. This is the dialer I use for my UUCP connections.

Dialcodes

The Dialcodes file is an optional file that equates some string with a series of numbers to be dialed. Although UUCP is perfectly happy to have a sequence such as 1028801144716194550,,2354 to reach a distant computer in the city of London, for a human being glancing at the file it may not be obvious. So Dialcodes permits the human to tie a string, innerlondon, to a dialing sequence 102880114471.

Because I have only one number, I don't use a Dialcodes file, but if you call many places nationwide, it might be useful.

Permissions

System security is one of the most pressing issues in the computer industry, and in UUCP it is no exception. Originally, UUCP allowed any user to write to any directory on the remote system, as long as the user ID for UUCP had write permissions. Similarly, reading files was also possible. This had the ugly effect of enabling users to steal remote password files with a simple UUCP command, and if any accounts weren't protected with passwords, those systems were definitely compromised. Similarly, with incorrect permissions, a remote user could do significant damage by moving or destroying important files.

The way around this problem is to use the Permissions file. This mechanism ties remote systems and accounts to specific read, write, and execute permissions. There are 13 different Permissions file entries, each with the format Option=Value. They must all be on the same line, although these lines may be broken with a backslash. Multiple values for an option are separated by colons. The 13 options are LOGNAME, MACHINE, REQUEST, SENDFILES, READ, WRITE, NOREAD, NOWRITE, CALLBACK, COMMANDS, VALIDATE, MYNAME, and PUBDIR.

The meaning of each option are described below.

LOGNAME refers to a specific login name used by the remote site to gain access. By specifying the LOGNAME, you can tie various options to the login call.

MACHINE refers to the machine name of the remote UUCP site. Specific permissions can be tied to a LOGNAME or to a MACHINE.

REQUEST is a yes/no flag indicating whether a remote machine can request files from your machine. The default is no. By permitting a remote system to request files, a command such as uucp mymach!myfile anotherfile can be executed from a remote machine. On a trusted network, that may be fine, but it is an invitation to trouble if set up on a link where you don't always know who is on the other end.

SENDFILES is another yes/no flag, but it is only tied to the LOGNAME. If set to yes, your system will send files to the remote system even if the remote system initiates the call. If you set the value to no, you will never send out files, and if you set it to call, you will send out files only when you have initiated the call.

READ specifies the directories from which uucico can access files for transfer. The default is /var/spool/ucppublic.

WRITE specifies the directories to which uucico may write files. Again, the default is /var/spool/uucppublic. These two options are designed to keep harm from uucp restricted to a public file system.

NOREAD and NOWRITE are exceptions to the other directories. For example, on a trusted network, you may want to set your directory open to reading, by setting READ=/home/james. However, you might have your own private directory that you don't want anyone to touch. To set this, you can have the options read READ=/home/james NOREAD=/home/james/.Private.

CALLBACK is another yes/no option. When set to yes, your system must call the remote system back before any transactions may take place. The default value is no. Be particularly careful using this option, because if both machines set CALLBACK to yes, they will never communicate. Also, if one system sets SENDFILES to call, and the other has CALLBACK as yes, the first system will never transfer files to the second. CALLBACK is definitely a security feature, because a remote site could always fake a machine name and steal a password, so by calling back you know with whom you are talking. It is also useful if one site has a particularly cheaper phone rate than the other.

COMMANDS is a very important option. The default is usually to permit rmail and rnews, the programs to receive mail and netnews. If set to ALL, any command that can be found in the local path of uuxqt will be executed. Because this often includes commands such as cat and rm, this is usually not recommended. The COMMANDS option is tied to a MACHINE name calling in.

VALIDATE is an option tied to the LOGNAME, and if set to yes, will validate the calling system's identity.

MYNAME is an option to provide another system name for the local name. This is useful if you need an alternate UUCP name.

PUBDIR is an option to specify a directory to be treated as the public directory for reading and writing. The default is /var/spool/uucppublic.

Although this may seem complicated, the default permissions are designed to keep a system secure, and it is only when you want to loosen permissions that you need to edit the Permissions file.

My Permissions file is rather simple, with a single entry:

```
MACHINE=netcomsv COMMANDS=rmail:rnews SENDFILES=yes
```

It enables the machine netcomsv to execute rmail and rnews, and it enables me to send files to them.

Sysfiles

Sysfiles is a special addition that allows the system to specify different Systems files for different services. It also allows for multiple Systems, Devices, and Dialers files, should these become long.

The format is simple. There are four keywords: service, systems, devices, and dialers. The format is always keyword=value. The service keywords can be uucico or cu, the two commands that access the UUCP files. The other three are files that replace the Systems, Devices, and Dialers files for that service. Each field is separated by a colon.

Poll

The Poll file is a list of times to poll a remote system. It is accessed by an administrative daemon to establish a fake request and force a UUCP call at a specific time. Its format is a system name followed by a tab, and a space-separated list of integers from 0 to 23, representing the hours of a 24-hour clock.

Supporting Files

UUCP creates many different files and file types. Briefly, they are work files, data files, status files, lock files, log files, and temporary files.

Work files are located in /var/spool/uucp/*machine name*, and are prefixed with the letter C. They are the workhorse for UUCP, because they list the specific files to be transferred, including the local and remote names, permissions, and owner. A request to send remote mail may look like this:

```
S D.dukeb3ae48e D.dukeb3ae48e james - D.dukeb3ae48e 0666 james
S D.netco0c7f621 X.dukeNb3ae james - D.netco0c7f621 0666 james
```

This indicates that two files are to be transferred.

The data files are kept in the same directory, but are prefixed with D. Even the files that specify remote execution are prefixed with D. In this request are two data files being transferred, one to become a data file on the remote machine, the other to become an execute file.

Execute files are identified by the prefix X. This prefix is sought by uuxqt, which is the program that actually runs the requested commands. These have their own format, indicating the command to be run and the input file to use.

Status files are kept in /var/spool/uucp/.Status, and have a specific format. There is a single status file per system, with six fields. The first is a type field, the second is a count field (used to indicate the number of retries, for example). The third field is a UNIX time to identify the last connection attempt. The fourth is the number of seconds before a retry attempt may be taken, the fifth is ASCII text to describe the status, and the sixth is the machine name. Status files are usually accessed by the uustat command.

Lock files are created when a call is attempted, and the lock files are in /var/spool/locks. These files contain the process ID of the uucico request that has locked the system.

Log files are kept in /var/spool/uucp/.Log. They are cleaned out daily by a daemon to prevent them from growing beyond control. Separate logs are kept for the uucico, uucp, uux, and uuxqt commands, each in a file named for the remote system. These are often accessed with the uulog command.

Finally, temporary files may be created by UUCP. These are in the directory with the work files and are prefixed with TM.

UUCP Daemons

There are four UUCP daemons that should be invoked on a regular basis. They are the admin daemon, the cleanup daemon, the polling daemon, and the hourly daemon. These are all started out of cron.

The *admin* Daemon

The admin daemon is a daemon that should be invoked at least once a day. It will give, by e-mail, a brief image of the state of UUCP, including a snapshot of the running processes and a listing of the job queue. It will also check the log files to see if there have been any attempts to transfer the passwd file.

The *cleanup* Daemon

The `cleanup` daemon is one of the hardest workers. It should be invoked daily, at a time when few users are likely to be on the system. It will back up all the log files and save them for three days. It will then make the current log files zero length. Other administrative files not discussed here are also backed up.

The `cleanup` daemon will invoke the `uucleanup` command. This command removes old jobs from the queue, based on a command line argument. On my system, I have stuck with the defaults, seven days until a delete, and one day until a warning.

The daemon then removes old files, empty subdirectories, and core files. When it finishes this, it sends e-mail to the UUCP administrator announcing what it has done.

The *polling* Daemon

This daemon quickly examines the Poll file to create polling requests for `uucico`. This is essentially touching a file in the spool directory. It should be executed hourly.

The *hourly* Daemon

The `hourly` demon should be invoked each hour. It just runs the `uusched` command, which examines the spool to find any queued jobs, and if it finds jobs, it runs `uucico` for that system. When it finishes, it runs `uuxqt` to execute any incoming jobs.

Using UUCP

Earlier in this chapter you were introduced to the commands `uucp` and `uux`, which are two of the most common commands for UUCP. There are two alternate commands, `uuto` and `uupick`, which ease the process.

The `uucp` command is the basic command for the transportation of files from one machine to another. The basic form allows for the specification of two paths to files, one being the original file, the other being the destination. `uucp` can take a number of arguments to help facilitate the transfer. By default, `uucp` will use the source file for originating the transfer. This means that if the source file is changed before the transfer is completed, the changed file will be sent. If that is not desired, the file can be copied to a temporary file for `uucp`, which is done by specifying the `-C` option. By default, `uucp` will also create the necessary destination directories, if it has permission to do so. This is the `-d` option and is turned off by `-f`. `uucp` also will assign a job ID to the transfer with the `-j` option. The `-m` option can be used to let the sender know when the job is complete (`uucp` will send a mail message to the requestor). The -g option enables the user to set the transfer grade (a single character from 0 to 9, A to Z, or a to z. 0 is highest, and z is lowest).

Similar to the -m option, the -n option followed by a user name will notify the user at the remote machine when the transfer is complete. Debugging information can be found with -x. To prevent an immediate start of uucico, use -r.

So if I want to copy a file, data, but might change it later, and I am not worried about speed, I might try this:

```
uucp -r -C -gz data remote!data
```

If I also want to know when it is done and want to send mail to my friend Joe at the remote machine, I'd expand it to this:

```
uucp -r -C -gz -m -njoe data remote!data
```

That's an ugly command, to say the least!

uux is another command frequently used to execute remote programs. Most remote sites restrict this command, but imagine that you are on a very friendly network. At minimum, you need a command string, which is just a machine name followed by an exclamation point and a command. The command is the same as a command typed on the system in the uucppublic directory. At minimum, you need this:

```
uux remote!date
```

That will run the date command on the remote system. Standard output is sent back to you. Assume that you want to put a message on your friend Joe's screen. If you were on the system, you'd use the command write joe and type something in. What you've typed in is standard input, but you can't type on Joe's machine. uux will accept standard input on your screen, if we include the - on the command line. So you'd type this:

```
uux - remote!write joe
```

Then you'd enter your message. Note that you don't need to quote the command because anything after the command is considered an argument.

> **NOTE:** Filenames for uux commands can be machine specified, as well. uux will attempt to get all the files needed to the remote machine before executing the command there.

uux also takes some other arguments. The -b option tells uux to return the standard input if the remote execution failed. Files may be copied to the spool with -c, and -j controls the ID string. The -n option tells uux not to return any indication of success or failure by mail. By default, uux will send mail to the originator, letting that person know whether the command worked. Standard input can also be used with -p, and -r doesn't immediately start uucico. The grade can be set with -g, and -x controls debugging. The originator name can be altered with -a.

uuto and uupick

These commands are complicated and can baffle the novice user. Fortunately, UNIX provides two friendlier commands, uuto and uupick, for transferring files. These two commands work together. The syntax for uuto is simple:

```
uuto file file file machine!user
```

Any number of files can be listed on the line—they'll all be transferred to the remote machine using uucp. Note that a user on the remote machine must be specified. This way, the file is placed in a directory on the remote machine identified by the user's name. Only two arguments are accepted for uuto: -m says to send mail to the originator when the transfer is complete, and -p says to copy the file to the spool before transmission. In the case of transferring a file to my friend Joe, I'd set up this command:

```
uuto -m file1 remote!joe
```

This is all I need to do. The uuto command will convert it to this:

```
uucp -d -m -njoe file1 remote!~/receive/joe/duke
```

The remote machine will then have a directory hierarchy for my friend Joe, under the receive directory, and with a subdirectory duke. A short time later, I'll get some e-mail that says (SYSTEM remote) copy succeeded and I will find a reference to the file in the header.

On the other machine, Joe will also receive some e-mail, saying /usr/spool/uucppublic/receive/james/duke/file1 from duke!james arrived, which lets him know that he has a file in the uucppublic directory.

Getting that file is easy using uupick. This is another shell script that searches the public directory for files under your name in a receive directory. If it finds any files, it prompts you for what you want to do. The actions are fairly straightforward:

New line:	Go to the next entry
d	Delete the file
m [dir]	Move the file to a directory dir
a [dir]	Move all files from the present system to a directory
p	Print the file
q	Quit

Control+D	Quit
!command	Run the command
*	Print the command summary

So if you enter `uupick`, Joe will be prompted with this:

```
from system duke: file file1 ?
```

If he types `m`, the file is placed in his current directory, and the transfer is complete.

> **TIP:** With `uuto` and `uupick`, the user is completely removed from the messy details of `uucp`. Furthermore, on many systems `uuto` and `uupick` are all most users need to know.

UUCP Utilities

There are two notable UUCP utilities available to the user. One examines log files, the other provides transfer status information.

UUCP keeps some very detailed log files in `/var/spool/uucp/.Log`. The `uulog` command is designed to access the two busiest of those logs. It always takes a system name as an argument. By default, or with the `-s` flag, it will display the transfer information for a given system. Here is a sample:

```
uucp remote  (5/14-19:18:42,9604,0) CONN FAILED (CALLER SCRIPT FAILED)
uucp remote  (5/14-19:48:40,9792,0) SUCCEEDED (call to remote )
uucp remote  (5/14-19:48:43,9792,0) OK (startup)
uucp remote  (5/14-19:48:44,9792,0) REMOTE REQUESTED (remote!D.netco56c3c71\
 -> duke!D.netco56c3c71 (netnews))
uucp remote  (5/14-19:48:55,9792,1) REMOTE REQUESTED (remote!D.duke4f4de04\
 -> duke!X.netcomsd56c3 (netnews))
uucp remote  (5/14-19:48:57,9792,2) REMOTE REQUESTED (remote!D.netcobeb02bd\
 -> duke!D.netcobeb02bd (netnews))
uucp remote  (5/14-19:49:14,9792,3) REMOTE REQUESTED (remote!D.duke4f4e043\
 -> duke!X.netcomsdbeb0 (netnews))
uucp remote  (5/14-19:49:17,9792,4) OK (conversation complete ttya 136)
uucp remote  (5/14-20:18:41,9972,0) FAILED (LOGIN FAILED)
uucp remote  (5/14-20:18:41,9972,0) CONN FAILED (CALLER SCRIPT FAILED)
```

From this log you can see that a connection failed at 7:18 PM, succeeded at 7:48, and failed again at 8:18. Normally this file would be fairly long, but I used the `-N` option to cut it to the last 10 lines of the file. If I wanted to wait on the file, I could have used `-f`. This is the same flag as for `tail`.

The only other option is `-x`. It gives details of the commands executed on the local system from UUCP. An example of the output (again, truncated to just the last 10 lines) is this:

```
uucp remote duked4f46 (5/14-17:32:37,9158,0) remote!remote!uucp-bounce XQT\
 (PATH=/bin:/usr/bin  USER=uucp UU_MACHINE=remote UU_USER=remote!uucp-bounce\
 export UU_MACHINE UU_USER PATH; rnews )
uucp remote duked4f43 (5/14-17:32:38,9158,0) remote!remote!uucp-bounce XQT\
 (PATH=/bin:/usr/bin  USER=uucp UU_MACHINE=remote UU_USER=remote!uucp-bounce\
 export UU_MACHINE UU_USER PATH; rnews )
uucp remote duked4f47 (5/14-17:52:08,9225,0) remote!remote!uucp-bounce XQT\
 (PATH=/bin:/usr/bin  USER=uucp UU_MACHINE=remote UU_USER=remote!uucp-bounce\
 export UU_MACHINE UU_USER PATH; rnews )
uucp remote duked4f48 (5/14-18:32:49,9287,0) remote!remote!uucp-bounce XQT\
 (PATH=/bin:/usr/bin  USER=uucp UU_MACHINE=remote UU_USER=remote!uucp-bounce\
 export UU_MACHINE UU_USER PATH; rnews )
uucp remote duked4f49 (5/14-18:32:50,9287,0) remote!remote!uucp-bounce XQT\
 (PATH=/bin:/usr/bin  USER=uucp UU_MACHINE=remote UU_USER=remote!uucp-bounce\
 export UU_MACHINE UU_USER PATH; rnews )
uucp remote duked4f4a (5/14-18:32:51,9287,0) remote!remote!uucp-bounce XQT\
 (PATH=/bin:/usr/bin  USER=uucp UU_MACHINE=remote UU_USER=remote!uucp-bounce\
 export UU_MACHINE UU_USER PATH; rnews )
uucp remote duked4f4b (5/14-18:32:52,9287,0) remote!remote!uucp-bounce XQT\
 (PATH=/bin:/usr/bin  USER=uucp UU_MACHINE=remote UU_USER=remote!uucp-bounce\
 export UU_MACHINE UU_USER PATH; rnews )
uucp remote duked4f4c (5/14-18:32:53,9287,0) remote!remote!uucp-bounce XQT\
 (PATH=/bin:/usr/bin  USER=uucp UU_MACHINE=remote UU_USER=remote!uucp-bounce\
 export UU_MACHINE UU_USER PATH; rnews )
uucp remote duked4f4d (5/14-19:49:19,9793,0) remote!remote!uucp-bounce XQT\
 (PATH=/bin:/usr/bin  USER=uucp UU_MACHINE=remote UU_USER=remote!uucp-bounce\
 export UU_MACHINE UU_USER PATH; rnews )
uucp remote duked4f4e (5/14-19:49:20,9793,0) remote!remote!uucp-bounce XQT\
 (PATH=/bin:/usr/bin  USER=uucp UU_MACHINE=remote UU_USER=remote!uucp-bounce\
 export UU_MACHINE UU_USER PATH; rnews )
```

Every command executed has been rnews, for transmission of netnews. To examine the other two files, my uux requests on a remote system, and my uucp requests to a remote system, I'd need to examine the files using an editor or other UNIX tools.

The other notable command is the uustat command. It has a lot of power, including the ability to delete jobs. There are several options.

The command uustat -a will give a listing of all jobs currently in the queue. Here is a sample:

```
netcomsn0000  05/14-20:45:00  (POLL)
remoteNb1ae  05/14-19:53  S  remote  james 48871\
 /home/james/Docs/Sams/Uucp/file1
```

This indicates that a poll request is in for netcom, and a file transfer request for remote.

To check the accessibility of machines, use uustat -m. It will give a listing such as this:

```
netcomsv   05/14-20:18 CALLER SCRIPT FAILED
remote     05/14-20:20 LOGIN FAILED  Count: 2
```

This indicates that there are presently problems reaching both machines. The command uustat -p will perform a ps command for every PID found in a lock file. uustat -q will give a listing of the state of the queue for each machine. It is similar to uustat -m, but it also includes a count of outstanding jobs.

Detailed job information, similar to that obtained with uustat -a, can be found for a given system or a given user with uustat -s*system* or uustat -u*user*. Finally, a user may kill a job or rejuvenate a job. The uustat -a command will give a job ID in the first field. By specifying that job with a -k option, it will be removed from the queue. By using the -r option, it will be touched, and spared from any administrative daemons.

With these two commands, a user can determine the status of jobs already sent but not yet complete.

Summary

This chapter has provided a brief overview of the use and administration for UUCP. The uucp, uux, uuto, and uupick commands are used for data and command transfers. The uustat and uulog commands are used to check on the status and actions of UUCP. Different files are used to administer the UUCP system, with the power to restrict types of access and facilitate data transfers.

UNIX System Security

44

By Jeff Smith

IN THIS CHAPTER

How secure is your UNIX system? Consider this: In the three years 1991 through 1993, the Computer Emergency Response Team Coordination Center (CERT/CC) issued more than 60 advisories describing UNIX insecurities and ongoing cracking incidents. That's almost two per month for the last three years. Many of these advisories described serious security flaws that allowed unprivileged users to gain superuser access, or worse, allowed unauthorized users access to the computer. If you haven't done anything to improve the security of your UNIX system, it's probably vulnerable.

The original developers of UNIX used it in a friendly, collegial environment that required only basic security features. Computer networks were a future dream. Since then UNIX has become one of the most popular operating systems in the world, installed on hundreds of thousands of networked computers. As it has evolved, security features have been added, but so have new facilities that have brought new security threats.

Why would someone break in to your computer? It boils down to access to services and information. Computers provide a variety of attractive services, such as access to networks and other computers, computing time, and disk storage. Most people use computers to store and organize valuable information. This information has potential value to those who don't have it, and unscrupulous people will do whatever it takes to get it.

Does your computer system contain information that someone else can use? Your company's trade secrets? A description of an academic research project or a grant proposal that you want to keep secret until it's in the mail? Most people can answer yes to these or similar questions—after all, you wouldn't be storing information on a computer if you didn't have something worth saving.

This chapter can't tell you everything you need to know about UNIX system security. That would take an entire book, and there are references to several "nuts and bolts" security books in the section "Finding More Information" later in this chapter. This chapter *does* give you a broad overview of UNIX security concerns, help you evaluate your security needs, tell you about tools you can use to improve your system's security, and tell you how to get more information. It may also help keep your hair from turning various shades of gray.

Kinds of Attacks and Their Consequences

Although it may seem like a naive question, you should ask yourself why you care whether your system is attacked. What are the consequences if someone breaks in? If a cracker breaks in to your system, he may do the following:

- Use system resources (disk space, CPU cycles, network bandwidth) you want for you or other users

- Deny services to you or other users, either maliciously or because he's using the resources himself

- Steal valuable information

- Destroy files, either maliciously or to cover his tracks

- Use your computers to break in to other sites

- Cause you to lose staff time (read: *money*) in tracking him down and putting compromised systems back in order

You must analyze your own situation and decide how important these consequences are to you. You may have CPU cycles and disk space to spare, no information to protect. You may not really care if other system administrators spit on the ground when they hear your name, and therefore decide to run a completely open system. On the other hand, you might lose your job if your company loses a contract because of industrial espionage. Most security needs fall somewhere between these two extremes, but you can see that security is a continuum, and you're in the best position to decide your own security requirements.

All attacks depend on gaining initial access to the computer. You should put yourself in the cracker's shoes and think about how you could attack your own system. Is it used by you alone or by many people? Is it accessible via a phone line, or connected to a private or public network? If it's connected to a network, is the network physically secure? Are your computers locked up or in a public site? Where are your backup tapes stored? Can a cracker get access to them, thereby gaining access to your files without ever breaking into your computer? If you're responsible for administering a multiuser system, how wise are your users? What will they do if they receive a phone call from the "system administrator" asking for their passwords for "special maintenance?"

These questions cover many—but not all—of the approaches a cracker might use to gain access to your computer or data. The attacks fall into four basic categories: physical security attacks; social engineering attacks; Dumpster-diving attacks; and network- and phone-based attacks.

The point of any attack is to gain access to a legitimate user's account, or to exploit bugs in system programs to get a command shell without actually compromising an account.

> **NOTE:** Computer viruses are programs that attach themselves to other programs and replicate when the infected programs are executed. Some viruses are relatively benign, but some *malware* can erase or damage disk files. Viruses are a big problem in the MS-DOS and Macintosh world because personal computers lack the sophisticated memory and file protection mechanisms of mature operating systems like UNIX.
>
> Although a few theoretical UNIX viruses have been presented in academic journals, to date there have been no widespread outbreaks of UNIX viruses. There are plenty of things to worry about regarding the security of your UNIX system, but viruses are not one of them.

Physical Security

If your computer is locked in a room with a guard who checks IDs at the door, and isn't connected to a network or a phone line, you can skip to the next chapter. Unfortunately, computers are pretty useless when they're sitting in locked rooms, and most of them aren't. A cracker who gains physical access to your computer or the network to which it's attached may be able to tap the physical network and snoop legitimate users' passwords or data, reboot the computer with a different version of UNIX, or modify values in RAM memory to gain privileged access.

The first type of attack is becoming difficult to prevent. Laptop computers now have pocket-size EtherNet cards that plug into PCMCIA slots, and there is free, public-domain software that captures all packets on an EtherNet and saves them on a computer's hard disk. A cracker can unplug one of your computers from the EtherNet, attach his laptop, record packets for a while, and analyze them later to find valid login names and passwords. Even worse, if your users log in to remote systems with `ftp`, `telnet`, or `rlogin`, the cracker doesn't need access to the physical network at your site—anyplace between your site and the remote one will do. One-time passwords, Kerberos, and encrypting EtherNet hubs can help solve these problems.

Many workstations have a *ROM-monitor* mode that is entered by typing a special key combination. This mode suspends the normal operation of UNIX to allow you low-level access to the computer's hardware. It may allow you to reboot the computer or alter memory locations and resume running UNIX.

If a cracker can boot an operating system of her choice and masquerade as the legitimate computer, she can do any number of bad things. If your workstations have CD-ROMs, floppy disks, or tape drives and can be booted from those devices, the door may be open.

A cracker who can boot an operating system of his choice while retaining a computer's identity can trick that computer or others on your network into providing illicit access or services.

A workstation that allows the user to change system memory while in ROM-monitor mode gives a cracker who has gained access to an unprivileged account the chance to promote it to the superuser account by changing the numeric user ID in RAM to 0.

Most workstations provide a way to prevent users other than the system administrator from entering ROM-monitor mode such as a password. Check your system administration manual to ensure that you've enabled whatever ROM-monitor security features are available, and avoid buying workstations that allow unrestricted access to this mode.

Social Engineering

Social engineering is a euphemism for the phenomenon P.T. Barnum had in mind when he said "There's a sucker born every minute." More kindly, most people are trusting, and that trust can be exploited by system crackers.

Social engineering might be a seemingly innocuous offer to "help set up your account," or the gift of a free program that purports to do one thing but does something else (a *Trojan horse*). Either offer gives the cracker the chance to alter a legitimate user's files so he can later gain access to the account. Another popular approach is to send e-mail to naive users, saying that system security has been compromised, and the victim must change her password to one specified by the cracker. Calling a legitimate user on the phone, claiming to be the system administrator, and asking for the user's password on a pretext is another example of social engineering. Social engineering approaches shouldn't be taken lightly—they are surprisingly effective.

As you may guess, the best defense against social engineering is user and staff education. Your users should know, for instance, that since you have superuser privileges you never have any reason to ask for their passwords, and that any such request should be reported to you immediately. Part of the goal of a security policy (see the section "Security Policies" later in this chapter) is to educate your users.

Dumpster-Diving Attacks

Rummaging through your company's trash bins may produce good results for a cracker: unlisted modem numbers, lists of valid accounts, passwords, discarded diskettes or tapes, and other helpful information. You may want to review how your organization disposes of waste paper, storage media and used computer equipment, and make changes if you feel that crackers can get a helping hand from your discards.

Network- and Phone-Based Attacks

If your computer system is attached to a network it is both a more attractive target and easier to crack. Physical access to the computer is no longer necessary, since the cracker can connect with a modem or over the network. If you are connected to the Internet (network of networks), your system can be attacked from anyplace in the world.

Physical network-based attacks like those described earlier in this chapter in the section "Physical Security" are a form of network-based attack. However, physical access to the network is not necessary for network or phone-based attacks—all you need is (legitimate or illegitimate) access to a computer on the Internet, or a terminal and a modem.

Attacks of this kind fall into two general categories: breaking into a user or system account by guessing its password, and tricking a network server program into giving you information about the system (for instance, the password file) or into executing commands to give you access to the computer.

You can thwart the first attack by ensuring that all system accounts (for example, the `ftp` account) have strong passwords or are shut off; and by educating, cajoling, and coercing your users into choosing good passwords, or switching to one of the *one-time* password schemes described in the section "User Authentication" later in this chapter.

The second attack is harder to stop because it depends on something over which you have little control—the quality of vendor software. Your best defense is to keep abreast of current bugs by joining mailing lists, reading the appropriate USENET newsgroups, tracking CERT/CC and other advisories, and taking advantage of any security alerts your vendor may offer. This gives you the information you need to patch problems quickly. The various ways of keeping up with the crackers are explained later in this chapter in the section "Finding More Information."

You may also want to run public-domain replacements for some vendor software, for instance the public-domain Version 8 `sendmail` program. (See Chapter 41, "Mail Administration.") Most public-domain programs come with complete source code, which allows you to fix bugs without waiting on the vendor. Further, the authors of public-domain programs are often quicker to fix bugs than vendors.

Phone-based attacks either attempt to guess passwords, or (if you run it) trick a program like UUCP (UNIX to UNIX File Copy). The first problem is solved by the methods mentioned in the previous paragraph. Dial-back modems help with either attack and are covered in the section "Hardware Solutions" later in this chapter.

Security Policies

If your computer or network of computers is used by someone other than you, then you need a security policy (also known as a *proper use* policy.) Your security policy is your chance to do a little social engineering of your own, and it educates your users, garners support from management, and sets standards of proper behavior for users *and* system administrators.

User education is important because security is often inconvenient and users are devious— they will thwart your best-laid plans unless they understand the *reasons* for the inconvenience. Many users may feel that their account security is a personal matter, similar to the choice of whether to wear seat belts while driving. However, a multiuser computer system is a community of sorts, and one weak account is all a cracker needs to compromise an entire system.

Because security is inconvenient, you also need the support of management to enforce potentially unpopular security policies. Management will be more receptive to user inconvenience if you present evidence of the costs of a break-in, for instance an estimate of how much staff time it would take to restore your systems to a clean state after a break-in, or the cost to your company of theft of information.

Finally, a security policy tells users how you expect them to use the system, the consequences of misuse, and what actions you may take to investigate alleged misuse.

Not so long ago, a system administrator who suspected a user of the slightest wrongdoing would put on his shiny jackboots and stomp through users' files and electronic mailboxes like a hog rooting for truffles, looking for "evidence." If he found any, the user got booted from the system. Then came the ECPA (Electronic Communications Privacy Act) of 1986, a federal law that provides criminal penalties for invading the privacy of users of computer systems and networks.

The ECPA legal waters are still murky because there hasn't yet been enough case law to clarify the intent of Congress. Since you probably don't want to be on the receiving end of such a clarification, you should act cautiously when gathering evidence. A security policy that clearly states what actions the systems administrator may take in investigating security incidents helps protect you from the possibly untoward consequences of "just doing your job." However, this is *not* legal advice—if you are concerned about how the ECPA may affect you, *consult a lawyer*, preferably one with expertise in computer law.

Before developing a security policy you should answer the following questions: What information and resources are you protecting? Who may want to break in? What are the likely consequences of a break-in?

If you don't know what you're protecting, you can't decide how strong your security profile should be. You have to have some idea of who the crackers may be because they come in all shapes and sizes. They vary from the kid in the basement with a Commodore 64, who wants to take your system for the computer equivalent of a joyride, to sophisticated industrial spies who may set up housekeeping on your system, covering their tracks by altering programs and log files. The consequences of a break-in depend on the value of the information and resources you're protecting, and the cost of recovery. Since a security policy usually imposes some inconveniences on your system's users and you want their cooperation in implementing it, you should tailor it to minimize inconvenience while maintaining the level of security your site needs.

A large collection of security policies is available for anonymous `ftp` from the host `ftp.eff.org` in the directory `pub/CAF/policies`. The USENET newsgroup `comp.admin.policy` is another good resource for getting feedback on a security policy.

User Authentication

Authentication is a fancy name for identifying yourself as a valid user of a computer system, and it's your first defense against a break-in. Until recently, UNIX user authentication meant typing a valid login name and password. This is known as *reusable* password authentication, meaning that you enter the same password each time you log in. Reusable password authentication is too weak for some systems and will eventually be replaced by *one-time* password systems in which you enter a different password each login.

Reusable passwords are strong enough for some sites as long as users choose good passwords. Unfortunately, many don't—research has shown that as many as 30%–50% of passwords on typical UNIX systems can easily be guessed. Your security policy should both require strong passwords and provide guidelines for choosing them.

Picking Good Passwords

Good passwords are 6–8 characters long, use a rich character set (upper- and lowercase letters, digits, punctuation, and control characters), are not in English or foreign-language dictionaries, and don't contain any public information about you, such as your name or license number. Detailed guidelines for choosing passwords are presented in the security books mentioned in the section "Finding More Information" later in this chapter, but one good method is to take a random phrase and modify it in ingenious ways. For instance, the phrase "If pigs had wings" could yield the password "1fpiGzhw." This password is a combination of a misspelled word ("1f" standing for "if"), a misspelled word with odd capitalization ("pigZ"), and the first letters of two more words. It's as secure as a reusable password can be since it isn't found in any dictionary and uses a fairly rich vocabulary (the digit "1" and capitalization), and it's easy to remember (but not to type).

Password choice is one of the areas in which users will deviously (and sometimes maliciously) thwart your security policies—some people can't be convinced that they should pick a good password. You have two alternatives for these recalcitrant users: proactive and retroactive password vetting.

Password screening

Retroactive password vetting puts you in the role of the cracker. You make your best effort to break your users' passwords, and if you succeed you notify the user and require her to change her password to something safer. The public domain program crack, written by Alec Muffett and available for anonymous ftp from ftp.cert.org and other sites, is one of the best. crack uses various tricks to permute login names and finger information into likely passwords and whatever word lists you specify. If you've got the disk space and CPU cycles you can feed crack the huge English and foreign-language word lists available for ftp from the host black.ox.ac.uk.

The problem with crack and similar programs is that users hate being told that you've cracked their passwords—it's kind of like having a neighbor say, "By the way, I was rattling doorknobs last night and noticed that yours wasn't locked." However, crack *is* useful for gathering information you can use to make a case to management for stronger password security. For instance, if you can show that 30 percent of your users' passwords are easily guessed, you may be able to persuade your boss that proactive password screening is a good idea. And if you do plan to crack passwords, your users may react more positively if you make that clear in your security policy.

Proactive password screening is more like a preemptive strike—if you prevent your users from choosing poor passwords, there's no reason to run crack. With proper education via your security policy users will react more positively (or at least less negatively) to being told they must choose a more secure password than to being told that you broke their current one. The passwd+ and npasswd programs screen passwords and can replace your standard passwd program. passwd+ is available for ftp from the host ftp.wustl.edu and others, and npasswd from ftp.luth.se.

If you have source code for your system's passwd program you can modify it to call the cracklib library of C functions. cracklib is also authored by Alec Muffett and makes checks similar to crack. A password that gets by cracklib's screening is not likely to be guessed, especially by crack. cracklib is available from ftp.cert.org and other hosts.

Password for System Accounts

The system administrator must take special care in choosing a good password for her account and the superuser account. The superuser account must be protected because of the power it gives a cracker, and the system administrator's account because it can give access to the superuser account in many ways. For instance, if a system administrator's account is broken, the cracker can install a fake su program in his private bin directory that records the root password, removes itself, and then invokes the real su program. The system administrator account may have other special privileges that a cracker can make use of; for instance, membership in groups that allow you to read—or worse, write—system memory or raw disk devices, and permission to su to the superuser account. The systems administrator and root passwords should be changed often and should be as strong as you can make them.

Password Aging

SVR4 UNIX also provides password *aging* facilities. Password aging places a time limit on the life of a password. The longer you keep the same password, the better the chance that someone will crack it, either by guessing it, watching you type it, or by cracking it offline on another computer. Changing passwords every 1–6 months is sufficient for many sites, and password aging enforces that policy by requiring users to change their passwords when they expire. However, a poor implementation of password aging is worse than none at all. Users should be warned a few days in advance that their passwords will expire, because they may choose poor passwords if forced to choose on the spur of the moment.

Shadow Passwords

SVR4 UNIX also provides *shadow* passwords. UNIX passwords are encrypted in the password file, but access to the encrypted version is valuable because it allows a cracker to crack them on her own computer. A fast personal computer can try thousands of guesses per second, which is a huge advantage for the cracker. Without access to the encrypted passwords, the cracker must try each of her guesses through the normal login procedure, which at best may take five to ten seconds per guess.

Shadow passwords hide the encrypted passwords in a file that is readable only by the superuser, thereby preventing crackers from cracking them offline. You should use them.

One-time Passwords

Reusable passwords may be a serious problem if your users use your site to connect to remote sites on the Internet or if your local network is not physically secure. On February 3, 1994, the CERT/CC issued advisory CA-94:01. Crackers had broken into several major Internet sites, gained superuser access, and installed software to snoop the network and record the first packets of telnet, ftp, and rlogin sessions, which contain login names and passwords. According to the CERT/CC advisory, "…all systems that offer remote access through rlogin, telnet, and FTP are at risk. Intruders have already captured access information for *tens of thousands* of systems across the Internet" (emphasis added).

Internet programs such as `telnet` send unencrypted passwords over the network, making them vulnerable to snooping. The only way to truly solve this problem is to change the protocols so that user authentication doesn't require sending passwords over the network, but that won't happen soon.

Reusable passwords are valuable precisely because they're reusable. One-time passwords get around this problem by requiring a new password for each use—the bad guys can sniff all they want, but it does them no good since the password that logs you in on Tuesday is different from the one you used Monday.

Smart Cards

Smart cards are one way to implement one-time passwords. Users are issued credit card–sized devices with numeric keypads and a PIN (personal identification number) that acts as the password for the card. When the user logs in to the computer it issues a *challenge*, which the user types into the smart card, along with her PIN. The smart card encrypts the challenge with other information such as the time, and displays a *response*, which the user types to the computer to log in. The computer generates a different challenge for each login. Each response is unique and can't be reused, so it doesn't matter if the challenge and response strings are sniffed. If the card is lost or stolen the login name and PIN are still required for the card to be used. Smart cards are a good solution to the reusable password problem, but they are too expensive for many sites.

S/Key

`S/Key` is a solution for sites that can't afford smart cards. `S/Key` generates a sequential list of unique passwords and uses a different one for each login, but without using a smart card. Suppose that you log in to your computer from home over a phone line, or perhaps from a commercial Internet service provider. Your home computer runs an `S/Key` program that takes the place of a smart card by producing a response to the computer's challenge string, which is also generated by `S/Key`. If you're using a terminal that can't run `S/Key`, or a computer that doesn't have `S/Key` installed, you can generate a list of passwords to be entered sequentially in future logins.

`S/Key` also provides a *duress* password that you enter to let the computer know that the bad guys have a gun to your head, and that although you want access now, you also want to invalidate the current password sequence. This is also useful if you lose your list of passwords and want to invalidate them until you can generate a new one.

The disadvantage of `S/Key` is that it may require you to carry around a list of valid passwords, which you could lose. However, as long as your login name doesn't appear on that list, a cracker still must guess that and the name of your computer. Further, since a list the size of a credit card can hold hundreds of passwords, and you only have to remember which one is next, the cracker still has to guess which of the passwords is next in the sequence.

An advantage of S/Key is that it doesn't require a smart card. It's available for anonymous ftp from the hosts thumper.bellcore.com and crimelab.com.

Equivalent Hosts and *.rhosts* Authentication

UNIX provides two mechanisms for authenticating yourself to other hosts on a network after you've logged in to one. Suppose that your organization has 10 workstations, named ws1, ws2,...ws10. Since the workstations are all administered by you, one should be as trustworthy as another. If you log in to ws3 you would like to get access to ws5 without providing a password, since you already gave one when you logged in to ws3. You can do this for your account alone with a .rhosts file, and for all the accounts on the computer (except the superuser account) with the file /etc/hosts.equiv.

A .rhosts file lists host/login name pairs that you want to give access to your account. Suppose that your main account *mylogin* is on the host money.corp.com, but sometimes you first login to the host lucre.corp.com and then use rlogin to get to money.corp.com. On money.corp.com you create a .rhosts in your home directory, readable and writable only by you and containing the line

```
lucre.corp.com mylogin
```

The .rhosts tells the rlogin daemon on money.corp.com that the account *mylogin* on the host lucre.corp.com should be allowed access *without a password*. You can add additional lines for other host/login name pairs, and the login name does not have to be the same on both hosts.

> **TIP:** While this is convenient, it carries a risk—if a cracker breaks into your account on lucre.corp.com, she can then break into your account at money.corp.com without a password. The .rhosts file also provides cracker clues. If your account on money.corp.com is broken, the cracker will see from your .rhosts the login name of your account on lucre.corp.com. On the other hand, .rhosts authentication avoids the problem of sending clear-text passwords over the network, which is an advantage if you're not using one-time passwords. You must decide whether the convenience outweighs the security risks.

The file /etc/hosts.equiv does on a global level what .rhosts files do on the account level. The 10-workstation site example could create an /etc/hosts.equiv file like this on each workstation:

```
ws1.corp.com
ws2.corp.com
[...]
ws10.corp.com
```

Now the ten workstations are mutually equivalent with respect to user authentication. Once you log in to one of the workstations, you can log in to any other without a password and without a .rhosts file. Again, while this may be convenient, when a single account on one of the 10 workstations is cracked, the other 9 are also compromised.

.rhosts and the superuser account

The superuser account (root) gets special treatment. Even if a host appears in /etc/ hosts.equiv, root at that host is not considered equivalent unless the file /.rhosts also exists and contains a line for that site's root account. While this may be convenient for software distribution using rdist, consider carefully the security implications before you create a /.rhosts; passwordless software distribution is also convenient for crackers. For instance, if a cracker gains superuser access on ws1.corp.com, he can install a special version of the login program on that host, use rdist to send it to the other nine, and break into those, too. It may be better to forgo /.rhosts files and do your software distribution the hard way with ftp.

.netrc authentication

The .rhosts and /etc/hosts.equiv files only work with the so-called *r-commands* (rsh, rlogin, rdist, rcp). The telnet and ftp will still ask for a login name and password. However, you can use the .netrc file to automate ftp access. The .netrc should reside in your home directory on the host from which you run ftp. It contains a list of host names, login names, and passwords, all *unencrypted*. Because it holds clear text passwords, the .netrc file must be readable *only* by its owner. Because the password is unencrypted, a .netrc is a worse security risk than a .rhosts. It is useful for anonymous ftp access, though. For instance, if you often log in to the host ftp.cert.org to look at the CERT/CC advisories, you could create a .netrc containing the following lines:

```
machine ftp.cert.org
login anonymous
password yourlogin@yourhost.domain
```

This is safe since you're not divulging anything that isn't already public knowledge, that ftp.cert.org supports anonymous ftp.

If possible, don't use .rhosts, .netrc, and /etc/hosts.equiv. Your security policy should specify whether your users are allowed to use the .rhosts and .netrc files. The COPS and chkacct programs (covered in the section "Security Tools" later in this chapter) check the security of your users' .rhosts and .netrc files.

File System Security

Despite your best efforts at establishing and implementing a good password security policy, your site may still be broken in to. Once a cracker has gained access to an account on your computer, his goal is to ensure continued access—if he's broken a user's password it may be changed to something more secure, or you might close whatever security hole he exploited to gain access. One way for crackers to ensure access is to install new accounts, or trapdoor versions of a system program such as `login`. Good file system security helps you prevent or detect these modifications and recover from a break-in.

As distributed, most vendors' operating systems are not secure. System configuration files may be writable by users other than root, device files may have insecure file permissions, and programs and configuration files may be owned by users other than `root`. Configuration files writable by non-root accounts may allow a cracker to trick the system into granting additional privileges, or allow him to trick other computers on the same network. Device files that are readable or writable by users other than root may allow the cracker to alter system memory to gain additional privileges, snoop terminal or network traffic, or bypass the normal UNIX file protections to read files from or alter information on disk or tape storage. The cracker can alter files owned by users other than root even without breaking the superuser account. These are just a few of the ways vendors help make your life more interesting.

Ideally you will both ensure that your newly installed UNIX system has proper file system security (intrusion *prevention*), and have a way to detect unauthorized file system changes (intrusion *detection*). There are several good tools for these jobs. You can use the COPS and TAMU Tiger programs to detect insecurities in newly installed systems, and the Tripwire and TAMU tiger packages can both detect subsequent file system modifications. These programs are covered later in this chapter in the section "Security Tools."

Backup Policies

You may not think of your system backups as a security tool. However, if crackers modify programs or destroy files, how will you recover? If you don't run Tripwire you may detect a break-in but not be able to tell which files the crackers changed. Your only recourse is to restore the system to its clean state from your backups. Even if you run Tripwire you must still be able to restore files that were removed or changed. Good backups are essential to both tasks. Backups may also be important as evidence in court proceedings.

You should answer the following questions about your backup strategy:

- ■ Are your backups physically safe? Can a cracker get your backup tapes and alter them or get information from them? Shadow passwords are useless if a cracker can retrieve the encrypted passwords from a backup tape and crack them offline.

A cracker who can alter a backup and trick you into reloading it can cause his own programs to be installed on your system.

■ Do you test your backups? Are you *certain* that you can restore your system? The worst time to find out there's a problem with your backup procedures is when you really need them. A good system administrator will periodically test-restore random files or entire file systems from her backup tapes to ensure that they will work in an emergency. This is especially important with 8mm helical scan tape systems because the tapes wear out after a few dozen passes.

WARNING: 8mm helical scan tape backups (e.g., Exabyte) are based on video recording technology. If you drop a few bits on your video of Johnny's fourth birthday party, it's no big deal, but a few missing bits on your backup tape may render the remainder unreadable. Helical scan technology may result in data loss after only a few dozen passes over a tape. This includes reads, writes, and even retensioning passes—in fact, anything that moves the tape over the capstan.

Further, tape formulations vary among manufacturers and even between production runs as vendors change their formulations. To make matters worse, buying "data grade" 8mm tapes may not guarantee better quality. Your best bet is to experiment with different brands of tapes to see which work the most reliably with your drives. Once you've found a brand that works well for you, buy it in bulk. You should also experiment to see how many read and write passes you can achieve before a tape goes bad. Cycle in new tapes as the old ones near their life expectancies.

4mm digital auto tape (DAT) drives were designed from the ground up for date recording, and the prices of DAT drives are dropping. You can now buy a DAT drive that will hold up to 8 GB of compressed data for about $1,500. If you're thinking about replacing your existing 8mm helical scan drives you should go with 4mm DAT.

■ Do you keep your tapes forever? Tapes and other media wear out and should be replaced on a set schedule and disposed of in a way that thwarts dumpster-diving attacks.

■ Are your backups kept onsite? What will you do if there's a fire or other natural disaster? Consider storing archival backups offsite in a safe-deposit vault.

■ Is your backup schedule sufficient for your security needs? How often do you run partial and full backups, and what is the chance that a file you create Monday and remove Tuesday will appear on a backup tape? Depending on the value of the information you back up, you may want to revise your schedule to run backups more frequently.

■ Should you make periodic archival backups of the entire system on a read-only medium like a WORM (write-once, read-many) drive?

Network Security

Attaching your computer to a network presents a host of new security threats—networked computers may be attacked from any host on the network or by tapping into the physical network, and if you are connected to the Internet your computer can be attacked from sites anywhere in the world. Networking software also introduces new threats. Most Internet software protocols were not designed with security in mind, and network server programs often run with superuser privileges that make them fruitful grounds for system cracking.

If you don't need a software service, do away with it. For instance, if you don't plan to use the UUCP software, remove both it and the UUCP account. However, you will want some network services, and you must ensure that those are as secure as you can make them. A few of the most important services are discussed in the following sections.

FTP

FTP is the Internet *File Transfer Protocol*, implemented on UNIX systems by the client program `ftp` and the server program `ftpd`. The `ftpd` server runs with superuser privileges and has been a rich source of bugs.

The `ftpd` server allows `ftp` clients to connect to a computer and transfer files back to the client computer. While the `ftp` protocol requires user authentication, most implementations also allow *anonymous* logins. There are two problems. First, normal `ftp` authentication sends passwords over the network in the clear, where they can be snooped. Second, if you run `ftpd`—and especially if you allow anonymous logins—crackers have a program to exploit that might give them superuser privileges.

If you run `ftpd`, make sure you're running a fairly recent version. If your vendor doesn't provide a sufficiently bug-free `ftpd`, you may want to get a public-domain replacement. The BSD and Washington University (WU) replacements are available on `ftp.uu.net` and other hosts. The WU `ftpd` is based on the BSD version with many additional features, but new features sometimes mean new bugs—if you don't need the features, the BSD version may be better.

Another possibility is to run `ftpd` in a `chrooted` environment. The `chroot` system call changes the root of the file tree from the directory / to one you specify. The process is trapped inside the directory tree below the new root, which allows you to insulate the rest of your file system from buggy software. You can use wrappers such as `tcpd` and `netacl` (described in the section "Program Wrappers" later in this chapter) to run a short program that changes to a secure directory and runs `chroot` before invoking `ftpd`.

`chroot` is not a panacea. A chrooted environment must be set up carefully, or a knowledgeable cracker may break out of it. Device files in the `chroot` directory are a particular risk since access to raw devices isn't affected by `chroot`. That is, if you create a device file in the `chroot` directory that allows access to the raw disk, a cracker can still access files outside the `chroot` file tree.

> **WARNING:** The chroot system call won't solve all your problems. While it limits the cracker's access to the part of the UNIX file tree you specify in the `chroot` call, a good cracker may still break in. For instance, if a buggy `setuid root` program allows a cracker to get a shell with superuser permissions inside the chrooted directory, she can create device files with read and write permission on system memory or raw disks. A knowledgeable cracker could then add new accounts to the password file or break your system in any number of other ways. The moral is that you shouldn't feel safe just because you're running a `setuid root` program inside a `chrooted` directory. `setuid root` programs should always be carefully inspected for bugs regardless of whether they're running in a restricted environment.

sendmail

The `sendmail` program is a mail router that implements the *Simple Mail Transfer Protocol* (SMTP). Because it is large, complex, and runs with superuser privileges, it has yielded a monotonous string of serious bugs. (The notorious *Internet worm* of November 1988 exploited a `sendmail` bug.) Worse, vendors often lag several versions behind the state of the art and fail to fix known bugs, or they add new, bug-producing "features."

Your most secure option is to toss your vendor's sendmail and run Version 8 `sendmail`, available from `ftp.cs.berkeley.edu` and other hosts. Eric Allman, the original author, has resumed work on `sendmail` and rewritten much of the code, and is actively maintaining it. The serious bugs detailed in the CERT/CC advisory of November 4, 1993, were not present in Version 8 `sendmail`, and would probably have been fixed more promptly by Allman than by vendors, some of whom took up to two months to produce fixes. See Chapter 41 for instructions on installing Version 8 `sendmail`.

For sites that need very high security, the TIS (Trusted Information Systems, Inc.) toolkit, available from the host `ftp.tis.com`, circumvents `sendmail` problems by providing an SMTP client, `smap`, that runs as an unprivileged user in a chrooted environment. `smap` implements a minimal version of SMTP and writes mail to disk for later delivery by `smapd`. `smap` also allows you to refuse mail that's too large, to prevent attackers from filling your disks.

Network File System (NFS)

NFS was invented by Sun Microsystems, which put the protocol specification in the public domain. This meant that anyone could write an NFS implementation that would interoperate with Sun's, and many vendors did. NFS is useful and popular, but does not offer strong security. It opens you to many attacks, and if you don't need it, you shouldn't run it.

If you run NFS, carefully read your vendor's documentation and make sure you've enabled all security features. Keep exported file systems to a minimum, and export them with the minimal set of permissions. The books mentioned in the section "Finding More Information" later in this chapter provide cookbook procedures for safely administering NFS.

Network Information System (NIS)

Sun Microsystems also created NIS (previously known as YP, or `yellow pages`). As with NFS, several vendors besides Sun have implemented NIS on their computers.

NIS allows you to share system administration data over the network, which is convenient if you have many hosts to administer. For instance, if you have a cluster of 50 workstations using the same password file, you can create a single copy and use NIS to share it among the workstations.

Although NIS is convenient, it is not secure. A poorly administered NIS may allow crackers to gather information about your site remotely, for instance by requesting your password file for offline cracking. As before, if you don't need it, don't run it. If you do need it, make sure that your NIS domain name isn't easily guessed, and refer to your vendor's documentation and one of the "nuts and bolts" books for detailed instructions on safe NIS administration.

finger

Although the `finger` program seems innocuous, it may be another you can do without. `finger` is the client, and `fingerd` the server. The client program is safe, but the server can give crackers information about your site. In particular, the time of last login is often included in `finger` output, which helps crackers find unused accounts to break. `finger`'s output format may also give clues to the kind of operating system you run. Since many crackers work from checklists of bugs particular to certain versions of UNIX, this information is valuable. Also, if your password policy doesn't prevent your users from choosing bad passwords, `finger` information may provide clues to crackers.

You should run `fingerd` as an unprivileged user—the login `nobody` is a good choice.

The Trivial File Transfer Protocol (TFTP)

TFTP is used by diskless workstations to load UNIX from a file server. It's called "trivial" because the normal security checks of FTP have been removed—accounts and passwords are not required. Some versions of the TFTP server allow crackers to grab any file on the system—for instance the shadow password file for offline cracking. Recent versions of the TFTP server offer better security by only allowing files to be retrieved from a specific directory. If you don't need TFTP service, disable it, and if you do, make sure you're using all its security features. Secure versions of the TFTP daemon are available from `ftp.uu.net` and other hosts.

Intrusion Detection

Despite your best efforts, your site may be cracked. How will you know when it happens? Sophisticated system crackers go to great lengths to cover their tracks.

If you administer a single computer, it helps to get to know it *and* your users. Run `ps` periodically to get an idea of what jobs are usually running, and look for unusual ones. Use `sa` to see what typical job mix your users run. Is a user who normally does only word processing suddenly compiling programs? Is an account being used while a user is on vacation? Either might indicate a break-in.

This kind of monitoring is very limited, though. You can't be logged in all the time, and if you have more than one computer to administer, this approach is impractical. How can you detect the telltale signs of crackers automatically?

Account auditing helps detect whether crackers have created new accounts. If you run a small system you may be able to print the entire password file and periodically compare it to the system password file. If you have too many users for this to be practical, you can store the current password file on a read-only medium (for example, a floppy disk that you can write-protect) and use `diff` to look for new, unauthorized accounts. Account auditing should also ensure that inactive or idle accounts are removed.

Message Digests

Message digests, also known as *file signatures*, are the preferred way to alert you when crackers alter files. A message digest is a cryptographic signature specific to a file—if the file changes, the signature changes, and if the signature is strong enough, it's not possible for a cracker to create another file with the same signature. If you compute a message digest for all your important system files, and a cracker changes one, you'll find out.

The public-domain Tripwire software automates detection of file system alterations. You can ftp Tripwire from ftp.cs.purdue.edu. Tripwire computes up to five different signatures for each file you specify. It reports deleted files and new files. You can configure it to ignore files you know will change, such as system log files.

If possible you should install Tripwire just after you've installed your vendor's operating system, *before* you install user accounts and connect it to a network. If you're installing Tripwire on an existing system, put it in single-user mode or detach it from the network, and then install Tripwire and compute the file signatures. If you can, keep Tripwire, its configuration file, and its database of file signatures offline or on read-only media.

Files change all the time on UNIX systems, and if you don't configure it correctly Tripwire may become your UNIX equivalent of "the boy who cried wolf." For instance, the /etc/ password file signature changes whenever a user changes her password. The danger is that warnings of illicit changes to files will be buried in the noise of valid changes. Spend some time configuring Tripwire until the signal-to-noise ratio is high enough that you won't miss valid reports.

Tripwire's message digests vary in their cryptographic strength. Read the documentation carefully and make sure you're using digests strong enough for your site's security needs.

C2 Auditing

The National Computer Security Center (NCSC) publishes the Trusted Computer Systems Evaluation Criteria (TCSEC, or *Orange Book*) to specify the security standards computers must meet for certification at various levels for government use. The *C2* level is one that vendors commonly claim to meet. Among other things, C2 security requires that *audit events* be logged to help track intrusions. For example, if the user joe runs the su command and becomes root at 14:23 on February 10, 1994, this information is recorded in an audit file.

Many other fairly routine events are audited, and audit logs become huge. The problem on large systems with many users is winnowing the chaff from the wheat, and few tools are available to automate the process. However, if you run a small system and you have time to inspect the logs, C2 auditing may help you discover intrusions.

Note that there is a difference between offering "C2 security features" (as many vendors claim) and actually being certified at a TCSEC level by the NCSC. The former is marketing hype, and the latter a lengthy process that leads to official certification. This doesn't mean that uncertified "C2 features" aren't valuable, but you should know the difference.

Program Wrappers

A *wrapper* is a program that offers additional security by surrounding a less secure program and running it in a more secure environment, making additional checks before running it, or logging information about who uses it.

For instance, suppose that you usually log in to your computer yourhost.zorch.com, but sometimes log in to zach.glop.org and then telnet to yourhost.zorch.com. Running a telnet server on yourhost.zorch.com makes it possible for anyone on the Internet to attempt a break-in. Since you know that the only Internet host that *should* have access is zach.glop.org, you can put a wrapper around telnetd that checks incoming connections and refuses ones from other hosts.

The tcpd wrapper is available from ftp.cert.org and other sites. tcpd sits between the Internet daemon inetd and the programs that inetd runs. For instance, instead of having inetd run telnetd directly, you can configure it to run tcpd. Based on the rules you give, tcpd can start telnetd or reject the connection request. For instance, in the previous example it could reject telnet connections from all hosts other than zach.glop.org. In either case it can log the attempt. tcpd can be used for any program run by inetd. The TIS firewalls toolkit provides a similar program, netacl (Network Access Control), available from ftp.tis.com.

Disaster Recovery

If you discover a break-in, what should you do? That depends on what the cracker is doing, whether you intend to catch and prosecute him, and how disruptive he is. You may want to monitor the cracker's activities to see how he got in, and gather information about other sites he may be using (or cracking from your site) so you can notify those sites' system administrators. You should also notify CERT/CC. (See the section "Finding More Information" later in this chapter.) Depending on your security needs and what you know about how the cracker got in, you may need to restore changed files, change the superuser and system administrator passwords, audit (your password file), install a secure version of a broken program or change system configuration files to remove insecurities, or even restore your entire system from the vendor's original distribution media and your own backups.

This list is not exhaustive, but it shows a broad range of post-intrusion options. Some of these options—such as requiring all your users to change their passwords—severely affect your users and staff. Things will go more smoothly if you have a written plan. Although you may not create a perfect plan the first time, having one helps keep you calm and provides some structure when things go wrong.

After your system is secure again, you should assess your security needs and strategies. Could the break-in have been prevented? How bad were the consequences? Should you revise your security policy or devote more staff time to security? Post-intrusion may be a good time to approach management with previously rejected security proposals.

Security Tools

Programmers have developed automated security tools (ASTs) to assess your system security. ASTs are sharp on both sides—if you don't use them to find insecurities, crackers may.

Many crackers work from checklists of known bugs, methodically trying each in turn until they find a way in or give up and move on to an easier target. ASTs automate this boring job and generate summary reports. If you close those holes, a checklist cracker may move on to less secure hosts, preferably ones you don't administer.

There are two problems with ASTs. First, you may gain a false sense of security when they cheerfully report "all's well." ASTs only report *known* insecurities, and new ones are discovered constantly. A second, related problem, is that if crackers break in to your system they may alter your AST to always report good news.

Despite these problems, you should run ASTs. They are good tools if you understand their limitations, and especially if you can install them on and run them from read-only media. You can also use tools like Tripwire to verify the integrity of your ASTs.

COPS

COPS (Computer Oracle and Password System) was written by Dan Farmer of Sun Microsystems. COPS has been ported to many different versions of UNIX. Most of it is written in Bourne shell scripts and `perl`, so it's easy to understand and to modify if it doesn't do exactly what you want. COPS performs comprehensive checks for user- and system-level insecurities, checks whether you've patched programs with known insecurities, and includes an expert system that tries to determine whether your computer can be cracked. If you don't run any other AST, you should run COPS.

TAMU Tiger

Texas A&M University (TAMU) developed a suite of *tiger team* programs to look for system insecurities in response to serious and persistent break-ins. A tiger team is a group of security experts hired to break in to your system and tell you how they did it. TAMU didn't have the staff resources for tiger teams, so they automated the process—if a host passed the TAMU tiger gauntlet, it was relatively immune to cracking.

In contrast to COPS, which makes many checks of user accounts, Tiger assumes that the cracker *already* has access to a legitimate account on your computer and looks for ways in which she can get superuser access. Tiger checks `cron` entries, mail aliases, NFS exports, `inetd` entries, and PATH variables. It also checks `.rhosts` and `.netrc` files, file and directory permissions, and files that shouldn't be there.

Tiger also computes message digests for important system files, and reports unpatched programs for which vendors have provided fixes. Tiger includes file signature databases for several standard UNIX distributions, which you can use rather than developing your own. You can `ftp` TAMUtiger from the host `net.tamu.edu` in the directory `pub/security/TAMU`. The TAMU tiger tar archive is named `tiger-2.2.3.tar.gz` (the extension ".gz" means the tar archive is compressed with the `gzip` program, available from `ftp.uu.net` and other `ftp` sites). The signature files are in the subdirectory `tiger-sigs`.

SATAN

SATAN (Security Analysis Tool for Auditing Networks) was promised for release by Dan Farmer, author of COPS, and Wietse Venema, author of `tcpd`, for the first half of 1994. According to the prerelease notes, SATAN will probe a host or set of hosts over a network, looking for information and potential insecurities in network services. It will either report the data or use an expert system to investigate further, based on the insecurities and information already discovered. SATAN will be a useful tool for both crackers and system administrators. Watch for an announcement in the USENET newsgroup `comp.security.announce`.

Firewalls and Bastion Hosts

Just as your car's firewall is designed to protect you from engine fires, a network firewall protects an internal, hidden network from the rest of the Internet. Firewalls are popular with sites that need heightened security, but are unpopular with users.

The basic idea of a firewall is to establish a single, heavily guarded point of entry to your local area network (LAN). The system administrator maintains a high level of security on the firewall (or *bastion host*), which may also be surrounded by *filtering routers* that automatically limit access to the firewall.

Firewalls (and the interior LANs they protect) can be made very secure, but they limit access to Internet services. In many firewall implementations, users who want access to the Internet must first log in to the firewall host.

If you plan to implement a firewall you should subscribe to the *Firewalls* mailing list to get a feel for the design issues (see the section "Finding More Information" later in this chapter). The TIS firewalls software and other information is available from `ftp.tis.com`. Firewall tutorials, theoretical papers, and information about commercial firewall vendors is available on `ftp.greatcircle.com`. You should also read the Cheswick and Bellovin book mentioned in the section "Finding More Information" in this chapter.

Kerberos

The problem of maintaining security on hundreds of workstations installed in insecure, public sites led the Massachusetts Institute of Technology's (MIT's) *Project Athena* programmers to develop Kerberos.

Kerberos solves some (but not all) of the problems inherent in physically insecure networks and computers. Kerberos network servers verify both their own identity and that of their clients *without* sending unencrypted passwords over the LAN where they may be snooped, and can provide privacy via data encryption. Persons using Kerberos services can be fairly sure that they're talking to the real service, and Kerberos services can be equally sure that when Joe asks the mail server for his electronic mail, it's really Joe. Kerberos is free, and source code is available from the host `athena-dist.mit.edu`. The USENET newsgroup `comp.protocols.kerberos` is devoted to discussion of the Kerberos system.

A disadvantage of Kerberos is that each network client and server program must be *Kerberized*, that is, modified to call the Kerberos subroutines. Kerberized versions of standard applications such as `telnet` are supplied with Kerberos, and if you have source code for your applications you can add calls to the Kerberos subroutines yourself. However, many third-party software vendors provide neither source code nor Kerberized versions of their software.

Kerberos has additional problems. Many Internet servers don't use it, and it does you no good to install a Kerberized `telnet` client if your users connect to remote hosts that run unKerberized `telnet` servers. Kerberos doesn't work with *dumb* (ASCII) terminals or most *X-terminals*, and on multiuser computers is only as strong as the superuser account because the superuser can find the secret keys. Kerberos also requires an otherwise-unused, secure host to maintain its database of *principals* and their secret keys.

Despite its limitations, Kerberos is useful in certain environments. For more information, `ftp` to the host `rtfm.mit.edu` and download the Kerberos FAQ (Frequently Asked Questions) document.

Hardware Solutions

Dial-back modems, encrypting EtherNet hubs, and filtering routers all help solve some of your security problems.

Dial-Back Modems

A dial-back modem stores a list of valid login names and phone numbers. You dial the modem, go through an authentication procedure, and hang up. The modem consults its list of phone numbers and users, and calls you back. A cracker who discovers your modem through random dialing can't connect to your computer unless he's calling from one of the listed numbers.

> **TIP:** Dial-back modems can be tricked by clever crackers who use special equipment to generate the proper tones to trick your modem into thinking the calling modem has hung up when it hasn't. If your dial-back modem then looks up the "secure" number of the good guy's phone and calls back on the same line, the bad guy's modem picks up the call and gets in anyway. The best defense against this attack is to use one line for incoming connection requests and a second line for the dial-back. Some telcos even provide a one-way line for its call-back, so it can't be tricked by the method described above.

Dial-back modems work well for organizations with relatively immobile users. They are also useful if you offer modem-based Internet access to users via the SLIP or PPP protocols. However, they don't work well for peripatetic users who need remote access to your system—S/Key is a better solution in that case.

Encrypting EtherNet Hubs

Encrypting hubs used with 10 BASE-T EtherNet can prevent snooping attacks. 10 BASE-T installations use a star topology, in which each station is on its own wire, connected to a central packet-routing hub. The EtherNet protocol requires that a packet destined for a certain host be sent to all hosts on the EtherNet, which is why packets can be snooped. An encrypting hub scrambles the contents of the packet for all the stations except the one for which the packet is intended, making snooping a waste of time.

> **TIP:** Some encrypting hubs also keep track of the EtherNet MAC addresses of the hosts on each wire, and can shut down a wire if a foreign host is introduced. This may help if a cracker unhooks one of your hosts and attaches his PC to your network, but it's not foolproof—most EtherNet cards allow you to set the MAC address in software, and a sophisticated cracker would set his to match the computer he's impersonating. However, some hubs can shut down a wire if the EtherNet heartbeat is interrupted, even momentarily. These hubs prevent the latter attack.

Filtering Routers

Filtering routers are often used in firewalls, placed between the Internet and the bastion host, or on both sides of the bastion host. They can be configured to discard packets based on the type of service requested, such as mail or `ftp`, or to discard some or all packets from specified hosts or networks. Routers are more difficult to break in to than are UNIX hosts because routers are single-purpose computers. Because they stop dangerous network connections before your bastion host ever sees them, the cracker's job is harder.

Finding More Information

The problem with printed security books is that they're soon out of date. Vendors release new versions of UNIX with new bugs, and crackers continually look for new ways to break in. If you rely on old information, you'll soon fall behind. The following list gives some good sources of up-to-date information and the "nuts and bolts" books that give detailed procedures for implementing security.

USENET News

If your site receives USENET news, you at least should read these: `comp.security.announce`, `comp.security.unix`, and `comp.security.misc`.

`comp.security.announce` postings warn you of newly discovered security problems. CERT/CC advisories are posted there. `comp.security.unix` is for general discussion of UNIX security. `comp.security.misc` is for general discussions of computer security. You may also want to read `comp.risks` for discussions of the risks of computers, and `comp.admin.policy` for system administration policy discussions.

CERT/CC

The Computer Emergency Response Team Coordination Center (CERT/CC) was formed by the Defense Advanced Research Projects Agency (DARPA) and is run by Carnegie-Mellon University (CMU). (Alphabet soup, anyone?) CERT/CC acts as a coordination center for computer security information and incidents. When a security problem is found, CERT/CC works with UNIX vendors to correct the problem, and then issues an advisory through electronic mail and `comp.security.announce`, describing the problem, its impact, and how to correct it. CERT/CC advisories do not include specific how-to details of security problems, but they are specific about the fixes.

FIRST

The Forum of Incident Response and Security Teams (FIRST) is a cooperative group of government and private organizations in North America and Europe. By sharing information among FIRST members, they hope to prevent or at least respond quickly to intrusions. CERT/CC is one FIRST member, and its advisories are usually circulated for comment among FIRST members before they are released to the general public. For current information about FIRST, `ftp` to `csrc.ncsl.nist.gov` and look in the directory `pub/first/gen-info`. This host also has a large archive of security information.

Vendor Contacts

Some vendors have become more responsive to security concerns over the years. Some have mailing lists for notifying their customers of new bugs and patches. Contact your vendor's salesperson to see what security information your vendor provides.

Mailing Lists

Special-interest groups maintain mailing lists to discuss specific security topics. One of the most useful is the `Firewalls` list, which is targeted at discussion of firewall implementations, but often contains good advice on other aspects of security. To join firewalls, send mail to `majordomo@greatcircle.com` and include the words `subscribe firewalls-digest` in the body of the message.

You can subscribe to the TAMU Tiger mailing list by sending mail to `majordomo@net.tamu.edu` and including the words `subscribe tiger` in the body of the message.

The *bugtraq* mailing list is a currently popular "full-disclosure" list. The signal-to-noise ratio is fairly low, but depending on your paranoia level, you may want to subscribe to it. Subscribe by sending a letter to `bugtraq-request@fc.net`, with a single line in the body of the message that says: `subscribe bugtraq` *yourlogin@your.host.domain.*

Periodically, someone dissatisfied with CERT/CC's vague advisories starts a security mailing list for public disclosure of security problems, including enough detail to exploit the problem. Some lists try to screen new members so only the "good guys" will get the hot tips, but some believe that the crackers already know the bugs, and the best defense for system administrators is full disclosure as soon as possible. This approach puts a burden on system administrators who don't have source code and must rely on their vendors to fix security bugs. You may want to monitor these lists so you'll be aware of new insecurities, even if you must rely on your vendor to fix them. Most of these lists are announced in `comp.security.unix`.

Conferences and Networking

Security conferences give you the opportunity to find out what other sites are doing to improve their security, to learn of new security software, and to see what theoretical work is being done. You can also meet other system administrators and share information with them. Systems administrators may tell you things in person that they wouldn't publish in the security newsgroups or mailing lists. Advance warning via a phone call from a friend at another site can give you the jump on the latest security problem. Most conferences are announced in the USENET newsgroups previously mentioned.

Online Information and Program Source Archives

Much security information resides on the Internet, accessible via `ftp` or one of the newer information protocols such as `gopher` or the `World-Wide-Web`. Many of these sources have been mentioned previously in this chapter. Good places to start are the archives on `ftp.cert.org`, `csrc.ncsl.nist.gov`, and `ftp.cs.purdue.edu`. Look for security software at the sites mentioned previously, or use an `archie` server such as `archie.ans.net` to find them. Mailing lists and USENET newsgroups frequently mention specific source or information archives. New security software is often posted to the USENET newsgroup `comp.sources.unix`.

FTP and Other Information Archives

A lot of security information is available on the net at `ftp.cert.org`, `csrc.ncsl.nist.gov`, and others. Recently the COAST (Computer Operations, Audit, and Security Tools) project of the Purdue University Computer Sciences department has set up an FTP archive that contains a large collection of security information and tools. You can access this archive via the `ftp` command by connecting to the host `coast.cs.purdue.edu`. Gopher and WWW (World-Wide-Web) access is planned soon.

Other Books

The following books give the detailed procedures you need in order to avoid common mistakes. The first two are basic UNIX security texts that anyone concerned with security should read. The third book covers basic system administration in detail, and includes a good section on security.

Firewalls and Internet Security: Repelling and Wily Hacker, William R. Cheswick and Steven M. Bellovin, Addison-Wesley, 1994.

Practical UNIX Security, Simson Garfinkel and Eugene Spafford, O'Reilly & Associates, 1991, Sebastopal, CA, ISBN 0-937175-72-2.

UNIX System Security: A Guide for Users and System Administrators, David Curry, Addison-Wesley, 1992, ISBN 0-201-56327-4.

UNIX System Administration Handbook, Evi Nemeth, Garth Snyder, and Scott Seebass, Prentice Hall, 1989, ISBN 0-13-933441-6.

Where to Go from Here?

Computer security is a full-time job for many people. As a system administrator you must decide how secure your system should be, what measures you should take to prevent, detect, and recover from intrusions, and then convince yourself (or your manager) to devote the necessary resources to the job. This chapter gives you a broad outline of security concerns, but doesn't tell you all you need to know. Running a secure system means evaluating your security needs, researching software and hardware security systems, and staying abreast of a rapidly changing field by taking advantage of all the resources available.

8

PART

UNIX Flavors and Graphical User Interfaces

UNIX Flavors

45

By S. Lee Henry

The UNIX operating system has clearly emerged as one of the primary software platforms for the '90s, providing distributed computing capabilities for even the most diverse networks. Its remarkable success has been due both to its portability and to its long history of innovation. In the more than 25 years that UNIX has been around, it has had plenty of time to "soak up" good ideas from some of the sharpest computer people in the business. From AT&T, the University of California at Berkeley, Sun Microsystems, and many other companies, UNIX has acquired a tremendous collection of powerful tools and maintained an open architecture that continues to invite development.

UNIX today runs on three or four million computers, maybe more. These computers range from very small personal computers to Crays. The concept of creating ad hoc "programs" by interconnecting commands is extremely powerful whether you're working on a laptop or a supercomputer.

Because of its portability and because of an elegant design that appeals to developers, UNIX has proliferated into many different "flavors" over the past couple decades. As much as this divergence has profited UNIX by providing many venues for innovation, it has also frustrated the growing need for portable applications. Without an adequate market share, any particular UNIX flavor has suffered from a dearth of software or, at least, a dearth of affordable software, especially compared with personal computer systems such as those built by IBM and Apple. The flavors of UNIX are different enough that it became difficult and, therefore, costly to port applications from one to the other. In addition, UNIX is not the same simple creature that it was back in Bell Labs. Windowing systems, graphical user interfaces, and years of innovation have complicated UNIX and dramatically affected the complexity of porting applications.

The need for simplified application portability was not, however, the only factor pushing for a more unified UNIX. Improvements in networking put interoperability among different UNIX systems, as well as between UNIX and non-UNIX systems, high on everyone's agenda. Today's businesses are demanding enterprise-wide computing solutions. These solutions entail a high degree of data sharing—both distributed applications and an ease of moving information and people expertise around the organization. Today's procurements are specifying standard interfaces and protocols to help meet this demand and leverage organizations' investments in computing technology.

As a result, the UNIX command sets and the programming interfaces are becoming increasingly standardized and a number of startling alliances between UNIX competitors are bringing a new unity to UNIX.

This chapter briefly reviews the history of UNIX, describes some of the main "flavors" of UNIX that are popular today, addresses the most important standards that are helping to bring unity to UNIX, and predicts what will happen to UNIX in the remainder of the '90s.

The Beginnings of UNIX

If you feel that you've cut your teeth on UNIX, its early history at Bell Labs may seem extremely remote. UNIX was created at AT&T's Bell Labs roughly 25 years ago, where technological innovation and engineering elegance seemed to reign over more worldly concerns such as proprietorship.

In those days, operating systems were difficult to use and programmers had to work hard to make their programs acceptable to the difficult-to-please computers. The convenient shell environments that you use today did not, for the most part, exist.

UNIX, first called UNICS, was built to run on the DEC PDP-7 and PDP-11 systems. It was not intended to be a product. Its designers, Ken Thompson and Dennis Ritchie, were after usability and had no thoughts about marketing it. They were simply looking to create a more hospitable programming environment, so they created and enhanced UNIX basically for their own use. In time, other people at Bell Labs contributed additional concepts and tools and, by 1969, the basics of UNIX were established.

Given this beginning, it is extremely ironic that UNIX has become not only one of the most successful operating systems ever but that it has influenced every other important operating system as well. For an operating system first developed by experts for experts, the impact that UNIX has had on the industry has been nothing short of staggering. UNIX has had a transforming influence on all computer operating systems since its first introduction into popular use. Even single-user operating systems such as DOS (in releases after 2.0) have taken on many of the characteristics and capabilities of UNIX. The hierarchical file system, which allows a much better way of organizing files than the previous "flat" file space, for example, is incorporated into DOS (except that it does not have a root directory). Search paths and pipes have also worked their way into DOS as has the more command for viewing subsequent pieces of a file.

The more modern Windows NT incorporates many characteristics of UNIX from the basic file metaphor (that is, virtually everything is a file) and hierarchical file system to support for named pipes for interprocess communication and the use of STREAMS in networking. Windows NT has also implemented many of the most important features of UNIX, including multitasking, multiprocessing, and security. Although UNIX has had enhancing effects on many other operating systems, its capabilities still continue to set it in a class by itself. Among these capabilities, its availability over a variety of hardware platforms, its multiuser character, and its support of parallel processing and distributed file systems make it ideal for large heterogeneous networks.

From Lab to Mainstream

The small group of people who created UNIX consisted of AT&T members of a development team looking at an operating system called MULTICS. MULTICS was a time-sharing and multitasking operating system developed at MIT in the '60s. It ran on computers built by General Electric. MULTICS had many important features, but it was complex and unwieldy. When AT&T eventually withdrew its participants, they were left without an operating system but with plenty of good ideas about what a modern time-sharing system should be like. In fact, despite the early disappearance of MULTICS, the astounding success of UNIX owes a considerable amount to several ideas of this then-aggressive operating system. MULTICS had the concept of the shell as command interpreter and a hierarchically arranged file system. Both of these features became features of the new UNIX system as well. Just as important, MULTICS was also one of the first operating systems to support more than one user at a time. This one feature made UNIX especially valuable in its early customer environments, most notably academic and research establishments, where the need to share computer systems was extremely important.

When AT&T decided to license UNIX on DEC minicomputers to educational institutions in 1974, it gave no-cost licenses and source code. Unlike companies such as Microsoft that maintain tight control over source code, AT&T practically gave UNIX away, complete with source code, for the asking. This early availability of UNIX source code to universities meant that hundreds of thousands of bright computer scientists and engineers who could use UNIX, support UNIX, and modify UNIX began flooding the market a few years later. Their expertise led to the early success of UNIX and to much of the divergence of UNIX into many custom versions. The further development of UNIX both within the universities and within the organizations that these UNIX experts began working for quickly began moving UNIX in many new directions at once.

By 1977, UNIX was ready for more commercial use. Digital Equipment was, at the time, emphasizing smaller systems with fewer users. The minicomputer era was getting off the ground, and UNIX had an ideal platform in the PDP series systems because even universities could afford to own them.

Within several years of its commercial availability, UNIX existed in so many different versions that, like the aftermath of the tower of Babel, its followers did not all speak the same language.

Many proprietary versions of UNIX came into being during these times. Some were based on the AT&T release and others on the Berkeley Software Distribution (BSD), often combining features of both. Digital Equipment's Ultrix, for example, was based on the Berkeley release but incorporated some System V features as well. SunOS was moving to the Berkeley release but incorporated System V features, too. Even HP-UX was primarily BSD but added some System V features. IBM's AIX, on the other hand, was based on

System V and added some BSD features, as did Apple's AUX. Users and administrators could move between these different versions of the UNIX operating system but not without a fair degree of stress and retooling. The command rsh, for example, was a remote shell command in the Berkeley release, but was the restricted shell command in System V. These differences, along with significantly different print subsystems, were enough to make the different flavors of UNIX an issue for just about anyone who had to move between them.

By the time UNIX realized it was without the stabilizing influence of standards, commercialism had taken over and many UNIX products were being sold and used in large quantity. UNIX had been thrown into the world of big business, government, and competition.

Factors Leading to UNIX's Early Success

The quick acceptance of UNIX and its move from the laboratory into big business and government was based on a number of compelling advantages that this powerful operating system offered to its users.

A few underlying concepts of UNIX really work well: the tree-structured file system, the fact that a file is a sequence of bytes, and the fact that objects can be accessed as files. UNIX also survived, even embraced, the advent of networks. Its survival made it the operating system of choice in many campus environments and gave it an early mandate for interoperability.

The features that most contributed to the success of UNIX include its model of computing, its portability, and events in its history that allowed its proliferation and encouraged innovation.

The UNIX Model of Computing

The UNIX kernel became the core of the operating system, which generally only UNIX wizards concern themselves with; the shells' environments became the messengers, making the wishes of users palatable before delivering them to the kernel; and the shells (Bourne and C) created the working environments of users. This organization of UNIX into a kernel surrounded by the shell and by user commands was a revolutionary concept in the early days of UNIX.

The UNIX kernel became the core of the system, interacting directly with the hardware while providing services to programs to insulate them from hardware details. The kernel provided essential control and support for the many processes needing to use the CPU. It managed the sequential sharing of the CPU to effect time sharing in such a way that it appeared to users that their processes were continuously running when, in fact, they were running only intermittently. The kernel also maintained the file system and handled interrupts (for example, devices requesting attention). Processes interacted with the kernel through system calls.

The UNIX shells act both as command interpreters and as mini programming languages. Shells read and interpret user commands, expanding filenames and substituting variables with their values before passing commands to the kernel for execution. Over the years, a number of shells have been added to UNIX. The Bourne shell (sh) is the standard UNIX shell; the C shell (csh) and Korn shell (ksh) bring many modern features. Other shells available in some UNIX systems provide limited-access environments with restricted shells such as rsh and process (that is, job) control with jsh. Additionally, public-domain utilities such as PERL and tcsh are used on many UNIX systems.

The simple yet powerful concepts of pipes and redirects are clearly two of the most important features of UNIX. The ability to string together commands to create new tools brings the extensibility of UNIX to every user. When a user feeds the output of a cat command into grep or sort, for example, and then to awk for reformatting or sed for string substitution, he or she is creating a new tool "on the fly."

UNIX also contains several hundred commands and utilities. Many of these, such as sed and awk, are languages with powerful capabilities. Others, such as fold, have a single, simple function.

Portability

From a technical point of view, portability was probably the most important factor in the overall success of UNIX. Users could move UNIX to many different platforms with very little change. Coded in the high-level language C, UNIX was easily ported to a variety of very different hardware platforms. For any large organization, the ability to run the same operating system on virtually all of its computers continues to have considerable appeal. The overhead associated with using and managing these systems is significantly reduced.

Extensibility

Another reason for the early success of UNIX was its extensibility and simplicity. UNIX was able to grow without losing its fundamental elegance and without excessive risk of introducing serious new bugs. Previously, as systems grew, they became increasingly complex and increasingly difficult to maintain. Each feature that was added affected other features, and the likelihood of introducing errors was considerable. It was nearly impossible to maintain or control a single feature without considering its effect on the rest of the operating system.

UNIX, on the other hand, with its simple modularity, allowed developers of new tools to code them fairly independently of other tools and commands. The developers merely had to build tools so that they worked with standard input, standard output, and standard error. In addition, many requirements for additional features could be answered by innovative use of existing UNIX commands. The "UNIX way" suggested simple robust tools that could be used almost like tinker toys to create command one-liners that could accomplish more than complex programs in any other operating system.

Additional Features

The multiuser and multiprocessing nature of UNIX greatly amplified the productivity of its users; they could work on several things at a time.

UNIX also became ready for networking at an early age. With the TCP/IP protocol suite that was derived from the Berkeley work, network-ready UNIX implementations arrived early and fulfilled important needs.

Although you may have heard complaints about UNIX security, the security of UNIX was, in fact, another key feature that helped it to make its way into business and government sites. Operating system security was almost totally lacking in earlier operating systems. In UNIX, file permissions and fairly secure passwords created a paradigm for privacy.

Appeal

Finally, the success of UNIX is based on its appeal to its users. Enthusiasm for UNIX is generally correlated with the time people spend with it. Users must get to a certain level of expertise before they can string together commands and "compose" their own functionality or embed their tricks into scripts that they use as if they were UNIX commands themselves. Once they've mastered this skill, however, UNIX is extremely powerful and compelling. UNIX wizards have many tricks up their sleeves and are always looking for that new clever combination to further streamline their work. The almost endless ways that commands can be combined and data extracted and manipulated is unique to UNIX.

UNIX is composed of many small pieces. UNIX commands don't try to do everything; instead, they do something simple well. Because UNIX offers so many commands, even those who consider themselves experts are constantly discovering new commands and new options. At the same time, much of the detail even the experts don't need to concern themselves with at all. They don't worry, for example, if their data is coming from a file or a device or even from another program. It doesn't matter. The experts can plug the pieces together whenever they need to without having to make allowances for the source or destination of the data.

The early creators of UNIX got to name all the tools that were added to the growing set of commands and utilities that was early UNIX. Some, with names such as sed and grep, are acronyms. Others were given names such as `biff` (after a dog) and `awk` (after its creators). The mix of meaningful and arbitrary command names gave an odd character to this revolutionary operating system. Interestingly, you might notice that UNIX has only advocates and enemies. Almost no one who knows anything about UNIX is neutral.

Some people are overwhelmed by the hundreds of commands and tools that comprise UNIX, and they consider UNIX to be a "four-letter word." It has a terse syntax and oddly named commands, some with an overwhelming set of options. Other people are fond of individual commands or tools. Talk to a UNIX devotee about `awk`, if you don't believe this devotion. UNIX people can talk at length about the power of the operating system and their favorite utilities.

Flavors: BSD and System V

By the time UNIX had become mainstream, there were two primary flavors, each with its own strengths and markets. For the most part, BSD has become firmly entrenched in the academic and research environments and has maintained a lead in innovation. The System V version has moved toward more strictly commercial applications and stresses robustness and rugged error handling. Each of the UNIX camps has become devoted to its own particular flavor of UNIX, and each has resisted standardization.

The BSD and System V versions differ in many ways. Many of the basic commands, such as `ls` and `cd`, are the same, but other major components are different. The print subsystems, for example, in BSD and System V are different. The files required to set up and provide access to printers and the commands to issue print requests and check the print queue also are different.

For system administrators, moving from one flavor of UNIX to another involves additional troubles. Many of the start-up and configuration files in the `/etc` directory are differently named or differently formatted so that administering a System V host is quite different from administering a BSD system. Files used during the bootup process include `/etc/rc.local` and `/etc/rc.boot` on BSD systems and `/etc/rc0` and `/etc/rc2` on System V. In addition, many scripts and utilities for facilitating system administration (for example, adding and removing users) exist in one and not the other. Enough differences exist that a system administrator always encounters some degree of difficulty moving between the two major flavors of UNIX.

Despite the fact that the BSD and AT&T UNIX flavors compete, they have benefitted from considerable cross-fertilization. This cross-fertilization helped both major versions of UNIX evolve but also proliferated many different proprietary UNIX implementations that included some features from both systems. Some System V versions of UNIX have BSD enhancements, and some BSD versions have System V support. Saying "I use UNIX" isn't enough anymore. The particular command set that you know may be a grab bag of features from both BSD and System V. The merge of the BSD and System V into SVR4 will end much of the stress involved in moving between versions of UNIX.

Among the many popular flavors of UNIX in use today are many BSD and System V representatives. SunOS 4.1, for example, is a BSD-based UNIX. SGI's IRIX is based on System V. SCO UNIX, a popular UNIX for personal computers, is based on System V. NeXTStep is based on Carnegie-Mellon's Mach, which is based on BSD.

The following factors differentiate the popular flavors of UNIX today: completeness of the command set, availability of different shells, support for diverse file systems, sophistication of system administration tools, networking features and support, user interface and desktop tools, support for internationalization, application development support, memory management, and adherence to standards

Open Systems

When the phrase *open systems* emerged, it caught on quickly. Soon, every computer vendor was using the term. After all, open systems had a ring of idealism and an appeal to buyers. Initially, however, vendors didn't all mean the same thing when they used the term. For some, *open* meant that an operating system ran on more than one vendor's equipment. For others, it meant that the systems could be purchased from more than one source.

The valid definition of *open systems* is the one that vendor consortiums use. An open system is one that uses published interface specifications to promote interoperability and portability. The standards groups that promote open systems pursue interoperability and portability to facilitate innovation and preserve the investment that both users and developers make in their systems. Once developers, for example, can spend less time worrying about porting their code between vastly different systems, they can spend more time working on improvements and new features.

Open can refer to licensing as well as to specifications. *Open licensing* means that technology produced by one company can be licensed for use by another, allowing for a good degree of interoperability. Open licensing, however, generally means that a single vendor is responsible for the technology. *Open specifications*, on the other hand, allow for many vendors to participate in defining the specifications and permit the creation of a vendor-neutral environment for development and innovation.

In contrast to *open* is the concept of *proprietary*. Proprietary systems do not use open specifications or open licensing. The Macintosh operating system is an example of a proprietary operating system; it is neither openly licensed nor openly specified. It isn't licensed to other vendors nor are its specifications determined by vendors outside of Apple. In sharp contrast, the TCP/IP protocol suite is both openly specified in extensive documents (RFCs) and influenced by a large population of users.

Software that is built to open standards, whether through open specifications or open licensing, promotes interoperability. Consider the example of the role that Sun Microsystems has had in promoting open systems. The published specifications for its network file system (NFS) have allowed it to be incorporated or otherwise made available in most every UNIX operating system and as an add-on utility for personal systems such as PCs and Macintosh systems. NFS was designed to provide distributed file systems between computers from different manufacturers running different operating systems. Sun, more than any computer corporation, has used the standards process both to its own strategic advantage and to promote open systems.

The Role of Standards and Consortiums

Slowly, the evolution of standards has begun to ease the work of UNIX developers and end users. Users of heterogeneous networks with computers from many different vendors are finding ways to share information effectively. Software products are finding easier ports to new platforms. Standards are also becoming big business as the specification of compliance with the emerging set of important standards is increasingly included in large contracts. If a federal procurement requires POSIX compliance, large vendors will scramble to make their offerings POSIX compliant. Standards affect the way that a UNIX system acts both on the outside (for example, the syntax of user commands) and on the inside (for example, how it does system calls).

Standards are important to end users because following standards leads to software becoming cheaper to produce, with a resultant drop in price and increase in availability. In the past, it may have cost ten times as much to buy a software product for most UNIX platforms simply because the ratio of development cost to customer base was too large. With effective standards, software can be ported at considerably less cost, resulting in a higher availability of inexpensive software for all UNIX systems.

Both SVR4 and OSF/1 include specification of an application binary interface (ABI), which allows compiled code to be run on diverse hosts if they can run the ABI interface software. The ABI promises shrink-wrapped software that says just "UNIX" on the box; this is certainly an ideal. The idea is not entirely new. The Pascal language included a very similar concept with its use of p-code. Pascal compiles to the intermediate p-code, which can then be compiled or interpreted by a small piece of machine-specific software. Software that runs using an ABI will take advantage of a similar technique.

UNIX vendors are not the only ones interested in standards. System administrators are interested in standards that facilitate management of large collections of often diverse systems. Administrators often have the superset of problems that face developers, end users, and system integrators. Standards of interest to systems administrators include distributed management of resources. Standards for network management, distributed systems administration, and distributed computing are high on their lists. Programmers, on the other hand, want standard interfaces to facilitate program development and standard development tools.

Indeed, the move toward a uniform UNIX has created some strange bedfellows. Alliances between previously bitter rivals have become commonplace as the drive to define a unified UNIX and the drive to maintain market leadership force UNIX vendors to take strange turns. The major UNIX vendors are all participating in efforts to end the UNIX feuds.

Some of the most important standards that apply to UNIX are described briefly in the following sections.

SVID

SVID, the System V Interface Definition and Verification Suite, has increasingly more clout as large backers, including the federal government, look to standards to protect their investment in computer technology and ease the work of managing huge information processing operations. SVID standards also include conformance testing. The System V Verification Suite is used to gauge adherence to SVID. SVR4 is, as you might have guessed, SVID-compliant.

POSIX

POSIX, a standard started by /usr/group, an organization made up of UNIX System users, and eventually IEEE-supported, sets a standard for a portable operating system interface for computer environments. POSIX defines the way applications interact with the operating system. It defines, for example, system calls, libraries, tools, and security.

X/Open

X/Open is a consortium that was started by European companies. X/Open publishes guidelines for compatibility leading to portability and interoperability. The X/Open portability guide was first published in 1985. At one time, both OSF and UI were members, but OSF has left the group. X/Open has a series of groups in areas such as the UNIX kernel, distributed processing, and security.

COSE/CDE

Another vendor-driven alliance, the Common Open Software Environment (COSE)—with partners IBM, HP, SunSoft, UNIX System Laboratories, Univel, and the Santa Cruz Operation—formed to work on a common graphical interface for UNIX based on

OSF/Motif. Sun's involvement in this coalition and its adoption of Motif ended a long-time standoff in the UNIX GUI battleground. A large part of what this group is defining is called the Common Desktop Environment (CDE).

The COSE efforts are bringing a unified look-and-feel and behavior model to the UNIX desktop. UNIX has always lacked a unified model even though the desktops of many popular versions of UNIX have been easy to use. To the extent that this effort is successful, the skills of UNIX end users can carry over from one UNIX system to the next.

CDE itself is based on a long list of standards that the UNIX community has been using and relying on for some time. These standards include the X11R5 windowing environment, the OSF/Motif GUI, and the ICCCM standard for interclient communications. COSE will also develop a style guide for CDE.

SunSoft's desktop tools, including a calendar manager, file manager, and mail tool, and SunSoft's ToolTalk for messaging between applications are also being incorporated into the CDE. HP's Visual User Environment and the windowing Korn shell will also be incorporated.

War and Peace

The stage was finally set for the development of a unified UNIX when, in 1988, AT&T purchased a percentage of Sun. Immediately following the fairly startling announcement of this purchase, a group of vendors, including IBM, DEC, and HP, set out to compete with the SVR4 direction that Sun and AT&T were taking. Calling themselves the Open Software Foundation (OSF), they were clearly reacting against the evidence of impending collaboration between Sun and AT&T that would unify UNIX and possibly give them a competitive advantage in marketing their products. OSF quickly raised $90 million for the development of their own standard, intent on avoiding licensing fees and possible "control" of UNIX by competitors.

AT&T and Sun Microsystems then reacted to the formation of OSF by establishing UNIX International, a set of System V endorsers that would be responsible for its future specifications. This consortium would oversee the development of the standard UNIX. Sun and AT&T hoped to ward off complications that would result from the establishment of yet another standard for UNIX. This move, apparently, did not appease the founders of OSF, and both organizations continued their efforts to bring about their own answer to the need for a unified UNIX.

OSF developed the Motif GUI and the OSF/1 version of UNIX. OSF/1 is based on the Mach system, which is, in turn, based on UNIX System V Release 3.

Although the ultimate success of OSF/1 was still in question, the division of UNIX into another pair of competing technologies threatened the unification of UNIX envisioned by the Sun/AT&T establishment of SVR4.

For years, these vendor groups were at odds. Sun swore that it would never endorse OSF's Motif GUI standard, and OSF steadfastly pursued development of its own technology, charging fees for licensing Motif. In March 1993, however, Sun adopted Motif as a windowing direction, promising to end the "GUI Wars," which complicated the lives of UNIX users looking for products that complied with Motif or Sun's Open Look, depending on their preferences, or living with a mixed-GUI desktop that sometimes made moving from one tool to another difficult.

When OSF reorganized in March 1994, however, it revised its charter to focus closely on specifications of vendor-neutral standards, rather than creating licensable technology. This change left participating vendors able to use these specifications to develop their own implementations (which they then own and don't have to license) and brings greater adherence to OSF's standards to most of the UNIX community.

The UNIX Future

UNIX is, in most ways, stronger than ever. The alliances that have formed to bring about a uniformity will dramatically simplify portability of applications and allow end users to develop transferable skills on most UNIX desktops.

UNIX rarely comes with source code anymore, and one effect of compliance with a myriad of standards is to slow innovation. You will never have UNIX quite the way it was in its formative years—small and pliable. Those times are lost, a necessary cost of UNIX's amazing success. Today, the UNIX system is not quite so simple as it was back then. When networking was added, followed by Windows and GUI support, UNIX became increasingly complicated. The exception, however, is the continued availability of the Berkeley version of UNIX through Berkeley Systems Design, Inc. Available with and without source code, BSDI's UNIX product runs on Intel systems.

At the same time, UNIX continues to provide stunning new capabilities. Real-time features, multi-threaded kernels, virtual file systems, and user desktops that provide intuitive access to the system not only to end users but to system administrators are only examples.

The strong appeal of interoperability is increasingly important as large companies and government agencies plan how they will tie their resources together in enterprise networks in what is left of the 1990s. End users want portability because it saves them money. Developers want it to reduce their workload and lower their costs. Big customers want to leverage their investments. You are likely to see many organizations running UNIX across the enterprise and many others with UNIX on servers and workstations and other operating systems on personal computers.

UNIX is becoming less and less a system that only wizards and programmers use and more a system that everyone—including businesspeople—use. UNIX has not sacrificed, however, any of its elegance but acquired a veneer that appeals to less system-savvy users. Users today want services transparently and, for the most part, don't really want to use computers so much as to get some job done. They are not the same people who made UNIX popular in the early days. UNIX has made it into big business and into big finance and sits on the desktop of CEOs and secretaries, not just programmers and engineers. These users want GUIs, desktop tools, and transparent access to remote and disparate systems without having to be conscious of the differences between their platforms.

The development of a common desktop will allow users to move easily from one UNIX system to another without "retraining their fingers." Until a true binary standard (ABI) appears, you will still be driven, in part, by applications that may be available on one platform and not another. Just as many personal computers were once sold because users wanted to use the Lotus spreadsheet, systems still sometimes sell on the strength of powerful or customer-specific software—such as Wolfram's Mathematica—that may not be available on every UNIX platform.

Another similar trend is the appearance of system-management tools that provide uniform management of diverse systems to even the most heterogeneous networks. Hiding the platform-specific details from the user relieves the systems administrator from having to be an expert on every different system on the network.

When you really get down to it, the differences between flavors of UNIX are not really all that great, given adherence to the current set of standards. Almost any current operating system with any relation to UNIX will conform to the standards such as SVID and POSIX and the X/Open guidelines. The cohesiveness of heterogeneous networks and the common desktop environment for UNIX systems are likely to be the factors that most heavily influence the future success of UNIX. At the same time, companies will be motivated to differentiate their versions of UNIX in spite of their support to the goals of a unified UNIX in order to sell their product.

The war is no longer UNIX vs. UNIX, even though battles will still be fought between vendors competing for your purchases with whatever added value they can bring to their products without violating the alliances they have joined to support the unified UNIX. The war will be between open and proprietary, between standards-backed UNIX and contenders such as Windows NT vying for the desktop in the enterprise network. If the open systems movement is to continue to bring value to the working lives of programmers, systems administrators, and end users of UNIX systems, they must continue to insist on adherence to open standards and the "plug and play" desktop.

Graphical User Interfaces for End Users

46

By Kamran Husain

IN THIS CHAPTER

In this chapter you will do the following:

- Learn about major components of a graphical user interface. Along the way you will get a brief history lesson on X Windows.

- Learn the major concepts required for using X Windows. This will introduce displays, windows, screens, and the client server architecture in X.

- Start an X Windows session from logging in and using the X Windows Manager (xdm) display manager.

- Get an introduction to window managers, specifically the Motif Window Manager (mwm).

- Learn to move about in mwm windows with the keyboard and mouse.

- Use widgets and the characteristics of these widgets.

- Customize your desktop with resource files and client applications.

- Understand how to set your environment to your liking.

- Use some standard tools available in X.

- See what's in the future with COSE, CDE, and X11R6, and how vendors support various interfaces for their UNIX systems.

What Is a GUI?

UNIX's user interface was character based when it was first developed. The curses window package was somewhat of a relief but offered nothing in the way of displaying complex graphics or pictures on a monitor. Something more was needed, something that would provide a graphical interface for the user.

This brought about the birth of the term graphical user interface (GUI). A GUI is the graphical interface to an underlying operating system.

The minimal components for a GUI are the following:

- A screen to show the data in a textual and/or graphical form.

- A keyboard interface for the user to type in information.

- A device to control the movement of a cursor or pointing device that the user can move on the screen. The devices for this interface could be a mouse, light pen, palette, or glove.

This list is by no means complete, but it illustrates some of the minimum requirements for a typical GUI.

UNIX's standard character-based interface is a reminder of its age. X Windows is UNIX's breaking into the GUI age. X Windows was developed to be a standard graphical user interface for UNIX platforms. The development work was done at the Massachusetts Institute of Technology (MIT). The MIT project was called Project Athena and was funded by many corporations. The largest contribution came from Digital Equipment Corporation (DEC).

> **TIP:** The X Window system is sometimes referred to as X, X Windows, X11R5, or X11, depending on what you happen to be reading.

X Window

The first commercial release of X Windows was X10.4 in 1986 and was the basis for some commercial applications. The next release was X11R1 in 1987, followed by X11R2 in 1988. Version 11 was a complete windowing package that outperformed X10 in its speed, flexibility of features, and styles for multiple screens. X11 and later versions have become the de facto standard GUI for UNIX systems and are therefore the focus of this chapter.

> **TIP:** The way to read X11R4 is *X version 11, Are Four.*

The main features offered by X Windows are the following:

- *Standard GUI for more UNIX workstations.* See Chapter 47, "Graphical User Interfaces for Programmers," which is on multiple windowing platforms and standards.
- *High portability.* It's written in C and is designed to be portable.
- *It's highly extensible.* New features can be implemented into the kernel, run as separate applications, or can use the pre-existing applications that come with X.
- *It's very flexible.* The number of features in X make it very complicated. However, you can do a lot more with it because you can modify it to your needs and you have access to the large collection of UNIX tools.

Displays, Screens, and Windows

X is typically run on a large screen with special graphics capabilities. X allows you to work with multiple processes, each in its own window. Next you'll look at a screen dump of a typical window. Depending on your installation, you might see a different screen. Figure 46.1 shows a typical X display running under Motif. The same window will look different under a different Tab Window Manager (TWM). (See Figure 46.2.) See the section "Introduction to Window Managers" for more details.

The operations on a particular window can vary greatly. Some windows are used only for

FIGURE 46.1.

A typical X display with the Motif Window Manager (mwm).

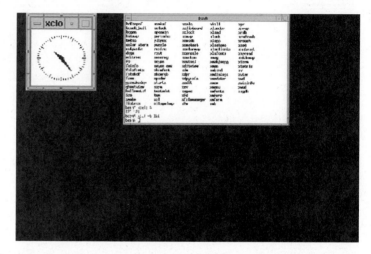

FIGURE 46.2.

A typical X window in the Tab Window Manager (TWM).

Tab Window Manager

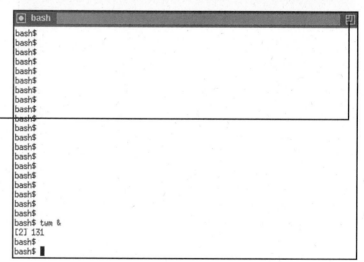

displaying data, some for input and output of data. Some windows can be resized or moved, or they can overlap or hide contents of another window. Each window is generally independent and contains information about its contents, including how to draw itself on the screen. The window does not have to care about itself being hidden from view by another window because its internal operations are not affected when it is overlapped by another window.

The display in Figure 46.1 shows a clock and an xterm. A clock simply shows the time of day. An xterm is a terminal emulator and provides a window into the UNIX operating system. You can have several X Windows open at one time on a display. Each xterm is a window independent of all other xterms on that display and contains a separate UNIX terminal session.

The fact that you can run separate processes in simultaneously displayed windows is one of the most powerful features of X. Also, since you have the full networking capabilities of UNIX, you can run remote sessions on several machines on separate windows on the same display. In fact, you can even force a window to be displayed on a remote UNIX machine running X Windows.

The background area is referred to as the root window. All application windows are displayed on top of this window. X maintains a hierarchical tree of all the windows on the root window. All applications that reside on the root window are its children. Their parent is the root window. The root window's parent is the root window itself. All components of windows also are child windows of the application window on which they reside.

For example, button and text widgets you see in an application are all windows on top of their controlling application's window. The depth of the tree is the number of elements in the tree and in some cases can be a very large number.

Stacking Order

The location of the windows relative to each other on the screen itself is referred to as their stacking order. You could compare this to stacking sheets of paper on a large canvas. The writing or pictures on each sheet are not changed when another sheet is stacked on top. Some parts of the lower sheet are visible while it is overlapped by the top sheet.

When the top sheet is moved around, the writing on the lower sheets is visible again. Changing the location and order of papers is analogous to moving windows around on the display.

The paper on the top of the stack is always fully visible. The topmost window is analogous to the top sheet of paper. Knowing which window is on top is very important when working in the X Window environment. The control of the windows, their placement, and their stacking order is handled by a special client called the window manager. See the section "Introduction to Window Managers" later in this chapter.

Pointers in X

All X displays require some sort of pointing device. This is generally a three-button mouse; however, you are not limited to a mouse. You can have many types of pointers, including pens, tablets, and so on. You can get by without a pointer in some very limited cases, but this is not the way X was designed and is therefore not recommended practice.

A cursor represents the pointer position on the screen. The cursor follows your movement of the pointer on the screen. As you slide the pointer across the screen, you should see the cursor move with your movements. Several cursors exist in the X Window environment for you to use in customizing. See the section "Customizing mwm" for details.

Keep in mind that Display and Screen are not equivalent in X. You can actually hook two monitors and have a screen on each of them hooked to a common display area. A display can have multiple screens. As you move the cursor to the edge of a screen, it will appear on the other screen. Screens are numbered from 0 up. By default, your screen 0 is hooked to display 0 for normal operations. You can also define two screens on the same monitor. See the installation instructions for your hardware vendor for more details.

The Client/Server Architecture

X Window was designed to be platform and kernel independent. Therefore, it is not part of any formal operating system. X's architecture is based on a client–server architecture. The server in the X Window system is very different from the network servers.

Servers provide the display capabilities to user applications clients. This is why they are referred to as display servers. The server sits between the client and the hardware. A client makes a request for display operations to the server. The server translates these requests into hardware directives for the underlying system. Figure 46.3 shows the logical relationship between servers and clients.

FIGURE 46.3.

The logical relationship of X servers and clients.

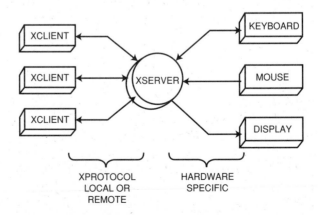

The requests are made via message queues, using the X protocol. The X protocol is the means of communication requests and responses between clients and servers. The X server tracks all the user input from the keyboard and pointer. It conveys this information via the X protocol back to the clients.

The division of work between the client and server allows each to run on completely different platforms connected via a network. This provides several advantages: If most of the computationally intensive work can be done on a remote site, you could run the server on another system to spare the already overloaded system from the overhead of graphics.

Also, only the server application has to be hardware specific. All client software can be designed to be platform independent and easier to port.

You can run several clients on several machines from your server. Each client can then take advantage of the machine on which it is running.

Clients can also communicate with other clients. The server can keep this information in a common place and have it available for all other clients. This information is referred to as properties. A property is simply a piece of information recorded by the server for a client. Refer to the xprop program offered by the X Window system for more information.

A lot of options exist for all the options available for customizing clients. Look at the man page for xterm as an example. X also provides another way of customizing appearances, using the resources file called .Xresources. This file is usually located in the home directory.

> **TIP:** The .Xresources file is sometimes called .Xdefaults.

Introduction to Window Managers

How the windows are arranged is a function of a special program called the window manager. The window manager controls the "look and feel" of all the windows on a particular display. The window manager allows the user to move, restack, resize, and iconify windows.

X Window comes with two window managers. These managers are called the Tab Window Manager (TWM) and the OPEN LOOK Window Manager (OLWM). The TWM is also referred to as Tom's Window Manager, after its author, Tom LaStrange. Earlier versions of X also offered the Universal Window Manager (UWM); however, this is no longer offered since it does not conform to the X Consortium's Inter-Client Communications Conventions Manual (ICCCM) standards.

Window managers in X are different from other windowing system managers because you are allowed to choose whichever manager you like. As long as a manager follows the ICCCM standard, it can serve as your window manager.

The most prevalent window manager today is the Motif Window Manager (mwm) from the OSF/Motif distribution. The Motif window manager is now more important than ever before since being adopted by Common Open Software Environment (COSE) as the standard interface for future UNIX GUIs. It's most famous for its borders around all the windows it displays. Figure 46.4 shows the frame mwm puts around each window.

FIGURE 46.4.

A typical Motif Frame.

Getting Started with X Window

> **NOTE:** The first thing to remember is that X is very flexible. You can customize almost anything in X. Therefore, be warned that even though this chapter attempts to describe the most common features of X, they may not work exactly as described. This is the price of flexibility. This is especially true for all the different versions of X and window managers offered in X.

On some systems, you may have to start X from the command line after you log in. On other systems you may have to interface through the xdm client. The case of the xdm manager already running on your system is easy, so that's a good place to begin.

Using xdm

The xdm utility stands for X Display Manager. It manages several X displays. It is designed to provide the same services as `getty`, `init`, and `login` on character terminals. This is where the system verifies your password and performs the login procedure. xdm runs in the background by default. It was first introduced in X11R4 and conforms to the X Display Manager Control Protocol (XDMCP) developed by the X Consortium.

When xdm is running on a system, a typical display would look like the one shown in Figure 46.5.

FIGURE 46.5.

A typical xdm display.

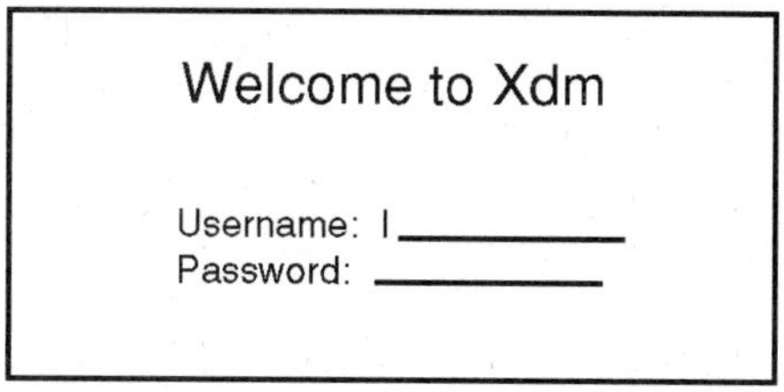

The xdm session will ask for your login id and password as with any character-based session. However, it would then bring up the X server with an xterm by default instead of just presenting the shell prompt. This book is written with the understanding that no customization has been done on your site or that particular machine. xdm emulates the login and getty programs and must be run from the /etc/rc system file. In UNIX, login verifies your password. Under xdm, the login and getty are replaced by xdm's own functionality.

By default, the mwm window manager should be running. See if the familiar borders exist around the xterm. If mwm is not running, type mwm & on the xterm prompt to invoke it. Later in this section you will learn more about how to invoke mwm.

The Hard Way to Start X

If you do not see any windows at all and you do not see a cursor, then you do not have the X server running. In this case you have to start X server yourself.

There are several steps to take before you start X:

1. If you are new to UNIX and X, contact your system administrator for help. If you are the system administrator, this chapter will only guide you in the right direction. Now would be a good time to read the hardware manual.
2. Confirm that xinit exists in your PATH. Use the echo $PATH command to see if /usr/bin/X11 is in your path.
3. Look for a file called Xconfig in /usr/lib/X11 or /usr/bin/X11. This file will contain hardware-specific information about your system. Contact your vendor if this file does not exist.

TIP: Always make a copy of Xconfig and save it before you modify it. Do not edit this file while you are already in X, because X may be reading it while you are trying to edit.

4. Look for a file starting with the letter X with a machine name after it. This is your X server. You will usually find X386 on PCs, Xsun on Suns, and so on.

5. Use the `which` command to find out the location of the `xinit` command. Use the following command on the `/usr` directory:

   ```
   find . -name xinit -print
   ```

6. Type the command `xinit` at your prompt.

7. Wait a few seconds (or minutes, depending on your hardware). You should see several messages whisk by, and the screen should change to that of a session without a window manager.

8. At this point, you could run with this somewhat crippled windowing system or you could start a window manager. For the Motif Window Manager, use the command in the `xterm`:

   ```
   mwm &
   ```

Note that you are running the mwm in the background. If you do not do this, you will not be able to issue any commands to the `xterm`.

> **TIP:** If you are in the Korn or C shell at this point and you forgot the `&`, then type `Ctrl+z` to put the job in the background. If you are not running the Korn or C shell, you can kill mwm with `Ctrl+c` and then restart it with the ampersand.

So now you are running Motif and X Window on your system. Remember that a lot of things can go wrong while you're getting to this point. Here are a few of the most common problems:

- You cannot find the correct files. Ensure that the path includes `/usr/bin/X11` or the like. On some systems, it could be `/usr/bin/X11R4` or `/usr/bin/X11R5`, or something similar. Use the `find` command to locate it.

- When working on Suns, some of your system files may reside in the `/usr/openwin` directories.

- You moved the cursor into the window, but now you have to click to be able to type commands to your `xterm`. By itself, X Window gives the focus to a window when a cursor is moved on to it. mwm, on the other hand, requires that you actually click the left mouse button (Button1) for that window to get focus. Focus means that all user input (keyboard and pointer) will now be sent to that window. mwm will change the color of the window border to show that it has received focus.

- You do not have enough memory to run the system. This is especially true if you are on a PC-based platform. Typically you can get away with 4 MB of dynamic RAM for a simple X Window system, but you will almost certainly require 8 MB or more to be able to get a reasonable response time on a PC. The memory upgrade to 8 MB is well worth it, given the performance on a 4 MB machine. Those who are patient can live with 4 MB.

- The configuration does not look right. You have to modify the default start-up parameters. See the section "Customizing mwm" for more information.

- Exiting the last command in your `xinit` file will terminate your entire X session. If your last command was an `xterm` and you logged off that `xterm`, your entire session will be terminated.

Congratulations! You are now running Motif.

Figure 46.6 shows a typical `xterm` window in Motif.

FIGURE 46.6.

A typical `xterm` window.

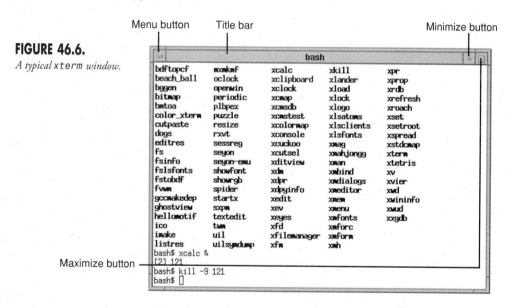

The title bar is the wide horizontal band on the top of the window. This contains the title for the application itself. In this case, this is the application itself, `xterm`. You can modify it to your needs. Try this:

```
xterm -name "I am here" &
```

You can use the minimize button to iconify this `xterm` or the maximize button to resize the window to occupy the entire display area. The sides and corners can be used to resize the window by using the mouse. Note the pseudo-3D appearance of the borders. The area of window that is used to display output and get input is also called the *window pane.*

Working with Motif Windows in mwm

This section deals with some of the Motif windows you have on the screen. Typically, you will work with a mouse for the pointer, so the text will refer to mouse devices at times. However, you can always substitute your device name for the word "mouse" or "pointer" and not lose any meaning of the discussion.

Using the Pointer

Pointers in the mwm environment typically use three buttons, called Button1, Button2, and Button3. Button1 is the most-used button of the three and is usually referred to as the "left button." The left button on a mouse is the one that is pressed with your righthand index finger.

When you take the pointer to an item and press a button, you are *clicking* the button. If you hold the pointer down with your finger and the object moves with your pointer movements, you are *dragging the object.* If you click twice or thrice in quick succession, you are *double-clicking* or *triple-clicking,* respectively. *Drag and drop* is when you drag an object to a new location and the object stays in the new location after you release the pointer button.

If you are left-handed, you can map your mouse or pointer buttons differently. See the section "Help for Left-Handed Users" later in this chapter.

Icons and Windows

The minimize button allows you to iconify an application. An icon is a small symbol that represents an inactive window. The contents of that window are not visible, although they may be updated internally by the processes running in that window. Icons can be moved around on a window, but they cannot be resized. Icons save you valuable screen space for applications that do not require your constant attention.

Iconifying a Window

Move the cursor to the minimize button and press the left mouse button. The window is removed from the screen and a smaller icon appears somewhere on the left of the screen.

To restore an icon to a screen, move the cursor to the icon and click on Button1 twice in quick succession. This is known as double-clicking the mouse. A typical Motif icon is shown in Figure 46.7.

FIGURE 46.7.

A typical Motif icon.

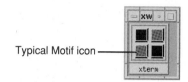

Typical Motif icon ——

Maximizing a Window

Move the cursor to the maximize window and press the pointer Button1. This enlarges the window to the size of the root window. This way you can have a huge clock on your screen. Some applications, such as older versions of `calc`, do not adjust their internal graphic areas when their frame is resized. This leads to annoying blank space on a screen.

Use the maximize button as a toggle. Clicking on an already maximized window causes it to revert to its size and position (also known as geometry) before it was maximized. Clicking on it again maximizes it (again).

> **TIP:** Avoid resizing a window when running a `vi` session under an `xterm`. This usually leads to unpredictable results and may cause `vi` to behave very strangely.

Sizing a Window

The entire frame on a Motif window is a control that allows you to resize the window. See Figure 46.8 for the size controls. You can use any of the four corners to stretch the window. You can use the mouse to move the edges of the window by dragging the four long bars.

FIGURE 46.8.

The eight sizing controls for windows.

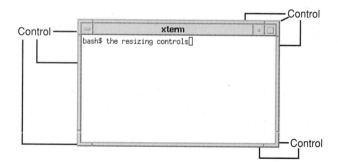

To stretch the window using a corner, move the mouse to that corner. Press Button1 and while keeping it pressed, move the mouse. The cursor changes its shape to a double-headed arrow. Size the window by moving the mouse while pressing Button1. Release the button when you have achieved the desired size.

Note that some applications do not have these sizing controls enabled. An example is the cute, but not very useful, pointer tracking program called xeyes. (See Figure 46.9.)

FIGURE 46.9.

A window of the Xeyes program without resize borders.

To move the edge of the window, move the mouse to that edge. You should see your cursor change shape to a vertical double-headed arrow if you are on a horizontal edge (top or bottom of the window). If you are on a vertical edge, the double-headed arrow will be horizontal. Press Button1 and while keeping it pressed move the pointer around. This moves the edge along with your pointer. Release the button when you have the edge where you want it.

While you are resizing this window, you will see a small box come up in the center of the display. This box contains the size of the window in pixels if it's a graphics image or in rows and columns (in the number of characters) if this is an xterm. On some systems you can use the arrow keys on your keyboard to achieve precision when resizing your windows. Remember to keep the button pressed while you use the arrow keys on your keyboard to do the precise adjustment.

Focus and Selecting a Window

You can select which window or icon gets focus by moving the pointer to that item and pressing the left button. This moves the window or icon to the top of the stack. This way the window or icon will not be obscured by any other screen item.

When a window has focus, it collects all the user input from the pointer and the keyboard. There are two types of focus for a window: click to type and explicit. The click to type focus requires a user to click a pointer button in a window for it to get focus. The explicit focus requires only that the cursor be in the window for the window to get focus. Explicit focus is sometimes referred to as real estate–driven focus.

In some cases you might want to have focus where the mouse was without having to click the pointer button. Sometimes this is not useful for touch typists, because a single movement of the pointer can have the keystroke sent to the wrong window.

TIP: Sometimes it's a good idea to click on the frame to get focus to a window since clicking in the window might accidentally press a button or other control in the window.

Once you give the focus to a client, the client window will collect all typed or graphics information until the user clicks elsewhere. It has the focus.

Getting focus also raises the window to the top of the stack. The window frame color also changes at this point. You can set the focus to an icon also by selecting it with a mouse. The name of the icon expands at that point, and you see the window menu for that icon. You can move the mouse away from the menu, but the icon will retain the focus until you click elsewhere.

NOTE: The color change scheme will depend on your site's default colors. In some cases you may not see any color change at all if the focused and out-of-focus colors are the same.

Moving a Window or an Icon

To move a window's location on the screen do the following:

1. Move the cursor on top of the title bar.
2. Press and hold down pointer Button1.
3. Move the pointer to the desired location. You should see an outline of the window border move with your pointer.
4. Move the outline to the part of the screen where you want your window to be. This is referred to as dragging the window.
5. Release Button1. The window now appears at the new location. It also is the window with the focus (by default).

This procedure can be duplicated for an icon. In the case of an icon, you would click and drag with the cursor in the icon itself.

While you are moving the window, you will see a small box in the center of the screen with two numbers in it. These are positive X and Y offsets of the top-left corner of the window from the top-left corner of the screen. This is very useful information when trying to precisely place a window on the screen.

On some workstations, you can achieve some fine precision by pressing the arrow keys on the numeric keypad to move the window one step at a time. You must keep the pointer button pressed while you use the arrow keys.

Adding a New Window

If you want to add a calculator to your screen, you can type

```
xcalc &
```

at the prompt. The calculator appears on the screen.

For an xterm, type this:

```
xterm &
```

Depending on your site, this can appear anywhere on the screen. Typically, the new window is placed in the upper-left corner (X=0,Y=0) of the root window or in the center of the root window.

The size and location of a window is referred to as the window's geometry.

Window Geometry

Almost all clients accept the `-geometry` command line option. This option tells the window manager where to locate the window on a screen. If you do not specify any geometry, the window manager will use its defaults.

The coordinate system for the root window is as follows:

- The origin is top left (0,0).
- The number of display units is pixels for graphics.
- The number of display units is character sizes for xterms.

A pixel is the smallest unit available on a screen. Usually screens are displayed in 1024×768 pixels, or 2048×2048 pixels, or something similar. The size of a pixel onscreen is very much hardware dependent. A 200×200 window appears as different sizes on monitors with different resolutions.

The geometry parameter is of the form

```
heightxwidth[{+-}xoff{-+}yoff]
```

The height and width is usually given in pixels. In the case of xterms it is given in lines for the height and characters per line for the width. It is common to have a 24×80 xterm.

The xoff and yoff are offsets from the start of left and top edges of the screen, respectively. These represent the location of the window on the root window. The curly braces represent either the - or the + character, but not both.

+xoff   A positive offset from the left edge of the screen to the left edge of the window-xoff. A negative offset from the right edge of the screen to the right edge of the window.

+yoff   A positive offset from the top edge of the screen to the top edge of the window-yoff. A negative offset from the bottom edge of the screen to the bottom edge of the window.

Figure 46.10 shows a visual representation of the geometry. For example,

```
xterm -geometry -50+50 &
```

places the xterm on the top-right corner, 50 pixels from the right edge of the screen and 50 pixels from the top of the screen.

FIGURE 46.10.

Window geometry.

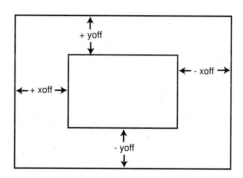

WINDOW GEOMETRY

The following parameters specify the edges of the screen:

-0-0   Lower-right corner
-0+0   Upper-right corner
+0-0   Lower-left corner
+0+0   Upper-left corner

Using the Window Menu

Using the Window menu requires you to focus on a window. Let's look at a typical Window menu. It may be different on your screen, but the basic functionality listed here should exist for all later versions of Motif. Take the cursor to the Window menu button and press the left button. The following menu (or something close to it) should appear:

Restore	Alt+F5
Move	Alt+F7
Size	Alt+F8
Minimize	Alt+F9
Maximize	Alt+F10
Lower	Alt+F3
Close	Alt+F4

Using the Keyboard and the Meta Key in X

It's important to bring up this point about the keyboard and its special keys under X. Keyboards come in different flavors, and the most important key for using keystrokes in X can be radically different from one keyboard to another. On the PC-based keyboards it is usually the Alt key, on Macintoshes it is the fan-shaped key, on Suns it's Left, Right, Alternate; on other keyboards it's completely different.

In short, when this chapter refers to the Meta key, it means *your* special key for *your* special keyboard. For a PC-based keyboard, this would be the Alt key. So do not look for a key called Meta on your keyboard. Where the chapter says Meta, use Alt, fan, or whatever your keyboard uses.

Now you can invoke any item on this Window menu one of two ways:

- Use the pointer. This is how you would click on the window menu and press Button1. Now do this:

  Move the cursor to the item you want and release Button1, or

  Press the Meta key and the character that is underlined in the menu. For moving a window you would press Meta+M. Note that this does not work on some Motif systems.

> **NOTE:** This may not always work. In Metro's version of Motif 1.2, the Meta+F7 key combination enables you to move a window, but the Meta+m key does not work at all. You may have a completely different experience with your keyboard.

- While the window has focus, press the Meta+function key combination. Then use the arrow keys on your keyboard to simulate the movement of the cursor, or just use the pointer.

Note that some of these functions may not be available for a menu shown for an icon. You will not be able to size or minimize an icon. You will, however, be allowed to move, maximize, or close it.

Using the *root* Menu

Click Button3 while the cursor is in the root window. You will see a menu pop up on top of all the windows. This is known as the root menu. Keep in mind that this menu is very customizable and may look radically different on your machine. You will learn all about creating your own menu later in this chapter in the section "Customizing mwm."

A typical root menu would list the following items:

```
"Root Menu"
New Window
Shuffle Up
Shuffle Down
Refresh
Utils >
Restart
Exit
```

While holding Button1 down, move the cursor down the list to the item you want to select. When you get to the menu item you want, release the button. If you do not want to select any items, move the cursor off the menu and release the button.

In the root menu list, the functionality could be as follows:

- New Window starts a new xterm and sets focus to it.
- Refresh redraws the entire screen and all windows.
- Restart kills mwm and restarts it.
- Shuffle up and down shuffles the stacking order of the windows up or down. The window with focus is moved down to the bottom when shuffling down, and the next highest window is given the focus. The last window in the stack is brought to the top and given the focus when shuffling up.
- The Utils item brings up another sub menu with more choices to select from. See the section "Customizing mwm" for details on how to set your menu items.
- Exit kills mwm and leaves you without a window manager. If this is the last command in your start-up script, your windowing session will terminate.

> **TIP:** On occasion, you will come across a vendor that will not allow you to back up to the operating system. In this case, you can try the Ctrl+Alt+Backspace key combination to get back to the prompt.

Working with Motif Clients

Most programmers find the X Windows system libraries too basic to work with, so they use the next building block, called Toolkits. The most common interface toolkit is called the XtIntrinsics toolkit from MIT. This is called Xt. On top of Xt, you can have other toolkits such as Motif or the OPEN LOOK Interface Toolkit (OLIT). When you are working with Motif, you are working with a Motif toolkit. In Motif you are working with Motif widgets.

Widgets help users program consistent user interfaces in Motif. By using widgets, users can quickly put together interfaces that have the same look and feel of all Motif applications.

Some widgets display information. Some widgets collect user input (mouse or keyboard) information. Some widgets react to user input by changing their appearance or by performing some programmed function. Some widgets are simply containers for other widgets. All widgets can be customized in one form or another, whether it is appearance, font size or style, colors, or whatever other parameter is required.

All widgets of the same type have two data structures with information that describes their attributes: instance and class. The instance data structure contains information for a specific widget on the screen. The class information contains information required for all widgets of the class.

Widgets are grouped into several classes. Each class depends on the type of functionality offered by the widget. Normally the internal functions of a widget are hidden from the applications programmer (encapsulation). A widget class shares a set of functions and data structures for all widgets in that class. A new widget class can be derived from an existing widget class.

The newly derived class can inherit all the parent class' data structures and functions. A widget is created and destroyed during a Motif program execution.

> **NOTE:** The destruction of a widget is a bit complicated and will be discussed in detail in Chapter 47, "UNIX Graphical User Interfaces for Programmers."

This should sound familiar to C++ programmers. True polymorphism is somewhat harder to find in widgets. This is all done in C. For C++ programmers, the `class` data structure is to the class of an object as the `instance` data structure is to the instance of an object.

A widget is really a pointer to a data structure when viewed in a debugger. This data structure is allocated on the creation of a widget and is destroyed when a widget is destroyed.

Let's look at a typical application screen to see some widgets in action. You will work with a demo application called xmdialogs, shown in Figure 46.11. The widgets shown here are described later in this chapter. The xmdialogs application can be found in the /usr/bin/ X11 directory. If you do not have this application, you can still learn about working with widgets by applying these concepts to different applications.

> **NOTE:** Don't worry if you can't find this application on your machine. You will develop the components for this application in the next chapter. If you have the Motif 1.2 release from Metro Link, (305) 938-0283, you will have this in your demos directory.

FIGURE 46.11.

The xmdialogs *demo application.*

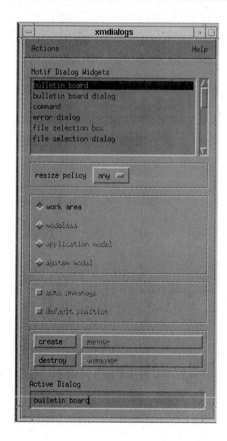

Figure 46.11 shows a menu bar, a file selection list with scroll bars, an option button, some radio and toggle buttons, some push buttons, labels, and a text display dialog.

The Actions and Help items are shown on a menu bar. By moving the pointer to either of these items and pressing Button1, you will be presented with a menu of options very similar in operation to the window and root menu.

Under this menu bar is a list of items in a scrollable list. This widget is of the type XmList. The XmList lets you keep a selection of items in a visible list. It has scroll bars to allow the user to scroll the list if the entire list is not visible. A programmer can set the number of items that are visible at one time. If you resize the window and if the list box sizes itself proportionately with the window, the number of visible items in the list may change.

To select an item, move the pointer to the item of your choice and press Button1 once. The item is highlighted in a darker color. Some lists allow you to select more than one item, some just one item. In this application you select only one type of dialog box. Figure 46.11 shows that the bulletin board item is the selected item.

The scroll bars on the side of the list widget are of the class XmScrollbar. A scroll bar is either a horizontal or vertical rectangle. There is a raised box in the rectangle, called the slider box. This slider moves within the larger rectangle. The moveable space for the slider bar is called the scroll region. The size of the slider bar to the scroll region is proportional to the size of the work area to the total area being viewed.

The XmScrollBar rectangle has an arrow at each end. The arrows point out from the rectangle and in opposite directions. You can use the arrow keys to move the slider bar within the scroll region.

1. Move the mouse to the slider bar arrow.
2. Click Button1.
3. The slider bar moves closer to the arrow. The slider moves as close as possible to the arrow being clicked in the scroll area.
4. Release Button1.

You can also move the slider bar by dragging with the mouse:

1. Move the pointer onto the slider bar.
2. Press Button1.
3. Move the pointer up or down for a vertical scroll bar. Move the pointer left or right for a horizontal scroll bar.

The contents of the work area as well as the slider bar should scroll with the movement of the pointer. The viewable portion is the work area.

4. Release Button1 when list area contains the desired viewing data.

Now move your cursor to the selection item of the resize policy button. When you click this button, you are presented with a pop-up menu containing the types of resize policies for the dialog box you want to create. When you press the button, a menu pops out and presents a list of options. You make the selection with your pointer by moving the pointer to that button and releasing it. The menu disappears and your selection is displayed in the box. In Figure 46.11 the resize policy is set to any. This is known as an Option Button.

Note the diamond-shaped buttons and selections below this current menu. This is a list of one of four possible selections for the dialog box. One of the items is shown in a lighter gray color. This is known as being grayed out, and the option is a not a valid option at the time. The option for the work area is disabled. You can select one of the other three options. These items are grouped together with a rectangular frame drawn around them. Usually buttons are grouped together in Motif this way when their functionality falls in the same group of actions. The actions are similar to the buttons on an old radio: Push one button and the rest in the row of buttons all come up. This is why these are referred to as radio buttons.

Look at the two buttons called auto manage and default position. These are toggle buttons for this application. When you select one button, the other is not influenced at all. The functionality provided by each button is completely independent of that of the other. Do you see the difference between radio buttons and toggle buttons?

Sometimes the scroll bar is used on either side of a drawing area. This is called a scrolled window and belongs to the `XmScrolledWindow` class. This widget can hold graphics instead of a list of items. The `XmScrolledWindow` is used primarily to view large graphics items in a small window, whereas `XmList` is used to show a list of items from which the user can select.

Under the toggle buttons, you will see four push buttons. When a push button is pressed, the colors on the border of the button reverse. Furthermore, the color of the pressed rectangle changes to show the user action. Push buttons are used to invoke some sort of action. When you select the file selection dialog from the list and press the push button to manage it, the display shown in Figure 46.12 appears. This is the standard file selection box under Motif, and you will see it for most applications.

FIGURE 46.12.

A typical File Selection dialog box.

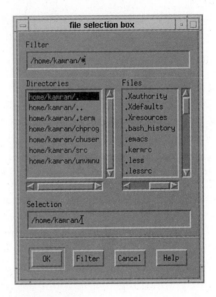

Other Types of Widgets

The Motif toolkit also supplies the widgets described in the following sections.

XmDialogShell

This is a subclass of TransientShell. Instances of this class are used from modal or modeless dialog boxes. Modality refers to whether the user may interact with other windows while the dialog box is being displayed. A modal dialog box prevents you from moving on until you are finished with the dialog box. A modeless dialog box lets you work with other boxes. A File Selection dialog box is a modeless dialog box.

XmMenuShell

Instances of this class are used to create menu panes for pop-up and pull-down menus. This is derived from the OverrideShell.

VendorShell

This is a subclass of WMShell. It provides the interface to a window manager. These are provided by specific systems vendors, hence the name.

Other Display Widgets

These display widgets are used to provide user interaction tools via buttons, arrows, scroll bars, etc. This list is by no means complete since vendors and end users can create their own versions of widgets or brand new widgets. Some examples of commercially available widgets include spreadsheet widgets, bar chart widgets, gauges, and so forth. These widgets provide a consistent interface and are therefore easy to include in Motif applications. Some of the standard widgets are listed here.

XmArrowButton

This is a directional arrow with a border around it. A programmer can modify the direction of the arrow, as well as the thickness and color of the border, by setting the widget's parameters. If you look at the ends of a scroll bar, you will see two examples of such a widget.

XmDrawnButton

A DrawnButton provides a rectangular area with a border for the programmer. The programmer can size, redraw, or reposition text or graphics within this window. This widget provides hooks to set parameters for its border appearance, as well as to attach functions for accepting user inputs.

XmLabel

This is a rectangular box consisting of either text or graphics. It is instantiated but is also used as a base class for all button widgets. A label's text can be multiline, multifont, or even multidirectional. In the `xmdialogs` example, this would be the labels Active Dialog and the Motif Dialog widgets.

Many features of labels can be modified such as fonts, foreground and background colors, and alignment (left, center, or right justification). In fact, this can even store a pixmap graphic image.

XmPushButton

This is a text label or pixmap with a border around it. This widget accepts keystrokes or mouse button presses. In the `xmdialogs` example these are the create, destroy, manage, and unmanage buttons. When a button has focus, it has a heavy border.

Press the Enter key or a pointer button when the button has focus. Move the cursor to the button. Press a key or button and hold it down. You have armed the button. The color on the button changes and the border colors reverse. This gives the impression that the button has been pressed inward. When you release the button, the button reverts to its original state.

When a mouse button is pressed in this widget, the foreground and background colors of the widget usually invert. This simulates the pressing of a button.

XmSeparator

This is used to create a line between functional sections of a screen. There is really not much users can do with this widget except position it on the screen.

XmText

This is used to create a fully functional multiline text editor on a screen. The user can select text by dragging the mouse from one location to another while Button1 is pressed. Users can also click anywhere on the widget to mark the insertion point. If the text widget is enabled for user input, the user can type at the insertion point and insert the text into the text widget.

Pull-down Menus

These are rectangular areas in the window that allow users to select from a group of items. The items are generally laid out in push buttons. You can select a push button either by moving the mouse to that selection or by pressing Alt+K, where K is the letter in the menu button that is underlined. In the `xmdialogs` function, the Meta+F key selects the file item, and Meta+H selects the Help item.

Pop-Up Menus

The Motif root window menu is a good example of a pop-up menu. When you press the mouse button, a menu is displayed. You can select the items in the menu by moving the cursor onto the item and pressing Button1.

Xmscale

The `Xmscale` widget is used to display the value of a data item between two extremes. It can also be used to accept user input. A scale widget has a scroll region very similar to the scroll bar. However, it does not have the arrow buttons at either end.

XmScrolledWindow

This is a combination of a horizontal scroll bar, vertical scroll bar, and a drawing area. If the size of the drawing area fits within the window, you will not see the scroll bars. If the size of the drawing area is greater than the visible area of the scrolled window, then you will see either the horizontal scroll bar, the vertical scroll bar, or both. You can then use the scroll bars to move the visible portion on top of the drawing area. This is known as panning the window.

XmFrame

This is a simple widget used to put a consistent border around one single widget. A frame can only hold one widget at a time.

XmRowColumn

This is a general-purpose widget organizer. The widget can lay out its widget collection in a variety of ways, including the following:

Row major	This is where all widgets on the row column widget are stored until one row fills up, and a new row is created when another widget is added that will not fit on this row. The creation of a new row is sometimes called wrap around.
Column major	This is the same as a row major, but it wraps around in a columnar fashion.

You can specify the width of each column to be that of the widest widget, the number of fixed columns, the packing (whether all widgets should be packed as closely as possible), or determined individually by each widget.

As mentioned earlier, there are several other widgets available in the Motif widget set. You can see the complete listing and their options in *The Programmers' Reference Manual* from the Open Software Foundation (OSF).

Gadgets

Motif widgets create a window in X Windows. A complex Motif application can create several X Windows very quickly. Each window uses X resources in the server and having many windows can slow your overall system performance.

Gadgets are windowless versions of widgets. Most gadgets have the same names as widgets but have the string gadget appended to their names. So `XmLabel` has an `XmLabelGadget` counterpart.

Gadgets do not have all the features of widgets. For example, gadgets share the foreground and background colors of their parents. Also, some gadgets actually turn out to be slower than the widgets they are trying to replace. Given the troubles you can get into by using gadgets, you would be better off not using them.

Customizing with Resources

Now that you are familiar with widgets, you need to know the parameters that affect them: resources.

What Are Resources?

As you saw in the previous sections, you can customize some aspects of an application from the command line prompt. X allows you to modify the aspects of an existing application every time a client runs that application. X does this by setting control variables for that client. These control variables are called resources and have a value associated with them.

For example, take the case of an xterm. An xterm's resources are its font size, its pointer shape, the foreground color for all displayed text, its background color, and so on. These are only a few of the resources for an xterm. Most of these resources exist as predefined defaults for all the common clients in a system.

You can specify resources on an application-specific basis or for all applications on your system. These resources are normally stored in an ASCII file called .Xresources in your home directory.

This file affects only those applications that you run. This file normally contains only those options that you would customize over those in the systemwide files.

You can always override these defaults specified in the systemwide file with defaults in your .Xresources file. In turn, your command line options for a single client override those in the .Xresources file. Keep in mind that the command line default applies only to a specific client; the .Xresources default setting becomes the default for all your clients.

Also remember that the command line operations override any default resources set in a file. Normally you set how you want your application to look under normal circumstances, then override the changes via command line options.

> **TIP:** In some systems, the .Xresources file can also be .Xdefaults. This text will use .Xresources by default.

To make your resource specifications available to all clients, use the X resource database manager program, or xrdb. This stores the resources directly on the server and makes the resource available to all clients on the system. This step takes some care since your change will affect all your clients, regardless of what platform they are running on.

Defining Resources

A resource definition file is basically a line-by-line list of all the resources in the file. Each line consists of two entries: one for the resource type and the other for the value for the resource. The two entries are separated by a colon.

The syntax for a resource definition is

```
client*variable:  value
```

where client is the name of the client. The variable for that client is set to value. Note that the colon follows the variable without any spaces.

Now look at the resource declaration for an xterm client.

```
XTerm*foreground: white
XTerm*background: blue
XTerm*font: 10x20
...
aixterm*foreground: white
aixterm*background: blue
aixterm*font: 10x20
```

On your system, you may see declarations for cterm, or in the case of IBM's AIX machine, aixterm, instead of xterm. These are simply names for xterm in other versions. When in doubt, search for the word XTerm, xterm, or term in your .Xresources file. If you do not already have an .Xresources file, you can create one yourself with an ASCII editor.

The values can be Boolean, numeric, or string values. They can be specified for widgets in an application, as well. For example, if you want to set the background color for all push buttons in an application called myWorld, you would set the following resource:

```
myWorld*PushButton.background: red
myWorld*background: blue
```

Note that the asterisk is used to represent the widgets between the actual myWorld application and all push buttons in that application. Had we specified

```
myWorld.mainForm.PushButton: blue
```

then only the buttons on the widget, mainForm, which in turn had to exist on myWorld, would be affected. This would be tight binding. Using the asterisk is loose binding since it allows for multiple levels of widget hierarchy between the objects on either side of the asterisk. If you had an application with a hierarchy of

```
myWorld.mainForm.subForm.PushButton
```

then the first two of the following declarations would affect the push buttons on the subForm, but the last one would not:

```
myWorld*PushButton.background: red
myWorld*background: blue
myWorld.mainForm.PushButton: blue
```

Another example would be the settings for an xterm. If you attempt to set the scroll bars using

```
XTerm.scrollbar: true
```

it will most likely not work. There will probably be a widget hierarchy between the top-level application and the scroll bar widgets. In this case, it will work if you use this:

```
XTerm*scrollbar: true
```

> **TIP:** When you use a very general setting for a widget in your resource files, say
> `*labelString`, you will affect all such occurrences of `labelString` in all files. So be
> careful!

After you have modified the `.Xresources` file, you will probably expect to see the changes occur immediately. Not so. You now have to inform the server of your defaults by using the `xrdb` command. Use the command

```
xrdb -load .Xresources
```

This will reflect the changes for all subsequent executions of your client. These changes will remain in effect until they are overridden or until your session terminates. If you saved your `.Xresources` file in your login directory, these changes will be loaded whenever you start X in the future if you run this:

```
xrdb -load .Xresources
```

This command is useful when creating `.Xresources` for the first time in a session. That is why in most cases this command is run when the windowing system is first created. If you want to keep the previous settings, use the `-merge` command option instead of `-load`, as in

```
xrdb -merge .myOwnResources
```

Also, you can use the exclamation point as the comment character at any point in the input line before any text begins. Therefore, the following lines are comments:

```
! This is a comment
! another one
! commented*labelString: This resource is not used.
```

You can also use the cpp preprocessor's directives #if, #ifdef, #else, and #endif. This is running through xrdb only. cpp is not run when the .Xresources file is parsed. You can override the run through cpp by using the -nocpp parameter on the command line. No other parameters are required. If you want to remove a resource, use the -remove operation:

```
xrdb -remove myOldResources
```

User and Class Resource Files

There are two types of resource files: user and class.

User files apply to each instance of all applications. These are the resources you would set in the .Xresources file.

Class files pertain to all the instances of a particular class. These will exist in files usually in your home directory or in your path. The name of the class file is the name of the class. The class name is the name of the application class with the first letter capitalized.

For example, all xterms belong to the class XTerm. Note that the class name is the name of a type of an application, with the first letter capitalized. XTerm is an exception in this regard since it has *XT* capitalized instead of only *X*.

Now look at setting the resources for a particular class of an application. The command line

```
*labelString: Hello World
```

will set the labelString resource for all widgets in every application in your session to Hello World. This may not be exactly what you want. The command line

```
Xapp*labelString: Hello World
```

will set the labelString resource for all widgets in every Xapp application in your session to Hello World. This will not affect widgets within other applications. This effect would be desirable if you were trying to set only one type of application resource.

You can also specify your own class for setting resources. This would be via setting the -name option on a client. For example, you could define all the resources for an xterm with 10 x 20 font to be of class hugeterm. Then whenever you run

```
xterm -name hugeterm &
```

it will use the resources in the class hugeterm. So now you can set the foreground color to whatever you want for terminals, with a name of hugeterm.

Note that the name of a resource cannot contain the * or . characters. These values will cause your resource setting to be ignored. mwm simply ignores bad syntax rather than informing the user to make corrections.

Customizing mwm

Customizing mwm is very similar to customizing the X resources. However, mwm offers a far greater set of features and allows the user to customize just about every item on the screen. The resources here can be set to maintain a consistent set of interfaces for all applications, without changing a line of code. For example, it's easy to change the background color of all the forms in your applications by simply editing the resources file rather than editing each source file individually. Here are some more methods for setting resources:

- Use hard code resource settings.
- Set command line parameters.
- Use the environment variables to specify class files.

Hard Coding Resource Setting

You can set resources by hard coding the values in your application source code. See Chapter 47.

Hard coding resource settings is justifiable in the following situations:

- When you do not want to give control to the end user for application-critical resources. A good example is the locations of all buttons on a data entry form. An end user is liable to shuffle them around to the point where the entry application may become unusable.
- When you do not have to worry about locations of resource files. The application is completely stand-alone.
- When you do not want user intervention in your program code.
- When you want to shield users from modifying their UNIX environment variables and having to learn the customization syntax.

Using the Command Line

You saw an example of this earlier when the chapter talked about customizing X applications and listed some of the resources that can be set from the command line. Motif applications usually list their options in man pages.

Use the `-xrm` command line option to set or override a particular resource. The syntax for this option is

```
xclient -xrm "resource*variable: value"
```

Note that you can concatenate several resource settings using the \ operator.

```
xclient -xrm "resource*variable: value" \
        -xrm "resource*variable: value"    \
        -xrm "resource*variable: value"
```

So, how do you know which resources to set? Look in the OSF/Motif *Programmers' Reference Manual* for the description of a widget's resources.

Looking at the Label widget, you will see resources grouped by the class and all its inherited resources. Some of the resources would be declared under the class `Core`, some under `Manager`, and so on. Now look at some of the resources for an `XmPushButton` widget. You will see these listed with the letters *XmN* in front of them. These letters signify that it is a Motif resource.

```
XmNinputCallback XcCallback    XtCallBackList NULL       C
XmNarmColor      XmCarmColor    Pixel     Dynamic        CSG
XmNarmPixmap     XmCArmPixmap   Pixmap    XmUNSPECIFIED_PIXMAP
CSG
XmNdefaultButtonThickness
XmCdefaultButtonShadowThickness Dimension 0 CSG
....
```

Note the letters *CSG* for the access description. The *C* signifies creation. This tells that the resource can be set upon creation. The *S* signifies that this value can be set at runtime. The *G* signifies that it can be read (`get`) at runtime.

In the case of the push button widget, the `XmNinputCallback` class can be set only at the time when it is created (that is, once at runtime). This is usually done in the code section where an address to a pointer is set for this widget.

The other values can be set at runtime. For example, the `XmNarmColor` can be set from a resource file since it does have the *S* set for it. Likewise, when programming widgets, this resource can be read from an application since the *G* value is specified for this resource.

Using Environment Variables

Motif uses several environment variables to hold its pointers to locations for resource files.

The `XENVIRONMENT` environment variable can hold the complete path to a file that holds the resource file. This must be the complete path of the application. If this variable is not set, then the Xt toolkit will look in `.Xresources-HostName` in the application's home directory.

The XUSERFILESEARCHPATH is a pointer to the locations of application resource files. This is a colon-delimited string. Each field is expanded into meaningful names at runtime. Some of the most common fields are these:

- %C   Customize color
- %l   Language part
- %L   Full language instruction
- %N   Application class name
- %S   Suffix

The RESOURCE_MANAGER variable is set by xrd. This xrd is executed at runtime. This usually happens at start-up.

The XFILESEARCH environment variable holds a colon-delimited list of directories for the app-defaults file. Usually these defaults are in the /usr/lib/X11/app-defaults directory. The files in this directory are interesting to see. See Listing 46.1.

Listing 46.1. Typical listing of /usr/lib/xii/app-defaults.

```
Bitmap
Bitmap-color
Chooser
Clock-color
Doc
Editres
Editres-color
Fileview
Ghostview
Mwm
Neko
Periodic
Viewres
X3270* XCalc
XCalc-color
XClipboard
XClock
XConsole
XDbx
XFontSel
XGas
XLess
XLoad
XLock
XLogo
XLogo-color
XMdemos
XMem
XMtravel
XTerm
Xditview
Xditview-chrtr
```

```
Xedit
Xfd
Xgc
Xmag
Xman
Xmh
Xtetris
Xtetris.bw
Xtetris.c
```

Note that some of the classes listed here have the first two letters of their names capitalized instead of just one (XTerm, XDbx, XMdemos). So if your class resource settings do not work as expected, look in this directory for some hints on what the resource class name might look like. Again, the contents of this directory depend on your installation of Motif and X.

The search for the missing .Xresources occurs in the following order:

■ Check in XUSERFILESEARCHPATH.

■ If not successful or if XFILEUSERSEARCHPATH is not set, check in XAPPLRESDIR.

■ If not successful or if XFILESEARCHPATH is not set, check user HOME directory.

Keep this advice in mind: In all but the most unavoidable cases you should not rely on environments to set your application resources.

The methods are too complicated to learn, especially for the end user. However, they can be a very powerful customization tool. Editing resource files is hard enough on the programmer, but it's even worse on the user. However, in order to be a good Motif user, you should know about the environment variables that affect applications that come from other vendors.

Listing an Application's Resources

There are two Motif applications that can assist you in determining an application's resources: appres and editres.

The appres program's syntax is this:

```
appress Class application
```

This will list all the resources in a given class for the named application.

The second command is a menu-driven GUI program, editres, that allows you to edit the given resources for an application. This is available for X11R5 and later. The program displays a tree-like representation of all the widget classes in a program and allows the user to move through the tree node by node. Search your release for this file. If you do not have this file, do not despair, contact your local hardware vendor for a complete X installation.

Using the *.mwmrc* File

Create this file from the system.mwmrc file by copying it into your $HOME directory as .mwmrc, and then edit it. (Look in the /usr/bin/X11 directory and search for the file system.mwmrc using the find command.)

Listing 46.1 on the CD-ROM shows a sample .mwmrc file. As stated earlier, when working with .Xresources, you start a comment with a ! character.

Listing 46.2. A sample .mwmrc file.

```
!!
!!        $HOME/.mwmrc
!!   Modified system.mwmrc for personal changes. kh.
!!


!!
!! Root Menu Description
!!

Menu DefaultRootMenu
{
     "Root Menu"            f.title
     "New Window"           f.exec "xterm &"
     "Shuffle Up"           f.circle_up
     "Shuffle Down"         f.circle_down
     "Refresh"         f.refresh
     "Pack Icons"           f.pack_icons
!    "Toggle Behavior..."       f.set_behavior
     no-label       f.separator
     "Restart..."           f.restart
!    "Quit..."        f.quit_mwm

}

Menu RootMenu_1.1
{
     "Root Menu"            f.title
     "New Window"           f.exec "xterm &"
     "Shuffle Up"           f.circle_up
     "Shuffle Down"         f.circle_down
     "Refresh"         f.refresh
!    "Pack Icons"           f.pack_icons
!    "Toggle Behavior"    f.set_behavior
     no-label          f.separator
     "Restart..."           f.restart
}
```

```
!!
!! Default Window Menu Description
!!

Menu DefaultWindowMenu
{
        Restore         _R   Alt<Key>F5      f.restore
        Move      _M   Alt<Key>F7     f.move
        Size      _S   Alt<Key>F8     f.resize
        Minimize  _n   Alt<Key>F9     f.minimize
        Maximize  _x   Alt<Key>F10    f.maximize
        Lower           _L   Alt<Key>F3      f.lower
        no-label                  f.separator
        Close           _C   Alt<Key>F4      f.kill
}



!!
!! Key Binding Description
!!

Keys DefaultKeyBindings
{
        Shift<Key>Escape      window¦icon       f.post_wmenu
        Alt<Key>space         window¦icon       f.post_wmenu
        Alt<Key>Tab           root¦icon¦window  f.next_key
        Alt Shift<Key>Tab     root¦icon¦window  f.prev_key
        Alt<Key>Escape        root¦icon¦window  f.circle_down
        Alt Shift<Key>Escape      root¦icon¦window    f.circle_up
        Alt Shift Ctrl<Key>exclam root¦icon¦window  f.set_behavior
        Alt<Key>F6            window            f.next_key transient
        Alt Shift<Key>F6      window            f.prev_key transient
        Shift<Key>F10         icon           f.post_wmenu
!    Alt Shift<Key>Delete      root¦icon¦window   f.restart
}


!!
!! Button Binding Description(s)
!!

Buttons DefaultButtonBindings
{
        <Btn1Down>    icon¦frame     f.raise
        <Btn3Down>    icon¦frame     f.post_wmenu
        <Btn3Down>    root      f.menu    DefaultRootMenu
}


Buttons ExplicitButtonBindings
{
        <Btn1Down>    frame¦icon     f.raise
        <Btn3Down>    frame¦icon     f.post_wmenu
        <Btn3Down>    root      f.menu    DefaultRootMenu
!    <Btn1Up>  icon      f.restore
        Alt<Btn1Down> window¦icon    f.lower
!    Alt<Btn2Down> window¦icon    f.resize
!    Alt<Btn3Down> window¦icon    f.move

}
```

continues

Listing 46.2. continued

```
Buttons PointerButtonBindings
{
     <Btn1Down>      frame¦icon     f.raise
     <Btn3Down>      frame¦icon     f.post_wmenu
     <Btn3Down>      root     f.menu     DefaultRootMenu
     <Btn1Down>      window         f.raise
!    <Btn1Up>  icon     f.restore
     Alt<Btn1Down>   window¦icon    f.lower
!    Alt<Btn2Down>   window¦icon    f.resize
!    Alt<Btn3Down>   window¦icon    f.move
}

!!
!!  END OF mwm RESOURCE DESCRIPTION FILE
!!
```

There are several key features here: key bindings, button bindings, and menu items.

A binding is a mapping between a user action and a function. The key bindings map keystrokes to actions, and the button bindings map button presses and releases to actions. Menus display the menu items and let you organize action items into sections.

The format for the all items is

```
Section_type Section_Title
{
.. definitions..
.. definitions..
}
```

where `Section_type` could be `Menu`, `Keys`, or `Buttons`. The `Section_Title` is a string defining the variable name. It's a name that can be used to refer to this section in other portions of the file.

The functions shown in the sample file begin with an `f.` keyword. Some actions are fairly obvious: `f.move`, `f.resize`, `f.maximize`, `f.minimize`, `f.title`, `f.lower`, and so on. Some actions are not: `f.separator` (displays a line on the menu item), `f.circle_up` (shuffles the window stacking order up), `f.circle_down` (shuffles the window stacking order down). Remember how windows are like sheets of paper stacked on a canvas. (See section "Stacking Order.")

See Table 46.1 for all the features available.

Table 46.1. Valid Window Manager Functions.

Function	Description
f.menu mm	Associates mm with a menu.
f.minimize	Changes the window to an icon.

Function	Description
`f.move`	Enables the interactive movement of a window.
`f.nop`	No operation—it's a filler only.
`f.normalize`	Restores a window to its original size.
`f.pack_icons`	Rearranges the icons on a desktop.
`f.pass_keys`	Toggles enabling and disabling key bindings.
`f.quit_mwm`	Terminates mwm.
`f.raise`	Raises a window to the top of the stack.
`f.refresh`	Redraws all windows.
`f.resize`	Enables the interactive sizing of a window.
`f.restart`	Restarts mwm.
`f.separator`	Draws a line.
`f.title nn`	Names the menu.

Adding Your Own Menu Items

Now you're ready to define your own menu items. Here are some examples of menu item names:

```
Menu MyGames
    {
    "Kamran Games" f.title
    no-label       f.separator
    "Tetris"       f.exec "xtetris &"
    "Mahhjong"     f.exec "xmahjong &"
    "Chess"        f.exec "xchess &"
    }
```

The `f.title` action specifies a heading for the submenu. The `f.separator` action draws a line under the title. The `f.exec` action fires up the command shown in double quotes.

> **TIP:** Note the ampersand in `f.exec` for starting these tasks in the background. Do not start a task that may never return and that may therefore hang up your mwm session.

Now you can add this new menu to the root menu by adding the line

```
"Utils"        f.menu    MyGames
```

in your `DefaultRootMenu` definitions.

More on Button and Key Bindings

The key and button bindings work in the same way as menus. The first obvious difference is the extra column with the words icon, frame, window, and root in it. These words force the bindings on the context. The root applies to any location of the pointer on the root window, the frame or window keywords apply binding only when the pointer is in a window or its frame, and the icon bindings apply to icons.

In your .Xresource or .Xresources file, you will refer to these key bindings for the class mwm as follows:

```
Mwm*keyBindings: DefaultKeyBindings
```

Here are some of the descriptions in the key bindings:

```
    Shift<Key>Escape  window¦icon    f.post_wmenu
    Alt<Key>space     window¦icon    f.post_wmenu
    Alt<Key>Tab       root     f.menu DefaultRootMenu
```

The syntax for a keystroke binding is

```
modifier<Key>key
```

where modifier is Alt, Control, or Shift. The key can be a keystroke or function key. The first two declarations describe the same action—Show the window menu—but use different keystrokes. The third key, binding, shows a method for displaying the root menu.

The button bindings are the bindings for your buttons. These are the three important bindings to remember:

```
Buttons DefaultButtonBindings
Buttons ExplicitButtonBindings
Buttons PointerButtonBindings
```

In your .Xresource or .Xresources file, you will refer to one of these button bindings for the class mwm in one of the following ways:

- ▪ Mwm*buttonBindings: DefaultButtonBindings
- ▪ Mwm*buttonBindings: ExplicitButtonBindings
- ▪ Mwm*buttonBindings: PointerButtonBindings

Customizing Your Desktop with Clients

You can customize your desktop using some of the client software that comes with your X11R5 distribution. This chapter covers the following applications:

- ▪ xsetroot

- ▪ xset
- ▪ xdpyinfo
- ▪ xmodmap

There are several more utilities in the /usr/bin/X11 directory for you to play with: bitmap, xmag, xcalc. Check each one out to customize your desktop. This chapter describes the ones that are not intuitively obvious.

xsetroot

This client customizes the root window characteristics. Some of the options available are the following:

- ▪ -cursor cursorfile maskfile. Changes the cursor to a displayed mask value. See the sidebar for creating your own cursor using bitmap.
- ▪ -cursor_name name. This is the name of the standard cursors in the X11 protocol.
- ▪ -bitmap filename. This creates a tiled surface on the root window with a bitmap. Check the /usr/lib/X11/bitmaps directory for a list of the standard bitmaps.
- ▪ -fg color foreground. The color for the bitmap on the root display.
- ▪ -bg color background. The color for the bitmap on the root display.
- ▪ -gray or -grey. Sets the background to a pleasant (for some) gray background.
- ▪ -rv. Reverses the foreground and background colors.
- ▪ -solid color. Sets the root window to a solid color.

Look in the /usr/lib/X11 directory for the file called rgb.txt for a list of files and look at the section called "Colors" in this chapter for more information.

See the man pages for additional features for xsetroot.

Creating a Cursorfile

The cursorfile is an ASCII file with arrays of characters. You create a bitmap using the bitmap utility. You then run this bitmap through bmtoa to convert a bitmap to an array. There is a reverse utility called atobm to convert a pre-existing array to bitmaps for use with the bitmap editor.

Using xset

The xset command sets up some of the basic options on your environment. Some of these options may not work on your particular system. It's worth it to check these out.

You can set the bell volume:

```
xset b volume frequency durationInMilliseconds.
```

For example, the command line

```
xset b 70 4000 60
```

sets the keyboard bell to about 70 percent of the maximum, with a frequency of 4,000 Hz, lasting 60 milliseconds.

To turn on the speaker, use xset b on. To turn it off, type xset off. Use xset c volume to set the keyclick volume in percentages. A volume setting of 0 turns it off. Any other number (1–100) turns it on at that percentage. Of course, for this command to work, you have to have your speaker turned on.

To set the mouse speed, type xset m acceleration threshold at the prompt.

The acceleration is the number of times faster to travel per mouse movement that is greater than the threshold. If your movement is below the threshold, the mouse will not accelerate. If the movement is greater than the threshold, each pointer movement on the screen will be greater than the physical movement by this accelerated factor. This way you can zip across the screen with a twitch. Use care in setting this feature unless you are very adroit.

Invoking the Screen Saver

Use xset s seconds to enable the screen saver. You can turn off the screen saver with the off option. The default option reverts to system default time for blanking the screen.

For more options type in xset q.

Using Fonts

To load your own fonts, use

```
xset.fp /user/home/myfont,/usr/lib/X11/fontsdir
xset fp rehash
```

The rehash command forces the server to reread its system files for your command to take effect.

To restore to normal, use

```
xset fp default
xset fp rehash
```

See the section called "Fonts" later in this chapter.

Getting More Information About Your Display: *xdpyinfo*

The `xdpyinfo` utility gives you more information about your X server. It is used to list the capabilities of your server and all predefined parameters for it. Some of these capabilities include the following:

- Name of display
- Version number
- Vendor name
- Extensions

The list is too exhaustive to include here and will be different for your installation. Pipe its output to a file and review it for information about the server.

Help for Left-handed Users: *xmodmap*

If you are a left-handed user, it might a bit uncomfortable to use the left mouse button with your third or second finger. The X designers kept you in mind. If you want to swap the functionality of the pointers on your mouse, or pointer, use the `xmodmap` command. First, display the current mappings with

```
xmodmap -pp
```

You will see the following display:

```
Physical  Button
Button    Code
1  1
2  2
3  3
```

This shows you that Button Code 1 is mapped to Physical Button 1, Button Code 2 is mapped to Physical Button 2, and Button Code 3 is mapped to Physical Button 3.

Now issue the command

```
xmodmap -e 'pointer = 3 2 1'
```

to reverse the mappings on the buttons. Now Physical Button 1 will be mapped to Button Code 3, and so forth. To confirm this, retype the `xmodmap -pp` command, and you'll see this:

```
Physical  Button
Button    Code
1  3
```

```
2  2
3  1
```

You can always revert to the default with `xmodmap -e 'pointer = default'`.

Useful Command Line Options

Some other standard input parameters that can be used from the command line to change the behavior of a window are the following:

- `-borderwidth` or `-bw`. The border width of the frame, in pixels. This may not be available for all clients.

- `-foreground` or `-fg`. The foreground color. For example, this could be the text color for an `xterm`.

- `-background` or `-bg`. The background color. For example, this could be the text color for an `xterm`.

- `-display`. The display on which the client will run.

- `-font` or `-fn`. The font to use for a particular text display.

- `-geometry`. The geometry of the window. See the section called "Geometry" earlier in this chapter.

- `-iconic`. Start the application in an iconic form.

- `-rv` or `-reverse`. Swap the foreground and background colors.

- `-title`. The title for the title bar.

- `-name`. The name for the application.

For example, you can make one terminal name, `editor`, and set your resources in the `.Xresources` file for the name `editor`. When you then invoke a new term with the `xterm -name editor` command, the server will apply the resources for `editor` to this `xterm`.

Logging In to Remote Machines

You can log in to remote machines using the `xterm -display` option. The remote system must allow you to open a display on its machine. This is done with the `xhost +` command on the remote machine.

```
-display nodename:displayname.ScreenName
```

This starts up a remote session on another node. `displayname` and `ScreenName` are optional and default to zero if not entered.

When you want to open an xterm on the remote machine, alma, you run the following command:

```
xterm -display alma:0.0 &
```

The format for the option into the display parameter is this:

```
[host]:[server][:screen]
```

If you are given permission to open a display, you will be logged in to the remote machine. You can verify this with the uname command. Check the DISPLAY with the echo $DISPLAY command.

When you log out with the exit command, the remote session and the xterm are terminated.

> **TIP:** One of the most common reasons for not being able to open a remote terminal is that the remote host does not allow you to open windows there. Ask the remote user to use the xhost command at the remote machine as a part of login.

Colors

All the colors in the X Windows system are located in the /usr/lib/X11/rgb.txt file. This file consists of four columns: the first three columns specify red, green, and blue values, and the last entry specifies the name that you can use in your parameters.

A partial listing of the rgb.txt file is shown in Listing 46.3.

Listing 46.3. An excerpt from the rgb.txt file.

```
255 250 250        snow
248 248 255        ghost white
248 248 255        GhostWhite
245 245 245        white smoke
245 245 245        WhiteSmoke
220 220 220        gainsboro
255 250 240        floral white
255 250 240        FloralWhite
253 245 230        old lace
253 245 230        OldLace
250 240 230        linen
250 235 215        antique white
255 239 213        PapayaWhip
255 235 205        blanched almond
255 235 205        BlanchedAlmond
```

continues

Listing 46.3. continued

```
255 218 185        peach puff
255 218 185        PeachPuff
255 222 173        navajo white
255 228 181        moccasin
255 248 220        cornsilk
255 255 240        ivory
255 250 205        lemon chiffon
255 250 205        LemonChiffon
255 245 238        seashell
240 255 240        honeydew
245 255 250        mint cream
255 240 245        LavenderBlush
255 228 225        misty rose
255 228 225        MistyRose
255 255 255        white
  0   0   0        black
 47  79  79        dark slate grey
 47  79  79        DarkSlateGrey
105 105 105        dim gray
105 105 105        DimGray
105 105 105        dim grey
105 105 105        DimGrey
112 128 144        slate gray
112 128 144        SlateGray
112 128 144        slate grey
112 128 144        SlateGrey
119 136 153        light slate gray
119 136 153        LightSlateGray
119 136 153        light slate grey
119 136 153        LightSlateGrey
190 190 190        gray
190 190 190        grey
211 211 211        light grey
```

Since the red, green, and blue have 256 values each, the number of possible colors is 16,777,216. Not many workstations can display that many colors at one time. Therefore, X uses a facility to map these colors onto the display, which is called a colormap. A color display uses several bits for displaying entries from this map. The xdpyinfo program gives you the number of bits for the display. This is a frame buffer. A 1 bit frame signifies a black-and-white display. An 8 bit frame buffer signifies 2^8 entries, or 256 possible colors.

Unfortunately, due to different phosphors on different screens, your color specification on one monitor may be completely different on another monitor. Tektronix provides a tool called xtici, an API and docs to counter such problems by using the international CIEXYZ standard for color specifications. This is called the Color Management System (CMS), which uses a model called HVC (hue-value-chroma). In the X11R5 (or later) release look for Xcms for more details, or contact Tektronix.

Fonts

Fonts in the X Windows system are designed for maximum flexibility. There are two good utilities to help you sift through some of the 400 or so font types on a basic system:

- ■ xlsfonts. Lists the fonts in your system.
- ■ xfontsel. Allows you to interactively see what fonts are available on your system and to see what they look like on the screen.

Using *xlsfonts*

First, let's examine the font names themselves. Use the xlsfonts command to list the fonts on your system. Type the command on an xterm, and since the listing from xlsfonts is very long, be sure to pipe to a text file for review. You should get a listing in which each line is of the form

```
-foundry-family-wt-sl-wd-p-pts-hr-vr-sp-ave-charset-style
```

The foundry is the company that first developed the font. The most common foundries are misc., Adobe, Bitstream, and B&H. You may see more on your system from the results of your xlsfonts command.

A font of the misc. foundry has a fixed width and height per character type of font; the rest of the fonts were donated by their respective manufacturers.

The family is the general type of font: Courier, Helvetica, New Century Schoolbook, Lucida, and so on. Some families are monospaced (that is, all their characters have the same width). The other families are proportionally spaced (that is, each character has a separate width). Courier and Lucida are monospaced fonts. New Century Schoolbook is proportionally spaced.

You would use monospaced information for tabular information or running text. This makes your text line up cleanly in running displays. Proportionally spaced fonts are helpful for text in buttons or menu items.

The wt and sl parameters are for weights and slants, respectively. The common weights are bold and medium. Bold text is drawn with a pen thicker than the normal pen. The common slants are roman (r), oblique (o), and italic (i). Roman text is upright, oblique text has characters sheared to the right. Italic text is similar to oblique text, but the characters show a smoother effect. You may also have a reverse oblique (ro) and reverse italic (ri) when the text leans to the left instead of to the right.

The p stands for the point size, which has traditionally been 1/72 inch. Most monitors traditionally support only 75 or 100 dots per inch (dpi) resolution. Since X fonts are bitmaps, it seems logical that the most common fonts within X are of two flavors: 75 dpi and 100 dpi. This is the number that is found in the two fields hr and vr, which stand for the horizontal and vertical resolution, respectively. In almost all cases you will specify either 75 or 100 in each of these fields.

The sp refers to the spacing between two characters on the screen. This could be m for monospaced, p for proportional, and c for fixed fonts where each character occupies a fixed box.

The ave is the 1/10 average width of all the characters in the set.

The character set and style is usually set to ISO8859-1. This refers to the ISO Latin-1 character set, which includes characters found in the ASCII and other European character sets.

Now that you have seen the large number of options just to define a font, you can rely on using wildcards to specify most of the options for a font. The server will match the first font name that matches your specification with a wild card. In other words, you only have to specify the parameters you want to change and use the asterisk for the rest.

For example, *courier-roman will get the first specification for the roman-weighted Courier font. However, *courier will get the bold Courier font. This is because the bold specification exists before the Roman specification in the fonts file.

> **TIP:** Use the xset fp=fontpath command to set the directory (75 dpi or 100 dpi) you want searched first in the front of the font path. This will guarantee that the correct-sized (in dpi) directory is searched first.

The font search path is the path used by the server to search for the fonts in your system. This path is usually set to the following value:

```
/usr/lib/X11/fonts/misc,/usr/lib/X11/fonts/75dpi,/usr/lib/X11/fon
ts/100dpi,
```

In each of these directories is a file called fonts.dir. This is a listing of all the fonts in the directory and has two entries per line. The first entry gives a font filename, the second entry gives the complete font description. The first line in the file gives the number of entries in the file.

> **TIP:** Font names are not case sensitive. *New Century Schoolbook* is the same as *new century schoolbook.*

You can create another file in the font path to alias your own font names. This file is called fonts.alias. The server uses only the first one it finds in its path, so just keep one such file in the first directory in your font path. The `fonts.alias` format is very similar to the `fonts.dir` file, except that the first entry is not a filename, it is an alias for a font name. So if you want to specify a special font type for all your editor `xterm`s, you would have a line such as this:

```
editterm  *lucida-medium-r-*-100*
```

Then you can invoke your `xterm` with the command

```
xterm -fn editterm &
```

to get an `xterm` window with the desired font. This is a lot better than typing in the full font specification. Also, by changing the alias once, you can change it for all scripts that use this alias, rather than modifying each script individually.

A good place to start is the `/usr/lib/X11/fonts/misc` directory, where a `fonts.alias` exists from your initial X installation. This file has the fixed and variable aliases defined for you to work with.

Using *xfontsel*

The `xfontsel` program helps you get a better feel for some of the parameters of a particular font. (See Figure 46.13.)

FIGURE 46.13.

Using `xfontsel`.

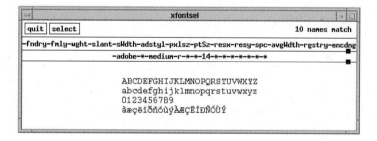

You can move your pointer to any one of the parameters in the first line, and click Button1. As you move the pointer on a field, the field will draw a box around itself to show that it has focus.

If any font options exist for your selection, you will be presented a pop-up menu to select from. Move the mouse to a selection and click on the selection. You will see your selection displayed in the font specification string, as well as a sample of what the font will look like on the fonts display screen below that.

Future Enhancements in X11R6

This book covers features up to X11R5. At the time of writing, X11R6 is about to be released. Here are some of its expected features:

- Enhanced support for serial lines with serial line protocol (SLIP) and low bandwidth (LBX) features. This involves removing unused bytes from messages, compressing images, and sending only differences across the network to the server.

- X image extensions (XIE). This includes compressed images being transmitted between the client and server.

- Support for Microsoft Windows NT. Most client applications will run, but not xterm or xdm. The server also will not be supported.

- Fresco, a C++ toolkit for developing object-oriented applications. This will support both X and Microsoft Windows.

- A session manager to record the status of all windows on a screen so that a user can return to the state they were in when they last exited X.

- Enhanced support for 2D fonts. This will include shading, mirroring, rotating, and variable x-heights on fonts. Also, you would be able to select subsets of an entire character set. This would reduce rasterization time, which is the means by which the graphics routines convert text or data to pixels on the screen.

- Recording of all X requests at the server for playback when debugging applications.

- Prioritization of the execution of clients.

- Direct communication between clients instead of going through the server.

Contact the X Consortium for details on availability.

GUI Front Ends to UNIX

There are many GUI fronts to X Windows and UNIX. This section will briefly introduce you to a few of the common commercially available front ends and their window managers.

Motif

Motif applications look more like a Mayan temple than a menu system. Almost every item on the screen is rectangular. A rectangular button rests on a rectangular menu bar, which may rest on another rectangular form, which sits on a square window.

The latest version, at the time of writing, is Motif 1.2. There are several updates to Motif (1.2.1, 1.2.3, and so on), but Motif 1.2 is a major release from the last major release, 1.0. The 1.2 release includes a lot of bug fixes and adds widgets to its list of convenience functions. Get an upgrade if you are running an older version. Some of your existing bugs may even disappear!

Sun MicroSystems OPEN LOOK and OLIT

OPEN LOOK is Sun Microsystems' windowing interface. It is perhaps the most popular interface for end users. Its Open Desktop is a set of tools for the desktop.

The most major difference between Motif and OPEN LOOK is that OPEN LOOK uses rounded corners, and in Motif almost everything is based on rectangles. See Figures 46.14 and 46.15 for xterm and menu, respectively.

FIGURE 46.14.

An xterm in OPEN LOOK.

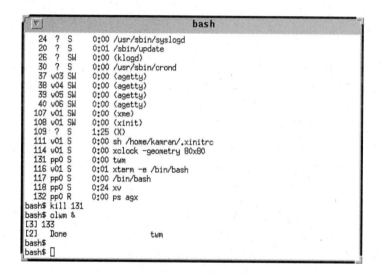

FIGURE 46.15.

An menu in OPEN LOOK.

Another major difference in functionality between Motif and OPEN LOOK is the use of mouse buttons. Motif uses the left mouse button (Button1) almost exclusively for all operations. OPEN LOOK, on the other hand, generally uses the left mouse button to select and the right mouse button to open menus.

Furthermore, the menu items offered by the window menus in OPEN LOOK give different functionality than those in Motif. See Table 46.2 for a comparison of some operations.

Table 46.2. Differences Between OPEN LOOK and Motif

Operation	OPEN LOOK	Motif
Exit application	"Quit"	"Close"
Iconify a window	"Close"	"Minimize"
De-iconify a window	"Open"	"Maximize"
Restore size	"Restore Size"	"Restore"
Push window down	"Back"	"Lower"

In OPEN LOOK the buttons have rounded edges, scroll bars are shaped like elevators, and menu items are rectangular. It also offers pinnable menus, a feature that lets you "pin" a menu anywhere on the screen. Notice how the pinnable main menu is overlapped by another window, indicating that it does not have focus but is still visible on the desktop.

Another feature carried into Motif is the ability to have a virtual backplane for all the sessions. The display manager in the common desktop environment provides the same functionality.

COSE and CDE

In March 1993, the Common Open Software Environment (COSE) was formed. Thus ended the war between OPEN LOOK and Motif, supposedly. The agreement set the basis for the common desktop environment (CDE).

CDE enables users to preserve their desktop configuration between logins. Users return to their exact user configuration when they log back in.

Online help is available with embedded graphics, multiple fonts, and hypertext capabilities. Applications are able to access the help system.

The CDE provides a standard text editing attachment widget. This provides functionality similar to the composition tool in Sun's OpenWindows mail tool. Users can drag and drop nontextual data into text, where the system will represent it as an icon. This text widget is expected to be Multipurpose Internet Mail Extensions (MIME) capable. The MIME feature will allow users to share nontextual data via e-mail.

The print features in CDE have been greatly enhanced. Users will be able to use drag-and-drop features to print files and manage print queues. Beyond these capabilities, COSE also specifies a standard method for printing X images and screen dumps. This is very similar to the capabilities in the now all-but-abandoned NeWS system. The standard calls for the X print server to convert the X protocol into a format acceptable to the user's connected printer. This allows users to create screen dumps and bitmap images from X applications much more easily.

One of the most powerful features of CDE is its scripting language. This language allows users to create shell scripts that have pop-up windows, alerts, and dialog boxes. Also, hooks will be included into the mail system, so users can create consistent help menus.

Other GUI Vendors

Hewlett-Packard (HP) calls its GUI environment the Visual User Environment (VUE). HP is perhaps the most influential corporation for the COSE user interface standard.

Unfortunately, the interface you see in Motif for a standard application may have a different look under VUE. HP has customized its Motif libraries to conform to its own way of doing things. For example, it overrides all attempts to set the background colors for menu items. At the time of writing, there is no way to override this using the xset's background commands.

VUE uses the Broadcast Message Server to dynamically change an application's colors. You request the VUE to change the application's colors dynamically in its palette. As a rule, all X applications must conform to the window manager's preferences on a system. The only time this causes problems is when you are porting color-sensitive non-COSE applications to an HP (or HP-conforming system).

There is a way around this problem. You can define your colors through the resource files. (See the section "Using Resources" earlier in this chapter.) This will work on HP systems with operating system Version HP9.01 or later. Contact HP for details.

NeXT's NextStep is a completely object-oriented system that has now been released for Intel's 486+ platforms. It is based on the multithreaded Mach kernel. NeXT initially developed hardware for their operating systems, but now they are only a software vendor.

One of the major problems with NeXTStep when it was first introduced was its lack of X Windows support. Presently, NeXT is working in conjunction with Sun on a GUI called OpenStep. This is at odds with the CDE proposed by COSE and is possibly Sun's way of resurrecting its OPEN LOOK Interface. NeXT is also working with HP and Silicon Graphics to port to their workstations.

NextStep's GUI is based on the Adobe Display PostScript Language. This approach gives excellent graphics capabilities on displays you get with PostScript plotter. Version 3.2 was the first POSIX-compliant release, but neither Motif nor OpenWindows was available for it.

Santa Cruz Operations (SCO) is the owner of IXI corp. IXI licenses its X.desktop product to Sun. X.desktop is the standard desktop for ODT. SCO is a founding member of COSE and supports the CDE.

IBM's AIX Windows is very similar to OSF/Motif. The later versions of AIX Windows have better icons and file management capabilities. If you use Motif, you will be able to use AIX. Some quirks exist in some AIX-specific areas. A good example is `aixterm`, which is used in place of `xterm`. Barring these minor quirks, the transition to IBM from another Motif system is easy.

Digital Equipment Corporation (DEC) is perhaps the oldest supporter of X Windows. Its version of DECWindows runs on Ultrix, DEC's version of UNIX. Contact (800)DIGITAL for more information.

People do not think of Apple Computer's Macs as UNIX platforms. With its pre-existing GUI, the Mac is a good candidate for a UNIX platform. Apple's A/UX provides a layer for native applications to work on.

You can work in three basic environments in A/UX:

- A tty-like console
- An X11 window manager
- The Mac file finder

The first two options are almost like a UNIX and X11 session. The last option is like a Mac Finder session. Look on the desktop for a disk with a label /. Click on it to open subdirectories and applications underneath it. You can use the mouse to invoke UNIX commands, such as `ls`, `ps`, and so on, from icons in windows.

Softland system's version of Linux is PC-based UNIX for free. Linux is a UNIX clone and comes with X11R5. You can quite painlessly and successfully port code between Linux and other Motif platforms. Contact SLS directly at (604)360-0188 for more information.

Porting Non-Motif Applications to Motif

Moving from other windows front ends to CDE should give Sun users a strange feeling. All Sun desktop tools will be available but will look different. All OPEN LOOK applications will have to be ported over to Motif eventually. Some Sun users will have to wait a while to get their pinnable menus back, for example. However, some relief is available in the upcoming Motif tear-away menus, which will offer about the same functionality.

Presently, some commercial vendors are working hard to get a foothold in this market. These are only a few applications of the development packages presently available for porting applications—no doubt you will find more as time passes.

For those developing applications in the xview marketplace, Qualix Corporation, San Mateo, California (800/245-UNIX), is developing a tool called XvM. This is an XView/Motif library that allows Xview-based applications to move to Motif by just recompiling. This library maps the Xview API into Motif calls.

Another vendor, Integrated Computer Solutions (ICS), Cambridge, Massachusetts (617/621-0200), provides tools to convert existing Xview applications into Motif. The GIL to UIL conversion tool converts the existing GIL files produced by Sun's DevGuide OPEN LOOK Interface builder into Motif UIL or directly to C or C++. You could also use their other tool, Xview/GIL, to convert the XView API into GIL. The GIL can then be moved into C, C++, or Motif UIL.

National Information Systems (NIS), San Jose, California (800/441-5758), offers a package called ACCENT consisting of four modules. The DevGuide conversion module converts DevGuide GIL files into C/C++. The XView Conversion module converts source code, using the Xview API into source. The OLIT converts source in the OPEN LOOK Interface Toolkit API into C/C++ source. The fourth module, the GUI builder itself allows the user to build Motif interfaces interactively. They have services to convert source code to Motif for a fixed fee, as well as training facilities.

Imperial Software Technology Ltd., Reading, England, offers a GUI builder that has built-in OPEN LOOK to Motif conversion. Its product is called X-Designer. With add-on options, users can convert DevGuide files into X-Designer files. With this conversion, users can modify the converted graphics images to their taste. After any modifications, the interface file can be saved in Motif UIL, C, or C++. The add-on options will be a part of the new release. Their distributor is VI Corporation, North Hampton, Massachusetts (800/732-3200).

Where to Go from Here

If you want more information about specific vendors, you can get a wealth of information from the Internet about the latest releases and sources of shareware utilities. Listed in Table 46.3 are some of the newsgroups that can provide more information about vendors.

Table 46.3. Some newsgroups with more information.

Function	Description
comp.os.linux	The UNIX clone used to develop this book.
comp.sources.x	Sources for X Windows system.
comp.sys.dec	DEC systems.
comp.unix.ultrix	DEC's Ultrix.
comp.sys.next.programmer	NeXT programming.
comp.sys.next.announce	NeXT latest news.
comp.sys.mac.programmer	Mac programming.
comp.windows.x.apps	X Windows apps.
comp.windows.x.motif	Motif programming issues.
comp.windows.x.pex	PEX, the 3D extensions to X.

Summary

In this chapter you learned about the following:

- The major components of a graphical user interface. Along the way you got a brief history lesson on X Windows.
- The major concepts required for using X Windows: displays, windows, screens, and the client server architecture in X.
- Starting an X Windows session from the prompt as well as using the xdm display manager.
- The Motif Window Manager, mwm.
- Moving about in mwm and working windows with the keyboard and mouse.
- Customizing your desktop with resource files and client applications.
- Setting your environment to your liking with resources.
- Using some standard tools available in X to further set up your desktop.

- What's in the future with COSE, CDE, and X11R6, and how vendors support their interfaces for their versions of UNIX.

- Where to look next for more information.

- Using widgets and the characteristics of these widgets. This provides the basis for learning how to program your own applications in the Motif environment.

Acknowledgements

I am indebted to Metro Link Software (305/938-0283) for providing me with their version of Motif 1.2 for developing all the routines and testing the sources in this chapter. Their software installed cleanly with no hassles on a Linux (1.02) system running on a 486DX. All libraries worked great at the time and presented no compatibility problems in porting sources to Sun and AIX.

UNIX Graphical User Interfaces for Programmers

47

By Kamran Husain

Writing Motif Applications

This chapter will serve as an introduction to event-driven programming. After reading this chapter, you will have enough information to write your own application. Keep in mind, though, that writing Motif applications is perhaps not the easiest task in the world, nor is it the most complex. As with any other system, you will learn new ways of doing things. In Motif, you have to get used to programming in an event-driven environment. A typical C application runs from start to finish at its own pace. When it needs information, it looks for it from a source such as a file or the keyboard, and gets the information almost as soon as it asks for it. However, in event-driven programming, applications are executed on an asynchronous basis. That is, the order and time of arrival of each event is not deterministic. The application waits for an event to occur and then proceeds based on that event. Thus the term "event-driven programming."

In the case of X Window programming, an application must wait for events on the input queue. Similarly, a server waits for an event from a client and then responds based on the type of event received. This event handling and other aspects of X programming are handled by a toolkit called the Xt ToolkitIntrinsics, or Xt for short.

In Xt, an application typically runs in a loop forever. This loop is called an event loop, and an application enters it by calling the function XtAppMainLoop. While in this event loop, the application will always wait for an event, and will either handle it itself or more likely "dispatch" the event to a window or widget.

A widget registers functions that it wants called when a type of event is received. This function is called a callback function. In most cases, a callback function is independent of the entire application. For example, some widgets will redraw themselves when a Pointer button is clicked in their display area. In this case, they would register a redraw callback function on a button click. Xt also supports "actions," which allow applications to register a function with Xt. An action is called when one or more sequences of specific event types are received. For example, Ctrl+X would call the exit function. The mapping of the action to an event is handled through a translation table within Xt. Functions which handle specific events are referred to as "event handlers."

Naming Conventions

By default, most X lib functions begin with the letter "X", but sadly this is not a rule to rely on. Several macros and functions do not begin with X, such as `BlackColor`, `WhiteColor`, etc. In general, if a name in Xlibrary begins with X, it's a function. If a name begins with any other capital letter, it's a macro.

With Xt, the naming conventions get better, but only slightly. In Xt, macros are not differentiated from functions.

> **TIP:** Do not rely on the name of a toolkit function to tell you whether it's a macro or not. Read the manual.

In Motif, almost all declarations begin with Xm. XmC refers to a class. XmR refers to a resource. XmN refers to a name. XtN refers to Xt resources used by Motif.

In Motif, declarations ending with the words WidgetClass define the base class for a type of widget. Other conventions to remember about parameters passed in most X library function calls are: Width is always to the left of height. x is to the left of y. Source is to the left of destination. Display is usually the first parameter.

With practice, you will be able to identify the types of parameters to pass and which toolkit a function belongs to, and you'll be able to "guess" what parameters an unknown function might expect.

Writing Your First Motif Application

 See 47_1.c on the CD-ROM for a complete listing showing the basic format for a Motif application.

The listing shows an application in which a button attaches itself to the bottom of a form. No matter how you resize the window, the button will always be on the bottom. The application does the following things:

- Initializes the toolkit to get a Shell widget.
- Makes a Form widget.
- Manages all widgets as they are created.
- Makes a Button widget and puts it on top of the Form widget.
- Attaches a callback function to the button.
- Realizes the widget (that is, makes the hierarchy visible).
- Goes into its event loop.

Let's look at the application in more detail. The #include files in the beginning of the file are required for most applications. Note the following files:

```
#include <X11/Intrinsic.h>
#include <Xm/Xm.h>
```

These declare the definitions for XtIntrinsics and Motif, respectively. Some systems may not require the first inclusion, but it's harmless to put it in there because multiple inclusions of `Intrinsic.h` are permitted. In addition, each Motif widget requires its own header file. In Listing 47.1, the two widgets Form and PushButton require the following header files:

```
#include <Xm/Form.h>
#include <Xm/PushB.h>
```

The variables in the program are declared in the following lines:

```
Widget top;
XtAppContext app;
Widget aForm;
Widget aButton;
int     n;
```

The `top`, `aForm`, and `aButton` represent widgets. Even though their widget types are different, they can all be referred to as widgets.

The `XtAppContext` type is an "opaque" type, which means that a Motif programmer does not have to be concerned about how the type is set up. Widgets are opaque types as well, because only the items that are required by the programmer are visible.

The first executable line of the program calls the `XtAppInitialize()` function. This will initialize the Xt toolkit and create an application shell and context for the rest of the application. This value is returned to the widget "top" (for top level shell). This widget will provide the interface between the window manager and the rest of the widgets in this application.

The application then creates a Form widget on this top-level widget. A Form widget places other widgets on top of itself. It is a Manager widget because it "manages" other widgets.

There are two steps for displaying a widget: Managing it and realizing it.

Managing a widget allows it to be visible. If a widget is unmanaged, it will never be visible. By managing a widget, the program gives the viewing control over to the windowing system so it can display it. If the parent widget is unmanaged, any child widgets remain invisible even if managed.

Realizing a widget actually creates all the subwindows under an application and displays them. Normally only the top-level widget is realized after all the widgets are managed. This call will realize all the children of this widget.

Note that realizing a widget takes time. A typical program will manage all the widgets except the topmost widget. This way the application will only call `XtRealizeWidget` on the topmost parent when the entire tree has to be displayed. You have to realize a widget at least once, but you can manage and unmanage widgets as you want to display or hide them.

In the past, the way to create and manage a widget was to call `XtCreate` and `XtManageChild` in two separate calls. However, this text will use a single call to create and manage a widget: `XtVaCreateManagedWidget`.

Note the parameters to this call to create the Form widget:

```
aForm = XtVaCreateManagedWidget("Form1", xmFormWidgetClass, top, XmNheight,90,
XmNwidth,200,
NULL);
```

The first parameter is the name of the new widget. The second parameter describes the class of the widget being created. Recall that this is simply the widget name sandwiched between `xm` and `WidgetClass`. In this case it's `xmFormWidgetClass`. Note the lowercase x for the class pointer. This class pointer is declared in the header files included at the beginning of the file, `Form.h`.

> **TIP:** As another example, a label's class pointer would be called `xmLabelWidgetClass` and would require the `Label.h` file. Motif programmers have to be especially wary of the case-sensitivity of all variables.

The next argument is the parent widget of this new widget. In this case `top` is the parent of `Form1`. The top widget was returned from the call to `XtAppInitialize`.

The remaining arguments specify the parameters of this widget. In this case you are setting the width and height of this widget. This list is terminated by a `NULL` parameter.

After the form is created, a button is placed on top of it. A Form widget facilitates placement of other widgets on top of it. In this application you will cause the button to "attach" itself to the bottom of the form. The three lines attach themselves to the form.

```
XmNleftAttachment,XmATTACH_FORM,
XmNrightAttachment,XmATTACH_FORM, XmNbottomAttachment,XmATTACH_FORM,
```

The class of this button is included in the `PushB.h` file and is called `xmPushButtonWidgetClass`. The name of this widget is also the string that is displayed on the face of the button. Note that the parent of this button is the `aForm` widget. Thus the hierarchy is: `top` is the parent of `aForm` is the parent of `aButton`.

The next step is to add a callback function when the button is pressed. This is done with the following call:

```
XtAddCallback( aButton, XmNactivateCallback, bye, (XtPointer) NULL);
```

In this call:

- ■ `aButton` is the pushbutton widget.
- ■ `XmNactivateCallback` is the action that will trigger this function.

■ bye is the name of the function called. You should declare this function before making this function call.

■ NULL is a pointer. This pointer could point to some structure meaningful to function bye.

This will register the callback function bye for the widget. Now the topmost widget, top, is realized. This causes all managed widgets below top to be realized. The application then goes into a forever loop while waiting for events.

The bye function of this program simply exits the application.

Compiling This Application

Read the compiler documentation for your machine. Almost all vendor supplied compilers now conform to the ANSI C standard. If your compiler is not ANSI compatible, get an upgrade—you'll need it.

Next, check the location of the libraries in your system. Check the /usr/lib/X11 directory for the following libraries: libXm.a, libXt.a, and libX11.a. If possible, use the shared library versions of these libraries with .so extensions followed by some numbers. The advantage of using shared libraries is that it results in a smaller Motif application. A typical application like the preceding one can be up to 1M in size because of the overhead of Motif.

The disadvantage of shared libraries is that your end user may not have the correct version of the library in his path. This does annoy some end users, especially if no fast method of acquiring this resource is available to them. Also, shipping a shared library with your application may require you to pay some licensing fees to the original library vendor. From a programmer's perspective, shared libraries are sometimes impossible to use with your debugger. Of course, if your debugger supports them, use them. Check your compiler documentation.

In most cases, if you intend to use shared libraries, use the static versions to do your debugging and testing and then compile the shared version. Always check your vendor's licensing agreement for details on how to ship shared libraries.

The application can be compiled with this command:

```
CC list1.c -o list1 -lXm -lXt -lX11
```

CC is your version of the ANSI compiler: gcc, acc, cc, or whatever. The program can be run from a command line; create a script file:

```
CC $1.c -o $1 -lXm -lXt -lX11
```

Now pass this script file; just the filename without the extension. The best way is to create a makefile, although this command will work with the examples in this text.

The Widget Hierarchy

The Motif widget set is a hierarchy of widget types. (See Figure 47.1.) Any resources provided by a widget are inherited by all its derived classes. Consider the three most important base classes: Core, XmPrimitive, and XmManager.

FIGURE 47.1.

The widget hierarchy.

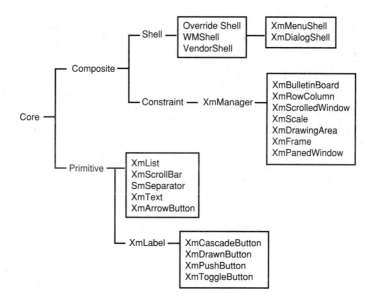

Core

The Core widget class provides the basis for all classes. It provides at least the following variables:

- XmNx, XmNy: This is a widget's position on the display.
- XmNheight, XmNwidth: This is a widget's size.
- XmNborderWidth: This is set to 1 by default.
- XmNsensitive: A Boolean resource that specifies whether this widget can receive input.
- XmNcolorMap: The default colormap.
- XmNbackground: The background color.

Check the Motif Programmer's reference manual for a complete listing.

XmPrimitive

The XmPrimitive widget class inherits all the resources from Core and adds more functionality.

- XmNforeground: The foreground color.
- XmNhighlightOnEnter: Changes color when the pointer is within the window of the widget.
- XmNhighlightThickness: If XmNhighlightOnEnter is True, changes the border to this thickness.
- XmNhighlightColor: The color to use when drawing the highlighted border.
- XmNshadowThickness: The number of pixels used to draw the psuedo-3D look that Motif is famous for. This is defaulted to 2.
- XmNtopShadowColor and XmNbottomShadowColor: Sets the color for top and bottom lines around a widget.
- XmNuserData: A pointer available for use to the programmer.

The XmPrimitive widget also provides the XmNdestroyCallback resource. This can be set to a function that does clean-up when a widget is destroyed. In Motif 1.2 or later, the XmPrimitive class also provides a XmNhelpCallback resource that is called when the F1 key is pressed in the widget's window. This is to allow specific help information for a widget.

XmManager

The XmManager class provides support for all Motif widgets that contain other widgets. This is never used directly in an application and works in a similar manner to the XmPrimitive class.

The Label Widget

The Label widget is used to display strings or pixmaps. Include the Xm/Label.h file in your source file before you use this widget.

Some of the resources for this widget include:

- XmNalignment: This resource determines the alignment of the text in this widget. The allowed values are XmALIGNNMENT_END, XmALIGNMENT_CENTER, and XmALIGNMENT_BEGIN, for right-, center-, and left- justification, respectively.
- XmNrecomputeSize: A Boolean resource. If set to TRUE, the widget will be resized when the size of the string or pixmap changes dynamically. This is the default. If set to FALSE, the widget will not attempt to resize itself.

- XmNlabelType: The default value of this type is XmSTRING to show strings. However, it can also be set to XmPIXMAP when displaying a pixmap specified in the XmNpixmap resource.

- XmNlabelPixmap: This is used to specify which pixmap to use when the XmNlabelType is set to XmPIXMAP.

- XmNlabelString: This is used to specify which XmString compound string to use for the label. This defaults to the name of the label. See the section "Strings in Motif: Compound Strings" later in this chapter.

 To get acquainted with left- and right-justification on a label, see file 47_2 on the CD-ROM. This listing also shows how the resources can be set to change widget parameters, programmatically and through the .Xresource files.

Avoid using the \n in the label name. If you have to create a multi-string widget, use the XmStringCreate call to create a compound string. (See the next section, "Strings in Motif: Compound Strings.") Another way to set the string is to specify it in the resource file and then merge the resources.

The listing shows the label to be right-justified. You could easily center the string horizontally by not specifying the alignment at all and letting it default to the center value. Alternatively, try setting the alignment parameter to XmALIGNMENT_BEGINNING for a left-justified label.

Strings in Motif: Compound Strings

A compound string is Motif's way of representing a string. For a typical C program, a null-terminated string is enough to specify a string. In Motif, a string is also defined by the character set it uses. Strings in Motif are referred to as compound strings and are kept in opaque data structures called XmString.

In order to get a compound string from a regular C string, use this function call:

```
XmString XmStringCreate( char *text, char *tag);
```

This returns an equivalent compound string, given a pointer to a null-terminated C string and a tag. The tag specifies which font list to use and is defaulted to XmFONTLIST_DEFAULT_TAG.

New lines in C strings have to be handled by special separators in Motif. To create a string and preserve the new lines, use this call:

```
XmString XmStringCreateLtoR( char *text, char *tag);
```

The compound strings have to be created and destroyed just like any other object. They persist long after the function call that created them returns. Therefore, it's a good idea to free all locally used XmStrings in a function before returning, or else all references to the strings will be lost.

Here's the definition of a call to free XmString resources:

```
XmStringFree( XmString s);
```

You can run operations on strings similar to those you would under ASCII programming, except that they are called by different names. Use Boolean XmStringByteCompare(XmString s1, XmString s2); for a strict byte-for-byte comparison. For just the text comparison, use XmStringCompare(XmString s1, XmString s2);.

To check if a string is empty, use the following:

```
Boolean XmStringEmpty( XmString s1);
```

To concatenate two strings together, use the following:

```
XmString XmStringConcat( XmString s1, XmString s2);
```

It creates a new string by concatenating s2 to s1. This new resource has to be freed just like s1 and s2.

If you want to use sprintf, use it on a temporary buffer and then create a new string. For example:

```
char str[32];
XmString xms;
......
sprintf(str," pi = %lf, Area = %lf", PI, TWOPI*r);
xms =  XmStringCreateLtoR( str,  XmFONTLIST_DEFAULT_TAG); ......
n = 0;
XtSetArg(arg[n],XmNlabelString,xms); n++; XtSetValues(someLabel, arg, n);
XmStringFree(xms);
```

If a string value is corrupted by itself over time, check to see if the widget is not making a copy of the passed XmString for its own use. Sometimes a widget may only be keeping a pointer to the XmString. If that string was "freed," the widget may wind up pointing to bad data.

One good way to check is to set an XmString resource. Then use the XtGetValues function to get the same resource from the widget. If the values of the XmStrings are the same, the widget is not making a copy for itself. If they aren't the same, it's safe to free the original because the widget is making a local copy. The default course of action is to assume that a widget makes copies of such resources for itself.

A similar test could be used to determine if a widget returns a copy of its resource to a pointer to it. Use the preceding listing, but this time use XTgetValues to get the same resource twice. Then do the comparison.

```
/**
*** This is a sample partial listing of how to check if the
*** data returned on an XtGetValues and an XtSetValues
*** call is a copy or a reference.
***/

#include "Xm/Text.h"
..
Widget w;
XmString x1, x2, x3;

x3 = XmStringCreateLtoR("test", XmFONTLIST_DEFAULT_TAG); XmTextSetString(w,x3);
...
x1 = XmTextGetString(w);
x2 = XmTextGetString(w);

XtWarning(" Checking SetValues");
if (x1 != x3)
    XtWarning("Widget keeps a copy ! Free original!");
else
XtWarning("Widget does not keep a copy! Do NOT free original");


XtWarning(" Checking GetValues");
if (x1 == x2)
    XtWarning("Widget returns a copy! Do NOT free");
else
XtWarning("Widget does not return a copy! You should free it ");
```

The XtWarning() message is especially useful for debugging the execution of programs. The message is relayed to the stderr of the invoking application. If this is an xterm, you will see an error message on that terminal window. If no stderr is available for the invoker, the message is lost.

TIP: The XtSetArg macro is defined as:

```
#define XtSetArg(arg,n,d) \
    ((void)((arg).name = (n).(arg).value = (XtArgVal)(d)))
```

Do *not* use XtSetArg(arg[n++], ... because this will increment n twice.

The PushButton Widget

XmPushButton is perhaps the most heavily used widget in Motif.

Listings 1 and 2 showed the basic usage for this class. When a button is pressed in the pushbutton area, the button goes into an "armed" state. The color of the button changes to reflect this state. This color can be set by using XmNarmColor. This color is shown when the XmNfillOnArm resource is set to TRUE.

> **TIP:** If the `XmNarmcolor` for a pushbutton does not seem to be working, try setting the `XmNfillOnArm` resource to TRUE.

The callback functions for a pushbutton are:

- `XmNarmCallback`: Called when a pushbutton is armed.
- `XmNactivateCallback`: Called when a button is released in the widgets area while the widget is armed. This is not invoked if the pointer is outside the widget when the button is released.
- `XmNdisarmCallback`: Called when a button is released with the pointer outside the widget area while the widget is armed.

> **TIP:** If a callback has more than one function registered for a widget, all the functions will be called but not necessarily in the order they were registered. Do not rely on the same order being preserved on other systems. If you want more than one function performed during a callback, sandwich them in one function call.

In Listing 47.2, you saw how a callback function was added to a pushbutton with the `XtAddCallback` function. The same method can be used to call other functions for other actions, such as the `XmNdisarmCallback`.

The Toggle Button Widget

The toggle button class is a subclass of the `XmLabel` widget class. There are two types of buttons: N of many and one of many. When using N of many, users can select many options. When using one of many, the users must make one selection from many items. Note the way the buttons are drawn; N of many buttons are shown as boxes and one of many buttons are shown as diamonds.

The resources for this widget include:

- `XmNindicatorType`: This determines the style and can be set to `XmN_OF_MANY` or `XmONE_OF_MANY` (the default).
- `XmNspacing`: The number of pixels between the button and its label.
- `XmNfillOnSelect`: The color of the button changes to reflect a "set" when the `XmNfillOnArm` resource is set to TRUE.

■ XmNfillColor: The color to show when "set."

■ XmNset: A Boolean resource indicating whether the button is set or not. If this resource is set from a program, the button will automatically reflect the change.

It's easier to use the convenience function XmToggleButtonGetState(Widget w) to get the Boolean state for a widget, and to use XmToggleButtonSetState(Widget w, Boolean b) to set the value for a toggle button widget.

Like the pushbutton class, the toggle button class has three similar callbacks:

■ XmNarmCallback: Called when the toggle button is armed.

■ XmNvalueChangedCallback: Called when a button is released in the widget area while the widget is armed. This is not invoked if the pointer is outside the widget when the button is released.

■ XmNdisarmCallback: Called when a button is released with the pointer outside the widget area while the widget is armed.

For the callbacks, the callback data is a structure of type:

```
typedef struct {
    int   reason;
    XEvent *event;
    int   set;
} XmToggleButtonCallbackStruct;
```

The reason for the callback is one of the following: XmCR_ARM, XmCR_DISARM, or XmCR_ACTIVATE. The event is a pointer to XEvent that caused this callback. The set value is 0 if the item is not set and non-zero if it's set. The buttons are arranged in one column through the RowColumn widget discussed later in this chapter. See file 47_3c on the CD-ROM for an example of how to use the toggle button.

By defining the DO_RADIO label, you can make this into a radio button application. That is, only one of the buttons can be selected at one time.

Convenience Functions

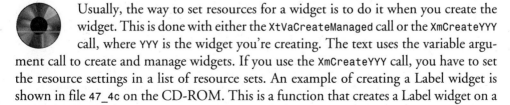

Usually, the way to set resources for a widget is to do it when you create the widget. This is done with either the XtVaCreateManaged call or the XmCreateYYY call, where YYY is the widget you're creating. The text uses the variable argument call to create and manage widgets. If you use the XmCreateYYY call, you have to set the resource settings in a list of resource sets. An example of creating a Label widget is shown in file 47_4c on the CD-ROM. This is a function that creates a Label widget on a widget given the string x.

Or you could use the variable argument lists to create this label, as shown in file 47_5c.

In either case, it's your judgment call as to which one to use. The label created with the variable lists is a bit easier to read and maintain. But what about setting values after a widget has been created? This would be done through a call to XtSetValue with a list and count of resource settings. For example, to change the alignment and text of a label, you would use the following:

```
n = 0;
XtSetArg(arg[n], XmNalignment, XmALIGNMENT_BEGIN); n++;
XtSetArg(arg[n], XmNlabelString, x); n++;
XtSetValues(lbl,arg,n);
```

Similarly, to get the values for a widget you would use XtGetValues:

```
Cardinal n; /* usually an integer or short... use Cardinal to be safe
*/ int align;
XmString x;
...
n = 0;
XtSetArg(arg[n], XmNalignment, &align); n++;
XtSetArg(arg[n], XmNlabelString, &x); n++; XtGetValues(lbl,arg,n);
```

In the case of other widgets, such as the Text widget, this setting scheme is hard to read, quite clumsy, and prone to typos. For example, to get a string for a Text widget, do you use x or address of x?

For this reason, Motif provides convenience functions. In the ToggleButton widget class, for example, rather than use the combination of XtSetValue and XtSetArg calls to get the state, you would use one call, XmToggleButtonGetState(Widget w), to get the state. These functions are valuable code savers when you're writing complex applications. In fact, you should write similar convenience functions whenever you cannot find one that suits your needs.

The List Widget

The List widget displays a list of items from which the user can select. The list is created from a list of compound strings. Users can select either one item or many items from this list. The resources for this widget include:

- XmNitemCount: This determines the number of items in the list.
- XmNitems: An array of compound strings. Each entry corresponds to an item in the list. Note that a List widget makes a copy of all items in its list when using XtSetValues; however, it returns a pointer to its internal structure when returning values to an XtGetValues call. So do *not* free this pointer from XtGetValues.

- ◼ XmNselectedItemCount: The number of items currently selected.

- ◼ XmNselectedItems: The list of selected items.

- ◼ XmNvisibleItemCount: The number of items to display at one time.

- ◼ XmNselectionPolicy: This is used to set single or multiple selection capability. If set to XmSINGLE_SELECT, the user will be able to select only one item. Each selection will invoke XmNsingleSelectionCallback. Selecting one item will deselect another previously selected item. If set to XmEXTENDED_SELECT, the user will be able to select a block of contiguous items in a list. Selecting one or more new items will deselect other previously selected items. Each selection will invoke the XmNmultipleSelection callback.

If set to XmMULTIPLE_SELECT, the user will be able to select multiple items in any order. Selecting one item will not deselect another previously selected item. Each selection will invoke the XmNmultipleSelection callback.

If the resource is set to XmBROWSE_SELECT, the user can move the pointer across all the selections with the button pressed, but only one item will be selected. This will invoke XmbrowseSelectionCallback when the button is finally released on the last item browsed. Unlike with the XmSINGLE_SELECT setting, the user does not have to press and release the button to select an item.

It is easier to create the List widget with a call to XmCreateScrolledList(), because this will automatically create a scrolled window for you. Also, the following convenience functions will make working with List widgets easier. However, they may prove to be slow when compared to XtSetValues() calls. If you feel that speed is important, consider using XtSetValues(). You should create the list for the first time by using XtSetValues.

- ◼ XmListAddItem(Widget w, XmString x, int pos): This will add the compound string x to the List widget w at the 1-relative position pos. If pos is 0, the item is added to the back of the list. This function is very slow. Do not use it to create a new list, because it rearranges the entire list before returning.

- ◼ XmListAddItems(Widget w, XmString *x, int count, int pos): This will add the array of compound strings, x, of size count, to the List widget w from the position pos. If pos is 0, the item is added to the back of the list. This function is slow too, so do not use it to create a new list.

- ◼ XmDeleteAllItems(Widget w): This will delete all the items in a list. It's better to write a convenience function:

```
n = 0;
XtSetArg(arg[n], XmNitems, NULL); n++;
XtSetArg(arg[n], XmNitemCount, 0); n++;
XtSetValues(mylist,arg,n);
```

- `XmDeleteItem(Widget w, XmString x)`: Deletes the item x from the list. This is a slow function.

- `XmDeleteItems(Widget w, XmString *x, int count)`: Deletes all the count items in x from the list. This is an even slower function. You might be better off installing a new list.

- `XmListSelectItem(Widget w, XmString x, Boolean Notify)`: Programmatically selects x in the list. If Notify is TRUE, the appropriate callback function is also invoked.

- `XmListDeselectItem(Widget w, XmString x)`: Programmatically deselects x in the list.

- `XmListPos( Widget w, XmString x)`: Returns the position of x in the list. 0 if not found.

See file `47_6c` on the CD-ROM.

The Scrollbar Widget

The Scrollbar widget allows the user to select a value from a range. Its resources include:

- `XmNvalue`: The value representing the location of the slider.

- `XmNminimum` and `XmNmaximum`: The range of values for the slider.

- `XmNshowArrows`: The Boolean value if set shows arrows at either end.

- `XmNorientation`: Set to `XmHORIZONTAL` for a horizontal bar or `XmVERTICAL` (default) for a vertical bar.

- `XmNprocessingDirection`: Set to either `XmMAX_ON_LEFT` or `XmMAX_ON_RIGHT` for `XmHORIZONTAL`, or `XmMAX_ON_TOP` or `XmMAX_ON_BOTTOM` for `XmVERTICAL` orientation.

- `XmNincrement`: The increment per move.

- `XmNpageIncrement`: The increment if a button is pressed in the arrows or the box. This is defaulted to 10.

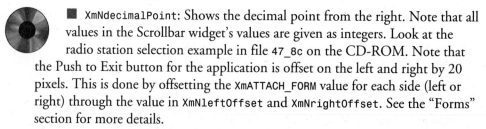

- `XmNdecimalPoint`: Shows the decimal point from the right. Note that all values in the Scrollbar widget's values are given as integers. Look at the radio station selection example in file `47_8c` on the CD-ROM. Note that the Push to Exit button for the application is offset on the left and right by 20 pixels. This is done by offsetting the `XmATTACH_FORM` value for each side (left or right) through the value in `XmNleftOffset` and `XmNrightOffset`. See the "Forms" section for more details.

For the case of FM selections, you would want the bar to show odd numbers. A good exercise for you would be to allow only odd numbers in the selection. Hint: Use `XmNvalueChangedCallback`:

```
XtAddCallback(aScale, XmNvalueChangedCallback, myfunction);
```

The callback will send a pointer to the structure of type `XMScaleCallbackStruct`. where `myfunction` is defined as:

```
/**
*** Partial listing for not allowing even numbers for FM selection.
**/
#define MAX_SCALE 1080
#define MIN_SCALE 800
static void
myfunction(Widget w, XtPointer dclient,  XmScaleCallbackStruct *p)
{
int k;

k = p->value;
if ((k & 0x1) == 0)  /** % 2  is zero ** check limits & increase **/
    {
    k++;
    if (k >= MAX_SCALE) k = MIN_SCALE + 1;
    if (k <= MIN_SCALE) k = MAX_SCALE - 1;
XmScaleSetValue(w,k);  /** this will redisplay it too
**/
}
}
```

The Text Widget

The Text widget allows the user to type in text. This text can be multi-line, and the Text widget provides full text editing capabilities. If you are sure you want only single-line input from the user, you can specify the TextField widget. This is simply a scaled-down version of the Text widget. The resources for both are the same unless explicitly stated. These include:

- ■ `XmNvalue`: A character string, just like in C. This is different from Motif 1.1 or older, where this value was a compound string. If you have Motif 1.2 or later, this will be C string.

- ■ `XmNmarginHeight` and `XmNmarginWidth`: The number of pixels between the widget border and the text. The default is 5 pixels.

- ■ `XmNmaxLength`: This sets the limit on the number of characters in the `XmNvalue` resource.

- ■ `XmNcolumns`: The number of characters per line.

- ■ `XmNcursorPosition`: The number of characters at the cursor position from the beginning of the text file.

■ `XmNeditable`: The Boolean value that, if set to TRUE, will allow the user to insert text.

The callbacks for this widget are:

■ `XmNactivateCallback`: Called when the user presses the Return key.

■ `XmNfocusCallback`: Called when the widget receives focus from the pointer.

■ `XmNlosingFocusCallback`: Called when the widget loses focus from the pointer.

There are several convenience functions for this widget:

■ `XmTextGetString(Widget w)` returns a C string (`char *`).

■ `XmTextSetString(Widget w, char *s)` sets a string for a widget.

■ `XmTextSetEditable(Widget w, Boolean trueOrFalse)` sets the editable string of the widget.

■ `XmTextInsert(Widget w, XmTextPosition pos, char *s)` sets the text at the position defined by `pos`. This `XmTextPosition` is an opaque item defining the index in the text array.

■ `XmTextShowPosition(Widget w, XmTextPosition p)` scrolls to show the rest of the string at the position `p`.

■ `XmTextReplace(Widget w, XmTextPosition from, XmTextPosition to, char *s)` replaces the string starting from the location `from` inclusive to the position `to`, with the characters in string s.

■ `XmTextRemove(Widget w)` clears the text in a string.

■ `XmTextCopy(Widget w, Time t)` copies the currently selected text to the Motif clipboard. The `Time t` value is derived from the most recent `XEvent` (usually in a callback), which is used by the clipboard to take the most recent entry.

■ `XmTextCut(Widget w, Time t)` is like `XmTextCopy`, but removes the selected text from the text's buffer.

■ `XmTextPaste(Widget w)` pastes the contents of the Motif clipboard onto the text area at the current cursor (insertion) position.

■ `XmTextClearSelection(Widget w, XmTextPosition p, XmTextPosition q, Time t)` selects the text from location `p` to location `q`.

In the following example, you could construct a sample editor application with the Text widget. For the layout of the buttons, you would use widgets of the XmManager class to manage the layout for you. These manager widgets are:

■ `XmBulletinBoard`

■ `XmRowColumn`

■ `XmForm`

The Bulletin Board Widget

The Bulletin Board widget allows the programmer to lay out widgets by specifying their XmNx and XmNy resources. These values are relative to the top left corner of the Bulletin Board widget. The Bulletin Board widget will not move the children widget around on itself. If a widget resizes, it's the application's responsibility to resize and restructure its widgets on the Bulletin Board.

The resources for the widget are:

- XmNshadowType: Specifies the type of shadow for this widget. It can be set to XmSHADOW_OUT (the default), XmSHADOW_ETCHED_IN, XmSHADOW_ETCHED_OUT, or XmSHADOW_IN.

- XmNshadowThickness: The number of pixels for the shadow. This is defaulted to 0 (no shadow).

- XmNallowOverlap: Allows the children to be overlapped as they are laid on the widget. This is a Boolean resource and is defaulted to TRUE.

- XmNresizePolicy: Specifies the resize policy for managing itself. If set to XmRESIZE_NONE, it will not change its size. If set to XmRESIZE_ANY, it will grow or shrink to attempt to accommodate all its children automatically. This is the default. If set to XmRESIZE_GROW, it will grow, but never shrink, automatically.

- XmNbuttonFontList: Specifies the font for all XmPushButton children.

- XmNlabelFontList: Specifies the default font for all widgets derived from XmLabel.

- XmNtextFontList: Specifies the default font for all Text, TextField, and XmList children.

It also provides the callback XmNfocusCallback, which is called when any children of the Bulletin Board receives focus.

The *RowColumn* Widget

The RowColumn widget class orders its children in a row or columnar fashion. This is used to set up menus, menu bars, and radio buttons. The resources provided by this widget include:

- XmNorientation: XmHORIZONTAL for a row major layout of its children; XmVERTICAL for a column major layout.

- XmNnumColumns: Specifies the number of rows for a vertical widget and the number of columns for a horizontal widget.

- XmNpacking: Determines how the children are packed. XmPACK_TIGHT allows the children to specify their own size. It fits children in a row (or column if

XmHORIZONTAL), and then starts a new row if no space is available. XmPACK_NONE forces Bulletin Board-like behavior. XmPACK_COLUMN forces all children to be the size of the largest column. This uses the XmNnumColumns resource and places all its children in an organized manner.

- XmNentryAlignment: Specifies which part of the children to use in its layout alignment. Its default is XmALIGNMENT_CENTER, but it can be set to XmALIGNMENT_BEGINNING for the left side or XmALIGNMENT_END for the right side. This is on a per column basis.

- XmNverticalEntryAlignment: Specifies the alignment on a per row basis. It can be assigned a value of XmALIGNMENT_BASELINE_BOTTOM, XmALIGNMENT_BASELINE_TOP, XmALIGNMENT_CONTENTS_BOTTOM, XmALIGNMENT_CONTENTS_TOP, or XmALIGNMENT_CENTER.

- XmNentryBorder: The thickness of a border drawn around all children, and is defaulted to 0.

- XmNresizeWidth: A Boolean variable that, if set to TRUE, will allow the RowColumn widget to resize its width when necessary.

- XmNresizeHeight: A Boolean variable that, if set to TRUE, will allow the RowColumn widget to resize its height when necessary.

- XmNradioBehaviour: Works with toggle buttons only. It allows only one toggle button in a group of buttons to be active at a time. The default is FALSE.

- XmNisHomogeneous: If set to TRUE, this specifies that only children of the type Class in XmNentryClass can be children of this widget. The default is FALSE.

- XmNentryClass: Specifies the class of children allowed in this widget if XmNisHomogeneous is TRUE. A sample radio button application was shown in file 47_5c. To see another example of the same listing but with two columns, see file 47_8c on the CD-ROM.

The Form Widget

The beginning of the chapter introduced you to the workings of the Form widget. This is the most flexible and most complex widget in Motif. Its resources include:

- XmNtopAttachment
- XmNleftAttachment
- XmNrightAttachment
- XmNbottomAttachment

These values specify how a child is placed. The following values correspond to each side of the widget:

XmATTACH_NONE: Do not attach this side to Form.

XmATTACH_FORM: Attach to corresponding side on Form.

XmATTACH_WIDGET: Attach this side to opposite side of a reference widget. For example, attach the right side of this widget to the left side of the reference widget. A reference widget is another child on the same form.

XmATTACH_OPPOSITE_WIDGET: Attach this side to same side of a reference widget. This is rarely used.

XmATTACH_POSITION: Attach a side by the number of pixels shown in XmNtopPosition, XmNleftPosition, XmNrightPosition, and XmNbottomPosition resources, respectively.

XmATTACH_SELF: Use XmNx, XmNy, XmNheight, and XmNwidth.

The following resources are set to the corresponding widgets for each side for the XmATTACH_WIDGET setting in an attachment:

- XmNtopWidget
- XmNleftWidget
- XmNrightWidget
- XmNbottomWidget

The following resources are the number of pixels a side of a child is offset from the corresponding Form side. The offset is used when the attachment is XmATTACH_FORM.

- XmNtopOffset
- XmNleftOffset
- XmNrightOffset
- XmNbottomOffset

Sometimes it is hard to get the settings for a Form widget just right, or the Form widget does not lay out the widgets in what seems to be the proper setting for a child widget. In these cases, lay the children out in ascending or descending order from the origin of the Form widget. That is, create the top left widget first and use it as an "anchor" to create the next child, then the next one to its right, and so on. There is no guarantee that this will work, so try using the bottom right, bottom left, or top right for your anchor positions.

If this technique does not work, try using two forms on top of the form you're working with. Forms are cheap, and your time is not. It's better to just make a form when two or more widgets have to reside in a specific layout.

When you're trying a new layout on a Form widget, if you get error messages about failing after 10,000 iterations, it means you have conflicting layout requests to one or more child widgets. Check the attachments very carefully before proceeding. This error message results from the Form widget trying different layout schemes to accommodate your request.

> **TIP:** At times, conflicting requests to a form will cause your application to slow down while it's trying to accommodate your request, not show the form, or both.

Designing Layouts

When you're designing layouts, think about the layout before you start writing code. Let's try an album search front-end example. See file **47_9c** on the CD-ROM.

The application is shown in Figure 47.9. Notice how the labels do not line up with the Text widget. There is a problem in the hierarchy of the setup. See the hierarchy of the application in Figure 47.10.

The Form widgets are created to maintain the relative placements of all widgets that correspond to a type of function. The RowColumn widgets allow items to be placed on them. The best route to take in this example is to lay one text and one label on one RowColumn widget and have three RowColumn widgets in all, one for each instance up to NUM_ITEMS. This will ensure that each label lines up with its corresponding Text widget.

FIGURE 47.9.

The output of Listing 47.9.

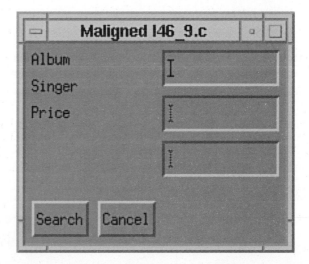

FIGURE 47.10.

The hierarchy of Listing 47.9.

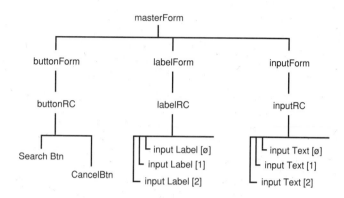

A couple of points to note about laying out applications:

- Think about what you want the form or dialog to do. Draw it on paper if you have to. Coding is the easy part; determining what to do is much harder.

- Be consistent. Users will love you for it. If Alt+x is a shortcut for "Exit" in one screen, do not make it a cut operator in another. Keep controls on the same side of all dialog boxes and forms. Use separators to separate different functions on the same window.

- Choose a color scheme for your end users. What may be cool to you may be grotesque to the end user. They may not even be using a color monitor in some rare cases. A combination of white, gray, and black may be your best bet if you don't want to deal with different color schemes in your code.

- Colors on your monitor may not be the same on the end user's monitor.

- Do not assume that the user's monitor has the same resolution as yours. Keep fonts (and buttons) big enough for a large cursor. Allow windows to be resizeable as much as possible to allow the user to customize his desktop.

- Assume nothing. If the user can size your window to an unworkable size, either limit the size in `resizeCallback` to the lowest size or don't allow sizing at all.

- Offer some help for the user. In the future, Help will be required as a standard option on menu bars, so plan ahead.

- Avoid clutter. Too many options and entries on one huge form tend to confuse and baffle the user. Consider two tiers or more. Default everything as much as possible.

- Make the program more forgiving. Sometimes an "Are you sure?" dialog with an option to change a list of parameters can be endearing to a user. On the other hand, some users hate this type of checking.

Menus

The way you design widget hierarchies is especially important when you're working with Motif menus. Motif menus are a collection of widgets, so there is no "menu" widget for a menu. You create menus using a hierarchy of different types of widgets: RowColumn, PushButton, CascadeButton, ToggleButton, Label, and Separator.

There are three kinds of menus in Motif:

- Popup: This appears as a list of items when a pointer button is pressed on a widget.
- Pulldown: This appears when a button on an existing menu is pressed.
- Option: This allows the user to select from a list of options, with the current selection visible at all times.

The procedure to create a menu is different for each type of menu.

Popup

To create a Popup menu, do the following:

1. Include the correct header files. You will need the header files for the menu:

   Label.h

   RowColumn.h

   PushB.h

   Separator.h

   BulletinB.h

   CascadeB.h

2. Create the menu pane with a call to `XmCreatePopupMenu`. This is a convenience call to create a RowColumn widget and a MenuShell widget with the proper settings.

3. Create the buttons on the menu pane. Use `XmPushbuttons`, `XmToggleButtons`, `XmSeparator`, and `XmCascadeButtons`.

4. Attach callback functions to the widgets.

 See file `47_10c` on the CD-ROM for a listing that sets up a pop-up menu.

Note three important items about this listing: You can use `printf` functions within Motif applications. The output goes to the controlling terminal by default. This is invaluable in debugging. The menu is not visible by itself. An event handler on the parent of the menu is registered before the menu can be displayed. This allows the menu to be displayed any time a button is pressed. The XmMenuPosition call sets the position of the Popup menu. It is then managed (after placement).

The Menu Bar

A menu bar is a horizontal bar that is continually available to the user. Motif uses the RowColumn widget as a bar, with cascading buttons for each option.

The procedure for creating a menu bar is as follows:

1. Include the correct header files. You will need the header files for the menu:

Label.h	RowColumn.h
PushB.h	Separator.h
BulletinB.h	CascadeB.h

2. Create the menu bar with a call to XmCreateMenuBar().

3. Create the pull-down menu panes with a call to XmCreatePulldownMenu().

4. For each pull-down pane, create a cascade button on the menu bar. Use the menu bar as the parent. A cascade button is used to link the items in a menu with the menu bar itself.

5. Attach the menu pane to its corresponding cascade button. Use the XmNsubMenuId resource of the cascade button on the appropriate menu pane.

6. Create the menu entries in the menu panes.

 File 47_1k on the CD-ROM shows how to set up a menu bar and pull-down menus.

Note that the Motif programming style requires you to make the Help button (if you have one) right-justified on the menu bar. This Help cascade button should then be set to the XmNmenuHelpWidget of a menu bar. The menu bar will automatically position this widget at the right-hand side of the visible bar.

 File 47_12c on the CD-ROM is another example of setting up a menu bar and pull-down menus.

The Options Menu

The Options menu allows the user to select from a list of items, and displays the most recently selected item. The procedure for creating an Options menu is similar to creating a menu bar.

1. Include the correct header files. You will need the header files for the menu:

`Label.h`	`Separator.h`
`RowColumn.h`	`BulletinB.h`
`PushB.h`	`CascadeB.h`

2. Create the menu bar with a call to `XmCreateOptionMenu()`.

3. Create the pull-down menu panes with a call to `XmCreatePulldownMenu()`.

4. For each pull-down pane, create a cascade button on the menu bar.

5. Attach the menu pane to its corresponding cascade button. Use the `XmNsubMenuId` resource of the cascade button on the appropriate menu pane.

6. Create the menu entries in the menu panes.

Accelerators and Mnemonics

A menu item's accelerator is a keystroke that invokes the callback for that particular item. For example, to open a file you could use Ctrl+O. The resource for this accelerator could be set in the resource file as the following:

`*Open*accelerator: Ctrl<Key>O`

The corresponding menu item should read "Open Ctrl+O" to make the user aware of this shortcut. You can also set this resource through the following command in the `.Xresources` file:

`*Open*acceleratorText: "Ctrl+O"`

Using the `.Xresource` file is the preferred way of setting these resources.

Mnemonics are a shorthand for letting users select menu items without using the mouse. For example, you could use <meta>F for invoking the File menu. These are usually set in the `.Xresources` file as well. The syntax for the File menu to use the <meta>F key would be as follows:

`*File*mnemonic: F`

Dialog Boxes

A dialog box conveys information about something to the user, and receives one of a limited number of responses. For example, a dialog box could read "Go Ahead and Print" with three buttons—OK, Cancel, and Help. The user would then select one of the three buttons.

A typical dialog box displays an icon, a message string, and (usually) three buttons. Motif provides predefined dialog boxes for the following categories: Errors, information, warnings, working, and question.

Each of the above dialog box types displays a different icon: a question mark for the Question dialog box, an exclamation mark for the Information dialog box, and so on. Convenience functions ease creation of dialog boxes:

- `XmCreateErrorsDialog`
- `XmCreateInformationDialog`
- `XmCreateWarningDialog`
- `XmCreateWorkingDialog`
- `XmCreateQuestionDialog`

 The infamous "Really Quit?" dialog box can be implemented as shown in Listing 47.13. There is another example in file `47_17c` on the CD-ROM.

Append this to the end of any listing to get instant verification before you actually quit the application.

Note that the `quitDlg` dialog box is set to NULL when the function is first called. It is only managed for subsequent calls to this function.

Modes of a Dialog Box

A dialog box can have four modes of operation, called modalities. The mode is set in the `XmNdialogStyle` resource. The possible values are as follows:

- Non-Modal: The user can ignore the dialog box and work with any other window on the screen. The resource value is `XmDIALOG_MODELESS`.
- Primary Application Modal: All input to the window that invoked the dialog box is locked out. The user can use the rest of the windows in the application. The resource value is `XmDIALOG_PRIMARY_APPLICATION_MODAL`.
- Full Application Modal: All input to all the windows in the application that invoked the dialog box is locked out. The user cannot use the rest of the windows in the application. The resource value is `XmDIALOG_FULL_APPLICATION_MODAL`.
- System Modal: All input is directed to the dialog box. The user cannot interact with any other window in the system. The resource value is `XmDIALOG_SYSTEM_MODAL`.

The dialog boxes provided by Motif are based on the `XmMessageBox` widget. Sometimes it is necessary to get to the widgets in a dialog. This is done by a call to the following:

```
Widget XmMessageBoxGetChild( Widget dialog, typeOfWidget);
```

Here, `typeOfWidget` can be one of these:

```
XmDIALOG_HELP_BUTTON      XmDIALOG_CANCEL_BUTTON
XmDIALOG_SEPARATOR        XmDIALOG_MESSAGE_LABEL
XmDIALOG_OK_BUTTON        XmDIALOG_SYMBOL_LABEL
```

The dialog box may have more widgets that can be addressed. Check the man pages for the descriptions of these widgets.

For example, to hide the Help button in a dialog box, use this call:

```
XtUnmanageChild(XmMessageBoxGetChild(dlg, XmDIALOG_HELP_BUTTON));
```

In the case of adding a callback, use this call:

```
XtAddCallback(XmMessageBoxGetChild(dlg, XmDIALOG_OK_BUTTON),
XmNactivateCallback, yourFunction);
```

A typical method of creating custom dialog boxes is to use existing ones. Then, using the `XmMessageBoxGetChild` function, you can add or remove any function you want. For example, replace the Message String widget with a Form widget and you have a place to lay out widgets however you need.

Events

An event is a message sent from the X server to the application that some condition in the system has changed. This could be a button press, a keystroke, a request for information from the server, or a timeout. An event is always relative to a window and starts from the bottom up. It propagates up the window hierarchy until it gets to the root window, where the root window application makes the decision whether to use or discard it. If an application in the hierarchy does use the event or does not allow propagation of events upwards, the message is used at the window itself. Only device events (keyboard or mouse) are propagated upwards, not configuration events.

An application must request an event of a particular type before it can begin receiving events. Each Motif application calls `XtAppInitialize` to make this request automatically.

Events contain at least the following information:

- The type of event
- The display where it happened
- The event window
- The serial number of the last event processed by the server

Look in the file `<X11/Xlib.h>` for a description of the union called `XEvent`, which allows access to these values. The file `<X11/X.h>` contains the descriptions of constants for the types of events.

All event types share this header:

```
typedef struct {
        int type;
unsigned long serial;    /* # of last request processed by server */
Bool send_event;         /* true if this came from a SendEvent request */ Display
*display;/* Display the event was read from */
        Window window;   /* window on which event was requested in event mask */ }
XAnyEvent;
```

The types of events include:

KeyPress	KeyRelease	ButtonPress
ButtonRelease	MotionNotify	EnterNotify
LeaveNotify	FocusIn	FocusOut
KeymapNotify	Expose	GraphicsExpose
NoExpose	VisibilityNotify	CreateNotify
DestroyNotify	UnmapNotify	MapNotify
MapRequest	ReparentNotify	ConfigureNotify
ConfigureRequest	GravityNotify	ResizeRequest
CirculateNotify	CirculateRequest	PropertyNotify
SelectionClear	SelectionRequest	SelectionNotify
ColormapNotify	ClientMessage	MappingNotify

Expose

The server generates an Expose when a window that has been covered by another is brought to the top of the stack, or even partially exposed.

The structure for this event type is as follows:

```
typedef struct {
    int type;       /* Type of event */
    unsigned long serial;      /* # of last request processed by server */
    Bool send_event;       /* true if this came from a SendEvent request */
    Display *display;      /* Display the event was read from */
    Window window;
    int x, y;
    int width, height;
    int count;      /* if non-zero, at least this many more */
} XExposeEvent;
```

Note how the first five fields are shared between this event and XAnyEvent. Expose events are guaranteed to be in sequence. An application may get several Expose events from one condition. The count field keeps a count of the number of Expose events still in the queue when the application receives this one. Thus, it can be up to the application to wait to redraw until the last Expose event is received (count == 0).

Pointer Events

A pointer event is generated by a mouse button press or release, or by any mouse movement. This type of event is called XButtonEvent. Recall that the leftmost button is Button1, but it can be changed. See the section "Left-Handed Users" in the previous chapter. The structure returned by a button press and release is the following:

```
typedef struct {
    int type;      /* of event */
    unsigned long serial;      /* # of last request processed by server */
    Bool send_event;      /* true if this came from a SendEvent request */
    Display *display;      /* Display the event was read from */
    Window window;      /* "event" window it is reported relative to */
    Window root;      /* root window that the event occured on */
    Window subwindow;      /* child window */
    Time time;      /* milliseconds */
    int x, y;      /* pointer x, y coordinates in event window */
    int x_root, y_root;      /* coordinates relative to root */
    unsigned int state;      /* key or button mask */
    unsigned int button;      /* detail */
    Bool same_screen;      /* same screen flag */
} XButtonEvent;


typedef XButtonEvent XButtonPressedEvent;
typedef XButtonEvent XButtonReleasedEvent;
```

The event for a movement is called XMotionEvent, with the type field set to MotionNotify.

```
typedef struct {
    int type;      /* MotionNotify */
    unsigned long serial;      /* # of last request processed by server */
    Bool send_event;      /* true if this came from a SendEvent request */
    Display *display;      /* Display the event was read from */
    Window window;      /* "event" window reported relative to */
    Window root;      /* root window that the event occured on */
    Window subwindow;      /* child window */
    Time time;      /* milliseconds */
    int x, y;      /* pointer x, y coordinates in event window */
    int x_root, y_root;      /* coordinates relative to root */
    unsigned int state;      /* key or button mask */
    char is_hint;      /* detail */
    Bool same_screen;      /* same screen flag */
} XMotionEvent;


typedef XMotionEvent XPointerMovedEvent;
```

Keyboard Events

A keyboard event is generated when the user presses or releases a key. Both types of events, KeyPress and KeyRelease, are returned in an XKeyEvent structure.

```
typedef struct {
    int type;      /* of event */
```

```
      unsigned long serial;      /* # of last request processed by server */
      Bool send_event;      /* true if this came from a SendEvent request */
      Display *display;       /* Display the event was read from */
      Window window;        /* "event" window it is reported relative to */
      Window root;        /* root window that the event occured on */
      Window subwindow;        /* child window */
      Time time;       /* milliseconds */
      int x, y;       /* pointer x, y coordinates in event window */
      int x_root, y_root;        /* coordinates relative to root */
      unsigned int state;        /* key or button mask */
      unsigned int keycode;       /* detail */
      Bool same_screen;       /* same screen flag */
} XKeyEvent;

typedef XKeyEvent XKeyPressedEvent;
typedef XKeyEvent XKeyReleasedEvent;
```

The keycode field presents the information on whether the key was pressed or released. These constants are defined in <X11/keysymdef.h> and may be vendor-specific. These are called KeySym and are generic across all X servers. For example, the F1 key could be described as XK_F1.

The function XLookupString converts a KeyPress event into a string and a KeySym (a portable key symbol). Here's the call:

```
int XLookupString(XKeyEvent *event,
            char *returnString,
            int max_length,
            KeySym  *keysym,
            XComposeStatus *compose);
```

The returned ASCII string is placed in returnString for up to max_length characters. The KeySym contains the key symbol. Generally, the compose parameter is ignored.

Window Crossing Events

The server generates crossing EnterNotify events when a pointer enters a window, and LeaveNotify events when a pointer leaves a window. These are used to create special effects for notifying the user that the window has focus. The XCrossingEvent structure looks like this:

```
typedef struct {
      int type;                 /* of event */
      unsigned long serial;      /* # of last request processed by server */
      Bool send_event;      /* true if this came from a SendEvent request */
      Display *display;      /* Display the event was read from */
      Window window;           /* "event" window reported relative to */
      Window root;           /* root window that the event occured on */
      Window subwindow;        /* child window */
      Time time;           /* milliseconds */
      int x, y;                 /* pointer x, y coordinates in event window */
      int x_root, y_root;       /* coordinates relative to root */
      int mode;                 /* NotifyNormal, NotifyGrab, NotifyUngrab */
```

```
    int detail;
    /*
        * NotifyAncestor, NotifyVirtual, NotifyInferior,
        * NotifyNonlinear,NotifyNonlinearVirtual
        */
    Bool same_screen;      /* same screen flag */
    Bool focus;            /* boolean focus */
    unsigned int state;      /* key or button mask */
} XCrossingEvent;
typedef XCrossingEvent XEnterWindowEvent;
typedef XCrossingEvent XLeaveWindowEvent;
```

These are generally used to change a window's color when the user moves the pointer in and out of it.

Event Masks

An application requests events of a particular type by calling a function XAddEventHandler.

```
XAddEventHandler( Widget ,
                  EventMask ,
                  Boolean maskable,
XtEventHandler handlerfunction,
                  XtPointer clientData);
```

The handler function is of this form:

```
void handlerFunction( Widget w, XtPointer clientData,
                XEvent *ev, Boolean *continueToDispatch);
```

The first two arguments are the client data and widget passed in XtAddEventHandler. The ev argument is the event that triggered this call. The last argument allows this message to be passed to other message handlers for this type of event. This should be defaulted to TRUE.

You would use the following call on a widget (w) to be notified of all pointer events of the type ButtonMotion and PointerMotion on this widget.

```
extern void handlerFunction( Widget w, XtPointer clientData,
            XEvent *ev, Boolean *continueToDispatch); ..
XAddEventHandler( w, ButtonMotionMask | PointerMotionMask, FALSE, handlerFunction, NULL
);
```

The possible event masks are the following:

NoEventMask	KeyPressMask	KeyReleaseMask
ButtonPressMask	ButtonReleaseMask	EnterWindowMask
LeaveWindowMask	PointerMotionMask	PointerMotionHintMask
Button1MotionMask	Button2MotionMask	Button3MotionMask
Button4MotionMask	Button5MotionMask	ButtonMotionMask
KeymapStateMask	ExposureMask	VisibilityChangeMask

StructureNotifyMask	ResizeRedirectMask	SubstructureNotifyMask
SubstructureRedirectMask	FocusChangeMask	PropertyChangeMask
ColormapChangeMask	OwnerGrabButtonMask	

 File 47_14c on the CD-ROM is a sample application that shows how to track the mouse position.

Managing the Queue

The XtAppMainLoop() function handles all the incoming events through the following functions:

- XtAppPending, which checks the queue to see if any events are pending.
- XtAppNextEvent, which removes the next event from the queue.
- XtDispatchEvent, which passes the message to the appropriate window.

The loop can do something else between checking and removing messages through the replacement code segment:

```
while (!done)
        {
        while (XtAppPending( applicationContext))
            {
XtAppNextEvent( applicationContext, &ev));
            XtDispatchEvent( &ev));
            }
        done = interEventFunction();
        }
```

There are some caveats with this scheme:

- This is a non-blocking function. It must be fed at all times with events or it will take over all other applications' time.
- There is no guarantee when your interevent function will be run if the queue is flooded with events.
- Note the while loop for checking messages. It's more efficient to flush the queue first and then call your function, rather than calling it once per check for messages.
- The interevent function must be fast or you will see the user interface slow down. If you want to give your user feedback about what's going on during a long interevent function, you can handle just the Expose events through a call to XmUpdateDisplay(Display *). This will handle only the Expose events in the queue so that you can update a status display.

> **Caution:** Consider using the select call to handle incoming events of file descrip-
> tors. This is a call that allows an application to wait for events from various file
> descriptors (in AIX, on UNIX message queues) on read-ready, write-ready, or
> both. This is done by setting the bits in 32-bit wide integer for up to 16 files (and
> 16 more message queues in AIX) to wait on input from. The setup scheme for
> select calls is different on different UNIX systems. Check the man pages for the
> select function on your system. The pseudo-code to handle select calls follows.
>
> Check your system's man pages for this code.
>
> Open all the files with an open call.
>
> Get the file descriptor for the event queue. Use the Select macros to set up the
> parameters for select call `ret = return` from the select function.
>
> ```
> switch (ret)
>    case0:
>
>            process the event queue.
>        case 1:    ...
>            process the file descriptor
> ```

Work Procedures

These are functions called by the event handler loop whenever no events are pending in
the queue. The function is expected to return a Boolean value indicating whether it has to
be removed from the loop once it is called. If TRUE, it will be removed. If FALSE, it will
be called again. For example, you could set up a disk file transfer to run in the "background" that will keep returning FALSE until it is done, at which time it will return TRUE.

The work procedures are defined as

```
XtWorkProc yourFunction(XtPointer clientdata);
```

The way to register a work procedure is to call

```
XtWorkProcId    XtAppAddWorkProc ( XtAppContext app,
XtWorkProc   functionPointer, XtPointer    clientData);
```

The return ID from this call is the handle to the work procedure. It is used to remove the
work procedure with a call to

```
XtRemoveWorkProc( XtWorkProcId id);
```

Using Timeouts

A timeout is used to perform some task at (almost) regular intervals. Applications set up a timer callback function, which is called when a requested time interval has passed. This function is defined as the following:

```
XtTimerCallbackProc thyTimerCallback( XtPointer clientdata, XtInterval *tid);
```

Here, `clientdata` is a pointer to client-specific data.

The setup function for the timeout returns the timer ID and is defined as the following:

```
XtIntervalId XtAppAddTimeOut ( XtAppContext app,
int milliseconds, XtTimerCallback TimerProcedure, XtPointer clientdata);
```

This call sets up a timer to call the `TimerProcedure` function when the requested milliseconds have passed. It will do this only once. If you want cyclic timeouts, say, in a clock application, you have to explicitly set up the next function call in the timer handler function itself. So generally the last line in a timer handler is a call to set a timeout for the next time the function wants to be called.

UNIX was not originally designed for real-time applications and you cannot expect a deterministic time interval between successive timer calls. Some heavy graphics updates can cause delays in the timer loop. For user interface applications, the delays are probably not a big drawback. However, consult your vendor before you attempt to write a time-critical control application. Your mileage may vary depending on your application.

File `47_15c` on the CD-ROM is a program that sets a cyclic timer.

Other Sources

The `XtAddInput` function is used to handle inputs from sources other than the event queue. Here is the definition:

```
XtInputId XtAddInput( XtAppContext app,
    int UNIXfileDescriptor,
 XtPointer  condition,
XtInputCallback inputHandler,
XtPointer clientdata);
```

The return value from this call is the handle to the `inputHandler` function. This is used to remove the call through the call:

```
XtAppAddInput( XtInput Id);
```

The input Handler function itself is defined as:

```
XtImportCallbackProc InputHandler(XtPointer clientdata, int *fd,
XtInputId *id);
```

Unlike timers, you must register this function only once. Note that a pointer to the file descriptor is passed into the function. The file descriptor must be a UNIX file descriptor. You do not have support for UNIX IPC message queues or semaphores through this scheme. The IPC mechanism is considered dated, and is limited to one machine. Consider using sockets instead.

Handling Output

The Graphics Context

Each widget draws itself on the screen using its set of drawing parameters, called the graphics context. For drawing on a widget, you can use the X primitive functions if you have its window and its graphics context. It's easier to limit your artwork to the DrawingArea widget, which is designed for this purpose. You can think of the GC as your paintbrush and the widget as the canvas. The colors and the thickness of the paintbrush are just two of the factors that determine how the paint is transferred to the canvas. The GC is your paintbrush.

Here is the function call to create a GC:

```
GC XCreateGC (Display dp, Drawable d, unsigned long mask, XGCValue *values);
```

For use with a widget, w, this call would look like the following:

```
GC gc;
XGCVvalue gcv;
unsigned long mask;

gc = XCreate(XtDisplay(w), XtWindow(w),
    mask, gcv);
```

Also, you can create a GC for a widget directly with a call to `XtGetGC`:

```
gc = XtGetGC (Widget w, unsigned long mask, XGCValue *values);
```

The values for the mask are defined as follows:

GCFunction	GCPlaneMask	GCForeground
GCBackground	GCLineWidth	GCLineStyle
GCCapStyle	GCJoinStyle	GCFillStyle
GCFillRule	GCTile	GCStipple
GCTileStipXOrigin	GCTileStipYOrigin	GCFont
GCSubWindowMode	GCGraphicsExposures	GCClipXOrigin
GCClipYOrigin	GCClipMask	GCDashOffset
GCDashList	GCArcMode	

The data structure for setting graphics context is shown here:

```
typedef struct {
     int function;        /* logical operation */
     unsigned long plane_mask;/* plane mask */
unsigned long foreground;/* foreground pixel */ unsigned long background;/* background
pixel */ int line_width;        /* line width */
     int line_style;        /* LineSolid, LineOnOffDash, LineDoubleDash */
     int cap_style;        /* CapNotLast, CapButt,
               CapRound, CapProjecting */
     int join_style;        /* JoinMiter, JoinRound, JoinBevel */
     int fill_style;        /* FillSolid, FillTiled,
               FillStippled, FillOpaeueStippled */
     int fill_rule;        /* EvenOddRule, WindingRule */
     int arc_mode;        /* ArcChord, ArcPieSlice */
     Pixmap tile;        /* tile pixmap for tiling operations */
     Pixmap stipple;        /* stipple 1 plane pixmap for stipping */
     int ts_x_origin;        /* offset for tile or stipple operations */
     int ts_y_origin;
     Font font;        /* default text font for text operations */
     int subwindow_mode;        /* ClipByChildren, IncludeInferiors */
Bool graphics_exposures;/* boolean, should exposures be generated */ int clip_x_origin;
/* origin for clipping */
     int clip_y_origin;
     Pixmap clip_mask;        /* bitmap clipping; other calls for rects */
     int dash_offset;        /* patterned/dashed line information */
     char dashes;
} XGCValues;
```

If you want to set a value in a GC, you have to take two steps before you create the GC:

1. Set the value in the XGCValue structure.

2. Set the mask for the call GCFunction. This determines how the GC paints to the screen. The dst pixels are the pixels currently on the screen, and the src pixels are those that your application is writing by using the GC.

```
GXclear   dst = 0
GXset     dst = 1
GXand     dst = src AND dst
GXor      dst = src OR dst
GXcopy    dst = src

GXnoop    dst = dst
GXnor     dst = NOT(src OR dst)
GXxor     dst = src XOR dst

GXinvert dst = NOT dst
GxcopyInverted dst = NOT src
```

The function for a GC is changed through a call XSetFunction (Display *dp, GC gc, int function), where function is set to one of the above values. The default value is GXcopy.

There are several other masks that you can apply. They are listed in the <X11/X.h> file.

■ GCPlaneMask: The plane mask sets which planes of a drawable can be set by the GC. This is defaulted to AllPlanes, thereby allowing the GC to work with all planes on a window.

■ GCForeground and GCBackground: These are the values of the pixels to use for the foreground and background colors, respectively. Here is the call to manipulate these:

```
XSetForeground(Display *dp, GC gc, Pixel pixel); XSetBackground(Display
*dp, GC gc, Pixel pixel);
```

■ GCLineWidth: This is the number of pixels for the width of all lines drawn through the GC. It is defaulted to 0, which is the signal to the server to draw the thinnest line possible.

■ GCLineStyle, GCDashOffset, and GCDashList: This determines the style of the line drawn on the screen. LineSolid draws a solid line using the foreground color, LineOnOffDash draws an intermittent line with the foreground color, and LineDoubleDash draws a line that is composed of interlaced segments of the foreground and background colors. The GCDashOffset and GCDashList values determine the position and length of these dashes.

■ GCCapStyle: This determines how the server draws the ends of lines. CapNotLast draws up to, but not including, the end point pixels of a line. CapButt draws up to the end points of a line (inclusive). CapRound tries to round off the edges of a thick line (3 or more pixels wide). CapProjecting projects the end point out a little.

■ GCJoinStyle: This is used to draw the end points of a line. It can be set to JointMiter for a 90-degree joint, JoinBevel for a beveled joint, or JoinRound for a rounded joint.

■ GCFillStyle, GCTile, and GCStipple: The fill style can be set to FillSolid, which specifies the foreground color as the fill color. FillTiled specifies a pattern set in the tile attribute. FillStipple specifies a pattern in the stipple attribute. It uses the foreground color when a bit is set to 1 and nothing when a bit is set to 0, whereas FillOpaqueStippled uses the foreground when a bit is set to 1 and the background when a bit is set 0.

■ GCFont: This specifies the font list to use. See the section "Using Fonts and FontLists" later in this chapter.

■ GCArcMode: This defines the way an arc is drawn on a screen. See the next section, "Drawing Lines, Points, Arcs, and Polygons."

Drawing Lines, Points, Arcs, and Polygons

Motif applications can access all the graphics primitives provided by Xlib. All Xlib functions must operate on a window or a pixmap; both are referred to as *drawable*. A widget has a window after it is realized, and you can access this window with a call to XtWindow().
An application can crash if Xlib calls are made to a window that is not realized. The way to check is through a call to XtIsRealized() on the widget, which returns TRUE if it's realized and FALSE if it's not. Use the XmDrawingArea widget's callbacks for rendering your graphics, because it is designed for this purpose. The following callbacks are available to you:

- XmNresizeCallback: Invoked when the widget is resized.
- XmNexposeCallback: Invoked when the widget receives an Expose event.
- XmNinputCallback: Invoked when a button or key is pressed on the widget.

All three functions pass a pointer to XmDrawingAreaCallbackStruct.

Drawing a Line

To draw a point on a screen, use the XDrawLine or XDrawLines function call.
Consider the example shown on the CD-ROM in file 47_16c.

The following code is an example of the primitives required to draw one line on the widget. Note the number of GCValues that have to be set to achieve this purpose. The XDrawLine function definition is shown here:

```
XDrawLine( Display *dpy,
    Drawable d,
    GC gc,
    int x1,
    int y1,
    int x2,
    int y2);
```

It's more efficient to draw multiple lines in one call. Use the XDrawLines function with a pointer to an array of points and its size.

The mode parameter can be set to:

- CoorModeOrigin: Use the values relative to the drawable's origin.
- CoorModePrevious: Use the values as deltas from the previous point. The first point is always relative to the drawable's origin.

To draw boxes, use the XDrawRectangle function:

```
XDrawRectangle( Display *display,
Drawable dwindow,
        GC       gc,
        int      x,
        int      y,
        unsigned int width,
        unsigned int height);
```

This will draw a rectangle at (x, y) of geometry (width, height). To draw more than one box at one time, use the XDrawRectangles() function. This is declared as the following:

```
XDrawRectangles( Display *display,
        Window   dwindow,
        GC       gc,
        XRectangle *xp,
int     number);
```

Here, xp is a pointer to an array of "number" rectangle definition structures.

For filled rectangles, use the XFillRectangle and XFillRectangles calls, respectively.

Drawing a Point

To draw a point on a screen, use the XDrawPoint or XDrawPoints function call. These are similar to line-drawing functions. Look at Listing 47.16.

Drawing Arcs

To draw circles, arcs, and so on, use the XDrawArc function:

```
XDrawArc(Display *display,
        Window   dwindow,
        GC   gc,
        int  x,
        int  y,
unsigned int    width; unsigned int    height; int    a1,
        int   a2);
```

This function is very flexible. It draws an arc from angle a1, starting at the 3 o'clock position, to angle a2. The unit of measurement for angles is 1/64 of a degree. The arc is drawn counterclockwise. The largest value is 64×360 units because the angle arguments are truncated. The width and height define the bounding rectangle for the arc.

The XDrawArcs() function is used to draw multiple arcs, given pointers to the array.

```
XDrawArcs (Display *display,
        Window   dwindow,
        GC   gc,
        XArc *arcptr,
        int   number);
```

To draw polygons, use the call:

```
XDrawSegments( Display *display, Window dwindow,
        GC    gc,
        XSegment *segments,
        int      number);
```

The XSegment structure includes four "short" members, x1, y1, x2, and y2, which define the starting and ending points of all segments. For connected lines, use the XDrawLines function shown earlier. For filled polygons, use the XFillPolygon() function call.

Using Fonts and Fontlists

Fonts are perhaps the trickiest aspect of Motif to master. See the section on Fonts in the previous chapter before you read this section to familiarize yourself with font definitions. The function XLoadQueryFont(Display *dp, char *name) returns an XFontStruct structure. This structure defines the extents for the character set. This is used to set the values of the Font field in a GC.

To draw a string on the screen, use the following:

```
XDrawString ( Display *dp, Drawable dw, GC gc,
     int x, int y, char *str, int len);
```

This only uses the foreground color. To draw with the background and foreground, use this:

```
XDrawImageString ( Display *dp, Drawable dw, GC gc,
        int x, int y, char *str, int len);
```

The X Color Model

The X color model is based on an array of colors called a colormap. Applications refer to a color by its index in this colormap. The indices are placed in an application's frame buffer, which contains an entry for each pixel of the display. The number of bits in the index define the number of bitplanes. The number of bitplanes define the number of colors that can be displayed on a screen at one time. For example, one bit per pixel displays two colors, four bits per pixel displays 16 colors, and eight bits per pixel displays 256 colors.

An application generally inherits the colormap of its parent. It can also create its own colormap by using the XCreateColormap call. The call is defined as:

```
Colormap XCreateColormap( Display *display,
            Window   dwindow,
            Visual   *vp,
            int      allocate);
```

This allocates the number of allocate color entries in a window's colormap. Generally the visual parameter is derived from this macro:

```
DefaultVisual (Display *display, int screenNumber);
```

Here `screenNumber` = 0 in almost all cases. See the previous chapter, "Screens, Displays, and Windows," for a definition of screens.

Colormaps are a valuable resource in X and must be freed after use. This is done through this call:

```
XFreeColormap(Display *display, Colormap c);
```

Applications can get the standard colormap from the X server by using the `XGetStandardColormap()` call, and can set it through the `XSetStandardColormap()` call. These are defined as

```
XGetStandardColormap( Display *display,
          Window   dwindow,
XStandardColormap *c, Atom      property);
```

and

```
XSetStandardColormap( Display *display,
Window  dwindow, XStandardColormap *c, Atom      property);
```

Once applications have a colormap to work with, you have to take two steps:

1. Define the colormap entries.

    The property atom can take the values of `RGB_BEST_MAP`, `RGB_GRAY_MAP`, or `RGB_DEFAULT_MAP`. These are names of colormaps stored in the server. They are not colormaps themselves.

2. Set the colormap for a window through this call:

```
XSetWindowColormap ( Display *display,
          Window   dwindow,
          Colormap c );
```

    For allocating a color in the colormap, use the XColor structure defined in `<X/Xlib.h>`.

    To see a bright blue color, use the segment:

```
XColor color;
color.red = 0;
color.blue = 0xffff;
color.green = 0;
```

    Then add the color to the colormap using the call to the function:

```
XAllocColor(Display *display,
      Window dwindow,
      XColor *color );
```

A sample function that sets the color of a widget is shown in file 47_17c on the CD-ROM.

The default white and black pixels are defined as the following:

```
Pixel BlackPixel( Display *dpy, int screen); Pixel WhitePixel( Display *dpy, int
screen);
```

These will work with any screen as a fallback.

The index (`Pixel`) returned by this function is not guaranteed to be the same every time the application runs. This is because the colormap could be shared between applications that each request colors in a different order. Each entry is allocated on the basis of next available entry. Sometimes if you overwrite an existing entry in a cell, you may actually see a change in a completely different application. So be careful.

Applications can query the RGB components of a color by calling this function:

```
XQueryColor( Display *display,
        Colormap *cmp,
        XColor  *clr);
```

For many colors at one time, use this:

```
XQueryColors( Display *display,
        Colormap *cmp,
        XColor  *clr,
        int number);
```

At this time the application can modify the RGB components and then store them in the colormap with this call:

```
XStoreColor( Display *display,
        Colormap *cmp,
        XColor  *clr);
```

Recall that X11 has some strange names for colors in `/usr/lib/rgb.txt file`. Applications can get the RGB components of these names with a call to this:

```
XLookupColor( Display *display,
        Colormap cmp,
        char    *name,
        XColor  *clr
        XColor  *exact);
```

The name is the string to search for in the rgb.txt file. The returned value `clr` contains the next closest existing entry in the colormap.

The exact color entry contains the exact RGB definition in the entry in `rgb.txt`. This function does not allocate the color in the colormap. To do that, use this call:

```
XAllocNamedColor( Display *display,
        Colormap cmp,
        char    *name,
        XColor  *clr
        XColor  *exact);
```

Pixmaps, Bitmaps, and Images

A pixmap is like a window but is off-screen, and is therefore invisible to the user. It is usually the same depth as the screen. You create a pixmap with this call:

```
XCreatePixmap (Display *dp,
Drawable dw, unsigned int width, unsigned int height, unsigned int depth);
```

A drawable can be either a window (on-screen) or a pixmap (off-screen). Bitmaps are pixmaps with a depth of one pixel. Look in /usr/include/X11/bitmaps for a listing of some of the standard bitmaps.

The way to copy pixmaps from memory to the screen is through this call:

```
XCopyArea( Display dp,
    Drawable Src,
    Drawable Dst,
    GC   gc,
    int  src_x,
    int  src_y,
    unsigned int width,
    unsigned int height,
    int  dst_x,
    int  dst_y);
```

The caveat with this call is that the Src and Dst drawables have to be of the same depth. To show a bitmap with a depth greater than one pixel on a screen, you have to copy the bitmap one plane at a time. This is done through the following call:

```
XCopyPlane( Display dp,
    Drawable Src,
    Drawable Dst,
    GC   gc,
    int  src_x,
    int  src_y,
    unsigned int width,
    unsigned int height,
    int  dst_x,
    int  dst_y,
    unsigned long plane);
```

The plane specifies the bit plane that this one-bit-deep bitmap must be copied to. The actual operation is largely dependent on the modes set in the GC.

For example, to show the files in the /usr/include/bitmaps directory, which have three defined values for a sample file called gumby.h:

- gumby_bits: Pointer to an array of character bits
- gumby_height:Integer Height
- gumby_width: Integer width

First create the bitmap from the data using the XCreateBitmapFromData() call. To display this one-plane-thick image, copy the image from this plane to plane 1 of the display. You can actually copy to any plane in the window.

A sample call could be set for copying from your pixmap to the widget's plane 1 in the following manner:

```
XCopyPlane( XtDisplay(w), yourPixmap, XtWindow(w), gc,
0,0, your_height, your_width, 0,0,1);
```

It copies from the origin of the pixmap to the origin of plane 1 of the window.

There are other functions for working with images in X. These include the capability to store device-dependent images on disk and the Xpm format.

Xpm was designed to define complete icons and is complicated for large pixmaps. The format for an Xpm file is as follows:

```
char *filename[] =
{
"Width Height numColors CharacterPerPixel",
"character colortypes"
..PIXELS..
};
```

A string of "8 8 2 1" defines a 8×8 icon with two colors and one character per color. The PIXELS are strings of characters: the number of strings equals the number of rows. The number of characters per string equals the number of columns.

The character represents a color. Colortypes are a type followed by a color name. So "a c red m white" would show a red pixel at every "a" character on color screens, and a white pixel on monochrome screens. See the following example:

```
char *someFig[ ] = {
"8 8 2 1",
"a c red m white",
". c blue m black",
"aa....aa",
"aa....aa",
"aa....aa",
"aaaaaaaa",

"aaaaaaaa",
"aa....aa",
"aa....aa",
"aa....aa"
};
```

See the man pages for more details on using Xpm files. Look for the functions XpmReadFileToPixmap and XpmWriteFileToPixmap for information on reading these images from or storing them to disk.

GUI Builders and Management Tools

The difference between a GUI interface builder and a GUI interface management tool is that if you generate new code from a GUI interface builder, it will not save any previous changes that you have made to previous versions of code. No backups are kept. A GUI interface management tool, however, will allow you to keep all your changes in the file.

Here are some ideas on selecting and using GUI builders:

They do save you time even if you don't intend to use the code generated by the builder. They can help you lay out all the widgets and set the appropriate placements to get the desired effect (colors, X,Y positions, and so on).

One of the failings of such software packages is that no backups are kept of the code that a developer has done to the callback stubs. Refer to the sections on using and writing Motif widgets for more information about callbacks. This software simply generates code from the interface that the user has designed. This code includes all stubs for the widgets that the user has designated. Therefore, regenerating code from an edited interface overwrites any modifications to any previously edited stubs. Some builders do this, some don't. Check this with your vendor.

Environments tend to lock you into a specific programming mode. For some developers, this may equate to lack of freedom, and may turn them away from what might well mean time to market. The time to try an environment out and test its flexibility is *before* you buy.

Code generated by GUI builders may not be the most efficient for your particular application. You should be able to easily modify the generated code.

Check to see if functionality can be added without going through special hoops (such as precompilers). For example, how easy is it to add your own C++ classes?

Does the builder generate native code, or do you have to use her libraries? If you have to ship shared libraries, check the licensing agreements or see if static versions are available.

A Few Commercial GUI Builders

This is a list of some of the GUI builders and environments on the market today. This list is by no means complete, and exists only as a guide to what's available. Contact your local vendor for more information.

- Imperial Software Technology Ltd., Reading, England, through VI Corporation (800-732-3200), offers a GUI builder, X-Designer, which has built-in OpenLook-to-Motif conversion.

■ Kinesix (713-953-8300) provides Sammi, an integrated GUI building environment.

■ LIANT (800-237-1873) offers a C++/Views visual programming tool that ports Motif applications to DOS text, OS/2, Windows, and so on.

■ Neuron Data (800-876-4900) lists an amazing 40 platforms that you can port your GUI application to.

■ XVT Design (800-678-7988) offers an Interactive Design Tool and the XVT Portability Toolkit, which will port Motif applications to DOS text, OS/2, Windows, and so on.

■ Zinc Software (801-785-8900) offers Zinc Designer and Applications Framework to build and port Motif applications to DOS text, OS/2, Windows, and so on.

What You Have Learned in this Chapter

This chapter covered the following topics:

■ The basics of writing Motif applications
■ Special naming conventions in Motif and X
■ Writing and compiling your first Motif application
■ Revisiting widget hierarchy
■ Working with various common widgets
■ Introduction you to designing layouts
■ Creating pop-up menus and menu bars
■ Creating simple dialog boxes
■ Learning how to use the mouse in event handling
■ Colors in X
■ Drawing lines and points
■ Introduction to GUI builders and management tools

Acknowledgements

I am indebted to Metro Link software for providing me with their version of Motif 1.2, which I used to develop all the routines and test the sources in this book. Their software installed cleanly with no hassles on a linux (1.02) system running on a 386DX. All librar-ies worked great at the time and presented no compatibility problems in going porting sources to Sun and AIX. There was no reason to call their support line, so I could not evaluate it. The price for all binaries and the development system is $208, which includes overnight shipping and my choice of Volume 3 or Volume 6 from the O'Reilly *X Window System User's Guide* manual set.

You can contact Metro at (305) 938-0283.

References

Quercia, Valerie and O'Reilly, Tim. *The Definitive Guides to the X Window System, X Window System User's Guide*, Volume Three, Motif Edition. O'Relly, March 1992.

Johnson, Eric F. and Reichard, Kevin. *Advanced X Window Applications Programming*. MIS:Press, 1990.

Johnson, Eric F. and Reichard, Kevin. *Power Programming ... Motif* Second Edition. MIS:Press, 1993.

OSF/Motif Programmers Guide. Prentice Hall, 1993.

OSF/Motif Style Guide. Prentice Hall, 1990.

Taylor, Dave. *Teach Yourself UNIX in a Week*. Sams Publishing, 1994.

Rost, Randi J. *X and Motif Quick Reference Guide*. Digital Press, 1990.

Young, Doug. *The X Window System Programming and Applications with Xt*, OSF/Motif Edition, 1994.

What's on the CD-ROM Disc

Installing the Software

Most of the software included with this CD-ROM is for the UNIX Operating System. Since there are several flavors of UNIX for every possible hardware configuration known to mankind, a simple installation program is not possible. If you are new to UNIX, you should contact the person responsible for installing software on your system to install your selected programs. This might be a support person or a system administrator. You will find a bag of M&Ms and a cola will probably get the job done faster.

If you are responsible for installing software on your system, this CD-ROM can be mounted with the mount command discussed in Chapter 40, "Device Administration." Please read the installation and configuration instructions that come with each package for further detail on how to install and configure the software for your particular operating system and hardware. Have fun!

Contents of the CD-ROM

Unless the authors of the software are noted at the end of the description, the programs listed here are distributed under the Free Software Foundation's General Public License. This license is in the file COPYING on the CD-ROM.

The CD-ROM is an ISO-9660 disc, which means that full UNIX file and directory names cannot be used. If you have the Rock Ridge CD-ROM extensions on your system, the YMTRANS.TBL files (included for most of the software) allow your system to automatically expand the ISO-9660 names to full UNIX names.

The listings follow this format:

program name (location on disc) ()-description

acm-4.5 (ACM_4_5)—acm is a LAN-oriented, multiplayer aerial combat simulation. Players engage in air-to-air combat against one another using heat-seeking missiles and cannons.

autoconf-1.11 (AUTOCONF)—autoconf is an extensible package of m4 macros that creates a noninteractive configuration script for a package from a template file. The template file lists the operating system features that the package can use, in the form of m4 macro calls, and can also contain arbitrary shell commands. Autoconf requires GNU m4.

bash-1.13.5 (BASH_1_1)—BASH (the Bourne Again SHell) is a Posix-compatible shell with full Bourne shell ('sh') syntax and some C-shell commands. BASH supports emacs-style command-line editing, job control, functions, and online help. Instructions for compiling BASH may be found in the file README.

binutils-2.4 (BINUTILS)—This is a beta release of a completely rewritten binutils distribution. These programs have been tested on various architectures. Most recently tested are sun3 and sun4s running sunos4, as well as Sony News running newsos3. This release contains the following programs: ar, demangle, ld (the linker), nm, objcopy, objdump, ranlib, size, strip, and gprof. BFD (the Binary File Descripter) library is in the subdirectory bfd and is built along with GDB (which uses bfd). See the README file for further instructions on where to look for building the various utilities.

bison-1.22 (BISON_1_)—Bison is an upwardly compatible replacement for the parser generator yacc, with more features. The file README gives instructions for compiling Bison; the files bison.1 (a man page) and bison.texinfo (a GNU Texinfo file) give instructions for using it.

calc-2.02c (CALC_2_0)—Calc is an extensible, advanced desk calculator and mathematical tool that runs as part of GNU Emacs. You can use Calc as a simple calculator, but it provides additional features including choice of algebraic or RPN (stack-based) entry, logarithmic functions, trigonometric and financial functions, arbitrary precision, complex numbers, vectors, matrices, dates, times, infinities, sets, algebraic simplification, differentiation, and integration. Instructions for installing Calc for Emacs are in the README file.

clisp-1994.01.08 (CLISP_19)—CLISP is a Common Lisp implementation by Bruno Haible and Michael Stoll. It mostly conforms to the version of Common Lisp described by *Common LISP: The Language* (1st edition) and supports CLOS as well. CLISP runs on many microcomputers and needs only 1.5 MB of memory. CLISP includes an interpreter, a compiler, and (for some machines) a screen editor.

cperf-2.1a (CPERF_2_)—This is a program to generate minimally perfect hash functions for sets of keywords. Programs that must recognize a set of keywords may also benefit from using this program. Instructions for compiling cperf may be found in the file README.

cvs-1.3 (CVS_1_3)—CVS is a collection of programs that provide for software release and revision control functions. CVS is designed to work on top of RCS version 4. It will parse older RCS formats, but cannot use any of its fancier features without RCS branch support. The file README contains more information about CVS.

diffutils-2.6 (DIFFUTIL)—diff compares files showing line-by-line changes in several flexible formats. GNU diff is much faster than the traditional UNIX versions. This distribution includes diff, diff3, sdiff, and cmp. Instructions for compiling these are in the README file.

dld-3.2.3 (DLD_3_2_)—Dld is a library package of C functions that performs *dynamic link editing*. Programs that use dld can add compiled object code to or remove such code from a process anytime during its execution. Dld works on VAX, Sun 3, SPARCstation, Sequent Symmetry, and Atari ST machines.

doschk-1.1 (DOSCHK_1)—This program is intended as a utility to help software developers ensure that their source filenames are distinguishable on MS-DOS and 14-character SYSV platforms.

ecc-1.2.1 (ECC_1_2_)—ECC is a Reed-Solomon error correction checking program. It is capable of correcting three byte errors in a block of 255 bytes, and is capable of detecting more severe errors.

emacs-18.59 (EMACS_18)—GNU emacs is an extensible, customizable full-screen editor. Read the README and INSTALL files for a full description of the parts of GNU emacs, and the steps needed to install it. This distribution includes the complete GNU emacs Manual.

emacs-19.24 (EMACS_19)—GNU emacs is an extensible, customizable full-screen editor. Read the README and INSTALL files for a full description of the parts of GNU emacs, and the steps needed to install it. This distribution includes the complete GNU emacs Manual.

es-0.84 (ES_0_84)—This is an extensible shell based on rc but with more features including first class functions, lexical scope, an exception system, and rich return values (functions can return values other than just numbers).

f2c-1994.05.10 (F2C_1994)—This is a Fortran-to-C converter program. Instructions for compiling it are in the src/README file.

fileutils-3.9 (FILEUTIL)—These are the GNU file-manipulation utilities. Instructions for compiling these utilities are in the file README. The fileutils package contains the following programs: chgrp, chmod, chown, cp, dd, df, dir, du, ginstall, ln, ls, mkdir, mkfifo, mknod, mv, rm, rmdir, touch, vdir.

find-3.8 (FIND_3_8)—This is a Posix-compliant implementation (with many extensions) of find, a program used for searching file systems for files that match certain criteria and performing operations (like showing the path) when they are found. Also included in this distribution are xargs and locate.

finger-1.37 (FINGER_1)—GNU finger is a utility program designed to allow users of UNIX hosts on the Internet network to get information about each other. Instructions for building finger itself are in the README file.

fontutils-0.6 (FONTUTIL)—These are the GNU font utilities. There are various programs for converting between various bitmaps and other graphical data formats, creating fonts using Ghostscript, and other such utilities. You will need GCC and GNU Make to compile these programs. For the programs that do online graphics, you will need an X11 server and the X11R4 or R5 libraries. Instructions for building the fontutils are in the README file.

gas-2.3 (GAS_2_3)—GAS is the GNU assembler. Version 2 has many changes over previous GAS releases. Most notable among the changes are the separation of host system, target CPU, and target file format (i.e. cross-assembling is much easier). Many CPU types and object file formats are now supported. Read the `gas-2.3/gas/README` file for instructions on building and using GAS.

gcc-2.5.8 (`GCC_2_5_`)—This is version 2 of GCC, the GNU C Compiler. In addition to supporting ANSI C, GCC Version 2 includes support for the C++ and Objective C languages. GCC extends the C language to support nested functions, non-local gotos, taking the address of program labels, and unnamed structures as function arguments (among other things). There are also many new warnings for frequent programming mistakes. GCC can be easily configured as a cross-compiler, running on one platform while generating code for another. A list of supported systems and instructions for compiling GCC are in the `INSTALL` file.

gcl-1.0 (`GCL_1_0`)—GNU Common Lisp (`GCL`) has a compiler and interpreter for Common Lisp. It is very portable and extremely efficient on a wide class of applications. It compares favorably in performance with commercial Lisps on several large theorem prover and symbolic algebra systems.

gdb-4.12 (`GDB_4_12`)—This is the GNU source-level debugger. A list of the machines supported as targets or hosts, as well as a list of new features, appears in `gdb-4.12/gdb/NEWS`. Instructions for compiling GDB are in the file `gdb-4.12/gdb/README`. BFD (the Binary File Descripter) library is in the subdirectory `bfd` and is built along with GDB (which uses it).

gdbm-1.7.3 (`GDBM_1_7`)—This is the beta-test version of the GNU DBM library. DBM is a set of library routines which implement a database using quick lookup by hashing. See the file `README` for further details.

ghost-2.6.1 (`GHOST_2_`)—This program is an interpreter for a language that is intended to be, and very nearly is, compatible with the PostScript language. It runs under X on UNIX and VMS systems, and also runs on MS-DOS machines. It will drive either displays or low-to-medium-resolution printers. Instructions for compiling Ghostscript are in the file `README`. Fonts for Ghostscript are in the directory `ghost-2.6.1/fonts`.

ghostview-1.5 (`GHOSTVIE`)—Ghostview allows you to view PostScript files on X11 displays. Ghostview handles the user interface details and calls the 'ghostscript' interpreter to render the image. Instructions for compiling Ghostview are in the `README` file.

glibc-1.08 (`GLIBC_1_`)—This directory contains a beta release of the GNU C Library. The library is ANSI C-1989 and POSIX 1003.1-1990 compliant and has most of the functions specified in POSIX 1003.2. It is upwardly compatible with the 4.4 BSD C library and includes many System V functions, plus GNU extensions. Version 1.08 adds support for Sun RPC, `mmap` and friends, and compatibility with several more traditional UNIX functions. See the file `INSTALL` for instructions on building the library.

gnats-3.2   (GNATS_3_)—GNATS (GNats: A Tracking System) is a bug-tracking system. It is based upon the paradigm of a central site or organization which receives problem reports and negotiates their resolution by electronic mail. Although it's been used primarily as a software bug-tracking system so far, it is sufficiently generalized so that it could be used for handling system administration issues, project management, or any number of other applications.

grep-2.0   (GREP_2_0)—This package contains version 2.0 of grep, egrep, and fgrep. They are similar to their UNIX counterparts, but are usually faster. Instructions for compiling them are in the file README.

groff-1.09   (GROFF_1_)—groff is a document formatting system, which includes drivers for Postscript, TeX dvi format, and typewriter-like devices, as well as implementations of eqn, nroff, pic, refer, tbl, troff, and the man, ms, and mm macros. groff's mm macro package is almost compatible with the DWB mm macros and has several extensions. Written in C++, these programs can be compiled with GNU C++ Version 2.5 or later.

gzip-1.2.4   (GZIP_1_2)—This is a new compression program (free of known patents) which the GNU Project is using instead of the traditional compress program. Gzip can uncompress LZW-compressed files but uses a different algorithm for compression, which generally yields smaller compressed files. This will be the standard compression program in the GNU system.

hp2xx-3.1.4   (???)—GNU hp2xx reads HP-GL files, decomposes all drawing commands into elementary vectors, and converts them into a variety of vector and raster output formats. It is also an HP-GL previewer.

indent-1.9.1   (INDENT_1)—This is the GNU modified version of the freely distributable indent program from BSD. The file indent.texinfo contains instructions on using indent.

ispell-3.1.04   (ISPELL_3)—Ispell is an interactive spell checker that finds unrecognized words and suggests "near misses" as replacements. Both system and user-maintained dictionaries can be used. Both a stand-alone and GNU Emacs interface are available.

libg++-2.5.3   (LIBG___2)—The GNU C++ library is an extensive collection of C++ forest classes, a new IOStream library for input/output routines, and support tools for use with G++. Among the classes supported are Obstacks, multiple-precision Integers and Rationals, Complex numbers, arbitrary length Strings, BitSets, and BitStrings. Instructions are in the file libg++-2.5.3/libg++/README.

m4-1.1   (M4_1_1)—m4 is a macro processor, in the sense that it copies its input to the output, expanding macros as it goes. Macros are either built-in or user-defined, and can take any number of arguments. Besides just doing macro expansion, m4 has built-in functions for including named files, running UNIX commands, doing integer arithmetic, manipulating text in various ways, recursion, etc. Instructions for building m4 are in the README file.

make-3.71 (MAKE_3_7)—This is GNU Make. GNU Make supports many more options and features than the UNIX make. Instructions for using GNU Make are in the file make.texinfo. See the file README for installation instructions.

mkisofs-1.01 (MKISOFS_)—mkisofs is a pre-mastering program to generate an ISO9660 file system. It takes a snapshot of a given directory tree, and generates a binary image which will correspond to an ISO9660 file system when written to a block device. mkisofs is also capable of generating the System Use Sharing Protocol records specified by the Rock Ridge Interchange Protocol. This is used to further describe the files in the ISO9660 file system to a UNIX host, and provides information such as longer filenames, uid/gid, Posix permissions, and block and character devices.

mtools-2.0.7 (MTOOLS_2)—Mtools is a public domain collection of programs to allow UNIX systems to read, write, and manipulate files on an MS-DOS file system (typically a diskette).

mule-1.1.4 (MULE_1_1)—Mule is a MULtilingual Enhancement to GNU Emacs 18. It can handle, not only ASCII characters (7 bits) and ISO Latin-1 (8 bits), but also Japanese, Chinese, Korean (16 bits) coded in the ISO2022 standard and its variants (e.g. EUC, Compound Text). For Chinese there is support for both GB and Big5. Thai (based on TIS620) and Vietnamese (based on VISCII and VSCII) are also supported.

netfax-3.2.1 (NETFAX_3)—This is a set of software which provides Group 3 fax transmission and reception services for a networked UNIX system. It requires a faxmodem which conforms to the new EIA-592 Asynchronous Facsimile DCE Control Standard, Service Class 2.

nihcl-3.0 (NIHCL_3_)—This is an object oriented program support class library with a portable collection of classes similar to those in Smalltalk-80. This library used to be known as OOPS (Object-Oriented Program Support). NIHCL does not presently work with G++ (GNU C++).

nvi-1.11 (NVI_1_11)—nvi is a free implementation of the vi/ex UNIX editor. It has most of the functionality of the original vi/ex, except open mode and the lisp option, which will be added. Enhancements over vi/ex include split screens with multiple buffers, ability to handle 8-bit data, infinite file and line lengths, tag stacks, infinite undo and extended regular expressions. It runs under BSD, Linux, NetBSD, FreeBSD, BSDI, AIX, HP-UX, DGUX, IRIX, PSF, PTX, Solaris, SunOS, Ultrix, and UNIXware and should port easily to many other systems.

oleo-1.5 (OLEO_1_5)—Oleo is a spreadsheet program (better for you than the more expensive spreadsheet). It supports X windows and character-based terminals, and can generate embedded PostScript renditions of spreadsheets. Keybindings should be familiar to Emacs users and are configurable by users. There is relatively little documentation for Oleo yet. The file USING contains what there is.

p2c-1.20 (P2C_1_20)—This is a Pascal to C conversion program, written by Dave Gillespie.

patch-2.1 (PATCH_2_)—patch will take a patch file containing any of the four forms of difference listing produced by the diff program and apply those differences to an original file, producing a patched version. Instructions for building patch are in the README file.

perl-4.036 (PERL_4_0)—This is version 4.036 of Larry Wall's perl programming language. Perl is intended as a faster replacement for sed, awk, and similar languages. The file README contains instructions for compiling perl.

rc-1.4 (RC_1_4)—rc is a shell which features a C-like syntax (much more so than csh) and far cleaner quoting rules than the C or Bourne shells. It's intended to be used interactively, but is great for writing scripts as well.

rcs-5.6.0.1 (RCS_5_6_)—This is the Revision Control System, a program to manage multiple versions of a software project. This program keeps the changes from one version to another rather than multiple copies of the entire file; this saves disk space. Instructions for compiling RCS are in the file README.

recode-3.3 (RECODE_3)—recode converts files between character sets and usages. When exact transliterations are not possible, it may get rid of the offending characters or fall back on approximations. This program recognizes or produces nearly 150 different charsets and is able to transliterate files between almost any pair. Most RFC 1345 charsets are supported.

regex-0.12 (REGEX_0_)—The GNU regex library routines. It is compliant with POSIX.2, except for internationalization features. It also includes a programmer's reference manual for the library (which is slightly out of date for version 0.12).

rx-0.05 (RX_0_05)—Rx is a pattern matcher compatible with GNU regex, but generally faster (when compiled with gcc -O or in some other way that supports the inline keyword). Version 0.05 is probably not stable.

sed-1.18 (SED_1_18)—sed is a text editor much like ed, but is stream-oriented. It is used copiously in shell scripts. Although GNU sed has fewer static limitations in terms of buffer size, command length, etc., it is a little slower than most implementations. Instructions for building GNU sed are in the file README.

sed-2.05 (SED_2_05)—This is a newer version of GNU sed, with many bug fixes. It also uses a beta test version of the rx library, instead of the older and slower regex library. (Because that library is still in beta testing, sed Version 1 is also included on this CD-ROM.) Instructions for building GNU sed are in the file README.

sh-utils-1.10 (SH_UTILS)—These are the GNU shell utilities, comprising small commands that are frequently run on the command line or in shell scripts. Instructions for compiling these utilities are in the file README. The sh-utils package contains the following programs: basename, date, dirname, echo, env, expr, false, groups, hostname, id, logname, nice, nohup, pathchk, printenv, printf, pwd, sleep, stty, su, tee, test, true, tty, uname, users, who, whoami, yes.

smalltalk-1.1.1 (SMALLTAL)—This is the GNU implementation of Smalltalk, an object-oriented programming language. Instructions for compiling it are in the file README.

superopt-2.3 (SUPEROPT)—The superoptimizer is a function sequence generator that uses an exhaustive generate-and-test approach to find the shortest instruction sequence for a given function.

tar-1.11.2 (TAR_1_11)—Tar is a program used for archiving many files in a single file, which makes them easier to transport. GNU tar includes multivolume support, the ability to archive sparse files, automatic archive compression/decompression, remote archives, and special features to allow tar to be used for incremental and full backups. Unfortunately GNU tar implements an early draft of the POSIX 1003.1 'ustar standard which is different from the final standard. Adding support for the new changes in a backward-compatible fashion is not trivial. Instructions for compiling GNU tar may be found in the file README.

termcap-1.2 (TERMCAP_)—This is a stand-alone release of the GNU Termcap library, which has been part of the GNU Emacs distribution for years but is now available separately to make it easier to install as libtermcap.a. The GNU Termcap library does not place an arbitrary limit on the size of termcap entries, unlike most other termcap libraries. Instructions for building the termcap library are in the README file.

TeX-3.1415 (TEX_3_14)—This is version 3.1415 of the C TeX translation from the original WEB version. Instructions for building TeX and references for further reading are in the file TeX-3.1415/web2c-6.1/README.

texinfo-3.1 (TEXINFO_)—This package contains a set of utilities related to Texinfo, which is used to generate printed manuals and online hypertext-style manuals (called info). Programs and interfaces for writing, reading, and formatting texinfo files are available both as stand-alone programs and as GNU Emacs interfaces. See the file README for directions on how to use the various parts of this package.

textutils-1.9 (TEXTUTIL)—These are the GNU text utilities, commands that are used to operate on textual data. Instructions for compiling these utilities are in the file README. The textutils package contains the following programs: cat, cksum, comm, csplit, cut, expand, fold, head, join, nl, od, paste, pr, sort, split, sum, tac, tail, tr, unexpand, uniq, wc.

tput-1.0 (TPUT_1_0)—tput provides a portable way of allowing shell scripts to use special terminal capabilities. Although its interface is similar to that of `terminfo`-based `tput` programs, this one uses `termcap`. Instructions for compiling `tput` are in the README file.

trn-3.5 (TRN_3_5)—Trn is Threaded RN, a newsreader that uses an article's references to order the discussions in a natural, reply-ordered sequence called threads. Having the replies associated with their parent articles not only makes following the discussion easier, but also makes it easy to backtrack and read a specific discussion from the beginning. By Wayne Davidson, based on `rn` by Larry Wall and Stan Barber.

uucp-1.05 (UUCP_1_0)—This version of UUCP was written by Ian Lance Taylor. It will be the standard UUCP system for GNU. It currently supports the f, g (in all window and packet sizes), G, t and e protocols, as well as `Zmodem` protocol and two new bidirectional protocols. If you have a Berkeley sockets library, it can make TCP connections. If you have TLI libraries, it can make TLI connections. Other important notes about this version of UUCP, and instructions for building it, are in the file README.

uuencode-1.0 (UUENCODE)—Uuencode and uudecode are used to transmit binary files over transmission mediums that do not support anything other than simple ASCII data.

wdiff-0.04 (WDIFF_0_)—wdiff compares two files, finding which words have been deleted or added to the first for getting the second. We hope eventually to integrate `wdiff`, as well as some ideas from a similar program called `spiff`, into some future release of GNU `diff`.

X11R6 (X11R6)—This is the X Window System. The complete "core" distribution is included, plus a preliminary release of the "contributed" distribution. The following patches from the X Consortium have already been applied to the core distribution: fix-01 Released 17 May 1994.

xvnews (XVNEWS)—An Openlook newsreader that uses the XView 3 toolkit. It has been tested using Sun OpenWindows Version 2 and Version 3 xnews servers along with `olvwm`, `olwm`, and `twm`. By J.J. deGraaff.

INDEX